World Directory of Trade and Business Associations

Euromonitor plc, 60-61 Britton Street, London EC1M 5NA

WORLD DIRECTORY OF TRADE AND BUSINESS ASSOCIATIONS

Second edition

Researched and published by
EUROMONITOR plc
60-61 Britton Street
London EC1M 5NA
Great Britain

Telephone: (0171) 251 8024
Telex: 262433
Fax: (0171) 608 3149

EUROMONITOR INTERNATIONAL Inc
122 South Michigan Avenue
Suite 1200
Chicago
Illinois 60603, USA

Tel: (312) 922 1115
Fax: (312) 922 1157

E-mail: info@euromonitor.com   http://www.euromonitor.com

British Library Cataloguing in Publication Data

A CIP catalogue record for this book is available from the British Library

Euromonitor is a member of the Directory Publishers Association and the European Association of Directory Publishers

ISBN: 0 86338 754 3

Printed in Great Britain by Antony Rowe Ltd., Chippenham, Wiltshire

Table Of Contents

Introduction

This is the second edition of our World Directory of Trade and Business Associations which grew out of our European editions of the same title. It forms part of a range of directories which cover business information sources and which are now also available on CD-ROM.

This edition has been completely updated and considerably expanded. We have concentrated on broadening both coverage and detail on trade associations in, primarily, the consumer market and service sectors: coverage of industrial sectors concentrates on those industries with a link with consumer markets, unless a particular sector is of paramount importance to a country's economy. In addition we have added substantial detail on the statistics and publications which the individual associations produce and we have aimed thereby to indicate the relative importance of the association within its market and its usefulness to the researcher. This edition also now includes E-mail and website addresses where they exist. We have included only trade associations and business bodies which have national representation.

The directory begins with the major international and pan-regional trade associations and then lists countries and associations on an A-Z basis. There are two indices including a full A-Z listing of trade associations and a listing by sector and sub-sector.

The directory as a whole covers 146 countries worldwide with substantially broadened coverage on less accessible regions such as Eastern Europe, the Far East and Latin America.

We are confident that this is the best available source of information on trade associations throughout the world: all contact details have been thoroughly checked through an extensive programme of primarily telephone and fax research. However if any errors or omissions were found we would very much like to hear of them. Finally we would like to thank all those organisations who responded so enthusiastically to our requests for information.

Section One

Major Pan-regional and International Trade and Business Associations

PAN-REGIONAL AND INTERNATIONAL

African Groundnut Council
Address: PO Box 3025, Trade Fair Complex, Km 15 Lagos, Badagry Expressway, Lagos, Nigeria
Telephone: +234 1 880 982

African Investment and Trade Association
Address: PO Box 103, Trade Fair Center, 2 Bridge Lane, Accra, Ghana
Telephone: +233 21 775 311
Fax: +233 21 776 711/2

African Petroleum Producers' Association (APPA)
Address: P O Box 1097, Brazzaville, Congo
Telephone: +242 836 438
Fax: +242 836 799
Year established: 1987
Activities: cooperation, coordination, exchanges and technical assistance
Chief officers: Mohamed Souidi (Executive Secretary), Albina De Assis Africano (President)
Publications:
● APPA Bulletin: *data, information and news covering a wide range of oil and gas industry activities in Africa - biannual: March and September*

African Publishers' Network (APNET)
Address: PO Box 43733, 11th Floor Megawatt House, 44 Samora Machel Avenue, Harare, Zimbabwe
Telephone: +263 4 706 196/739 681
Fax: +263 4 705 106/729 905
E-mail: apnet@mago.apc.org
Chief officers: Mr Victor Nwankwo (Director), Ms Gillian Nyambura (Executive Secretary)

American Management Association International (AMA International)
Address: Management Centre Europe (MCE), rue de l'Aqueduc 118, B-1050 Brussels, Belgium
Telephone: +32 2 543 2120
Fax: +32 2 543 2400
E-mail: sisa@mce.be
Activities: conferences, courses, seminars
Chief officers: John Doerr (Managing Director)
Notes: at the same location: Middle East Management Centre; internet address: www.mce.be/mce/

Arab Sugar Federation (ASF)
Fédération Arabe de Sucre
Address: PO Box 195, Khartoum, Sudan
Telephone: +249 11 769 28/737 83
Year established: 1977
Activities: research and educational programmes; library; database of sugar production data; exchange visits
Publications:
● Alsukaria: *annual*

ASEAN Bankers' Association
Address: 180 Cecil Street, 0106, Singapore
Telephone: +65 224 7155
Fax: +65 225 0727
Year established: 1976
Chief officers: Tay Kah Chye

ASEAN Federation of Glass Manufacturers
Address: c/o Malaysian Sheet Glass Berhad, 21 km, 4700 Sungei Buloh, Selangor, Malaysia
Telephone: +60 3 656 1001/656 5011
Fax: +60 3 656 2587/627 9587
Chief officers: Leslie Struys (Chairman), M Morgan (Secretary)

ASEAN Federation of Plastics Industries (AFPI)
Address: c/o Malaysian Plastics Manufacturers Association, 37 Jalan 20/14, Paramount Garden, 46300 Petaling Jaya, Selangor, Malaysia
Telephone: +60 3 776 3027/775 7423/777 4620
Fax: +60 3 776 8352
Year established: 1981
Chief officers: Liew Sew Yee (Chairman), Callum K S Chen (Secretary General)
Membership: 5 national associations: Indonesia, Malaysia, Philippines, Singapore and Thailand
Publications:
● AFPI Manufacturers Directory: *basic facts about each ASEAN country together with an overview of both the economy and the plastics industry. Also includes information on member companies - annual*

Asia-Pacific Broadcasting Union (ABU)
Address: POB 1164, Pej Pos Jalan, Pentai Bahru, Sec Gen's Office, Prog Dept/Tech Dept, 2nd floor, Bangunan IPTAR, 50614 Kuala Lumpur, Malaysia
Telephone: +60 3 282 3592/2480/3108
Fax: +60 3 282 5292
Year established: 1964
Chief officers: Dato' Jaafar Kamin (President), Mikio Kawaguchi, Mehdi Tabeshian (Vice Presidents), Hugh Leonard (Secretary General)
Membership: 37 full members, 24 additional members, 27 associate members
Publications:
● ABU News: *bi-monthly*
● ABU Technical Review: *bi-monthly*

Asian Federation of Advertising Associations
Address: c/o Vigil Management Sdn Bhd, No 75-B, 2/F, Jalan SS 21/1A, Damansara Utama, 47400 Petaling Jaya, Malaysia
Telephone: +60 3 719 8195
Fax: +60 3 719 7894
Activities: organises the biennial Asian Advertising Congress
Chief officers: Saburosuke Suzuki (Chairman), YB Dat' Jaffar bin Mohd Ali, Aristides Katoppo (Vice Chairman)

Association of Chocolate, Biscuit and Confectionery Industries in the EU (CAOBISCO)
Association des Industries de la Chocolaterie, Biscuiterie et Confiserie de l'UE
Address: Rue Defacqz 1, B-1000 Brussels, Belgium
Telephone: +32 2 539 1800
Fax: +32 2 539 1575
E-mail: caobisco@caobisco.be
Year established: 1959
Activities: liaises with the EU and UN; sets up trading systems; organises a sales scheme for surplus butter for biscuit and pastry products; compiles statistics on the industry
Chief officers: Mr Crombé (President), Arnold Van Hecke (Director)
Membership: 18 national associations from 16 countries (EU and AELE) representing 1,950 companies
Publications:
● IOCCC/CAOBISCO Statistical Review: *provides an international comparison of production, imports, exports and*

consumption of chocolate, sugar confectionery and biscuits for 20 countries world-wide - annual
Notes: member of IOCCC - International Office of Cocoa, Chocolate and Sugar Confectionery

Association of Corn Starch Industries of the EU (AAC)
Association des Amidonneries de Céréales de l'Union Européenne
Address: Boîte 10, 1 avenue de la Joyeuse Entrée, B-1040 Brussels, Belgium
Telephone: +32 2 230 2031
Fax: +32 2 230 0245
Chief officers: Mrs Iliana Axiotiades (Managing Director)
Membership: 18 manufacturing companies with 35 plants throughout Europe

Association of Dietetic Foods Industries of the EU (IDACE)
Association des Industries des Aliments Diététiques de l'UE
Address: 194 rue de Rivoli, F-75001 Paris, France
Telephone: +33 1 534 58787
Fax: +33 1 534 58780
E-mail: andrée.bronner@wanadoo.fr
Year established: 1959
Chief officers: Dr Andrée Bronner (Secretary General), Chris Collins (President)
Structure: national delegations, ad hoc working groups
Membership: 14 European associations
Notes: The Association does not produce any publications or statistics; see : International Association of Infant Food Manufacturers (IFM) and International Federation of Special Dietary Food Industries (ISDI)

Association of European Airlines (AEA)
Address: Boîte 4, Avenue Louise 350, B-1050 Brussels, Belgium
Telephone: +32 2 640 3175
Fax: +32 2 648 4017
Telex: 22918
Year established: 1952
Activities: databases of information supplied by members
Chief officers: Karl-Heinz Neumeister (Secretary General), G Bisignani (President)
Membership: 24 European airlines
Publications:
• Statistical Appendices (Association of European Airlines): extensive statistics on revenue, traffic capacity and production data for each airline - annual, coincides with yearbook
• Traffic Update: press release giving latest traffic results of AEA carriers with a short comment on influencing factors - monthly
• Yearbook: reviews trends and achievements of the AEA airlines in the preceding calendar year: technical developments, fleet, traffic and capacity, fares and yield, productivity and operating results, basic statistics, activities of AEA committees - annual

Association of European Chambers of Commerce (EUROCHAMBRES)
Address: 5 rue Archimède, B-1040 Brussels, Belgium
Telephone: +32 2 231 0715
Fax: +32 2 230 0038
Year established: 1958
Chief officers: Mr Friedrich (Secretary General)
Membership: National chambers of commerce associations in 18 European countries.

Association of European Co-operative and Mutual Insurers (ACME)
Association des Assureurs Coopératifs et Mutualistes Européens
Address: Boîte 19, Avenue Galilée 5, B-1210 Brussels, Belgium
Telephone: +32 2 250 9597
Fax: +32 2 250 9600
Chief officers: Jeannine Devuyst (Secretary General)
Membership: 33 European co-operative and mutual insurers
Publications:
• Ensemble-Together: monthly
Notes: The Association does not produce statistics.

Association of European Fruit and Vegetable Processing Industries (OEITFL)
Organisation Européenne des Industries Transformatrices de Fruits et Légumes
Address: Avenue de Roodebeek 30, B-1030 Brussels, Belgium
Telephone: +32 2 743 8730
Fax: +32 2 736 8175
Telex: 26246 SIA B
Year established: 1978
Activities: compiles statistics
Chief officers: P Keppeune (Secretary General)
Membership: 14 associations and federations representing the industry in Belgium, Denmark, Germany, France, Greece, Ireland, Italy, Netherlands, Spain, United Kingdom

Association of European Manufacturers of Instantaneous Gas Water Heaters and Wall-Hung Boilers (AFECI)
Association des Fabricants Européens de Chauffe-Eau Instantanés et de Chaudières Murales au Gas
Address: c/o FABRIMETAL, 21 rue des Drapiers, B-1050 Brussels, Belgium
Telephone: +32 2 510 2508
Fax: +32 2 510 2562
E-mail: afeci@fabrimetal.be
Year established: 1958
Activities: compiles technical, economic, industrial and social documentation; promotes the industry
Chief officers: Mr Hans-Joachim Lydecker (President), Felix Van Eyken (General Secretary)

Association of European Market Research Institutes (AEMRI)
Address: 35 Perrymead Street, London SW6 3SN, United Kingdom
Telephone: +44 171 736 4445
Fax: +44 171 371 9542
Year established: 1991
Activities: organises 2-3 conferences per year; publishes code of business practice and quality guidelines; maintains a database of market research buyers
Chief officers: Heather Dunn (Chairman); Philippa Gillies (Honorary Secretary)
Structure: a limited company headquartered in London; council of 12 directors representing many different European countries
Membership: over 80 members in 15 European countries
Publications:
• Handbook of Members: contains full details of all members - annual
• Synergie: newsletter containing articles by leading research practitioners, news of AEMRI conferences, etc. - quarterly

Association of European Operational Research Societies (EURO)

Address: CP 210/01, c/o ULB - SMG, Boulevard du Triomphe, B-1050 Brussels, Belgium
Telephone: +32 2 650 5674/2 650 5956
Fax: +32 2 650 5970
E-mail: euro@ulb.ac.be
Web site: www.ulb.ac.be/euro
Year established: 1975
Activities: promotes communication and cooperation among European operational researchers
Structure: President, a President-Elect, two Vice-Presidents, a Secretary, a Treasurer and an Executive Committee
Membership: 24 societies throughout Europe
Publications:
● EURO Bulletin: *information about current EURO activities and announcements of conferences, meetings etc. - monthly*
● European Journal of Operational Research (EJOR): *articles on operational research and book reviews etc. - bimonthly*
Notes: Euro is affiliated to the umbrella organisation the "International Federation of Operational Research Societies".

Association of European Tomato Processing Industries (OEICTO)

Organisation Européenne des Industries de la Conserve de Tomates
Address: Avenue de Roodebeek 30, B-1030 Brussels, Belgium
Telephone: +32 2 743 8730
Fax: +32 2 736 8175
Year established: 1963
Chief officers: P. Gomendio (President), M. Jones (Vice President), Pascale Keppenne (Secretary General)
Membership: 8 national associations
Publications:
● List of Members
Notes: The Association does not produce any statistics.

Association of Glucose Producers in the EU

Association des Producteurs de Glucose de l'UE
Address: Boîte 10, 1-5 Avenue de la Joyeuse Entrée, B-1040 Brussels, Belgium
Telephone: +32 2 230 2031
Fax: +32 2 230 0245
Year established: 1968
Chief officers: Iliana Axiotiades (Director General)
Membership: 19 companies in Belgium, Germany, Spain, France, United Kingdom, Greece, Italy, Ireland, Netherlands and Portugal

Association of Management Consulting Firms (AMCF)

Address: Avenue Marcel Thiry 204, B-1200 Brussels, Belgium
Telephone: +32 2 774 9528
Fax: +32 2 774 9690
E-mail: amcf@eyam.be or info@amcf.org
Web site: www.amcf.org
Year established: 1929
Activities: liaises between member companies and state, federal and international governmental bodies and agencies on matters involving taxation, regulation and world trade; organises conferences, seminars and symposiums; provides surveys and studies, carries out research, advocacy service, referrals
Chief officers: Alfons Westgeest (Director of European Office)
Membership: 50 leading firms representing over 50,000 management consultants: small firms as well as large, traditional management consultants and professional services providers, generalists and specialists in relevant industries and areas of practice
Publications:
● AMCF Surveys of United States and European Key

Management Information: *studies of the management consulting industry: fee arrangements, financial operating results, employee recruiting, compensation and benefits, billing procedures and other key management information*
● Critical Management Issues Report: *prioritises and analyses key issues that will affect the international business community by 2001. Also identifies the areas of consulting that will be in demand after the millennium*
● For Members Only: *updates member firms on association news and activities, trends and issues facing the profession - 10 times a year*

Association of National Organisations of Fishery Enterprises of the EU (ANOFEE)

Europêche
Address: Boîte 15, Rue de la Science 23-25, B-1040 Brussels, Belgium
Telephone: +32 2 230 4848
Fax: +32 2 230 2680
E-mail: europeche@free-way.net
Chief officers: Ervio Dobosz (President), Guy Vernaeve (Secretary General)
Publications:
● Statistiques (ANOFEE): *includes data on the number of fishing enterprises, fish catches, types of fish caught. Based on information supplied by members in various countries across Europe and some official data - annual*

Association of Natural Rubber Producing Countries (ANRPC)

Association des Pays Producteurs de Caoutchouc Naturel
Address: 7th floor, Bangunan Getah Asli Menara, 148 Jalan Ampang, 50450 Kuala Lumpur, Malaysia
Telephone: +60 3 261 1900/453 5851
Fax: +60 3 261 3014
Telex: 30953
Year established: 1970
Activities: workshops, seminars, meetings aimed at progress and development of smallholders; technical committee on South American Leaf Blight (SALB); improvement of statistics in member countries; contacts and marketing; studies, research and development in production, marketing and consumption of natural rubber
Chief officers: Mrs J. Lalithambika (Secretary General), Arumugam (Senior Research Officer), Tan Gaik Sim (Publication/Documentation Officer)
Structure: assembly, executive committee, committee of experts, committee on South American Leaf Blight, secreteriat, working groups as and when necessary
Membership: 7 countries: India, Indonesia, Malaysia, Papua New Guinea, Singapore, Sri Lanka and Thailand, which produce about 90% of the world's supply of natural rubber
Publications:
● ANRPC Statistical Review: *regular statistics on the production, output, consumption, imports, exports of rubber based on the returns from member organisations in various countries - quarterly*
● Newsletter: *regular*
● Proceedings of seminars and workshops
● South American Leaf Blight: *pamphlet*

Association of Plastics Manufacturers in Europe (APME)

Address: Boîte 3, 4 Avenue E Van Nieuwenhuyse, B-1160 Brussels, Belgium
Telephone: +32 2 675 3297/2 672 8259
Fax: +32 2 675 3935/2 675 4002
Chief officers: Ms François (Office Manager), Nancy Russotto (Director General), Fred Mader (Deputy Director General), Alan J Griffiths (Communications Director), Juha Rantanen

(President 95/6)
Membership: 41 European plastics companies
Publications:
• Annual Report of the Association of Plastics Manufacturers in Europe (APME): *annual*
• Newsletter of the Association of Plastics Manufacturers in Europe (APME)
• Putting Plastics in Print: *leaflet detailing all publications produced to date (47 books, magazines, bulletins and newsletters), as well as forthcoming publications*

Association of Telecommunications Businesses Party to the Andean Subregional Agreement (ASETA)
Asociación de Empresas de Telecomunicaciones del Acuerdo Subregional Andino
Address: Casilla 17-11-06042, La Pradera N° 510 y San Salvador, Quito, Ecuador
Telephone: +593 2 563 812/509 821
Fax: +593 2 562 499
Year established: 1974
Chief officers: Ing Marcelo López Arjona (Secretary General), Ing Eduardo Pichilingue (Director - International Relations), Ing Jairo Gómez (Director - Studies and Projects)
Structure: board of directors, secretariat
Membership: 5 members - Entel-Bolivia, Telecom-Colombia, Emetel-Ecuador, Telefonica del Peru, and Cantv-Venezuela
Publications:
• Enlace Andino: *telecommunications industry news, technological up dates, new services, association news. Covers the entire Andean region - quarterly*

Association of the Cider and Fruit Wine Industry of the EU (AICV)
Association des Industries des Cidres et Vins de Fruits de l'UE
Address: Avenue de Roodebeek 30, B-1030 Brussels, Belgium
Telephone: +32 2 743 8730
Fax: +32 2 736 8175
Chief officers: Jean-Pierre Stassen (President), Pieter Hatton (Vice President), Jan Hermans (Secretary General)
Membership: 11 associations and companies in Europe
Publications:
• List of Members
Notes: The Association does not produce statistics.

Association of the International Rubber Trade
Address: Wigham House, 16/30 Wakering Road, Barking, Essex 1G11 8PG, United Kingdom
Telephone: +44 181 594 5346
Fax: +44 181 507 8017
Year established: 1913
Activities: annual dinner (London)
Chief officers: J M Basto (Chairman), J M Hobbs (Executive Director)
Membership: 9 trading companies in 3 countries; 59 trade association members
Publications:
• Official Daily Prices: *daily prices for certain grades of natural rubber*

Association of Tin Producing Countries (ATPC)
Association des pays producteurs d'étain
Address: 4th floor, Menara Dayabumi, Jalan Sultan Hishamuddin, 50050 Kuala Lumpur, Malaysia
Telephone: +60 3 274 7620
Fax: +60 3 274 0669
Telex: 32721
Activities: supply rationalisation scheme; supervision of International Tin Research institute
Structure: conference of ministers; executive committee

Publications:
• Annual Report of the Association of Tin Producing Countries (ATPC): *a review of the Association's activities plus statistics on tin production and trade based on returns from member associations in specific countries - annual*

Association of West African Book Publishers
Address: PO Box 9400, University of Ibadan, Ibadan, Nigeria
Telephone: +234 22 411 429
Fax: +234 22 415 681

Australasian Soft Drinks Association Ltd (ASDA)
Address: Suite 3, Level 3, Westfield Tower, 100 William St, Woolloomooloo, NSW 2011, Australia
Telephone: +61 2 936 80200
Fax: +61 2 936 80095
Year established: 1945
Activities: produces statistics on production and per capita consumption of soft drinks by type in New Zealand and Australia
Chief officers: Tony Gentile (Chief Executive); Melanie McPherson (Technical and Environmental Manager); Joanne Thompson (Public Affairs Officer)
Structure: board; technical committee; public affairs committee; environmental committee
Membership: 19 members. Divided into National membership and Association membership
Publications:
• Mineral and Aerated Beverages Production Summary: *a statistical summary of the soft drinks industry in Australia. Covers per capita consumption, production by type and total production. Based on official data - annual*

Caribbean Association of Industry and Commerce (CAIC)
Association de l'Industrie et du Commerce des Caraibes
Address: POB 442, Room 351, Trinidad Hilton, Lady Young Road, St Anns, Trinidad & Tobago
Telephone: +1 868 623 4830
Fax: +1 868 623 6116
E-mail: caic@trinidad.net
Web site: www.trinidad.net/caic/index.shtml
Year established: 1917
Activities: supports implementation of CARICOM Enterprise Regime and the establishment of a Caribbean Stock Exchange; international trade negotiations; training and affiliate developments; communications and membership development; economic research and analysis; small enterprise assistance projects; export development
Chief officers: Pat Thompson (Executive Director)
Membership: 20 chambers of commerce or manufacturing associations, 65 organisations, firms and companies - covers all Caribbean territories, including Venezuela and Mexico
Publications:
• "CAIC Speaks" Bulletin: *Caribbean and Latin-American business news and short articles, activities of the association, issues related to business in Latin America and the Caribbean - monthly*

Caribbean Broadcasting Union (CBU)
Address: Wilkins Lodge, Two Mile Hill, Dayrell's Road, St Michael, Barbados
Telephone: +1 246 429 9146
Fax: +1 246 429 2171
Year established: 1970
Chief officers: Vic Fernandes (President), Neil Giuseppi (Vice President - radio), Ronald Abraham (Vice President - television), Michael Thompson (Vice President - engineering), Leo de León (Secretary General)

Membership: full members from 18 countries, associate members from 7 countries

Caribbean Hotel Association

Address: Suite 1A, 18 Marseille Street, 00907-1672 Santurce, Puerto Rico
Telephone: +1 809 725 9139/9167/9159
Fax: +1 809 725 9108/9166
Year established: 1962
Activities: publications, conferences, special interest programmes, training activities and regional market initiatives
Chief officers: Michael Williams ((President), John Bell (Executive Vice President)
Membership: 37 countries: Anguilla, Antigua and Barbuda, Aruba, Bahamas, Barbados, Belize, Bermuda, Cayman Islands, Colombia, Cuba, Curaçao, Dominica, Dominican Republic, French Guiana, Guadaloupe, Guyana, Haiti, Honduras, Jamaica, Martinique, Montserrat, Mexico, Puerto Rico, Saba, St Barthelemy, St Croix, St Eustatius, St John, St Martin, St Thomas, St Marteen, St Kitts and Nevis, St Lucia, St Vincent and the Grenadines, Trinidad and Tobago, Turks and Caicos Islands, Venezuela and Virgin Islands

Caribbean Tourism Organisation (CTO)

Address: Mer Vue, Marine Gardens, Christ Church, Barbados
Telephone: +1 246 4 275 242
Fax: +1 246 4 273 065
E-mail: ctosysop@caribtourism.com
Web site: www.caribtourism.com
Year established: 1989
Activities: maintains a comprehensive tourism information system, promotes tourism in the Caribbean, maintains links with regional institutes and international agencies
Membership: 32 countries in the Caribbean basin (including Mexico and Venezuela) as well as airlines, cruise ship companies, retail travel agencies, tour operators, travel writers, media, etc.
Publications:
● Caribbean Tourism Statistical Report: *details of visitors to and from 32 Caribbean countries plus data on the tourism infrastructure and transport modes. Based on information supplied by national tourist boards - annual*
● Statistical News (CTO): *quarterly updates of tourism trends in the Caribbean with data on visitors, mode of transport, accomodation, etc.. Based on information supplied by national tourist boards - quarterly*

Central Africa Textile Manufacturers' Association

Address: PO Box 2317, c/o CZI, Bulawayo, Zimbabwe
Telephone: +263 9 606 42
Fax: +263 9 608 14

Central American Association of Pharmaceutical Laboratories (FEDEFARMA)

Federación Centroamericana de Laboratorios Farmacéuticos
Address: Comercial El Patio 7ª Av, 7-07, Zona 4, Oficina 328, Guatemala, Guatemala
Telephone: +502 360 0662/360 0672
Fax: +502 332 28 04
Membership: national associations from Costa Rica, Guatemala, Honduras, Nicaragua, Panama and El Salvador

Committee of Cotton and Allied Textile Industries of the EU (EUROCOTON)

Comité des Industries du Coton et des Fibres Connexes de l'UE
Address: Rue Montoyer 24, B-1000 Brussels, Belgium
Telephone: +32 2 230 3239
Fax: +32 2 230 3622

Year established: 1960
Chief officers: José Vicente Rojo (Chairman), Bernard Hebbelyhek (Treasurer), Michèle Anselme (Secretary General)
Membership: 10 full members, 6 associate members

Committee of Sugar Using Industries (CIUS Europe)

Comité des Industries Utilisatrices de Sucre
Address: Rue Defacqz 1, B-1000 Brussels, Belgium
Telephone: +32 2 539 1800
Fax: +32 2 539 1575
Chief officers: Marcel Laubacher (President), Arnold van Hecke (Secretary General), Céline Anselme (Assistant)
Membership: 23 companies in Europe
Notes: The Committee does not produce any publications or statistics.

Committee of the Mayonnaise and Condiment Sauces Industries in the EU (CIMSCEE)

Comité des Industries des Mayonnaises et Sauces Condimentaires de l'UE
Address: Avenue de Roodebeek 30, B-1030 Brussels, Belgium
Telephone: +32 2 743 8730
Fax: +32 2 736 8175
Year established: 1961
Chief officers: J. Van de Wouwer (President), F. Sponza (Vice President), Michael Coenen (Secretary General)
Membership: 8 industry organisations and companies throughout the EU
Publications:
● List of Members
Notes: The Association does not produce statistics.

Committee of the Mustard Industries of the EU (CIMCEE)

Comité des Industries de la Moutarde de l'UE
Address: Avenue de Roodebeek 30, B-1030 Brussels, Belgium
Telephone: +32 2 743 8730
Fax: +32 2 736 8175
Year established: 1960
Chief officers: J. Alday (President), J. van de Wouwer (Vice President), Michael Coenen (Secretary General)
Membership: 7 national associations
Publications:
● List of Members
Notes: The Association does not produce any statistics.

Committee of the Wool Textile Industry in the EU (Interlaine)

Comité des Industries Lainières de l'UE
Address: Box 14, Rue du Luxembourg 19, B-1000 Brussels, Belgium
Telephone: +32 2 513 0620
Fax: +32 2 514 0665
E-mail: iwto@skynet.be
Activities: liaises between its members and EU authorities; collects statistics on wool production and foreign trade in Europe and worldwide
Chief officers: William H. Lakin (Secretary General), Ingrid van Ouytsel (Assistant Secretary General), Valérie Vandroost (Statistics Department)
Membership: members from eight European countries: Belgium, France, Germany, Italy, Portugal, Spain, Switzerland, UK
Publications:
● Statistics Brochure: *statistics are regularly collected on wool textile production and trade in EU countries. Based mainly on official sources with some input from associations in member countries - annual*

Commonwealth Broadcasting Association (CBA)

Address: Yalding House, 152-156 Great Portland St, London W1N 6AJ, United Kingdom
Telephone: +44 171 765 5144/51
Fax: +44 171 765 5152
E-mail: cba@bbc.co.uk
Web site: www.oneworld.org/cba
Year established: 1945
Chief officers: Elizabeth Smith (Secretary General)
Membership: 61 national broadcasting organisations in 51 commonwealth countries in Europe, Asia, Africa, Caribbean, Australasia, the Pacific and North and South America
Publications:
• CBA Handbook: *details of the association's history and its aims, as well as background information about each member organisation - biennial*
• COMBROAD: *programme production, engineering, management and training - quarterly*
• Who's Who in Commonwealth Broadcasting: *annual*

Confectionery Manufacturers of Australasia (CMA)

Address: PO Box 1307, Camberwell, Victoria 3124, Australia
Telephone: +61 3 981 31600
Fax: +61 3 988 25473
E-mail: spencer@cma.candy.net.au
Web site: www.candy.net.au
Web site notes: includes detailed statistics and analysis of the Australian confectionery market. Includes market size, trends, company profiles, market shares etc.
Year established: 1969
Activities: government liaison, education and training, compiles statistics on the industry
Membership: 200 member firms
Publications:
• Australian Confectionery Industry Profile: *detailed statistics and analysis of the Australian confectionery market. Includes market size, trends, company profiles, market shares etc.' - annual*
• CMA Members Directory: *description on the business activities of members, along with senior management and contact details - annual*
• Confectionery News: *information on the confectionery industry both in Australia, New Zealand and around the world. The CMA Newsletter provides information on legislative changes which could affect businesses, political news and views, convention and seminar information, education and training news, regular global confectionery reports - monthly*
• True Stories: *publication about the care of confectionery stock and the prevention from loss of stock. It deals with the prevention from loss of product through odour contamination, insects and rodents, heat and dampness and appropriate storage facilities - annual*

Confederation of European Paper Industries (CEPI)

Address: Boîte 4, 306 Avenue Louise, B-1050 Brussels, Belgium
Telephone: +32 2 627 4911
Fax: +32 2 646 8137
Year established: 1963
Activities: lobbying, quarterly statistics, communication among members, pulp, paper and board waste general assembly
Membership: 14 national paper associations
Publications:
• Annual Statistical Review: *annual*
• Capacity Report on Woodcontaining Grades: *annual*
• Production Statistics: *quarterly*
• Trade Statistical Annual: *annual*
• Voice for Paper in Europe: *a review of the European paper industry with statistics on production, consumption, recycling etc. Based on various sources - annual*

Confederation of International Soft Drinks Associations (CISDA)

Union Internationale des Associations de Boissons Gazeuses
Address: BP 14, Boulevard Louis Schmidt 35, B-1040 Brussels, Belgium
Telephone: +32 2 735 3749
Fax: +32 2 732 5102
E-mail: mail@unesda-cisda.org
Year established: 1959
Activities: collects statistics on consumption of soft drinks
Chief officers: Alain Beaumont (General Secretary)
Membership: 26 international soft drinks associations
Publications:
• Statistics: *annual*
Notes: see : Union of National European Soft Drink Associations (UNESDA)

Confederation of Latin American Tourist Organisations (COTAL)

Confederación de Organizaciones Turísticas de la América Latina
Address: Viamonte 640, 8° piso, 1053 Buenos Aires, Argentina
Telephone: +54 1 322 4061/4001/3562
Fax: +54 1 393 5696/325 6171
Year established: 1957
Activities: organises an annual congress in various Latin American countries which it supplements with tourism exhibitions and marketing meetings; maintains relations with official tourism bodies throughout the region; progress in establishing permanent dialogue with representatives of the world's airlines through high-level commissions as well as in eliminating restrictions to the free movement of tourists in Latin American countries
Chief officers: Alvaro de la Espriella (President), Lic Eduardo Pantano (Executive Secretary)
Structure: non-profit making organisation
Membership: Full members: national travel associations from 21 countries; active members: individual travel agencies throughout Latin America; adherent members: companies involved in the tourism trade, national and regional tourism organisations, chambers of tourism and travel agencies outside Latin America; there are 16 Chapters (made up of members outside Latin America) throughout Europe, Asia, Africa, the Middle East, Australasia and North America
Publications:
• COTAL: La Revista del Turismo Total: *travel and tourism industry news - monthly*

Confederation of the Food and Drink Industries of the EU (CIAA)

Confédération des Industries Agro-Alimentaires de l'UE
Address: Boîte 9, Avenue des Arts 43, B-1040 Brussels, Belgium
Telephone: +32 2 514 1111
Fax: +32 2 511 2905
E-mail: ciaa@hebel.net
Year established: 1959
Activities: provides statistics on production, structure, trade and employment in the industry in the EU; represents the interests of the food and drink manufacturing industries active in the EU from a commercial, legal, scientific and technical point of view; presents CIAA policies and provides information on the industry to EU community and international organisations
Chief officers: Raymond Destin (Director General), Francis Gautier (President), Elisabeth Reynolds (Communication)
Membership: national federations from the 15 member countries of the EU and 36 sectorial organisations
Publications:
• European Packaging Waste Legislation
• Food and Drink Industry : a constant need, a constant challenge: *historical study of the industry*

● Food and Drink Industry in Figures: *statistics on production, structure, trade and employment in the food and drink industry in the EU - annual*
● Status Report on Food Legislation in the EU: *update of food and drink law current and pending - quarterly*

Confederation of the National Associations of Hotels, Restaurants and Cafés in the EU (Hotrec)
Confédération des Associations Nationales de l'Hôtellerie, de la Restauration et des Cafés de l' UE
Address: Boîte 4, Boulevard Anspach 111, B-1000 Brussels, Belgium
Telephone: +32 2 513 6323
Fax: +32 2 502 4173/2 513 8954
E-mail: hotrec@skynet.be
Activities: to maximise pan-European co-operation between members; to defend the interests of the European Horeca (hotels, restaurants, cafés) industry
Chief officers: Pierre Alax Turpault (President), Marguerite Sequaris (Secretary General), Niel Datta (Assistant Secretary General)
Membership: 31 national trade and employer associations
Publications:
● 100 Union measures affecting the HORECA Sector
● HORECA Sector and the European Union: *defines the role of Hotrec vis-à-vis the Institutions of the Union*
● Live from Brussels
● Training practices for and training needs of managers in the HORECA sector
Notes: The Association does not produce any statistics.

EuroCommerce
Address: Rue Froissart 123-133, B-1040 Brussels, Belgium
Telephone: +32 2 230 5874 /231 0799
Fax: +32 2 230 0078
E-mail: lobby@eurocommerce.be
Web site: www.eurocommerce.be
Year established: 1993
Activities: compiles general and limited statistics on multiple retailing in member countries; information service for members only on topical EU questions
Chief officers: Henrik H. Kröner (Secretary General)
Membership: the membership spans 20 countries in Europe, including national trade associations, companies and national and European sectorial trade associations of the retail, wholesale and international trade sectors
Publications:
● Annual Report of EuroCommerce: *available to members only - annual*
● EuroCommerce Newsletters: *in special cases made available to non-members - monthly*
● EuroCommerce Press Releases: *international trade, food law, social affairs, fiscal affairs… - annual*

European Adhesive Tapes Manufacturers' Association
Address: c/o Centre Français des Caoutchoucs et Polymères, 60 rue Auber, F-94408 Vitry-sur-Seine Cedex, France
Telephone: +33 1 496 05757
Fax: +33 1 452 10350
Year established: 1957
Activities: standardisation of test methods for adhesive tapes; determination of size standards for European production; annual meetings; seminars; contacts between manufacturers and their suppliers of raw materials
Chief officers: G Brisson (General Secretary/Treasurer), Ms Lechowicz (Assistant)
Structure: national groups, general assembly, steering committee; management secretariat
Membership: ca. 150 active members (European pressure sensitive tape manufacturers undertaking their own coating); honorary members (suppliers of raw materials etc.)

Publications:
● Glossary of Technical Terms
● List of Members
● Standards for Sizes
● Test Methods

European Adhesives Manufacturers' Federation (FEICA)
Fédération Européenne des Industries des Colles et Adhésifs/Verband Europäischer Klebstoffindustrien
Address: PO Box 23 01 69, Ivo-Beucker-Strasse 43, D-40237 Düsseldorf, Germany
Telephone: +49 211 679 3130
Fax: +49 211 679 3188
E-mail: mats.hagwall@feica.com
Web site: www.feica.com
Activities: General Assembly in September including an adhesives conference, working groups for the different fields of the adhesives business, e.g. hazardous products, packaging, standardisation
Chief officers: Mr Mats Hagwall (Permanent Secretary), Ansger Van Halteren (General Secretary)
Membership: adhesives associations in Austria, Belgium, Denmark, Finland, France, Germany, Italy, Netherlands, Norway, Portugal, Spain, Sweden, Switzerland and United Kingdom
Publications:
● Adhesives and Sealants
● Adhesives Classification Manual
● FEICA in brief: *annual*
● FEICA Newsletter: *quarterly*
● Statistics: *sales statistics for the member countries divided into market and product segments, usually completed in August each year - annual*

European Aluminium Association (EAA)
Association Européenne de l'Aluminium/Europäische Aluminium Vereinigung
Address: POB 1207, Avenue de Broqueville 12, B-1150 Brussels, Belgium
Telephone: +32 2 775 6311
Fax: +32 2 779 0531/2 779 2559
Year established: 1981
Activities: annual general assembly; annual press conference; quarterly statistics; information brochures; PR; standardisation; health and environment
Chief officers: D Dermer (President), M G Labberton (Public Relations Manager)
Membership: over 100 companies and associations throughout Europe, Japan and North America
Publications:
● EAA Aluminium News: *a review of trends in the European aluminium sector with statistics covering production, trade, and consumption. Based on returns from national member associations - quarterly*
● EAA Europe and Aluminium: *brochure*
● European Aluminium Statistics: *annual statistics, by country, on aluminium production, foreign trade, consumption, prices with comparative data for earlier years. Based on returns from national member associations - annual*

European Apparel and Textile Organisation (EURATEX)
Organisation Européenne de l'Habillement et du Textile
Address: Rue Montoyer 24, B-1000 Brussels, Belgium
Telephone: +32 2 285 4880
Fax: +32 2 230 6054
Year established: 1961
Activities: policy-making; research and technology; statistics and economic research; statistical enquiries; economic analyses; training
Chief officers: Guy Arnould (Director General), Ms Noël (Assistant Director General), Dominique Jacomet (President)

Membership: 57 members : national associations and companies
Publications:
• EURATEX-Bulletin: *news, articles, and some statistics on the textile industry and trade in European countries - five issues per year*

European Association for Festivals
Association Européenne des Festivals
Address: 120B rue de Lausanne, CH-1202 Geneva, Switzerland
Telephone: +41 22 732 2803
Fax: +41 22 738 4012
Year established: 1952
Chief officers: Frans de Ruiter (President), Henry Siegwart (Secretary General)
Membership: 63 European festival organisers (music, theatre, dance)
Publications:
• Annual List of European Arts Festivals: *annual*

European Association of Advertising Agencies (EAAA)
Address: 5 rue Saint-Quentin, B-1000 Brussels, Belgium
Telephone: +32 2 280 1603
Fax: +32 2 230 0966
Year established: 1959
Activities: annual conference (May); EAAA fact file - database on advertising legislation in member countries, compiles statistics on advertising expenditure in Europe
Chief officers: Albert Winninghoff (President)
Structure: council with representatives from all members, president; day to day running by director general
Membership: 19 multinational agencies and 24 national associations (this represents around 2,000 agencies in total; about 80% of all marketing communications in Europe)
Publications:
• Laws and Regulations on Advertising in Europe: *legislative, administrative and voluntary controls on advertising in 21 European countries - 2 volumes loose-leaf*

European Association of Automotive Suppliers (CLEPA)
Address: Boîte 1, Boulevard Brand Whitlock 87, B-1200 Brussels, Belgium
Telephone: +32 2 743 9130
Fax: +32 2 732 0055
E-mail: clepa@pophost.eunet.be / eaas@pophost.eunet,be
Web site: www.clepa-eaas.org
Year established: 1959
Activities: JAMA-CLEPA conferences; training programmes
Chief officers: Raip Bergner (Managing Director), Dr Motele Kalk (Secretary General), Marie Siraut (Communication)
Membership: 13 national associations including: Belgium; Denmark; France; Germany; Italy; Netherlands; Poland; Spain; Sweden and the United Kingdom as well as 60 corporate members

European Association of Canned and Preserved Fruit and Vegetable Industries (AIFLV)
Association de l'Industrie des Fruits et Légumes au Vinaigre, en Saumure, à l'Huile et des Produits Similaires de l'UE
Address: Avenue de Roodebeek 30, B-1030 Brussels, Belgium
Telephone: +32 2 743 8730
Fax: +32 2 736 8175
Chief officers: C.J.J. Koeleman (President),Michael Coenen (Secretary General)
Membership: 6 organisations throughout the EU representing the canned and preserved fruit and vegetables industry

Publications:
• List of Members
Notes: The Association does not produce any statistics.

European Association of Co-operative Banks
Groupement Européen des Banques Coopératives/Europäische Vereinigung der Genossenschaftsbanken
Address: Boîte 9, Rue de la Science 23-25, B-1040 Brussels, Belgium
Telephone: +32 2 230 1124
Fax: +32 2 230 0649
Year established: 1970
Activities: takes part in European Conference on Social economy; co-founded the International Cooperative Banking Association in 1992; statistics; active member of the Coordinating Committee of EU Cooperative Associations (CCACC)
Chief officers: Mr W. Grüger (President), Johann-G. von Süsskind (Secretary General), Olivier Rohlfs (Assistant Secretary General), W. Meijer (Vice President), E. Pflimlin (Vice President)
Membership: 24 co-operative banks in 14 EU member states, 6 associate members in 5 other European countries, 2 correspondent members
Publications:
• Activity Report: *biennial*
• Information Leaflet

European Association of Consumer Electronics Manufacturers (EACEM)
Address: Boîte 6, Avenue Louise 140, B-1050 Brussels, Belgium
Telephone: +32 2 644 2681
Fax: +32 2 640 4409
E-mail: info@eacem.be
Web site: www.eacem.be
Year established: 1979
Activities: collects industry statistics
Chief officers: Gerard J. Nauwelaerts (Secretary General), Rony van Haegenbergh (Technical Director)
Membership: 22 consumer electronics manufacturers and 7 trade associations
Publications:
• European Production and Market Figures
• Newsletter: *monthly*
• Statistical Document: *annual statistics, collected by the Association, covering production, sales, and imports and exports for various product categories. Some data for earlier years given - annual*

European Association of Directory Publishers (EADP)
Association Européenne des Editeurs d'Annuaires
Address: Box 17, Avenue Louise 363, B-1050 Brussels, Belgium
Telephone: +32 2 646 3060
Fax: +32 2 646 3637
E-mail: 10145.2661@compuserve.com
Web site: www.worldyellowpages.com:80/eadp/
Year established: 1966
Activities: organises a congress each year attended by directory publishers world-wide
Chief officers: Anne Lerat (Secretary-general), Ken Burton (President)
Membership: 150 members in 24 countries: directory publishing houses based in Europe, national associations of directory publishers and directory publishers outside Europe, as well as suppliers of products and services to the industry
Publications:
• Directories in Europe: *list of members - annual*
• Newsletter of the European Association of Directory Publishers: *quarterly*

European Association of Flexible Polyurethane Foam Blocks Manufacturers (EUROPUR)

Association des Producteurs de Blocs de Mousses Souples de Polyuréthane

Address: c/o Fédération des Industries Chimiques de Belgique, Square Marie-Louise 49, B-1000 Brussels, Belgium
Telephone: +32 2 238 9869
Fax: +32 2 238 9998
Telex: B23167
Year established: 1968
Activities: research on environment and security; collects statistics on production of flexible polyurethane foam blocks
Chief officers: Théo Speeleveld (Secretary General)
Membership: 14 national associations from Belgium, Denmark, France, Germany, Italy, Netherlands, Portugal, Spain, Sweden, United Kingdom
Publications:
● Directory: *lists all members - annual*

European Association of Fruit and Vegetable Juice Industries (AIJN)

Association de l'Industrie des Jus et Nectars de Fruits et de Légumes de l'UE

Address: Avenue de Roodebeek 30, B-1030 Brussels, Belgium
Telephone: +32 2 743 8730
Fax: +32 2 736 8175
Year established: 1958
Chief officers: Pieter Eckes (President), J. Roclore (Vice President), Jan Hermans (Secretary General)
Membership: 14 national associations from Belgium, Denmark, Germany, Greece, Ireland, Italy, Netherlands, Portugal and UK
Publications:
● Code of Practice: *legislation affecting the European fruit and vegetable juice industry*
Notes: The Association does not produce any statistics.

European Association of Industries of Branded Products (AIM)

Association des Industries de Marques

Address: Avenue des Gaulois 9, B-1040 Brussels, Belgium
Telephone: +32 2 736 0305
Fax: +32 2 734 6702
E-mail: brand@aim.be
Chief officers: Alain Galaski (Director General), Frans Tummers (President)
Membership: 51 companies and 17 national associations in Europe
Notes: The Association does not produce statistics. Publications are only available to members.

European Association of Livestock Markets (AEMB)

Association Européenne des Marchés aux Bestiaux

Address: Rue de la Loi 81a, B-1040 Brussels, Belgium
Telephone: +32 2 230 8698
Fax: +32 2 230 9400
E-mail: uecbv@pophost.eunet.be
Chief officers: Gilles Rousseau (President), Jean-Luc Meriaux (Communication)
Membership: 15 national federations
Publications:
● Reportoire des Marchés aux Bestiaux Membres de l'AEMB: *a review of the animal production and meat markets in Europe based on data supplied by member organisations - annual*

European Association of Manufacturers of Business Machines and Information Technology Industry (EUROBIT)

Europäischer Verband der Büro- und informationstechnischen Industrie

Address: POB 710109, Lyoner Strasse 18, D-60528 Frankfurt am Main, Germany
Telephone: +49 69 6603 1530
Fax: +49 69 6603 1510
E-mail: FVIT@FVIT-eurobit.de
Web site: www.fvit-eurobit.de/def-euro.htm
Year established: 1947
Chief officers: Dr. Bruno Lamborghini (President), Günther E. W. Möller (Secretary General)
Membership: almost 100 per cent of European manufacturers in the field of business machines, information technology and telecommunications terminal equipment, including hardware, software and services. It is the only association in Western Europe providing comprehensive representation for the whole IT sector on a European and international basis
Publications:
● Statistics (EUROBIT) (Statistik): *statistics are collected on the production and markets for business machines and electronic data processing equipment. National organisations across Europe are members - annual*

European Association of Manufactures of Processed Cheese (ASSIFONTE)

Association de l'Industrie de la Fonte de Fromage de l'UE

Address: Godesberger Allee 157, D-53175 Bonn, Germany
Telephone: +49 228 959 690
Fax: +49 228 371 535
Chief officers: Mr Eberhard Hetzner

European Association of Perfumery Retailers

Federation Europeenne des Parfumeurs Detaillants

Address: An de Engelsburg 1, D-45657 Recklinghausen, Germany
Telephone: +49 236 19248
Fax: +49 236 1924888
Chief officers: Werner Hariagel (Director)

European Association of Refrigeration Enterprises (AEEF)

Address: Avenue de Broqueville 272, Bte 4, 1200 Brussels, Belgium
Telephone: +32 2 771 3635
Fax: +32 2 762 9425
Chief officers: Philippe Binard (Secretary General)

European Association of Syrups Manufacturers (EASM)

Association Européenne des Fabricants de Sirops

Address: Avenue de Roodebeek 30, B-1030 Brussels, Belgium
Telephone: +32 2 743 8730
Fax: +32 2 736 8175
Chief officers: Mr van Dijkman (President); Jan Hermans (Secretary General)
Membership: 8 companies and associations in Europe
Publications:
● List of Members
Notes: The Association does not produce statistics.

European Association of the Margarine Industry (IMACE)

Association des Industries Margarinières des Pays de l'Union Européenne
Address: Boîte 3, 74 rue de la Loi, B-1040 Brussels, Belgium
Telephone: +32 2 230 4810
Fax: +32 2 230 2274
Year established: 1958
Activities: annual conference, technical working groups: hygiene, claims and fat spreads
Chief officers: Janet Nunn (Secretary General)
Membership: 11 national associations in Belgium, Germany, Denmark, Spain, France, Greece, Italy, Ireland, Norway, Portugal and United Kingdom
Publications:
• Annual Report (European Association of the Margarine Industry): *commentary and statistics on trends in the margarine industry in the EU with some data on production and trade - annual*
• Newsletter of the European Association of the Margarine Industry: *quarterly*
• Trade Sources: *annual*

European Broadcasting Union (EBU)

Union Européenne de Radio-Télévision
Address: Case Postale 67, Ancienne Route 17A, CH 1218 Grand-Saconnex (GE), Switzerland
Telephone: +41 22 717 2719
Fax: +41 22 717 2727
E-mail: dvb@ebu.ch
Web site: www.ebu.ch
Year established: 1950
Activities: Eurovision and Euroradio news and programmes, technical documents and information sheets, technical monographs, reports of conferences and seminars; data and reference centre; communications division
Chief officers: Albert Scharf (President), X. Goyou-Beauchamps, I Mathhé, E Forde (Vice Presidents), Jean-Bernard Münch (Secretary General)
Membership: European broadcasting associations and companies - 63 active members in 48 countries, 52 associate members in 32 countries
Publications:
• Diffusion: *quarterly*
• EBU Technical Review: *quarterly*
• European Transmitter Lists: *long and medium wave, FM and television*
• Statistics (EBU): *based on replies from active members - annual*
Notes: OIRT (former Soviet Bloc Broadcasting Union) merged with EBU in 1993

European Brush Federation (FEIBP)

Fédération Européenne de l'Industrie de la Brosserie et de la Pinceauterie
Address: 109-111 rue Royale, B-1000 Brussels, Belgium
Telephone: +32 2 217 6365
Fax: +32 2 217 5904
Chief officers: Mr van Steertegen (Director)

European Business Aviation Association (EBAA)

Address: Building 28, Brussels National Airport, B-1930 Zaventem, Belgium
Telephone: +32 2 721 4272
Fax: +32 2 721 2158
Year established: 1977
Activities: annual meeting
Chief officers: Fernand M Francois (Chief Executive officer), Carine Jacobs (administrative Manager)
Membership: ca. 200 members, including national associations and companies

Publications:
• Bulletin: *bi-monthly*
• Worldwide Business Aviation Fleet: *statistics - annual*

European Car and Truck Rental Association (ECATRA)

Europäischer Verband für PKW und LKW Vermietung
Address: Grafenberger Allee 363, D-40235 Düsseldorf, Germany
Telephone: +49 211 685 373
Fax: +49 211 660 571
Year established: 1964
Activities: promotes the mutual exchange of experience, influences legislation;coordinates and supports the work and profitability of national associations and their member companies on an international level; organises annual assembly of delegates
Chief officers: Frederick H Aldous (President), Klaus Langmann-Keller (Secretary General)
Membership: 18 national associations from Austria, Belgium, Denmark, France, Germany, Greece, Ireland, Israel, Italy, Luxembourg, Malta, Netherlands, Norway, Portugal, Spain, Sweden, Switzerland, United Kingdom
Publications:
• ECATRA Brochure
• ECATRA News: *bi-monthly*
• ECATRA Statistical Survey: *general statistics on car and truck rental - biennial*
• European Statistical Survey: *a regular report with data on the vehicle rental sector in specific countries. Based on a survey by the Association in its 19 member countries across Europe - biennial*
• Membership List

European Carpet Association (ECA)

Address: Rue Montoyer 24, B-1000 Brussels, Belgium
Telephone: +32 2 280 1813
Fax: +32 2 280 1809
Activities: collects statistics on production and sales
Chief officers: Simon van de Vrande (Director)
Membership: national associations representing the carpet industry
Notes: The Association does not produce any publications.

European Chemical Industry Federation (CEFIC)

Conseil Européen des Fédérations de l'Industrie Chimique
Address: POB 1, Avenue Van Nieuwenhuyse 4, B-1160 Brussels, Belgium
Telephone: +32 2 676 7211
Fax: +32 2 676 7300
Telex: 62444
E-mail: mail@cefic.be
Web site: www.cefic.be/
Year established: 1972
Activities: conference; library; information service; statistics
Chief officers: Hugo Lever (Director General); Jean-Marie Devos (Secretary General); Mike Cockburn (Director Communications)
Structure: secretariat; steering committees, high level strategy groups, task forces, working parties and working groups
Membership: national chemical industry federations of 22 countries in Europe and large international companies, representing about 30,000 large, medium and small chemical companies in Europe
Publications:
• Annual Report of the European Chemical Industry Federation: *review of year, includes overview of CEFIC priorities and activity of statutory bodies, activity report, some statistics and list of members - annual*
• Basic Economic Statistics of the European Chemical Industry: *production data for various European countries*

based on national statistical sources - annual
● CEFIC Focus: *outline of the organisation, including its objectives and role, statutory bodies, secretariat, committees and groups, affiliated organisations, related organisations*
● Economic Bulletin: *quarterly*
● Facts and Figures: *basic statistics on European Chemical industry trends, including production, consumption, and trade - annual*
● ICE News: *news on the european chemical industry - ad hoc*
● Publications List: *includes monographs, periodicals, position papers and annual reports*
● Situation and Outlook of the European Chemical Industry: *a review of the European chemical industry with an appraisal of the future prospects for the sector - annual*
● Statutes and By-Laws
Notes: Member of the International Council of Chemical Associations (ICCA)

European Chilled Food Federation

Address: c/o ETL, PL115, Pasilankatu 2, Helsinki, SF-00241, Finland
Telephone: +358 9 1488 7228
Fax: +358 9 1488 7201
Membership: trade organisation for manufacturers in the European chilled food sector

European Chips and Snacks Association (ECSA)

Address: Swiss Centre, 10 Wardour Street, London W1V 3HG, United Kingdom
Telephone: +44 171 439 2567
Fax: +44 171 439 2673
Membership: national organisations in Germany, Netherlands, United Kingdom

European Committee for Private Hospitals (CEHP)

Comité Européen de l'Hospitalisation Privée
Address: 5 Avenue A Solvay, B-1700 Brussels, Belgium
Telephone: +32 2 660 3550
Fax: +32 2 647 7283
Year established: 1972
Activities: information service; sector studies
Chief officers: M Frova (Secretary General)
Membership: 7 national associations of private health care institutions
Publications:
● Monographs

European Committee of Manufacturers of Domestic Electrical Equipment (CECED)

Address: c/o ANIE, Via Alessandro Algardi 2, I-20148 Milan, Italy
Telephone: +39 2 326 4299
Fax: +39 2 326 4212
Year established: 1959
Activities: studies and research
Chief officers: Mr Hasse (President)
Membership: 12 national associations

European Committee of Sugar Manufacturers

Comité Européen des Fabricants de Sucre
Address: Avenue de Tervueren 182, B-1150 Brussels, Belgium
Telephone: +32 2 762 0760
Fax: +32 2 771 0026
E-mail: cefs@infoboard.be
Web site: www.ib.be/cefs/
Year established: 1954
Activities: collects statistics on beet yield, sugar yield, beet processing, beet production, cane sugar, consumption, duties and taxes, import, export, number of factories, number of sugar and refinery companies, sugar factories and daily capacity, production of molasses, production of pulp and white sugar production
Chief officers: Jules Beauduin (General Manager)
Membership: the CEFS represents all beet-sugar manufacturers in the European Union, plus Switzerland and refiners processing raw cane-sugar imported from overseas into white sugar (France, Portugal, United Kingdom); its members are the national trade associations and sugar companies themselves when a Member State has only one or two such companies
Publications:
● Statistics Booklet (European Committee of Sugar Manufacturers): *statistics on sugar production, consumption, and foreign trade based on data collected by the Committee. Data on specific European countries - annual*

European Computer Manufacturers' Association (ECMA)

Address: Rue du Rhone 114, CH-1204 Geneva, Switzerland
Telephone: +41 22 849 6000
Fax: +41 22 849 6001
Web site: www.ecma.ch

European Confederation of Brewers (CBMC)

Confédération des Brasseurs du Marché Commun
Address: Boîte 20, Chaussée de la Hulpe 181, B-1170 Brussels, Belgium
Telephone: +32 2 672 2392
Fax: +32 2 660 9402/2 675 1729
E-mail: infos@cbmc.org
Web site: www.cbmc.org
Web site notes: site includes comprehensive statistics on the European beer industry including production, consumption, sales by type, imports, exports, beer duty etc.
Year established: 1958
Activities: government and EU liaison, collects statistics on production, consumption, import, export, number of breweries, etc.
Chief officers: Dr Richard Weber (President), Rodolphe de Looz-Corswarem (Secretary General)
Structure: Council of Delegates, Heads of Delegation, Secretaries General
Membership: 17 national brewing associations including 15 European Union members as well as Switzerland and Norway
Publications:
● Beer in Figures (La Bière en Chiffres): *statistics on the European beer industry - annual*
● Statistiques CBMC: *a statistical brochure with basic data on brewing and beer including data on production, consumption, foreign trade, and taxes - annual*

European Confederation of Linen and Hemp Industries

Confédération Européenne du Lin et du Chanvre
Address: 27 boulevard Malesherbes, F-75008 Paris, France
Telephone: +33 1 426 65005
Fax: +33 1 426 66365
Chief officers: Benoît Hubert (Secretary General)

European Confederation of Paint, Printing Ink and Artists' Colours Manufacturers' Associations (CEPE)

Confédération Européenne des Associations de Fabricants de Peintures, Encres et Couleurs d'Art
Address: BP 10, Avenue Van Nieuwenhuyse 4, B-1160 Brussels, Belgium
Telephone: +32 2 676 7480
Fax: +32 2 676 7490
Year established: 1951
Chief officers: Jean Schöder (Secretary General), Pr Rankl

(President)
Membership: 22 national associations in 16 countries and 16 corporate associate members, representing a total of over 1,200 paint and 200 printing ink companies
Publications:
• CEPE - a Multicoloured Europe: *brochure about the association and the industries it represents*

European Confederation of Spirits Producers (CEPS)

Confédération Européenne des Producteurs de Spiritueux
Address: Boîte 3, Avenue de Tervueren 192, B-1150 Brussels, Belgium
Telephone: +32 2 779 2423
Fax: +32 2 772 9820
Year established: 1993
Activities: collects statistics on production
Chief officers: Clive Wilkinson (President), Valérie Corre (Director)
Membership: 35 national associations from 19 countries including the 15 EU countries
Publications:
• Annual Report: *annual*
• Newsflash: *monthly*
Notes: Previously part of the Union Européenne des Alcools, Eaux-de-Vie et Spiritueux, which represented both alcohol and spirits producers.

European Confederation of the Footwear Industry (CEC)

Confédération Européenne de l'Industrie de la Chaussure
Address: 53 rue François Bossaerts, B-1030 Brussels, Belgium
Telephone: +32 2 736 5810
Fax: +32 2 736 1276
Year established: 1958
Activities: produces annual statistics leaflet - available to non-members
Chief officers: Roeland Smets (Managing Director), L Rossi (President)
Membership: national associations from Belgium, Denmark, France, Germany, Ireland, Italy, Netherlands, Portugal, Spain, United Kingdom
Publications:
• Statistical Leaflet: *annual*
• Statistics (CEC): *statistics on footwear production and the footwear market in various European countries. The Confederation comprises footwear associations in various countries - annual*

European Confederation of Tobacco Retailers (CEDT)

Confédération Européenne des Distributeurs de Tabac
Address: Avenue Marcel Thiry 204, B-1200 Brussels, Belgium
Telephone: +32 2 774 9610
Fax: +32 2 774 9690
Chief officers: Poul Hansen

European Confederation of Woodworking Industries (CEI Bois)

Confédération Européenne des Industries du Bois
Address: Rue Royale 109-111, B-1000 Brussels, Belgium
Telephone: +32 2 217 6365
Fax: +32 2 217 5904
Telex: 64143
E-mail: euro.wood.fed@skynet.be
Year established: 1952
Chief officers: Dr Guy Van Steertegem (Secretary General), Filip De Jaeger (Assistant Secretary General), V. Aelterman (Secretary)
Membership: 14 national woodworking federations
Notes: statistics and publications only for members

European Cosmetic, Toiletry and Perfumery Association (COLIPA)

Address: Rue du Congrès 5-7, B-1000 Brussels, Belgium
Telephone: +32 2 227 6610
Fax: +32 2 227 6627
E-mail: colipa@colipa.be
Year established: 1962 ~ 2002 40th
Activities: general assembly; limited statistical data compiled annually in September covering ex-factory sales for EU markets, distribution channels, product categories; publishes guidelines and information
Chief officers: Robert Vanhove (Secretary General), Rory Macmillan (Communication & Information Manager), John Sharpe (President), Spyros Georgantos (Vice President)
Membership: 22 national associations and 24 multinationals
Publications:
• Colipa Annual Report: *contains statistics - annual*
• COLIPA News: *quarterly*
• COLIPA Statistics: *detailed statistics on the cosmetics, toiletry, and perfumery sectors in Europe with data for specific countries - annual*

European Council of Vinyl Manufacturers (ECVM), PVC Information Council

Address: Box 4, Avenue E Van Nieuwenhuyse 4, B-1160 Brussels, Belgium
Telephone: +32 2 675 2971
Fax: +32 2 675 3935
Web site: www.pvc.org
Year established: 1988
Activities: provides an information resource for organisations and individuals interested in environmental, technical and socio-economic issues surrounding PVC and its role in society; collects market figures
Chief officers: Frédéric Sevenster (Chairman), John R Svalander (Director)
Membership: 12 leading European manufacturers of PVC
Notes: ECVM is a division of the Association of Plastics Manufacturers in Europe (APME). Both APME and ECVM in turn fall under the umbrella of the European chemical industry body, the European Chemical Industry Council (CEFIC).

European Crop Protection Association (ECPA)

Address: 79a Avenue Albert Lancaster, B-1180 Brussels, Belgium
Telephone: +32 2 375 6860
Fax: +32 2 375 2793
Telex: 62120
Year established: 1992
Activities: statistics, various publications covering plant protection, organic farming, health effects of pesticides
Chief officers: Konstantinos P Vlahodimos (Director General), Alain Godard (President), Gordon Baker (Chairman), Andrée Dooms (communications officer), Dr Ron Gardiner (technical Director), Dick Oosthuizen (Policy and Trade Director)
Structure: secretariat, board of directors, working groups
Membership: 18 national associations and 15 member companies in EU, other Europe, Hungary and Turkey
Publications:
• Annual Report of the European Crop Protection Association (ECPA): *general information on the association's activities in the year, details about the association, its publications, some industry statistics, etc. - annual*
• Membership List
• Publications List (European Crop Protection Association): *contains a range of easy to read publications which summarise the results of studies carried out by outside experts on behalf of the organisation. Each provides a detailed résumé of its topic and no prior knowledge is assumed*

European Dairy Association (EDA)

Association Laitière Européenne
Address: Rue Montoyer 14, B-1000 Bruxelles, Belgium
Telephone: +32 2 549 5040
Fax: +32 2 549 5049
E-mail: eda@arcadis.be
Activities: collects statistics on dairy products, available only to members
Chief officers: A.J. Van de Ven (Secretary General), Bénédicte Masure (Trade and Economic Officer), Christophe Wolff (Legislation Officer)
Membership: 15 European national associations
Publications:
● Dairy Telegraph: *fortnightly*
● Rapport Annuel: *annual*

European Dessert Mixes Manufacturers' Association (EDMMA)

Association des Fabricants Européens de Poudres pour Entremets, Desserts et Produits Divers
Address: Avenue de Roodebeek 30, B-1030 Brussels, Belgium
Telephone: +32 2 743 8730
Fax: +32 2 736 8175
Chief officers: J. Holt (President), J. van de Wetering (Vice President), Michael Coenen (Secretary General)
Membership: 4 European dessert mixes manufacturers
Publications:
● List of Members
Notes: The Association does not produce statistics.

European Disposables and Nonwoven Association (EDANA)

Address: Avenue E. Plasky 157, B-1030 Brussels, Belgium
Telephone: +32 2 734 9310
Fax: +32 2 733 3518
Year established: 1971
Activities: INDEX exhibition and congress every 3 years; statistics on production, consumption of raw materials
Chief officers: Guy Massenaux (Secretary General), Pierre Wiertz (Industry Affairs Director), Henri Potier (Technical Director)
Membership: 150 members in 21 countries (manufacturers of non wovens, disposable soft goods and suppliers of raw materials)
Publications:
● INDEX Congress papers: *set of 14 volumes (can be ordered separately)*

European Economic Union Fish Processors' Association (AIPCEE)

Association des Industries du Poisson de l'UE
Address: Avenue de Roodebeek 30, B-1030 Brussels, Belgium
Telephone: +32 2 743 8730
Fax: +32 2 736 8175
Year established: 1959
Activities: collects statistics on white fish
Chief officers: A. Thomas (President), G. Pieters (Vice President), Michael Coenan (Secretary General)
Membership: 20 national associations - Belgium, Denmark, France, Germany, Ireland, Italy, Netherlands, Portugal, Spain, United Kingdom
Publications:
● Etude Poissons Blancs: *statistical survey on white fish - annual*

European Electronic Component Manufacturers' Association (EECA)

Address: Boîte 6, Avenue Louise 140, B-1050 Brussels, Belgium
Telephone: +32 2 646 5695/ 2646 1151
Fax: +32 2 644 4088
Activities: collects statistics on the European market (twice a year) and on production, imports, exports (once a year)
Chief officers: Harry L. Tee (President), Eckhard Runge (Secretary General)
Membership: 10 national associations in Europe
Publications:
● European Electronic Components Industry Report: *annual*

European Employers Federation of Yeast Manufacturers

Comité des Fabricants de Levure de Panification de l'UE
Address: 15 rue du Louvre, F-75001 Paris, France
Telephone: +33 1 450 85482
Fax: +33 1 422 10214
Chief officers: André de Schepper (Chairman), M. Jongejan (Treasurer), J.P. Loup (Secretary)
Membership: 12 associations of yeast manufacturers from 12 European countries

European Federation of Aerosol Associations (FEA)

Address: Square Marie-Louise 49, B-1040 Brussels, Belgium
Telephone: +32 2 238 9877
Fax: +32 2 280 0929
Year established: 1959
Activities: conferences, exhibitions, information service for members; import/export, production and consumption data
Chief officers: Pierre Costa (Secretary General), Ms Gomez (Communication Manager)
Structure: 4 committees: public relations, environment, packaging, industrial security
Membership: 17 national aerosol associations including Austria, Belgium, Denmark, Finland, France, Germany, Greece, Italy, Ireland, Netherlands, Norway, Portugal, Spain, Sweden, Switzerland and the UK
Publications: ·
● Aerosol Europe: *monthly*
● FEA Bulletin: *monthly*
● FEA Yearbook: *includes statistics on the number of aerosols filled in Europe, by product type. Based on returns from member associations in various countries - annual*
● Spray Report: *8 p.a.*
● Statistics: *annual*

European Federation of Associations of Health Product Manufacturers (EHPM)

Europäische Vereinigung der Verbände der Reformwarenhersteller
Address: POB 2445, Schwedenpfad 2, D-61348 Bad Homburg, Germany
Telephone: +49 6172 240 64
Fax: +49 6172 215 98
Web site: www.ehpm.org
Year established: 1975
Activities: two general meetings a year; circulation of research and information of relevance to the health product industry; representation to the council and commissions of the EU
Chief officers: Maurice Hanssen (President), R A Wolfgang Reinsch (General Secretary)
Membership: 15 national associations in Europe, 5 associate members outside Europe. The Association is comprised of 750 health product manufacturers throughout Europe and 2500 companies world-wide manufacturing health promoting products, including: food supplements in tablet, capsule or liquid form, vitamins and minerals, other nutrients and/or

herbs; natural and traditional remedies; whole foods and foods for special diets; natural cosmetics; organic products
Publications:
• EHPM - Federation News

European Federation of Associations of Particleboard Manufacturers (FESYP)

Fédération Européenne des Syndicats de Fabricants de Panneaux de Particules/Europäische Föderation der Verbände des Spanplattenindustrie
Address: Rue de l'Association 15, B-1000 Brussels, Belgium
Telephone: +32 2 223 1144
Fax: +32 2 219 4444
E-mail: euro.wood.fed@skynet.be
Year established: 1958
Activities: supplies its members with quarterly statistics on production and foreign trade in Europe; collects statistics on production, imports, exports, consumption (apparent and real), stocks, structure of sales, breaks down production data into raw and surface improved particleboard as well as raw wood consumption
Chief officers: Guy Van Steertegem (Secretary General), Ilse van den Akker (Economic Advisor), Kris Wijnendaele (Advisor of Technical and Environemental Affairs)
Membership: 18 national associations
Publications:
• Annual Report of the European Federation of Associations of Particle Board Manufacturers: *contains extensive statistics on production, export, import, employment etc. of the woodworking industry in Europe; addresses of all members, associated members and collaborating institutes; business cards for each FESYP member country - annual*
• FESYP Info: *information brochures - 6 p.a.*
• Statistics: *quarterly*

European Federation of Building Societies (EFBS)

Fédération Européenne d'Epargne et de Crédit pour le Logement - Europäische Bausparkassenvereinigung
Address: POB 15 01 55, D-53040 Bonn, Dottendorfer Straße 82, D-53129 Bonn, Germany
Telephone: +49 228 239 041
Fax: +49 228 239 046
Year established: 1962
Activities: congresses; advice and support to fledgling states of Eastern and Central Europe in the development of a working housing finance system
Chief officers: Dr Paul Oppitz (President), Andreas J Zehnder (Managing Director)
Structure: general assembly, council of management, legal affairs committee, housing policy and marketing committee
Membership: 16 participating members and 51 corresponding members in 17 countries
Publications:
• Annual Report of the European Federation of Building Societies (EFBS): *includes some statistics - annual*
• Circulars
• Directory of Members
• Newsletter of the European Federation of Building Societies (EFBS): *quarterly*

European Federation of Chemical Trade (FECC)

Address: Square Marie-Louise 49, B-1000 Brussels, Belgium
Telephone: +32 2 238 9711
Fax: +32 2 230 8288
Year established: 1959
Activities: annual conference; information service for members
Chief officers: Dr B Stephan (Secretary General), Pierre Costa (Head of Permanent Office to EU), Mr de Beco (President)
Membership: 20 national associations

Publications:
• European Federation of the Chemical Trade Newsletter: *bi-monthly*
Notes: The Association does not produce any statistics.

European Federation of Corrugated Board Manufacturers (FEFCO)

Fédération Européenne des Fabricants de Carton Ondulé
Address: 37 rue d'Amsterdam, F-75008 Paris, France
Telephone: +33 1 532 06680
Fax: +33 1 428 29707
Year established: 1952
Activities: biennial technical seminar, marketing seminar, congress, compiles statistics
Chief officers: Jean Pierre Lardillon (General Secretary), Bernard Rossmann (President)
Membership: 20 active members (national associations) and 300 associate members (suppliers)
Publications:
• Annual Report of the European Federation of Corrugated Board Manufacturers (FEFCO): *includes statistics on corrugated board over a nine year review period. Covers average production of corrugated board per capita and total shipments for 19 European markets - annual*

European Federation of Frozen Food Products (Syndigel)

Fédération Européenne du Commerce de Produits Surgelés
Address: 18 rue de la Pépinière, F-75008 Paris, France
Telephone: +33 1 530 43343
Fax: +33 1 530 43346
Year established: 1973
Activities: information service for members
Chief officers: Danielle Lo Stimolo (Managing Director)
Membership: 100 wholesalers and retailers
Notes: The Federation does not produce any statistics or publications.

European Federation of Glass Packaging (FEVE)

Fédération Européenne du Verre d'Emballage
Address: Avenue Louise 89, B-1050 Brussels, Belgium
Telephone: +32 2 539 3434
Fax: +32 2 539 3752
Year established: 1977
Chief officers: A Smoggi (Secretary General)
Membership: manufacturers of glass packaging

European Federation of Medium-Sized and Major Retailers (FEMGED)

Fédération Européenne des Moyennes et Grandes Entreprises de Distribution
Address: Avenue Edouard Lacomblé 17, B-1040 Brussels, Belgium
Telephone: +32 2 736 0404
Fax: +32 2 732 5360
Year established: 1959
Activities: no statistical services; publishes occasional circulars and newsletters
Chief officers: Claude Droulans (Secretary General), Theodor Althoff (Chairman)
Membership: 3 national federations and 20 companies
Publications:
• Circulars and Newsletters: *monthly*

European Federation of Perfumery Retailers (FEPD)

Address: POB 103-246, D-33532 Bielefeld, Germany
Telephone: +49 521 964 470
Fax: +49 521 964 4770

Year established: 1960
Activities: annual congress, internal information service
Chief officers: Reinhard Dieterwolf (President)
Membership: 12 national perfumery retailers' associations from Austria, Belgium, Denmark, France, Germany, Italy, Luxembourg, Netherlands, Norway, Spain, Sweden, Switzerland

European Federation of Pharmaceutical Industries Association (EFPIA)

Address: Boîte 91, Avenue Louise 250, B-1050 Brussels, Belgium
Telephone: +32 2 640 6815
Fax: +32 2 626 2566
Year established: 1978
Activities: represents the pharmaceuticals industry in Europe through contact with international governmental organisations; bi-annual conference (open to the public)
Chief officers: Brian Ager (Director General)
Membership: 16 national associations in Austria, Belgium, Denmark, Finland, France, Germany, Greece, Ireland, Italy, Netherlands, Norway, Portugal, Spain, Sweden, Switzerland, United Kingdom
Publications:
• Annual Report of the European Federation of Pharmaceutical Industries Association (EFPIA): *annual*
• Brief Guide to EU Directives Concerning Medicines: *overview of the existing legislation and existing and soon to be presented proposals*
• Completing the International Market for Pharmaceuticals: *memoranda on restoration of effective patent terms for pharmaceticals*
• EFPIA in Figures: *a general review of trends in the European pharmaceutical industry with data on specific countries. Based on returns from national associations - annual*
• Flash : *quarterly*

European Federation of Vending Machine Associations (Euromat)

Fédération Européenne des Associations de l'Automatique
Address: Boîte 4, Place Princesse Elisabeth 44, B-1030 Brussels, Belgium
Telephone: +32 2 245 5604
Fax: +32 2 245 5370
Year established: 1980
Activities: collects statistics on trading
Chief officers: Hans Rosenzweig (President), Nathalie Laglae (Secretary)
Membership: 22 national associations of manufacturers and traders of vending machines
Publications:
• Newsletter of the European Federation of Vending Machine Associations: *monthly*

European Federation of Wine and Spirit Importers and Distributors (Wine and Spirits Importers Group)

Address: Van Eeghenlaan 27, NL-1071 EN Amsterdam, Netherlands
Telephone: +31 20 673 0331/673 1654
Fax: +31 20 664 5466
Year established: 1973
Activities: statistics; standardisation; legalisation; marketing and training
Structure: general assembly, board
Membership: national associations in 7 countries, each representing over 60% of its countries' imports

European Federation of Wooden Pallet and Packaging Manufacturers (FEFPED)

Fédération Européenne des Fabricants de Palettes et Embalages en Bois
Address: POBox 90154, NL-5000 LG Tilburg, Netherlands
Telephone: +31 13 594 4802
Fax: +31 13 594 4749
E-mail: fefpeb@vsam.spaendonck.nl
Year established: 1946
Activities: produces statistics on production
Chief officers: Mr Alphonse JM Ceelaert (Secretary General)
Membership: 10 national associations representing wooden pallet, packaging and export packing companies
Publications:
• Newsbox

European Feed Manufacturers' Association (FEFAC)

Address: Boîte 3, Rue de la Loi 223, B-1040 Brussels, Belgium
Telephone: +32 2 285 0050
Fax: +32 2 230 5722
E-mail: 106456.3373@compuserve.com
Year established: 1959
Activities: collects statistics on production, consumption, prices
Chief officers: Alexander Döring (Secretary General), Pat Lake (President)
Membership: 15 national associations
Publications:
• Chiffres-Clé de l'Industie Européenne des Aliments Composés: *key figures of the European feed industry*
• Feed & Food: *statistics on production, consumption, prices*
• Guide Tarifaire GATT de la FEFAC pour l'industrie des aliments composés: *guide for prices*
• L'Importance Economique de l'Elevage dans l'Union Européenne
• Liste d'Adresses des Associations Membres: *member associations' addresses*
• Rapport sur les Besoins Prioritaires RDT des PME dans le Secteur des Aliments Composés: *report on small and medium sized companies in Research, Development and Technology*
• Séminaire FEFAC "Gestion de Crise"

European Fertiliser Manufacturers' Association (EFMA)

Address: 4 Avenue E Van Nieuwenhuyse, B-1160 Brussels, Belgium
Telephone: +32 2 675 3530
Fax: +32 2 675 3961
E-mail: main@etma.be
Activities: carries out research, produces statistics on the industry, government liaison
Chief officers: Mr Helmul Aldinger (Director General), Mr Tom Jago (President)
Membership: 13 fertiliser manufacturers representing 85% of total production capacity in the European Union
Publications:
• Annual Review: *a review of the activities of the Association as well as an overview of the industry with statistics on the consumption, production, utilisation, and imports of fertilizers. Based largely on returns from national associations - regular*

European Financial Management and Marketing Association (EFMA)

Association Européenne de Management et de Marketing Financiers
Address: 16 rue d'Aguesseau, F-75008 Paris, France
Telephone: +33 1 474 25272
Fax: +33 1 474 25676
Year established: 1971
Activities: maintains an information centre, (access free of charge). Undertakes surveys, studies, study groups; study tours; seminars. Annual Convention (March); Annual

Congress (October); various international conferences on topical matters per year
Chief officers: Michel Barnich (Managing Director), Patrick Desmarès (Director of business development), Martha Ilic (Director of communication), Myriam Rault (Director of Publications), Hélène Schmidt (Director of Finance and Administration)
Structure: non-profit making association with board of directors and permanent staff
Membership: 150 financial institutions in 15 European countries (this represents two-thirds of the main European financial institutions); associate members in North and South America, the Far East, the Middle East and the Maghreb
Publications:
• European Financial Management and Marketing Association newsletter: *news on EFMA, in-depth articles and news items on innovations and new initiatives in the financial world - bi-monthly*
• Facts and Figures (EFMA): *document covering the major bank card systems in every country of the world, providing data on the different types of cards, the numbers of holders, branches accepting the card, ATMs, transactions and retailers accepting the card - annual; March*
• International Press Review: *weekly*
• Product Profiles: *each covers a specific topic; up-to-date information on the products and services of EFMA member institutions; presentation of the policy adopted by each institution in the field concerned; detailed description of products or services offered, figures and original copies of brochures and promotional advertising - annual*
• Workbooks: *based on EFMA proceedings and a selection of the best studies and articles on the subject concerned, in the original language*

European Food Brokers' Association
Address: Fair Winds, Vicarage Lane, Steeple Claydon, Bucks, MK18 2PR, United Kingdom
Telephone: +44 1296 730 850
Fax: +44 1296 738 724
Year established: 1977
Activities: organises an annual conference and provides information
Chief officers: Ms M A Reynolds, (Secretary/Treasurer)
Membership: 57 member companies
Publications:
• Directory of Members: *member contact details as well as information on products and retail outlets - annual*
• Newsletter: *the activities of the Association and developments in the industry - bi-monthly*
Notes: The Association does not produce statistics.

European Fresh Produce Importers' Association (CIMO)
Address: Boîte 4, Avenue de Broqueville 272, B-1200 Brussels, Belgium
Telephone: +32 2 771 3635
Fax: +32 2 762 9425
E-mail: webmaster@www.cimo.be
Web site: www.cimo.be
Web site notes: site includes some data on European fresh produce production and imports into the EU
Year established: 1972
Activities: bi-annual congress relating to the fruit and vegetable trade, monitors legislation affecting the industry
Chief officers: Mr Stulcken (President), Philippe Binard (Managing Director)
Membership: 47 corporate members (fresh fruit and vegetable importers)

European Furniture Manufacturers' Association (UEA)
Union Européenne de l'Ammeublement
Address: 109-111 rue Royale, B-1000 Brussels, Belgium
Telephone: +32 2 218 1889
Fax: +32 2 219 2701
Year established: 1950
Chief officers: Bart de Turck (Secretary General), Jurgen Engels (President)
Membership: members from European countries, including France, Italy, Netherlands, Norway, Portugal, Spain, Sweden
Publications:
• European Furniture Manufacturers' Association Newsletter: *information of interest to the sector - bi-monthly*
• Furniture Industry in Western Europe - a Statistical Digest: *annual*

European Group of Packaging Paper Producers (EMBALPACK)
Europäischer Verband der Hersteller von Verpackungspapieren/Groupement Européen des Fabricants de Papier d'Emballage
Address: Jahnstraße 93, D-64285 Darmstadt, Germany
Telephone: +49 6151 44501
Fax: +49 6151 421702
Telex: 419571
Activities: information, statistics
Chief officers: Manfred Sulzmann (Director General), H Mosert (Secretary General)

European Healthcare Management Association (EHMA)
Address: Vergemount Hall, Clonskeagh, Dublin 6, Ireland
Telephone: +353 1 283 9299
Fax: +353 1 283 8653
E-mail: ehma@iol.ie
Web site: homepages.iol.ie/~ehma
Activities: organises conferences; disseminates information; liaises with international organisations and national governments
Chief officers: Philip C. Berman (Director), John McMahon (Secretary)

European Landscape Contractors' Association (ELCA)
Gemeinschaft des europäischen Garten-, Landschafts- und Sportplatzbaues
Address: Alexander von Humbolt Straße 4, D-53604 Bad Honnef, Germany
Telephone: +49 2224 770 720
Fax: +49 2224 770 777
Year established: 1963
Activities: annual congress
Chief officers: Lothar von Wurmb (President), Klaus Kobold (Secretary)
Membership: 12 national associations
Publications:
• Directory of Members

European Liquid Petrol and Gas Association (LPG)
Association Européenne de Gaz de Pétrole Liquéfiés
Address: 6 rue Galilée, F-75782 Paris Cedex 16, France
Telephone: +33 1 472 35274
Fax: +33 1 472 35279
Activities: annual general assembly; study groups, triennial congress and exhibition; provides statistics to members only
Chief officers: M P Taupin (Secretary General)
Membership: 17 members

European Livestock and Meat Trading Union (UECBV)
Union Européenne du Commerce du Bétail et de la Viande
Address: Boîte 9, Rue de la Loi 81a, B-1040 Brussels, Belgium
Telephone: +32 2 230 4603

Fax: +32 2 230 9400
E-mail: uecbv@pophost.eunet.be
Web site: uecbv.eunet.be
Year established: 1952
Activities: Annual General Assembly Meeting
Chief officers: Antonio Anoro (President), Jean-Luc Mériaux (Secretary General)
Structure: non-profit-making organisation
Membership: 40 national federations, representing 13,500 enterprises
Publications:
• Lists of Importers and Exporters
• Reportoire de l'UECBV: *a report on the livestock, meat production and meat trade in Europe based on various sources - annual*
Notes: Also represents the European Association of Livestock Markets.

European Mail Order Traders' Association (EMOTA-AVEPC)
Association Européenne de Vente par Correspondance
Address: 13 Avenue Edouard Lacomblé, B-1040 Brussels, Belgium
Telephone: +32 2 736 0348
Fax: +32 2 736 0542
Year established: 1971
Activities: compiles key statistics for Europe and individual member countries; promotes the interests of the mail order trade at the level of the EU and other international organisations
Chief officers: Dr Peter Frische (General delegate)
Membership: 13 national associations
Publications:
• Annual Statistics (EMOTA): *basic data on the size of the European mail order sector with statistics for specific countries. Based on returns from member organisations in various countries - annual*
• Membership List

European Mortgage Federation
Fédération Hypothéquaire Européenne/Europäischer Hypothekenverband
Address: Box 2, Avenue de la Joyeuse Entrée 14, B-1040 Brussels, Belgium
Telephone: +32 2 285 4030
Fax: +32 2 285 4031
E-mail: ernf.be@skynet.be
Activities: collects statistics on real estate and mortgage loans; publishes various studies on the sector
Chief officers: Judith Hardt (Secretary General), Annik Lambert (Assistant Secretary General), Tobias Mackie (Economic Department Director)
Membership: 40 members
Publications:
• Annual Report of the European Mortgage Federation: *an annual report with statistics on mortgage credit and its funding in specific European countries. There are also sections with general economic data and construction and property market data - annual*
• Hypostat 1983-1994: *statistics in the 12 European countries, Norway and Sweden on mortgage interest rates, net and gross credit, housing building, transactions and price index*
• Répertoire des Etablissements de Crédit Hypothécaire dans l'UE
• Statistiques Trimestrielles: *statistics on mortgage interest rates, net and gross credit, housing building, transactions and price index - quarterly*

European Organisation of the Dehydrated Fruit and Vegetable Industries (AIFLD)
Association des Industries des Fruits et Légumes Déshydratés de l'UE
Address: Avenue de Roodebeek 30, B-1030 Brussels, Belgium
Telephone: +32 2 743 8730
Fax: +32 2 736 8175
Chief officers: Hubert Darbonne (President), F. Brückner (Vice President), Pascale Keppenne (Secretary General)
Membership: industry organisations from five EU countries
Publications:
• List of Members
Notes: The Association does not produce statistics.

European Petroleum Industry Association (Europia)
Address: Madou Plaza, Place Madou 1, B-1210 Brussels, Belgium
Telephone: +32 2 226 1911
Fax: +32 2 219 9551
Chief officers: Mr W.J. Thompson (Assistant Secretary General)
Notes: The Association does not produce statistics.

European Proprietary Medicines Manufacturers' Association (AESGP)
Association Européenne des Specialités Pharmaceutiques Grand Public
Address: Avenue de Tervueren 7, B-1040 Brussels, Belgium
Telephone: +32 2 735 5130
Fax: +32 2 735 5222
E-mail: aesgp@innet.be
Web site: www.club.innet.be/~pub00568
Web site notes: site includes statistics on pharmaceuticals and OTC healthcare in Europe with individual breakdowns covering 15 European countries
Year established: 1963
Activities: organises annual meetings; collects statistics on sales of OTC products in Europe
Chief officers: Dr Hubertus Cranz (Director)
Membership: national associations and manufacturers of non-prescription medicines; 24 full members, 12 associate members
Publications:
• AESGP Proceedings from Annual Meetings
• Developing Self-Medication in Central and Eastern Europe
• Economic and Legal Framework for Non-Prescription Medicines in Europe
• Self-Medication and the Pharmacist
• Summary of Product Characteristics for Non-prescription Medicines in the EU: *new proposals for key OTC substances*
Notes: European member contries include the following: Austria, Belgium/Luxembourg, Bulgaria, France, Germany, Greece, Hungary, Ireland, Italy, Latvia, Netherlands, Norway, Portugal, Slovenia, Spain, Sweden, Switzerland, Turkey and the United Kingdom.

European Regional Airlines Organisation (ERA)
Address: The Baker Suite, Fairoaks Airport, Chobham, Nr Woking, Surrey GU24 8HX, United Kingdom
Telephone: +44 1276 856 495
Fax: +44 1276 857 038
E-mail: info@eraa.org
Web site: www.eraa.org
Web site notes: site includes statistics on annual passenger growth, average seating capacity, aircraft type and average distance travelled
Year established: 1981
Activities: the Association produces statistics on punctuality, passanger growth etc.
Chief officers: Mike Ambrose (Director General), Chris

Holliday (Corporate Communications Manager)
Structure: council, directorate, committees
Membership: 190 members including 65 airlines, 30 airports, 25 aircraft, engine and equipment manufacturers and a large number of members in other associated industries
Publications:
• ERA Regional Performance: *detailed statistics on regional airline traffic - quarterly*
• ERA Regional Report: *news and views from the Association. Regular features include detailed profiles of ERA member airlines and the views of sponsoring associate members. - monthly*
• ERA Yearbook: *news and views on the main issues facing Europe, details on ERA's activities, statistics and data on regional airline and aircraft development. Also includes comprehensive details about all ERA airline and associate members, including contact details, fleet summaries and descriptions of products and services that they offer - annual*

European Secretariat of Light Metal Packaging (SEFEL)
Address: Rue des Drapiers 21, B-1050 Brussels, Belgium
Telephone: +32 2 510 2503
Fax: +32 2 510 2301
E-mail: sefel@fabrimetal.be
Year established: 1959
Activities: collects statistics on production, sales, exports, etc.
Chief officers: Pierre Diederich (Secretary General)
Membership: 10 national associations and 3 individual companies in Europe
Publications:
• Directory of Members
• Presentation Brochure
• Statistical Brochure: *annual*

European Society for Opinion and Marketing Research (ESOMAR)
Address: J J Viottastraat 29, NL-1071 JP Amsterdam, Netherlands
Telephone: +31 20 664 2141
Fax: +31 20 664 2922
E-mail: email@esomar.nl
Web site: www.esomar.nl
Publications:
• Congress and Seminar Proceedings: *in book form*
• ESOMAR Handbook: *directory of member companies - annual*
• International Codes and Guidelines: *13 issues*
• Marketing and Research Today: *mainly papers from seminars - quarterly*
• NewsBrief (European Society for Opinion and Marketing Research): *news on conferences; book reviews; calendar of events; company developments - monthly*
• Report of ESOMAR Annual Industry Survey: *statistics and commentary on market research trends in ESOMAR member countries. Includes statistics on turnover, type of work undertaken, employment in the market research industry, etc. Based on data collected from the membership - annual*

European Telecommunications Satellite Organisation (EUTELSAT)
Organisation Européenne de Télécommunications par Satellite
Address: 70 rue Balard, F-75502 Paris Cedex 15, France
Telephone: +33 1 539 84747
Fax: +33 1 539 83788
E-mail: voconnor@eutelsat.fr
Web site: www.eutelsat.org
Year established: 1977
Chief officers: Jean Grenier (Director General), Giuliano Berretta (Commercial Director), Andreas Langemeyer (Technical Director), D G Hardman (Finance Director), Jesús Domingo Laborda (Operations Director), Vanessa O'Connor

(Head of Press and Public Relations)
Membership: private and public telecommunication operations in 45 European countries
Publications:
• Annual Report of the European Telecommunications Satellite Organisation (EUTELSAT): *annual*
• Newsletter of the European Telecommunications Satellite Organisation (EUTELSAT): *quarterly*

European Timeshare Federation (ETF)
Address: c/o Market Access Europe, Rue d'Arlon 50, B-1000 Brussels, Belgium
Telephone: +32 2 230 0545
Fax: +32 2 230 5706
E-mail: ingrid.tondeur@gpcmae.com
Activities: to represent the interests of the timeshare industry at European level to European legislators and administration
Chief officers: Willemien Bax (Secretary General), Ingrid Tondeur (Secretary)
Membership: 15 members
Publications:
• Newsletter
Notes: The Association does not produce statistics.

European Trade Institute (EHI)
EuroHandelsinstitut
Address: Spichernstraße 55, D- 50672 Cologne, Germany
Telephone: +49 221 579 93/0
Fax: +49 221 579 9345
Activities: supported by wholesale and retail associations and companies, EHI carries out research into economic problems facing the trade sector and distribution of goods
Chief officers: Jürgen Tantzen (President), Dr Bernd Hallier (General Director),
Membership: retail and wholesale companies; retail and wholesale associations
Publications:
• Dynamik im Handel: *monthly*
• Newsletter Reports and Specialist Books

European Union Cocoa Trade Organisation
Address: Commodity Quay, St. Katharine Dock, London E1 9AX, United Kingdom
Telephone: +44 171 481 2080
Fax: +44 171 702 9924
Membership: 9 organisations throughout the EU

European Union Committee for the Aromatic, Sparkling and Fortified Wine Industry
Comité de la Communauté Economique Européenne des Industries et du Commerce des Vins, Vins Aromatisés, Vins Mousseux, Vins de Liqueur
Address: Boîte 4, 9 Rond-Point Schuman, B-1040 Brussels, Belgium
Telephone: +32 2 230 9970
Fax: +32 2 230 4323
Activities: prepares trade statistics
Chief officers: Dominique Emirelt (Chairman), Mme Marion Wolfers (Secretary General)

European Union of Alcoholic Drinks Producers
Union Européenne des Producteurs d'Alcool
Address: 192 Avenue de Tervueren, B-1150 Brussels, Belgium
Telephone: +32 2 772 9830
Fax: +32 2 772 9824
Year established: 1993
Chief officers: Jean-louis Van de Wouwer (Secretary General), Knut Elmendorf (President)
Membership: 23 member countries

European Union of Dairy Traders (Eucolait)
Union Européenne du Commerce des Produits Laitiers et Dérivés
Address: Avenue Livingstone 26, B-1000 Brussels, Belgium
Telephone: +32 2 230 4448
Fax: +32 2 230 4044
E-mail: eucolait@skynet.be
Chief officers: Annelie Gehring (Secretary General), Brigitte Gilmont, Lisa Zenner, Inge Clerens
Membership: 13 national associations, 4 direct members and 7 associated members
Publications:
● Eucolait Information: *monthly*
Notes: The Association does not produce statistics.

European Union of Eggs, Egg Products, Poultry and Game Wholesalers
Europäische Union der Großhandels mit Eiern, Eiprodukten, Geflügel und Wild/ Union Européenne du Commerce en Gros des Oeufs, Produits d'Oeufs, Volaille et Giber
Address: POB 503, Utrechtseweg 31, NL-3704 HA Zeist, Netherlands
Telephone: +31 0313404 672 03
Fax: +31 0313404 672 47
Telex: 47 326 pluei nl
Year established: 1959
Chief officers: Richard Protzel (President), A Mijs (General Secretary)
Membership: national associations in 7 EU countries (Denmark, France, Germany, Italy, Netherlands, Spain, UK)

European Union of Fruit and Vegetable Wholesale, Import and Export Trade (EUCOFEL)
Address: Rue Jenneval 29, B-1000 Brussels, Belgium
Telephone: +32 2 736 1584/2 736 1654
Fax: +32 2 732 1747
Telex: 24395
E-mail: eucofel.fruittrade.org@skynet.be
Year established: 1958
Activities: statistical monitoring
Chief officers: Manfred Stülcken (President); Vincent van Dijk (Secretary General)
Membership: 22 national associations of fruit and vegetable traders, representing 150 000 companies in Europe, and 16 associated members
Publications:
● Annual Report of the European Union of Fruit and Vegetable Wholesale, Import and Export Trade (EUROFEL): *commentary and some figures on the trade in fruit and vegetables in Europe. Based on returns from members in various countries - annual*
● Newsletter of the European Union of Fruit and Vegetable Wholesale, Import and Export Trade (EUCOFEL): *monthly*

European Vegetables Protein Federation (EUVEPRO)
Fédération Européenne des Protéines Végétales
Address: Avenue de Roodebeek 30, B-1030 Brussels, Belgium
Telephone: +32 2 743 8730
Fax: +32 2 736 8175
Chief officers: P.S. Rasmussen (President), Y. Goemans (Vice President), J. Hallaert (Secretary General)
Membership: 9 full members and 3 associated members
Publications:
● List of Members
Notes: The Association does not produce statistics.

European Vending Association (EVA)
Address: Rue Belliard 15-17, B-1040 Brussels, Belgium
Telephone: +32 2 512 0075
Fax: +32 2 502 2342
E-mail: vending@eva.be
Year established: 1976
Chief officers: David Hoskin (President), Catherine Piana (Secretary General), Nathalie Storme (Assistant Secretary General)
Membership: 49 national vending trade associations from Belgium, Denmark, France, Germany, Netherlands, Italy, Spain, United Kingdom
Publications:
● Annual Report: *annual*
● EVA-DTS: *data transfer standard - annual*
Notes: The Association does not produce statistics at present but is planning to introduce them in the near future.

European Venture Capital Association (EVCA)
Address: Box 6, Keibergpark, Minervastraat 6, B-1930 Zaventem, Belgium
Telephone: +32 2 715 0020/2 720 6010
Fax: +32 2 725 0704
E-mail: evca@evca.com
Web site: www.evca.com
Activities: promotion of dynamic entrepreneurship in Europe; advice on stockmarkets for growth companies; development of relationships with institutional investors worldwide; development of private equity in Central and Eastern Europe and the Commonwealth of Independent States; proposals for supportive European policies and best national practices; organises symposiums, business seminars, technology investment & early-stage conferences, instistute management development course, workshops
Chief officers: Gaëlle Jadoul (Office Manager), Serge Raicher (Secretary General)
Membership: 330 members
Publications:
● Central & Eastern Europe Directory: *Central European venture capital listing major organisations active in Central and Eastern Europe and the CIS*
● Directory: *contains comprehensive listings of all members and their activities*
● Performance Measurement Study: *pan-European study of performance of private equity and venture capital*
● Yearbook: *comprehensive venture capital survey, reporting and analysing venture capital in 17 countries - annual*

Federation of Soup Industries Associations (FAIBP)
Föderation der Suppen-Industrie -Verbände der EG/Federation des Associations de l'Industries des Bouillons et Potages de la CEE
Address: Reuterstraße 151, D-53113 Bonn, Germany
Telephone: +49 228 212 017
Fax: +49 228 229 460
Year established: 1959
Activities: annual meeting, general assembly, technical commission, working groups, legal and technical advice, analysis, market development
Chief officers: Dr Hans-Joachim Mürau (Secretary General)
Membership: 11 national associations - all producers of soups, broth, seasonings, sauces and similar products
Publications:
● Analytical methods for the Soup Industry
● Circulars

Federation of European Bakery Products Ingredients Manufacturers (FEDIMA)
Fédérations des Industries des Produits Intermédiaires pour la Boulangerie et la Pâtisserie de l'Espace Economique Européen
Address: Rue Defacqz 1, B-1000 Brussels, Belgium
Telephone: +32 2 539 1800
Fax: +32 2 539 1575

Chief officers: Arnold van Hecke (Secretary General)
Membership: 11 national associations
Notes: The Association does not produce any statistics or publications.

Federation of European Chemical Societies (FECS)

Address: c/o Royal Society of Chemistry, Burlington House, Piccadilly, London W1V 0BN, United Kingdom
Telephone: +44 171 437 8656
Fax: +44 171 437 8883
E-mail: mcewane@rsc.org
Web site: www.worldserver.pipex.com/rsc/fecs.htm
Activities: working groups including cosmetics and toiletries
Membership: 40 member societies which in total represent some 200,000 individual chemists in academia, industry and government in 32 countries across Europe

Federation of European Direct Marketing (FEDMA)

Address: Avenue de Tervueren 439, B-1150 Brussels, Belgium
Telephone: +32 2 779 4268
Fax: +32 2 779 4269
E-mail: info@fedma.org
Web site: www.fedma.org
Year established: 1997
Activities: undertakes appropriate research and provides a regular flow of business information to FEDMA members to allow them to operate legally, and in a commercially positive environment; publishes member activities and achievements; organises an annual forum
Chief officers: Carel Rog (President), Melanie Vritschan (Membership Services Officer)
Membership: 600 members in 40 countries; represents 10,000 companies directly or through national direct marketing associations
Publications:
• FEDMA Statistics: *size of the direct marketing sector in Europe based on data supplied by member organisations in individual countries - regular*
• FEDMAGRAM: *monthly*
Notes: FEDMA was created by the merger of EDMA (est. 1976) and FEDIM (est. 1992)

Federation of European Direct Selling Associations (FEDSA)

Fédération Européenne pour la Vente et le Service à Domicile
Address: Avenue de Tervueren 14, B-1040 Brussels, Belgium
Telephone: +32 2 736 1014
Fax: +32 2 736 3497
E-mail: fedsa@fedsa.be
Year established: 1983
Activities: biennial survey of member companies; collects statistics on production, salesforce, sales, turnover, part time/full time
Chief officers: Marie Andrée Vander Elst (Director)
Membership: 25 national associations; also 12 companies (associate members) in EU, Europe and Hungary
Publications:
• Annual Report of the European Direct Selling Federation: *a review of the Association's activities and direct selling in Europe with some statistics on volumes and turnover supplied by national associations - annual*
• Direct Selling in Europe: *list of members with a brief statistical section based on survey carried out by the Association - biennial*

Federation of European Publishers (FEP)

Fédération des Editeurs Européens
Address: Avenue de Tervueren 204, B-1150 Brussels, Belgium
Telephone: +32 2 770 1110
Fax: +32 2 771 2071
E-mail: fep.vonalemann@linkline.be
Web site: www.editeur.org/FEP.html
Year established: 1967
Activities: working groups; book and reading promotion; statistics; publications for members only; taxation, copyright, information society, international trade, market rights; provides training on writing, publishing, marketing, translation, bookselling and librarianship
Chief officers: John Clement (President), Ulrico Hoepli (Vice President), Mechthild von Alemann (Secretary General), Jean Vandeveld (Treasurer)
Membership: 17 national associations of book publishers of 15 countries members of the European Union and of Norway
Publications:
• Annual Report: *annual*
• European Statistics: *various statistics are published at regular intervals on European publishing trends with data collected from member organsiations in 15 European countries - regular*
• Newsletter: *weekly*

Federation of European Stock Exchanges

Fédération des Bourses Européennes
Address: Rue du Lombard 41, B-1000 Brussels, Belgium
Telephone: +32 2 551 0180
Fax: +32 2 512 4905/2 514 5581
E-mail: detry@fese.be
Web site: www.fese.be
Activities: produces statistics for equity markets (monthly and annualy) showing stock exchange price index movements, total return index movements, market capitalisation: main 2 parallel markets, value of equity trading, listed shares, value of bond turnover, listed bonds, exchange rates, stock index options and future turnover, bond options and future turnover
Chief officers: Cathy Detry (Executive Assistant), Jeffrey Knight (Special Advisor), Sharon Neill (Communication)
Membership: 18 member countries
Publications:
• Annual Directory: *list of all members and other important addresses - annual*
• Booklet: *the role of the Federation of European Stock Exchange*
• European Stock Exchange Statistics: *annual summary data based on the monthly statistics. Includes data from 17 European stock exchanges with information on share prices, equity turnover, and market capitalisation. Based on returns from the individual stock exchanges - annual*
• Newsletter: *news and details on the member exchanges and FESE itself and on other Eastern European markets - monthly*

Federation of International Mechanical Engineering and Electronics Industries

Fédération des Entreprises Internationales de la Mécanique et de l'Electronique
Address: 25-27 rue d'Astorg, F-75008 Paris, France
Telephone: +33 1 445 11460
Fax: +33 1 426 53949
Chief officers: Mr Salva (General Director)

Federation of International Trade Associations (FITA)

Address: 1851 Alexander Bell Drive, Reston Virginia 22091, USA
Telephone: +1 703 620 1588
Fax: +1 703 391 0159
E-mail: FITA@mcimail.com
Web site: www.fita.org
Year established: 1984
Publications:
• Exporter Magazine: *in-depth articles on all aspects of*

exporting including: legislation; trade finance; operations, distribution and logistics; markets and marketing - monthly

Federation of Latin American Pharmaceutical Industries Associations (FIFARMA)

Federación Latinoamericana de la Industria Farmacéutica
Address: Casilla de Corro 22-9, c/o Cámara de la Industria Farmacéutica de Chile - CIF, Hernando de Aguirre 1981, Providencia, Chile
Telephone: +56 2 225 2959/225 2461
Fax: +56 2 205 2060

Federation of Oils, Seeds and Fats Associations Ltd (FOSFA International)

Address: 20 Dunstains Hill, London EC3R 8HL, United Kingdom
Telephone: +44 171 283 5511
Fax: +44 171 623 1310
Year established: 1971
Activities: training, seminars, consultancy and advisory service, legal, scientific and technical information service, research, annual trade education course, annual general meetings, price settlement committees. FOSFA publishes International Trading Contracts and related technical publications
Chief officers: Stuart Logan (Chief Executive and Secretary)
Membership: over 600 members in 55 countries
Notes: The Association does not produce any statistics.

Federation of the Associations of EU Frozen Food Producers (FAFPAS)

Fédération des Associations de Fabricants de Produits Alimentaires Surgelés de l'UE
Address: Avenue de Roodebeek 30, B-1030 Brussels, Belgium
Telephone: +32 2 743 8730
Fax: +32 2 736 8175
Activities: collects statistics on consumption
Chief officers: Léo de Bruijn (President), G. Molloy (Vice President), Michael Coenen (Secretary General)
Membership: 9 national frozen food manufacturing associations of the EU
Publications:
• List of Members

Federation of the European Cutlery, Flatware, Hollowware and Cookware Industries (FEC)

Fédération de l'Industrie Européenne de la Coutellerie, des Couverts de Table, de l'Orfèvrerie et des Articles Culinaires
Address: 58 rue du Louvre, F-75002 Paris, France
Telephone: +33 1 423 36133
Fax: +33 1 402 62951
Year established: 1952
Activities: Biennial congress; statistics on sales and production; research and development; relationship with professional press; branch related statistical information release
Chief officers: Giuseppe Moroni (President), Emmanuel Descheemaeker (Secretary General), John Price (Vice President)
Membership: 400 trade associations and companies from 12 European countries: Belgium, Denmark, Finland, France, Germany, Italy, Netherlands, Norway, Spain, Sweden, Switzerland, UK
Publications:
• Annuaire FEC: *FEC members*
• Circulars

Federation of the Meat Stock and Soup Industry Associations of the EU

Address: Reuterstrasse 151, D-53113 Bonn 1, Germany
Telephone: +49 228 212017
Fax: +49 228 229460
Year established: 1959
Activities: information service and working groups
Membership: industry associations in Belgium, Denmark, France, Germany, Ireland, Italy, Spain, United Kingdom

Federation of Tourism Associations of Central America (FEDECATUR)

Federación de Cámaras de Turismo de Centroamérica
Address: PO Box 62, 10 North Park Street, Belize City, Belize
Telephone: +501 2 757 17/787 09/711 44
Fax: +501 2 787 10
Activities: quarterly meetings, coordinates activities at a regional level
Chief officers: Godsman Ellis (President)

Flavour and Fragrance Association of Australia and New Zealand

Address: Private Bag 938, Level 4, 140 Arthur Street, North Sydney 2059, Australia
Telephone: +61 2 992 77500
Fax: +61 2 995 50032
Chief officers: Bill Torrey (President), John Arrowsmith (Secretary)

Food Business Forum (CIES)

Address: 8 place d'Iéna, F-75783 Paris Cedex 16, France
Telephone: +33 1 443 46900
Fax: +33 1 443 46939
Activities: organises management programmes made up of international congresses, conferences and "modules" or smaller meetings dealing with specific topics: strategic management, executive development, marketing and merchandising, supply chain management, information technology and environment; periodically commissions research into trends and topical developments in the food industry; provides an international business forum for member company chief executives and their senior management
Chief officers: Paul-Louis Halley (President), Henry Mestdagh (Treasurer), Etienne P. Laurent (Managing Director), Daniela Menzel (Assistant)
Structure: international headquarters in Paris and sub-offices in Brussels, Washington, Tokyo and Singapore
Membership: 250 major food retailing chains and an equal number of their suppliers drawn from 45 countries
Publications:
• CIES Yearbook: *members directory, statistics on companies members, information on services and events provided by CIES - annual*
• Euro Food Focus: *news on European Community and its impact on trade - monthly*
• Food Business News: *information on world distribution and the food industry - monthly*
• WasteLine: *innovation in packaging and waste management - quarterly*
• Window on the World: *information and ideas for company managers*
Notes: Official languages are English, French, German and Spanish.

Food Distributors' International (FDI)

Address: NAWGA/IFDA, 9 Jay Gould Court, Waldorf MD 20604, USA
Telephone: +1 301 843 3084
Fax: +1 301 843 0159
E-mail: foodorg@aol.com

Web site: www.nawga-ifda.org
Chief officers: Van Stekelenburg (Chairman)
Membership: food distribution companies which primarily supply and service independent grocers and foodservice operations throughout the US, Canada and more than 20 other countries
Publications:
• Activity Based Costing for Food Wholesalers and Retailers: *ABC and its application in the food distribution arena*
• Analysis of Wholesale Inventory: *describes national warehouse inventory by product category, and identifies current and potential problem areas or trends*
• Cash-and-Carry Survey: *operating results and statistical data from the cash-and-carry sector throughout North America and abroad; includes details on type of operation, sales volumes, trading areas, customer service, advertising/promotion, and future plans - annual*
• Distributor Productivity and Financial Report: *profiles wholesale grocery and foodservice distributors; includes comparative financial ratios and statistics*
• Trade Practice Recommendations for Grocery and Non-Food Products: *a summary of the current industry practices and the joint industry committee recommendations, with details on technology and systems in the industry*
• Transportation: The Critical Link in the Grocery Industry Supply Chain: *presents the argument for concentrating on improving the grocery industry's transportation system*
• Wholesale Food Distribution: Today and Tomorrow: *focuses on the background and current role of the grocery wholesaler, key issues facing the wholesale-supplied system, and potential responses and roles for wholesalers in the future*
Notes: Food Distributors International is the umbrella name for the National American Wholesale Grocers' Association (NAWGA) and the International Foodservice Distributors' Association (IFDA).

Foreign Trade Association (FTA)

Address: Avenue de Janvier 5, B-1200 Brussels, Belgium
Telephone: +32 2 762 0551
Fax: +32 2 762 7506
Year established: 1977
Activities: compilation of trade and price statistics (available to members only)
Chief officers: Jacqueline Peltier (Chairman), Dr Konrad Neundörfer (Delegate General)
Membership: 15 European retail trade organisations and 61 retail trade firms
Publications:
• Annual Report of the Foreign Trade Association (FTA): *annual*
• Circulars: *occasional*

Freight Forward Europe (FFE)

Address: Avenue Marcel Thiry 204, B-1200 Brussels, Belgium
Telephone: +32 2 774 9639
Fax: +32 2 774 9690
E-mail: ffe@ey.be
Chief officers: Poul Hansen (European Representative)
Membership: 9 companies (ASG, BTL, Dachser, Danzas, Kühne & Nagel, LEP, Paralpina, Scherker, THL)
Notes: The Association does not produce any statistics or publications.

Industrial Fabrics Association International (IFAI)

Address: 1801 County Road B West, Roseville MN 55113-4060, USA
Telephone: +1 612 222 2508/800 225 4324
Fax: +1 612 631 9334
E-mail: mrktresearch@ifai.com
Web site: www.ifai.com
Year established: 1912
Activities: technical services, market research, legislative updates, business services, certification and awards programs, and educational programs, workshops and conferences
Chief officers: Alex Strzetelski (Market Research Director), Juli Case (Information and Technical Services Manager)
Membership: manufacturers and suppliers of a wide range of fabrics used in industrial and technical sectors, including architectural structures, awnings, automotive, banners and flags, casual furniture, geosynthetics, marine, medical, narrow fabrics, recreation, rental tents, safety and protective, tarps and truck covers, transportation etc.
Publications:
• Buyer's Guide: *directory of 1,200+ companies that supply chemicals, compounds, fabrics, fibres, films, hardware, findings, accessories, equipment, tools and end products - annual*
• Fabrics and Architecture: *showcases industrial fabric applications to architects. Featured works include awnings, canopies, flags, banners, tension structures and other fabric end products in commercial and residential application - bi-monthly*
• Geosynthetics International: *all aspects of materials, research, behavioural research and applications technology relating to geosynthetics*
• Geotechnical Fabrics Report: *latest information on design techniques and developments in geotextiles, geomembranes, geosynthetic clay liners, geogrids, geocomposites and erosion-control products - 9 p.a.*
• IFAI's Marine Fabricator: *MFA news, beginning and advanced cut-and-sew articles, photo showcases, fabricator profiles, business tips and solutions to source of supply problems - quarterly*
• In Tents: *use of tents and accessories to the special event and general rental industries - quarterly*
• Industrial Fabrics Products Review: *reports on emerging and traditional end markets, including airbags, awnings, marine products, rental tents and truck covers. Industry updates also feature new technical developments of fibres, fabrics and treatments, general interest articles on growth-oriented products and companies, and features on sewing, seaming and cutting equipment - monthly*
• Safety and Protective Fabrics: *includes news, updates, information on new products, publications and events - quarterly*

Inter-African Coffee Organisation (IACO)

Address: BP V 210, Abidjan 01, Côte d'Ivoire
Telephone: +225 2 161 31/216 185
Fax: +225 2 162 12
Year established: 1960
Activities: annual meetings and seminars; research network; studies of marketing problems and market trends; creates Coffee Information Centres in consumer countries
Chief officers: Arega Worku (Secretary General)
Membership: 25 members (representing 99% of coffee produced annually in Africa, which produces 33% of the world's coffee consumption): Angola, Benin, Burundi, Cameroon, Central African Republic, Democratic Republic of Congo, Republic of Congo, Côte d'Ivoire, Equatorial Guinea, Ethiopia, Gabon, Ghana, Guinea, Kenya, Liberia, Madagascar, Malawi, Nigeria, Rwanda, Sierra Leone, Tanzania, Togo, Uganda, Zaïre, Zambia, Zimbabwe
Publications:
• African Coffee: *bulletin - quarterly*
• Exporter Directory of African Coffee: *biennial*
Notes: Member of the International Coffee Organisation (ICO).

Interamerican Publishers' Group

Grupo Inter-Americano de Editores
Address: Cámara Argentina del Libro, Belgrano 1580, piso 4, 1093 Buenos Aires, Argentina

Telephone: +54 1 371 5546
Fax: +54 1 375 1659
Chief officers: Mr F del Carril, Ms Ana M Cabanellas (Director)

International Advertising Association (IAA)

Address: 251 Fifth Avenue, Suite 1807, New York, NY 10175, USA
Telephone: +1 212 557 1133
Fax: +1 212 983 0455
E-mail: enet@ibnet.com
Web site: www.iaaglobal.org
Year established: 1938
Activities: world council every two years; world congress; education and training; campaign for advertising
Chief officers: Luis Carlos Mendiola Codina (President), Senyon Kim (Senior Vice President), Michel Reinarz (Secretary), Leon Hertz (Treasurer), Normal Vale (Director General), Richard Cornen (Executive Director)
Membership: 3,457 advertisers, agencies and media in 87 countries
Publications:
• Ad hoc publications: *government regulations; industry self-regulation; smoking; sexism and decency; sponsorship etc. - various*
• Annual Report and Membership Directory: *annual*
• International Advertising Association News World: *newsletter - bi-monthly*
• World Advertising Expenditures: *trends in advertising expenditure worldwide with data by media type, category of advertising, product areas, etc. Figures for earlier years - annual*
Notes: The Association is the only global partnership of advertisers, agencies, media and other services.

International Air Transport Association (IATA)

Address: Box 672, IATA Centre, Route de l'Aéroport 33, CH-1215 Geneva 15 Airport, Switzerland
Telephone: +41 22 799 2525
Fax: +41 22 799 2685
E-mail: Sales@iata.org
Web site: www.iata.org
Web site notes: site includes various statistics on air transport
Year established: 1945
Chief officers: Pierre J. Jeanniot (Director General)
Membership: 137 companies worldwide
Publications:
• Monthly International Statistics: *monthly statistics on approximately 30 airlines with data on traffic, capacity, passenger loads. Monthly and cumulative data based on returns from Association members - monthly*
• North Atlantic Traffic Report: *traffic trends on North Atlantic airline routes in total and for individual airlines. Based on data from members - annual*
• Total Market Freight Traffic Forecasts: *forecasts of international freight tonnes by world regions and by country. Based on data from members - annual*
• Total Market Passenger Transport Forecasts: *a collective view of the airlines of passenger traffic growth in 32 world regions including Europe - annual*
• World Air Transport Statistics: *a review of trends in every IATA airline with statistics on routes, passengers, cargo, traffic, loads and finances. Includes historical data and based on returns from association members - annual*

International Article Numbering Association (EAN International)

Address: Rue Royale 145, B-1000 Bruxelles, Belgium
Telephone: +32 2 227 1020
Fax: +32 2 227 1021
E-mail: info@ean.be

Web site: www.ean.be
Year established: 1977
Activities: manages a world-wide system that allows the identification and communication of products, services, utilities, transport units and locations; develops and maintains coding standards for all users, and has the aim of developing a global, multi-sectorial standard with the objective of providing a common language for international trade
Membership: 79 Numbering Organisations covering 86 countries

International Association for the Development of Agri-Business (Adepta)

Association pour le Développement des Echanges Internationaux de Produits et Techniques Agro-Alimentaires
Address: 41 rue de Bourgogne, F-75007 Paris, France
Telephone: +33 1 441 80888
Fax: +33 1 441 80889
E-mail: adepta@adepta.com
Web site: www.adepta.com
Year established: 1977
Activities: agro-development, agro-industry; fisheries and packaging. Attends international exhibitions
Chief officers: Jean Ayral (President), Claude Caustier (Vice-President), Jean-Philippe Moulin (Vice-President), Jean-Laurent Cascarano (General Secretary)
Membership: 210 members : Public bodies; unions; regional development bodies
Publications:
• Objectif export: *annual*
• The Guide (Le Guide): *guide to national and international financial programmes*

International Association for the Distributive Trades

Address: 34 rue Marianne, B-1180 Brussels, Belgium
Telephone: +32 2 345 9923
Fax: +32 2 346 0204
Publications:
• Retail Trade Statistics: *statistics for retail trade sales and structure based on data supplied by national member organisations - regular*
• Sectoral Analysis of the Retail Trade: *a detailed review of the international retail trade with data on retailing structure, outlets, sales etc. Based on various sources. - regular*
• Statistics (International Association for the Distributive Trades): *regular statistics are compiled covering retail structure, sales, and consumer expenditure in various countries. Based largely on returns from national associations - regular*

International Association for the Study of Insurance Economics (The Geneva Association)

Address: 18 Chemin Rieu, CH-1208 Geneva, Switzerland
Telephone: +41 22 347 0938
Fax: +41 22 347 2078
E-mail: geneva.association@iprolink.ch
Year established: 1973
Chief officers: Mr JH Holsboer (President), Mr Orio Giarini (Secretary General and Director)
Membership: 80 members
Publications:
• Four Pillars Bulletin (Les Quatre Piliers): *research programme on social security, insurance, savings and employment*
• Newsletter: *the Geneva Group of Risk and Insurance Economists*
• Risk Management Bulletin
• World Fire Statistics Bulletin: *regular statistics on fire insurance claims and premiums in various countries around the world, based on returns from members - annual*

International Association of African French-Speaking Publishers (AIEAF)

Association Internationale des Editeurs Africans Francophones
Address: BP 541, c/o Edition CEDA, Abidjan 04, Côte d'Ivoire
Telephone: +225 246 510/246 511
Fax: +225 250 567

International Association of Airport Duty Free Shops (IAADFS)

Address: Suite 300, 1200 19th Street NW, Washington, DC 20036-2422, USA
Telephone: +1 202 857 1184
Fax: +1 202 429 5154
Web site: www.iaadfs.org
Year established: 1966
Activities: government liaison, runs an exchange programme for members to exchange information on products and their duty-free market potential, sponsors the annual "Duty Free Show of the Americas"
Chief officers: Michael Payne (Executive Director), Steven Antolick (Director of Membership)
Membership: 500 operators of airport duty-free stores and their suppliers

International Association of Amusement Parks and Attractions (IAAPA)

Address: 1448 Duke St, Alexandria VA 22314, USA
Telephone: +1 703 836 4800
Fax: +1 703 836 4801
E-mail: ihunnewe@iaapa.org
Web site: www.iaapa.org
Chief officers: John Graff (Executive Director), Mandy McCullough (Secretary), Sarah Wholey (Research Manager)
Membership: education and training, government relations, conventions and trade shows
Publications:
• Amusement Industry Abstract: *operational and financial statistics on the amusement industry in the USA, and internationally. Data on attendances, income, costs, marketing, catering etc. - Annual*
• Family Entertainment Centre: *the US and international entertainment industry. Includes in-depth company profiles and industry trends - monthly*
• Funworld: *international news and trends in the leisure and amusement park industry - monthly*
• International Directory and Buyers' Guide: *contact information on individual management, suppliers, parks and attractions - annual*

International Association of Audio-visual Copyright Producers (AGICOA)

Association de Gestion Internationale Collective des Oeuvres Audiovisuelles
Address: Rue de Saint Jean, 26, CH-1203 Geneva, Switzerland
Telephone: +41 2 234 032 00
Fax: +41 2 234 034 32
E-mail: info@agicoa.org
Web site: www.agicoa.org
Year established: 1981
Activities: negotiates the payment of royalties to producers with the appropriate cable bodies
Chief officers: Rodolphe Egli (Managing Director), Magali Barman (Secretary), Luigi Cattaneo (Director of Legal Services)
Membership: 32 major producers associations from 18 countries
Notes: International non-governmental organisation.

International Association of Department Stores (IADS)

Association Internationale des Grands Magasins
Address: 4 rue de Rome, F-75008 Paris, France
Telephone: +33 1 429 40202
Fax: +33 1 429 40204
E-mail: iads@worldnet.fr
Year established: 1928
Activities: annual general meeting; 8 conferences per year for members; information exchange for members; annual confidential operating statistics and information; research
Chief officers: Maarten de Groot van Embden (General Secretary), Mr Knee (Assistant General Secretary)
Membership: 18 members
Publications:
• Digest and Comments on World Retailing
• Retail Newsletter: *monthly*

International Association of Financial Planning (IAFP)

Address: Suite 800, 2 Concourse Parkway, Atlanta, GA 30328, USA
Telephone: +1 800 945 4237
E-mail: info@iafp.org
Web site: www.iafp.org
Year established: 1969
Activities: promotes business ethics and professional conduct; conducts continuing education programmes; compiles statistics
Chief officers: Janet Crane (Director)
Structure: permanent staff; councils
Membership: 15,000 financial advisors and companies that provide financial products and services in 23 countries
Publications:
• Financial Planning: *industry-specific news, products and services, retirement planning, asset management and investment strategies, tax planning, asset protection and estate planning - monthly*
• Planning Matters: *current trends and developments in the financial planning industry, provides practice management and professional development guidance, and interprets legislative and regulatory changes affecting the financial planning profession - monthly*

International Association of Food Distribution (AIDA)

Address: Rue Marianne 34, B-1180 Brussels, Belgium
Telephone: +32 2 345 9923
Fax: +32 2 346 0204
Year established: 1950
Activities: provides retailing information services for member companies and organises two conferences a year
Chief officers: Mario Bertolini (President), Léon F. Weguez (Director General)
Publications:
• Le Bulletin International de l'AIDA: *quarterly*

International Association of Food Industry Suppliers (IAFIS)

Address: 1451 Dolley Madison Boulevard, McLean, Virginia McLean, Virginia, USA
Telephone: +1 703 761 2600
Fax: +1 703 761 4334
E-mail: info@iafis.org
Web site: www.iafis.org
Year established: 1911
Activities: education and training, provides an information service to members, organises an annual trade show
Notes: Formerly the Dairy and Food Industries Supply Association.

International Association of Infant Food Manufacturers (IFM)

Association Internationale des Fabricants d'Aliments pour l'Enfance
Address: 194 rue de Rivoli, F-75001 Paris, France
Telephone: +33 1 534 58787
Fax: +33 1 534 58780
E-mail: andrée.bronner@wanadoo.fr
Year established: 1984
Chief officers: Dr Andrée Bronner (Secretary General), Véronique Clignet (Assistant Secretary General)
Membership: 21 companies
Notes: The Association does not produce any publications or statistics; see : Association of Dietetic Foods Industries of the EU (IDACE) and International Federation of Special Dietary Food Industries (ISDI)

International Association of Packaging Research Institutes (IAPRI)

Address: Emiel Verséstraat 24, B-1070 Brussels, Belgium
Telephone: +32 2 521 2709
Fax: +32 2 521 2709
E-mail: flox@meko.vub.ac.be
Web site: vub.vub.acbe/-flox/iapri.html
Year established: 1971
Activities: organisation of Symposia (only for members) and International Congresses (each bi-yearly); exchange of knowledge, expertise and information in general on packaging testing, research and education; each member-institute collects data for statistics
Chief officers: Dr A. Söräs (President), Prof. Dr. F. Lox (Secretary General)
Membership: 42 institutes
Publications:
● IAPRI-Handbook: *every two years*
● IAPRI-Newsletter: *twice a year*

International Association of Purchasing and Marketing Groups (IVE)

Internationale Vereinigung von Einkaufs- und Marketingverbände
Address: Lindenstraße 20, D-5000 Cologne 1, Germany
Telephone: +49 221 219456
Chief officers: Martin G G Oostvogel (President), Günter Olesch (General Secretary)
Membership: voluntary buying groups

International Association of Refrigerated Warehouses (IARW)

Address: Suite 1200 North, 7315 Wisconsin Avenue, Bethesda, MD 20814, USA
Telephone: +1 301 652 5674
Fax: +1 301 652 7269
Web site: www.iarw.org
Web site notes: site includes a database of member companies
Year established: 1891
Activities: monitors government regulations and legislation; public relations; collection and dissemination of statistical information
Chief officers: J William Hudson (President)
Structure: permanent staff; board; committees
Membership: 1,000 warehouses representing 85% of the public refrigerated warehousing industry
Publications:
● Cold Facts: *newsletter - 10 p.a.*
● Directory of Public Refrigerated Warehouses: *annual*

International Association of the Bread Industry (AIBI)

Association Internationale de la Boulangerie Industrielle/Internationaler Verband der Backwaren-Industrie
Address: POB 30440, In den Diken 33, D-40472 Düsseldorf, Germany
Telephone: +49 211 653 086/7
Fax: +49 211 653 088
Year established: 1956
Activities: AIBI Congress (biennial); statistics twice a year for members
Chief officers: Paul van Maele (President), Helmut Martell (General Secretary)
Membership: 9 national federations; 47 direct members
Publications:
● AIBI Bulletin: *quarterly*
● AIBI Presidium: *Bread consumption, production, bakery market shares, company information*
● European Food Law for Bakeries

International Association of the Soap Detergent and Maintenance Products Industry (AISE)

Association Internationale de la Savonnerie, de la Détergence et des Produits d'Entretien
Address: Square Marie-Louise 49, B-1000 Brussels, Belgium
Telephone: +32 2 230 8371
Fax: +32 2 230 8288
E-mail: a.i.s.e@euronet.be
Activities: collects statistics on production, consumption, import and export of soap and cleaning products sector worldwide; publishes a wide range of relevant publications
Chief officers: Pierre V. Costa (Secretary General), Anne-Marie Rodeyns (Deputy Secretary General), Liliane Van Sichelen (Executive Secretary), Hansrudolf Bircher (Chairman)
Membership: 32 national associations worldwide
Publications:
● AISE Statistics: *detailed statistics, including production, consumption, import and export data, for Western European countries broken down by product categories such as toilet products, household and industrial soaps,washing products, etc. Some data for earlier years is included and based largely on data supplied by the national associations - annual*

International Bottled Water Association (IBWA)

Address: 1700 Diagonal Road, Suite 650, Alexandria, VA 22314, USA
Telephone: +1 703 683 5213
Fax: +1 703 683 4074
Web site: www.bottledwater.org
Year established: 1982
Activities: conducts research; offers seminars; monitors government regulation and legislation; compiles statistics
Chief officers: Sylvia E Swanson (Executive Vice President), Jennifer Levine (Communications Director)
Structure: board; committees; permanent staff
Membership: IBWA's member companies produce and distribute 85 percent of the bottled water sold in the US. Membership includes more than 1,200 US-based and international bottlers, distributors and suppliers
Publications:
● Bottled Water Reporter: *magazine, statistics and other information - bi-monthly*
● International Bottled Water Association Member Roster: *annual*
● International Bottled Water Association Newsletter: *bi-monthly*

International Bureau of Social Tourism (BITS)

Bureau International du Tourisme Social
Address: Rue de la Loi 63, B-1040 Brussels, Belgium
Telephone: +32 2 230 7530
Fax: +32 2 230 7509

Year established: 1963
Activities: provides studies and surveys; collects statistics
Chief officers: Raymond Stelandre (Secretary General), Hans Teuscher (President), David Al-Hamruni (Permanent Secretary)
Structure: general assembly; board of directors, secretariat
Membership: 100 national associations, 11 government associates, 2 international members
Publications:
• BITS-Information: *quarterly*

International Bureau of Tyre Dealers' and Retreaders' Associations (BIPAVER)
Bureau Internationale Permanent des Associations de Vendeurs et Rechapeurs de Pneumatiques
Address: Elsinore House, Buckingham Street, Aylesbury, Bucks HP20 2NQ, United Kingdom
Telephone: +44 1296 399 837
Fax: +44 1296 88675
E-mail: bipaver@ndirect.co.uk
Year established: 1954
Activities: the Association produces statistics on retread sales in Europe (only available to members)
Chief officers: Richard Edy (Secretary General)
Structure: non-profit making lobbying organisation
Membership: full members: national associations in most European countries; also corresponding, supplier and extraordinary members
Publications:
• Directory of Members: *contact details of member companies - annual*
• Newsletter (BIPAVER): *covers the activities of the Association and European tyre industry with emphasis on distribution - periodically*

International Cablemakers' Federation (ICF)
Address: Graben 30, A-1010 Vienna, Austria
Telephone: +43 1 532 964 9/5329640
Fax: +43 1 532 9769
Year established: 1990

International Cargo Handling Co-ordination Association (ICHCA)
Address: ICHCA International Secretariat, 71 Bondway, London SW8 1SH, United Kingdom
Telephone: +44 171 793 1022
Fax: +44 171 820 1703
Year established: 1952
Activities: organises a biennial conference; disseminates information on current trends and issues that directly affect the profitability of business; assistance on every aspect of cargo movement, from production to consumer, by air, sea, road or rail
Chief officers: Jean Michel Tessier (President), Mike Butcher (Chairman)
Membership: members from over 80 countries
Publications:
• Bulletin: *quarterly*
• Buyers' Guide to Manufacturers
• ICHCA Journal: *monthly*
• ICHCA's Membership Directory: *who's who in cargo handling*
• International Bulk Journal: *official dry bulk journal - monthly*
• World of Cargo Handling

International Cocoa Organisation (ICCO)
Address: 22 Berners Street, London W1P 3DB, United Kingdom
Telephone: +44 171 637 3211
Fax: +44 171 631 0144
E-mail: Library@icco.org

Web site: www.icco.org
Web site notes: site includes a statistical summary of the cocoa market including statistics on the following: world cocoa bean production and grindings; cocoa bean prices in current and constant terms; monthly and annual averages of daily prices of cocoa beans since 1971
Year established: 1973
Activities: compiles statistics, disseminates information on cocoa, conducts research, liaises with member governments
Chief officers: Mr. Edouard Kouamé (Executive Director)
Membership: 40 member countries as well as the European Union representing over 91% of world cocoa production and over 62% of world cocoa consumption
Publications:
• Annual Report of the International Cocoa Organisation: *general commentary on the world cocoa industry but also includes statistics on production, exports, imports, and consumption with data for individual countries - annual*
• Cocoa Newsletter: *economic, scientific and technical information relating to the world cocoa economy and general ICCO news - monthly*
• Quarterly Bulletin of Cocoa Statistics: *production and exports of cocoa from the producing countries and imports, consumption, prices in the importing countries. Historical data is included - quarterly*
• World Cocoa Directory: *annual*

International Coffee Organisation
Address: 22 Berners Street, London W1P 4DD, United Kingdom
Telephone: +44 171 580 8591
Fax: +44 171 580 6129
E-mail: dubois@intercafe.win-uk.net
Year established: 1963
Activities: annual International Coffee Council meeting ; maintains a comprehensive collection of statistics on coffee trade, production, consumption and prices from 1963. Library of 20,000 volumes and 400 periodical titles (access by appointment only). Coffeeline bibliographical database service
Membership: 42 countries
Publications:
• Monthly Library Entries Bulletin: *documents - monthly*

International Committee of Paper and Board Converters of the EU (CITPA)
International Konföderation der Verarbeiter von Papier und Pappe in Europa
Address: Arndstraße 47, D-6000 Frankfurt, Germany
Telephone: +49 69 743 011
Fax: +49 69 747 714
Telex: 411925
Year established: 1961
Activities: seminars, statistics
Chief officers: Volkmar Wulf (Director), Dr H Kohl (General Delegate)
Membership: national associations of EU/EFTA paper and board converting industries
Publications:
• Annual Statistics (CITPA): *detailed statistics on the production, consumption, foreign trade, prices of paper and board plus some industry structure data. Based on a combination of official data and returns from member associations in various countries - annual*
• Circulars
• Foreign Trade Statistics: *annual*

International Communications Industries' Association (ICIA)
Address: Suite 200, 11242 Waples Mill Road, Fairfax, Virginia 22030, USA
Telephone: +1 800 659 7469/703 273 7200

Fax: +1 214 233 2813
E-mail: icia@icia.org
Web site: www.icia.org
Year established: 1948
Membership: 1,500 dealers, manufacturers, suppliers of telecom equipment
Publications:
● Communications Industries Report: *covers the following markets: A/V, audio, video, multi-media, teleconferencing, presentation, interactive, computers. Includes stories on industry developments, new products, technologies and applications. Also covers industry legislation, mergers, alliances and joint ventures - monthly*
● Directory of Multimedia Equipment, Software and Services: *annual*
● ICIA Membership Directory: *annual*

International Confederation for Printing and Allied Industries (INTERGRAF)

Address: Boîte 25-27, Square Marie-Louise 18, B-1040 Brussels, Belgium
Telephone: +32 2 230 8646/2 230 2672/2 230 2678
Fax: +32 2 231 1464
Year established: 1976
Activities: conferences, annual congress
Chief officers: Jean-Pierre Bouillot (Secretary General)
Membership: national federations from 15 countries
Publications:
● Annual Statistical Survey (INTERGRAF): *an annual survey of production and market trends in the international printing sector. Based largely on returns from national associations in 21 countries - annual*

International Confederation of Furnishing Fabric Manufacturers (CITTA)

Internationale Verband der Möbelstoff-Fabrikanten/Confédération International des Fabricants de Tapis et de Tissus d'Ameublement
Address: Hans Böckler Straße 205, D-42109 Wuppertal 1, Germany
Telephone: +49 202 759 710/750 035
Fax: +49 202 759 797/755 254
Year established: 1960
Chief officers: Emile Rasson (President), J Giersfeld (Secretary)
Membership: 12 national furnishing fabric federations, 6 regional German associations (Landesverbände)
Publications:
● CITTA Bulletin

International Council of Shopping Centres (ICSC)

Address: 11th Floor, 665 Fifth Avenue, New York, NY 10022-5370, USA
Telephone: +1 212 421 8181
Fax: +1 212 421 6464
E-mail: mbaker@icsc.org (Statistics)
Web site: www.icsc.org
Web site notes: site includes various basic economic statistics such as retail sales, price index etc.
Year established: 1957
Activities: publishes a monthly newsletter and holds meetings twice a year
Chief officers: Lisa Barskey, Pauline Cauldwell, Robert Mallia
Membership: 32,000 members in 62 countries worldwide
Publications:
● Scope USA: *shopping centre growth, shopping centre impact on state or provincial economies, per capita square feet of shopping centres, key comparative economic indicators, selected major metropolitan areas. Also includes data on new construction, retail sales and employment in shopping centres - annual*
● Shopping Centers Today (SCT): *developments and trends in international retailing with emphasis on the USA and Canada - monthly*

International Customer Service Association (ICSA)

Address: 401 N. Michigan Ave., Chicago, IL, 60611, USA
Telephone: +1 800 360 4272
Fax: +1 312 245 1084
E-mail: ICSA@sba.com
Web site: www.icsa.com
Publications:
● Benchmarking Study: *key benchmarks in customer service, includes information on customer service functions, personnel/training, order processing, complaint handling etc. based on a survey of member companies - annual*
● ICSA News: *organisation news, ideas and business trends in customer service - monthly*
● Industry Surveys: *a series of industry surveys examining different aspects of customer service. Past survey reports include studies of customer satisfaction, compensation, performance measurements and benchmarking - annual*

International Dairy Federation (IDF-FIL)

Fédération Internationale de Laiterie
Address: Square Vergote 41, B-1030 Brussels, Belgium
Telephone: +32 2 733 9888
Fax: +32 2 733 0413
E-mail: info@fil-idf.org
Web site: www.fil-idf.org
Year established: 1903
Activities: International Dairy Congress every 4 years, annual sessions, seminars, symposia, workshops, consultations
Chief officers: Jerry Kozak (President), Edward Hopkin (Secretary General)
Membership: 38 full members
Publications:
● Books: *with chapters dealing with different aspects of the same subject, by different authors. Some are monographs written by a group of international experts, others are the proceedings of an international symposium or seminar - special issues*
● Dairy: *newsletter*
● IDF Catalogue: *IDF publications' list - annual*
● IDF News
● IDF Standards: *mostly dealing with methods of sampling and analysis of milk and milk products*
● Packaging: *newsletter*
● World Dairy Situation Bulletin: *summary of production, utilization, consumption, international trade and policy developments in 1995. Forecasts for 1996-1997 for production, utilization, consumption, demand, international trade, policy developments. World tables 1994-1995-1996 of cow numbers, total milk production, milk supplies, liquid milk, butter, cheese, skim milk powder, whole milk powder, condensed milk, fresh products, world exports and world imports of dairy products, international prices. Dairy situation in 37 individual countries*

International Dairy Foods Association (IDFA)

Address: Suite 900, 1250 H Street NW, Washington DC 20005, USA
Telephone: +1 202 737 4332
Fax: +1 202 331 7820
E-mail: jrice@idfa.org
Web site: www.foodexpo.com/orgs/idfa/
Year established: 1990
Activities: continuing education; monitors government regulations on trade, labelling, quality insurance, sanitation
Chief officers: E Linwood Tipton (President and CEO)
Structure: permanent staff; board; committees
Membership: 800 dairy foods processors, manufacturers,

marketers, distributors and industry suppliers, all across the US and in 22 countries
Publications:
• Cheese Facts: *an annual report covering the trends in the cheese industry and market in the USA. Detailed production, consumption, supply, and utilisation statistics by product type plus import and export data. Other tables cover prices, stocks, and the number of cheese plants. Most tables have historical data. Sources include official statistics and trade association data - annual*
• Latest Scoop: *statistics on ice cream market in US, Canada and other countries; published by International Ice Cream Association (part of IDFA) - annual*
• Milk Facts: *an annual review of the milk industry and market in the USA. Detailed statistics on production, consumption, utilisation, dairy products, imports, exports. Other tables cover prices, stocks, herds, farms. Historical statistics are included in most tables and data comes from a mixture of official sources and trade associations - annual*
Notes: umbrella organization for three separate associations - the Milk Industry Foundation (MIF), the National Cheese Institute (NCI), and International Ice Cream Association (IICA)

International Dairy Products Council
Conseil International des Produits Laitiers
Address: Centre William Rappard, Rue de Lausanne 154, CH-1211 Geneva, Switzerland
Telephone: +41 22 739 5111
Fax: +41 22 739 5760
Year established: 1980
Chief officers: Jorge A Ruiz (Chairman), Kim Luotonen (Vice Chairman), Mrs Gretchen Stanton (Secretary)
Membership: member states of the EU and representatives from a further 15 countries
Publications:
• World Market for Dairy Products: *the most important developments in global production, consumption and trade of milk products; tables and charts - annual*

International Egg Commission
Address: Suite 105, Albany House, 324-326 Regents Street, London WIR 5AA, United Kingdom
Telephone: +44 171 580 7425
Fax: +44 171 580 7430
Chief officers: Neil McKenzie (Executive Officer)
Publications:
• Monthly Chick Placement Bulletin: *annual*
• Promotion and Marketing Survey: *annual*
• Situation Outlook Report: *6 monthly*

International Federation of Consulting Engineers (FIDIC)
Fédération Internationale des Ingenieurs-Conseils
Address: PO Box 86, Avenue du Temple 13C - Chailly, CH-1012 Lausanne, Switzerland
Telephone: +41 21 654 4411
Fax: +41 21 653 5432
E-mail: fidic@pobox.com
Web site: www.fidic.org
Year established: 1913
Activities: ca. 50 publications on general information, agreements, tendering procedure, standard contract conditions, endorsement and software, all available on request; seminars, conferences, exchange of views and information service
Chief officers: Ernst Hofmann (President), Marshall Gysi (Managing Director), Gerda Paschoud (Administration Director), Peter van der Togt (Publications Manager)
Membership: 56 national associations worldwide; ca. 12 correspondent and affiliate members

Publications:
• Conference and seminar proceedings
• FIDIC International Directory: *assists clients, owners, bankers and international funding agencies to select consulting engineers. It contains information about major consulting engineering firms working internationally that are members of FIDIC member associations*
• Forms, Documents and Agreements

International Federation of Fruit Juice Producers (IFU)
Fédération Internationale des Producteurs de Jus de Fruits
Address: 10 rue de Liège, F-75009 Paris, France
Telephone: +33 1 487 43116
Fax: +33 1 532 19588
Year established: 1948
Activities: organises international congresses, symposia, workshops; provides annual statistics
Chief officers: Philippe Dardonville (Secretary General), H.U. Daepp (President), J.P. Roclore (Deputy Chairman), P.E. Eckes (Vice President), R. di Leonardo (Vice President)
Membership: 48 national associations, professional organisations and companies from 24 countries
Publications:
• Annual Activity Report of the International Federation of Fruit Juice Producers: *report on the activities of the various commissions; situation of the fruit juice industry in the member countries; statistical data on production and consumption; federation membership directory - annual*
• Bulletins: *extracts of articles appearing in the specific press on trade, acquisitions, mergers, statistics,...*
• Congresses, Symposia and Workshops Reports
• Newsletter
• Scientific Brochures

International Federation of Glucose Industries (IFG)
Fédération Internationale des Industries de Glucose
Address: Boîte 10, 1 Avenue de la Joyeuse Entrée, B-1040 Brussels, Belgium
Telephone: +32 2 230 2031
Fax: +32 2 230 0245
Telex: 22283 AACCEEB
Year established: 1968
Chief officers: Iliana Axiotiades (Secretary General)
Membership: manufacturers of starch derived sweeteners in 17 countries

International Federation of Grocers' Associations
Address: Postfach 2740, Falkenplatz 1, CH-3001 Bern, Switzerland
Telephone: +41 31 237 646
Fax: +41 31 237 646
Year established: 1927
Activities: biennial conference
Membership: 30 food retailers and food retail associations from 15 countries

International Federation of Independent Film Producers' Associations (FIAPF)
Fédération Internationale des Associations de Producteurs de Film
Address: 33 avenue des Champs-Elysées, F-75008 Paris, France
Telephone: +33 1 422 56214
Fax: +33 1 425 62386
Year established: 1973
Activities: statistics on cinema, video and television, available to members only
Structure: directorate
Membership: 50 national film producers associations

International Federation of Library Associations and Institutes (IFLA)

Address: Postbus 95312, Koninklijke Bibliotheek, Prins Willem-Alexanderhot 5, NL-2509 CH The Hague, Netherlands
Telephone: +31 70 314 0884
Fax: +31 70 383 4827
E-mail: lfla.hq@lfla.nl
Web site: www.nlc-bnc.ca/ifla/home.htm
Chief officers: Leo Voogt (Secretary General), Winston Roberts (coordinator of professional activities), Carol Hentry (Executive officer)
Publications:
• IFLA Directory: *biennial*
• Newsletter: *regular*

International Federation of Margarine Associations (IFMA)

Address: Boîte 4, 74 rue de la Loi, B-1040 Brussels, Belgium
Telephone: +32 2 230 4910
Fax: +32 2 230 2274
Telex: Olma 23628
Year established: 1987
Activities: statistics - annual trade sources (for members only)
Chief officers: Janet Nunn (Secretary General)
Membership: 29 national associations
Publications:
• Annual General Meeting Report: *annual*
• Circulars
• Newsletter of the International Federation of Margarine Associations (IFMA): *6 pa*

International Federation of Pharmaceutical Manufacturers' Associations (IFPMA)

Fédération Internationale de l'Industrie du Médicament
Address: PO Box 9, 30 Rue de Saint-Jean, CH-1211 Geneva 18, Switzerland
Telephone: +41 22 340 1200
Fax: +41 22 340 1380
E-mail: admin@ifpma.org   f.redard@ifpma.org (Secretary)
Web site: www.pharmweb.net:80/pharmweb/ifpma.html
Year established: 1968
Activities: central role in the exchange of information within the international industry and in the development of policy statements
Chief officers: Mr Séan Lance (President), Dr Richard Arnold (Executive Vice President), Mrs France Redard (Secretary)
Structure: General Assembly; 13-member Council, Secretariat, Permanent Committees as follows: Intellectual Property Co-ordination, Biologicals, Public Affairs, Advisory Committee on Health Economics, and various sub-Committees
Membership: 57 national pharmaceutical industry associations representing ca. 200 research-based pharmaceutical companies and ca. 200 national manufacturing companies in approximately 51 countries
Publications:
• GATT TRIPs and the Pharmaceutical Industry: a Review: *booklet which summarises the main issues of the Trade Related Intellectual Property Rights (TRIPs) Agreement*
• Health Horizons: *updates on the latest progress in medical and pharmaceutical research; news on health legislation; information on public health matters; and exclusive interviews with key figures in the healthcare field - 3 p.a.*
• IFPMA Code of Pharmaceutical Marketing Practices: *irregular*
• IFPMA Compendium on Regulation of Pharmaceuticals for Human Use: *two volume ring-binder with information on the system for the registration of pharmaceutical products in over 70 countries*
• Pharmaceutical Industry Issues Handbook: *irregular*
• Providing Quality Medicines for Health Care: *annual*
• Quality Assurance of Pharmaceutical Products: *annual*

International Federation of Pharmaceutical Wholesalers (IFPW)

Address: Suite 22A, 3915 Old Lee Highway, Fairfax Virginia 22030, USA
Telephone: +1 703 352 0808
Fax: +1 703 352 6905
E-mail: ifpwusa@ifpw.com
Web site: www.ifpw.com
Web site notes: the site includes a directory of members
Chief officers: William G. Goetz (President)

International Federation of Roofing Contractors (IFD)

International Föderation des Dachdeckerhandwerks
Address: POB 511067, Fritz-Reuter Straße 1, D-5000 Cologne 51, Germany
Telephone: +49 221 372058
Fax: +49 221 384336
Year established: 1952
Activities: organises triennial international Convention, as well as annual congress, regular work meetings and training
Chief officers: Henri Flener (President), Hans-Joachim Müssig (Secretary General), Klaus Jobke (Deputy Secretary)
Membership: 13 national organisations from 10 European countries
Publications:
• Circulars
• Dictionary
• Handbooks
• Recommendations

International Federation of Sewing Thread Manufacturers

Fédération Internationale de la Filterie
Address: BP 15, c/o Maisons des Professions, 40 rue Eugène Jacquet, F-59708 Marcq en Baroeul Cedex, France
Telephone: +33 3 208 97510
Fax: +33 3 206 50638
Year established: 1960
Activities: annual general assembly; information service for members
Chief officers: Jacques Dufour (Secretary General)

International Federation of Societies of Cosmetic Chemists (IFSCC)

Address: GT House, 24-26 Rothesay Road, Luton, Beds LU1 1QX, United Kingdom
Telephone: +44 1582 726 661
Fax: +44 1582 405 217
Year established: 1959
Activities: biennial conference; KOSMET database;1998 IFSCC Congress Paris, France; 1999 IFSCC Conference - South Africa; 2000 IFSCC Congress - Berlin, Germany; 2002 IFSCC Congress - Edinburgh, Scotland
Chief officers: Mrs Lorna Weston (General Secretary)
Membership: national associations from 31 countries representing 11,500 individuals
Notes: The Association does not produce any statistics or publications.

International Federation of Special Dietary Food Industries (ISDI)

Fédération Internationale des Industries des Aliments Diététiques
Address: 194 rue de Rivoli, F-75001 Paris, France
Telephone: +33 1 534 58787
Fax: +33 1 534 58780
E-mail: andrée.bronner@wanadoo.fr
Year established: 1965
Activities: technical expertise; advice to members, governments and international organisations; develops policies on codes of practice; collects and disseminates

information
Chief officers: Dr Andrée Bronner (Secretary General),
Véronique Clignet (Assistant Secretary General)
Membership: 25 national associations and companies from
19 countries
Notes: The Federation does not produce any publications or
statistics; see : Association of Dietetic Foods Industries of the
EU (IDACE) and International Association of Infant Food
Manufacturers (IFM)

International Federation of Stock Exchanges (FIBV)

Fédération Internationale des Bourses de Valeurs
Address: 22 boulevard de Courcelles, F-75017 Paris, France
Telephone: +33 1 440 10545
Fax: +33 1 475 49422
E-mail: fibv@mail3.imaginet.fr
Web site: www.fibv.com
Activities: produces statistics on stock exchanges and
finance around the world
Chief officers: Gerrit H. de Marez Oyens (General Secretary),
Renée Pouillon (Administrator), Lorenzo Gallai
(Economist-Statistics), Véronique Hayoun (Assistant)
Membership: 51 full members, covering over 97% of world
stock exchange market capitalization
Publications:
• A Study of the Market Structure for Small and Medium Sized
Businesses: *key issues and initiatives*
• Directory: *lists member stock exchanges*
• Focus: *monthly*
• Market Information on Member Stock Exchanges
• Statistical Year-Book: *annual*
• Statistics Report (International Federation of Stock
Exchanges): *statistics on stock exchange trends around the
world over the last year including share and stock price
changes. Based on returns from various member exchanges -
annual*

International Federation of the Independent Shoe Trade (INTERSHOE)

Fédération des Détaillants en Chaussures
Address: 44 boulevard du Magenta, F-75010 Paris, France
Telephone: +33 1 420 67930
Fax: +33 1 420 65209
Membership: national associations of shoe manufacturers

International Federation of the Periodical Press (FIPP)

Address: Queens House, 55/56 Lincoln's Inn Fields, London,
WC2A 3LJ, United Kingdom
Telephone: +44 171 404 4169
Fax: +44 171 404 4170
E-mail: info1@fipp.com
Web site: www.ppa.co.uk/fipp/
Year established: 1925
Chief officers: Per R. Mortensen (President and Chief
Operating Officer), Helen Bland (General Manager)
Membership: 33 national associations and 91 international
publishing companies and associate members representing
some 3,000 publishing companies, including approximately
50,000 titles in 37 countries
Publications:
• FIPP Membership Directory: *directory of FIPP members
including National Association, Publisher and Associate
members' contact details - annual*
• International Handbooks - Germany, Italy, Japan, UK, US:
*in-depth reports based on extensive data collection and
interviews. Includes distribution information and details about
entering these markets - irregular*
• International Media Guides: *five directories totalling 1,750
pages with 17,000 publications in over 200 countries. Lists
addresses, phone and fax numbers, key personnel, sales
contacts and representatives - annual*

• Magazine World: *international review of periodical publishing
trends - six times p.a.*
• Publishers Advertising Sales Information Group (PASIG
Research Abstracts): *dissemination of information on research
carried out by member companies for advertising selling
purposes - quarterly*
• Willings Press Guide: *media directory with full contact details
plus advertising rates and sizes, frequency, circulation,
subscription rates, summary of content and target audience -
annual*
• World Magazine Trends Handbook: *primary data source of
worldwide magazine publishing trends covering 37 countries
and includes: demographic data, number of consumer and
business titles; average issue readership; top 10 magazine
titles etc - annual*

International Federation of the Phonographic Industry (IFPI)

Address: 54 Regent Street, London W1R 5PH, United
Kingdom
Telephone: +44 171 878 7900
Fax: +44 171 878 7950
E-mail: info@ifpi.org
Year established: 1933
Activities: campaigns for the introduction and enforcement of
copyright and related legislation and co-ordinates the
industry's anti-piracy activities. The Association also
produces statistics on international retail sales of recorded
music
Chief officers: Catrin Hughes (Communications Director),
Nicholas Garnett (Director and CEO), David Fine (Chairman)
Membership: 1,300 record producers in 70 countries
world-wide
Publications:
• IFPI Annual Review: *a general review of the audiovisual
market with some statistics on specific markets in various
member counries. Based on returns from national associations
- annual*
• IFPI Newsletter: *industry issues and IFPI activities - quarterly*
• IFPI Pirate Sales: *estimates of illegal sales of pirated records
by type in over 65 countries world-wide - annual*
• IFPI World Sales: *statistics on retail sales of records by type
in over 65 countries world-wide - annual*
• Interim Sales Data: *statistics on retail sales of records by
type in over 65 countries world-wide - annual*
• Recording Industry in Numbers: *annual*
• World Record Sales by Year: *statistics on retail sales of
records by type in over 65 countries world-wide - annual*

International Federation of the Seed Trade

Address: Chemin du Reposoir 7, CH-1260 Nyon, Switzerland
Telephone: +41 22 361 9977/14
Fax: +41 22 361 9219
Year established: 1924
Activities: organises annual general assembly
Chief officers: Dr Bernard le Buanec (Secretary General)
Membership: 39 national associations; also individuals, full,
extraordinary and honorary life members from 52 countries
Publications:
• Annual Bulletin: *annual*
• Arbitration Procedure Rules for the International Trade in
Seeds
• Newsletter of the International Federation of the Seed Trade:
bi-monthly
• Rules and Usages for the International Trade in Seeds

International Federation of Tour Operators (IFTO)

Address: 170 High Street, Lewes, East Sussex BN7 1YE,
United Kingdom

Telephone: +44 1273 477 722
Fax: +44 1273 483 746
Year established: 1970
Activities: monthly closed meetings
Chief officers: Martin Brackenbury (President)
Membership: national tour operator associations in 19 countries
Publications:
● Planning for Sustainable Tourism: *summary of research carried out to develop a model of sustainable tourism - irregular*
Notes: Formerly known as Tour Operators Study Group, changed to present title in 1994.

International Federation of Wines and Spirits (FIVS)

Fédération Internationale des Vins et Spiritueux
Address: 116 boulevard Haussmann, F-75008 Paris, France
Telephone: +33 1 429 41827
Fax: +33 1 429 41446
Year established: 1951
Activities: annual general meeting, autumn meeting, annual symposium in February on the problems of the international drinks trade; laws and regulations
Chief officers: Donna Reitano Fenelon (Managing Director), Ernö Péter Botos (Vice President, Hungary), Alastair Eadie (President, UK)
Structure: general assembly of delegates from member associations, executive committee, standing committees on: alcohol and society, general trade policy, laws and regulations, intellectual property, environment
Membership: 59 national and regional associations whose members cover those involved in the production, export, import and distribution of wines and spirits in 28 countries
Notes: The Federation does not produce any publications or statistics.

International Feed Industry Federation (IFIF)

Address: 214 Prestbury Road, Cheltenham GL52 3ER, United Kingdom
Telephone: +44 1242 579 570
Fax: +44 1242 579 411
E-mail: 100544.2147@compuserve.com
Year established: 1987
Activities: feed industry technology transfer; annual conference; statistics on international feed production and stock production
Chief officers: Roger Gilbert (Secretary General)
Structure: general assembly, governing council, presidium, formation committee, advisory panel
Membership: ca. 60 national associations and individuals from approximately 17 countries
Publications:
● IFIF News: *news on the international feed industry - quarterly*

International Fertiliser Industry Association (IFA)

Association Internationale de l'Industrie des Engrais
Address: 28 rue Marboeuf, F-75008 Paris, France
Telephone: +33 1 539 30500
Fax: +33 1 539 30547
Year established: 1926
Activities: reports and statistics
Membership: ordinary, affiliate and associate members in 71 countries
Publications:
● Conference Proceedings
● Fertilizers and Agriculture
● Scientific and Technical Reports

International Flavour and Fragrance Industry Association (IFRA)

Address: Rue Charles-Humbert 8, CH-1205 Geneva, Switzerland
Telephone: +41 22 321 3548
Fax: +41 22 781 1860
Year established: 1973
Chief officers: Dr C Skopalik (President), Dr F Grundschober (Secretary General)
Membership: national associations in 14 countries
Publications:
● Bulletins
● Code of Practice for the Fragrance Industry: *defines good manufacturing practices for the use of fragrance ingredients*
● Newsletter

International Foodservice Manufacturers' Association (IFMA)

Address: Two Prudential Plaza, Suite 4400, 180 N. Stetson Avenue, Chicago, IL 60601, USA
Telephone: +1 312 540 4400
Fax: +1 312 540 4401
E-mail: IFMA@prodigy.com
Web site: www.foodserviceworld.com/ifma/
Year established: 1952
Activities: compiles statistics; marketing and market research; monitors government regulations and legislation; conducts seminars
Chief officers: Michael J Licata (President), Mary Neil Crosby (Communications Manager)
Structure: permanent staff; board; committees
Membership: over 600 food, beverage, equipment and supply manufacturers
Publications:
● International Foodservice Manufacturers' Association World: *newsletter - 9 p.a.*
● Membership Directory: *annual*

International Franchise Association (IFA)

Address: Suite 900, 1350 New York Avenue NW, Washington, DC 20005-4709, USA
Telephone: +1 202 628 8000
Fax: +1 202 628 0812
E-mail: ifa@franchise.org
Web site: www.franchise.org/
Year established: 1960
Activities: maintains library and information service; represents members
Chief officers: William B Cherkasky (President)
Structure: permanent staff; board; committees; councils
Membership: 850 firms in 58 countries using franchise method of distribution
Publications:
● 50 Best Low-Investment, High-Profit Franchises
● Answers to the 21 Most Commonly Asked Questions About Franchising
● College of Franchise Knowledge
● Complete Guide to Franchising in Canada
● Financing Your Franchise
● Franchise Bible
● Franchise Insider: *monthly*
● Franchise Legal Digest: *bi-monthly*
● Franchise Opportunities Guide: *semi-annual*
● Franchise Success System
● Franchise Survival Guide
● Franchises: Dollars & Sense
● Franchising Statistics: *the Association compiles regular statistics on franchise numbers, outlets, and types of businesses. These statistics cover various countries, but particularly North American and European areas - regular*
● Franchising World: *bi-monthly*

• Franchising: The Business Strategy that Changed the World
• Franchising: The Inside Story
• Investigate Before Investing
• Public Relations for the Franchisee: How to Create Your Own Publicity
• Running a Successful Franchise
• Tips & Traps When Buying a Franchise
• Wealth Within Reach
Notes: To order publications e-mail tanya@franchise.org. Research and information e-mail nancyw@franchise.org.

International Frozen Food Association (IFFA)

Address: 2000 Corporate Ridge, Suite 1000, McLean VA 22102-7805, USA
Telephone: +1 703 821 0770
Fax: +1 703 821 1350
Year established: 1973
Chief officers: Steven C. Anderson (Director General)
Publications:
• IFFA World Review: *news and statistics on the frozen foods market with data on specific foods and specific national markets - monthly*

International Grains Council (IGC)

Address: Canada Square, Canary Wharf, London E14 5AE, United Kingdom
Telephone: +44 171 513 1122
Fax: +44 171 513 0630
E-mail: igc-fac@igc.org.uk
Web site: www.igc.org.uk
Web site notes: site includes a summary of the Grain Market Report
Activities: organises a grain trade convention, annual conference. Produces statistics on production, trade, consumption and ocean freight rates
Chief officers: A.W. De Maria (Assistant Executive Director)
Membership: 32 member governments
Publications:
• Food Aid Shipments: *40 pages of data itemising individual donor shipments of wheat, wheat products, rice, maize (corn) and other grains. It contains information on food aid channelled by members through multilateral channels and records "triangular" transactions and "local purchases" - annual*
• Grain Market Report: *market commentary plus statistics on production, foreign trade, prices, consumption and stocks of grain - eleven issues a year*
• Ocean Freight Rates: *weekly freight rates for grain transported by sea for the major countries - weekly*
• Report for the Fiscal Year: *mainly commentary on the world wheat situation and Council activities but some statistics on production and trade - annual*
• Wheat and Coarse Grain Shipments: *50 pages of tables, the report contains detailed statistics on commercial and non-commercial world trade in wheat (including wheat flour, durum and semolina) and coarse grains (including maize (corn), barley, sorghum, oats and rye) - annual*
• World Grain Statistics: *production, foreign trade, stocks, prices, freight, etc. in the major countries with detailed data for a number of years - annual*

International Hotel and Restaurant Association (IH&RA)

Association Internationale de l'Hôtellerie
Address: 251 rue du Faubourg St Martin, F-75010 Paris, France
Telephone: +33 1 448 93400
Fax: +33 1 403 67330
E-mail: infos@ih-ra.com
Web site: www.ih-ra.com
Activities: information, training, regional cooperation programmes; international employment service for qualified

hotel staff; advice; study carried out twice a year on economic trends in the hotel industry worldwide; provides research reports.
Chief officers: Christiane Clech (Secretary General), Ken Hine (Director General & CEO), Ellen Mollay Director, Events Department), George Dommering (Treasurer), Allan Nyren (Secretary), Michael B. Peceri (President), Eric E. Pfeffer (Vice President)
Membership: 2 000 establishments in 150 countries including: chain headquarters, chain hotels, independent hotels and restaurants, national hotel and restaurant associations, suppliers to the international hospitality industry, educational centres for the hospitality industry, Individual members and hospitality students
Publications:
• Action: *reports on the association's achievements - quarterly*
• Careers & Choices
• Dialogue: *newsletter - bi-monthly*
• Environmental Action Pack: *guide for hotels on how to start and develop an environmental programme*
• Environmental Good Practice in Hotels: *case studies*
• Eurhotec Resource Book
• Hotels and Restaurants International: *official journal of the IHA - monthly*
• Hotels of the Future: *IHA commissioned report by Horwath & Horwath*
• IHA International Hotel Guide: *annual*
• Impact: *bulletin on current issues affecting international hospitality industry*
• InnDependent: *quarterly*
• Into the New Millennium: *white paper on the global hospitality industry*
• Opportunities: *information on hotel development and investment - bi-monthly*
• The IH&RA Tax Survey
• World Directory of Travel Agencies
Notes: IHA Asia Pacific Office, Contact: Andrew Jones, 2nd floor 36 Magazine Gap Rd. Hong Kong Tel: (852) 2849.8306 Fax: (852) 2849.8325, Email: hotel@asiaonline.net

International Ice Cream Association (IICA)

Address: Suite 900, 1250 High Street NW, Washington DC 20005, USA
Telephone: +1 202 737 4332
Fax: +1 202 331 7820
E-mail: jrice@idfa.org
Web site: www.foodexpo.com/orgs/iica/
Publications:
• Latest Scoop: *covers USA, Canadian, and international production of ice cream and related products and, for the USA, data is given for specific states and regions. Other statistics cover ice cream consumption, supermarket sales, sales by flavours, industry structure, etc. - annual*
Notes: Constituent organisation of the International Dairy Foods Association (IDFA)

International Institute for Synthetic Rubber Producers (IISRP)

Address: Suite 133, 2077 S Gessner Road, Houston TX 77063-1123, USA
Telephone: +1 713 783 7511
Fax: +1 713 783 7253
E-mail: iisrp@website.att.net
Web site: www.iisrp.com
Year established: 1961
Activities: symposia, conferences, annual general meeting
Chief officers: W E Tessmer (Director)
Structure: board of directors, executive committee, operating committees
Membership: 53 companies in 19 countries

Publications:
- Mooney Viscometer Measurement Video Kit
- Proceedings of annual meeting
- Story of an Industry
- Synthetic Rubber End-Use Survey
- Synthetic Rubber Manual
- Worldwide Rubber Statistics: *includes ten-year production figures by type and area and five-year forecasts by product type and area. Also includes details of the world's synthetic rubber plants and gives a statistical history of motor vehicle and tyre production in major markets. Based on various sources - annual*

International Mass Retail Association (IMRA)

Address: 10th floor, 1901 Pennsylvania Avenue, NW, Washington, DC 20006, USA
Telephone: +1 202 861 0774
Fax: +1 202 785 4588
Web site: www.imra.org
Year established: 1966
Activities: conducts research and educational programmes; liaison with state and federal government; compiles statistics
Chief officers: Robert J Verdisco (President)
Structure: permanent staff; board; committees
Membership: 800 members representing discount department stores, home centres, category dominant or speciality discounters, catalogue showrooms, and warehouse clubs, as well as 600 suppliers to the retail industry
Publications:
- IMRA Membership Directory and Exposition Guide: *annual*
- Mass Retailers' Merchandising Report: *annual*
- Operating Results of Mass Retail Stores: *review of the retail discount industry, including data on sales, earnings expenditure and key operating ratios - annual*
- Prerequisites in Mass Retailing: *semi-annual*

International Meat Trade Association

Address: 217 Central Markets, London EC1A 9LH, United Kingdom
Telephone: +44 171 489 0005
Fax: +44 171 248 4733
Year established: 1895
Activities: information service on meat stocks; arbitration service available to members
Chief officers: A G Gordon (Executive Director); C J Gadsden (Secretary General)
Membership: 62 corporate members (ordinary and associate)
Publications:
- Conditions of Sale for C.I.F. and F.O.B.: *contracts for imported meat, delivered terms, ex store terms, export terms and arbitration rules*
Notes: The Association does not produce statistics.

International Milling Association (IMA)

Address: c/o ECCO, Avenue des Gaulois 9, B-1040 Brussels, Belgium
Telephone: +32 2 736 5354
Fax: +32 2 732 3427
Year established: 1931
Activities: compiles statistics
Membership: national associations from 17 countries
Publications:
- IMA Bulletin: *irregular*

International Newspaper Marketing Association (INMA)

Address: 12770 Merit Drive, Suite 330, Dallas, Texas, USA
Telephone: +1 972 991 5900
Fax: +1 972 991 3151
E-mail: inma@connect.net

Web site: www.inma.org
Chief officers: Earl J. Wilkinson (Executive Director), Andrea Loubier (Membership Manager)
Membership: 1,000 member network of newspaper marketing professionals in more than 40 countries
Publications:
- IDEAS Magazine: *all aspects of newspaper marketing - monthly*

International Office of Cocoa, Chocolate and Sugar Confectionery (IOCCC)

Office International du Cacao, Chocolat et Confiserie
Address: Rue Defacqz 1, B-1000 Brussels, Belgium
Telephone: +32 2 539 1800
Fax: +32 2 539 1575
E-mail: sweets@ioccc.be
Year established: 1930
Activities: provides an international comparison of production, import/export and consumption of products of the chocolate, sugar confectionery and biscuit industries; organises a worldwide forum for associations and companies; supports research in all related fields
Chief officers: Hilde Van Gerwen (Secretary General), Nathalie Gyselinck (Publications)
Membership: represents 2000 companies in 23 countries
Publications:
- Cocoa Archive: *information on the cocoa industry; in particular the original scientific reports on which the research programme about Witches' Broom disease is based, or the report on research campaigns in Indonesia - 3 volumes*
- Factsheets: *review the state of scientific knowledge on various subjects, and are designed for use by scientists and interested readers in IOCCC member countries. They provide scientific information to the industry on various subjects such as: Dental caries - Diet and behaviour - Edible fats - Food additives/allergy & intolerance - Heavy metals - Methalyxanthines - The microbiology of confectionery - Nutritional goals & guidelines - Obesity - Pesticides - Role of diet in exercise - Salt - Sweeteners - Sugars*
- GMP - Code of Good Manufacturing Practice: *general aspects of hygiene and food safety as well as with specific aspects of the cocoa, chocolate and sugar confectionery industry*
- HACCP: *describes the principles of the HACCP (Hazard Analysis Critical Control Point) system as implemented in the cocoa, chocolate and sugar confectionery industry*
- IOCCC/CAOBISCO Statistical Review: *provides an international comparison of production, import/export and consumption of products of the chocolate, sugar confectionery and biscuit industries - annual*
- Methods of Analysis: *these relate to both commercial and Quality Assurance aspects; some have been approved as ISO or AOAC methods*
Notes: IOCCC is a merger of IOCC (International Office of Coffee and Chocolate) which was founded in 1930, and ISCMA (International Sugar Confectionery Manufacturers' Association), founded in 1953. Both organisations collaborated closely from 1980 to 1985, and they merged in January 1986 under the name of IOCCC.

International Office of Wine and Vineyards (OIV)

Office International de la Vigne et du Vin
Address: 11 rue Roquepine, F-75008 Paris, France
Telephone: +33 1 449 48080/426 50464
Fax: +33 1 426 69063
Year established: 1924
Activities: conferences, information services, statistics and research
Chief officers: Georges Dutruc-Rosset (Director General)
Membership: 42 wine producing and/or consuming countries
Publications:
- Bulletin de L'OIV: *codes for practice for wine growing and*

numerous scientific publications - bi-monthly
• La Lettre de L'OIV: *monthly*

International Organisation and European Union of Natural Mineral Water Springs (UNESEM-GISEMES)

Groupement International et Union Européenne des Sources d'Eaux Minérales Naturelles et des Eaux de Source
Address: 10 rue de la Trémoille, F-75008 Paris, France
Telephone: +33 1 472 03110
Fax: +33 1 472 02762
Year established: 1959
Activities: provides annual statistics
Chief officers: Jésus Perez Diaz (President), Helmut Ruhrmann (Vice President), Françoise de Buttet (General Secretary)
Membership: international associations of natural mineral water springs

International Organisation of Hotel and Restaurant Association (International HORECA)

Address: Blumenfeldstrasse 20, CH-8046 Zürich, Switzerland
Telephone: +41 1 377 5111
Fax: +41 1 372 0081
Chief officers: Dr Xavier Frei (Secretary General)

International Organisation of Motor Vehicle Manufacturers (OICA)

Organisation Internationale des Constructeurs d'Automobiles
Address: 4 rue de Berri, F-75008 Paris, France
Telephone: +33 1 435 90013
Fax: +33 1 456 38441
Year established: 1919
Activities: compiles statistics on world automobile production; liaises at international level between national associations in the automotive industry and intergovernmental and international law bodies
Chief officers: A Dieksmann (President), C Espinoza de los Monteros (1st Vice President), K H Chuo and R Huser (Vice Presidents), J M Muller (Secretary General)
Structure: technical committee (est 1956), industrial and economic policy committee (est 1975), exhibition committee (est 1976)
Membership: 35 national organisations, of which 20 represent the major manufacturing countries in Europe, America and Asia.
Publications:
• OICA Yearbook of the World's Motor Industry: *includes key statistics on vehicle production, registrations, trade, etc. based on various sources - annual*

International Organisation of the Flavour Industry (IOFI)

Address: Rue de Charles-Humbert 8, CH-1205 Geneva, Switzerland
Telephone: +41 22 321 3548
Fax: +41 22 781 1860
Year established: 1969
Activities: deals with the safety evaluation and regulation of flavouring substances
Chief officers: P van Berge (President), Dr F Grundschober (Secretary General)
Structure: general assembly, board of directors, committee of experts, working groups
Membership: 21 national associations

International Pepper Community

Address: 3rd Floor, Jalan H.R. Rasuna Said, Kav. 13.1 Kuningan, Jakarta, Indonesia
Telephone: +62 21 520 0401
Fax: +62 21 520 0401

Publications:
• Pepper Statistical Yearbook: *statistics on the international production and consumption of pepper with additional data on import and export trends and flows - annual*

International Pharmaceutical Federation (FIP)

Fedration Internationale Pharmaceutique
Address: Andries Bickerweg 5, 2517 JP The Hague, Netherlands
Telephone: +31 70 363 1925
Fax: +31 70 363 3914
E-mail: Pauline@fip.nl
Web site:
www.pharmweb.net/pwmirror/pw9/fip/pharmweb925.html
Year established: 1912
Membership: 250,000 pharmacists or pharmaceutical scientists around the world

International Publishers' Association (IPA)

Union Internationale des Éditeurs/International Verleger-Union
Address: Ave de Miremont 3, CH-1206 Geneva, Switzerland
Telephone: +41 22 346 3018
Fax: +41 22 347 5717
E-mail: secretariat@ipa-uie.org
Web site: www.ipa-uie.org
Web site notes: online publications, copyright information, links to publishing organisations worldwide
Year established: 1896
Activities: helps secure signatories to Berne Convention and Universal Copyright convention; takes part in the revisions and drafting of new Copyright Conventions; keeps the flow of books from one country to another free of tariffs and other obstructions; sections, groups, committees (specialised), and affiliated associations; care for special needs of members; International Copyright Symposium; organises regular international Congress ; seminars, trade fairs; statistics
Chief officers: Alain Gründ (President), J Alexis Koutchoumow (Secretary General)
Structure: international committee composed of the representatives of member associations, executive committee of 15 members, president and vice-president elected for a four-year term, secretary general responsible for the administration of the association, specialised sub-committees: copyright, electronic publishing, freedom to publish, reading committee
Membership: 69 member organisations in 60 countries
Publications:
• Calendar of International Book Fairs: *annual*
• Compilation of Statistics: *annual*
• Congress Proceedings
• Creative Role of the Professional or STM Publisher: *a detailed book about professional publishing, the business of publishing and the importance of printing - series*
• International Publishers' Bulletin: *quarterly*
• IPA 25th Congress Special Edition- Index on Censorship: *annual*
• IPA Newsflashes: *news from member associations, diverse events, copyright information and articles - monthly*
• IPA Online Publications on Copyright
• Reports
Notes: President's address: Alain Gründ, Librairie Gründ , 60 rue Mazarine, 75006 Paris;   tel : +33 1 43 29 87 40/ fax : +33 1 43 29 49 86

International Pulse Trade and Industry Confederation (IPTIC)

Confédération Internationale du Commerce et des Industries des Légumes Secs
Address: 286 Bourse du Commerce, 2 rue de Viarmes, F-75040 Paris Cedex 01, France

Telephone: +33 1 423 68435
Fax: +33 1 422 10371/1 423 64493
Year established: 1963
Activities: biennial general assembly
Chief officers: Jacques Gauthier (Executive Officer)
Structure: executive and 5 standing committees
Membership: national associations, companies and organisations in 25 countries

International Railway Congress Association (AICCF-IRCA)

Association Internationale du Congrès des Chemins de Fer/Internationale Eisenbahn-Kongreßvereinigung
Address: Section 10, Rue de France 85, B-1060 Brussels, Belgium
Telephone: +32 2 520 7831
Fax: +32 2 525 4084
Telex: (46) 20424 BERAIL B
Year established: 1885
Activities: organises congresses, conferences
Chief officers: E. Schouppe (President), A. Martens (Secretary General), P. Jacquemin (Head of Secretariat)
Membership: 27 governments; 15 organisations, ca. 90 railway administrations
Publications:
• IRCA Brochure: *explains what the association is about*
• Rail International/Schienen der Welt: *original papers dealing with all branches of railway science and management; technical, economic, financial and social matters; technical documents; information on UIC and IRCA activities; international news - monthly*
Notes: The Association does not produce statistics.

International Rayon and Synthetic Fibres Committee (CIRFS)

Comité International de la Rayonne et des Fibres Synthétiques
Address: Avenue E. Van Nieuwenhuyse 4, B-1160 Brussels, Belgium
Telephone: +32 2 676 7455
Fax: +32 2 676 7454
Activities: represents the European man-made fibres industry; collects a wide range of statistics on the man-made fibres sector
Chief officers: Monique Gerritsma (Secretary), Colin M. Purvis (Director General)
Membership: 40 members
Publications:
• Statistical Yearbook: *detailed statistics, by country and region, covering the production, consumption, imports and exports of rayon and synthetic fibres. Also data on sector structure and employment. Many tables have historical data over 5, 10, or 15 years and there are summary world figures. Based on data from various national associations and agencies - annual*

International Road Federation (IRF)

Address: 63 rue de Lausanne, CH-1202 Geneva, Switzerland
Telephone: +41 22 731 7150
Fax: +41 22 731 7158
E-mail: IRF@dial.eunet.ch
Web site: www.eunet.ch/Customers/irf
Web site notes: statistical information, data on road projects worldwide, press releases
Activities: organises seminars, conferences, produces statistics covering export, production, road taxation, etc, library, joint road projects
Chief officers: MW Westerhuis (Director General), A Sinding (Deputy Director General), S Woods (Director for Communications)
Membership: 600 members: associations, trade and sectoral organizations, construction equipment distributors, construction equipment manufacturers, road building, educational and research institutions, governmental organizations, highway systems technology, motor vehicle manufacturers, national road associations, oil and bitumen industry, road construction materials manufacturers, road infrastructure operators, traffic and safety devices, tyre and automotive accessories manufacturers
Publications:
• IRF Bulletin: *monthly*
• World Highways: *bimonthly*
• World Road Statistics: *statistics on road networks, production, export of motor vehicles, first registration and imports of motor vehicles, vehicles in use, road traffic, multimodal traffic comparisons, motor fuels, road accidents, rates and basis of assessment of road user taxes, annual receipts from road user taxation, road expenditure, energy, consumption. All major countries are covered with data collected from national agencies - annual*

International Rubber Association (IRA)

Address: PO Box 10531, 3rd & 4th Floors Bangunan Getah Asli, 148 Jalan Ampang, 50716 Kuala Lumpur, Malaysia
Telephone: +60 3 261 5566
Fax: +60 3 261 3179
Telex: MA 30220
Year established: 1971
Activities: rubber contracts; shipping/freight; palletisation of rubber; biennial general meeting
Chief officers: Frank J Ranioto (Chairman); Abdul Rasip Latiff (Executive Secretary)
Structure: management committee (8 members), secretariat
Membership: ca. 30 national and international associations from 15 countries

International Self-Service Organisation (ISSO)

Association Internationale du Libre Service/Internationale Selbstbedienungs-Organisation
Address: c/o EuroHandelsinstitut eV, Spichernstraße 55, D-50672 Cologne, Germany
Telephone: +49 221 579 93-0
Fax: +49 221 579 9345
Year established: 1960
Activities: collects statistics on worldwide self-service trends
Chief officers: Dr Bernd Hallier (President and Chief Executive)
Membership: Research institutes and associations in 17 countries, plus 3 guest members

International Silk Association (ISA)

Association Internationale de la Soie
Address: 34 rue de la Charité, F-69002 Lyon, France
Telephone: +33 4 784 21079
Fax: +33 4 783 75672
Chief officers: Mr Currie (General Secretary)
Membership: silk manufacturers and dealers

International Society of Violin and Bowmakers (ISVBM)

Address: Innere Margarethenstrasse 10, CH-4501 Basel, Switzerland
Telephone: +41 61 226 9191
Fax: +41 61
Year established: 1950
Membership: members in 18 countries

International Sugar Organisation (OIS)

Organisation Internationale de Sucre
Address: Canada Square, Canary Wharf, London E14 5AA, United Kingdom
Telephone: +44 171 513 1144

Fax: +44 171 513 1146
E-mail: iso@sugar.org.uk
Web site: www.sugarinfo.co.uk:80/ISO/isoconts.html
Year established: 1968
Activities: administers the international sugar agreement; produces statistics and information on the industry;organises seminars
Membership: governments of 43 countries
Publications:
• Monthly Report and Press Summary: *commentary on the world sugar market and a detailed, comprehensive summary of events and news during the month as published in the world commodity press - monthly*
• Pocket Sugar Yearbook: *production, consumption, stocks and foreign trade statistics for sugar over an eight year period. Covers all the major sugar producing and sugar importing countries - annual*
• Quarterly Market Review: *in depth analysis of the sugar market as well as the detailed country-by-country, short-term estimates of supply and demand and the world sugar balance - quarterly*
• Statistical Bulletin (International Sugar Organisation): *production, consumption, stocks and foreign trade data for the sugar producing and sugar importing countries. Data for the latest year and two or three earlier years - monthly*

International Tea Committee Limited

Address: Sir John Lyon House, 5 High Timber Street, London EC4V 3NH, United Kingdom
Telephone: +44 171 248 4672
Fax: +44 171 329 6955
Activities: compilation of statistics including acreage, production, imports, exports, quantities sold and prices realised at various auction centres
Chief officers: M J Bunston (Chairman); Peter Abel (Chief Executive)
Membership: 15 members representing producing and consuming governments/associations
Publications:
• Bulletin of Statistics: *comprises a section on tea-producing countries and exports followed by a section on tea-importing countries with trade by country of origin, quantities sold, prices and tea consumption per capita. Data for a number of years. A supplement reviews the world tea situation - annual; November*
• Monthly Statistical Summary: *general statistics on tea production and trade in producing countries, plus trade, consumption and prices in the consuming countries - monthly*
• World Tea Statistics: *an historical compendium of tea statistics with data over an 80 year period - regular*

International Telecommunication Satellite Organisation (INTELSAT)

Address: 3400 International Drive NW, Washington DC 20008-3098, USA
Telephone: +1 202 944 6800
Fax: +1 202 944 7898
E-mail: marketing.communications@intelsat.int
Web site: www.intelsat.com
Year established: 1964
Activities: establishes technical and operating standards
Chief officers: Irving Goldstein (Director General and CEO)
Membership: 135 member nations
Notes: INTELSAT is the world's largest commercial satellite communications services provider.

International Telecommunication Union (ITU)

Address: Place des Nations 1211, CH-Geneva 20, Switzerland
Telephone: +41 22 730 5111/969
Fax: +41 22 733 7256

Year established: 1865
Activities: organises and disseminates information for the planning and operation of telecommunication netwoks and services
Chief officers: Pekka Tarjanne (Secretary General), Jean Jipguep (Deputy Secretary General)
Membership: over 180 countries
Publications:
• African Telecommunications Statistics: *statistics on trends in the African telecommunications sector based on returns from national telecommunications distributors - annual*
• American Telecommunications Indicators: *statistics on trends in the US telecommunications sector based on returns from national and state telecommunications distributors - annual*
• European Telecommunications Indicators: *statistics on trends in the major European countries based on returns from national telecommunications distributors - annual*
• Yearbook of Common Carrier Telecommunications Statistics: *statistics on approximately 200 countries with data on system sizes, demand, traffic, equipment and staff. Figures for a number of years are given - annual*
Notes: the oldest intergovernmental organisation in the world

International Textile Manufacturers' Federation (ITMF)

Fédération Internationale des Industries Textiles/Internationale Vereinigung der Textilindustrie
Address: Am Schanzengraben 29, CH-8002 Zürich, Switzerland
Telephone: +41 1 201 7080
Fax: +41 1 201 7134
E-mail: secretariat@itmf.org
Web site: www.itmf.org/
Year established: 1904
Activities: information; subcommittees: cotton, spinners, technical, statistical, man-made fibres; official liaison with various intergovernmental organisations and with private and international textile and fibre organisations
Chief officers: Hervé Giraud (President), Herwig M Strolz (Director General), Peer Munkholt (Deputy Director), Edmund Travis Gartside (Honorary Treasurer)
Structure: management committee with proportionate representation from full and associate members (closed meetings)
Membership: 35 national associations, 16 associate members; from ca. 48 countries
Publications:
• Ad-hoc reports and studies
• Cotton Contamination Survey: *survey on the subject among spinning mills affiliated with its world-wide membership - biennial*
• International Cotton Industry Statistics: *contains data on the productive capacity (spindles and looms), machinery utilization and raw materials consumption in the short-staple sector of the textile industries in all countries - annual*
• International Production Cost Comparison - Spinning/Weaving/Knitting: *examines the cost structure in the spinning, weaving and knitting industries in selected countries, presenting a comparison of manufacturing costs and a breakdown of the major cost elements - biennial*
• International Textile Machinery Shipment Statistics: *shows shipments by country of destination, of spinning, weaving, draw texturing and knitting machines by manufacturers, provides a comprehensive picture of textile machinery investments in all countries and identifies investment trends - annual*
• International Textile Manufacturing: *this report contains the full text of the papers presented at the Federation's annual conference - annual*
• ITMF Country Statements: *review of the current state of the textile industry in each member country; included are data related to the general economic situation, textile*

manufacturing capacities, activity levels and trade in textiles. Both short-staple sector and pan-textile data are shown in tabular form, accompanied by a commentary for each country - annual
- ITMF Directory: *biennial*
- State of Trade Report: *compiled from reports received by ITMF from its member associations shows country-by-country changes in the spinning and weaving sectors for production, outstanding orders and sotcks during the last 12 quarters - quarterly*

International Tobacco Growers' Association (ITGA)

Address: PO Box 125, East Grinstead, West Sussex RH18 5FA, United Kingdom
Telephone: +44 1342 823 549
Fax: +44 1342 825 502
E-mail: 106227,2700@Compuserve.com
Web site: www.tobacoleaf.org
Year established: 1984
Activities: Annual General Meeting, advice and information available on request
Chief officers: David J Walder (Chief Executive)
Membership: national associations or cooperatives in 17 countries; producers of all types of tobacco: flavoured, burley, oriental, air- and flue-cured. Members account for over 80% of the world's traded tobacco
Publications:
- Tobacco Courier
- Tobacco Farming Sustainable Alternatives
- Tobacco Forum
- Tobacco in the Developing World: *annual, ad hoc*
- Tobacco Trade or Aid?
- Tobbacco in the Developing World: *irregular*
Notes: The asociation does not produce statistics on the industry.

International Trade Federations (ITF-FIP)

Fédérations Internationales Professionelles
Address: 33 rue de Trèves, B-1040 Brussels, Belgium
Telephone: +32 2 230 6295
Fax: +32 2 230 8722
Telex: 26966 CMTWCL B
Activities: instrumental in setting up the World Committee for Trade Action

International Trademark Association (INTA)

Address: 1133 Avenue of the Americas, New York, NY 10036-6710, USA
Telephone: +1 212 768 9887
Fax: +1 212 768 7796
E-mail: communications@inta.org
Web site: www.inta.org
Web site notes: site includes a listing of 4,000 registered trade marks/brand names
Year established: 1878
Activities: promotes the use of trademarks
Membership: 3200 corporations and firms in 117 countries. INTA's members are in every major industry, from aerospace to consumer goods, alcoholic beverages to textiles, electronics to financial services
Publications:
- Country Guides: *information on trademark filing, prosecution, registration, maintenance and enforcement on a country-by-country basis - annual*

International Union of Confectioners, Pastry Cooks and Ice Cream Makers

Union Internationale des Patissiers-Confiseurs et Glaciers
Address: 41 rue Glesener, L-1631 Luxembourg, Luxembourg
Telephone: +352 400 0221

Fax: +352 492 380
Telex: 2215 CHMET W
Year established: 1954
Chief officers: Ralph Weis (Secretary General)
Membership: national associations in 17 countries

International Union of Public Transport (UITP)

Union Internationale des Transports Publics/Internationaler Verband für Öffentliches Verkehrswesen
Address: Avenue de l'Uruguay 19, B-1000 Brussels, Belgium
Telephone: +32 2 673 6100
Fax: +32 2 660 1072
Telex: 046 63916
E-mail: administration@uitp.com
Web site: www.uitp.com
Year established: 1885
Activities: congresses, exhibitions; library service and database; studies all aspects of urban and regional public transport and overall mobility, considering the effects of economic and social changes, the consequences of shifting major business centres and all issues concerning public transport worldwide
Chief officers: Dr Pierre Laconte (Secretary General), J.P. Bailly (President)
Structure: 10 commissions and technical committees
Membership: 1,700 members
Publications:
- Biblio-Express: *bi-monthly*
- Congress Reports: *biennial*
- EuroExpress: *monthly*
- International Public Transport: *bi-monthly*
- Rapport d'Activité de l'UITP: *annual report - annual*
- Recueil UITP des Transports Publics 1985- 1986: *statistical information on over 1 100 public transport network worldwide*
- UITP Express: *bi-monthly*
Notes: Founded in 1885 as International Union of Tramways, Local Railways and Public Motor Transport. Present name adopted in 1939.

International Union of Railways (UIC)

Union Internationale des Chemins de Fer
Address: 16 rue Jean Rey, F-75015 Paris, France
Telephone: +33 1 444 92050/1 444 92020
Fax: +33 1 444 92059/1 444 92029
E-mail: uic-comm@imaginet.fr
Web site: www.uic.asso.fr
Activities: collects statistics on lines, traffic results for passengers and freight, revenues, etc.
Chief officers: Paul Véron (Communication), Stig Larsson (Chairman), Philippe Roumeguère (Chief Executive)
Membership: 119 railway companies, companies involved with in rail transport, etc.
Publications:
- Annual Report: *annual report*
- International Railway Statistics: *statistics collected from approximately 70 railway companies around the world with data for specific countries on lines, passengers, stock, freight trends, staff, financial data, and technical operating results - annual*

International Union of Roofing and Plumbing Contractors

Union Internationale de la Couverture et Plomberie/Internationale Union für Spenglerei und Sanitäre Installationen
Address: 9 rue La Pérouse, F-75784 Paris Cedex 16, France
Telephone: +33 1 406 95307
Fax: +33 1 450 21880
Year established: 1949
Activities: collects statistics on salaries, comparisons of costs in different branches, working time; no statistics concerning production and turn-over; economic and social activities;

vocational training; technical advice and information
Chief officers: Eduard Kull (President -Switzerland), Gerard
Laurent (Vice President -Paris), Max Meyer (Managing
Director -Switzerland)
Membership: 11 national associations in 12 countries
Notes: No external publications, only internal communications.

International Union of the Associations of Heating, Ventilating and Conditioning Contractors (GCI)

Génie Climatique International
Address: Boîte 5, Rue Brogniez 41, B-1070 Brussels, Belgium
Telephone: +32 2 520 7300
Fax: +32 2 520 9749
Year established: 1935
Chief officers: Paul Reckinger (President), Mike Burgoyne
(Vice President), Gerard Broeders (Treasurer), Jozef
Vantieghem (Secretary General)
Membership: 14 national associations in Europe representing
over 20 000 companies
Publications:
• Membership Directory
• Presentation and Historical Survey of the GCI
Notes: member of the CEETB (European Technical
Contractors Committee for the Construction Industry) based in
Brussels

International Vine and Wine Office

Address: 18 rue d'Aguesseau, F-75008 Paris, France
Telephone: +33 1 449 48080
Fax: +33 1 426 69063
Chief officers: Mr Dutruc-Rosset (Director General)
Publications:
• Situation de la Viticulture dans le Monde: *a review of the
world wine industry with data on grape growing trends,
cultivation, etc. Specific data on certain countries important as
wine producers - annual*

International Wood Products' Association (IHPA)

Address: 4214 King Street, West, Alexandria, Virginia 22302,
USA
Telephone: +1 703 820 6696
Fax: +1 703 820 8550
E-mail: info@ihpa.org
Web site: www.ihpa.org
Activities: sponsors trade fairs, disseminates information on
importing wood products, monitors government legislation
Membership: represents companies that handle imported
wood products
Publications:
• IHPA Membership Directory: *listing of all members, by
classification of membership, with complete contact
information, products and species imported.*
• IHPA NEWS: *trends in the wood products industry - monthly*
• Import Statistics: *imports of wood products based on official
data from the Commerce Department - annual*

International Wool Secretariat (IWS)

Address: Valley Drive, Ilkley LS29 8PB, United Kingdom
Telephone: +44 1943 601555
Fax: +44 1943 601521
Year established: 1964
Activities: research, technical, styling, fashion and marketing
services; attends fabric fairs
Chief officers: Mac Drysdale (Chairman)
Membership: woolgrowers in 4 countries
Publications:
• International Wool Secretariat Annual Review
• Wool Facts: *statistics and data*

International Wool Textile Organisation

Address: 63 Albert Drive, London SW19 1LB, United Kingdom
Telephone: +44 181 788 8876
Fax: +44 181 788 5171
E-mail: whlarkinlon@msn.com
Activities: produces statistics on production, external trade,
capacities and prices
Membership: National Associations in 23 countries
Publications:
• International Wool Textile Overview: *bi-annual*
• Wool Statistics: *data on wool production, international trade
and the consumption of wool. Data for individual countries and
some tables have historical runs of data - bi-annual*

Latin American Association of Advertising Agencies (ALAAP)

Associação Latino Americana de Agencias de Publicidade
Address: Rua Alvaro Chaves 665, 90220-040 Porto Alegre
RS, Brazil
Telephone: +55 51 222 5429/222 5222
Fax: +55 51 222 5490
E-mail: alap@pro.via-rs.com.br
Web site: www.procergs.com.br/alap/alap.html
Year established: 1983
Activities: holds a Data Bank, which provides information on
advertising rates of the main newspapers, magazines,
television and radio stations, billboards and suppliers of the
advertising business
Chief officers: Edmar Costa (President), Joao Firme de
Oliveira (General Secretary)
Membership: advertising agencies in Latin America

Latin American Association of the Pharmaceutical Industry (CAPLA)

Asociación Latinoamericana de las Industrias Farmacéuticas
Address: CP 1405, A Coite 520, Buenos Aires, Argentina
Telephone: +54 1 903 4440
Fax: +54 1 903 4440
Year established: 1980
Chief officers: Dra Mirta Leve (Executive Secretary)
Structure: general assembly, board of directors

Latin American Federation of Marketing (FELAM)

Federación Latinoamericana de Marketing
Address: Viamonte 723, 7° piso, oficina 27, 1053 Buenos
Aires, Argentina
Telephone: +54 1 382 4005/382 4006
Fax: +54 1 383 6799
E-mail: info@aam-ar.com
Year established: 1997
Activities: exchange of information; information service,
training courses, seminars and conferences
Chief officers: Sergio Smith (President), Delfina Balestra
(Secretary)
Membership: marketing associations from Argetina, Bolivia,
Brazil, Colombia, Ecuador, Mexico, Paraguay, Peru, Uruguay
and Venezuela
Publications:
• FELAM Bulletin (Gacetilla de la Federación Latinoamericana
de Marketing): *news and issues related to marketing in Latin
America - monthly*

Liaison Group of the European Mechanical, Electrical, Electronic and Metalworking Industries (ORGALIME)

Organisme de Liaison des Industries Mécaniques, Métalliques,
Electriques et Electroniques Européennes
Address: Rue de Stassart 99, B-1050 Brussels, Belgium
Telephone: +32 2 511 3497/2 511 3484
Fax: +32 2 512 9970
E-mail: secretariat@orgalime.be

Year established: 1954
Activities: annual conference in October for members; information service for members; bi-annual statistics on production, import, export, investment, employment; international economic studies; coordination of the European engineering industry's views on EU initiatives, lobbying, etc in most areas of interest to the industry, with the exception of industrial relations (dealt with by a seperate organisation).
Chief officers: Ed de Haas (President), Heinz Rashka (Chairman of Council), Patrick Knox-Peebles (Secretary General)
Structure: president's committee, executive committee, management committee; 3 liaison committees for main sectors: MELC (mechanical), EELC (electrical and electronic), MALC (metalworking); 4 working groups: legal, trade policy, environment, economics and statistics
Membership: 25 national federations and associations from 16 EU countries; each member covers the entire engineering industry or one of its main branches
Publications:
● Annual Report of the European Mechanical, Electrical, Electronic and Metalworking Industries (ORGALIME): *includes list of members - annual*
● Conditions for contract: *general conditions for the supply of mechanical, electrical and associated products S92 / General conditions for the supply and erection of mechanical, electrical and associated electronic products SE94 / Conditions for the provision of technical personnel abroad / International conditions of contract for the repair of machinery and equipment*
● Contract price adjustment
● Drawings & technical documents, Ownership and protection against improper use
● Guides: *international commercial arbitration / Bank guarantees / Product liability in Europe - a practical guide for industry / For drawing up an international research and development contract (Eng/Ger) / Commercial agency law in Europe (Eng/Fr) /For preparing a know-how contract (Eng) / Council directive on electromagnetic compatibility EMC (Eng) - various*
● Information Bulletin: *monthly*
● Law on General Conditions in Western Europe
● Model forms: *agency contract - International agency on an exclusive basis / Exclusive agreement with distributors abroad / International patent licence contract / Maintenance contract / Processing contract / Consortium agreement / OEM (Original equipment manufacturer) contract (English and French only) - various*

Liaison Office of the European Ceramic Industry (CERAME-UNIE)

Address: 18-24 rue des Colonies, B-1000 Brussels, Belgium
Telephone: +32 2 511 3012/511 7025
Fax: +32 2 511 5174
Year established: 1962
Chief officers: 6 national federations

Mailleurop

Comité des Industries de la Maille de l'UE
Address: Rue Montoyer 24, B-1000 Brussels, Belgium
Telephone: +32 2 285 4894
Fax: +32 2 230 8669
Chief officers: Jean-Marie Costermans (Secretary General)
Membership: representatives of the knitwear industry in Europe

Marques (Association of European Brand Owners)

Address: 852 Melton Rd, Thurmaston, Leicester LE4 8BN, United Kingdom
Telephone: +44 116 264 0080

Fax: +44 116 264 0141
E-mail: marques@martex.co.uk
Year established: 1986
Activities: produces a monthly newsletter available to members only
Chief officers: Colin Grimes (Secretary General)

North American Automotive Products Industry European Office (NAAPIEO)

Address: Avenue Marcel Thiry 204, B-1200 Brussels, Belgium
Telephone: +32 2 774 9606
Fax: +32 2 774 9690
Year established: 1992
Activities: introductory business advices, initial contact buildings, regulatory information; provides listings, publications database, international show listings to its members
Chief officers: Wills Hughes-Wilson (Secretary General), Poul Hansen
Membership: representative office of MEMA and SEMA so a combination of their members
Publications:
● Europe Automotive Insight: *developments in the automotive OE and aftermarkets, technological developments and EU news - monthly*

Oil Companies International Study Group for Conservation of Clean Air and Water in Europe (CONCAWE)

Address: Madouplein 1, B-1210 Brussels, Belgium
Telephone: +32 2 220 3111
Fax: +32 2 219 4646
Web site: www.concawe.be/
Year established: 1963
Activities: technical and economic studies relevant to oil refining, distribution and marketing in Europe
Chief officers: Peter Gill (Chairman), Gundolf Goethel (Vice Chairman)
Membership: 29 members companies and 1 associate member
Publications:
● Catalogue of Concawe reports
● Catalogue of CONCAWE special interest reports
● European downstream oil industry safety performance: *statistical summary of reported incidents*
● Performance of cross country pipelines in Western Europe: *statistical summary of reported spillages*
● Streamline: *a database on petroleum substance classification for use on a personal computer (programme being tested, to be issued later)*

Organisation of Asia Pacific News Agencies (OANA)

Address: c/o Antara, Wisma Antara, Jalan Merdeka Selatan 17, Jakarta, Indonesia
Telephone: +62 21 344 379
Fax: +62 21 363 052
Year established: 1961
Activities: news agencies' association

Pacific Asia Travel Association (PATA)

Address: Telesis Tower, 1 Montgomery Street, San Francisco CA 94104, USA
Telephone: +1 415 986 4646
Fax: +1 415 986 3458
E-mail: patahq@ix.netcom.com
Web site: www.pata.org
Chief officers: Lakshman Ratnapala (President and CEO)
Membership: 2,100 worldwide travel industry organisations, including 101 government, state and city tourism bodies, 76

airlines and cruise lines and approximately 2,060 industry members serving the Pacific Asia region
Publications:
• Annual Statistical Report (Pacific Asia Travel Association): *tourism and travel statistics covering 30 countries including data by country of arrival, purpose of visit, age and sex of tourists, outbound travel of residents, etc. Statistics usually cover the last two years - annual*
• Cooperative Market Studies: *a series of market studies on various countries in the region with information on the following: motivations for taking an overseas holiday, importance ratings of various factors in choosing a destination; knowledge and perceptions of various holiday destinations; the trip planning process; sources of information; television, radio, magazine, and newspaper consumption: preferred type of holiday, expected duration of trip; anticipated accommodations: type of travel arrangements made; travel expenditures; cruising: familiarity with airline; factors important in selecting an airline; image of various airlines; market segmentation by cluster analysis. Based on a survey conducted by the Association and on other secondary sources*
• Market Intelligence Reports: *provide analysis of the political, economic, demographic and travel trends in selected markets. These reports describe each country's overall political structure and the factors which are likely to affect their political stability and future outlook especially as they relate to tourism issues*
• Quarterly Statistical Report (Pacific Asia Travel Association): *a quarterly update of the annual statistics contained in the Annual Statistical Report - quarterly*

Pan-American Dairy Federation (FEPALE)
Federación Panamericana de Lechería
Address: Information System, Ituzaingó 1324/503, 11000 Montevideo, Uruguay
Telephone: +598 2 965 356
Fax: +598 2 957 670
Year established: 1991
Activities: national and international statistics; congresses, fairs, workshops, training and seminars; gives technical advice; promotes business; technology updateand cooperation in the dairy sector of the Americas
Chief officers: Fabio Scarcelli (President), Dr Eduardo Fresco Leon (General Secretary), Jose P Urraburu (information Manager)
Structure: non-governmental and non-profit organisation
Membership: dairy companies and institutions from Argentina, Bolivia, Brazil, Colombia, Costa Rica, Cuba, Dominican Republic, Guatemala, Mexico, Paraguay, Peru, Uruguay and Venezuela
Publications:
• Panamerican Dairy Federation Newsletter: *general information regarding the Panamerican and international dairy sectors - bi-monthly*

Photo Marketing Association International (PMA)
Address: 3000 Picture Place, Jackson, MI 49201, USA
Telephone: +1 517 788 8100
Fax: +1 517 788 8371
E-mail: PMA_Business_Resources@pmai.org
Web site: www.pmai.org
Year established: 1974
Activities: maintains library; compiles statistics, conducts research programs
Chief officers: Neil D. Cohen (President)
Structure: permanent staff; regional and local groups
Membership: represents 17,000 members in over a hundred countries. PMA members represent almost every segment of the photo/imaging industry: photo/video retailers; wholesale and mail-order photofinishers; retail minilabs; photo

retail/studio operators; electronic imaging service centres; commercial, people and corporate/institutional labs; professional school portrait companies; and photo/video repair technicians
Publications:
• PMA Canadian Consumer Photographic Survey: *survey of 1,500 households across Canada. Covers ownership and use of cameras and video equipment; use of film and film processing, including one-hour processing; plans to purchase new equipment; storage of prints; use of professional portrait services; camera and video repair; and household buying behaviour - annual*
• PMA Industry Trends Report: *provides a performance and trend analysis of the U.S. photographic market, with a chapter on international trends. Areas covered in-depth include consumer markets, professional markets, channels of distribution, and international markets - annual*
• PMA U.S. Consumer Photographic Survey: *numerous breakdowns by demographic categories of age, income, household composition, and region. Topics covered in detail include: camera and camcorder ownership, consumer photographic behaviour, camera and camcorder purchase in the previous 12 months, camera and camcorder used most, camera and camcorder future purchase plans, one-time-use cameras, film use, photofinishing use, fast photo processing, video equipment ownership and use, camera repair, professional portrait photography, print storage and display, advertising awareness etc. - annual*
• PMA UK Consumer Photographic Survey: *in-depth photographic survey examining camera ownership and usage, single-use cameras, film usage, photo processing usage, picture taking activities, spending on photo and video goods and services, advertising awareness, professional portrait services, and consumer use of computers and electronic imaging services - annual*
• Who's Who in Photographic Management: *PMA membership directory contains alphabetical and geographical listings of more than 16,000 key industry people worldwide - annual*

Photo Marketing Association International (UK) Ltd
Address: Peel Place, 50 Carver Street, Birmingham B1 3AS, United Kingdom
Telephone: +44 121 212 0299
Fax: +44 121 212 0298
Publications:
• PMA United Kingdom Consumer Photographic Survey: *based on a panel of 1,000 households, the results provide an analysis of the photographic market in the UK. Statistics on camera ownership, types of cameras used, distribution channels, films used and types of films purchased, use of professional services - every five years*

Private Label Manufacturers' Association
Address: WTC, Stravimsky Laan 705, 1077 XX Amsterdam, Netherlands
Telephone: +31 20 575 3032
Fax: +31 20 575 3093
Activities: information sevice; trade shows; general statistics
Chief officers: 40 key personnel
Membership: 2,500 companies worldwide
Notes: Publications are unavailable to non-members.

Regional Book Promotion Centre for Africa (CREPLA)
Centre Regional du Promotion du Livre en Afrique
Address: BP 1646, Yaoundé, Cameroon
Telephone: +237 224 782/222 936
Chief officers: William Moutchia (Director)

Retail Codification Institute of Central America (ICCC)

Instituto Centroamericano de Codificación Comercial
Address: Edificio Cámara de Industria, Nivel 10, Ruta 6, 9-21
Zona 4, Guatemala, Guatemala
Telephone: +502 2 341 327
Fax: +502 2 326 658

Sea Fish Industry Authority

Address: 18 Logie Mill, Logie Green Road, Edinburgh EH7
4HG, United Kingdom
Telephone: +44 131 558 3331
Fax: +44 131 558 1442
E-mail: seafish.co.uk
Activities: research & development, marketing, training;
collects statistics on all areas in relation to fish industry
Chief officers: E. Davey (Chairman), Alasdair Fairbairn (Chief
Executive), R.M. Kennedy (Marketing Director)
Publications:
• Annual Report: *annual*
• European Supplies Bulletin: *data on fish landings, values,
markets, and sales of fish and fish products. Data for
individual European countries (16 countries) and based on
data collected by the authority - quarterly*
• Fisheries Economics Newsletter
• Household Fish Consumption in Great Britain: *a review of
fish sales broken down by type of fish: fresh/chilled and
frozen, based on a sample survey of households - quarterly*
• Key Indicators (Sea Fish Industry Authority): *basic statistics
on supplies, demand, household consumption, foreign trade,
prices. Based largely on official sources - quarterly*
• Technical Reports: *ad hoc*
• Trade Bulletin (Sea Fish Industry Authority): *imports and
exports of fresh and frozen fish, with data by value and
volume. Figures for the latest month, year-to-date,and
comparative figures for the previous year. Based on official
sources - monthly*

Society of Publishers in Asia

Address: Room 502-503, Admiralty Centre Tower 1, 18
Harcourt Road, Admiralty, Hong Kong
Telephone: +852 286 54007
Fax: +852 286 52559

Software Publishers' Association Europe (SPA)

Address: 57, Rue Pierre Charron, 75008 Paris, France
Telephone: +33 1 537 76377
Fax: +33 1 537 76378
E-mail: info@spa-europe.org
Web site: www.spa-europe.org
Web site notes: site includes quarterly and annual software
sales data for Western Europe for the latest year
Chief officers: Gerard Gabella (Managing Director), Jim
Sanders (Research Director)
Membership: 200 European software developers, publishers,
republishers, distributors, hardware manufacturers, and other
industry-related firms, from more than 20 different countries.
SPA Europe caters to the business, consumer and education
software markets
Publications:
• SPA Membership Directory: *1200 companies in the software
industry (publishers, developers, distributors, service
companies, with contact information, company description,
product list etc.*
Notes: SPA Europe is an affiliate of the Software Publishers
Association in the United States which has a membership of
over 1,200 firms.

Standing Committee of the Glass Industries of the EU (CPIV)

Comité Permanent des Industries du Verre de la CEE
Address: Boîte 2, Avenue Louise 89, B-1050 Brussels,
Belgium
Telephone: +32 2 538 4446
Fax: +32 2 537 8469
Year established: 1962
Activities: collects statistics on production, import, export
Chief officers: Dr W G A Cook (President), Gilbert Maeyaert
(Secretary General), Frédéric van Houte (Assistant Secretary
General), Véronique Faury-Dupuis (Assistant)
Structure: standing committee
Membership: 16 national glass federations
Publications:
• CPIV-Info: *monthly*
• Panorama of the EU Glass Industry: *commentary and
statistics on the glass industry in the European Union with
some statistics on specific countries, and by type of glass.
Based largely on data collected by the association - annual*

Sugar Association of the Caribbean

Address: PO Box 719C, Bridgetown Barbados;, 80
Abercromby Street, Port of Spain, Trinidad & Tobago
Telephone: +1 868 4 250 010/623 6106/636 2449
Fax: +1 868 4 250 007/636 2847
Year established: 1942
Activities: exchange and dissemination of information,
associated with the Commonwealth Sugar Exporters and the
Caribbean Cane Farmers' Association; finances and
administers the West Indies Central Sugar Cane Breeding
Station; conducts scientific and other research in the industry;
exchanges and disseminates information; publishes material
in regard to the industry
Chief officers: Harold B Davis (Chairman), Sheridan Race
(Secretary)
Structure: board of directors composed of one director
nominated by each member association
Membership: national sugar associations from Barbados,
Belize, Guyana, Jamaica, St Kitts-Nevis, Trinidad and Tobago
Publications:
• Annual Report of the Sugar Association of the Caribbean:
annual
• Research Papers
Notes: Although the physical offices and street address are in
Trinidad and Tobago, the postal address is in Barbados

Tea Council Limited (The)

Address: 5 High Timber Street, London EC4V 3NJ, United
Kingdom
Telephone: +44 171 248 1024
Fax: +44 171 329 4568
E-mail: tea@teacouncil.co.uk
Web site: www.teacouncil.co.uk
Web site notes: site includes statistics on tea sales in the UK,
as well as information on brand shares and on tea's share of
the total drinks market
Year established: 1967
Chief officers: Ken Pringle (Chairman), IL Lewis (Executive
Director and Secretary)
Membership: members include the Tea Board of India, Sri
Lanka Tea Board, Tea Board of Kenya, Tea Association of
Malawi, Tea Packers Association
Publications:
• Annual Report: *covers the activities of the Association and
various statistics on the world market for tea. Includes
statistics on annual production, supply and demand, exports,
apparent consumption in the United Kingdom, average per
capita consumption and percentage of population drinking
daily - annual*

Technical Association of Latin American Newspapers (ATDL)

Asociación Técnica de Diarios Latinoamericanos
Address: Casilla Postal 09-01-0531, Guayaquil, Ecuador
E-mail: jaimep@telconet.net or cgi95532@icepr.com
Web site: www.atdl.com/
Year established: 1982
Activities: seminars and training courses, collects statistics
Chief officers: Jaime Pérez (Executive President), Fernando Guerrero (Executive Director)
Membership: 30 newspapers
Notes: Executive Director's address: Apartado Postal 297, San Juan, Puerto Rico 00902.

Textile Industry Federation of Africa and Madagascar (FITAM)

Fédération de l'Industrie Textile Africaine et Malgache
Address: 13 rue de Peronne, F-80200 Cartigny, France
Telephone: +33 3 228 696 42
Fax: +33 3 228 693 09
Year established: 1978
Chief officers: Hugues Bouvard (Secretary General)
Membership: 15 countries: Benin, Burkina Faso, Cameroon, Central African Republic, Chad, Democratic Rep of Congo, Rep of Congo, Gabon, Ivory Coast, Madagascar, Mali, Mauretania, Niger, Senegal and Togo
Publications:
• Textile Industry Federation of Africa and Madagascar Newsletter: 5 p.a.

Textile Institute

Address: 10 Blackfriars Street, Manchester M3 5DR, United Kingdom
Telephone: +44 161 834 8457
Fax: +44 161 835 3087
E-mail: tiihq@textileinst.org
Web site: www.texi.org
Activities: education and training, dissemination of information, information service, maintains a library. The Textile Institute is the World's leading publisher of periodicals and books for every part of the industry from fiber engineering to fashion retailing, including marketing, design, technology, production and financial management of yarns and fabrics, clothing and footwear, interior and technical textiles
Chief officers: Paul Daniels, (Publications Manager)
Membership: individuals and companies worldwide from all industry sectors including: fibre, yarn and fabric manufacturing; dyeing and finishing; production of knitwear and making-up of clothing; footwear production; manufacture of carpets, soft furnishings and other household textiles; manufacture of textile products used in engineering, agriculture, medicine and other fields; and the distribution and retailing of textile products to personal and commercial markets
Publications:
• Journal of The Textile Institute: *papers presenting the results of research in Fiber Science and Textile Technology, Textile Economics, Management and Marketing - quarterly*
• Textile Horizons: *covers every sector of fiber-based activity. Contains articles on topics of current interest and new developments in the industry - bi-monthly*
• Textiles Magazine: *each issue focuses on a particular fiber, process and product, with regular features including technology, book reviews, career guides, profiles of individuals and companies - quarterly*

Toy Industries of Europe (TIE)

Address: Avenue de Tervueren 13a, B-1040 Brussels, Belgium
Telephone: +32 2 732 7040

Fax: +32 2 736 9068
E-mail: european.strategy@infoboard.be
Year established: 1990
Activities: annual conference; research on play value and effects of video games
Chief officers: Maurits Bruggink (Secretary General), Graham Benison (President)
Membership: 24 members - companies and national associations
Publications:
• Advertising, Children and Adolescents
• Brochure TIE
• TIE Against Conterfeit Toys
• TIE Bulletin: *monthly*
• Value of Toys and Play
Notes: The Association does not produce statistics.

Tropical Growers' Association (TGA)

Address: Wigham House, 16/30 Wakering Road, Barking, Essex 1G11 8PG, United Kingdom
Telephone: +44 181 594 5346
Fax: +44 181 507 8017
Year established: 1907
Activities: technical advice to members; compilation of statistics for members only
Chief officers: P D Gatland (Director)
Structure: non-profit making organisation; London council, Malaysia council; finance, trade and technical committees
Membership: 80 tropical plantation owners. The major crops include palm oil, coconut, rubber, tea, coffee, fruit, sugar, cotton, bananas, spices, etc.
Publications:
• Annual Report and Financial Statements of the Tropical Growers' Association (TGA): *includes country reports - annual*
• Newsletter (Tropical Growers' Association): *includes statistics on tropical crops - every two months*

Union of Associations of Semolina Manufacturers of the EU (SEMOULIERS)

Union des Associations des Semouliers des Communautés Européennes
Address: Via del Croceferi N 44, 00187 Rome, Italy
Telephone: +39 6 678 5409/679 4425
Fax: +39 6 678 3054
Telex: 621487 MOL PAS
Year established: 1961
Activities: annual conference
Chief officers: Dr Fabrizio Vitali (Secretary General)
Membership: 10 national associations

Union of European Independent Retail Groups

Union des Groupements de Commercants Détaillants Indépendants de l'Europe
Address: Avenue des Gaulois 3, B-1040 Brussels, Belgium
Telephone: +32 2 732 4660
Fax: +32 2 735 8623
E-mail: ugal@optinet.be
Year established: 1963
Activities: collects statistics covering members' turnover, profit, number of outlets etc. Also provides an information service and operates sector working groups
Chief officers: Denis Labatut (Secretary General), Anne Sophie Piavaux (Assistant)
Structure: general assembly, head committee, secretariat
Membership: 20 retail buying groups, representing over 120,000 retailers from 12 European Union countries plus Norway and Switzerland
Publications:
• Annual Report: *annual*

Union of Industrial and Employers' Confederations of Europe (UNICE)

Union des Confédérations de l'Industrie et des Employeurs d'Europe
Address: Boîte 4, Rue Joseph II 40, B-1000 Brussels, Belgium
Telephone: +32 2 237 6511
Fax: +32 2 231 1445
E-mail: main@unice.be
Year established: 1958
Activities: documentation centre - visits by appointment only
Chief officers: Z.J.A. Tyszkiewicz (Secretary General), François Perigot (President)
Membership: 33 central industry and employers' federations from 25 European countries
Publications:
● CBI European Business Handbook: *comprehensive information on the political background as it is expected to evolve in 1997; an up-to-date survey of local economies and business conditions in the countries of the European Union and Eastern Europe; sources of further information*
● Compendium of Position Papers: *over 100 important papers along with press releases, speeches and other public documents - 2 p.a.*
● UNICE Information: *overview of future trends and immediate past work - every 2 months*
Notes: The Association does not produce statistics.

Union of International Associations (UAI)

Union des Associations Internationales
Address: Rue Washington 40, B-1050 Brussels, Belgium
Telephone: +32 2 640 1808
Fax: +32 2 646 0525
Telex: 65080 INAC B
E-mail: uiaweb@uia.be
Web site: www.uia.org/
Year established: 1907
Activities: publishes data on over 30,000 international governmental and non-governmental organisations, their meetings, publications and strategies, and on over 13,000 world problems with which they are preoccupied
Chief officers: Marcel Merle (President), Jacques Raeymaeckers (Secretary General), Paul Hiernaux (Treasurer-General)
Membership: ca. 130 members in 35 countries
Publications:
● Annuaire des organisations internationales
● Who's Who in International Organizations: *13,000 eminent individuals associated with international organizations*
● Yearbook of International Organizations: *Organization Descriptions and Cross-references; International Organization Participation (Country Directory of Membership); Global Action Networks (Subject Guide and Index); International Organizations Bibliography & Resources*

Union of National European Soft Drink Associations (UNESDA)

Union Européenne des Associations de Boissons Gazeuses
Address: BP 14, Boulevard Louis Schmidt 35, B-1040 Brussels, Belgium
Telephone: +32 2 735 3749
Fax: +32 2 732 5102
E-mail: mail@unesda-cisda.org
Activities: collects statistics on consumption of soft drinks
Chief officers: Alain Beaumont (General Secretary)
Membership: 18 national soft drink associations
Publications:
● Statistics: *annual*

Union of Potato Starch Factories of the EU (UFE)

Union des Féculeries de Pommes de Terre de la CE
Address: Avenue de Roodebeek 30, B-1030 Brussels, Belgium
Telephone: +32 2 743 8730
Fax: +32 2 736 8175
Activities: technical committee meetings; praesidium
Chief officers: Ms P. De Sloovere (Secretary General), Dr B. J. Roosjen (President)
Membership: 21 potato starch factories within the EU
Notes: The Association does not produce any statistics or publications.

Working Committee of the EU Malting Industry

Euromalt
Address: Avenue des Gaulois 9, B-1040 Brussels, Belgium
Telephone: +32 2 736 5354
Fax: +32 2 732 3427
Year established: 1959
Activities: representation, advice, coordination, information, meetings, reports; collects statistics on number of malting, capacity, investments planned, export, import, energy
Chief officers: Alain Galaski (Secretary General), Hans-Georg Sarx (President), Harald Relander (Vice President)
Membership: 13 national maltster associations

World Airline Entertainment Association (WAEA)

Address: 401 N. Michigan Avenue, Chicago, IL, 60611-4267, USA, USA
Telephone: +1 312 245 1034
Fax: +1 312 321 5144
E-mail: assochq@aol.com
Web site: www.waea.org
Web site notes: site includes a market review of in-flight entertainment with commentary and statistics on the industry, including: estimated annual airline expenditure on IFE and communications, top 5 in-flight movies by year, etc. The site also includes a list of members
Year established: 1979
Activities: evaluation and promotion of technical and programming innovations; promotes industry standards; monitors industry trends and passenger preferences in inflight entertainment and communications
Membership: 90 airlines, 200 airline suppliers and related companies providing inflight entertainment (IFE), communications and services
Publications:
● AVION Magazine: *industry news, airline/vendor profiles, programming trends, technology reviews, airline movies bookings, upcoming theatrical releases. - quarterly*
● WAEA Membership Directory: *members contact details - annual*

World Association of Newspapers (FIEJ)

Association Mondiale des Journaux
Address: 25 rue d'Astorg, F-75008 Paris, France
Telephone: +33 1 474 28500
Fax: +33 1 474 24948
E-mail: fiej.nemo@nemo.geis.com
Web site: www.fiej.org
Year established: 1948
Activities: manages the Newspaper Management & Marketing Bureau, the Fund for Press Freedom Development and the Newspaper in Education Programm; organises the World Editor Forum; provides 50 publications on newspaper trends, strategies and operations
Chief officers: Timothy Balding (Director General); Jayme Sirotsky (President); Bengt Braun (Vice President)
Structure: board; executive committee; various specialist committees
Membership: 53 newspaper publishers associations in 50

countries, individual newspaper executives in 73 nations, 16 national and international news agencies, a media foundation and 7 affiliated regional press organisations
Publications:
• FIEJ Newsletter: *association activities, newspaper market information and important events*
• World Press Trends: *detailed information from almost 50 countries, covers: newspaper circulation, readership, advertising and sales revenues, classified advertising, advertising expenditures per media, VAT and other taxes, and regulations on ownership - annual*
Notes: represents the newspaper industry at UNESCO, the United Nations and the Council of Europe

World Association of Travel Agencies (WATA)
Address: 14, rue Ferrier, CH-1202 Geneva, Switzerland
Telephone: +41 22 731 4760
Fax: +41 22 732 8161
E-mail: watahq@iprolink.ch
Web site: www.worldyellowpages.com:80/wata/
Year established: 1949
Activities: annual general assembly (autumn)
Chief officers: Marco Agustini (Secretary General)
Structure: general assembly, executive committee
Membership: 200 members from 175 cities in 82 countries
Publications:
• Master Key: *manual of all inbound services of WATA members*
• Who's Who in WATA

World Federation of Advertisers (WFA)
Address: box 6, Rue des Colonies 18/24, B-1000 Brussels, Belgium
Telephone: +32 2 502 5740
Fax: +32 2 502 5666
E-mail: info@wfa.be
Web site: www.wfa.be/wfa/index.html
Year established: 1953
Activities: lobbying and other representational activity with appropriate governmental and institutional bodies in order to influence the various legislative processes affecting advertising; public presentations and guest appearances at major trade fairs, conferences, seminars, think-tanks etc; active participation in expert working groups on key advertising-related issues; dissemination of Position Papers; targeted PR and press relations; sponsoring of key advertising events; the forging of strategic alliances with other supranational or cross-industry organisations....
Chief officers: Bernhard Adriaensens (Director General), Henry d'Anethan (Executive Manager), Karine Lesuisse (responsible for the Secretariat)
Membership: national associations of advertisers in nearly 40 countries in addition to several corporate members - which are major international corporations, representing over 170 billion US dollars of annual advertising investment, roughly 85 % of the world's total media advertising spend
Publications:
• WFA Focus: *provides an insight into the global activities of WFA and its members, as well as information that is of significance or general interest to companies engaged in commercial communications - quarterly*

World Federation of the Sporting Goods Industry (WFSGI)
Address: P.O. Box 480, Le Hameau, CH-1936 Verbier, Switzerland
Telephone: +41 2 777 53 57 0
E-mail: 100736.1547@compuserve.com
Web site: www.sportlink.com/international/index.html
Web site notes: includes information on the industry including

market research reports on sporting goods in various countries
Year established: 1976
Activities: annual general assembly
Chief officers: André Gordemans (Secretary General)
Membership: manufacturers, distributors and retailers
Publications:
• International Handbook: *annual*
• News Bulletin: *bi-monthly*

World Gold Council
Address: 13th Floor, Printing House, 6 Duddell Street,, Central, Hong Kong
Telephone: +852 2 521 0241
Fax: +852 2 810 6038
Web site: www.jewelrynet.com:80/WorldGold/index.html
Membership: non-profit association of the world's leading gold producers
Publications:
• Gold Demand Trends: *a review of the demand and supply of gold split between developed and developing markets. Also includes data on prices, gold interest rates, and Central Bank holdings. Individual countries are covered. The report is compiled and produced in-house by the World Gold Council - quarterly*

World Institute of Electronic Commerce
Address: World Trade Centre, 380, rue Saint-Antoine Ouest, Bureau 3280, Montréal, Québec, H2Y 3X7, Canada
Telephone: +1 514 288 3555
Fax: +1 514 288 6355
E-mail: institute@ecworld.org
Web site: www.ecworld.org
Chief officers: André Vallerand (President), Sylvie Labrèche (Director Information and Internet Services)

World Packaging Organisation
Address: 481 Carlisle Drive, Herndon VA 20170 USA, USA
Telephone: +1 703 318 5512
Fax: +1 703 318 0310/814 4961
E-mail: info@pkgmatters.com
Web site: PackInfo-World.org/wpo
Chief officers: William C Pflaum (General Secretary), Raul C Fernandez (President)
Membership: 39 national packaging institutes and regional packaging federations: 25 corporate members; 257 individual members
Publications:
• News and Views Magazine
• Packaging Technology International: *international technology, new developments, applications, trends, exhibits and more - annual*

World Travel and Tourism Council
Address: 20 Grosvenor Place, London SW1X 7TT, United Kingdom
Telephone: +44 171 838 9400
Fax: +44 171 838 9050
E-mail: 100435.3140@compuserve.com
Web site: www.wttc.org
Web site notes: site includes some statistical data including various individual country reports
Publications:
• Annual Report of the World Travel and Tourism Council: *an annual report with data on the economic contribution travel and tourism makes to the total economy - annual*
• Travel and Tourism Report: *in-depth analysis of the world market for travel and tourism. Includes analyses and forecasts for 11 world regions as well as detailed reports on 24 individual countries - annual*

Notes: The World Travel and Tourism Council (WTTC) is a global coalition of over 80 Chief Executive Officers from all sectors of the travel and tourism industry, including accommodation, catering, cruises, entertainment, recreation, transportation and travel-related services.

Section Two

Major National Trade and Business Associations

AFGHANISTAN

Afghanistan Carpet Exporters' Guild
Address: PO Box 3159, Kabul
Telephone: +93 93 417 65

Afghanistan Tourist Organisation
Address: Ansari Wat, Shar-I-Nau, Kabul
Telephone: +93 93 303 23
Year established: 1958

ALGERIA

Algerian Article Numbering Association
Address: CACQUE, 2, Rue des Frères Ziata, El Mouradia
Telephone: +213 2 591 436
Fax: +213 2 592 241

National Institute of Manufacturing Industries
Institut National des Industries Manufacturiéres
Address: 35000 Boumerdes
Telephone: +213 2 816 271
Fax: +213 2 825 662
Year established: 1973

Newspapers Editors' Association
Associaiton des Editeurs de Journaux
Address: 100 rue Hassiba Ben Bouali, Alger
Telephone: +213 2 660 942
Fax: +213 2 651 341
Chief officers: Mr Zoubir Souissi (President)

ANTIGUA AND BARBUDA

Antigua Hotel and Tourist Association (AHTA)
Address: PO Box 454, Newgate Street, St John's
Telephone: +1268 462 0374
Fax: +1268 462 3702

ARGENTINA

Argentine Advertising Agencies' Association (AAAP)
Asociación Argentina de Agencias de Publicidad
Address: Hipólito Yrigoyen 1968, 1889 Buenos Aires
Telephone: +54 1 951 9630/954 2346/2357
Fax: +54 1 951 0575
Year established: 1933
Activities: education and training
Chief officers: Juan Carlos Colonnese (President), Hugo Zicari (General Manager)
Structure: non-commercial professional organisation
Membership: over 60 advertising agencies
Publications:
• Advertising Directory (Directorio Publicitario): *a directory of publishing companies affiliated to the association, contact names, clients etc. - annual*
• Publicidad Magazine

Argentine Association of Industry and Trade for Meat and Derivatives
Cámara de Industria y Comercio de Carnes y Derivados de la República Argentina
Address: Perú 746, piso 1, 1068 Buenos Aires
Telephone: +54 1 362 9437
Fax: +54 1 361 5941

Argentine Association of Books
Cámara Argentina del Libro
Address: Av Belgrano 1580,4° piso, 1093 Buenos Aires
Telephone: +54 1 381 8383/9277
Fax: +54 1 381 9253
E-mail: carl@editores.com
Chief officers: Ms AM Cabanellas (President), Mr R Chwat, Mrs C Surace (Director)

Argentine Association of Electrical Material Distributors (CADIME)
Cámara Argentina de Distribuidores de Materiales Eléctricos
Address: Alberti 1074, 1223 Buenos Aires
Telephone: +54 1 982 8642
Fax: +54 1 982 8642
Membership: electrical goods distributors
Publications:
• Avance Eléctrico: *bi-monthly*

Argentine Association of Electronics Industries (CADIE)
Cámara Argentina de Industrias Electrónicas
Address: Bdo. de Irigoyen 330, Piso 5, Of. 121, 1072 Buenos Aires
Telephone: +54 1 334 6672/334 7763/334 4159/334 5752
Fax: +54 1 334 5752/334 7753/334 6672
Membership: electronics industries

Argentine Association of Exporters (CERA)
Cámara de Exportadores de la República Argentina
Address: Av Presidente Roque Saenz Peña 740, 1° piso, 1035 Buenos Aires
Telephone: +54 1 328 9583/8556
Fax: +54 1 328 1003
E-mail: contacto@cera.satlink.net
Web site: www.cera.org.ar
Year established: 1943
Activities: market research and economic analysis, education and training, development of international export strategies
Chief officers: Dr Enrique Matilla (President)
Membership: exporters

Argentine Association of Limited Companies
Cámara Argentina de Sociedades Anónimas
Address: Florida 1, 3° piso, Buenos Aires
Telephone: +54 1 331 0981/342 9013/9225/9272
Fax: +54 1 342 9013
Chief officers: Jorge Enrique Rivarola (President), Adalberto Zelmar Barbodsa (Manager)
Membership: businesses from all sectors

Argentine Association of Manufacturers of Office Machinery and Equipment
Cámara Argentina de Fabricantes de Equipos y Máquinas de Oficinas
Address: Alsina 1607, 1° piso, 1088 Buenos Aires
Telephone: +54 1 371 5063/5055/5071
Membership: office equipment and machinery manufacturers

Argentine Association of Non-Alcoholic Beverages Producers

Cámara Argentina de Bebidas sin Alcohol
Address: Rivadavia 1823, Piso 3, Of. A, Buenos Aires
Telephone: +54 1 952 5375/953 7982
Fax: +54 1 952 5375
Membership: producers of non-alcoholic drinks

Argentine Association of Poultry Products (CAPIA)

Cámara Argentina de Productores Avícolas
Address: Bouchard 454, 6° piso, 1106 Buenos Aires
Telephone: +54 1 312 2000/9/313 5666 x333/x334
Fax: +54 1 312 2000/9
Membership: poultry producers
Publications:
• CAPIA Informa: *bi-monthly*

Argentine Association of Refrigeration and Air Conditioning Industries (ACAIRE)

Cámara Argentina de Industrias de Refrigeración y Aire Acondicionado
Address: Av de Mayo 1123, Piso 5, A, 1085 Buenos Aires
Telephone: +54 1 382 144/381 862/7544
Fax: +54 1 362 2517
Chief officers: Roberto Ricardo Aguilo (President)
Membership: manufacturers of refrigeration equipment and air conditioners

Argentine Association of the Brewing Industry

Cámara de la Industria Cervecera Argentina
Address: Av. Roque Sáenz Peña 637, Piso 5, 1393 Buenos Aires
Telephone: +54 1 362 5767/326 0125
Fax: +54 1 326 5767

Argentine Association of the Meat Processing Industry

Cámara Argentina de la Industria Frigorífica
Address: Lavalle 710, piso 1-A, 1047 Buenos Aires
Telephone: +54 1 392 4539/322 6131/393 5579
Fax: +54 1 325 8993
Membership: meat processors

Argentine Association of the Toy Industry

Cámara Argentina de la Industria del Juguete
Address: Cochabamba 4067, 1262 Buenos Aires
Telephone: +54 1 922 1537/0169
Fax: +54 1 923 6658/312 3699
Membership: toy manufacturers

Argentine Autoparts Manufacturers' Association (CIFARA)

Cámara Industrial de Fabricantes de Autopiezas
Address: Viamonte 1393, 1053 Buenos Aires
Telephone: +54 1 495 784/496 029/496 889
Fax: +54 1 496 724

Argentine Building and Construction Association

Cámara Argentina de la Construcción
Address: Av Paseo Colón 823, 9° piso, 1063 Buenos Aires
Telephone: +54 1 361 5537/5035/5845/5939/5839
Fax: +54 1 361 8778
Membership: building firms

Argentine Cable TV Association (ATVC)

Asociación Argentina de Televisión por Cable
Address: Av de Mayo 749, 2° piso, Of. 10, 1084 Buenos Aires
Telephone: +54 1 342 3362/5074/5075
Fax: +54 1 343 1716/342 1130
E-mail: atvc@satlink.com
Web site: www.atvc.org.ar
Year established: 1980
Activities: education and training; information service; organisation of the annual "Jornadas y Exposición International de la Insudtria del Cable"; publishes technical books and summaries of conferences
Chief officers: Dr. Horacio Guibelalde (President), Sr. Serafin Guillani (Secretary General)
Membership: cable TV operators and cable television stations
Publications:
• Circular (Circular): *news and information on legislation affecting the industry - monthly*

Argentine Chamber of Importers

Cámara de Importadores de la República Argentina
Address: Av. Belgrano 427, Piso 7, 1092 Buenos Aires
Telephone: +54 1 342 1101/0523
Fax: +54 1 331 9342/ 345 3003
Chief officers: Ing. Diego Pérez Santiesteban (Director)

Argentine Chamber of the Clothing Industry

Cámara Industrial Argentina de la Indumentaria
Address: Av Leandro N Alem 1067, piso13 - oficina 41, 1001 Buenos Aires
Telephone: +54 1 313 6006/6107
Fax: +54 1 313 6206
Membership: clothing manufacturers

Argentine Coffee Association

Cámara Argentina del Café
Address: Santiago del Estero 508, 1° piso A, 1075 Buenos Aires
Telephone: +54 1 383 3037
Fax: +54 1 381 6199
Year established: 1918
Activities: statistics, information
Chief officers: Rubén H Pellegrini (Manager)
Membership: 55 companies - coffee processors and importers

Argentine Council of Industry

Consejo Argentino de la Industria
Address: Piedras 83, Piso 3, Of. E, 1070 Buenos Aires
Telephone: +54 1 343 9977/2081032/2081398
Fax: +54 1 331 280
Telex: 17155

Argentine Detergent Manufacturers' Association

Cámara de Fabricantes de Detergentes
Address: Av. Leandro N. Alem 1067, Piso 12, 1001 Buenos Aires
Telephone: +54 1 312 4605

Argentine Edible Oils and Fats Association (CIARA)

Cámara de la Industria Aceitera de la República Argentina
Address: Tucumán 637, Piso 6, 1049 Buenos Aires
Telephone: +54 1 322 3990/322 7908/393 8322
Fax: +54 1 393 7685

Argentine Fish Industry Association

Cámara Argentina de Industriales del Pescado
Address: Barquina de Pescadores/Puerto, 7600 Mar de Plata
Telephone: +54 23 800 991/0638
Fax: +54 23 800 655

Argentine Fish Processing Industry Association
Cámara Argentina de Procesadores de Pescado
Address: Av Leandro N Alem 3251, 7600 Mar del Plata
Telephone: +54 23 518 148/861402
Fax: +54 23 518 148/861402

Argentine Franchising Association
Asociación Argentina de Franchising
Address: Santa Fe 995, piso 4, 1059 Buenos Aires
Telephone: +54 1 393 5263
Fax: +54 1 393 9260
Chief officers: Richaard Rivera (President)

Argentine Fruit Producers' Association
Asociación de Productores de Frutas Argentinas
Address: Lavalle 3161, PB, Of C, 1190 Buenos Aires
Telephone: +54 1 884 445/862 8333
Fax: +54 1 862 833
Membership: fruit growers

Argentine Household Cleaning and Related Products' Association (ALPHA)
Asociación Industrial Artículos de Limpieza del Hogar y Afines
Address: Av. Leandro N. Alem 1067, Piso 12, 1001 Buenos Aires
Telephone: +54 1 312 4605

Argentine Importers' and Exporters' Association (AIERA)
Asociación de Importadores y Exportadores de la República Argentina
Address: Av Belgrano 124, 1° piso, oficina A, 1092 Buenos Aires
Telephone: +54 1 342 0010/18/19
Fax: +54 1 342 1312
Year established: 1966
Chief officers: Héctor Marcelo Vidal (President), Estelia D de Amati (Manager)
Membership: importers and exporters

Argentine Industry Association
Unión Industrial Argentina
Address: Avda Leandro N. Alem 1067, Piso 10, 1001 Buenos Aires
Telephone: +54 1 313 2012/313 2512/313 2561
Fax: +54 1 313 2413
Telex: 21749
Membership: 95% of industrial corporations

Argentine Insurance Companies' Association
Asociación Argentina de Compañías de Seguros
Address: 25 de Mayo 565, 1002 Buenos Aires
Telephone: +54 1 313 6974
Fax: +54 1 312 6300
Chief officers: Daniel R Salazar
Membership: insurance companies

Argentine Marketing Association (AAM)
Asociación Argentina de Marketing
Address: Viamonte 723, 7° piso, oficina 27, 1053 Buenos Aires
Telephone: +54 1 382 4005/382 4006
Fax: +54 1 383 6799
E-mail: aam@aam-ar.com
Web site: www.aam-ar.com
Year established: 1965
Activities: courses, seminars and conferences; monthly meetings with associates; promotes marketing techniques, exchanges export information

Chief officers: Sergio Smith (President), Enrique D'Alessandro (Secretary), Jorge Castrillo (General Manager)
Membership: over 1,200 members

Argentine Meat Industries' Association
Asociación de la Industria Argentina de Carne
Address: Paraguay 776, 2° piso, 1057 Buenos Aires
Telephone: +54 1 393 8049/322 0587/392 5422
Membership: companies and individuals involved in the meat industry

Argentine Meat Industry Union
Unión de la Industria Cárnica Argentina
Address: Avda de Mayo 981, piso 2, 1084 Buenos Aires
Telephone: +54 1 345 1993/2491/0582/4943/0354
Fax: +54 1 345 1864

Argentine Packaging Institute (IAE)
Instituto Argentino del Envase
Address: Av Jujuy 425, 1083 Buenos Aires
Telephone: +54 1 957 0350/0968
Fax: +54 1 956 1368
Activities: organises Envase trade fair
Chief officers: Enrique Schcolnik (President), Francisco Albini (Vice President), Jorge Acevedo (Manager)
Membership: 16 packaging companies

Argentine Personal Care and Toiletry Products Industry Association
Cámara Argentina de la Industria de Productos de Higiene y Tocador
Address: Paraguay 1857, 1121 Buenos Aires
Telephone: +54 1 425 925

Argentine Pharmaceutical Confederation
Confederación Farmacéutica Argentina
Address: Alsina 655, Piso 2, 1087 Buenos Aires
Telephone: +54 1 343 5632

Argentine Pharmaceutical Drug Producers' Association (CAPDROFAR)
Cámara Argentina de Productores de Drogas Farmacéuticas
Address: Florida 274, 6° piso, of 64, 1005 Buenos Aires
Telephone: +54 1 457 918/4520/403 370
Fax: +54 1 325 8817
Chief officers: Lina Gomes Figueiredo (Technical Secretary)
Membership: drugs companies

Argentine Pharmacies' Association
Cámara Argentina de Farmacias
Address: Uruguay 60, 1015 Buenos Aires
Telephone: +54 1 381 4141/4945/5213
Fax: +54 1 381 5213

Argentine Plastic Industry Association
Cámara Argentina de la Industria Plástica
Address: Jerónimo Salguero 1939/41, 1425 Buenos Aires
Telephone: +54 1 821 9603/5/826 8498/6060
Fax: +54 1 826 6060/826 5480

Argentine Sugar Association
Centro Azucarero Argentino
Address: Reconquista 336, 12° piso, 1335 Buenos Aires
Telephone: +54 1 394 0257/0358/0459
Fax: +54 1 394 0358/322 9358
Chief officers: Enrique A Urien (President)
Membership: companies involved in the sugar industry

Publications:
• La Industria Azucarera: *news on the sugar industry - bi-monthly*

Argentine Supermarkets' Association
Cámara Argentina de Supermercados
Address: Viamonte 342, piso 3, 1053 Buenos Aires
Telephone: +54 1 313 1812/1822/1835
Fax: +54 1 313 1897

Argentine Television and Radio Association (ATA)
Asociación de Teleradiodifusoras Argentinas
Address: Av Córdoba 323, 6° piso, 1054 Buenos Aires
Telephone: +54 1 312 4219/312 4533
Fax: +54 1 312 4208
Chief officers: Eduardo Oscar Farley (President), Luis Humberto Tacitarno (Secretary)
Membership: private television and radio stations

Argentine Textile Industries' Association (ADITA)
Asociación de Industriales Textiles Argentinos
Address: Uruguay 291, 4° piso, 1015 Buenos Aires
Telephone: +54 1 373 2256
Year established: 1945
Membership: 250 textile manufacturers
Publications:
• Base Textil Informativa: *monthly*

Argentine Tobacco Industry Association
Cámara de la Industria Tabacalera
Address: Reconquista 656, Piso 3, 1003 Buenos Aires
Telephone: +54 1 313 7705/8/312 8207
Fax: +54 1 312 8205
Membership: tobacco processors

Argentine Wholesalers' Federation (ADDIF)
Federación de Comerciantes Argentinos
Address: Paraguay 515 1 Piso (1057), Capital Federal 1428
Telephone: +54 1 312 1834
Fax: +54 1 312 0534

Argentine Wine Producers' Association
Asociación de la Industria Vitivinícola Argentina
Address: Guemes 4464, 1425 Buenos Aires
Telephone: +54 1 774 1887/3370
Fax: +54 1 776 2529

Association of Alcoholic Drinks Producers
Cámara de Alcoholes
Address: Maipú 267, 12° piso, 1084-Buenos Aires
Telephone: +54 1 465 953/326 0058
Fax: +54 1 326 5953/0058/0083
Chief officers: Susanna Elena Teigeiro
Membership: alcoholic drinks producers

Association of Argentine Banks (ADEBA)
Asociación de Bancos Argentinos
Address: San Martín 229, 10° piso, 1004 Buenos Aires
Telephone: +54 1 394 1430/3941737/3941836
Fax: +54 1 394 6340/3939764
Publications:
• Boletín ADEBA: *banks - bi-monthly*

Association of Argentine Textile Industries
Asociación de Industriales Textiles Argentinos
Address: Uruguay 291, 4° piso, 1015 Buenos Aires
Telephone: +54 1 492 256/373 2256/2502/2154
Fax: +54 1 492 351
Publications:
• Informe de Coyuntura (Association of Argentine Textile Industrialists): *regular statistics on textile production, consumption, end-users, and foreign trade plus details of the structure of the industry in Argentina. Based largely on data collected by the Association - regular*

Association of Food Manufacturers
Cámara de Industriales de Productos Alimenticios
Address: Av Leandro N Alem 1067, piso 12, 1001 Buenos Aires
Telephone: +54 1 312 1929/312 3508
Fax: +54 1 312 1929/312 3508

Association of Furniture Manufacturers
Cámara de Empresarios Madereros y Afines
Address: Maza 578, 3° piso, 1220 Buenos Aires
Telephone: +54 1 931 111/976 940/954 1111/954 2046
Fax: +54 1 971 556
Membership: furniture manufacturers and dealers

Association of Housewares Manufacturers
Cámara de Industriales de Artefactos para el Hogar
Address: Paraguay 1855, Buenos Aires
Telephone: +54 1 813 2673/812 0232
Fax: +54 1 814 2650

Association of Refreshment Manufacturers
Cámara de Fabricantes de Refrescos y Afines
Address: Av. Leandro N. Alem 734, Piso 7, 1001 Buenos Aires
Telephone: +54 1 311 4271/311 2882

Association of Special Medicine Distributors
Asociación de Distribuidores de Medicamentos Especiales
Address: Avda de Mayo 1353 2do. piso, 1085 Capital Federal
Telephone: +54 1 383 4925
Fax: +54 1 383 4925

Automotive Manufacturers' Association (ADEFA)
Asociación de Fábricas de Automóviles
Address: Marcelo T de Alvear 636, 5° piso, 1058 Buenos Aires
Telephone: +54 1 312 1306/312 3483
Fax: +54 1 315 2990
Chief officers: Horacio Losoviz (President), Guillermo Franchelli (Executive President), Mario Dasso (Director), Rolando Tettamanzi (Secretary General)
Membership: vehicle assembly plants

Baby and Children's Clothing Association
Cámara Argentina de Indumentaria para Bebés y Niños
Address: Junín 347, piso 4 - oficina B, 1026 Buenos Aires
Telephone: +54 1 953 9540
Membership: baby and children's clothing manufacturers

Banks' Association of the Argentine Republic
Asociación de Bancos de la República Argentina
Address: Reconquista 458, piso 2, 1358 Buenos Aires
Telephone: +54 1 394 6452
Fax: +54 1 322 9642

Bovine Meat Producers' Association
Cámara de Productores de Carne Vacuna
Address: Córdoba 1525, piso 6, 1055 Buenos Aires
Telephone: +54 1 813 9751
Fax: +54 1 813 9571

Buenos Aires Travel and Tourism Agencies' Association (AVIABUE)
Asociación de Agencias de Viajes y Turismo de Buenos Aires
Address: Viamonte 640, 6° piso, 1053 Buenos Aires
Telephone: +54 1 325 8173/325 8177/394 3093/325 4691
Fax: +54 1 322 9641
Membership: travel and tourism agencies in Buenos Aires
Publications:
• Revista: *bi-monthly*

Candy and Confectionery Distributors' Association
Asociación de Distribuidores de Golosinas y Afines
Address: Teniente Gral JD Perón 1610, piso 2, 1037 Buenos Aires
Telephone: +54 1 382 3350/0780/3218
Fax: +54 1 382 3218

Cereal Exporters' Office
Centro de Exportadores de Cereales
Address: Bouchard 454, 7° piso, 1106 Buenos Aires
Telephone: +54 1 311 1697/4627/312 6924
Fax: +54 1 312 6924
Telex: 18644
Year established: 1943
Chief officers: Pedro E Garcia Oliver (President)
Membership: grain exporters

Citrus Fruit Industries' Association
Cámara de Industriales Cítricos de la República Argentina
Address: Florida 140, piso 4, 1005 Buenos Aires
Telephone: +54 1 326 9673

Consumer Products Codification Association (CODIGO)
Asociación Argentina de Codificación de Productos Comerciales
Address: Viamonte 340/342, 1° piso, 1053 Buenos Aires
Telephone: +54 1 313 1719
Fax: +54 1 313 1765
E-mail: aapcomer@starnet.net.ar
Web site: www.codigo.com.ar

Corporation of Argentine Meat Producers (CAP)
Corporación Argentina de Productores de Carne
Address: Avda de Córdoba 883 - piso 12, 1054 Buenos Aires
Telephone: +54 1 312 1014/9683

Cotton Textile Manufacturers' Association
Asociación de Fabricantes de Tejidos de Algodón
Address: Av Leandro N Alem 1067, piso 8, 1001 Buenos Aires
Telephone: +54 1 311 0499
Fax: +54 1 311 7602
Year established: 1960
Membership: cotton textiles manufacturers

Electronic and Electrical Industry Association
Asociación de la Pequeña y Mediana Industria Electrónica y Eléctrica
Address: Gascón 62, 1181 Buenos Aires
Telephone: +54 1 981 2335

Federal Commission for Broadcasting (COMFER)
Comité Federal de Radiodifusión
Address: Suipacha 765, 1008 Buenos Aires
Telephone: +54 1 394 1149/4309/4274/4549
Activities: controls technical aspects of broadcasting in Argentina
Chief officers: León Guinzburg (President)
Membership: radio stations

Federation of Argentine Textile Industries (FITA)
Federación de Industriales Textiles Argentinos
Address: Av Leandro N Alem 1067, Piso 8, 1001 Buenos Aires
Telephone: +54 1 311 0499/0599/6899/7776
Fax: +54 1 311 7602
Structure: umbrella organisation for Asociación de Fabricantes de Tejidos de Algodón (Cotton Fabric Manufacturers' Association); Asociación de Fabricantes de Tejidos de Lana (Wool Fabric Manufacturers' Association); Asociación de Hilanderías de Algodón (Cotton Spinning Mills Association); Asociación de Tintorerías de Establecimientos Textiles (Textile Dyeing Establishments' Association); Asociación Peinadurías e Hilanderías (Combing and Spinning Mills Association); Asociación Texturizadores de Hilados Sintéticos y Afines (Synthetic Yarn Texturisers' Association); Cámara Industrial de la Seda y de las Fibras Sintéticas (Silk and Synthetic Fibre Industries' Association): Asociación de Fabricantes de Hilos de Coser (Sewing Thread Manufacturers' Association); Asociación de Fabricantes de Medias (Hosiery Manufacturers' Association); Asociación de Fabricantes de Tejidos de Lino y Cáñamo (Linen and Hemp Fabrics Manufacturers' Association)
Membership: textile manufacturers and clothing industries
Notes: All of the associations listed above are located at the same address.

Flexible Packaging Association
Asociación Argentina de Productos de Envases Flexibles
Address: Bacacay 1789, 1405 Buenos Aires
Telephone: +54 1 825 4120
Fax: +54 1 205 2276

Food Products' Industries Association (COPAL)
Coordinadores de Industriales de Productos Alimenticios
Address: Oficina 513, Florida 537, 2° piso, 1005 Buenos Aires
Telephone: +54 1 325 8643/394 1653/322 5245/322 5260
Fax: +54 1·325 1483
Publications:
• Industria Alimentaria: *every 2 months*

Furniture and Carpet Manufacturers' Association (CAFYDMA)
Cámara de Fabricantes de Muebles, Tapicerías y Afines
Address: Manuel Ricardo Trelles 1961/87, 1416 Buenos Aires
Telephone: +54 1 583 5606/7
Fax: +54 1 583 5608

Hotels and Catering Enterprises' Federation (FEHGRA)
Federación Empresaria Hotelera-Gastronómica de la República Argentina
Address: Tucumán 1610, piso 5, 1050 Buenos Aires
Telephone: +54 1 372 6846/6705
Fax: +54 1 371 8815
Activities: close links with its affiliated bodies
Chief officers: German Luis Perez (President)
Membership: groups together entrepreneurs who operate hotels, restaurants, cafeterias, bars and similar establishments

Hotels, Restaurants, Confectioners and Cafés Association

Asociación de Hoteles, Restaurantes, Confiterias y Cafés
Address: Tucumán 1610 PB, 1050 Buenos Aires
Telephone: +54 1 372 7295
Fax: +54 1 405 108
Membership: privately owned hotels, restaurants, cafés and tea rooms
Notes: Member of Cámara Argentina de Turismo.

National Viticulture Institute

Instituto Nacional de Vitivinicultura
Address: A. Julio A. Roca 651, Piso 5, Of. 22, 1067 Buenos Aires
Telephone: +54 1 343 3846/349 4272
Fax: +54 1 343 3846/343 3846

Pulp and Paper Manufacturers' Association

Asociación de Fabricantes de Celulosa y Papel
Address: Av Belgrano 2852, piso 1, Of. 04, 1209 Buenos Aires
Telephone: +54 1 970 051/2/4
Fax: +54 1 970 053
Activities: statistical reports and analyses on production, trade and consumption, assistance with air and water contamination control
Chief officers: Rafael Gaviola (President), César Etchemendy (R&D Director)
Membership: 50 pulp and paper manufacturers

Shoe Industry Association (CIC)

Cámara Argentina de la Industria del Calzado
Address: Av Rivadavia 4323, 1205 Buenos Aires
Telephone: +54 1 981 9609/4524/0818/0732/2303/5992
Fax: +54 1 981 3203
Year established: 1916
Activities: national and international exhibitions, courses and seminars
Chief officers: Carlos A Litzmann (Manager), Graciela Boeri (Deputy Manager)
Membership: 460 footwear manufacturers
Publications:
• La Industria Argentina del Calzado: *footwear magazine*

Spirits Industry Federation

Federación de la Industria Licorista
Address: Av Leandro N Alem 1067, piso 7, 1001 Buenos Aires
Telephone: +54 1 311 2882/4271

Tourist Hotels' Association (AHT)

Asociación de Hoteles de Turismo
Address: Av Rivadavia 1157/9, 9° piso, Of C, 1033 Buenos Aires
Telephone: +54 1 383 2039/1160
Fax: +54 1 383 0669
Chief officers: Gomes Losada (President)
Notes: Affiliated with the International Hotel Association.

Vegetable and Fruit Cooperatives' Association

Asociación de Cooperativas Hortícolas, Frutihortícolas Argentinas Cooperativas Limitadas
Address: Mercado Central, piso 3 - oficina 332, Villa Celina, 1761 Buenos Aires
Telephone: +54 1 622 1028
Membership: fruit and vegetable manufacturers

ARMENIA

Article Numbering Association of Armenia

Address: PO Box 51, Komitas Avenue 49/2, 375051 Yerevan
Telephone: +7 4 223 4778
Fax: +7 4 285 620
E-mail: sarm@arminco.com

ARUBA

Aruba Trade and Industry Association

Address: Pedro Gallegostraat 6, Oranjestad
Telephone: +297 8 215 66
Fax: +297 8 330 68

AUSTRALIA

Advertising Federation of Australia Limited (AFA)

Address: POB 166, Level 1, 201 Miller St, North Sydney, NSW 2060
Telephone: +61 2 995 73077
Fax: +61 2 995 73952
Year established: 1975
Activities: provides a range of member services including education and training; sets up and implements rules and standards on advertising; also produces statistics on the industry (available to members only)
Chief officers: Beverley Dyke (Federal Director); Hilary Chatterton (Member Services Manager); Helga Diamond (Research and Communications Manager); Janet Fish (Special Projects Manager); Bill Atkinson (AFA Advisory Service)
Membership: 75 advertising agencies
Notes: The association publishes a number of advertising casebooks.

Air-Conditioning and Refrigeration Equipment Manufacturers' Association (AREMA)

Address: P.O. Box 7622, Melbourne, Victoria 3004
Telephone: +61 3 280 0111
Fax: +61 3 280 0199
Chief officers: Ian Binger (National Secretary)

Association of Liquid-paperboard Carton Manufacturers Inc. (ALC)

Address: Level 3, 121 Walker Street, North Sydney NSW 2059
Telephone: +61 2 995 44588
Fax: +61 2 995 44546
E-mail: office@ecomall.com.au
Web site: www.ecomall.com.au
Activities: government liaison, public relations
Membership: manufacturers of liquidpaperboard milk and juice cartons and their paperboard suppliers

AUS-MEAT

Address: MTQ House, 41 Logan Road, Woolloongabba QLD 4102
Telephone: +61 7 3307 3333
Fax: +61 7 3391 4015
E-mail: gmcloughlin@ausmeat.com.au
Web site: www.ozemail.com.au/~gmclough/
Activities: education and training, setting standards for accreditation, providing solutions and publications for Industry
Notes: Umbrella organisation of the meat and livestock industry. Member organisations include: Australian Meat and

Livestock Corporation (AMLC); Australian Pork Corporation (APC); Australian Meat Council (AMC); National Meat Association (NMA); Cattle Council of Australia (CCA); Sheepmeat Council of Australia (SCA); Australian Supermarkets Institute (ASI); Agricultural and Resource Management Council of Australia and New Zealand (ARMCANZ)

Australian Automobile Association (AAA)
Address: GPO Box 1555, 212 Northbourne Avenue, Canberra, ACT, 2601
Telephone: +61 6 247 7311
Fax: +61 6 257 5320
E-mail: aaa@aaa.asn.au
Web site: www.aaa.asn.au
Web site notes: site includes various statistics on automotives, transport and petroleum in Australia
Year established: 1924
Publications:
● Motoring Directions: *transport policy, road infrastructure, safety, new motor vehicle technology, the environment, tourism, and the activities and view points of AAA itself - quarterly*
● Motoring Facts: *importance of road transport in the Australian economy, vehicle sales and production, the road network, expenditure and consumption, number of passenger motor vehicles on register, the environment and road safety. Compiled from the AAA Transport Statistics Database - annual*

Australian Automotive Aftermarket Association Ltd.
Address: 8th Floor, Sir John Monash Drive, Caullifield East, Victoria 3145
Telephone: +61 3 957 22686
Fax: +61 3 957 22956
Activities: maintains a database of sales imports and exports based on voluntary returns from members. Does not publish statistics on sales of aftermarket products at present but plans to introduce them in the near future
Chief officers: David Wright (Executive Director)

Australian Bankers' Association
Address: Level 42/55, Collin St, Melbourne, VIC 3000
Telephone: +61 3 965 45422
Fax: +61 3 965 01756
Activities: government liaison, development of industry standards and protocol
Chief officers: Mark Addis (Chief Executive)
Membership: 30 member banks
Notes: The association does not produce any statistics or publications.

Australian Canegrowers Council (CANEGROWERS)
Address: GPO Box 1032, Brisbane Qld 4001
Telephone: +61 7 3864 6444
Fax: +61 7 3864 6429
Web site: www.farmwide.com.au/nff/canegrowers/cane.htm
Activities: provides information and comment on sugar industry issues to the media, provides information about the canegrowing industry
Chief officers: H.R. Bonanno (Chairman), Senior Vice Chairman J.E. Pedersen (Senior Vice-Chairman)
Structure: Council of 25 elected members representing all canegrowing areas
Membership: sugarcane growers who produce over 95% of Australia's sugar

Australian Chamber of Fruit and Vegetable Industries
Address: PO Box 70, Brisbane Market 4106
Telephone: +61 7 337 93061
Fax: +61 7 337 93792
Chief officers: Don Alroe (President), Chris Box (Executive Officer)
Membership: confined to 6 state and regional chambers; fruit and vegetable merchants and agents in Australian wholesale markets

Australian Chemical Specialties Manufacturers' Association (ACSMA)
Address: 4th Floor, Royal Domain Centre, 380 St Kilda Road, Melbourne 3004
Telephone: +61 3 969 08588
Fax: +61 3 969 07522
E-mail: acted@vianet.net.au
Web site: www.vianet.net.au/~acted/acsma.htm
Year established: 1975
Activities: government liaison
Chief officers: K.D. Fuller (Executive Director)
Membership: represents companies that formulate (blend) chemicals to the needs of the markets

Australian Chicken Meat Federation
Address: PO Box 579, North Sydney 2059
Telephone: +61 2 9929 4077
Fax: +61 2 9925 0627
Chief officers: Mrs G. Marven (President)

Australian Citrus Growers' Inc. (ACG)
Address: Level 10, 118 King William Street, Adelaide, SA 5000
Telephone: +61 8 821 24245
Fax: +61 8 823 13413
E-mail: austcitrus@msn.com
Web site: www.farmwide.com.au/nff/Acg/acg.htm
Web site notes: site includes production and export statistics on the Australian citrus industry as well as figures for land under cultivation and number of growers
Year established: 1948
Activities: promotion of citrus fruits and juices, compiling and circulating statistical data (production)
Chief officers: Michael Crook (President), Bob Curren (Executive Director)
Publications:
● Annual Report: *summary of developments in the Australian citrus growing industry over the past year - annual*
● Australian Citrus News: *the Australian citrus growing industry - monthly*
● Citrus Export and Import Statistics: *imports and exports of citrus fruit and juices, based on official statistics - quarterly*

Australian Citrus Industry Council Inc.
Address: 10th Floor, 118 King William Street, Adelaide SA 5000
Telephone: +61 8 821 24245
Fax: +61 8 823 13413
Activities: collection and collation of industry statistics and information (production, plantings, market distribution, exports, imports) advice to governments and statutory bodies on citrus industry issues, administration of industry codes of practice for the Australian fruit juice industry
Chief officers: Michael Crook (President), Hugh Cope (Executive Director), Rolf Schufft (Executive Secretary)
Notes: The Citrus Council is the umbrella organisation of the Australian citrus industry. Member organisations include Australian Citrus Growers, Australian Citrus Processors Association, Australian Fruit Juice Association and the National Citrus Packers Association.

Australian Council of Shopping Centres

Address: Level 26, Australia Square Tower, 264-278 George Street, Sydney 2000
Telephone: +61 2 925 23111
Fax: +61 2 925 23103
Chief officers: Jim Service (President), Alan Briggs (Chairman)

Australian Council of Wool Exporters

Address: Level 8, 530 Little Collins St, Melbourne, VIC 3000
Telephone: +61 3 962 94527
Fax: +61 3 961 46529
E-mail: acwemelb@ozemail.com.au
Web site: www.ozemail.com.au/~acwemelb/index.html
Web site notes: site includes statistics on Australian shorn wool production as well as market indicators, statistics on wool international stockpile sales and forthcoming sales details
Membership: 51 member firms involved with the purchase, export, early stage processing and marketing of over 80% of Australian wool production
Publications:
• Wool Market Review: *statistical review of the Australian wool industry - annual*

Australian Dairy Corporation

Address: PO Box 5000, 1601 Malvern Road, Glen Iris, VIC 3146
Telephone: +61 3 980 53777
Fax: +61 3 988 55885
E-mail: webenquiries@adc.aust.com
Web site: www.adc.aust.com
Web site notes: site includes comprehensive statistics on the Australian dairy industry including domestic sales trends for the latest year
Year established: 1926
Activities: promotes consumption; assists in marketing; controls exports; provides financial assistance.
Chief officers: K P Baxter (Chairman); John Gibson (Managing Director)
Structure: Board appointed by Minister for Primary Industries
Publications:
• Annual Report of the Australian Dairy Corporation: *the report includes sections on the domestic market, industry trends, and the export market. Each section has relevant statistics - annual*
• Dairy Moves: *trends in the Australian and international dairy industry - monthly*
• Market Review: *statistics and analysis of the Australian and international dairy markets - monthly*
• Update (Australian Dairy Corporation): *commentary and statistics on the Australian dairy products industry. Includes a broad sector breakdown of production statistics for milk and cheese by volume over a six year period. Also includes a section on Australian and international trends as well as data on imports-exports - monthly*

Australian Dairy Farmers' Federation Limited (Australian National Committee of the International Dairy Federation

Address: Level 6, 84 William Street, Melbourne, Victoria 3000
Telephone: +61 3 964 280 66/964 280 33
Fax: +61 3 964 281 66/964 281 33
Chief officers: Ms H. Dornom (Secretary)
Publications:
• Issues Watch: *summary of developments in the Australian dairy industry. Includes information on legislation, world trade developments etc. - annual*

Australian Dairy Industry Council Inc.

Address: 6th Floor, 84 William St, Melbourne, VIC 3000
Telephone: +61 3 964 28044
Fax: +61 3 988 51526
E-mail: adic@dairy.com.au
Web site: www.dairy.com.au/adic/index.htm
Year established: 1977
Chief officers: Patrick Rowley (Chairman); Peter Gallagher (Chief Executive Officer)
Structure: management committee of 4, executive of 18, full council of 46
Membership: 5 national dairy industry associations and federations
Publications:
• Australian Dairy Farmer: *6 p.a.*
• Milk Matters: *articles and features on developments in the Australian and international dairy industry - 10 p.a.*

Australian Dairy Products Federation (ADPF)

Address: 6th Floor, 84 William Street, Melbourne 3000
Telephone: +61 3 964 28033
Fax: +61 3 964 28144
E-mail: adpf@dairy.com.au
Web site: www.dairy.com.au/adic/
Activities: the ADPF collects statistics from the State Dairy Authorities and statutory marketing bodies and conducts government liaison
Chief officers: John Hughes (President), Helen Dornom (Executive Officer)
Membership: 31 member companies
Publications:
• Annual Report: *activities of the association and information on the Australian dairy industry - annual*
Notes: Affiliated with the Australian Dairy Industry Council.

Australian Egg Industry Association Inc.

Address: PO Box 569, Suite 404, 12-14 Ormonde Parade, Hurtsville NSW 2220
Telephone: +61 2 9570 9222
Fax: +61 2 9570 9763
Chief officers: Malcolm Peacock (President), Hugh McMaster (Executive Director)

Australian Electrical and Electronic Manufacturers' Association Ltd

Address: Po Box 1966, Suite 404, 10 Moore Street, Canberra, ACT 2601
Telephone: +61 6 247 4655
Fax: +61 6 247 9840
Year established: 1969
Activities: promotes best practices and quality standards in terms of manufacturing facilities, product innovations and customer service; promotes development of electrical/electronic industries in Australia
Chief officers: Alex Gosman(Executive Director) Peter Janssen (President), Judy Watkinson (Administration Manager)
Membership: 230 member companies

Australian Federation of Travel Agents (AFTA)

Address: 3rd Floor, 309 Pitt St, Sydney, NSW 2000
Telephone: +61 2 926 43299
Fax: +61 2 926 41085
E-mail: gina@afta.net.au
Web site: www.afta.com.au
Year established: 1957
Activities: government liaison; 'watchdog' services; active promotion of AFTA by media-tagging; provides members with negotiated special low merchant fee rates, legal assistance, dispute assistance and regular news updates on industry matters; education and training; seminars; annual convention;

travel insurance; ID cards; annual 'Talkabout'; industrial relations; terms of trade
Chief officers: John Dart (Chief Executive); Marie Allom (Australian Manager)
Structure: federal office and 8 state/territory chapters
Membership: represents a majority of travel agents in Australia with over 2,300 outlets and 500 allied industry organisations, hotels, wholesalers, tour operators etc
Publications:
• AFTA Frontline: *every 2 months*

Australian Food Brokers' Association

Address: Suite 3, Level 1, 410 Church Street, North Parramatta NSW 2151
Telephone: +61 2 989 01077/01314
Fax: +61 2 989 01377
Chief officers: Keith Quigg (President), David Burton (Executive Director)

Australian Food Council (AFC)

Address: Level 2, Salvation Army Building, 2-4 Brisbane Avenue, Barton 2600
Telephone: +61 6 273 1466
Fax: +61 6 273 1477
E-mail: harbecke@afc.org.au
Web site: www.afc.org.au
Web site notes: site includes a brief overview of the Australian food industry including some general statistics and a list of members
Year established: 1995
Chief officers: W Murray Rogers (Chairman), Mitchell H Hooke (Executive Director)
Structure: the Council, comprising all member companies, is the supreme governing body of the AFC and is responsible for overall policy direction
Membership: 80 small, medium and large companies, subsidiaries and associates, representing over 80% of the gross value of the highly processed food and beverages sector in Australia. Approximately 30% of the membership are small to medium enterprises and around 45% are Australian owned companies.
Publications:
• Annual Report: *information on the association's activities as well as a brief profile of the Australian food industry. Includes some general statistics on the industry - annual*

Australian Foodservice Manufacturers' Association

Address: POBox 168, Crows Nest 2065
Telephone: +61 2 943 83255
Fax: +61 2 943 83255
Activities: seminars, market research, government lobbying and salary surveys. Also compiles statistical data based on member returns.
Chief officers: Lyn Winneke (President), Philip Lee (Executive Director)
Membership: 53 food manufacturers and wholesalers
Notes: Also publishes a member newsletter (not available to non-members).

Australian Fruit Juice Association

Address: Level 12, Australian Business Centre, 140 Arthur Street, North Sydney 2059
Telephone: +61 2 992 77416
Fax: +61 2 995 67004
Chief officers: Rolf Schufft (Secretary)

Australian Information Industry Association (AIIA)

Address: 12 Campion Street, Deakin ACT 2600
Telephone: +61 11 616 282 4700

Fax: +61 11 616 285 1408
E-mail: s.burns@aiia.com.au
Web site: www.aiia.com.au
Activities: government lobbying, produces statistics on revenues, exports, research and development, and salaries expenditure of the information technology and telecommunications (IT&T) market in Australia
Chief officers: Sandy Burns (Membership Services Manager)
Membership: medium and large companies involved in developing, producing and distributing computer and telecommunications hardware, infrastructure, software and services. Membership encompasses more than 80% of the total turnover of the IT industry in Australia
Publications:
• AIIA Salary and Remuneration Survey: *comprehensive information on salaries and remuneration packages. Monitors some 115 job positions within the information technology and telecommunications (IT&T) industry - annual*

Australian Institute of Food Science and Technology

Address: PO Box 319, Noble Park
Telephone: +61 3 958 06182
Fax: +61 3 958 06933
Chief officers: Prof Ken Buckle (President), Christine Harfield (Executive Secretary)

Australian Institute of Packaging Inc. (AIP)

Address: 54 Blackwall Point Road, Chiswick, NSW 2046
Telephone: +61 2 912 33269
Fax: +61 2 971 23282
E-mail: office@ecomall.com.au
Web site: www.ecomall.com.au
Year established: 1963
Activities: seminars; training courses; conferences (biannual)
Chief officers: Helen Swinton (Chief Executive Officer), Terry Waterson (President), Professor Harry Lovell (Vice President)
Structure: board of directors and a chief executive officer with branch committees in each state
Publications:
• AIP News, Events & People: *monthly*

Australian Library and Information Association (ALIA)

Address: PO Box E441, Kingston ACT 2604
Telephone: +61 6 285 1877
Fax: +61 6 282 2249
E-mail: enquiry@alia.org.au
Web site: www.alia.org.au
Year established: 1937
Chief officers: Virginia Walsh (Executive Director), Marie Murphy (Membership Services)
Membership: 7,500 members
Publications:
• InCite Magazine: *news from around the world for library and information professionals - monthly*
Notes: Professional organisation for the Australian library and information services sector.

Australian Market Research Society (MRSA)

Address: PO Box 697, North Sydney NSW 2059
Telephone: +61 2 9955 4830
Fax: +61 2 9955 5746
E-mail: sydney@bigpond.com.au
Web site: www.mrsa.com.au
Web site notes: the site includes a database of market research agencies in Australia
Activities: promotes market research; education and training
Membership: 1,300 market research professionals
Publications:
• Research News: *the activities of the Association as well as developments in the Australian market research industry*

Australian Meat and Livestock Corporation (AMLC)

Address: 327 Elizabeth Street, Sydney, NSW 2000
Telephone: +61 2 926 03111
Activities: promotion of Australian meat to overseas markets
Publications:
• Australian Meat and Livestock Corporation Statistics: *an annual report with detailed statistics on livestock, slaughterings, meat production, domestic consumption of meat, world trends, and some forecasts. Historical data in most tables - annual*

Australian Olive Oil Association

Address: Legion House, 145 Park Street, South Melbourne 3205
Telephone: +61 3 969 62143
Fax: +61 3 969 62127
Chief officers: E A Garing (President), A Rossi (Secretary)

Australian Pharmaceutical Manufacturers' Association Inc. (APMA)

Address: 2nd Floor, 77 Berry St, North Sydney, NSW 2060
Telephone: +61 2 992 22699
Fax: +61 2 995 94860
Year established: 1965
Chief officers: P.R. Clear (Chief Executive Officer), Merv Mitchell (Chairman)

Australian Pork Corporation (APC)

Address: Level 5, 174 Pacific Highway, St Leonards 2065
Telephone: +61 2 943 93688
Fax: +61 2 943 83913
E-mail: pork@apc.gov.au
Activities: compiles statistics on the industry including volume and value of retailers' purchases of fresh pork for the latest year
Chief officers: Hilda Meo (Statistical Services Manager)

Australian Poultry Industry Association

Address: PO Box 579, Suite 4, 30th Floor, 100 Miller St, North Sydney, NSW 2059
Telephone: +61 2 992 94077
Fax: +61 2 992 50627
Chief officers: Jack Ingham (Chairman), Dr Jeff Fairbrother (Executive Director)

Australian Publishers' Association Ltd

Address: 89 Jones Street, Ultimo NSW 2007
Telephone: +61 2 928 19788
Fax: +61 2 928 11073
Chief officers: Mr P Donougue, Ms S Blackwell (Director)

Australian Retailers' Association

Address: Level 2, 20 York St, Sydney, NSW 2000
Telephone: +61 2 929 03766
Fax: +61 2 929 97154
Activities: exhibitions and trade fairs
Chief officers: Antony Coote (President)

Australian Seafood Industry Council (ASIC)

Address: Unit 1, 6 Phipps Close, Deakin 2600
Telephone: +61 6 281 0383
Fax: +61 6 281 0438
Chief officers: Nigel Scullion (Chairman), Paul Jones (Secretary)

Australian Supermarket Institute (ASI)

Address: 20 York St, Sydney, NSW 2000
Telephone: +61 2 929 96126
Fax: +61 2 929 01045
E-mail: office@ecomall.com.au
Web site: www.ecomall.com.au
Year established: 1990
Activities: education and training, public opinion research, organises an annual trade show
Chief officers: Bruce Bevan (Executive Director), Ken Henrick (Assistant Director), Raeleen Ronan (Coordinator)
Membership: representative body for the nation's major supermarket chains and grocery wholesaling companies. Members operate or supply 5800 supermarkets and food stores throughout Australia, accounting for about 95 per cent of the nation's annual grocery sales

Australian Toy Association Ltd (ATA)

Address: P.O. Box 355, Suite 23, Moriton House, 432 Chapel Road, Bankstown, NSW 2200
Telephone: +61 2 979 64933
Fax: +61 2 970 96685
Activities: collects statistics on the market for toys and games in Australia
Chief officers: John Peddie (Executive Secretary)
Notes: Affiliated with the International Coucil of Toy Industries.

Australian United Fresh Fruit and Vegetable Association

Address: PO Box 82, Flemington Markets 2129
Telephone: +61 2 976 31767
Fax: +61 2 974 63008
Chief officers: Jeremy Gaylard (Chairman), Eric Kime (Secretary)

Australian Wine and Brandy Corporation

Address: POB 595, Wine Industry House, 55 The Parade, Magill, SA 5072
Telephone: +61 8 364 2828
Fax: +61 8 364 5151
Year established: 1929
Chief officers: Michael Boswell (General Manager), John Pendrigh (Chairperson)
Structure: statutory marketing authority
Membership: serves all Australian wine producers
Publications:
• Annual Report/Export Market Grid of the Australian Wine and Brandy Corporation: *annual*

Australian Wine Export Council

Address: PO Box 622, Magill South Australia 5072
Telephone: +61 8 364 1388
Fax: +61 8 364 2290

Canned Food Information Service Inc.

Address: PO Box 284, South Melbourne, Victoria 3205
Telephone: +61 3 9696 1366
Fax: +61 3 9696 2018
E-mail: D.Hall@cfis.com.au
Web site: www.cfis.com.au/
Web site notes: site provides a comprehensive listing of canned food brands by manufacturer together with company contact details. It also includes information on the canning process itself
Activities: provides information to all consumers of canned food, educators, health professionals, the media and the retail trade
Chief officers: David Hall (Executive Director)

Notes: The information service is sponsored by BHP Packaging Products, which manufactures Australia's tin plate, and the two principal can makers, Containers Packaging Food Can Group and Southcorp Packaging, Rigid Packaging Division, Beverage and Food.

Carpet Institute of Australia
Address: GPO Box 1469N, Melbourne 3001
Telephone: +61 3 9698 4474
Fax: +61 3 9698 4473
Chief officers: Ian Cox (Executive Director)

Cattle Council of Australia (CCA)
Address: 3rd Floor, NFF House, 14-16 Brisbane Avenue, Barton ACT
Telephone: +61 6 273 3688
Fax: +61 6 273 2397
E-mail: cattlecouncil@msn.com
Web site: www.farmwide.com.au/nff/cattlecouncil/index.htm
Web site notes: site includes various statistics on the beef industry in Australia, including domestic consumption
Year established: 1979
Activities: consultation, policy development and market intelligence
Chief officers: Mr Justin Toohey (Executive Director), Mrs Kerry Collins (Secretary)
Publications:
• National Cattle Market Bulletin (NCMB): *market intelligence in regular segments on cattle prices and trends; major overseas market trends; seasonal and pasture conditions; retail demand in Australia; trade access issues and cattle turnoffs - monthly*
• Off-the-Hoof: *summary of activities undertaken by the Cattle Council - monthly*

Cosmetic, Toiletry and Fragrance Association of Australia Inc.
Address: Private Bag 938, Level 4, 140 Arthur Street, North Sydney, NSW 2059
Telephone: +61 2 9927 7500
Fax: +61 2 9955 0032
Chief officers: Karen Wilson (President), John Arrowsmith (Secretary)

Distilled Spirits Industry Council of Australia (DSICA)
Address: 117 Ferrars Street, South Melbourne Victoria 3205
Telephone: +61 3 9696 4466
Fax: +61 3 9696 6648
Chief officers: Gordon J. Broderick (Executive Director)

Food and Beverage Importers' Association
Address: 181 Drummond Street, Carlton Victoria 3053
Telephone: +61 3 9639 3644
Fax: +61 3 9639 0638
Activities: government liaison, advice to members on all aspects of government regulation of food and beverage imports, regular circulars to members (24 per annum)
Chief officers: Mark Humphries (President), Tony Beaver (Secretary)
Membership: 40 food importers
Notes: The Association does not produce any statistics on the industry.

Food Industry Council
Address: 3rd Floor, Commerce House, Brisbane Avenue, Barton Act 2600
Telephone: +61 6 273 2311
Fax: +61 6 273 3286/3196

Chief officers: Fred Stauder (Chairman), Graham Chalker (Executive Director)

Grains Council of Australia
Address: NFF House, 16 Brisbane Avenue, Barton ACT 2600
Telephone: +61 6 273 3000
Fax: +61 6 273 3756
Activities: collects information and provides market analysis to the industry, lobbies the government, liaises with media, consumer, environmental, manufacturing, mining and other industry groups
Structure: Wheat, Coarse Grains, Oilseeds and Grain Legumes and Seeds committees, Executive Committee, Council
Membership: represents 60,000 growers

Grocery Manufacturers of Australia
Address: 3rd Floor, NCPA Building, 10-12 Brisbane Avenue, Barton 2600
Telephone: +61 6 273 3144
Fax: +61 3 273 3405
E-mail: gma@iaccess.com.au
Activities: government liaison, public relations
Chief officers: Ross Peterson (Chairman)

Jewellers Association of Australia Ltd
Address: Unit 2A/JAA House, 19 Napier Close, Deakin, ACT 2600
Telephone: +61 6 282 3211
Fax: +61 6 282 2725
Chief officers: MS Kim Hilliard, (Executive Director)
Publications:
• Jewellers Association of Australia: *quarterly*

Liquor Merchants' Association of Australia (LMA)
Address: PO Box 5575, 7 Help St, Chatswood, NSW 2067
Telephone: +61 2 941 51199
Fax: +61 2 941 51080
Year established: 1897
Activities: sales and marketing services for wine, spirits and liquors. Maintains a database of statistics on the industry
Chief officers: Ross Burns (Executive Director)
Membership: 30 major supply houses
Publications:
• Annual Statistics Yearbook: *annual*
Notes: Trade Association owned by suppliers of alcoholic beverages.

Motor Trades' Association of Australia (MTAA)
Address: PO Box E368, Kingston, Canberra, ACT 2604
Telephone: +61 6 273 4333
Fax: +61 6 273 2738

National Association of Retail Grocers
Address: 23 Wardell Road, Dulwich Hill 2203
Telephone: +61 2 9559 4471
Fax: +61 2 9799 1421
Chief officers: Ian Baldock (Director), Keith Billington (Chairman)
Membership: independent food retailers and supermarket owners

National Farmers' Federation Australia (NFF)
Address: PO Box E10, Kingston ACT 2604
Telephone: +61 6 273 3855
Fax: +61 6 273 2331
E-mail: rleason@nff.org.au

Membership: 120,000 farmers through 29 affiliated organisations

National Footwear Retailers' Association
Address: 50 Burwood Road, Hawthorn 3122
Telephone: +61 3 9810 6333
Fax: +61 3 9818 3686
Chief officers: Peter Parkinson (President), Christiane Darmann (Executive Officer)

National Meat Association
Address: PO Box 1208, 1st Floor, 25-27 Albany St, Crows Nest, NSW 2065
Telephone: +61 2 990 67767
Fax: +61 2 990 68022
Year established: 1928
Activities: training; business management advice; enterprise bargaining assistance; award enquiries; technical advice; health and hygiene issues; general insurance; superannuation and workers' compensation
Chief officers: Dr Stephen Carroll (Chief Executive Officer); Colin Morley (Executive Officer); Joy Allen (Manager Public Affairs); Garry Johnston (National Director Human Resources); Russell Jones (Business Manager)
Structure: National Management Committee; 4 councils
Membership: 3,800 export and domestic meat processors, small goods manufacturers and meat retailers.
Publications:
• Australian Meat Industry Bulletin: *monthly*

National Pharmaceutical Distributors' Association
Address: 102 Briens Road, Northmead New South Wales, 2152
Telephone: +61 2 843 5299
Fax: +61 2 843 5031

Packaging Council of Australia (PCA)
Address: GPO Box 1469N, Melbourne 3001
Telephone: +61 3 9698 4278/9
Fax: +61 3 9690 3514
Activities: education and training, environmental and pakaging information
Chief officers: Gavin Williams (Chief Executive Officer)
Membership: packaging raw materials suppliers, package designers and consultants, wholesalers and retailers, packaging converters, and associated sectors

Pharmaceutical Society of Australia
Address: POB 21, Curtin, ACT 2605
Telephone: +61 6 283 4777
Fax: +61 6 285 2869
E-mail: psa.nat@psa.org.au
Web site: www.hen.au/psa/natoffice.htm
Chief officers: Bruce Jenkin (National Director)
Membership: 8,500 member pharmacists
Publications:
• Australian Pharmacist: *covers various pharmaceutical and medical issues, legislation, conferences etc. - monthly*

Pharmacy Guild of Australia
Address: PO Box 36, 14 Thesiger Ct, Deakin, ACT 2600
Telephone: +61 6 281 0911
Fax: +61 6 282 4745/285 1969
E-mail: guild.nat@guild.org.au
Web site: www.hcn.net.au/guild
Year established: 1928
Activities: industrial relations; marketing; staff training; product and economic information; negotiation with

governments, manufacturers, wholesalers and other organisations
Chief officers: Stephen Greenwood (Executive Director), Mr Vasken Demirian (Director, Economic Analysis)
Membership: 4,500 pharmacies throughout Australia
Publications:
• Community Pharmacy: *an annual survey of independent pharmacy operations in Australia with commentary and statistics on outlet numbers, sales, income, profit, employment, prescriptions. Data by type of drug and type of store. Also local information for states and major metropolitan areas. Based largely on the Guild's own survey - annual*
• Pharmacy Review: *quarterly*

Plastics and Chemicals Industry Association (PACIA)
Address: GPO Box 1610M, 380 St Kilda Rd, Melbourne, VIC 3000
Telephone: +61 3 969 96299
Fax: +61 3 969 96717
E-mail: pacia@c031.aone.net.au
Year established: 1994
Activities: publishes statistics
Chief officers: Michael MacKellar (Chief Executive Officer), Robert Bryce (Chemicals Sector and Commercial Manager), Mike Martin (Plastic Sector Services Manager)
Membership: 600 chemicals importers and exporters
Publications:
• Annual Report: *annual*
• Facts and Figures: *relates only to the component of manufacture of industrial chemicals and synthetic resins by participating companies. All data relates to calendar year - annual*
• Inside PACIA: *monthly*
• Looking Ahead: *bi-monthly*

Pork Council of Australia (PCA)
Address: 2nd Floor, 16 National Cct, Barton, ACT 2600
Telephone: +61 6 273 5222
Fax: +61 6 273 5022
E-mail: PorkCouncil@msn.com
Web site: www.farmwide.com.au/nff/PORK/PCA.htm
Year established: 1992
Activities: industry communications and image management, research and development of export markets, training
Chief officers: Dr Paul Higgins (President), Mr Brian Ramsay (Executive Officer)

Proprietary Medicines Association of Australia Inc.
Address: Level 4, 140 Arthur Street, North Sydney NSW 2060
Telephone: +61 2 992 25111
Fax: +61 2 995 93693
E-mail: juliet@pmaa.com.au
Activities: annual general meeting and conference; industry self-regulation; advertising preclearance; lobbying and information tracking and dissemination; collects confidential data on members and data on consumer attitudes toward self-medication
Chief officers: Juliet Seifert (Executive Director), Bronwyn Capanna (Technical Manager)
Membership: 39 manufacturers of OTC medicines and 25 related companies
Publications:
• Annual Report: *annual*
• Conference Proceedings and Executive Summaries for Research
• PMAA Newsletter: *fortnightly*

Refrigerated Warehouse and Transport Association

Address: Level 1, 8-10 Palmer Street, North Parramatta 2151
Telephone: +61 2 989 02426
Fax: +61 2 989 02415
Chief officers: Ross S Bell (Chairman), Paul Burn (Vice Chairman)

Retail Confectionery and Mixed Business Association

Address: 250-252 Canterbury Road, Surrey Hills, VIC 3127
Telephone: +61 3 983 66566
Fax: +61 3 983 63452
Activities: collects statistics on sales, rent values, etc
Chief officers: Andrew Baker (Executive Director), Allen Roberts
Membership: 3,500 small independently owned food shops
Publications:
● Food Shop: *business information and education for small shop owners. Principal subjects covered include: prices; wages; legislation; merchandising techniques; hygiene and advice on how to run and improve a small business - monthly*

Retailer Traders' Association of Australia

Address: 2nd Floor, 20 York St, Sydney, NSW 2000
Telephone: +61 2 929 03766
Fax: +61 2 926 21464
Year established: 1903
Activities: education and training
Chief officers: Laurie Elliot (President), Bill Healey (Executive Director)
Structure: council of 25 elected retailers who set policy; executive director who is a full time employee of the association
Membership: 4,242 members
Publications:
● Australian Retailer Business: *quarterly*
● Retail Trader: *monthly*

Small Business Combined Associations

Address: Level 3, 20 York Street, Sydney 2000
Telephone: +61 2 929 03766
Fax: +61 2 926 21464
Chief officers: Geoffrey Hughes (President), Scott Arnold (Secretary)

Small Retailers Association

Address: 321 Port Rd, Hindmarsh, SA 5007
Telephone: +61 8 8340 1722
Fax: +61 8 8340 1007
Year established: 1958
Chief officers: Max Baldock (President), John Brownsea (Executive Director)
Publications:
● Independent Food Retailer (The): *association news, new product releases, comprehensive pricing for small independent food retailers, training news, product relaunch or promotion and award rates information - monthly*

Textile, Clothing and Footwear Union of Australia (TCFUA)

Address: Ground Floor, 28 Anglo Road, Campsie, NSW 2194
Telephone: +61 2 9789 4188
Fax: +61 2 9789 6510
E-mail: helen@tcfua.org.au
Web site: www.@tcfua.org.au
Activities: collects statistics on production, retail sales, imports and exports
Chief officers: Tony Woolgar
Membership: 29,569 members

Publications:
● Statistics (Textile, Clothing and Footwear Union of Australia): *regular statistics on the production of clothing and footwear and the markets for specific types of clothing and footwear - annual*

Wine Makers' Federation of Australia Inc.

Address: PO Box 647, Wine Industry House, 55 The Parade, Magill, SA 5072
Telephone: +61 8 364 1122
Fax: +61 8 364 4489
Year established: 1990
Activities: compiles statistics on the Australian wine industry
Chief officers: Ian Sutton (Chief Executive), Stephen Strachan (Senior Analyst)
Structure: executive council consisting of 10 chief executives representing small, medium and large producers
Membership: winemakers
Publications:
● Sales of Domestic Wine Statistics: *monthly*
● Statistical Report: *annual*

Wool Council of Australia

Address: NFF House, 14-16 Brisbane Avenue, Barton ACT 2600
Telephone: +61 6 273 2531
Fax: +61 6 273 1120
Web site: www.farmwide.com.au/nff/wool/wool.htm
Year established: 1979
Activities: management of the stockpile and debt; quality; the wool selling system; wool testing and measurement; animal health and quarantine; shipping freight rate negotiations; research development and promotion
Chief officers: Rod Thirkell-Johnston (President), Greg Evans (Executive Director)
Membership: Australian wool growers

AUSTRIA

Association of Pharmaceutical Products Wholesalers (ARGE Pharmaceuticals)

ARGE Pharmazeuticals - Arbeitsgemeinschaft des Pharmazeutischen Großhandels
Address: Prinz Eugen Straße 16/30, A-1040 Vienna
Telephone: +43 1 504 445 2
Fax: +43 1 504 445 340
Activities: consulting, produces statistics (members only)
Chief officers: Dkfm. Friedrich Pfleger (President), Mag. Heinz Krammer (Managing Director)
Membership: 10 members
Publications:
● ARGE Intern (ARGE Intern): *summary of newspaper cuttings about the pharmaceutical market - monthly*

Association of the Austrian Vehicle Industry

Fachverband der Fahrzeugindustrie Österreichs
Address: Wiedner Hauptstrasse 63, A-1045 Vienna
Telephone: +43 1 501 054 801
Fax: +43 1 502 062 89
E-mail: fahrzeuge@wk.or.at
Web site: www.wk.or.at/fahrzeuge
Web site notes: the site provides a link to the Associations statistical department
Activities: economic promotion, general assistance to members, promotion of foreign trade, maintenance of member files and statistical information
Chief officers: Dr. Richard Daimer, (President), Franz Rottmeyer, (Vice President), Mag. Erik Baier (General Manager), Mag. Walter Linszbauer (Assistant Manager)

Membership: 230 member companies: manufacturers of vehicles, two-wheelers, surface mountings, trailers and car bodies, motor vehicle parts and components (especially motors and gear boxes), motor vehicle repair work and aircraft
Publications:
• Statistical Yearbook (Fahrzeugindustrie: Kurzbericht): *statistical information covering production, exports, investment - annual*

Association of the Electric and Electronics Industry
Fachverband der Elektro- und Elektronikindustrie Oesterreichs
Address: Mariahilfer Strasse 37-39, A-1060 Vienna
Telephone: +43 1 588 390
Fax: +43 1 586 6971
E-mail: fv19@feei.wk.or.at
Chief officers: Dkfm. Dr.Walter Wolfsberger (Chairman), Dr Heinz Raschka (Director)

Association of the Tourist Trade
Fachverband der Freizeitbetriebe
Address: Postfach 1045, Wiedner Hauptstrasse 63, A-1045 Vienna
Telephone: +43 1 501 05 3308
Fax: +43 1 502 062 32
Year established: 1946
Activities: information and advice service to members; service agency for members; statistics; promotes quality and consistency
Chief officers: Komm. Rat Dkfm. Karl Hofbauer (President), Mag. iur.Peter-Christian Dorner (Director)
Membership: 8,651 corporate members from a range of service firms including car hire, tennis courts, squash, tour guides, camp sites, boat hire, fitness centres, golf clubs (membership obligatory by law)

Austrian Association for the Petroleum Industry
Austrian Association for the Petroleum Industry
Address: Erdbergstrasse 72, A-1031 Vienna
Telephone: +43 1 713 2348
Fax: +43 1 713 0510
Publications:
• Annual Report of the Austrian Association for the Petroleum Industry (Jahresbericht): *mainly commentary on the Austrian oil and gas sectors but there is a statistical section with tables on production, exploration, imports, and consumption of specific products. A separate section covers natural gas and most tables have five-year runs of data - annual*

Austrian Automotive and Bicycle Association (ARBÖ)
Address: Mariahilfer Strasse 180, A-1150 Vienna
Telephone: +43 1 891 21260
Fax: +43 1 891 21286

Austrian Book Traders' Association
Hauptverband der Österreichischen Buchhändels
Address: Grünangergasse 4, A-1010 Vienna
Telephone: +43 1 512 1535/10
Fax: +43 1 512 8482
Year established: 1859
Activities: bibliographical references; advice on all aspects of bookselling
Chief officers: Michael Kernstock (Chairman), Mr M Puhringer (Director), Dr Otto Mang (General Secretary)
Membership: 360 booksellers
Publications:
• Anzeiger des Osterreichischen Buchhandels: *newsletter - fortnightly*

Austrian Branded Goods' Association
Österreichischer Verband der Markenartikel Industrie
Address: Am Heumarkt 12, A-1030 Vienna
Telephone: +43 1 713 3288
Fax: +43 1 713 8328
Year established: 1946
Activities: advice and information service (for members only)
Chief officers: Dr Thomas Oliva (Executive Director)
Membership: 160 manufacturers of branded goods
Publications:
• Newsletter of the Austrian Branded Goods Association: *weekly*

Austrian Brewers' Association (VOEB)
Verband der Brauereien Österreichs
Address: Zaunergasse 1-3, A-1037 Vienna
Telephone: +43 1 713 1505
Fax: +43 1 713 3946
E-mail: bier-fruchtsaft-limonade@getraenkeverband-austria.telecom.at
Web site: bier.oesterreich.com
Web site notes: site includes various statistics on the beer industry in Austria as well as product information and a list of members, etc.
Chief officers: Mr G Berner (Statistical Director), Leopold Wurstbauer (Director)
Membership: all Austrian breweries
Publications:
• Austropack (Austropack): *packaging, logistics and transportation; market data and statistics published on ad hoc basis including articles and profiles - monthly*
• Drinks (Getränke): *issues affecting drinks industry in general; some market data - monthly*

Austrian Clothing Industry Association
Fachverband der Bekleidungsindustrie Österreichs
Address: Schwarzenbergplatz 4, A-1030 Vienna
Telephone: +43 1 712 1296/7123203
Fax: +43 1 713 9204
Web site: www.fashion.at
Year established: 1946
Chief officers: KR Ing. Wilhelm Ehrlich (President), Christoph Haidinger (Director)
Membership: membership is obligatory for manufacturers; ca. 320 companies
Publications:
• Fachverbandsnachrichten (Austrian Clothing Industry Association): *monthly newsletter for members only - monthly*
Notes: State organisation.

Austrian Coffee Manufacturers' Association
Verband der Kaffeemittelindustrie
Address: Zaunergasse 1-3, A-1030 Vienna
Telephone: +43 1 712 2121
Fax: +43 1 713 1802
Chief officers: Dr Vejpustek (Director)
Dr Smolka (Chairman of Whole Food Association)
Structure: part of the umbrella association Fachverband der Lebensmittel und Nährungsindustrie
Membership: manufacturers of instant coffee

Austrian Drink Manufacturers' Association
Verband der Getränkehersteller Österreichs
Address: Zaunergasse 1-3, A-1030 Vienna
Telephone: +43 1 713 1505
Fax: +43 1 713 3946
E-mail: bier-fruchtsaft-limonade@getraenkeverband-austria.
Activities: statistical information and reference service for members and non-members
Chief officers: KR Dlug. Ferdinand Ganther (President), Mag.

Leopold Wurstbauer (Secretary), IA Werner (Statistical Information)
Membership: 75 alcohol, alcohol free and soft drinks manufacturers
Publications:
● Drinks Magazine (Die Getränkezeitung): *soft drinks, mineral water and beer, issues affecting alcoholic and non-alcoholic drinks industry - 11 p.a.*
● Statistics: *regular statistics are published by the association covering soft drinks and alcholic sales and consumption, broken down by type of drink - regular*

Austrian Frozen Food Association
Österreichisches Tiefkühl Institut
Address: Neuwaldeggerstrasse 1, Top 9, A-1170 Vienna
Telephone: +43 1 484 2220
Fax: +43 1 484 2221

Austrian Hotel Association
Österreichischer Hoteliervereinigung (ÖHV)
Address: Hofburg, A-1010 Vienna
Telephone: +43 1 533 0952
Fax: +43 1 588 707121
Year established: 1953
Chief officers: Gunther Ronacher (President); Dr Wolfgang Grassl (Executive Director)
Membership: 860 corporate members; 20 individual members. Membership confined to hotels and institutions connected with the hotel industry

Austrian Leather Industry Association
Fachverband der ledererzeugenden Industrie
Address: Wiedner Hauptstraße 63, A-1045 Vienna
Telephone: +43 1 501 053 453
Chief officers: KR Helmut Schmidt (Chairman), Dr.Heinrich Leopold (Director)

Austrian Magazines' Association (OZV)
Österreichischer Zeitschriftenverband
Address: Hoerglasse 18/5, A-1090 Vienna
Telephone: +43 1 319 7001
Fax: +43 1 319 7001

Austrian Pet Food Association (ÖHTV)
Österreichischer Heimtierfuttermittel Vereinigung
Address: c/o Master Foods Austria, Industriestrasse 20, A-2460 Bruck Leitha
Telephone: +43 216 2601
Fax: +43 216 2601601
Activities: research and statistics department for members only
Chief officers: Mrs Gerda Strass-Hortwig (Secretary)
Membership: 20 firms

Austrian Professional Hotel Association (APHA)
Fachverband der Hotellerie
Address: Postfach 342, Wiedner Hauptstrasse 63, A-1045 Vienna
Telephone: +43 1 501 053 555
Fax: +43 1 501 053 568
E-mail: Austrian@hotel-fed.co.at
Web site: www.wk.or.at/bstf
Activities: press conferences and participation in exhibitions, fairs; information bulletin four times per year; publishes newsletters and directives concerning classification of hotels; training; statistics covering economic forecasts, hotel classification, types of members, etc.
Chief officers: Dr Michael Raffling (Director)
Structure: national committee, steering committees on hotels,

pensions and guest houses
Membership: 18,400 members of the hotel industry
Publications:
● Annual Report (Jahresbericht): *annual*

Austrian Spirits Producers' Association
Verband der Spirituosenindustrie
Address: Postfach 144, Zaunergasse 1-3, A-1037 Vienna
Telephone: +43 1 712 5248
Fax: +43 1 715 4819
Activities: information service, fair competition, contacts with the government, production statistics
Chief officers: Dr Bruno Mayer (Director)
Membership: 29 members
Notes: part of the larger Fachverband des Nahrungs- und Genussmittelindustrie Österreichs (Austrian Food Industries Association)

Austrian Textile Industry Association
Fachverband der Textilindustrie Österreichs
Address: Rudolfsplatz 12, A-1000 Vienna
Telephone: +43 1 533 3726
Fax: +43 1 533 372 640
Chief officers: Günter Rhomberg (President), Dr Peter Schinzel (Director)
Publications:
● Annual Report of the Austrian Textile Industry Association (Jahrbuch): *includes a statistical supplement with the latest year's data on production, imports, and exports. Based on various sources - annual*
● Statistical Bulletin of the Austrian Textile Industry Association (Statistischer Bericht): *monthly, quarterly, and year to date figures on trends in the Austrian textile industry. Data on production, consumption, foreign trade, etc. - quarterly*

Austrian Wine Producers' Association
Bundesverband der Weinbautreibenden Österreichs
Address: Löwelstraße 12, A-1014 Vienna
Telephone: +43 1 534 41
Fax: +43 1 534 414 11
Chief officers: Josef Glatt (Director)

Banks' and Bankers' Association of Austria
Verband Österreichischer Banken und Bankiers
Address: Postfach 132, Börsegasse 11, A-1013 Vienna
Telephone: +43 1 535 177 10
Fax: +43 1 535 177 138
Activities: collaboration with the European Banking Federation, deposit guarantee facilities, all kinds of member information and statistics
Chief officers: Dr Hermann Bell (President), Helmut Elsner, Dr Erich Hampel, Dr Heinrich Wiesmüller (Vice Presidents), Franz Ovesny (Secretary General)
Membership: 54 member banks and 27 associate member banks
Publications:
● Annual Report (Jahresbericht): *annual report on financial trends and the banking sector in Austria with data for the latest year and some earlier years, based on data collected by the Association - annual*
● Banks and Conjecture (Banken and Konjunktur): *monthly*

Coffee and Tea Federation of Austria
Kaffee- und Tee- Verband
Address: Alser Straße 45, 4, A-1080 Vienna
Telephone: +43 1 405 7472
Fax: +43 1 408 7811
Year established: 1952
Activities: information by circular letters and conferences, sales statistics on coffee and tea, press releases

Chief officers: W Zieger (President), H Dany (Vicepresident), P Reinecke (Vicepresident), W Steinnendtner (Vicepresident), H Vejpustek (Executive Director)
Membership: 50 importers, processors and retailers of tea and coffee
Publications:
• Circular Letters: *internal communication of diverse events, meetings, seminars - on a regular basis*
• Trade Statistics (Coffee and Tea Association): *detailed trade statistics for coffee and tea with the latest month's figures and comparative data for earlier years - monthly*

Economic Chamber of Austria (Foreign Trade Department)

Wirtschaftskammer Österreich
Address: Postfach 354, Wiedner Hauptstrasse 63, A-1045 Vienna
Telephone: +43 1 501 05/4419
Fax: +43 1 502 06250
E-mail: inforef1@aw.wk.or.at
Year established: 1946
Activities: information on legislation and assistance with funding; as the Wirtschaftskammer is a state organisation, market information is restricted
Chief officers: Representatives: Leopold Maderthaner (President); General trade: Werner Hutschinski, Industry: Engelbert Wenckheim, Retail: Ernst Steidl, Banking and finance: Dr Guido Schmidt-Chiari, Travel: Helmut Friedrich, Tourism: Dr Günter Puttinger
Structure: the association comprises several sub-associations, dealing with all aspects of industry, trade and business representation
Membership: incorporates divisions covering general trade, industry, business, finance, transport and tourism
Publications:
• Der Unternehmer: *business advice to new businesses - 8 p.a.*
• Statistik und Dokumentation: *bi-monthly*
• Zeitschrift für Arbeits- und Sozialrecht: *employees' information and issues affecting employees' rights - bi-monthly*
Notes: membership is compulsory for all Austrian enterprises.

Federal Association for Dairy and Cheese Production

Bundesinnung der Molkereien und Käsereien
Address: Wiedner Hauptstrasse 63, A-1045 Vienna
Telephone: +43 1 501 053 277
Fax: +43 1 502 062 93
Year established: 1946
Chief officers: Walter Loibl (Director), Gerhard Woerle (President)
Structure: national committee drawn from leading companies in the field
Membership: cheese and dairy product retailers (ca. 100 members)
Notes: State oganisation.

Federal Association for Leather Goods, Toys and Fitness Equipment

Bundesgremium des Lederwaren-, Spielwaren- und Sportartikelhandels
Address: Postfach 440, Wiedner Hauptstrasse 63, A-1045 Vienna
Telephone: +43 1 501 053 370
Fax: +43 1 502 062 92
E-mail: bggr3@wkoesk.wk.or.at
Year established: 1946
Activities: conferences as needed on all areas of interest to the trade, information service and formal consultation on legislative matters, lobbying at national and international level
Chief officers: Komm. Rat Heimo Hütter (President), Dr Manfred Kandelhart (General Secretary)
Structure: national steering committee, standing committees on toys, sporting goods and leather goods, advertising council for leather articles and 9 regional chapters in all federal states
Membership: 14,965 companies (membership is obligatory by law)
Publications:
• Sport Play Free Time (Spiel Sport Freizeit Mode): *toys, games, leisure and accessories, fashion - monthly*

Federal Association of Distributors of Perfumes and Cosmetics

Budesgremium des Parfümeriewarenhandels
Address: Postfach 440, Wiedner Hauptstrasse 63, A-1045 Vienna
Telephone: +43 1 501 053 331/3208
Fax: +43 1 501 053 043
Activities: provides advice, service and training for entrepeneurs
Chief officers: Komm Rat Peter Haidinger (President), Ma. Johann Varga (Managing Director)
Structure: national committee of 24 members
Membership: 4,000 members, central state association of perfume traders, with equivalent provincial registers (membership is obligatory)
Publications:
• Perfume and Cosmetics Magazine (Parfümerie und Drogerie Magazin): *issues pertinent to perfumery and toiletries trade - monthly*
Notes: State organisation.

Federal Association of the Chemical Trade

Bundesinnung der Chemischen Gewerbe
Address: Wiedner Hauptstrasse 63, A-1045 Vienna
Telephone: +43 1 501 053 283
Fax: +43 1 502 06249
Year established: 1946
Chief officers: Dr Walter Smetana (President); Dr Robert Zoch (Director)
Membership: small-scale manufacturers of perfumery and cosmetics, cleaning products, other chemical products, pharmaceuticals; membership is obligatory for all firms
Notes: State organisation.

Federal Association of the Furniture and Wallpaper Trade

Bundesgremium des Handels mit Möbeln, Waren der Raumausstattung und Tapeten
Address: Postfach 354, Wiedner Hauptstrasse 63, A-1045 Vienna
Telephone: +43 1 501 053 322
Fax: +43 1 502 062 74
E-mail: bggr6@wkoesk.wk.or.at
Year established: 1948
Activities: giving expert opinion on law projects, intervention on behalf of members with ministries and other authorities, organisation of training programmes, legal counselling for members, negotiation of free agencies, edition of information brochures and model contracts
Chief officers: Komm. Rat Heimold Schorghofer (Chairman), Dr Gerhard Bacovsky (Managing Director)
Membership: ca. 6,300 members (membership is obligatory by law)
Notes: State organisation.

Federal Association of the Radio and Electrical Trade

Bundesgremium des Radio- und Elektrohandels
Address: Postfach 440, Wiedner Hauptstrasse 63, A-1045 Vienna
Telephone: +43 1 501 053 352
Fax: +43 1 502 062 92

Activities: conferences as needed, information service on all subjects, formal consultation on legislative matters
Structure: national steering committee and standing committees on retail trade (lighting), wholesale trade (importers), audio media (video rental); 10 regional chapters in all federal states
Membership: 10,000 companies; membership is obligatory by law
Publications:
• ERH: *retail and wholesale trade - monthly*
Notes: State oganisation.

Federal Association of the Shoe Trade
Schuhverband Österreich
Address: Postfach 440, Wiedner Hauptstrasse 63, A-1045 Vienna
Telephone: +43 1 501 053 453
Fax: +43 1 502 062 78
Structure: national committee with 14 members
Membership: obligatory membership for all shoe retailers
Publications:
• Schuh-Revue: *fortnightly*
• Schuh-Zeitung: *fortnightly*
Notes: State oganisation.

Federal Association of the Textile Trade
Bundesgremium des Textilhandels
Address: Postfach 440, Wiedner Hauptstrasse 63, A-1045 Vienna
Telephone: +43 1 501 053 320
Fax: +43 1 502 062 94
Year established: 1946
Chief officers: Dr Oskar Rick (Director)
Structure: national committee with 30 members chosen from leading companies in the industry
Membership: membership is obligatory for all shoe retailers
Publications:
• Österreichische Textil-Zeitung: *textiles - weekly*
Notes: State oganisation.

Federal Bakers' Association
Bundesinnung der Bäcker
Address: Postfach 357, Wiedner Hauptstrasse 63, A-1045 Vienna
Telephone: +43 1 501 053 191
Fax: +43 1 504 3613
Year established: 1946
Chief officers: Dr Ulrich Christalon (Director)
Structure: national committee chosen from leading companies in the field
Membership: membership is obligatory for all retail bakers
Notes: State oganisation.

Federal Butchers' Association
Bundesinnung der Fleischer
Address: Postfach 357, Wiedner Hauptstrasse 63, A-1045 Vienna
Telephone: +43 1 501 053 192
Fax: +43 1 504 3613
Year established: 1946
Chief officers: Anton Karl (President); Dr Ulrich Christalon (Director)
Structure: national committee drawn from leading companies in the field
Membership: retail butchers; membership is obligatory
Notes: State oganisation.

Federal Confectionery Association
Bundesinnung der Konditoren
Address: Postfach 354, Wiedner Hauptstrasse 63, A-1045 Vienna
Telephone: +43 1 501 053 652
Fax: +43 1 504 3613
Year established: 1946
Chief officers: Anton Harrer (President); Dr Ulrich Christalon (Director)
Structure: national committee drawn from leading companies in the field
Membership: the pastry and ice cream industry; membership is obligatory by law
Notes: State oganisation.

Federal Department Store Association
Bundesgremium der Warenhäuser
Address: Postfach 440, Wiedner Hauptstrasse 63, A-1045 Vienna
Telephone: +43 1 501 053 320
Fax: +43 1 502 062 94
Chief officers: Dr Peter Böck (President); Dr Oskar Rick (Director)
Membership: 30 department stores; membership is obligatory
Publications:
• Membership List: *annual*
Notes: State oganisation.

Federal Food Retailing Association
Bundesgremium des Lebensmittelhandels
Address: Postfach 440, Wiedner Hauptstrasse 63, A-1045 Vienna
Telephone: +43 1 650 530 00/3002
Fax: +43 1 502 062 90
Chief officers: Dr Johannes Mraz (Director)
Structure: 43 members comprising national committee; 16 regional committees
Membership: comprises membership of associations covering food, agricultural produce, meat and wine and spirits
Notes: Affiliated associations include: Bundesgremium des Landesprodukten-Handels (agricultural produce); Bundesgremium des Viehhandels und des Fleischgrosshandels (meat); Bundesgremium des Wein - und Spirituosengrosshandels (wine and spirits).

Federal Hardware Association
Bundesgremium des Eisenhandels
Address: Postfach 354, Wiedner Hauptstrasse 63, A-1045 Vienna
Telephone: +43 1 501 053 322
Fax: +43 1 502 062 87
E-mail: bggr6@wkoesk.wk.or.at
Year established: 1948
Activities: giving expert opinion on law projects, intervetion on behalf of members with ministries and all other administrative authorities; legal counselling for members, organisation of education programmes, negotiation of free agencies, edition of information brochures and model contracts
Chief officers: Komm. Rat Kurt Ehernberger (Chairman), Dr Gerhard Bacovsky (Managing Director)
Membership: ca. 13,000 members (membership is obligatory by law)
Publications:
• EWH: *monthly*
• Hartwarenmarkt
Notes: state organisation belonging to central Wirtschaftskammer (Federal Chamber of Austria)

Federation of Chemical Industry (FCIO)

Fachverband der Chemischen Industrie Österreichs
Address: Postfach 325, Wiedner Hauptstrasse 63, A-1045
Vienna
Telephone: +43 1 501 053 371
Fax: +43 1 502 062 80
E-mail: fcio@wkosk.wk.or.at
Web site: www.wk.or.at/fcio
Year established: 1947
Activities: chemical production and trade statistics,
negotiations with unions
Chief officers: Techn.Rat Dipl.-Ing. Josef Frick (Managing
Director), Dr Harald Strassnitzky (Director)
Membership: 550 companies
Publications:
• Austrian Chemical Annual Report (Österreichs Chemie
Jahresbericht): *mainly commentary reviewing trends in the
chemical sector but a statistical section includes data on total
production, production by product, foreign trade, and
employment. Figures for the last two or three years - annual*
• Handbooks about the Chemicals Industry: *triennial*
• Handbooks about the Pharmaceuticals Industry
• Handbooks about the Plastics Industry: *triennial*
Notes: State oganisation.

Federation of the Food Industry

Fachverband der Lebensmittel- und Nährungsindustrie
Address: Zaunergasse 1-3, A-1037 Vienna
Telephone: +43 1 712 212 10
Fax: +43 1 713 1802
Activities: information and statistics for members publishes
newsletters and brochures
Chief officers: Herr Domsitz (Director)
Structure: umbrella organisation for sub-associations dealing
with specific food sectors
Publications:
• Ernährung: *issues affecting food industry - monthly*

Federation of the Glass Industry

Fachverband der Glasindustrie
Address: Postfach 328, Wiedner Hauptstrasse 63, A-1045
Vienna
Telephone: +43 1 501 053 428
Fax: +43 1 502 062 81
Year established: 1946
Chief officers: Dipl. Ing. Rudolf Schraml (Chairman), Dr Peter
Schöpf (Director)
Membership: membership obligatory by law for all glass
manufacturers
Notes: State oganisation.

Federation of the Paper Industry (AUSTROPAPIER)

Fachverband der Papierindustrie
Address: Gumpendorferstraße 6, A-1061 Vienna
Telephone: +43 1 588 860
Fax: +43 1 588 862 22
E-mail: fvpapier@fvpapier.wk.or.at
Year established: 1866
Activities: education and training for pulp, paper and board
industries
Chief officers: KR Dr.Robert Launsky-Tieffenthal (Chariman),
Gerolf Ottawa (Director)
Membership: membership is obligatory by law for all paper,
pulp and board manufacturers
Publications:
• Austrian Paper (Papier aus Österreich): *monthly*
Notes: State organisation.

Federation of Travel Agencies

Fachverband der Reisebüros
Address: Postfach 1045, Wiedner Hauptstrasse 63, A-1045
Vienna
Telephone: +43 1 501 053 308
Fax: +43 1 502 062 32
Activities: service agency for members; legal representation;
collects statistics of members, incoming tourism and
apprentices
Chief officers: Komm. Rat Rudolf Kadanka (President), Mag.
iur. Peter-Christian Dorner (Director)
Membership: 2,353 travel agencies (obligatory membership
by law)
Publications:
• Info-brochures: *tourist information on Austria, places of
interest, hotels, camping sites, etc. - regularly*
• Membership List (Mitgliederlist): *compilation of contact
details of members (name, address, phone, fax, type of
license) - annual*
• Text Books: *text books for license-tests - annual*
Notes: State oganisation.

Film and Audiovisual Industry Association of Austria

Fachverband der Audiovisions- und Filmindustrie
Address: Postfach 327, Wiedner Hauptstrasse 63, A-1045
Vienna
Telephone: +43 1 501 053 010
Fax: +43 1 502 062 76
Year established: 1947
Activities: information service for members, sends out
professional association notices, issues membership lists,
prepares and conducts press interviews, press conferences,
seminars, undertakes public relations, concludes collective
agreements with the Art, Media and Freelance Professionals'
Union, provides legal information in relation to commercial law,
trade regulations, financial and tax and copyright law
Chief officers: Michael Wolkenstein (President), Dr Elmar A
Peterlunger (General Manager)
Membership: over 1480 members: companies dealing with
the manufacture of moving pictures on video, carriers of all
kinds (film/video production), film and video distributing
companies, copying and reversal shops, studios, sound
studios, video finishing firms, firms involved in recording,
pressing and CD manufacture; membership is obligatory
Publications:
• Membership Address Book: *names and addresses of all
members of the association - annual*
• Roundletter: *monthly*
• Statistics: *production*
Notes: State oganisation.

Food and Delicatessen Food Association of Austria (FIAA)

Fachverband des Nahrungs- und Genussmittelindustrie
Österreichs
Address: Postfach 144, Zaunergasse 1-3, A-1037 Vienna
Telephone: +43 1 712 2121/36/713 1505
Fax: +43 1 713 1802/713 3946
Chief officers: Gen.Dir. Dkfm. Dr. Erwin Bundschuh
(Chairman), Dr. Klaus Smolka (Director)
Membership: general food industry association incorporating
specialist groups which represent most sectors, e.g.
bread-baking, dairy products and retail meat handling

Foreign Trade Association

Bundesgremium des Aussenhandels
Address: Postfach 440, Wiedner Hauptstrasse 63, A-1045
Vienna
Telephone: +43 1 501 053 561
Fax: +43 1 502 062 92
E-mail: bggr3@wkoesk.wk.or.at

Year established: 1946
Activities: formal consultation on legislative matters, statistical information available to members
Chief officers: Dr Karl-Heinz Dernoscheg (President), Dr Manfred Kandelhart (General Secretary)
Structure: national committee (15 members) and 10 regional committees in federal states
Membership: 15 committee members, 2,900 full members
Notes: State organisation belonging to central Wirtschaftskammer (Federal Chamber of Austria).

Fruit and Vegetable Processing Industry Association

Verband der Obst- und Gemüseverwertungsindustrie
Address: Zaunergasse 1-3, A-1037 Vienna
Telephone: +43 1 712 2121
Fax: +43 1 713 1802
Chief officers: Herr Domsitz
Structure: the Association comes under the general umbrella organisation Fachverband der Lebernsmittelindustrie
Membership: fruit and vegetable processors

Hardware and Kitchen Equipment Traders' Association

Verband Österreichischer Eisenwaren- und Küchengerätehändler
Address: Karl-Meisslstrasse 2, A-1200 Vienna
Telephone: +43 1 332 4436
Fax: +43 1 330 7751
Year established: 1905
Chief officers: Barbara Fürst (Director)
Membership: 260 members from the retail trade
Publications:
● EWH: *trade issues, some statistics covering developments in the housewares market - monthly*

Hotel and Catering Association of Austria

Fachverbände Gastronomie und Hotellerie der Wirtschaftskammer Österreich
Address: Augasse 2-6, A-1090 Vienna
Telephone: +43 1 313 36/4586
Fax: +43 1 317 1205
E-mail: karl.woeber@wu-wien.ac.at
Web site: www.wu-wien.ac.at/inst/tourism/bv

National Committee of the International Dairy Federation

Oesterreichisches Nationalkomitee des IMV
Address: Lilienbrunng. 11, 1020 Wien
Telephone: +43 1 216 25 22
Fax: +43 1 216 25 22/15
Chief officers: Dr Franz Hoche (Secretary)

Newspaper Publishers' Association (VÖZ)

Verband Österreichischer Zeitungsherausgeber und Zeitungsverleger
Address: Schreyvogelgasse 3, A-1010 Vienna
Telephone: +43 1 533 6178
Fax: +43 1 533 617822
Year established: 1946
Activities: central information point for all details on press and media industry in Austria; publishes handbook
Chief officers: Dr Walter Schaffelhofer (Secretary General)
Membership: 86 newspapers
Publications:
● Pressehandbuch: *list of all newspapers, newsletters, journals, magazines, and other published media including advertising companies and concerns; includes some German listings - annual*

Paper and Pulp Processing Industry Association

Fachverband der Papier und Pappe verarbeitenden Industrie
Address: Brucknerstraße 8, 1040 Wien
Telephone: +43 505 53 82-0
Chief officers: KR Gustav Glöckner (Chairman), Mag. Rudolf Bergolth (General Director)

Soft Drinks Producers' Association

Verband der Hersteller Alkoholfreier Erfrischungsgetränke
Address: Zaunergasse 1-3, A-1037 Vienna
Telephone: +43 1 713 1505
Fax: +43 1 713 3946
Membership: alcohol free and soft drinks manufacturers

Textile Industry Association (VTI)

Vereinigung Textilindustrie
Address: Postfach 114, Rudolfsplatz 12, A-1013 Vienna
Telephone: +43 1 532 9751
Fax: +43 1 532 7289
Year established: 1948
Activities: produces production, import and export statistics and statistical publications (internal use only)
Chief officers: Werner Dünser (Director)
Membership: 42 companies

BANGLADESH

Bangladesh Computer Society

Address: House #2 (2nd Flr), Road 32 (New), Dhanmondi Dhaka-1209
Telephone: +880 231 8312
Fax: +880 281 3186

BARBADOS

Barbados Hotel and Tourism Association

Address: P.O. Box 711C, Bridgetown W.I.
Telephone: +1 246 4 265 041
Fax: +1 246 4 292 845
E-mail: sales@sandlinx.bajan.com
Web site: www.bajan.com/barbados/bhta/bhta.html
Year established: 1957
Activities: information service, education and training
Chief officers: Jeff Kinch (President)
Membership: ca. 100 members from the hotel and catering industry

Barbados Manufacturers' Association (BMA)

Address: Building #1, Pelican Industrial Park, St Michael
Telephone: +1 246 4 264 474/427 9898
Fax: +1 246 4 365 182
Web site: www.b-m-a.org
Year established: 1964
Activities: promotes and regulates manufacturing industry through the cooperation, understanding and closer association of manufacturers in Barbados
Chief officers: Bobby Khan (President), Rita Atkins (Executive Secretary)
Membership: full members from the following sectors: 19 food, 7 clothing, 7 furniture, 10 plastics and packaging, 11 construction, 6 miscellaneous; also 14 associate and 4 affiliate members
Publications:
● Membership Directory: *annual*

Caribbean Publishing and Broadcasting Association

Address: BHA Building, 4th Ave, Belleville, St Michael
Telephone: +1 246 436 5889
Year established: 1962
Activities: monitors press freedom, provides an information service
Membership: umbrella organisation for media related enterprises

BELGIUM

Association of Belgian Breakfast Cereals Manufacturers

Association Belge des Fabricants de Céréales pour le Petit Déjeuner/Belgische Vereniging van Fabrikanten van Ontbijtgranen
Address: Avenue de Roodebeek 30, B-1030 Brussels
Telephone: +32 2 743 8730
Fax: +32 2 736 8175

Association of Belgian Distribution Firms (AGED)

Association des Groupements et Entreprises de Distribution de Belgique
Address: 60 rue Saint-Bernard, B-1060 Brussels
Telephone: +32 2 537 3060
Fax: +32 2 539 4026
Year established: 1921
Chief officers: Gui de Vaucleroy (President)
Structure: non-profit-making organisation
Membership: large-scale distributors, including department stores, multiples, mail order groups

Association of Belgian Frozen Food Industries (ABEPAS)

Association Belge des Entreprises de Produits Alimentaires Surgelés/Belgische Vereniging van Ondernemingen van Diepvries-Voedingsprodukten
Address: Avenue de Roodebeek 30, B-1030 Brussels
Telephone: +32 2 743 8730
Fax: +32 2 736 8175
Chief officers: Johan Hallaert, Ms P. de Sloovere
Notes: Member of the Federation of the Associations of EU Frozen Food Producers (FAFPAS) based in Brussels.

Association of Belgian Manufacturers and Importers of Pet Foods and Accessories (CPAF)

Chambre Professionnelle Belge de Fabricants et Importateurs d'Aliments et Accessoires pour Animaux de Compagnie
Address: c/o Wolfs S.A., 10, rue du Bosquet, B-1400 Nivelles
Telephone: +32 678 87560
Fax: +32 678 87570
Year established: 1969
Chief officers: Mr Dany Dupont
Structure: independent non-profit-making organisation
Membership: manufacturers and importers of pet foods and accessories

Association of Belgian Pulp, Paper and Board Manufacturers (COBELPA)

Association des Fabricants de Pâtes, Papiers et Cartons de Belgique
Address: Avenue Louise 306, B-1050 Brussels
Telephone: +32 2 646 6450
Fax: +32 2 646 8297
Year established: 1940
Activities: statistical services, compilation of sector data (not usually available to non-members)
Chief officers: Firmin François (Managing Director), Cristina Mariages-Janssens (Assistant Director)
Structure: non-profit independent organisation
Membership: 14 pulp and paper manufacturers

Publications:
• Annual Statistics (COBELPA): *a general overview of the Belgian pulp, paper and board sector is followed by a general statistical survey and detailed data on production, imports, exports, consumption, and raw materials. The report also contains a list of COBELPA members. Mainly figures for the latest year based on a combination of trade association data and official statistics - annual*

Association of Belgo-Luxembourg Manufacturers and Distributors of Soaps, Detergents and Hygiene Products (DETIC)

Association Belgo-Luxembourgeoise des Producteurs et des Distributeurs de Savons, Détergents, Produits d'Entretien, d'Hygiène et de Toilette, Colles et Produits Connexes
Address: Square Marie-Louise 49, B-1000 Brussels
Telephone: +32 2 238 9711
Fax: +32 2 230 8288
E-mail: d.e.t.i.c@infoboard.be
Year established: 1977
Activities: DETIC has a well established research department (free service to members) offering technical as well as legal and commercial information
Chief officers: Pierre Costa (Director), J.A. De Smedt (Advisor)
Membership: 180 manufacturing and distributing firms belonging to the soap/detergent, cosmetic/perfumery, adhesive/sealant and household product sectors
Publications:
• Advertising Code for Cosmetics (Code de Publicité pour les Produits Cosmétiques): *advertising law for cosmetic products*
• DETIC-CONTACT: *journal of DETIC, the Belgo-Luxembourg Association of Manufacturers and Distributors of Soaps, Detergents, Household Cleaning Materials, Hygiene and Toiletry Products, Adhesives and Related Products - monthly*
• List of Members (Liste des Membres): *list of DETIC members*
• Répertoire des Marques
Notes: Member of AISE (International Association of the Soap Detergent and Maintenance Products Industry) based in Brussels.

Association of General Food Wholesalers

Association des Entreprises de Gros en Alimentation Générale
Address: Avenue Louis Gribaumont 3, B-1150 Brussels
Telephone: +32 2 771 9191
Fax: +32 2 771 3252
Membership: general food wholesalers

Association of Manufacturers and Distributors of Concentrated Soup and Meat Stock

Association des Fabricants et Distributeurs de Bouillons et Potages Concentrés/Associatie van Fabrikanten en Producenten van boullions en geconc. soepen
Address: Avenue de Roodebeek 30, B-1030 Brussels
Telephone: +32 2 743 8730
Fax: +32 2 736 8175
Year established: 1982
Chief officers: Michael Coenen (Secretary General)
Structure: member of LIV (Landbouw en Voedings Industrie - the agriculture and food sector's umbrella organisation)
Membership: 4 soup and meat stock manufacturers and distributors

Association of Pasta Manufacturers and Importers (AFISPA-VIVED)

Association des Fabricants et Importateurs de Spécialités et de Pâtes Alimentaires/Vereniging van Producenten en Invoerders van Voedingsspecialiteiten en Deegwaren
Address: Avenue de Roodebeek 30, B-1030 Brussels
Telephone: +32 2 743 8730
Fax: +32 2 736 8175

Belgian Aerosols' Association (ABA)

Association Belge des Aérosols
Address: 49 Square Marie-Louise, B-1040 Brussels
Telephone: +32 2 280 4090
Fax: +32 2 280 0929
Year established: 1982
Activities: conducts research, compiles statistics
Chief officers: Mr Anis
Structure: non-profit-making organisation
Membership: 57 aerosol manufacturers

Belgian Association of Baby and Dietetic Food (ABSAED)

Association Belge du Secteur des Aliments de l'Enfance et des Aliments Diététiques/Belgische Vereniging van de Sektor der Kinder en Dieetvoeding
Address: Avenue de Roodebeek 30, B-1030 Brussels
Telephone: +32 2 743 8730
Fax: +32 2 736 8175

Belgian Association of Insurance Companies (UPEA)

Union Professionnelle des Entreprises d'Assurances
Address: Maison de l'Assurance, Square de Meeûs 29, B-1040 Brussels
Telephone: +32 2 547 5611/513 6845
Fax: +32 2 547 5600/514 2469
Publications:
● Belgian Insurance Market (Le Marché Belge de l'Assurance): *commentary and statistics on the Belgian insurance market with sections on the main insurance areas. Mainly text with some statistics - annual*
● Insurance in Belgium: *a summary of the union's annual report with commentary and statistics on Belgian insurance - annual*

Belgian Association of Multiple Food Traders (ABEAS)

Association Belge des Entreprises d'Alimentation à Succursales
Address: 60 rue Saint-Bernard, B-1060 Brussels
Telephone: +32 2 537 3060
Fax: +32 2 539 4026
Membership: food multiples

Belgian Bakery, Pastry, Confectionery and Ice Cream Confederation (BPCG)

Confédération de la Boulangerie, Patisserie, Confiserie, Glacerie de Belgique
Address: Boîte 42, 83 Boulevard Louis Mettewie, B-1080 Brussels
Telephone: +32 2 469 2908
Fax: +32 2 469 2140
Year established: 1982
Chief officers: Willy Claes (General Secretary)
Structure: independent non-profit-making organisation
Membership: 5,500-6,000 local unions that have bakeries as their members

Belgian Bankers' Association (ABB-BVB)

Association Belge des Banques/Belgische Vereniging van Banken
Address: Boîte 5, Rue Ravenstein 36, B-1000 Brussels
Telephone: +32 2 507 6811
Fax: +32 2 512 5861
E-mail: abb-bvb@abb-bvb.be
Web site: www.abb-bvb.be
Web site notes: site includes various statistics on the banking sector in belgium
Year established: 1936
Activities: provides statistical services; data about Belgian banking sector: activities, trends, interbank activity; the association also provides information to its members and to the public in general through publishing, regular conferences and seminars for a corporate and teaching audience
Chief officers: W. Breesch (President), C. Henriksen (Vice President), M. Tilmant (Vice President), Jacques Zeegers (Secretary-General of Communication Department)
Membership: 124 banks and 17 representative offices; the banks' group includes 84 banks under Belgian law (53 banks with purely Belgian interest, 31 banks under Belgian law with foreign majority interest) and 40 branches of foreign banks
Publications:
● Administrative Inventory of Banks (Recueil Administratif des Banques): *twice a year*
● Annual Report: *annual*
● banks in 1995 - Individual data (Les banques en 1995 - Données individuelles): *list of the Belgium-based banks and their individual data*
● Vade-mecum statistique du secteur bancaire: *aggregate data on the banking sector plus statistics for specific banking sectors, employment data, investments, money supply, credit, international banking, banking services. Based mainly on data from the association and other associations in the financial sector - annual*

Belgian Central Committee of Wool and Associated Fibres

Comité Central Belge de la Laine et des Fibres Associées/Centraal Belg. Commitere voor Wol en aanverwante weefsels
Address: Boîte 13, Rue du Luxembourg 19-21, B-1000 Brussels
Telephone: +32 2 513 0620
Fax: +32 2 514 0665
Year established: 1930
Activities: provides statistics
Chief officers: Dimitri Orekhoff (Director General)
Structure: non-profit-making organisation in association with FEBELTEX
Membership: 40 members: manufacturers and wholesalers of wool and textiles

Belgian Clothing Association

Fédération Belge des Industries de l'Habillement
Address: Rue Montoyer 24, B-1000 Brussels
Telephone: +32 2 238 1011/44
Fax: +32 2 230 4700
E-mail: belfashion@glo.be
Web site: www.vbo-feb.be:80/fashion/
Year established: 1916
Chief officers: Bernard Siau (President), Eric Magnus (Secretary General)
Membership: 400 clothing and apparel companies representing 90% of the Belgian fashion sector
Publications:
● Fashion from Belgium: *alphabetical listing of all affiliated ready-to-wear manufacturers, including address, telephone and fax number, showroom address, the company's manager and the sales manager, a description of the collection, the customer segment, the brands, the export markets and the specialised fairs in which the different companies participate - annual*

Belgian Coffee Office

Office Belge du Café
Address: Avenue de Roodebeek 30, B-1030 Brussels
Telephone: +32 2 743 8730
Fax: +32 2 736 8175
Publications:
● Coffee Consumption in BELUX: *total consumption, in tons, and per capita consumption, in kilograms, of coffee in Belgium and Luxembourg for a number of years. Based on data collected by the Belgian Coffee Office - annual*
● Exported Roasted Coffee/Imported Roasted Coffee: *two*

separate publications show exports and imports respectively of roasted coffee in tons for a number of years. Based on official statistics - annual

Belgian Direct Marketing Association (BDMV-ABMD)
Association Belge du Marketing Direct/Belgisch Direct Marketing Verbond
Address: Avenue Edouard Lacomblé 17, B-1040 Brussels
Telephone: +32 2 736 4583
Fax: +32 2 735 8725
Web site: www.bdma.be
Activities: organises events; collects statistics on turnover
Chief officers: Paul van Lil (Director), Patrick Marck (Office Manager)
Membership: 425 members
Publications:
• Brochure "Comment avez-vous eu mon nom?"
• Le Guide du Marketing Direct: *annual*
• Les Guides de l'ABMD
• Objet Direct/In Direct: *monthly*

Belgian Distribution Committee
Comité Belge de la Distribution/Belgisch Comité voor de Distributie
Address: 34 rue Marianne, B-1180 Brussels
Telephone: +32 2 345 9923
Fax: +32 2 346 0204
Year established: 1954
Activities: collects data on distribution of food products and general consumer goods (accessible to non-members); library of 4,000 books and 200 European and US periodicals relevant to the distribution of food products and general consumer goods; organisation of seminars, workshops, study tours in Belgium and abroad; market research; professional exhibitions (Visumat; Franchising; Vending)
Chief officers: Prof J. Leunis (President); Léon F. Wegnez (Director General)
Structure: independent non-profit making organisation
Membership: 11,000 members; manufacturers; retailers and wholesalers; consultants; executive officers from Belgian universities and institutions
Publications:
• Annuaire Libre-Service: *annual directory of self-service sector - annual*
• Atlas Commercial de Belgique: *9 volume series*
• Distribution d'Aujourd-hui/Distributie Vandaag: *a monthly journal with regular features and surveys on Belgian retailing plus annual surveys of the food and retailing sectors. Based on various sources - 10 p.a.*
• Habitudes d'Achat
• Informations Specialisées: *monograph series - quarterly*
• J'Installe, Je Modernise mon Magasin
• La Promotion au Lieu de Vente: *point of sale advertising*
• Le Marché Belge en Chiffres
• Manuel de la Distribution
• Marges de Distribution
• Répertoire de la Distribution Belge
• Restauration d'Aujourd'hui/Restauratie Vandaag: *6 pa*
• Superettes et Supermarchés de Petite Surface
Notes: The Comité is the Belgian Section of the International Association for the Distribution of Food Products and General Consumer Goods (AIDA) (qv)

Belgian Editors' Association (ADEB)
Association des Editeurs Belges/Verening van Uitgevers van Nederlandstalige Boeken
Address: Boîte 1, Boulevard Lambermont 140, B-1030 Brussels
Telephone: +32 2 241 6580
Fax: +32 2 216 7131

Year established: 1922
Activities: collects statistics on production and turnover
Chief officers: J P Michaud (President), Cr. Cremer (Administrations Officer), Bernard Gérard (Director), Nicole Larock (Assistant Dorector), Mr G Hoyos (General Secretary)
Structure: independent non-profit-making organisation
Membership: 94 books editors
Publications:
• Annuaire des Editeurs Belges
• Statistics: *production and turnover*

Belgian Federation of Bus and Coach Operators (FBAA)
Fédération Belge des Exploitants d'Autobus et d'Autocars et des Organisatuers de Voyages
Address: Avenue de la Métrologie 8, B-1130 Brussels
Telephone: +32 2 245 3570
Fax: +32 2 245 2050
Chief officers: Paul Laeremans (Deputy Administrator), Luc Glorieux (Administrator), Yves Mannaerts (Director), Luc Jullet (Director)
Structure: non-profit independent organisation
Membership: 600 bus and coach companies
Publications:
• Car & Bus: *ten p.a.*
• Guide Car & Bus: *annual*
• Hebdo/Nieuws in het Kort: *weekely*
• La Bourse du Transport: *fortnightly*
• Travel News: *fortnightly*
Notes: The Association does not produce statistics.

Belgian Federation of Distribution (FEDIS)
Fédération Belge des Entreprises de Distribution/Belgische Federatie van de Distributie Onderdelen
Address: rue Saint-Bernard 60, B-1060 Brussels
Telephone: +32 2 537 3060
Fax: +32 2 539 4026
E-mail: fedis@fedis.be
Year established: 1978
Activities: collects sector statistics on number of enterprises, consumption, prices, labour trends and trends by type of outlet and product areas (summary published in annual report); information service
Structure: member of umbrella organisation VBO
Membership: 16 associations; wholesalers and retailers
Publications:
• Annual Report (Belgian Federation of Distribution Firms) (Rapport Annuel): *largely text on the retailing and distributive trades but various tables on number of enterprises, consumption, prices, labour trends, and trends by type of outlet and product areas. Data for earlier years in most tables and based on a combination of sources - annual*

Belgian Federation of the Car and Bicycle Industries (FEBIAC)
Fédération Belge des Industries de l'Automobile et du Cycle
Address: Boîte 6, Boulevard de la Woluwe 46, B-1200 Brussels
Telephone: +32 2 778 6400
Fax: +32 2 762 8171
E-mail: web@febiac.be
Web site: www.febiac.be
Activities: marketing and publishing of statistical data on the Belgian motor vehicles sector; macro-economic survey; promotion of the members; organisation of the Car Show
Chief officers: René Fabry (Director General), Gabriel Leman (Administrative Manager), Jaques Soenen (Director of the Car Show)
Structure: independent non-profit organisation
Membership: 200 manufacturers, distributors etc in the automotive sector and governement representatives concerned with transport in general

Publications:
• Annual Report (FEBIAC) (Rapport Annuel): *an annual report, with statistics, on the motor vehicle, motorcycle, and cycle sectors in Belgium. Most of the data is collected by the association itself - annual*
• Data Digest: *annual*
• Febiac Info: *quarterly*

Belgian Federation of Wines and Spirits (FBVS-BFWG)
Fédération Belge des Vins et Spiritueux/Belgische Federatie van Wijn en Gedistileerd
Address: Boîte 5, Rue de Livourne 13, B-1050 Brussels
Telephone: +32 2 537 0051
Fax: +32 2 537 8156
Year established: 1950
Activities: promotes and defends its members' interests (trade, taxation, production & definitions, alcohol & society, environnement; collects statistics on import and export
Chief officers: Mieke Leys-Bailleul (Secretary General), Jean-Jaques Delhaye (Deputy Secretary General)
Structure: non-profit making organisation associated with LIV (agricultural and food-industry association)
Membership: 185 wine merchants, wine bottlers, spirits producers, brand distributors in Belgium
Publications:
• Import/Export Statistics (Cahier des Statistiques): *imports and exports of wine and spirits by type*
• Newsletter: *monthly*
• Wines and Spirits Bulletin of Statistics (Bulletin Economique de Vins et Spiritueux): *basic data on trends in the wine and spirits sector including data on production, foreign trade, demand - ten issues a year*

Belgian Franchise Federation
Fédération Belge de la Franchise
Address: Boîte 2, Boulevard de l'Humanité 116, B-1070 Brussels
Telephone: +32 2 523 9707
Fax: +32 2 523 3510
Chief officers: Pierre Jeanmart (Chairman), Carine Schryers (Executive Secretary), Reinhilde Hendrickx (Managing Secretary)
Membership: 52 members
Publications:
• Newsletter: *four p.a.*
Notes: The Association does not produce statistics.

Belgian Institute of Packaging (IBE-BVI)
Institut Belge de l'Embalage/Belgisch verpakkings instituut
Address: Rue Picard 15, B-1000 Brussels
Telephone: +32 2 427 2583
Fax: +32 2 425 9975
Year established: 1954
Activities: operates a technical and commercial information centre and a scientific and technical centre for research and testing (laboratory tests, study office, quality control, expert surveys); training courses and in-service training, committees, seminars; collects statistics on production, imports, exports, etc.
Chief officers: Dr F. Lox (President), Maxence Wittebolle (Technical Director), M. Calcoen (Co-ordination Director)
Structure: independent (parastatal) non-profit making organisation
Membership: 229 packaging manufacturers, distributors, professional associations, government authorities
Publications:
• Annuaire: *annual*
• Pack Newsletter: *fortnightly*
• Packnews: *monthly*
• Vademecum de l'Emballage

Belgian Royal Association of Biscuit and Confectionery Industries (ROYAL SWEETS)
Association Royale Belge des Industries du Biscuit, du Chocolat, de la Confiserie et de la Praline/Koninklijke Belgische Vereniging van de Biscuit, Chocolade, Suikergoed en Praline Industrie
Address: Avenue de Roodebeek 30, B-1030 Brussels
Telephone: +32 2 743 8744/2 743 8730
Fax: +32 2 736 8175
Chief officers: Myriam Goffings (Secretary General)

Belgian Union of International Trade Companies
Association Belge des Sociétés de Commerce International/Belgisch Vereniging van Uitvoer en Invoerhandelaars
Address: Israëlietenstraat 7, B-2000 Antwerpen
Telephone: +32 3 226 0712
Fax: +32 3 231 9969/3 226 2967
Structure: independent non-profit organisation
Membership: 50 commodity traders
Notes: The Association does not produce any statistics or publications.

Belgian Union of Professional Beauty Consultants
Union Professionnelle reconnue des Esthéticiennes-Techniciennes de Beauté de Belgique/Beroepsvereniging van schoonheidsspecialisten, technici van Belgie
Address: 169 Avenue Molière, B-1060 Brussels
Telephone: +32 2 343 2096
Fax: +32 2 346 5316
Year established: 1960
Chief officers: Madame Richard (President)
Membership: beauty consultants

Belgian Union of Professional Food Product Importers (Belgafood)
Union Professionnelle Belge pour l'Importation de Denrées Alimentaires/Belgische Beroepsvereniging voor de Invoer van Voedingswaren
Address: Bus 3, Leopoldplaats 10, B-2000 Antwerp
Telephone: +32 3 231 8556
Fax: +32 3 226 3498
Year established: 1971
Chief officers: J. Ploegaerts (President), F Vaerewijck (Secretary)
Membership: 50 general food importers
Publications:
• Bulletin d'Information
Notes: The Association does not produce statistics.

Belgium Federation of Fuel Wholesalers (ASBL)
Fédération Belge des Negotiants en Combustibles et Carburants/Belgische Federatie der brandstoffen grosshandelaars
Address: Rue Léon LePage 4, 1000 Brussel
Telephone: +32 2 502 4200
Fax: +32 2 502 5446
E-mail: euooo453@pophost.eunet.be
Year established: 1946
Chief officers: Mr Antoine Mornie (President), Rene Metrgen (Administration Representative), Marc Devos (Administration Representative)
Structure: independent VZW
Membership: 10 trade unions
Publications:
• Fuel Info (Combustibles/Brandstoffen Info): *11 p.a.*
• Fuel Magazine (Combustibles/Brandstoffen): *10 p.a.*

Belgo-Luxembourg Federation of Tobacco Industries (FEDETAB)

Fédération Belgo-Luxembourgeoise des Industries du Tabac
Address: Boîte 1, Avenue Lloyd Georges 7, B-1050 Brussels
Telephone: +32 2 646 0420
Fax: +32 2 646 2213
Year established: 1947
Chief officers: Francis De Vroey (President)
Structure: independent non-profit-making organisation
Membership: 51 manufacturers and 9 importers
Publications:
• FEDETAB: *annual review of the tobacco sector with commentary and statistics on production, consumption, trade. Statistics for the last two or three years - annual*
• Monthly Bulletin (FEDETAB) (Bulletin Mensuel): *production data for various tobacco products for the latest month plus the corresponding month in the last year and cumulative year-to-date figures. Also includes consumption and import-export data by product - monthly*

Central Food Association

Association Centrale de l'Agro-Alimentaire/Centrale der Levensmiddelenbedrijven
Address: 8 rue de Spa, B-1040 Brussels
Telephone: +32 2 238 0511
Fax: +32 2 230 9354
Telex: 24745
Structure: independent non-profit
Membership: central association for food and beverage companies
Publications:
• Alimentation et Distribution/Voedingsblad (Het): *food and beverage retailing and distribution - 10 p.a.*

Central Organisation of Food Retailers (CLB)

Nationale Centrale voor Kleine en Middelgrote Levensmiddelenbedrijven
Address: Rue de Spa 8, B-1000 Brussels
Telephone: +32 2 338 0622
Fax: +32 2 230 9354
Year established: 1967
Chief officers: Luc Ardies (Secretary General); E. De Woy (President); Karina Stockinan (Administration); Luc Vogels (Public Relations)
Structure: independent non-profit-making organisation
Membership: 10,000 small to medium-sized food retailers and occupational organisations
Publications:
• Alimentation & Distribution: *food distribution - 9 p.a.*
• V-Inform: *socioeconomic subjects - monthly*
• Vademecum: *food distribution regulations*

CHOBISCO

Address: Boîte 3, Rue de la Bourse 22, B-1000 Brussels
Telephone: +32 2 511 0030
Fax: +32 2 512 6890
Activities: regular production, sales and trade statistics covering biscuits, chocolate confectionery and snacks
Chief officers: Paul de Backer (National Secretary)
Structure: independent
Membership: 200 manufacturers, importers and wholesalers
Publications:
• Echo de votre Confiseur: *six-monthly*
• Market Guide (Guide du Marché): *contact details of the main biscuits, confectionery, and snack manufacturers and importers - annuel*
• Périodique Chobisco: *monthly*

Coffee Roasters' Union (UTC-VVK)

Union des Torréfacteurs de Café/Verbond van Koffiebranders
Address: Avenue de Roodebeek 30, B-1030 Brussels
Telephone: +32 2 743 8730
Fax: +32 2 736 8175
Year established: 1943
Activities: collects comprehensive statistics on coffee; provides legal advice for members
Chief officers: Ivan Rombouts (Director); Charles Van der Kelen (Secretary General)
Membership: 35 (individuals and corporate)

Confederation of Belgian Breweries (CBB)

Confédération des Brasseries de Belgique/Confederatie der Brouwerijen van Belgie
Address: Maison des Brasseurs, Grand'Place 10, B-1000 Brussels
Telephone: +32 2 511 4987
Fax: +32 2 511 3259
E-mail: cbb@beerparadise.be
Web site: www.beerparadise.be
Year established: 1971
Activities: produces statistics and analyses of the Belgian beer market; publishes statistics in Le Journal du Brasseur
Chief officers: Paul de Keersmaeker (President), Michel Brichet (Chief Executive Officer)
Structure: non-profit-making organisation associated with VBO
Membership: 115 breweries
Publications:
• Le Journal du Brasseur: *information on the Belgian beer sector. Each issue of Le Journal du Brasseur deals with a particular theme, such as beer and gastronomy, exports of Belgian beer, the Arnoldus Group, or the annual results of the Belgian brewery sector - quarterly*

European Newspaper Publishers' Association (ENPA)

Address: Bte 8, Rue Des Pierres 29, 1000 Brussels
Telephone: +32 2 551 0190
Fax: +32 2 551 0199
E-mail: enpa@nemo.geis.com
Web site: www.enpa.be
Web site notes: site includes back issues of "The Monthly Review"
Chief officers: Michel Vander Straeten (Director)
Membership: ENPA represents 1,800 daily and weekly in European newspapers

FABRIMETAL

Address: Rue des Drapiers 21, B-1050 Brussels
Telephone: +32 2 510 2521
Fax: +32 2 510 2561
E-mail: herman.looghe@fabrimetal.be
Activities: information service for members
Chief officers: Ch. Franzen (General Secretary), P Demin (General Director - Flanders), P Vandercryse (General Director - Wallonie)
Structure: non-profit-making association
Membership: 1,200 companies
Publications:
• Annual Statistics (FABRIMETAL) (Annuaire Statistique): *international statistics on the motor vehicle sector with specific data on most European countries. Statistics usually cover the latest two years - annual*
Notes: FABRIMETAL is a member of The Federation of Belgian Companies (VBO - FEB) and of the EECA (European Electronic Component Manufacturers Association) based in Brussels.

Federation of Belgian Chemical Industries (FECHIMIE)
Fédération des Industries Chimiques de Belgique/Federatie der Chemische Nijverheid van Belgie
Address: Square Marie-Louise 49, B-1040 Brussels
Telephone: +32 2 238 9711
Fax: +32 2 231 1301
Year established: 1919
Activities: provides information, compiles research and statistics; organises conferences
Chief officers: N Martin (Chairman)
Structure: non-profit-making organisation associated with VBO (entrepreneurs umbrella organisation)
Membership: 750 manufacturers of chemical products, retailers and grocers

Federation of Belgian Clothing Manufacturers (Syncobel)
Syndicale kamer der fabrikanten van confectie van Belgie
Address: Avenue Louise 500, B-1050 Brussels
Telephone: +32 2 396 2500
Fax: +32 2 396 2299
Year established: 1947
Activities: collects statistics on ready-to-wear clothing
Chief officers: Ms T. Battaille (President)
Structure: independent non-profit-making organisation
Membership: textile and clothing manufacturers
Publications:
• Newsletter of the Employers' Federation of Belgian Clothing Manufacturers: *occasional*
• Syncobel: *monthly*

Federation of Belgian Enterprises (FEB)
Fédération des Entreprises de Belgique
Address: Rue Ravensteinstraat 4, B-1000 Brussels
Telephone: +32 2 515 0811
Fax: +32 2 515 0999
E-mail: red@vbo-feb.be
Web site: www.vbo-feb.be
Activities: promotes the interests of business in particular vis-…-vis government, public services and trade unions; represents the professional federations and their member firms in many institutions and bodies; negotiates inter-professional agreements which apply to all private sector workers and companies; represents and promotes companies' interests in international organisations; organises seminars
Chief officers: Karel Boone (President), Tony Vandeputte (Managing Director), Wilfried Beirnaert (Director-General Manager), Guy Keutgen (Director-Secretary-General), Didier Malherbe (Director of the Communication Department)
Membership: 35 professional federations plus 29 different associations with affiliated or associate member status, representing a total of more than 30.000 companies; members represent all sectors of manufacturing and service industries: banking and credit, breweries, building, cement, chemicals, cleaning, clothing and outfitting, concrete, distribution, energy, fibre cement, the graphic industry, food, glass, insurance, iron and steel, leather, the lime, metal working, oil, paper, ports, quarries, shipowners, sugar, terra cotta, temporary employment agencies, textiles, tobacco and wood
Publications:
• Annual Report of FEB: *annual*
• Bulletin FEB: *information, advice on economic, financial, legal and general business matters - monthly*
Notes: member of the Union of Industrial and Employers' Confederations of Europe (Unice), the International Employers' Organisation (IEO), the OECD Business and Industry Advisory Committee (Biac), and the International Chamber of Commerce (ICC)

Federation of Food Industries (FIA)
Fédération de l'Industrie Alimentaire
Address: avenue de Cortenbergh 172, B-1040 Brussels
Telephone: +32 2 743 0800
Fax: +32 2 733 9426
Chief officers: Paul Verhaeghe (Assistant Administrator)

Federation of Malt Suppliers
Fédération Belge des Malteurs
Address: Rue André Fauchille 10, B-1150 Brussels
Telephone: +32 2 762 7550
Fax: +32 2 762 7230
Year established: 1962
Activities: collects statistics on production, imports and exports in both Belgium and the rest of Europe
Chief officers: Jean-Louis Dourcy (President), Jean-Pierre de Kerchove (Secretary General)
Membership: 7 belgian malt suppliers
Publications:
• Annual Report (Rapport Annuel de la FBM): *annual*

Federation of the Belgian Footwear Industry (FEBIC)
Fédération Belge de l'Industrie de la Chaussure/Federatie van de Belgische Schoeiselindustrie
Address: 53 rue François Bossaerts, B-1030 Brussels
Telephone: +32 2 735 2701/2 735 2215
Fax: +32 2 736 1276
E-mail: febic@tornado.be
Year established: 1968
Chief officers: Mr Smets (Chairman)
Structure: independent non-profit-making organisation
Membership: 47 footwear manufacturers

Federation of the Belgian Textile Industry (FEBELTEX)
Fédération de l'Industrie Textile Belge/Belgische Federatie van de textiel industrie
Address: Rue Montoyer 24, B-1000 Brussels
Telephone: +32 2 287 0811
Fax: +32 2 230 6585
Web site: www.vbo-feb.be:80/textile/texen.html
Year established: 1945
Activities: provides statistics for members only; advice and information about the textile industry; organises meetings, provides consultation and information
Chief officers: Jean-François Quix (General Director)
Membership: 600 textile companies and their associations
Publications:
• Info: *economic, legal and tax matters related to the Belgian textile industry - weekly*
• Les répertoires: *contact details of Belgian manufacturers as well as a detailed list of their products (textiles, clothing textiles, interior textiles, technical textiles, wool textiles, filaments and yarns)*
• Rapport Annuel: *examines trends in the textile industry over the past year; a seperate issue gives a statistical overview of the industry - annual*
Notes: Member of the Federation of Belgian Companies (FEB).

Federation of the Paper and Board Converting Industries (FETRA)
Fédération des Industries Transformatrices de Papier et Carton
Address: Box 25, Chaussée de Waterloo 715, B-1180 Brussels
Telephone: +32 2 344 1962
Fax: +32 2 344 8661
Web site: www.vbo-feb.be:80/fetra/en/
Activities: disseminates information and individual consultancy in the social, economic and environmental field; produces statistics on the sector; organises regular meetings of the different subsector-associations
Chief officers: Isidoor Thijs (President), Philippe della Faille

de Leverghem (Director), Michel Léonard (Vice President), Freddy Semoulin (Vice President)
Membership: 99 manufacturers
Publications:
• Annual Report of FETRA: *annual*

Flemish Publishers' Association (VBVB)
Vereniging ter Bevordering van het Vlaamse Boekwezen
Address: Hof ter Schrieklaan 17, B-2600 Berchem- Antwerpen
Telephone: +32 3 230 8923
Fax: +32 3 281 2240
Activities: collects statistics
Chief officers: Mr Wim de Mont (Secretary General),
Membership: 170 publishers, 285 booksellers, 50 distributors

Food Industries' Federation (FIA-LVN)
Fédération des Industries Agricoles et Alimentaires/Verbond der Landbouw- en Voedingsnijverheden
Address: Avenue de Roodebeek 30, B-1030 Brussels
Telephone: +32 2 743 8730
Fax: +32 2 736 8175
Year established: 1946
Chief officers: Ms Jans; Mr Verhuyen
Membership: general food and agricultural producers
Publications:
• Statistics (Food Industries Federation) (Statistiques): *figures on the production and turnover of the Belgian food industry with data on specific food sectors. Based largely on statistics collected and analysed by the federation - annual*

General Association of Grain Milling Companies
Association Générale des Meuliers Belges/Algemene Vereniging der Belgische Maalders
Address: PO Box 3, 172 Avenue de Cortenbergh, B-1040 Brussels
Telephone: +32 2 735 8170
Fax: +32 2 732 0296
Year established: 1890
Activities: statistical service available to members only
Chief officers: Karel van den Bossche (President); J M Copinne (Secretary General)
Structure: non-profit-making organisation in association with VBO (Entrepreneurs Confederation) and LVI (Agricultural and Food-Industry Association)
Membership: 40 grain milling companies
Notes: Affiliated to the International Milling Association and the Groupement des Meuneries de la UE.

Horeca Brussels/Horeca Flanders (HBHV)
Horeca Brussel-Horeca Vlaanderen
Address: Boîte 4, 111 Boulevard Anspach, B-1000 Brussels
Telephone: +32 2 513 7814
Fax: +32 2 513 8954
Year established: 1837
Activities: provides information to hotel and catering associations
Chief officers: L de Bauw (General Secretary)
Membership: 20,000 companies in the Flemish and Brussels catering business
Publications:
• L'Horeca Officiel/De Officiele Horeca

Ice Cream Industry Group
Groupement de l'Industrie des Crèmes Glacées/Groepering van de Roomijsindustrie
Address: Avenue de Roodebeek 30, B-1030 Brussels
Telephone: +32 2 743 8730
Fax: +32 2 736 8175

ICODIF, EAN Belgium Luxembourg
Address: Rue Royale 29, B-1000 Brussels
Telephone: +32 2 229 1880
Fax: +32 2 217 4347
E-mail: eanbelgilux@ibm.net
Activities: standardisation
Chief officers: Henri Gutman (President), Jacques Mahieu (Vice President), Etienne Boonet (Director General)
Membership: 3000 companies
Publications:
• ICODIF Bulletin: *quarterly*

Medicines Industry Association (AGIM)
Association Générale de l'Industrie du Médicament
Address: Square Marie-Louise 49, B-1000 Brussels
Telephone: +32 2 238 9711/2 238 9972
Fax: +32 2 231 1164
Chief officers: Ms Baekeland (Communication)

National Association of Clothing and Leather Retailers (NAVETEX-ANDT)
Association Nationale des Détaillants en Textile et Habillement/Nationaal Verbond Textiel en Kleding Detaillisten
Address: Rue de Spa 8, B-1000 Brussels
Telephone: +32 2 238 0651
Fax: +32 2 230 6444
E-mail: imfo@ncmv.be
Web site: www.ncmv.be
Year established: 1949
Activities: organises seminars; collects statistics on production and sales
Chief officers: Ward Bohé (Secretary General)
Structure: non-profit-making organisation affiliated to the NCMV
Membership: 3 000 clothing and leather retailers
Publications:
• MODIS: *fashion and distribution - bi-monthly*
• Vademecum Professionnel: *trade figures and statistics - annual*

National Committee for Jewellers, Goldsmiths, Makers of Clocks, Medals, Insignia and Precious Metals, and Related Professions
Comité National de la Bijouterie, Horlogerie, Joaillerie, Orfèvrerie, Medailles et Insignes, Métaux Précieux et des Professions Connexes
Address: 290A Boulevard de Smet de Naeyer, B-1090 Brussels
Telephone: +32 2 428 2245
Fax: +32 2 428 3078
Year established: 1941
Activities: statistical services for members only, import and export data
Structure: independent non-profit organisation
Membership: 31 jewellers, clock/watch-makers and gold/silversmiths, including importers, wholesalers, repairers and retailers
Publications:
• Technica: *the jewellery and watch sector - 11 p.a.*

National Committee of the International Dairy Federation
Comité Belge de la FIL
Address: Boulevard Simon Bolivar 30, 4e étage, 1000 Bruxelles
Telephone: +32 2 208 35 52
Fax: +32 2 208 35 65
Chief officers: Mr M. Van Belleghem (Secretary)

National Federation of Beer and Soft Drink Wholesalers

Fédération Nationale des Négociants en Bières et Eaux de Boisson

Address: Boîte 1, 83 Boulevard Edmond Machtens, B-1080 Brussels
Telephone: +32 2 410 3347
Fax: +32 2 410 3545
Activities: government liaison, information service to members, annual conference
Chief officers: Dirk Van Waesberge (Director)
Membership: 570 of the largest beer and soft drinks wholesalers in Belgium (representing one third of all companies in the sector)
Publications:
• Monthly Bulletin (Bulletin d'Information Mensuel/Nieuwsbrief): *activities of the Association, industry trends, legislation and new product information - monthly*
Notes: The Association does not compile statistics.

National Federation of Belgian Butchers and Meat Processors

Fédération Nationale des Bouchers, Charcutiers et Traiteurs de Belgique/Algemene Landsbond der Beenhouwers en Spekslagers en Traiteurs van België
Address: Avenue de Cortenbergh 116, B-1000 Brussels
Telephone: +32 2 735 2470
Fax: +32 2 736 6493
Year established: 1894
Activities: collects non-published statistics
Chief officers: Wim van der Aa (General Director), R Van Lerberge, J Walraevens (Chairman)
Structure: independent occupational organisation; organised into 9 provincial unions and 86 local unions
Membership: 4,995 butchers and meat processors
Publications:
• La Boucherie Belge/De Belgische Beenhouwerij: *fortnightly*

National Federation of Chilled and Canned Meat (FENAVIAN)

Fédération Nationale des Fabricants de Produits et de Conserves de Viande/Nationale Federatie der Fabricanten van Vleeswaren en Vleeskonserven
Address: Avenue de Roodebeek 30, B-1030 Brussels
Telephone: +32 2 743 8730
Fax: +32 2 736 8175

National Union of Footwear Retailers

Union Nationale des Détaillants en Chaussure/Nationale Beroepsvereniging van Detaillisten in Schoeisels
Address: 8 rue de Spa, B-1040 Brussels
Telephone: +32 2 238 0651
Fax: +32 2 230 9354
Year established: 1962
Activities: conferences, research, library, information
Chief officers: Mr Bohe (Secretary General)
Structure: non-profit-making organisation affiliated to the NCMV
Membership: footwear retailers

Pastry, Preserves and Jams Manufacturing and Import Group

Groupement des Fabricants et Importateurs de Confitures, Sirops à Tartiner, Compotes et Conserves de Fruits/Groepering der Fabrikanten & Invoerders van Konfituren, Vruchtensiroop, Compotes & Fruitkonserven
Address: Avenue de Roodebeek 30, B-1030 Brussels
Telephone: +32 2 743 8730
Fax: +32 2 736 8175
Year established: 1945
Chief officers: Mevr. Keppen (Secretary)
Structure: member of Belgian agriculture and food-industry federation (LVI)
Membership: manufacturers and importers of jams and preserves

Perfume, Essences and Aromatic Products Manufacturing Group (AROMA)

Groupement des Fabricants d'Essences, Huiles essentielles, Extraits, Produits chimiques aromatiques et Colorants
Address: 49 Square Marie-Louise, B-1040 Brussels
Telephone: +32 2 230 4568
Fax: +32 2 230 4090
Telex: 23167 FECHIM B
Membership: perfume manufacturers, manufacturers and importers of essences and aromatic products

Personal Computer Memory Card International Association (PCMCIA)

Address: Avenue Marcel Thiry 204, B-1200 Brussels
Telephone: +32 2 774 9620
Fax: +32 2 774 9690
E-mail: pcmcia@eyam.be
Web site: www.pc-card.com
Year established: 1989
Chief officers: Sabine Henssler (European Representative), Bill Lempesis (Chief Executive Officer)
Membership: 500 members worldwide
Publications:
• PC Card Ressource Directory: *comprehensive ressource for locating PC Card related products and services*
• PC Card Standard: *contains the physical, electrical and software specifications for the PC Card technology*
Notes: The Association does not produce statistics.

Professional Confederation of Sugar and its By-Products (SUBEL)

Confédération Professionnelle du Sucre et de ses Dérivés/Beroepsconfederatie voor Suiker en Bijprodukten
Address: Boîte 4, Avenue de Tervueren 182, B-1150 Brussels
Telephone: +32 2 775 8065
Fax: +32 2 775 8075
Year established: 1977
Activities: collects statistics on production
Chief officers: Marc Rosiers (Director General)
Membership: 3 manufacturers of sugar and sugar products
Publications:
• La Sucrerie Belge: *sugar industry - annual*
Notes: Member of the VBO (cross-sector employer-owner associaton).

Royal Federation of Water and Soft Drinks Industry

Fédération Royale de l'Industrie des Eaux et des Boissons Rafraîchissantes
Address: Boîte 5, 51 Avenue du Général de Gaulle, B-1050 Brussels
Telephone: +32 2 649 1286
Fax: +32 2 646 1339
Year established: 1902
Chief officers: Karine Lambert (Secretary General)
Structure: non-profit-making organisation associated with LIV and VBO, member of European UNESDA
Membership: manufacturers and importers of water and soft-drinks

Union of Manufacturers and Importers of Bakery and Ice Cream Ingredients (UNIFA)

Union des Fabricants et Importateurs de Matières Premières pour la Boulangerie, Pâtisserie et Glacerie
Address: Bus 8, Nieuwdreef 101, B-2170 Merksem
Telephone: +32 3 645 6004
Fax: +32 3 645 5518

Chief officers: MR Van Stridonck (President), F de Keukeleer (Secretary General)
Membership: bakery and ice cream ingredients manufacturers and importers

BELIZE

Belize Hotel Association
Address:
Telephone: +501 2 318 57
Fax: +501 2 788 08
E-mail: fortst@btl.net
Chief officers: Teresa Parkey (President), Susan Fuller (Secretary), Einer Gomez (Director)

Belize Tourism Industry Association (BTIA)
Address: P.O. Box 62, 10 North Park Street, Belize City
Telephone: +501 2 757 17/711 44
Fax: +501 2 787 10
E-mail: fortst@btl.net or bzadventur@btl.net
Web site: www.belize.com/btia/btia.html
Chief officers: Teresa Parkey (President), Susan Fuller (Secretary), Einer Gomez (Director)

BENIN

Association of Manufacturers of Benin (ASNIB)
Association Nationale des Industriels du Bénin
Address: BP 412, Cotonou
Telephone: +229 331 121
Fax: +229 331 126
Chief officers: Raffet O. Loko (President)
Membership: 529 manufacturers and importers

Banks' Association (APBEF)
Association Professionnelle des Banques et Etablissements Financiers au Bénin
Address: BP 08 0879
Telephone: +229 313 228
Chief officers: Paul Derreumaux (President), Rizwan Haider (Vice President)
Membership: 7 banks

Coffee Board of Benin (SONAPRA)
Address: PO Box 933, Cotonou
Telephone: +229 330 820
Fax: +229 331 948

BERMUDA

Bermuda Bar Association
Address: P.O. Box HM 125, Hamilton HMAX, Reid House, 31 Church Street, Hamilton HM 12
Telephone: +1 441 2 954 540
Fax: +1 441 2 954 540

Bermuda Insurance Management Association
Address: P.O. Box HM 681, Hamilton
Telephone: +1 441 2 950 265
Fax: +1 441 2 924 910
Chief officers: Alan C. Cossar (President)

Bermuda International Business Association (BIBA)
Address: 41 Victoria Street, Hamilton HM BX
Telephone: +1 441 2 920 632
Fax: +1 441 2 921 797
Year established: 1970
Activities: research into customer needs and possible new areas of service
Chief officers: Richard D Butterfield (Chairman), Cummings V Zuill, Glen Titterton & Frank Mutch (Vice Chairman), Wendy Davis-Johnson (President), Peter Watsom (Treasurer)
Membership: banks, law firms, accounting and management service companies

BOLIVIA

Article Numbering Association
Asociación de Codificación de Productos
Address: PO Box 180, Cámara de Industria y Comercio de Santa Cruz, Suarez Figueroa 127, 3° y 4° piso, Santa Cruz
Telephone: +591 3 334 555
Fax: +591 3 342 353

Bolivian Association of Insurance Companies
Asociación Boliviana de Aseguradoras
Address: 4804 LP, Edificio Castilla, piso 5, Calle Loayza, N° 250, La Paz
Telephone: +591 2 310 056/328404
Fax: +591 2 379 154

Bolivian Book Association
Cámara Boliviana del Libro
Address: Casilla 682, Edificio Las Palmas, oficina 5 - planta baja, Avda 20 de Octubre 2005, La Paz
Telephone: +591 2 327 039
Fax: +591 2 391 817
Chief officers: Mr R Condori (Director)

Bolivian Federation of Medium Size Industries
Federación Boliviana de la Pequeña Industria
Address: Casilla 8847 LP, Edificio Chuquiago, piso 2, Calle México, n° 1554, La Paz
Telephone: +591 2 391 463
Fax: +591 2 391 463

Bolivian Federation of Small Industries
Federación Boliviana de la Pequeña Industria
Address: 8847 LP, Edificio Chuquiago, piso 2, Calle México, N° 1554, La Paz
Telephone: +591 2 391 463
Fax: +591 2 391 463

Bolivian Pharmaceutical Association (CBM)
Cámara Boliviana del Medicamento
Address: Edificio Casa Bernardo, Avenida Camacho 1280, Piso 3, Oficina, 02, La Paz
Telephone: +591 2 361 570
Fax: +591 2 326 797

Milling Industries Association
Asociación de Industriales Molineros
Address: Casilla 8688 LP, Edificio Mariscal de Ayacucho, piso 13, oficina 1301, Calle Loayza, La Paz
Telephone: +591 2 358 280/322 882/377 909
Fax: +591 2 391 239

National Chamber of Exporters (CANEB)

Cámara Nacional de Exportadores de Bolivia
Address: Casilla 20744 LP, Avda. Arce esquina Goitia, n°
2017, La Paz
Telephone: +591 2 361 491/322 943
Fax: +591 2 361 491
Year established: 1970
Activities: trade fairs, statistics, contacts, legal and technical
advice, contacts, registers, training
Chief officers: ic. Adhemar Guzmán Valdivia (President), Lic
Andrés Saldías Pozo (Executive Director), Lic José K Khun
Poppe (Marketing and PR Director)
Structure: non-profit-making association
Membership: 160 companies linked to the export sector
Publications:
• Trade Magazine: *covers the Bolivian export trade - monthly*

National Chamber of Freight Forwarders

Cámara Nacional de Despachantes de Aduana
Address: 8804 LP, Edificio 16 de Julio, piso 10, Oficina 1008,
Av. 16 de Julio, N° 1566, La Paz
Telephone: +591 2 392 830/327 231
Fax: +591 2 316 325

National Confederation of Private Enterprises of Bolivia

Confederación de Empresarios Privados de Bolivia
Address: Casilla 4239 LP, Edificio Cámara Nacional de
Comercio, 7° piso, Avda Mariscal Santa Cruz 1392, La Paz
Telephone: +591 2 356 831/358 366/371 293
Fax: +591 2 379 970/1
Year established: 1962
Chief officers: Lic. Manuel Arana (Director Economics
Department)
Structure: confederation of private enterprise organisations
Membership: 33 associations and chambers of private
commerce

National Exporters' Association of Bolivia

Cámara Nacional de Exportadores de Bolivia
Address: Casilla 12145 LP, Av Arce esquina Goitia, n° 2017,
La Paz
Telephone: +591 2 361 491/322 943
Fax: +591 2 361 491

National Hotels' Association

Cámara Nacional de Hotelería
Address: Casilla 12827 LP, Edificio Hermann, piso 9, oficina
4, Av Mariscal Santa Cruz, La Paz
Telephone: +591 2 375 867/318 259
Fax: +591 2 318 259

Supermarkets and Self-Service Association

Asociación Departamental de Supermercados y Autoservicios
Address: 3-12399 San Miguel-LP, Edificio Futura, piso 1, Av.
Mariscal Montenegro, N° 778, La Paz
Telephone: +591 2 799 964
Fax: +591 2 799 941

Travel and Tourism Agencies' Association (ABAVYT)

Asociación Bolivariana de Agencias de Viajes y Turismo
Address: Casilla 8737, Calle Colon, 161- piso 3, La Paz
Telephone: +591 3 523 88
Fax: +591 3 511 113

Article Numbering Association

Address: Chamber of Economy of Bosnia and Herzegovina,
Mis Irbina 13, 71000 Sarajevo
Telephone: + 387 71 663 370
Fax: + 387 71 663 633

Union of Independent Newspaper Publishers of Bosnia and Herzegovina

Address: P Goranina Street, Sarajevo
Telephone: + 387 71 441 837
Fax: + 387 71 441 837
Chief officers: Sead Domirookolovic (President)
Notes: Satellite fax: +871 111 4101; via USA: +141 2339 4724

Exporters' Association of Botswana (EAOB)

Address: Private Bag 167, Gaborone
Telephone: +267 313 974
Fax: +267 309 482
Activities: provides specialised service to existing and
potential exporters by identifying foreign markets for locally
produced exportable merchandise and by making
representation to the government on behalf of the exporting
community of Bostwana
Membership: umbrella organisations for exporters in
Bostwana
Publications:
• Bostwana Export Directory: *country profile and a list of
Bostwana exporters with contact names, addresses and
telephone numbers - biannual*

Alcoholic Drinks Manufacturers' Association

Sindicato da Indústria da Fabricação do Alcool
Address: Rua Boa Vista 280, 5° andar, 01014-000 São Paulo,
SP
Telephone: +55 11 605 1141
Fax: +55 11 605 5913

Artificial and Synthetic Fibres Fabrics Manufacturers' Association

Associação Brasileira dos Produtores de Fibras Artificiais e
Sintéticas
Address: A. Bri. Faria Lima 1886, 14° andar, cj. 11,
01452-918 São Paulo, SP
Telephone: +55 11 814 6133
Fax: +55 11 814 6240

Brazilian Aluminium Association (ABAL)

Associação Brasileira do Aluminio
Address: Av República do Líbano 671, 04501-000 São Paulo
SP
Telephone: +55 11 885 0222
Fax: +55 11 885 5822
Telex: 31116 ABLM
Chief officers: Carlos Ermirio de Moraes (President)
Membership: aluminium manufacturers and distributors
Notes: Rua Humberto I, 220 4° andar - CEP 04118-030 - São
Paulo/SP Tel: (011) 5084-1544 - Fax: (011) 549-3159

Brazilian Article Numbering Association
Associaçã da Codificação
Address: Av Paulista 2644, 10° andar, 01310.300 São Paulo
Telephone: +55 11 259 3444
Fax: +55 11 231 2808
E-mail: ean@eanbrazil.org.br

Brazilian Association of Advertisers (ABA)
Associação Brasileira de Anunciantes
Address: Av Paulista 352, 6° andar, conj 64/45, 01310-000
São Paulo SP
Telephone: +55 11 283 4588
Fax: +55 11 283 1457
Chief officers: Avelar Vascolcelos (Vice President), Ronaldo
Marques, Celso Traco, Horacio Rocha (Directors)

Brazilian Association of Advertising Agencies (ABAP)
Associação Brasileira de Agências de Propaganda
Address: 8° andar, Rua Pedregoso Alvarenga 1208,
04531.004 São Paulo SP
Telephone: +55 11 852 6966
Fax: +55 11 647 668
E-mail: abaprio@uninet.com.br
Web site: www.abap-rio.com.br
Year established: 1964
Chief officers: Roberto Duailibi (President), Julio Ribeiro (Vice
President)
Membership: 28 advertising agencies representing 60% of
the industry in Brazil
Notes: ABAP-RIO: Praia de Botafogo, 210 sala 806,
22250-040 - Rio de Janeiro - RJ - Tel.: (021) 551-7849/Fax:
(021) 552-0496 / Secretária Executiva: Maria Lúcia Egito

Brazilian Association of Drinks Producers (ABRABE)
Associação Brasileira de Bebidas
Address: Av Nove de Julho 5017, 1° andar, 01407-903
SãoPaulo SP
Telephone: +55 11 883 6144
Fax: +55 11 646 381
Chief officers: Fadrizio Fasano (President)
Membership: drinks producers and distributors

Brazilian Association of Flexible Packaging Manufacturers (ABIEF)
Associação Brasileira das Indústrias de Embalagens Flexíveis
Address: Rua Fuchal 573, 8° andar, conj 81, 04551-060 São
Paulo SP
Telephone: +55 11 820 6011
Fax: +55 11 829 7989
Chief officers: Israel Sverner (President)
Membership: manufacturers of flexible plastic containers

Brazilian Association of Metals and Metallurgy (ABM)
Associação Brasileira de Metais e Metalurgical
Address: Rua Antonio Comparato 218, 04605-030 São Paulo
SP
Telephone: +55 11 531 5333/536 4333
Fax: +55 11 287 9893/2404273
Telex: 57116
Chief officers: Fernando Cosme Rizzo Assunçao (President)
Membership: companies from the metal and metallurgy
industries

Brazilian Association of Motor Vehicles Manufacturers (ANFAVEA)
Associação Nacional dos Fabricantes de Veículos Automotores
Address: Av Indiánopolis 496, 04062-900 São Paulo SP
Telephone: +55 11 549 4044
Fax: +55 11 549 4044, ext 225

Web site: www.anfavea.com.br
Year established: 1956
Activities: organises and promotes fairs and other events;
maintains the library the Centro de Documentação da
Indústria Automobilística (Cedoc- Alameda dos
Nhambiquaras, 367, Moema, São Paulo - SP - Brasil -
04090-010 fax: 55 011 549-4044), which holds national and
international information on the automotive sector
Chief officers: Adelar Scheuer (President), R L Bogus (Vice
President)
Membership: motor vehicle manufacturers and assemblers
Publications:
• Anfavea Newsletter (Carta da Anfavea): *statistical
information including production, sales, export of the
automotive industry and agriculture machinery in Brazil -
monthly*
• Statistical Report of the Brazilian Automotive Industry
(Anuário de Estatística da Indústria Automobilística Brasileira):
*analysis and statistics of the Brazilian automotive industry,
includes international comparisons - annual*
Notes: Member of the Organisation Internationale des
Constructeurs d'Automobiles (OICA) Branch in Brasilia: SHIS,
quadra 1-15, cj 14, casa 5, Lago Sul, Brasilia DF 71600-340
Tel: 61 2480390/542, Fax: 61 2405078.

Brazilian Association of Shopping Centres (ABRASCE)
Associação Brasileira de Shopping Centers
Address: Rua da Quitanda, 52 - 10° Andar, 20011-030 Rio de
Janeiro - RJ
Telephone: +55 21 221 7371
Fax: +55 21 224 7158
E-mail: abrasce@abrasce.com.br
Web site: www.abrasce.com.br
Year established: 1976
Activities: in close contact with foreign organisations;
participates in different international fairs and conferences;
organises the 'Congressos Internacionais de Shopping
Centers', seminars, quarterly meetings with its members;
produces publications on topics related to the industry and
translates foreign publications; collates and publishes
statistical data covering retail, production, etc.; its library,
open to members and non-members, holds national and
international publications on the shopping industry sector
Chief officers: Henrique Falzoni (President), José Zobaran
(Executive Director)
Membership: shopping centres
Publications:
• Shopping Centers Magazine (Revista Shopping Centers):
*management, marketing and technical matters and a section
covering statistical data - bimonthly*
Notes: Rua Dr. Sampaio Viana, 277- 6° Andar, 04.004-000
São Paulo/Tel. (011) 884 - 928/Fax: (011) 889 -
9358/E-Mail:abrasp@abrasce.com.br

Brazilian Association of Software Companies (ABES)
Associação Brasileira das Empresas de Software
Address: Av Brig Faria Lima 1766, 3° andar, cj 33/34,
01451.001 São Paulo SP
Telephone: +55 11 813 2057/9511/9704
Fax: +55 11 815 0359
Chief officers: Carlos Alberto Lima Sacco (President)
Membership: software manufacturers and suppliers
Notes: Rua Barão de Itapetininga, 255 - Conj. 709 CEP
01042-000 - São Paulo/SP - Tel: (011) 259-0765.

Brazilian Association of the Automated Glass Industry (ABIVIDRO)
Associação Brasileira das Indústrias Automáticas de Vidro
Address: Rua Geral Jardim 482, 16° andar, Vila Buarque,
01223-010 São Paulo SP
Telephone: +55 11 255 3336/256 5140/255 3033

Fax: +55 11 255 4457
Telex: 32918 ATVB
Chief officers: Roberto Luiz da Silva Prado (President) Ana
Lia Fernandes de Castro (Executive Secretary)
Membership: automated glass manufacturers

Brazilian Association of the Construction Industry (CBIC)
Cámara Brasileira da Indústria de Construção
Address: Edifiço Ariston, 31° andar, Sector Comercial Sul,
Quadra 02, 70300-500 Brasília DF
Telephone: +55 61 321 4949
Fax: +55 61 321 9771
Web site: www.horizontes.com.br/infoserv/cbic/3.html
Year established: 1957
Activities: liaises with national and international organisations
on behalf of the industry
Chief officers: Marcos Villela de Sant'anna (President),
Gilberto Morand Paixao (Secretary)
Membership: 155 trade associations, 37 regional trade
associations and 20 construction companies
Notes: Member of Federação Internacional da Indústria da
Construção (FHC), Rio de Janeiro branch: Av Alm Barroso,
63, sala 1817, 20031-003 Rio de Janeiro, RJ Tel: 21 2406790,
Fax: 21 2629521

Brazilian Association of the Electric and Electronics Industry (ABINEE)
Associação Brasileira da Indústria Elétrica e Eletrônica
Address: Av Paulista 1439, 6° andar, 01311-200 São Paulo SP
Telephone: +55 11 251 1577/289 2692
Fax: +55 11 285 0607
E-mail: bandeira@abinee.org.br
Web site: www.abinee.org.br
Year established: 1963
Activities: represents the following sectors: industrial
automation, electric and electronic components, industrial
equipment, domestic electrical appliances, electric power
generation, transmission and distribution, information
technology, telecommunications, audio visual
telecommunications
Chief officers: Nelson Peixoto Freire (President), Ruy de
Salles Cunha (General Secretary)
Membership: 700 electrical and electronics manufacturers
Publications:
● ABINEE Directory (Guía ABINEE): *information on members'
products - bi-annual*
● General Evaluation of the Electrical and Electronic Industry
(Avaliação Conjuntural da Indústria Eletroeletrônica): *monthly*

Brazilian Association of the Footwear Industry (ABICALÇADOS)
Associação Brasileira das Industrias de Calçados
Address: Rua Alvisto de Azevedo, 60, sala 6, Novo
Hamburgo-Porto Alegre, 93520-300
Telephone: +55 51 593 4844
Fax: +55 51 593 4446
Chief officers: Rogerio Dreyer, (Executive Director)
Membership: footwear manufacturers

Brazilian Association of the Medical and Dental Equipment Industry (ABIMO)
Associação Brasileira da Industria De Artigos Equipamentos
Médicos, Odontologicos Hospitalares E De Laboratórios
Address: Sala 806, Avenida Paulista 1313, 8°Andar, cj. 806,
São Paulo SP
Telephone: +55 11 285 0155
Fax: +55 11 285 0018

Brazilian Association of the Pharmaceutical Industry (ABIFARMA)
Associação Brasileira das Indústrias Farmacêuticas
Address: Rua Beira Rio 57, 7° andar, Vila Olimpia, 04548-050
São Paulo SP
Telephone: +55 11 820 3775
Fax: +55 11 822 6628
Web site: www.quattro.com.br/abifarma/
Year established: 1948
Chief officers: José Eduardo Bandeira de Mello (President),
Serafim Branco Neto (Executive Secretary)
Membership: pharmaceutical companies
Publications:
● Directory of the Brazilian Pharmaceutical Industry (Diretório
Brasileiro da Indústria Farmacêutica): *lists pharmaceutical
companies which produce on an industrial scale*

Brazilian Association of the Textile Industry (ABIT)
Associação Brasileira da Indústria Têxtil
Address: Rua Marques de Itú, 968, 01223-000 São Paulo SP
Telephone: +55 11 660 101
Fax: +55 11 678 209
Chief officers: Luiz Américo Medeiros (President)
Membership: textile manufacturers

Brazilian Book Chamber (CBL)
Câmara Brasileira do Livro
Address: Av Ipiranga, 1267 - 10° Andar, 01039-907 São Paulo
Telephone: +55 11 225 8277
Fax: +55 11 229 7463
Web site: www.cbl-net.com.br/
Year established: 1946
Activities: organises an international biennial book fair in São
Paulo, provides training courses
Chief officers: Mr A Weiszflog (President), MS C Rodriguez
(Director)
Membership: publishers, book sellers, distributors and
importers; also individual members, such as writers, literary
agents etc.
Publications:
● Boletim informativo: *general statistics covering books
production, books retail, etc. and statistical information on the
readers' profile - annual*

Brazilian Ceramics' Association
Associação Brasileira de Cerâmica
Address: Rua Leonardo Nunes Clementino 82, 04039-010
São Paulo SP
Telephone: +55 11 549 3922
Fax: +55 11 573 7528
Chief officers: Geraldo Agosti (President)
Membership: ceramics and tile manufacturers

Brazilian Chemical and Chemical Derivative Products' Association (ABIQUIM)
Associação Brasileira da Indústria Química e de Produtos
Derivados
Address: PO Box 640, Rua Santo Antônio, 184- 17°/18°
andares, 01314-900 São Paulo SP
Telephone: +55 11 232 1144/373 481
Fax: +55 11 232 0919/377 791
E-mail: abiquim@abiquim.org.br
Web site: www.abiquim.org.br
Year established: 1966
Chief officers: Carlos Mariani Bittencourt (President),
Eduardo Eugênio Gouvêa Vieira (1st Vice President), Otto
Vicente Perrone (2nd Vice President)
Membership: 111 chemical companies
Publications:
● Brazilian Chemical Industry Directory (Guia da Indústira

Química Brasileira): *directory of chemical companies listing products and key personnel - annual*
• Brazilian Chemical Industry Yearbook (Anuário da Indústria Química Brasileira): *detailed statistical profile of the Brazilian chemical sector. Includes data on production, national sales, exports as well as financial information on companies in the sector. Also includes consumer products prices; status and development of different projects and information on Mercosul - annual*
• Relatório de Acompanhamento de Preços - RAP: *main product prices of the chemical sector and relevant information on petroleum, natural gas, fuels and other petrochemical products, as well as overseas market information - monthly*
• Relatório de Acompanhamento Conjuntural - RAC: *a report analysing prices, domestic sales, production as well as product information - monthly*

Brazilian Chocolate, Cocoa and Confectionery Manufacturers' Association (ABICAB)
Associacão Brasileira da Indústria de Chocolate, Cacau, Balas e Derivados
Address: Av Pauliste 1313, 8° Ander, São Paulo
Telephone: +55 11 287 5633
Fax: +55 11 287 5287
Chief officers: Gestulio Ursulino Netto (President)

Brazilian Corrugated Cardboard Association (ABPO)
Associação Brasileira do Papelão Ondulado
Address: Rua Brigadeiro Gavião Peixoto 646, 05078-000 Lapa São Paulo, SP
Telephone: +55 11 831 9844/2616201
Fax: +55 11 261 6801
Telex: 82004
Chief officers: Milton Ferrari (President)
Membership: paper manufacturers

Brazilian Dairy Products' Association
Associação Brasileira dos Produtores de Leite
Address: Rua Bento Freitas, 178, 9 Andar, Cep 01220-905
Telephone: +55 11 221 3599
Fax: +55 11 222 6495
Chief officers: Edson Rosolen

Brazilian Direct Selling Association (DOMUS)
Associação Brasileira de Empresas de Vendas Diretas
Address: rua Tabapuã, 649 - Conj. 33, CEP 05433-012 - São Paulo
Telephone: +55 11 822 5316
Fax: +55 11 822 5316
Web site: www.domusvendadiret.com.br
Web site notes: site includes statistics on Brazilian and world direct sales markets
Membership: 10 companies representing 70% of the national direct sales market from various sectors, including: cosmetics; cleaning products; frozen food; magazines and newspapers; plastic containers for food; nutritional supplements etc.
Notes: Associated to the World Federation of Direct Selling Associations.

Brazilian Federation of Coffee Exporters (FEBEC)
Federação Brasileira dos Exportadores de Café
Address: Rua da Quitanda, 191 - 11o andar, 20091-000 Rio de Janeiro RJ
Telephone: +55 21 263 6730
Fax: +55 21 263 6331
Web site: www.magicweb.com.br/febec/
Web site notes: site includes statistics on coffee exports for the latest month
Year established: 1988
Activities: Febec maintains a database of statistics on

Brazilian coffee exports which is updated daily
Chief officers: Oswaldo Aranha Neto (President), Usr Walter Wegmann (Vice President)
Membership: 110 exporting firms, accounting for 61% of foreign trade in green coffee

Brazilian Food Industry Association (ABIA)
Associação Brasileira da Industria da Alimentaçao
Address: Av Brigadeiro Faria Lima 2003,, 11° Andar, Conj. 1104, Baja 1116, Pinheiros, 01451-001 São Paulo SP
Telephone: +55 11 814 8733/816 5733
Fax: +55 11 814 6688
Telex: 80982
Year established: 1963
Chief officers: Dr Edmundo Klotz (President), Armando Soares dos Reis (Vice President and Coordinator of the Commission for International Trade)
Membership: food manufacturers, food and drink suppliers
Publications:
• ABIA Informa
• Apoio
• Circulars
• Specialised Publications

Brazilian Franchising Association (ABF)
Associação Brasileira de Franchising
Address: Av. Prof. Ascendino Reis, 1548, 04027-000 São Paulo SP
Telephone: +55 11 573 9496
Fax: +55 11 575 5590
E-mail: connect@amcham.com.br
Web site: www.abf.com.br
Activities: public relations, publishes industry information, information on the Association's activities and other information of public interest; conducts monthly meetings with its members
Chief officers: Fabio Paiva Guimarães (Director President), Romoaldo Destro (Executive Director),
Membership: 700 franchise consulting and business associations
Publications:
• Agenda ABF Rio: *bimonthly*
• Franchising Census (Censo do Franchising): *statistics on the franchising sector in Brazil - annual*
• Franchising Directory (Guia do Franchising Anual): *a relation of all the franchising companies in Brazil - annual*
Notes: Associação Brasileira de Franchising: Rua da Candelária, 9 - 413, Rio de Janeiro Fax/Tel: 263-2525 / E-mail: abfrj@ism.com.br

Brazilian Meat Manufacturers' Association
Associação Profissional da Indústria de Carnes
Address: Alameda Barão de Limeira 539, 2° andar, 01202-902 São Paulo, SP
Telephone: +55 11 220 1205
Fax: +55 11 220 5160

Brazilian Mineral Water Association (ABINAM)
Associação Brasileira das Indústrias de Água Mineral
Address: Av. Brig. Faria Lima, 2003 - Conj. 203, 01451-001 São Paulo/SP
Telephone: +55 11 816 0484
Fax: +55 11 814 3296

Brazilian Packaging Association (ABRE)
Associação Brasileira de Embalagem
Address: Rua Oscar Freire 379, 16° andar, cj 161, 01426-001 São Paulo SP
Telephone: +55 11 282 9722

Fax: +55 11 282 9091
E-mail: abre@sanet.com.br
Activities: courses, seminars, congresses, statistics, library, information services, sponsors the Brazilian Packaging Congress (every 3 years), co-sponsors the Packaging, Paper and Graphics Exhibition (every 2 years)
Chief officers: Alberto Barbagallo (President)
Membership: 130 packaging companies and companies related to the packaging industry
Publications:
• Membership List

Brazilian Personal Care, Perfume and Cosmetics Industries' Association (ABIHPEC)
Associação Brasileira da Indústria de Higiene Pessoal, Perfumaria e Cosméticos
Address: Av. Paulista, 1313 - Conj. 901, 01311-923 São Paulo/SP
Telephone: +55 11 251 1999
Fax: +55 11 287 9207

Brazilian Pharmaceutical Industry Association (INTERFARMA)
Associação da Industria Farmaceutica do Brasil
Address: Av Almirante Barroso no 63, GR 2417, 20031-003 Rio de Faneiro RJ
Telephone: +55 21 240 7575
Fax: +55 21 262 7112

Brazilian Public Relations Association (ABRP)
Associação Brasileira de Relaçoes Publicas
Address: Rua Rafael de Barros 505, 04003.043 São Paulo SP
Telephone: +55 11 885 8619
Fax: +55 11 885 4568
E-mail: abrp@rio.com.br
Web site: www.rio.com.br/abrp/
Year established: 1954
Activities: education and training
Chief officers: Ires Fernandes Tito (President), Carlos Vechiatti (planning Vice President), Adelaide Giordano (PR Director)
Membership: public relations agencies

Brazilian Statistical Association
Associacao Brasileira de Estatistica
Address: C.P. 66281, O5389-970-Sao Paulo,SP, Brasil
Telephone: +55 11 818 6261/212 5067
Fax: +55 11 814 4135/212 5067
E-mail: abe@ime.usp.br
Web site: www.ime.usp.br/~pam/abe.html
Year established: 1984
Chief officers: President: H. Bolfarine, Secretary: D. A. Botter; Executive Editor: REBRAPE: Lucia P. Barroso(lbarroso@ime.usp.br), Editor, Newsletter: Monica C. Sandoval(sandoval@ime.usp.br)
Membership: 1,000 individual members and institutions

Brazilian Supermarkets' Association (ABRAS)
Associação Brasileira de Supermercados
Address: Rua Cristiano Viana 80, Casa 4/5, 05411-090 São Paulo SP
Telephone: +55 11 883 2244
Fax: +55 11 852 312
Telex: 25341 ABDS
E-mail: abrasrs@abrasnet.com.br
Web site: www.abrasnet.com.br/
Chief officers: Levi Mogueira (President)
Publications:
• SuperHiper: *monthly*

Notes: Av. Diógenes Ribeiro Lima, 2.872 - CEP 05083-010 São Paulo/SP - Tel: (011) 837-9922 Fax: (011) 837-9933.

Brazilian Wood Packaging Manufacturers' Association (ABRAPEM)
Associação Brasileira dos Produtores de Embalagens de Madeira
Address: Rua Coronel Xavier de Toledo, 220 11° Andar, 01048-000 São Paulo/SP
Telephone: +55 11 255 8566
Fax: +55 11 255 8566

Confederation of Commercial Associations of Brazil
Confederação das Associações Comerciais do Brasil
Address: Rua da Calendaria9, 12 andar, 20091-020 Rio de Janeiro
Telephone: +55 21 291 1229
Fax: +55 21 263 7613
E-mail: acrj@openlink.br
Web site: www.openlink.com.br
Chief officers: Humberto Mota (President)

Confederation of National Commerce (CNC)
Confederação Nacional de Comercio
Address: Av Gal Justo 307, 20021-130 Rio de Janeiro
Telephone: +55 21 240 7070/297 0011
Fax: +55 21 240 6920
Chief officers: Antonio Oliveira Santos (President)

Dairy Products Manufacturers' Association
Sindicato da Indústria de Lacticínios e Produtos Derivados
Address: Pça. Dom José Gaspar 30, 10° andar, 01047-901 São Paulo, SP
Telephone: +55 11 259 3251
Fax: +55 11 259 8482

Edible Oils and Fats Industry Association (SINDOLEO)
Sindicato da Indústria de Azeite e Óleos Alimentícios
Address: Alameda Barão de Limeira 539, 2° andar, 01202-902 São Paulo, SP
Telephone: +55 11 220 9822
Fax: +55 11 220 5802

Frozen Food Industry Association
Sindicato da Indústria Alimentar de Congelados, Supercongelados, Sorvetes, Concentrados
Address: Av. Paulista 1313, 8° andar, cj. 803, 01311-923 São Paulo, SP
Telephone: +55 11 251 3455
Fax: +55 11 251 3524

Furniture Industry Association
Associação Indústria do Mobiliário
Address: George Eastman 140, 03830-000 São Paulo, SP
Telephone: +55 11 844 6222
Fax: +55 11 844 6222

Jewellery and Watch Industry Association
Sindicato da Indústria da Jaolheria e Ourivesaria de São Paulo
Address: R. Teixeira da Silva 654, 04002-033 São Paulo, SP
Telephone: +55 11 887 2280
Fax: +55 11 887 2332

Machinery Manufacturers' Association (ABIMACQ)
Associação das Indústrias de Máquinas e Equipamentos
Address: Av Jabaquara, 2925, 04045-902 São Paulo SP
Telephone: +55 11 579 5044/558 26311

Fax: +55 11 579 3498/558 26312
Telex: 21217 SMSP-BR
Chief officers: Sergio Paulo Pereira de Magalhaes (President)
Membership: machinery manufacturers
Publications:
• Máquinas e Equipamentos Brasileiros para Madeira

Magazine Editors' Association

Associação Nacional de Editores de Revistas
Address: SCS-Quadra 06, Ed Bandeirantes, Salas 201/204, 70300-910 Brasilia DF
Telephone: +55 61 223 5846
Fax: +55 61 321 8348

National Association of Book Publishers

Sindicato Nacional dos Editores de Livros
Address: Av Rio Branco 37, 15º andar - salas 1503-6 e 1510, 120090-003 Rio de Janeiro
Telephone: +55 21 233 6481
Fax: +55 21 253 8502
Chief officers: Mr SA da C Machado (President), Ms L Alves (Director)

National Association of Pulp and Paper Manufacturers

Associação Nacional dos Fabricantes de Papel e Cellulose
Address: Rua Alfonso Freitas 499, 04006-900 Paraiso, São Paulo SP
Telephone: +55 11 885 1845
Fax: +55 11 885 3689
E-mail: anfpcsip@ruralsp.com.br
Web site: www.homeshopping.com.br/~anfcsip
Activities: statistics, library, information service, education and training
Chief officers: José Carlos Bim Rossi (Secretary), Horacio Cherkassy (President), Mario Higino Neves Mello Leonel (Executive Director), Omar Elias Zogbi (Vice President)
Membership: 100 pulp and paper manufacturers
Publications:
• Membership List

National Electronic Products Manufacturers' Association (Eletros)

Associação Nacional de Fabricantes de Produtos Eletroeletrônicos
Address: Rua Alexandre Dumas, 1901, Bl. B, 4º, 04717-004 São Paulo SP
Telephone: +55 11 521 8018/521 8918
Fax: +55 11 521 8867
E-mail: connect@amcham.com.br
Chief officers: Roberto Macedo (President), Luiz Fernando Brandão (Administrative and Financial Director)

National Newspapers' Association

Associação Nacional de Jornais
Address: SCS Edificio Oscar Niemeyer, Salas 603/604, Brasilia
Telephone: +55 61 223 7488
Fax: +55 61 226 3698
Chief officers: Edgar Lisboa (Executive Director)

Paper Processors' Association

Associação Brasileira dos Convertedores de Papel Rotoflexo
Address: Av. Prestes Maia, 241 27º Andar, Conj. 2706, 01031-001 - São Paulo/SP
Telephone: +55 11 228 6183
Fax: +55 11 227 8010

Sao Paulo Association of the Sugar and Alcohol Industry (AIAA)

Associação das Indústrias de Açúcar e Alcool do Estado de Sao Paulo
Address: PO Box 3095, Rua Boa Vista 280, 5º andar, 01014-000 São Paulo SP
Telephone: +55 11 229 0611/6051141
Fax: +55 11 355 913/606 5659/605 5913
Chief officers: José Pilon (President)
Membership: sugar and alcohol refiners and processors

Tobacco Growers' Association of Brazil (AFUBRA)

Associação dos Fumicultores do Brasil
Address:
E-mail: afubra@empresa.unisc.br
Web site: www.unisc.br/afubra
Year established: 1955
Activities: conducts a survey on production costs (result is used as a parameter for price negotiations with the industry); carries out research
Chief officers: Hainsi Gralow (President), Jorge Kämpf (Secretary), Benício Albano Werner (Treasurer)
Membership: tobacco growers

Toy Manufacturers' Association (ABRINQ)

Associação dos Fabricantes de Brinquedos
Address: Av Pedroso de Morais 2219, 05419-001 São Paulo SP
Telephone: +55 11 816 3644
Fax: +55 11 211 0226
Membership: toy manufacturers

BULGARIA

Association of Wine and Spirits Manufacturers and Traders

Address: 19 Lavele St., BG-1080 Sofia
Telephone: +359 2 873 520
Fax: +359 2 873 520
Chief officers: Bogdan Madjukov

Bulgarian Article Numbering Association

Address: Bulgarian Chamber of Commerce and Industry, 42 P. Partchevitch Str, 1000 Sofia
Telephone: +359 2 872 631
Fax: +359 2 873 209
E-mail: bcci@bis.bg

Bulgarian Association of Newspapers Publishers

Address: PO Box 114, c/o The Open Society Fund, NDK Office Building, 11th floor, 1 Bulgaria Square, Sofia
Telephone: +359 2 890 428
Fax: +359 2 492 1097
Chief officers: Mr Evgenii Dainov (President)

Bulgarian Association of Travel Agents

Address: 1 Sv. Nedelya Square, BG-1000 Sofia
Telephone: +359 84131
Fax: +359 83254

Bulgarian Book Publishers' Association (BBPA)

Address: PO Box 1046, 1000 Sofia
Telephone: +359 2 878 965
Chief officers: Mr I Chipev (Secretary General), Ms G Parashkevanove (Director)

Bulgarian Construction Industry Chamber
Address: 17 Kiril i Metodii St., BG-1000 Sofia
Telephone: +359 2 730 237
Fax: +359 2 835 653
Chief officers: Dimo Guguchkov

Bulgarian Industrial Association
Address: 16-20 Alabin Str, Sofia 1000
Telephone: +359 2 871990, 879611, 884308
Fax: +359 2 872 604
E-mail: BIA@BULMAIL.Sprint.com
Year established: 1980
Activities: assistance to Bulgarian enterprises wishing to enter foreign markets in the form of promotion and contacts; analysis of economy; assistance with the development of small and medium-sized firms
Chief officers: Bodijar Danev (Chairman), Milena Staikova (General Secretary), Tonio Dimitrov (Director International Relations)

Chamber for the Telecommunications Industry
Address: 6 Stefan Karadja St - TUSTTS, BG-1000 Sofia
Telephone: +359 2 833 412
Fax: +359 2 802 728
Chief officers: Stoicho Stoichov

Chamber of Foreign Trade Companies
Address: 1 Tzar Ivan Asseni St. - VTD " Raznoiznos ", BG-1000 Sofia
Telephone: +359 2 879 084
Chief officers: Maxim Swartz

Chamber of the Electronics and Computer Science Industry
Address: Akademik G,Bonchev St, Blok 25 A, BG-1113 Sofia
Telephone: +359 2 708 494
Fax: +359 2 777 104
Chief officers: Kiril Boianov

Chamber of the Ferrous and Non-Ferrous Metallurgy
Address: 13 Serdika St., 2E, BG-1000 Sofia
Telephone: +359 2 896 903
Fax: +359 2 877 620
Chief officers: Vassil Zlatanov, Elizabeta Stoikova

Chamber of the Food and Bio-Machine Building Industry
Address: " Hraninvest " AD, 23 Patriarh Eptimii St., BG-6000 Stara Zagora
Telephone: +359 42 252 16
Fax: +359 42 431 63
Chief officers: Borislav Vassilev

Chamber of the Leather, Fur, Footwear and Accessories Industry
Address: Blvd. " Al.Stamboliiski " 125 - 2, II, BG-1000 Sofia
Telephone: +359 2 220 124
Fax: +359 2 267 239
Chief officers: Miroslav Pantaleev

Chamber of the Machine-Building Industry
Address: 34 Alabin St.,Floor 4, BG-1000 Sofia
Telephone: +359 2 525 148
Fax: +359 2 700 784
Chief officers: Ilia Keleshev

Chamber of the Materials Handling, Automotive, Construction and Agricultural Machine-Building Industry
Address: " Elmot " AD, 73 N. Gabrovski St., BG-5000 Veliko Turnovo
Telephone: +359 62 41931
Fax: +359 62 44861
Chief officers: Dancho Danchev

Trade Research and Promotion Institute (Wool Trade)
Address: zh k Izgreva Str. 165 3a, BG-1797 Sofia
Telephone: +359 700 100
Fax: +359 700 131
Activities: trade research and promotion

Union of Flour Manufacturers
Address: Grain and Cereals Institute, BG-2230 Kostinbrod
Telephone: +359 2 871 293
Fax: +359 2 871 293

Union of Fodder Manufacturers
Address: 15 Vitosha Blvd., BG-1000 Sofia
Telephone: +359 2 882 331
Fax: +359 2 882 332
Chief officers: Emil Todorov

Union of Poultry Breeders
Address: BG-2230 Kostinbrod
Telephone: +359 9 711 322 01
Fax: +359 2 741 844

Union of Sugar Manufacturers
Address: 19 Ekzarh Losif St. -" Zaharimpexserviz ", BG-1000 Sofia
Telephone: +359 2 833 972
Fax: +359 2 831 839
Chief officers: Luben Lotov

BURKINA FASO

Association of Automotive Components Traders
Address: BP 2482, Ouagadougou
Telephone: +226 334 644/307 299/03 084
Year established: 1993
Chief officers: Soumaila El Hadj Kafando (President), Saydou Bagagnan (Vice President), N. François Gansonre (Secretary)

Association of Retailers
Association des Petites Commercants
Address: BP 6125, Ouagadougou
Telephone: +226 310 199/306 354/312 198
Chief officers: Hamdo Yanogo (President), Salif Oudraogo (Vice President), Benoit Kouda (Secretary General)

Bakery Products' Association
Address: BP 9050, Ouagadougou
Telephone: +226 307 345
Year established: 1994
Chief officers: Sekou Ouedraogo (President), Koké Dembele (Vice President), François Konseiga (Secretary General)

Banking and Finance Enterprises' Association
Address: D.G. BIB, Ouagadougou
Telephone: +226 306 169/332 255/335 238

Chief officers: Gaspard Ouedraogo (President), Mahamadi Napon (Secretary General)

Cereal Traders' Association
Association des Commerçants de Cereals
Address: BP 11008, Ouagadougou
Telephone: +226 314 497/302 699
Chief officers: K. Harouna Kabore (President), Sahanouna El Hadj Sanfo (Vice President)

Hotel and Catering Association of Burkina Faso
Address: c/o Hotel Indépendance, Ouagadougou
Telephone: +226 306 061/304 811
Chief officers: S. Paul Ouedraogo (President), Ben Adama Traore (Secretary General)

BURUNDI

Coffee Exporters' Association of Burundi (ABEC)
Association Burundaise des Exportateurs de Café
Address: PO Box 2441, Bujumbura
Telephone: +257 2 224 553
Telex: 5089 BDI

CAMEROON

Cocoa and Coffee Exporters' Association (GEX)
Groupement des Exportations Cacao-Café
Address: BP 4216, Douala
Telephone: +237 426 911
Fax: +237 427 583
Telex: 5163
Year established: 1973
Activities: promotes export activities
Chief officers: Emile Engamba Engamba (President)

National Book Development Council (NBDC)
Address: PO Box 364, Buea, South West Province
Telephone: +237 322 586
Fax: +237 322 232
Chief officers: George Ngware (Chairman)

National Coffee and Cocoa Board
Address: BP 3018, Douala
Telephone: +237 425 936/934
Fax: +237 420 002
Telex: 5260 KN
Chief officers: Hope Sona Ebai, Etienne Essame Ndongo (Executive Officers)

Timber Producers and Exporters of Cameroon (TPEC)
Address: BP 570, Yaoundé
Telephone: +237 202 722
Fax: +237 202 722
Telex: 8998 KN
Chief officers: R Laheuguere (Secretary General)

CANADA

Aerospace Industries' Association of Canada (AIAC)
Address: Suite 1200, 60 Queen Street, Ottawa, ON K1P 5Y7
Telephone: +1 613 232 4297

Fax: +1 613 232 1142
E-mail: aiac@fox.nstn.ca
Web site: www.aiac.ca
Year established: 1962
Chief officers: Peter R Smith (President)
Structure: board; committees; permanent staff
Membership: 215 manufacturers and suppliers
Publications:
• Annual Report of the Aerospace Industries Association of Canada: *annual*
• Newsletter of the Aerospace Industries Association of Canada: *quarterly*
• Products and Services Guide: *annual*

Alliance of Manufacturers and Exporters Canada
Address: 75 International Boulevard, Suite 400, Toronto, Ontario, M9W 6L9
Telephone: +1 416 798 8000
Fax: +1 416 798 8050
E-mail: orders@the-alliance.com. (Publications)
Web site: www.palantir.ca/the-alliance/
Publications:
• Advantage Canada Magazine: *Canadian products and services and international trade - monthly*
Notes: The organisation was formed by an alliance of the Canadian Manufacturers' Association and the Canadian Exporters' Association.

Association for the Export of Canadian Books (AECB)
Address: 504-1 Nicholas Street, Ottawa Ontario, K1N 7B7
Telephone: +1 613 562 2324
Fax: +1 613 562 2329
Web site: www.aecb.org
Year established: 1972
Activities: provides financial assistance and market intelligence
Membership: publishers and distributors

Association of Canadian Advertisers (ACA)
Address: South Tower, Suite 307, 175 Bloor Street East, Toronto, Ontario M4W 3R8
Telephone: +1 416 964 3805
Fax: +1 800 565 0109
E-mail: aca@sympatico.ca
Web site: www3.sympatico.ca/aca/aca.htm
Web site notes: site includes a complete list of members
Membership: represents companies that spend over 80% of the national advertising expenditure in Canada

Association of Canadian Distillers
Address: Suite 1100, 90 Sparks Street, Ottawa, ON K1P 5T8
Telephone: +1 613 238 8444
Fax: +1 613 238 3411
Year established: 1947
Activities: lobbying (federal, provincial and municipal)
Chief officers: Ron Veilleux (President)
Structure: board of directors; permanent staff (11)
Membership: 10 distillers
Publications:
• Annual Statistical Report (Association of Canadian Distillers): *annual statistics covering the Canadian distilling sector with data on specific product areas and figures for earlier years - annual*

Association of Canadian Publishers
Address: 2 Gloucester Street, Suite 301, Toronto, Ontario, M4Y 1L5
Telephone: +1 416 413 4929
Fax: +1 416 413 4920

Association of Canadian Travel Agents (ACTA)
Association Canadienne des Agents de Voyages
Address: Suite 201, 1729 Rue Bank Street, Ottawa, ON K1V 7Z5
Telephone: +1 613 521 0474
Fax: +1 613 521 0805
Web site: www.acta.net
Year established: 1977
Activities: education courses; insurance; national and provincial conferences and trade shows
Structure: board of directors; committees; 7 permanent staff; regional associations
Membership: 3,000 travel agencies, tour operators, travel wholesalers, national and international travel service suppliers such as airlines, hotels, tourist boards, cruise lines, railways, car rental companies and other members of the travel industry

Association of International Automobile Manufacturers of Canada
Address: Suite 700, 210 Dundas Street West, Toronto, ON M5G 2E8
Telephone: +1 416 595 5333
Fax: +1 416 595 8226
Web site: www.importers.ca
Year established: 1973
Chief officers: Donald McCarthur (Executive Director)
Structure: executive committee, 8 sub-committees
Membership: 26 manufacturers, importers and distributors of cars, trucks, vans and special purpose vehicles
Publications:
• International Automobile Manufacturers' Update: *monthly*

Automotive Industries Association of Canada (AIA)
Association des Industries de l'Automobile du Canada
Address: 1272 Wellington Street, Ottawa, ON K1Y 3A7
Telephone: +1 613 728 5821
Fax: +1 613 728 6021
E-mail: yaro@mail.craigtech.com
Web site: www.aftmkt.com/associations/AIA
Year established: 1941
Activities: government relations, market research, education and training, export and trade promotion. Also organises the Canadian International Automotive Show
Chief officers: Dean Wilson (President), Yaroslaw Zajac, (Vice President), Denise Faguy, (Manager, Communication Services)
Structure: board of directors
Membership: 1,200 manufacturers, wholesalers, distributors, retailers
Publications:
• Aftermarket Outlook Study, Dynamics of a Market: *current size and structure of the industry, trends that influence the way aftermarketers go to market, and the general economic factors that affect the health of the industry - biennial*
• Aftermarket Watch Newsletter - Annual Review (Automotive Industries Association of Canada): *statistics and trends on the automotive aftermarket industry including information on vehicle registrations, cost of vehicle repairs, and characteristics of the current market place - annnual*
• Business Management Review: *information on wholesalers, warehouse distributors, manufacturers, rebuilders and retailers' salaries, employee benefits, and compensation - annual*

Automotive Parts Manufacturers' Association of Canada (APMA)
Associations des Fabricants de Pièces d'Automobile
Address: Suite 516, 195 West Mall, Toronto, ON M9C 5K1
Telephone: +1 416 620 4220
Fax: +1 416 620 9730
Year established: 1952
Chief officers: Pete Mateja (President)
Structure: board and several committees
Membership: 350 manufacturers of automotive parts, equipment, tools, supplies and services
Publications:
• APMA Directory of Automotive Parts Manufacturers: *key corporate information as well as information on the products they produce. Also included is a list of associate members, international automotive associations and major vehicle manufacturers - annual*

Bakery Association of Canada
Association Canadienne de la Boulangerie
Address: Suite 301, 885 Don Mills Road, Don Mills, ON M3C 1V9
Telephone: +1 416 510 8041
Fax: +1 416 510 8043
Year established: 1939
Activities: education and training, liaises with government, publishes statistics
Chief officers: Paul Hetherington (President), Christina Montford, (Co-ordinator, Member Services)
Structure: executive committee; board
Membership: membership of around 4,000 wholesale and retail bakers and their suppliers
Publications:
• BAC Comuniqué: *industry information - quarterly*
• Retail News and Views: *6 p.a.*

Beef Information Centre (BIC)
Address: 2233 Argentia Road, Suite 100, Mississauga, Ontario, L5N 2X7
Telephone: +1 905 821 4900
Fax: +1 905 821 4915
Web site: www.royalbank.com/english/agri/livestoc/beef
Activities: responsible for beef promotion and consumer education
Notes: The Beef Information Centre (BIC) is a division of the Canadian Cattlemen's Association.

Book Publishers' Association
Association Nationale des Éditeurs de Livres
Address: 2514 bd Rosemont, Montreal H1Y 1KA
Telephone: +1 514 273 8130
Fax: +1 514 273 9657
Web site: www.cam.org/~anel/index.htm
Chief officers: Mr R Vezina (General Secretary), Ms L Oligny (Director)

Brewers' Association of Canada
Address: Suite 1200, 1200-155 Queen Street, Ottawa, ON K1P 6L1
Telephone: +1 613 232 9601
Fax: +1 613 232 2283
E-mail: office@brewers.ca
Web site: www.brewers.ca
Web site notes: site includes statistics on domestic beer sales over a five year review period. Also includes data on exports to the USA, consumption of imported beer by province and per capita consumption
Year established: 1943
Activities: lobbying at federal level; information; programmes on responsible drinking
Chief officers: R A Morrison (President)
Structure: board; committees
Membership: 25 Canadian beer and malt producers accounting for over 98 per cent of domestic beer sales
Publications:
• Annual Statistical Bulletin: *an in-depth statistical profile of the*

market for beer in Canada. Covers domestic beer sales over a five year review period, per capita consumption, imports and exports, production, trends in the industy and legislation - annual
• Brewing in Canada: covers the brewing process and the history of the industry. Also includes a listing of all Canadian beer brands - annual
• Micro Breweries in Canada: list of Canadian breweries that produce less than 60,000 hectolitres of beer per year
• On Tap: a brief newsletter covering the activities of the Brewers Association and developments in the Canadian and international brewing industry - 5 p.a.
• Sales Bulletin: latest available data on beer sales by type and by province - monthly

Business and Institutional Furniture Manufacturers' Association of Canada

Address: c/o Teknion Furniture Systems Inc., 1150 Flint Road, Downsview, Ontario, M3J 2J5
Telephone: +1 416 661 3360
Fax: +1 416 661 4586
Chief officers: Mr. Monty Brown (Acting President)

Canada Beef Export Federation (Canada Beef)

Address: 235, 6715 - 8th Street, N.E. Calgary, Alberta, Canada T2E 7H7
Telephone: +1 403 274 0005
Fax: +1 403 274 7275
E-mail: canada@cbef.com
Web site: www.cbef.com
Year established: 1989
Activities: trade facilitation, detailed market intelligence, comprehensive market research studies and product inquiry information
Chief officers: Cam Daniels (Marketing Manager)
Membership: producers, packers, processors, exporters and suppliers

Canada Pork International

Address: 75 Albert, Suite 1101, Ottawa, Ontario
Telephone: +1 613 236 9886
Fax: +1 613 236 6658
E-mail: cpi@fox.nstn.ca
Web site: www.cfta.ca/cpi/cpi.html
Web site notes: site includes detailed statistics on the Canadian pork industry
Year established: 1991
Activities: providing foreign customers with information on Canadian pork products and the Canadian pork industry. Working with the Canadian Government and trading partners to resolve specific foreign market access issues impacting on Canadian pork exports. Developing, coordinating and implementing the generic international promotional efforts of the Canadian pork industry; and keeping the Canadian industry appraised of changes taking place in export markets
Membership: pork producers, pork packers and trading companies
Notes: Canada Pork International is the export promotion agency of the Canadian pork industry. It is a joint initiative of the Canadian Meat Council, representing the pork packers and trading companies, and of the Canadian Pork Council, which is the national pig producer organisation.

Canadian Advertising Foundation (CAF)

Address: Suite 402, 350 Bloor Street East, Toronto, ON M4W 1H5
Telephone: +1 416 961 6311
Fax: +1 416 961 7904
E-mail: webmaster@canad.com

Year established: 1957
Chief officers: Linda Nagel (President and CEO), Susan Morgan, (Director Food Section)
Structure: board of directors; permanent staff; standing committees
Membership: 300 advertisers, agencies, media organisations, and suppliers to the advertising sector
Publications:
• Annual Report of the Canadian Advertising Foundation: annual
• Pulse: issues and statistics - quarterly

Canadian Apparel Federation

Address: Suite 605, 130 Slater Street, Ottawa, ON K1P 6E2
Telephone: +1 613 231 3220
Fax: +1 613 231 2305
E-mail: 76470.3143@compuserve.com
Web site: www.apparel.org
Year established: 1976
Activities: promotes the apparel industry; provides discount programs to members; publishes and distributes reference materials; matches retailers and consumers with manufacturers; promotes Canadian suppliers to new markets in the U.S. and abroad; promotes best practices in labour issues; and links manufacturers with training expertise
Chief officers: Jack Kivenko (President); Stephen Beatty (Executive Director)
Structure: board
Membership: 600 members including clothing manufacturers, designers and their suppliers
Publications:
• CAF Bulletin: provides updates on the federal government's policy and regulatory programmes, trade developments in Canada and abroad as well as information on developments in technology, company news, and Federation activities - monthly
• Directory of International Apparel Trade Shows: listing of more than 600 apparel trade shows in Canada, the United States, Mexico, Europe, and Asia - annual
• Directory of North American Apparel Trade Shows: listing of nearly 200 apparel trade shows in Canada, the United States, and Mexico. Listings are grouped by menswear, womenswear, childrenswear, sports, textiles and technology - annual
• Marketing Newsletter: reports on trade shows, outlines what's selling where, and describes the successful campaigns of leading clothing marketers - monthly
• STYLE Buyers' Guide: information about manufacturers, wholesalers and importers of apparel plus industry suppliers and other related businesses. Listings include full address and contact for all companies. Listings are also cross-referenced by product - annual

Canadian Appliance Manufacturers' Association (CAMA)

Address: 10 Carlson Court, Suite 500, Rexdale, ON M9W 6L2
Telephone: +1 416 674 7410 Ext. 220
Fax: +1 416 674 7412
Chief officers: Ms. Alda Murphy (Manager)

Canadian Association of Animal Breeders (CAAB)

Address: 150 Research Lane, Suite 307, Guelph, Ontario, N1G 4T2
Telephone: +1 519 767 9660 ext. 302
Fax: +1 519 767 6768
E-mail: info@caab.com
Web site: www.caab.com
Chief officers: Information Director (Karen Hunt)

Canadian Association of Chain Drug Stores (CACDS)
Address: Suite 1210, 121 Bloor Street East, Toronto, ON M4W 3M5
Telephone: +1 416 922 1976
Fax: +1 416 922 6532
Membership: retail drug store chains in Canada, and their associate member partners who supply goods and services to the industry

Canadian Association of Chemical Specialities Manufacturers (CMCS)
L'Association Canadienne des Manufacturiers de Spécialités Chimiques
Address: 56 Sparks Street, Suite 702, Ottawa, Ontario, K1P 5A9
Telephone: +1 613 232 6616
Fax: +1 613 233 6350
E-mail: assoc@cmcs.org
Web site: www.cmcs.org
Membership: trade association for companies who manufacture, market, process, package and distribute: soaps and detergents; pest control products; waxes and polishes; antiseptics sanitizers; disinfectants; aerosols; antimicrobial chemicals; automotive chemicals; deodorizers; flame retarding chemicals and water treatment chemicals

Canadian Association of Fish Exporters (CAFE)
Address: Suite 212, 1770 Woodward Drive, Ottawa, ON K2C 0P8
Telephone: +1 613 228 9220
Fax: +1 613 228 9223
E-mail: csmith@seafood.ca
Web site: www.seafood.ca
Year established: 1978
Activities: market intelligence and promotion
Chief officers: Jane Barnett (President)
Membership: 66 seafood exporters and processors
Publications:
● World Seafood Market Report: *monthly*

Canadian Association of Footwear Importers Inc.
Address: #700 - 210 Dundas Street West, Toronto ONT M5G 2E8
Telephone: +1 416 595 5333
Fax: +1 416 595 8226
E-mail: caf:@importers.ca
Membership: 20 member companies

Canadian Association of Marketing Research Organisations (CAMRO)
Address: Suite 1105, 191 The West Mall, Etobicoke, ON M9C 5K8
Telephone: +1 416 620 7420
Fax: +1 416 620 5392
E-mail: bbandc@enterprise.ca
Year established: 1975
Activities: monitors government actions; collects financial information from its members on both a quarterly and annual basis. The results are only available to member companies
Chief officers: Amanda Curtis, (Executive Director), Melissa Roche, (Administrator)
Structure: board of directors; permanent staff; committees
Membership: 23 full service marketing research companies
Publications:
● CAMRO News: *articles on industry trends and highlights from the annual financial survey - twice-yearly*

Canadian Association of Speciality Foods (CASF)
Address: 19 Burlingame Rd., Etobicoke, ON, CA. M8W 1Y7
Telephone: +1 416 255 7071
Fax: +1 416 253 6571
Web site: www.cfta.ca/casf/casf.html
Web site notes: site includes a list of members
Activities: government relations, seminars, organises the Canadian Fine Food Show
Membership: members include retailers, wholesalers, manufacturers, importers, trade organisations, government agencies, as well as suppliers of accessories, servicing and equipment
Publications:
● Communiqué: *industry-related information - monthly*
Notes: Formally Canadian Specialty Food Assocation. "Specialty Foods" are defined as premium-quality foods of some uniqueness with good presentation and select distribution.

Canadian Association of Warehousing and Distribution Services (CAWDS)
Address: Suite 111, 1300 W Higgins Road, Park Ridge, IL 60068-5764
Telephone: +1 847 292 1891
Fax: +1 847 292 1896
E-mail: Logistx@aol.com
Web site: www.iwla.com/Gen-Info/cawds-bio.html
Year established: 1920
Activities: education and training, government liaison and public relations
Chief officers: Mike Jenkins (President and CEO), Janette Teevan (Marketing/Public Relations Coordinator)
Structure: board of directors; permanent staff
Membership: 41 companies engaged in public and contract warehousing and third-party logistics
Publications:
● Logistics Today: *the North American distribution system*
● Newsgram: *covers the activities of the Association and industry news - monthly*
● Warehouse Supervisor: *monthly*

Canadian Bankers' Association
Address: Suite 3000, Commerce Court West, Toronto, ON M5L 1G2
Telephone: +1 416 362 6092
Fax: +1 416 362 5668
Year established: 1891
Activities: education and lobbying; provides information, research, advocacy, education and operational support to its members
Chief officers: Helen K Sinclair (President and CEO)
Structure: board of directors; professional staff; standing committees
Membership: 60 banks
Publications:
● Bank Facts: *general statistics on the activities of Canadian banks and trends in the financial and monetary sectors. Some statistics for earlier years - annual*
● Canadian Banker/Le Banquier: *banking news and analysis - 6 p.a.*

Canadian Bottled Water Association
Address: 203-1, 70 East Beaver Creek Rd., Richmond Hill, ON, CA. L4B 3B2
Telephone: +1 905 886 6928
Fax: +1 905 886 9531

Canadian Carpet Institute

Address: Suite 605, 130 Slater Street, Ottawa, ON K1P 5H9
Telephone: +1 613 232 7183
Fax: +1 613 232 3072
Year established: 1942
Chief officers: Michael B Kronick (Executive Director)
Structure: permanent staff; board, committees
Membership: 34 manufacturers
Publications:
• Canadian Consumers Guide to Carpet: *irregular*

Canadian Chemical Producers' Association

Address: Suite 805, 350 Sparks Street, Ottawa, ON K1R 7S8
Telephone: +1 613 237 6215
Fax: +1 613 237 4061
E-mail: info@ccpa.ca
Web site: www.ccpa.ca
Year established: 1962
Chief officers: Jean Belanger (President)
Structure: board; committees; permanent staff
Membership: 64 manufacturers accounting for more than 90 per cent of the chemicals manufactured in Canada
Publications:
• CCPA Annual Report: *a short statistical section gives sales, consumption, foreign trade data for the chemicals industry in total and for petrochemicals, inorganic chemicals, and organic and speciality chemicals. Also statistics on the chemicals balance of trade, assets, capital expenditure, number of sites, profit, income, and employment. Statistics mainly for the last five years and based largely on Association data - annual*
• Newsletter of the Canadian Chemical Producers' Association

Canadian Cosmetic, Toiletry and Fragrance Association (CCTFA)

Association Canadienne des Cosmetiques, Produits de Toilettes et Parfums
Address: 5090 Explorer Drive, Suite 510, Mississauga, Ontario L4W 4TN
Telephone: +1 905 629 0111
Fax: +1 905 629 0112
E-mail: ccarter@cctfa.ca
Year established: 1928
Chief officers: Charles A Low (President)
Structure: executive committee; board of directors; permanent staff
Membership: 200 manufacturers, distributors, suppliers
Publications:
• CCTFA Membership Directory: *complete listing of member companies which includes contact information, description of products and services - annual*
• Sales of Cosmetic, Toiletry and Fragrance Products in Canada: *summarises industry sales, by category. The report is supplemented by senior management commentary and additional data where available. Participating companies are listed in the report - annual*

Canadian Council of Furniture Manufacturers

Address: c/o Accro Furniture Industries, 211 Hutchings Street, Winnipeg, Manitoba, R2X 2R4
Telephone: +1 204 633 5872
Fax: +1 204 694 1281
Chief officers: Mr. Terry Clark (Acting President)

Canadian Council of Grocery Distributors

Address: PO Box 1082, Place du Parc, Montréal, PQ H2W 2P4
Telephone: +1 514 982 0267
Fax: +1 514 849 3021
E-mail: ccgd@magi.com
Web site: www.cfta.ca/ccgd/ccgd.html
Year established: 1987

Activities: public policy, trade relations and member education and development. Council members have access to up-to-date technical, legislative, regulatory, educational and research information
Chief officers: John F Geci (President), Monika Simon (Vice-President, Communications and Development)
Structure: board of directors; permanent staff; 4 officers
Membership: 23 distributors and marketers of food and grocery-related products accounting for 80% of the food distribution industry in Canada. Membership includes both large and small retail and wholesale enterprises and grocery chain operators. There are also Allied Members, persons or companies which provide support services to regular members in fields such as banking, data processing, equipment procurement, marketing, research and transportation
Publications:
• Annual Report of the Canadian Council of Grocery Distributors: *annual*
• Canadian Food Retailing Industry at a Glance
• Industry Survey (Canadian Council of Grocery Distributors): *a survey of the trends in the Canadian and US food distribution sectors based partly on a survey by the Council (50%) and partly on other sources. A brief commentary accompanies the data - annual*
• Precis: *3 p.a.*
• State of the Industry: *annual*
• Trends in Canada: *survey on consumer shopping - bi-annual*

Canadian Dairy and Food Industries' Supply Association (CDFISA)

Address: 1148 Vanier Drive, Mississauga, ON L5H 3X1
Telephone: +1 416 278 6496
Fax: +1 416 278 6496
Year established: 1943
Structure: board; committees
Membership: CDFISA is an association of professional suppliers to the food industry made up of 51 member companies from the food processing sector, government and academia
Publications:
• Window: *monthly*

Canadian Dietetic Association

Address: Suite 601, 601-480 University Avenue, Toronto, ON M5G 1VZ
Telephone: +1 416 596 0857
Fax: +1 416 596 0603
Year established: 1935
Activities: lobbying (federal and provincial); continuing education programs; data collection; annual conference
Chief officers: Marsha Sharp (CEO)
Structure: board of directors; permanent staff; committees
Membership: 5,100 dietitians
Publications:
• Annual Report of the Canadian Dietetic Association: *annual*
• Canadian Dietetic Association Journal: *quarterly*
• Communiqué (Canadian Dietetic Association): *newsletter - bi-monthly*
Notes: Annual conference

Canadian Direct Marketing Association (CDMA)

Address: Suite 607, 1 Concorde Gate, Don Mills, ON M3C 3N6
Telephone: +1 416 391 2362
Fax: +1 416 441 4062
E-mail: kbrasch@cdma.org
Web site: www.cdma.org
Web site notes: site includes statistics on Canadian Direct Response Marketing including total market size, per capita

sales and number employed by the industry. Also includes supplier listings and a glossary of direct marketing terms
Year established: 1967
Activities: education and training, sponsors trade shows
Chief officers: John Gustazson (President and CEO), Scott McClellan (Director Communications)
Structure: board of directors; permanent staff
Membership: 650 member companies including Canada's major financial institutions, publishers, cataloguers and charities as well as various suppliers of goods and services to the industry. Members responsible for over 80 percent of annual direct response marketing sales in Canada
Publications:
• Annual Fact Book: *in-depth commentary and statistics on the Canadian direct marketing industry. Includes the results of several surveys commissioned by the Association - annual*
• CDMA Membership Directory: *contains contact details of member companies - annual*
• Communicator (The): *articles on direct marketing in Canada - quarterly*

Canadian Drug Manufacturers' Association (CDMA)
L'Association Canadienne des Fabricants de Produits Pharmaceutiques
Address: Suite 606, 4120 Yonge Street, North York, ON M2P 2B8
Telephone: +1 416 223 2333
Fax: +1 416 223 2425
Year established: 1981
Chief officers: Brenda Drinkwater (President), Jim Keon (Vice President Research and International Affairs), Jack Kay (Chairman)
Structure: executive committee; board (quarterly)
Membership: 15 members representing the Canadian pharmaceutical industry. Members specialise in the production of generic drugs, fine chemicals and alternatives to brand name prescription drugs
Publications:
• Drug News and Views: *newsletter - quarterly*

Canadian Egg Marketing Agency
Address: Suite 1900-320, 320 Queen Street, Ottawa, ON K1R 5A3
Telephone: +1 613 238 2514
Fax: +1 613 238 1967
E-mail: info@canadaegg.ca
Publications:
• Annual Report of the Canadian Egg Marketing Agency: *includes commentary on activities during the year and some statistics covering egg production and deliveries in Canada. Based on data collected by the agency - annual*

Canadian Federation of Agriculture (CFA)
Address: Suite 1101, 75 Albert Street, Ottawa, ON K1P 5E7
Telephone: +1 613 236 3633
Fax: +1 613 236 5749
E-mail: cfafca@fox.nstn.ca
Web site: www.cfa-fca.ca
Web site notes: site includes general information on Canadian agriculture and agricultural exports
Year established: 1935
Chief officers: Sally Rutherford (Executive Director)
Structure: executive board of directors; committees
Membership: 20 provincial organisations and marketing groups
Publications:
• CFA Bulletin: *bi-weekly*
• CFA Update: *policy statement - quarterly*
• Issue Papers: *irregular*
• On the Hill: *proceedings in parliament - weekly*

Canadian Film and Television Association
Address: North Tower, Suite 806, 175 Bloor Street East, Toronto, ON M4W 3R8
Telephone: +1 416 927 8942
Fax: +1 416 922 4038
Year established: 1948
Activities: promotes interests of members by lobbying governments on policy matters; negotiates labour agreements on behalf of independent producers; sponsors conferences, seminars and workshops
Chief officers: Sandra MacDonald (President)
Structure: board of directors; permanent staff; 2 offices in Toronto and Vancouver
Membership: 250 independent producers and distributors (production facilities and services)
Publications:
• ACTION (Canadian Film and Television Production Association): *newsletter, activities - quarterly*
• CFTPA
• Directory of Members
• Guide: *production handbook - annual*

Canadian Food Brokers' Association (CFBA)
Address: 70 Aitken Circle, Unionville, ON L3R 7LI
Telephone: +1 905 477 4644
Fax: +1 905 477 9580
E-mail: kbray@idirect.com
Web site: web.idirect.com/~cfba/
Year established: 1943
Chief officers: Keith Bray (President)
Structure: volunteer board; committees
Membership: manufacturers to the grocery, foodservice, mass merchandisers, drug, warehouse and convenience trade, accounting for 25% of food sold in Canada
Publications:
• Canadian Food Brokers' Association News: *newsletter - quarterly*
• Membership Directory: *annual*

Canadian Food Service Executives' Association (CFSEA)
Address: 1531 Bayview Avenue, Suite 3529, Toronto, Ontario M4G 4G8
Telephone: +1 416 421 5045
Fax: +1 416 421 5045
E-mail: cfsea@foodservice.ca
Web site: www.foodserviceworld.com
Chief officers: Grant Thompson, (President)
Membership: food service management

Canadian Gift and Tableware Association (CGTA)
Address: Suite 301, 265 Yorkland Blvd., North York Ontario M2J 1S5
Telephone: +1 416 497 5771
Fax: +1 416 497 3448
E-mail: 104033.735@compuserve.com
Year established: 1974
Activities: advocacy on trade issues (federal and provincial); collects statistics on members; provides information to members
Chief officers: Yvonne Bridgman (President)
Structure: board of directors; permanent staff; standing committees
Membership: 1,300 manufacturers, importers, distributors, sales agents. Product lines range from novelty and souvenir items through to formal tableware settings
Publications:
• Annual Report of the Canadian Gift and Tableware Association (CGTA): *annual*

• Canadian Gift and Tableware Association Newsletter: *issues, summary of association activity - annual*

Canadian Hardware and Housewares Manufacturers' Association (CHHMA)

Address: Suite 101, 1335 Morningside Avenue, Scarborough, ON M1B 5M4
Telephone: +1 416 282 0022
Fax: +1 416 282 0027
Year established: 1966
Activities: lobbying, data collection, education and training, networking sesions with key customers
Chief officers: Vaughn W Crofford (President), Kathryn Lee (Communications Manager)
Structure: board of directors; permanent staff
Membership: 250 manufacturers of hardware and housewares products
Publications:
• Annual Report of the Canadian Hardware and Housewares Manufacturers' Association: *annual*
• Canadian Hardware and Housewares Manufacturers' Association News: *quarterly*

Canadian Importers' Association Inc.

Address: Suite 700, 210 Dundas Street West, Toronto, ON M5G 2E8
Telephone: +1 416 595 5333
Fax: +1 416 595 8226
E-mail: webmaster@premenos.com
Year established: 1932
Chief officers: Donald R McArthur (President)
Structure: board of directors; committees; permanent staff
Membership: 700 retailers, manufacturers, distributors, service companies
Publications:
• Import Canada: *guide on importing into Canada - annual*
• Import Week: *current information on emerging world trade issues, trade regulations and tariffs, customs policy changes, and upcoming government reviews and hearings - weekly*
• Importworld: *annual*

Canadian Independent Record Production Association

Address: Suite 202, 144 Front Street West, Toronto, Ontario, M5J 2L7
Telephone: +1 416 593 1665
Fax: +1 416 593 7563
Chief officers: Mr. Brian Chater (Executive Director)

Canadian Information Processing Society

Address: Suite 106, 430 King Street West, Toronto, ON M5V 1L5
Telephone: +1 416 593 4040
Fax: +1 416 593 5184
E-mail: info@cips.ca
Web site: www.cips.ca
Year established: 1958
Activities: annual convention and meeting
Chief officers: Mary Jean Kucerak (Executive Director), Michele Sura (Coordinator, Internet Services)
Structure: board of directors; permanent staff; standing committees, regional offices
Membership: 6,500 individuals in information technology
Publications:
• National Newsletter (Canadian Information Processing Society): *bi-monthly*
• News from National: *Electronic - bi-weekly*

Canadian Institute of Plumbing and Heating

L'Institut Canadien de Plomberie et de Chauffage
Address: Suite 330, 295 The West Mall, Etobicoke, ON M9C 4Z4
Telephone: +1 416 695 0447
Fax: +1 416 695 0450
Web site: www.ciph.com
Year established: 1933
Activities: conducts seminars and workshops, regional trade shows on plumbing, heating, cooling and piping
Chief officers: E P Hordison (President and CEO)
Structure: elected board of directors and executive/ finance committee; staff; 4 active councils
Membership: 200 manufacturers, wholesaler distributors, manufacturers' agents and service companies who manufacture, distribute and sell plumbing, hydronic heating, industrial, waterworks and other environmental products
Publications:
• CIPH Membership Directory: *annual*
• Pipeline: *newsletter*

Canadian Jewellers' Association

Address: Ste 600-27 Queen Street East, Toronto ONT M5C 2M6
Telephone: +1 416 368 7616
Fax: +1 416 368 1986
E-mail: cjaa@cycor.ca
Web site: cja.worldgate.com
Chief officers: Mr. James Biss (General Manager)
Membership: 1000 retailers and suppliers

Canadian Juvenile Products' Association

Address: P.O. Box 294, 10435 Islington Avenue, Kleinburg, Ontario, L0J 1C0
Telephone: +1 905 893 1689
Fax: +1 905 893 2392
Chief officers: Mr. Wayne Glover (Executive Director)

Canadian Lamp and Fixture Manufacturers' Association Inc.

Address: c/o Barclay Lamps Inc, 1780 Alstep Drive, Mississauga, Ontario, L5S 1W1
Telephone: +1 905 672 8400
Fax: +1 905 672 8461
Chief officers: Mr. Claude Barclay (National President)

Canadian Library Association (CLA)

Address: 200 Elgin Street, Ottawa, ON K2P 1L5
Telephone: +1 613 232 9625
Fax: +1 613 563 9895
E-mail: ai077@freenet.carleton.ca
Web site: www.cla.amlibs.ca/
Membership: 3,800 individuals and companies

Canadian Magazine Publishers' Association (CMPA)

Address: 2 Stewart Street, Toronto, Ontario, M5V 1H6
Telephone: +1 416 362 2546
Fax: +1 416 362 2547
E-mail: cmpainfo@cmpa.ca
Web site: www.cmpa.ca
Chief officers: Mrs. Catherine Keachie (Executive Director)

Canadian Meat Council

Address: Dow's Lake Court,, 875 Carling Avenue, Suite 410, Ottawa, ON K1S 5P1
Telephone: +1 613 729 3911
Fax: +1 613 729 4997
E-mail: cmvcabrw@acamcs.com

Web site: www.canswine.ca/pack.html
Year established: 1919
Activities: the Council maintains a library that provides economic, technical, nutritional and statistical information on the industry
Chief officers: Wayne Unbas (President)
Structure: board
Membership: 52 packers and processors; 41 suppliers
Publications:
● Canada's Meat Processing Industry: *data on trends in the meat processing sector with specific tables on various types of meat and livestock. Some tables include figures for earlier years - annual*

Canadian Natural Health Products' Association (CNHPA)

Address: 550 Alden Road, #205, Markham, ON L3R 6A8
Telephone: +1 905 479 6939
Fax: +1 905 479 1516
Membership: represents natural health food stores across Canada

Canadian Newspaper Association (CNA)

Association Canadienne Des Journaux
Address: 890 Yonge St., Suite 200, Toronto, Ontario M4W 3P4
Telephone: +1 416 923 3567
Fax: +1 416 923 7206
E-mail: bcantley@cna-acj.ca
Web site: www.cna-acj.ca
Web site notes: site includes circulation data on every newspaper in Canada; who owns them; information on who is reading daily newspapers; Canadian daily newspapers by province. The site also includes a list of the top 200 Canadian daily newspaper advertisers and their advertising expenditure for the latest year
Year established: 1996
Activities: government lobbying, public policy, marketing and member services
Chief officers: Richard Dicerni, (President and Chief Executive Officer), Gary Masters, (Vice-President, Marketing)
Membership: 101 Canadian daily newspapers (English and French). Membership represents 99% of newspapers distributed daily across Canada
Notes: The Canadian Newspaper Association was founded in 1996, following a decision to wind down operations of the Canadian Daily Newspaper Association and the Newspaper Marketing Bureau.

Canadian Office Products' Association (COPA)

Address: Suite 911, 1243 Islington Avenue, Toronto, ON M8X 1Y9
Telephone: +1 416 239 2737
Fax: +1 416 239 1553
Web site: www.copa.com
Year established: 1933
Activities: research and statistics; conferences and education; member programs and services; government lobbying
Chief officers: Lorne Wight (Chairman), Bart Sullivan (Vice-Chairman)
Structure: board of directors; permanent staff; manufacturer council; dealer council
Membership: 1,000 office product (furniture, stationery) manufacturers, retailers, sales agents and affiliates
Publications:
● Canadian Market Trends Report (Canadian Office Products Association): *sales statistics and trends in the office products market in Canada - monthly*
● Canadian Purchaser: *new product profiles and case application articles - quarterly*
● COPA Confidential (Canadian Office Products Association):

regular features on the industry, news and updates on legislative issues, association programs and statistics - 8 p.a.
● COPA Conversation: *market developments in the office products industry as well as issues affecting COPA members and the industry at large - quarterly*
● North American Business Product Sourcing Guide: *comprehensive product sourcing guide for the North American office products industry. The guide also features a listing of brand names - annual*
● SOHO Update Report: *comprehensive survey of the small office and home based business market including buying habits and tendencies - annual*
● Your Office: *focuses on the needs of small and home offices. Includes product application articles, general interest articles and product feature comparisons - quarterly*

Canadian Petroleum Products' Institute (CPPI)

Address: Suite 1000, 275 Slater Street, Ottawa, ON K1P 5H9
Telephone: +1 613 232 3709
Fax: +1 613 236 4280
Year established: 1989
Activities: conducts research, develops policy positions; liaises with government
Chief officers: Alain Perez (President), Brendan Hawley (Vice President of Public Affairs)
Structure: board of directors; permanent staff; core committee
Membership: 17 refiners and marketers
Publications:
● Annual Report of the Canadian Petroleum Products Institute: *statistics and issues - annual*
● Communiqué (Canadian Petroleum Products Institute): *newsletter - bi-monthly*

Canadian Pharmaceutical Association (CPhA)

Address: 1785 Alta Vista Drive, Ottawa, ON K1G 3Y6
Telephone: +1 613 523 7877
Fax: +1 613 523 0445
E-mail: cpha@cdnpharm or requests@cdnpharm.ca
Web site: www.cdnpharm.ca
Year established: 1907
Chief officers: Mr. Bev Allen (President), Mr. Leroy Fevang (Executive Director)
Structure: board of directors (decisions); council of delegates (policy making)
Membership: 11,000 pharmacists
Publications:
● Canadian Pharmaceutical Journal: *current practice issues, changes in the profession and new products - 10 p.a.*
● Compendium of Non-Prescription Products (CNP): *600 product monographs and product tables with a summary of the condition, possible signs and symptoms, diagnosis and pharmacological and non-pharmacological treatment options - annual*
● Compendium of Pharmaceutical Specialities: *generic and brand name drugs; an index of drug manufacturers, colour photographs of drug products and clinical tips - annual*

Canadian Plastics Industry Association

Address: Suite 500, 5925 Airport Road, Mississauga, ON L4V 1W1
Telephone: +1 905 678 7748
Fax: +1 905 678 0774
Year established: 1942
Structure: board of directors; committees; permanent staff; branch offices (in Montreal and Vancouver)
Membership: 400 members
Publications:
● Reporter: *newsletter - bi-monthly*
● Survey Series: *labour, finance, operating ratios, salary - irregular*

Canadian Pork Council (CPC)

Address: Suite 1101, 75 Albert Street, Ottawa, ON K1P 5E7
Telephone: +1 613 236 9239
Fax: +1 613 236 6658
E-mail: cpc@fox.nstn.ca
Web site: www.canpork.ca/
Web site notes: site includes statistics on the Canadian Pork industry over an eleven year review period including: total number of pigs by province; exports of pigs and pork; per capita consumption of meat and poultry products
Year established: 1966
Chief officers: Jim Smith (President)
Structure: board of directors, executive committee
Membership: 9 provincial hog marketing organisations
Publications:
• CPC Update: *news on the canadian pork industry - 6 p.a.*
• Statistical Review: *statistical profile of the Canadian pork industry - annual*

Canadian Poultry and Egg Processors' Council (CPEPC)

Conseil Canadien des Transformateurs d'Oeufs et de Volailles
Address: Suite 600, 2 Gurdwara Road, Ottawa, ON K2E 1A2
Telephone: +1 613 224 0001
Fax: +1 613 224 2023
E-mail: cpepc@magi.com
Web site: www.cfta.ca/cpepc/cpepc.html
Activities: lobbying and advocacy, promotes awareness and consumption of poultry and egg products; monitors legislation and regulation
Chief officers: Robert M. Anderson (President and CEO)
Structure: board of directors, executive committee
Membership: 200 member companies consisting of processors, egg graders, egg further processors, hatcheries and suppliers
Publications:
• Highlighter: *overview of industry issues - bi-weekly*
• Poultry Stock Report: *storage, stocks and supplies figures and forecasts - monthly*
• Processed Eggs: *industry statistics - monthly*

Canadian Printing Industries' Association

Address: Suite 906, 75 Albert Street, Ottawa, ON K1P 5E7
Telephone: +1 613 236 7208
Fax: +1 613 236 8169
Year established: 1958
Activities: public relations; technological and management information; lobbying; data collection
Chief officers: Mr. Michael F. Makin (President)
Structure: board of directors, regional associations, permanent staff
Membership: 630 commercial printing companies, suppliers
Publications:
• Canadian Printing Industries' Association National Communiqué: *newsletter - 5 p.a.*
• National Impressions: *newsletter - monthly*
Notes: Annual convention in September

Canadian Produce Marketing Association

Address: Suite 310, 1101 Prince of Wales Drive, Ottawa, ON K2C 3W7
Telephone: +1 613 226 4187
Fax: +1 613 226 2984
E-mail: question@cpma.ca
Web site: www.cpma.ca/
Year established: 1924
Activities: government lobbying, promotes consumption of fresh produce, provides members with a resource and communication centre
Chief officers: Peter Austin (President)

Structure: board of directors, 3 committees
Membership: 500 fruit and vegetable packers, shippers, importers, exporters, wholesalers, retailers, brokers, fresh cut processors
Publications:
• Agriculture Canada Produce Inspection and Licensing Manuals: *irregular*
• Fresh Fruits and Vegetables Nutrition Encyclopedia
• Fresh News: *covers developments in the Canadian fresh produce industry - quarterly*
• Membership Directory: *annual*

Canadian Publishers' Council

Address: 250 Merton Street, Suite 203, Toronto, Ontario, M4Y 1S2
Telephone: +1 416 322 7011
Fax: +1 416 322 6999
E-mail: lcharter@pubcouncil.ca
Web site: www.pubcouncil.ca
Web site notes: site includes a section on sources of Canadian publishing statistics as well as links to sources of information on publishing world-wide
Year established: 1910
Chief officers: Gayle Metson Director, (Public Affairs, School Group) Mrs. Jacqueline C. Husion (Executive Director)
Membership: 30 companies who publish books and other media for elementary and secondary schools, colleges and universities, professional and reference, retail, and library markets
Publications:
• Annual Report: *activities of the Association - annual*

Canadian Pulp and Paper Association (CPPA)

Address: 19th Floor, 1155 Metcalfe Street, Montréal, PQ H3B 4T6
Telephone: +1 514 866 6621
Fax: +1 514 866 3035
E-mail: communic@cppa.ca
Web site: www.open.doors.cppa.ca/
Year established: 1913
Chief officers: E.F. Boswell (Chairman), Esther Szynkarsky (Vice President Communications)
Structure: board, executive committee
Membership: 42 pulp and paper manufacturers
Publications:
• Annual Review: *comprehensive commentary and statistics on the Canadian pulp and paper industry - annual*
• At A Glance Key Statistics (Canadian Pulp and Paper Association): *concise statistics on paper and pulp mills, forestry resources, production, recycling, and some international comparisons. Based on various sources - annual*
• Pulp and Paper From Canada: *trade directory - annual*

Canadian Recording Industry Association

Address: Suite 400, 1250 Bay Street, Toronto, Ontario, M5R 2B1
Telephone: +1 416 967 7272
Fax: +1 416 967 9415
Chief officers: Mr. Brian Robertson (President)

Canadian Restaurant and Foodservice Association (CRFA)

Address: Suite 1201, 80 Bloor Street West, Toronto, ON M5S 1W5
Telephone: +1 416 923 8416
Fax: +1 416 923 1450
Activities: collects statistics; provides information and conducts research on the industry; lobbies government; provides group buying service; organises 2 trade shows (Including HostEx the largest foodservice trade show in

Canada); conducts training programs for food service managers
Chief officers: Douglas Needham (President)
Structure: board of directors
Membership: 13,500 members with an estimated 35,000 food, beverage and accommodation establishments across Canada. Members include full service and quick service restaurants, contract and institutional foodservice, hotels, motels, airline caterers and clubs
Publications:
● CRFA News: *information on the foodservice sector in Canada - 5 per annum*
● Eating Out Quarterly: *consumers dining out attitudes and behaviour. Includes market share information; average bill; top ten food and beverage items ordered as well as data on number of outlets by sector and by province - quarterly*
● Foodservice Facts: *general statistics on trends and the growth in the food service industry with statistics for earlier years and projections for the coming year. Based on a combination of sources including original research and official data - annual*
● Industry Operations Report: *financial operating results of a wide range of foodservice outlets in Canada - annual*
● Infostats Quarterly Report: *detailed analysis of sales statistics. Data is available by sector and by province and is represented monthly, quarterly, and for the year to-date. Forecasts, number of outlets and bankruptcy figures are also included. Based on official statistics - quarterly*

Canadian Retail Hardware Association (CRHA)
Address: 6800 Campobello Road, Mississauga, ON L5N 2L8
Telephone: +1 416 821 3470
Fax: +1 481 821 8946
E-mail: crha@crha.com
Web site: www.crha.com
Activities: CRHA owns and operates Canada's premier hardlines industry trade show "A World of Innovation"
Chief officers: Thomas M Ross (Executive Director), Margaret Goulding (Communications Coordinator)
Membership: Canadian hardware, housewares and home improvement retailers
Publications:
● CRHA Reporter: *current trends in the industry, education, training and legislation - monthly*
● Do-It-Yourself Retailing: *trends in Do-It-Yourself retailing in the United States and Canada - monthly*
● Financial Survey for Hardware Stores: *aggregate income and expenditure data for hardware and building supply stores with information given by state. Figures for the latest year and previous year. Also gives total sales figures for specific product categories. Based on a survey by the Association - biennial*

Canadian Shirt Manufacturers' Association
Address: c/o John Forsyth Co. Inc., 36 Horner Avenu, Toronto, Ontario, M8Z 5Y1
Telephone: +1 416 251 9618
Fax: +1 416 252 6231

Canadian Soft Drinks' Association (CSDA)
Address: Suite 330, 55 York Street, Toronto, ON M5J 1R7
Telephone: +1 416 362 2424
Fax: +1 416 362 3229
E-mail: 102005.1662@compuserve.com
Year established: 1942
Activities: produces statistics
Chief officers: Paulette Vinette (President)
Structure: permanent staff; regional divisions
Membership: 64 soft drink bottlers, distributors, franchise houses and industry suppliers

Publications:
● Perspectives (CSDA): *text and some statistics on trends in the Canadian soft drinks sector with data on specific drinks and markets - biannual*
● Product Stewardship Annual Report (Canadian Soft Drinks Association): *product packaging, solid waste - annual*

Canadian Sporting Goods' Association
Address: Suite 510, 455 St Antoine West, Montréal, PQ H2Z 1J1
Telephone: +1 514 393 1132
Fax: +1 514 393 9513
E-mail: sportind@cgsa.ca
Year established: 1945
Activities: organises the Sporting Goods Trade Show
Chief officers: Yves Paquette (President and CEO)
Structure: board of directors; executive committee; permanent staff
Membership: 1,702 companies, suppliers, wholesalers, retailers, sales representatives
Publications:
● Sports Vision: *statistics - bi-annual*

Canadian Sugar Institute (CSI)
Address: 10 Bay Street, Suite 620, Toronto, Ontario, M5J 2R8
Telephone: +1 416) 368-8091
Fax: +1 416) 368-6426
E-mail: info@sugar.ca
Web site: www.redpath.com/CSI/CSI_Page8.html
Year established: 1966
Activities: government lobbying
Membership: Canada's refined sugar manufacturers

Canadian Textiles Institute
Address: Suite 1720, 66 Slater Street, Ottawa, ON K1P 5H1
Telephone: +1 613 232 7195
Fax: +1 613 232 8722
Year established: 1935
Activities: data collection; deals with federal government on international trade matters
Chief officers: Eric Barry (President)
Structure: board of directors
Membership: 60 fibre and yarn producers, processers, fabric producers, dyers and finishers
Publications:
● Texnotes: *newsletter - weekly*

Canadian Tobacco Manufacturers' Council (CTMC)
Address: Suite 701, 99 Bank Street, Ottawa, ON K1P 6B9
Telephone: +1 613 238 2799
Fax: +1 613 238 4463
E-mail: pgordon@ecto.com
Year established: 1963
Activities: definition of products and standards, exchange of statistical information, support for technical research, liaison with other sectors of the tobacco industry, and international relations
Chief officers: Robert R Parker (President), Marie-Josee Lapointe (Vice-President Communications)
Structure: permanent staff; board
Membership: 3 Canadian tobacco manufacturers
Publications:
● Tobacco File (Le Dossier Tabac): *addresses public policy issues with respect to tobacco - 2-3 times p.a.*

Canadian Toy Manufacturers' Association
Address: PO Box 294, 10435 Islington Ave., Kleinburg, ON L0J 1C0

Telephone: +1 905 893 1689
Fax: +1 905 893 2392
Year established: 1932
Activities: liaises between government and industry, particularly on issues relating to tariffs; taxation, packaging and labelling, advertising guidelines and environmental issues; develops toy safety standards
Chief officers: Ms. Sheila Edmondson (General Manager)
Structure: board of directors; 12 committees; permanent staff
Membership: 185 manufacturers, distributors, importers
Publications:
• Insider: *issues - 3 p.a.*
• Membership and Show Directory: *annual*

Canadian Turkey Marketing Association
Address: 102-969 Derry Rd. E., Mississauga, ON, CA. L5T 2J7
Telephone: +1 905 564 3100
Fax: +1 905 564 9356
E-mail: ctma@idirect.com

Canadian Wine Institute
Address: 35 Maywood Avenue, St Catharine's, ON L2R 1L5
Telephone: +1 905 684 8070
Fax: +1 905 684 2993
Publications:
• Statistical Report (Canadian Wine Institute): *data on trends in the Canadian wine industry and market with tables on specific types of wine. Some figures for earlier years - annual*

Canadian Wood Council
Address: 1730 St Laurent Blvd Ste 350, Ottawa ON K1G 5L1
Telephone: +1 613 247 0777
Fax: +1 613 247 7856
E-mail: cwc@hookup.net
Web site: www.cwc.ca

Children's' Apparel Manufacturers' Association (CAMA)
Association des Manufacturiers de Mode Enfantine
Address: Suite 3110, Decanie Square, 6900 boul. Decarié, Montréal, Quebec, H3X 2T8
Telephone: +1 514 731 7774
Fax: +1 514 731 7459
Activities: operates a credit reporting service to members through a database of of 5,000 retail accounts in Canada
Chief officers: Murray Scwartz (Executive Director)
Membership: represents 85 childrenswear manufacturers
Publications:
• Kids Creations: *covers the Canadian children's clothing industry - quarterly*

Coffee Association of Canada
Address: Suite 301, 885 Don Mills Road, Don Mills, ON M3C 1V9
Telephone: +1 416 510 8032
Fax: +1 416 510 8044
Year established: 1991
Activities: membership networking and education; member services
Chief officers: David Wilkes (President)
Structure: board of directors; small permanent staff
Membership: 60 roasters, green coffee importers, suppliers, retailers
Publications:
• Media Report: *bi-monthly*
• Newsletter of the Coffee Association of Canada: *monthly*
• Resource Book: *annual*
• Statistical Report: *quarterly*

Confectionery Manufacturers' Association of Canada (CMAC)
Address: Suite 301, 885 Don Mills Road, Don Mills, ON M3C 1V9
Telephone: +1 416 510 8034
Fax: +1 416 510 8044
Year established: 1919
Activities: statistics gathering; programs with wholesale and retail trade
Chief officers: Carol Hochu (President)
Structure: board of directors; committees; permanent staff (2)
Membership: 25 manufacturers, 60 suppliers
Publications:
• CMAC News Clips: *business calendar - monthly*
• Confectionery Communiqué: *newsletter - quarterly*

Envelope Makers Institute of Canada
Address: P.O. Box 2339, c/o National Paper Goods Ltd., 144 Queen Street North, Hamilton, Ontario, L8N 4E1
Telephone: +1 905 527 3641
Fax: +1 905 527 0667
Chief officers: Chip Holton (President)

Food and Consumer Product Manufacturers of Canada (FCPMC/FPACC)
Fabricants de Produits Alimentaires et de Consommation du Canada
Address: 301-885 Don Mills Rd., Don Mills, ON, CA. M3C 1V9
Telephone: +1 416 510 8024
Fax: +1 416 510 8043
E-mail: Info@Fcpmc.Com
Web site: www.fcpmc.com
Chief officers: George Fleischmann, (President and CEO), Christina Bisanz (Vice President Corporate Communications)
Membership: 180 major companies engaged in the manufacturing and marketing of branded consumer packaged products available through retail and food service outlets

Food Beverage Canada (FBC)
Address: 17313 - 107 Avenue Edmonton, Alberta T5S 1E5
Telephone: +1 403 486 9679/800 493 9767
Fax: +1 403 484 0985
E-mail: pmurphy@foodbeveragecanada.com
Web site: www.foodbeveragecanada.com
Chief officers: Paul Murphy (President), Allan Cote (Director Member Programs and Services)
Membership: 400 food and beverage processors and producers
Publications:
• Exportfolio: *export related information on the Canadian food and beverage industry - quarterly*
• Industry Souce Directory-Overseas Buyers Guide: *food and beverage producers and processors, listed by product category. Data includes product descriptions, size of company and sales, markets in which they are operating, and those in which they are interested - annual*

Food Institute of Canada (FIC)
Address: Suite 415, 1600 Scott Street, Ottawa, ON K1Y 4N7
Telephone: +1 613 722 1000
Fax: +1 613 722 1404
E-mail: fic@foodnet.fic.ca
Web site: foodnet.fic.ca
Year established: 1989
Structure: board of directors; ad hoc committees; permanent staff
Membership: 150 manufacturers, distributors, processors, retailers etc

Footwear Council of Canada
Address: 799 Euclid Avenue, Toronto, Ontario, M5G 2E8
Telephone: +1 416 588 1603
Fax: +1 416 588 0486

Fur Council of Canada
Address: 1435 St. Alexandre Street, Suite 1270, Montreal, Quebec, H3A 2G4
Telephone: +1 514 844 1945
Fax: +1 514 844 8593
Chief officers: Mr. Del Haylock (Executive Vice-President)

Further Poultry Processors' Association of Canada (FPPAC)
Address: 203-2525 St. Laurent Blvd, Ottawa, Ontario, Canada K1H 8P5
Telephone: +1 613 738 1175
Fax: +1 613 733 9501
E-mail: fppac@sympatico.ca
Web site: www.cfta.ca/fppac/fppac.html
Web site notes: site includes a summary of trends in the industry for the latest year. Also includes brief member profiles and contact details
Chief officers: Lem Janes (Chairman)
Membership: 24 active further processors and 8 associated members. Members are engaged in adding value to chicken, turkey, and fowl meat by way of sizing, marinating, breading, cooking, forming and adding other ingredients to make ready-to-eat meals
Publications:
• FPPAC: *legislation, industry trends and company news relating to the poultry processing sector in Canada - monthly*

Heating, Refrigerating and Air Conditioning Institute of Canada (HRAI)
Address: Building 11, Suite 300, 5045 Orbitor Drive, Mississauga, Ontario L4W 4Y4
Telephone: +1 905 602 4700
Fax: +1 905 602 1197
Year established: 1948
Chief officers: Warren J Heeley (President)
Structure: 4 divisions; board of directors; committees; local chapters; permanent staff
Membership: 1,100 manufacturers and suppliers, wholesalers, contractors
Publications:
• HRAI News
• Membership Directory: *annual*

Hotel Association of Canada (HAC)
Address: Suite 1016, 130 Albert Street, Ottawa, ON K1P 5G4
Telephone: +1 613 237 7149
Fax: +1 613 238 3878
E-mail: info@hotels.ca
Web site: www.hotels.ca
Year established: 1913
Activities: government relations (federal level); data collection; education and training; national conferences
Chief officers: Anthony P Pollard (President)
Structure: board of directors; executive committee; committee; permanent staff
Membership: provincial and territorial hotel associations, as well as corporate hotel companies, who collectively represent more than 6,658 properties
Publications:
• Cross-Border Statistics: *statistics - monthly*
• Hotel Association of Canada Newsletter: *developments in the international hospitality industry - quarterly*
• Lodging Outlook: *statistics - monthly*

• Systems Directory: *information on hotel companies in Canada - annual*

Independent Toy Store Association of Canada (ITSAC)
Address: Retail Council of Canada, 121 Bloor Street East, Suite 1210, Toronto, ON   M4W 3M5
Telephone: +1 416 922 6678
Fax: +1 416 922 8011

Information Technology Association of Canada (ITAC)
Address: 2800 Skymark Ave Ste 402, Mississauga ON L4W 5A6
Telephone: +1 905 602 8345
Fax: +1 905 602 8346
E-mail: info@itac.ca
Web site: www.e-Commerce.Com/ITAC/
Year established: 1953
Activities: policy development, advocacy, research, government and member relations; initiates and participates in major research programs and policy development focusing on the information infrastructure; advocacy on government IT policies such as procurement, free trade, economic policy and tax changes, financing high tech companies, privacy, standards; and international policy development with representation on major global IT alliances
Structure: 13-14 permanent staff; large board of directors; executive committee; 10-15 member-driven taskforces and committee
Membership: 1200 companies in the computing and telecommunications hardware, software, services, and electronic content sectors
Publications:
• Fax Flash: *newsletter - every 3-4 weeks*
• Policy Papers: *irregular*

International Dairy Federation Committee of Canada
Address: c/o Dairy Division, Agriculture Canada, 2200 Walkley Road, Ottawa, Ontario K1A OC5
Telephone: +1 613 957 7078
Fax: +1 613 957 9073
E-mail: doylep@em.agr.ca
Chief officers: Mr P. Doyle (Secretary)

Magazine Association of Canada
Address: 777 Bay Street, 7th Floor, Toronto, Ontario, M5G 2C8
Telephone: +1 416 596 5306
Fax: +1 416 596 5707
Chief officers: Mr. Brian Segal (Chairman)

Music Industries' Association of Canada
Address: Suite 109, 1210 Sheppard Avenue East, North York, ON M2K 1E3
Telephone: +1 416 490 1871
Fax: +1 416 490 9739
Year established: 1971
Activities: government relations; MIAC Conference and Trade Show
Chief officers: Al Kowalenko (Executive Director)
Structure: board of directors; executive committee
Membership: 70 manufacturers of musical instruments and accessories and distributors

National Association of Tobacco and Confectionery Distributors (NACTD)
Association Nationale des Distributeurs de Tabac et de la Confiserie
Address: 3090 Le Carrefour Blvd., Suite 504, Laval QC H7T 2J7

Telephone: +1 514 682 6556
Fax: +1 514 682 6732
Chief officers: Mr. Luc Dumulong, (Chief Executive), Mark Tobenstein (Chairman)
Membership: 400 members
Publications:
• Contact: *covers management issues as well as regional reports - monthly*

National Dairy Council of Canada

Conseil National de l'Industrie Laitière du Canada
Address: 221 Laurier Avenue East, Ottawa, ON K1N 6PI
Telephone: +1 613 238 4116
Fax: +1 613 238 6247
Web site: www.dairyinfo.agr.ca
Web site notes: site includes comprehensive statistics on the Canadian dairy industry as well as some international data
Year established: 1918
Activities: non-profit-making association of Canadian processors and marketers of dairy products
Structure: 29 directors on board; 9 of these form the executive committee; 7 permanent staff
Membership: producers of fluid milk, creamery butter, natural and processed cheese, condensed milk, skim milk powder, ice cream, yoghurt and a variety of products with dairy ingredients
Publications:
• Direction: *newsletter - bi-monthly*

National Snow Industries Association

Address: 245 Victoria Ave., Suite 810, Westmount, Quebec, H3Z 2M6
Telephone: +1 514 939 7370
Fax: +1 514 939 7371

Packaging Association of Canada

Address: Suite 330, 2255 Sheppard Avenue East, Willowdale, ON MZJ 4Y1
Telephone: +1 416 490 7860
Fax: +1 416 490 7844
Year established: 1951
Activities: education programme (technical seminars); provincial and federal lobbying (regulation issues and labelling, recycling, procurement, definitions; health protection, transportation); standards; limited collection of statistics
Structure: board of directors; regional chapters; 2 officers; permanent staff
Membership: 1,800 manufacturers and some retailers
Publications:
• Bulletin: *monthly*
• Update: *features - quarterly*

Pharmaceutical Manufacturers' Association of Canada (PMAC)

Address: Suite 302, 1111 Prince of Wales Drive, Ottawa, ON K2C 3T2
Telephone: +1 613 727 1380
Fax: +1 613 727 1407
E-mail: info@pmac-acim.org
Web site: www.pmac-acim.org
Year established: 1914
Chief officers: Honorable Judy Erola (President) Robert Andrews (Coordinator, Publications and Information Services)
Structure: board of directors
Membership: 68 manufacturers of brand name drugs
Publications:
• PMAC Annual Review: *overview of industry statistics and issues - annual*

• PMAC News: *industry oriented activities - 10 p.a.*
• Provincial Fax Sheets: *annual*

Retail Council of Canada

Le Conseil Canadien du Commerce de Détail
Address: 121 Bloor St. E., Suite 1210, Toronto, Ontario, M4W 3M5
Telephone: +1 416 922 6678
Fax: +1 416 922 8011
E-mail: jchurch@sympatico.ca
Web site: www.retailcouncil.org
Year established: 1963
Activities: lobbying; trade show, provides information on retailing
Structure: board of directors; permanent staff; 40 committees
Membership: 6,500 retailers (grocery, apparel, hardware)
Publications:
• Canadian Retailer: *inside stories on technology, financial management, success profiles, visual merchandising, advertising and marketing, loss prevention, and retail operations - bi-monthly*
• Operating Survey of Canadian Retailing: *annual statistics on Canadian retailing in general plus data on specific retailing sectors. Turnover, sales, operating ratios are included. Based on a survey by the Council - annual*
• Retail Executive: *quarterly*
• Retail Sales: *monthly journal - monthly*
• Store Sales: *monthly journal - monthly*
Notes: The Association incorporates the Retail Footwear Alliance of Canada.

Shoe Suppliers' Association of Canada

Address: 4101 Sherbrooke Street W., Montreal, Quebec, H3Z 1A8
Telephone: +1 514 937 8118
Fax: +1 514 937 7066
Chief officers: Ms. Shirley Laliberte (President)

Tea Council of Canada/Tea Association of Canada

Address: Suite 301, 885 Don Mills Rd., Don Mills, ON, CA. M3C 1V9
Telephone: +1 416 510 8647
Fax: +1 416 510 8044
Web site: www.tea.ca
Web site notes: site includes statistics on tea in Canada including retail sales value by type
Activities: public relations, education and training, compiles statistics on the market for tea
Membership: tea packers, blenders, importers and retailers
Publications:
• Market Statistics: *detailed statistics and analysis of the tea market in Canada. Based on a survey commissioned by the Council and official sources - annual*
• Membership Directory: *contact details and activities of member companies - annual*
• Tea Zone (La Zone du thé): *preparation and serving ideas, market trends, health information - quarterly*

Tourism Industry Association of Canada (TIAC)

Address: Suite 1016, 130 Albert Street, Ottawa, ON K1P 5GA
Telephone: +1 613 238 3883
Fax: +1 613 238 3878
E-mail: tiac@magi.com
Year established: 1931
Activities: advocate for policies and programmes that enhance viability and profitability of Canada's tourism industries; exists to form consensus in action on tourism issues and foster effective communication with government
Chief officers: Debra Ward (President)
Structure: board of directors; standing committees;

permanent staff
Membership: 200 hotels and travel firms
Publications:
• TIAC Update: *monthly*
Notes: Linked to provincial organisations.

CAYMAN ISLANDS

Cayman Insurance Managers' Association
Address: P.O. Box 69, George Town, Grand Cayman

Cayman Islands Bankers' Association
Address: PO Box 676, George Town
Telephone: +1 809 9 490 330
Fax: +1 809 9 490 220
Chief officers: Rosaleen Corbin (President), Daniel Haase (Vice President), David Sargison (Treasurer), Larry Ingraham (Secretary)

Cayman Islands Hotel and Condominium Association
Address: PO Box 1367, George Town
Telephone: +1 809 9 474 057
Fax: +1 809 9 474 143
Chief officers: Lissa Adam (President), Jon Tremellen, Betty Wood (Vice Presidents), Bill Myers (Treasurer), Barbara Daily (Secretary), Lorraine Ebanks (Executive Director)

Cayman Islands Real Estate Brokers' Association
Address: P.O. Box 497, George Town, Grand Cayman
Telephone: +1 809 9 497 099
Fax: +1 809 9 496 819

Cayman Islands Restaurant Association
Address: P.O. Box 1000, George Town
Telephone: +1 809 9 477 377
Fax: +1 809 9 490 220

CHILE

Association of Chilean Hotels
Asociación de Empresarios Hoteleros de Chile
Address: Casilla No. 3410, Elías Fernández Albano No. 171 Piso 3, Santiago
Telephone: +56 2 698 8765/671 1937
Fax: +56 2 698 8850
Chief officers: Enrique Carvajal (President), Colin Turner (Vice President), Hanja Razmilic (Secretary)

Association of Cosmetic and Toiletries Companies (AEA)
Asociación de Empresas de Aseo
Address: Huérfanos No. 714, oficina 303, Santiago
Telephone: +56 2 639 5481
Chief officers: Jesús Rico R (President), Lorena Navarrete (Secretary)

Association of Dried Plum Producers (ASPROCICA)
Asociación de Productores de Ciruelas Secas
Address: Casilla 9442, Santiago, Avda Ramón Subercasseaux 1712, Pirque
Telephone: +56 2 850 3122/3257/0265/3578/1220
Fax: +56 2 850 5134
Telex: 244379 ASP CL

Year established: 1941
Activities: sorts, processes, packs and exports its members' produce
Membership: over 70 prune growers and driers

Association of Estate Agents and Construction Contractors
Asociación de Corredores de Propiedades y Promotores de la Construcción
Address: Avda. Providencia No. 2008, Piso 2 - oficina A, Santiago
Telephone: +56 2 231 6548/ 252 0167
Fax: +56 2 233 5110
E-mail: acopasoc.gremd001@chilnet.cl
Chief officers: José F Montalva O (President), Pablo Bauer J (Vice President), Leonardo Carvallo (Secretary General), Ricardo Anwandter Fernandez (General Manager)
Membership: estate agents

Association of Exporters of Non-Traditional Manufactured Goods (ASEXMA)
Asociación de Exportadores de Productos Manufacturados No Tradicionales AG
Address: Las Hortencias 2710, Providencia, Santiago
Telephone: +56 2 233 2465/2315823
Fax: +56 2 233 1843
Chief officers: Roberto Fantuzzi (President), Andrés Vicens (Vice President), Sergio Sarmiento Torres (Treasurer), Rose Marie Gei Concha (General Manager)
Membership: exporters of non-traditional manufactured goods

Association of Footwear Traders (ACOMCAL)
Asociación de Comerciantes de Calzados
Address: Casilla no. 4011, Huérfanos nº 757- oficina 316, Santiago
Telephone: +56 2 638 1542
Chief officers: Segundo Barranco C (President), Antonio Montes O (Vice President), Felix Aparicio B (Secretary)
Membership: footwear retailers

Association of Fuel Distributors
Asociación de Distribuidores de Combustibles
Address: Casilla nº 1086, Regina Paci nº 767, Nuñoa, Santiago
Telephone: +56 2 204 9646
Fax: +56 2 274 0527
Chief officers: Fernando Rodríguez (President)

Association of Producers and Exporters of Fine Wines
Asociación de Productores de Vinos Finos de Exportación
Address: Manuel Rodriguez 229, Isla de Maipo, Casilla 47, Isla de Maipo
Telephone: +56 2 819 2809/2959
Fax: +56 2 819 2986
E-mail: vinos@uva.cl
Web site: www.chilevinos.cl
Activities: coordinates export of wine, advises in relation to overseas commerce and law, publishes quarterly information in national press, produces monthly statistics of wine exports
Chief officers: Rodrigo Alvarado (Executive Director), Paula Valdivieso (Secretary)

Association of Professional Organisers of Conferences, Seminars and Exhibitions (OPCE)
Organizadores Profesionales de Congresos, Exposiciones y Seminarios de Chile, Asociación Gremial
Address: Toledo No. 1991, Santiago
Telephone: +56 2 225 6888/274 6714/251 4268
Fax: +56 2 274 2789

Chief officers: Ana María Montes C (President)

Association of the Chilean Cosmetics Industry
Cámara de la Industria Cosmética de Chile AG
Address: PO Box 2946, Avda General Bustamante 24, oficina E, piso 3, Santiago
Telephone: +56 2 274 3816/251 8749/2049501
Fax: +56 2 204 9501
E-mail: camarade.laind001@chilnet.cl
Year established: 1945
Chief officers: Rene Haug-Gallagher (Manager)
Membership: 42 manufacturers, importers and suppliers of cosmetics, and representatives of foreign companies
Publications:
• Boletín Informativo: *monthly*

Association of the Chilean Pharmaceutical Industry (CIF)
Cámara de la Industria Farmacéutica de Chile AG
Address: PO Box 22 Correo 9, Hernando de Aguirre 1981, Providencia, Santiago
Telephone: +56 2 225 2959/225 2461
Fax: +56 2 205 2060
E-mail: camarade.laind002@chilnet.cl
Membership: pharmaceutical companies

Association of Traders in Agricultural Produce and Livestock (ACOPAG)
Asociación de Corredores de Productos Agrícolas y Ganado
Address: Huérfanos nº 1022 - oficina 1009, Santiago
Telephone: +56 2 698 7412
Fax: +56 2 698 65682/ 698 6568
Chief officers: Roberto Baltra B (President), Santiago Arenas (Vice President), Fernando Yañez F (General Manager)
Membership: agricultural traders

Canned Products Manufacturers' Association (Asfacc)
Asociación de Fabricantes de Conservas de Chile
Address: Ahumada 254 - oficina 1209, Santiago
Telephone: +56 2 698 0682

Chemical Industrialists' Association (ASIQUIM)
Asociación Gremial de Industriales Químicos
Address: Avda Bello 2777, of 501, Santiago
Telephone: +56 2 203 3350/1
Fax: +56 2 231 0097/2033351
E-mail: asiquim.asiq001@chilnet.cl
Chief officers: Sergio Robledo Escudero (President), Juan Sarraf Canessa (Vice President), Francisco Muñoz Carrasco (Vice President), Stelio Cembrano Carniglia (General Manager)
Membership: chemicals companies

Chilean Advertising Agencies' Association (ACHAP)
Asociación Chilena de Agencias de Publicidad AG
Address: Guardia Vieja 181, Providencia. Santiago
Telephone: +56 2 231 0935/231 3644
Fax: +56 2 231 2354
Chief officers: Henry Nothcote (President), Mario Lübbert Pérez (Vice President), Alfonso Pérez (Treasurer), Fernando Gardella Brusco (Secretary General)
Membership: advertising agencies

Chilean Article Numbering Association
Asociación Chilena de Codificación Comercial
Address: Vecianl 140, Las Condes, Santiago
Telephone: +56 2 231 3024
Fax: +56 2 233 3516
E-mail: eanchil@ibm.net

Chilean Association of Air Freight Agencies (ACHIAC)
Asociación Chilena de Agencias de Carga AG
Address: Luis Thayer Ojeda nº 0115 - oficina 1002, Santiago
Telephone: +56 2 231 5970
Fax: +56 2 233 8232
E-mail: alacat@entel chile.net
Chief officers: David Kimber (President), Pedro Costas (Vice President), Hans Erasmy (Secretary)
Membership: air freight agencies

Chilean Association of Automobile Dealers and Businessmen
Asociación Gremial Chilena de Comerciantes e Industriales en Automoviles
Address: Santa Lucía No. 302 Piso 3, Santiago
Telephone: +56 2 632 1232 x 33
Chief officers: Fernando de Carcer (President)

Chilean Association of Legal Administrators
Asociación Chilena de Administradores de Consorcios
Address: Avda. Bernardo O'Higgins no.884, Santiago
Telephone: +56 2 633 5753/638 0236
Fax: +56 2 633 0708
Telex: 2 241143 CREDS-CL
Chief officers: Patricio Millas N (President), Gerald Howard (Vice President)

Chilean Association of Supermarkets
Asociación Gremial de Supermercados de Chile
Address: República de Cuba 1474, Santiago de Chile
Telephone: +56 2 209 4166
Fax: +56 2 274 6564

Chilean Association of Tyre Distributors (ASODIN)
Asociación Gremial de Distribuidores de Neumáticos
Address: Luis Thayer Ojeda No.183, oficina 201, Santiago
Telephone: +56 2 231 3547
Fax: +56 2 231 3547
Chief officers: Michael Cheetham (President), José M. Cuevas (Vice President), Julio León (Secretary General)

Chilean Banking and Financial Institutions' Association
Asociación de Bancos e Instituciones Financieras de Chile AG
Address: Agustinas 1476, 10°, Santiago
Telephone: +56 2 671 7149/672 7062
Fax: +56 2 699 3634/698 8945
Telex: 340958
E-mail: asocdeba.ncose001@chilnet.cl
Chief officers: Adolfo Rojas Gandulfo (President), Hernán Somerville Senn (Vice President), Gonzalo Valdés (Vice President), Edward Dreyfus (Vice President), Arturo Tagle Quiroz (General Manager)
Membership: banks and financial institutions

Chilean Books' Association
Cámara Chilena del Libro
Address: Avda Bernardo O'Higgins 1370, oficina 502, 13526 Santiago
Telephone: +56 2 698 9519/698 9226/672 4088
Fax: +56 2 698 9226/687 4271
E-mail: camlibro@reuna.cl or camarach.ilena018@chilnet.cl
Activities: collects statistics, information service
Chief officers: MR E Castillo (General Secretary), Carlos Cuneo Lommatzsch (General Manager)
Membership: bookshops, publishers, etc.

Chilean Construction Association

Cámara Chilena de la Construcción
Address: Marchant Pereira 10, 3° piso, Santiago
Telephone: +56 2 233 1131
Fax: +56 2 232 7600
E-mail: camara@mailnet.puc.cl
Web site: www.reuna.cl/camarach/cover.html
Year established: 1951
Activities: in close contact with the Universities, seminars and conferences, edition of a large number of publications which they distribute to its members and diverse authorities and academic entities throughout the country, among them videos (recorded during the Technologic Conferences)
Chief officers: Hernán Doren Lois (President), Blas Bellolio Rodriguez (General Manager)
Structure: 16 branches throughout the country
Membership: over 3,000 members: construction companies, industrials, suppliers, estate agents, all professionals related to the sector
Publications:
• Boletín Estadístico (Statistical Bulletin): *monthly summaries of the activities of the institution, statistical information covering the construction sector and other sectors at a national level - monthly*
• Boletín Tecnológico- BIT (Technological Bulletin): *innovation and technological transference of materials related to the sector - three times a year*
• Catálogo Chileno de la Construcción (Chilean Construction Catalog): *5 volummes with aprox 1800 pages describing existing materials of the country, updated every year enclosing new products related to the sector - annual*
• Catastro de Infraestructura Sanitaria (Sanitary Infrastructure Compilation): *book related to the sector's activities*
• Legislación completa sobre "Leasing Habitacional" (Lease Holders' Legislation): *book related to the sector's activities*
• Reglamento de Instalaciones Domiciliarias de Agua Potable y
Alcantarillado (Regulations of Water and Sewage Installations): *book related to the sector's activities*
Notes: member of the Confederación de la Producción y el Comercio de Chile (Chilean Production and Trade Confederation) and of the Federación Interamericana de la Industria de la Construcción (Interamerican Construction Industry Federation), based in Mexico email:camara@xxxxx.cl

Chilean Direct Sales Association

Cámara de Venta Directa de Chile
Address: Casilla No. 16427 - Correo Providencia, Apoquindo No. 4240, Santiago
Telephone: +56 2 246 7755
Chief officers: Carlos Hurtado R (President)

Chilean Egg Producers' Association

Asociación de Productores de Huevos de Chile
Address: Av Providencia 187, piso 4, Santiago
Telephone: +56 2 204 4440
Fax: +56 2 204 4440

Chilean Estate Agents' Association (COPROCH)

Asociación Gremial de Corredores de Propiedades de Chile
Address: Avda. Providencia No. 2019, Oficina 41A, Santiago
Telephone: +56 2 233 3139/242 8089/242 8797/8
Fax: +56 2 233 3139/232 7209
E-mail: coproch.copr001@chilnet.cl
Chief officers: Roger de Barbieri O (President), Carlos Aviles P (Vice President), Carlos Bravo G (Secretary General)
Membership: estate agents

Chilean Franchising Association

Asociación de Franchising de Chile
Address: Hernando Aguirre 162, oficina 904, Providencia, Santiago
Telephone: +56 2 234 4189
Fax: +56 2 334 5719
E-mail: 70501.2671@compuserve.com

Chilean Fresh Fruit Association

Address: P.O. Box 2410, c/o Caryl Saunders Associates, Sausalito, CA 94966-2410
Telephone: +56 415 331 8313
Fax: +56 415 331 1258
E-mail: Chilefruit@aol.com
Web site: www.fruitnet.com/FruitnetDirectoryFR.html
Activities: The association manages the advertising, merchandising and public relations activities in North America for the exporters and growers of fresh fruits from Chile

Chilean Fruit Exporters' Association (ASOEXPOR)

Asociación de Exportadores de Fruta de Chile
Address: Casilla 10096, Correo 21, Cruz del Sur 133, Piso 2, Las Condes, Santiago
Telephone: +56 2 206 6604
Fax: +56 2 206 4163
E-mail: asoex@netup.cl or asocdeex.porta001@chilnet.cl
Web site: nexus.chilenet.cl/export/index.html
Activities: collects export statistics on the industry
Chief officers: Ronald Brown Fernández (President), Sergio Barrios Freire (Vice President), Juan Paez Ceroni (Foreign Trade Manager)
Membership: 40 fruit and vegetable exporters
Publications:
• Informative Bulletin (Boletín Informativo): *news on the industry and the activities of the association, legislation, export statistics - quarterly*

Chilean Fruit Producers' Federation (FEDEFRUTA)

Federación de Productores de Fruta de Chile AG
Address: San Antonio 220 - oficina 301/302, Santiago
Telephone: +56 2 632 5224/ 632 5274
Fax: +56 2 632 7322/ 632 7327
E-mail: fedefrut.a001@chilnet.cl
Membership: fruit producers

Chilean Insurance Brokers' Association

Asociación de Aseguradores de Chile AG
Address: Casilla 2630, Correo Central, Moneda 920, piso 10, of 1002, Santiago
Telephone: +56 2 696 7431/5178/672 1172/671 4668
Fax: +56 2 698 4820
Chief officers: Francisco Serquiera Abarca (President), Gastón Aguirre Silva (Vice President), Jorge Cañas Suárez (General Manager)
Membership: insurance companies

Chilean Plastics Manufacturers' Association (ASPILA)

Asociación Gremial de Industriales del Plástico de Chile
Address: Casilla 14610, Correo 21, Avda Pedro de Valdivia 1481, Providencia, Santiago
Telephone: +56 2 223 4546/205 2231
Fax: +56 2 223 4546
Telex: 340412
Chief officers: Gastón Burgos Ilufi (President), Ricardo Schwartz Racz (Vice President), Julio Compagnon Ahumada (Vice President), Sergio Ramírez Muñoz (General Manager), Ledda Aste Escobar (Treasurer)
Membership: plastics processors
Notes: other office: Av A Bello 2777, oficina 50, Santiago/ Tel (2) 203 33 42/3

Chilean Poultry Producers' Association
Asociación de Productores Avícolas de Chile
Address: Dr C Charlín 1468, Santiago
Telephone: +56 2 236 0240

Chilean Refrigeration and Climatisation Association
Cámara Chilena de Refrigeración y Climatización
Address: Casilla 14771, Avda. Salvador No. 716, Piso 3,
Santiago
Telephone: +56 2 204 7517
Fax: +56 2 204 7517
Chief officers: Hector Fernandez Perez (President)

Chilean Retailing Association
Cámara de Comercio Minorista de Chile AG
Address: Casilla 9004, Correo Central, Santo Domingo 1845,
Santiago
Telephone: +56 2 698 1224/7230
Chief officers: E Llaneza Jove (President), S Cortés Cortés
(Vice President)
Membership: retailers from all sectors

Chilean Salmon and Trout Farmers' Association
Asociación de Productores de Salmón y Trucha de Chile AG
Address: Casilla 453, C de Casillas, Avda Libertador B
O'Higgins 949, of 2502, Santiago
Telephone: +56 2 699 2825/696 8899/697 3326
Fax: +56 2 671 3765
Year established: 1986
Activities: all members' products display the association's
mandatory seal of quality; statistics, marketing, international
food and seafood shows; daily reports for members on supply,
demand and price fluctuations around the world
Chief officers: Arnoldo Macaya Moreno (President), Alfonso
Muena Rodriguez (Vice President)
Membership: 46 salmon and trout breeding companies

**Chilean Small and Medium-Sized Industries'
Association (AMPICH)**
Asociación Gremial de la Mediana y Pequeña Industria de Chile
Address: Avda República 371, Santiago
Telephone: +56 2 689 6363/689 4260
Fax: +56 2 689 4260
E-mail: asocgrem.delam001@chilnet.cl
Chief officers: Chaquib Sufán Aidar (President), Leonardo
Opazo Troncoso (Vice President)
Membership: small and medium-sized businesses

Chilean Society of Information Technology Companies
Asociación Chilena de Empresas de Tecnología de Información
Address: Avenida Santa María nº 0508, Santiago
Telephone: +56 2 735 5754/55
Fax: +56 2 735 5754/55
Chief officers: Osvaldo Schaerer (President), Raúl Ciudad
(Vice President), Alejandro Vallarino (Secretary)
Membership: information technology companies

Chilean Spirits Manufacturers' Association
Asociación Gremial de Licoristas de Chile
Address: Av Gral Bustamante 130 - oficina 204, Santiago
Telephone: +56 2 222 6603
Fax: +56 2 634 3662
E-mail: asocgrem.ialde005@chilnet.cl
Year established: 1951

Chilean Tourism Agencies' Association (ACHET)
Asociación Chilena de Empresas de Turismo
Address: Casilla 3402, Correo Central, Moneda 973, oficina
647, Santiago
Telephone: +56 2 696 5677/699 2140/695 3888/598 5677
Fax: +56 2 699 4245
Telex: 242114 ACHET CL
E-mail: asocchil.enade002@chilnet.cl
Chief officers: Onofre Urrutia Blanco (President), Luis
Enrique Besa (Vice President)
Membership: companies in the tourism industry

Chilean Tourism Confederation
Confederación Gremial del Comercio Detallista y Turismo de
Chile AG
Address: Merced 380 , oficina. 74, Santiago
Telephone: +56 2 639 5719
Fax: +56 2 638 0338
E-mail: confeder.acion007@chilnet.cl
Chief officers: Marco Veragua Contreras (General Manager)

Chilean Wood Corporation
Corporación Chilena de la Madera
Address: Agustinas 814, oficina 407, Santiago
Telephone: +56 2 633 5728/638 4194
Fax: +56 2 639 7485
E-mail: corma.corm001@chilnet.cl
Chief officers: Eladio Susaeta Sainz de San Pedro
(Chairman), Giamberto Bisso Capurro (General Manager)
Membership: 400 members

Confederation of Manufacturers and Traders
Confederación de la Producción y del Comercio
Address: Casilla 9984, Monseñor Nuncio S Saenz de Villalba
182, of 507, Santiago
Telephone: +56 2 333 690/231 9764
Fax: +56 2 231 9808
E-mail: procomer@entelchile.net
Chief officers: Walter Riesco Salvo (President), Cristian
Pizarro Allard (General Manager), José Antonio Guzman Matta
(Legal Advisor), Maria Gatica Cortes (Accounts Manager)
Membership: manufacturers and traders
Notes: e-mail: confeder.acion003@chilnet.cl

**Food Processing and Agricultural Industry Federation
(FEPACH Ltda)**
Federación de Procesadores de Alimentos y Agroindustriales de
Chile Ltda
Address: Ahumada 254, oficina 1209, Santiago
Telephone: +56 2 699 5400
Fax: +56 2 696 3506
E-mail: asaco.asac001@chilnet.cl

Footwear Manufacturers' Trade Association (ASINCAL)
Asociación de Industriales del Calzado de Chile
Address: Casilla 14209, Correo 21, Teatinos 248, oficina 23,
Santiago
Telephone: +56 2 672 4527
Chief officers: Maximiliano Obach González (President), Raul
Urbina Pugin (Manager)

Fruit Traders' and Grocers' Association
Asociación de Comerciantes en Frutos del País y Abarrotes AG
Address: Huérfanos 1117, oficina 734, Santiago
Telephone: +56 2 696 7755/696 2878
Fax: +56 2 696 2878
Chief officers: Jorge León Parro (President), José Garcia
Baretto (Vice President), Lorenzo Antillo Escobar (Treasurer),

Jorge Goles Papic (General Manager)
Membership: fruit sellers and grocers

National Chamber of the Automobile Industry (CAVEM)

Cámara Nacional de Comercio Automotriz
Address: Huelén 132, Dpto 2, Providencia, Santiago
Telephone: +56 2 223 0294/235 6095/2741793
Fax: +56 2 223 0294
E-mail: cavemag.cave001@chilnet.cl
Chief officers: Omar Oyarce Caviedes (President), Alberto Lanas Bunster (Vice President)

National Corporation of Exporters

Corporación Nacional de Exportadores
Address: Nueva Tajamar 481, oficina 101, Providencia, Santiago
Telephone: +56 2 339 7003
Fax: +56 2 339 7001
Activities: promotes exports and Chile in general
Chief officers: Cristóbal Valdés (President)
Membership: 22 trade associations and companies from the following sectors: agriculture, forestry, fishing, manufacturing, chemicals, mining and services, representing more than 90% of private exporters in the country
Publications:
• Chile Review (Revisón de Chile): *general information about Chile, reports on exports, economy and investment - annual*

National Importers' Association

Asociación Nacional de Importadores AG
Address: Santa Lucía 302, piso 5, Santiago
Telephone: +56 2 639 7859
Fax: +56 2 639 7859
E-mail: asocnaci.onald007@chilnet.cl
Chief officers: William McKendrick Bastien (President), Florencio Ortúzar (1st Vice President), Hernán Pizarro (2nd Vice President)

National Press Association (ANP)

Asociación Nacional de Prensa
Address: Bandera 84, oficina 408, Santiago
Telephone: +56 2 696 6431/698 7699
Fax: +56 2 698 7699
E-mail: asocnaci.onald009@chilnet.cl
Chief officers: Carlos Raúl Lamas (President), Jorge Babarovic Novakovic (1st Vice President), Roberto Fuenzalida González (2nd Vice President), Fernando Silva Vargas (Secretary General)
Membership: newspaper proprietors

Pork Producers' Association (ASPROCER)

Asociación Gremial de Productores de Cerdos de Chile
Address: Manuel Rodriguez 83, Santiago
Telephone: +56 2 695 7725
Fax: +56 2 696 6616
E-mail: asprocer.aspr001@chilnet.cl

Rubber Industries Association (ASIGOM)

Asociación Gremial de Industriales de la Goma
Address: Cóndor 968, piso 2 - oficina A, Santiago
Telephone: +56 2 639 3789
Fax: +56 2 633 1594
E-mail: asigom@cmet.net
Web site: www.altavoz.cl/asigom/
Web site notes: membership directory, trade fair information for October '97
Year established: 1956
Activities: manufactured products for mining, construction, footwear, automotive sector, capital goods manufacturers and

business graphics
Chief officers: Alejandro Miralles Guthmann (President), Alvaro Barriga Allende (Vice President), José Campos (General Manager), Patricio Besnier Caceres (Treasurer)
Membership: 72 companies: industrial companies, suppliers, rubber companies

Small and Medium-Size Industrials' Association (CORMETAL)

Asociación Gremial de Medianos y Pequeños Industriales
Address: Av Ejército Libertador 426, Santiago
Telephone: +56 2 671 0873
Fax: +56 2 671 0873
E-mail: cormetal.corm001@chilnet.cl

Wine Bottlers' and Exporters' Association

Asociación de Exportadores y Embotelladores de Vinos AG
Address: Avda Manuel Montt 037 - oficina 308-309, Providencia, Santiago
Telephone: +56 2 235 1812/2205
Fax: +56 2 235 7105
E-mail: asocdeex.porta002@chilnet.cl
Chief officers: Alfonso Larrain Santa Maria (President), Alfonso Undurraga McKenna (Vice President), Elizabeth Díaz Retamal (Executive Secretary)
Membership: wine merchants and exporters

CHINA

Article Numbering Centre of China

Address: 9830, East Gate No. 46, Yuzhongxili Dewai, Xicheng District, Beijing 10009
Telephone: +86 10 620 24528
Fax: +86 10 620 24523
E-mail: ancc@public3.bta.net.cn

Association of Radio and TV Equipment Industry of China

Address: 12/F, Tongguang Mansion, Nongzhanguan South Road, Beijing 100026
Telephone: +86 10 650 01144
Fax: +86 10 650 05233
Year established: 1986
Activities: organises technological exchanges, cooperation and implementation; provides consulting services and organises exhibitions of the industry and related products

China Arts and Crafts Association

Address: 101 Fuxingmenwai Street, Beijing 100031
Telephone: +86 10 660 13020
Fax: +86 10 660 13029
Year established: 1988
Activities: promotes economic relations among the trades and corporations; organises international exchange activities and exhibitions at home and abroad; provides consulting services and personnel training
Chief officers: De Shang Dai (General Manager)

China Association for Medical Equipment Industry

Address: A-38, Beilishilu Road, Xicheng District, Beijing 100810
Telephone: +86 10 683 13344
Fax: +86 10 683 15675
Activities: provides domestic and international economic and marketing information; improves clinical and medical apparatus standards and management standards
Chief officers: Jia Jing Xu (General Manager)

China Association of Automotive Enterprises

Address: 46 Fucheng Road, Beijing 100036
Telephone: +86 10 681 23210
Fax: +86 10 681 27562
Year established: 1990
Activities: provides consulting services; promotes exchange and cooperation within the industry; studies and investigates general and specific policies related to the industry
Chief officers: Bo Luo Teng (General Manager)

China Association of Enterprises with Foreign Investment

Address: 14 Dongzhimen Nandajie, Beijing 100027
Telephone: +86 10 650 01188
Fax: +86 10 650 19361
Activities: develops the foreign investment market and offers consulting and information related to investment outside China
Chief officers: Qun Rong Zhu (Director)

China Association of Fragrance, Flavour and Cosmetics Industries

Address: 6 Chang'an E. Street, Beijing 100740
Telephone: +86 10 652 29449
Fax: +86 10 652 41619
Year established: 1984
Activities: undertakes investigation, statistics and forecasts of the industry; formulates quality standards and organises quality grading
Chief officers: Ding Yi Zhang (Chairman)
Publications:
• Statistics (China Association of Fragrance, Flavour and Cosmetics Industries): *the Association regularly compiles statistics on the Chinese cosmetics sector. Detailed statistics in Chinese with some basic data available in English - regular*

China Association of Industrial Economics

Address: 9 Xi Huang Cheng Gen Nan Jie, Xicheng District, Beijing 100032
Telephone: +86 10 660 34061
Fax: +86 10 660 13887
Year established: 1986
Activities: studies policies concerning industrial development and provides information to enterprises and trades; coordinates the activities of different industrial trade associations; promotes economic ties among regions and enterprises
Chief officers: Da Qi Dong (Director)

China Association of the Electronic Equipment Industry

Address: Room 109, 23 Shijingshan Road, Beijing 100043
Telephone: +86 10 688 65302
Fax: +86 10 688 65302
Year established: 1986
Activities: provides consulting services; undertakes international and domestic technological exchange; participates in formulating technological standards
Chief officers: Yuan Chang Dong (General Manager)

China Association of the Electronic Vacuum Industry

Address: A-65, Fuxinglu, Beijing 100036
Telephone: +86 10 682 11166
Fax: +86 10 682 17517
Year established: 1988
Activities: provides technical consultation; organises technical exchange
Chief officers: Qing He Li (General Manager)

China Audio Industries' Association

Address: 1442 Hongqiao Road, Shanghai 200335
Telephone: +86 21 627 58236
Fax: +86 21 627 58236
Year established: 1983
Activities: organises exchange of technology and management; strengthens the relations between related trade at home and abroad; improves product technology and standards of quality in the industry

China Automotive Engineering Association

Address: 46 Fucheng Road, Beijing 100036
Telephone: +86 10 681 27156
Fax: +86 10 632 63605
Chief officers: Xing Yie Zhang (Director)

China Bakery Products Industry Association

Address: 22 Fuwaida Street B, Beijing 100833
Telephone: +86 10 683 96646
Fax: +86 10 652 38090
Chief officers: Xiu Zheng Zhang (Director)

China Batteries' Association

Address: 6 Dongchangan Street, Beijing 100740
Telephone: +86 10 652 28520
Fax: +86 10 652 28520
Chief officers: Jing Zhong Wang (Director)

China Beverage Industry Association

Address: 22 Fuwaida Street B, Beijing 100833
Telephone: +86 10 685 81755
Fax: +86 10 685 81756
Chief officers: Qi Lu Qi (Director)

China Bicycle Industry Association

Address: 6 Dong Changan Street, Beijing 100740
Telephone: +86 10 651 24336
Fax: +86 10 651 21876
Chief officers: Hai Yan Guo (Director)

China Brewery Industry Association

Address: 34 Fuwaida Street, Xicheng Dist., Beijing 100833
Telephone: +86 10 685 75069
Fax: +86 10 685 75069
Chief officers: Shao Lin Geng (Director)

China Canned Food Industry Association

Address: 22 Fuwaida Street B, Beijing 100833
Telephone: +86 10 683 96648
Fax: +86 10 683 96661
Chief officers: Zhong Kang Yang (Director)

China Ceramic Industry Association

Address: 6 Dongchangan Street, Beijing 100740
Telephone: +86 10 651 24684
Fax: +86 10 651 24672
Chief officers: Gong du Yan (Director)

China Chamber of Medicine and Health Products Importers and Exporters

Address: 12 Jianguomenwai Street, Beijing 100022
Telephone: +86 10 650 01022
Fax: +86 10 650 01150
Year established: 1988
Activities: organises trade activities; coordinates prices,

markets and clients; promotes cooperation and exchange; offers consulting services and personnel training

China Clocks and Watches Industry Association
Address: 6 Dongchangan Street, Beijing 100740
Telephone: +86 10 651 22650
Fax: +86 10 651 22650
Chief officers: Xia Ling Zhang (Director)

China Commercial Enterprises Management Association
Address: 45 Fuxingmennei Da Street, Beijing 100801
Telephone: +86 10 660 95626
Fax: +86 10 661 79897
Chief officers: Jian Ming Zhang (Director)

China Commission Trade Society
Address: 47 Heping Road, Heping District, Tianjin 300021
Telephone: +86 22 2735 3296
Fax: +86 22 2735 1541
Activities: promotes the development of China's commission trade industry. Disseminates market information and sponsors trade fairs and sales exhibitions
Chief officers: Huan Zhe Geng (Director)

China Daily Merchandise Industry Association
Address: 6 Dongchangan Street, Beijing 100740
Telephone: +86 10 651 22394
Fax: +86 10 651 22394
Chief officers: Guo Wei Yin (Director)

China Dairy Federation
Address: 75 Gulou Xidajie, Xicheg District, Beijing 100009
Telephone: +86 10 640 31310
Fax: +86 10 640 33841
Publications:
• Dairy Statistics: *an annual review of the Chinese dairy sector with data on specific dairy products. Figures included on production, trade, sales - annual*

China Dairy Products Industry Association
Address: 22 Fuwaida Street B, Beijing 100833
Telephone: +86 10 683 96646
Fax: +86 10 652 75330
Chief officers: Kun Gang Song (Director)

China Department Store Commercial Association
Address: 45 Fuxingmennei Da Street, Beijing 100801
Telephone: +86 10 660 24633
Fax: +86 10 660 23998
Chief officers: Zhan Yong Li (Director)

China Domestic Electrical Appliances Association
Address: 45 Fuxingmennei Da Street, Beijing 100801
Telephone: +86 10 660 32533
Fax: +86 10 660 32533
Chief officers: Zhong Bin Gong (Director)

China Electrical Industry Association
Address: 26 Yuetan S. Street, Beijing 100825
Telephone: +86 10 685 31167
Fax: +86 10 685 31167
Year established: 1989
Activities: promotes economic and technological exchange among enterprises
Chief officers: Da Zheng You (Director)

China Exhibition Centres' Association
Address: 135 Xizhimenwai Dajie, Beijing 100044
Telephone: +86 10 683 16677
Fax: +86 10 683 52716
Activities: promotes the exhibitions industry. Provides consulting services and educational programmes
Chief officers: Shao Ji Shen (Director)

China Feather Industry Association
Address: 6 Dongchangan Street, Beijing 100740
Telephone: +86 10 652 37296
Fax: +86 10 652 73201
Chief officers: Yong Xu (Director)

China Fermentation Industry Association
Address: 11 Fuwaida Street A, Beijing 100037
Telephone: +86 10 685 84959
Fax: +86 10 685 84959
Chief officers: Xin You (Director)

China Food Additives Industry Association
Address: 32 Dongxiaoyun Road, Sanhuanqiao, Beijing 100027
Telephone: +86 10 646 72233
Fax: +86 10 646 17853
Chief officers: Xin You (Director)

China Food and Packaging Machinery Industry Association
Address: 26 Yuetan Nanjie, Xicheng District, Beijing 100045
Telephone: +86 10 685 23242
Fax: +86 10 685 33077
Year established: 1989
Activities: formulates standards for the industry; organises international and domestic exhibitions; provides consulting services and training

China Food Marketing and Development Committee
Address: 45 Fuxingmennei Da Street, Beijing 100801
Telephone: +86 10 660 95027
Fax: +86 10 660 13385
Chief officers: Xiao Pei Xiang (Director)

China Furniture Industry Association
Address: Building No. 6, Dixingju, Ande Road, Andingmenwai, Beijing 100011
Telephone: +86 10 642 60244
Fax: +86 10 642 60544
Chief officers: Qing Wen Jia (Director)

China Glass Association
Address: 6 Dongchangan Street, Beijing 100740
Telephone: +86 10 652 48399
Fax: +86 10 652 48399
Chief officers: Shu Feng Ma (Director)

China Hardware and Chemical Industry Association
Address: 45 Fuxingmennei Da Street, Beijing 100 801
Telephone: +86 10 660 32533
Fax: +86 10 660 32533
Chief officers: Zhong Bin Gong (Director)

China Household Electrical Appliances Association
Address: 6 Dongchang'anjie, Dongchang District, Beijing 100740

Telephone: +86 10 651 21567
Fax: +86 10 651 21567
Year established: 1988
Activities: promotes the household electrical appliance industry; seeks the development of advanced manufacturing and product technologies; establishes quality standards; fosters exchange with manufacturers in other countries; participates in national and international exhibitions and shows
Chief officers: Fu Zhong Liu (General Manager)

China Interior Decorating Association
Address: Building No. 6, Dixingju, Ande Road, Andimenwai, Beijing 100011
Telephone: +86 10 642 60711
Fax: +86 10 652 60711
Chief officers: Quan Zai (Director)

China International Trade Association
Address: 2 East Chang'an Avenue, Beijing 100731
Telephone: +86 10 652 41816
Fax: +86 10 651 28257
Activities: promotes China's international trade. Provides information and educational programmes
Chief officers: Deng Li Gao (Director)

China Leather Industry Association
Address: 6 Dongchangan Street, Beijing 100740
Telephone: +86 10 652 64589
Fax: +86 10 652 31698
Chief officers: Shu Hua Zhang (Director)

China Leisure Goods and Stationery Association
Address: 6 Dongchangan Street, Beijing 100740
Telephone: +86 10 651 21122
Fax: +86 10 652 67873
Year established: 1990
Activities: provides consulting services; undertakes information exchange, personnel training and exhibitions; develops cooperation in the trade at home and abroad
Chief officers: Peng Cheng Xu (General Manager)

China Light Industry Enterprise Management Association
Address: 6 Dongchangan Street, Beijing 100740
Telephone: +86 10 651 22604
Fax: +86 10 651 22604
Chief officers: Zheng Yu (Director)

China Lighting Industry Association
Address: 6 Dongchangan Street, Beijing 100740
Telephone: +86 10 651 35872
Fax: +86 10 651 35872
Chief officers: Yao Zhang Zheng (Director)

China Marketing Promotion Association
Address: 45 Fuxingmennei Da Street, Beijing 100801
Telephone: +86 10 660 94504
Fax: +86 10 660 30199
Chief officers: Jing Ying Zhou (Director)

China Musical Instruments Industry Association
Address: 6 Dongchangan Street, Beijing 100740
Telephone: +86 10 651 22058
Fax: +86 10 651 22058
Chief officers: Hong Zheng Li (Director)

China National Association for Foreign Economic Relations and Trade
Address: 7 Liufang Beili, Xiangheyuan, Chaoyang District, Beijing 100028
Telephone: +86 10 640 81118
Chief officers: Xingqiao Zhang (President), Hong Jiang (Secretary General)

China Optical Goods Industry Association
Address: 6 Dongchangan Street, Beijing 100740
Telephone: +86 10 651 22084
Fax: +86 10 652 34376
Chief officers: Yun Yuan Xu (Director)

China Packaging and Printing Industry Association
Address: 22 Liulichang East Street, Xuanwu Dist., Beijing 100050
Telephone: +86 10 630 37488
Fax: +86 10 630 13945
Chief officers: Jian Du (Director)

China Packaging Technology Association
Address: 31 E Chang'an Avenue, Beijing 100005
Telephone: +86 10 652 46160
Fax: +86 10 651 24123
Publications:
• China Yearbook of Packaging: *although primarily a directory of the packaging industry, it also includes a statistical section with data on packaging market and industry trends - annual*

China Paper Industry Association
Address: 22 Fuwaida Street B, Beijing 100833
Telephone: +86 10 683 96636
Fax: +86 10 683 96633
Chief officers: Shi Liang Cheng (Director)

China Pen Making Industry Association
Address: 6 Dongchangan Street, Beijing 100740
Telephone: +86 10 651 24689
Fax: +86 10 651 24689
Chief officers: Chong He Zhang (Director)

China Plastics Industry Association
Address: 6 Dongchangan Street, Beijing 100740
Telephone: +86 10 651 22056
Fax: +86 10 652 25254
Chief officers: Zheng Ping Liao (Director)

China Porcelain Industry Association
Address: 6 Dongchangan Street, Beijing 100740
Telephone: +86 10 651 22138
Fax: +86 10 651 22138
Chief officers: Xia Ju Ying (Director)

China Refrigeration and Air Conditioning Industry Association (CRAA)
Address: No. 77 Bei Li Shi Street, Western District, Beijing 100044
Telephone: +86 10 834 3506
Fax: +86 10 834 3502
Chief officers: Song Guoqiang (Secretary General), He Yong Heng (Director of Foreign Affairs)

China Salt Industry Association

Address: 55 Taoranting Road, Beijing 100054
Telephone: +86 10 635 20042
Fax: +86 10 635 20894
Chief officers: Zhi Hua Dong (Director)

China Sewing Machine Industry Association

Address: 6 Dongchangan Street, Beijing 100740
Telephone: +86 10 652 42231
Fax: +86 10 651 35820
Chief officers: Cheng Kang Wang (Director)

China Silk Association

Address: Room 339 & 341, Building 3, 82 Donganmen Street, Beijing 100747
Telephone: +86 10 651 23338
Fax: +86 10 651 28685
Year established: 1986
Activities: conducts research; provides consulting services; strengthens international and domestic connections and cooperation within the trade
Chief officers: Zhuang Mu Wang (Director)

China Soaps and Detergents Industry Association

Address: 6 Dongahangas Street, Beijing 100740
Telephone: +86 10 651 21880
Fax: +86 10 651 21880
Chief officers: Yun Yan Wu (Director)

China Sugar Industry Association

Address: Dajue Hutong, Xicheng Dist., Beijing 100035
Telephone: +86 10 630 99952
Fax: +86 10 630 99515
Chief officers: Xue Zhi Lian (Director)

China Textile Federation

Address: 12 Dongchangan Street, 100742 Beijing
Telephone: +86 10 630 812 07
Fax: +86 10 651 295 45
Chief officers: Wen Ying Wu (Chairman)

China Tobacco Association

Address: 11 Hufang Road, Xuanwu Dist., Beijing 100052
Telephone: +86 10 635 33399
Chief officers: Dong Fen Qu (Director)

China Toothpaste Industry Association

Address: 6 Dongchangan Street, Beijing 100740
Telephone: +86 10 652 60062
Fax: +86 10 652 60062
Chief officers: Dian Yi Zhang (Director)

China Tourism Association

Address: A9 Jianguomennei Dajie, Beijing 100740
Telephone: +86 10 651 22907
Fax: +86 10 651 35383
Activities: promotes tourism in China. Fosters cooperation with tourism organisations in other countries. Organises education programmes and conducts research
Chief officers: Wei Yu Li (Director)

China Toy Industry Association

Address: 101 Fuxingmennei Da Street, Beijing 100085
Telephone: +86 10 660 13019
Fax: +86 10 660 13029
Chief officers: De Gao Dai (Director)

China Transportation and Communications Association

Address: 31 Dong Chang'an Street, Dongcheng District, Beijing 100005
Telephone: +86 10 670 29973
Fax: +86 10 670 29972
Telex: 22552 SEC CN
Year established: 1982
Activities: helps the government to coordinate different means of transportation; organises domestic and international economic and technological cooperation and exchanges on transportation; communications
Chief officers: De Rong Wang (Director)

Chinese Garment Association

Address: A9 Beisanhuan E. Road, Beijing 100028
Telephone: +86 10 642 39139
Fax: +86 10 642 39134
Activities: promotes the clothing industry; represents and protects members' interests; conducts survey and research programmes; fosters exchange with clothing producers in other countries
Chief officers: Zong Yao Yu (General Manager)

Chinese National Committee of the International Dairy Federation

Address: 337 Xuefu Road, Harbin 150086
Telephone: +86 451 666 1588
Fax: +86 451 667 7612
E-mail: mhuang@hope.hit.edu.cn
Chief officers: Mrs M. Huang (Secretary)

National Federation of New Shopping Arcades

Address: No. 290, Heping Road, Heping District, Tianjin
Telephone: +86 22 2670 4546
Fax: +86 22 2670 2378

COLOMBIA

Colombian Association of Air-conditioning and Refrigeration (ACAIRE)

Asociación Colombiana del Acondicionamiento y de la Refrigeración
Address: Calle 90 #13A-31, Oficina 405, Santafe de Bogota, D.C.
Telephone: +57 511 222 8419
Fax: +57 511 222 8470
Chief officers: Luis Bernardo Velez

Colombian Association of Banking and Finance Institutions (ASOBANCARIA)

Asociación Bancaria y de Entidades Financieras de Colombia
Address: Apdo Aéreo 13994, Carrera 9, 74-08 9 #17 - 01, 3°, Santafé de Bogotá
Telephone: +57 1 282 1066/341 1100/2813017/211 4087
Fax: +57 1 341 1161/211 9915/217 5594
Year established: 1936
Activities: economic, judicial and technical activities, finance information centre, regional committees, statistics, database of clients, annual Banking Convention, symposium on Financial Markets every 2 years
Chief officers: César González Muñoz (President), Mauricio Cabrera Galvis (President of board of Directors)
Membership: all banks, 17 financial corporations, 8 savings and buildings societies, 9 general deposit warehouses, 4 fiduciary societies, 1 pensions administrative society

Publications:
• Financial and Legal Bulletin
Notes: Other branch: P O Box 13994, Carrera 9 #74 - 08, piso 9, Santafé de Bogotá. Tel: 1 2114811. Fax: 1 2119915. Telex: 44300 ABC

Colombian Association of Construction (CAMALCO)
Cámara Colombiana de la Construcción
Address: Calle 70A #10-22, Santafé de Bogotá
Telephone: +57 1 217 0929/3130/210 4588
Fax: +57 1 211 9559/346 2287
Chief officers: Alberto Vasquez (President), Yolanda Azouth Roa (Secretary General)
Membership: construction companies

Colombian Auto Components Manufacturers' Association
Asociación Colombiana de Fabricación de Autopartes
Address: Carrera 10, 27-27 - oficina 1010, Bogotá
Telephone: +57 1 284 2409

Colombian Book Association
Cámara Colombiana del Libro
Address: Carrera 17A, nº 37-27/ 31, Bogotá
Telephone: +57 1 288 6188/0023
Fax: +57 1 287 3320
Chief officers: Mr G Arboleda Palacio (General Secretary), Mr J Buitrago (Director)

Colombian Cooperatives' Association (ASCOOP)
Asociación Colombiana de Cooperativas
Address: Apdo 11575, Transversal 29, 35 A-29, Bogotá
Telephone: +57 1 268 0450
Fax: +57 1 268 4230
Publications:
• Revista Colombiana Cooperativa

Colombian Federation of Edible Oils and Fats Manufacturers
Federación Colombiana de Fabricantes de Grasas y Aceites Comestibles
Address: Carrera 9 #74-08 - oficima 403, Bogotá
Telephone: +57 1 211 1285

Colombian Federation of Mango Producers (FEDEMANGO)
Federación Colombiana de Cultivadores de Mango
Address: Carrera7, #72-64, ofic 216, Santafé de Bogotá
Telephone: +57 1 310 1896
Fax: +57 1 235 5220

Colombian Flower Exporters' Association (ASOCOLFLORES)
Asociación Colombiana de Exportadores de Flores
Address: Apdo Aéreo 55151, Carrera 9A #90-53, Santafé de Bogotá
Telephone: +57 1 257 9311
Fax: +57 1 218 3693/3693
Membership: flower growers and exporters

Colombian Food Industry Association
Asociación Colombiana de Ingeniería de Alimentos
Address: Cra 50, nº 27-70 - oficina 6, 408 Santafé de Bogotá
Telephone: +57 1 221 7429
Fax: +57 1 410 1464

Colombian Hotel Association
Asociación Hotelera de Colombia
Address: Cotelco, Calle 61, 5-83, Bogotá
Telephone: +57 1 310 3583
Fax: +57 1 310 3509

Colombian Leather Producers' Association
Asociación Colombiana de Manufactureros del Cuero
Address: Carrera 4A #25C - 71, Santafé de Bogotá
Telephone: +57 1 281 6171/62/6602/6400
Fax: +57 1 281 6187/8995
Chief officers: Maria Angela Tavela (Executive Director), Mario Hernandez (President)
Membership: leatherworkers

Colombian Livestock Breeders' Association (FEDEGAN)
Federación Colombiana de Ganaderos
Address: Apdo Aéreo 9709, Carrera 14, No 36-65, Santafé de Bogotá, DC
Telephone: +57 1 245 3041/4010/6923
Fax: +57 1 232 7253/7153
Year established: 1963
Chief officers: José Raimundo Sojo Zambrano
Membership: ca. 350,000 cattle breeders

Colombian National Advertising Association (ANDA)
Asociación Nacional de Anunciantes de Colombia
Address: Apdo Aéreo 90565, Calle 98 #9-03, of 606/607, Santafé de Bogotá
Telephone: +57 1 218 2773/2931/35
Fax: +57 1 218 2294
Year established: 1979
Activities: conferences, forums, seminars, workshops, research
Chief officers: Luis Hernando Dueñas (President), Ana Patricia Villota (Vice President)
Membership: 85 companies advertising agencies
Publications:
• ANDA: *information on marketing, ethics, advertising, communication, includes interviews and company news*
Notes: member of International Union of Advertising Associations and the World Federation of Advertisers

Colombian Newspapers' Association (Andiarios)
Asociación de Diarios Colombianos
Address: Apdo Aéreo 13663, Calle 61, 5-20, Bogotá
Telephone: +57 1 211 4181/4450
Fax: +57 1 212 7894
Telex: 41261
Chief officers: María Isabel Silve Nigrinis (Excutive Director)
Membership: daily newspapers

Colombian Pharmaceutical Industries' Association (ASINFAR)
Asociación de Industrias Farmacéuticas Colombianas
Address: Calle 38, 8-62 - oficina 1002, Bogotá
Telephone: +57 1 285 6261/8629
Fax: +57 1 285 8894

Colombian Pharmaceutical Wholesalers' Association (FECOLDROGAS)
Federación Colombiana de Droguistas Farmacéuticos
Address: Carrera 19, nº 39B-68, Santafe de Bogota, D.C.
Telephone: +57 1 285 4524/4924
Fax: +57 1 285 4560

Colombian Plastics Industry (ACOPLASTICOS)
Asociación Colombiana de Industrias Plásticas
Address: Apdo Aéreo 29844, Calle 69 #5 - 33, Santafé de Bogotá
Telephone: +57 1 346 0655/249 3697/6997
Fax: +57 1 249 6997/283 6207/249 6997
Chief officers: Alfredo Frohlich (President), Hans U Steinhauser (Vice President)
Membership: plastics manufacturers and dealers

Colombian Publishing Industry Association
Cámara Colombiana de la Industria Editorial
Address: Carrera 17 A #37-27, Bogotá
Telephone: +57 1 288 6188
Fax: +57 1 287 3320

Colombian Retail Pharmacists' Association (ASOCOLDRO)
Asociacion Colombiana de Droguistas Detallistas
Address: 77071, Av Carrera 27A, 53A-33, Bogota
Telephone: +57 1 310 4936/312 6542/248 3370
Fax: +57 1 310 4469
Membership: retail chemists

Colombian Spirits Industries' Association (ACIL)
Asociación Colombiana de Industrias Licoreras
Address: PO Box 56529, Calle 72 #6-44, ofic 502, Santafé de Bogotá
Telephone: +57 1 211 0425/0306
Fax: +57 1 212 8318
Chief officers: Lucía Carmenta Mora (Director)
Membership: alcoholic drinks manufacturers

Colombian Textile Producers' Society (ASCOLTEX)
Asociación Colombiana de Productores Textiles
Address: Calle 72 no.9-55, oficina 903, Santafé de Bogotá
Telephone: +57 1 211 5887/212 6234
Fax: +57 1 210 3894
Chief officers: Marcos Jara (Secretary General)

Colombian Tobacco Exporters' Association (ASOTABACO)
Asociación Colombiana de Exportadores de Tabaco
Address: 89585, Calle 95 #11-51, of 404, Santafé de Bogotá
Telephone: +57 1 616 0890/218 7422/251 6
Fax: +57 1 218 8707
Membership: tobacco exporters

Colombian Travel and Tourism Agencies' Association
Asociación Colombiana de Agencias de Viajes y Turismo
Address: Carrera 21, 83-63, Bogotá
Telephone: +57 1 256 2290/610 7099/258 2290
Fax: +57 1 218 7103

Federation of Milk Producing Cooperatives (FEDECOLECHE)
Federación Colombiana de Cooperativas de Productores de Leche
Address: Apdo 466, Calle 26, 13 A- 23 P-5, Bogotá
Telephone: +57 1 282 5664/243 8897
Fax: +57 1 243 8347

National Association of Leather Products Manufacturers
Asociación Nacional de Manufactureros de Artículos de Cuero
Address: Carrera 4A, 25C-71 Ap 701, Bogotá
Telephone: +57 1 281 9183

National Cocoa Workers' Association (FEDECACAO)
Federación Nacional de Cacaoteros
Address: Apdo Aéreo 17736, Carrera 17, #30-39, Santafé de Bogotá DC
Telephone: +57 1 288 7288/7188/232 0806
Fax: +57 1 288 4424
Chief officers: Dr Miguel Uribe
Membership: cocoa growers

National Coffee Workers' Federation
Federación Nacional de Cafeteros de Colombia
Address: PO Box 3938, Calle 73 No 8-13, Santafé de Bogotá
Telephone: +57 1 217 0600/4074/0010
Fax: +57 1 217 1021/1306/7613/1048
Telex: 44723
Year established: 1927
Chief officers: J Cárdenas Gutierrez (President), H Uribe (Vice President)
Membership: 203,000 coffee processors and dealers
Notes: Other branches: Carrera 6 #13-46, Piso 13, Calí; Tel + 57 23 823256, Fax +57 23 831487, Calle 49 #50-21, Piso 13, Medellín Tel +57 4 511550, Fax + 57 4 2514623

National Colombian Coffee Exporters' Association
Asociación Nacional de Exportadores de Café de Colombia
Address: Calle 72 No 10-07, oficina 1101, Santafé de Bogotá
Telephone: +57 1 210 2181/2109/2072/2302
Fax: +57 1 210 2072
Year established: 1938
Chief officers: Gabriel Rosas Vega (President), Piedad Gómez Ramírez (Vice President), Roberto Junguito Bonet
Structure: private association
Membership: coffee exporters
Notes: Other branch: Carrera 7 #32-33, of 25-01, Santafé de Bogotá Tel: 1 2830669, Fax 1 2830699, Telex 44802

National Cotton Workers' Association
Federación Nacional de Algodoneros
Address: Apdo Aéreo 8632, Carrera 8A, No 15-73, 5°, Santafé de Bogotá, DC
Telephone: +57 1 234 3221/282 4116/411 7/4129
Fax: +57 1 283 3162
Telex: 44864
Year established: 1953
Chief officers: Antonio Albello Roca
Membership: 14,000 cotton growers
Notes: Cartagena branch: Calle 35 #88-05, Centro. Fax 53 646146, Barranquilla branch: Fax 58 319207, Girardot branch : Fax 834 26796, Zarzal branch: 2220 206523

National Exporters' Association (ANALDEX)
Asociación Nacional de Exportadores
Address: Apdo Aéreo 29812, Edificio Bachué, Oficina 902, Carrera 10, No 27-27, int 137, Santafé de Bogotá, DC
Telephone: +57 1 342 0788/284 6577/354
Fax: +57 1 284 6911/3237
E-mail: analdex@colomsat.net.co
Year established: 1971
Activities: advisors to national government, technical advice, analyses of economic conditions, promotion of trade fairs in Colombia and overseas
Chief officers: Ricardo Sala Gaitan (President), Jorge Ramirez Ocampo (Executive President)
Structure: non profit-making corporation
Membership: exporters
Publications:
● Export Guide-Colombian Exporters (La Guía de Comercio Exterior - Exportadores de Colombia): *information on members of the Association as well as general information on Colombia and Colombian exports*

National Financial Institutions' Association (ANIF)

Asociación Nacional de Instituciones Financieras
Address: Apdo Aéreo 29667, Calle 70A #7-86, Santa Fé de Bogotá
Telephone: +57 1 212 8200/832/188/312 4514
Fax: +57 1 235 5947
Year established: 1974
Activities: research, seminars, forums, conferences, annual assembly of members
Chief officers: Javier Fernández Riva (President), Andres Lancebaek Rueda (Vice President), Luis Carlos Sarmiento (President of council)
Membership: financial institutions
Publications:
• Carta Financiera: *financial news and information - bi-monthly*
• Guía Empresarial ANIF: *detailed macroeconomic information*
• Informe Macroeconómico Sectorial: *analyses of economic and socio-political situation, world economics, especially Venezuela, Mexico and Ecuador - 2 p.a.*
• Informe Semanal de ANIF: *analysis of most recent information - weekly*

National Industrialists' Association (ANDI)

Asociación Nacional de Industriales
Address: Apdo Aéreo 997, Edificio Coltejer, Calle 52, n° 47-48, pisos 4-8-9, Medellín
Telephone: +57 4 251 4444/511 1177
Fax: +57 4 251 8830/511 7575
Year established: 1944
Chief officers: Fabio Echeverri Coréa (President), Dra Magdalena Uribe Rivas
Membership: 756 industrial companies
Notes: Address in Bogotá: Carrera 13 #26-45, 6° piso, Santafé de Bogotá Tel: 1 2810600 / fax: 1 2813188

National Rice Growers' Association (Fedearroz)

Federación Nacional de Arroceros
Address: Apdo Aéreo 52772, Calle 72 # 13 - 23, 12° piso, Santafé de Bogotá
Telephone: +57 1 210 0911/210 0252
Fax: +57 1 255 0477/255 8843
Publications:
• Revista Arroz

National Traders' Federation (FENALCO)

Federacion Nacional de Comerciantes
Address: Apdo Aéreo 4405, Carrera 4 n° 19-85, 7° piso, Santafé de Bogotá
Telephone: +57 1 286 0600
Fax: +57 1 282 7573/3462287
Telex: 44706 FN CO
Year established: 1945
Activities: information service, assistance with marketing strategy, etc
Chief officers: Sabas Prefelt de la Vega (President)
Membership: 15,000 member companies
Publications:
• Anuario: *directory of members - annual*
• Avances del Comercio: *monthly*
• Boletín del Comercio Exterior: *fortnightly*
• Boletín FENALCO: *fortnightly*
• Comercio: *compiled from different bulletins from various regions - Bi-monthly*
• Informes de Labores: *annual*
Notes: Provides economic studies and perspectives for retailing businesses

Pasta Manufacturers' Federation

Federación Nacional de Fabricantes de Pastas Alimenticias
Address: Calle 14 # 12-50- oficina 501, Bogotá
Telephone: +57 1 342 8828

Pharmaceutical Product Manufacturers' Association (AFIDRO)

Asociación de Fabricantes de Productos Farmacéuticos
Address: Apdo Aéreo 5461, Transversal 6ª, No 27-10, 6° piso, Santafé de Bogotá, DE
Telephone: +57 1 334 1580/85
Fax: +57 1 334 6139

Soap and Detergent Manufacturers' Association (ANALJA)

Asociación Nacional de Jaboneros y Productores de Detergentes
Address: Apdo 4550, Carrera 7, 24-89 - oficina 1801, Bogotá
Telephone: +57 1 284 4162
Fax: +57 1 284 0649

COSTA RICA

Advertising Agencies' Association

Asociación de Agencias de Publicidad de Costa Rica
Address: Oficina 2, Restaurante Rio los Doce, 25m al este, Altos de Video, Hollywood, San José
Telephone: +506 234 9715
Fax: +506 234 9715
Chief officers: Mr. Dennis Aguiluz Milla (Executive Director)

Association of Representatives of Overseas Businesses, Distributors and Importers (CRECEX)

Cámara de Representantes de Casas Extranjeras, Distribuidores e Importadores
Address: Apdo 3738, 1000 San José, De McDonald's Plaza del Sol, Crta. a Curridabat 900 metros Sur, 25 metros oeste y 25 metros sur, Edificio Blanco, al lado izdo., San José
Telephone: +506 2 530 126/253 2964/224 6944
Fax: +506 2 342 557
E-mail: crecex@sol.racsa.co.cr
Year established: 1952
Activities: advice, national and international databases, mutual cooperation agreements with similar bodies in other countries, legal services; bilateral trade agreements with the Chambers of Commerce of: Romania, Hialea Latin (USA), London, Puerto Rico, Taipei, Zamora (Argentina), Peru, Mexico; seminars, training courses; statistical analysis
Chief officers: Marco Antonio Gómez Leiva (President), Walter Marín Levy (Executive Director), Jazmín Carpenter (Foreign Trade), Alvaro Chaves Chavarría (Secretary)
Structure: members' assembly, board of directors, council of directors, executive directors
Membership: 1,000 distributors, importers and representatives of foreign companies
Publications:
• Commercial Opportunities (Oportunidades Comerciales): *bulletin with details of overseas companies interested in establishing themselves in Costa Rica; advertisements of local companies - quarterly*
• CRECEX Official Guide (Guía Oficial Crecex): *information on Costa Rica's international trade, statistics, information about CRECEX's services to national and foreign companies, legislation, etc; directory of members - annual*
• Representative (El Representante): *bulletin with information on activities and achievements in CRECEX; articles on current affairs*

Automotive Businesses' Association
Cámara Costarricense de Empresas Automovilísticas y Similares
Address:
Telephone: +506 223 7343
Fax: +506 223 7343
Chief officers: Ms. Lilliana Aguilar Rojas (Executive Director)

Balanced Foods Manufacturers' Association
Cámara de Fabricantes de Alimentos Balanceados
Address: Carrera San Rafael Heredia, San José
Telephone: +506 293 0191
Fax: +506 293 0191
Chief officers: Mr. Miguel Rodríguez (Executive Director)

Car Components Importers' Association
Asociación de Importadores de Partes de Coches
Address:
Telephone: +506 222 8168
Fax: +506 222 8168
Chief officers: Mr. Jorge Enrique Peña (Executive Director)

Cars and Machinery Importers' Association
Asociación de Importadores de Coches y Maquinaría
Address: De la Esquina Noreste de la Corte 25, Norte, San José
Telephone: +506 222 5513
Fax: +506 233 5432/223 6173
Chief officers: Mr. Julio Barquero Salazar (Executive Director)

Clothing and Textiles Industries' Association (CATECO)
Cámara de Industrias Textiles y de Confección
Address: Apdo 1512, BO La California, 1002 Paseo Estud, San José
Telephone: +506 253 5936
Fax: +506 225 1078
Chief officers: Ms Gabriela Lobo (Executive Director)

Coffee Processing Plants' Association
Cámara Nacional de Plantas Procesadoras de Café
Address:
Telephone: +506 221 8207
Fax: +506 222 9936
Chief officers: Mr. Joaquín Valverde Berrocal (Executive Director)

Costa Rica National Chamber of Tourism (CANATUR)
Cámara Nacional de Turismo de Costa Rica
Address: Apdo 828, Oficinas Centrales, 200 EITAN Carrera Zapote, San José
Telephone: +506 234 6222
Fax: +506 253 8102
E-mail: Canatur@tourism.co.cr or Canatur@sol.rasca.co.cr
Web site: www.toruism.co.cr/canatur
Activities: Tourist Information Centre -CIT- with important data on tourist development, both in the country and worldwide; organises the National Tourism Congress (biannual);
Chief officers: Ms María Martha Calvo (Executive Director)
Membership: airlines, hotels, restaurants, travel agencies, media companies, car rental companies, entertainment companies, transport companies

Costa Rican Association of Industries
Cámara de Industrias de Costa Rica
Address: Apdo 1003, Avda 6, Calles 13 y 15, 1000 San José
Telephone: +506 256 2826
Fax: +506 222 1007
E-mail: camind@sol.racsa.co.cr

Web site: www.cicr.or.cr
Year established: 1943
Activities: country profiles, export guides, information on fairs and conventions, market profiles, statistics, legal and technical advice, chamber credit card, etc
Chief officers: Samuel Yankelewitz Berger (President), José León Desanti, Gabriel González Fonseca (Vice Presidents), Ms.Licda Mayi Antillón Guerrero (Executive Director), Miguel Schyfter (Secretary), Marco Vinicio Ruiz (Treasurer)
Membership: 600 national associations and organizations: plastics, metals, automotives, coffee, transport, clothing, knitwear, pharmaceuticals, manufacturing, food, industry, textiles, graphics
Publications:
● Bulletin (Agenda Industrial): *information on new legislation, economic indicators, chamber's activities, studies and research, industrial news - monthly*
● Business Investigation: Industrial Sector (Encuesta Coyuntural de Negocios: Sector Industrial): *statistcal analysis of the industrial sectors in Costa Rica, prospects and development of the industry - quarterly*
● Industrial Directory (Guía Industrial): *general members' profiles, maps, economic reports, statistics - annual*
● Industry Magazine (Revista Industria): *current affairs, economic reports and analysis - bi-monthly*

Costa Rican Exporters' Association (CADEXCO)
Cámara de Exportadores de Costa Rica
Address: Apdo Postal 213-2010 San José, Oficentro la Virgen #2, Pavas, Costa Rica
Telephone: +506 296 4485/231 7366
Fax: +506 296 4684
E-mail: cadebid@sol.racsa.co.cr
Web site: www.cadexco.or.cr
Web site notes: list of Costa Rican export products and search form for suppliers of specific products
Year established: 1981
Activities: training seminars, technical assistance programme, commercial promotion activities, training, data-base, trade fairs
Chief officers: Rodolfo Castro (President), Ms Gabriela Sánchez P (Executive Director)
Membership: Costa Rican exporting companies

Dairy Products Manufacturers' Association
Cámara Nacional de Fabricantes de Productos Lácteos
Address:
Telephone: +506 253 5720
Fax: +506 253 6573
Chief officers: Mr. Erick Montero V (Executive Director)

Flexible Packaging Producers' Association
Asociación de Fabricantes de Envases Flexibles de Costa Rica
Address:
Telephone: +506 221 7442
Fax: +506 272 0214
Chief officers: Mr. Numa Estrada (Executive Director)

Food Industry Association
Cámara Costarricense de la Industria Alimentaria
Address: Apdo 7097, 1000 San José, Los Yoses, 75 m sur del Restaurante Río, San José
Telephone: +506 234 0966/234 1127
Fax: +506 225 0901/234 6783
Chief officers: Mr. Erick Quirós Quirós (Executive Director)

Hotels and Related Businesses' Association
Asociación Costaricensa de Hoteles y Empresas Relacionadas
Address: 50 Mts. Norte de Sterling Prods., La Paulina de Mdec, San José

Telephone: +506 253 3086/2246572
Fax: +506 224 6572
Activities: statistics and analysis of the sector, information available to the members
Chief officers: Manuel Bustamante (President), Luis Diego Echeverría (Executive Director)
Membership: over 100 hotels
Publications:
• Bulletin (Boletín): *general information on the industry - fortnightly*

Independent Banana Producers' Association
Asociación de Productores Independientes de Bananas
Address: Apdo 4642, 1000 San José
Telephone: +506 224 1130
Fax: +506 253 6027
Activities: collects statistics on production area, exports, importing countries, productivity, consumption, etc.
Chief officers: Mr Víctor E. Herrera (President), Mr Luis Umaña Aguilar (Executive Director)
Membership: 80 banana plantations
Publications:
• ANAPROBAN Bulletin (Boletín ANAPROBAN): *monthly*
• ANAPROBAN Magazine (Revista ANAPROBAN): *news and opinion articles on the sector, association's activities, statistics - quarterly*

Melon Producers' and Exporters' Association
Cámara Nacional de Productores y Exportadores de Melones
Address:
Telephone: +506 443 2454
Fax: +506 443 2276
Chief officers: Mr. Claudio Zumbado (Executive Director)

Mountain and Fruit Producers' Association
Asociación de Productores de Mora y Frutales de Altura
Address: Tejar del Guarco, Cartago, San José
Telephone: +506 5 522 769
Fax: +506 5 522 769

National Association of Banana Producers'
Cámara Nacional de Productores de Plátanos
Address:
Telephone: +506 222 7891
Fax: +506 233 1268
Chief officers: Mr. Alejandro Bejarano (Executive Director)

Restaurants and Affiliated Businesses' Association
Cámara Costarricense de Restaurantes y Empresas Relacionadas
Address:
Telephone: +506 283 2579
Fax: +506 283 2580
Chief officers: Mr. Juan Carlos Delgado (Executive Director)

Sugar Processing Industries' Association
Cámara de Industrias Azucareras
Address: Calle 3, entre Avda Central y 1ª, San José
Telephone: +506 221 2103
Fax: +506 222 1358
Chief officers: Ms. Virginia Chavarría (Executive Director), Edgar Mata (Secretary)

Travel Agencies' Association (ACAV)
Asociación Costarricense de Agencias de Viaje
Address: Apdo 7182, 1000 San José, Edifico Edificio Teresa, Del Hotel Aurola Holiday Inn, 100 Norte, 50 Oeste y 25 Norte, San José

Telephone: +506 233 9751/257 3285
Fax: +506 233 2921
Activities: promotes the Costa Rican travel industry, public relations, training, seminars, advertising and marketing, link to national and international bodies
Chief officers: Juan Manuel Borloz (Executive Director)
Membership: 100 travel agencies and tourism related enterprises
Publications:
• INFOCAV Newsletter (Boletín INFOCAV): *opinion articles, news and tourism related matters, information about the activities of the Association - quarterly*

Union of Costa Rican Chambers and Associations of Private Companies (UCCAEP)
Unión Costarricense de Cámaras y Asociaciones de la Empresa Privada
Address: Apdo 539, 1002 Paseo de Estudiantes, San José
Telephone: +506 253 4412/290 5594
Fax: +506 234 6603/290 5597
Year established: 1974
Chief officers: Alberto José Amador (President), José Arturo Montero Chavarria
Structure: business federation

CROATIA

Croatian Article Numbering Association
Address: Croatian Chamber of Economy, Rooseveltov Trg 2, 10000 Zagreb
Telephone: +385 5 146 515 55
Fax: +385 5 144 8618

CUBA

Association of Commerce of the Republic of Cuba
Cámara de Comercio de la Republica de Cuba
Address: Apdo 4237, Zona 4, Calle 21 Nº 661/701, esquina A. Vedado, Ciudad de la Habana 10400
Telephone: +53 7 304 436/3356/8
Fax: +53 7 333 042
Telex: 51-1752 camar cu
E-mail: camara@ceniai.inf.cu
Web site: www.wtca.org/wtc/havana.html
Year established: 1963
Activities: Havana International Trade Fair; exhibitions, information, statistics, publication of bulletins, pamphlets, directories; annual best product/service award; contacts for foreign business people, conferences, seminars, etc; legal department, court of foreign commerce arbitration; research on international trade techniques, world market trends, etc; annual general assembly; translating services
Chief officers: Carlos Martinez Salsamend (President), Jose Miguel Diaz Mirabal (Vice President)
Membership: commerce, industry, agriculture, fishing, National Bank of Cuba, etc
Publications:
• Cuba - Foreign Trade: *magazine - quarterly*
• Directorio Comercial: *information on Cuba, details of members, information on the chamber and its services, Cuban economy, statistics*
• Information (Información): *trade newsletter with general information on Cuba and foreign trade market - monthly*
Notes: member of WTCA - World Trade Centres Association, West Indies Committee, ASTRO - Association of Trade Organisations of Developing Countries, FAN, APPI

Cuban Export Association (EXPOCUBA)

Asociación de Exportación de Cuba
Address: Carretera del Rocio Km. 5,5, Arroyo Naranjo
Telephone: +53 7 944 6250/6259

CYPRUS

Cyprus Aerosol, Detergents and Cosmetics Manufacturers' Association

Address: PO Box 1455, CY-Nicosia
Telephone: +357 2 445 900
Fax: +357 2 467 593

Cyprus Article Numbering Association

Address: PO Box 1455, Cyprus Chamber of Commerce and Industry, 39, Grivas Digheis Avenue and Deligiorigis 3, Nicosia
Telephone: +357 2 449 500
Fax: +357 2 365 685

Cyprus Milk Industry Organisation (CMIO)

Address: P.O. Box 2418, 39, Dem Severies Ave, 1521 Nicosia
Telephone: +357 2 475 697
Fax: +357 2 467 313
Chief officers: Dr. S. Papadopoulos (Secretary)

Cyprus Newspapers and Magazines Publishers' Association

Address: 13 Dramas Street, Nicosia
Telephone: +357 2 37 64 87
Fax: +357 2 37 71 57
Chief officers: Mr N Ph Hadjinicolas (Executive Director)

CZECH REPUBLIC

Article Numbering Association of Czech Republic

Address: EAN Czech, Na Pankraci 30, 140 00 Prague 4
Telephone: +420 2 610 011 45
Fax: +420 2 610 011 47
E-mail: eancz@mbox.vol.cz

Association of Accommodation and Tourism Industry Entrepreneurs

Address: Na Sedive 5, CS-180 00 Prague 8
Telephone: +420 2 663 111 68/663 108 45
Fax: +420 2 663 111 68
Year established: 1990
Activities: advisory services, requalification courses, legislative activity
Chief officers: Jaroslav Smicka (Chairman)
Membership: 920 members
Publications:
• Information Bulletin

Association of Advertising Agencies

Address: 28. rijna 13, CS-112 79 Prague 1
Telephone: +420 2 241 953 49
Fax: +420 2 241 954 81
Year established: 1992
Activities: represents Czech advertising industry at the European Association of Advertising Agencies
Chief officers: Jiri Mikes (Vice-President and Executive Director)
Membership: 57 Czech advertising agencies

Publications:
• ARA Bulletin

Association of Banks

Bankovni asociace
Address: Vodickova 30, CS-110 00 Prague 1
Telephone: +420 2 242 259 26
Fax: +420 2 242 259 57
Year established: 1990
Activities: banking legislation and regulation, information and tax services, representation abroad, various publications
Chief officers: Jan Velek (President)
Membership: 48 banks

Association of Consulting Businesses

Address: PO Box 44, Veletrzni 27, CS-170 01 Prague 7
Telephone: +420 2 879 043
Fax: +420 2 879 043
Activities: mediation for clients, information service
Chief officers: Ivo Ulrich
Structure: independent organisation
Membership: 550 consulting firms: 100 large firms and 450 independent consultants

Association of Czech Booksellers and Publishers

Address: Jan Masaryka 56, 120 00 Prague 2
Telephone: +420 2 242 353 02
Fax: +420 2 242 353 02
E-mail: book@login.cz
Web site: www.centraleurope.com
Chief officers: Mr J Kanzelsberger (General Secretary), Mr J Cisar (Director)

Association of Czech Entrepreneurs

Address: Skretova 6/44, CS-120 59 Prague 2
Telephone: +420 2 242 305 80
Fax: +420 2 242 104 34
Year established: 1990
Activities: advisory services for taxes and loans; establishes contacts between Czech and foreign firms; participates in creating legislative regulations; consultancy services
Chief officers: Bendrich Danda (Chairman)
Membership: 220,000 small and medium-sized companies

Association of Czech Travel Agents (ACSCK)

Associace Ceskych Soukiomych Cestovnich Kancelari
Address: c/o Floratour, Novostrasnicka 58, CS-100 00 Prague 10
Telephone: +420 2 781 7419/781 7429
Fax: +420 2 781 7419

Association of Electronics

Address: Pobrezni 46, CS-186 37 Prague 8
Telephone: +420 2 286 6320/286 6433
Fax: +420 2 2481 3142
Chief officers: Frantisek Hybner (Director)

Association of Private Broadcasters

Address: Zelena 14A, CS-160 00 Prague 6
Telephone: +420 2 320 582
Fax: +420 2 321 867
Year established: 1992
Activities: organises seminars, workshops and educational programs
Chief officers: Michal Zelenka (President)
Membership: 58 members
Publications:
• Annual Report

Association of Producers of Paints and Varnishes

Address: Kodanska 46, CS-100 10 Prague 10
Telephone: +420 2 671 541 47
Fax: +420 2 673 112 62
Chief officers: Milan Maxa (President)
Membership: 10 companies

Association of Textile, Clothing and Leather Industries (ATOK)

Address: Slezská 13, CZ-120 00 Prague 2
Telephone: +420 2 210 017 31/111
Fax: +420 2 210 017 21
Chief officers: Jiri Kohoutek (Director)

Association of the Pulp and Paper Industry

Address: Skretova 6, CS-120 59 Prague 2
Telephone: +420 2 242 132 08
Fax: +420 2 242 132 08
Year established: 1990
Activities: business, economic and social promotion
Chief officers: Josef Zboril (President)
Membership: 54 producers, manufacturers and suppliers of paper, cardboard and cellulose in the Czech Republic
Publications:
• Paper and Cellulose (Papir a Celulozy): *monthly*

Association of the Textile, Clothing and Leather Industry

Address: Slezska 13, CS-120 00 Prague 2
Telephone: +420 2 210 017 32
Fax: +420 2 210 017 21
Year established: 1990
Activities: publishing, advisory functions, organises trade fairs and exhibitions
Chief officers: Stanislav Nosek (President)
Membership: 96 companies, research institutions, schools and trade organisations
Publications:
• Annual Report

Association of Travel Agencies of the Czech Republic (ACK CR)

Address: Zitná 12, CS-121 05 Prague 2
Telephone: +420 2 242 165 69
Fax: +420 2 297 380
Year established: 1991
Activities: cooperation and creation of legislative and economic rules regarding the tourism industry, link to international non-governmental organisations
Chief officers: Michal Seba (President), Oldrich Freidinger (Secretary General)
Membership: 187 travel agencies
Publications:
• Membership Directory: *list of members with adresses, telephone and fax numbers and contact names - annual*

Car Industry Association

Sdruzeny Automoboliveho Prumyslu
Address: Opletalova 29, CS-110 00 Prague
Telephone: +420 2 242 121 00
Fax: +420 2 242 121 00
Year established: 1989
Activities: legal advice and support, advisory service, organises exhibitions, business and economic promotion, compiles statistics, publishes production programmes
Chief officers: Vlatislav Kulhanek (President), Vlastimil Devera (Vice President)
Membership: 89 companies in the Czech Republic, 43 in the Slovak Republic: manufacturers of vehicles; producers of car parts and accessories; and organisations involved in research; trade; advisory and engineering activities
Publications:
• Yearbook: *annual*

Chamber of Tax Advisors

Address: PO Box 121, CS-657 21 Brno 2
Telephone: +420 5 423 213 06
Fax: +420 5 422 103 28
Structure: a self-governing professional organisation with compulsory membership
Membership: tax advisors who have passed the required exams and have been entered in the Tax Advisors' Register

Czech Agrarian Chamber

Address: Dlouhá Str.13, CS-116 78 Prague
Telephone: +420 2 232 8209
Fax: +420 2 231 8868

Czech and Moravian Dairy Association

Address: V Olsinach 75, 100 98 Praha 10
Telephone: +420 2 660 42730
Fax: +420 2 782 1759
Publications:
• Information on the Czech Dairy Industry: *statistics on production and consumption and information on the market structure*

Czech Soap and Detergent Products' Association (CSDPA)

Address: V Olsinach 75, CS-100 00 Prague 10
Telephone: +420 2 573 213 63
Fax: +420 2 573 214 13
Chief officers: Mrs Mati Kleinova
Membership: 5 companies

Electrical and Electronic Association

Address: Pobrezni 46, CS-186 00 Prague 8 - Karlin
Telephone: +420 2 286 632 0
Fax: +420 2 242 186 48
Chief officers: Josef Hybs (President)
Membership: 45 companies

National Association of Hotels and Restaurants

Narodni Federace Hotelu a Restauraci CR
Address: Senovazne nam. 23, CS-112 82 Prague 1
Telephone: +420 2 241 426 76
Fax: +420 2 241 426 81
Year established: 1990
Activities: participates in tourism fairs, sponsors conventions twice a year, organises seminars, publishes information bulletins and professional publications
Chief officers: Jan Filip (President)
Membership: 165 enterprises

Union of the Chemical Industry

Address: Kodanska 46, CS-100 10 Prague 10
Telephone: +420 2 671 841 31/6
Fax: +420 2 671 541 30
Year established: 1990
Activities: laises with international institutions, publishes an information bulletin for members
Chief officers: Miroslav Krejci (President), Karel Voldrich (Director)
Membership: 18 chemical, rubber and pharmaceutical companies

Publications:
• Annual Report

Union of Industry and Transport

Address: Mikulandska 7, CS-113 61 Prague 1
Telephone: +420 2 249 156 79
Fax: +420 2 297 896
Year established: 1990
Activities: advocacy service to government, trade unions and other institutions, liases with international institutions
Chief officers: Stepan Popovic (President)
Membership: 1,742 members

Union of Wood Processors

Address: Na Florenci 7-9, CS-111 71 Prague1
Telephone: +420 2 261 212
Fax: +420 2 261 212
Year established: 1991
Activities: legislative activities, establishes foreign contacts
Chief officers: Tomas Hubec (President)
Membership: 75 organisations

DENMARK

Association of Danish Advertisers

Address: Laederstraede 32-34, DK-1201 Copenhagen K
Telephone: +45 33 14 43 46
Fax: +45 33 14 05 03
Year established: 1947
Activities: information and advice; communication; negotiation; government liaison; cooperation with agencies and media; various publications
Chief officers: Bent Vindelin Peterson (Director)
Structure: board, standing committees, ad hoc committees
Membership: 125
Publications:
• List of Agencies and Suppliers: *annual*
• Newsletter of the Association of Danish Advertisers: *4-6 p.a.*

Association of Danish Bakers

Danske Bagerstands Fællesorganisation
Address: Bjerregårdsvej 16, DK-2500 Valby
Telephone: +45 3617 2300
Fax: +45 3617 2772
Year established: 1895
Activities: compiles limited sector statistics; information service available
Chief officers: Carsten Wickmann (Secretary), Eigeld Nicolaisen (President)
Membership: 1,040 retailers, bakers and confectioners
Publications:
• Bager Konditor: *monthly*

Association of Danish Cosmetics, Toiletries, Soap and Detergent Industries

SPT Brancheforeningen for Sæbe-, Parfumeri-, Toilet- og Kemisk-teknisk Artikler
Address: Falkoner alle 53, 4th Floor, DK-2000 Frederiksberg
Telephone: +45 381 40414
Fax: +45 381 40415
E-mail: spt@danbbs.dk
Web site: www.danbbs.dk/~spt
Activities: main trade organisation for the cosmetics and detergents markets in Denmark. The organisation holds all relevant information on their members and products, and is able to provide trade publications, product brochures and general information. It does not, however, hold any significant statistical data on market trends.

Chief officers: Henrik Malmos (Managing Director)
Membership: 96 manufacturing companies in the field of cosmetics and toiletries and household chemicals plus two associate members. The membership is divided into six sections depending on their main activity, as follows: soaps and detergents, institutional produce and utensils, cosmetics and toiletries, hairdressers' articles, perfume and cosmetics, and industrial hygiene and processing systems.
Publications:
• Newsletter of the Association of Soap, Perfumes, Toiletries and Chemical Articles

Association of Danish Finance Companies

Danske Finansieringsselskabers Forening
Address: Dr. Tvaergade 16, DK-1302 Copenhagen K
Telephone: +45 33 15 15 32
Fax: +45 33 12 24 24
Year established: 1984
Activities: information dissemination on the leasing market in Denmark and abroad; information on legislation affecting the leasing industry; special meetings as required
Chief officers: Kjeld Regnarsen (Chairman), Palle Nielsen (Vice Chairman)
Structure: board of directors, several sub-committees
Publications:
• Nyhedsorentering: *news and information on leasing - quarterly*

Association of Danish Furniture Industries

Address: Center Boulevard 5, DK-2300 Copenhagen S
Telephone: +45 325 18000
Fax: +45 325 18332
E-mail: dmi@fdmi.dk
Web site: www.furniture.fdmi.dk
Activities: advisory service for members, seminars and information campaigns, co-ordination of participation by Danish manufacturers in foreign fairs. Each year the association also organises the Scandinavian Furniture Fair. Maintains a database of Danish furniture manufacturers and supplies as well as other information on the furniture industry in Denmark. Collects statistics on furniture production, exports and imports
Chief officers: Keld Korsager (Managing Director), Count Preben Ahlefedt-Laurvig (Chairman)
Membership: 500 Danish furniture manufacturers and retail companies
Publications:
• DANMARK - The Furniture Industry: *news on the furniture industry - 4 p.a.*
• Danske Mobler: *news on the furniture trade in Denmark - monthly*

Association of Danish Horticultural Producers (DEG)

Dansk Erhvervsgartnerforening
Address: Hvidkærvej 29, DK-5250 Odense SV
Telephone: +45 66 171 714
Fax: +45 66 171 715
E-mail: degodvirk@cybernet.dk
Web site: www.inet.unic.dk/~degarhus
Activities: test and laboratory activities; consulting; information services; collect statistics covering production, area, numbers of growers, product variety and value, energy, export and import
Chief officers: Mr Poul Thage (Chairman), Mr Jan Hassing (Managing Director)
Membership: approx. 2,500 members
Publications:
• Gartner Tidende: *horticulture in Denmark and foreign countries - weekly*
Notes: Umbrella organisation of the Danish horticultural industry.

Association of Danish Pharmacists
Danmarks Apotekerforening
Address: PO Box 2181, Bredgade 54, DK-1017 Copenhagen K
Telephone: +45 33767600
Fax: +45 33767699
Year established: 1844
Activities: negotiate with the health authorities and political bodies regarding regulation of the trade, price policies; provides comprehensive services to individuals
Chief officers: Peter J Kielgast (Director General), Kurt Thingler Olsen (Director)
Membership: 300 pharmacists
Publications:
• Farmaceutisk Tidende: *pharmaceuticals and drugs - weekly*
• Farmacy: *magazine - monthly*

Association of Danish Shoe Retailers
Danmarks Skohandlerforening
Address: Spotorno Alle 8, DK-2630 Taastrup
Telephone: +45 43 714 607
Fax: +45 43 714 650
Activities: education; governmant lobbying; publishes a trade magazine; provides an information service to members; holds classes and conferences; collects statistics covering the retail footwear market
Chief officers: Leif Bernth (Manager), Bente Mikkelsen (Secretary)
Membership: 450 footwear retailers
Publications:
• SKO: *fashion and shoe business; leather business; trade magazine - 10 p.a.*
• Sko Magasinet: *monthly*

Association of Danish Travel Agents and Tour Operators
Danmarks Rejsebureau Forening
Address: Falkoner Alle 58 B, DK-2000 Frederiksberg
Telephone: +45 31 356 611
Fax: +45 31 358 859
E-mail: drf@travelassoc.dk
Year established: 1938
Activities: advisory service; training
Chief officers: Mrs Karin Aagesen (Secretary General)
Membership: 281 active members and 62 associate members
Publications:
• Newsletter: *current update on relevant information, new rules - monthly*
Notes: The Association does not produce any statistics.

Association of Manufacturers and Importers of Electrical Household Appliances (FEHA)
Address: Postboks 1336, Naverland 34, DK-2600 Glostrup
Telephone: +45 434 34646
Fax: +45 434 35272

Association of Pharmaceutical Wholesalers (MEGROS)
Foreningen af Medicingrossister
Address: Amagertorv 11, DK-1160 Copenhagen K
Telephone: +45 33 12 6040
Fax: +45 33 14 1933
Chief officers: H Ostergaard (President), V Jessen Nielsen (Vice-President)
Membership: 3 pharmaceutical wholesalers
Notes: Does not collect statistics nor produce publications.

Association of Refrigeration and Air-Conditioning Companies (FAV)
Foreningen af Ventilationsfirmaer Jern-og Metalindustriens Sammenslutning
Address: Norre Voldgade 34, DK-1358, Copenhagen K
Telephone: +45 33 143 414
Fax: +45 33 936 240
Chief officers: Tom Rytlander

Association of the Chocolate and Confectionery Industry
Chokolade- og Konfekture-Industriens Brancheforening
Address: Dansk Industri, DK-1787 Kobenhavn
Telephone: +45 3 377 3377
Fax: +45 3 377 3300
Chief officers: Mrs B Staerk (Secretary)
Membership: 8 manufacturers of chocolate and confectionery

Association of the Danish Ice Cream Industry
Iskremindustriens Sammenslutning
Address: Industriens Hus, Vesterbrogade 2 B, DK-1620 Copenhagen V
Telephone: +45 333 64000
Fax: +45 333 64001
Chief officers: Ebbe M Loiborg (President), Jorgen Maltha Rasmussen (General Secretary)
Membership: 5 members
Notes: The Association does not produce any publications or statistics..

Association of the Danish Tobacco Industry
Tobaksindustrien
Address: Svanemollevej 62, DK-2900 Hellerup
Telephone: +45 396 26899
Fax: +45 396 24321
Year established: 1875
Activities: collects statistics on imports, domestic production and sales but does not produce any publications
Chief officers: Peter T H Madsen (Director)
Membership: 7 companies

Association of Wine Merchants
Vinhandlerforeningen for Danmark
Address: Magstræde 7, DK-1204 Copenhagen K
Telephone: +45 331 45200
Fax: +45 339 50506

Council for the Danish Textile Industry
Dansk Textil Union
Address: HC Andersens Boulevard 48, DK-1553 Copenhagen V
Telephone: +45 33121708
Fax: +45 33931708
Year established: 1915
Activities: arranges a home and household textiles fair (TEXPO) in Bella Center, Copenhagen
Chief officers: Jan Hammerich (Director)
Membership: textile retailers
Publications:
• Textil: *17 p.a.*

Council of the Danish Frozen Food Industries
Dybfrostrådet
Address: Vesterbrogade 6D, DK-1620 Copenhagen V
Telephone: +45 33 33 9500
Fax: +45 33 33 9505
Chief officers: Mr L. Olsen
Publications:
• Frozen Foods in Denmark: *sales and consumption trends for*

frozen foods in Denmark with data divided into specific product areas and consumer groups, eg retail, catering, etc. Also some statistics on freezer sales and capacity. Some tables have figures for earlier years - annual

Danish Article Numbering Association
Address: Aldersrogade 6d, DK-2100 Copenhagen
Telephone: +45 3 927 8527
Fax: +45 3 927 8510
E-mail: info@ean.dk

Danish Association of Car Dealers
Automobilforhandlerforening Danmarks
Address: Alhambravej 5, DK-1826 Frederiksberg C
Telephone: +45 313 14555
Fax: +45 313 13075
Chief officers: Jette Noes (Director)
Publications:
● Bil og Motor: *all aspects of the automotive trade - 8 pa*

Danish Association of Retailers of Sports Equipment
Danmarks Sportshandlerforening
Address: Naverland 34, DK-2600 Glostrup
Telephone: +45 434 34646
Fax: +45 429 67515
Year established: 1939
Activities: conferences, information service and research
Chief officers: Poleaik Pidisen (Director)
Membership: 340 sports retailers
Publications:
● Handel & Sport: *monthly*

Danish Bacon and Meat Council
Danske Slagterier
Address: Axelborg, 3 Axeltorv, DK-1609 Copenhagen 5
Telephone: +45 331 16050
Fax: +45 331 16814
E-mail: KF@ds-data.dk
Web site: www.landbrug.dk/ds/ds.htm

Danish Bankers' Association
Finansradet - Danske Pengeinstitutters Forening
Address: Amaliegade 7, DK-1256 Copenhagen K
Telephone: +45 33 120 200
Fax: +45 33 930 260
E-mail: f@finansraadet.dk
Year established: 1990
Activities: information; training and education; financial and economic advice and consultation service
Chief officers: Lars Barfoed (Managing Director), Klaus Willerslev-Olsen (Deputy Managing Director)
Membership: 173 banks, savings banks and cooperative banks
Publications:
● Annual Report of the Danish Bankers' Association: *partly reports the activities of the association and partly summarises the focused political and economic events of the year - annual*
● Facts about the Danish Bankers' Association: *basic statistics on the banking sector in Denmark with data on the number of banks, branches, transactions, employees, payment cards, terminals, balance sheets. Basic financial data for the major banks plus a list of member banks is also included - annual*
● Finans & Samfund: *articles covering finance and banking - monthly*
Notes: In addition to the publications, the Association produces pamphlets about different aspects of the banking industry.

Danish Booksellers' Association
Danske Boghandlerforening
Address: 3rd Floor, Siljangade 6, DK-2300 Copenhagen S
Telephone: +45 315 42255
Fax: +45 315 72422
Year established: 1963
Activities: annual general assembly; a wide range of data processing and networking services; annual survey of the membership's financial results; marketing
Chief officers: Anker Hedoegaard (Deputy Manager), Olaf Winsloev (Accounts Manager)
Structure: deputy committee, marketing committee
Membership: 440 booksellers
Publications:
● Newsletter of the Association of Danish Booksellers: *approx. 8 p.a.*

Danish Brewers' Association
Bryggeriforeningen
Address: Frederiksberggade 11, DK-1459 Copenhagen K
Telephone: +45 3 312 6241
Fax: +45 3 314 2513
Year established: 1899
Activities: national and EU legislation and decisions of importance to the breweries; service functions for member companies; collects statistics on beer sales, exports and imports, consumption, excise duty, tax revenue and lists of members' products
Chief officers: Mr Niel Hald (Secretary General), Mr Per Schou Christiansen (Head of Division)
Membership: 10 members
Publications:
● Statistics from the Danish Brewers' Association: *annual*

Danish Brewers' Association
Address: Frederiksberggade 11, DK-1459 Copenhagen
Telephone: +45 331 26241
Fax: +45 331 42513
Publications:
● Tal fra Bryggeriforeningen: *pocket book with statistics on brewing and beer in Denmark. Includes production, consumption, foreign trade statistics - annual*

Danish Butchers' Association
Danske Slagtermestres Landsforening
Address: Postbox 709, Poppelvej 83, DK-5230 Odense M
Telephone: +45 661 28730
Fax: +45 661 28794
Year established: 1915
Activities: Interfair; training courses; biennial international competition for butchers
Chief officers: Lars Bode (Managing Director), Jonna Hugger (Vice Director)
Structure: standing committee consisting of seven butchers plus the director
Membership: 1,500 retail butchers
Publications:
● Den Rigtige Slagter: *issues pertaining to the meat trade; profiles of members and individuals; price issues; European meat trade - 10 p.a.*
● Kodbranchen: *news for retail butchers, covers new trends including product information - 10 p.a*

Danish Chemical Industries' Association (FDKI)
Address: Nørre Voldgade 48, DK-1358 Copenhagen K
Telephone: +45 331 51748
Fax: +45 331 51722
Chief officers: J Jessen (Director)
Membership: manufacturers of chemical products

Danish Consumer Goods Suppliers' Association (DLF)
Dansk Dagligvareleverandoer Forening
Address: Kronprinsessegade 34, DK-1306 Copenhagen K
Telephone: +45 33 139 292
Fax: +45 33 911 375
Activities: collects statistics covering retail sales for
chocolate, sweets, spirits, petfoods and catering
Chief officers: Erling Petersen (Managing Director)
Membership: 138 members
Notes: No publications produced.

Danish Dairy Board
Mejeriforeningen
Address: Frederiks Allé 22, DK-8000 Århus C
Telephone: +45 873 120 00
Fax: +45 873 120 01
E-mail: ddb@mejeri.dk
Web site: www.landbrug.dk/dmf/dmf.htm
Year established: 1912
Activities: collects production statistics, export statistics,
profit and loss accounts, milk quality data (some data
available to non-members); administration of trade political
interests in relation to the EU concerning agricultural and dairy
policy issues; co-ordination of joint research activities of the
Danish dairy industry; supervision of efforts to combat cattle
diseases and handling veterinary and other cattle health issues
Chief officers: Knud Harck (Chairman), Kaj Ole Pedersen
(Vice Chairman), Mr J.H. Christensen (Secretary)
Structure: 4 product and market committees for cheese,
butter, preserved milk and consumer milk
Membership: 30 dairy companies receiving more than 99% of
the Danish milk production
Publications:
• Aarsstatistik: *statistics - annual*
• Annual Report of the Danish Dairy Board: *an annual report
with some statistics on trends in the dairy industry in Denmark.
Dairy production and consumption statistics are included
based on data collected by the Board - annual*
• Producentorientering fra Mejeriforeningen: *political issues,
milk quota administration and veterinary health services -
fortnightly*
• Scandinavian Dairy Information (SDI): *dairies, dairy
production and technology in and outside Scandinavia -
quarterly*
• UgeNyt fra Mejeriforeningen (Newsletters from the Danish
Dairy Board): *dairy production, exports and political issues -
weekly*

Danish Fish Processing Industries' and Exporters' Association
Danmarks Fiskeindustri- og Eksportforening
Address: Konprinsessegade 8B 4th floor, DK-1306
Copenhagen K
Telephone: +45 331 49999
Fax: +45 333 27757
Chief officers: Peder Hyldtoft (President), Bent Buch (Chief
Executive)
Membership: 120 fish processors and exporters
Publications:
• Annual Report: *annual*
Notes: Association does not collect statistics.

Danish Fruit Juice and Fruit Drinks Industry Association
Danmarks Juice-, Saft- og Frugdrikindustriforening Industrifagene
Address: Norre Voldgade 34, DK-1358 Copenhagen K
Telephone: +45 33 773 377
Fax: +45 33 773 320
Membership: fruit juice manufacturers

Danish Livestock and Meat Board
Køedbranchens Faellesråd
Address: Vesterbrogade 6 D, 7, DK-1620 Copenhagen V
Telephone: +45 33 914 446
Fax: +45 33 323 503
Web site: www.landbrug.dk/kfr/kfr.htm
Activities: collect annual statistics covering production,
prices and trade for cattle in Denmark
Chief officers: H R Thomsen (General Director), E Franzen
(Vice Director)
Membership: 10 cattle slaughter companies; 25 traders and
processing companies; 1 organisation for trade with live cattle;
Farmers' Union; Family Farmers' Association
Publications:
• Orientering: *production, trade, EU policy - monthly*

Danish Marketing Association
Dansk Markedsforingsforbund
Address: St Strandstraede 21, 1255 Copenhagen
Telephone: +45 31 118 787
Fax: +45 31 119 797
E-mail: dmf@d-m-f.dk
Web site: www.d-m-f.dk
Activities: courses, seminars and conferences
Chief officers: Chris Hahn-Evers (Director)
Membership: 6,500 members
Publications:
• Markedsforing: *bi-monthly*

Danish Newspapers' Association
Danske Dagblades Forening
Address: Pressens Hus, Skindergade 7, 1159 Copenhague k
Telephone: +45 33 12 21 15
Fax: +45 33 14 23 25
Chief officers: Mr Ebbe Dal (Managing Director), Mr Henrik
Marstrand Dahl (Director)

Danish Paper Wholesalers' Association
Dansk Papirhanolerforening
Address: Borsen, 1217 Copenhagen K
Telephone: +45 33 950 500
Fax: +45 33 325 216
E-mail: bo.green@commerce.dk
Chief officers: Mr Bo Green, Ms Winnie Christiansen
Membership: 90 member companies
Notes: The Association does not produce any publications or
statistics..

Danish Pharmaceutical Industry Association (LIF)
Lægemiddlelindustriforeningen
Address: Strødamvej 50A, DK-2100 Copenhagen Ø
Telephone: +45 392 76060
Fax: +45 392 76070
Year established: 1997
Activities: annual conference; publications forwarded on
request to any interested company/organisation
Chief officers: Jørgen Jørgensen (Director)
Structure: board of directors and 6 permanent working
parties dealing with law, economy, research etc
Publications:
• Annual Report of the Association of the Danish
Pharmaceutical Industry: *annual*
• Drug Consumption Denmark: *annual statistics on the use of
pharmaceuticals in Denmark with analysis by type of drug and
purpose of use - annual*
• Made in Denmark: *information covering Danish
pharmaceutical companies - annual*
• Medicine and Health Care (Talog og Data Medicin og
Sundhedsvaesen): *a statistical yearbook with figures on
pharmaceuticals production, investment, prices, consumption*

by drug type, advertising, taxes, and research trends. Also
data on general health trends. Various time series over five,
ten, and fifteen years - annual
Notes: The Association was established in September 1997
as a result of the merger between MEDIF and MEFA which
ceased to exist at that date.

Danish Plastics Industry Association
Plastindustrien i Denmark
Address: Nørre Voldgade 48, DK-1358 Copenhagen K
Telephone: +45 33 133 022
Fax: +45 33 910 898
Year established: 1947
Activities: liaison with government; meetings; education and
research
Chief officers: Mrs Jette Rasmussen (Managing Director),
Mrs Joan Boegh (Consultant)
Membership: 340 members including producers and
suppliers
Notes: No statistics collected and publications are
unavailable to non-members.

Danish Poultry Meat Association
Dansk Slagtefjerkrae
Address: 5, Trommesalen, DK-1614 Copenhagen V
Telephone: +45 33 254 100
Fax: +45 33 253 014
E-mail: dsf@poultry.dk
Activities: collects statistics covering production,
consumption, sales, imports and exports
Chief officers: Mr Terkildsen (General Manager),
Marie-Louise Madsen (Information Manager)
Membership: 30 members
Notes: No publications produced.

Danish Publishers' Association
Danske Forlæggerforening
Address: Købmagergade 11, 1150 København K
Telephone: +45 33 15 66 88
Fax: +45 33 15 65 88
Chief officers: Mr OA Busck (President), Mr EC Lidgren
(General Secretary), Mr EV Krustrup (Director)

Danish Soft Drinks Manufacturers' Association
Danske Laeskedrik Fabrikanter
Address: Frederiksberggade 11, DK-1459 Copenhagen K
Telephone: +45 331 26241
Fax: +45 331 42513
Year established: 1910
Activities: produces statistics on the following: total sales,
imports and exports, consumption etc., Also provides
information on taste developments; legal advice on food, law
and the environment
Chief officers: Mr Niel Hald (Secretary General), Mr Per
Schou Christiansen (Head of Division)
Membership: 10 manufacturers of carbonated soft drinks
Publications:
• Statistics from the Danish Soft Drinks Association: *annual*

Danish Tea and Coffee Association
Address: Hammerensgade No 1, Copenhagen
Telephone: +45 331 32323
Fax: +45 333 22005
Telex: 27208
Chief officers: Niels Gade, Karsten Blom
Membership: 16 member companies
Notes: Contact Dansk Kaffe Information (Public Relations
bureau) for publications and statistics. Tel: +45 396 30037.

Danish Toy Trade Association
Legetojsbranchens Faellesrad
Address: Hjortevej 15, DK-8900 Randers
Telephone: +45 86 434 309
Fax: +45 86 434 309
Activities: provide services including information and advising
Chief officers: Steen J Selbach (Chairman)
Membership: 1,300 members including retailers, chains,
wholesalers, agents, factories (accounting for 85% of the
Danish market)
Notes: The Association does not produce any publications or
statistics..

Danish Wine and Spirits Association (VSOD)
Vin og Spiritus Organisationen i Denmark
Address: Magstraede 7, DK-1204 Copenhagen K
Telephone: +45 33 145 200
Fax: +45 33 135 013
Year established: 1977
Activities: statistical and other information services (in
principle available to members and non-members)
Chief officers: John Chrietensen (President)
Membership: 50 companies (spirits
importers/producers/retailers)
Publications:
• Newsletter of the Danish Wine and Spirits Association
• Statistical Service (Danish Wine and Spirits Association): *the
association provides a statistical service on the wine and
spirits markets in Denmark. The service includes various
publications and on-demand services - regular*

Federation of Danish Retail Grocers (DSK)
Samvirkende Koebmandsforeningen i Danmark
Address: PO Box 122, Svanemollevej 41, DK-2900 Hellerup
Telephone: +45 396 21616
Fax: +45 396 20300
Activities: annual conferences and seminars; collects
statistics on number of stores, market share and turnover
Chief officers: John Wagner (Director), Paul F Nonnecke
(President)
Structure: 18 regions with 33 local associations
Membership: 1500 members (including 500 supermarkets)
Publications:
• Dansk Handelsblad: *information on grocery trade in
Denmark - weekly*
• Erit Koebmandskab: *quarterly*

Federation of Danish Shoe Manufacturers
Skofabrikantenforeningen i Danmark
Address: Norre Voldgade 34, DK-1358 Copenhagen
Telephone: +45 33 773 377
Fax: +45 33 773 440

Federation of Danish Textile and Clothing Industries
Textil- og Beklaedningsindustrien
Address: PO Box 507, Bredgade 41, DK-7400 Herning
Telephone: +45 992 77200
Fax: +45 971 22350
E-mail: info@textile.dk
Web site: www.textile.dk
Year established: 1895
Activities: 30-40 conferences p.a. (members only); collection
and dissemination of information to member firms; export
statistics twice a year; market analyses (findings available to
members only); articles; fashion papers; newsletters
Chief officers: Jens Bollerup-Jensen (Managing Director),
Soeren Holm Pedersen (Deputy Director), Preben W Friis
(Administrative Head), Niels Ole Vestegaard-Poulson
(Chairman)

Membership: 350 private Danish textile and clothing companies
Publications:
• Danish Textile amd Clothing Industry: *an annual survey of the textiles and clothing sector with data on production, consumption, imports, exports, employment. Based on a combination of official and non-official sources - annual*
• Export Guide: *guide to Danish contractors in textile and clothing - annual*
• Prognosis (Textil- og Beklaedningsindustrien): *trends and the forecasted outlook for Danish textile and clothing sectors. Based on a combination of official and non-official sources - biannual*
• Textil & Beklaedning: *information on the textile industry - 10 p.a.*

IT Industry Association
Address: Boersen, Glas og Porcelaensbrnachen, DK-1217 Copenhagen K
Telephone: +45 33 950 500
Fax: +45 33 325 216
Telex: 19520 CHAMCO DK
E-mail: itb@dk
Web site: www.itb.dk
Year established: 1939
Chief officers: Jakob Lyngso (Director)
Membership: 130 members
Notes: The Association does not produce any publications or statistics.. Incorporates Hardware Association.

National Association of Danish Fish Retailers
Landsorganisationen af Danmarks Detailfiskehandlere
Address: Peblinge Dosseringen 36, DK-2200 Copenhagen N
Telephone: +45 35 372 023
Fax: +45 35 371 788
Year established: 1917
Activities: information for members; sales campaigns; public relations; collect statistics covering retail sales
Chief officers: Carl Ahrenkiel (President), Hans Erik Hansen (Managing Director)
Membership: 150 independent fishmongers
Publications:
• Detailfiskehandleren: *seafood, seafood retailing, seafood production - 6 p.a.*

DOMINICA

Dominica Association of Industry and Commerce
Address: PO Box85, Roseau
Telephone: +1 809 4 482 874
Fax: +1 809 4 486 868

Dominica Eco-Tourism Association
Address: PO Box 244, Corner Queen Mary & King George Streets, Roseau
Telephone: +1 809 4 481 800
Fax: +1 809 4 481 801

Dominica Export and Import Agency (DEXIA)
Address: PO Box 173, Bay Front, Roseau
Telephone: +1 809 4 482 780/483 494/ 483 495
Fax: +1 809 4 486 308

Dominica Hotel and Tourism Association
Address: 111 Bath Road, Roseau
Telephone: +1 809 4 486 565
Fax: +1 809 4 480 299

DOMINICAN REPUBLIC

Article Numbering Association
Asociación de Codificación Comercial
Address: Edificio Plaza Compostela, Suite 3-I-5, Ave. John F. Kennedy esq. Calle 7, Santo Domingo
Telephone: +1 809 476 0829
Fax: +1 809 476 0828
E-mail: eanrd7@tricom.net

Commerce and Production Association
Cámara de Comercio y Producción de Santiago, Inc.
Address: Apartado Postal 44, Edificio Empresarial, Avda Las Carreras # 7, Santiago
Telephone: +1 809 582 2856
Fax: +1 809 241 4546
Web site: www.hispanet.com/camara
Year established: 1914
Activities: seminars. conferences and forums, maintains a library specialising in economics with statistical data, directories, national and international press; sources of information
Chief officers: Lic. Juan Alfonso Mera (President), Lic. Jose Cario Suarez (Secretary), Ivan Reynoso (Executive Director)
Membership: law firms, hotels, travel agencies, chemical and pharmaceutical companies, food industry, book shops, clothing and textiles companies

Dominican Newspapers Association
Sociedad Dominicana de Diarios
Address: PO Box 416, Santo Domingo
Fax: +1 809 688 3019
Chief officers: German Emilio Ornes (President)

Dominican Traders' Federation
Federación Dominicana de Comerciantes
Address: Carretera Sanchez Km 10, Santo Domingo DN
Telephone: +1 809 350 553 2666
Structure: federation of retailers

Dominican Travel Agencies' Association (ADAVI)
Asociación Dominicana de Agencias de Viajes
Address: Padre Billini No. 263, Santo Domingo
Telephone: +1 809 541 3488
Fax: +1 809 682 9927

ECUADOR

Association of Finance Companies (ASOFIN)
Asociación de Sociedades Financieras del Ecuador
Address: Ed. Banco La Previsora, Torre B, Av. Naciones Unidas, Quito
Telephone: +593 2 462 107
Fax: +593 2 463 358

Association of Manufacturers and Importers of Pharmaceutical Products (ASOPROFAR)
Asociación Ecuatoriana de Industriales e Importadores de Productos Farmacéuticos
Address: PO Box 17078842, Edf Gabriela 3, Of 101, Avs República de El Salvador 733 y Portugal, Quito
Telephone: +593 2 469 139/454 212
Fax: +593 2 454 212
Membership: pharmaceutical manufacturers and importers

Association of Private Banks of Ecuador (ABPE)
Asociación de Bancos Privados del Ecuador
Address: Apdo 17-11-6708, Edificio Delta, piso 7, Av
República de El Salvador 898, Quito
Telephone: +593 2 566 670/566 674
Fax: +593 2 466 702/466 701
Chief officers: Ernesto Chinbogo B (Executive Director)
Membership: private banks
Notes: Other branch: Av 10 de Agosto 850 y Patria, Edif
Banco de Prestamos, piso 18, Quito Tel 2
567611/554210/554410 Fax 2 567612

Banana Producers' Association (APROBANA)
Asociación de Productores Bananeros del Ecuador
Address: Malecón, 2002, Guayaquil
Telephone: +593 4 522 580
Membership: banana growers

Business Association : Cosmetics Section
Cámara de Industrias: Grupo Seccional de Cosméticos
Address: PO Box 4007, Av 9 de Octubre #910 y Rumichaca,
Guayaquil
Telephone: +593 4 562 705/305 150
Fax: +593 4 320 924
Membership: cosmetics companies

Cosmetic Chemicals' Association
Asociación Ecuatoriana de Químicos Cosméticos
Address: Apdo 09-01-00430, 10 de Agosto Nº 637 y Garcia
Aviles, Guayaquil
Telephone: +593 4 516 575
Fax: +593 4 328 735
Activities: seminars
Chief officers: Dra Isabel de Luque (President)
Membership: 50 members

Dairy Products Manufacturers' Association
Asociación de Industriales de Productos Lácteos del Ecuador
Address: Robles 653, Quito
Telephone: +593 1 547 310

Domestic Automobile Association (AEADI)
Asociación Automotriz del Interior
Address: piso 6, oficina 6, Av Colón 535 y 6 de Diciembre,
Quito
Telephone: +593 2 527 110/527 912
Fax: +593 2 509 473
Membership: motor vehicle manufacturers and dealers

Ecuadorian Advertisers' Association (AEA)
Asociación Ecuatoriana de Anunciantes
Address: Edificio Valladolid, piso 2, Paez 370 y Robles, Quito
Telephone: +593 2 528 653/543 304/540 708
Fax: +593 2 503 210
Chief officers: Alberto García (President), Samuel Castro
(Vice President), Sr Armando Sobalvarro
Membership: advertisers - Proesa, Life Laboratories, Nestlé,
Adams, Daca, La Reforma, Atlantic Ind, Nutrinsa,
Fleischmann, Jaboneria Nacional, Licoresa, Banco
Continental, Atlantic Industries, Pronaca

Ecuadorian Book Association
Cámara Ecuatoriana del Libro
Address: Casilla nº 17-01-3329, Guayaquil 1629, piso 4, Quito
Telephone: +593 2 212 226
Fax: +593 2 512 286
Chief officers: Ms E Loaize de Arias (General Secretary), Mr
P Mena (Director)

Ecuadorian Product Codification (ECOP)
Ecuatoriana de Código de Producto
Address: Edificio Conde Ruiz de Castilla, 3º piso, oficina 3,
Ruiz de Castilla 763 y Andagoya, Quito
Telephone: +593 2 507 580
Fax: +593 2 507 584
E-mail: ecop@uio.telconet.net

Ecuadorian Textile Association (AITE)
Asociación de Industriales Textiles del Ecuador
Address: Casilla 17-01-2893, Edificio Las Cámaras 8º, Avs
República y Amazonas, Quito
Telephone: +593 2 249 434/451 286/451 350
Fax: +593 2 445 159
Year established: 1938
Chief officers: Diego Terán Dammer (President), Richard C
Handal
Membership: 33 textile manufacturers

Ecuadorian Tobacco Industry Association
Asociación Ecuatoriana de la Agroindustria Tabacalera
Address: Edf Belmonte, piso 6, Corea 126 y Av Amazonas,
Quito
Telephone: +593 2 458 703
Fax: +593 2 435 361
Activities: promotes the cultivation and commercialisation of
cigarettes and tobacco; market reports on tobacco
consumption; reports on education, culture and health in
relation to tobacco; laws relating to the industry; technical and
professional training
Chief officers: Armando Sobalvarro Conde (Presidente), Ana
María Molina de Silva (Executive Secretary), Dr Manuel
García-Jaen (Director)
Membership: 6 tobacco growers
Publications:
• ÁGORA (ÁGORA): *opinion articles and news on the tobacco
and food industry; legislation and information on taxation -
quarterly*
• White Book ASOTAB (Libro Blanco ASOTAB): *information on
the projects and activities over the past year and the future
plans of ASOTAB - annual*

Exporters' Association of Ecuador (FEDEXPORT)
Federación Ecuatoriana de Exportadores
Address: Apdo 17-15-0187-B, Edificio las Cámaras, 8 piso,
Avenida de la República y Amazonas, Quito
Telephone: +593 2 452 769/452 770
Fax: +593 2 440 74
Year established: 1976
Activities: trade information database, access to international
databases, library, organises trips for members to overseas
trade fairs, contacts with overseas business people
Chief officers: José Augusto Bermeo (President), Hernán
León Guarderas (Executive Director)
Membership: exporters
Publications:
• Directorio Oficial de Exportadores Ecuador: *information on
exporting companies, their products and services, to promote
Ecuador abroad - annual*
• Ecuador Exporta: *up-to-date information on exports,
research, trade opportunities, legislation, regimes, etc. -
bi-monthly*
• Suplemento a la Revista Ecuador Exporta: *information on
Fedexpor's main activities; trade fairs, events and seminars,
both national and international, and other news of interest to
exporters - monthly*

Flower Producers' and Exporters' Association (EXPOFLORES)

Asociación de Productores y Exportadores de Flores
Address: Apdo 8049, República 1331 y Alemania, Quito
Telephone: +593 2 251 036/037/038
Fax: +593 2 449 691
Chief officers: Mauricio Davalos Guevara
Membership: flower cultivators and exporters

Hotel Association of Ecuador (AHOTEC)

Asociación Hotelera del Ecuador
Address: Av América 5378 - piso 2, Quito
Telephone: +593 1 453 942/443 425
Fax: +593 1 453 942
Membership: hotels

National Businessmen's' Association (ANDE)

Asociación Nacional de Empresarios
Address: Apdo 3489, Edif España 6°, of 67, Avda Colón y Amazonas, Quito
Telephone: +593 2 238 507/550 879
Fax: +593 2 503 271/509 806
Telex: 22298
Membership: businesses from all sectors

National Sugar Growers' Association (AZTRA)

Federación Nacional de Azucareros
Address: PO Box 09-01-5895, Sucre 203 y Pichincha, piso 8, Guayaquil
Telephone: +593 4
Fax: +593 4 320 353
Telex: 43220
Chief officers: G Echeverria (President)
Membership: sugar processors and dealers

Newspaper Editors' Association (AEDEP)

Asociación Ecuatoriana de Editores de Periódicos
Address: Mariscal Foch 510 y Diego Almagro, piso 3 - oficina 3, Quito
Telephone: +593 2 564 348/9
Fax: +593 2 564 363
Chief officers: Jaime Mantilla (President), Guadalupe Mantilla (Executive Director), Andrés Carrion (Permanent Executive Secretary)
Membership: 7 daily newspapers

Traders' and Industrialists' Association

Asociación de Comerciantes e Industriales
Address: Boyaca 1416, Guayaquil
Telephone: +593 4 527 204
Membership: association of merchants, retailers and manufacturers

Travel and Tourism Agencies' Association (ASECUT)

Asociación Ecuatoriana de Agencias de Viajes y Turismo
Address: PO Box1210, Av Amazonas 720 y Veintimilla, piso 5, Quito
Telephone: +593 2 562 397/560 550
Fax: +593 2 505 402/564 655
Membership: travel agencies and tourism centres
Notes: Airport branch: Aeropuerto Mariscal Sucre (Tel 2 462977)

EGYPT

Egyptian Article Numbering Association

Address: PO Box 64, T3A, 6A Giza Street, Giza, El Orman
Telephone: +20 2 571 9302
Fax: +20 2 571 5161
E-mail: tza@ritseel.com.eg

Egyptian Businessmen's Association (EBA)

Address: P.O. Box: 265 Orman, Nile Tower 21 Giza St, Giza
Telephone: +20 2 573 6030/572 3020/5723855
Fax: +20 2 573 7258/568 1014
E-mail: eba@ritsec1.com.eg

Egyptian Federation of Tourist Chambers

Address: 8 El Sad El Aaly Street Dokki, Giza
Telephone: +20 360 8487/348 3313
Fax: +20 361 4286
Activities: human resource development; sponsors tourism studies and travel research; co-ordinates work carried out by the different tourist associations; promotes and develops Egyptian tourism; gives advice to the authorities on legislation and regulations
Chief officers: Mr Ahmad Zaki abdel Hamid (President), Mr Hamdy Saleh (Director General)
Membership: Egyptian tourism business sector including the Egyptian Travel Agents' Association, Egyptian Hotel Association, Chamber of Tourist Establishments, Egyptian Chamber of Tourist Commodities, Egyptian Tourism Marketing Fund

Egyptian Textile Manufacturers' Federation (ETMF)

Address: PO Box 359 - Code 11511, 43, Sherif Street, Cairo
Telephone: +20 2 392 693 2
Fax: +20 2 390 000 5
Chief officers: Shetata S. Semida (Director General)

Federation of Egyptian Industries

Address: PO Box 251, Immobilia Bldg, 26a Sharia Sherif Pasha, Cairo
Telephone: +20 2 392 8317/392 8075
Fax: +20 2 392 8075
Web site: www.exporter.com/egypt/index.htm
Chief officers: Mr H Mattawi (Director General)
Publications:
• Industrial Egypt: *quarterly*

EL SALVADOR

Exporters Association of El Salvador (COEXPORT)

Corporación de Exportadores de El Salvador
Address: Apdo 05-235, Condominios del Mediterráneo Edificio A #23, Colonia Jardines de Guadalupe, San Salvador
Telephone: +503 224 4019/223 1888/243 3110
Fax: +503 298 0951/243 1329
E-mail: silvia@coexp.euromaya.com
Year established: 1985
Activities: foreign trade advice service; national and international trade information; management and promotion; services; training; publicity, videos of members' products
Chief officers: Mario Molina (President), Edgardo Vides Limus (Vice President), Lic.Silvia M Cuellar Sicilia (Executive Director), Lorezo Rivera (Secretary)
Structure: general assembly, board of directors, executive board
Membership: 300 export companies and export service companies

Publications:
• Boletín Informativo
• El Exportador: *export market information*
• El Salvador Export Products Catalogue (Catálogo de Productos Exportables de El Salvador): *directory of the majority of the country's producers and exporters of non traditional products and services in various sectors including: food, agriculture, aquaculture, chemicals and pharmaceuticasl, apparel and accessories, paper, handicrafts, plastics, metals, wood products etc. - annual*

Manufacturers Association of El Salvador
Asociación Salvadoreña de Industriales
Address: Calles Roma y Liverpool, Colonia Roma, San Salvador
Telephone: +503 279 2488
Fax: +503 279 2070

National Association of Private Businesses
Asociación Nacional de la Empresa Privada
Address: Apdo 1204, 1ª Calle Poniente y 71ª Ave Norte #204, Colonia Escalón, San Salvador
Telephone: +503 224 1236/0563
Fax: +503 223 8932
Chief officers: Roberto Vilanova (President)
Membership: privately owned companies

Travel Agencies' and Tourism Enterprises' Association of El Salvador (ASAV)
Asociación Salvadoreña de Agencias de Viajes y Empresas de Turismo
Address: Edificio Beethoven, Paseo General Escalón 3913, San Salvador
Telephone: +503 242 034
Fax: +503 242 529

Union of El Salvadoran Businesses
Unión de Dirigentes de Empresas Salvadoreñas
Address: Condominio Mediterráneo, Edificio C, nº 22, Jardines de Guadalupe, San Salvador
Telephone: +503 243 2746
Fax: +503 243 3145
Activities: promotes export in El Salvador, training courses to members
Chief officers: Ing. Raúl Soto Ramírez (President)

EQUATORIAL GUINEA

Chamber of Agriculture of Bioko
Cámara de Agricultura de Bioko
Address: Malabo
Telephone: +240 240 923

ESTONIA

Estonian Article Numbering Association
Address: Estonian Chamber of Commerce and Industry, 17 Toom-Kooli Street, EE0106 Tallinn
Telephone: +372 2 443 482
Fax: +372 2 443 656

Estonian Breweries' Association
Address: Tahtve Re 56/62, Tartu EE2400
Telephone: +372 7 422 553
Fax: +372 7 421 993

Activities: internal communication
Chief officers: Madis Paddar (Chairman of the Board)
Membership: 7 breweries

Estonian Clothing Manufacturers' Association
Address: Tartu mnt. 63, Tallinn EE0001
Telephone: +372 2 429 324
Fax: +372 2 430 554
Activities: legal advice and support, education, organises seminars, collects statistical data on the clothing industry
Chief officers: Andres Soosaar (Chairman of the Board), Katrin Klein-Näppi (Executive Manager)
Membership: 215 manufacturers
Publications:
• Infolest: *monthly*

Estonian Dairy Association
Address: Vilmsi 53, EE 0001 Tallinn
Telephone: +372 2 427 468
Fax: +372 2 643 0418
Chief officers: Rein Reisson (Director), Enn Sokk (Chairman of the Board)
Membership: 20

Estonian Food Industry Association
Address: Gonsiori 29, Tallinn EE001
Telephone: +372 2 422 246
Fax: +372 2 312 718
Activities: monitors legislation, collects and disseminates information, compiles statistics on production and consumption
Chief officers: Helve Remmel (Managing Director)
Membership: 21 members including the Estonian Fishing Industry Association, Estonian Dairy Association, Estonian Meat Association, Union of Estonian Breweries

Estonian Meat Association
Address: Lai 39/4, Tallinn EE0001
Telephone: +372 2 609 125
Fax: +372 2 448 345
Chief officers: Peeter Maspanov (Chairman of the Board)

Estonian Newspapers' Association
Eesti Ajalehtede Liit
Address: Pärnu mnt. 67a, EE0 001 Tallinn
Telephone: +372 646 1005
Fax: +372 631 1210
Chief officers: Mr Tarmu Tammerk (Managing Director)

Estonian Publishers' Association
Address: Pärnu mnt. 10, pk 3366, EE0090 Tallinn
Telephone: +372 2 666 925
Fax: +372 2 445 720
Chief officers: Mr T Koger (General Secretary), Mr A Tarvis (Director)

Estonian Soap and Detergent Industry Association (EKTL)
Eesti Keemiatööstuse Liit
Address: 19, Tulika, Eat-EE0006 Tallinn
Telephone: +372 659 1040
Fax: +372 650 5010
Chief officers: Mrs Helgi Rôôs

Estonian Union of Automobile Enterprises
Address: Magasini 31, Tallinn EE0001
Telephone: +372 2 439 476
Fax: +372 2 443 345

Chief officers: Mati Magi (President), Lembit Ojavere (Director)
Membership: 55

Estonian Woodwork Federation
Address: Gonsiori 29, Tallinn EE0001
Telephone: +372 2 499 546
Fax: +372 2 421 591
Chief officers: Olev Nigul (President), Erhard Toots (Director)
Membership: 27

Federation of Estonian Chemical Industries
Address: Tulika 19, Tallinn EE0006
Telephone: +372 650 5140
Fax: +372 650 5010
Chief officers: Rein Reile (Chairman of the Board), Helgi Roos (Managing Director)
Membership: 20

Union of Estonian Wine Producers
Address: Karksi, Viljandima EE294
Telephone: +372 43 315 33
Fax: +372 43 315 33
Activities: coordinates different activities
Chief officers: Juri Kert (Chairman of the Board)
Membership: 7 wine producers

ETHIOPIA

Coffee and Tea Development Board
Address: PO Box 3222, Addis Ababa
Telephone: +251 1 518 088/159 243
Fax: +251 1 517 933

Wholesale and Retail Traders' Association
Address: PO Box 1489, Addis Abeba
Telephone: +251 750 477
Membership: wholesalers and retailers

FALKLAND ISLANDS

Association of the Falkland Islands Fishing Industry
Address: c/o Fortuna Ltd, Waverley House, Philomel Street, Stanley
Telephone: +500 226 16
Fax: +500 226 17
Chief officers: Stuart Wallace (Chairman)
Membership: fishing and fish processing companies in Falkland Islands

Falkland Islands Textile Association
Address: Fox Bay Village, Stanley
Telephone: +500 420 98/215 72
Chief officers: Carol Cant, Grizelda Cockwell (Information Officer)
Membership: machine and hand knitters, weavers, spinners and anyone interested in crafts

Spinners and Weavers Handicrafts Guild
Address: Guild Room, Ross Road, Stanley
Telephone: +500 21106
Activities: promotion of hand-crafts
Chief officers: Mrs Marj McPhee (Chairman), Mrs Liz Burnett (Treasurer)

Membership: wool spinners and weavers and other textile manufacturers

FINLAND

Article Numbering Association
Address: PO Box 1000, Central Chamber of Commerce of Finland, World Trade Center Helsinki, Aleksanterinkatu 17, 00101 Helsinki
Telephone: +358 0 696 969
Fax: +358 0 650 303
E-mail: sven-gustaf.lindroos@wtc.fi

Association of Automobile Spare Parts Retailers
Address: Mannerheimintie 76 B, 00250 Helsinki
Telephone: +358 9 407 355
Fax: +358 9 449 419
Chief officers: Matti Räisänen (Ombudsman)

Association of Electronics Wholesalers
Address: PO Box 150, Mannerheimintie 76 A, 00250 Helsinki
Telephone: +358 9 441 651
Fax: +358 9 496 142
E-mail: etk@megabaud.fi
Activities: economic policy, trade policy, legislation, taxation, logistics, statistics, research, education
Chief officers: Pentti Karhu (Managing Director)
Membership: 54 companies

Association of Finnish Advertisers
Mainostajien L
Address: Meritullinkatu 3D, 00170 Helsinki
Telephone: +358 9 662 622
Fax: +358 9 665 030
E-mail: me@mainostajat.fi
Web site: www.mainostajat.fi
Web site notes: site includes information on publications and the advertising industry
Activities: consultation, newsletters, research, publications, seminars and workshops
Chief officers: Kristiina Suhonen (Managing Director), Janne Haivala (Publishing Manager)
Membership: 377 member companies
Publications:
• Advertiser's Directory: *advertising agencies and other service companies - annual*

Association of Finnish Flower Wholesalers
Address: PO Box 150, Mannerheimintie 76 A, 00251 Helsinki
Telephone: +358 2 250 7000
Fax: +358 2 247 1402

Association of Finnish Pharmacies
Suomen Apteekkailitto/Finlands Apotekareförbund
Address: Pieni Rbbbertinkatu 14 C, SF-00120 Helsinki
Telephone: +358 9 228 711
Fax: +358 9 647 167
Web site: www.apteekkariliitto.fi
Year established: 1897
Activities: education and training, developed of the computer based ELIAS customer information system, organises the annual national pharmacy campaign "Pharmacy Awareness Week"
Chief officers: Reijo Purasmaa (Chairman), Reijo Kärkkäinen (Managing Director)
Membership: 580 individual members

Publications:
• Finnish Journal of Proprietary Pharmacists (Suomen Apteekkarilehti - Finlands Apotekartidning): *professional pharmaceutical journal - trade and industry news, new products and developments, research, association news - 15 p.a.*
• Terveydeksi! (The Magazine for Your Health!): *current information on medicines, self- care and treatments of illnesses - 2 p.a.*

Association of Finnish Retailers
Kauppiaitten Kustannus Oy
Address: Rauhankatu 15, SF-00170 Helsinki
Telephone: +358 9 228 821
Fax: +358 9 175 426
Chief officers: Kari Hagfors (Managing Director)
Membership: ca. 3,000 retailers affiliated to the Kesko retail and wholesale group
Publications:
• Elintarvikeuutiset: *case studies of K-stores, new products and marketing information - every other week*
• Kehittyvae Kauppa: *fortnightly*
• Pirkka: *monthly*

Association of Finnish Shoe and Leather Industries
Address: Etelaranta 10, SF-00130 Helsinki
Telephone: +358 9 172 841
Fax: +358 9 179 588
Chief officers: S. Vannela (Managing Director)

Association of Finnish Travel Agents (AFTA)
Address: Vilhonkatu 4B, 00100 Helsinki
Telephone: +358 9 170 112
Fax: +358 9 170 331
Activities: produces a market trend survey on package tours based on charter and scheduled flights (4 p.a.)
Chief officers: Mr Hannu Hamalainen (Managing Director), Ms Elina Peltonen (Deputy Director)
Membership: 173 full members (including travel agents, tour operators, incoming agencies); 73 associate members
Publications:
• Smal Info: *3-4 p.a.*

Association of Importers and Wholesalers of Photographic Supplies
Address: PO Box 150, Mannerheimintie 76 A, 00251 Helsinki
Telephone: +358 9 441 651
Fax: +358 9 496 142
Chief officers: Sinikka Häkkinen (Manager)

Association of Laboratory and Health Care Products Suppliers (SAI-LAB)
Address: PO Box 150, Mannerheimintie 76 A, 00251 Helsinki
Telephone: +358 9 441 651
Fax: +358 9 496 142
Chief officers: Antti Vatanen (Manager)

Association of Opticians in Finland
Address: Mannerheimintie 76 A, 00250 Helsinki
Telephone: +358 9 492 134
Fax: +358 9 492 147
Chief officers: Ilkka Liukkonen (Managing Director)

Association of Pharmaceutical Distributors
Apteekkitavaratukkukauppiaat ry aty
Address: PO Box 150, 00251 Helsinki
Telephone: +358 9 441 651
Fax: +358 9 496 142

Activities: collects statistics (only available to members)
Chief officers: Seppo Morri (President), Antti Vatanen (Manager)
Membership: 2 member companies

Association of Suppliers of Electronic Instruments and Components (ELKOMIT)
Elektroniikan Komponentti- ja Mittalaitetoimittajat ry
Address: PO Box 150, Mannerheimintie 76 A, 00251 Helsinki
Telephone: +358 9 441 262
Fax: +358 9 496 142
E-mail: elkomit@megabaud.fi
Web site: www.electroind.fi/elkomit
Year established: 1972
Activities: economic policy; trade policy; legislation; taxation; logistics; publishes a bulletin for members containing current trends and events
Chief officers: Pentti Karhu (Managing Director)
Membership: 45 member companies importing electronic instruments and components
Publications:
• Buyers Guide: *product register comprising around 13,000 lines of products from 350 companies - annual*

Association of Support Service Industries
Address: Etelaranta 10, SF-00130 Helsinki
Telephone: +358 9 172 841
Fax: +358 9 179 588
Chief officers: Peter Forsstrom (Managing Director)

Association of Textile and Footwear Importers and Wholesalers
Tekstiili-Jalkinetoimittajat ry
Address: PO Box 150, Mannerheimintie 76 A, FIN-00251 Helsinki
Telephone: +358 9 441 651
Fax: +358 9 496 142
Web site: www.tradepoint.fi/ads/jalkine/skl5.html
Year established: 1986
Activities: economic policy, trade policy, legislation, environmental issues, 2 conferences p.a.; brochures; statistics on performance
Chief officers: Mr. Antti Aartela (Managing Director), Miss Maria Vataja (Secretary)
Structure: board
Membership: 100 member companies incorporating importers, wholesalers and traders of textiles, clothing, shoes and boots
Publications:
• List of Members: *annual*
• Statistics
Notes: Member of the Federation of Finnish Commercial Trade.

Association of Watch and Jewellery Wholesalers
Address: PO Box 150, Mannerheimintie 76 A, 00251 Helsinki
Telephone: +358 9 441 651
Fax: +358 9 496 142
Chief officers: Juhani Pursiainen (Managing Director)

Booksellers' and Stationers' Association
Kirja-ja Paperikauppojen Liitto ry
Address: Eerikinkatu 15-17 D 43, FIN-00100 Helsinki
Telephone: +358 9 694 4822
Fax: +358 9 694 4900
E-mail: kplry@kplry.pp.fi
Web site: www.booknet.cultnet.fi/yhdistykset/kplry/
Year established: 1903
Activities: information service; investigations concerning the

book trade
Chief officers: Olli Eräkivi (Managing Director)
Membership: 225 members (accounting for 325 bookstores)
Publications:
• Kirja-ja Paperialan Kalenteri (Calendar of the Book and Paper Trade): *listings of bookstores, publishers and wholesalers in Finland - annual*
• Kirjakauppalehti : *market trends and development in the book and stationery trade - 7 p.a.*

Central Organisation of the Health Food Trade in Finland
Luontaistuotealan Keskusliitto ry
Address: Manerheimintie 76 A, FIN-00250
Telephone: +358 9 449 212
Fax: +358 9 454 4588
Activities: organises education for those in health food trade; co-operation with Finnish authorities and Scandinavian countries
Membership: 2 associations (Heath Product Wholesalers' and Manufacturers' Association and Finnish Health Product Retailers' Association)

Domestic Electrical Appliances and Consumer Electronics Retailers' Association
Address: Vuorimiehenkatu 21, 00140 Helsinki
Telephone: +358 9 174 233
Fax: +358 9 624 474
Chief officers: Teijo Talka (Managing Director)

Employers' Association of the Finnish Furniture and Joinery Industries
Address: Etelaesplanadi 2, SF-00130 Helsinki
Telephone: +358 9 13261
Fax: +358 9 657923
Chief officers: Martti Uoti (Ombudsman)

Federation of Finnish Commerce and Trade
Kaupan Keskusliitto
Address: P.O. Box 150, Mannerheimintie 76 A, 00251 Helsinki
Telephone: +358 9 441 651
Fax: +358 9 496 142
E-mail: guy.wires@kaupankl.fi
Web site: www.kaupankl.fi
Chief officers: Guy Wires (Managing Director), Stig Henriksson (Deputy Managing Director)
Membership: 14,000 wholesalers and retailers
Publications:
• Membership List: *annual*

Federation of Finnish Fisheries Associations (FFFA)
Kalatalouden Keskuslutto kkl
Address: Repslagaregatan 7 B 23, 00180 Helsinki
Telephone: +358 9 640 126
Fax: +358 9 608 309
E-mail: kalastus@kala.fi
Web site: www.kala.fi
Year established: 1891
Activities: information service to members
Chief officers: Hannele Pokka (President), Markku Myllyla (Managing Director)
Membership: 16 provincial centres for agriculture instruction and registered associations (inland); 8 regional associations of commercial fishermen (coastal)
Publications:
• Fiskeritidsskrift for Finland: *fishing technology, fish farming, fishery administration etc. - 5 per year*
• Kalastaja: *fishing technology, fishery economy, fishery biology, etc. - 5 per year*

• Suomen Kalastuslehti: *fishing, fish farming, fishery studies, fish processing, and marketing - 8 per year*

Federation of Finnish Furniture Retailers
Finlands Möbelhandelns Förbund r.f.
Address: Kannussillankatu 10, FIN-02770 Espoo
Telephone: +358 9 859 3914
Fax: +358 9 859 3951
E-mail: taisto.eronen.shl@pp.kolumbus.fi
Activities: collect statistics including furniture sales in Finland
Chief officers: Mr Timo Vepsäläinen (President), Mr Taisto Eronen (Secretary General)
Membership: 150 members who account for 40% of the total number of furniture retailers in Finland and 80% of the total furniture sales
Publications:
• Huonekalukauppa (Furniture Retail): *trade orientated information about developments in the furniture retailing sector and interior design - monthly*

Federation of Finnish Textile and Clothing Industries
Tekstiili-ja Vaatetusteollisuus ry
Address: Etelaranta 10, FIN-00130 Helsinki
Telephone: +358 9 686 121
Fax: +358 9 653 305
E-mail: name@finatex.ttliitot.fi
Web site: www.interteva.fi/.., www.finatex.fi, www.vateva.fi
Chief officers: Matti Jarventie (Managing Director, Tampere Office), Jussi Peitsara (Director, Helsinki Office)
Membership: 280 member companies
Publications:
• List of Members: *contact details of member companies - annual*
• Textile Industry Statistics: *an English language pocketbook of statistics with basic data on production, foreign trade, consumption. Data presented in tables and graphs - annual*
• Textile Industry Yearbook: *a yearbook with statistics on production, imports, exports, consumption, labour trends, and prices. Data for the latest year and comparisons with earlier years in most tables - annual*
Notes: Head office: PO Box 50, FIN-33211 Tampere Tel: +358 3 388 9111 fax: +358 3 388 9120

Federation of the Finnish Chemical Industry
Kemianteollisuus ry
Address: PO Box 4, SF-00131 Helsinki
Telephone: +358 9 172 841
Fax: +358 9 630 255
Year established: 1993
Activities: business and industrial affairs and labour market policy; collects statistics (only available to members)
Chief officers: Hannu Vornamo (Director General)
Membership: 233 companies
Publications:
• Directory of Chemical and Plastics Industries in Finland: *annual*

Finnish Association for the Trade of Alcoholic Beverages
Address: PO Box 150, Mannerheimintie 76 A, 00251 Helsinki
Telephone: +358 9 441 651
Fax: +358 9 496 142
Chief officers: Antti Vatanen (Ombudsman)

Finnish Association of Advertising Agencies
Mainostoimistojen Liitto MTL
Address: Vuorikatu 22 A 3, 00100 Helsinki
Telephone: +358 9 625 300

Fax: +358 9 625 305
E-mail: sinikka.virkkunen@mtl.fi
Web site: www.mtl.fi
Year established: 1942
Activities: arranges meetings, lobbies the government, conducts research; collects statistics on the industry
Chief officers: Mrs Sinikka Virkkunen (Managing Director), Mrs Paivi Aitkoski-Catani (Chairman)
Structure: committee of publications and public relations, training, media and research committees
Membership: 41 advertising agencies
Publications:
● List of Members: *annual*

Finnish Association of Bakeries

Suomen Leipuriliitto ry
Address: PO Box 115, Pasilankatu 2, SF-00241 Helsinki
Telephone: +358 9 148 87300
Fax: +358 9 148 87301
E-mail: olli.kuhta@et.ttliitot.fi
Activities: information service; lobbying; publishing; staistics on production
Chief officers: Olli Kuhta (Managing Director), Juhani Enkovaara (Chairman)
Membership: 450 bakeries or bakery companies
Publications:
● Leipuri: *includes production and sector statistics, issues, trends and developments in the Finnish bakery industry - 8 p.a.*

Finnish Association of Consulting Firms (SKOL)

Address: Pohjantie 12 A, FIN-02100 Espoo
Telephone: +358 9 460 122
Fax: +358 9 467 642
E-mail: skol.ry@pp.kolumbus.fi
Web site: www.enef.fi/skol/
Activities: collects statistics on invoices, cost indices, trends and salaries
Chief officers: Mr Timo Myllys (Managing Director)
Structure: professional and employers' organisation for independent and private consulting engineering companies
Membership: 230 firms
Publications:
● Information Letter: *regular*
● Member List: *annual*

Finnish Association of Office Technology Trade

Address: Mannerheimintie 76 A, SF-00250 Helsinki
Telephone: +358 9 441 651
Fax: +358 9 496 142
E-mail: peritalo@megabaud.fi
Activities: information technology; statistics; publications
Chief officers: Eero Peritalo (Managing Director)
Membership: 80 members
Notes: Statistics and publications for members only.

Finnish Association of Pipe Retailers

Suomen Putkikauppiasyhdistys
Address: PO Box 22, Kaarelantie 12, SF-00431 Helsinki
Telephone: +358 9 348 340 0
Fax: +358 9 348 341 00
Activities: monthly statistics to members only
Chief officers: Timo Peltola (President), Jan-Olof Grönlund (Director), Timo Lahtinen (Manager of Info Systems)
Membership: 4 companies
Publications:
● Newsletter: *biannual*

Finnish Automotive Importers' Association

Autotuojat ry
Address: Lönnrotinkatu 36 B, 00180 Helsinki
Telephone: +358 9 680 32010
Fax: +358 9 680 32022
Year established: 1955
Chief officers: Pekka Puputti (Managing Director)
Membership: 22 member companies
Publications:
● Press Release (Finnish Automotive Importers' Association): *summary of new registrations; vehicles in use by make, model and year of new registration; also includes a membership list - monthly*

Finnish Book Publishers' Association

Suomen Kustannusyhdistys ry
Address: PO Box 177, Lönnrontinkatu 11A, SF-00120 Helsinki
Telephone: +358 9 228 77250
Fax: +358 9 612 1226
Web site: www.edita.fi/sky
Web site notes: site includes statistics and commentary on book publishing in Finland including data on production and sales volume by genre over a two year review period. The site also includes a list of members
Year established: 1858
Chief officers: Mr Veikko Sonninen (Managing Director), Mr MA Siljola (Secretary), Mr O Arrakoski (Secretary)
Membership: 65 companies

Finnish Cosmetics, Toiletries and Detergents Association

Teknokemian Yhdistys ry
Address: PO Box 311, Eteläranta 10, FIN-00131 Helsinki
Telephone: +358 9 172 841
Fax: +358 9 666 561
Year established: 1942
Activities: provides an information service (national information to consumer organisations, press and authorities); organises conferences; collects annual statistics on domestic sales of cosmetics, toiletries, detergents and maintenance products for household and industrial use
Chief officers: Mr Jarl Storgärds (President), Mr Kaj Svahn (Managing Director)
Structure: technical committee; 5 sections for companies concerned with oral hygiene products; cosmetics; grocery trade products; detergents for consumers; detergents for industrial and institutional use
Membership: 44 company members
Publications:
● Bulletins
● List of Members

Finnish Council of Hotels and Restaurants (HRN)

Hotelli ja ravintolaneuvosto
Address: Merimiehenkatu 29, SF-00150 Helsinki
Telephone: +358 9 632 488
Fax: +358 9 632 813
Year established: 1946
Activities: information service to members only; statistics (free); various types of research for members only
Chief officers: Jorma Latvus (Managing Director), Pekka Roppowen (Consultative Manager)
Structure: committees: hotel and travelling, restaurant and cafeteria, research and catering
Publications:
● Finnish Hotel and Restaurant Industry: *statistics*
● Hot Utiset: *6 p.a.*

Finnish Electrical Wholesalers' Federation
Suomen Sähkötukkuliikkeiden Liitto (SSTL)
Address: PO Box 30, Särkiniementie 3, FIN-00211 Helsinki
Telephone: +358 9 696 3700
Fax: +358 9 621 7710
E-mail: markku.waltari@sstl.fi
Year established: 1931
Activities: collects sales statistics monthly; imposes code numbers on all electrical articles in Finland
Chief officers: Markku Waltari (Managing Director)
Membership: 53 members (11 electrical wholesalers, accounting for over 95% of the Finnish electrical wholesale market, and 42 manufacturers or importers)
Publications:
• Product Catalogue: *listings of products with code numbers*

Finnish Federation of Brewing and Soft Drink Industries
Panimo-ja Virvoitusjuomateollisuusliitto
Address: PO Box 115, Pasilankatu 2, FIN-00241 Helsinki
Telephone: +358 9 148 871
Fax: +358 9 148 87201
E-mail: sirpa.rinne@et.ttliitot.fi
Activities: publishes statistics
Chief officers: Mr Risto Saarinen (Managing Director), Ms Sirpa Rinne (Communication Manager)
Membership: 4 members
Publications:
• Brewing Industry Statistics: *in-depth statistical analysis of the Finnish market for beer, soft drinks and mineral water with references to other alcoholic beverages. Includes details on: number of employees in the industry; sales in volume terms; consumption per capita; broad sector breakdown of consumption of alcoholic beverages in Finland, sales of beer by container type; imports-exports; sales of soft drinks and mineral water by container type; consumption of beverages in nordic countries; beer excise and VAT rates in various countries; international comparisons and a list of members - annual*

Finnish Federation of Periodical Publishers
Address: Lönnrotinkatu 11A, 00121 Helsinki
Telephone: +358 9 228 77280
Fax: +358 9 603 478
E-mail: fppa@aliitto.pp.fi
Year established: 1946

Finnish Federation of Petrol Retailers
Suomen Bensiinikauppiaitten Liitto ry
Address: Mannerheimintie 40D 84, SF-00100 Helsinki
Telephone: +358 9 441 675
Fax: +358 9 442 465
Year established: 1961
Activities: business counselling; annual congress; annual conference (April/May); a combined congress and exhibition; statistics available for pricing of petrol and diesel (retail and wholesale) and service station profitability
Chief officers: Veikko Anola (Managing Director), Hannu Laitinen (Secretary for organisational affairs)
Structure: board (Chairman, 2 Vice-Chairmen, 11 members); Board of Directors (Chairman, 2 Vice-Chairmen, Managing Director); 25 regional associations, 5 nationwide (brand) associations
Membership: 750 members and 25 affiliated local organisations
Publications:
• Bensiiniuutiset (Petrol News): *service stations and petroleum products retailing; car servicing equipment and materials - monthly*
• Outcomes: *monthly; except July*

Finnish Fish Farmers' Association
Suomen Kalankasvattajaliitto
Address: Cygnaeuksenkatu 5 A 3, SF-40100 Jyväskylä
Telephone: +358 14 218 222
Fax: +358 14 218 858
Chief officers: Kaisa Rossi (Editor)
Publications:
• Suomen Kalankasvattaja Fiskodlaren (Finnish Fish Farmer): *articles on issues affecting Finnish fish farmers. International fishing industry news and analysis - 5 per year*

Finnish Flour Milling Association
Kauppamyllyjen Yhdistys ry
Address: PO Box 115, FIN-00241 Helsinki
Telephone: +358 9 148 871
Fax: +358 9 148 87201
Year established: 1943
Activities: collects statistics on grain in Finland
Chief officers: Mr Pekka Kulonen (Chairman of the Board), Mr Antero Leino (Secretary General)
Structure: board of directors from 5 members
Membership: 5 milling companies
Notes: No publications produced.

Finnish Food and Drink Industries' Federation
Elintarviketeollisuus
Address: PL 115, Pasilankatu 2, FIN-00241 Helsinki
Telephone: +358 9 148 871
Fax: +358 9 148 87201
E-mail: irmeli.mustonen@ttliitot.fi
Year established: 1944
Activities: collects statistics on domestic sales of Finnish food products, exports and imports of foodstuffs
Chief officers: Mr Pekka Hämäläinen (Managing Director), Mrs Irmeli Mustonen (PR Manager)
Membership: 400 enterprises and 3 industry associations in the food sector
Publications:
• Annual Report of the Finnish Food and Drink Industries Association: *annual*
• Catalogue of the Branch Associations: *list of the 26 branch associations*
• Facts about Finnish Food Industry: *general statistical brochure - annual*
• List of Members
Notes: Federation is divided into 26 branch associations operating under FFDIF and at the same address; member of the Federation of the Associations of EU Frozen Food Producers (FAFPAS) based in Brussels (Belgium)

Finnish Food Marketing Association
Kaupan Keskusliitto
Address: PO Box 150, Mannerheimintie 76A, FIN-00250 Helsinki
Telephone: +358 9 441 651
Fax: +358 9 441 674
E-mail: pty@www.inefcom.fi
Web site: www.zaupankl.fi/pty
Activities: collects statistics including retail sales of food and groceries
Chief officers: Osmo Laine (Managing Director)
Membership: 10 members
Notes: Incorporates Association of Department Stores.

Finnish Forest Industries Federation (FFIF)
Address: P.O.Box 316, Eteläesplanadi 2, 1st floor, SF-00131 Helsinki
Telephone: +358 9 132 61
Fax: +358 9 174 479/132 6630

Web site: www.forestforum.fi
Year established: 1927
Activities: government lobbying
Chief officers: Matti Korhonen (Managing Director), Marja-Leena Lohi (Secretary)
Membership: 105 companies representing 95 % of Finland's wood-processing industry
Publications:
● Facts and Figures (Finnish Forest Industries Federation): *a compilation of statistics including forest area, ownership, products, foreign trade, capital formation, raw material costs, earnings, operating rates, labour force, and recycling trends. Historical data for the last 15 years in many tables - annual*

Finnish Hardware and Builders Merchants' Association

Suomen Rauta-Ja Koneliikkeiden Yhdistys ry
Address: PO Box 150, Mannerheimintie 76 B, SF 00251 Helsinki
Telephone: +358 9 441 651
Fax: +358 9 491 707
Chief officers: Kari Kulmala (Managing Director)
Publications:
● Kodinrakentaja: *information on: hardware and household goods; building materials; raw materials; accessories and tools for the construction industry; furnishing materials; DIY; machines; glass; porcelain and sports goods*

Finnish Health Product Retailers' Association

Address: Mannerheimintie 76 B, 00250 Helsinki
Telephone: +358 9 449 216
Fax: +358 9 449 419

Finnish Marketing Federation

Address: PO Box 119, 00131 Helsinki
Telephone: +358 9 651 500
Fax: +358 9 179 498
E-mail: kari.hamalainen@mark.fi
Web site: www.mar.fi
Chief officers: Mr Kari Hamalainen (Managing Director)
Membership: 4,800 individual members and 70 company members
Publications:
● Mark Markkinoinnin Ammattilehti: *marketing and advertising - 10 p.a.*
Notes: The Association does not produce statistics.

Finnish National Committee of International Dairy Federation

Address: P.O. Box 390, 00101 Helsinki 10
Telephone: +358 10 381 3008
Fax: +358 10 381 3019
E-mail: mona.soderstrom@rd.valio.fi
Chief officers: Mrs Mona Söderström (Secretary)

Finnish Newspaper Association

Sanomalehtien Liitto - Tidningarnas Förbund
Address: PO Box 415, Lönnrotinkatu 11, 00121 Helsinki
Telephone: +358 9 228 77 300
Fax: +358 9 607 989
E-mail: info@sanomalehdet.fi
Web site: www.sanomalehdet.fi
Activities: education and training, conducts surveys and studies, distributes statistical information and promotes the industry
Chief officers: Mr Veikko Loyttyniemi (Managing Director)
Structure: board, executive committee
Membership: 171 member companies, which publish 214 newspaper titles. Members of the Association represent all Finnish newspapers

Publications:
● Finnish Press (Suomen Lehdistö): *news and trends in the Finnish newspaper publishing industry - monthly*

Finnish Packaging Association

Address: Ritarikatu 3 B A, SF-00170 Helsinki
Telephone: +358 9 651 344
Fax: +358 9 666 899
Activities: education, publications, public relations, information, services; collects statistics on packaging, exports and imports
Chief officers: Jorma Hämäläinen (Chief Executive)
Membership: 200 companies
Publications:
● Pakkaus: *covers the packaging and distribution industry in general - monthly*

Finnish Pharmaceutical Industry Federation (FPIF)

Finlands Farmaciförbund
Address: P. O. Box 108, Sornaisten rantatie 23, FIN-00501 Helsinki
Telephone: +358 9 584 2400
Fax: +358 9 584 24728
E-mail: Erkki.Alanko@sll.fimnet.fi.
Web site: www.fimnet.fi/fpif
Web site notes: site includes the publication "Pharma Facts Finland" which includes statistics and analyses of the Finnish Pharmaceutical market. Includes data on the both the prescription and OTC market and includes information on: market size; top ten pharmaceutical companies; leading brands; sales by type of outlet etc.
Year established: 1991
Activities: Finnish Pharmaceutical Data Ltd. (owned by FPIF) provides statistics on the sale of medicinal products by pharmacies and the use of medicinal products in hospitals (updated monthly)
Chief officers: Mr Jarmo Lehtonen (Managing Director), Mr Matti Lievonen (Chairman)
Membership: 55 member companies
Publications:
● Laakeopas Pharmaca Fennica: *medicinal products marketed in Finland - every second year*
● Medicines and Health: *medicinal products, the pharmaceutical industry in Finland - every second year*
● Pharma Facts Finland: *statistics and analyses of the Finnish Pharmaceutical market. Includes data on the both the prescription and OTC market and includes information on: market size; top ten pharmaceutical companies; leading brands; sales by type of outlet etc. - annual*
● Pharmaca Fennica: *medicinal products marketed in Finland - annual*
● Pharmaca Fennica Veterinaria: *veterinary medicinal products marketed in Finland - every second year*

Finnish Photo Dealers' Association

Suomen Fotokauppiaat ry
Address: Mannerheimintie 76 B, 00250 Helsinki
Telephone: +358 9 441 627
Fax: +358 9 441 683
E-mail: lea.herttua@photoas.pp.fi
Activities: sales survey statistics including information on retail sales, profit and loss accounts, number of photo shops
Chief officers: Ms Lea Herttua (Managing Director)
Membership: 195 members
Publications:
● Foto Magazin: *4 p.a.*

Finnish Shoe Retailers' Association

Suomen Kenkäkauppiaiden Liitto ry
Address: Fredrikinkatu 67 E 42, SF-00100 Helsinki
Telephone: +358 9 443 390
Fax: +358 9 409 563
E-mail: yrjo.gorski@kenkaliitto.inet.fi
Web site: www.tradepoint.fi/ads/jalkine/
Web site notes: site includes statistics on the shoe trade in Finland including retail sales of shoes by type, production, imports, exports and sales by type of outlet
Year established: 1917
Activities: compiles statistics on the industry including retail, production, imports and exports; foundation carries out research in retailing; courses are organised annually
Chief officers: Yrjo Gorski (Managing Director)
Membership: 250 members, with 400 retail outlets
Publications:
• Kenkälusikka: *magazine for Finnish shoe retailers serving the needs of manufacturing, export and import as well as wholesale and retail business - bi-monthly*
• Pocket Diary of the Finnish Shoe Retailers' Association: *information and contact details of suppliers and retailers - annual*
Notes: The Association is a member of the Speciality Goods Retailers' Association, the Federation of Finnish Commerce and Trade, the Finnish Entrepreneurs and the Finnish Publishers' Association.

Finnish Swedish-Speaking Retailers' Association

Address: PO Box 41, 21601 Parainen
Telephone: +358 2 4589 780
Fax: +358 2 4585 130
Chief officers: Ralf Juslin (Managing Director)

Finnish Textile Retailers' Association

Address: Mariankatu 26 B 14, 00170 Helsinki
Telephone: +358 9 135 1288
Fax: +358 9 135 1384
Activities: provides assistance, information and education; collects statistics including retail sales and forecasts
Chief officers: Aimo Virtanen (Managing Director)
Membership: 430 member companies accounting for 1,600 shops
Publications:
• TEKSI: *forecasts for the coming season for the textile and clothing sectors; relevant news and features; colour and fashion trends; fashion fair reports - 11 p.a.*

Finnish Toy Industry Association

Address: Huopalahdentie 5 A, 00330 Helsinki
Telephone: +358 9 480 012
Fax: +358 9 480 014

Finnish Travel Association

Suomen Matkailulitto
Address: PL 776, SF-00101 Helsinki
Telephone: +358 9 622 6280
Fax: +358 9 654 358
E-mail: matkailuliitto@matka.pp.fi
Web site: www.sml.fta.softavenue.fi
Year established: 1887
Activities: publishing activities including local travel guides and brochures; travel service for members
Chief officers: Jussi Yrjola (Director General), Sirpa Vuontela (International Affairs Executive), Ari Niemi (Book Sales)
Membership: 20,000 individual members through 66 member clubs
Publications:
• Hotel Guide Finland: *hotels, motels, inns, hostels, booking centres, conference rooms, bathing establishments, prices, services, conveniences, facilities, etc. - annual*
• Matkailu: *professional travel and tourism journal - bi-monthly*
• Suomen Kulkuneuvot/Finlands Kommunikationer: *railway traffic, coach services, ship services, air services and public transport in the Helsinki metropolitan area - 3 p.a.*
Notes: The Association does not produce statistics.

Finnish Watch and Jewellery Retailers' Association

Address: Ajurinkatu 3, 02600 Espoo
Telephone: +358 9 513 755
Fax: +358 9 518 833
Chief officers: Tapio Suomi (Managing Director)

Forma-Association/Forma Hair

Address: Mechelininkatu 28 A, 00100 Helsinki
Telephone: +358 9 454 2520
Fax: +358 9 454 25211
Activities: gathering information of the trade, information and advice service to members, collects statistics on retail and wholesale sales
Chief officers: Ms Arja Tammi (Managing Director)
Membership: 200 members
Publications:
• Forma Uutlset Magazine (Forma Uutlset Magasine): *4 p.a.*

General Retailers' Group

Address: Mannerheimintie 76 B, 00250 Helsinki
Telephone: +358 9 407 355
Fax: +358 9 449 419
Chief officers: Tiina Oksala-Leino (Ombudsman)

Health Product Wholesalers' and Manufacturers' Association in Finland

Luontaistuotealan Tukkukauppiaiden Liitto ry
Address: Mannerheimintie 76 A, FIN-00250 Helsinki
Telephone: +358 9 449 214
Fax: +358 9 454 4588
Activities: collects statistics and information on the health food product trade
Chief officers: Pekka Harvia (Managing Director)
Membership: 18 importers, manufacturers and wholesalers of health food products
Publications:
• Specialist Health Food Product Trade in Finland: *statistics and information on the health product trade including product groups, retail and wholesale trade, legislation and rules of advertising*

Information Technology Services Association (TIPAL)

Address: Tekniikantie 12, FIN-02150 Espoo
Telephone: +358 9 435 43510
Fax: +358 9 435 43511
E-mail: valtonen@tipal.fi

Optical Goods Wholesalers' Association

Address: Mannerheimintie 76 A, 00250 Helsinki
Telephone: +358 9 492 042
Fax: +358 9 490 275
Chief officers: Rauno Paavola (Chairman)

Organisation for Motor Trade and Repairs

Autoalan Keskusliitto ry
Address: Hietalahdenkatu 4 A, 00180 Helsinki
Telephone: +358 9 680 3200
Fax: +358 9 680 32011
Chief officers: Harri Nykanen (Managing Director)

Organisation of Clothing and Fur Traders
Address: Mannerheimintie 76 B, 00250 Helsinki
Telephone: +358 9 407 355
Fax: +358 9 449 419
Chief officers: Tiina Oksala-Leino (Ombudsman)

Speciality Goods Retailers' Association
Address: Mannerheimintie 76 B, 00250 Helsinki
Telephone: +358 9 407 355
Fax: +358 9 449 419
Chief officers: Tiina Oksala-Leino (Managing Director)

Sport and Leisure Wholesalers' Association
Address: PO Box 150, Mannerheimintie 76 A, 00251 Helsinki
Telephone: +358 9 441 651
Fax: +358 9 496 142
Chief officers: Juhani Pursiainen (Managing Director)

Stationary Wholesalers' Association (KONPAP)
Address: PO Box 150, Mannerheimintie 76 A, 00251 Helsinki
Telephone: +358 9 441 651
Fax: +358 9 496 142
Chief officers: Antti Aartela (Managing Director)

FRANCE

Alliance 7
Alliance 7
Address: 194 rue de Rivoli, F-75001 Paris
Telephone: +33 1 447 78585
Fax: +33 1 426 19534
Year established: 1991
Activities: statistics on production, export, import, consumption, sales, for the French toast, biscuits, breakfast cereals, chocolate, sugar, baby and dietetic food, chilled and processed dessert sectors, (usually only available to members)
Chief officers: Hélène Sartiaux (Information Manager), Sylvain Margou (General Director), Jean-Marie Detrez (President)
Membership: Syndicat des Industries de la Biscotterie (Association of French Toast Industry), Syndicat des Industries de la Biscuiterie (Association of Biscuit Manufacturers), Syndicat des Industries des Céréales Prêtes à Consommer ou à Préparer (Association of Breakfast Cereals Manufacturers), Syndicat des Industries de la Chocolaterie (Association of Chocolate Manufacturers), Syndicat des Industries de la Confiserie (Association of Sugar Confectionary), Syndicat des Industries des Aliments de l'Enfance et de la Diététique (Association of Baby and Dietetic Food), Syndicat des Industries des Préparations pour Entremets et Desserts Ménagers (Association of Chilled and Processed Dessert Industries).

Association for Development and Innovation of the Furniture Industry (VIA)
Valorisation et Innovation de l'Ammeublement
Address: 29-37 avenue Daumesnil, F-75012 Paris
Telephone: +33 1 462 81111
Fax: +33 1 462 81313
Year established: 1979
Chief officers: Mr Mayer (President), Gérard Laizé (General Director), Sophie Lupoglazoff (Press Attaché)
Membership: 35 members

Association for the Promotion of French Perfumery Products
Prestige de la Parfumerie Française
Address: 8 place du Général Catroux, F-75017 Paris
Telephone: +33 1 441 58383
Fax: +33 1 441 58384
Activities: the organisation is primarily involved in international public relations; in Japan it organises awards, produces films for the industry and runs a perfume school in large department stores in Tokyo
Chief officers: Danièle Michelet (Secretary General)
Notes: The Associationaffiliated to the Federation of Perfumery Industries (FIP)

Association of Advertising and Communication Companies (AACC)
Association des Agences-Conseils en Communication
Address: 40 boulevard Malesherbes, F-75008 Paris
Telephone: +33 1 474 21342
Fax: +33 1 426 65990/1 474 20132
E-mail: aacc@aacc.fr
Web site: www.aacc.fr
Activities: statistics on employment, market information, legal information, advertising, direct marketing and sales promotion
Chief officers: Jacques Bille (Vice-Président, Managing Director), Philippe Legendre (Director), Michelle Gross (General Secretary)
Structure: board, delegations with representatives of specialised agencies
Membership: over 200 French Agencies working in the field of commercial communications : advertising, direct marketing, sales promotion and healthcare advertising.
Publications:
● Lettre: *every two month*
● Members Directory: *annual*

Association of Alsatian Wine Producers
Association des Viticulteurs d'Alsace
Address: BP 1225, 12 avenue de la Foire aux Vins, F-68012 Colmar Cedex
Telephone: +33 3 892 01650
Fax: +33 3 892 01660
Activities: organisation of wine tasting for the annual agricultural conference in Paris. The defence of members interests, economic cooperation, information and training
Chief officers: Raymond Battenweck (President), Jean-Paul Goulby (Director)
Structure: President, Director, administrative unit of 6
Membership: 6,000 members from 99 local associations

Association of Bakery Industries
Syndicat des Industries de Boulangerie Pâtisserie
Address: 2 rue de Châteaudun, F-75009 Paris
Telephone: +33 1 532 03888
Fax: +33 1 402 39116
Year established: 1959
Structure: general assembly

Association of Biscuit Manufacturers (L'Alliance 7)
Syndicat National de la Biscuiterie Française
Address: 194 rue de Rivoli, F-75001 Paris
Telephone: +33 1 447 78585
Fax: +33 1 426 19534
Activities: produces statistics, mainly on sales
Chief officers: Gilles Cantreau (President), Jean-Jacques Jarrosson (Treasurer), Jean-Michel Barraud (Vice President), Gérard Lebaudy (Vice President), Laurence Daniel-Legris (General Secretary)
Membership: 184 companies
Notes: The Association is a member of Alliance 7

Association of Bordeaux Wine and Alcohol Wholesalers
Syndicat des Négociants en Vins et Spiritueux de Bordeaux et de la Gironde
Address: 1 cours du 30 juillet, F-33000 Bordeaux
Telephone: +33 5 560 02290
Fax: +33 5 568 13743
Activities: advises on legislation; produces statistics on marketing, operating results and production
Chief officers: F. Cruse (Director), Ms Guillard (Assistant Director)
Membership: over 100 companies representing 95% of the market
Publications:
- "Bordeaux Négoce": *quarterly*
- "Le Guide": *covers product legislation, evaluation and marketing*
- Wholesalers' Directory

Association of Champagne Producers
Union des Maisons de Champagne
Address: 218 551 081 Reims Cedex, 1 rue Marie Stuart, F-51100 Reims
Telephone: +33 3 264 72689
Fax: +33 3 264 74844
E-mail: umch@ebc.net
Activities: internal statistics
Chief officers: Yves Lombard (General Manager), Yves Bénard (President)
Membership: 100 Champagne french and international producers
Notes: The Association does not produce any publications

Association of Chocolate Manufacturers (L'Alliance 7)
Chambre Syndicale Nationale des Chocolatiers
Address: 194 rue de Rivoli, F-75001 Paris
Telephone: +33 1 447 78585
Fax: +33 1 426 19534
Activities: produces statistics, mainly on sales
Chief officers: Jean-Pierre Proponnet (President), Patrick Bendavid (Vice President), Jean Cauchefert (Vice President), Jean Valentin (Treasurer), Sylvain Margou (General Secretary)
Membership: 102 companies
Notes: The Association is a member of Alliance 7

Association of Cognac Exporters
Syndicat des Exportateurs de Cognac
Address: 102 avenue Victor Hugo, F-16103 Cognac
Telephone: +33 5 453 63232
Fax: +33 5 453 63228
Chief officers: Mr Raguenaud (President)
Membership: 10 producers
Notes: The Association does not produce any publications or statistics.

Association of Food Industries (L'Alliance 7)
Syndicat des Industries Alimentaires Diverses
Address: 194 rue de Rivoli, F-75001 Paris
Telephone: +33 1 447 78585
Fax: +33 1 426 19534
Activities: produces statistics, mainly on sales
Chief officers: Pascal Jouannet (President), Jean-Pierre Ballanger (Vice President), Luc Foulonneau (Vice President), Yves de Garidel (Vice President), Jean-Peirre Dumont (Treasurer), Maurice Delaporte (General Secretary)
Membership: 37 companies
Notes: The Association is a member of Alliance 7

Association of French Dairy Processors (ATLA)
Association de la Transformation Laitière Française
Address: Maison du Lait, 34 rue de Saint-Petersbourg, F-75382 Paris Cedex 08
Telephone: +33 1 497 07272
Fax: +33 1 428 06362
Chief officers: Xavier Paul-Renard (President), Marcel Urion (General Secretary), Philippe Ansel (Economic Director)
Membership: 400 private an cooperative industries
Notes: Atla is composed of the National Federation of Dairy Co-operatives (FNCL) and the National Federation of the Dairy Industry (FNIL); see National Interprofessional Centre for the Dairy Economy (CNIEL) for publications and statistics

Association of French Toast Industry (L'Alliance 7)
Syndicat National de la Biscotterie et de la Panification Fine
Address: 194 rue de Rivoli, F-75001 Paris
Telephone: +33 1 447 78585
Fax: +33 1 426 19534
Activities: produces statistics, mainly on sales
Chief officers: Gérard Pananceau (President), Olivier Poigny (Vice President), Laurent Jubert (Vice President), Daniel Baujean (Treasurer), Jean-Michel Bottineau (General secretary)
Membership: 19 companies
Notes: The Association is a member of Alliance 7

Association of Fruit and Vegetable Packers
Association Emballages Fruits et Légumes
Address: 8 bis Cité Trevise, F-75009 Paris
Telephone: +33 1 424 68263
Fax: +33 1 448 39584
Year established: 1976
Activities: the study, promotion, organisation and control of fabrication of reusable packaging for fruit and vegetables. Provides statistics on sales of fruit and vegetables.
Chief officers: André Saillard (Managing Director)
Membership: 400 fruit and vegetable producers and distributors
Notes: Open Monday to Thursday

Association of International Trading Companies in Audio-Visual Equipment and Public Information Services (SECIMAVI)
Syndicat des Entreprises de Commerce International de Materiel Audio/Video et Inform. Grand Public
Address: 25-27 rue d'Astorg, F-75008 Paris
Telephone: +33 1 445 11460
Fax: +33 1 426 53949
Year established: 1984
Activities: consumer electronics (brown goods)
Chief officers: Mr Sedaoun (President), B.Eteve (General Secretary)
Membership: 40 companies

Association of International Trading Companies in Photographic, Cinema and Video Equipment (SIPEC)
Syndicat des Entreprises de Commerce International de Matériels Photo et Cinéma-Vidéo
Address: 25-27 rue d'Astorg, F-75008 Paris
Telephone: +33 1 445 11460
Fax: +33 1 426 53949
Activities: statistics on sales networks
Chief officers: Michel Develay (President), Jean-Pierre Faucher (Vice President), Michel Gaillard (General director), Michel Chartus (General Secretary), Edouard Cabasse (Administrator), Jacques Guasti (Administrator)
Membership: 21 companies

Association of Manufacturers of Household Appliances (GIFAM)
Groupement Interprofessionnel des Fabricants d'Appareils d'Equipment Ménager
Address: 39 avenue d'Iéna, F-75783 Paris Cedex 16
Telephone: +33 1 532 30653
Fax: +33 1 472 02073
Year established: 1968
Activities: provides statistics on production and sales; organises Confortec International (trade show for houshold appliances)
Chief officers: Michel Malnoy (Managing Director)
Membership: 80 companies
Publications:
• Annual Report of the Interprofessional Group of Manufacturers of Household Appliances: *annual*
• Statistics on French Household Appliance Market: *monthly*

Association of Petfood Manufacturers (FACCO)
Chambre Syndicale des Fabricants d'Aliments pour Chiens, Chats, Oiseaux et autres Animaux Familiers
Address: 46 boulevard de Magenta, F-75010 Paris
Telephone: +33 1 480 32911
Fax: +33 1 401 81543
Year established: 1965
Chief officers: Mr Pierre Bonnavaud (Director)
Structure: president, elected every other year, board of directors, and three committees: Technical Committee, External Relations Committee, and Small Pets Committee
Membership: 21 pet food manufacturers
Publications:
• Les Chiffres-Clés: *annual*
Notes: The Association is a member of the Association Nationale des Industries Agro-Alimentaires (ANIA), and the Fédération Européenne de L'industrie des Aliments pour Animaux Familers (FEDIAF)

Association of Risk Management and Insurance (AMRAE)
Association pour le Management des Risques et des Assurances de l'Entreprises
Address: 9-11 avenue Franklin Roosevelt, F-75008 Paris
Telephone: +33 1 428 93316
Fax: +33 1 428 93314
E-mail: amrae@wanadoo.fr
Web site: perso.wanadoo.fr/amrae
Activities: research into risk management with regard to the automotive industry, construction, the environment, legislation, transportion, fire, human resources and information systems. The organisation organises an annual conference which assembles the leading members of the profession as well as heads of French industry. The association is also engaged in education and training, awarding a diploma in risk management
Chief officers: Thierry van Santen (President), Michel Cournier (Vice President) Guy Lamand (Vice President), Alain Lemaire (Secretary General), Yvan Moellinger (Treasurer), Florence Métairie (Managing Director)
Structure: board of six appointed members and nine advisors
Membership: 350 members from 200 different companies
Publications:
• Internal Letter

Association of Study and Statistics for the Textile Industry (ESITEX)
Association d'Etudes et de Statistiques pour l'Industrie Textile
Address: BP 249, 37-39 rue de Neuilly, F-92113 Clichy Cedex
Telephone: +33 1 475 63041
Fax: +33 1 475 63049
Chief officers: Denis Chaigne (President)

Association of Sugar Confectionery (L'Alliance 7)
Chambre Syndicale Nationale des Fabricants de Confiserie
Address: 194 rue de Rivoli, F-75001 Paris
Telephone: +33 1 447 78585
Fax: +33 1 426 19534
Activities: produces statistics, mainly on sales
Chief officers: Georges Verquin (President), René Ciseri (Treasurer), Didier Renou (Vice President), Bruno Luisetti (Vice President), Jean-Loup Allain (General Secretary)
Membership: 134 companies
Notes: The Association is a member of Alliance 7

Association of Sugar End-User Industries (CIUS)
Comité des Industries Utilisatrices de Sucre
Address: 194 rue de Rivoli, F-75001 Paris
Telephone: +33 1 447 78585
Fax: +33 1 426 19534
Year established: 1992
Chief officers: Sylvain Margou (President), Jean-Michel Bottineau (General Secretary)
Membership: 10 companies and 10 professional organisations
Notes: The Commitee is a member of Alliance 7

Association of the French Furniture Industry (UNIFA)
Union Nationale de l'Industrie Française de l'Ammeublement
Address: 28 bis avenue Daumesnil, F-75012 Paris
Telephone: +33 1 446 81800
Fax: +33 1 446 81801
E-mail: furniture-of-france@compuserve.com
Chief officers: Henri Griffon (President), Georges Cambour (Managing Director)
Membership: furniture manufacturers

Association of the Regional Daily Press (SPQR)
Syndicat de la Presse Quotidienne Régionale
Address: 17 place des Etats-Unis, F-75116 Paris
Telephone: +33 1 407 38020
Fax: +33 1 472 04894
E-mail: spqr-france@pobox.com
Year established: 1952
Activities: provides statistics on sales
Chief officers: Jean Viansson-Ponté (Director), Jean-Pierre Delivet (Assistant Director), Ms de la Clergerie (Documentation)
Membership: 38 regional daily newspapers

Association of the Soap and Detergent Industries (AISD)
Association des Industries des Savons et des Détergents
Address: 118 avenue Achille Peretti, F-92200 Neuilly-sur-Seine
Telephone: +33 1 474 76000
Fax: +33 1 474 70751
Chief officers: Patrick Miot (Secretary General)
Membership: c.a 60 soap and detergent manufacturers
Notes: The Association is a member of the AISE based in Brussels (Belgium)

Association Telexport
Association Telexport
Address: Chambre de Commerce et d'Industrie de Paris, 92 bis rue Cardinet, F-75017 Paris
Telephone: +33 1 556 56400
Fax: +33 1 556 56382
E-mail: telexport@ccip.fr
Web site: www.worldchambers.com
Web site notes: or: http://www.ccip.fr
Year established: 1985
Activities: provide information on French exporters and importers, and on cross-border business opportunities
Chief officers: Phillippe Do (Product Manager)

Structure: composed of French chambers of commerce
Membership: French Chambers of Commerce and Industry
Publications:
• France Telexport Directory: *French, Spanish, Italien, Portuguese, Austrian exporters and importers - annual*
Notes: Telexport does not collect statistics

Bourgogne Wine Producers' Association (BIVB)
Bureau Interprofessionnel des Vins de Bourgogne
Address: BP 150, 12 boulevard Bretonnière, F-21204 Beaune Cedex
Telephone: +33 3 802 50480
Fax: +33 3 802 50490/3 802 50481
Year established: 1989
Activities: produces statistics on stocks, consumption, exports
Chief officers: Louis Trébuchet (President), A. Ségala (Director), Jean-Charles Servant (Public Relations Director)
Membership: 72 members (wine growers, merchants)
Publications:
• Bourgogne Wines News (Bourgogne Vins Actualités): *news and statistics on stocks, consumption, exports - monthly*
• En direct de la Bourgogne (En direct de la Bourgogne): *monthly*

Central Committee for Wool and Related Fibres (CCLFA)
Comité Central de la Laine et des Fibres Associés
Address: BP 249, 37-39 rue de Neuilly, F-92113 Clichy Cedex
Telephone: +33 1 475 63141/1 475 63040
Fax: +33 1 473 70620/1 475 63049
Year established: 1948
Activities: Expofil (spinners exhibition, 2 p.a.; members only) Premiere Vision (weavers exhibition, 2 p.a.; members only); statistics
Chief officers: Camille Amalric (President), Denis Chaigne (Managing Director), Hubert du Potet (Assistant Managing Director)
Membership: 200+
Publications:
• Informations Lanières: *monthly*
• Note de Conjoncture: *economic information on wool - monthly*
• Rapport d'Assemblée Générale: *annual*
• Statistiques de la Production Lanière
• Statistiques du Commerce Exterieur Lanières
Notes: Sectors covered include wool pulling, wool top making, woollen spinning and wool weaving.

Central Committee of French Shipowners
Comité Central des Armateurs de France
Address: 47 rue de Monceau, F-75008 Paris
Telephone: +33 1 538 95252
Fax: +33 1 538 95253
Year established: 1903
Activities: provides statistics on prices, export, merchant fleets on order
Chief officers: Philippe Poirier d'Angé d'Orsay (President), Edouard Berlet (Managing Director), Alix Daujart (Public Relations)
Membership: 104 shipowners
Publications:
• Annuaire de la Marine Marchande (Merchant Navy Directory): *french shipowners, members or not - annual*
• Le Cahier Statistique Maritime: *commentary and statistics on maritime transport in France, Europe and worldwide, including data on shipping stock, shipping activity, traffic, passenger transport, and goods transport. Historical series in many tables. - annual*

Committee of French Automobile Manufacturers (CCFA)
Comité des Constructeurs Français d'Automobiles
Address: 2 rue de Presbourg, F-75008 Paris
Telephone: +33 1 495 25100/1 495 25124
Fax: +33 1 472 37473/1 472 00246
Year established: 1909
Activities: provides statistics on vehicle production, registrations, motor vehicle parc, imports, exports, fuels, taxes
Chief officers: Yves de Belabre (President), Jean-Pierre Reynier (Vice President), Laurence Massenet (International Business), Jean-Pierre Mercier (Public Relations), Béatrice de Castelnau (Economical and Statistical Business)
Membership: French automobile manufacturers : Alpine, Citroën, Heuliez, Matra, Panhard & Levassor, Peugeot, Renault, Renault V.I.
Publications:
• French Automotive Industry Statistics (L'Industrie Automobile en France): *annual statistics on vehicle production, registrations, motor vehicle parc, imports, exports, fuels, taxes. Based on various sources - annual*
• Notes de Conjoncture (Committee of French Automobile Constructors): *market shares for the various makes and models of motor vehicles plus production and foreign trade data for the latest month and year to date. Comparable figures for the previous year. Also some regional analysis - monthly*

Confederation of Ceramic Industries of France
Confédération des Industries Céramiques de France
Address: 15 avenue Victor Hugo, F-75016 Paris
Telephone: +33 1 450 01856
Fax: +33 1 450 04756
Chief officers: M. De la Tour (General Secretary)
Publications:
• Statistiques (Confederation of Ceramic Industries of France): *annual statistics on the production, deliveries, foreign trade for ceramics and earthenware based largely on data collected by the association - annual*

Confederation of French Wholesale and International Trade (CGI)
Confédération Française du Commerce de Gros Interentreprises et du Commerce International
Address: 18 rue des Pyramides, F-75001 Paris
Telephone: +33 1 445 53500
Fax: +33 1 428 60183
Year established: 1947
Chief officers: Mr de Morcourt (General Director), Guy Laporte (President)
Membership: wholesale and international trade federations

Confederation of the French Ceramics Industry
Confédération des Industries Françaises de la Poterie
Address: 44 rue Copernic, F-75016 Paris
Telephone: +33 1 450 01856
Fax: +33 1 450 04756
Activities: provides statistics on the ceramics sector
Chief officers: Mr Riou (President)
Membership: 10 federations

Cotton Federation
Fédération du Coton
Address: 37-39 rue de Neuilly, F-92113 Clichy Cedex
Telephone: +33 1 475 63040
Fax: +33 1 475 63049

Employers Federation of Distribution of Oil Products (CSDPP)
Chambre Syndicale de la Distribution des Produits Pétroliers
Address: 4 avenue Hoche, F-75008 Paris
Telephone: +33 1 405 37000/1 405 37024
Fax: +33 1 405 37049
Chief officers: Ms Muller (Public Relations)
Notes: see : French Union of Petroleum Industries (UFIP)

European Packaging Federation (EPF)
Fédération Européenne de l'Emballage
Address: Délégation Nationale, 33 rue Louis Blanc, 93 582 Saint-Ouen Cédex
Telephone: +33 1 401 12212
Fax: +33 1 401 10106
E-mail: ifec@marisy.fr
Web site: www.marisy.fr/ifec
Activities: takes part in most important packaging exhibitions in the world
Chief officers: Jean-Paul Pothet (General Director), Annette Freidinger-Legay (Director)
Membership: 15 national institutes of packaging
Notes: see : French Institute of Packaging and Conditioning (IFEC Promotion) and World Packaging Organisation

Federation of Automobile Distribution Associations (FEDA)
Fédération des Syndicats de la Distribution Automobile
Address: 10 rue Pergolèse, F-75016 Paris Cedex 16
Telephone: +33 1 450 03971
Fax: +33 1 450 09360
Chief officers: Mr Morel (Public Relations)
Publications:
● Le Distributeur Automobile: *10 p.a.*
● Press Information Kit

Federation of Bordeaux Wine Associations
Fédération des Syndicats des Grands Vins de Bordeaux
Address: 1 cours du 30 Juillet, F-33000 Bordeaux
Telephone: +33 5 560 02299
Fax: +33 5 564 85379
Chief officers: Xavier Carreau (President), Jean-Marie Garde (Managing Director), Catherine Barbier (Assistant Director)
Membership: wine associations
Publications:
● L'Union Girondine des Vins de Bordeaux: *commentary and statistics on wine - monthly*

Federation of Canning Industries (FIAC)
Chambre Syndicale de la Conserve
Address: 44 rue d'Alésia, F-75682 Paris Cedex 14
Telephone: +33 1 539 14444
Fax: +33 1 539 14470
Chief officers: Mr Michelon (General Director)
Membership: ca. 300 manufacturers
Publications:
● Fruits, Appertisés et Confitures Production: *annual statistics on the production of canned and preserved fruits and jams with data broken down into specific product areas. Includes both value and volume figures and based on data collected by the Association - annual*
● Rapport Économique: *review of the sector with commentary and statistics on production and markets - annual*
● Statistiques du Commerce Exterieur: *import and export statistics for canned and preserved foods with data for the latest two years in both value and volume terms. Based on an analysis of national trade statistics - annual*

Federation of Diverse Clothing Industries (FIDH)
Fédération des Industries Diverses de l'Habillement
Address: 8 rue Montesquieu, F-75001 Paris
Telephone: +33 1 429 60350
Fax: +33 1 428 68202
Web site: www.lamodefrancaise.tm.fr/fidh
Activities: government liaison, promotion of exports, information service to members
Notes: The Association is made up of four constituent organisations: Chambre Syndicale Nationale du Bouton; Syndicat Français des Fabricants de Ceinture-Bretelles; Comité des Fabricants Français de Cravates; Union Intersyndicale des Manufactures de Parapluies et Ombrelles de France.

Federation of French Electric, Electronic and Communication Industries (FIEEC)
Fédération des Industries Electriques, Electroniques et de Communication
Address: 11-17 rue Hamelin, F-75783 Paris Cedex 16
Telephone: +33 1 450 57070
Fax: +33 1 455 30393
E-mail: info@esigetel.fr / fieecomm@freenet.fr
Web site: fiee.freenet.fr/fieec/fiee_eng.html
Activities: provides statistics on sales, exports and imports
Chief officers: Jean-Pierre Desgeorges (President), Jacques Buzenet (Vice President), Robert Mahler (Vice President)
Membership: 26 trade associations representing 900 firms - large, medium-sized and small companies
Publications:
● Annual Statistics: *annual*
● Directory of the French Electrical, Electronics and Communication Companies: *900 French electrical, electronics and communication companies (management, major subsidiaries in the world and list of products in English) - annual*
● Economic Term Letters: *booklet on the organization and trade associations*
● Guide of Small French Enterprises Telecommunications Products: *annual*

Federation of French Ladies Fashion (FAPF)
Fédération Française du Prêt-à-Porter Féminin
Address: 5 rue Caumartin, F-75009 Paris
Telephone: +33 1 449 47000
Fax: +33 1 449 47004
Activities: statistics on production, consumption, foreign trade
Chief officers: David Pisanti (President), Gérard Roudine (Managing Director), Catherine Coudoux (Financial Director)
Membership: associations of manufacturers

Federation of French Maltsters (MALT)
Malteurs de France
Address: 33 rue du Louvre, F-75002 Paris
Telephone: +33 1 530 09450
Fax: +33 1 530 09459
E-mail: malteursfr@aol.com
Web site: www.siebel-institute.com:80/malteurs.html
Web site notes: some statistics on malt barley and French exports of malt
Activities: provides statistics on production, sales, export
Chief officers: Ms Deshayes (Communication Manager), Pierre-André Masteau (Managing Director)
Membership: 7 members

Federation of French Trade Fairs and Exhibitions (FFSF)

Fédération des Foires & Salons de France
Address: 31 rue de Billancourt, F-92771 Boulogne Cedex
Telephone: +33 1 482 56655
Fax: +33 1 482 50455
Year established: 1925
Activities: promoting the interests of the members through the association's publications and by political lobbying. Organising a competition for the trade fair of the year and for the best promotional campaign. Providing companies with information on fairs in their respective sectors and educating members through the organisation of seminars
Chief officers: Jean Taelman (President), Marlène Vamvakidès (General Secretary)
Structure: president, board of directors
Membership: 104 private members, 230 trade fairs and conference organisers, 57 exhibition venues
Publications:
• Annual Calender (Calendrier Annuel): *dates of the exhibitions organised by members - annual*
• Booklet (Brochure Foires, Salons et Parcs d'Expositions): *trade fairs, exhibitions and exhibitions parc - annual*
Notes: The Federation does not produce any statistics; see : Office de Justification des Statistiques

Federation of French Wine Exporters (FEVS)

Fédération des Exportateurs de Vins et Spiritueux de France
Address: 95 rue de Monceau, F-75008 Paris
Telephone: +33 1 452 27573
Fax: +33 1 452 29416
Activities: regular sector statistics (production, sales, export) are available to members; also annual publications available to non-members
Chief officers: Louis-Régis Affre (Managing Director), Nicolas Ozanam (Assistant Managing Director), Antoine Rinaldi (Export Manager)
Membership: 550 members
Publications:
• Cahier de Statistiques: *statistics on the French wine industry - annual*
• Flash Export: *periodicly by fax*
• Le Bulletin: *economical information - fortnightly*

Federation of Paints, Inks, Glues and Adhesives Industries (FIPEC)

Fédération des Industries des Peintures, Encres, Couleurs, Colles et Adhesifs
Address: 42 avenue Marceau, F-75008 Paris
Telephone: +33 1 532 30000
Fax: +33 1 472 09030
Year established: 1880
Activities: statistical analysis; education and training; monthly, quarterly and annual statistics on sales available only for members
Chief officers: Michel Magnan (President), C. Saunier (Vice-President), JP Bourillon (Assistant Director), P Pierremont (Treasurer)
Structure: president, commitee of directors, general assembly and regional associations
Membership: 10 trade associations representing 220 individual members
Publications:
• Rapport d'Activités Annuel: *economic, social and technical reports; statistics - annual*
Notes: FIPEC is a member of the European Association of Paints, Printing Inks and Artistic Colours Manufacturers based in Belgium.

Federation of Paper Products' Manufacturers

Fédération d'Articles de Papeterie
Address: 71 avenue Marceau, F-75116 Paris
Telephone: +33 1 472 09012
Fax: +33 1 495 20588
Activities: produces statistics on production (usually only available to members)
Chief officers: Robert de Caumont (Managing Director)
Membership: 5 trade associations representing 80 manufacturers
Notes: The Federation does not produce any publications.

Federation of Particle Board Manufacturers

Syndicat des Fabricants de Panneaux de Particules
Address: 30 avenue Marceau, F-75008 Paris
Telephone: +33 1 472 01732/9
Fax: +33 1 472 07631
Notes: The Federation is a member of FESYP (European Federation of Associations of Particleboard Manufacturers) based in Brussels.

Federation of Perfumery Industries (FIP)

Fédération des Industries de la Parfumerie
Address: BP 104.04, 8 place du Général Catroux, F-75814 Paris Cedex 17
Telephone: +33 1 441 58383
Fax: +33 1 441 58384
Activities: formulation of codes of practice; political lobbying; research; developing European wide initiatives; education; public relations. International relations; provides statistics on production; turnover, and distribution trends for perfumes and beauty products
Chief officers: Michel Mosser (President), Jean-François Tanneur (Technical Director), Danièle Michelet (Communications Director)
Structure: president, board of directors, general assembly, 6 affiliated organisations
Membership: 6 associations representing 201 member companies (95% of the Industry)
Publications:
• List of Members (Liste des Adhérents): *230 perfume, cosmetics, toiletries companies and pharmaceutical laboratories*
• Statistical Digest (Dossier Statistiques): *production, turnover, and distribution trends for perfumes and beauty products; based on returns from members - annual*
Notes: The Federation consists of six affiliated organisations, the Syndicat Français de la Parfumerie (SFP), Syndicat Français des Produits de Beauté (SFPB), the Syndicat Français des Produits Cosmétiques et de la Tiolette (SFCT), the Syndicat Français des Produits de Parfumerie et de Beauté en Vente Directe (SFVD), the Syndicat Français des Fournisseurs pour Coiffeurs et Coiffeurs Parfumeurs (SFFCCP), Syndicat Français des produits Cosmétiques de Conseil Pharmaceutique (SFPCP).

Federation of Sugar Refiners

Chambre Syndicale des Raffineurs de Sucre
Address: 23 avenue d'Iéna, F-75783 Paris Cedex 16
Telephone: +33 1 495 26696
Fax: +33 1 407 00255
Year established: 1901
Activities: compilation of sector statistics
Chief officers: Anne-Marie Guerin (President), Jean Airiau (Secretary General)
Membership: 9 sugar refining companies
Notes: The Federation does not produce any publications.

Federation of Suppliers and Distributors of Mineral Water
Chambre Syndicale des Eaux Minérales
Address: 10 rue de la Trémoille, F-75008 Paris
Telephone: +33 1 472 03110
Fax: +33 1 472 02762
Chief officers: Françoise de Buttet (President)
Membership: suppliers and distributors of bottled waters

Federation of the French Ceramics Industries
Chambre des Industries Françaises de la Poterie
Address: 15 avenue Victor Hugo, F-75116 Paris
Telephone: +33 1 450 01856
Fax: +33 1 450 04756
Year established: 1937
Activities: provides economic, legal and technical information to members; collects statistics on production, sales, exports, employment etc.
Chief officers: Jaques Henry (President), Françoise Labarre (Secretary General)
Membership: 15 companies

Federation of Vehicle Equipment Manufacturers (FIEV)
Fédération des Industries des Equipments pour Vehicules
Address: 79 rue Jean-Jacques Rousseau, F-92158 Suresnes Cedex
Telephone: +33 1 462 50230
Fax: +33 1 469 70080
Activities: organises the World Auto-Equipment Show; promotion of member companies products; lobbying
Chief officers: Amaury Halna du Fretay (President), Jean Pages (Managing Director SFEPA), Raymond Guasco (Director), Pierre Foret (Statistics), Fabienne Sourau-Parault (Communication)
Structure: president, commitee, general assembly, regional sections and special working groups
Membership: 200 member companies of the Automotives division (SFEPA) which is composed of components and equipment manufacturers for both automotives and service stations
Publications:
● Key Statistics (Chiffres Clefs): *covers the French automotive equipment and components industry. Contains statistics on sales, sales by channel, sales per household, geographical location of premises and staff, imports and exports by destination and country of origin - annual*
● Statistical Brochure (Plaquette Statistique): *statistics on car and motorcycle equipment for the latest year and four or five earlier years. Data on turnover, sales by product, labour, imports, exports, and locations. Based on a combination of official and non-official statistics with some commentary - annual*
Notes: The Federation is composed of three closely affiliated organisations which represent equipment manufacturers in the fields of automotives, bicycles and motorcycles. The Syndicat des Fabricants D'Equipments pour Automobiles (SFEPA), the Conseil National des Professions du Cycle (CNPC), and the Chambre Syndicale Nationale du Motocycle (CSNM).

Federation of Wine and Spirit Merchants
Chambre Syndicale des Industries et Commerces en Gros des Vins et Spiritueux
Address: 103 boulevard Haussmann, F-75008 Paris
Telephone: +33 1 447 53326
Fax: +33 1 447 53348
Chief officers: Mr Bazin
Membership: wine and spirits producers and wholesalers, incorporating regional associations

Food Processing Industry Association (AIA)
Agro-Industrie Avenir
Address: 8 rue d'Athènes, F-75009 Paris
Telephone: +33 1 445 31535
Fax: +33 1 445 31549
Year established: 1993
Activities: produces surveys; consultancy services; organises meetings and debates; provides advice on marketing and exporting; mailing lists
Chief officers: Carl Venables (Deputy Director), Dominique Emanuely (Managing Director), Hervé Jégou (Deputy Director)
Membership: 50 members in agriculture, the food industry, distribution as well as hotel and catering
Publications:
● GRIAL: *details on most French food groups including: firm's name and address; capital and major shareholders; turnover, number of employees; board of directors; activities; list of the main brands; home market shares; production facilities (addresses, capacities), overview charts showing the financial links of companies within groups; lists and addresses of main subsidiaries - every 2 years*

French Advertisers Association
Union des Annonceurs
Address: 53 avenue Victor Hugo, F-75116 Paris
Telephone: +33 1 450 07910
Fax: +33 1 450 05579
Year established: 1916
Activities: seminars for members
Chief officers: Alain de Cordemoy (President)
Membership: 1,000 companies and associations
Publications:
● Annual Report of the Union of Announcers: *annual*
● La Lettre des Annonceurs: *newsletter - monthly*

French Air-Conditioning Association (UCF)
Union Climatique de France
Address: 9 rue la Pérouse, F-75784 Paris Cedex 16
Telephone: +33 1 406 95294
Fax: +33 1 407 09529
Chief officers: Guy Trebulle (President), Paul Genin (Managing Director), Bertrand Rivain (Secretary General)
Membership: 4650 companies
Publications:
● Lettre de l'UCF: *quarterly*
Notes: The Association is a member of GCI (Génie Climatique International) based in Brussels (Belgium); the Association does not produce any statistics.

French Article Numbering Association
Gencod EAN France
Address: 13 boulevard Lefèbvre, F-75015 Paris
Telephone: +33 1 536 80560
Fax: +33 1 482 81681
E-mail: infos@gencod-ean.fr
Year established: 1972
Activities: definition of communication standards
Membership: 19,000 members in the wholesaling and retailing industry
Publications:
● Des Normes pour Harmoniser les Relations entre l'Industrie et le Commerce: *presentation of GENCOD-EAN France*
● Familiarisez vous avec le Code à Barres: *presentation of the bar code system and its use*
● Le Petit Livre du Code à Barres EAN: *different bar codes (EAN8, EAN13, UPC)*

French Association for Commerce and Electronic Trade (AFCEE)

Association Française pour le Commerce et les Echanges Electroniques
Address: 2 rue de Viarnes, F-75040 Paris Cedex 01
Telephone: +33 1 402 66336
Fax: +33 1 402 67092
E-mail: Julien.Dufour@Utopia.Eunet.fr
Web site: www.afcee.asso.fr/
Year established: 1996
Chief officers: Jean-Claude Pelissolo (President), Georges Fischer (International Relations)

French Association of Petroleum Technicians and Professionals (AFTP)

Association Française des Techniciens et Professionnels du Pétrole
Address: 45 rue Louis Blanc, F-92038 Paris-La-Défense Cedex
Telephone: +33 1 471 76732
Fax: +33 1 471 76744
Year established: 1930
Activities: organises meetings, conferences
Chief officers: Danièle Leyrahoux (Assistant Managing Director)
Membership: 2,500 french petroleum technicians and professionals from 300 companies in the petroleum, petroleum equipment and services, and chemical industries
Publications:
• Pétrole et Technique: *six per year*
Notes: The Association does not produce any statistics.

French Association of Beauty Products (SFPB)

Syndicat Français des Produits de Beauté
Address: 8 place du Général Catroux, F-75017 Paris
Telephone: +33 1 441 58383
Fax: +33 1 441 58384
Membership: 61 producers of beauty products sold through selective channels, 11 companies manufacturing raw materials, packaging, etc.
Notes: The Association does not produce any statistics; the Association is a member of the Federation of Perfumery Industries (FIP).

French Association of Cocoa Traders (AFCC)

Association Française du Commerce des Cacaos
Address: Bourse de Commerce, 2 rue de Viarmes, F-75001 Paris
Telephone: +33 1 423 31500
Fax: +33 1 402 84705
Activities: provides statistical services and information
Chief officers: J.C. Ramadier (Managing Director), M. Barry (Secretary), I. Zouhour (Secretary), A. Touton (President), S. Orebi (Vice President), J.B. Pofana (Treasurer)
Membership: 88 European members
Notes: The Association does not provide any statistics anymore

French Association of Cosmetic Products (SFPCP)

Syndicat Français des Produits Cosmétiques de Conseil Pharmaceutique
Address: 8 place du Général Catroux, F-75017 Paris
Telephone: +33 1 441 58383
Fax: +33 1 441 58384
Membership: 9 members
Notes: The Association does not produce any statistics; The Association is a member of the Federation of Perfumery Industries (FIP)

French Association of Direct Sellers of Perfumery and Beauty Products (SFVD)

Syndicat Français des Produits de Parfumerie et de Beauté en Vente Directe
Address: 8 place du Général Catroux, F-75017 Paris
Telephone: +33 1 441 58383
Fax: +33 1 441 58384
Year established: 1974
Membership: 9 companies engaged in direct sales of perfumery and beauty products
Notes: The Association does not produce any statistics; The Association is a member of the Federation of Perfumery Industries (FIP)

French Association of Edible Oils and Oilcakes Manufacturers (SGFHTF)

Syndicat Général des Fabricants d'Huile et de Tourteaux de France
Address: 118 avenue Achille Peretti, F-92200 Neuilly sur Seine
Telephone: +33 1 463 72206
Fax: +33 1 463 71560
Activities: provides monthly statistics on imports and exports for France and Europe only to members
Chief officers: Jean Claude Barsaq (General Secretary)
Membership: 6 french oil manufacturers (Astra Clave SA; Robbe; Lesieur Alimentaire; Cereol; Sté Industrielle des Oléagineux; Cargill)
Publications:
• Annual Report (Rapport Général): *contains statistics on edible oils in France including: production; imports; exports; consumption and prices - annual*

French Association of Finance Companies (ASF)

Association Francaise des Sociétés Financières
Address: 24 avenue Grande Armée, F-75854 Paris Cedex 17
Telephone: +33 1 538 15151
Fax: +33 1 538 15150
Activities: produces statistics on the following: equipment, real estate, leasing, finance, sales finance, consumer credit and hire purchase securities
Chief officers: Michel Lecomte (President), Gilbert Mourre (Managing Director), Jean-Claude Nasse (Assistant Managing Director)
Structure: General Assembly, board of directors, sectorial committees, horizontal committee
Membership: 724 (financial companies and specialist banks)
Publications:
• Annual Activity Report (Rapport Annuel d'Activité): *annual*
• La Lettre de l'ASF (La Lettre de l'ASF): *2 per month*
• List of Members of the Association (Liste des Membres de l'Association): *six-monthly*

French Association of Fruit and Vegetable Committees (AFCOFEL)

Association Française des Comités Economiques Agricoles des Fruits et Légumes
Address: 4 bis rue de Cléry, F-75002 Paris
Telephone: +33 1 448 23000
Fax: +33 1 448 23001
Activities: statistics on production, exports, consumption
Chief officers: André Potel (President), Bernard Cabiron (General Director), Philippe Renaud (Assistant Director)
Membership: 320 producers of fruits and vegetables
Publications:
• AFCOFEL Information Folder: *general information covering the organisation structure and market information*
• Statistiques: *regular statistics on fruits and vegetables in France including data on production, consumption, foreign trade. Based on data collected by the association - annual*

French Association of the Baby and Dietetic Food Industry (L'Alliance 7)
Syndicat Français des Aliments de l'Enfance et de la Diététique
Address: 194 rue de Rivoli, F-75001 Paris
Telephone: +33 1 447 78585
Fax: +33 1 426 19534
Activities: produces statistics, mainly on sales
Membership: 56 companies
Notes: The Association is a member of Alliance 7.

French Banks' Association
Association Française des Banques
Address: 18 rue La Fayette, F-75440 Paris Cedex 09
Telephone: +33 1 480 05252
Fax: +33 1 424 67640
E-mail: afbdif@iplus.fr
Web site: www.afb.fr
Year established: 1976
Activities: monitors legislative, regulatory, administrative and judicial developments; public relations; education and training; carries out research on the banking sector; maintains a library
Chief officers: Michel Freyche (Chairman), Patrice Cahart (Managing Director), Charles Cornut (Deputy Managing Director), Serge Rechter (General Secretary), Robert de Bruin (Public Relations Director)
Membership: 424 banks
Publications:
• Actualité Bancaire: *weekly*
• Le Catalogue: *list of the association's publications*
• Lettre Entreprendre en France

French Breakfast Cereals Association (L'Alliance 7)
Syndicat Français des Céréales Prêtes à Consommer ou à Préparer
Address: 194 rue de Rivoli, F-75001 Paris
Telephone: +33 1 447 78585
Fax: +33 1 426 19534
Activities: produces statistics, mainly on sales
Chief officers: Philip Donne (President), Joël Saint-Vanne (Vice President), Thierry Plassais (Treasurer), Catherine Chapalain-Wallin (General Secretary)
Membership: manufacturers of breakfast cereals
Publications:
• L'Alliance 7: *objectives of the alliance together with membership details*
Notes: The Association is a member of Alliance 7.

French Brewers' Association (ABF)
Association des Brasseurs de France
Address: 25 boulevard Malesherbes, F-75008 Paris
Telephone: +33 1 426 62927
Fax: +33 1 426 65279
Activities: provides statistics on production in both France and Europe as well as data on consumption and retail sales in France
Chief officers: Jean-Paul Shmidt (President Managing Director), Louis Delalande (General Secretary), Elisabeth Pierre (Public Relations Manager)
Membership: 16 brewers
Publications:
• Statistics: *production and consumption of beer in France based on data collected from member organisations - annual*

French Coffee Association
Comité Français du Café
Address: 3 rue de Copenhague, F-75008 Paris
Telephone: +33 1 452 27023
Fax: +33 1 452 21542

Chief officers: Ms Rault
Membership: coffee wholesalers and distributors

French Committee for Beauty Products (CFPB)
Comité Français des Produits de Beauté
Address: 57 avenue de Villiers, F-75017 Paris
Telephone: +33 1 441 58383
Fax: +33 1 476 69762
Year established: 1974
Activities: publishes educational material and organises an annual awards ceremony (Mercure de la Beauté) to recognise excellence in the industry
Chief officers: Gérard Delcour (President), Marie-Hélène Gourmelon (Secretary General), Lilliane Wickersheim (Assistant)
Publications:
• Beauté Contact: *newsletter giving information on new developments in the beauty products' industry*
Notes: The Committee is affiliated to the Federation of Perfumery Industries (FIP).

French Committee for Perfume (CFP)
Comité Français du Parfum
Address: 57 avenue de Villiers, F-75017 Paris
Telephone: +33 1 441 58383
Fax: +33 1 476 69762
Activities: publishes perfume classifications and offers advice on how to sell perfume; produces training films for the industry as well as running promotional campaigns on TV and radio; offers a CD-Rom providing information on different products for distributors and customers
Chief officers: Gérard Delcour (President), Marie-Hélène Gourmelon (Secretary General), Lilliane Wickersheim (Assistant)
Publications:
• Comment Conseiller et Vendre un Parfum
• La Classification des Parfums
Notes: The Committee is affiliated to the Federation of Perfumery Industries (FIP).

French Confederation of Poultry Farming (CFA)
Confédération Française de l'Aviculture
Address: 28 rue du Rocher, F-75008 Paris
Telephone: +33 1 452 26240
Fax: +33 1 438 74613
Chief officers: Mr Darvogne (Director)
Membership: poultry farmers and processors, egg producers
Publications:
• Tendance des Marchés: *market trends and prices for poultry and eggs - weekly*

French Confederation of the Pulp, Paper and Board Industry (COPACEL)
Confédération Française des Producteurs de Papiers, Cartons & Celluloses
Address: 154 boulevard Haussmann, F-75008 Paris
Telephone: +33 1 538 92400
Fax: +33 1 538 92401
E-mail: copacel@msn.com
Year established: 1960
Activities: forms working groups to examine issues such as the competitiveness of the industry and the effect on the environment (particularly in relation to forest depletion); organises an international paper industry conference
Chief officers: Philippe Montel (Chairman), Jean-Paul Franiatte (General Director), Anne-Sophie Japiot (Head of Communications)
Membership: 110 companies
Publications:
• Annual Report of the French Paper Industry (Rapport Annuel

de l'Industrie Papetière Française): *commentary and statistics on the production, consumption, and general markets for paper and cardboard plus foreign trade statistics for pulp and paper. Historical data is included in many tables - annual*
• Bulletin Economique: *statistics - monthly*
• Fiches Techniques
• Plaquette "Papier Nature": *training document*

French Cosmetic and Toiletry Products Association (SFCT)
Syndicat Français des Produits Cosmétiques et de Toilette
Address: 8 place du Général Catroux, F-75017 Paris
Telephone: +33 1 441 58383
Fax: +33 1 441 58384
Year established: 1974
Membership: 65 producers of cosmetics and toiletries
Notes: The Union does not produce any statistics; The Union is a member of the Federation of Perfumery Industries (FIP).

French Dairy Association (ALF)
Association Laitère Française
Address: Maison du Lait, 34 rue de Saint-Petersbourg, F-75382 Paris Cedex 08
Telephone: +33 1 497 07111
Fax: +33 1 428 06345
Chief officers: Dominique Burel (General Secretary)
Notes: The Association is a member of International Dairy Federation (FIL) based in Belgium.

French Electrical and Electronics Industries Association (FIEE)
Fédération des Industries Electriques et Electroniques
Address: 11-17 rue Hamelin, F-75783 Paris Cedex 16
Telephone: +33 1 450 57070
Fax: +33 1 455 30393
E-mail: info@esigetel.fr / fieecomm@freenet.fr
Web site: www.esigetel.fr
Web site notes: site includes a database of French electrical manufacturers with contact details, number of employees, turnover and product information (including brand names when applicable)
Activities: provides statistics on sales and exports
Chief officers: Jean-Pierre Desgeorges (President), Jean-Claude Karpeles (Managing Director)
Membership: regroups 26 trade associations; represents 900 firms - large, medium-sized and small companies. Main product areas covered include: cables and wires, computer and business equipment, electrical equipment for power generation, transmission and distribution, electrical and electronic consumer goods, electronic components, Equipment and systems for process, measurement and control, lighting equipment, medical technologies, professional defence electronics, telecommunications, voice, image and data communications equipment
Publications:
• Annual Statistical Report: *statistics for the major product areas in the electronics industry in France. Figures on industry structure, turnover, production, imports, exports, employment, earnings, with most tables containing figures for earlier years - annual*
• Directory of the French Electrical and Electronics Industries Association: *900 French electrical, electronics and computer companies (management, major subsidiaries in the world and English, German and Spanish list of products) - annual*
• Guide to Small French Telecommunications Products Manufacturers: *annual*

French Federation of Cotton Industries
Fédération Française des Industries Cotonières
Address: 37-39 rue de Neuilly, F-92113 Clichy Cedex
Telephone: +33 1 475 63040
Fax: +33 1 475 63049
Activities: provides statistics
Chief officers: Denis Chaigne (Vice President)
Publications:
• Statistiques: *annual statistics on French textile production, sales, and foreign trade. Based on data collected by the association - annual*

French Federation of Haute Couture
Address: 100 - 102, Faubourg Saint-Honoré, 75008 Paris
Telephone: +33 1 426 66444
Fax: +33 1 426 69463
Web site: www.lamodefrancaise.tm.fr/couture
Membership: 15 fashion houses: Pierre Balmain; Chanel; Christian Dior; Christian Lacroix; Emanuel Ungaro; Givenchy; Hanae Mori; Jean Louis Scherrer; Lecoane Hemant; Louis Feraud; Nina Ricci; Paco Rabbane; Lapidus; Torrente; Yves Saint Laurent

French Federation of Image Industries
Fédération Française des Industries de l'Image
Address: 5 bis rue Jacquemont, F-75017 Paris
Telephone: +33 1 402 59665
Fax: +33 1 422 90222
E-mail: sipi@wanadoo.fr
Year established: 1889
Activities: statistics on sales
Chief officers: Alain Joffrin (President), Jean Pierre Baux (Managing Director), Jacqueline Develay (Vice President), Patrick Posso (Vice President)
Membership: 140 members

French Federation of Insurance Companies (AFSA)
Fédération Française des Sociétés d'Assurance
Address: 26 boulevard Haussmann, F-75311 Paris Cedex 09
Telephone: +33 1 424 79000/1 424 79309
Fax: +33 1 424 79311
Web site: www.ffsa.fr / www.ffsa.com
Web site notes: site includes some data on the French insurance industry including global premium income for the latest year
Year established: 1937
Activities: statistics on the insurance sector
Chief officers: Jean Arvis (President), Patrick Werner (Vice President, Managing Director), Gilles Wolkowitsch (General Secretary)
Structure: board, standing committees,technical groups and associations
Membership: 332 companies that represent 92% of the market
Publications:
• Annual Report: *presentation of the French insurance market with statistics on the industry - annual*
• Assurer: *monthly*
• Directory of French Insurance Companies Abroad (Annuaire de l'Implantation des Sociétés Françaises à l'Etranger): *foreign-based French firms - annual*

French Federation of Lingerie Manufacturers
Fédération Française des Industries de la Corseterie
Address: 8 rue Montesquieu, F-75001 Paris
Telephone: +33 1 429 62235
Fax: +33 1 428 60485
Web site: www.lamodefrancaise.tm.fr/Corseterie.Lingerie
Web site notes: site includes a list of members
Activities: information service to members
Chief officers: Claude Pasquier (President), Jean-Jacques

Béna (Vice President), Alain Arnaud (Treasurer),
Jean-Léonard Bonzon (Acting managing director)
Membership: 22 companies
Notes: The Federation does not produce any statistics or
publications.

French Federation of Specialised Trade Fairs (FSS)

Fédération Française des Salons Specialisés
Address: 4 place de Valois, F-75001 Paris
Telephone: +33 1 428 68299
Fax: +33 1 428 68297
E-mail: salons@wcube.fr
Web site: salons.wcube.fr
Year established: 1954
Activities: promotion of international trade fairs organised by
member companies, monitors and publishes each year the
attendance figures for fairs and shows organised in France
Chief officers: John Shaw (President), Michel François
(Managing Director)
Membership: 44 organisers, representing 80% of the French
market for trade shows in terms of M^2 rented, exhibitors and
visitors

French Federation of Spirits

Fédération Française des Spiritueux
Address: 8 rue de l'Isle, F-75008 Paris
Telephone: +33 1 530 43030
Fax: +33 1 530 43029
Chief officers: Alain Tocquemé (President)

French Federation of the Brush Trade (FFB)

Fédération Française de la Brosserie
Address: 11 rue de l'Arsenal, F-75004 Paris
Telephone: +33 1 488 76777
Fax: +33 1 488 73266
Chief officers: Gérard Droulers (Secretary General)
Publications:
• Annuaire Professionnel de la Fédération Française de la
Brosserie: *annual*

French Federation of the Jewellery and Jewel Trade

Fédération Française de la Bijouterie, Joaillerie, Orfèvrerie
Address: 58 rue du Louvre, F-75002 Paris
Telephone: +33 1 423 36133
Fax: +33 1 402 62951
Activities: statistics for members
Chief officers: Mr Roux (President), Mr Benoît (General
Secretary)
Structure: executive committee; extended executive
committee; 3 commissions
Membership: jewellery manufacturers

French Federation of the Knitwear and Hosiery Industry

Fédération Française de l'Industrie de la Maille et de la Bonneterie
Address: 37-39 rue de Neuilly, F-92113 Clichy Cedex
Telephone: +33 1 475 63232
Fax: +33 1 475 63299
Chief officers: Corrine Volpelier
Publications:
• Lingerie and Underwear Directory: *an annual directory
which includes production statistics for most EU countries plus
detailed data for the French hosiery industry - annual*

French Franchise Federation

Fédération Française de la Franchise
Address: 60 rue de la Boétie, F-75008 Paris
Telephone: +33 1 537 52225
Fax: +33 1 537 52220
E-mail: fff@club-internet.fr

Year established: 1971
Activities: franchise exhibition (annual); franchising
information centre; collects statistics on turnover and numbers
of point of sale
Chief officers: Phillipe Jambon (President), Chantal Zimmer
(Executive Director), Florent Lamoureux (Export Department),
Xavier Legrand-Ferronnière (Information)
Membership: 100 members
Publications:
• Annuaire de la Franchise
• Franchising in Figures (La Franchise en Chiffres): *statistics
on the French franchising sector*
• La Lettre de la FFF: *annual*

French Hardware and DIY Traders Association (AFQB)

Association Française des Commerces de Quincaillerie et
Bricolage
Address: 91 rue de Miromesnil, F-75008 Paris
Telephone: +33 1 456 19944
Fax: +33 1 422 57752
Activities: publishes financial ratios of member companies
Membership: 400 hardware/DIY traders
Notes: The Association does not produce any publications.

French Institute of Packaging (IFEC)

Institut Français de l'Emballage et du Conditionnement
Address: 33 rue Louis-Blanc, F-93582 Saint-Ouen Cedex
Telephone: +33 1 401 12212
Fax: +33 1 401 10106
E-mail: ifec@marisy.fr
Web site: www.marisy.fr/ifec
Year established: 1955
Activities: provides industrial marketing studies and business
to business studies, technical studies, expert evaluations,
regional studies, forecasting studies, annual statistics on
packaging, forum reports and documentary studies; organises
events like the International Packaging Congress, International
Meetings, Packaging Forums
Chief officers: Jean-Paul Pothet (General Director), Annette
Freidinger-Legay (Director)
Membership: 700 members: designers, raw materials
suppliers, packaging manufacturers, machines
manufacturers, packaging users (food and drink industry),
beauty and health industry, distribution, logistics, services, etc.
Publications:
• Newsletter (Lettre): *specific studies*
• Packaging Statistics (Les Chiffres Clés de L'Emballage):
statistics on consumer packaging by sector - annual

French Institute of Self-Service and Modern Distribution Techniques (IFLS)

Institut Français pour le Développement des Liens
Industrie-Commerce
Address: 46 rue de Clichy, F-75009 Paris
Telephone: +33 1 487 43280/1 428 04212
Fax: +33 1 401 69020
Activities: research and compilation of statistics on all
aspects of retail distribution, with particular emphasis on
hypermarkets, shopping centres, supermarkets and
superstores. It also publishes a regular newsletter.
Chief officers: Bernard Bresson (Secretary General)
Membership: self-service store operators
Publications:
• Newsletter of the French Institue of Self-Service and Modern
Distribution Techniques: *retailing*
• Statistiques (French Institue of Self-Service and Modern
Distribution Techniques): *regular statistical series on retail
distribution and retailing structure in France with particular
emphasis on hypermarkets, supermarkets and shopping
centres - regular*

French Lighting Association (AFE)
Association Française de l'Eclairage
Address: 52 boulevard Malesherbes, F-75008 Paris
Telephone: +33 1 438 72121
Fax: +33 1 438 71698
Chief officers: Isabelle Arnaud (Secretary), Catherine Fraudeau (Public Relations)

French Optical Industries' Group (GIFO)
Groupement des Industries Françaises de l'Optique
Address: 39-41 rue Louis Blanc, F-92400 Courbevoie
Telephone: +33 1 471 76400
Fax: +33 1 471 76398
E-mail: gifo@gifo.org
Web site: www.gifo.org
Activities: collects statistics on the optical goods sector including production, sales, imports and exports
Chief officers: Bertrand de Lime (President), Hélène Morcrette (Communication Director)
Membership: 4 optical industries associations
Publications:
• GIFO Info: *six-monthly*

French Petroleum Institute (IFP)
Institut Français du Pétrole
Address: BP 311, 1-4 avenue du Bois Préau, F-92506 Rueil Malmaison Cedex
Telephone: +33 1 475 26000
Fax: +33 1 475 27096

French Plastic Packaging Board (CSEMP)
Chambre Syndicales des Emballages en Matière Plastique
Address: 5 rue de Chazelles, F-75017 Paris
Telephone: +33 1 462 23366
Fax: +33 1 462 20235
Activities: provides information about prices and statistics on sector
Chief officers: Marc Lebosse (President)
Membership: 61 plastic packaging manufacturers
Publications:
• Bulletin d'Informations: *bimonthly*
• L'Emballage Plastique: *presentation of the plastic packaging sector*
• Prix de Vente Industriels: *industrial sales prices - quarterly*
• Prix des Matières Plastiques: *prices of plastics - monthly*

French Refrigeration Association (AFF)
Association Française du Froid
Address: 17 rue Guillaume Apollinaire, F-75006 Paris
Telephone: +33 1 454 45252
Fax: +33 1 422 20042
Year established: 1908
Chief officers: Michel Barth (President), François Billiard (Vice President), Louis Millot (General Secretary)
Membership: 1100 members
Publications:
• La Revue Générale du Froid: *frozen food review - 10 issues per year*
Notes: The Association does not produce any statistics.

French Textile Centre (CTCOE)
Centre Textile de Conjoncture et d'Observation Economique
Address: BP 121, 37-39 rue de Neuilly, F-92113 Clichy Cedex
Telephone: +33 1 475 63030
Fax: +33 1 475 63016
Year established: 1967
Activities: statistics on production, consumption, distribution, sales; market reports covering France and Europe; trade and economic database SINTEX (qualitative and quantitative);

organises an annual seminar
Chief officers: Dominique Jacomet (President)
Publications:
• Annuaire des Chaînes Spécialisées: *directory of distributors*
• Guide du Textile et de l'Habillement: *menswear, womenswear,sportswear, underwear and nightwear, fabrics*
• La Lettre du CTCOE

French Textiles Manufacturers' Institute (UIT)
Union des Industries Textiles
Address: BP 249, 37-39 rue de Neuilly, F-92113 Clichy Cedex
Telephone: +33 1 475 63107
Fax: +33 1 473 02528
E-mail: 100645,45@compuserve.com / journoud@imaginet.fr
Web site: www.textile.fr
Activities: provides regularly updated statistics on the French textile industry including: imports, exports, production
Chief officers: Georges Jollès (President), Guillaume Sarkozy (Vice-President), Suzanne Baumeige (Vice-President)
Membership: 60 professional organisations including 9 companies
Publications:
• Brochure Annuelle: *annual*
• General Statistics on the French Textile Industry (Statistique Générale de l'Industrie Textile Française): *general statistics on textiles in France with data on production, sales, imports, exports etc.. Based on various sources - regular*
• Texpress: *every 2 or 3 month*

French Union of Artificial and Synthetic Textiles (SFTAS)
Syndicat Francais des Textiles Artificiels et Synthétiques
Address: 37-39 rue de Neuilly, F-92113 Clichy Cedex
Telephone: +33 1 475 63100
Fax: +33 1 473 02528
Activities: collects statistics on production and sales
Chief officers: Mr Troy (President), Ms Milon (Assistant President)
Membership: 17 companies
Publications:
• Statistics: *commentary and statistics on the French synthetic fibres and textile industry - annual*

French Union of Clothing Industries (UFIH)
Union Française des Industries de l'Habillement
Address: 8 rue de Montesquieu, F-75001 Paris
Telephone: +33 1 429 62415
Fax: +33 1 429 64841
E-mail: ufih@wanadoo.fr
Web site: www.lamodefrancaise.tm.fr
Web site notes: site includes some basic data on the French clothing industry including imports and exports by value
Chief officers: Phillipe-Jean Lecas (Managing Director), Phillipe Adec (President)
Membership: 5 clothing industries federations and 25 associations
Publications:
• Clothing Industry Statistics (Les Chiffres-Clés de l'Habillement): *key figures on the French clothing sector with data on production, imports, exports, sales and data for specific clothing sectors - annual*
Notes: The Union does not produce any publications; The Union is a member of Euratex.

French Union of Perfumery (SFP)
Syndicat Français de la Parfumerie
Address: 8 place du Général Catroux, F-75017 Paris
Telephone: +33 1 441 58383
Fax: +33 1 441 58384

Year established: 1974
Activities: informs, advises and assists members
Chief officers: Bruno Giry (President); Janine Delmaire (Secretary General)
Membership: 63 producers of perfume products sold through selective channels; 28 raw material, packaging, etc manufacturers
Publications:
• Newsletter of the French Union of Perfumery
Notes: The Union does not produce any statistics; The Union is a member of the Federation of Perfumery Industries (FIP).

French Union of Petroleum Industries (UFIP)

Union Française des Industries Pétrolières
Address: 4 avenue Hoche, F-75008 Paris
Telephone: +33 1 405 37000
Fax: +33 1 405 37049
Activities: organises specific events, publishes reference works
Chief officers: Bernard Calvet (President)
Membership: Chambre Syndicale de la Recherche et de la Production du Pétrole et du Gaz Naturel (Employers Federation of Study and Production of Petroleum and Gas), Chambre Syndicale du Raffinage du Pétrole (Employers Federation of the Oil Refining Industry), Chambre Syndicale des Transports Pétroliers (Employers Federation of Oil Transportation), Chambre Syndicale de la Distribution des Produits Pétroliers (Employers Federation of Oil Products Distribution)
Publications:
• French Petroleum Industry (L'Industrie Française du Pétrole): *commentary and statistics on the oil industry with sections on natural gas and petroleum, production, consumption etc.. Mainly concerned with France but there is a section on world trends - annual*

French Union of Suppliers of Hairdressing and Perfumery Products (SFFCCP)

Syndicat Français des Fournisseurs pour Coiffeurs et Coiffeurs Parfumeurs
Address: 8 place du Général Catroux, F-75017 Paris
Telephone: +33 1 441 58383
Fax: +33 1 441 58384
Year established: 1974
Membership: 20 suppliers of hairdressing and perfumery products
Notes: The Union does not produce any statistics; The Union is a member of the Federation of Perfumery Industries (FIP).

General Confederation of Small and Medium Businesses (CGPME)

Confédération Générale des Petites et Moyennes Entreprises
Address: 10 terrasse Bellini, F-92806 Puteaux Cedex
Telephone: +33 1 476 27373
Fax: +33 1 477 30886/1 477 61749
Year established: 1944
Chief officers: Lucien Rebuffel (President), René Bernasconi (Honorary President), Jaques Pinet (Vice President), Pierre Gilson (Vice President), Pierre Gauthier (Vice President, Treasurer)
Membership: 400 federations
Publications:
• Flash PME: *monthly*
• La Volonté: *monthly*

Hospitality and Catering Association (SNRT)

Syndicat National des Résidences de Tourisme
Address: 178 boulevard Haussman, F-75008 Paris
Telephone: +33 1 537 51275
Fax: +33 1 537 51276

Year established: 1982
Activities: tourist guides; market statistics
Chief officers: Jacques Pancera (President), Pascale Jallet (Managing Director)
Membership: 61 companies
Publications:
• Activity Statistics: *2 p.a.*
• La Lettre SNRT: *2 or 3 times per year*
• Le Guide des Residences de Tourismes SNRT: *biannual*

Institute of Furniture's Promotion and Study

Institut de Promotion et d'Etude de l'Ammeublement
Address: 37 avenue Daumesnil, F-75012 Paris
Telephone: +33 1 462 82121
Fax: +33 1 462 82204
Activities: provides statistics
Chief officers: Mr Gazel (Director), Mr Estassy (Sales Manager)

Lighting Union

Syndicat de l'Eclairage
Address: 52 boulevard Malesherbes, F-75008 Paris
Telephone: +33 1 438 70441
Fax: +33 1 429 30755
E-mail: lux@wanadoo.fr
Activities: conventions; standards; regulation; customer service; quality control; research and development
Chief officers: Jean-Claude Eberling (President); Jean-Pierre Achale (1st Vice-President); Christian Remande (Treasurer), Dominique Ouvrard, (Assistant Managing Director), Catherine Fraudeau (Public Relations)
Structure: professional organisation
Membership: 30 members
Notes: Affiliated to Fédération des Industries Electriques et Electroniques.

Mail-Order and Direct-Marketing Association (SEVPCD)

Syndicat des Entreprises de Vente par Correspondance et à Distance
Address: 60 rue la Boétie, F-75008 Paris
Telephone: +33 1 425 63886
Fax: +33 1 456 39195
E-mail: bs12@calva.net
Web site: www.sevpcd.com
Year established: 1957
Activities: mail order/direct marketing; 1 exhibition p.a.; several conferences for members; information centre; monthly statistics on mail order (members only)
Chief officers: Bernard Siouffi (Managing Director), Dominique du Chatelier (General Secretary)
Membership: 245 companies
Publications:
• Bulletin Syndical: *monthly*
• Lettre d'Information: *includes statistics on the mail order sector in France and other European countries - monthly*
• Revue de Presse: *the mail order market in France - monthly*
• Statistiques (Trade Union of Long-Distance and Mail-Order Sales): *detailed statistics on the mail order and direct mail sectors in France based on returns from members - annual*

National Association of Bleach and Related Products (CSNEJ)

Chambre Syndicale Nationale de l'Eau de Javel et des Produits Connexes
Address: 125 boulevard Malesherbes, F-75017 Paris
Telephone: +33 1 422 75945
Fax: +33 1 426 79316
Chief officers: Dominique Auzou (Managing Director)
Notes: The Commitee is a member of AISE (Association Internationale de la Savonnerie, de la Détergence et des Produits d'Entretien) based in Brussels (Belgium)

National Association of Farm Produce Industries (ANIA)
Association Nationale des Industries Alimentaires
Address: 155 boulevard Haussmann, F-75008 Paris
Telephone: +33 1 538 38600
Fax: +33 1 456 19664
Activities: collects annual statistics on farm produce industries
Membership: 30 agribusinesses, food and drinks manufacturers
Publications:
• Annuaire ANIA: *annual*

National Association of Frozen Food Manufacturers
Syndicat National des Fabricants de Produits Surgelés et Congelés
Address: 18 rue de la Pépinière, F-75008 Paris
Telephone: +33 1 534 21330
Fax: +33 1 534 21332
Activities: statistics on production and sales
Chief officers: Alain Delamort (General Secretary), Michel Figeac (President)
Membership: 37 companies
Notes: The Association is a member of the Federation of the Associations of EU Frozen Food Producers (FAFPAS) based in Brussels (Belgium).

National Committee of Trade
Conseil National du Commerce
Address: 8 place d'Iéna, F-75783 Paris Cedex 16
Telephone: +33 1 443 46834
Fax: +33 1 475 51854
Activities: collects statistics on all sectors
Chief officers: Jacques Dermagne (President), Marie Dardayrol (Secretary General), Jean-Pierre Léonard (Director)
Membership: 110 wholesalers, retailers and international traders federations
Notes: Publications exclusively for members.

National Confederation of Butchers and Delicatessen Retailers
Confédération Nationale de la Boucherie et Boucherie-Charcuterie Française
Address: Maison de la Boucherie, 98 boulevard Pereire, F-75850 Paris Cedex 17
Telephone: +33 1 405 34750
Fax: +33 1 438 02385
Chief officers: Mr Chesnaud (President)
Membership: ca. 16,000 retail butchers
Publications:
• Boucherie Française: *covers the meat and meat products sector; includes market information, trade fairs, product and company news - monthly*

National Confederation of French Bakers and Pastry Cooks
Confédération Nationale de la Boulangerie et de la Pâtisserie Française
Address: 27 avenue d'Eylau, F-75016 Paris
Telephone: +33 1 537 01625
Fax: +33 1 472 71577
Membership: retail bakers and pastry cooks, industrial bakeries

National Confederation of French Meat Processors
Confédération Nationale de la Triperie Française
Address: 60 rue des Prouvaires, F-94535 Rungis
Telephone: +33 1 467 59320
Fax: +33 1 456 09171
Membership: meat processors
Publications:
• Etude Statistique et Economique sur les Abats: *data on the tripe and offal industry in France - annual*
• La Triperie Française: *weekly*

National Confederation of French Pastry, Confectionery and Ice-Cream Manufacturers
Confédération Nationale de la Pâtisserie, Confiserie et Glacerie de France
Address: 4 rue de Hanovre, F-75016 Paris
Telephone: +33 1 474 24137
Fax: +33 1 474 25304/5 630 33208
Chief officers: Jean Millet (President); Robert Marty (Secretary)
Membership: pastry, ice cream and confectionery manufacturers

National Confederation of Hardware Traders
Confédération Nationale des Commerces de Quincaillerie
Address: 91 rue de Miromesnil, F-75008 Paris
Telephone: +33 1 456 19944
Fax: +33 1 422 57752
Membership: 6 hardware traders associations
Publications:
• Confédération Service
Notes: The Confederation does not produce any statistics.

National Confederation of Ice Cream Manufacturers
Confédération Nationale des Glaciers de France
Address: 64 rue de Caumartin, F-75009 Paris
Telephone: +33 1 487 47228
Fax: +33 1 499 50344

National Confederation of Manufacturers and Retailers of Chocolate, Confectionery and Biscuits
Confédération Nationale des Détaillants et des Détaillants-Fabricants de la Confiserie, Chocolaterie, Biscuiterie
Address: 103 aue La Fayette, F-75010 Paris
Telephone: +33 1 428 51820
Fax: +33 1 401 60145
Membership: chocolate, confectionery and biscuit manufacturers and retailers

National Confederation of Wine Distilleries
Confédération Nationale des Distilleries Vinicoles
Address: 12 rue Mairan, F-34500 Béziers
Telephone: +33 4 674 92202
Fax: +33 4 674 92847

National Drinks Federation
Fédération Nationale des Boissons
Address: 49 rue de la Glacière, F-75013 Paris
Telephone: +33 1 458 72141
Fax: +33 1 458 71169
Chief officers: Pascal Sanson (General Secretary)
Membership: manufacturers and distributors
Publications:
• Boissons de France: *covers beer, mineral water, soft drinks, fruit juice and cider including new product information, market reports, statistics on the production of various drinks and data on trade and prices, market trends, financial and company news, technical information; some coverage of wine, spirits and food - 11p.a.*

National Federation of Dairy Cooperatives (FNCL)
Fédération Nationale des Coopératives Laitières
Address: Maison du Lait, 34 rue de Saint-Petersbourg, F-75382 Paris Cedex 08
Telephone: +33 1 497 07290
Fax: +33 1 428 06398

Chief officers: Jean Le Vouch (President)
Membership: 300 dairy cooperatives
Notes: The Federation does not produce any publications or statistics.

National Federation of Dairy Producers (FNPL)
Fédération Nationale des Producteurs de Lait
Address: Maison du Lait, 34 rue de Saint-Petersbourg, F-75382 Paris Cedex 08
Telephone: +33 1 497 07190
Fax: +33 1 428 06380
Chief officers: Mr Beche (Communication)

National Federation of Fruit Producers
Fédération Nationale des Producteurs de Fruits
Address: 4 bis rue de Clery, F-75002 Paris
Telephone: +33 1 448 23060
Fax: +33 1 448 23061
Year established: 1945
Chief officers: Pierre Blanc (President), Luc Boucher (Director)
Membership: 60 federations of fruit producers

National Federation of Gardening Products Distributors
Fédération Nationale des Distributeurs Spécialistes Jardin
Address: 22 rue Esquirol, F-75013 Paris
Telephone: +33 1 442 49697
Fax: +33 1 442 40124
Chief officers: Mr Alleton (Director)

National Federation of Hairdressers
Fédération Nationale de la Coiffure
Address: 17 rue des Victoires, F-75002 Paris
Telephone: +33 1 426 15324
Fax: +33 1 426 00208
Membership: hairdressers
Publications:
• Coiffeur de France: *monthly*
• Voix de la Coiffure Française: *quarterly*
Notes: The Fédération Coiffeur de France and Fédération Officiel de la Coiffure also share these premises (telephone 42615324 and 47707130 respectively).

National Federation of Hardware Wholesalers' Associations
Fédération Nationale des Syndicats de Droguistes en Gros
Address: 42 avenue Marceau, F-75008 Paris
Telephone: +33 1 472 36448
Fax: +33 1 472 39388
Activities: organises conference, compiles statistics and provides information service
Membership: ca. 20 regional wholesale druggists' associations comprising 350 member companies

National Federation of Jam and Fruit Preserve Manufacturers' Associations
Fédération Nationale des Syndicats de Confituriers et Conserveurs de Fruits
Address: 3 rue de Logelbach, F-75017 Paris
Telephone: +33 1 422 74302
Fax: +33 1 405 40079
Chief officers: René Walther (President), Mr Penanhoat

National Federation of Lingerie Retailers
Chambre Nationale des Détaillants en Lingerie
Address: 46 boulevard Magenta, F-75010 Paris
Telephone: +33 1 424 04990
Fax: +33 1 424 05046

Chief officers: Nelly Servais (Chairman)
Membership: lingerie retailers
Publications:
• L'Officiel de la Corseterie: *quarterly*

National Federation of Perfume Retailers
Fédération Nationale de la Distribution en Parfumerie
Address: 14 terrasse Bellini, F-92807 Puteaux Cedex
Telephone: +33 1 477 80044
Fax: +33 1 477 84025
Activities: provides fiscal and legal assistance to members. Compiles statistics on the industry and produces consumer trends forecasts. Offers arbitration services, defence of the French perfume industry in Europe, maintains a database (3615 Parkod), and organises an annual National Perfume Congress
Chief officers: Daniel Guyon (President), François Yung (Vice President), Christiane Manfredi (2nd Vice President), Jean Benoit (Honoury President), Noëlle Ménard (Administrative Secretary)
Structure: president, vice presidents, administrative staff and 13 regional branches
Membership: perfumery and beauty products retailers

National Federation of Producers for Horticulture and Nurseries (FNPHP)
Fédération Nationale des Producteurs pour Horticulture et les Pépinières
Address: 19 boulevard de Magenta, F-75010 Paris
Telephone: +33 1 424 09922
Fax: +33 1 424 09253
Chief officers: Micheline Sallès (Administrative Director)
Publications:
• Horticulture Ornementale: *economic data*

National Federation of Radio, Television and Domestic Electrical Appliance Associations (FENACEREM)
Fédération Nationale des Syndicats du Commerce Electronique-Radio-Télévision et de l'Equipement Ménager
Address: 1 rue Richer, F-75009 Paris
Telephone: +33 1 410 29440
Fax: +33 1 477 81382
Chief officers: M L Herbier (President); M Leleup (Secretary General)
Membership: dealers in radio, television and domestic electrical appliances
Publications:
• Quarterly Review: *quarterly*

National Federation of Rum Producers
Fédération Nationale des Producteurs de Rhum
Address: 4 rue Arsène Houssaye, F-75008 Paris
Telephone: +33 1 435 94147
Fax: +33 1 456 25329
Chief officers: Luc Domergue (Managing Director), Jean-Pierre Bourdillon (President)
Membership: 20 spirits producers

National Federation of Shirt and Lingerie Industries
Fédération Française des Industries de la Chemiserie-Lingerie
Address: 18 rue des Bons Enfants, F-75001 Paris
Telephone: +33 1 426 14088
Fax: +33 1 426 10460
Web site: www.lamodefrancaise.tm.fr/chemiserie.lingerie
Year established: 1884
Activities: government liaison, information service to members, export promotion
Chief officers: Mme De Medeiros, Alain Damamme (President)
Membership: 130 manufacturers of shirts and under-wear

National Federation of the Clothing Trade

Fédération Nationale du Négoce du Tissu
Address: 15 rue de la Banque, F-75002 Paris
Telephone: +33 1 429 65542
Fax: +33 1 492 70893
E-mail: fentiss@isp.fr
Web site: www.selectiss.tm.fr
Year established: 1945
Activities: Salon du Tapis; Biennale des Textiles
d'Ammeublement; answering enquiries from members and the
general public
Chief officers: P Lasseigne (President), Ms Bourdrel de
Contes (General Secretary)
Structure: managing committee, social affairs committee
Membership: 164 wholesalers of fabrics, rugs, carpets and
household linen
Publications:
• Newsletter of the National Federation of the Clothing Trade:
monthly

National Federation of the Dairy Industry (FNIL)

Fédération Nationale de l'Industrie Laitière
Address: Maison du Lait, 34 rue de Saint-Petersbourg,
F-75382 Paris Cedex 08
Telephone: +33 1 497 07285
Fax: +33 1 428 06394
Chief officers: Xavier Paul-Renard (President)
Membership: 100 milk and dairy products manufacturers
Notes: The Federation does not produce any publications or
statistics; see : French Dairy Association (ATLA) and National
Interprofessional Centre for the Dairy Economy (CNIEL)

National Federation of the Dairy Product and Poultry Trade (FNCPLA)

Fédération Nationale du Commerce des Produits Laitiers et
Avicoles
Address: Centra 402, 3 rue de la Corderie, F-94616 Rungis
Cedex
Telephone: +33 1 468 64164
Fax: +33 1 468 70373
Chief officers: Mr Koubbi (General Secretary)
Membership: dairy product and poultry distributors

National Federation of the Edible Oils and Fats Industry

Fédération Nationale des Industries des Corps Gras
Address: 118 avenue Achille Peretti, F-92200 Neuilly sur Seine
Telephone: +33 1 463 72025
Fax: +33 1 474 77489/1 463 71560
Membership: 7 members

National Federation of the French Footwear Industry

Fédération Nationale de l'Industrie de la Chaussure de France
Address: 2 avenue Hoche, F-75008 Paris
Telephone: +33 1 441 51515
Fax: +33 1 462 27152
Chief officers: Olivier Bouissou

National Federation of the Hotel Industry (FNIH)

Fédération Nationale de l'Industrie Hotelière
Address: 22 rue d'Anjou, F-75383 Paris Cedex 08
Telephone: +33 1 449 41994
Fax: +33 1 426 51621
E-mail: fnih@imaginet.fr
Activities: informs and advises its members and resolves
their difficulties; develops and promotes tourism products and
conducts education and training
Chief officers: Jacques Thé (President), Michelle Mangen
(General Secretary), Constance Perrin de Nelle (Public
Relations Manager)

Structure: 6 branches; committees, working groups
Membership: 80,000 individual members, 34 hotel chains
Publications:
• L'Industrie Hotelière: *the French hotel industry - monthly*
Notes: The Federation is a member of the World Tourism
Organisation (WTO) based in Madrid (Spain).

National Federation of Tourism and Delivery Firms (CSNERT)

Chambre Syndicale Nationale des Entreprneurs de Remise et de
Tourisme
Address: 9 rue Montera, F-75012 Paris
Telephone: +33 1 446 78154
Fax: +33 1 531 70860
Activities: education and training, information service to
members
Chief officers: Bernard Durand
Publications:
• Grande Remise: *activities of the Association - quarterly*
Notes: The Association does not produce statistics.

National Federation of Toy Industries

Fédération Française des Industries du Jouet
Address: 103 rue La Fayette, F-75481 Paris Cedex 10
Telephone: +33 1 401 62570
Fax: +33 1 401 62571
Activities: toys and games
Chief officers: Mr Aboaf (Secretary General)

National Federation of Vegetable Producers

Fédération Nationale des Producteurs de Légumes
Address: 4 bis rue de Clery, F-75002 Paris
Telephone: +33 1 448 23065
Fax: +33 1 448 23061
Year established: 1945
Chief officers: Jean Sales (President), Anne Prudhomme
(Director)
Membership: 60 federations of vegetable producers

National Federation of Vending Machine Sales and Services (NAVSA)

Chambre Syndicale Nationale de Vente et Services Automatiques
Address: 34 rue Boursault, F-75017 Paris
Telephone: +33 1 438 77191
Fax: +33 1 438 75378
Year established: 1955
Activities: advice, information on all areas of automatic
vending services
Chief officers: François Saint-Rémy (Managing Director),
Jean-François Coyon (President), Benoît Marotte (Vice
President), Guillaume Borione (Vice President), Elisabeth
Deloche (Treasurer)
Structure: commission; sectoral committees; working
committees
Membership: 190 vending professionals
Publications:
• L'Officiel de la Distribution Automatique: *information about
NAVSA, its members, and the vending machines sector -
annual*

National Federation of Wholesale Potato and Vegetable Traders

Fédération Nationale des Négociants en Pommes de
Terre/Légumes en Gros
Address: 62 bourse de Commerce, F-75040 Paris
Telephone: +33 1 423 35749
Fax: +33 1 423 34993
Chief officers: Mr Touzin
Membership: wholesale potato and vegetable traders

National Furniture Federation (FNA)

Fédération Nationale du Négoce de l'Ameublement
Address: 59 rue St-Lazare, F-75009 Paris
Telephone: +33 1 428 58755
Fax: +33 1 428 06884
Year established: 1936
Activities: conferences and exhibitions held annually in departments; legal information
Chief officers: Jean-Pierre Walter (General Secretary), Georges Cayzac (General Secretary)
Structure: 48 associations and 12 sectoral groups that represent 4000 sales outlets
Membership: 4000 furniture wholesalers and retailers
Publications:
● La Fiche Commerciale
● La Fiche Fiscale
● La Fiche Sociale

National Interprofessional Centre for the Dairy Economy (CNIEL)

Centre National Interprofessionel de l'Economie Laitière
Address: Maison du Lait, 34 rue de Saint-Petersbourg, F-75382 Paris Cedex 08
Telephone: +33 1 497 07111
Fax: +33 1 428 06345
Activities: statistics on French and international dairy economy
Chief officers: Jean-Paul Jamet (Director), Jean-Michel Lemetayer (President)
Membership: 3 members : National Federation of Dairy Industry (FNIL), National Federation of Dairy Co-operatives(FNCL), National Federation of Dairy Producers (FNPL)
Publications:
● Dairy Economy in Figures (L'Economie Laitière en Chiffres): *detailed statistics on the dairy sector including data on industry structure, production, sales, prices, foreign trade, consumption. Data for the last ten years in many tables. Also includes some EU and world data - annual*
● Practical Guide of the Organisation of the Market of Milk and Dairy Products in the European Union (Guide Pratique de l'Organisation du Marché du Lait et des Produits Laitiers dans l'UE): *annual*

National Interprofessional Office of Cognac (BNIC)

Bureau National Interprofessionnel du Cognac
Address: BP 18, 23 allées du Champ de Mars, F-16101 Cognac Cedex
Telephone: +33 5 453 56000
Fax: +33 5 458 28654
E-mail: 100350.224@compuserve.com
Activities: research; information service; training; collects statistics on exports, sales, prices, production
Chief officers: Alain Philippe (Director), Jaques Guibé (President), Claire Coates (Communication)
Membership: 10,000 Cognac wines manufacturers, co-operatives, wholesalers
Publications:
● Cognac Market (Le Marché du Cognac): *statistics on the Cognac market in France - annual*
● Cognac Markets (Les Marchés du Cognac): *analysis of the Cognac market in the EU; statistics on sales in 50 Cognac importer countries - annual*
● Statistics on Cognac-Pineau-Brandy-Wines (Statistiques Cognac-Pineau-Brandy-Vins): *statistics on export, sales, prices, production for Cognac, Pineau, Brandy, Wines - monthly*

National Interprofessional Office of Fruits, Vegetables and Horticulture

Office National Interprofessionel des Fruits et Légumes et de l'Horticulture
Address: 164 rue de Javel, F-75739 Paris Cedex
Telephone: +33 1 442 53636
Fax: +33 1 455 43169
Year established: 1983
Activities: statistics on exports-imports production; marketing research
Chief officers: Mr Laneret (Director)
Structure: public organisation related to the Ministry of Agriculture in France
Publications:
● Annual Report of the National Interprofessional Office of Fruits, Vegetables and Horticulture: *annual*

National Interprofessional Office of Wine (ONIVINS)

Office National Interprofessionel des Vins
Address: 232 rue de Rivoli, F-75001 Paris
Telephone: +33 1 428 63200
Fax: +33 1 401 50696
Activities: collects statistics on production, consumption, foreign trade
Chief officers: Georges Bourgeais (Director), Patrick Soulé (Assistant Director), Jean-Louis Boër (Assistant Director)
Publications:
● ONIVINS-Infos: *market situation, EU news, foreign trade, distribution - 8 to 10 per year*
● Statistics of the Wine Sector (Statistiques de la Filière Viti-Vinicole): *statistics on the wine sectors evolution*
● Wholesale Production Market of French Wine (Marché de Gros des Vins de Table et Vins de Pays à la Production en France): *prices analisys and market segmentations*
● Wine Sector in GMS (La Filière Vins en GMS): *survey on supplying modes and French bid policies*

National Leather Council

Conseil National du Cuir
Address: 109 rue du Faubourg-Saint Honoré, F-75373 Paris Cedex 03
Telephone: +33 1 435 90569
Fax: +33 1 435 93002
Publications:
● Foreign Trade of French Leather Industries (Commerce Exterieur des Industries Françaises du Cuir): *annual foreign trade statistics for leather and leather goods with data for specific products and sectors - annual*
● French Leather Industries (Les Industries Françaises de Cuir): *an annual review of the leather industry in France with data on production, trade, markets and products - annual*

National Union of Bakery, Pastry and Related Industries

Syndicat National des Industries de Boulangerie-Pâtisserie
Address: 10 rue du Débarcadère, F-75852 Paris Cedex 17
Telephone: +33 1 406 80202
Fax: +33 1 406 80980
Activities: collects statistics on production, sales, consumption
Chief officers: Alain Rabreau (President)
Membership: 170 bakery and pastry manufacturers
Publications:
● Information Circulars (Circulaire d'Information): *bimonthly*
● Objectives and Performance (Objectifs et Performances): *presentation of the organisation and the sector*

National Union of Footwear Traders
Syndicat National du Commerce de la Chaussure
Address: 53 boulevard de la Reine, F-78000 Versailles
Telephone: +33 1 302 14061
Fax: +33 1 406 77296
Chief officers: Guy Puiservert
Membership: 40 footwear retailers

National Union of French Importers of Poultry and Dairy Products
Syndicat National des Importateurs Français en Produits Laitiers et Avicoles
Address: Centra 402, 3 rue de la Corderie, F-94616 Rungis Cedex
Telephone: +33 1 468 64164
Fax: +33 1 468 70373
Chief officers: Mr Koubbi (General Secretary)
Membership: wholesale dairy product and poultry distributors

National Union of French Porcelain
Syndicat National de la Porcelaine Française
Address: 44 rue Copernic, F-75166 Paris
Telephone: +33 1 450 01856
Fax: +33 1 450 04756
Chief officers: Mr De la Tour (Director)

National Union of Fruit Juice and Fruit Drink Producers (UNPJF)
Union Nationale des Producteurs de Jus de Fruits, de Nectars et de Boissons aux Fruits
Address: 10 rue de Liège, F-75009 Paris
Telephone: +33 1 487 43116
Fax: +33 1 428 06058
Year established: 1936
Activities: compiles statistics, provides members with information, political lobbying
Chief officers: Philippe Dardonville (Secretary General)
Structure: general secretary, board of 24 members, commission, working groups determined according to members concerns
Membership: 65 producers and distributors of fruit and vegetable juices and drinks
Publications:
• Statistics on Soft Drinks and Fruit Juices (Statistiques Industrielles Mensuelles Jus de Fruits et Boissons aux Fruits): *detailed statistics on the soft drinks sector with data on fruit juices and fruit drinks. Based on various sources - monthly*

National Union of Pharmacies (UNPF)
Union Nationale des Pharmacies de France
Address: 57 rue Spontini, F-75016 Paris
Telephone: +33 1 536 56171
Fax: +33 1 470 47015
Publications:
• Pharmaceutical Evolution (L'Evolution Pharmaceutique): *pharmaceutical industry, drugs legislation, pharmacy management, market news - monthly*

National Union of Phonographic Publishing (SNEP)
Syndicat National de l'Edition Phonographique
Address: 27 rue du Docteur Lancereau, F-75008 Paris
Telephone: +33 1 441 36666
Fax: +33 1 537 60733
Activities: develops economic tools like statistics, database; provides statistics on sales
Chief officers: Patricia Sarrant (Public Relations), Hervé Rony (General Director), Jean-Yves Mirski (Economic Business), Antoine Cartier (Economic Business)
Membership: 51 international companies

Publications:
• L'Economie du Disque: *annual*
• Lettre: *4 per year*

National Union of Publishing (SNE)
Syndicat National de l'Edition
Address: 115 boulevard Hausmann, F-75279 Paris 06
Telephone: +33 1 444 14050
Fax: +33 1 444 14060
Activities: statistics
Chief officers: Serge Eyrolles (President), Jean Sarzana (Director General)
Membership: 400 members
Publications:
• L'Edition de Livres en France: *statistics on the production, imports and exports of books in France. - annual*

National Union of Soft Drinks
Syndicat National des Boissons Rafraîchissantes
Address: 10 rue de La Trémollie, F-75008 Paris
Telephone: +33 1 472 03110
Fax: +33 1 472 02762
Year established: 1963
Chief officers: Michel d'Ornano (President)
Membership: producers and distributers of soft drinks
Notes: The Union is a members of the Union of National European Soft Drink Associations (UNESDA) based in Brussels, the Association Nationale des Industries Agro-Alimentaires (ANIA) and the Comité des Industries Utilisatrices de Sucre (CIUS)

National Union of the Coffee Industry
Syndicat National de l'Industrie et du Commerce du Café
Address: 17 rue de Constantinople, F-75008 Paris
Telephone: +33 1 429 36170
Fax: +33 1 400 80061
Activities: provides statistics on production
Chief officers: J.L. Davon (President), J.C. Frankel (Managing Director), M. Vincent (Administrative Secretary)
Membership: 23 members

National Union of the Pharmaceutical Industry (SNIP)
Syndicat National de l'Industrie Pharmaceutique
Address: 88 rue de la Faisanderie, F-75782 Paris Cedex 16
Telephone: +33 1 450 38888
Fax: +33 1 450 44771/1 450 38842
Activities: statistical service for French pharmaceutical industry with some international comparisons
Chief officers: Françoise Buhl (Public Relations Manager), Bernard Lemoine (General Director), Bernard Mesuré (President)
Membership: 261 laboratories
Publications:
• Annual Report (Rapport d'Activité): *annual activities and figures of the pharmaceutical industry - annual*
• L'Industrie Pharmaceutique : *annual*

National Union of Tourism and Outdoor Associations (UNAT)
Union Nationale des Associations de Tourisme et de Plein Air
Address: 8 rue César-Franck, F-75015 Paris
Telephone: +33 1 478 32173/1 430 68821
Fax: +33 1 456 66990
E-mail: unat@loffice.org
Year established: 1920
Activities: manages an economic database on tourism; Salon Mondial du Tourisme (annual - March)
Chief officers: Jean-Marc Mignon (Managing Director)
Membership: combines the 53 main tourism trade associations

Publications:
• Annuaire Unat
• Flash UNAT: *monthly*
Notes: The Union is a member of the World Tourism Organisation (WTO) based in Madrid (Spain)

National Union of Vending Machine Sales and Services (NAVSA)
Syndicat National de Vente et Services Automatiques
Address: 34 rue Boursault, F-75017 Paris
Telephone: +33 1 438 77191
Fax: +33 1 438 75378
Publications:
• L'Officiel de la Distribution Automatique: *vending industry directory including distributors, producers, associations, etc - annual*

National Wine Labelling and Classification Institute (INAO)
Institut National des Appellations d'Origine des Vins
Address: 138 avenue des Champs Elysées, F-75008 Paris
Telephone: +33 1 538 98000
Fax: +33 1 422 55797/1 538 98044
Publications:
• Bulletin (periodical)

Perfumery Statistics Centre (CISPAR)
Centre d'Information Statistique de la Parfumerie
Address: 8 place du Général Catroux, F-75017 Paris
Telephone: +33 1 441 58383
Fax: +33 1 441 58384
Activities: compiles statistics on the perfume and beauty products market in France, as well as maintaining a products database
Chief officers: Michèle-Dominique Moizo (Secretry General), Josiane Eggimann (Assistant)
Notes: The Centre affiliated to the Federation of Perfumery Industries (FIP)

Petroleum Executive Association (CPDP)
Comité Professionnel du Pétrole
Address: BP 282, Tour Corosa, 3 rue Eugène et André Peugeot, F-92505 Rueil Malmaison Cedex
Telephone: +33 1 471 69460
Fax: +33 1 470 81057
Activities: provides statistics on oil production, freight, storage, foreign trade, refining, consumption, prices, trends, and energy production and consumption for France and the world
Chief officers: Mr Le Crocq (President)
Publications:
• Annuaire Statistique: *detailed statistics on the oil industry in France and worldwide including data on oil reserves, foreign trade, prices, consumption, drilling, refining, trends, etc.. French sector includes the use of oil by sector. Data for the last four or five years is usually included in the tables - annual*
• Bulletin Analytique Pétrolier: *analysis of articles and surveys published in French an foreign trade journals - bimonthly*
• Bulletin Mensuel: *analysis of statistics on sales; covers market trends, production, imports, exports, refining, transport, prices and some internal data - monthly*
• Le Marché Pétrolier Français: *statistical summary of the oil market in France followed by data by region and local areas. Includes sales for the major product groups, ie motor oil, diesel fuel, etc.. Summary data for earlier years and detailed data for the latest year - annual*
Notes: see : French Union of Petroleum Industries (UFIP)

Pharmaceutical Distribution Association
Chambre Syndicale de Répartition Pharmaceutique
Address: 47 rue de Liège, F-75008 Paris
Telephone: +33 1 429 40125
Fax: +33 1 429 41984
Chief officers: Mr Le Guisquet (General Director)

SITELE
Address: 11 rue Hamelin, F-75783 Paris Cedex 16
Telephone: +33 1 450 57070
Fax: +33 1 450 57037
E-mail: 101517.1755@compusrve.com
Activities: produces production and sales statistics on the industry
Chief officers: Gerard Ollivier (Managing Director), Nicole Scholtz (Statistics)
Membership: 20 member companies
Notes: The Association is a member of the EECA (European Electronic Component Manufacturers Association) based in Brussels (Belgium)

Union of Audio-Visual Equipment Industries (SIMAVELEC)
Syndicat des Industries de Matériels Audiovisuels Electroniques
Address: 17 rue Hamelin, F-75783 Paris Cedex 16
Telephone: +33 1 450 57181
Fax: +33 1 450 57172
Structure: professional body
Membership: audiovisual equipment manufacturers
Publications:
• Annual Report of the Union of Audio-visual Equipment Industries: *annual*

Union of French Pasta Manufacturers (SIFPAF)
Syndicat des Industriels Fabricants de Pâtes Alimentaires de France
Address: 23 rue d'Artois, F-75008 Paris
Telephone: +33 1 456 39544
Fax: +33 1 456 33766
Chief officers: Serge Mouzay (Managing Director)

Union of French Tobacco Growers' Co-operatives
Union des Coopératives des Planteurs de Tabac de France
Address: 19 rue Ballu, F-75009 Paris
Telephone: +33 1 445 34800
Fax: +33 1 428 11686
Chief officers: Jacques Beaudoin (President), Mr Haein (Director)

Union of Fruit and Vegetable Wholesalers (Rungis Market)
Union Générale des Syndicats de Grossistes du Marché d'Interêt National de Rungis
Address: 2C rue de Perpignan-Fruleg 115, F-94512 Rungis
Telephone: +33 1 468 60488
Fax: +33 1 467 50819
Chief officers: Mr de Lisle (General Secretary)
Membership: food importers

Union of Housewares Manufacturers (UNITAM)
Union Intersyndicale des Fabricants d'Articles pour la Table, le Ménage et Activités Connexes
Address: 39-41 rue Louis Blanc, F-92400 Courbevoie
Telephone: +33 1 471 76460
Fax: +33 1 471 76461
Activities: provides statistics on production
Chief officers: Laurent Martin (Vice-President, Managing Director), Marcelle Le Poulichet (Secretary)
Membership: 50 housewares manufacturers

Publications:
• Les Chiffres Clés: *production, foreign trade, and market data for the latest year with figures for specific products and housewares. Based on various sources - annual*

Union of Industrial Ice Cream Manufacturers (SFIG)
Syndicat des Fabricants Industriels de Glaces, Sorbets et Crèmes Glacées
Address: 18 rue de la Pépinière, F-75008 Paris
Telephone: +33 1 534 21330
Fax: +33 1 534 21332
Activities: annual production statistics
Chief officers: Alain Delamort (General Secretary), Hervé Cathelin (President)
Membership: 13 members
Notes: The Union does not produce any publications.

Union of Public Transport (UTP)
Union des Transports Publics
Address: 5-7 rue d'Aumale, F-75009 Paris
Telephone: +33 1 487 46351
Fax: +33 1 401 61172
Chief officers: Mr Soupault (Managing Director)
Publications:
• Statistiques et Ratios (Union of Public Transport, UTP): *statistics on transport trends with data for the latest year and comparative data for the previous year - annual*

Union of the Plastics and Rubber Industries (UCAPLAST)
Union des Industries et de la Distribution des Plastiques et du Caoutchouc
Address: 1 square la Bruyère, F-75009 Paris
Telephone: +33 1 428 21022
Fax: +33 1 428 05545
Activities: provides statistics on production, export, import, and annual economic results
Chief officers: Jean Peyronnet (President), Patrick Mercier (Managing Director)
Membership: 13 associations represnting 450 companies
Publications:
• Bilan Economique Caoutchouc et Plastiques: *economic results; surveys on prices, consumption, production; french and international markets; statistics on production and export; economic outlook - annual*
• Guide Caoutchouc et Plastiques d'UCAPLAST: *directory of the plastics and rubber professionals - every two year*
• Informations Mensuelles: *monthly*

GERMANY

Federation of the Chemical Industry (VCI)
Verband der Chemischen Industrie eV
Address: 111943, Karlstrasse 21, D- 60329 Frankfurt
Telephone: +49 69 255 6321
Fax: +49 69 561 471
Web site: www.chemische-industrie.de
Web site notes: list of publications, links to chemical industries who are members of VCI, information on organised events, diverse information on the sector
Year established: 1877
Activities: represents the economic interests of member companies on a national and international level vis-à-vis government, other associations and the general public; maintains archives, compiles economic information
Chief officers: Professor Dr Helmut Sihler (President), Dr Wolfgang Munde (Managing Director)
Membership: ca. 1,500 firms; membership is divided into regional and sector associations/groups,

Publications:
• Chemical Industry in Figures, Chemie-Journal (periodical), topic series of per: *chemical industry and environment; technical*
• Chemie-Report: *monthly*
• Chemiewirtschaft in Zahlen: *basic chemical industry figures with statistics on production, sales, imports, exports, prices, investment. Usually, a table covers a ten-year time span. Based on various sources - annual*
• Chemische Industrie: *monthly*
• Chemische Industrie International: *gives an overview of the international chemical industry with the focus on Germany; in-depth reports on specific markets and market trends covering both chemical processes and manufactured products and giving figures for trade, production, and prices - quarterly*
• Chemische Industrie, Die: *brief reports on developments in the international chemical industry; in-depth reports on the industry, both German and international, which include key indices, figures for imports and exports, production and trade in specific chemicals - monthly*
• Europa Chemie: *gives an overview of the European chemical industry with the focus on Germany; in-depth reports on specific markets and market trends covering both chemical processes and manufactured products and giving figures for trade, production, prices and turnover - every 10 days*
• Europe-Chemie: *3 times/month*

Association for Modern Kitchen Research (AMK)
Arbeitsgemeinschaft der Moderne Küche
Address: Dannstadler Straße 6-8, D-68171 Mannheim 24
Telephone: +49 621 850 6100
Fax: +49 621 850 6101
Year established: 1956
Activities: public relations (PR and Media Committee), provision of brochures, press releases and public addresses
Chief officers: Hans-Joachim Adler (Secretary)
Membership: 124 companies
Publications:
• DMK (die Deutsche Moderne Küche): *articles on issues affecting the modern German kitchen, new product development, some market data, international news - monthly*

Association of Building Societies
Verband der Privaten Bausparkassen
Address: Dottendorfer Straße 82, D-5300 Bonn 1
Telephone: +49 228 239 041
Fax: +49 228 239046
Chief officers: Andreas J Zehnder (General Diretor)
Membership: 22 building societies
Publications:
• Bericht über das Geschäftsjahr (Verband der Privaten Bausparkassen): *commentary and statistics on the housing market and the activities of private banks and building credit banks in Germany. Data usually over a ten-year period - annual*
• Privates Bausparwesen Jahrbuch (Verband der Privaten Bausparkassen): *detailed text and statistics on the activities of private banks and building credit banks in Germany. - annual*

Association of Catering and Vending Companies (BDV)
Bundesverband Deutscher Verpflegungs- und Vending-Unternehmen eV
Address: c/o Weisshausstraße 23, D-50939 Cologne
Telephone: +49 221 447 968
Fax: +49 221 422 522
Chief officers: Pierre Pernet (President), Norbert Moßen Secretary)
Membership: 240 catering and vending firms

Association of Companies involved in the Cocoa Trade
Verein der am Rohkakaohandel beteiligten Firmen eV
Address: Gotenstraße 21, D-20097 Hamburg
Telephone: +49 40 236 016/0
Fax: +49 40 236 01610
Year established: 1911
Activities: compiles industry data for member companies
only; library and information service for member companies
only
Chief officers: Franz-Alfred Wooge (President), Raven
Karalus (Secretary)
Membership: 38 corporate members (importers, agents,
warehouse operators, banks and others)
Publications:
● Annual Report of the Registered Association for Companies
involved in the Cocoa Trade: *annual*

Association of German Air and Space Equipment Industry (BDLI)
Bundesverband der Deutschen Luftfahrt-Raumfahrt und
Ausrüstungsindustrie eV
Address: Konstantinstraße 90, D- 5300 Bonn 2
Telephone: +49 228 849 07/0
Fax: +49 228 330 778
Chief officers: Wolfgang Piller (President), Dr Hans-Eberhard
Birke (General Director)
Publications:
● BDLI Jahresbericht: *mainly commentary and details of
members in the aerospace and aerospace equipment
industries but a small section covers turnover and employment
in the industry with figures for earlier years - annual*

Association of German Gas and Water Industries (BGW)
Bundesverband der Deutschen Gas und Wasserwirtschaft
Address: 140154, Josef-Wirmer Straße 1, D-53056 Bonn
Telephone: +49 228 2598-0
Fax: +49 228 2598-120
Chief officers: Hans-Otto Schwarz (President), Dr Wolf Pluge
(General Director)
Membership: 7 Landesgruppen and 2 Landesverbände
Publications:
● Bundesverband der Deutschen Gas und Wasserwirtschaft
Jahresbericht: *a two-volume annual report with one volume
giving facts about the German gas industry and a second
volume including data on the water industry - annual*

Association of German Market Research Institutes (ADM)
Arbeitskreis Deutscher Markt- und Sozialforschungsinstitute eV
Address: Marktplatz 9, D-63065 Offenbach
Telephone: +49 69 814 325
Fax: +49 69 814 388
Activities: represents the interests of market research
companies and institutes
Chief officers: Dr Klaus Haupt (Chairman)
Membership: members account for around 80% of total
German turnover in the field of market research and opinion
polls

Association of Life Insurance Companies
Verband der Lebensversicherungs Unternehmen
Address: Eduard-Pflüger Straße 55, D- 53113 Bonn
Telephone: +49 228 530 08/0
Fax: +49 228 530 0820
Chief officers: Klemens Wesselkock (Chairman), Dr Hans
Jörg Ehler (Director)
Membership: 133 companies
Publications:
● Jahrbuch (Verband der Lebensversicherungs
Unternehmen): *an annual yearbook with some statistics*

*covering the life insurance sector. Figures are largely based
on a survey by the association but some central government
figures are also included - annual*

Association of Metal Packaging Manufacturers for the Cosmetics and Pharmaceutical Industries
Gruppe Feinstblechverpackungen für Kosmetische und
Pharmazeutische Erzeugnisse
Address: Kaiserwertherstraße 135, D-40474 Düsseldorf
Telephone: +49 211 434 104
Fax: +49 211 454 9369
Telex: 8584985
Chief officers: Rolf Zöllner (Section Director)
Notes: cosmetic/pharmaceutical section of the German
packaging association (Verband Metallverpackungen eV).
There is also an aerosol group: all share the same address.

Association of the Cigar Industry (BdZ)
Bundesverband der Zigarrenindustrie eV
Address: 200626, Körnerstraße 18, D-53175 Bonn
Telephone: +49 228 364 026/27
Fax: +49 228 361 659
Chief officers: Dr Lothar Gabriel (Secretary)
Membership: 50 companies

Association of the German Automotive Industry (VDA)
Verband der Automobilindustrie eV
Address: 170563, Westendstraße 61, D- 60325 Frankfurt/Main
Telephone: +49 697 5700
Fax: +49 697 570 261
Web site: pluto.messe.de:8000/iaa96/vda/index_e.html
Year established: 1945
Activities: organisation of the International Automobile Show
(IAA)
Chief officers: Erika Emmerich (President), Dr. Kunibert
Schmidt (Secretary)
Membership: 550 manufacturers of vehicles and engines,
trailers, semitrailers, containers and vehicle parts or
accessories
Publications:
● Auto Aktuell: *new product information and some trade data;
mostly articles on issues affecting German automobile industry
- irregular*
● Das Auto International in Zahlen/Tatsachen und Zahlen:
*production stats; new vehicle registrations, both domestic and
international*
● Tatsachen und Zahlen aus der Kraftverkehrswirtschaft:
*detailed statistics on motor vehicles covering production,
shipments, imports, exports, stocks, licences, traffic, roads,
fuels etc.. Many series give data by make, model, region.
Historical data in some tables for the last 20 years. A section
with international data is also included - annual*

Association of the German Book Trade
Börsenverein des Deutschen Buchhandels
Address: Postfach 10 04 42, Grosser Hirschgraben 17-21, D-
60311 Frankfurt
Telephone: +49 69 1306 292/130 6324
Fax: +49 69 1306 201/130 6399
Web site: www.darmstadt.gmd.de/BV/
Year established: 1825
Activities: provides statistics on German book market with
some international comparisons; press and information
department
Chief officers: Gerhardt Kurtze (Director and President), Mr
W von Lucius, Mr A Langenscheidt, Mr F von Notz (Director)
Membership: 6,500 members: 2,100 publishers, 4,300 retail
booksellers, 80 firms from the intermediate book trade
Publications:
● Börsenblatt für den Deutschen Buchhandel: *official organ of*

the Börsenverein - twice weekly
• Buch und Buchhandel in Zahlen 1997: statistics and analysis of the German book trade - annual
• BuchJournal: overview of current titles - quarterly

Association of the German Dairy Trade

Arbeitsgemeinschft Deutscher Milchhandels-verbände
Address: Baumschulallee 6, D-53115 Bonn
Telephone: +49 228 637 605
Fax: +49 228 637 354
Chief officers: Ottmar Burska (Secretary)
Membership: approximately 5,000 retail and distributing companies

Association of the German Soft Drinks Industry

Bundesverband der Deutschen Erfrischungsgetränke-Industrie
Address: Königswinterer Strasse 300, D-5300 Bonn 3
Telephone: +49 228 441 072
Fax: +49 228 440 019
Year established: 1882
Chief officers: Carl J Bachem (General Director), Eduard Herder (Secretary)
Membership: soft drink producers and mineral water manufacturers
Publications:
• Das Erfrischungsgetränk/Mineralwasser-Zeitung: soft drinks and mineral water
• Die Statistikn (Federal Association of the German Soft Drinks Industry): production, import and export statistics for the soft drinks industry - annual

Berlin Brewing Industry Academy (VLB)

Versuchs- und Lehranstalt für Brauerei in Berlin
Address: Seestraße 13, D-1000 Berlin 65
Telephone: +49 30 459 245
Fax: +49 30 453,6069
Year established: 1883
Chief officers: Herr H Bayer (Director)
Publications:
• Brauerei-Forum: new products, company and financial news, trade publications - 3 per month
• Tageszeitung für Brauerei (periodical)
Notes: Member of Arbeitsgemeinschaft industrieller Forschungsvereinigung "Otto von Guericke" eV (Union of Industrial Research "Otto von Guericke")

Branded Goods' Association

Markenverband eV
Address: 4149, Schöne Aussicht 59, D-65193 Wiesbaden
Telephone: +49 611 586 70
Fax: +49 611 586 727
Telex: 4186753
Year established: 1903
Activities: compilation of industry data (available to non-members); special consulting service; library (for members only)
Chief officers: Peter Lips (General Director), Horst Priesznitz (Senior Director)
Membership: manufacturers of branded products
Publications:
• Markenartikel: monthly

Central Association of German Pork Producers

Zentralverband der Deutschen Schweineproduktion
Address: Adenauerallee 174, D- 5300 Bonn 1
Telephone: +49 228 211 069
Fax: +49 228 211 777
Chief officers: Dr Jens Ingwersen (Secretary)
Publications:
• Zahlen aus der Deutschen Schweineproduktion: annual

statistics on pig meat production, consumption, imports, exports, prices, and industry organisation. Some comparative European data and based on a combination of sources - annual

Central Association of German Retail Trade (HDE)

Hauptgemeinschaft des Deutschen Einzelhandels
Address: 250425, Höninger Weg 106a, D- 50969 Cologne
Telephone: +49 221 936 55/02
Fax: +49 221 936 55/909
Year established: 1919
Activities: central organisation for German retail trade, to which all relevant associations are affiliated. Publishes statistics based on official data, data compiled by the Institut für Handelsforschung of the University of Cologne and own research, as well as directories on German retail sector
Chief officers: Hermann Franzen (President); Holgar Wenzel (Director)
Membership: 16 regional and 30 national commodity associations
Publications:
• Annual Report of the Central Association of the German Retail Trade (HDE) (Jahresbericht): annual
• Retail Journal (Handel Journal): collates data on retail trends from each region (Land) in Germany into a central source of retail data - monthly
• Statistical Bulletin: monthly
• Statistical Report (Arbeitsbericht): mainly text on the retailing sector in Germany but there is some data on the number of enterprises, turnover and employment. Most tables have figures for earlier years - annual

Central Association of the Electronic Industry (ZVEI)

Zentralverband Elektrotechnik- und Elektronikindustrie eV
Address: Stresemannallee 19, D-60596 Frankfurt am Main
Telephone: +49 69 630 2-280
Fax: +49 69 630 2317
Chief officers: Ernst Georg Stöckl (Chairman), Franz-Josef Wissing (General Director), Norbert Knaup (Secretary)
Membership: ca. 1400, represents 90% of the sector
Publications:
• Die Elektrotechnische Industrie: turnover, imports, exports, investment, employment, and earnings data for the electronics and electrical equipment sectors with some data on worldwide trends - annual
• Elektroindustrie in Zahlen: basic statistics on the electronics and electrical equipment sectors in pocket book format - annual

Central Association of the German Building Industry

Hauptverband der Deutschen Bauindustrie
Address: Abraham Lincoln Strasse 30, D- 65189 Wiesbaden
Telephone: +49 611 217720
Fax: +49 611 772240
Chief officers: Christian Roth (President)
Publications:
• Baustatistisches Jahrbuch (Central Association of the German Building Industry): trends in the German construction industry with statistics on new buildings, orders, completions, etc. Based on returns from member organisations in the various federal states - annual

Central Association of the German Shoe Industry

Hauptverband des Deutschen Schuhindustrie eV
Address: 100761, Waldstraße 44, D- 63065 Offenbach am Main
Telephone: +49 69 829 7410
Fax: +49 69 812 810
Activities: information and statistics regarding the German shoe industry; ad hoc research conducted for set fee

Chief officers: Friedrich Ross(Chairman), Philipp Urban (General Director)
Structure: umbrella association for 16 regional associations (Landesverbände)
Publications:
• Production, Import and Export Statistics: *annual*
• Shoe (Schuhe): *statistics on the German footwear industry including data on production, sales, imports, exports, prices. Largely based on official statistics - annual*

Central Association of the Paper, Pulp and Synthetics Processing Industry (HPV)
Hauptverband der Papier-, Pappe und Kunststoffe verarbeitenden Industrie eV
Address: Arndstraße 47, D- 60325 Frankfurt
Telephone: +49 69 975 735/0
Fax: +49 69 975 73530
Chief officers: Lutz Boeder (President), Dr Horst Kohl (General Director)
Structure: 10 regional associations (Landesverbände), 20 trade associations
Membership: 30 paper manufacturers
Publications:
• HPV Foreign Trade Statistics (HPV Außenhandelsstatistik): *import and export statistics in the paper and board industry by product and by country and region; latest year and previous year's data usually given; based on official statistics - annual*
• HPV Statistics (HPV Statistik): *statistics on the paper and board industry with historical data often going back over a 10 to 20 year period; covers production by product, turnover, investment, prices, imports, exports, labour, wages etc; based on a combination of original survey data, central government data, and data from various non-official bodies - annual*

Central Federation of German Bakers
Zentralverband des Deutschen Bäckerhandwerks eV
Address: 1808, Bondorfer Straße 23, D- 53588 Bad Honnef
Telephone: +49 2224 71058
Fax: +49 2224 75978
Year established: 1946
Activities: legal advice; advice on technology, business, public relations and advertising
Chief officers: Hans Baum (President), Dr Eberhard Groebel (General Director)
Membership: ca. 27,000 retail bakers
Publications:
• Allgemeine Bäckerzeitung: *weekly*
• Bäckermeister: *weekly*
• Bäko-Information: *monthly*
• Deutsche Bäckerzeitung: *weekly*

Central Federation of German Electronics Workers (ZVEH)
Zentralverband der Deutschen Elektrohandwerke
Address: 900370, Haus der Deutschen Elektrohandwerke, Lilienthalallee 4, D- 60487 Frankfurt
Telephone: +49 69 247 747/0
Fax: +49 69 247 747/19
Chief officers: Karl Hagedorn (President), Heinz-Werner Schult (GeneralDirector)
Membership: 16 regional associations (Landesverbände) and 60,000 members
Publications:
• Brochures and Information Leaflets: *production and trade statistics*

Central Federation of German Fruit Importers and Exporters
Zentralverband des Deutschen Früchte-Import und Grosshandels eV
Address: Schedestraße 11-13, D-53113 Bonn
Telephone: +49 228 213 267
Fax: +49 228 213 265
Telex: 8869625
Year established: 1948
Chief officers: G Schmack (Secretary); Frau Legenburger (Secretary)
Membership: 408 importers and wholesalers of fruit

Central Federation of German Hairdressers
Zentralverband des Deutschen Friseurhandwerks
Address: 140104, Weißenburgstraße 74, D- 50670 Cologne
Telephone: +49 221 724 376
Fax: +49 2211 973 03
Telex: 7/30
Chief officers: Bernd Müller (General Director), Rainer Röhr (Secretary)
Membership: central hairdressers' trade association with over 30,000 individual members; 11 regional groups are affiliated

Central Federation of German Pig Producers (ZDS)
Zentralverband der Deutschen Schweineproduktion eV
Address: Adenauerallee 174, D-53113 Bonn
Telephone: +49 228 211 069/211 060
Fax: +49 228 211 777
Chief officers: Dr Jens Ingversen (Director)
Structure: central association
Membership: 14 associations of pig breeders and pork dealers, 85 companies
Publications:
• Pig Production (Schweinezucht und Schweinemast): *monthly*
• Pig Production in Germany (Schweineproduktion in der Bundesrepublik Deutschland): *annual*

Central Federation of German Potato Traders
Zentralverband des Deutschen Kartoffelhandels eV
Address: 301655, Beueler Bahnhofsplatz 18, D- 53225 Bonn
Telephone: +49 228 975 85/22
Fax: +49 228 975 85/30
Telex: 228345
Chief officers: Dr Herwig Elgeti (President), Robert Künzel (Secretary)
Structure: 11 regional associations (Landesverbände)
Membership: wholesale potato merchants

Central Office for Information on German Ice Cream Brand Manufacturers (ICE)
Informations-Centrale Eiskrem der Deutschen Markeneishersteller
Address: Schumannstraße 4-6, D-53113 Bonn
Telephone: +49 228 260 0751
Fax: +49 228 260 0789
Activities: PR activity and information for international exchange
Membership: 34 companies with ice cream brands

Central Organisation of German Trade Agents and Trade Brokers (CDH)
Zentralvereinigung Deutscher Handelsvertreter- und Handelsmakler- Verbände
Address: CDH-Haus, Geleniusstraße 1, D- 50931 Cologne 41
Telephone: +49 221 514 043/44
Fax: +49 221 525 767
Telex: 8881743
Chief officers: N Hopf (President); E H Hanmann (Managing Director)
Structure: 14 regional associations, 26 trade associations

Membership: central organisation of German trade agents and brokers representing approx. 30,000 individuals and covering all industry sectors including foods and drinks

Chewing Gum Association
KAUGUMMI Verband eV
Address: 12 55, Kelkheimer Staße 10, D- 61350 Bad Homburg v.d. Höhe
Telephone: +49 6172 330 16
Fax: +49 6172 306 847
Chief officers: Heinz Wenner (Director), Grudun Steitz (Secretary)
Membership: 9 manufacturers
Publications:
• Kaugummi Presseinformation: *statistics on international and national market development, market data - annual*

Chocolate Union
Schoko-Verband
Address: Ulrich-von-Hasseltstraße 64, D-53123 Bonn
Telephone: +49 228 919 200
Fax: +49 228 919 2010
Chief officers: Friedrich Janz (Chairman), Klaus Warzecha (Secretary)
Structure: trade association part of the umbrella organisation Bundesverband des Deutschen Lebensmittel Einzelhandels eV (BVL)

Cigarette Industry Association
Verbanfd der Cigarettenindustrie
Address: Königswinterer Straße 550, D-53227 Bonn
Telephone: +49 228 449 060
Fax: +49 228 442 582
Chief officers: Paul Hendrys (Chairman), Dr Harald König (General Director)
Membership: 11 companies

Confederation of German Trade Fair and Exhibition Industries (AUMA)
Ausstellungs- und Messe-Ausschuß der Deutschen Wirtschaft e.V.
Address: Lindenstraße 8, D- 50674 Cologne
Telephone: +49 221 20907/0
Fax: +49 221 20907/12
Year established: 1907
Chief officers: Dr Claus Boener (General Director), Peter Neven (Secretary)

Dairy Products Manufacturers' Association
Bundesfachverband der Marktmolkereien eV
Address: Godesberger Allee, D-53175 Bonn
Telephone: +49 228 959 6930
Fax: +49 228 371 233
Activities: organises conferences and exhibitions
Chief officers: Max Bialek (President), Winfried Meier (Secretary)
Membership: 670 firms
Publications:
• Annual Report of the Dairy Products Manufacturers' Association: *issues affecting retailing of milk - annual*

Employers Union for Wholesalers and Importers
AGA Unternehmens- und Arbeitgeberverband Großhandel, Aussenhandel, Diensteilung eV
Address: 100329, Kurze Mühren 2, D-20095 Hamburg 1
Telephone: +49 40 308 101
Fax: +49 40 308 01107
Chief officers: Dr Uwe Mehrtens (President)
Membership: 3,300 general importers and wholesalers

Federal Association for Entertainment and Communication (BVU)
Bundesverband des Unterhaltungs und Kommunikationselektronik-Einzelhandels eV
Address: 250363, Höninger Weg 106a, D- 50969 Cologne
Telephone: +49 221 936 55/821
Fax: +49 221 936 55/838
Chief officers: Dieter Argenton (Chairman), Willy Fischel (Secretary)
Structure: part of the Hauptverband des Deutschen Einzelhandels
Membership: over 10,000 retailers of electronic goods
Publications:
• RF Briefe/RF Zeitung: *circulars which bring members up to date with latest developments in the industry and within the association. RF Zeitung is the official trade journal of the association - fortnightly/monthly*

Federal Association for Jewellers and Watch Retailers
Bundesverband der Juweliere, Schmuck- und Uhrenfachgeschäfte in der Hauptgemeinschaft des Deutschen Einzelhandels eV
Address: Altkönigstraße 9, D- 61462 Königstein
Telephone: +49 6174 404 1/2
Fax: +49 6174 225 87
Year established: 1948
Activities: circulars to members; annual report to members; statistical data
Chief officers: Bodo Jonda (Director)
Membership: 2,500 retailers and organisations
Notes: the Zentralverband der Juweliere etc, which represents manufacturers and workshops for jewellery, watches and clocks is also at this address

Federal Association of Coffee Manufacturers
Bundesverband der Kaffeemittelindustrie eV
Address: Reuterstraße 151, D- 53113 Bonn
Telephone: +49 228 212 017
Fax: +49 228 229 460
Telex: 8869489
Activities: information on instant coffee production and substitute coffee drinks production
Chief officers: F J Strehle (Chairman)
Membership: 8 coffee manufacturers

Federal Association of Confectionery Wholesalers, Importers and Exporters
Bundesverband des Süßwaren- Groß- und Außenhandels eV
Address: Grillparzerstraße 38, D- 81675 Munich
Telephone: +49 89 470 6093
Fax: +49 89 470 3783
Chief officers: Heiner Ernst (Director)
Structure: umbrella organisation for 16 regional associations (Landesverbände)
Membership: wholesale confectioners and importers
Publications:
• Süßwarenhandel: *issues affecting German confectionery retailing industry; some market data - twice monthly*

Federal Association of Exporters of Pearls and Precious Stones
Bundesverband der Importeure und Exporteure von Edelsteinen und Perlen eV
Address: Martinskirchstraße 51, D- 60529 Frankfurt
Telephone: +49 69 605 29/357302
Fax: +49 69 357 304
Activities: conferences and statistical information
Chief officers: Curt -Albert Neumetzger (Chariman), Dr Lothar M Schmid (Secretary)
Membership: precious stones and pearls trade

Federal Association of Fruit Spirit Distilleries

Bundesverband der Obstverschlußbrenner eV
Address: Kaiser-Joseph-Straße 243, D- 79098 Freiburg
Telephone: +49 761 325 12
Fax: +49 761 326 12
Chief officers: Nicolaus Schladere-Ulmann (Chairman),
Harald Brugger (Secretary)
Membership: fruit spirits producers; includes 2 trade
associations

Federal Association of Game and Poultry Wholesalers and Exporters

Bundesverband des Wild- und Geflügel- Groß- und Außenhandels
Address: 240134, Buschstraße 2, D- 53113 Bonn
Telephone: +49 228 959 600
Fax: +49 228 959 6050
Telex: 886429
Activities: dissemination of statistics and information
concerning the retail market
Chief officers: Peter Biegi (Chairman), Kaspar von der Crone
(Secretary)
Membership: 115 poultry wholesalers and exporters

Federal Association of German Banks

Bundesverband deutscher Banken eV
Address: 100555, Kattenburg 1, D- 50667 Cologne
Telephone: +49 221 166 30
Fax: +49 221 1663 222/280
Activities: represents interests of major German banks; acts
as central information point for legislative consultation
Chief officers: Dr Karl-Heinz Wessel (President), Dr Manfred
Weber (General Director)
Membership: approximately 300 banks
Publications:
• Die Bank: *banking and finance issues; membership lists;
new product development - monthly*
• Membership List

Federal Association of German Beer and Beverage Wholesalers

Bundesverband des Deutschen Bier und
Getränkefachgroßhandels
Address: Humboldstraße 7, D- 40237 Düsseldorf
Telephone: +49 211 683 938
Fax: +49 211 683 602
Year established: 1950
Activities: information service for members only
Chief officers: Heinrich Hahn (President), Heinz Graffmann
(Director)
Structure: the organisation is an umbrella group for regional
associations and exists mainly as a headquarters
Membership: 1,500 members and 16 regional associations
(Landesverbände)
Publications:
• Der Biergrosshandel: *fortnightly*
• Jahresbericht (Annual Report) and Newsletter of the Federal
Association of German Beer and Beverage Wholesalers:
information on wholesale beer trade - annual; monthly

Federal Association of German Butchers and Meat Wholesalers (BGF)

Bundesverband der Deutschen Großschlächter und
Fleischgroß-händler eV
Address: Landfriedstraße 1a, D- 6900 Heidelberg
Telephone: +49 6221 23644
Fax: +49 6221 181438
Structure: 16 regional associations (Landesverbände)
Membership: slaughterhouses and meat wholesalers
Publications:
• Rundschreiben: *monthly*

Federal Association of German Corn Distillers

Bundesverband Deutscher Kornbrenner
Address: Westfalendamm 59, D- 44141 Dortmund
Telephone: +49 231 433 764/430144
Fax: +49 231 422 037
Year established: 1884
Activities: information and conferences; some statistics
Chief officers: Knut Elmendorf (President), Josef Cornelissen
(General Director), Ökonom Peter Pilz (Secretary)
Membership: 450 distillers and 8 Landesverbände
Publications:
• Brennerei-Informationen: *information on the sector*

Federal Association of German Fast Food Restaurants

Bundesverband Schnellgastronomie und Imbissbetriebe e.V.
Address: Klettenbergguertel 51, 50939 Cologne
Telephone: +49 221 461 020
Fax: +49 221 465 882

Federal Association of German Food Retailers (BVL)

Bundesverband des Deutschen Lebensmittel-Einzelhandels
Address: 140164, Ulrich-von-Hassell Straße 64, D- 53056
Bonn
Telephone: +49 228 919 200
Fax: +49 228 919 2010
Activities: central organisation for all the German food retail
trade; represents the interests of companies in the retail
grocery trade in dealings with the government, public
authorities and the general public at national and EU levels
Chief officers: Gerd Härig (General Director), Dr
Johann-Anton Pernice
Structure: 16 regional associations (Landesverbände)
Membership: member associations cover the delicatessen,
fish trade, chocolate, game and poultry, and mobile shop
sectors
Publications:
• Die Kennzeichnungselemente von fertigverpackten
Lebensmitteln
• Die Sorgfaltspflichten des Lebensmittel-Kaufmanns
• Jahresbericht (Federal Association of German Food
Retailers): *annual report on association's activities;
membership list - annual*
• Lebensmittel Einzelhandel 1992

Federal Association of German Fruit Liqueur Distillers

Bundesverband der Deutschen Klein- und Obstbrenner
Address: Saarlandstraße 2, D- 77652 Offenburg
Telephone: +49 7804 97940
Fax: +49 7804 979416
Chief officers: Dr G Erdrich (Secretary)
Structure: umbrella organisation for 8 regional associations
(Landesverbände)
Membership: fruit spirits producers and small distilleries

Federal Association of German Fruit Wholesalers (BVF)

Bundesverband Deutscher Fruchthandelsunternehmen
Address: Oberhafenstraße 3, Fruchthof 5th floor, D-20097
Hamburg
Telephone: +49 40 335 162
Fax: +49 40 337 775
Telex: 2161367
Activities: represents importers and wholesalers of fresh fruit
and vegetables
Chief officers: Manfred Stülcken (President/Munich), Rolf
Volkmann (Vice President/Munich), Michael Krebs
(Secretary/Munich), Ulrich Boisen (Secretary)
Structure: 3 branches, in Berlin, Hamburg and Munich
(headquarters)
Membership: 500 wholesale fruit and vegetable dealers

Federal Association of German Newspaper Publishers (BDZV)

Bundesverband Deutscher Zeitungsverleger eV
Address: Riemenschneiderstraße 10, D- 53175 Bonn 2
Telephone: +49 228 810 040
Fax: +49 228 810 0415
Year established: 1954
Activities: provides legal advice, training programmes
Chief officers: Wilhelm Sandmann (President), Dr Dirk Michael Barton (Managing Director), Mr Volker Schulze (Director), Mr Alexander von Kuk (Director)
Membership: 331 newspapers and 12 Landesverbände
Publications:
• BDZV Jutem: *weekly*
• Die Zeitung : *monthly*
• Yearbook : *examine the affect of legislation on the industry and produces analysis of future prospects in the market - annual*

Federal Association of German Textile Retailers (BTE)

Bundesverband des Deutschen Textileinzelhandels eV
Address: Sachsenring 69, D- 50677 Cologne
Telephone: +49 221 33699/0
Fax: +49 221 336 99/10/915
Telex: 882953
Chief officers: Klaus J Stange (President), August Möller (General Director)
Structure: umbrella organisation for 16 regional associations (Landesverbände)
Membership: approx 30,000 retail outlets
Publications:
• BTE Textil-Berater: *monthly*
• Taschenbuch des Textil Lederwaren Einzelhandels: *a yearbook covering general trends in the textiles and leather products industries and markets. Information on industry structure, investment, sales by product groups, prices, costs etc.. Many tables have data for earlier years - annual*
• Textil-Wirtschaft: *weekly*

Federal Association of German Wine Distributors and Wholesalers

Bundesverband der Deutschen Weinkommissionäre eV
Address: Große Bleiche 29, D- 55116 Mainz
Telephone: +49 6131 232 392
Fax: +49 6131 235 947
Chief officers: Hans Jung (President), Hermann Böckel (Secretary)
Structure: umbrella organisation for 16 regional associations (Landesverbände)
Membership: 500 wine distributors and retailers
Publications:
• Annual Report of the Federal Association of German Wine Distributors and Wholesalers: *in-house publication including membership directory - annual*

Federal Association of German Wine Producers and Retailers

Bundesverband der Deutschen Weinkellereien und des Weinfachhandels eV
Address: Baumschulallee 6, D- 53115 Bonn
Telephone: +49 228 630 333
Fax: +49 228 696 042
Activities: information to members
Chief officers: R A Heinrich Fenner (Secretary)
Membership: over 600 wine retailers, distributors and producers

Federal Association of German Yeast Processors

Bundesverband der Deutschen Hefeindustrie und der Melasseverarbeitenden Brennereien
Address: 650560, Schaumkrautweg 2-4, D- 22395 Hamburg
Telephone: +49 40 601 9247
Fax: +49 40 601 0767
Telex: 2173660
Activities: information to members; statistics, legislative consultation
Chief officers: Dr Günter Moormann (Chairman), Werner Matthes (Secretary)
Membership: 15 firms; yeast producers
Publications:
• Brennerei Information: *monthly*

Federal Association of Glass, China and Ceramic Retailers

Bundesverband des Glas-, Porzellan- und Keramik-Einzelhandels
Address: 250363, D- 50519 Cologne
Telephone: +49 221 936 5502/831
Fax: +49 221 936 55839
Chief officers: Thomas Grothkopp (Secretary)
Structure: 16 regional associations (Landesverbände)
Membership: ceramics, glass and porcelain retailers
Publications:
• Porzellan und Glas: *monthly*

Federal Association of Instant Coffee Manufacturers (BLK)

Bundesverband der Hersteller von löslichem Kaffee
Address: Am Sandtorkai 4, D- 20457 Hamburg
Telephone: +49 40 365 134
Fax: +49 40 364 311
Telex: 214144
Activities: organises conferences and publishes statistical data
Chief officers: Thomas Köhler (Secretary)
Membership: 10 companies

Federal Association of Jewellery Wholesalers

Bundesverband des Schmuc- Großhandels eV
Address: Höslinstraße 18, D- 72587 Römerstein
Telephone: +49 7382 5366
Fax: +49 7382 5310
Chief officers: Reinhardt Schmohl (Secretary)
Membership: 90 jewellery wholesalers
Publications:
• Annual Report of the Federal Association of Jewellery Wholesalers: *annual*

Federal Association of Perfume Retailers

Bundesverband Parfümerien eV
Address: Am Lohtor 14, D-45657 Recklinghausen
Telephone: +49 2361 25078
Fax: +49 2361 182565
Chief officers: Rheinard-Dieter Wolf (Chairman), Werner Hariegel (Secretary)
Membership: 3,000 perfumery retailers
Publications:
• Parfumerie Nachrichten/Parfumerie Aktuell: *sector news - monthly*
Notes: This is the perfume section of the Hauptgemeinschaft des Deutschen Einzelhandels, the German Retailers' Association.

Federal Association of Private Dairies

Bundesverband der Privaten Milchwirtschaft eV
Address: Kaiser-Ludwig-Platz 2, D- 80336 Munich
Telephone: +49 89 531 158
Fax: +49 89 530 9615

Year established: 1949
Activities: conferences on independent milk production and information service to members and non-members
Chief officers: Horst Ziegenhain (President), Gernot Werner (Secretary)
Membership: includes 4 regional organisations

Federal Association of Retail and Self-service Department Stores (BFS)

Bundesverband der Filialbetriebe und Selbstbedienungs-Warenhäuser eV
Address: 320340, Büchelstrasße 50, D- 53227 Bonn
Telephone: +49 228 449 08/0
Fax: +49 228 449 08/88
Telex: 2283734
Year established: 1988
Chief officers: Eugen Viehof (President), Uwe Schepers (General Director), Werner Wiitting (Deputy Director)
Membership: 45 food chain stores and self-service stores
Publications:
• Lebensmittelfilialbetriebe Jahresgeschäftsbericht: *trends and activities in food retailing multiples - annual*
Notes: Formed in June 1988 from a merger of the Arbeitsgemeinschaft der Lebensmittel-Filialbetriebe and the Bundesverband der Selbstbedienungs- Warenhäuser.

Federal Association of Shoe Retailers

Bundesverband des Deutschen Schuheinzelhandels eV
Address: Sachsenring 69, D- 50677 Cologne
Telephone: +49 221 327 051
Fax: +49 221 327 058
Year established: 1945
Chief officers: Wilhelm Boss (Chairman), Winfried Toubartz (Secretary)
Structure: 11 regional associations (Landesverbände)
Membership: 6,000 shoe retailers
Publications:
• Schuhmarkt: *weekly*

Federal Association of the Clothing Industry

Bundesverband Bekleidungsindustrie eV
Address: Mevissenstraße 15, D-50668 Cologne
Telephone: +49 221 774 40
Fax: +49 221 774 4118
Year established: 1962
Activities: information service and advice to members and non-members
Chief officers: Dr Fritz Goost (President), Sartois Friedhelm (Director), Marlies Temme (Secretary)
Structure: umbrella group for 16 regional associations (Landesverbände)
Membership: clothing manufacturers', importers' and distributors' associations
Publications:
• Die Deutsche Bekleidungsindustrie: *annual document detailing all association activities with reports on new business trends, market data and statistics - annual*

Federal Association of the Diamond and Precious Stones Industry

Bundesverband der Edelstein und Diamantenindustie
Address: Mainzerstraße 34, D- 55743 Idar-Oberstein
Telephone: +49 6781 439 89
Fax: +49 6781 412 69
Year established: 1950
Activities: organises conferences, exhibitions and statistical service for members
Chief officers: Jochen Müller (Chairman), Michael Engel (Joint-Director), Rolf Goerlitz (Joint-Director), Dieter Hahn

(Joint-Director), Dr Bodo Bachmeyer (Secretary)
Membership: approx 250 members

Federal Association of the Fruit and Vegetable Processing Industry

Bundesverband der Obst- und Gemüseverarbeitenden Industrie eV
Address: Von-der-Heydtstraße 9, D- 53177 Bonn
Telephone: +49 228 354 026
Fax: +49 228 361 889
Activities: information service and advice to members and , non-members
Chief officers: Hans-Egbert Brinkmann (General Director), Erick Demarrez (Secretary)
Membership: 80 manufacturers and importers of preserved fruit and vegetables
Publications:
• Jahresbericht (Federal Association of the Fruit and Vegetable Processing Industry): *in-house report on association activities for members only - annual*

Federal Association of the German Confectionery Industry

Bundesverband der Deutschen Süßenwarenindustrie
Address: Schumannstraße 4-6, D- 53113 Bonn 1
Telephone: +49 228 260 07/0
Fax: +49 228 260 0789
Activities: basic statistics on production and markets for sugar and chocolate confectionery in Germany (published in pocket book format); information service; conference; training
Chief officers: Dr Klaus Schutze (Director)
Membership: ca. 300 manufacturers
Publications:
• Geschäftsbericht: *annual*
• Statistisches Taschenbuch: *annual*
• Süsswarentaschenbuch: *a pocketbook of statistics on sugar confectionery and chocolate confectionery with detailed data on production and consumption trends in specific markets. Most tables have long runs of annual data, based on various sources - annual*

Federal Association of the German Fish Wholesaling Industry

Bundesverband der deutschen Fischindustrie und des Fischgroßhandels eV
Address: Groß Elbstraße 133 II, D- 22767 Hamburg 50
Telephone: +49 40 381 811
Fax: +49 40 389 8554
Telex: 212578
Chief officers: Jan Pickenpack (Chairman), Dr Matthias Keller (Director)
Membership: ca. 100 firms
Publications:
• Annual Report of the Federal Association of the German Fish Wholesaling Industry: *issues affecting wholesale trade of fish - annual*

Federal Association of the German Spirits Industry (BSI)

Bundesverband der Deutschen Spirituosen-Industrie eV
Address: 120539, Urstadtstraße 2, D- 5300 Bonn 1
Telephone: +49 228 238 061/63
Fax: +49 228 234 351
Year established: 1974
Activities: statistical services provided: available only to member companies. Telephone information service; written queries should be addressed to Arbeitskreis Alkohol at the address above
Chief officers: Nicolaus Schladerer-Ulmann (President)Dr

Martin Kieffer (Executive Director)
Membership: 51 spirits manufacturers
Publications:
• Die Spirituosen Industrie: Daten aus der Alkoholwirtschaft: *a pocket book with basic data on spirits and liqueurs in Germany plus comparative data for the other EU countries - annual*
• Die Spirituosenindustrie Jahresbericht: *commentary and statistics on the German spirits and liqueurs industries with data on sales, employment, prices, numbers of firms. Some data on specific product areas and historical data. Based on a combination of sources - annual*

Federal Association of the Spirit-Based Cleaning Products Industry
Bundesverband der Spiritus-Reinigungswerke eV
Address: 2180, Kaiser-Wilhelm-Ring 14, D-48145 Münster
Telephone: +49 251 308 50/13130
Fax: +49 251 378 525/13130
Chief officers: Paul-Josef Meyer (Secretary)
Membership: 6 members

Federal Association of Toys and Games Retailers (BVS)
Bundesverband des Spielwaren-Einzelhandels
Address: Höninger Weg 106a, D- 50969 Cologne
Telephone: +49 221 936 55820
Fax: +49 221 936 55838
Chief officers: Willy Fische (Secretary)
Structure: 15 regional associations
Membership: over 4,000 toy retailers
Publications:
• Jahresbericht (Federal Association of Toys and Games Retailers)
Notes: releases information to press, which is also available to non-members on application to the association

Federal Association of Wholesalers and Importers of Dairy Products
Bundesverband des Groß- und Außenhandels mit Molkereiprodukten
Address: Buschstraße 2, D- 53113 Bonn
Telephone: +49 228 213 266
Fax: +49 228 214 301
Chief officers: Dr G Wollin (Director)
Membership: 4 organisations

Federal German Car Rental Association
Bundesverband der Autovermieter Deutschlands
Address: Grafenberger Allee 363, D- 40235 Düsseldorf
Telephone: +49 211 685 373
Fax: +49 211 660 571
Activities: information for members
Chief officers: Joachim Döring (President), Klaus Langmann-Keller (Director)
Membership: ca. 1000 members
Publications:
• Der Autovermieter (The Car Rental Agent): *official publication of the association; trade activities - 3/4 p.a.*
Notes: central association for car rental in Germany; the international association for car rental is also based at this address

Federal German Cosmetics Manufacturers' Association (BDK)
Bundesverband Deutscher Kosmetikerinnen eV
Address: Liesegangstraße 10, D-40231 Düsseldorf
Telephone: +49 211 365 891
Fax: +49 211 350 020
Year established: 1966
Chief officers: Verena Grzimek (Director)

Membership: 2,000 independent cosmeticians, manufacturers of cosmetic products and retailers
Publications:
• INFO: *newsletter - quarterly*
• Kosmetik Journal: *monthly*

Federal German Wholesalers' and Importers' Association (BGA)
Bundesverband des Deutschen Groß- und Außenhandels
Address: 1349, Kaiser Friedrichstraße 13, D-53113 Bonn 1
Telephone: +49 228 260 04-0
Fax: +49 228 260 04-55
Telex: 886621
Year established: 1949
Chief officers: Dr Peter Spary (General Director), Uwe Schwarting (Deputy Director)
Structure: umbrella organisation for 67 sub-associations
Membership: 28 general importers and wholesalers

Federal Office of the German Bakery and Pastry Cooperatives
Bundeszentrale deutscher Baecker- und Bundeszentrale deutscher Baecker- und
Address: Rhoendorfer Straße 87, 53604 Bad Honnef
Telephone: +49 2224 92230
Fax: +49 2224 922 318

Federal Print Association
Bundesverband Druck eV
Address: Biebricher Allee 79, D-65187 Wiesbaden
Telephone: +49 611 803/0
Fax: +49 611 803 113
Chief officers: Hans-Otto Reppekus (President), Dr Walter Hesse (General Director)
Structure: 12 regional associations (Landesverbände)
Publications:
• Die Deutsche Druckindustrie in Zahlen: *data for a four year period on the printing industry. Covers production, prices, turnover, imports/exports, employment etc. Produced in pocket book format - annual*
• Jahresbericht (Federal Print Association): *mainly text and commentary on the printing industry but a statistical appendix contains data for the last ten years on turnover, employment, production, wages in the industry - annual*

Federal Trade Association for Cattle and Meat
Bundesmarktverband für Vieh und Fleisch
Address: Godesberger Allee 142-148, D- 53175 Bonn
Telephone: +49 228 819 80
Fax: +49 228 819 8205
Year established: 1952
Chief officers: Welhelm Niemeyer (Chairman), Richard Bröcker (General Secretary)
Structure: umbrella organisation for 12 regional associations

Federal Trade Association of the Fishing Industry
Bundesmarktverband der Fischwirtschaft eV
Address: Große Elbstraße 133, D- 22767 Hamburg 50
Telephone: +49 40 385 931
Fax: +49 40 389 8554
Chief officers: Kirk Ahlers, (President), Folkert Marr (Director)
Membership: 13 firms

Federal Union of the German Food Industry (BVE)
Bundesvereinigung der deutschen Ernährungsindustrie eV
Address: Winkelsweg 2, D- 53175 Bonn 2
Telephone: +49 228 373 041
Fax: +49 228 376 176
Telex: 885679

Year established: 1949
Activities: conferences, information and statistics concerning production and trade figures
Chief officers: Dr Matthias Horst (Director)
Structure: umbrella group for 16 regional associations and 13 assorted trade bodies
Membership: food manufacturers; around 40 members
Publications:
• Jahresbericht (Federal Union of the German Food Industry): *an annual report from the Association which begins with a large statistical section covering turnover, turnover by branch, production, exports, imports, prices, enterprises. Figures usually given for the latest five years and data on specific foods - annual*

Federal Union of Wine and Spirits Importers
Bundesvereinigung Wein- und Spirituosenimport eV
Address: Sonnenberger Straße 46, D-65193 Wiesbaden
Telephone: +49 611 521 033
Fax: +49 611 599 775
Chief officers: Hans-Jürgen Hertzberg (President), Ursula Schmitt (Secretary)
Membership: wine and spirits importers and distributors

Federation of Cosmetics, Toiletries and Detergents Manufacturers (IKW)
Industrieverband Körperpflege- und Waschmittel eV
Address: Karlstraße 21, D-60329 Frankfurt
Telephone: +49 69 255 613 23
Fax: +49 69 237 631
Telex: 414299 VCIF D
Year established: 1968
Chief officers: Dr Adalbert Schlitt, Dr Peter Olschewski (Directors), Bernd Stroemer (Secretary)
Membership: manufacturers of cosmetics, toiletries and detergents
Publications:
• Annual Report of the Registered Industrial Federation for Cosmetics, Toiletries and Detergents: *annual*
• Daten und Fakten brochure: *annual*
• IKW-Informationen: *topics such as animal testing, legal matters, etc.*

Federation of German Chemists (VDD)
Verband Deutscher Drogisten eV
Address: Friedrich-Schmidt Straße 53, D- 5000 Cologne 41 Lindenthal
Telephone: +49 221 401 038
Fax: +49 221 404 436
Telex: 8882752 DDDVD
Chief officers: Günter Kleinemas (President), Norbert Fecke (General Director), Michael Bastian (Secretary)
Structure: 6 group associations (Landesgruppe), 10 regional associations(Landesverbände) and 5 trade associations (Fachausschüsse)
Membership: approx 3,000 retail chemists
Publications:
• Die Deutsche Drogerie: *monthly*
• Drogerie und Parfümerie

Federation of German Cosmetics Associations (ADKV)
Arbeitsgemeinschaft Deutscher Kosmetik-Verbände
Address: Brabanterstraße 18-20, D-1000 Berlin 31
Chief officers: Renate Debold (Chairman), Karin Kruppa (Chairman), Wolfgang Streit (Vice Chairman)
Membership: national federation of 8 regional cosmetic (trade and industry) associations

Federation of German Fruit Juice Producers (VdF)
Verband der deutschen Fruchtsaftindustrie
Address: Mainzerstrasse 253, D- 53179 Bonn
Telephone: +49 228 954 600
Fax: +49 228 954 6020/30
Chief officers: Dr Frank Schobert (President), Herr Albrecht Korth (Director)
Membership: 208 domestic manufacturers, 78 foreign manufacturers and importers
Publications:
• Circulars

Federation of German Paper Manufacturers (VDP)
Verband Deutscher Papierfabriken eV
Address: Schauburg Lippestraße, 5, D-53113 Bonn 1
Telephone: +49 228 915 270
Fax: +49 228 915 2799
Chief officers: Christopher Sieber-Rilke (President), Dr Peter Otzen (Secretary), Dr Manfred Kühn (Secretary), Dr Reinhardt (Secretary), Klaus Windhagen (Secretary)
Structure: 7 regional associations (Landesverbände)
Membership: 130 members
Publications:
• Leistungsbericht der Deutschen Zellstoff und Papierindustrie: *commentary followed by statistics on the cellulose and paper industry. Data on turnover, consumption, production, foreign trade, investment, raw materials, prices etc. Some international data is also included. Based largely on statistics collected by the association - annual*
• Statistische Kurzinformation : *monthly*

Federation of German Perfume Manufacturers (VDRH)
Verband Deutscher Riechstoff-Hersteller eV
Address: Meckenheimer Allee 87, D- 53113 Bonn
Telephone: +49 228 653 729
Fax: +49 228 637 940
Year established: 1983
Chief officers: Dietrich Fuhrmann (Chairman), Hanns-Erwin Muermann (Secretary)
Membership: 25 perfume manufacturers
Publications:
• Rundschreiben (circulars)

Federation of German Savings Banks
Verband der Deutschen Freien Öffentlichen Sparkassen eV
Address: Am Brill 1, D- 28195 Bremen
Telephone: +49 421 179/2047
Fax: +49 421 179/2986
Year established: 1920
Activities: information for members; statistical and market data
Chief officers: Heinrich Frick (President), Thomas Rohver-Kahlmann (Director), Dr Rüdiger Kamp (Secretary)
Membership: 39 international and 9 domestic members
Publications:
• Verbandsbericht: *annual report on activities of association - annual*

Federation of German Sparkling Wine Producers
Verband Deutscher Sektkellereien eV
Address: Sonnenberger Straße 46, D- 65193 Wiesbaden
Telephone: +49 611 521 033
Fax: +49 611 599 775
Year established: 1892
Activities: statistical and information services for members only
Chief officers: Hans Christof Wegeler-Deinhard (President), Ursula Schmitt (Joint Director), Ralf Peter Müller (Joint Director)
Membership: 101 producers of sparkling wines

Federation of German Textile Wholesalers

Gesamtverband der Deutschen Textilgroßhandels eV
Address: 100164, Hohenzollernring 89-93, D-50672 Cologne
Telephone: +49 221 511 928
Fax: +49 221 512 147
Activities: organises information for association members; central association for textile wholesalers
Chief officers: Karl-Heinz Hauser (Secretary)
Structure: umbrella group for 16 regional associations
Membership: 150 textile wholesalers

Federation of German Travel Agents (DRV)

Deutscher Reisebüro-Verband eV
Address: Mannheimer Straße 15, D- 60329 Frankfurt
Telephone: +49 69 273 907/0
Fax: +49 69 236647
Year established: 1950
Activities: information service for members; legislative consultation
Chief officers: Gerd Hesselmann (President), Burkhard Nipper (General Director), Leonhard Reeb (Secretary)
Membership: 4,400 independent travel agents
Publications:
• Das Reisebüro: *issues affecting travel agents and tourism industry; some market data - monthly*
• Fakten und Zahlen (Federation of German Travel Agents): *a regular general survey with basic data on travel trends of Germans - regular*
• Geschaftsbericht (Federation of German Travel Agents): *an annual review of the German travel sector with data on accomodation, travel trends, tourists, expenditure etc based on data from official and non-official sources - annual*

Federation of German Watch Manufacturers (VDU)

Verband der Deutschen Uhrenindustrie eV
Address: 3728, Dauchinger Straße 20, D-78056 Villingen-Schwenningen
Telephone: +49 7720 7005/0
Fax: +49 7720 7007
Activities: production statistics, import and export data
Chief officers: Berthold Korzus (President), Karl Wahl (Secretary)
Membership: 250 manufacturers
Publications:
• Einfuhr-und Ausfuhr Statistik (Federation of German Watch Manufacturers): *various issues per year with data on the imports and exports of watches and clocks. Based on official statistics - regular*

Federation of German Wickerwork, Wicker Furniture and Pushchair Manufacturers

Verband der Korbwaren-, Korbmobel- und Kinderwagenindustrie eV
Address: Bahnhofstraße 11, D- 96465 Neustadt
Telephone: +49 9568 850 19
Fax: +49 9568 799 3
Chief officers: Wolfram e Salzer (Secretary)
Membership: 80 manufacturers

Federation of German Wine Exporters (VDW)

Verband Deutscher Weinexporteure eV
Address: Dorotheenstraße 241, D-53113 Bonn
Telephone: +49 228 262 888
Fax: +49 228 263 878
Activities: monthly and annual statistics on the international wine trade; information service to support export activity
Chief officers: Dr Hans-Rudolf Schmidt (President); Dr Rudolf Nickenig (Director)
Membership: 110 wine producers and exporters

Publications:
• Newsletter of the Federation of German Wine Exporters
• Statistisches (Federation of German Wine Exporters): *monthly and annual statistics on the international wine trade based largely on an analysis of official statistics - annual and monthly*

Federation of Pharmaceutical Wholesalers

Address: Savignystraße 42, D- 6000 Frankfurt 1
Telephone: +49 69 740477
Fax: +49 69 740470

Federation of the German Bakery Products Industry

Verband der Deutschen Brot und Backwarenindustrie
Address: In den Diken 13, D- ,40472 Düsseldorf
Telephone: +49 211 653 086
Fax: +49 211 653 088
Year established: 1903
Activities: information service for members only
Chief officers: Armin Juncker (Director)
Membership: 100 bakers
Publications:
• Jahresbericht (Federation of the German Bakery Products Industry): *in-house publication giving details of association activities and list of members - annual*
Notes: annual report for members and non-members

Federation of the German Dairy Industry (VDM)

Verband der Deutschen Milchwirtschaft eV
Address: Meckenheimer Allee 137, D- 53115 Bonn 1
Telephone: +49 228 982 430
Fax: +49 228 982 4320
Year established: 1874
Chief officers: Ernst Geprägs (President), Michael Schauff (Director), Thomas Kützemeier (Secretary)
Membership: 15 (farming, processing, trade research)
Publications:
• Jahresgeschäftsbericht: *annual*

Federation of the German Household Textiles Industry

Confédération International des Fabricants de Tissus d'Ameublement
Address: Hans Böckler Straße 205, D-42109 Wuppertal
Telephone: +49 202 759 720
Fax: +49 202 759 797
Chief officers: Peter Trepte (Director General)
Publications:
• Jahresbericht (Federation of the German Household Textiles Industry): *data on the household textiles industry and market with specific data on carpets, furnishing fabrics, curtains, bedroom fabrics etc. Mainly production and foreign trade data with some figures for earlier years. Based largely on official statistics - annual*

Federation of the German Margarine Industry

Verband der Deutschen Margarineindustrie
Address: Winkelsweg 2, D- 53175 Bonn
Telephone: +49 228 372 023
Fax: +49 228 372 025
Activities: information service for members only
Chief officers: Alfred Lakowski (President); Gerhardt Gnodtke (Joint Managing Director); Karl-Heinz Legendre (Joint Managing Director)
Membership: 20 manufacturers of margarine

Federation of the German Motorcycle and Bicycle Industry (VFM)

Verband der Fahrrad- und Motorradindustrie eV
Address: 1549, Otto-Volgar Straße 19, 65843 Suizbach/TS
Telephone: +49 6196 50770
Fax: +49 6196 507720
Year established: 1948
Chief officers: Susanne Dietrich (Statistics)
Publications:
• Federation of the German Motorcycle and Bicycle Industry Geschaftsbericht: *an annual report on the bicycle and motorcycle market with statistics on production, sales, import, and export trends. Figures by type of vehicle and data, in most tables, for a number of years. A mixture of official statistics and data from the association's members - annual*
• Zweirad Report - ZR: *monthly*

Federation of the German Sparkling Wine Industry (VdFw)

Verband der deutschen Fruchtwein- und Fruchtschaumwein-Industrie eV
Address: Mainzerstraße 253, D- 53179 Bonn
Telephone: +49 228 340 729
Fax: +49 228 347 53/95460
Year established: 1968
Chief officers: Albrecht Korth (Joint Director), Karsten Sennewald (Joint Director)
Membership: 72 manufacturers of fruit based wines (excl. grapes)

Federation of the Mineral Oil Industry (MWV)

Mineralölwirtschaftsverband
Address: Steindamm 55, D- 20099 Hamburg
Telephone: +49 40 248 49-0
Fax: +49 40 248 49-253
Year established: 1946
Activities: statistical information to members only
Chief officers: Dr Peter Schlüter (General Director), Barbara Meyer-Bukow
Membership: 18 mineral oil producers
Publications:
• Statistik Mineralölzahlen: *statistics on mineral oil production; only available to members of the association - annual*

Federation of the Soup Industry

Verband der Suppenindustrie
Address: Reuterstrasse 151, D-53113 Bonn
Telephone: +49 228 212 017
Fax: +49 228 229 460
Chief officers: Hans-Joachim Rieber (Chairman), Hans-Joachim Mürau (General Director), Dirk Radermacher (Secretary)
Membership: ca. 30 manufacturers
Publications:
• Marktentwicklung der Suppenindustrie: *industry review, market trends for soups, broths, seasonings, gravies. A commentary is followed by concumption, production, and foreign trade. Production data is broken down by product type. Based on central government data with figures for earlier years in most tables - annual*

Film Industry Organisation (SPIO)

Spitzenorganisation der Filmwirtschaft eV
Address: 5129, Kreuzberger Ring 56, D- 65205 Wiesbaden
Telephone: +49 611 778 9114
Fax: +49 611 778 9139
Chief officers: Franz Seitz (President), Peter Franz (General Director)
Membership: 9 associations

Publications:
• Filmstatistisches Taschenbuch: *tables and graphs on the number of films produced, cinema attendances, visits, turnover of the film industry, film hire, and television viewing. Historical series given in most tables and some comparative international data is also included - annual*

Garden Equipment Manufacturers' Federation (IVG)

Industrievereinigung Gartenbedarf eV
Address: Gothaer Straße 27, D- 40880 Ratingen
Telephone: +49 2102 497 1400
Fax: +49 2102 497 1414
Year established: 1973
Activities: information and advice to members; membership list
Chief officers: Eberhard Kastner (Chairman), Dr Gerd Müller-van Ißen (Secretary)
Membership: 84 producers of garden products
Publications:
• IVG Nachrichten (Garden Equipment Manufacturers' Federation): *statistical and market information published for members only - annual*

German Article Numbering Association (CCG)

Centrale für Corganisation
Address: Spichernstrasse 55, D-50672 Köln
Telephone: +49 2 215 749 02
Fax: +49 2 215 749 159
E-mail: admin@ccg.de or comsys@eancom.de

German Association of Manufacturers, Wholesalers and Exporters of Optical Precision Instruments (DGA)

Deutscher Groß und Außenhandelsverband Augenoptik-Feinmechanik eV
Address: Hensteigstraße 19, D- 70182 Stuttgart
Telephone: +49 711 233 211
Fax: +49 711 247 788
Activities: provides information on technical and scientific developments
Chief officers: Peter Wolf (Chairman), Helge Fehrmann (Secretary)
Membership: 45 manufacturers
Publications:
• List of members
• Newsletter of the German Association of Manufacturers, Wholesalers and Exporters of Optical Precision Instruments

German Brewing Union

Deutscher Brauer-Bund eV
Address: 200452, Annaberger Straße 28, D- 53175 Bonn
Telephone: +49 228 959 060
Fax: +49 228 959 0618
Web site: www.brauer-bund.de
Web site notes: statistical information covering exports, imports, consumption, types of bier, production, etc.; news on the bier industry at a national and international level; information of promotional publications: title, coverage and price
Year established: 1871
Activities: training courses, seminars, conferences, exhibitions; participates in trade fairs; collects statistics on exports, imports, consumption, types of bier, production, etc.; publishes a range of promotional brochures, leaflets, etc.
Chief officers: Dr Michael Dietzsch (President), Peter Stille (General Director), Erich Dederichs (Media Relations)
Structure: umbrella organisation covering 16 regional associations (Landesverbände)
Membership: brewers

Publications:
• Bier Aktuell: *news and opinion articles on the bier industry in Germany - monthly*

German Confectionery Industry Association

Bundesverband der Deutschen Süßwarenindustrie eV
Address: Schumannstraße 4-6, D-53113 Bonn
Telephone: +49 228 260 070
Fax: +49 228 260 0789
Chief officers: Bernd Monheim (Chairman), Klaus Schütze (General Director)
Membership: 300 sweet products manufacturers

German Distillers' Academy (VLSF)

Versuchs- und Lehranstalt für Spiritusfabrikation und Fermentationstechnologie
Address: Seestraße 13, D-1000 Berlin 65
Telephone: +49 30 450 91
Fax: +49 30 453 6067
Chief officers: R Klaus-Dieter Schünemann (Director)
Membership: spirits manufacturers
Publications:
• Die Branntweinwirtschaft

German Federation of High Quality Wine Producers

Verband Deutscher Prädikats- und Qualitätsweingüter eV
Address: Schloß Wallhausen, D-55595 Wallhausen
Telephone: +49 6706 289
Fax: +49 6706 6017
Chief officers: Michael Prinz zu Salm-Salm (President)
Membership: producers of quality wines

German Franchise Association

Deutscher Franchise-Verband eV
Address: Schwanthalerstraße 51, D- 80336 Munich
Telephone: +49 89 535 027
Fax: +49 89 531 323
Year established: 1978
Chief officers: Oskar D Biffar (President), Eberhard Abé (General Secretary), Hans Lang (General Manager)
Membership: ca. 350 members
Notes: member of the European Franchise Federation (Brussels)

German Frozen Food Association

Deutsches Tiefkühlinstitut eV
Address: An der Flora 11, D- 50735 Cologne
Telephone: +49 221 762 064
Fax: +49 221 767 860
Activities: information and advice to members
Chief officers: Otto Rasch (Chairman), Manfred Sassen (Secretary)
Membership: 140 manufacturers, importers and distributors of frozen food

German Mineral Water Federation

Verband Deutscher Heilbrunnen eV
Address: Kennedyalle 28, D-53175 Bonn
Telephone: +49 228 959 900
Fax: +49 228 373 453
Chief officers: Dr Martin Hirsch (Chairman), Dr Christian Fink (Secretary), Dr Helmut Ruhrmann
Membership: 61 mineral water producers, spring water suppliers
Publications:
• Mineral Water (Der Mineralbrunnen): *monthly*

German Mortgage Banks' Association

Verband Deutscher Hypothekenbanken
Address: 120640, Holbeinstrße 17, D- 5300 Bonn 1
Telephone: +49 228 959 020
Fax: +49 228 959 0244
Year established: 1902
Chief officers: Dr Helmut Scholz (Chairman), Dr Dieter Bellinger (General Director)
Membership: 50 members
Publications:
• Annual Report of the Verband Deutscher Hypothekenbanken: *includes a set of statistics on housing finance in Germany plus a review of the market. Based on returns from member organisations - annual*
• Pfandbrief News: *information on capital markets, economy, politics*

German Music Publishers' Association (DMV)

Deutscher Musikverleger-Verband
Address: Friedreich-Wilhelm-Strasse 31, D-53113 Bonn
Telephone: +49 2 282 385 65
Fax: +49 2 282 359 16
Chief officers: Maja-Maria Reis (President), Dr Hans Wilfred Sikorski (Vice President), Wolfgang Mewes (Secretary)
Membership: 480 member companies

German Petfood Manufacturers Association (IVH)

Industrieverband Heimtierbedarf
Address: Postfach 11 06 26, D-40506 Düsseldorf
Telephone: +49 211 594 074
Fax: +49 211 596 045
Chief officers: Mr Alfred Siessegger

German Registered Coffee Union (DKV)

Deutscher Kaffee-Verband eV
Address: Pickhuben 3, D- 20457 Hamburg
Telephone: +49 40 367 510/366256
Fax: +49 40 365 414
Year established: 1946
Activities: compiles statistics on coffee available on request to members and third parties; arbitration
Chief officers: Dr Frieder Rotzoll (Managing Director); Cuno Rothfos (President)
Membership: 101 roasters, agents and importers
Publications:
• Jahresbericht (German Registered Coffee Union): *commentary and statistics on the coffee industry and market with data on production, foreign trade, consumption by local area and prices. Data for earlier years included. Based mainly on central government data - annual*

German Registered Malt Federation

Deutscher Mälzerbund eV
Address: Dechant-Heimbach Straße 21, D- 53177 Bonn
Telephone: +49 228 311 062
Fax: +49 228 312 385
Chief officers: Gottfried Bauer (President), Dr Dieter Kühn (Director)
Membership: 70 company members of the malt industry, 16 regional associations (Landesverbände)

German Sporting Goods Manufacturers' Association (BSI)

Bundesverband der Deutschen Sportartikelindustrie eV
Address: Muehlenweg 12, 53581 Bad Honnef
Telephone: +49 2224 763 81
Fax: +49 2224 759 40
Year established: 1910
Chief officers: Ernst-Albert Holzapfel (President), Siegfried

Höhne (Secretary)
Membership: 250 companies

German Sweets Export Association

German Sweets Süßwarenexportförderung eV
Address: Schumannstrasse 4-6, D-53113 Bonn
Telephone: +49 228 260 07-0
Fax: +49 228 260 0789
Web site: www.germansweets.de
Web site notes: list of membership, exhibition list for 1997
Year established: 1977
Activities: supplies the names of clients and interested
parties worldwide to exporting German manufacturers of
confectionery products (candy, chocolate products, cookies
and biscuits, snacks and ice cream)
Chief officers: Rüdiger Larssen (Chairman), Klaus Reingen
(General Director)
Membership: 100 German industrial manufacturers
Publications:
• International Confectionery Export Catalogue: *annual*

German Transport Businesses' Association (VDV)

Verband Deutscher Verkehrsunternehmen
Address: Kamekestraße 37-39, D- 50672 Cologne
Telephone: +49 221 579 79/0
Fax: +49 221 514 272
Year established: 1895
Chief officers: Dieter Bollhöfer (President)
Membership: ca. 530 transport companies
Publications:
• Jahresbericht (Verband Deutscher Verkehrsunternehmen):
*statistics on various transport sectors including railways, bus
and truck lines, tramways, ski lifts, not operated by the federal
authorities. Based on returns from various operating
companies - annual*

German Union of Butchers (DFV)

Deutscher Fleischer-Verband
Address: Kennedyallee 53, D-60596 Frankfurt
Telephone: +49 69 639 043
Fax: +49 69 631 1060
Activities: information and advice to members
Chief officers: Albert Pröller (President), Theo Wershoven
(Director)
Membership: 2,700 butchers
Publications:
• Allgemeine Fleischer Zeitung: *trade journal dealing with
issues affecting meat retailing - weekly*
• Geschaftsbericht (German Union of Butchers): *the annual
review of the German Butchers Association with statistics on
meat supply, consumption, prices, retailing trends, industry
structure. A commentary accompanies the data and historical
series are included in many tables. Based on various sources
- annual*

Hamburg Frozen and Canned Food Association

Waren-Verein der Hamburger Börse eV
Address: Große Bäckerstraße 4, D-20095 Hamburg 1
Telephone: +49 40 326414
Fax: +49 40 322639
Telex: 162680
Year established: 1900
Chief officers: Christian Krogmann (Chairman), Dr Klaus
Hanebuth (General Director), Sigrid Schnelle (Secretary)
Membership: ca. 200 frozen and canned foods importers
Publications:
• Jahresbericht (Hamburg Frozen and Canned Food
Association): *includes import and consumption statistics, price
data - annual*

Industrial Federation of Yarn and Fabrics Manufacturers

Industrieverband Garne und Gewebe eV
Address: 5369, Frankfurter Straße 10-14, D- 65760 Eschborn
Telephone: +49 6196 472 30/472 45
Fax: +49 6196 472 340/472 370
Telex: 4072587
Chief officers: Klaus-Jürgen Kraatz (Director)
Membership: 100 companies and 6 associations

Magazine Publishers' Association

Verband Deutscher Zeitschriftenverlger
Address: Winterstrasse 50, D-53177 Bonn
Telephone: +49 228 382 0321
Fax: +49 228 382 0340

National Association of the Hotel and Catering Services (DEHOGA)

Deutscher Hotel- und Gaststaettenverband eV
Address: 200455, Kronprinzenstraße 46, D-53173 Bonn
Telephone: +49 228 820 080
Fax: +49 228 820 0846
Year established: 1949
Chief officers: Dr Erich Kaub (President), Christian Ehlers
(General Director)
Membership: ca. 95,000 members, 19 trade associations
Publications:
• Allgemeine Hotel- und Gaststätten-Zeitung (AHGZ)
• Das Gastgewerbe (DGa)

Non-Alcoholic Drinks Industry Association (AFG)

Vereinigung Alkoholfreie Getränke-Industrie eV
Address: Kennedyallee 28, D- 53175 Bonn
Telephone: +49 228 959 900
Fax: +49 228 373 453
Year established: 1989
Membership: mineral water, juices, soft drinks manufacturers

Opticians Association

Zentralverband der Augenoptiker
Address: Alexanderstraße 25a, D-40210 Düsseldorf
Telephone: +49 211 320 697
Fax: +49 211 324 453
Year established: 1951
Chief officers: Manfred L Müller (Chairman), Joachim Goerdt
(Director)
Membership: ca. 7,200 opticians, 12 regional associations
Publications:
• ZVA-Report: *annual*

Pharmaceutical Industry Association (BPI)

Bundesverband der Pharmazeutischen Industrie
Address: Karlstrasse 21, D- 60329 Frankfurt
Telephone: +49 69 2556-1266
Fax: +49 69 2556-1603
E-mail: Presse@pharma-bpi.com
Web site: www.pharma-bpi.com
Web site notes: site includes statistics on the German
pharmaceutical market including information on OTC products
Chief officers: Prof. Dr. Hans Rüdiger Vogel (General
Director), Alex Sander (Secretary)
Publications:
• BPI Annual Report (BPI Jahresbericht): *annual*
• Medicine and Opinion (Medikament und Meinung): *medicine
and health sectors - monthly*
• Phamaceutical Data (Pharma Daten): *brochure with detailed
data on the pharmaceutical and health sectors - annual*
Notes: cschulte@bpiffm.mhs.compuserve.com
gkienitz@bpiffm.mhs.compuserve.com

Registered Federal Association of Lighting and Electrical Retailers

Bundesverband des Beleuchtungs- und Elektro- Einzelhandels eV
Address: Höninger Weg 106a, D-50969 Cologne
Telephone: +49 221 936 5502
Fax: +49 221 936 55909
Year established: 1947
Activities: turnover data, company comparisons, retail structure data
Chief officers: Paul Flösch (President), Holger Wenzel (Executive Director)
Membership: over 600 firms and 16 regional associations (Landesverbände)
Publications:
• Elektrofach & Elektrobrief: *issues affecting electric fittings retail trade - monthly*
Notes: part of the umbrella organisation Hauptverband des Deutschen Einzelhandels

Registered German Wine Producers' Association

Deutscher Weinbauverband eV
Address: Heussallee 26, D-53113 Bonn
Telephone: +49 228 221 401
Fax: +49 228 261 683
Year established: 1874
Activities: organises INTERVITIS INTERFRUCTA trade fair (every 3 years)
Chief officers: Dr Reinhard Muth (President), Dr Rudolf Nickenig (Secretary General)
Structure: 34 regional associations (Landesverbände)
Membership: regional wine producers groups
Publications:
• Annual Report (Jahresbericht): *covers association's activities and publishes some market data - annual*
• German Wine Production (Der Deutsche Weinbau): *3-monthly*

Sugar Industry Association

Verein der Zuckerindustrie
Address: 2545, Am Hofgarten 8, D- 5300 Bonn
Telephone: +49 228 2285-0
Fax: +49 228 228 5100
Year established: 1850
Chief officers: Dieter Langendorf (General Director), Klaus von Briskorn (Secretary)
Membership: 13 sugar manufacturers associations
Publications:
• Jahresbericht (Verein der Zuckerindustrie): *an annual report with statistics covering sugar production and consumption in Germany. Based largely on the association's own survey with some data from official sources - annual*
• Zuckerwirtschaft: *detailed statistics on the sugar economy with sections covering production, consumption, foreign trade, prices, and sugar balances worldwide. Most tables contain figures covering a number of years - annual*

Textile Industry Association of the German Federal Republic (GESAMTTEXTIL)

Gesamtverband der Textilindustrie in der Bundesrepublik Deutschland eV
Address: Postfach 5340, Frankfurter Straße 10-14, D-65760 Eschborn
Telephone: +49 6 196 966 0
Fax: +49 6 196 421 70
Chief officers: Christian Georgi (President), Dr Wolf-Rüdiger Baumann (Director), Dr Klaus Schmidt (Director)
Structure: 11 regional associations (Landesverbände)
Membership: textile manufacturers and trade associations
Publications:
• Textil-Konjunkturbericht: *an annual review of the textile sector is followed by tables on the number of enterprises,* turnover, prices, production, foreign trade, products, retailing, and textile machinery. Historical figures in many tables and based on a mixture of official and non-official sources - annual
• Zahlen zur Textilindustrie: *statistics for the last 15 years covering the textile sector with tables on production, turnover, establishments, imports, exports, investment, etc.. Some comparative figures for other European countries - annual*

Union for the Export of Dairy Products

Export-Union für Milchprodukte eV
Address: Schedestraße 11, D-53113 Bonn
Telephone: +49 228 959 924
Fax: +49 228 371 534
Year established: 1964
Chief officers: H Strothmann (Director), Eckhard Heuser (Secretary)
Membership: 115 members

Union of Agriculture Machinery Manufacturers (LAV)

Die Landmaschinen-und Ackerschleppervereinigung
Address: 710864, Lyoner Straße 18, D- 60528 Frankfurt
Telephone: +49 69 660 31595
Fax: +49 69 660 31611
Chief officers: Dr Bernard Krone (Chairman), Dr Bernd Scherer (Director)
Publications:
• Jahresbericht (LAV): *a statistical yearbook with data on agricultural machinery and tractors. Includes tables covering supplies, turnover, imports, exports. Commentary is included and the statistics cover the latest three years - annual*
Notes: Member of Verband Deutscher Maschinen- und Anlagenbau eV (Association of German Machinery and Building)

Union of the Federal Associations of German Jewellers

Vereinigung der Bundesverbände des deutschen Schmuck- und Silberwarengewerbes eV
Address: 470, Poststraße 1, D-75172 Pforzheim
Telephone: +49 7231 330 41
Fax: +49 7231 3558 87
Chief officers: Joachim Köhle (President); Dr Alfred Schneider (Managing Director)
Membership: 9 associations representing export, manufacture, retailing and wholesaling

Union of Wholesalers for Writing Paper and Stationary (GVS)

Großhandelsverband Schreib-, Papierwaren- und Bürobedarf eV
Address: Kaiser Wilhelm Ring 13, D-50672 Cologne
Telephone: +49 221 951 591 0
Fax: +49 221 951 59115
Year established: 1906
Chief officers: Jürgen Höhfeld (Chairman), Hans-Karl Gamerschlag (Secretary)
Membership: 3 cooperatives, 103 writing paper and stationary wholesalers, 8 guest members
Publications:
• pbs-aktuell

Varnish/Painting Industry Association

Verband der Lackindustrie
Address: Karlstraße 21, D-60329 Frankfurt
Telephone: +49 69 255 61411
Fax: +49 69 255 61358
Chief officers: Dr Manfred Bode (General Director), Dr Dietmar Eichstädt (Secretary)
Publications:
• Jahresbericht (Verband der Lackindustrie): *statistics on total production, production of key products, turnover, foreign trade, and prices. A commentary accompanies the statistics*

and there is some data on European production and foreign trade - annual

Vocational Association for Market and Social Researchers (BVM)

Berufsverband Deutscher Markt- und Sozialforscher eV
Address: 100312, Frankfurter Straße 22, D- 63065 Offenbach/Main
Telephone: +49 69 800 1552
Fax: +49 69 800 3143
Year established: 1955
Chief officers: Dr Gerhard Breunig (Chairman), Gwendolin Hübner-Blos (Secretary)
Membership: ca. 800 members

GHANA

Association of Manufacturers of Ghana

Address: PO Box 8624, Ghana International Trade Fair Centre, Accra North
Telephone: +233 21 777 283
Telex: 3027
Year established: 1957
Chief officers: John K Richardson (President)
Membership: umbrella association for various industry sectors: food, drinks, clothing and textlies, pharmaceuticals, cosmetics, metals, packaging, automotives, etc
Publications:
● Ghana Manufacturer: *quarterly*

Coffee and Sheanuts Exporters' Association

Address: PO Box 226, c/o Mr J.W. Biney, Agrotrade Limited, Abavana Junction, Kotobabi, Accra
Telephone: +233 21 224 820
Fax: +233 21 224 564

Federation of Associations of Ghanaian Exporters (FAGE)

Address: PO Box M378, c/o Kiku Limited, South Industrial Area, Accra
Telephone: +233 21 223 215/229 064
Fax: +233 21 776 755
Membership: umbrella organisation for exporters of Ghana

Federation of Ghanaian Jewellers

Address: PO Box 5626, Loc. H/No. C894/3, Behind North Ridge School, North Ridge, Accra
Telephone: +233 21 225 346

Ghana Assorted Foodstuffs Exporters' Association

Address: PO Box 10673, Loc. Block no.3, 3rd Crescent Road, Abeka Junction, Airport, Accra
Telephone: +233 21 220 746
Fax: +233 21 223 663

Ghana Book Publishers' Association

Address: PO Box M 430, Accra
Telephone: +233 21 229 178
Fax: +233 21 220 271
Chief officers: Peter Kokoi (Executive Officer)

Ghana Booksellers' Association (GBA)

Address: PO Box 10367, Accra
Telephone: +233 21 224 829
Fax: +233 21 773 242

Ghana Cocoa Marketing Board

Address: POB 933, Accra
Telephone: +233 21 221 212
Telex: 20822311 GH

Ghana Export Promotion Council

Address: PO Box M 146, Republic House, Accra
Telephone: +233 21228 813/228 820/228 830/228 541
Fax: +233 21 668 263
Year established: 1969
Chief officers: Tawia Akyea (Executive Secretary)
Publications:
● Exporters' Directory: *information about export enterprises in Ghana - annual*

Ghana Furniture Producers' and Exporters' Association

Address: PO Box 32, Trade Fair Centre, Accra
Telephone: +233 21 775 311/774 251

Ghana National Association of Handicraft Exporters

Address: PO Box M146, c/o Ghana Export Promotion Council, Accra
Telephone: +233 21 228 813/830/620/541
Fax: +233 21 668 263

Ghana National Association of Salt Exporters (GNASE)

Address: PO Box 16175, Near Neoplan Station, Accra
Telephone: +233 21 225 542
Telex: 2289 EXPORT GH

Ghana Palm Oil, Palm Kernel and Coconut Oil Exporters' Association

Address: PO Box K597, Loc. H/No. E44/2, Op. Lorry Park, Tudu, Accra New Town, Accra
Telephone: +233 21 669 491

Ghana Yam Producers' and Exporters' Association

Address: PO Box 5233, Trade Fair Center, Accra
Telephone: +233 21 775 311/773 860
Fax: +233 21 668 263

Guild of Newspaper Publishers

Address: PO Box 11 924, Scoa House , Derby Avenue, On Kwame Nkrumah Avenue, Accra - North
Telephone: +233 21 699 111
Fax: +233 21 667 500
Chief officers: Magnus Rex Danquah (President)

Horticulture Association of Ghana

Address: PO Box 9303, Trade Fair Center, Accra
Telephone: +233 21 772 139/773 860
Fax: +233 21 772 350

Organisation for Export Development of Seafood

Address: PO Box 13588, c/o Signotrade Limited, Thema Fishing Harbour, Accra North
Telephone: +233 21 712 762
Fax: +233 21 668 263

Precious Minerals Marketing Corporation

Address: P Box M108, Diamond House, Accra
Telephone: +233 21 664 931/4
Fax: +233 21 668 263

Vegetable Exporters' Association
Address: PO Box M146, c/o Ghana Export Promotion Council, Accra
Telephone: +233 21 221 212/221 866
Fax: +233 21 668 263

West African University Booksellers' Association (WAUBA)
Address: PO Box 1, c/o The General Secretary's Office, University Bookshop, Legon, Accra
Telephone: +233 21 753 81 ext 2287

GREECE

Association of Baby Food Companies of Greece
Syndesmos etaireion Paidikon Trofon Ellados
Address: 17th km of Athens-Lamia National Road, GR-145 64 Nea Kifissia
Telephone: +30 1 807 2156
Fax: +30 1 807 7891
Chief officers: Mr. Vasilis Apazoglou
Membership: 8 companies
Notes: Based at the Nutricia head offices. No official publications (other than bulletins to members).

Association of Car Importers and Representatives
Syndesmos Eisagogeon Antiprosopon Autokiniton
Address: 108 Kifisias Avenue, GR-115 26 Athens
Telephone: +30 1 648 1365 / 648 7482
Fax: +30 1 693 2743
Chief officers: Sergios Sakellaropoulos (Director)
Notes: car sales statistics available by various breakdowns (including by make and model) but usually cost about $100.00

Association of Detergent and Soap Manufacturers (SAVOS)
Syndesmos Ellinikon Viomihanion Apporypandikon kai Sapounion
Address: 14-16 Vervenon Str, GR-115 27 Athens
Telephone: +30 1 777 2780
Fax: +30 1 775 4066
Year established: 1981
Activities: organisation of conferences, cooperation in legislative matters, public relations
Chief officers: Mr. P. Pavlidis (President),Theo Michaelidis (Secretary)
Membership: 12 companies
Publications:
• Annual Statistical Report: *statistics and analysis of the Greek market for household cleaning products - annual*
Notes: The association does not provide statistical information to non-members without permission from the board. Requests for information are dealt with on an individual basis. There are also irregular bulletins intended for environmentalist groups.

Association of Greek Brewers
Enosi Zythopion Ellados
Address: PO Box 383, 107 Kifissou Ave, Aegaleo, GR-122 41 Athens
Telephone: +30 1 538 4911
Fax: +30 1 538 4437/545 0848
Chief officers: Mr. Minas Tanes (President)
Membership: 3 domestic brewing companies
Notes: Based in premises of Athenean Breweries SA (Amstel-Heineken). No official publications other than bulletins to members.

Association of Greek Cereals Merchants (SEEDYZ)
Syndesmos Ellinon Emporon Dimitriakon
Address: 9 Vissarionos Street, Athens
Telephone: +30 1 364 3084
Fax: +30 1 364 3092
Chief officers: Mrs. Varitou (Secretary)
Notes: The Association does not produce publications or statistics.

Association of Greek Chocolate Industries
Syndesmos Ellinikon Viomihanion Sokolatas
Address: 69 Ethnikis Antistaseos and 2 Eptanisou, GR-152 31 Halandri
Telephone: +30 1 671 1177/672 3215
Fax: +30 1 671 1080
Chief officers: Anastasios Anastasiadis (Director)
Notes: Formally known as the 'Association of Biscuit, Rusk and Sugar Products' (Syndesmos Biskotopiias, Friganopiias, Zacharodon Proionton). Do not have publications or data of their own, use CAOBISCO publications.

Association of Greek Exporting and Consignment Enterprises for Fruit, Vegetables and Fruit Juice
Address: 7-9 Sophokleous Street, GR-105 59 Athens
Telephone: +30 1 324 9992/324 9003/321 5581
Fax: +30 1 325 3997
Activities: produces statistics on exports
Membership: 100 member companies
Notes: No official publications but regular bulletins to members plus news of exhibitions.

Association of Greek Flour Manufacturers
Syndesmos Alevroviomichanion tis Elladas
Address: 6 Fidiou Street and Genadiou Street, GR-106 78 Athens
Telephone: +30 1 382 0074
Fax: +30 1 380 0794
Year established: 1932
Activities: provides an information service
Chief officers: Mr Onik Atzemian
Structure: 7 member presidium with permanent secretariat (elections every 2 years)
Membership: 48 flour producing companies
Notes: The Association does not produce any publications.

Association of Greek Honey Processors and Exporters
Syndesmos Ellinon Typopoiiton Exagogeon Meliou
Address: 69 Ethnikis Antistaseos and 2 Eptanisou, GR-152 31 Halandri
Telephone: +30 1 671 1177 / 672 3215
Fax: +30 1 671 1080
Chief officers: George Pittas (President)

Association of Greek Manufacturers of Children's' Toys and Vehicles
Syndesmos Ellinon Viotehnon - Kataskeuaston Paidikon Paihnithion kai Amaxon
Address: 5 Karysti Street, Athens
Telephone: +30 1 324 3468/325 1296
Notes: The Association does not produce statistics or publications.

Association of Greek Milk and Dairy Products Industries (SEVGAP)
Syndesmos Ellinikon Viomichanion Galactokomikon Proionton
Address: 69 Ethnikis Antistaseos and 2 Eptanisou, GR-152 31 Halandri
Telephone: +30 1 671 1177 / 672 3215
Fax: +30 1 671 1080

Chief officers: Dimitrios Koronakis (General Director)

Association of Greek Olive Oil Processors (SEVITEL)

Syndesmos Ellinikon Viomichanion Typopiisis Elaioladou
Address: 15a Xenofontos Street, GR-105 57 Athens
Telephone: +30 1 323 8856/3223165
Fax: +30 1 324 6408
Chief officers: Paraskevas Tokouzbalidis (President)
Membership: 80 member companies
Notes: The Association does not produce any publications other than a members Bulletin, but does compile some market information.

Association of Greek Pharmaceuticals' Companies (SFEE)

Address: 15-17 Tsoha Street, GR-115 21 Athens
Telephone: +30 1 644 7271/643 0104
Fax: +30 1 641 1463
Chief officers: Mr. Manolis Neiadas (President)

Association of Greek Soft Drinks Industries (SEVA)

Syndesmos Ellinikon Viomichanion Anapsytikon (SEVA)
Address: 69 Ethnikis Antistaseos and 2 Eptanisou, GR-152 31 Halandri
Telephone: +30 1 671 1177/672 3215
Fax: +30 1 671 1080
Chief officers: Lukas Comis (Director)

Association of Greek Tobacco Industries (SEK)

Syndesmos Ellinikon Kapnoviomihanion
Address: 6 Panepistimiou Street, GR-106 71 Athens
Telephone: +30 1 363 4230
Fax: +30 1 363 4230
Activities: cooperation with government over legislative and taxation matters
Chief officers: Spyros Fleggas (Director)
Membership: 5 member manufacturing companies
Notes: No official publications except total sales figures to members and National Statistical Agency.

Association of Greek Tourist Enterprises (AGTE)

Address: 572, Vouliagmenis Avenue, GR-164 51 Athens
Telephone: +30 1 996 7002/003
Fax: +30 1 996 7003
Year established: 1992
Activities: promoting member activities and Greek tourism by participating in international forums and tourism exhibitions; proposing tourism development projects to state and tourism professionals; organising seminars, conferences and training programmes; conducting research on tourism subjects and supporting researchers from various educational institutions; media, press releases and newsletters
Chief officers: Mr Theodore Vassilakis (Secretary General)
Membership: tourism industry

Association of Greek Wine and Spirits Industries (SEVOP)

Syndesmos Ellinon Viomihanon Oinon Poton (SEVOP)
Address: 15a Xenofontos Street, GR-105 57 Athens
Telephone: +30 1 322 6053/324 9027
Fax: +30 1 323 7943
Year established: 1949
Activities: participates in most international drinks fairs
Chief officers: Mrs Koveou (Director)
Membership: 52 wine and spirits producing and bottling companies

Association of Hellenic Food Industries

Syndesmos Ellinikon Viomihanion Trofimon
Address: 69 Ethikis Antistaseos and 2 Eptanisou, GR-15231 Halandri
Telephone: +30 1 671 1177/672 3215
Fax: +30 1 671 1080
Chief officers: Mrs Papadimitriou (Director), Mrs Raptopoulou (Secretary)
Structure: umbrella organisation for most food industry trade associations

Association of Management Consultancy Companies of Greece

Address: 25 Filellinon Street, GR-10557 Athens
Telephone: +30 1 3221127
Chief officers: Yiannis Hastas

Association of Meat Product Processing Industries

Syndesmos Viotehnon kai Viomihanon Typopoiiseos Kreatoskeuasmaton
Address: 23 km of Athens-Lamia Road, GR-145 65 Kryoneri
Telephone: +30 1 816 1886/816 1912
Chief officers: N Kolovisteas (President)
Notes: no publications

Association of Pasta Product Industries

Panellinios Syndesmos Viomihanon Zymarikon
Address: 23 Sokratous Street, GR-105 52 Athens
Telephone: +30 1 522 4227
Chief officers: Theodore Haralambopoulos (President)
Membership: pasta producing companies

Association of Petroleum Products Trading Companies of Greece

Syndesmos Etaireion Emporeias Petraileoeidon Ellados
Address: 4 Thetidos Street, GR-115 23 Athens
Telephone: +30 1 729 1050/729 1051
Fax: +30 1 724 5172
Chief officers: Mr. I. Bitounis (President)
Membership: 13 member trading companies
Notes: No publications or information to non-members.

Association of Producers & Exporters of Vineyard Products (SYVEPA)

Syndesmos Viomihanon Exagogeon Proionton Ampelou (SY.V.E.P.A.)
Address: 178 Vouliagmenis Avenue, GR-172 35 Dafni, Athens
Telephone: +30 1 723 9913-14
Chief officers: Mr. V. Spiliopoulos (President)

Association of Retail Trade Companies (SELPE)

Syndesmos Epicheiriseon Lianikis Poliseos Ellados
Address: 1 Streit Street and Kratinou, GR-10551 Athens
Telephone: +30 1 3241410/3241743
Fax: +30 1 3216649
Year established: 1975
Chief officers: G A Meimarides
Membership: 100 companies

Athenian Meat Traders' Union

Enosis Emporon Kreatos Athenas
Address: 21 Sophokleos Street, GR-105 59 Athens
Telephone: +30 1 321 6148
Fax: +30 1 321 6252

Federation of Alcohol Manufacturers

Syndesmos Viomihanon Inopnevmatos
Address: 19 Patriarchou Ioakim, GR-106 75 Athens
Telephone: +30 1 723 913/724 2149
Chief officers: Mr Hatzidimas (President)

Federation of Hellenic Information Technology Enterprises

Address: Lagoumitze 23, Athens GR-17671
Telephone: +30 1 924 9540
Fax: +30 1 924 9524
E-mail: sepe@compulink.gr

Federation of Tobacco Processing Industries

Omospondia Viomihanion Epexergasias Kapnou
Address: 25 Voukourestiou Street, Athens
Telephone: +30 1 361 1105/361 5027
Activities: bargaining body between tobacco processors and cigarette manufacturers
Chief officers: Mr. Alex Mihailidis (President0
Membership: tobacco leaf processing companies - NB not cigarette manufacturers
Notes: no publications

Greek Association of Importers of European Tobacco Products

Ellinikos Syndesmos Kapnikon Etaireion Europis
Address: 21 Aigialias and 1 Halepa Street, GR-151 25 Paradeissos Amaroussiou
Telephone: +30 1 681 6918
Fax: +30 1 684 4053
Activities: co-operation with state over legislative issues, prices, taxation and public relations
Chief officers: Mr. Walter Bentrup (President)
Membership: 7 importing companies
Notes: Financial data is provided to national bodies such as the National Statistical Service of Greece and ICAP. Mr. W. Bentrup is Managing Director of Reemtsma Hellas SA

Greek Canners' Association

Enosis Conservopion Elladas
Address: 60 Solonos Street, GR-106 72 Athens
Telephone: +30 1 360 7816/363 4935
Fax: +30 1 360 9075
Chief officers: Mr. Vasilis Platon (President)
Membership: 42 tomato canning companies (manufacturers and exporters)
Notes: The Association does not produce any publications.

Greek Poultry Industry Association

Syndesmos Ptinotrofikon Epiheiriseon Ellados
Address: 54 Menandrou Street, GR-104 31 Athens
Telephone: +30 1 523 8190
Fax: +30 1 522 7370
Activities: operates information department, carries out research and compiles statistics
Chief officers: Mr. Spiros Nonikas (president)
Membership: poultry farmers and processors (poultry and eggs)
Notes: data supplied to ministry of agriculture - also monthly bulletin to members

Hellenic Aerosol Association

Syndesmos Aerozol Ellados
Address: Proektasi Souri Street, Peristeri, GR-121 31 Athens
Telephone: +30 1 574 1411-7
Fax: +30 1 574 1419
Year established: 1963
Chief officers: Mr. G. Pispinis (President)

Structure: elections every 2 years for presidency and secretariat. Both based in private companies. No autonomous offices
Membership: 15 aerosol producing, importing, supplying and packaging companies
Notes: no regular publications but occasional newsletters for members

Hellenic Association of Footwear Manufacturers and Exporters

Ellinikos Syndesmos Ergostasiarhon, Viotehnon, Viomihanon, Exagogeon Ypodimaton
Address: 27 Pinelopis Delta Street, GR-154 51 Neo Psychiko
Telephone: +30 1 672 5295
Fax: +30 1 674 4497
Chief officers: D. Paleokostas (Director)

Hellenic Centre of Article Numbering (HELLCAN)

Address: 5 Aghiou Dimitriou Square and 2 Diom. Kyriakou Street, GR-145 62 Kifissia, Athns
Telephone: +30 1 801 7224
Fax: +30 1 801 9156
E-mail: hellcan@elkeshp.ath.forthnet.gr

Hellenic Chamber of Hotels

Address: 24, Stadiou Str - 105 64, Athens
Telephone: +30 321 0022/26
Fax: +30 322 5449/323 6962
Web site: www.topnet-computers.com/greekhotels
Web site notes: statistics on Greek hotel capacity
Activities: supply of information and statistical data
Publications:
• Xenia: *monthly*

Hellenic Clothing Industries' Association

Syndesmos Kataskeuaston Etoimon Endymaton
Address: 3rd Floor, 51 Ermou Street, GR-10563 Athens
Telephone: +30 1 322 3979/323 4811
Fax: +30 1 323 9159
Chief officers: Mr. Theodore Paraskevopoulos (President), M. Karabinis (Director)
Publications:
• Clothing and Techniques Yearbook: *includes statistics on the Greek clothing industry with data on production and consumption. Figures for the latest year and the previous year - annual*

Hellenic Federation of Bakers

Omospondia Artopoion Ellados
Address: 15 Veranzelou, GR-106 77 Athens
Telephone: +30 1 382 4194/384 0530
Fax: +30 1 380 6289
Activities: until recently, the price of bread was state-controlled. The Federation was the means of communication between members and government.
Chief officers: Mr. P. Pavlopoulos (President)
Membership: independent bakers
Notes: no publications

Hellenic Federation of Publishers and Booksellers

Syndesmos Ekdoton Vivliou
Address: Book House, 73 Themistokleus Str., 106 83 Athens
Telephone: +30 1 330 0924/330 3942/330 1956
Fax: +30 1 330 1617/330 3942/330 1956
Chief officers: Mr G Dardanos (General Secretary), Mr G Doudoumis (Director)
Membership: 275 publishing companies
Notes: Information available from the National Book Centre (tel. 1 625 0264).

National Dairy Committee of Greece

Address: c/o Agricultural University of Athens, 75 Iera Odos-Votanikos, 11855 Athens
Telephone: +30 1 529 46 51
Fax: +30 1 529 46 51
Chief officers: Mr E. Doxanakis (Secretary)

National Tobacco Organisation

Ethnikos Organismos Kapnou
Address: 46 Veranzelou Street, GR-104 38 Athens
Telephone: +30 1 524 7311
Fax: +30 1 524 7318
Chief officers: Mr. N. Malisiovas (President)
Notes: no publications

Pan-Hellenic Association of Meat Processing Industries

Panellinios Syndesmos Viomihanon-Viotehnon Allantikon
Address: 15a Xenofontos Street, GR-105 57 Athens
Telephone: +30 1 325 3237
Fax: +30 1 325 4460
Year established: 1965
Chief officers: Mr. Dim. Papagiannis (President)
Structure: presidency, secretariat, members
Membership: about 35 meat processing companies
Notes: no publications

Pan-Hellenic Association of Clothes Manufacturers

Panellinios Syndesmos Kataskeuaston Etoimon Endymaton
Address: 51 Ermou Street, GR-105 63 Athens
Telephone: +30 1 322 3979
Fax: +30 1 323 9159
Chief officers: Mr. D. Charisis
Membership: approx. 300
Publications:
● Clothing and Technics (Endyma kai Techniki): *annual or bi-annual*
Notes: No statistical data or publications.

Pan-Hellenic Association of Cosmetics and Perfume Industries and Representatives

Panellhnios Syndesmos Viomihanon kai Antiprosopon Aromaton kai Kallyntikon
Address: 28 Académias Street, GR-106 71 Athens
Telephone: +30 1 361 2776
Fax: +30 1 363 7498
Telex: 214593
Chief officers: Mr. Dimitrios Spiliotopoulos (Director)
Membership: 80 - 85 member companies from manufacturing, importing and distribution sectors
Publications:
● Beautiful Industry: *letter from the president - legislative matterts - quantitive market figures - monthly*

Pan-Hellenic Association of Pharmacists

Panellinios Syndesmos Pharmacopoion
Address: 57 Marne Street, GR-10437 Athens
Telephone: +30 1 524 5820
Year established: 1928
Activities: information service covering pharmaceutical law, salaries, production, education. Cooperation with state over legislative matters.
Chief officers: Christos Skaidiotis (President), Manolis Agelakas (General Secretary)
Membership: 1,600
Publications:
● Pharmakeutika Chronika : *quarterly*
Notes: No statistical activities.

Pan-Hellenic Pharmaceutical Industries Union

Address: 12 Deligiorgi Street, GR-104 37 Athens
Telephone: +30 1 524 7139
Fax: +30 1 524 7139
Chief officers: Mr. Constantine Generakis (President)
Membership: 27 member companies - all Greek manufacturers or importers-representatives

Pan-Hellenic Union of Exporters of Table Olives

Panellinia Enosis Exagogeon Vrosimon Elaion
Address: See: record 27290
12 Agiou Constantinou Street, GR-10 431 Athens
Telephone: +30 1 522 7356/523 2036
Fax: +30 1 522 6616
Telex: 219318
Chief officers: Mr. Nikos Gatos (President)

Pan-Hellenic Union of Greek Cosmetic and Beauty Care Products, Industries and Handicrafts

Address: 351 Mesogion Avenue, GR-152 31 Athens
Telephone: +30 1 653 2811-3
Fax: +30 1 651 0694
Chief officers: Mr. Nikolaos Koveos (President)

Union of Artisan Confectionery Producers (EVZE)

Enosi Viotechnion Zacharodon Ellados (EVZE)
Address: 2nd floor, 8 Christopoulou Street, GR-184 54 Nikea
Telephone: +30 1 495 6990
Fax: +30 1 495 6990
Chief officers: Mr. Dimitrios Maloyannis (Director)

Union of Greek Cotton Industries

Address: 5 Xenofontos Street, GR-105 57 Athens
Telephone: +30 1 323 4775
Fax: +30 1 322 4429
Chief officers: Mr. Charalambos Sepentzis (Vice President), Mr. J. Argitos (Director)

Union of Processors of Agricultural Produce

Enosi Konservopopion Ellados - Enosi Metapoiiton Agrotikon Proionton
Address: 49 Megalou Alexandrou Street, Skydra Pierrias, GR-58 500
Telephone: +30 381 82349
Fax: +30 381 82329
Chief officers: Mr. K. Apostolou (President)
Membership: 25 member companies - processors and canners of fruit (mainly apricots)
Notes: No official publications - statistical data provided to the National Statistical Service of Greece.

Union of Refrigeration Industries

Enosis Viomichanion Psyhous
Address: 51 Stadiou Street, GR-105 59 Athens
Telephone: +30 1 3214900
Chief officers: Mr. Dimitrios Vamvakopoulos (Director)

Union of Wood Industries of Greece

Address: 12-14 Mitropoleos Street, GR-105 63 Athens
Telephone: +30 1 324 5306
Chief officers: Mr. Andreas Kyriazis (Director)

GRENADA

Grenada Cocoa Association
Address: Scott Street, St Georges
Telephone: +1 809 440 2234/2933
Fax: +1 809 440 1470

Grenada Hotel Association
Address: PO Box 440, Belmont, St Georges
Telephone: +1 809 444 1353
Fax: +1 809 444 4847

Marketing and National Importing Board
Address: PO Box 652, Young Street, St Georges
Telephone: +1 809 440 1791/3111/3191
Fax: +1 809 440 4152
Membership: exporters of agricultural products, fruit and vegetable suppliers

GUADELOUPE

Employers' Association of Guadeloupe
Union Patronale de la Region Guadeloupe
Address: Immeuble SCI BTB, Voie Principale, Z.I. de Jarry, 97122 Baie-Mahault
Telephone: +590 268 358
Fax: +590 268 367
E-mail: uprg@netguacom.fr
Web site: www.intel-media.fr/intermed/up.htm
Activities: information service, training, legal and social consulting, conferences, debates and seminars
Chief officers: Mr Lionel de Lavigne (President), Mr Christophe Naimi (Secretary General)
Membership: 14 Trade associations, 360 individual members

Small and Medium-Sized Enterprises' Association of Guadeloupe
Association des Moyennes et Petites Industries
Address: WTC, Zone de Commerce International, Pointe Jarry, 97122 Baie-Mahault
Telephone: +590 2 506 28
Fax: +590 2 506 29

GUATEMALA

Guatemalan Association of Exporters of Non-Traditional Products (GEXPRONT)
Asociación Guatemalteca de Exportadores de Productos No Tradicionales
Address: Edif Cámara de Industrias, 5º Nivel, Ruta 6, 9 - 21, Zona 4, Guatemala
Telephone: +502 2 346 872/7
Fax: +502 2 347 183/323 590
E-mail: gexpront@pronet.net.gt
Web site: www.quetzalnet.com/gexpront
Year established: 1982
Activities: AGRITRADE - convention and exhibition, annual Central American fair, visited by importers from Europe, USA and the rest of America; Apparel Sourcing Show (biannual convention and exhibition for Central America and the Caribbean, organised by GEXPRONT specialising in clothing and textiles; EXPOMUEBLE annual exhibition and convention for Central America specialising in furniture, accessories and services; international handicraft fair FOLKLORE; National fair AGROENCUENTRO; information, training, trade promotion services; CEDIME (Centro de Documentación e Información

de Mercados) founded in 1990 to gather documentation and identify information sources for Guatemalan business. Provides commercial information, training and technical assistance; market strategies; promotional events; investment promotion and access to technology
Chief officers: Juan Sánchez Bolván (President), Fanny de Estrada (Executive Director), Ing Bernardo Roehrs (Manager), Licª Lorena Colom (Information Officer)
Structure: private non-profit organisation; 6 departments; agriculture; apparel; textiles; shellfish and fish; handicrafts; wood products; manufacturers
Membership: 833 members: 294 agriculture, 221 clothing and textiles, 154 manufacturing, 81 traditional handicrafts, 25 fish and seafood, 90 wooden furniture, 77 services
Publications:
• Annual Exports' Analysis (GEXPRONT) (Análisis Anual de las Exportaciones): *statistical analysis of exports and trends of non-traditional Guatemalan products - annual*
• Bibliographic Bulletin (Boletín Bibliográfico): *notification of CEDIME's latest documentation*
• Data Export Magazine (Revista Data Export): *technical information; general pointers on markets and export products; vehicle for GEXPRONT to gather support among members for political action and the management of the organisation - monthly*
• Directories (Directorios): *there are separate directories for: clothing and textiles, handicrafts, and agriculture; they include details of exporting companies*
• Export Opportunities (Oportunidades de Exportación): *complete collection of contacts and export opportunities which GEXPRONT receives from around the world*
• Guatemalan Exporters' Directory: *general information on Guatemala and GEXPRONT; directory of members and products - annual*
• Me ... Exporter? (Yo...Exportador?): *basic guide to exporting*
Notes: Affiliated to the Chamber of Industries.

Travel Agencies' Association of Guatemala (AGAV)
Asociación Guatemalteca de Agencias de Viajes
Address: Apartado 2735, Guatemala City
Telephone: +502 2 310 320
Fax: +502 2 319 032

GUYANA

Guyana Manufacturers' Association
Asociacion de Guyana ded Productores
Address: 157 Waterloo Steet, Georgetown
Telephone: +592 2 742 95
Fax: +592 2 706 70/556 15
Year established: 1967
Chief officers: Mr Mohabir Singh (President), Trevor Sharples (Executive Secretary), Ms Inge Nathoo (Executive Director)

Tourism Association of Guyana
Address: 157 Waterloo Street, Cummingsburg, Gerogetown
Telephone: +592 2 508 07
Fax: +592 2 508 17

HAITI

Association of Manufacturers of Haiti (ADIH)
Association des Industries
Address: PO Box 2568, Port-au-Prince
Telephone: +509 4 645 09/4510
Fax: +509 4 622 11

Haitian Hotel and Tourism Association (AHTH)
Address: BP 2562, Hotel Montana, Port-au-Prince
Telephone: +509 5 719 20
Fax: +509 5 761 37

HONDURAS

Federation of Agricultural Producers and Exporters
Asociación de Productores y Exportadores Agrícolas y
Agroindustriales
Address: PO Box 1442, San Pedro Sula
Telephone: +504 5 267 95/94
Fax: +504 5 278 52

**Foundation for Investment and Development of
Exports (FIDE)**
Address: PO Box 2029, Tegucigalpa
Telephone: +504 3 293 45
Fax: +504 3 118 08

National Associations of Exporters (ANEXHON)
Asociación de Exportadores de Honduras
Address: Edificio Cámara de Comercio, Avda Circunvalación,
San Pedro Sula
Telephone: +504 5 336 26
Fax: +504 5 336 26

**Travel and Tourism Agencies' Association of Honduras
(ANAVYTH)**
Asociación Nacional de Agencias de Viajes y Turismo de
Honduras
Address: Apartado Postal 2068, Tegucigalpa
Telephone: +504 378 207
Fax: +504 375 294

HONG KONG

**Air-Conditioning and Refrigeration Association of
Hong Kong**
Address: 10158, General Post Office
Telephone: +852 2 694 5333
Chief officers: Raymond Chan (President), Eric Ng (Hon.
Secretary)
Membership: 52 members

**Association of Accredited Advertising Agents of Hong
Kong**
Address: 604 McDonald's Building, 48 Yee Wo Street,
Causeway Bay, Hong Kong
Telephone: +852 2 882 8161
Fax: +852 2 890 5083
Activities: annual 4As Creative Awards Presentation; training
programmes; bi-monthly members' general meeting
Chief officers: Peter Stening (Chairman), Stefanie
Cross-Wilson (Vice Chairman), Margaret Wong (Administrative
Secretary)

Association of Hong Kong Glove Trades Ltd.
Address: Room 1705, 17/F; Emperor Group Centre, 288
Hennessy Road, Wanchai
Telephone: +852 2 572 8224, 572 8225
Fax: +852 2 838 2229
Chief officers: Tsang Poa-kau (President), Austin K. S. Pang
(Vice President)
Membership: 120 member companies

Association of Photographic Equipment Importers
Address: PO Box 31373, Causeway Bay Post Office
Telephone: +852 2 827 7288
Fax: +852 2 311 7830
Chief officers: Mui Chung-chi (Chairman), Andrew Lee
(Secretary)
Membership: 27

Beverage Manufacturers' Association of Hong Kong
Address: 37/F, Wu Chung House, 213 Queen's Rd East, HK
Telephone: +852 2 838 0099
Fax: +852 2 838 0211
Chief officers: Steve Mason (President); Winston Lo (Vice
President); Eric Lam (Honorary Secretary)
Membership: 10

Chinese Manufacturers' Association of Hong Kong
Address: Ist Floor CMA Building, 64 Connaught Rd, Central
Telephone: +852 2 545 6166
Fax: +852 2 541 4541/8154
E-mail: cma@hkstar.com
Year established: 1934
Activities: sponsorship of and participation in a number of
trade and industrial exhibitions and conferences annually,
both local and overseas; trade information through trade
enquiries service; handling of local and overseas trade
enquiries; training courses; trade mediation; product
development; employment relations; operates testing and
certification laboratories
Chief officers: Irene Tse (Trade Enquiries Officer)
Structure: secretariat; 28 sub-committees; 15 standing
committees
Membership: approximately 3,600 corporate members
Publications:
● Business Journal: *articles on specific topics related to
economy, trade and industrial development, news on CMA
activities and services, etc. - monthly*
● Investment Opportunities Bulletin: *monthly*
● Membership Directory: *2 p.a.*
● Trade Enquiries Bulletin: *bi-weekly*

Chinese Paper Merchants' Association
Address: 4th Floor, 132-136 Des Voeux Road West, Hong
Kong
Telephone: +852 2 548 1969
Chief officers: Wong Yeung-ming (Chairman); Chin Wai-kao,
Louie Kam Fong (Vice Chairman); Wong Kam-chiu (Secretary)
Membership: 185

Computer Club Hong Kong Ltd.
Address: Room 9A, 9/F, Go-Up Commercial Bldg, 998
Canton Road, Mongkok
Telephone: +852 2 374 1328
Fax: +852 2 374 0859

**Cosmetic and Perfumery Association of Hong Kong
Ltd.**
Address: Room 308 Winning Commercial Building, 46-48
Hillwood Road, Tsimshatsui
Telephone: +852 2 366 8801
Fax: +852 2 312 0348

Costume Jewellery Association
Address: 16th Floor, Alma Link Building, 25 Ploenchit Road,
Soi Childlom, Bangkok
Telephone: +852 2 255 7169-70
Fax: +852 2 255 6990

Electronic Association

Address: Umawar Centre 1st Floor, Jl. Kapten Tendean Kav. 28, Jakarta 12710
Telephone: +852 21 522 5362
Fax: +852 21 522 5363

Employers' Federation of Hong Kong

Address: 12th Floor, Unit 3C, United Centre, 95 Queensway, Hong Kong
Telephone: +852 2 528 0536
Fax: +852 2 865 5285
Year established: 1947
Chief officers: Mark Leese (Chairman), Ms Mary Chow (Vice Chairman)
Membership: 280

Federation of Fur Manufacturers and Dealers

Address: Room 603, 6th Floor Chevalier House, 45-51 Chatham Road South, Tsim Cha Sui, Kowloon
Telephone: +852 2 367 4646
Fax: +852 2 739 0799
Year established: 1979
Activities: Hong Kong International Fur and Fashion Fair; organises training programmes to foster new blood; coordinates social activities to promote inter-member relationships; liaises and contacts representatives of various government bodies, overseas fur associations etc.
Chief officers: Ole Borresen (Chairman); Wan Sze Wah, Michael Woo (Vice Chairman)
Membership: 142 member companies
Publications:
• Programme for the Hong Kong International Fur & Fashion Fair

Federation of Hong Kong Cotton Weavers

Address: Flat B, 14th Floor, Astoria Building, 23-24 Ashley Road, Kowloon
Telephone: +852 2 367 2383
Fax: +852 2 721 3233
Chief officers: Edwin Y C Bien (Chairman); Sam Chen Tong-sang (Vice Chairman); Lui Chun-fan (Honorary Secretary)
Membership: 29

Federation of Hong Kong Garment Manufacturers

Address: 4th Floor, 25 Kimberley Road, Tsim Sha Tsui, Kowloon
Telephone: +852 2 721 1383
Fax: +852 2 311 1062
Chief officers: Ernest Kwan Man-kam (President); Choi Hin-to, Chan Wing-kee, Norman Tam, Daniel C M Chu (Vice Presidents); Anthony Tang
Membership: 280

Federation of Hong Kong Industries

Address: Room 407-411, Hankow Centre, 5-15 Hankow Road, Tsimshatsui, Kowloon
Telephone: +852 2 732 3188
Fax: +852 2 721 3494
Chief officers: Henry Y. Y. Tang (Chairman), V. C. Davies (General Director)
Membership: 2600

Fresh Milk Marketing Association

Address: c/o No. 1 Kin Wong Street, Tuen Mun, New Territories
Telephone: +852 2 468 9327, 466 0333
Fax: +852 2 456 3441

Chief officers: Winston Lo (President)
Membership: 3

Hong Kong Advertisers' Association

Address: 6A Capital Building, 6-10 Sun Wui Road
Telephone: +852 2 882 2555
Fax: +852 2 882 4673
Chief officers: Nancy Pang (Chairman), Pauline Yu (Secretary)
Membership: 107

Hong Kong Advertising Association

Address: 22/F Hang Lung Centre, 2-20 Paterson Street, Causeway Bay, Hong Kong
Telephone: +852 2 577 7176
Fax: +852 2 890 7047
Chief officers: John Dollison (President)

Hong Kong and Kowloon Cinema and Theatrical Enterprises Free General Association

Address: Flat A-B, 9th fl, 88 Nathan Rd, Kowloon
Telephone: +852 2 3674451
Fax: +852 2 7219225
Chief officers: Huang Yah-bai (Chairman)

Hong Kong and Kowloon Electric Trade Association

Address: 6th Floor, Cheong IP Building, 350-354 Hennessy Road
Telephone: +852 2 573 7007
Fax: +852 2 573 7005
Chief officers: Wong Wan Pui (President), H. S. Loo (Secretary)
Membership: 527

Hong Kong and Kowloon Electrical Appliances Merchants' Association Ltd

Address: 4th Floor, 732 Nathan Road, Mongkok, Kowloon
Telephone: +852 2 394 2135, 394 9991
Fax: +852 2 398 0147
Chief officers: Leo T H Lee (Presidents); Wong Ping-fu (Secretary)
Membership: 481

Hong Kong and Kowloon European Dress Merchants' Association

Address: Flats C-D, 9th Floor, 129-133 Johnston Road, Hong Kong
Telephone: +852 2 573 3371
Chief officers: Ng Yick-kwong (Chairman); Poon Ng-kan, Leung Tai-shing (Vice Chairman); Tang Cheung-fook (Secretary)
Membership: 154

Hong Kong and Kowloon Footwear Manufacturers' Association

Address: 3rd Floor, Flat D Kam Fung Building, 8 Cleverly Street, Sheung Wan
Telephone: +852 2 541 4499
Fax: +852 2 541 4499
Chief officers: Lok Wai-to (President), Lee Sum-hung (Secretary)
Membership: 102

Hong Kong and Kowloon Fruit and Vegetable Employees' and Employers' Guild

Address: Flat B, 3rd Floor, Kamwa Building, 382-388 Des Voeux Road West, Hong Kong
Telephone: +852 2 547 4223
Fax: +852 2 547 4223
Chief officers: Ip Yeuk-lam (Chairman); Yang Yoi-kwan, Fung Kum-hoi, Au Yim, Tse Choi (Vice Chairman); Tsang Kai-shui (Secretary)
Membership: 826

Hong Kong and Kowloon General Association of Liquor Dealers and Distillers

Address: Flat A, 7/F, New Lucky Building, 300 Nathan Road, Kowloon
Telephone: +852 2 385 1257
Fax: +852 2 854 3229
Chief officers: Kung Shui Chan (Chairman), Ho Kui Hung (Secretary)
Membership: 74 members

Hong Kong and Kowloon Glass Merchants' and Mirror Manufacturers' Association

Address: Room 1808, 18th Floor, Sun Hing Building, 607 Nathan Road, Kowloon
Telephone: +852 2 374 2772
Fax: +852 2 374 2774
Chief officers: Hui Kam-tong (Chairman); Tang Wah, Lee Kin Wah (Vice Chairmen); Ho Bok-kee (Secretary)
Structure: annual elections (July/September)
Membership: 175

Hong Kong and Kowloon Provisions, Wine and Spirits Dealers' Association

Address: 2nd Floor, Block B, Fu Lok Building, 131-133 Wing Lok Street, Hong Kong
Telephone: +852 2 854 2544/2514
Fax: +852 2 854 3816
Chief officers: Chow Cheung (Chairman); Lai Bun, Wong Cheuk-ting (Vice Chairman); Kwan Yi (Honorary Secretary)
Membership: 594

Hong Kong and Kowloon Tea Trade Merchants' Association Ltd

Address: Flat A, 3rd Floor, 196 Des Voeux Road West, Hong Kong
Telephone: +852 2 547 3306
Chief officers: Cheung Yuet-sing (Chairman); Kwok Wan-lung, Luk Wai-chan (Vice Chairman)
Membership: 125

Hong Kong and Kowloon Timber Merchants' Association

Address: 1st Floor, 50 Portland Street, Kowloon
Telephone: +852 2 385 0465
Chief officers: Wai Kam-chiu (Chairman); Ho Man-kit (Vice Chairman); Cho Mang-keung (Secretary)
Membership: 63

Hong Kong Article Numbering Association

Address: Unit B, 23/F United Centre, 95 Queensway
Telephone: +852 2 861 2819
Fax: +852 2 861 2423
E-mail: hkana@ibm.net

Hong Kong Association of Banks

Address: 11391 Prince's Building, Room 525, Hong Kong
Telephone: +852 2 521 1169
Fax: +852 2 868 5035
Year established: 1981
Activities: establishes banking policies
Chief officers: I R Wilson (Chairman); P R Lowndes (Secretary)
Membership: 163 banks

Hong Kong Association of the Pharmaceutical Industry

Address: 13th Floor, Room A, Trust Tower, 68 Johnston Road, Wanchai
Telephone: +852 2 528 3061
Fax: +852 2 865 6283
Chief officers: Thomas Lau (President); Simon Braden (Vice President); Joy Ottway (Executive Secretary)
Membership: 61

Hong Kong Association of Travel Agents

Address: Room 1003,Tung Bldg, 40 Des Voeux Road, Central
Telephone: +852 2 869 8624
Fax: +852 2 869 8632

Hong Kong Baby and Children Products' Industrial and Commercial Association

Address: Unit J, 7/F, Block A, Marvel Industrial Building, Kwai Fung Crescent, Kwai Chung, New Territories
Telephone: +852 2 422 2101
Fax: +852 2 489 1092
Chief officers: Yuen Man-Ho (Chairman), Charles Y. S. Chan (Vice-Chairman)
Membership: 9 members

Hong Kong Cargo-Vessel Traders' Association Ltd

Address: 2nd Floor, 21-23 Man Wai Building, Ferry Point, Kowloon
Telephone: +852 2 384 7102
Fax: +852 2 782 0342
Chief officers: Pang Yiu-son (Chairman); Yip Wing-chiu, Chow Yat Tak (Vice Chairman); Chan Bak (Secretary)
Membership: 978

Hong Kong Chinese Importers' and Exporters' Association

Address: 7-8F, Champion Bldg, 287-291 Des Voeux Road, Central
Telephone: +852 2 544 8474/2 545 5998
Fax: +852 2 544 4677

Hong Kong Chinese Press Association

Address: 3rd Floor, 48 Gage St, Hong Kong
Telephone: +852 2 5439477
Chief officers: Hue Pue-Ying (Chairman)

Hong Kong Computer Society

Address: Uit D, 1/F, Luckifast Building, 1 Stone Nullah Lane, Wanchai
Telephone: +852 2 834 2228
Fax: +852 2 834 3003
Chief officers: Agnes Mak (Chairman), W. K. Chan (General Secretary)
Membership: 2200 members

Hong Kong Construction Association Ltd

Address: 3rd Floor, 180-182 Hennessy Road, Wanchai
Telephone: +852 2 572 4414
Fax: +852 2 572 7104
Chief officers: Peter Lam (President); K K Chan, Peter Nie, Jimmy Tse, J J McNaught (Vice Presidents); Peter Mok Kwok-woo (Honorary Secretary)
Membership: 350

Hong Kong Corrugated Paper Manufacturers' Association Ltd

Address: 15th Floor, Kiu Kin Building, 568 Nathan Road, Kowloon
Telephone: +852 2 385 6894
Fax: +852 2 770 3898
Chief officers: Peter Chu Shu-kit (Chairman); Cowen Loh, Ong Koc-Chuan, Ma Wai-mo, Chan Kam-hung, H H Lau (Vice Chairman); Dr The Hon. Phillip Y Wong (Honorary Secretary)
Membership: 100

Hong Kong Cotton Made-Up Goods Manufacturers' Association Ltd

Address: 12th Floor, Flat D, 739 Nathan Road, Kowloon
Telephone: +852 2 394 3128
Fax: +852 2 394 4546
Chief officers: Sin Hon-pun (Chairman); Joe Y P Lau, Pang Hing-cheung (Vice Chairman); Wong Hay-tuck (Secretary)
Membership: 30

Hong Kong Diecasting Association

Address: c/o Dr WC Kung, HKPC Building, 78 Tat Chee Ave, Yau-Yat Chuen, Kowloon
Telephone: +852 2 788 5511
Fax: +852 2 788 5522
Telex: 32842 HKPC HX
Year established: 1985
Activities: diecasting Exhibition and Symposium (annually in April); circular to members
Chief officers: Dr W C Keung (honorary Chairman and advisor);S S Liu (Chairman); C.H. Tam (Secretary)
Membership: 120 (company and individual members)
Publications:
• Hong Kong Diecasting Association
• Membership Directory

Hong Kong Economic Association

Address: PO Box 4004, GPO Hong Kong
Telephone: +852 2 609 7046
Fax: +852 2 603 5805
Chief officers: Dr V Mok (President)

Hong Kong Electrical Contractors' Association Ltd

Address: 8th Floor, Kwong Ah Building, 195-197 Johnston Road, Wanchai
Telephone: +852 2 572 0843
Fax: +852 2 838 2532
Chief officers: Lau Chun-kay (Chairman); Tam Shang-too, Kwok Sze, Li Kun-tai (Vice Presidents); Bosco Lau, William Chan, Tam Kar-chuen, Wong Shek-choi (Vice Chairman); Raymond Sin (Honorary Secretary)
Membership: 541

Hong Kong Electronics' Association (Kowloon)

Address: HK Industrial Technology Centre, Unit 208-209, 72 Tat Chee Ave, Kowloon
Telephone: +852 2 778 8328
Fax: +852 2 788 2200

Hong Kong Electronics' Association (Wanchai)

Address: Rooms 1806-8, Beverley House, 93-107 Lockhart Road, Wanchai
Telephone: +852 2 866 2669
Fax: +852 2 865 6843
Year established: 1980
Activities: trade enquiries; library reference; newsletter
Chief officers: Dr M W Lui, JP Chairman); Victor Lo, Y K So, Anthony Lam, Dr C C Chang, Cheng Kit (Vice Chairman); Charles Chapman (Executive Director); Kenneth Tam (Sales Manager)
Structure: 38 committee members; 7 sub-committees
Membership: 429 traders and manufacturers
Publications:
• Annual Directory of Hong Kong Electronics Industry: *contains almost all the electronics companies in Hong Kong - annual*
• Hong Kong Electronics News: *news of electronics industry, trade fairs schedules, new products spotlight, trade fair reports etc. - bi-monthly*

Hong Kong Enamelware Manufacturers' Association

Address: 11th Floor, Front Portion, 550 Nathan Road, Kowloon
Telephone: +852 2 385 2874
Fax: +852 2 765 7607
Chief officers: Cheung Ian-chak (Chairman); Anthony Fu (Vice Chairman); Fan Chai (Honorary Secretary)
Membership: 5

Hong Kong Executives' Association

Address: c/o Hong Kong Commercial Broadcasting, 3 Broadcast Drive, Hong Kong
Telephone: +852 2 3365111
Chief officers: Leung Tin Wai (Chairman)

Hong Kong Exporters' Association

Address: Room 825, Star House, 3 Salisbury Road, Tsimshatsui, Kowloon
Telephone: +852 2 730 9851
Fax: +852 2 730 1869
Year established: 1955
Activities: Liaison; representation; information; seminars; library service
Chief officers: Willy S M Lin (Chairman), Mimi Yeung (Chief Executive Officer)
Structure: 18 member general committee, Chairman, Vice-Chairman
Membership: 350 full members and 100 associate members
Publications:
• Exporters' Bulletin: *current trade information - quarterly*
• Hong Kong Exporters' Association Members Directory: *members address, telephone and fax number as well as activities and markets served - annual*
Notes: members account for one third of Hong Kong's export and re-export trade

Hong Kong Federation of Insurers (HKFI)

Address: 9th Floor, First Pacific Bank Centre, 56 Gloucester Road, Wanchai
Telephone: +852 2 520 1868
Fax: +852 2 520 1967
Year established: 1988
Activities: collects statistical information, conducts research into technical issues and also responsible for arbitration
Chief officers: Louisa Leung (Senior Manager Public Relations), Mr Steven Lau (Chairman 96-97), Mr Frank Chan (Deputy Chairman)
Structure: the HKFI is managed by a governing committee formed by five nominees from the General Insurance Council and Life Insurance Council

Membership: 151 registered insurers (119 general insurance members, 42 life insurance members) reresenting 90% of gross premiums written in the Hong Kong market
Notes: the HKFI is composed of a number of organisations including : Fire Insurance Association; Accident Insurance Association; Marine Insurance Association; Reinsurers Forum; Chinese Insurance Association of Hong Kong and the Medical Insurance Association

Hong Kong Federation of Watch Trades and Industries Ltd

Address: Room 604, Peter Building, 58-62 Queen's Road, Hong Kong
Telephone: +852 2 523 3232/0576
Fax: +852 2 868 4485
Year established: 1947
Activities: Hong Kong International Watch and Clock Fair
Chief officers: Wong Kam Shing (Chairman); Kenneth Kwow, Daniel Chan (Vice Chairman)
Structure: board; chairmen; vice chairmen; 24 directors; 8 divisions
Membership: 4,000 corporate members, 380 personal members
Publications:
• Clock & Watch: *Annual Report*

Hong Kong Flour Merchants' Association

Address: G/F,, 203 Des Voeux Road West
Telephone: +852 2 546 4615
Fax: +852 2 541 4541
Chief officers: Poon Pik-kin (President), Yung Ying-kwong (Secretary)
Membership: 8

Hong Kong Food Council

Address: 1/F, CMA Building, 64 Connaught Road Central
Telephone: +852 2 545 6166
Fax: +852 2 541 4541
Chief officers: Lee Kwong-lam (Chairman), Lau Tat-ming (Secretary)
Membership: 74

Hong Kong Franchise Association

Address: 22/F United Centre, 95 Queensway
Telephone: +852 2 823 1295
Fax: +852 2 527 9843
Chief officers: Charlotte Chow (Senior Manager)

Hong Kong Fresh Fruit Importers' Association

Address: 401-403, Prosperous Building, 48, Des Voeux Road, Central
Telephone: +852 2 521 1228
Fax: +852 2 868 4402
Year established: 1964
Chief officers: Patrick Kam (Chairman), Fung Yan Yee(Secretary)
Membership: 22 member companies

Hong Kong Furniture and Decoration Trade Association Ltd

Address: 10th Floor, Kwong-ah Building, 114 Thomson Road, Wanchai
Telephone: +852 2 575 2755
Fax: +852 2 834 4643
Chief officers: Teo Boon-teong (Chairman); Denny Y Y Yung, Sidney Lin, Samson Wong (Vice Chairmen); Chow Yat-on (Secretary)
Membership: 230

Hong Kong General Association of Edible Oil Importers and Exporters Ltd.

Address: 1/F, Mandarin Building, 35-43 Bonham Strand East, Sheung Wan
Telephone: +852 2 815 8788
Fax: +852 2 815 5220
Chief officers: Leung Chi-bun (Chairman), Lo Cheong-ming (Hon. Secretary)
Membership: 17 members

Hong Kong Glass and Mirror Merchants' and Manufacturers' Association Co. Ltd.

Address: Room 1808, 18/F, Sun Hing Building, 607 Nathan Road, Kowloon
Telephone: +852 2 374 2772
Fax: +852 2 374 2774
Chief officers: Lee Kin-wah (Chairman), Ho Bok-kee (Secretary)
Membership: 68

Hong Kong Hat Manufacturers' Association Ltd.

Address: 1/F, 40-42 Gough Street, Central
Telephone: +852 2 545 2487
Chief officers: Kenneth Chiu (Chairman), Bobby C. M. Chow (Hon. Secretary)
Membership: 58

Hong Kong Hide and Leather Traders' Association Ltd, The

Address: 1st Floor, 33 Portland Street, Kowloon
Telephone: +852 2 388 7644
Fax: +852 2 783 0804
Chief officers: Wong King-hang (Chairman); Yeung Hung-kwan, Cheung Shiu-wah, Liu Chi-ming, Ng Siu-sek (Vice Chairman)
Membership: 180

Hong Kong Hotels' Association

Address: 508-511 Sivercord Tower Two, 30 Canton Road, Kowloon
Telephone: +852 2 375 3838
Fax: +852 2 375 7676
Year established: 1961
Activities: government lobbying, training
Chief officers: Leslie Davies (Executive Secretary), James Lu (Executive Director)
Membership: 75 member hotels
Publications:
• Concierge Magazine: *the hotel industry in Hong Kong - every two months*

Hong Kong Information Technology Federation Ltd.

Address: Suite 25A, One Capital Place, 18 Luard Road, Wanchai
Telephone: +852 2 527 2127
Fax: +852 2 252 1960

Hong Kong Institute of Marketing

Address: Room 1902 19/F AT Tower, 180 Electric Road, North Point
Telephone: +852 2 881 6682
Fax: +852 2 881 6057
E-mail: hkim@hkim.org.hk
Web site: www.hkim.org.hk
Year established: 1982
Activities: the institute has been active in the development of Hong Kong's marketing skills and provided members with a

range of quality services
Chief officers: Stephen Lau (Chief Executive officer)

Hong Kong Jewellers' and Goldsmiths' Association Ltd.
Address: 13/F, Hong Kong Jewellery Building, 178-180 Queen's Road Central
Telephone: +852 2 543 9633
Fax: +852 2 850 7361
Chief officers: Leung Sik-wah (Chairman), Ho Pak-tao (Vice-Chairman)
Membership: 310

Hong Kong Jewellery Manufacturers' Association
Address: Room 906, Block A, Focal Centre, 21 Man Lok Street, Hunghom, Kowloon
Telephone: +852 2 766 3002
Fax: +852 2 362 3647
E-mail: hkjma@hkstar.com
Year established: 1988
Activities: conferences and seminars; exhibitions; information service; liaison with government and official organisations; trade information; ATA carnet bond service; credit service
Chief officers: Shin Siu-kau (Chairman), Jimmy Chang (Honorary Secretary)
Membership: 185 member companies
Publications:
• HKJMA Year Book & Jewellery Business Directory: *provides up-to-date information about members as well as their merchandise - annual*
• Industry News: *news on the global jewellery industry - monthly*

Hong Kong Knitwear Exporters' and Manufacturers' Association
Address: 3rd Fl, Clothing Ind Training Authorit, Kowloon Bay Training Centre, 63 Tai Yip Street, Kowloon
Telephone: +852 2 755 2621
Fax: +852 2 756 5672
Chief officers: Willy Lin (Chairman); Peter Law, Lawrence Leung, Michael Yip, Linda Fung (Vice Chairman); Shirley Liu (Executive Secretary)
Membership: 107

Hong Kong Management Association
Address: 14/F Fairmont House, 8 Cotton Tree Drive
Telephone: +852 2 526 6516
Fax: +852 2 868 4387
Telex: 81903
Activities: offers management education and training programmes, management consultancy, library and information services, translation, conducts surveys
Chief officers: Elizabeth Shing (Secretary)
Publications:
• Hong Kong Manager: *articles by leading local and overseas executives and management educationists - bi-monthly*
• Management & Finance Weekly: *weekly*

Hong Kong Medicine Dealers' Guild
Address: 5th Floor Blocks E&F, Hennessy Apartment, 488 Hennessy Road, Hong Kong
Telephone: +852 2 577 6424
Chief officers: Lui Sin-kwok (Chairman); Chu See-chun, Wong Ying-lau (Vice Chairman); Cheung Tai-kai (Secretary).
Membership: 190

Hong Kong Oil Merchants' Association Ltd.
Address: 11/F, Block J, Sun On Building, 490 Queen's Road West
Telephone: +852 2 547 4334
Chief officers: Wong Luen-fai (Chairman)
Membership: 20

Hong Kong Optical Manufacturers' Association Ltd
Address: 2nd Floor, 11 Fa Yuen Street, Mongkok, Kowloon
Telephone: +852 2 332 6505
Fax: +852 2 770 5786
Year established: 1982
Activities: sponsor of Hong Kong Optical Fair (biennial, organised by Hong Kong Trade Development Council)
Chief officers: Harvey W.H. Fung (President); Chow Ching-lam (Vice President); William Hui (Honorary Secretary)
Structure: President, Vice Presidents, Members; Biennial Elections (November)
Membership: 101, including spectacle frame manufacturers, lens manufacturers, spectacle raw materials and parts importers, exporters and manufacturers
Publications:
• HKOMA Issue: *biennial*

Hong Kong Pacific Asia Travel Association (PATA)
Address: Room 1003, Tung Ming Building, 40 Des Voeux Road, Central
Telephone: +852 2 869 8624
Fax: +852 2 869 8632

Hong Kong Packing Institute Limited
Address: 98536, T. S. T., Kowloon
Telephone: +852 2 805 2811
Fax: +852 2 805 1931
Chief officers: C. K. Chan (Chairman), Tony Wong (Hon. Secretary)
Membership: Approx.100

Hong Kong Petroleum, Chemicals and Pharmaceutical Materials Merchants' Association Ltd
Address: Room 1102, Sunbeam Commercial Building, 469-471 Nathan Road, Kowloon
Telephone: +852 2 780 9241
Fax: +852 2 771 5176
Chief officers: Chong King-fan (Chairman); Lam Tung, Lee Chung-pui, Liu Ju-ching, Hung Tong, Chow Hung-yuan (Vice Chairman); Yeung Sik-cheong (Secretary)
Membership: 270

Hong Kong Pharmaceutical Manufacturers' Association Ltd
Address: 17/F, Jing Ho Industrial Building, 78-84 Wang Lung Styreet, Tsuen Wan, New Territories
Telephone: +852 2 407 3271
Fax: +852 2 407 5707
Telex: 61743 NEOPL HX
Year established: 1977
Activities: promotes the welfare of members; fosters a high standard of manufacturing practice; ensures the production of high-quality pharmaceutical products; liaises with other international bodies
Chief officers: Sin Lam Kong (President); Louisa Poon(Hon. Secretaries)
Membership: 36 companies

Hong Kong Plastic Material Suppliers' Association
Address: 5/F Interlanche House, 39-41 Hanow Road, TST
Telephone: +852 2 375 2686
Fax: +852 2 317 1129

Hong Kong Plastics Manufacturers' Association Ltd
Address: 1st Floor, Flat B, Fu Yuen, 39-49 Wanchai Road
Telephone: +852 2 574 2230
Fax: +852 2 574 2843
Chief officers: Kenneth Ting (President); Lam Hui (Chairman); Cliff Sun, Lee Kin-fong, Jeffrey Lam, Leung Ching-yee, Lun Lum Kwan, Augusta Cheung (Vice Chairmen); Peter Cheng (Honorary Secretary)
Membership: 120

Hong Kong Press Club
Address: 175 Lockhart Rd, 3/F, Hong Kong
Telephone: +852 2 5112626
Chief officers: Nigel Walker (General Manager)

Hong Kong Printers' Association
Address: 1st Floor, 48-50 Johnston Road, Wanchai
Telephone: +852 2 527 5050
Fax: +852 2 861 0463
Year established: 1939
Chief officers: Yip Yu-bun (Chairman); Yan Wan-pun, Ho Ka-hun (Vice Chairman); Ho Man-kit (Executive Director); Hsu Wen-cheng (Secretary)
Membership: 428

Hong Kong Publishers' and Distributors' Association
Address: National Building, 4th Floor, 240-246 Nathan Rd, Kowloon
Telephone: +852 2 567 4412

Hong Kong Retail Management Association
Address: Unit B, 23/F, United Centre, 95 Queensway
Telephone: +852 2 866 8311
Fax: +852 2 866 8380
Chief officers: Ma King-huen (Chairman), P. C. Yu (Vice-Chairman)
Membership: 288

Hong Kong Rice Importers' and Exporter' Association
Address: 301 Chiu Chow Association Building, 81-85 Voeux Road W
Telephone: +852 2 547 7323
Fax: +852 2 541 5134

Hong Kong Rubber and Footwear Manufacturers' Association Ltd
Address: Block A, 2nd Floor, 185 Prince Edward Road, Kowloon
Telephone: +852 2 381 2297
Fax: +852 2 397 6927
Chief officers: Tony M Chau (Chairman); Tang Kim-kwan (President); So Keng-ching, Wu Yau-tak, Lin Tat-sang, Chik Shum-kim, Cheung Kam, Yim Chan Chee (Vice Presidents); Wendy Lai (Secretary)
Membership: 220

Hong Kong Sugar Merchants' Association
Address: Flat E, G, 2/F; Nam Pak Hong Building, 22-24 Bonham Strand West
Telephone: +852 2 544 0298

Chief officers: Chiu Kam-cheu (Chairman), Tong Long-wah (Vice-Chairman)
Membership: 36

Hong Kong Telecom Association
Address: PO Box 13461
Telephone: +852 2 881 2333
Fax: +852 2 881 2332
Year established: 1983
Activities: quarterly luncheons; exhibitions; seminars/forums; new products/services presentation; representation on Hong Kong Telecommunications Board
Chief officers: Waleed Hanafi (Chairman); Prudence Chan, Patricia Yeung (Vice Chairmen); Henry Goldstein (Honorary Secretary); Iain Steele (Honorary Treasurer)
Membership: 60
Publications:
● Official Guide to Telecommunications in Hong Kong: *annual*

Hong Kong Tourist Association (HKTA)
Address: 11th Floor, Citicorp Centre, 18 Whitfield Road, North Point
Telephone: +852 2 807 6543
Fax: +852 2 806 0303
E-mail: info@hkta.org
Year established: 1957
Activities: coordinates travel industry activities; advises Hong Kong government on tourist-related matters; compiles visitor arrival statistics; training courses; conventions and meetings
Chief officers: Lo Yuk-sui (Chairman); Amy Chan (Executive Director)
Membership: 1,700
Notes: Web site: www.hkta.org. Information Service (multilingual): +852 2807 6177

Hong Kong Toys Council
Address: 4th Floor, Hankow Centre, 5-15 Hankow Road, Tsim Sha Tsui, Kowloon
Telephone: +852 2 732 3188
Fax: +852 2 721 3494
E-mail: fhki@fhki.org.hk
Year established: 1986
Activities: participates in trade fairs and exhibitions, liaises with the government, provides a consultancy service to the toy industry
Chief officers: Edmund Young (Chairman); Warren Kwok (Secretary General)
Structure: Chairman, Vice Chairman, Executive Committee members
Membership: 200 member companies
Notes: Member of the Asian Committee of Toy Industries and the International Council of Toy Industries.

Hong Kong Trade Fair Group
Address: 44th Floor, China Resources Building, 26 Harbour Road, Hong Kong
Telephone: +852 2 827 6211
Fax: +852 2 827 7831
Telex: 68444 HKTF HX
Activities: Organises Asia-Pacific Leather Fair
Notes: Member of United Newspapers Group

Hong Kong Watch and Clock Council
Address: Room 407-411, Hankow Centre, 5-15 Hankow Road, Tsimshatsui, Kowloon
Telephone: +852 2 732 3188
Fax: +852 2 721 3494

Chief officers: Eddie Leung (Chairman); Jackson Fong (Secretary)
Membership: 100

Hong Kong Watch Importers' Association
Address: PO Box 5311
Telephone: +852 2 722 6868
Fax: +852 2 739 8648
Chief officers: David Sun (President); Frank Chau (Secretary)
Membership: 42

Hong Kong Watch Manufacturers' Association Ltd.
Address: 3A/F and 11/F, Yu Wing Building, 64-66 Wellington Street, Central
Telephone: +852 2 522 5238
Fax: +852 2 810 6614
Chief officers: Ng Kam-wing Kenneth (President); Lau Chin-ho (General Secretary)
Membership: 634

Hong Kong Woollen and Synthetic Knitting Manufacturers' Association Ltd
Address: Room 506 C, Harbour Crystal Centre, 100 Granville Road, Kowloon
Telephone: +852 2 368 2091
Fax: +852 2 369 1720
Chief officers: Andrew K Y Leung (President); Michael H K Chan, Silas Chou Kei-fong, Hung Kar-wah (Vice Presidents); Yuen Man-hoi (Secretary)
Membership: 200

Hong Kong Yee Yee Tong Chinese Medicine Merchants' Association Ltd
Address: Blocks A7D, 3rd Floor, 22-28 Bonham Strand West, Hong Kong
Telephone: +852 2 543 5845
Fax: +852 2 543 2074
Chief officers: Chang Wei-chung (President); Choy Zee-chi, Yuen Kam-too, Ng Ming-chit (Vice Presidents); Yau Kai-fun (Honorary Secretary)
Membership: 65

Industrial Chemical Merchants' Association Ltd
Address: 84-86 Des Voeux Road, Central Hong Kong
Telephone: +852 2 545 3977
Fax: +852 2 854 3461
Chief officers: Hui In-ying MBE (President); Hong Tong, Tang Shiu-fu (Vice Presidents); Hui In-wai (Honorary Secretary)
Membership: 71

International Association of Business Communicators
Address: PO Box 1427, GPO Hong Kong
Telephone: +852 2 869 6536
Fax: +852 2 869 6556
Activities: organises bi-monthly professional development seminars and runs an information service
Chief officers: Fiona Mulliner (President), Suzi Ledger (secretariat)

Mail Order Association of Hong Kong
Address: PO Box 97098, Tsim Sha Tsui PO, Kowloon
Telephone: +852 2 721 2444

Motor Traders' Association of Hong Kong
Address: 37/F, Wu Chung House, 213 Queen's Road East, Wanchai

Telephone: +852 2 838 0099
Fax: +852 2 838 0211
Year established: 1958
Chief officers: B. H. Chow (Chairman), Mike Rushworth (Vice Chairman)
Structure: 8 member general committee manages the Association; monthly meetings
Membership: 18 full members, 18 subsidiary members, 10 associate members

New Territories Manufacturers' Association
Address: Tuen Mun Rural Committee, Admin Centre, San Ching Road, Tuen Mun, New Territories
Telephone: +852 2 459 4701-6
Fax: +852 2 404 1932
Chief officers: Leung Chi (Chairman); Mo Chi-sing (Vice Chairman); Yip Kin-wing (Secretary)
Membership: 80

Newspaper Society of Hong Kong
Address: PO Box 46, c/o Ming Pao, 651 King's Road, Hong Kong
Telephone: +852 2 548 0882/565 2400
Fax: +852 2 565 7545

Pharmaceutical Trade Federation Ltd.
Address: Room 3905, 39F, Hong Kong Plaza, 186-191 Connaught Road West
Telephone: +852 2 548 0068
Fax: +852 2 559 5689

Public Relations Association of Hong Kong
Address: PO Box 1264, GPO Hong Kong
Telephone: +852 2 5417976
Fax: +852 2 8155163
Chief officers: Anthony Chung (Chairman)

Rice Merchants' Association of Hong Kong Ltd.
Address: 3/F,, 77-78 Connaught Road West
Telephone: +852 2 548 4714
Fax: +852 2 559 5891
Chief officers: Cheung Hon-kit (Chairman), Lim Fai-yau (Secretary)
Membership: 31

Society of Builders Hong Kong
Address: Room 801-802, On Lok Yuen Building, 25 Des Voeux Road, Central
Telephone: +852 2 523 2081
Fax: +852 2 845 4749

Tobacco Institute of Hong Kong Ltd
Address: Room 1807 Harbour Centre, 25 Harbour Road, Wanchai
Telephone: +852 2 827 7383
Fax: +852 2 827 4799
Year established: 1983
Activities: compilation of statistics, government liaison, ensuring that members comply with government legislation, advisory service to members
Chief officers: Robert Fletcher (Chairman), Ms Hayley Kan (Executive Director)
Membership: 14 member companies
Publications:
• Duty Paid and Trade Statistics for Tobacco: *a press release of detailed statistics on the Hong Kong tobacco industry over a six year review period. Includes a broad sector breakdown*

by volume and value covering cigarettes, cigars, and chinese prepared tobacco. Also included is a section on imports, exports and re-exports of tobacco by volume. The statistics are based on a variety of sources including the Custom and Excise Department and Census and Statistics Department - annual

Toys Manufacturers' Association of Hong Kong Ltd.

Address: Level 12, Metroplaza, Tower 2,, 223 Hing Fong Road, Kwai Chung, New Territories
Telephone: +852 2 422 1209
Fax: +852 2 422 1639
Chief officers: C. L. Luk (President); Becky To (Secretary)
Structure: Annual Election: October
Membership: Over 150

Travel Industry Council of Hong Kong

Address: Room 1706-1709, Fortress Tower, 250 King's Road, North Point
Telephone: +852 2 807 1199
Fax: +852 2 510 9907

HUNGARY

Association of Construction Contractors (EVOSZ)

Address: Kuny Domokos u. 13-15, H-1012 Budapest
Telephone: +36 155 8203
Fax: +36 155 8203
Publications:
• Membership Directory: *list of members with contact name, telephone and fax numbers, address and a list of the main activities of the Association*

Association of Hungarian Body Hygiene and Detergent Industry

Address: Erzsébet Királyne útja 1/c, H-1146 Budapest
Telephone: +36 1 343 4359
Fax: +36 1 343 7458

Association of Hungarian Contractors

Magyar Fovallalkozok Orszagos
Address: Paulay Ede utca 52, H-1061 Budapest
Telephone: +36 142 0729
Fax: +36 122 0900
Telex: 202503
Publications:
• Membership Directory: *list of members and main activities*

Association of Hungarian Light Industries

Magyar Konnyuioaru Szovetseg
Address: Rozsa Ferenc u. 55, H-1064 Budapest
Telephone: +36 141 4790
Fax: +36 141 4790
Telex: 224131
Chief officers: Dr Jozsef Csen (Secretary General)
Publications:
• Membership Directory: *lst of members and main activities*

Association of Hungarian Packaging and Materials Handling Companies

Address: Rigó u. 3, 1st Floor, H-1058 Budapest
Telephone: +36 1 113 7034
Fax: +36 1 113 8170

Federation of Hungarian Food Industries and Agromarketing Ltd (EFOSZ)

Address: Kuny D. u. 13-15, H-1012 Budapest
Telephone: +36 1 175 9722/202 5586
Fax: +36 1 155 5057
Publications:
• Hungarian Food Catalogue

Hotels Association of Hungary

Magyar Szallodaszövetseg
Address: Szt. Gellert ter 1, H-1111 Budapest
Telephone: +36 166 9282
Fax: +36 1 224 363
E-mail: hah@mail.matav.hu
Web site: 1800travel.com.449
Chief officers: G. Lombosi (General Secretary), L Bochsak (President 1997-98), A.Rubovkszy (President 1998-1999)
Membership: 308 hotels and hotel chains

Hungarian Chamber of Real Estate Dealers

Address: POB 688, H-1356 Budapest
Telephone: +36 266 2076
Fax: +36 118 9857
Publications:
• List of Members and main activities

Hungarian Fashion Institute

Address: POB 13, H-1428 Budapest
Telephone: +36 113 5620
Fax: +36 133 7937
Telex: 224593
Publications:
• List of Members and main activities

Hungarian Franchise Association

Address: POB 446, Margit Krt. 15-17, H-1537 Budapest
Telephone: +36 1 212 4124
Fax: +36 1 212 5712
E-mail: Franchise.Ass.@mail.datanet.hu
Web site: www.datanet.hu/mfsz
Activities: promotion of franchising, franchise market management
Chief officers: E. Pincesi (President), Istvan Kiss (Secretary General)
Membership: 60 members
Publications:
• Franchise News

Hungarian Marketing Association

Address: Kuny D. u. 13-15, H-1012 Budapest
Telephone: +36 1 155 7721
Fax: +36 1 175 7843
E-mail: mmsq@maol.datanet.hu
Activities: helps the Hungarian marketing profession to enter international network, provides trade opportunities, seminars, training courses
Chief officers: Marta Tungli (Secretary General)
Membership: 300

Hungarian National Committee of International Dairy Federation

Address: P.O.B. 31, c/o Hungarian Dairy Research Institute, 1450 Budapest
Telephone: +36 1 215 0133
Fax: +36 1 217 0130
Chief officers: Dr F. Ketting (Secretary)

Hungarian Publishers' and Booksellers' Association

Magyar Konyvkiadók es Konyvterfesztök Egyesülése
Address: Pf 130, Vörösmarty tér 1, H-1367 Budapest
Telephone: +36 1 118 4758
Fax: +36 1 118 4581
Chief officers: István Bart (President), Péter Zentai (Director)

National Professional Association of Timber Industries (FAGOSZ)

Address: POB 106, H-1238 Budapest
Telephone: +36 155 6539
Fax: +36 155 6539
Publications:
• List of Members and main activities

Newspapers Publishers' Association

Magyar Lapkiadok Edeyesulete
Address: PO Box 1960, Bécsi út 122-124, Budapest
Telephone: +36 1 250 1680/410/411/168 8674
Fax: +36 1 188 6707
Chief officers: Mr J Pet (General Secretary)

ICELAND

Article Numbering Association (EAN Iceland)

Address: Icetec, Keldnaholt, 112 Reykjavik
Telephone: +354 5 877 000
Fax: +354 5 877 409
E-mail: ean@iti.is

Association of Icelandic Importers, Exporters and Wholesale Merchants

Address: Kringlunni 7, 103 Reykjavic
Telephone: +354 588 8910
Fax: +354 568 8441
E-mail: fis@centrum.is

Federation of Icelandic Industries

Address: POBox 1450, Hallveigarstig 1, 121 Reykjavic
Telephone: +354 511 5555
Fax: +354 511 5566
E-mail: gudmundur.asmunndsson@skima.is

Icelandic National Committee of International Dairy Federation

Osta - og Smjörsalan SE
Address: P.O. Box 10.100, 130 Reykjavik
Telephone: +354 45 191 600
Fax: +354 45 673 465
Chief officers: Dr T. Karlsson (Secretary)

Icelandic Publishers' Association

Address: Sudurlandsbraut 4A, 108 Reykjavik
Telephone: +354 553 8020
Fax: +354 588 8668
Chief officers: Mr O Ragnarsson (General Secretary), Mrs V Hardardottir (Director)

Retailers' Association of Iceland

Address: Kringlunni 7, 103 Reykjavik
Telephone: +354 568 7811
Fax: +354 568 5569
E-mail: kaupmann@mmedia.is

INDIA

All India Association of Industries (AIAI)

Address: 106 Uttam House, 69 P.D. D'Mello Road, Carnac Bunder, Majid, Bombay 400 009
Telephone: +91 22 341 2632/341 2643
Fax: +91 22 341 5685
E-mail: aiai@giasbm01.vsnl.net.in
Year established: 1956
Activities: organises trade fairs; collects relevant statistics, provides services to members; organises seminars, workshops and training programmes on subjects of topical importance; discusses members' problems with senior government officials; provides advisory and consultative services on various aspects of trade, industrial development, standard planning and implementation of policies
Chief officers: Vijay G Kalantri (President), Kamal M. Morarka Sr (Vice President), S.P. Bhansali Sr (Vice Pesident), P.R. Damani (Treasurer), Sushil Jiwarajka (Executive Committee member), Vikas Kasliwal (Executive committee member), Rajendra Miglani (Executive committee member)
Structure: governing body, executive committee
Membership: a cross section of manufacturers, traders, professionals, market and service intermediaries representing trade and industry sectors
Notes: The AIAI is one of the apex trade associations in India, whose primary task is to foster industrial development. It maintains excellent business relations with leading associations and trade bodies in India and abroad and has been involved in areas such as foreign collaboration and export promotion.

All India Manufacturers' Organisation (AIMO)

Address: Jeevan Sahakar, Sir P. M. Road, Fort, Mumbai-400 001
Telephone: +91 22 266 1016/266 1272 /266 5239
Fax: +91 22 266 0838
E-mail: navin@massiver.com
Web site: www.indialog.com/aimo/
Year established: 1941
Activities: Conferences and exhibitions held from time to time
Chief officers: Shri Kamalkumar R. Dujodwala (President)
Structure: central committee is the principal policy making and decision making organ
Membership: 1,000 members
Publications:
• AIMO Directory of Indian Manufacturers and Exporters: *members contact details and activities classified by sector. Also covers relevant business and industrial policies, laws, incentives, programmes, etc. - annual*
• Indian Economic Miracle
• Virtues of A Good Manager

Apparel Export Promotion Council (APEC)

Address: 15 NBCC Tower, Bhikaji Cama Place, New Delhi 110 066
Telephone: +91 11 618 3351/616 9394/616 9356
Fax: +91 11 616 8584
Web site: 206.252.12.4/aepc/default.htm
Web site notes: site includes detailed export statistics for the Indian textiles
Membership: 33,000 registered members

Association of Indian Automobile Manufacturers (AIAM)

Address: Core 4B, Zone IV, 5th Floor, India Habitat Centre, Lodhi Road, New Delhi- 110002
Telephone: +91 11 464 7810-12 /464 8555
Fax: +91 11 464 8222
Web site: www.planetindia.net/aiam/
Web site notes: site includes various statistics on the Indian

automotive industry including foreign investment, exports, production and retail sales. Also includes a list of members
Activities: provides information and services to members; advises members on upgrading technology; helps members to deal with problems of policies and infrastructure at industry level; carries out research and development on fuels, roads, traffic, materials and components
Chief officers: Mr. Rajat Nandi (Executive Director)
Membership: vehicle and vehicle engine manufacturers
Notes: Research & Publications Office, Maitri Shopping Centre, Sahyog Bhandar Building V.N. Purav Marg, Sion, Mumbai 400 022, Tel 22 522 0509, Fax 22 522 2725

Clothing Manufacturers' Association of India

Address: 90 Mahalaxmi Chambers, 22 Bhulabhai Desai Road, Bombay 40006
Telephone: +91 22 492 8245/494 5908
Fax: +91 22 493 8547
Year established: 1963
Activities: runs National Garment Fairs (2 p.a.); and export fairs (2 p.a. with other associations)
Chief officers: Mr Rahul N.Mehta (President), Mohan Sandhwani, (Vice President), H H Shah (Honorary General Secretary)
Structure: managing committee assisted by the fair sub-committee, export sub-committee, finance sub-committee, managing sub-committee and payment default sub-committee
Membership: 2,000
Publications:
• Apparel: *fashion information for consumers as well as manufacturers of clothing - monthly*

Confederation of Indian Industry (CII)

Address: 105 Kakad Chambers 1st Floor, 132 Dr Annie Besant Road, Worli Mumbai 400018
Telephone: +91 22 493 1790
Fax: +91 22 494 5831
Web site: 206.252.12.4/cii/default.htm
Web site notes: site includes a database of member companies
Year established: 1895
Activities: Indian Engineering Trade Fair and sectoral trade fairs; International Mining Machinery Exhibition
Chief officers: Dr Jamshed J Irani (President), Jamshed N Godrej (Vice President), Tarun Das (Secretary and Director General)
Structure: national council, regional councils, states and zonal councils; specialised committees, industry divisions and affiliated associations/institutions
Membership: 3600 member companies
Publications:
• Annual Report of the Confederation of Indian Industry (CII): *annual*
• Directory of Members
Notes: Formerly Confederation of Engineering Industry.

Federation of Freight Forwarders' in India (FFI)

Address: 73, "C" Wing, 7th Floor, Mittal Tower, Nariman Point, Mumbai - 400 021.
Telephone: +91 22 282 4618 /283 0117/282 4760
Fax: +91 22 285 2561
Web site: 206.252.12.4/ffi/default.htm
Year established: 1962
Chief officers: Mr. Vinod K. Chowdhry (President), Mr. Pravin K. Kanakia (Hon. Secretary)
Membership: 2500 customs house agents operating in India

Federation of Indian Publishers (FIP)

Address: 18/1C, Institutional Area, Aruna Asaf Ali Marg, New Delhi 110067
Telephone: +91 11696 4847685 2263
Fax: +91 11 686 4054
Activities: organises conferences; information service and library
Chief officers: Mr DN Malhotra (President), Mr Shakti Malik (Director),Mr AK Ghosh (Executive Secretary)
Publications:
• Directory of Members: *annual*
• Indian Book Industry Journal: *bi-monthly*
• Information Service Bulletin: *monthly*
• Newsletter of the Federation of Indian Publishers (FIP): *monthly*

Indian Article Numbering Association (EAN India)

Address: PO Box 9432, c/o Indian Institute of Packaging, E-2, MIDC Area, Andheri (East), 400 093 Bombay
Telephone: +91 22 821 9803
Fax: +91 22 837 5302

Indian Cotton Mills' Federation

Address: Amba Deep, 17th floor, 14, Kasturba Gandhi Marg., New Dehli 110 001
Telephone: +91 11 332 4655
Fax: +91 11 332 7245

Indian Institute of Packaging

Address: PO Box 9432, E-2 MIDC Area, Andheri (East), 400 093 Bombay
Telephone: +91 22 821 9803
Fax: +91 22 837 5302

Indian Newspaper Society

Address: PO Box 69, IENS Buildings, Rafi Marg, New Delhi 110001
Telephone: +91 11 371 5401/5950/5246
Fax: +91 11 372 3800
Year established: 1939
Chief officers: Mr S Bhushan Jain (Secretary)

Indian Tea Association

Address: Royal Exchange, 6 Nataji Subhas Road, Calcutta 700 001
Telephone: +91 33 220 8393
Fax: +91 33 243 4301
Year established: 1881
Chief officers: Mr S.K Bhasin (Chairman), Mr R. Das (Secretary General)
Membership: 459 member companies
Publications:
• Tea India: *all aspects of tea production in India - monthly*

National Association of Software and Service Companies

Address: #109 Ashok Hotel, Chanakyapuri, New Delhi, 110 021
Telephone: +91 11 688 5474
Fax: +91 11 688 5475

National Dairy Development Board - Indian National Committee of the International Dairy Federation

Address: Anand 388 001
Telephone: +91 2 692 401 48/40149/40157
Fax: +91 2 692 401 56/401 65
E-mail: nkc@anand.nddb.ernet.in

Chief officers: Dr N.K. Chawla (Secretary)

Organisation of Pharmaceutical Producers of India (OPPI)
Address: Cook's Building, 324 Dr Dadabhoy, Naoroji Road, Fort Bombay 400 001
Telephone: +91 22 204 5509/204 4518
Fax: +91 22 204 4705
Year established: 1965
Activities: seminars and workshops held periodically e.g. Quality Assurance and Safety, Health and Environment, Compensation and Field Staff Management; communicates information on vital aspects of the industry including government laws and rules to the members through periodical circulars; newspaper articles are circulated with appropriate comments; statistics are compiled on production, imports and exports and are included in the annual report
Chief officers: Anil S Mehta (President), R D Joshi (Secretary General)
Structure: executive committee consisting of 18 elected and 5 co-opted members; assisted by special advisory committees on pricing, taxation, exports, R&D, employee relations, medical affairs and communications.
Membership: 71 member companies
Publications:
• Annual Report of the Organisation of Pharmaceutical Producers of India (OPPI): *details of the associations activities as well as an overview of the industry over the past year. Includes statistics on production, imports and exports - annual*

Plastics and Linoleum's Export Promotion Council (PLEXCONCIL)
Address: World Trade Centre, Cuffe Parade, Colaba, Bombay 400 005
Telephone: +91 22 218 4474/218 4569
Fax: +91 22 218 4810
E-mail: plexcon@giasbm01.vsnl.net.in

INDONESIA

Article Numbering Association (EAN Indonesia)
Address: c/o Yasayan Codex Universalis, JL RP Suroso No.26, 10350 Jakarta
Telephone: +62 21 325 800
Fax: +62 21 310 3357

Association of Apparel Manufacturers
Address: Jakarta Design Center fl.6, Jl. Gatot Subroto no.53, Jakarta 10260
Telephone: +62 21 530 4636
Fax: +62 21 549 5173

Association of Automotive Parts and Component Industries
Address: Artamas Complex Gd. VI. 1. rg. 6-7-8, Jl. Jend. A Yani no 2, Jakarta 13210
Telephone: +62 21 489 8118, 489 8979
Fax: +62 21 471 4785

Association of Indonesian Alcohol Spirit Manufactures
Address: KPB Perkebunan Pusat, Jl. Cut Mutiah 11, Jakarta Pusat
Telephone: +62 21 310 6685
Fax: +62 21 331 883

Association of Indonesian Automotive Industries (GAIKINDO)
Address: Jalan HOS Cokroaminoto 6, Jakarta Pussat 10350
Telephone: +62 21 314 2100, 315 7178
Fax: +62 21 314 2100

Association of Indonesian Beverage Industries
Address: 10 th, Matru Pasarbrlu, Jalan H. Hamrnhude, Jakarta Pusat 10710
Telephone: +62 21 344 1222/1223
Fax: +62 21 384 2294

Association of Indonesian Bicycle Industries
Address: Jl. Kebon Sirih 40 Flat 18, Jakarta 10340
Telephone: +62 21 384 1359, 350 1294
Fax: +62 21 348 1359

Association of Indonesian Bookstores
Address: Jalan Gunung Sahari III/7, Jakarta 10610
Telephone: +62 21 354 700/420 4402

Association of Indonesian Coffee Exporters (AICE)
Asosiasi Eksportir Kopi Indonesia
Address: Jalan RP Soeroso 20, Jakarta 10350
Telephone: +62 21 384 2385, 310 6765
Fax: +62 21 314 4115
Telex: 61173 AEKI IA
Chief officers: M. Noer Madjid (Executive Secretary)

Association of Indonesian Corrugated Packaging Industries (PICCI)
Address: c/- PT Guru Indonesia, Jalan Raya, Jakarta Bogor Km 26, JakartaTimur
Telephone: +62 21 871 0621
Fax: +62 21 871 0625

Association of Indonesian Food and Beverage Industries
Address: Gedung Trade Mart 2nd Floor, 257-258 APRJ Kemayoran, Jakarta Pusat 10620
Telephone: +62 21 421 8436, 421 8437
Fax: +62 21 570 3472, 570 7209

Association of Indonesian Furniture and Handicraft Manufacturers
Address: Manggala Wanabakti, Blok 4-8th Floors, Jl. Gatot Subroto, Jakarta Pusat 10270
Telephone: +62 21 587 888/570 0249/3265 ext 5455
Fax: +62 21 570 4619

Association of Indonesian Garment Industries
Address: Jl. Blora21, Jakarta Pusat
Telephone: +62 21 331 407

Association of Indonesian Handicraft Producers and Exporters
Address: c/o PT Sarinah Jaya, Jalan Tirtayasa IX/12, Jakarta
Telephone: +62 21 720 7201
Fax: +62 21 739 0695

Association of Indonesian Inorganic Chemical Industries
Address: Jalan Tanah Abang II/63, Jakarta 10160
Telephone: +62 21 384 0949
Fax: +62 21 384 1994

Association of Indonesian Leather Exporters
Address: c/o Gedung AKA 1st Fl, Jalan Bangka No.2, Jakarta
Telephone: +62 21 799 4507 ext 225
Fax: +62 21 799 1444

Association of Indonesian Motor Cycle Assemblers and Manufacturers
Address: c/o PT Daan Motor Vespa Indonesia, Jl. Perintis Kemerdekaan, Kelapa Gading, Jakarta 14250
Telephone: +62 21 452 342/425 6500 ext 180
Fax: +62 21 452 3535

Association of Indonesian Pepper Exporters
Address: c/o PT Kerta Niaga fl.2, Jl. Roa Malaka Selatan no.35, Jakarta 11230
Telephone: +62 21 692 6401/679 765
Fax: +62 21 692 6401/291 2123

Association of Indonesian Recording Companies
Address: Glodok Plaza Blok C no.1, Jl. Pinangsia Raya, Jakarta 11110
Telephone: +62 21 659 7836/3453/9851

Association of Indonesian Shoe Manufacturers
Address: Duta Merlin 4th Fl, Blok F/11-12, Jalan Gajah Mada 3-5, Jakarta
Telephone: +62 21 380 7701
Fax: +62 21 380 7706

Association of Indonesian Watch Assemblers' and Suppliers'
Address: Jl. Kramat Kosambi 25, Cipinang Timur Rawamangum, Jakarta Timur
Telephone: +62 21 489 2096/ 4711695

Association of Synthetic Fibre Producers
Address: Jl. Raya Kebayoran Lama 33, Jakarta Barat
Telephone: +62 21 530 5414
Fax: +62 21 530 5415

Association of Tour and Travel Agencies
Address: 7 Jalan Iskandarsyah Raya, Jakarta 12120
Telephone: +62 21 722 1312
Fax: +62 21 725 1710

Federation of Indonesian Pharmaceutical Industries
Address: Jl. Mangga Besar Raya No. 183, Jakarta Barat
Telephone: +62 21 639 5031
Fax: +62 21 639 5031

Federation of Plastic Industries Association
Address: Jl. Cempaka Putih Tengah 20B/no.8, Jakarta 10510
Telephone: +62 21 420 9126
Fax: +62 21 489 1888

Federation of Rubber Industries
Address: Graha Purna Yudha fl.6, Jala. Jend Sudirman 50, Jakarta 12939
Telephone: +62 21 510 909 ext 1260-2
Fax: +62 21 514 123

Federation of Textile Industries Association
Address: Jalan Iskandarsyah II no.90, Jakarta 12160
Telephone: +62 21 720 6165/6163, 21 840 0775

Importers Association of Indonesia
Gabungan Importir Nasional Seluruh Indonesia (GINSI)
Address: Bank Niaga Building LT.1, J.L. M.H. Thamrin No 55, Jakarta 10350
Telephone: +62 21 391 1057/8
Fax: +62 21 391 1060
Year established: 1946
Activities: compiles statistics and market information, circulates trade offers to member importers, offers assistance to foreign importers for contacting member companies. Also offers advice on foreign trade regulations
Chief officers: H. Amirudin Saud
Membership: 2,000 member companies
Publications:
• Membership Directory: *contact details and activities of member companies - annual*

Indonesia Leasing Association
Address: Gedung BUN Lt.3, Jalan Senin Raya No.135, Jakarta 10410
Telephone: +62 21 385 6608/09
Fax: +62 21 385 6673
Year established: 1982
Activities: leasing industry representatives
Chief officers: Mustafa I. Jatim (Chairman); Sumkaka Takagi (Vice Chairman); Albertus Banunaek (Secretary General); Budi Purwanto (Secretary); Enrique V. Bernardo (Treasurer)
Membership: 160

Indonesia Marketing Association
Address: Duta Merlin Complex, E-18 Jl Gajah Mada 3-5, Jarkata 10130
Telephone: +62 21 634 9432
Fax: +62 21 633 7936
E-mail: ima@indosat.net.id
Year established: 1987
Activities: organises seminars and workshops for members, as well as for the public, by inviting experts in the fields of sales and marketing and other management skills in relation to marketing, such as public relations, from Indonesia and elsewhere

Indonesian Association of Fisheries Entrepreneurs
Address: Jl. Harsono R. M. No 3, Ragunan, Pasar Minggu Jakarta 12550
Telephone: +62 21 780 6131-4, 780 4116-7
Fax: +62 21 780 4019

Indonesian Association of Forestry
Address: Gedung Manggala Wanabakti, 9th Floor, Wing C, Block IV, Jalan Jenderal Gatot Subroto, Jakarta Pusat 10270
Telephone: +62 21 583 010
Fax: +62 21 583 017
Telex: 46977
Year established: 1974
Chief officers: M. Hasan (President)
Membership: 9

Indonesian Battery Manufacturers' Association
Address: Jalan Gunung Sahari No. 37, Jakarta 10410
Telephone: +62 21 600 8762
Fax: +62 21 600 6729

Indonesian Cane Sugar Association
Address: Jl. Salemba Raya no 16, Jakarta 104430
Telephone: +62 21 314 2334/314 3487
Fax: +62 21 314 2334/314 3487

Indonesian Caterers' Association
Address: Jl. cempaka Putih Raya 55, Jakarta 10510
Telephone: +62 21 415 184/410 960/420 4481

Indonesian Ceramics Manufacturers' Association
Address: c/o PT Serpih Mas, Jalan Martadinata no.1, Blok C 17, Jakarta
Telephone: +62 21 691 0813
Fax: +62 21 691 0815

Indonesian Cigarette Producers' Association
Address: Jalan RS Fatmawati Raya 33-A, Jakarta 12140
Telephone: +62 21 717 344
Fax: +62 21 717 344

Indonesian Cocoa Association
Address: Jl. Brawijaya VII/5, Kebayoran Baru, Jakarta 12160
Telephone: +62 21 771 721/739 8320
Fax: +62 21 720 3487

Indonesian Cold Storage Industries Association
Address: c/o Landmark Center 8th Fl, Tower A, Jalan Jenderal Sudirman No.1, Jakarta 12910
Telephone: +62 21 571 2945
Fax: +62 21 571 2828/571 2957

Indonesian Confectionery Manufacturers' Association
Address: Jalan Taman Kebon Sirih III/20, Jakarta 10160
Telephone: +62 21 799 3360/799 1366
Fax: +62 21 799 4283

Indonesian Corrugated/Cardboard Industry Association
Address: c/o PICCI, Jalan Raya Bekasi Km.22, Jakarta 13910
Telephone: +62 21 460 4716
Fax: +62 21 460 0940

Indonesian Cosmetics Industries' Association
Address: Jl. Sapta 68-A, Jakarta 12870
Telephone: +62 21 829 3501/830 3501

Indonesian Electronics and Domestic Electrical Appliances Industries' Association
Address: Gedung Umawar Fl.1, Jalan Kapten Tendean No.28, Jakarta 12710
Telephone: +62 21 522 5362
Fax: +62 21 522 5363

Indonesian Exporters' Association
Address: PO Box 4571, c/o PT Dian Matra Karya, Jl. Kwini I Blok B.9, Jakarta
Telephone: +62 21 344 0389/351 8019
Fax: +62 21 380 2788

Indonesian Fertiliser and Petrochemical Manufacturers' Association
Address: Umawar Centre, Jalan Kapt Tendean 28, Jakarta 12710
Telephone: +62 21 520 4234/4235
Fax: +62 21 520 4235
Telex: 62287

Indonesian Food and Beverages Producers' Association
Address: Jalan Kav. Bulak Tengah II/2, Klender, Jakarta
Telephone: +62 21 861 4535

Indonesian Footwear Manufacturers' Association
Address: Jl. Muara Karang Raya 291, Jakarta 14450
Telephone: +62 21 669 7508

Indonesian Forwarders' Association
Address: Jalan Iskandarsyah Raya No 7, Kebayoran Baru, Jakarta
Telephone: +62 21 359 591
Fax: +62 21 380 1424
Telex: 47376
Chief officers: Chris Kanter (President)

Indonesian Hotel and Restaurant Association
Address: Gedung Bank Pacific Lt.3, Jl. Sudirman 8, Jakarta 10220
Telephone: +62 21 570 6909

Indonesian Insurance Council
Address: Jl. NMajapahit 38 Blok V/17, jakarta 10160
Telephone: +62 21 363 264/354 307
Fax: +62 21 354 307

Indonesian Leather and Leather Goods Exporters' Association
Address: Jl. Bangka No. 2 Kebayoran Baru, Jakarta selatan
Telephone: +62 21 799 4507 ext. 255
Fax: +62 21 799 1444, 719 2761
Telex: 47127 IA

Indonesian National Contractors' Association
Address: Jl. Raya Pasar Minggu Km.17, No.11-A, Jakarta 12740
Telephone: +62 21 798 1670/797 4301
Fax: +62 21 797 4302

Indonesian Newspapers' Association
Serikat Penerbit Sukatkabar
Address: Gedung Dewan Pers, Jalan Kebonsirih 34, floor VI, Jakarta Pusat
Telephone: +62 21 36 73 38
Fax: +62 21 38 62 373
Chief officers: M r Bagjo Purwantho (Secretary General)

Indonesian Optical Association
Address: Jl. Panglima Polim Rayano. 125 A, Jakarta 12160
Telephone: +62 21 739 3617, 739 2853
Fax: +62 21 724 4787

Indonesian Packaging Federation
Address: Jl. Kamboja 62, Jakarta 11440
Telephone: +62 21 598 917/592 266
Fax: +62 21 567 2266

Indonesian Paint Manufacturers' Association
Address: Jl. Menteng raya 27, Jakarta 10340
Telephone: +62 21 390 9018
Fax: +62 21 375 3043

Indonesian Private Broadcasting Association
Address: Jl. KH Mansyur No.25 A, Jakarta 10230
Telephone: +62 21 314 5737
Fax: +62 21 327 443

Indonesian Pulp and Paper Association
Address: Flat 1/2, Jalan Cimandiri No 6, Jakarta Pusat
Telephone: +62 21 326 084
Fax: +62 21 320 168
Chief officers: Abubakar Soetikno (Chairman); Kahar Haryopuspito (Executive Director)

Indonesian Real Estate Association
Address: Jakarta Design Center, Jl. S Praman no.54, Jakarta 10260
Telephone: +62 21 549 5190

Indonesian Retailers' Association
Address: Gedung Alfa Gloria 4th Floor, Jalan Pegangsaan, Timur 1, Jakarta 10310
Telephone: +62 21 330 131
Fax: +62 21 330 131

Indonesian Sugar Association
Address: Jl. Salemba No. 16, Jakarta pusat
Telephone: +62 21 314 2334, 314 3487
Fax: +62 21 314 2334, 314 3487
Telex: 61137 SETDGI IA

Indonesian Synthetic Fibre Producers' Association
Address: Jl. Raya kebayoran Lama 33, Jakarta 11560
Telephone: +62 21 530 5414
Fax: +62 21 530 5415

Indonesian Telecommunications Association
Address: Ariobimo Central Building, 2th Floor, Jl. H. R. Rasuna Said X-2 Kav. 5, Jakarta 12950
Telephone: +62 21 252 5802
Fax: +62 21 231 5803

Indonesian Textile Association
Address: Gedung Adhi Graha 16th Floor, Jl. Jend. Gatot Subroto Kav. 56, Jakarta Selatan 12950
Telephone: +62 21 527 2171
Fax: +62 21 527 2166
Chief officers: Benny Soetrisno (Secretary)

Indonesian Tourism Promotion Board
Address: 4th Floor, Bank Pacific Building, Jalan Jendral Sudirman 8, Jakarta 10220
Telephone: +62 21 570 4917/4879
Fax: +62 21 570 4855

Indonesian Toys Association
Address: Gajah Mada Tower 10th Floor, Jl. Gajah Mada No. 19-26, Jakarta 10130,
Telephone: +62 21 231 1018
Fax: +62 21 231 1070

International Pharmaceutical Manufacturers' Group (G.P. Farmasi-IPMG)
Address: P. O. Box 3014/jkt, Bina Mulia II, 3th Floor, Jl. H. R. Rasuna Said Kav. 11, Jakarta 12950
Telephone: +62 21 520 1195
Fax: +62 21 520 1195

Milk Processing Industries' Association
Address: Jalan Pulomas Raya 31, Jakarta 13210
Telephone: +62 21 489 0230

National Private Banks' Association
Address: Jalan Perbanas Karet Kuningan, Jakarta 12940
Telephone: +62 21 522 3038, 522 3037
Fax: +62 21 515 731

Natural Fibre Industries' Association
Address: Gedung Artamas I/3, Jl. Ahmad Yani 2, Jakarta 10520
Telephone: +62 21 489 8118 ext.268

Photographic Goods Manufacturers' Association
Address: c/o PT Interdelta, Jl. Gaja Motor Barat, Sunter II, Jakarta
Telephone: +62 21 430 1340
Fax: +62 21 493 473

Press Foundation of Indonesia
Address: Jalan Jatinegara Barat 3/6, Jakarta Timur
Telephone: +62 21 819 4994

Shopping Centres' Association
Address: Jl. Agus Salim no 44 fl.4, Jakarta 10340
Telephone: +62 21 769 4592
Fax: +62 21 314 0594/769 4592

Soybean-Cheese Tofu/Tempe Producers Association
Address: Jl. Tebet Timur Dalam 11/12, Jakarta Selatan
Telephone: +62 21 829 5629, 829 8303
Fax: +62 21 829 8629

Tea Producers' Association
Address: Jalan Juanda 107, Bandung 40132
Telephone: +62 22 250 2049
Fax: +62 22 250 0587

Telecommunication Industries and Services Association
Address: Wijaya Grand center C-28, Jalan Darmawangsa raya no.2, Jakarta 12160
Telephone: +62 21 720 6896
Fax: +62 21 720 6896

Toothbrush and Nylon Manufacturers' Association
Address: Jl. Raya Boulevard kelapa Gading Pat no.12A, Jakarta
Telephone: +62 21 455 2553

Toothpaste Manufacturers' Association
Address: Jl. Melayu Kecil I no.28, Tebet, Jakarta 1284
Telephone: +62 21 829 6645

Tyre Manufacturers' Association
Address: Gedung Graha Purna Yudha Fl.6, Jl. Sudirman no.50, Jakarta 12930
Telephone: +62 21 520 3313 ext 1261
Fax: +62 21 520 7772

Union of Automotive Accessories Industries
Address: 4th Floor, Case Building, Jl. Jend, Gatot Subroto 12, Jakarta, Selatan
Telephone: +62 21 510 097

IRAN

Article Numbering Association (EAN Iran)
Address: C/o Institute for Trade Studies and Research, ITSR Building, 240 North Kargar St, Tehran
Telephone: +98 21 920 781
Fax: +98 21 927 236

Association of Knitwear Exporters of Iran
Address: 254 Aleghani Ave, Tehran
Telephone: +98 21 884 6031/9
Fax: +98 21 882 5111

Iran Dried Fruit Exporters' Association
Address: 4th Floor, 254 Taleghani Avenue, 15814 Tehran
Telephone: +98 21 838 334
Fax: +98 21 838 334/882 5111
Membership: fruit producers and traders

Iran Fruits, Vegetables and Flower Exporters' Association
Address: 3rd Floor, 254 Taleghani Avenue, Tehran
Telephone: +98 21 836 124
Fax: +98 21 836 124
Chief officers: F Fourfar (President) Mr Faramarz (Vice President)
Membership: fruit, vegetables and horticulture producers and traders

Iran Handicrafts Organisation
Address: 663 Valie-Asr Square, 15966 Tehran
Telephone: +98 21 892 122/1224/899 601
Fax: +98 21 898 281

Iran Horticultural Products Exporters' Association
Address: 254 Taleghani Avenue, 15814 Tehran
Telephone: +98 21 884 6031/6039/836 124
Fax: +98 21 882 5111

Iran National Committee of International Dairy Federation
Address: P.O. Box 14155-1467, c/o Iran Dairy Industries Company, 9 East Roudsar St., South Aban Ave., Tehran 15986
Telephone: +98 21 449 2403
Fax: +98 21 893 469/893 063
Chief officers: Mr A R Haghshenass (Secretary)

Iran Skins, Pickled Skins and Leather Exporters' Association
Address: 5th Floor, Seirafi Building, 42 Emam Khomeini Avenue, Amir Kabir Avenue, 11449 Tehran
Telephone: +98 21 311 9915
Fax: +98 21 311 9915

Iran Tragacanth, Gums, Herbal Roots and Seed Exporters' Association
Address: 4th Floor, 254 Avenue, Taleghani, Tehran
Telephone: +98 21 836 031/39
Fax: +98 21 836 039

Iranian Association of Handicrafts Exporters
Address: 254 Aleghani Ave, Tehran
Telephone: +98 21 884 6031/9
Fax: +98 21 882 5111

Iranian Textile Industry Association
Address: 5 Kandovan Alley, Opp. Vila Street, Enghelab Ave, Tehran
Telephone: +98 21 675 450/770

National Iranian Industry Organisation
Address: On the Corner of Parvich, 133 Etesami Street, Fateni Ave, Tehran
Telephone: +98 21 656 031/40
Fax: +98 21 658 000
Membership: umbrella organisation of the Iranian industry

Syndicate of the Iranian Woollen Textile Industry
Address: Keshmir Building, 3rd Floor, Jomhoori Crossroad, Valiagr Ave, Tehran
Telephone: +98 21 640 3172

Tea Organisation of Iran
Address: 11 Behrouz St, Mohseni Sq, Mirdamad Av, Tehran
Telephone: +98 21 808 8614
Fax: +98 21 200 9361

IRELAND

Article Numbering Association (EAN Ireland)
Address: c/o IBEC, Confederation House, 84/86 Lower Baggot Street, Dublin 2
Telephone: +353 1 660 1011
Fax: +353 1 660 1717
E-mail: ean.ireland@ibec.ie
Web site: wilde.iol.ie:80/ibec/Sectors/AFFILIAT/ean.htm
Activities: sets the standards for, and promotes the use of article numbering, bar coding, scanning and electronic commerce, including electronic data interchange (EDI), using EAN numbering systems
Chief officers: Tommy McCabe (Director)
Membership: over 550 members
Notes: Member of the Irish Business and Employers Confederation (IBEC). Fomerly the the Article Number Association of Ireland (ANAI).

Association of Advertisers in Ireland Ltd.
Address: Rock House, Main Street, Blackrock, Co Dublin
Telephone: +353 1 278 0499
Fax: +353 1 278 0488
E-mail: assadvis@indigo.ie
Activities: provides an advisory and information service for advertisers; collects statistics on media expenditures; conducts media research through involvment in industry research programmes; commissions and publishes ad hoc research on various topics of interest to members
Chief officers: M T Corcoran (President); D N Henderson (Vice President/Honorary Treasurer); P L Sweetman (Vice President/Honorary Secretary); Aidan Burns (Chief Executive)
Membership: 100 advertisers in Ireland
Notes: member of World Federation of Advertisers

Association of Independent Radio Stations
Address: Rock Court, 40 Main Street, Blackrock, Co Dublin
Fax: +353 1 283 4163

Chief officers: Charlie Collins (Chairman); Michael Crawley (Secretary); Eamonn Buttle (Treasurer); Ian O'Leary (Chief Executive)
Membership: 18 independent local radio stations

Audiovisual Federation
Address: Confederation House, 84/86 Lower Baggot Street, Dublin 2
Telephone: +353 1 660 1011
Fax: +353 1 660 1717
Activities: provides trade statistics, sector surveys and profiles, customised research and specialist databases, technical standards information and promotional literature; provides market information and forecasting services; acts as a direct link to European or international trade associations; training, workshops and seminars; export promotion; trade exhibitions
Chief officers: Tommy McCabe (Director)
Membership: broadcasters, animation studios, independent producers, facilities, marketing distribution companies, corporate video producers, legal/ financial companies, as well as other affiliated organisations from the sector

Building Materials Federation (BMF)
Address: Confederation House, 84/86 Lower Baggot Street, Dublin 2
Telephone: +353 1 660 1011
Fax: +353 1 660 1717
Web site: wilde.iol.ie:80/ibec/Sectors/BMF/
Chief officers: Derek Maynard (Director)
Notes: The interests of product groupings are represented through the Concrete Manufacturers' Association of Ireland, Polystyrene Moulders' Association (Insulation), and the Irish Plastic Pipe Manufacturers' Association.

Car Rental Council of Ireland
Address: 5 Upper Pembroke Street, Dublin 2
Telephone: +353 1 676 1690
Fax: +353 1 661 9213
E-mail: simi@iol.ie
Web site: www.iol.ie/simi/
Chief officers: Robert D.E. Prole (Chief Executive), John Smith (Chairman)
Membership: members
Publications:
● List of Approved Car Hire Operators: *annual*
Notes: The Association does not produce statistics.

Cereals Association of Ireland Limited
Address: 18 Herbert Street, Dublin 2
Telephone: +353 1 661 4696
Fax: +353 1 661 6774
Activities: collection, collation and dissemination of statistical information relevant to the grain trade
Chief officers: P Jones (Chairman); H F Beirne (Promotions and Marketing Director); S A Funge (Secretary)

Chartered Association of Certified Accountants (Irish Region)
Address: 9 Leeson Park, Dublin 6
Telephone: +353 1 496 3144
Fax: +353 1 496 3615
Year established: 1972
Chief officers: Joseph O'Leary (President)
Membership: 2,200

Chartered Institute of Transport in Ireland
Address: 1 Fitzwilliam Place, Dublin 2
Telephone: +353 1 676 3188/1 676 4290
Fax: +353 1 676 4099
Activities: education courses
Chief officers: T Ferris (President); J O'Hara, M Gallagher (Vice Presidents); D Lonergan (Honorary Secretary); M I Coleman (Honorary Treasurer)

Construction Industry Federation
Address: Federation House, Canal Road, Dublin 6
Telephone: +353 1 497 7487
Fax: +353 1 496 6953/1 496 6611
Activities: industrial relations service; government liaison; publication of contract documents, negociations on contract documents; management courses; group training and safety schemes; housing guarantee scheme; management of pension and mortality schemes
Chief officers: Pat Harrington (President); Liam B Kelleher (Director General); Eugene P O'Neill (Secretary/Financial Controller)
Structure: management association for the construction industry
Membership: 2,300+
Publications:
● Construction

Consumer Electronics Distributors' Association
Address: c/o IBEC, Confederation House, 84/86 Lower Baggot Street, Dublin 2
Telephone: +353 1 660 1011
Fax: +353 1 660 1717
Notes: Formerly known as Radio and Television Setmakers and Distributors' Association

Electrical and Electronic Retailers' Association of Ireland
Address: Temple Hall, Blackrock, Dublin
Telephone: +353 1 283 1021
Fax: +353 1 288 9483
E-mail: fm@iol.ie
Chief officers: John Kilkelly (President), Patrick O'Mara (Secretary)
Membership: electrical and electronic retailers
Notes: The Association does not produce statistics. Publications are only available to members.

Electrical Industries Federation of Ireland (EIFI)
Address: c/o ETCI, Parnell Avenue, Harold's Cross, Dublin 12
Telephone: +353 1 454 5819
Fax: +353 1 454 5821
Year established: 1934
Chief officers: Hugh McGee (President), Tony Carroll (Secretary), Lucie Brady (Administrator), Cel O'Reilly (Vice President)
Membership: 100 manufacturers, importers and distributors of electrical goods
Notes: The Association does not produce any statistics or publications.

Fashion and Footwear Federation
Address: Confedration House, 84/86 Lower Baggot Street, Dublin 2
Telephone: +353 1 660 1011
Fax: +353 1 660 1717/1 660 1917
Chief officers: Ultan Courtney (Director)

Federation of Aerospace Enterprises in Ireland (FAEI)

Address: Confederation House, 84/86 Lower Baggot Street, Dublin 2
Telephone: +353 1 660 1011
Fax: +353 1 660 1717
Web site: wilde.iol.ie:80/ibec/Sectors/AFFILIAT/aero.htm
Chief officers: Tommy McCabe (Director)

Federation of Electronic and Computer Science Industries (FEII)

Address: Confederation House, 84/86 Lower Baggot Street, Dublin 2
Telephone: +353 1 660 1011
Fax: +353 1 660 1717
E-mail: feii@ibec.ie
Web site: wilde.iol.ie:80/ibec/Sectors/FEII/index.html
Chief officers: Katherine Lucey (Director)

Federation of Irish Chemical Industries (FICI)

Address: Franklin House, 140 Pembroke Road, Dublin 4
Telephone: +353 1 660 3350
Fax: +353 1 668 6672
Activities: library, information service and other services accessible to members only; statistical services provided for members only (but see under Publications)
Chief officers: A Nolan (Secretary); M A Granville (President); Una Rushe (Office Co-ordinator)
Membership: 125 manufacturers of chemicals, pharmaceuticals, household chemicals, cosmetics and toiletries
Publications:
• Annual Report of the Federation of Irish Chemical Industries (FICI): *includes some statistical series with data on production, consumption, trade plus some comparative data from other EU countries. Also includes a list of members - annual*
Notes: The Federation comprises the following specialist committees, working parties and groups: Cosmetics, Toiletries and Household Maintenance Products; Chemical Industries Group Council; Pharmaceutical Division; Proprietary Medicines Division; Animal Health Division; Medical Diagnostics, Instruments and Devices Division; Agricultural Chemicals Division; Industrial and Fine Chemicals Division; Environmental Affairs (WP); Manpower (WP); Distribution of Chemicals (WP)

Federation of Jewellery Manufacturers of Ireland

Address: Temple Hall, Blackrock, Co Dublin
Telephone: +353 1 283 1021
Fax: +353 1 288 9483
Chief officers: Matt Murphy (Chairman); Ronald Finlay-Mulligan (Secretary)

Film Makers Ireland (FMI)

Address: The Studio Building, Meeting House Square, Temple Bar, Dublin 2
Telephone: +353 1 671 3525
Fax: +353 1 671 4292
E-mail: jcilmmi@iol.ie
Year established: 1987
Chief officers: Ed Guiney (Chairman), Gemma Dolan (Administrator)
Structure: executive committee
Membership: 90 members : all production companies
Publications:
• FMI News: *quarterly*

Financial Services Industries' Association (FSIA)

Address: Confederation House, 84/86 Lower Baggot Street, Dublin 2
Telephone: +353 1 660 1011
Fax: +353 1 660 1717
E-mail: fsia@ibec.ie
Web site: wilde.iol.ie:80/ibec/Sectors/FSIA/
Chief officers: Torlach Denihan (Director), Jacqueline Williams (Executive)

Food, Drink and Tobacco Federation (FDT)

Address: c/o IBEC, Confederation House, 84/86 Lower Baggot Street, Dublin 2
Telephone: +353 1 660 1011
Fax: +353 1 660 1717
Chief officers: Ciaran Fitzgerald (Director)
Membership: comprises 140 individual members and 16 product-related associations or groupings: Coffee Industry Association of Ireland; Federation of Irish Renderers; Food Processors and Suppliers Group; Irish Association of Pigmeat Processors; Irish Bread Bakers' Association; Irish Breakfast Cereals' Association; Irish Brewers' Association; Irish Cream Liqueurs Producers' Association; Irish Dairy Industry Association; Irish Duty Free Association; Irish Meat Industry Association; Irish Refrigeration Enterprises' Association; Margarine Manufacturers' Association of Ireland; Petfood Manufacturers' Association of Ireland; Soup Manufacturers' of Ireland; Spiritous Beverages Group; Sugar Users Group; Ground Limestone Producers' Association
Notes: Member of the Irish Business and Employers Confederation.

Institute of Advertising Practitioners in Ireland

Address: 8 Upper Fitzwilliam Street, Dublin 2
Telephone: +353 1 676 5991
Fax: +353 1 661 4589
E-mail: info@iapi.com
Activities: trade body for advertising agencies in Ireland; collects statistics on advertising expenditure
Chief officers: Brendan Bonass (President), Ian Fox (Chief Executive)
Membership: 38 advertising agencies representing 95% of Irish agencies
Publications:
• Business Readership in Ireland: *bi-annual*
• Changing Attitudes in Ireland

Institute of Bankers in Ireland

Address: Nassau House, Nassau Street, Dublin 2
Telephone: +353 1 679 3311
Fax: +353 1 679 3504
E-mail: instbank@indigo.ie
Web site: www.instbank.ie
Year established: 1898
Activities: operates a joint programme with University College Dublin on a distance learning basis, providing Bachelors Degree in Financial Services
Chief officers: E F McElroy (President); P W McDowell (Vice President); Patrick J. Rock (Chief Executive and Secretary); J. Frank Rooney (Director of Education)
Structure: council of 33 representatives of all banks in Ireland; 13 regional committees
Membership: 15,000 members working in the banking and financial services sector in Ireland
Publications:
• Banking Ireland: *quarterly*
Notes: The Association does not produce statistics.

Institute of Fisheries Management (Irish National Branch)

Address: The Marine Institute, Fisheries Research Centre, Abbotstown, Dublin 15
Telephone: +353 1 821 0111
Fax: +353 1 820 5078
E-mail: cmoriarty@fcr.ie
Year established: 1987
Activities: organises seminars and excurtions on matters relating to inland fisheries management
Chief officers: Eamon Cusak (Chairman), Dr Christopher Moriarty (Honorary Secretary), Dr K. Whelan (joint secretaries), E Twomey (Treasurer)
Membership: 76 members
Notes: The Association does not produce any statistics or publications.

Institute of Freight Forwarders of Ireland (IOFF)

Address: Merchamp House, Vernon Avenue, Dublin 3
Telephone: +353 1 833 1429
Fax: +353 1 832 7856
E-mail: ioff@ioff.ccs400.ie
Web site: www.ccs.ie/ioff.hom.htm
Activities: collects statistics only privately from member companies, mainly used for lobbying purposes
Chief officers: Sean Sandford (President), Fergus Treacy (Vice-President), Tony O'Hanlon (Chief Executive)
Membership: 90 corporate members and 80 professional members
Publications:
• Newsletter: *monthly*
Notes: member of FIATA (the International Federation of Freight Forwarders' Associations)

Institute of International Trade of Ireland

Address: Holbrook House, Holles Street, Dublin 2
Telephone: +353 1 661 2182
Fax: +353 1 661 2315
E-mail: iiti@exporters.itw.ie
Web site: www.itw.ie\exporter\iiti.htn
Activities: research of trade practice issues; general statistics
Chief officers: Lawrence Crowley (President); Colum MacDonnell (Director)
Membership: 300 members
Publications:
• Impact of Air Transport on Ireland's Export Performance
• International Trade Practice: A Practical Guide to Exporting

Institute of Petroleum (Irish Branch)

Address: Hugh Munro and Company Limited, Tramway House, Dartry Road, Rathgar, Dublin 6
Telephone: +353 1 497 5716
Fax: +353 1 497 5886
Year established: 1913
Chief officers: J G McManus (Chairman); B A Sheehan (Honorary Secretary)
Membership: 300

Insurance Institute of Ireland

Address: Insurance House, 39/45 Molesworth Street, Dublin 2
Telephone: +353 1 677 2582/2753/2844
Fax: +353 1 677 2621
Activities: education and training, annual national conference
Chief officers: Mr Dennis Hevey (Chief Executive)
Structure: national council elected by 6 local bodies
Membership: 3,500 members from insurance and related financial services sectors
Notes: The Institute does not produce any publications or statistics.

Irish Aquaculture Association

Address: Irish Farm Centre, Naas Road, Bluebell, Dublin 12
Telephone: +353 1 450 8755
Fax: +353 1 455 1043/ 1 456 5146
Chief officers: Dr John Joyce (Secretary)
Membership: individuals, cooperatives and companies
Publications:
• Aquaculture Ireland: *bi-monthly*

Irish Association of Distributive Trades (IADT)

Address: Rock House, Main Street, Blackrock, Co Dublin
Telephone: +353 1 288 7584/1 288 8274
Fax: +353 1 283 2206
Year established: 1979
Chief officers: Michael G Campbell (Director General), Sinead Creamer (Personal Assistant)
Membership: 68 food wholesalers

Irish Book Publishers' Association

Address: The Writers' Centre, 19 Parnell Square, Dublin 1
Telephone: +353 1 872 9090
Fax: +353 1 872 2035
Web site: www.book-publishers.ie
Activities: publishes a survey on the Irish book world
Chief officers: Michael Gill (President), Orla Martin (Administrator)

Irish Bread Bakers' Association

Address: Confederation House, 84/86 Lower Baggot Street, Dublin 2
Telephone: +353 1 660 1011
Fax: +353 1 660 1717
Chief officers: Peter Wood (Chairman)
Notes: Member of the Irish Business and Employers Confederation (qv).

Irish Brewers' Association

Address: c/o Confederation House, 84/86 Lower Baggot Street, Dublin 2
Telephone: +353 1 660 1011
Fax: +353 1 660 1717
E-mail: paddy.jordan@ibec.ie

Irish Business and Employers Confederation (IBEC)

Address: Confederation House, 84/86 Lower Baggot Street, Dublin 2
Telephone: +353 1 660 1011
Fax: +353 1 660 1717
E-mail: Tony.Barry.@ibec.ie
Web site: www.iol.ie/ibec
Activities: provides advice and assistance in different areas (management, employee/recruitment policies, trade union matters, etc.); information and general services
Chief officers: Tony Barry (President), John Dunne (General Director), Deirdre Quinn (Secretary)
Membership: ca. 6,000 companies and organisations from all sectors of economic and commercial activity
Publications:
• Directory of Services to Members: *description of the Confederations activities and services*

Irish Cattle Traders' and Stockowners' Association (ICSA)

Address: Unit 9, Lyster House, Portlaoise, Co.Laois
Telephone: +353 5 026 2120
Fax: +353 5 02 62121
E-mail: icsa@tinet.ie

Activities: monitors and analyses government and EU policies and legislation affecting drystock farmers; briefs and educates ICSA members on their best interests; lobbies politicians at local, national and international level; promotes knowledge and understanding among decision-makers and organisations whose policies affect the future of drystock farming; collects statistics on sale prices of sheep and cattle, on operation of national and EU supports for drystock farming, on socio-economic aspects of drystock farming and rural development
Chief officers: Albert Thompson (National Chairman); Patrick Lalor (National Secretary); Peter Austin (National Treasurer); Eddie Collins-Hughes (General Secretary)
Membership: 4500 members
Publications:
• Drystock Farmer: *bi-monthly*

Irish Clothing Manufacturers' Association and Irish Textiles' Federation (ICMF-ITF)
Address: Confederation House, 84/86 Lower Baggot Street, Dublin 2
Telephone: +353 1 660 1011
Fax: +353 1 660 1717
Web site: wilde.iol.ie:80/ibec/Sectors/ICMF/
Year established: 1993
Activities: lobbying; advice and information services; newsletter
Chief officers: Jacqueline Harrison (Director)
Structure: executive committee, subcommittees: training, retailer contacts, technical
Membership: 80
Notes: The Irish Clothing Manufacturers' Federation works to develop a more competitive manufacturing environment for the clothing sector and to ensure that appropriate policies are put in place to maximise the possibilities for growth and development.

Irish Concrete Society
Address: Stillorgan Road, Stillorgan, Co Dublin
Telephone: +353 1 206 4069
Fax: +353 1 206 4001
Activities: organises information evenings, lectures, seminars; disemination of information, publications
Chief officers: Owen Lewis (Chairman), Mark Prendergast (Honorary Secretary), Edward Hanlon (Honorary Treasurer), Roger West (Vice-Chairman)
Membership: 240 construction industries
Publications:
• Newsletter
Notes: The Association does not produce statistics.

Irish Cream Liqueur Producers' Association
Address: c/o IBEC, Confederation House, 84/86 Lower Baggot Street, Dublin 2
Telephone: +353 1 660 1011
Fax: +353 1 660 1717
Telex: 93502
Chief officers: C Fitzgerald (Chairman), J Harrison (Secretary)

Irish Dairy Industries' Association Limited
Address: Confederation House, 84-86 Lower Baggot Street, Dublin 2
Telephone: +353 1 660 1011
Fax: +353 1 660 1717
Web site: www.iol.ie:80/ibec/Sectors/FDT/
Year established: 1971
Chief officers: Pat Ivory (Director)
Notes: Member of the Irish Business and Employers' Confederation (qv).

Irish Detergent and Allied Products' Association (IDAPA)
Address: Burgess Galvin, Jamestown Road, Dublin 3
Telephone: +353 1 834 2255
Fax: +353 1 836 1399
Activities: represents member companies in Ireland operating in the detergent, hygiene and cleaning products sector, covering both household and institutional requirements, along with industrial applications
Chief officers: D C Reynolds (Director), Tom Taylor (Secretary General)
Notes: IDAPA is affiliated to the international trade associations for soap and detergents (AIS) and for cleaning and maintenance products (FIFE), both based in Brussels

Irish Direct Marketing Association
Address: The Powerhouse, Pigeon House Harbour, Dublin 4
Telephone: +353 1 668 7155
Fax: +353 1 668 7945
E-mail: bmoss@indigo.ie
Activities: trade association for companies that engage in any form of direct marketing, or that provide a service to the direct marketing industry
Chief officers: Pat Cody (Chairman); Jim Kid (Vice Chairman); Bill Moss (Secretary); Kathleen Treanor (Treasurer)
Membership: 280 members
Publications:
• Directory of Members: *annual*
• Go Direct: *bi-monthly*
• Newsletter: *monthly*

Irish Exporters' Association
Address: Holbrook House, Holles Street, Dublin 2
Telephone: +353 1 661 2182
Fax: +353 1 661 2315
E-mail: lea@exporters.itw.ie
Web site: www.itw.ie\exporter
Activities: government liaison; technical advice; statistics including freight movement, currency fluctuations, customs procedure satisfaction
Chief officers: John Whelan (President); Colum MacDonnell (Chief Executive)
Membership: 350 members representing manufacturers, service providers, transport companies, freight forwarders and logistics specialists
Publications:
• Exporting Today: *bi-monthly*

Irish Farmers' Association
Address: Irish Farm Centre, Bluebell, Dublin 12
Telephone: +353 1 450 0266
Fax: +353 1 455 1043
Chief officers: John Donnelly (President); Michael Berkery (General Secretary); Michael Slattery (Deputy President)
Structure: 900 branches and 29 county executives, each county executive represented on the national council, the governing body of the organisation, and on 22 national committees
Membership: 85,000 farm families

Irish Fish Producers' Organisation
Address: 11 Elgin Road, Dublin 4
Telephone: +353 1 668 7077
Fax: +353 1 668 4466
E-mail: jghurley@iol.ie
Activities: management of fisheries; operation of EU-funded market price support scheme; contribution to policy formulation through government and EU committees
Chief officers: Mark Lochrin (Chief Executive), David Owens

(Office Manager), John Hurley (Researcher)
Membership: 210 owners of commercial sea fishing vessels
Publications:
• Newsletter: *six p.a.*
Notes: The Association does not produce statistics.

Irish Hardware Association

Address: Elmville, Upper Kilmacud Road, Dundrum, Dublin 14
Telephone: +353 1 298 0969
Fax: +353 1 298 6103
E-mail: iha@iol.ie
Web site: www.iol.ie/iha
Activities: government liaison, management services, education and training etc. The Association collects statistics on various topics but these are normally only available to members. They do not produce information on production or sales
Chief officers: James Goulding (Secretary)
Membership: retailers, wholesalers, agents and manufacturers in the hardware, building materials, fancy goods, housewares and decorating sectors. Members represent 800 outlets
Notes: The Association produces occasional guides in areas of management but does not produce any regular publications.

Irish Hotel and Catering Institute

Address: Mespil House, Sussex Road, Dublin 4
Telephone: +353 1 668 8278
Fax: +353 1 660 5566
Activities: certification of courses; year-round programmes covering information and awareness
Chief officers: John D Carroll (President); Sheila Matthews (Deputy President); Alexis Fitzgerald (Secretary General); Tina Maree (administration)

Irish Hotels' Federation

Address: 13 Northbrook Road, Dublin 6
Telephone: +353 1 497 6459
Fax: +353 1 497 4613
Activities: development of business opportunities for members
Chief officers: Gerry O'Connor (President); John Horan (Chief Executive); Donal O'Meara (Secretary/Treasurer); Ben Deane (Marketing Executive)

Irish Master Printers' Association

Address: 33 Parkgate Street, Dublin 8
Telephone: +353 1 679 3679
Fax: +353 1 677 9144
Chief officers: J Gleeson (President); P Henderson (Vice President); Una Sheridan (Secretary)

Irish Meat Association

Address: 11 Merrion Square, Dublin 2
Telephone: +353 1 661 0422
Fax: +353 1 661 0427
Telex: 91684
E-mail: info@ima.ie
Activities: information service for its members; macro and micro policy issues
Chief officers: Tom McAndrew (Chairman), John Smith (Chief Executive)
Membership: beef and lamb export companies

Irish Organic Farmers' and Growers' Association (IOFGA)

Address: 56 Blessington Street, Dublin 7
Telephone: +353 1 830 7996
Fax: +353 1 830 0925
Activities: publishes reports on sales, production types, etc.; inspection and certification; training; advice on organic farming; publications; promotion; assistance with marketing
Chief officers: Noreen Gibney (National Co-ordinator), Shirley Cully (National Administrator)
Structure: voluntary organisation
Membership: 530 registered producers, mainly livestock producers, with 100 vegetable growers, 8 processors and 2 industrialists

Irish Pharmaceutical and Chemical Manufacturers' Association (IPCMF)

Address: Confederation House, 84/86 Lower Baggot Street, Dublin 2
Telephone: +353 1 660 1011
Fax: +353 1 660 1717
Web site: wilde.iol.ie:80/ibec/Sectors/IPCMF/index.html

Irish Pharmaceutical Union (IPU)

Address: Butterfield House, Butterfield Avenue, Rathfarnham, Dublin 14
Telephone: +353 1 493 6401
Fax: +353 1 493 6407
E-mail: ipu@iol.ie
Chief officers: Mr Diarmuid O'Donovan (President), Mr Brendan Quinn (Vice President), Mr Enda A. Ryan (Secretary General)
Membership: 1,300 self-employed community pharmacists, hospital and public pharmacists, academics, army, industry
Publications:
• IPU Review: *11 p.a.*
• IPU Yearbook and Diary: *annual*
Notes: The Union do not produce any statistics.

Irish Road Haulage Association

Address: 40 Lower Leeson Street, Dublin 2
Telephone: +353 1 661 8549
Fax: +353 1 662 0382
Year established: 1973
Activities: represents the majority of licensed road hauliers in Ireland
Chief officers: Sheila McCabe (President); Jimmy Quinn (Vice-President); Sean Murtagh (Deputy Vice-President); Audrey Shorten (Honorary Treasurer)

Irish Salmon Growers' Association

Address: The Farm Centre, Naas Road, Bluebell, Dublin 12
Telephone: +353 1 450 8755
Fax: +353 1 450 4182
Activities: quality control scheme
Chief officers: Tony Fox (Chairman); Dr John Joyce (Chief Executive)
Notes: Affiliated to the Irish Farmers' Association.

Irish Timber Council

Address: 7 Mount Street Crescent, Dublin 2
Telephone: +353 1 678 5733/1 678 5976
Fax: +353 1 678 5976
Activities: marketing of Irish timber, domestically and internationally
Chief officers: Liam McGrath (President); Pat Naughton, Declan Hutchinson (Vice Presidents); John Kerrigan (Director); Anne Jeffries (Secretary)

Irish Tourist Industry Confederation

Address: Alliance House, Adelaide Street, Dun Laoghaire, Co. Dublin
Telephone: +353 1 284 4222
Fax: +353 1 280 4218
Activities: identification of critical strategic issues affecting tourism; representation to government, Bord Failte and the public; participation in the formulation of government and EU tourism policy; information services for industry, media and members
Chief officers: Brendan Leahy (Chief Executive)
Membership: 22 members : Access Transport, Internal Transport, Accomodation Providers, Tour Operators, Tourism Services Companies
Publications:
• Economic Reports: *economic reports on tourism*

Irish Travel Agents' Association

Address: 3rd Floor, Heaton House, 32 South William Street, Dublin 2
Telephone: +353 1 679 4089
Year established: 1971
Activities: makes representations on travel-related matters to government bodies and to the principal carriers
Chief officers: Jim Sharkey (President); John O'Donoghue (Treasurer); Brendan Moran (Chief Executive)
Membership: 340

Irish Whiskey Distillers' Association

Address: Bow Street Distillery, Smithfield, Dublin 7
Telephone: +353 1 872 5566
Fax: +353 1 872 3109

Licensed Vintners' Association

Address: Anglesea House, Anglesea Road, Ballsbridge, Dublin 4
Telephone: +353 1 668 0215/1 668 4433
Fax: +353 1 668 0448
Year established: 1817
Activities: Services provided: economic, commercial, industrial relations and trade relations services
Chief officers: Frank Towey (Chairman); C F Fell (Chief Executive); Edwin Finnegan (Vice Chairman); Eamon McCormack (Treasurer)
Membership: ca. 650 licensed premises
Publications:
• Licensed Vintners' Association Newsletter

Music Industry Group

Address: Confederation House, 84/86 Lower Baggot Street, Dublin 2
Telephone: +353 1 660 1011
Fax: +353 1 660 1717
Web site: wilde.iol.ie:80/ibec/Sectors/AFFILIAT/music.htm
Chief officers: Tommy McCabe (Director)

National Dairy Council

Address: Grattan House, Lower Mount Street, Dublin 2
Telephone: +353 1 661 9599
Fax: +353 1 662 0379
Activities: advertising campaigns; promotional and educational activities; sponsorship programmes; information centre on nutrition and health
Chief officers: Billy Nagle (Chairman)
Structure: NDC is a company limited by guarantee and does not have a share capital

National Federation of Retail Newsagents

Address: 17 Greenmount House, Greenmount Office Park, Harold's Cross Road, Dublin 6
Telephone: +353 1 453 5822/1 453 7991
Activities: contacts with government on matters of legislation, trading practices and labour relations
Chief officers: M Moran (President); J A Holmes (regional Manager)
Publications:
• Irish Newsagent: *bi-monthly*

National Wholesale Grocers' Alliance

Address: 1 Cian Park, Drumcondra, Dublin 9
Telephone: +353 1 837 9238
Fax: +353 1 837 9562
Telex: 32219
Chief officers: J Kearney (President), Michael Shannon (Chief Executive); G Cooke, F Devins (Vice Presidents)
Membership: food wholesalers

Pharmaceutical Distributors' Federation

Address: 46 Merrion Square, Dublin 2
Telephone: +353 1 676 1803
Fax: +353 1 676 1803

Plastics Industries' Association (PIA)

Address: Confederation House, 84/86 Lower Baggot Street, Dublin 2
Telephone: +353 1 660 1011
Fax: +353 1 660 1717
Web site: wilde.iol.ie:80/ibec/Sectors/PIA/
Activities: represents the plastic industry, including processors and suppliers of plastics raw materials and seeks to promote its members' interests at all levels
Chief officers: Reg McCabe (Director)
Notes: Incorporates the Federation of Print Paper and Board Industries Irish Corrugated Packaging Association.

PRCA Ireland-Public Relations Consultants' Association of Ireland

Address: 62 Merrion Square, Dublin 2
Telephone: +353 1 661 8004
Fax: +353 1 676 4562
Chief officers: Jim Walsh (Chairman); Roddy Guiney (Vice Chairman); Betty Griffin (Company Secretary); Padraig Slattery (Honorary Treasurer)

Radio and Television Retailers' Association of Ireland (RTRA)

Address: 4th Floor, Dollard House, Wellington Quay, Dublin 2
Telephone: +353 1 283 1021
Fax: +353 1 288 9483
Activities: representative body for retailers of electrical and electronic consumer goods
Chief officers: Maeve Costello (President)
Membership: 300 retailers

Restaurants Association of Ireland

Address: 11 Bridge Court, City Gate, St Augustine Street, Dublin 8
Telephone: +353 1 677 9901
Fax: +353 1 671 8414
Year established: 1971
Chief officers: Tom Williams (President); Kay Caball (Vice President); Henry O'Neill (Chief Executive); Mairead Flanagan (Secretary)

Retail Grocery, Dairy and Allied Trades' Association (RGDATA)

Address: Rock House, Main Street, Blackrock, Co Dublin
Telephone: +353 1 288 7584
Fax: +353 1 283 2206
Year established: 1942
Activities: annual conference; various publications; co-operation with manufacturers, wholesalers, importers and other suppliers
Chief officers: Geraldine Joyce (President); M G Campbell (Director General)
Structure: national executive committee
Membership: independent retail stores

Small Firms Association (SFA)

Address: 84/86 Lower Baggot Street, Dublin 2
Telephone: +353 1 660 1011
Fax: +353 1 661 2861
E-mail: sfa@iol.ie
Web site: wilde.iol.ie:80/sfa/
Year established: 1972

Society of Irish Foresters

Address: c/o Royal Dublin Society, Dublin 4
Telephone: +353 1 278 1874
Year established: 1942
Activities: educational, including study tours of forest areas at home and abroad, field days and an annual symposium
Chief officers: Eugene Hendrick (President); Gerhadt Gallagher (Vice President); Pat O'Sullivan (Secretary); Richard Jack (Treasurer)
Membership: 700+

Society of Irish Maltsters

Address: c/o Minch Norton Malt Ltd, Athy, Co Kildare
Telephone: +353 5 074 0300
Fax: +353 5 073 1046
E-mail: minch@iol.ie
Web site: www.iol.ie/-minch/
Year established: 1947
Chief officers: Patrick J Murphy (Chairman); Michael McCarthy (Secretary)
Membership: 3 members
Notes: Affiliated to Euromalt, Brussels. The Association does not produce any statistics or publications.

Society of Manufacturing Engineers, Ireland District

Address: c/o CAMMS (Matt Cotterell), Regional Technical College, Rossa Avenue, Bishopstown, Co Cork
Telephone: +353 2 154 5222
Fax: +353 2 154 5343
Chief officers: Brian McCoy (National Chairman); Matt Cotterell (National Secretary)
Structure: national district with active chapters in 4 main centres

Society of the Irish Motor Industry (SIMI)

Address: 5 Upper Pembroke Street, Dublin 2
Telephone: +353 1 676 1690
Fax: +353 1 661 9213
E-mail: simi@iol.ie
Web site: www.iol.ie:80/~simi/
Activities: publishes industry statistics; industrial relations; complaints service
Membership: motor vehicle distributors, petroleum companies, wholesalers of spare parts, accessories and suppliers of garage equipment, motor factors, retail garages, vehicle specialist body repairers, petrol retailers, vehicle testers and engine manufacturers

Publications:
• Irish Motor Industry: *monthly*

Soft Drinks and Beer Bottlers' Association Ltd

Address: 13 Adelaide Street, Dun Laoghaire, Co Dublin
Telephone: +353 1 284 4374
Fax: +353 1 284 4375
Year established: 1928
Activities: annual statistics on soft drinks (carbonates, bottled waters, squash and cordial): available to non-members
Membership: 69 corporate members (soft drinks manufacturers; beer and cider bottlers; wholesale beverage distributors)
Publications:
• Annual Statistics (Soft Drinks and Beer Bottlers' Association): *detailed statistics on the soft drinks sector with data on the volume of production, consumption, imports, exports, packaging trends, and distribution channels - annual*

Wholesale Fruit, Potato and Produce Merchants' Association of Ireland Ltd

Address: 28 Dale Road, Kilmacud, Blackrock, Co Dublin
Telephone: +353 1 288 7959
Fax: +353 1 288 6406
Year established: 1930
Activities: coordination of negotiations with unions, government departments etc.
Chief officers: Michael J Byrne (Chairman); Thomas Downs FCA (Secretary); P Dolan, A. Gray (Directors)
Membership: 20 importers and wholesalers

Wine and Spirit Association of Ireland

Address: 33 Clarinda Park West, Dun Laoghaire, Co Dublin
Telephone: +353 1 280 4666
Fax: +353 1 280 7566
E-mail: winedb@iol.ie
Web site: www.e-maginet.com/wine
Year established: 1976
Activities: runs the wine promotion board; organises training courses; compiles sector statistics including consumption of wine and spirits
Chief officers: Jean Smullen (Diploma Administrator); Michelle Lyne (Office Manager)
Membership: 37 corporate members (producers, importers, wholesalers, distributors and merchants)
Notes: Publishes various general leaflets.

Wine Development Board of Ireland

Address: 33 Clarinda Park West, Dun Laoghaire, Co Dublin
Telephone: +353 1 280 4666
Fax: +353 1 280 7566
E-mail: winedb@iol.ie
Web site: www.e-maginet.com/wine
Year established: 1977
Activities: wine educational courses
Chief officers: Jean Smullen (Diploma Administrator); Michelle Lyne (Office Manager)
Membership: 37 members representing producers, importers, wholesalers and retailers
Notes: Publish various general leaflets.

ISRAEL

Advertisers' Association of Israel

Address: PO Box 20440, 117 Ha'hashmonaim Street, 61204 Tel Aviv

Telephone: +972 3 561 5310
Fax: +972 3 561 5281
Year established: 1961
Chief officers: Yair Feldmann (General Manager)
Membership: 340 companies (industry, finance, retail etc)
Publications:
• OTOT: *advertising, marketing, communication - monthly*

Association of Banks in Israel

Address: 12 Levontin Street, 65112 Tel Aviv
Telephone: +972 3 560 9332/569 019/624 332
Fax: +972 3 566 0317
Year established: 1959
Chief officers: Moshe Sambar (Chairman), Fred Vider (Executive Director)
Membership: 36 members: umbrella organisation for commercial, mortgage and investment banks operating in Israel

Association of Grocery Traders

Address: 4 Herzl, Haifa
Telephone: +972 4 867 2524
Membership: grocery traders and producers

Association of Israeli Journalists

Address: 27 Hill el Agron House, Jerusalem
Telephone: +972 2 625 4351

Book Publishers' Association of Israel

Address: PO Box 20123, 29 Carlebach Street, 67132 Tel Aviv
Telephone: +972 3 561 4121/4124
Fax: +972 3 561 1996
Year established: 1939
Activities: general book promotion and publicity; organises annual Hebrew Book Week; translation rights; information centre on publishing abroad for foreign publishers on matters concerning Israel
Chief officers: Racheli Edelman (Chairman), Mr S Hausman (President), Mr Amnon Ben Shmuel (Director)
Membership: 84 publishing firms

Citrus Marketing Board of Israel

Address: PO Box 80, 50250 Beit Dagan
Telephone: +972 3 968 3820/3 968 3819
Fax: +972 3 968 3838
Web site: www.ibc.co.il/c50.5.html
Year established: 1942
Activities: licenses the private exporters of Jaffa citrus and all Jaffa trademarks; research and development for the Israeli citrus industry; global advertising and promotion campaigns for Jaffa; internal and external relations of the citrus industry
Membership: central co-ordinating body of the country's citrus growers and exporters

Egg and Poultry Board

Address: 2 Kaplan Street, 61071 Tel Aviv
Telephone: +972 3 695 2335
Fax: +972 3 696 0151
Activities: statistics on poultry and egg consumption
Chief officers: Yonatan Basi (Chairman), Naphtali Ben Sira (Executive Director)
Membership: 1,900 poultry and egg producers

Fish Breeder's Association

Address: PO Box 33750, Haifa
Telephone: +972 4 862 3444
Fax: +972 4 867 3809

Fruit Board of Israel

Address: 17 Ha'hashmonaim Street, 61070 Tel Aviv
Telephone: +972 3 563 2929
Fax: +972 3 561 4672
Year established: 1960
Chief officers: D Litvak (Director General)

Fruit Growers' Organisation

Address: 8 Shaul Hamelech Boulevard, Tel Aviv
Telephone: +972 3 696 6267
Fax: +972 3 691 7625

General Merchants' Association of Israel

Address: 4 Herzl, Haifa
Telephone: +972 4 867 2526
Membership: 30,000 in 60 branches

International Federation of Producers of Phonograms and Videograms- The Israel National Group

Address: 1 Twins Building, 6th floor, 33 Jabotinsky Street, 52511 Ramat-Gan
Telephone: +972 3 613 071 5/6
Fax: +972 3 575 6747

Israel Association of Electronics Industries

Address: P.O.Box 50026, 29 Hamered Street, 61500 Tel Aviv
Telephone: +972 3 516 3986/519 8862
Fax: +972 3 516 1003
E-mail: elec_har@netvision.net.il
Web site: www.iaei.org.il/
Year established: 1972
Activities: collects and analyses information and data derived from sources in Israel and abroad and disseminates such data as required; builds and strengthens bilateral relations with similar organisations worldwide, aimed at promoting international cooperation; major part of the Associations activities are done through various forums to which all interested companies are invited
Chief officers: Mr Hanan Achsaf (Chairman), Mr. Uri Har (Director General)
Membership: 107 companies, nearly 100% of total industry (membership comprises government-owned, private and public companies, as well as subsidiaries of foreign companies)

Israel Association of the Periodical Press

Address: 93 Arlozorov St, 62098 Tel Aviv
Telephone: +972 3 692 1238
Fax: +972 3 696 0155

Israel Coding Association (ICA)

Address: Industry House, 29 Hamered Street, 61500 Tel Aviv
Telephone: +972 3 519 8839
Fax: +972 3 516 2082
E-mail: food@industry.org.il

Israel Dairy Board

Address: PO Box 20035, 14 Karlibach Street, 61200 Tel Aviv
Telephone: +972 3 561 9324
Fax: +972 3 561 6118
Year established: 1962
Activities: sector statistics: production, value, consumption, etc
Chief officers: Dalia Harel (Chairman), Zvi Reich (Executive Director)

Israel Diamond Manufacturers' Association
Address: 3 Jabotinsky Street, 52130 Ramat Gan
Telephone: +972 3 575 2483
Chief officers: Zvi Shur

Israel Export Institute
Address: P.O. Box 50084, 29 Hamered Street, 68125 Tel Aviv
Telephone: +972 3 514 2830
Fax: +972 3 514 2902
Activities: promotes the export sector and provides information about Israel's export capabilities, products and processes, and marketing and sales support; publishes a variety of catalogues of companies and their products by sector (e.g. software); sponsors trade fairs abroad to support its members' outreach to foreign markets; serves Israeli exporters with seminars, training programs and marketing assistance; its Business Opportunities Department supports a data service, PAMA, which matches foreign companies with suitable Israeli suppliers, contractors and/or manufacturers
Chief officers: Dan Meiri (Director of Agricultural and Equipment Machinery), Kinneret Ben-Amram (Executive Director of Cosmetics and Toiletries Department), Muli Flint (Director of Food Department), Mira Richman (Director of Healthcare and Biotechnology Department), Amnon Toren (Executive Director of the Plastics and Packaging Division)
Structure: Agricultural Equipment and Machinery Department, Building and Construction Department, Cosmetics and Toiletries Department, Food Department, Healthcare and Biotechnology Department, Plastics and Packaging Division, Marketing Division
Membership: importers and exporters

Israel Franchising and Distribution Association
Address: PO Box 3093, Herzeliya, 46590 Israel
Telephone: +972 9 576 631
Fax: +972 9 576 631
E-mail: emmers@netvision.net.il
Chief officers: Mike Emery (President)

Israel Groundnuts Production and Marketing Board
Address: 119 Hahashmona'im, Tel Aviv
Telephone: +972 3 561 0788
Fax: +972 3 561 6118

Israel Honey Board
Address: 121 Hahashmona'im, Tel Aviv
Telephone: +972 3 561 0395

Israel Hotel Association
Address: PO Box 50066, 29 Hamered Street, 61500 Tel Aviv
Telephone: +972 3 517 0131
Fax: +972 3 510 0197
E-mail: infotel@israelhotels.org.il
Web site: www.israelhotels.org.il/index.htm
Year established: 1962
Chief officers: Mickey Federman (Chairman), Avi Rosenthal (Executive Director)
Structure: 300 members
Publications:
• Hamionai (The Hotelier): *monthly*
• Hotel and Tourism Industry of Israel
• Israel Hotel Guide

Israel Insurance Association
Address: PO Box 2622, 65124 Tel Aviv
Telephone: +972 3 567 7333

Israel National Committee of International Dairy Federation
Address: P.O.Box 7083, c/o Central TNUVA Ltd, 61070 Tel Aviv
Telephone: +972 3 693 2543
Fax: +972 3 693 2719
Chief officers: Mr Z. Paikowsky (Secretary)

Israel Optics Products Importers' and Manufacturers' Association
Address: PO Box 5449, Haifa
Telephone: +972 4 862 6150

Israel Pharmaceutical Association
Address: 12 Levontin Street, 65112 Tel Aviv
Telephone: +972 3 566 1815
Fax: +972 3 560 5085
Year established: 1935
Chief officers: Howard Rice (Chairman)
Membership: 420 pharmacies

Israel Vegetable Growers' Organisation Ltd
Address: 8 Shaul Hamelech Boulevard, Tel Aviv
Telephone: +972 3 695 9311
Fax: +972 3 691 9176
Membership: fruit and vegetables producers and distributors

Israel Vinegrowers' Board
Address: 25 Carlebach, Tel Aviv
Telephone: +972 3 561 4416
Fax: +972 3 561 6872

Israeli Association of Software Houses
Address: Industry House, 29 Hamered Street, 68125 Tel Aviv
Telephone: +972 3 512 8863
Fax: +972 3 662 026
Chief officers: Arik Zur (Director)

Manufacturers' Association of Israel
Address: PO Box 50022, Industry House, 29 Hamered Street, 68125 Tel Aviv
Telephone: +972 3 512 8800
Fax: +972 3 516 2026/519 8770/519 8555
Activities: supports the various sectors of the industry in the following fields: regulatory affairs, quality control, price control, standards, government regulations and requirements, industry research by sector, vocational youth training; initiates and maintains contacts with organisations and institutes abroad
Chief officers: Mr Dan Proper (President), Mr Moshe Nahum (Director Department of Foreign Trade and International Relations), Mr Sima Amir (Investments and Industrial Cooperation), Mr Amnon Nadel (Director of Chemical and Pharmaceutical Division), Mr Baruch Sagiv (Director of the Textile Division), Mr Meir Bar (Furniture and Wood Products Division)
Structure: Chemical and Pharmaceuticals Division, Furniture and Wood Products Division, Metal Products Division, Textile Division
Membership: 100 members

Manufacturers' Association of Israel - (MAI) Chemical and Pharmaceutical Division
Address: P.O. Box 50022, 29 Hamered Street, 61500 Tel Aviv
Telephone: +972 3 512 8857/512 8858
Fax: +972 3 519 8718
E-mail: chemical@industry.org.il
Notes: See Manufacturers' Association of Israel.

Ministry of Industry and Trade, Centre for Business Promotion
Address: 8 King David St, 94101 Jerusalem
Telephone: +972 2 220 601
Fax: +972 2 236 303
E-mail: cbp_mit1@netvision.net.il
Web site: www.cbp.gov.il/Cbp/about.html
Chief officers: Noah Shani (Deputy Director General and Director)

National Association for Commerce in Israel
Address: 14 Ahad Haam, Haifa
Telephone: +972 4 862 1305

National Federation of Hotel Industry
Federation National de l'Industrie Hoteliere
Address: Tour Atlas Place Zallaqa, 20 000 Casablanca
Telephone: +972 2 319 083/447 270
Fax: +972 2 445 758
Activities: contributes to the promotion of the hotel and tourism industry; information, counselling, and assistance service; participates in the training of technicians and hotel executives; contributes in the cleaning up of the tourism environment
Chief officers: Mohamed Belghmi (President), Azzelarab Kettani (Secretary General)

Ornamental Plant Production and Marketing Board
Address: 2 Kaplan, Tel Aviv
Telephone: +972 3 691 8111
Fax: +972 3 695 9766

Vegetables Board of Israel
Address: PO Box 20130, 2 Karlibech Street, 67132 Tel Aviv
Telephone: +972 3 561 2711
Fax: +972 3 561 2717
Activities: collects statistics covering fresh vegetable consumption, local production, price/indexes, wholesale and retailing prices, revenue, etc

ITALY

National Federation of the Chemical Industry (FEDERCHIMICA)
Federazione Nazionale delle Industrie Chimiche
Address: Via Accademia 33, I-20131 Milan
Telephone: +39 2 268101
Fax: +39 2 26810310
Year established: 1945
Activities: government lobbying, co-ordination and information service
Chief officers: dott. Benito Benedini (President), dott. Guido Venturini (Director General)
Membership: sub-groups of specialist manufacturers including Gruppo Cosmetici Profumi e Prodotti di Igiene Personale (qv)
Publications:
● General Analysis with Statistical Data and Statistical Compendium: *the chemicals industry and the main chemical-consuming industries - twice a year*

Association for the Coffee, Spices and the Groceries Trade (ASSOCAF)
Associazione Commercio Caffe Droghe e Coloniali
Address: PO Box 1369, Via Caesarea 8, I-16100 Genoa
Telephone: +39 10 59 2161
Fax: +39 10 59 2161
Chief officers: Enrico Fantoni (President), Silvana Ruggiero (Secretary)

Association of Agricultural Produce Processing Companies (ASSI.TRA.PA)
Associazione Italiana Trasformatori Prodotti Agricoli
Address: Via Aureliana 53, I-00197 Rome
Telephone: +39 6 488 0708/487 3811
Fax: +39 6 488 0138
Year established: 1981
Chief officers: dott. Antonio Tenuta (President) , dott. Antonino Timpone(Vice President) dott. Roberto Rossi (Director)

Association of Beer and Malt Manufacturers (ASSOBIRRA)
Associazione Degli Industriali Della Birra e del Malto
Address: Via di Val Fiorita 90, 00144 Rome
Telephone: +39 6 543 932
Fax: +39 6 591 2910
E-mail: birra.viva@assobirra.it
Web site: www.assobirra.it
Web site notes: site includes the ASSOBIRRA Annual Report with data on production, consumption, imports and exports etc.
Year established: 1946
Activities: provides statistics on trade, production and price trends
Chief officers: dott.Rodolfo Peroni (President)dott. Aldo Bassetti (Director Genaral), dott. Daniele Rossi (Director)
Membership: 6 brewing and malt-producing firms
Publications:
● Annual Report: *review of the Italian beer sector with data on production, consumption, imports and exports etc. - annual*
● Birra e Malto: *includes statistics on beer and malt production, foreign trade, and prices with data for earlier periods - quarterly*

Association of Cotton, Linen and Related Fibres (ACI)
Associazione Cotoniera Liniera e delle Fibre Affini
Address: Viale Sarca 223, I-20126 Milan
Telephone: +39 2 661 03838/39
Fax: +39 2 661 03863/65
Year established: 1877
Chief officers: dott. Alberto Archetti (President): dott. Valerio Astolfi (Director General)
Publications:
● Industria Cotoniera: *commentary and statistics on the Italian cotton industry with information on production, prices, imports, exports, machinery used and productivity - 11 issues per year*
● Statistical Report on the Cotton and Linen Industries (Rapporto e Statistiche Industria Cotoniera e Liniera): *an appendix to the annual report contains statistics on production, imports, and exports with historical data in many tables. Some international data is also included - annual*

Association of Direct Marketing Agencies (ASSODIRECT)
Associazione delle Agenzie di Direct Marketing
Address: Via Larga 13, 20122 Milano, Piazza Borromeo 10, I-20123 Milan
Telephone: +39 2 861 725/583 05498
Fax: +39 2 890 0272/583 07642
Year established: 1984
Activities: co-ordinating study centre for direct marketing activities
Chief officers: dott. Ida Augusta Giuliano (President)
Membership: 20 direct marketing agencies
Publications:
● Filo Diretto col Consumatore

Association of Fruit and Vegetable Wholesalers (AGO)
Associazione Grossisti Ortofrutticoli
Address: Via Cesare Lombroso 54, I-20137 Milan
Telephone: +39 2 550 10310
Fax: +39 2 551 95614
Year established: 1945
Chief officers: dott. Giovanni Francesco Biffi (President), Liliana Gnaccarini (Secretary)
Membership: 157 fruit and vegetables wholesalers

Association of Italian Flour and Pasta Industries (ITALMOPA)
Associazione Industriali Mugnani e Pastai d'Italia
Address: Via dei Crociferi, 44, 00187 Roma
Telephone: +39 6 678 5409/679 4768
Fax: +39 6 678 3054
Year established: 1958
Chief officers: pof.Luigi Costato (President), dott. Vitali Fabrizio (Director)

Association of Italian Manufacturers of Chocolate/Sugar Confectionery, Ice-cream, Sweet Biscuits and Cakes (AIDI)
Associazione Industrie Dolciarie Italiane
Address: Via Barnaba Oriani, 92, 00197 Roma
Telephone: +39 6 807 5735/807 5643/807 5661
Fax: +39 6 807 3186
E-mail: aidi@foodarea.it
Web site: www.foodarea.it
Activities: collects statistics, co-ordinates trade fairs
Chief officers: dott. Gianfranco Faina (President), dott. Romano Chiavegatti (Director)
Membership: 100 Members
Publications:
● Report on the Italian Confectionery Industry (L'Industria Dolciaria Italiana): *production, consumption, imports, exports of chocolate confectionery, biscuits, baked goods - annual*

Association of Italian Rice Industries (AIRI)

Associazione Industrie Risiere Italiane
Address: Via Bernardino da Feltre, 6, 27100 Pavia
Telephone: +39 382 35375
Fax: +39 382 35376
Year established: 1964
Chief officers: Ing. Elio Scaramuzza (President) Dott. Robero Carriere (Director)
Membership: rice and rice products processors

Association of Petroleum Product Retailers (COMPETROL)

Commercianti Prodotti Petrolifieri
Address: c/o Confesercenti, Via Farini 5, I-00185 Rome
Telephone: +39 6 472 5
Fax: +39 6 474 6556
Year established: 1982
Chief officers: Renzo Tatini (President) , Paolo Piva (Secretary)

Association of Pharmaceutical Distributors (ADF)

Associazione Distributori Farmaceutici
Address: Via Milano 58, I-00184 Rome
Telephone: +39 6 487 0148
Fax: +39 6 482 8606
E-mail: adf.roma@agora.stm.it
Year established: 1987
Activities: collection of data
Chief officers: dott. Piero Navarro (President), Sergio Sparacio (Director)
Membership: 180 members
Publications:
• Il Quaderno della Distribuzione Farmaceutica: *Monthly*

Association of PR Agencies (ASSOREL)

Associazione Agenzie di Relazioni Pubbliche a Servizio Completo
Address: c/o Hill & Knowlton srl, Via Manzoni 38, I-20121 Milan
Telephone: +39 2 760 02276
Fax: +39 2 781 168
Year established: 1982
Chief officers: dott. Cesare Valli, (President) , ing. Giampaolo Doveri (Director General)

Association of the Italian Wine Industry

Unione Italiana Vini
Address: Via S Vittore al Teatro 3, I-20123 Milan
Telephone: +39 2 801 595
Fax: +39 2 866 226
E-mail: vinicolo@telemacus.it
Year established: 1895
Chief officers: dott. Vittorio V. Gancia (President), Pietro Cavigilia (Director General)
Membership: 13 regional offices
Publications:
• Corriere Vinicolo: *weekly*

Association of Tobacco Processors (APTI)

Associazione Professionale Trasformatori Tabacchi Italiani
Address: Via Collina 48, 00187 Rome
Telephone: +39 6 482 7770/474 4886
Fax: +39 6 482 7767
Year established: 1946
Chief officers: avv. Rinaldo Chidichimo (President), dott. Fabio Parboni (Director General)

Confederation of Italian Industry (CONFINDUSTRIA)

Confederazione Generale dell'Industria Italiana
Address: Viale dell'Astronomia 30, I-00144 Rome
Telephone: +39 6 590 31
Fax: +39 6 591 9615
Web site: www.confindustria.it
Year established: 1972
Activities: produces the "Statistiche del Commercio Estero dell'Italia" an online service giving import and export data on a range of products; regular updates; available via the host system GIANO
Chief officers: dott. Giorgio Fossa (President), prof. Innocenzo Cipoletta (Director General)
Publications:
• Small Business Journal (Gazzetta della Piccola Industria): *produced for the Comitato Nazionale Piccola Industria (National Committee for Small Businesses - part of CONFINDUSTRIA) - monthly*
Notes: 21 regional officers also Brussels office at: Ave de la Joyeuse Entrée 1 (bte 11), B-1040.

Federation of Distribution Companies (Faid Federdistribuzione)

Federazione Associazioni Imprese Distribuzione
Address: Corso di Porta Nuova 3, 20121 Milan
Telephone: +39 2 653 333/654 656
Fax: +39 2 655 1169
Year established: 1973
Chief officers: dott. Livignol Buttignol (President), dott. Cesare Motta (Secretary General)
Structure: federation of national associations
Membership: various retailer associations with a total of 3,500 sales outlets including: AISA (Associazione Italiana Supermercati Alimentari) (supermarkets); AICID (Associazione Italiana Commercio Imprenditoriale al Dettaglio); ANADIS (Associazione Nazionale Aziende di Distribuzione Specialistica a Succursali) (specialist chain stores); AICC (Associazione Italiana Centri Commerciali) (shopping centres); ADIS (Associazione Distribuzione Ingrosso a Self-Service) (cash and carry); AVEDISCO (Associazione Nazionale Vendite Dirette Servizio Consumatori) (direct selling of consumer services); AIF (Associazione Italiana del Franchising); ANVED (Associazione Nazionale Vendite per Corrispondenza e a Distanza) (mail order companies)
Publications:
• Statistics (FAID) (Annuario Statistico): *statistics on large retailers in Italy including: number of outlets; annual sales and selling space. Includes information on hyper-markets, supermarkets, and superstores. Based largely on an analysis of official data - annual*

Federation of Italian Jewellery Manufacturers and Wholesalers (CONFEDORAFI)

Unione Italiana delle Federazioni di Associazioni Nazionali di Categoria tra Industriali, Artigiani, Commercianti all'ingrosso, Commercianti Rappresentanti ed Agenti di Commercio in Oreficeria, Gioielleria, Argenteria, Orologeria, Metalli Preziosi
Address: Via Tancredi 8, 00162 Rome
Telephone: +39 6 442 36586/442 36726
Fax: +39 6 442 35981
Web site: www.confedorafi.com
Year established: 1946
Activities: represents the entire Italian gold and silver sector to international, national and local organisations; organises professional training, works closely with major Italian trade fairs and promotion boards for gold, platinum and diamonds
Chief officers: Emanuele de Giovanni (President), Claudio Tommasini (Director)
Membership: associations of jewellery traders, manufacturers and craftsmen: Assocoral, Associazione Orafa Valenzana, Federbanchi, Federgrossisti, Federpietre, Federdettaglianti, Federargentieri, Fedorafi, Federappresentanti

Publications:
• Primapagina Confedorafi: *every two months*

Federation of Mineral Water and Soft Drinks Manufacturers (MINERACQUA)

Federazione delle Industrie delle Acque Minerali e delle Bevande Analcooliche
Address: Via delle Tre Madonne, 12, 00197 Roma
Telephone: +39 6 807 9950/807 9969
Fax: +39 6 807 9946
Year established: 1990
Activities: data collection and analysis on production, consumption, imports and exports
Chief officers: dott. Ettore Fortuna (President), dott. Pierangelo Grippo (General Director)
Notes: No publications produced.

Federation of Textile and Clothing Industry Associations (FEDERTESSILE)

Federazione fra le Associazioni delle Industrie Tessili e Abbligliamento
Address: Vie Sarca 223, I-20126 Milan
Telephone: +39 2 661 034 40
Fax: +39 2 661 034 55
Year established: 1975
Chief officers: Angelo Pavia (President), dott. Alfredo Ciampini (Secretary General)

Food and Tobacco Federation (FAT CISL)

Federazione Alimentazione e Tabbaco
Address: Via Milazzo 23, I-00185 Rome
Telephone: +39 6 494 1293
Fax: +39 6 446 9750
Year established: 1951
Membership: convenience store proprietors (20 regional offices)

Italian Association of Advertising Agencies (ASSAP)

Associazione Italiana Agenzie Pubblicità a Servizio Completo
Address: Via Larga 19, 20122 Milan
Telephone: +39 2 583 07450
Fax: +39 2 583 07147
E-mail: informazioni@assap.it
Web site: www.assap.it
Year established: 1949
Activities: consultancy; legal; press relations; past campaigns and clients database; price lists; education and training, monthly analysis of advertising expenditure
Chief officers: Alberto Contri (President) , dott. Fidelio Perchinelli (Director General)
Membership: 54 Advertising Agencies
Notes: No publications produced.

Italian Association of Automotive Servicing Equipment Manufacturers (AICA)

Associazione Italiana Costruttori Autoattrezzature
Address: Via A G Ragazzi 9, I-40011 Anzola Dell'Emilia (BO)
Telephone: +39 51 733 000
Fax: +39 51 731 886
Year established: 1976
Chief officers: Giorgio Cometti (President) , dott. Renzo Servadei (Secretary General)
Membership: 105 automotive servicing equipment manufacturers

Italian Association of Beer and Malt Technicians

Associazione Italiana Tecnici Birra e Malto
Address: Via Trento 79, I-32034 Pedavena
Telephone: +39 431 60634
Fax: +39 431 60634
Year established: 1959
Activities: conferences, meetings, visits to breweries and related industries
Chief officers: Tullio Zangrando (Director)
Membership: 120 individuals (brewing industry)
Publications:
• Beer and Malt (Birra e Malto): *brewing technology, new equipment and market news - 3 p.a.*

Italian Association of Edible Oil Producers (ASSITOL)

Associazione Italiana dell'Industria Olearia
Address: Ascat Assitol, Piazza di Campitelli, 6, 00186 Roma
Telephone: +39 6 699 40058
Fax: +39 6 699 40118
E-mail: assitol@foodarea.it
Year established: 1972
Chief officers: dott. Demetrio Corno (President), dott. Giorgio Cilenti
Membership: producers, refiners and exporters of olive, vegetable and animal oils and fats as well as manufacturers of packaging for the industry

Italian Association of Food Product Manufacturers (AIIPA)

Associazione Italiana Industriali Prodotti Alimentari
Address: Ascat Aiipa, Corso di Porta Nuova, 34, I-20121 Milan
Telephone: +39 2 654 184
Fax: +39 2 654 822
Year established: 1945
Chief officers: Ms Franca Peron, Dott.Emilio Lavazza (President) Dott. Giovanni Franco Crippa (Director)
Structure: Chips and Snacks Division, Camomile Tea and Herbal Infusions Division, Cereals Division, Yeast Division, Mayonnaise, Sauces and Ketchup Division, Delicatessen Food Division, Spices, Herbs and Aromatic Plants Division, Sauces and Seasoning Products Division, Pre-cooked and Fast Food Division
Publications:
• Italian Foreign Trade of Horticulture and Fresh Products Manufacturers (Il Commercio Estero Italiano dei Prodotti Ortofrutticoli Trasformati): *Export Statistics - annual*
Notes: Member of the Federation of the Associations of EU Frozen Food Producers (FAFPAS) based in Brussels (Belgium).

Italian Association of Leather and Leather Substitute Manufacturers (AIMPES)

Associazione Italiana Manifatturieri Pelli e Succedanei
Address: Corso Italia 17, I-20122 Milan
Telephone: +39 2 890 10020
Fax: +39 2 890 10345
E-mail: aimpes.mipel@iol.it
Year established: 1966

Italian Association of Milk and Cheese Producers (ASSOLATTE)

Associazione Italiana Lattiero-Casearia
Address: Corsa di Porta Romana 2, 20122 Milan
Telephone: +39 2 720 21817/720 21867
Fax: +39 2 720 21838
Year established: 1945
Activities: compiles production, price, import and export statistics for the Italian dairy industry (published in the Annual Report)

Chief officers: Avv. Adriano Hribal (President/Director General)
Publications:
• Annual Report (Associazione Italiana Lattiero Casearia) (Relazione Annuale): *annual data, with figures for previous years, for milk and milk products covering domestic production and foreign trade. Based largely on data collected by the Association with some data from central government and international sources - annual*
• Milk Industry World (Il Mondo del Latte): *imports and exports of milk and milk products with data for the latest month and some earlier months. Based on an analysis of official trade statistics - monthly*

Italian Association of Producers and Distributors of Natural Health Products (PRO.SA.NA.)

Associazione Italiana Produttori e Distributori di Sostanze e Prodotti Salutistici Naturali
Address: Corso Venezia 47/49, I - 20121 Milan
Telephone: +39 2 775 0575
Fax: +39 2 775 0480
Web site: www.ehpm.org/members/prosana.htm
Web site notes: site includes links to members web sites
Year established: 1991
Activities: government liaison, information and guidance to members regarding labelling, legal and regulatory assistance; promotion of health products
Chief officers: Carlo Zonato (President), Rinaldo Canofari (General Secretary)
Structure: President, Vice President, Board of Directors, General Secretary
Membership: manufacturers, distributors and importers of dietetic products, food supplements, herbal health products and natural cosmetics
Publications:
• Newsletter: *latest news and market developments in the natural health products sector - monthly*

Italian Association of Soft Drinks Manufacturers (ASSOBIBE)

Associazione Italiana fra gli industriali delle Bevande Analcoliche
Address: Viale Umberto Tupini 103, I-00144 Rome
Telephone: +39 6 592 4668/591 8891
Fax: +39 6 592 4751/592 4751
Year established: 1987
Chief officers: dott. Giuseppe Turrin (President), Avv. Gianluca Volpi (Director General)
Membership: non-alcoholic drinks manufacturers

Italian Association of Toy Manufacturers (ASSOGIOCATTOLI)

Associazione Italiana Fabbricanti Giocattoli, Giochi, Hobby e Modellismo, Ornamentali Natalizi ed Articoli per la Prima Infanzia
Address: Via Petitti, 16, 20149 Milan
Telephone: +39 2 324 846
Fax: +39 2 330 03819
Year established: 1945
Chief officers: dott. Gianluca Perego (President), dott. Umberto Maltagliati (Director General)

Italian Banking Association (ABI)

Associazione Bancaria Italiana
Address: Piazza del Gesu 49, 00186 Rome
Telephone: +39 6 67671
Fax: +39 6 767457
E-mail: mc0469@mclink.it
Year established: 1919
Chief officers: dott. Bianchi Tancredi (President), dott. Giuseppe Zadra (Director General)
Membership: public credit institutions, big commercial banks, private banks and bankers, cooperative banks, savings banks, foreign bank branches, bank associations
Publications:
• Bancaria: *monthly*
• Lettera Marketing

Italian Booksellers' Association (ALI)

Associazione Librai Italiani
Address: Via Nizza 22, 00198 Rome
Telephone: +39 6 853 019
Fax: +39 6 853 01975
Year established: 1946
Chief officers: dott. Francesco Flaccovio (President), Francesco Fiorani (Secretary General)
Membership: book retailers
Publications:
• L'Informatore Librario Solathia
Notes: No publications produced.

Italian Clothing and Hosiery Manufacturers' Association (MODAINDUSTRIA)

Associazione Italiana Industriali Abbigliamento e della Magliera
Address: Viale Sarca 223, 20126 Milan
Telephone: +39 2 661 03566
Fax: +39 2 661 03667
E-mail: promoda@modaindustria.it/ecomomic@modaindustria.it
Web site: www.modaindustria.it
Year established: 1945
Chief officers: dott. Vittorio Giulini (President) , dott. Gaetano Marzotto (Vice President)
Publications:
• Conjectural Review (Indicatori Congiunturali): *general statistics on the textiles and clothing sector in Italy including data on production and foreign trade - ten issues a year*
• Newsletter (Notiziario): *weekly*

Italian Commerce and Tourism Confederation (CONFCOMMERCIO)

Confederazione Generale Italiana del Commercio e del Turismo
Address: Piazza GG Belli 2, I-00153 Rome
Telephone: +39 6 586 6244/6208
Fax: +39 6 588 2550
Chief officers: Francesco Colucci (President)
Membership: groups together various Italian professional federations and associations from the commercial sector of tourism

Italian Committee of the International Dairy Federation

Comitato Italiano della FIL-IDF
Address: 2, C. di Porta Romana, I- 20100 Milano
Telephone: +39 2 720 011 95
Fax: +39 2 720 010 65
Chief officers: Dr C. Emaldi (Secretary)

Italian Editors' Association (AIE)

Associazione Italiana Editori
Address: Via delle Erbe 2, I-20121 Milan
Telephone: +39 2 864 63091/62342
Fax: +39 2 890 10863
Year established: 1869
Chief officers: Mr G Merlini (President), Mr I Cecchini (Director), Mrs G Mursia (General Secretary)
Membership: book publishers

Italian Federation of Bakers and Pastry Cooks (FIPPA)

Federazione Italiana Panificatori, Panificatori-Pasticceri ed Affini
Address: Via Alessandria 159/D, 00198 Rome
Telephone: +39 6 854 7261

Fax: +39 6 853 51968
E-mail: fippa1@pronet.it
Year established: 1946
Chief officers: Antonio Marinoni (President),
Membership: bakers and confectioners
Notes: The Association does not produce any publications.

Italian Federation of Building Materials (FEDERMACO)
Federazione Italiana dei Materiali Costruzione
Address: Via di S. Teresa 23, 00198 Rome
Telephone: +39 2 855 4314
Fax: +39 2 841 6176
Year established: 1994
Chief officers: Alessandro Buzzi (President) , dott. Raffaella Di Ciccio (Secretary)
Membership: construction materials manufacturers and wholesalers
Notes: No publications produced.

Italian Federation of Furniture Traders (FEDERMOBILI)
Federazione Nazionale Commercianti Mobili
Address: Corso Venezia 49, 20121 Milan
Telephone: +39 2 775 0272
Fax: +39 2 775 0480
Chief officers: dott. Enrico Pirovano (President), Sergio Lolli (General Director)
Membership: furniture wholesalers and retailers

Italian Federation of Goldsmiths, Jewellery and Silver Retailers and Wholesalers (FEDERGROSSISTI)
Federazione Nazionale Commercianti Grossisti Orafi Gioiellieri Argentieri
Address: Via S. Baldacchini 11, 80133 Naples
Telephone: +39 81 287 266
Fax: +39 81 287 461
Year established: 1971
Chief officers: dott. Gaetano Cavalieri (President), cav. rag. Francesco Siciliani (General Secretary)
Membership: jewellery traders, wholesalers, gold and silversmiths
Notes: No publications produced.

Italian Federation of Soft Drinks Wholesalers (ITALGROB)
Federazione Italiana Grossisti Distributori Bevande
Address: Corso Venezia 49, 20121 Milano
Telephone: +39 2 775 0447
Fax: +39 2 760 14392

Italian Federation of Travel Operators (FIAVET)
Federazione Italiana delle Imprese Viaggi e Turismo
Address: Via Livenza 7, 00198 Rome
Telephone: +39 6 854 3246
Fax: +39 6 854 0062
Year established: 1961
Chief officers: Alis Maccarini (President), Nino Alinovi (General Secretary)
Membership: travel and tourism companies
Notes: No publications produced.

Italian Federation of Tyre Retailers (FEDERPNEUS)
Federazione Nazionale Rivenditori Specialisti di Pneumatici
Address: Via AG Ragazzi 9, 40011 Anzola Emilia
Telephone: +39 51 733 000
Fax: +39 51 731 886
E-mail: fedpneus@iperbole.bologna.it
Year established: 1970
Activities: trade representation, data research, consultancy
Chief officers: dott. Guido schiavon (President), Renzo

Servadei (General Secretary)
Membership: 600 companies; specialised tyre dealers and their suppliers
Publications:
• Tyre Magazine (Pneurama Magazine): *bi-monthly*

Italian Federation of Wine, Spirits, Syrups and Vinegar, Manufacturers, Importers and Exporters (FEDERVINI)
Federazione Italiana Industriali Produttori Esportatori ed Importatori di Vini, Acquaviti, Liquori, Sciroppi, Aceti ed Affini
Address: Ascat Federvini, Via Mentana, 2/B, 00185 Roma
Telephone: +39 6 446 9421/494 1630
Fax: +39 6 494 1566
Year established: 1944
Chief officers: Conte Luigi Rossi di Montelera (President), dott. Federico Castellucci (Director General)
Membership: producers, exporters and importers, of wine, fortified wines, vermouth, sparkling wines, spirits, acquaviti, syrups and vinegar

Italian Food Industry Federation (FEDERALIMENTARE)
Federazione Italiana dell'Industria Alimentare
Address: c/o Confindustria, Viale dell'Astronomia 30, I-00144 Rome
Telephone: +39 6 59031
Fax: +39 6 590 3342
Web site: www.fiere.parma.it:80/cibus/gb/EPAFEFD1.htm
Chief officers: Gianfranco Carlone (Chairman), Dr. Giuseppe Villani (Research), dott. Raffaella Maroncelli (Director)
Notes: The Federation consists of the following associations: Associazione Italiana Industriali Prodotti Alimentari (AIIPA), Associazione degli Industriali Mugnai e Pastai d'Italia (ITALMOPA), Unione Industriali Pastai Italiani (UNIPI), Associazione Industrie Risiere Italiane (AIRI), Associazione Industrie Dolciarie Italiane (AIDI), Associazione degli Industriali delle Carni (ASSICA), Associazione Italiana Lattiero Casearia (ASSOLATTE), Unione Nazionale dell'Avicoltura (UNA), Associazione Nazionale Conservieri Ittici e delle Tonnare (PESCACONSERVE), Associazione Nazionale Industriali Conserve Alimentari Vegetali (ANICAV), Associazione Italiana dell'Industria Olearia (ASSITOL), Associazione Nazionale tra i Produttori di Alimenti Zootecnici (ASSALZOO), Associazione Nazionale fra gli Industriali dello Zucchero, dell'Alcool e del Lievito (ASSOZUCCHERO), Federazione Italiana Industriali Produttori Esportatori ed Importatori di Vini, Acquaviti, Liquori, Sciroppi, Aceti ed Affini (FEDERVINI), Associazione degli Industriali della Birra e del Malto (ASSOBIRRA) e Associazione Italiana fra gli Industriali delle Bevande Analcooliche (ASSOBIBE), nonchè dalla Federazione delle Industrie delle Acque Minerali e delle Bevande Analcooliche (MINERACQUA).

Italian Franchising Association (ASSOFRANCHISING)
Associazione Italiana del Franchising
Address: Corso di Porta Nuova 3, I-20121 Milan
Telephone: +39 2 290 03779
Fax: +39 2 655 1169
Year established: 1971
Chief officers: dott. Nicola Fabbri (President), dott. Michele Scardi (Secretary General)
Membership: ca. 70 individuals, 50 franchise companies
Publications:
• Associazione Italiana Franchising News
• Directory of Italian Franchising: *annual*
• Franchising Journal (Il Giornale del Franchising): *quarterly*

Italian Frozen Food Institute (IIAS)

Istituto Italiano Alimenti Surgelati
Address: Via Firenze 32, Rome
Telephone: +39 6 487 740
Fax: +39 6 486 755
Publications:
• Annual Report: *statistics on consumption and retail sales of frozen food by type. Includes data by both volume and value - annual*

Italian Furs Association (AIP)

Associazione Italiana della Pellicceria
Address: Corso Venezia 49, 20121 Milan
Telephone: +39 2 775 0311
Fax: +39 2 760 21349
Year established: 1949
Chief officers: Giuseppe Balducci (President) , dott. Alessandra Dagnino (Secretary)

Italian Investment Banking Association (AIFI)

Associazione Italiana delle Finanziarie d'Investimento
Address: Via Cornaggia 10, I-20123 Milan
Telephone: +39 2 805 5901
Fax: +39 2 805 5926
Year established: 1986
Chief officers: prof. dott. Marco Vitale (President) , prof Anna Gervasoni (Secretary General)

Italian Newspapers Editors' Federation (FIEG)

Federazione Italiana Editori Giornale
Address: Via Piemonte 64, 00187 Rome
Telephone: +39 6 488 1683
Fax: +39 6 487 1109
E-mail: fiegroma@iol.it
Activities: promotes sales of member newspapers
Chief officers: dott. Giovanni Giovannini (President), dott. Sebastiono Sortino (Director General)
Membership: newspaper editors
Publications:
• Editor (L'Editore): *monthly*

Italian Oenologists' and Winetechnicians' Association (AEI)

Associazione Enologi Enotecnici Italiani
Address: Viale Murillo 17, 20149 Milan
Telephone: +39 2 400 72460
Fax: +39 2 487 04951
Year established: 1891
Activities: provides technical and legal information on the viti- and viniculture sector; keeps members up to date with latest scientific and technical developments
Chief officers: Pietro Pittaro (President) , dott. Giuseppe Martelli (Director)
Publications:
• Enotecnico: *10 p.a.*

Italian Packaging Institute

Istituto Italiano Imballaggio
Address: Via Cosimo del Fante 10, 20122 Milan
Telephone: +39 2 583 19624
Fax: +39 2 583 9677
Membership: Italian packaging maufacturers
Publications:
• Packaging Figures (Imballaggio in Cifre): *volume and value statistics on the Italian packaging industry by sector and by type of packaging - annual*

Italian Paper, Cardboard and Pulp Association (ASSOCARTA)

Associazione Italiana Industriali della Carta, Cartoni e Paste per Carta
Address: Bastioni di Porta Volta, 7, 20121 Milan
Telephone: +39 2 290 03018
Fax: +39 2 290 03369
Year established: 1962
Chief officers: ing. Giuseppe Fedrigoni (President), Roberto Taranto (Secretary General)
Membership: about 100 members
Publications:
• L'Industria della Carta: *the italian paper industry*

Italian Pasta Makers' Union (UNIPI)

Unione Industriali Pastai Italiani
Address: Ascat Unipi, Via Po 102, 00198 Rome
Telephone: +39 6 854 3291/841 6473
Fax: +39 6 841 5132
E-mail: unipi@foodarea.it
Year established: 1968
Chief officers: Giseppe Menconi (President), Raffaello Ragaglini (General Director)
Membership: pasta manufacturers

Italian Pharmacists Federation (FOFI)

Federazione Ordini Farmacisti Italiani
Address: Via Palestro 75, 00185 Rome
Telephone: +39 6 445 0361/445 362
Fax: +39 6 494 1093
Year established: 1946
Chief officers: dott. Giacomo Leopardi (President)
Membership: pharmacy owners
Publications:
• Federfarma Notizie: *weekly*

Italian Pharmacists' Federation (FOFI)

Federazione Ordini Farmacisti Italiani
Address: Via Palestro 75, I-00192 Rome
Telephone: +39 6 445 0361/445 0362
Fax: +39 6 494 1093
Year established: 1946
Chief officers: dott. Giacomo Leopardi (President) , dott. Antonio Mastroianni (Director)
Membership: pharmacists organisations and retailers
Publications:
• Il Giornale dei Farmacisti: *fortnightly*

Italian Phonographic Association (AFI)

Associazione dei Fonografici Italiani
Address: Via Vittor Pisani, 10, 20124 Milano
Telephone: +39 2 669 6263
Fax: +39 2 670 5059
Year established: 1948
Chief officers: Franco Donato (President),

Italian Professional Association of Tobacco Processors (APTI)

Associazione Professionale Trasformati Tabacchi Italiani
Address: Via Collina 48, 4 piano, 00187 Rome
Telephone: +39 6 482 7770
Fax: +39 6 482 7767
Year established: 1946
Chief officers: Dott, Fabio Parboni (Director General), Rinaldo Chidicino (President)
Notes: No publications produced

Italian Public Relations Federation (FERPI)
Federazione Relazioni Pubbliche Italiana
Address: Corso Vittorio Emanuele 37/B pal. del Toro, I-20122 Milan
Telephone: +39 2 760 21039
Fax: +39 2 781 537
Year established: 1970
Chief officers: dott. Claudio Maffei (President), dott. Serenella Salgarelli (General Secretary)

Italian Tobacconists' Federation (FIT)
Federazione Italiana Tabaccai
Address: Via Leopoldo Serra 32, I-00153 Rome
Telephone: +39 6 589 7151-4
Fax: +39 6 855 1439
Chief officers: Franco Ragni (President) , dott. Sergio Baronci (General Secretary)
Membership: retail tobacconists
Publications:
● La Voce del Tabaccaio

Italian Union of Beef Producers' Associations (UNICAB)
Unione Italiana Associazioni Produttori Carni Bovine
Address: Lungotevere Michelangelo 9, 00192 Rome
Telephone: +39 6 361 2441
Fax: +39 6 361 2892
Year established: 1989
Chief officers: Delfo Cavallini (President), dott. Renzon Fossato (Secretary General)
Membership: beef cattle producers
Notes: No publications produced

Italian Vending Machines' Association (ANIDA)
Associazione Nazionale Distributori Automatici
Address: Viale Zara 9, 20159 Milan
Telephone: +39 2 689 8014/689 9333
Fax: +39 2 689 9308
Year established: 1968
Chief officers: dott. Ettore Marzolo (President), dott.ssa Barbara Bassi (General Secretary)
Membership: vending machine operators and suppliers
Notes: No publications produced.

Meat Industries' Association (ASSICA)
Associazione degli Industriali delle Carni
Address: Ascat Assica, Strada 4 - Palazzo Q8 - Milanofiori, 20089 Rozzano (MI)
Telephone: +39 2 575 10257
Fax: +39 2 575 10607
Year established: 1946
Chief officers: Dott. Giuseppe Villani (President), dott. Gianni Gorreri (Director General)
Membership: meat processors
Publications:
● Meat Industry (L'Industria delle Carni): *fortnightly*

Media Buyers Agencies' Association (ACP)
Associazione Concessionarie Pubblicità
Address: Corso Venezia 51, I-20121 Milan
Telephone: +39 2 794 961
Fax: +39 2 780 368
Year established: 1951
Chief officers: dott. Giuliano Re (President) , Franco Rotta (Secretary)
Membership: 24 associations

National Association for Cycles, Motorcycles and Accessories (ANCMA)
Associazione Nazionale Ciclo Motociclo e Accessori
Address: Via Mauro Macchi 32, 20124 Milan
Telephone: +39 2 669 81818
Fax: +39 2 669 82072
Year established: 1920
Chief officers: dott. Costatino Ruggiero (General Secretary), dott. Claudio Castiglioni (President)
Membership: 200 manufacturers and suppliers of bicycle and motorcycle accessories
Publications:
● Annuario ANCMA: *Italian Motorcycle Industry and Accessories - annual*
● Notizario ANCMA: *bi-monthly*

National Association for Electronic Distribution (ASSODEL)
Associazione Nazionale Distribuzione Elettronica
Address: Via Alghero 20, 20128 Milan
Telephone: +39 2 255 2600/255 0207
Fax: +39 2 255 3094
Telex: 334022
E-mail: laura@visto.it
Web site: www.visto.it
Year established: 1985
Chief officers: Paolo Stefanelli (President), Cristina Lombardi (Secretary General)
Membership: 800 distributors of electronics products
Publications:
● A&V Elettronica (Buying and Selling Electronics): *Italian Electronic Trading - monthly*

National Association of Banks
Associazione Nazionale fra le Banche Popolari
Address: Via Nazionale 230, I-00184 Rome
Telephone: +39 6 488 4444/488 4445
Fax: +39 6 488 4447
Chief officers: dott. Aniceto Vittorio Ranieri (President), dott. Giorgio Carducci (Director General)

National Association of Beer Importers (GIBE)
Gruppo Importatori Importatori Birre Estere
Address: Corso Venezia 47-49, 20121 Milan
Telephone: +39 2 775 01/775 0320
Fax: +39 2 775 0329/760 05543
E-mail: ance.italy@iol.it
Year established: 1983
Chief officers: dott. Piero Piccardi (President), dott. Italo Bussoli (Secretary General)
Membership: foreign beer importers

National Association of Car Manufacturers (ANFIA)
Associazione Nazionale fra Industrie Automobilistiche
Address: Corso Galileo Ferraris 61, 10128 Turin
Telephone: +39 11 554 6511
Fax: +39 11 545 986
Year established: 1912
Chief officers: dott. Piero Fusaro (President), dott. Emilio di Camillo (Director General)
Membership: 229 companies in the automotives industry
Publications:
● Automobile Figures (Automobile in Cifre): *data on motor vehicle production, sales, registration by make and model with additional information on imports and exports and a regional analysis; a summary of historical tables is also included - annual*
● Statistical Review (ANFIA) (Notizario Statistico): *regular statistics on motor vehicle production, sales, registrations - monthly*

National Association of Cereal Producers

Associazione Nazionale Cerealisti
Address: Via Po 102, 00198 Rome
Telephone: +39 6 884 0296
Fax: +39 6 884 0877
Year established: 1946
Chief officers: dott. Romano Venturi (President) , dott. Lorenzo Fineschi (Director)
Membership: cereal manufacturers
Notes: No publications produced.

National Association of Cinematography and Audiovisual Industries (ANICA)

Associazione Nazionale Industrie Cinematografiche ed Audiovisive
Address: Viale Regina Margherita 286, 00198 Rome
Telephone: +39 6 442 5961
Fax: +39 6 440 4128
Year established: 1944
Chief officers: comm. Carmine Cianfarani (President), Andrea Marcotulli (General Director)
Publications:
• Cinema Industry Statistics (Statistiche dell'Industria Cinematografica): *published annually in the trade journal "Cinema d'oggi" and covering the production and imports of films, costs of production, and the origins of imported films - annual*

National Association of Exporters and Importers of Fruit, Vegetables and Citrus Fruits (ANEIOA)

Associazione Nazionale Esportatori Importatori Ortofrutticoli e Agrumari
Address: Via Sabotino 46, 00195 Rome
Telephone: +39 6 375 16721/375 15147
Fax: +39 6 384 128/372 3659
E-mail: aneioa@mail.nexus.it
Year established: 1949
Activities: disseminates information
Chief officers: Giuseppe Calcagni (President), rag. Franco Solidoro (Director)
Membership: importers, exporters, retailers and processors of fruit and vegetables
Publications:
• Bollettino Settimanale d'Informazione ANEIOA (Weekly News Bulletin ANEIOA): *Trade news - weekly*

National Association of Fertiliser Manufacturers (ASSOFERTILIZANTI)

Associazione Nazionale Produttori Fertilizanti
Address: Via Tomacelli 132, I-00186 Rome
Telephone: +39 6 687 8683
Fax: +39 6 687 8337/688 04829
Year established: 1985
Chief officers: dott. Cesare Puccione (President), dott. Narciso Salvo (Director)
Membership: producers of fertilisers

National Association of Fish Canneries (ANCIT)

Associazione Nazionale Conservieri Ittici e delle Tonnare
Address: Corso di Porta Nuova 34, 20121 Milano
Telephone: +39 2 655 1938
Fax: +39 2 659 0977
Year established: 1965
Chief officers: dott. Sergio Luoni (President)
Notes: No publications produced

National Association of Fish Processors, Importers and Exporters (ANTIEPI)

Associazione Nazionale Trasformatori, Importatori, Esportatori Prodotti Ittici
Address: Corso Venezia 47-49, 20121 Milan
Telephone: +39 2 775 0320
Fax: +39 2 760 05543
Year established: 1965
Chief officers: dott. Mario Seno (President), dott. Italo Bussoli (General Secretary)
Notes: No publications produced

National Association of Food Manufacturers

Associazione Nazionale dei Produttori di Alimenti Vari
Address: Via San Giovanni in Laterano 152, 00184 Rome
Telephone: +39 6 703 741
Fax: +39 6 704 54320
Year established: 1991
Chief officers: Luciano Lauteri (President)

National Association of Glass Manufacturers (ASSOVETRO)

Associazione Natizionale Degli Industriali del Vetro
Address: Via Bissolati 76, 00187 Rome
Telephone: +39 6 488 0947/487 11301
Fax: +39 6 488 5683
Year established: 1946
Activities: collects statistical data on production and trade
Chief officers: dott. Franco Todisco (President), dott Claudio Riccioni (Director)
Membership: Glass manufacturers
Notes: No publications produced.

National Association of Household Cleaning Products (ASSOCASA)

Associazione Nazionale Fabbricanti Prodotti per la Casa
Address: Via Accademia 33, I-2013 Milan
Telephone: +39 2 268 10235
Fax: +39 2 268 10320
Year established: 1984
Activities: Production of statistics
Chief officers: dott. Arturo Sutter (President), dott. Francesco Pedilarco (Director)

National Association of Importers of Preserved Fish Products (ANIPESCA)

Associazione Nazionale Importatori Prodotti della Pesca Conservati
Address: Via Giuseppe Avezzana 45, 00195 Rome
Telephone: +39 6 360 02889
Fax: +39 6 323 0536
Year established: 1947
Chief officers: dott. Antonello La Rocca (President), dott. Antonio Mignone (Director)
Membership: importers and distributors of canned and preserved fish products
Notes: No publications produced.

National Association of Italian Perfume Wholesalers (ANGIP)

Associazione Nazionale Grossisti Italiani Profumeria
Address: Lungotevere Portuense 158, 00153 Rome
Telephone: +39 6 581 4347
Fax: +39 6 589 4889
Chief officers: dott. Luciano Lazzari (President), dott Giorgio Giordano (National Secretary)
Membership: perfume wholesalers

National Association of Italian Shoe Manufacturers (ANCI)

Associazione Nazionale Calzaturifici Italiani
Address: Via Dogana 1, 20123 Milan
Telephone: +39 2 809 721
Fax: +39 2 720 20112
Year established: 1945
Chief officers: Pizzuti Maurizio (President) , dott. Leonardo Soana (Director)

National Association of Mail Order Companies (ANVED)

Associazione Nazionale Vendite per Corrrispondenza e a Distanza
Address: Via Melchiorre Gioia 70, 20125 Milan
Telephone: +39 2 688 4525/668 2464
Fax: +39 2 688 4525
Activities: production of statistics
Membership: Mail order companies
Publications:
• Annual Review ANVED (Relazione Annuale): *statistics on the Italian mail order market. Includes data on sales by value, as well as by sector and sub-sector - annual*

National Association of Optical Goods' Manufacturers (ANFAO)

Associazione Nazionale Fabbricanti Articoli Ottici
Address: Via Pettiti 16, 20149 Milan
Telephone: +39 2 324 846
Fax: +39 2 330 03819
Year established: 1954
Chief officers: dott. Leonardo Del Vecchio (President), dott. Umberto Maltagliati (Director General)
Membership: optical equipment manufacturers
Notes: No publications produced.

National Association of Pet Food and Animal Feed Manuafacturers and Producers (ASSALZOO)

Associazione Nazionale tra i Produttori di Alimenti Zootecnici
Address: Via Lovanio, 6, 00198 Roma
Telephone: +39 06 854 1641
Fax: +39 06 854 164
Year established: 1945
Activities: organises a trade fair called Zoomark in April each year; produces market reports for members
Chief officers: dott. Giordano Veronesi (President), dott. Emilio Minetti (Director General)
Notes: The asociation also has an office in Milan at:20123 Milano Vicolo 5, Maria Alla Porta 1 Tel: 02-871655 Fax: 02-8690180

National Association of Preserved Vegetable Industries (ANICAV)

Associazione Nazionale Industriali Conserve Alimentari Vegetali
Address: Viale della Costituzione Centro Direzionale di Nap, 80143 Naples
Telephone: +39 81 734 7020
Fax: +39 81 734 7126
Year established: 1945
Chief officers: dott. Pasquale D'Acunzi (President), dott. Nicola De Dilectis (Director)
Membership: food canning and bottling companies
Notes: No publications produced

National Association of Private Banks (ASSBANK)

Associazione Nazionale Banche Private
Address: Via Domenichino 5, 20149 Milan
Telephone: +39 2 480 10278
Fax: +39 2 481 7834

Year established: 1954
Chief officers: Professor Tancredi Bianchi (President), dott. Edmondo Fontana (Director General)

National Association of Producers, Wholesalers and Retailers of Dried Vegetables (ASSOLEGUMI)

Associazione Nazionale Operatori Legumi Secchi
Address: Piazza della Costituzione 8, 40128 Bologna
Telephone: +39 51 503 881
Fax: +39 51 355 166
Year established: 1989
Chief officers: Gaudenzio Melandri (President)
Notes: No publications produced.

National Association of Radio, Television, Domestic Electrical Appliances, Records and Related Products Retailers (ANCRA)

Associazione Nazionale Commercianti Radio, TV, Elettrodomestici, Dischi e Affini
Address: corso A Gramsci 34, 51100 Pistoia
Telephone: +39 573 328 54
Fax: +39 573 364590
Year established: 1969
Activities: information and representation in dealings with government and the authorities
Chief officers: dott. Francesco Panerai (President)
Membership: 8,000 retailers

National Association of Retailers and Wholesalers of Dairy Products (ASSOCASEARI)

Associazione Nazionale Del Commercio dei Prodotti Lattiero-Caseari
Address: Viale Milanofiori str.7 Palazzo S, 20089 Rozzano (MI)
Telephone: +39 2 824 3141
Fax: +39 2 575 02070
Year established: 1945
Chief officers: Dott.ssa Maria Antonia Pigozzi Rossini (President)
Membership: 110 members comprising wholesalers and retailers of dairy products
Notes: The Association does not produce any publications.

National Association of Retailers Cooperatives (ANCD)

Associazione Nazionale Cooperative fra Dettaglianti
Address: Via Chiana 38, I-00198 Rome
Telephone: +39 6 855 7961
Fax: +39 6 854 1419
Year established: 1973
Chief officers: dott. Roberto Dessi (Secretary General)
Membership: cooperative retailers

National Association of Shellfish and Tuna Processors and Canners (ANCIT)

Associazione Nazionale Conservieri Ittici e delle Tonnare
Address: V.le Pasteur,10, 00144 Roma
Telephone: +39 6 591 0544
Fax: +39 6 591 0711
Year established: 1961
Chief officers: Dott. Sergio Luoni (President) Dott. Valerio Bordoni (General Secratary)
Notes: Member of the Associazione delle industrie conserviere ittiche della UE - AIPCEE.

National Association of Spirits and Brandy Distillers (ANIDAA)
Associazione Nazionale Industriali Distillatori di Alcoli e di Acquaviti
Address: Via Barberini 86, I-00187 Rome
Telephone: +39 6 474 0851
Fax: +39 6 487 0904
Year established: 1946
Chief officers: dott. Francesco Castaldo (President), dott. Giorgio Semperlotti (Director)

National Association of Sportswear Manufacturers (ASSOSPORT)
Associazione Nazionale Produttori di Articoli Sportivi
Address: Via Petitti 16, I-20149 Milan
Telephone: +39 2 392 15282/330 01135
Fax: +39 2 311 182
Chief officers: dott. Attilio Pronzati (President)

National Association of Sportswear Retailers (ADAS)
Associazione Nazionale Dettaglianti Articoli Sportivi
Address: Corso Venezia 42-47, 20121 Milan
Telephone: +39 2 775 0272
Fax: +39 2 775 0480
Chief officers: Giorgio Brigatti (President), dott. Sergio Lolli (General Secretary)
Membership: 2,190 retailers
Notes: No publications produced.

National Association of Stationery Manufacturers (ASSOSCRITTURA)
Associazione Nazionale Produttori Articoli per Scrittura e Affini
Address: Via Petitti 16, 20149 Milan
Telephone: +39 2 324 846
Fax: +39 2 330 03819
Year established: 1945
Chief officers: dott. Alberto Candela (President), dott. Umberto Maltagliati (General Secretary)
Membership: 17 companies in the writing instruments field
Notes: No publications produced.

National Association of Sugar, Alcohol and Yeast Manufacturers (ASSOZUCCHERO)
Associazione Nazionale Fra gli Industriali dello Zucchero dell'Alcool e del Lievito
Address: Via Bartolomeo Bosco, 57/4, 16121 Genova
Telephone: +39 10 565 491/543 571
Fax: +39 10 553 1267
Year established: 1945
Chief officers: Dott. Renato Picco (President), dott. Marco Laganà
Membership: sugar manufacturers, alcohol manufacturers and yeast manufacturers

National Association of the Foreign Trade (ANCE)
Associazione Nazionale del Commercio con l'Estero
Address: Corso Venezia 47/49, 20121 Milan
Telephone: +39 2 775 0320
Fax: +39 2 760 05543
E-mail: ance.italy@iol.it
Year established: 1970
Chief officers: dott. Piero Piccardi (President) , dott. Italo Bussoli (Director General)
Membership: 800 trading companies
Publications:
• Foreign Trade Newsletter (Notiziario del Commercio con l'Estero): *fortnight*

National Association of the Pharmaceutical Industry (AGROFARMA)
Associazione Nazionale Industrie Fitofarmaci
Address: Via Accademia 33, 20131 Milan
Telephone: +39 2 681 01
Fax: +39 2 681 0331
Year established: 1987
Chief officers: Emmanuele Barracchia (President), dott. Piero Catelani (Director)

National Association of the Pharmaceutical Industry (FARMAINDUSTRIA)
Associazione Nazionale dell'Industria Farmaceutica
Address: Piazza di Pietra 34, 00186 Rome
Telephone: +39 6 675 801
Fax: +39 6 678 6494/679 7960
Activities: research and statistical department
Chief officers: dott. Francesco Costantini (President), Franco Zacchia (Director General)
Publications:
• Pharmaceutical Indicators (Indicatori Farmaceutici): *annual statistics on the pharmaceutical sector in Italy with data on production, sales, foreign trade, and consumption - annual*

National Association of Toys Importers (ANIG)
Associazione Nazionale Importatori Giacattoli e Modellismo
Address: Via M.F. Quintiliano 24, 20138 Milan
Telephone: +39 2 502 254
Fax: +39 2 502 254
Year established: 1960
Activities: import data elaboration
Chief officers: Renato Malavasi (President), Giuseppe Bardelli (Secretary)
Membership: 47 companies
Notes: No publications produced.

National Bakers' Association
Associazione Nazionale Panificatori
Address: Via San Giovanni in Laterano 152, 00184 Rome
Telephone: +39 6 703 741
Fax: +39 6 704 54320
Year established: 1991
Chief officers: Gilberto Sbrighi (President)
Notes: No publications produced.

National Federation of Associations for the Electrical and Electronics Industry (ANIE)
Federazione Nazionale delle Imprese Elettrotechniche ed Elettroniche
Address: Via A Algardi 2, 20148 Milan
Telephone: +39 2 326 41
Fax: +39 2 326 4212
Year established: 1945
Chief officers: cav. del lav. Roberto Bettazzani (President), dott. Daniel Kraus (General Secretary)
Membership: 17 National Associations (650 electronics companies)
Publications:
• Annual Report ANIE (Relazione Annuale ANIE): *Italian Electronic Industry - annual*

National Federation of Butchers (FEDERCARNI)
Federazione Nazionale Macellai
Address: Piazza G Belli 2, 00153 Rome
Telephone: +39 6 581 7032/588 3175
Fax: +39 6 588 1512
Year established: 1947
Activities: information, research and statistical services
Chief officers: dott. Giorgio Guazzaloca (President), dott.

Ortenzi Lorenzo (Director General)
Membership: retail butchers
Notes: No publications produced.

National Federation of Fishing Companies (FEDERPESCA)

Federazione Nazionale delle Imprese di Pesca
Address: Corso d'Italia 92, I-00198 Rome
Telephone: +39 6 854 1125/855 4198
Fax: +39 6 853 52992
Year established: 1969
Membership: fisheries

National Federation of Florists (FEDERFIORI)

Federazione Nazionale Fioristi
Address: Via Massena 3, 10128 Turin
Telephone: +39 11 547 051
Fax: +39 11 542 095
Chief officers: Sprocatti Carlo (President), Sartore Adriano (General Secretary)
Membership: wholesale and retail florists

National Federation of Italian Perfume Retailers (FENAPRO)

Federazione Nazionale Profumieri Italiani
Address: Corso Venezia 47-49, 20121 Milan
Telephone: +39 2 775 0203/08
Fax: +39 2 775 0480
Year established: 1948
Chief officers: Paolo Campion (President), dott. Mario Verduci (General Secretary)
Membership: c. 4,700 perfume retailers
Publications:
● Allure Beauty: *monthly ; 10 p.a.*
● Imagine: *official magazine of the perfumery trade*

National Federation of Stationers (FEDERCARTOLAI)

Federazione Nazionale Cartolai
Address: Corso Mazzini 27, I-57126 Livorno
Telephone: +39 586 807 387
Fax: +39 586 805 481
Chief officers: Piero Santini (President), Daniele Pracchia (Secretary)
Membership: stationers
Publications:
● La Cartoleria

National Federation of Textile, Clothing and Home Furnishing Retailers (FEDERABBIGLIAMENTO)

Federazione Nazionale Dettaglianti Tessili Abbigliamento Arredemento
Address: Via Palestro 24, I-20121 Milan
Telephone: +39 2 760 15212
Fax: +39 2 796 668
Year established: 1949
Chief officers: dott. Ingino Sogaro (President), Franco Tomelli (Secretary General)
Membership: clothing, textile and fabric retailers
Notes: No publications produced.

National Federation of the Electrical Material Wholesalers and Distributors

Federazione Nazionale Grossisti Distributori di Materiale Elettrico
Address: Corso Venezia 47-49, 20121 Milan
Telephone: +39 2 775 0289
Fax: +39 2 775 0480
Year established: 1970
Chief officers: dott. Rodolfo Bellentani (President), dott. Luigi

D'Alo (Secretary)
Membership: electrical wholesalers
Notes: No publications produced.

National Federation of the Goldsmiths (FEDERORAFI)

Federazione Nazionale Orafi Gioiellieri Fabbricanti
Address: Piazza Michelangelo Buonarroti 32, 20149 Milan
Telephone: +39 2 481 5364
Fax: +39 2 481 5118
Chief officers: Agostino Roverato (President), dott. Stefano de Pascale (General Secretary)
Notes: No publications produced.

National Federation of the Travel and Tourism Industry (FEDERTURISMO)

Federazione Nazionale dell'Industria dei Viaggi e del Turismo
Address: Viale Astronomia 30, 00144 Rome
Telephone: +39 6 590 3311
Fax: +39 6 590 3583
Year established: 1993
Chief officers: dott. Pier Vittorio Tugnoli (President), Fulvio Nannelli (Secretary)
Membership: associations in the travel and tourism industry
Notes: No publications produced.

National Federation of Wholesale Paper Distributors (FENCA)

Federazione Nazionale Distributori Ingrosso Carta
Address: Corso Venezia 49, 20121 Milan
Telephone: +39 2 775 0288
Fax: +39 2 775 0480
Year established: 1986
Chief officers: Giorgio Stizzoli (President), dott. Luigi D'Alo (Secretary)
Membership: paper wholesalers and distributors

National Poultry Union (UNA)

Unione Nazionale dell'Avicoltora
Address: Via Vibio Mariano 58, I-00189 Rome
Telephone: +39 6 33254015
Fax: +39 6 33252427
Year established: 1958
Chief officers: Rino Celadon (President), Rita Pasquarelli (Director General)
Membership: poultry farmers

National Road Transport Association (A.N.I.T.A.)

Associazione Nazionale Imprese Trasporti Automobilistici
Address: Via Oglio n° 9, Rome
Telephone: +39 6 855 0263
Fax: +39 6 855 4066
E-mail: anita@evolutionweb.it
Web site: www.evolutionweb.it/Servizi/anita.htm

National Trade Press Association (ANES)

Associazione Nazionale Editoria Specializzata
Address: Via Pantano 9, 20122 Milan
Telephone: +39 2 583 70348
Fax: +39 2 583 05050

National Union of Automotive Distributors (UNRAE)

Unione Nazionale Distributori Automotoveicoli
Address: Via Di Villa Albani 12a, 00198 Rome
Telephone: +39 6 854 3526
Fax: +39 6 854 1115
Year established: 1950
Chief officers: dott. Walter Walcher (President)

Publications:
• Italian Automobile (L'Auto in Italia): *general data on the motor vehicles sector covering production, registrations, imports, exports, vehicle parc for cars, commercial vehicles, buses, and other vehicles. Some data for earlier years given. Based largely on data collected by the Union - annual*
• Monthly Bulletin (Bollettino Mensile): *home production and imports for motor vehicles by make, model and engine type. Data for the latest month, cumulative year-to-date, and comparative figures for the corresponding period in the previous year. Based largely on data collected by the Union - monthly*

National Union of Milk Producers' Associations (UNALAT)
Unione Nazionale fra le Associazioni Produttori di Latte Bovine
Address: Via Modena 5, 00184 Rome
Telephone: +39 6 487 2194
Fax: +39 6 482 7571
Year established: 1987
Chief officers: dott. Carlo Venino (President), Enrico Bussi (Director)
Membership: dairy farmers and milk producers
Notes: No publications produced.

National Union of Small and Medium-Sized Food Industries (UNIONALIMENTARI)
Unione Nazionale Piccola e Media Industria Alimentare
Address: Via del Caucaso 49, 00144 Rome
Telephone: +39 6 591 4538
Fax: +39 6 591 5004
Year established: 1992
Chief officers: rag. Giorgio Zubani (President), dott. Leonardo Cullurà (Director General)
Membership: small and medium-size food manufacturers
Notes: No publications produced.

National Union of the Leather Industry (UNIC)
Unione Nazionale Industria Conciaria
Address: Via Brisa 3, 20123 Milan
Telephone: +39 2 801 026
Fax: +39 2 860 032
Year established: 1946
Chief officers: dott. Mario Di Stefano (President), dott. Salvatore Mercogliano (Director)
Membership: 500 companies
Notes: No publications produced.

National Union of the Perfume, Cosmetics, Soap and Allied Industries (UNIPRO)
Unione Nazionale delle Industrie di Profumeria Cosmesi, Saponi da Toeletta e Affini
Address: Via F. Juvara 9, 20129 Milan
Telephone: +39 2 706 31013/706 31010
Fax: +39 2 706 02093
Activities: represents the cosmetics, perfume, toilet soap and related industries; compiles statistics on the sector
Chief officers: Dr Florio Terenzi (Secretary General)
Membership: soap and cosmetics manufacturers
Publications:
• Annual Review UNIPRO (Relazione Annuale): *production, import-export, consumption and distribution breakdown - annual*

National Union of the Small and Medium-Sized Textile and Clothing Companies (UNIONTESSILE)
Unione Nazionale Piccola e Media Industria Tessile e dell'Abbigliamento
Address: Via della Colonna Antonina 52, 00186 Rome
Telephone: +39 6 699 1530
Fax: +39 6 679 1488
Year established: 1974
Chief officers: Carlo Soldano (President)
Membership: small and medium-sized textile and clothing manufacturers
Notes: No publications produced.

National Wine Trade Federation (FNCV)
Federazione Nazionale del Commercio Vinicolo
Address: Via S. Vittore al Teatro 3, 20123 Milan
Telephone: +39 2 801 595
Fax: +39 2 866 226
Year established: 1964
Chief officers: dott. Gianni Zonin (President), Pietro Caviglia (Director General)
Membership: wine traders
Notes: No publications produced.

Olive Growers' National Co-operative (CNO)
Consorzio Nazionale degli Olivicoltori
Address: Via Alessandria 199, 00198 Rome
Telephone: +39 6 841 3504
Fax: +39 6 884 8240
Year established: 1967
Chief officers: Massimo Pacetti (President)

Petroleum Association (UNIPETROL)
Unione Petrolifera
Address: Via del Giorgione 129, 00147 Rome
Telephone: +39 6 596 02939
Fax: +39 6 596 02924
Year established: 1948
Activities: promotes research into economic and technical problems affecting the industry
Chief officers: dott. Gian Marco Moratti (President), ing. Bruno Dattilo (Director General)
Membership: 38 companies
Publications:
• Annual Report (Unione Petrolifera) (Relazione Annuale): *commentary and statistics on the Italian and world oil and energy situation. Italian data covers production, consumption by sector, trade, prices. Data for some earlier years - annual*
• Annuario Statistico (Unione Petrolifera): *various tables on the world and Italian oil and energy markets - annual*

Product Coding Association (INDICOD)
Instituto Nazionale per la Diffusione della Codifica dei Prodotti
Address: Via Serbelloni 5, 20122 Milano
Telephone: +39 2 795 994
Fax: +39 2 784 373
E-mail: indicod@indicod.it

Radio and Television Federation (FRT)
Federazione Radio Televisioni
Address: Viale Regina Margherita 286, 00198 Rome
Telephone: +39 6 440 2096
Fax: +39 6 440 2723
Year established: 1984
Chief officers: Filippo Rebecchini (President), Stefano Selli (Director General)
Membership: national broadcasting association
Notes: No publications produced.

Technical Association of the Automotive Industry (ATA)

Associazione Tecnica dell'Automobile
Address: Strade Torino 32, I-10043 Orbassano
Telephone: +39 11 902 3638
Fax: +39 11 902 3637
Year established: 1948
Chief officers: Dott. Ing. Carlo Eugenio Rossi (President) ,
Prof. Ettore Pannizza (General Secretary)

Wool Industry Association

Associazione dell'industria Laniera Italiana
Address: Viale Sarca 223, 20126 Milan
Telephone: +39 2 661 03853
Fax: +39 2 661 03878
Year established: 1877
Chief officers: dott. Paolo Negri (President), dott. Giancarlo
Comuzzi (Director)
Notes: No publications produced

JAMAICA

Jamaica Exporters' Association (JEA)

Address: PO Box 9, 13 Dominica Drive, Kingston 5
Telephone: +1 876 9 291 292/960 2375/926 0586
Fax: +1 876 9 293 831
E-mail: jea@infochan.com. or sbed@infochan.com.
Year established: 1965
Activities: Small Business Exporter Development Project
SBED (technical assistance, training and market information);
Agricultural Export Services Project (grant funding to assist
small and medium-sized farmers); monthly board of directors'
meeting open to all members; quarterly luncheon; seminars
and workshops; trade fairs, missions, exhibitions, etc.; library;
National Export Week; Expo; collects export statistics
Chief officers: Rita Hilton (President), Beverly Morgan, Robert
McDonald, Leighton Ashley, Bruce Terrier (Vice Presidents),
Deryck Rose (Honorary Treasurer), Pauline Gray (Executive
Director)
Membership: 280 member companies representing a range
of commercial sectors, including agribusiness, apparel,
building products, chemicals, cosmetics and
pharmaceuticals, electronics, furniture and crafts, and allied
service industries
Publications:
• Export Manual
• Export Update: *newsletter: details of events, trade
opportunities, etc. - quarterly*
• Jamaican Exporter: *official yearbook and membership
directory; general information on Jamaica and its economy,
the association's activities, etc. - annual*

Jamaica Hotel and Tourist Association (JHTA)

Address: 2 Ardenne Road, Kingston 10
Telephone: +1 876 9 263 635/6/926 2796
Fax: +1 876 9 291 054
Year established: 1961
Activities: trade and promotional events; market information;
training and seminars; annual general meeting and trade
exhibition; legal and professional advice;
Chief officers: Lionel Reid (President), Camille Needham
(Executive Director)
Structure: board of directors, president, 4 vice presidents, 25
councillors; executive director, deputy executive director, 6
staff members
Membership: hoteliers, air and ground transport operators,
travel agents, entertainment companies, banks, suppliers of
specialised equipment, etc - 115 hotels, 173 allied members
(those who provide goods and services to the hotel industry),
33 affiliate members, 12 overseas allied members

Publications:
• Brochure: *how to become a member of the JHTA*
• Bulletins
• Front Desk: *newsletter - quarterly*
Notes: All members must be licensed by the Jamaica Tourist
Board or the appropriate authority as a prerequisite to joining;
also a member of Caribbean Hotel Association, the American
Society of Travel Agents, the American Hotel and Motel
Association and the International Hotel Association.

Jamaica Manufacturers' Association (JMA)

Address: 85A Duke Street, Kingston
Telephone: +1 876 9 228 880/1/922 0788
Fax: +1 876 9 229 205
Year established: 1947
Chief officers: Major Anthony Robinson (Chairman), Mrs.
Velma Sharpe (Executive Director)

Private Sector Organisation of Jamaica (PSOJ)

Address: POB 236, The Carlton Alexander Building, 39 Hope
Road, Kingston 10
Telephone: +1 876 9 276 786/6957/8/6238
Fax: +1 876 9 275 137
Year established: 1976
Activities: publishes occasional papers on economic issues
as well as topics of national importance
Chief officers: Charles Ross (Executive Director), Delroy
Lindsay (President), William McConnell, Elon Beckford,
Charles Johnson (Vice Presidents), Betty-Ann Jones-Kerr
(Honorary Secretary), Clifton Cameron (Honorary Treasurer)
Structure: council elected by general membership every 2
years
Membership: ca. 361 members (individuals, corporations and
associations)
Publications:
• Business Survey of Jamaican Companies
• PSOJ Enterprise: *newsletter - quarterly*
• Report of the Executive Committee: *annual*
• Report on the Jamaican Economy: *annual*

Professional Societies' Association of Jamaica (PSAJ)

Address: 23/4 Ruthven Road, Kingston 10
Telephone: +1 876 9 262 434
Fax: +1 876 9 269 741
Membership: 34 professional associations from various
sectors, including health and medical, construction, finance,
agriculture, law, administration and media

Small Business Association of Jamaica (SBAJ)

Address: 2 Trafalgar Road, Kingston
Telephone: +1 876 9 277 071
Fax: +1 876 9 782 733
Year established: 1974
Chief officers: Abe Williams (President)
Structure: private non-profit organisation

JAPAN

All Japan Advertising Federation

Zen Nippon Kokoku Renmei
Address: Kochiwa Building, 4-8-12 Ginza, Chuo-ku, Tokyo 104
Telephone: +81 3 3562 2966
Fax: +81 3 3535 4766
Chief officers: Rokuro Ishikawa (Chairman), Saburosuke
Suzuki (President)
Membership: 5,631 companies, 8,461 individuals
Notes: The Association does not produce any publications or
statistics.

All Japan Coffee Association

Address: 5th floor, Kitamura Building, 1-17-15, Nishi Shinbashi, Minato-ku, Tokyo 105
Telephone: +81 3 3580 9870
Fax: +81 3 3580 1516
Structure: monthly standing committees; 6 groups: Japan Coffee Federation, Japan Instant Coffee Association, Japan Home Regular Coffee Association, Japan Coffee Imports Association, Japan Green Coffee Association, individual members (company)
Membership: 39 companies and associations
Publications:
• Coffee Related Statistics: *a review of the history of coffee is followed by statistics on the coffee industry, foreign trade, the international coffee market, and general statistics on the catering sector, vending machines, import restrictions, and taxes - annual*
• Survey on Trends of Demand for Coffee: *includes a consumer survey of coffee with data on number of cups drunk, places where purchased, age of consumers, prices, choice of drinks etc. Also has a section on the coffee shop industry in Japan and the future outlook for consumption, by type of coffee, sex, age - annual*

All Japan Federation of Dry Noodle Manufacturers' Associations

Address: Seifunkaikan, 15-6 Nihonbashi Kabutocho, Chuo-ku, Tokyo 103
Telephone: +81 3 3634 2255
Fax: +81 3 3634 1930
Activities: compiles statistics on the industry

All Japan Health and Natural Food Association

Address: Sankyo Building 706, 2-1-2-11 Koishikawa, Bunkyo-ku, Tokyo 112
Telephone: +81 3 3814 6052
Membership: around 500 corporate members

All Japan Liquor Merchants' Association

Address: 2-1-26 Naka Meguro,Meguro-ku, Tokyo 153
Telephone: +81 3 371 40171
Fax: +81 3 371 08230
Chief officers: Koji Oshima (Chairman)

All Japan Rent-a-Car Association

Shadan Hojin Zenkoku Rent-a-car Kyokai
Address: 7th floor, Nakanishi Building, 2-5-6, Nishi Kanda, Chiyodo-ku,, Tokyo 101
Telephone: +81 3 3262 3076
Fax: +81 3 3262 5047
Activities: surveys and guidance on the car rental industry; guidance on traffic safety and research into repair management of rental cars; information on the industr; advertising and PR; dealing with complaints from rental car users and advising them; lobbying the government and politicians; issuing certificates to rental car companies; producing statistics and data on the car rental industry
Chief officers: Takeshi Kumahiro (President), Kazumi Wakayabashi (Vice President)
Membership: 142 member associations, including 53 regional associations with approximately 4500 companies nationwide
Publications:
• Automobile Rental and Lease Yearbook (Jidosha Rentarisu Nenkan): *yearly*

All Japan Thermos Flask Association

Zenkokou Mahoobin Kobyo Kumiai
Address: 9-13 Nishinakajima 3-chome, Yodogawa-ku, Osaka 532

Telephone: +81 6 390 5330
Fax: +81 6 390 5332
Year established: 1953
Activities: attends displays at the International Housewares Show (Tokyo), Frankfurter Messe, and Chicago Gift Show
Chief officers: Shigehiro Yamanaka (Chairman), Teruaki Nakaue (Secretary General)
Membership: 19 member companies

All Japanese Federation of Bakers' Associations

Zen Nihon Pan Kyodo Kumiai
Address: 1-34-9 Shinjuku, Shinjuku-ku, Tokyo 160
Telephone: +81 3 335 23341
Fax: +81 3 335 23344
Year established: 1956
Membership: 65 (Baker's Union)

All Nippon Confectionery Association

Address: Japan Biscuit Bldg, 6-9-5 Shinbashi, Minato-ku, Tokyo 105
Telephone: +81 3 343 13115
Fax: +81 3 343 21660

All Nippon Non-wovens' Association (ANNA)

Nihon Fushokufu Rengokai
Address: Soto Kanda 6-chome Building, 9-2 Soto Kanda 6-chome, Chiyoda-ku, Tokyo 101
Telephone: +81 3 5688 4041
Fax: +81 3 5688 4042
Year established: 1992
Chief officers: Shozo Iwakuma (Chairman),Teruo Yoshimura (Secretary General)
Notes: established in 1992 from the Nippon Non-wovens Association, the Nippon Engineered Fabrics Association, the Non-wovens Research Committee in the Textile Machinery Society of Japan. The Association is a member of the Association of Non-woven Fabrics Industry (INDA).

Brewers Association of Japan

Address: Showa Building 4F, 8-18, Kyobashi 2-chome, Chuo-ku, Tokyo 104
Telephone: +81 3 3561 8386
Fax: +81 3 3561 8380
Chief officers: Kenzo Edamoto (Chairman)
Publications:
• Beer Industry of Japan: *details of sales of beer, exports, imports, and consumption of alcoholic beverages. Also includes information on the location of breweries, taxation, and a history of beer production - annual*

Brewing Society of Japan

Nippon Jozokyokai
Address: 6-30 Takinogawa, 2-chome, Kita-ku, Tokyo 114
Telephone: +81 3 3910 3853
Fax: +81 3 3910 3748
Chief officers: Yuichi Akiyama (Chairman), Makoto Tadenuma (Executive Director)
Publications:
• Journal of the Brewing Society of Japan (Nippon Jozo Kyokaishi): *covers brewing and distilling methods for beer, spirits, soy sauce and sake - monthly*

Ceramic Society of Japan

Nihon Ceramics Kyokai
Address: 22-17 Haykunin-cho 2-chome, Shinjuku-ku, Tokyo 169
Telephone: +81 3 3362 5232
Fax: +81 3 3362 5714
E-mail: books@ceramic.or.jp

Web site: www.ceramic.or.jp
Year established: 1881
Activities: research and investigation into ceramics, holding lecture courses and symposiums, publication of monthly journals and a number of books, as well as cooperation on related scientific articles in Japan and abroad
Chief officers: Yoshiro Suzuki (President), Kunihiko Nomura (Secretary General)
Membership: 500 ceramics companies
Publications:
● Journal of the Ceramics Society of Japan: *news about the society, articles on ceramics from the theoretical to the practical, aesthetic to the scientific - monthly*

Chocolate and Cocoa Association of Japan

Nihon Chocolate and Cocoa Kyokai
Address: Tomita Building, 8-3-10 Chome Ginza, Chuo-ku, Tokyo 104
Telephone: +81 3 3572 8271
Fax: +81 3 3289 4598
Year established: 1952
Activities: promotion of consumption of chocolate and chocolate products; ensuring supply of raw materials; improvement of product quality; friendship among members; liaison with the Authorities; disseminating information; contributing to the development of the industry
Chief officers: Masahisa Uchino (Director General), Sasai Akira (Chairman, Meiji Confectionery Ltd.)
Membership: 26 private companies, 1 organisation
Publications:
● Chocolate Story: *the history of chocolate and the background to the industry*
● Cocoa Statistics of Japan: *comprehensive statistics on production, imports, exports and consumption of chocolate and chocolate products in Japan. Includes international comparisons - annual*

Cocoa Importers' Association of Japan

Nihon Kakao Yunyu Kyokai
Address: c/o Toshuku Ltd, 4-3 Nihonbashi-Muromachi 2-chome, Chuo-ku, Tokyo 103
Telephone: +81 3 324 52211
Fax: +81 3 324 52760
Year established: 1973
Activities: collects statistics on the industry
Chief officers: Akira Tachikawa
Membership: 10 members

Communications Industry Association of Japan (CIAJ)

Tsushin Kikai Kogyokai
Address: Sankei Building, Annex, 1-7-2 Otemachi, Chiyoda-ku, Tokyo 100
Telephone: +81 3 323 13005
Fax: +81 3 324 63110
Year established: 1948
Chief officers: Setsuji Takahashi (President), Shiko Sawamura (Chairman), E Tamura, T Tanida (International Affairs Department)
Membership: 256 member companies
Publications:
● CIAJ Annual Report: *annual*
● CIAJ Directory: *lists the Association's members*
● CIAJ Quarterly: *quarterly*

Dairy Farmers' Association of Japan

Address: 5th Floor, Zenkoku Biscuit Kaikan, 9-5 Shinbashi 6-chome, Minato-ku, Tokyo 151
Telephone: +81 3 337 05341
Fax: +81 3 337 03892

Electronic Industries' Association of Japan (EIAJ)

Nihon Denshi Kikai Kogyokai
Address: Tokyo Chamber of Commerce Building, 2-2 Marunouchi 3-chome, Chiyoda-ku, Tokyo 100
Telephone: +81 3 3211 2765
Fax: +81 3 3287 1712
E-mail: pao@eiaj.org.jp
Web site: www.eiaj.or.jp
Web site notes: site includes a series of press releases on the Japanese electronics industry with statistics on production of consumer electronics, industrial electronics and components as well as imports and exports
Year established: 1948
Activities: conducting surveys on the electronics industry world-wide through activities such as the dispatch of study missions; collects, evaluates and analyses statistics; arranges and participates in international conferences
Chief officers: Iwao Ojima (Secretary General), Norio Ohga (Chairman)
Membership: 565 member companies
Publications:
● Directory of Members: *detailed information on member companies, including addresses, telephone and fax numbers, main products and overseas facilities - annual*
● Electronic Industries Association of Japan Newsletter: *news, global trends, Japanese industry profiles, statistical digest - monthly*
● Facts and Figures on the Japanese Electronics Industry: *a general overview of the industry and a commentary on its position in the worldwide market is followed by detailed statistics on the production, sales and exports of specific products. A number of the tables give historical data and statistics are presented in value and volume terms. - annual*
● Perspective on the Japanese Electronics Industry: *overview of the Japanese electronics industry, comprising production, exports, imports and overseas production facilities - annual*

Federation of Bankers' Associations of Japan

Address: 3-1 Marunouchi 1-chome, Chiyoda-ku, Tokyo 100
Telephone: +81 3 3216 3761
Fax: +81 3 3201 5608
Chief officers: Shunsaku Hashimoto (Chairman)
Publications:
● Banking System in Japan: *a detailed survey of the Japanese banking system based on returns from the banks and an analysis of published data - regular*
● Japanese Banks: *commentary and statistics on the banking sector in Japan with data on loans, new markets, income, securities, electronic banking, internationalisation of Japanese banks etc. - annual*

Federation of Pharmaceutical Manufacturers' Associations of Japan (FPMAJ)

Address: Tokyo Yakugyo Kaikan, 1-5 Nihonbashi Hon-cho 2-chome, Chuo-ku, Tokyo 103
Telephone: +81 3 3270 0581
Fax: +81 3 3564 4766
Year established: 1948
Chief officers: Shigeo Moriaka (President)

Flour Millers' Association

Nihon Seifun Kyokai
Address: 15-6 Nihonbashi, Kabuto-cho, Chuo-ku 103
Telephone: +81 3 3669 1011
Fax: +81 3 3667 1673

Glass Manufacturers' Association of Japan

Glass Seihin Kogyokai
Address: 1-9 Shinbashi 3-chome, Minato-ku, Tokyo 105
Telephone: +81 3 3591 2697
Fax: +81 3 3595 2719
Chief officers: Mr Yamada

International Development Association of the Furniture Industry of Japan (IDAFIJ)

Shadanhojin Kokusai Kagu Sangyo Shinkokai
Address: Karukazako-Tanaka Building, 16-1 Kagurazaka 2-chome, Shinjuku-ku, Tokyo 162
Telephone: +81 3 5261 9401
Fax: +81 3 5261 9404
Year established: 1957
Chief officers: Kyoji Kageyama (Chairman); Katsuhiko Shirasu (Secretary General)
Membership: 79 member companies
Publications:
• Furniture Export and Import of Japan by Items: *annual*
• General Situation of the Household Furniture Market in Japan
• General Situation of the Imported Furniture Market in Japan
• List of Furniture Importers in Japan

Japan Adhesive Tapes Manufacturers' Association

Nihon Nenchaku Tape Kogyokai
Address: Naka Building, 1-1-3, Iwamoto-cho, Chiyoda-ku, Tokyo 101
Telephone: +81 3 3863 5347
Fax: +81 3 3865 2958
Year established: 1961
Chief officers: Naotake Okubo (Chairman), Yoshiaki Ohmachi (Secretary General)
Membership: 22 member companies
Publications:
• Members' List: *list of members*

Japan Association of Travel Agents

Address: Zen Nittu Building, 3-3-3 Kasumigaseki, Chiyoda-ku, 100 Tokyo
Telephone: +81 3 359 212 71
Fax: +81 3 359 212 68
Activities: collection and dissemination of information concerning the travel agency business to members and the public; dealing with complaints from travellers and/or the servicing side; professional training; advice centres; research, study and publicity for the sound development of travel agencies; coooperation with other organisations
Chief officers: Mr Shunishi Sumita (President), Mr Kaoru Sakurada (Director and Secretary General)
Membership: travel and tourism business sector

Japan Audio Society

Address: 14-34, Jingumae 1-chome, Shibuya-ku, Tokyo 150
Telephone: +81 3 3403 6649
Fax: +81 3 3403 6549
Year established: 1952
Activities: manages Japan Audio Fair
Chief officers: Heitaro Nakajima (President), Itaru Watanabe (Executive Director)
Membership: 1000 individual members, 100 member companies

Japan Auto Accessories Manufacturers' Association

Zenkoku Jidosha Yohin Kogyokai
Address: Nakamura Building, 3-36-2, Yushima, Bunkyo-ku, Tokyo 113
Telephone: +81 3 3833 7921
Fax: +81 3 3833 7922

Year established: 1969
Chief officers: Kinichi Ohno (Chairman), Hitoshi Takahashi (Secretary General)
Membership: 86 member companies
Publications:
• Member Lists: *lists the Association's members*

Japan Auto Parts Industries' Association (JAPIA)

Address: 1-16-15 Takanawa, Minato-ku, Tokyo 108
Telephone: +81 3 3445 4211
Fax: +81 3 3447 5372
Year established: 1948
Activities: publishes information and data concerning the improvement of management, technology, and productivity, as well as promoting international trade and cooperation
Chief officers: Shohei Hamada (Chairman); Kazunori Shibasaki (Vice Chairman and Executive Managing Director); Toshio Uchiyama (Managing Director); Akira Gyobu (General Manager, International Department)
Membership: 532 member companies
Publications:
• Guide to JAPIA
• JAPIA Membership Lists

Japan Auto-body Industries' Association

Address: Kishimoto Bldg., 2-2-1 Marunouchi, Chiyoda-ku, Tokyo 100
Telephone: +81 3 3213 2031
Fax: +81 3 3213 2034
Year established: 1948
Activities: research into improving management, engineering, technology, and efficiency in the auto-body industry
Chief officers: Saburo Bito (Chairman), Hiromasa Soeda (Managing Director)
Membership: 222 member firms

Japan Automobile Dealers' Association

Address: 5-7-17 Minami Aoyama,, Minato-ku, Tokyo 107
Telephone: +81 3 3400 8404
Fax: +81 3 3400 8413
Chief officers: Keishin Kato (President)

Japan Automobile Importers' Association (JAIA)

Address: Akiyama No7 Bldg., 5-3 Kojimachi Chiyoda-ku, Tokyo 102
Telephone: +81 3 3222 5421
Fax: +81 3 3222 1730
Year established: 1965
Activities: surveying conditions in Japan and overseas related to the import of foreign automobiles. Compiling statistics on automobile imports, improving the price and trade conditions of imported automobiles, sponsoring shows, fairs and other promotional activities relating to the import of foreign automobiles
Chief officers: Jiro Yanase (Chairman)
Structure: board of directors, Market Policy Committee, Public Relations Committee, Technical Committee, Service and Parts Committee
Membership: Japanese automotive importers
Publications:
• Imported Car Market of Japan: *detailed statistics and commentary on imports of foreign automotives by volume, value, make and model. Covers distribution, the motor vehicle inspection and certification system and user profiles. Also examines legislation affecting the industry and procedures from importation to registration - annual*

Japan Automobile Manufacturers' Association, inc. (JAMA)

Nihon Jidosha Kogyokai
Address: Ohtemachi Building 2F, 1-6-1 Ohtemachi, Chiyoda-ku, Tokyo 100
Telephone: +81 3 3216 5771
Fax: +81 3 3287 2073
Telex: 222 3410
Year established: 1967
Chief officers: Yoshifumi Tsuji (Chairman);Takao Tominaga (Executive Managing Director)
Membership: 13 companies
Publications:
● JAMA Forum
● Motor Industry of Japan

Japan Automobile Tyre Manufacturers' Association

Address: 1-1-12 Toranomon, Minato-ku, Tokyo 105
Telephone: +81 3 3503 0191
Fax: +81 3 3503 0199
Chief officers: Yoichiro Kaizaki (Chairman)

Japan Automotive Products' Association (JAMA)

Nihon Jidosha Kogyokai
Address: Enatsu Building, 3-19-17, Shinbashi, Minato-ku, Tokyo 105
Telephone: +81 3 3433 1658
Fax: +81 3 3433 1063
Year established: 1969
Chief officers: Kakuhei Iwanami (Chairman), Shigeo Miyoshi (Secretary General)
Membership: 26 wholesalers and dealers of automotive and motorcycle parts
Publications:
● Members' List: *lists the Association's membership*

Japan Automotive Service Equipment Association (JASEA)

Nihon Jidosha Kikai Kogu Kyokai
Address: 23-5 Shinjuku 7-chome Shinjuku-ku, Tokyo 160
Telephone: +81 3 3203 5131
Fax: +81 3 3208 2157
Year established: 1948
Activities: automotive service equipment, tools and testing, as well as organising the Auto Service Show
Chief officers: Yuhiko Yanagida (Chairman), Uichiro Matsuda (Secretary General)
Membership: 33 companies

Japan Baking Industry Association

Address: 6th Floor, Seifun Kaikan, 15-6 Kabuto-cho, Nihonbashi, Tokyo 103
Telephone: +81 3 3667 1976
Fax: +81 3 3667 2049
Year established: 1963
Chief officers: Nobuhiro Iijima (President)
Structure: yearly general committee, monthly regular committee
Membership: 27

Japan Banana Importers' Association

Nihon Banana Yunyu Kumiai
Address: 5th Floor Zenkyoren Building, 2-7-9 Hirakawa-cho, Chiyoda-ku, Tokyo 102
Telephone: +81 3 3263 0461
Fax: +81 3 3263 0463
Year established: 1965
Chief officers: Nobutsugu Shimuzu (Chairman), Kinichi

Yamazaki (Director)
Membership: 26 companies
Publications:
● Bulletin of Banana Statistics: *monthly*
● Member List of The Japan Banana Importers' Association
● Report on Banana Statistics: *Annual*

Japan Battery and Appliance Industries' Association

Nihon Kandenchi Kogyokai
Address: No. 9 Mori Building, 2-2 Atago 1-chome, Minato-ku, Tokyo 105
Telephone: +81 3 3436 2471
Fax: +81 3 3436 2617
Year established: 1948
Chief officers: Tokio Tatsuta (Chairman), Akira Ikegami (Secretary General)
Membership: 50 companies

Japan Biscuit Association

Nihon Bisukitto Kyokai
Address: Japan Biscuit Bldg, 6-9-5 Shinbashi Minato-ku, Tokyo 105
Telephone: +81 3 343 36131
Fax: +81 3 343 36473
Chief officers: Akira Ito (President)
Membership: 29 members
Publications:
● Biscuit Statistics: *statistics on production and retail sales of biscuits in Japan based on data produced by the Food Supplies Bureau - annual*
● Japan Biscuit Association News: *news of the association and the industry - irregular*

Japan Book Importers' Association (JBIA)

Address: Chiyoda Kaikan, 21-4-1 Nihonbashi, Chuo-ku, Tokyo 103
Telephone: +81 3 3271 6901
Fax: +81 3 3271 6920
Activities: imports overseas publications; promotes and protects members' interests; collects and disseminates information; works to improve customs clearance of publications; contacts with various governmental authorities; organises exhibitions
Chief officers: Mitsuo Shibata (Secretary)
Membership: 115 importers and distributors of overseas publications
Publications:
● Bulletin of the JBIA: *members only - 12 p.a.*

Japan Book Publishers' Association

Address: 6 Fukuro-machi, Shinjuku-ku, Tokyo 162
Telephone: +81 3 3268 1301
Fax: +81 3 3268 1196
Web site: www.jbpa.or.jp
Year established: 1957
Activities: holds the Tokyo International Book fair every year; carries out research projects to help the publishing industry to expand; promotes ties between members; acts as a representative to government authorities concerning current legislation and business practices in the publishing world and preserving copyright laws; conducts studies with distributors and wholesalers to improve distribution
Chief officers: T. Watanabe (President), K. Maeda, T. Gomi (Director)
Membership: 501 members
Publications:
● An Introduction to Publishing in Japan: *summary and introduction to Japanese publishing world, and general directory of Japanese publications in foreign languages. - biennial*

• Japanese Books in Print (Nihon Shoseki Soumokuroku): *directory of books currently available in Japan - Annual*
• JBPA Bulletin and Information (Shokyo): *news on the Japan Book Publishers' Association - monthly*
• List of Forthcoming Books (Korekara Deru Hon): *forthcoming books from JBPA members - 6 p.a.*
• Publishing PR (Shuppan Koho): *major topics concerning the publishing industry*

Japan Business Machine Makers' Association
Nihon Jimukikai Kogyokai
Address: Shuuwa Dai-ni Toranomon Building, 1-21-19 Toranomon, Minato-ku, Tokyo 105
Telephone: +81 3 350 39821
Fax: +81 3 359 13646
Year established: 1960
Activities: publication of statistical journal for members, market research on domestic and foreign markets, studies on office automation and other technical developments of business machines, decisions on standards of business machinery
Chief officers: Atsushi Asada (President), Munehiro Tokugawa (Executive Director)
Membership: 45 companies
Publications:
• Estimated Demand for Business Machines: *statistics on the business machine industry, covering previous years and estimates for the coming year - annual*

Japan Camera Industry Association
Address: JC11 Bldg, 25 Ichiban Cho, Chiyoda-ku, Tokyo 102
Telephone: +81 3 5276 3891
Fax: +81 3 5276 3893
Chief officers: Toru Matsumoto (President)

Japan Canners' Association
Nihon Kanzume Kyokai
Address: Marunouchi Building, 2-4-1 Marunouchi, Chiyoda-ku, Tokyo 100
Telephone: +81 3 3213 4751
Fax: +81 3 3211 1430
Chief officers: Yoshinobu Kanie (President)
Publications:
• Canners' Notebook: Members' Directory: *lists the members of the Japan Canners' Association*
• Cannery Review: *statistical data on production, imports and exports - monthly*

Japan Carbonated Beverage Inspection Association
Nihon Tansan Inryo Kensa Kyokai
Address: Mochizuki Building, 2-6-16 Shibaura, Minato-ku, Tokyo 108
Telephone: +81 3 3455 6851
Fax: +81 3 3455 6852
Year established: 1975
Chief officers: Kenjiro Nishimura (Chairman), Yoshimi Horibe (Secretary General)

Japan Cereals Importers' Association
(Nihon P and B Kyokai)
Address: Daiichi Suzumaru Building, 2-39 Nishishimbashi, Minato-ku, Tokyo 105
Telephone: +81 3 3431 3895
Fax: +81 3 3431 3882

Japan Chain Stores' Association
Address: Toranomon 40 Mori Building, 5-13-1 Toranomon, Minato-ku, Tokyo 105

Telephone: +81 3 3433 1290
Fax: +81 3 3433 1297
Chief officers: Katsuhiro Fujiseki (Chairman)

Japan Clock and Watch Association
Address: Kudan TS Building, 1-9-16 Kudan-kita, Chiyoda-ku, Tokyo 102
Telephone: +81 3 5276 3411
Fax: +81 3 5276 3414
Chief officers: Michio Nakajima (Chairman)

Japan Cosmetic Industry Association
Address: Hatsumei Kaikan, 2-9-14 Toranomon, Minato-ku, Tokyo 105
Telephone: +81 3 3502 0576
Fax: +81 3 3502 0829
Year established: 1959
Chief officers: Yoshiharu Fukuhara (Chairman)
Publications:
• Cosmetic Industry Annual Report: *contains reports on the industry, including statistics on production, imports and exports of cosmetic products - annual*

Japan Dairy Products' Association
Address: Komodo Kudan Building, Nyugyo-Kaikan, 1-14-19 Kudan-kita, Chiyoda-ku, Tokyo 102
Telephone: +81 33 264 3731
Fax: +81 33 264 3732
Year established: 1954
Chief officers: Mr T. Hirota (Secretary General)
Membership: 18 companies
Publications:
• Dairy Milk: *monthly*

Japan Data Communications' Association
Address: 5-14-3 Nishi Nippori, Arakawa-ku, Tokyo 116
Telephone: +81 3 3801 0111
Fax: +81 3 3801 0115
Year established: 1973
Activities: research, education, training, consultation on data communications and distribution of materials and information on data communications
Chief officers: Minoru Shioya (Director General), Atsu Konishi (Executive General)
Membership: 74 members

Japan Department Stores' Association
Address: Yanagiya Building, 2-1-10, Nihonbashi, Chuo-ku, Tokyo 103
Telephone: +81 3 3272 1666
Fax: +81 3 3281 0381
Chief officers: Yoshiaki Sakakura (Chairman)

Japan DIY Industry Association
Shadan Hojin DIY Kyokai
Address: No. 2 Kaono Building, 2-16-7 Higashi Nihonbashi, Chuo-ku, Tokyo 103
Telephone: +81 3 5687 4475/6
Fax: +81 3 5687 4487
Year established: 1980
Chief officers: Toshiakai Tanzawa (Chairman), Michiaki Yamamoto (Secretary General)
Membership: 860 companies
Publications:
• Brochure for Japan DIY Show
• Exhibitors List Only: *gives names of exhibitors at Japan DIY show in Tokyo and Osaka*

- Member Lists
- Our Project Profile

Japan Electric Association
Nihon Denki Kyokai
Address: Yurakucho Electric Building (North), 1-7-1 Yurakucho, Chiyoda-ku, Tokyo 100
Telephone: +81 3 3216 0555
Fax: +81 3 3214 6005
Chief officers: Kiyoji Mori (President)
Publications:
- Journal of the Japan Electric Association (Nihon Denki Kyokai Zasshi): *as well as trade news, there are reports from the Association and special reports and articles contributed by those in the industry - monthly*

Japan Electric Heater Co-operative Association
Address: Dennetsu Building, 2-18-8 Nakazato, Kita-ku, Tokyo 114
Telephone: +81 3 3576 1123
Fax: +81 3 3576 1124
Chief officers: Kiyoshi Watanabe (Chairman), Sadahiro Ishizaki (Vice-Chairman)
Membership: 150 companies

Japan Electric Lamp Manufacturers' Association
Address: Yurakucho Denki Bldg, North wing, 7-1, Yurakucho 1-chome, Chiyodo-ku, Tokyo 100
Telephone: +81 3 3201 2641
Fax: +81 3 3201 2644
Chief officers: Kinichi Kadono (president), Seinosuke Ito (Executive Director)
Membership: 110 members

Japan Electrical Manufacturers' Association
Nihon Denki Kogyokai
Address: Denki Kogyo Kaikan, 2-4-15 Nagatacho, Chiyoda-ku, Tokyo 100
Telephone: +81 3 3581 4841
Fax: +81 3 3593 3198
Year established: 1948
Activities: financial and legal support for new technologies, promotion of standardisation in the industry, both in Japan and overseas, and the promotion of safety within the industry
Chief officers: Yoshihiko Nakazato (Chairman)
Membership: 262 companies
Publications:
- Electrical Industries in Japan: *a review, with statistics, of trends in the Japanese electrical sector with data on heavy electrical machinery and domestic electrical appliances - annual*
- JEMA Report: Production, Exports, Imports: *commentary and statistics on the production of heavy electrical machinery, electrical home appliances and other electrical goods. Also import and export data for the above products. Statistics for the last few years are given - annual*

Japan Electronic Industry Development Association (JEIDA)
Nihon denshi Kogyo Shinko Kyokai
Address: Kikai Shinko Kaikan Building, 5-8 Shibakoen 3-chome, Minato-ku, Tokyo 105
Telephone: +81 3 3433 6296/1922
Fax: +81 3 3433 2003/6350
Year established: 1958
Activities: organises the "Embedded Systems Solutions" and "Data Show" trade fairs in Tokyo
Chief officers: Tsutomu Kanai (Chairman), Seishun Sato

(Managing Director)
Membership: 175 companies
Publications:
- Computer Industry in Japan (brochure)
- Guide to JEIDA
- JEIDA Memeber Lists

Japan Electronic Products Importers' Association
Nihon Denshi Kiki Yunyu Kyokai
Address: c/o Hakuta Co. Ltd, 1-13 Shinjuku 1-chome, Shinjuku-ku, Tokyo 160
Telephone: +81 3 3225 8069
Fax: +81 3 3225 9060
Year established: 1976
Chief officers: Shigeo Takayama (Chairman), Toshihiro Moriya (Secretary General)
Membership: 54 companies
Publications:
- JEPIA Member Lists

Japan Federation of Consumer Credit Companies
Address: Toshin Kanda Bldg., 14 Kanda Higashi Matsushitacho, Chiyoda-ku, Tokyo 101
Telephone: +81 3 5296 2971
Fax: +81 3 5296 2979
Chief officers: Nobutaka Shibuya (President)

Japan Federation of Economic Organisations
Keidanren
Address: 1-9-4, Otemachi, Chiyoda-ku, Tokyo 100
Telephone: +81 3 327 91411
Fax: +81 3 525 56255
E-mail: webmaster@keidanren.or.jp
Web site: www.keidanren.or.jp
Chief officers: Shimamoto Akinori, (Director International Relations Bureau)
Membership: 970 corporations and 123 association members

Japan Federation of Employers' Associations
Nikkeiren
Address: 4-6 Marunouchi 1-chome, Chiyoda-ku, Tokyo 130
Telephone: +81 3 3213 4474
Year established: 1948
Activities: represents almost all private industry except agriculture and forestry; deals with labour and social issues from employers viewpoint
Chief officers: Jiro Nemoto (Chairman)
Membership: includes 47 regional associations, and 55 industrial associations

Japan Fine Ceramics Association
Address: Halifax Onarimon Building, 6th Floor, 24-10 Nishinbashi 3-chome, Minato-ku, Tokyo 105
Telephone: +81 3 3437 3781
Fax: +81 3 3437 3790
Year established: 1986
Chief officers: Toshihito Kohara (Chairman), Hitosito Watanabe (Executive Director)

Japan Fine Ceramics Centre (JFCC)
Nihon Fain Seramikkusu Senta
Address: 2-4-1 Mutsuno, Atsuta-ku, Nagoya 456
Telephone: +81 52 871 3500
Fax: +81 52 871 3505
Year established: 1985
Activities: activities connected with the advanced ceramics industry, as well as organising the Fine Ceramics Fair (Nagoya)
Chief officers: Takeshi Hijikata (Chairman), Nobufumi Ito

(Secretary General)
Membership: 253 member companies
Publications:
• Japan Fine Ceramics Center Today

Japan Fisheries Association

Address: Sankaido Building, 9-13 Akasaka 1-chome, Minato-ku, Tokyo 107
Telephone: +81 3 3585 6683
Fax: +81 3 3582 2337
Chief officers: Hiroya Sano (President)

Japan Food Additives' Association

Address: Nihonbashi-Sanei Building, 3rd Floor, 3-9 Nihonbashi Horidome-cho 1-chome, Chuo-k, Tokyo 103
Telephone: +81 3 3667 8311
Fax: +81 3 3667 2860
Year established: 1982
Chief officers: Sabourouke Suzuki (President), Akio Kawamoto (Executive Managing Director)

Japan Food Service Association

Nihon Food Service Kyokai
Address: Hamamatsu-cho Central Building, 1-29-6 Hamamatsu-cho, Minato-ku, Tokyo
Telephone: +81 3 3573 3231
Fax: +81 3 3572 5099
E-mail: jfnet@itjit.ne.jp
Web site: www.itjit.ne.jp/~jfnet/
Activities: education and research to improve the food service industry, communication between members of the industry and researchers into food products and food ingredients, management service for members, and PR work for the industry
Chief officers: Ohkawara Takeshi (President)
Membership: 731 members (419 regular members, 312 backing members)
Publications:
• JF Yearbook: *includes an outline of the Association's member companies - annually*

Japan Frozen Food Association

Address: No.2 Katsuraya Building, 10-6 Nihonbashi, Kofune-cho, Chuo-Ku, Tokyo 103
Telephone: +81 3 366 76671
Fax: +81 3 366 92117
Year established: 1969
Chief officers: Kozo Kaneda (President), Mr Tsutomu Hisa (Director General)
Structure: annual general meeting, many standing committees
Membership: 985 companies, associations and organisations
Publications:
• Frozen Food Statistics (Japan Frozen Food Association): *detailed statistics on the Japanese frozen food industry - annual*

Japan Fruit Juice Association

Address: Nihonbashi Fuji Building, 2-5-13 Nihonbahi, Chuo-ku, Tokyo 103
Telephone: +81 3 3275 1031
Fax: +81 3 3275 1067
Chief officers: Akiteru Okada (President)
Publications:
• Japan Fruit Juice Industry: *monthly data on the production of fruit drinks (volume) plus production of fruit juice, imports, and the harvest of the main fruits as well as consumption - monthly*

Japan Golf Goods' Association (JGGA)

Nihon Gorufu Yohin Kyokai
Address: Kanda Kobayashi Building, 6-11-11, Soto Kanda, Chiyoda-ku, Tokyo 101
Telephone: +81 3 3832 8589
Fax: +81 3 3832 8594
Year established: 1982
Activities: organises the Japan Golf Fair (Tokyo), and the Japan Golf Fair Autumn (Osaka)
Chief officers: Masato Mizuno (Chairman), Akira Kida (Secretary General)
Membership: 601 companies
Publications:
• JGGA Newsletter: *news on the activities of the Association as well as company profiles and product information*

Japan Health Food and Specialist Nutrition Association

Nihon Kenko Eiyo Shokuhin Kyokai
Address: Shokuhin Eisei center Building, 2-6-1 Jingumae, Shibuya-ku, Tokyo 150
Telephone: +81 3 5410 8231
Fax: +81 3 5410 8235
Year established: 1992
Activities: coordinates activities related to health food and special nutrition foods
Publications:
• Guide To Health Foods: *a publication aimed at consumers with information on healthy eating and health food products - irregular*
• Japan Health Food Authorisation (JHFA): *catalogues JHFA approved products*
• Survey on Awareness on Health Foods: *in-depth survey on attitudes to health foods. Includes statistics on the Japanese health food market by product type - biannual*

Japan Ice Cream Association

Address: Nyugyo Kaikan 7F, 1-14-19 Kudan-kita, Chiyoda-ku, Tokyo 102
Telephone: +81 3 3264 3104
Fax: +81 3 3230 1354
Year established: 1966
Activities: produces statistics on the Japanese ice-cream industry
Chief officers: Akira Ono
Membership: 276

Japan Information Service Industry Association (JISA)

Joho Service Sangyo Kyokai
Address: Time 24 Bldg, 2-45 Aomi, Koto-ku, Tokyo 135-73
Telephone: +81 3 5500 2610
Fax: +81 3 5500 2630
Year established: 1984
Chief officers: Tomoo Takahara (Chairman), Hirotake Oshio (Secretary General)
Membership: 542 companies
Publications:
• JISA Membership Directory
• JISA Newsletter
• JISA Profile

Japan Laser Disk Association

Nihon Laser Disk Kyokai
Address: 1-4-1, Meguru, Meguru-ku, Tokyo 153
Telephone: +81 3 349 38990
Fax: +81 3 349 56329
Chief officers: Mr Yamashita

Japan Leather and Leather Goods Industries' Association

Address: 2nd Floor, Meiyu Building, 4-9 Kaminarimon
2-chome, Taito-ku, Tokyo 111
Telephone: +81 3 3847 1451
Fax: +81 3 3847 1510

Japan Lighting Association

Nihon Shomeikigu Kogyokai
Address: Fujio Building, 2-1 Ueno 3-chome, Taito-ku, Tokyo
110
Telephone: +81 3 3833 5747
Fax: +81 3 3833 8455
Year established: 1942
Activities: dissemination of information
Chief officers: Tadao Kano (Chairman), Yusaku Matsushima
(Secretary General)
Membership: 115 member companies
Publications:
• Member List of Japan Luminaires Association: *lists the
Association's members*

Japan Magazine Publishers' Association (JMPA)

Address: 1-7 Kanda Surugadai, Chiyoda-ku, Tokyo 101
Telephone: +81 3 329 107 75
Fax: +81 3 329 362 39
Web site: www.j-magazine.or.jp
Web site notes: site includes data on the Japanese magazine
market with statistics on the following: total number of
magazines; magazine sales; sales revenue; current trends in
magazine publishing; distribution
Year established: 1956
Activities: conducts magazine related surveys and research;
liaises with legislative bodies and other organisations
Chief officers: Kengo Tanaka (Chairman), Sadami Akita
(Executive Director)
Membership: 84 magazine publishers who account for 85%
of total Japanese magazine circulation

Japan Management Association

Address: 3-1-22 Shiba Koen, Minato-ku, Tokyo 105
Telephone: +81 3 3434 6211
Fax: +81 3 3434 1087
Chief officers: Tatsuki Mikami (Chairman)

Japan Margarine, Shortening and Lard Association

Address: 27-8 Nihonbashi Hama-cho 3-chome, Chuo-ku,
Tokyo 103
Telephone: +81 3 3666 6159
Fax: +81 3 3666 6150
Year established: 1947
Chief officers: Toshiyuki Miki (Chairman), Nobuji Saito
(Secretary General)

Japan Medical Products International Trade Association

Nihon Iyakuryohin Yushutsu Kumiai
Address: Ninjin Building, 7-1 Nihonbashi Hon-cho, 4-chome,
Chuo-ku, Tokyo 103
Telephone: +81 3 3241 2106
Fax: +81 3 3241 2109
Year established: 1953
Chief officers: Tadashi Suzuki (President), Kuniichiro Ohno
(Managing Director), Tokuji Kasamatsu (Secretary General)
Membership: 160 companies involved in pharmaceuticals,
OTC Drugs, surgical dressings, dental and medical
equipment and instruments
Publications:
• Japan Medical Instruments Catalogue (JMC)
• Japan Medical News

• Japan Pharmaceutical Reference (JPR)
• Member Lists

Japan Mineral Water Association

Address: 3F Tomomi Bldg, 5-11-19 Shinjuku, Shinjuku-ku,
Tokyo
Telephone: +81 3 335 09100
Fax: +81 3 335 07960
Publications:
• Production of Domestic Mineral Water: *detailed statistics on
production of mineral water in Japan - annual*

Japan Motor Industrial Federation

Address: Otemachi Building, 1-6-1 Otemachi, Chiyoda-ku,
Tokyo 100
Telephone: +81 3 3211 8731
Fax: +81 3 3211 5798
Web site: www.motorshow.or.jp
Web site notes: site includes statistics on Japanese
passenger car sales by market sector; domestic registrations
by manufacturer; new motor vehicle registrations; domestic
demand for motorcycles; production; imports and exports
Year established: 1958
Activities: the association functions as a PR agency for the
Automotive Industry of Japan, and its main undertaking is the
organising of the Tokyo Motor Show, as well as publishing
books and films
Chief officers: Yoshifumi Tsuji (Chairman), Yoshio Komiya
(Executive Managing Director)

Japan National Tourist Organisation (JNTO)

Address: 2-10-1, Yurakucho, 2-chome, Chiyoda-ku, Tokyo 100
Telephone: +81 3 321 619 02/2905
Fax: +81 3 321 476 80
E-mail: jnto@jnto.go.jp
Web site: www.jnto.go.jp
Year established: 1964
Activities: operates tourist information centres for foreign
visitors to Japan, consolidation of reception facilities for
overseas visitors, promotion of international conventions and
international events, international tourism-related research and
publication of printed materials, dissemination of information
on recommended health and safety precautions for Japanese
travellers overseas, conducting annual National Examination
for Guide-interpreters
Chief officers: Mr Akira Niwa (President), Mr Satoshi
Nakamura (Executive Vice President)
Membership: tourism business sector
Publications:
• Statistics on Tourism: *statistics on visitor arrivals and
Japanese overseas travellers, travel receipts, and payments.
Other tables cover visitor arrivals by nationality, purpose of
visit, month of arrival, and Japanese overseas travellers by
destination and month. Most tables give historical data over a
five or ten year period. Based on Japanese official data and
data from overseas tourist offices - annual*

Japan Newspaper Association

Nihon Shimbun Kyokai
Address: 7th Floor Nippon Press Centre Building, 2-1
Uchisaiwai-cho 2-chome, Chiyoda-ku, Tokyo 100
Telephone: +81 3 35914401
Fax: +81 3 3591 6149
Year established: 1946
Chief officers: Yosoji Kobayahi (President), Toshie Yamada
(General Secretary), Asano Osamu (Managing Director and
Secretary General)

Japan Optical Industry Association

Address: Kikai Shinko Kaikan, 3-5-8 Shiba Koen, Minato-ku, Tokyo 105
Telephone: +81 3 3431 7073
Chief officers: Koji Sho (Chairman)

Japan Paint Manufacturers' Association

Address: Tokyo Toryo Kaikan, 3-12-8 Ebisu, Shibuya-ku, Tokyo 150
Telephone: +81 3 3443 2011
Fax: +81 3 3443 3599
Year established: 1986
Chief officers: Masuo Tanaka (Chairman), Seiya Hoshino (President)

Japan Paper Association

Nihon Seishi Rengokai
Address: Kami-Parupu Kaikan Building, 9-11 Ginza 3-chome, Chuo-ku, Tokyo 104
Telephone: +81 3 3248 4801
Fax: +81 3 3248 4826
Year established: 1972
Chief officers: Masahiko Ohkuni (Chairman), Seiya Hoshino (Secretary-General)
Membership: 56 companies
Publications:
• Pulp and Paper Statistics: *a general review is followed by pulp and paperboard statistics covering production, demand, imports, exports, employment, earnings, raw materials use, and advertising. Graphs and tables cover the last ten years in most instances - annual*

Japan Petrochemical Industry Association

Address: Iino Building, 1-1 Uchisaiwai-cho 2-chome, Chiyoda-ku, Tokyo 100
Telephone: +81 3 350 12151
Fax: +81 3 350 13895
Year established: 1958
Chief officers: Reiichi Yumikura (Chairman), Hiroshi Goto (Senior Managing Director)

Japan Pharmaceutical Manufacturers' Association (JPMA)

Address: Torii Nihonbashi Building, 3-4-1 Nihonbashi Honcho 3-chome, Chuo-ku, Tokyo 103
Telephone: +81 3241 0326
Fax: +81 3242 1767
E-mail: jpma@ppp.bekkoame.or.jp
Year established: 1968
Chief officers: Tomokichiro Fujisawa (President)

Japan Recording Media Industries' Association

Address: Toranomon Chiyoda Building, 1-16-2 Toranomon, Minato-ku, Tokyo 105
Telephone: +81 3 3501 0631
Fax: +81 3 3501 0630
Year established: 1953
Activities: market research and technical trend research into magnetic recording tapes, video tapes, floppy disks and optical media; publication of Association Standard (MTS), research and distribution of production statistics among members
Chief officers: Minoru Ohnishi (President), Kyohei Kimura (Managing Director)
Membership: 79 companies (14 regular members, 64 supporting members, 1 organisation)

Japan Refrigeration and Air Conditioning Industrial Association

Shadanhojin Nihon Reito Kucho Kogyokai
Address: Kikai Shinko Kaikan, 5-8 Shiba-koen 3-chome, Minato-ku, Tokyo 105
Telephone: +81 3 3432 1671
Fax: +81 3 3438 0308
Year established: 1949
Chief officers: Hiroyuki Fujimura (Chairman of the Board), Tsuguhiro Amano (President)
Publications:
• Refrigeration and Air-Conditioning: *statistics and indices on refrigeration and air conditioning, details of the association's news, upcoming seminars and trade fairs - monthly*

Japan Retailers' Association

Nihon Kouri Gyosha Kyokai
Address: 3-2-2, Marunouchi, Chiyoda-ku, Tokyo Shokpkaigisho Building 4F, Tokyo 100
Telephone: +81 3 3283 7920
Fax: +81 3 3215 7698

Japan Rubber Manufacturers' Association

Address: Tosen Building, 5-26 Motoakasaka 1-chome, Minato-ku, Tokyo 107
Telephone: +81 3 3408 7101
Fax: +81 3 3408 7106
Year established: 1950
Chief officers: Shizuo Katsurada (President)

Japan Securities Dealers' Association

Address: 1-5-8 Nihonbashi Kayabacho, Chuo-ku, Tokyo 103
Telephone: +81 3 3667 8451
Fax: +81 3 3666 8009
Chief officers: Masashi Suzuki (Chairman)

Japan Semi-Baked Confectionery Association

Nihon Hannama Kashi Kyokai
Address: Shirainagotomido, 54 Mibumatsubara-cho Nakagyo-ku, Kyoto 604
Telephone: +81 7 5311 3692
Fax: +81 7 5321 5710

Japan Sesame Oil Industry Association

Address: 1-7-11 Nihonbashi, Chuo-ku, Tokyo 103
Telephone: +81 3 3271 4402
Fax: +81 3 3274 0830
Chief officers: Takemoto
Membership: 11

Japan Silk and Synthetic Textiles Exporters' Association

Nihon Kinukasen Yushutsu Kumiai
Address: 4-9 Bingo-machi 3-chome, Chuo-ku, Osaka 541
Telephone: +81 6 201 1812
Fax: +81 6 201 1819
Year established: 1952
Chief officers: Kazuo Haruna (Chairman), Takao Kobayashi (Secretary-General)
Membership: 157 companies involved in staples, yarns and fabrics of silk and man made fibers
Publications:
• JSSTEA Members List

Japan Small Vehicle Association

Address: 3-20-4 Nishi Shinbashi, Minato-ku, Tokyo 105
Telephone: +81 3 3436 2381
Fax: +81 3 3436 2385

Japan Smoking Articles Corporate Association (JSACA)

Nihon Kitsuengu Kyokai
Address: Nihon Kitsuenga Kyokai Building, 19-5 Kotobuki 3-chome, Taito-ku, Tokyo 111
Telephone: +81 3 3845 6121
Fax: +81 3 3845 6128
Year established: 1976
Chief officers: Susumu Maruyama (Chairman), Tamotsu Kuroiwa (Secretary-General)
Membership: 145 manufacturers of smoking goods such as cigarette lighters, cases, holders, and pipes

Japan Soap and Detergent Association (JSDA)

Nihon Sekken Senzai Kogyokai
Address: Yushi Kogyo Kaikan, 13-11 Nihonbashi, 3-Chome, Chuo-Ku, Tokyo 103
Telephone: +81 3 3271 4301
Fax: +81 3 3281 1870
Year established: 1950
Chief officers: Fumikatsu Tokiwa (Chairman), Dr. Yoshiaki Komeda (Executive Director)
Publications:
• Annual Environmental Report: *data on water quality, sewerage and pollution in key Japanese localities. Includes reports on synthetic detergents and the reduction of packaging materials - annual*
• Annual Report: *detailed statistics and analysis of the Japanese market. Includes information on production of soaps and detergents, sales of skin cleansers, shampoos, soaps, detergents and other household products. Also includes data on imports and exports - annual*
• Soap and Detergent Industry Statistics: *production, consumption, and sales of products for the latest year. Also includes information on imports and exports and international trends - annual*

Japan Soft Drinks' Association

Address: Kurosebia Hongo Building 5-F,, 3-23-1 Hongo, Bunkyo-ku, Tokyo 113
Telephone: +81 3 3814 0666
Fax: +81 3 3813 9739
Chief officers: Michinori Kuwabara (President)
Publications:
• Soft Drinks Statistics Book: *annual trends in the production of various types of soft drinks, volume of imported soft drinks, brands, drinks expenditure per family, production of soy milk, and some related statistics for the USA and Europe - annual*

Japan Spinners' Association

Address: Mengyo Kaikan Building, 2-5-8 Bingomachi, Chuo-ku, Osaka 541
Telephone: +81 6 231 8431
Fax: +81 6 229 1590
Chief officers: Akihiro Mochizuki (President), Kan-ichi Itoh (Executive Director)
Publications:
• Annual Statistical Review (Japan Spinners Association): *a detailed commentary on the cotton and allied textile industry in Japan is followed by statistical tables on industry capacity and equipment, raw materials consumed and imported, production of specific textiles, imports, exports, and a summary table on the demand/supply position. Most tables give data over a five year period with an emphasis on data from official sources - annual*

Japan Spirits and Liquor Makers' Association

Nihon Joryu Shuzo Kumiai
Address: Kouru Dai 1 Building, 1-6 Nihombashi, Kabayo-cho 1-chome, Chuo-ku, Tokyo 103

Telephone: +81 3 3281 5316
Fax: +81 3 3281 5310

Japan Sports Industries' Federation

Sports Sangyo Dantai Rengokai
Address: Nogakushorin Building 3F, 3-6 Kanda Jinbo-co, Chiyoda-ku, Tokyo 101
Telephone: +81 5 5276 0141
Fax: +81 5 5276 0288
Year established: 1988
Activities: organises the International Trade Fair for Sports and Leisure
Chief officers: Yutaka Takeda (Chairman), Toru Terayama (Secretary General)
Membership: 91 companies

Japan Storage Battery Association

Address: Kikai Shinko Kaikan, 3-5-8 Shiba Koen, Minato-ku, Tokyo 105
Telephone: +81 3 3434 0261
Fax: +81 3 3434 2691
Year established: 1972
Activities: promotion of storage batteries; provides certification tests for approval of storage batteries as an emergency power source; research; studies on production and marketing; examination of environmental safety checks
Chief officers: Teruhisa Yuasa (President), Masahiko Sakatani (Executive Director)
Membership: 11 member companies

Japan Tea Association

Address: J C Building, 3-6-22 Shibakoen, Minato-ku, Tokyo 105
Telephone: +81 3 3431 6509
Fax: +81 3 3431 6711
Year established: 1971
Chief officers: Yoshiaki Nakade
Structure: regular standing committees
Membership: 58 companies (including tea boards from India, Kenya, Sri Lanka)
Publications:
• Tea: *monthly*

Japan Textile Importers' Association

Nippon Sen-i Yunyu Kumiai
Address: 9th Floor, Nihonbashi Daiwa Building, 1-9-4 Nihonbashi Honcho, Chuo-ku, Tokyo 103
Telephone: +81 3 3270 0791
Fax: +81 3 3243 1088
Year established: 1972
Activities: conducts surveys of foreign markets and profiles foreign manufacturers, produces textile-related statistics, provides information on importing and offers an arbitration service
Chief officers: Iwao Toriumi (President), Yutaka Shimamine (Executive Managing Director)
Membership: 160 member companies
Publications:
• Japan Textile Imports Statistics Monthly: *a summary of trade is followed by detailed statistics on the imports of yarns, fabrics and garments. Imports cover specific products and specific countries. Statistics cover the latest month and are based on official figures - monthly*
• Japanese Apparel Market Imports: *a regular review of the Japanese apparel market concentrating on the role of imported products with data on specific products - regular*
• List of Members: *lists the Association's members*

Japan Toothpaste Manufacturers' Association (JDMA)

Nihon Hamigaki Kogyokai
Address: Primo-KS No.2 Building 6F, 2-9-2 Higashi
Nihonbashi, Chuo-ku, Tokyo 103
Telephone: +81 3 3866 6586
Fax: +81 3 3866 6574
Year established: 1971
Chief officers: Michinao Takahashi (Chairman), Seiichiro
Kaga (Secretary General)
Membership: 13 member companies, 19 associate members
Publications:
• General Products Catalog: *covers products available in the
oral hygiene market*
• JDMA Member List: *lists the Association's members*

Japan Toy Association

Nihon Gangu Kyokai
Address: 22-4 Higashi Komagata 4-chome, Sumida-ku, Tokyo
130
Telephone: +81 3 3829 2513
E-mail: toys@fjt.co.jp
Web site: www.fjt.co.jp/TOYS/indexe.htm
Web site notes: site includes some information and statistics
on the Japanese toy market
Year established: 1967
Activities: government liaison, public relations and the
compilation of industry statistics
Chief officers: Makoto Yamashina (Chairman), Taizo Okano
(Director)
Membership: 537 member companies

Japan Trade and Investment Insurance Organisation

Address: Akasaka Twin Tower Main Building, 2-17-22
Akasaka, Minato-ku, Tokyo 107
Telephone: +81 3 3224 1201
Fax: +81 3 3224 0527
Chief officers: Takashi Okabe (President)

Japan Vending Machine Manufacturers' Association

Address: Shinbashi Tanaka Building, 2-37-6 Nishi Shinbashi,
Minato-ku, Tokyo 105
Telephone: +81 3 3431 7443
Fax: +81 3 3431 1967
Year established: 1963
Chief officers: Masayoshi Ushikubo (Chairman), Hisae Onoe
(President), Shori Sawatori (Director General)
Membership: 88 members

Japan Vinyl Goods Manufacturers' Association

Address: Tobu Building, 1-5-26 Moto Akasaka, Minato-ku,
Tokyo 107
Telephone: +81 3 5413 1311
Fax: +81 3 3401 9351
Chief officers: Tsuneo Kondo (Chairman)

Japan Wool Importers' Association

Address: c/o Mengyo Kaikan, 5-8 2-chome, Bingo-machi,
Chuo-ku, Osaka 541
Telephone: +81 6 231 6201
Fax: +81 6 231 6276

Japan Wool Spinners' Association

Address: Ueno DK Building, 1-15-4 Ueno, Taito-ku, Tokyo 110
Telephone: +81 3 3837 7916
Fax: +81 3 3837 7918
Chief officers: Mitsuo Shiraha (Chairman)

Japan Woollen and Linen Textiles Exporters' Association

Address: 4-9 Bingo-machi 3-chome, Chuo-ku, Osaka 541
Telephone: +81 6 202 5067
Fax: +81 6 231 1045
Telex: 5222614 KEASAO J
Year established: 1952
Activities: activities related to woollen and linen textile
industry, and organising stands at various trade fairs
worldwide
Chief officers: Akira Nishio (Chairman), Shogo Asahina
(Secretary General)
Membership: 61 companies

Japanese Advertising Agencies' Association (JAAA)

Nihon Kokokugyo Kyokai
Address: 8-12, Ginza 4-Chome, Chuo-ku Tokyo
Telephone: +81 3 3562 0876
Fax: +81 3 3562 0889
Web site: www.inter.co.jp/JAAA/english.html
Year established: 1950
Activities: government liaison, information service for
members, organises conferences and maintains a small library
Chief officers: Eijiro Sakurai (Executive Director), Yoshikazu
Ishibashi (International Service Manager)
Membership: 155 agencies representing approximately 78%
of total advertising expenditure in Japan
Publications:
• JAAA Reports: *monthly*

Japanese Association of Refrigeration

Nihon Reito Kyokai
Address: San-ei Building, 8 San-ei-cho, Shinjuku-ku, Tokyo
160
Telephone: +81 3 3359 5231
Fax: +81 3 3359 5233
Year established: 1951
Publications:
• Refrigeration: *trade journal covering both refrigeration and
air-conditioning: includes statistics related to the consumer
market, as well as new technological developments in
manufacturing and production, foreign articles translated into
Japanese, and details of national and international
conferences, and news of events in the industry - monthly*
• Transactions of the Japanese Refrigeration Society: *scientific
and technical articles on refrigeration - three issues p.a.*

Japanese Consumers' Co-operative Union

Address: Seikyo Kaikan, 4-1-13 Sendagaya, Shibuya-ku,
Tokyo 151
Telephone: +81 3 3497 9111
Fax: +81 3 3402 8246
Chief officers: Shigenori Takemoto (President)

Life Insurance Association of Japan

Address: Shinkokusai Building, 3-4-1 Marunouchi,
Chiyoda-ku, Tokyo 100
Telephone: +81 3 3286 2624
Fax: +81 3 3201 6713
Chief officers: Kenjiro Hata (Chairman)

Marine and Fire Insurance Association of Japan

Address: Non-Life Insurance Building, 9 Kanda Awajicho,
2-chome, Chiyoda-ku, Tokyo 101
Telephone: +81 3 3255 1211
Fax: +81 3 3255 1270
Chief officers: Takeo Inokuchi (Chairman)
Publications:
• Fact Book Non-Life Insurance in Japan: *an annual market*

report on the non-life insurance industry in Japan with data on premiums, revenue, types of insurance, etc - annual

National Association of Commercial Broadcasters in Japan

Address: 3-23 kioicho, Chiyoda-ku, Tokyo 100
Telephone: +81 3 5213 7711
Fax: +81 3 5213 7703
Chief officers: Seiichiro Ujiie (President)

National Paper Merchants' Association of Japan

Address: 2-42-10 Nihonbashi, Hama-cho, Chuo-ku, Tokyo
Telephone: +81 3 3669 5171
Fax: +81 3 3664 7163
Chief officers: Akira Seki (Chairman), Shizuka Kuroko (Executive Director)

National Rice Association

Address: Shokuryo Kaikan, 3-3-6 Kojimachi, Chiyoda-ku, Tokyo 102
Telephone: +81 3 3222 9581
Fax: +81 3 3264 1771
Chief officers: Hiroyuki Noake (Chairman)

Petroleum Association of Japan

Address: Keidanren Kaikan, 1-9-4 Otemachi, Chiyoda-ku, Tokyo 100
Telephone: +81 3 3279 3811
Fax: +81 3 3242 5688
Chief officers: Yuji Idemitsu (President)

Petroleum Energy Centre (PEC)

Sekiyu Sangyo Kasseika Center
Address: 3-9 Toranomon 4-chome, Minato-ku, Tokyo 105
Telephone: +81 3 5402 8500
Fax: +81 3 3402 8511
Year established: 1986
Activities: research and technical development in all areas connected with the refining and marketing of petrolem
Chief officers: Kazushige Nagashima (Chief Director), Shigeyuki Sasaki (Secretary General and Executive Director), Kanae Niwa (Senior Managing Director)
Membership: 122 member companies

Recording Industry Association of Japan

Address: 2-8-9 Tsukiji, Chuo-ku, Tokyo 104
Telephone: +81 3 3541 4411
Fax: +81 3 3541 4460
Year established: 1942
Activities: carries out studies into all the problems common to member companies that exist or arise out of the production, pressing, copyright sound and audio-visual recordings, the sale and promotion of the product, and looks at suitable solutions for these problems
Chief officers: Shugo Matsuo (President), Ikuo Kato (Executive Director), Saburo Kimura (Managing Director and General Manager)
Membership: 27 members
Publications:
• RIAJ Yearbook: *a yearbook for the recording industry in Japan with company data and other industry information plus some statistics on industry trends - annual*

Society of Japanese Aerospace Companies (SJAC)

Address: Hibiya Park Building, Suite 518, 8-1 Yuraka-cho 1-chome, Chiyoda-ku, Tokyo 100

Telephone: +81 3 3211 5678
Fax: +81 3 3211 5018
Year established: 1952
Chief officers: Kentaro Aikawa (Chairman), Toshihiko Nakamura (President)
Membership: 177 Japanese companies involved in the manufacture of aerospace equipment
Publications:
• Aerospace Industry in Japan: *bi-annual*
• Aerospace Statistics: *a summary of the sector is followed by statistics on production by type of product, demand, imports, exports, manpower. Tables cover both complete aircraft and aircraft parts and engines - annual*
• Nihon Koku Uchu Kogyokai Kaiho: *monthly*

Sporting Goods Importers' Association of Japan (SGIA JAPAN)

Nihon Sports Yohin Yunyu Kyokai
Address: Misaki Building 9F, 3-28-9, Kanda-Ogawamachi, Chiyoda-ku, Tokyo 101
Telephone: +81 3 3219 2532
Fax: +81 3 3219 2533
Year established: 1971
Activities: matters relating to the importing of sporting goods; displays at the Sporting Goods Trade Fair (Sports Japan, Spring and Autumn)
Chief officers: Kenji Koike (Chairman), Hirotaka Miyaji (Director General)
Membership: 28 member companies
Publications:
• SGIA Japan Member List: *lists the Association's members*

Tanners' Council of Japan

Nihon Tanners Kyokai
Address: c/o Himeji Palacio II Building, 100, Minami-Ekimae-cho, Himeji City, Hyogo 670
Telephone: +81 792 82 6701
Fax: +81 792 82 6703
Year established: 1978
Activities: activities related to the leather tanning industry
Chief officers: Masashi Yamura (Chairman), Kiminaga Deguchi (Executive Director)
Structure: 593 member companies
Publications:
• Japan Leather Industry News

Tokyo International Trade Fair Commission

Address: 4-7-24 Harumi, Chuo-ku, Tokyo 104
Telephone: +81 3 3531 3371-9
Fax: +81 3 3531 1344
Activities: organising trade fairs, in particular the Tokyo International trade fair, the Tokyo International Good Living Show, Japan International Machine Tool Fair, Firesafety Frontier, Tokyo Flower Show, Tokyo International RV Show, Measurements and Quality Control Exhibition (Micro Tech)
Chief officers: Shunichi Suzuki (Chairman), Takeji Sekioka (Director General),

Tokyo Stationery Industry Association

Tokyo Bunbogu Kogyokai
Address: 3-14, Asakusabashi 1-chome, Taito-ku, Tokyo 111
Telephone: +81 3 3864 4391
Fax: +81 3 3864 4393

JORDAN

Agricultural Products Wholesalers' Association
Address: PO Box 326 or PO Box 621295, Amman
Telephone: +962 6 791 229/756 344
Fax: +962 6 649 496/756 344
Chief officers: Salim Jadoun (Chairman); Hammed Schoubaki (Manager)

Association of Banks in Jordan
Address: PO Box 926174, Amman
Telephone: +962 6 662 258
Fax: +962 6 687 011
Web site: www.arab.net/abj/
Year established: 1978
Activities: information service; develops and modernises the banking services; publishes bulletins and periodicals dealing with various aspects of banking activities; organises seminars, panel discussions and lectures on economic issues in general and banking topics in particular; establishes institutes and centres for banking training and studies; prepares and circulates studies and research related to the banking business
Structure: General Assembly and Board of Directors
Membership: banks, financial companies, specialised credit institutions and representative offices working in Jordan

Foodstuff Merchants' Association
Address: PO Box 7664, Al-Shemesani, Amman
Telephone: +962 6 690 540/539
Fax: +962 6 690 539
Chief officers: Ilya Noukoul (President)

General Association for Clothing and Textiles
Address: PO Box 182229, Amman
Telephone: +962 6 624 251/623 442
Fax: +962 6 655 409/655 409
Chief officers: Salah Amin Ihmidan (President)

General Association of Automotive Agents, Spare Parts and Accessories Traders
Address: PO Box 4462, Amman
Telephone: +962 6 651 763/743 773
Fax: +962 6 651 736
Chief officers: Mohammed Maddani (President)

General Syndicate of Bakery Products
Address: PO Box 183966, Amman
Telephone: +962 6 692 393
Fax: +962 6 692 394

Housewares Sector Committee
Address: PO Box 7193, Amman
Telephone: +962 6 636 830/657 663
Fax: +962 6 647 630

Jordan Insurance Federation
Address: PO Box 1990, Jabal Al-Hussein, Amman
Telephone: +962 6 689 510
Fax: +962 6 689 266

Jordan Trade Association
Address: PO Box 830432, Amman
Telephone: +962 6 685 603
Fax: +962 6 685 605

Web site: www.arab-business.net/jta/
Year established: 1988
Activities: information service: local and international databases and library facilities on topics such as world export markets, trade opportunities, market distribution channels, international trade and legal regulations, etc.; gathers, analyses and exchanges information relating to Jordanian industry; conducts economic and marketing studies for developing Jordanian exports; participates in trade fairs and exhibitions; seminars and specialised courses related to export interests and local and international market forces; publishes a number of materials for foreign and local distribution including a quarterly newsletter, directories, and special market reports
Chief officers: HE Dr. Bassam Saket (Chairman), Mr. Halim Abu Rahmeh (Executive Manager), Mr. Mansour Ghishan (Secretary)
Membership: members of various industry sectors: agricultural, food and supply, chemical, furniture, clothing and spinning, pharmaceutical and medical, construction, plastic and rubber, cosmetics, printing, paper and stationery, engineering, services
Publications:
• Newsletter: *quarterly*

Jordanian Businessmen Association
Address: PO Box 926182, Amman
Telephone: +962 6 680 855
Fax: +962 6 680 663
Year established: 1985
Activities: conducts studies on Jordanian investment laws and regulations; acts as spokeman for Jordanian businessmen in communications and meetings with foreign associations
Chief officers: Hamidi Tabbaa (Chairman), Faghri Bil Bieisi
Membership: 350 members of different Jordanian economic sectors including industry, commerce, agriculture, banking, insurance, construction, tourism, transport etc.
Publications:
• JBA Members' Directory: *directory listing all the firms which are members of the Association, with contact names, addresses and telephone numbers - annual*
• Monthly Symposium Series: *monthly*

Jordanian Society of Tourist and Travel Agencies
Address: Alsayegh Commercial Block , 5th Floor, 20 King Hussein Street Abdaly, Amman
Telephone: +962 6 638 599/611 304
Fax: +962 6 611 302
Activities: liaises with airlines and package tour operators and presents information on behalf of the Jordanian travel and tourism industries
Chief officers: Abdul Mallik el Ahmar (President)
Membership: travel agencies and tourist related enterprises

Union of Confectionery and Restaurant Enterprises
Address: PO Box 1274, Amman
Telephone: +962 6 692 448
Fax: +962 6 692 448

KAZAKHSTAN

Article Numbering Association (EAN Kazakhstan)
Address: Baizkov Street, 299, 480070 Almaty
Telephone: +7 72 457 578
Fax: +7 72 455 932
E-mail: root@ean.almaty.kz

Kazakhstan Association of Food Enterprises

Address: 62, Aiteke Bi St., Room 52, Almaty
Telephone: +7 72 330 096
Fax: +7 72 330 096
E-mail: SMorozov@online.ru
Web site: www.online.ru/people/smorozov/
Activities: provides financial, technical, organisational support; professional training; up-to-date information on food trade in Kazakhstan and abroad; food marketing research; promotes trade relations in Kazakhstan and abroad; information service
Chief officers: Sergei Morozov (General Director)
Membership: 17 companies, which own about 70 food stores dealing with food production, processing, sales, storage and transportation

KENYA

Coffee Board of Kenya

Address: PO Box 30566, Exchange Lane, Nairobi
Telephone: +254 2 332 896/897/898
Fax: +254 2 330 546
Telex: 22190 COBOK
Chief officers: Aggrey Ole Murunga, Mzee Hamisi Ngutu (Executives)
Publications:
• Kenya Coffee: *analysis of the Kenyan market, statistics on exports, consumption, production - monthly*

Fresh Produce Exporters' Association of Kenya (FPEAK)

Address: PO Box 39504, Nairobi
Telephone: +254 2 448 297
Fax: +254 2 445 795

Horticultural Crops Development Authority (HCDA)

Address: PO Box 42601, Nairobi
Telephone: +254 2 337 381/82/83/311 150
Fax: +254 2 228 386

Kenya Association of Manufacturers (KAM)

Address: PO Box 30225, Nairobi
Telephone: +254 2 746 005/7
Fax: +254 2 746 028
Year established: 1959
Chief officers: AC Juma (Chairman), JW Kuria (Chief Executive)
Structure: Board of Directors, 10 Committees for Export Development, Textile Manufacturers, Cereals Sector, Pharmaceutical Sector, Printing and Packaging Sector, Paint Sector, Cosmetic Sector, Plastics and Rubber Sector, Motor Vehicle Components Manufacturers Sector, Furniture Sector
Membership: umbrella association for all sectors of the industry: clothing and textiles; cosmetics and toiletries; pharmaceuticals; food; printing; packaging; chemicals; plastic and rubber; automotives; furniture
Publications:
• KAM Directory: *contact details of members of the association - annual*

Kenya Association of the Pharmaceutical Industry (KAPI)

Address: P.O. Box 41578, Nairobi
Telephone: +254 2 521 578

Kenya Booksellers' and Stationers' Association (KBSA)

Address: PO Box 20373, Nairobi
Telephone: +254 2 226 543
Chief officers: Joseph Njorge Mwenda (Chairman)

Kenyan Publishers' Association

Address: PO Box 18650, c/o Phoenix Publishers Ltd, Nairobi
Telephone: +254 2 222 309/223 626
Fax: +254 2 339 875
Chief officers: Mr Gacheche Waruingi (Chairman), Mr H Chakava (Director)

Tea Board of Kenya

Address: PO Box 20064, Nairobi
Telephone: +254 2 569 102
Fax: +254 2 331 650

KOREA (SOUTH)

Agricultural and Fishery Marketing Corporation

Address: Central POB 3212, 191 Hangangno 2-ga, Yongsan-gu, Seoul
Telephone: +82 2 795 8201/795 8205
Fax: +82 2 790 8010/798 7513
Year established: 1967
Activities: price stabilisation; export/import business; marketing; food industry promotion programme
Chief officers: Shin Dae-jin (President)

Association of Foreign Trading Agents of Korea (AFTAK)

Address: Donjin Building, 218 Hanggangno 2-ga, Yongsan-gu Seoul
Telephone: +82 2 792 1581/4
Fax: +82 2 780 4337/749 1830
Year established: 1970
Activities: registration and approval of offer-issuing businesses, government liaison
Chief officers: Choi Seung-woong (President)
Membership: 12,000 firms, including 449 foreign firms from more than 18 countries including the US, Japan, the UK and Germany

Canning Fisheries' Cooperative

Address: Room 502, Sungji Building, 538 Tohwa 2-dong, Map'o-gu, Seoul
Telephone: +82 2 715 1057/1060
Fax: +82 2 702 0408
Year established: 1962
Chief officers: Cha Suk-hong (President)
Membership: 40 members

Construction Association of Korea

Address: 8th Floor, Construction Building, 71-2 Nonhyon-dong, Kangnam-gu, Seoul
Telephone: +82 2 547 6101/7/548 7101
Fax: +82 2 542 6264
Year established: 1947
Chief officers: Choi Won-suk (President)
Membership: 2929

Electronic Industries' Association of Korea (EIAK)

Address: 648 Yoksam-dong, Kangnam-gu, Seoul
Telephone: +82 2 553 0941/7/555 6187
Fax: +82 2 555 6195/563 7371
E-mail: eiak@eiak.org

Web site: www.eiak.org
Year established: 1976
Activities: monitors import and export trends, analyses trade enquiries, organises trade fairs, government liaison, trade promotion, industrial research, statistics and information service
Chief officers: Koo Cha Hak (Chairman), J.K. Jeong (Manager International Cooperation)
Structure: Chairman, Managing Dirctor, Board of Directors, Committees, various departments including: General Affairs; Trade and Exhibitions; Research; Consumer Electronics; Information and Electronic Components
Membership: 600 member companies, 220 affiliated organisations
Publications:
• Directory of Korean Electronic Parts and Components: *directory of Korean manufacturers with detailed information on electronic parts and components produced - annual*
• Electronic and Electrical Manufacturers in Korea Directory: *company directory with full contact details, number of employees, capital, annual production figures, value of exports and main activities - annual*
• Electronic Industries Association of Korea Annual Report: *the associations activities in the past year. Also includes a summary of the performance of the Korean electronics industry with commentary and statistics covering: overseas investment by Korean electronic companies; employment in the industry; international comparisons; R&D expenditure over a three year period; production by sector and exports by value - annual*
• Electronics Industry: PR Booklet: *features on the industry with analysis of current and future trends - irregular*
• Korean Electronics: *news and analysis of trends in various sectors of the Korean electronics industry. Also includes production and export statistics (by value) for various product sectors - monthly*
• Statistics of the Electronics and Electrical Industries: *in-depth commentary and sector by sector statistics covering the Korean electonics industry - irregular*

Federation of Korean Industries

Address: Central POB 6931, 28-1 Yoido-dong, Yongdungpo-gu, Seoul 150
Telephone: +82 2 780 0821/30, 1801/6
Fax: +82 2 784 1640
Year established: 1961
Chief officers: Choi Jong-Hyun (Chairman)
Membership: 436

Korea Agriculture and Fisheries Food Trade Association

Address: Room 1905, KWTC Building, 159 Samsung-dong, Kangnam-gu, Seoul
Telephone: +82 2 551 1936/9
Fax: +82 2 551 1940
Year established: 1964
Chief officers: Kim Doo-man (President)
Membership: 53

Korea Alcohol and Liquor Industry Association

Address: 7th Floor, Sewoo Hoekwan, 10 Youido-dong, Yongdungpo-gu, Seoul
Telephone: +82 2 780 6411/5
Fax: +82 2 783 8787
Year established: 1980
Chief officers: Bae Jhong-kyu (President)
Membership: 68

Korea Apparel Industry Association

Address: Room 801, KWTC Building, 159 Samsong-dong, Kangnam-gu, Seoul
Telephone: +82 2 551 1451
Fax: +82 2 551 1519
Year established: 1963
Chief officers: Park Sei-young (President)
Membership: 8,603

Korea Apparel Sub-Material Association (Association of Manufacturers)

Address: 2A-1, KOEX Building, 159 Samsong-dong, Kangnam-gu, Seoul
Telephone: +82 2 551 6000/3
Fax: +82 2 551 6006
Year established: 1984
Activities: distribution consultancy
Chief officers: Young You (Managing Director)
Membership: 120 factories

Korea Association of Advertising Agencies

Address: 410 Hyndal Cheil B/D, Cheokseon-Dong, Chongro-gu, Seoul
Telephone: +82 2 733 1201
Fax: +82 2 738 7824
Chief officers: Sang-Jo Nahm (President)

Korea Audio and Video Association

Address: Room 201, UIL Building, 255-56 Yongdu-dong, Tongdaemun-gu, Seoul
Telephone: +82 2 922 6612/922 6614
Fax: +82 2 967 6615
Year established: 1972
Chief officers: Shin Hyun-taek (President)
Membership: 167

Korea Auto Industries' Cooperative Association

Address: 1638-3 Socho-dong, Socho-gu, Seoul
Telephone: +82 2 587 0014/8/587 3416
Fax: +82 2 583 7340
Year established: 1962
Chief officers: Ryu Hee-chun (President)
Membership: 405

Korea Automobile Manufacturers' Association

Address: 8th Floor, KLI 63 Building, 60 Youido-dong, Yongdeungpo-gu, Seoul
Telephone: +82 2 782 1360/1
Fax: +82 2 782 0464
Year established: 1988
Activities: survey and research activities on the future development of the auto-industry; government liaison; organising exhibitions and trade fairs
Chief officers: Han Seung-jun (Chairman)
Structure: Chairman, Executive Vice Chairman, Director, Board of Directors, Standing Committee, General Committee
Membership: 6 member companies: Hyundai Motor Company; Kia Motors; Daewoo Motor Company Limited; Asia Motors; Ssangyong Motor; Hyundai Precision and Industrial Company Ltd.
Publications:
• KAMA Booklet: *the associations activities; list of member companies with contact information; turnover; annual production; main products; sales, exports etc. Also includes a map showing the location of all automotive production facilities in Korea - annual*

Korea Bag and Luggage Industry Cooperative

Address: 44-35 Youido-dong, Yongdungpo-gu, Seoul
Telephone: +82 2 782 2159/2161
Fax: +82 2 782 2161
Year established: 1974
Chief officers: Kim Soo-tae (President)
Membership: 64

Korea Battery Industry Cooperative

Address: 1304-4 Socho-dong, Socho-gu, Seoul
Telephone: +82 2 553 2401/2403
Fax: +82 2 556 1290
Year established: 1972
Chief officers: Ro Sang-kook (President)
Membership: 12 member companies producing rechargable, storage and automotive batteries

Korea Bicycle Industry Association

Address: Room 604 Sanjung Building, 15-16 Youido-dong, Yongdungpo-gu, Seoul
Telephone: +82 2 784 2582/3/786 7270
Fax: +82 2 785 7270
Year established: 1975
Chief officers: Cho Hyung-lai (President)
Membership: 38 manufacturers of bicycles and parts

Korea Can Industry Cooperative

Address: 6th Floor, Daekwang Bldg, 7-15, Nonhyon-dong, Kangnam-gu, Seoul
Telephone: +82 2 543 0140
Fax: +82 2 548 0640
Year established: 1984
Chief officers: Lee Chul-soon
Membership: 21

Korea Ceramic Industry Cooperative

Address: 53-20 Taehyon-dong, Sodaemun-gu, Seoul
Telephone: +82 2 363 0361
Fax: +82 2 392 8149
Year established: 1962
Chief officers: Hwang Ho-yeon (President)
Membership: 115

Korea Computers Cooperative

Address: 14-8 Youido-dong, Yongdungp'o-gu, Seoul
Telephone: +82 2 780 0511/3
Fax: +82 2 780 7509
Chief officers: Min Kyung-hyun (President)
Membership: 230

Korea Consumer Goods Exporters' Association

Address: Room 1802, KWTC Building, 159 Samsong-dong, Kangnam-gu, Seoul
Telephone: +82 2 551 1858/67
Fax: +82 2 551 1870
Year established: 1986
Activities: supports export of consumer goods
Chief officers: Shin Yong-woog (President)
Membership: 110

Korea Cosmetic Industry Association

Address: 17-1 Youido-dong, Yongdungpo-gu, Seoul
Telephone: +82 2 785 7984/7985, 782 0948
Fax: +82 2 782 6659/784 7639
Year established: 1949
Chief officers: Yu Sang-ok (President)
Membership: 70

Korea Dairy and Beef Farmers' Association

Address: 4th Floor, Livestock Centre Building, 1516/5, Socho-dong, Socho-gu, Seoul
Telephone: +82 2 588 7055-6/584 5143
Fax: +82 2 584 5144
Year established: 1981
Activities: supply of grass seed
Chief officers: Kang Seong-won(President)
Membership: 20,000

Korea Dairy Industrial Association

Address: 1031-1 Pangbae 3-dong, Sacho-gu, Seoul
Telephone: +82 2 584 3631
Fax: +82 2 588 1459
Year established: 1978
Activities: import promotion
Chief officers: Kim Young-jin (President)
Membership: 16 member companies

Korea Department Stores Association

Address: Central POB 10571, Rm 643, KCCI Building, 45, Namdaemunro 4-ga, Chung-gu, Seoul
Telephone: +82 2 754 6054
Fax: +82 2 776 9528
Year established: 1983
Chief officers: Han Jien-yoo (President)
Membership: 37

Korea Dyestuff and Pigment Industry Cooperative

Address: 17-1 Youido-dong, Yongdungpo-gu, Seoul
Telephone: +82 2 783 0721
Fax: +82 2 786 1888
Year established: 1978
Chief officers: Lee Chong-man (President)
Membership: 60

Korea Edible Oils and Fats Industry Cooperative

Address: Room 304, Nakwin Building, 284-6 Nahwon-dong, Chongno-gu, Seoul
Telephone: +82 2 742 2687-8
Fax: +82 2 745 0444
Year established: 1962
Chief officers: Lee Jae-tae (President)
Membership: 15

Korea Electrical Contractors' Association

Address: 533-2 Tungchon 2-dong, Kangso-gu, Seoul
Telephone: +82 2 653 0161/3
Fax: +82 2 653 3173
Year established: 1960
Chief officers: Park Woon-hee (President)
Membership: 9184

Korea Electrical Manufacturers' Association (KOEMA)

Address: 9/F, Taekyong Building, 51-5 Panp'o-dong, Soch'o-gu, Seoul
Telephone: +82 2 347 60271
Fax: +82 2 347 60275
Chief officers: Lee Hee-chong (President)
Membership: 170

Korea Electrical Manufacturers' Cooperative

Address: 103-10 Shingil 2-dong, Yongdungpo-gu, Seoul
Telephone: +82 2 849 2811/9
Fax: +82 2 848 8337

Year established: 1962
Chief officers: Lim Do-soo (President)
Membership: 538

Korea Electronic Industries Cooperative

Address: 925-9 Pangbae-dong, Socho-gu, Seoul
Telephone: +82 2 597 9411/9417
Fax: +82 2 597 9418/9419
Year established: 1967
Chief officers: Kim Young-woo (President)
Membership: 570

Korea Employers' Federation

Address: 276-1Tohwa-dong, Map'o-gu, Seoul
Telephone: +82 2 327 07300
Fax: +82 2 706 1059
Year established: 1970
Activities: represents Korean employers at the International
Organisation of Employers; makes recommendations
regarding labour policy on behalf of business circles
Chief officers: Lee Dong-chan (President)
Membership: 3,550

Korea Export Association of Textiles

Address: Room 1803-4, 18th Floor, KWTC Building, 159
Samsong-dong, Kangnam-gu, Seoul
Telephone: +82 2 551 1876/1895
Fax: +82 2 551 1896
Year established: 1981
Chief officers: Park Chang-ho (President)
Membership: 715

Korea Federation of Advertising Associations

Address: 4th Floor Cheokseon Hyundai Chell Bldg, 80
Cheokseon-Dong, Chongro-gu, Seoul
Telephone: +82 2 733 1201/02
Fax: +82 2 738 7824
Chief officers: Eung-Doek Chun (Chairman), Eung Bae Lim
(Executive Managing Director)

Korea Federation of Banks

Address: 33 Sorin-dong, Chung-gu, Seoul
Telephone: +82 2 399 5811
Fax: +82 2 399 5810
Year established: 1928
Chief officers: Lee Sang-chul (President)
Membership: 35

Korea Federation of Furniture Industry Cooperatives

Address: 374-2 Changan-dong, Tongdaemun-gu, Seoul
Telephone: +82 2 215 8838/9
Fax: +82 2 215 9729
Year established: 1962
Chief officers: Lee Jae-sun (President)
Membership: 1200

Korea Federation of Knitting Industry Cooperatives

Address: 48, 1-ga. Shinmunno, Chongno-gu, Seoul
Telephone: +82 2 735 5951-3
Fax: +82 2 735 1447
Year established: 1962
Chief officers: Kim Kyung-o (President)
Membership: 14

Korea Federation of Printing Industry Co-operatives

Address: 352-26 Sogyo-dong, Mapo-gu, Seoul
Telephone: +82 2 335 6161
Fax: +82 2 334 6773
Year established: 1962
Chief officers: Kim Jick-seung (President)
Membership: 2,780

Korea Feed Association

Address: Central POB 3473, 1581-13 Soch'o-dong,
Soch'o-gu, Seoul
Telephone: +82 2 581 5721/581 5733
Fax: +82 2 587 2911
Year established: 1961
Chief officers: Lee Byung-suk (President)
Membership: 47

Korea Fishery Exporters' Association

Address: Room 1904, KWTC Building, 159-1 Samsong-dong,
Kangnam-gu, Seoul
Telephone: +82 2 551 1925/30
Fax: +82 2 551 1931
Year established: 1986
Activities: export promotion
Chief officers: Kim Myung-nyun (President)
Membership: 192

Korea Flour Mills Industrial Association

Address: 118 Namdaemunno 5-ga, Chung-gu, Seoul
Telephone: +82 2 777 9451/4
Fax: +82 2 757 7125
Year established: 1955
Chief officers: Lee Joon-yong(President)
Membership: 11

Korea Foods Industry Association

Address: 1002-6, Pangbae-dong, Seocho-gu, Seoul
Telephone: +82 2 585 5052/5053
Fax: +82 2 586 4906
Year established: 1969
Activities: research for the food industry; examination of food
additives
Chief officers: Chun Myung-ki (President)
Membership: 106

Korea Garment Industry Cooperative

Address: 105-238 Kongdok-dong, Mapo-gu, Seoul
Telephone: +82 2 717 3191/715 8998
Fax: +82 2 718 3192
Year established: 1962
Chief officers: Lee Sung-ik (President)
Membership: 400

Korea Garments and Knitwear Export Association

Address: PO Box 8790, Rom 801, KWTC Building, 159
Samsong-dong, Kangnam-gu, Seoul
Telephone: +82 2 551 1456
Fax: +82 2 551 1467
Year established: 1981
Activities: promotes exports of textile goods
Membership: 697

Korea Glass Industry Association

Address: 53-20 Taehyon-dong, Sodaemun-gu, Seoul
Telephone: +82 2 364 7799
Fax: +82 2 312 8838

Year established: 1962
Chief officers: Yoon Kook-hyun (President)
Membership: 67

Korea International Foreign Trade Association (KITA)
Address: Central POB 100, 159-1 Samsong-Dong, Kangnam-Gu, Seoul
Telephone: +82 2 551 5114/0114
Fax: +82 2 551 5100/5200/5161
E-mail: stwheel@sol.nuri.net
Year established: 1946
Activities: trade promotion; provides information services including statistics on a range of industries; pursues policies to accelerate foreign investment
Chief officers: Pyong-Hwoi Koo (Chairman)
Membership: 54,000 member companies
Publications:
● Korea Export: *comprehensive product catalogue - bi-annual*
● Korea Trading Post: *features the latest trends in major export industries and a selected listing of Korean suppliers - monthly*
Notes: Formerly known as the Korea Foreign Trade Association. The address for publications subscriptions is: Korea Trade Information Centre, Trade Centre PO Box 100, Seoul, Korea; Tel +82 2 551 52535, Fax +82 2 551 5249

Korea Kitchen Furniture Co-operative
Address: 910-14 Pangbae-dong, Socho-gu, Seoul
Telephone: +82 2 586 2451/3
Fax: +82 2 586 2454
Year established: 1983
Chief officers: Lim Joong-soon (President)
Membership: 123

Korea Lighting Fixtures Industry Cooperative
Address: Room 621, KFSB Building, 16-2, Youido-dong, Yongdungp'o-gu, Seoul
Telephone: +82 2 786 9876
Fax: +82 2 782 0944
Year established: 1982
Chief officers: Panrk Wan-kyo (President)
Membership: 111

Korea Listed Companies Association
Address: 33 Yoido-dong, Youngedeungpo-ku, Seoul 150-010
Telephone: +82 2 783 6501/782 5651
Fax: +82 2 785 5171
Year established: 1973
Activities: maintains a database of information on Korean listed companies and provides rankings of Korean listed companies
Chief officers: Park Sung-bok (President)
Membership: 725

Korea Management Association
Address: 544 Tohwa-dong, Mapo-gu, Seoul
Telephone: +82 2 719 8225
Fax: +82 2 719 7047
Year established: 1962
Activities: industrial training; inter-company training; management consulting
Chief officers: Song In-sang (President)
Membership: 1,800

Korea Marketing Association
Address: Central POB 3774, 45 Namdaemunno 4-ga, Chung-gu, Seoul
Telephone: +82 2 753 5011/752 8074
Fax: +82 2 752 6156

Year established: 1965
Activities: dissemination of marketing knowledge; co-operative projects with international marketing institutions
Chief officers: Cho Hai-hyung (President)
Membership: 350
Publications:
● Management and Marketing: *monthly*

Korea Musical Instrument Industry Association
Address: Room 306, Songwoo Building, 51-1 Tohwa-dong, Mapo-gu, Seoul
Telephone: +82 2 719 5037/8
Fax: +82 2 718 0493
Year established: 1983
Chief officers: Chu Kyo-uk (President)
Membership: 32

Korea National Tourism Corporation
Address: CPO Box 4893, 10 Ta Dong, Chung-gu, Seoul
Telephone: +82 2 757 6030
Fax: +82 2 757 6046
Chief officers: Lee Ke-ik (President)

Korea Newspapers' Association
Address: Korea Pres Center Building, 25 Taepyong-ro 1-ga, Chung-ku, Seoul
Telephone: +82 2 733 2251
Fax: +82 2 720 3291
Chief officers: Sun-kyu Sohn (Secretary General)

Korea Non-Life Insurance Association
Address: 80 Susong-dong, Chongno-gu, Seoul
Telephone: +82 2 739 4161/4170
Fax: +82 2 739 3769
Year established: 1946
Activities: research; analysing statistics and market trands; education and training
Chief officers: Lee Suk-Lyong (President), Su-Ung Cho (Executive Mangaing Director), Jong-Chan Jang (Manging Director)
Structure: Chairman, Executive Managing Director, Managing Director, Secreteriat
Membership: 14 full member companies, 3 associate foreign members (11 non-life insurance companies, 2 fidelity and surety insurance companies, 1 re-insurance company
Publications:
● Annual Report: *annual*
● Monthly Magazine of the Korea Non-Life Insurance Association: *the non-life insurance market in Korea - monthly*

Korea Noodle Industry Cooperative
Address: Room 301-4, Tongnam Officetel, 104-10 Kuro 5-dong, Kuro-gu, Seoul
Telephone: +82 2 830 2091
Fax: +82 2 830 2095
Chief officers: Kwak Jae-sub (President)
Membership: 126

Korea Optical Industry Cooperative
Address: 616-13 P'ongni 5-dong, So-gu, Tae-gu
Telephone: +82 53 562 0991
Fax: +82 53 562 0993
Year established: 1962
Chief officers: Yuk Dong-chang (President)
Membership: 108

Korea Paint and Printing Ink Industry Co-operative
Address: 204-6 Nonhyon-dong, Kangnam-gu, Seoul
Telephone: +82 2 549 3321-5
Fax: +82 2 549 3326
Year established: 1962
Chief officers: Lee Byung-suh (President)
Membership: 54

Korea Paper Industry Cooperative
Address: 831 Yoksam-dong, Kangnam-gu, Seoul
Telephone: +82 2 567 5912/5913
Fax: +82 2 567 6984
Year established: 1962
Chief officers: Ryoo Hie-yoon (President)
Membership: 56

Korea Paper Manufacturers' Association
Address: Room 302, Songpa Building, 505 Shinsa-dong, Kangnam-gu, Seoul
Telephone: +82 2 549 0981/5
Fax: +82 2 549 0980
Year established: 1952
Chief officers: Lee Jong-dae (President)
Membership: 26

Korea Pharmaceutical Manufacturers' Association (KPMA)
Address: Je - Yak Building, 990-2, Bangbae-1 Dong, Seochu-ku, Seoul 137-061
Telephone: +82 2 581 2101
Fax: +82 2 581 2106
E-mail: kpma@nextel.net
Year established: 1945
Chief officers: Lee Kum-ki (President)
Membership: 265

Korea Pharmaceutical Traders' Association
Address: Trade Centre POB 14, Room 1801, KWTC Building, 159 Samsong-dong, Kangnam-gu, Seoul
Telephone: +82 2 551 1841
Fax: +82 2 551 1850
Year established: 1957
Chief officers: Koo Ja-choon (President)
Membership: 423

Korea Plywood Industries' Association
Address: Room 906, KFSB Building, 16-2 Youido-dong, Yongdungpo-gu, Seoul
Telephone: +82 2 780 3631
Fax: +82 2 780 3634
Year established: 1963
Chief officers: Park Young-ju (President)
Membership: 11

Korea Refrigeration and Air Conditioning Industry Association
Address: 13-06 Youido-dong, Yongdungpo-gu, Seoul
Telephone: +82 2 369 7500-17
Fax: +82 2 785 1195
Year established: 1975
Chief officers: Won Yun-hi (President)
Membership: 99

Korea Rubber Industry Cooperative
Address: 7, 1-ga Sinmun-ro, Jomgro-gu, Seoul
Telephone: +82 2 733 8584-6
Fax: +82 2 730 3355

Year established: 1962
Chief officers: Wan Yun-hi (President)
Membership: 90

Korea Soap and Detergent Industry Co-operative
Address: Room 406, Haech'on Building, 831-47 Yoksam-dong, Kangnam-gu, Seoul
Telephone: +82 2 553 3241
Fax: +82 2 553 3243
Year established: 1977
Chief officers: Kim Man-heung (President)
Membership: 16 member companies

Korea Soy Sauce Industry Cooperative
Address: 248-13 Chamshil-dong, Songp'aa-gu, Seoul
Telephone: +82 2 424 3141
Fax: +82 2 424 3145
Year established: 1962
Chief officers: Yang Byung-tak (President)
Membership: 70

Korea Sporting Goods Industry Association
Address: Rm 814, Life Officetel, 61-3 Youido-dong, Yongdungpo-gu, Seoul
Telephone: +82 2 786 7761/3
Fax: +82 2 786 7764
Year established: 1970
Chief officers: Shim Yong-Kyu (President)
Membership: 90

Korea Stationery Industry Cooperative
Address: Stationery Building, 36-3, 5-ga, Chungmu-ro, Chung-gu, Seoul
Telephone: +82 2 278 7891-5
Fax: +82 2 275 1065
Year established: 1962
Chief officers: Woo Dong-seok (President)
Membership: 338

Korea Stationery Wholesaler Cooperative
Address: Room 107, Kunshin Building, Annexe 2, 250-4 Tohwa-dong, Map'o-gu, Seoul
Telephone: +82 2 704 4635-7
Fax: +82 2 706 9146
Year established: 1985
Chief officers: Park Yong-sun (President)
Membership: 265

Korea Sugar Manufacturers' Association
Address: Central POB 6576, Room 501, Choyang Building, 49-17 Ch'ungmuro 2-ga, Chung-gu, Seoul
Telephone: +82 2 275 6071-3
Fax: +82 2 277 5858
Year established: 1955
Chief officers: Sohn Kyung-shick (President)
Membership: 3

Korea Super Chainstores' Association (KOSCA)
Address: 1536-6 Seoch'o-dong, Seoch'o-ku, Seoul 137-070
Telephone: +82 2 522 1271
Fax: +82 2 522 1275
Year established: 1975
Activities: education, research, publications and exhibitions for retailers and wholesalers in Korea
Chief officers: Lee Seok-hyung (President)
Structure: chairman, vice-president, executive director,

operation, editorial, education, exhibition department
Membership: 71 retailers, wholesalers, manufacturers
Publications:
• Chainstore: *monthly*

Korea Tanners' Association

Address: Room 805, Samhwa Building, 204-4,
Nonhyon-dong, Kangnam-gu, Seoul
Telephone: +82 2 549 5432-3
Fax: +82 2 549 6733
Year established: 1981
Chief officers: Han Kwan-dong (President)
Membership: 68

Korea Tobacco Association

Address: 100 Phongchon-dong, Taedeog-gu, Taejon City
306-130
Telephone: +82 42 939 5113
Fax: +82 42 633 0551/2
Chief officers: Kim Kyu-Tae (President)

Korea Tourist Association

Address: Kangnam POB 1130, 945 Daech'i-Dong,
Kangnam-gu, Seoul
Telephone: +82 2 556 2356
Fax: +82 2 556 3818-9
Year established: 1963
Activities: develops the tourism industry; promotes the
industry through publications and publicity; analyses
tourism-related statistics; provides initial and continuing
training for industry employees; operates a mutual aid society
for members; conducts qualification examinations; operates
the tourism information centre; furnishes management
guidance for the tourism industry; conducts research and
study programmes
Chief officers: Chang Chul-hi (Chairman); Lee Dong-Hee
(Executive Vice Chairman)
Membership: 4370

Korea Toy Industry Cooperative

Address: POBox 2692, 361-1, Hangangno 2-ga, Yongsan-gu,
Seoul
Telephone: +82 2 795 9505/9818
Fax: +82 2 795 0401
Year established: 1967
Chief officers: Kim Yang-muk (President)
Membership: 142

Korea Tyre Manufacturers' Association

Address: Room 1910, KWTC Building, 159 Samsong-dong,
Kangnam-gu, Seoul
Telephone: +82 2 551 1903-7
Fax: +82 2 551 1910
Year established: 1956
Chief officers: Hong Geun-hi (President)
Membership: 9

Korea Watch and Clock Industry Cooperative

Address: Central POB 8496, 11th Floor, Samsung Building,
169-2, Namchang-dong, Chung-gu, Seoul
Telephone: +82 2 779 1761-3
Fax: +82 2 779 1763
Year established: 1966
Chief officers: Kim Young-ho (President)
Membership: 130

Korean Bakers' Association

Address: 120-3 Ch'ungmuro 4-ga, Chung-gu, Seoul
Telephone: +82 2 273 1830
Fax: +82 2 271 1822
Year established: 1963
Chief officers: Lee Hong-kyung (President)
Membership: 8603

Korean Chapter of the International Advertising Association

Address: 4th Floor, Samtan Building, 947-7 Daechi-dong,
Kangnam-gu, Seoul
Telephone: +82 2 564 0064
Fax: +82 2 565 2676
Chief officers: Myung-Ha Him (President)

Korean Ginseng Products Manufacturers' Association (The)

Address: 30-6 Chamwon-dong, Soch'o-gu, Seoul
Telephone: +82 2 549 4330
Fax: +82 2 511 4533
Year established: 1973
Chief officers: Choi Ki-sun (President)
Membership: 78

Korean Institute of Industrial Design and Packaging

Address: Central POB 2325, Design Centre Building, 128-8
Yongong-dong, Changno-gu, Seoul
Telephone: +82 2 708 2033/8
Fax: +82 2 745 5519
Year established: 1970
Activities: promotion and research for design and packaging
Chief officers: Yoo Ho-min (President)

Korean Jewellery Industry Cooperative

Address: 224-2, Yongdung-dong, Iri-shi, Chonbuk
Telephone: +82 653 835 0363/4
Fax: +82 653 835 7275

Korean Printers' Association

Address: 352-26, Sogyo-dong, Map'o-gu, Seoul
Telephone: +82 2 335 5881
Fax: +82 2 338 9801
Year established: 1973
Activities: promotion of printing culture, Korean printing
research institute
Chief officers: Park Cheung-il (President)
Membership: 400

Korean Publishers Cooperative

Address: 448-6 Sinsu-dong, Mapo-gu, Seoul
Telephone: +82 2 716 5621-3/5616-9
Fax: +82 2 716 999
Year established: 1962
Chief officers: Park Ki-bong (President)
Membership: 400

Life Insurance Association of Korea

Address: 60-1 Chungmu-ro 3-ka, Chung-ku, Seoul
Telephone: +82 2 275 0121/6
Fax: +82 2 275 7696
Year established: 1950
Chief officers: Lee Kang-hwan (President)
Membership: 33

KUWAIT

Kuwait Committee of the International Dairy Federation
Address: P.O. Box 835, c/o Kuwaiti Danish Dairy Company Ltd, Safat 13009
Telephone: +965 471 7911
Fax: +965 474 7029

LATVIA

Article Numbering Association (EAN Latvia)
Address: Latvian Chamber of Commerce and Industry, 21 Brivibas Boulevard, LV-1849 Riga
Telephone: +371 7 333 227
Fax: +371 7 820 092
E-mail: liene@sun.lcc.org.lv

Latvian Book Publishers' Association
Address: Aspazijas bulvaris 24, 1050 Riga
Telephone: +371 7 225 843/336 332
Fax: +371 7 228 482
Chief officers: Mr M Ozolins (Secretary)

Latvian Publishers' and Editors' Association
Address: Balasta Dambis 3, 702, Riga 226081
Telephone: +371 2 220 019/465 375
Fax: +371 2 786 0169
Chief officers: Ms Ilvija Zvaigzne (Office Manager)

LEBANON

Article Numbering Association (EAN Lebanon)
Address: PO Box 11, Beirut Chamber of Commerce and Industry, Elias Abdel Nour Building Sassine-Ashrafieh, George Haimary Street, 1801 Beirut
Telephone: +961 1 218 120
Fax: +961 1 218 121

LESOTHO

Lesotho Publishers' Association (LPA)
Address: PO Blox Roma 180, Institute of Southern African Studies, Lesotho
Telephone: +266 340 601/640 247
Fax: +266 340 000
E-mail: isas@isas.nil.is

Poultry Association of Lesotho
Address: Box 15, Butha-Buthe
Telephone: +266 460 257

LITHUANIA

Article Numbering Association (EAN Lithuania)
Address: PO Box 995 ARP-3, Association of Lithuanian Chambers of Commerce and Industry, 18 V. Kurdirkos, 2600 Vilnius
Telephone: +370 2 614 562
Fax: +370 2 222 621
E-mail: lppra@post.omnitel.net

Association of Commercial Banks of Lithuania
Address: J. Basanaviciaus 45, 2009 Vilnius
Telephone: +370 2 650 841
Fax: +370 2 651 267
Year established: 1993
Activities: financial leasing and other credits
Chief officers: Algis Dobrovolskas (Chairman)
Membership: 10 members

Business and Market Research Association
Address: Kanto 6-1, 3000 Kaunas
Telephone: +370 7 705 715
Fax: +370 7 705 733
Year established: 1994
Activities: market research; business consultations; legal and social activities
Chief officers: Raimundas Petrikas (President)

Lithuanian Breweries' Association
Address: Aludariu 1/2, 2649 Vilnius
Telephone: +370 2 222 495
Fax: +370 2 628 816
Activities: liaises with governmental organisations and institutions; provides contacts with foreign companies; technological support to members; collects information and statistics on production; retail sales; imports/exports and pricing
Chief officers: P.Poskus (President), A. Vydzys (Vice President)
Membership: 10 breweries

Lithuanian Dairy Association (PIENOCENTRAS)
Address: A.Jaksto 9, 2699 Vilnius
Telephone: +370 2 790 894
Fax: +370 2 790 894/ 221 247
Year established: 1991
Activities: advice on new technologies; consultancy services; practical help to members
Chief officers: Vladas Lasas (President)

Lithuanian Meat Processors' Association
Address: I. Savickio 4, 2001 Vilnius
Telephone: +370 2 222 009
Fax: +370 2 222 009
Year established: 1991
Activities: liaison with governmental institutions; practical help in applying new technologies; organises seminars; collects monthly statistics on meat production
Chief officers: Gintaras Valancius (President)
Membership: 20 meat processing factories

Lithuanian Publishers' Association
Address: K. Sirvydo, 62600 Vilnius
Telephone: +370 2 628 945
Fax: +370 2 619 696
Chief officers: Mr A Andrjauskas (Secretary), Mr A Krasnovas (Director)

LUXEMBOURG

Association of Agricultural and Food Product Manufacturers and Traders
Union Interprofessionnelle du Commerce et de la Fabrication de Produits Agricoles et Alimentaires
Address: Rue Glesener 41, L-1631 Luxembourg
Telephone: +352 488 051
Membership: food retailers and wholesalers

Association of Bakers, Confectioners and Ice Cream Makers

Association des Patrons Patissiers-Confiseurs et Glaciers
Address: Rue Glesener 41, L-1631 Luxembourg
Telephone: +352 400 0221
Fax: +352 492 380
Chief officers: Norbert Nicolas (President); Ralph Weis (Secretary)
Membership: retail bakers, confectioners and ice cream makers

Association of Pasta Manufacturers

Groupement des Fabricants de Pâtes Alimentaires
Address: BP 1304, 7, rue A. de Gasperi, L-1013 Luxembourg
Telephone: +352 43 536 6/1
Fax: +352 43 232 8
E-mail: unice-fedil@mcr1.poptel.org.uk
Membership: 2 members
Notes: The Association does not produce any publications.

Association of Public Works and Construction

Groupement des Entrepeneurs du Bâtiment et des Travaux Publics
Address: BP 1304, 7, rue A. de Gasperi, L-1013 Luxembourg
Telephone: +352 436 024
Fax: +352 432 328
E-mail: unice-fedil@mcr1.potel.org.uk
Chief officers: Christian Thiry (President)
Membership: 38 members
Notes: No publications nor statistics produced.

Association of Temporary Employment Agencies (ULEDI)

Union des Entreprises de Travail Intérimaire
Address: BP 1304, 7, rue A. de Gasperi, L-1013 Luxembourg
Telephone: +352 435 366/1
Fax: +352 132 328
E-mail: unice-fedil@mcr1.poptel.org.uk
Chief officers: Thierry Vermulen (President)
Membership: 19 member agencies
Notes: The Association does not produce any publications or statistics.

Book Editors' Federation of Luxembourg

Fédération Luxembourgeoise des Éditeurs de Livres
Address: BP 482, 7 rue Alcide de Gasperi, L-2014 Luxembourg
Telephone: +352 439 444
Fax: +352 439 450
Chief officers: Mr G Zangerle (Director)

Federation of Luxembourg Brewers

Fédération des Brasseurs Luxembourgeois
Address: Box 1304, 7 Rue Alcide de Gasperi, L-1013 Luxembourg-Kirchberg
Telephone: +352 435 366/61
Fax: +352 432 328
E-mail: unice-fedil@mcr1.poptel.org.uk
Activities: collects statistics on production and sales; publishes a press release of statistics on the brewing industry in Luxembourg available annually at the end of March
Chief officers: Rene Gredt (President), Lucien Jung (Director), Mrs Liliane Fisch (Directors Secretary)
Membership: 5 brewers

Federation of Luxembourg Food Industries

Fédération des Industries Agro-Alimentaires Luxembourgeoises
Address: BP 1304, 7, Rue A. de Gasperi, L-1013
Telephone: +352 43 5366/1

Fax: +352 43 2328
E-mail: unice-fedil@mcr1.poptel.org.uk
Chief officers: M. Edmond Muller (President)
Membership: 19 member companies
Notes: The Association does not produce any publications or statistics.

Federation of Luxembourg Wholesalers

Fédération Luxembourgeoise des Négociants en Gros
Address: Rue Alcide de Gasperi 7, L-2981 Luxembourg-Kirchberg
Telephone: +352 439 444
Fax: +352 439 450
Membership: general wholesalers

Federation of Manufacturers (FEDIL)

Fédération des Industriels Luxembourgeois
Address: PO Box 1304, 7 Rue Alcide de Gasperi, L-1013 Luxembourg
Telephone: +352 435 366/1
Fax: +352 432 328
E-mail: unice-fedil@mcr1.poptel.org.uk
Chief officers: M. Marc Assa (President), M.Nicholas Soisson (Director)
Membership: 400 member companies
Publications:
● Fedil Annual Report (Rapport Annuel FEDIL): *compilation of information on the food industry with statistical data - annual*
● Industry's Echo (Echo de L'Industrie): *monthly*

Federation of Retail Bakers and Pastry Cooks

Fédération des Patrons Boulangers-Patissiers
Address: Rue Glesener 41, L-1631 Luxembourg
Telephone: +352 400 0221
Fax: +352 492 380
Chief officers: Norbert Geisen (President), Ralph Weis (Secretary)
Membership: retail bakers and pastry-cooks

Federation of Wine and Spirits Wholesalers

Fédération Luxembourgeoise des Industries et du Négoce des Vins Liqueurs et Spiritueux
Address: See: Confédération du Commerce
Case Postale 30, 7 rue Alcide de Gasperi, L-1013 Luxembourg/Kirchberg
Telephone: +352 439 444
Fax: +352 439 450
Chief officers: Pierre Desom (Chairman)
Membership: wholesalers, distributors, exporters of wines and spirits

Federation of Wine Producers

Fédération des Associations Viticoles
Address: Route de Trèves 23, Grevenmacher
Telephone: +352 751 39
Fax: +352 758 882
Year established: 1911
Activities: conferences; exhibitions; information services; statistics; library activities
Chief officers: Lucien Gretash
Membership: wine producers

Federation of Wine Producers

Vinmoselle
Address: 12 Route du Vin, 5450 Stadtbredimus
Telephone: +352 698 314
Fax: +352 629 189
Chief officers: Mr Infalt (Director)

Luxembourg Association of Sparkling Wine Producers

Groupement des Producteurs de Vins Mosseux et Crémants Luxembourgeois
Address: BP 1304, 7, rue A. de Gasperi, L-1013 Luxembourg
Telephone: +352 43 536 6/1
Fax: +352 43 232 8
E-mail: unice-fedill@mcr1.poptel.org.uk
Chief officers: M. Hubert Clasen (President)
Membership: 6 wine producers
Notes: The Association does not produce any publications.

National Committee of the International Dairy Federation

Comité National Luxembourgeois de la Fédération Internationale du Lait
Address: B.P. 1904, c/o Administration des Services Techniques de l'Agriculture, Route d'Esch, 16, 1019 Luxembourg
Telephone: +352 443 232
Fax: +352 45 717 2341
Chief officers: Mr H. Theves (Secretary)

Newspapers Publishers' Association

Association Luxembourgeoise des Editeurs de Journaux
Address: BO Box 147, c/o Tageblatt, 44 Rue du Canal, 4050 Esch-Alzette
Telephone: +352 547 131
Fax: +352 547 130
Chief officers: Alvin Sold (President)

Retailers' Federation

Confédération du Commerce Luxembourgeois
Address: 7 rue Alcide de Gasperi, L-2014 Luxembourg
Telephone: +352 439 444
Fax: +352 439 450
Chief officers: Thierry Nothum (Secretary General), Norbert Friob (President)
Membership: 48 professional federations
Publications:
• Handelsblat: *bimonthly*
Notes: The Association does not produce statistics.

MACEDONIA

Article Numbering Association (EAN-MAC)

Address: PO Box 324, c/o Economic Chamber of Macedonia, Dimitrie Cupovski 13, 91000 Skopje
Telephone: +389 91 118 088
Fax: +389 91 116 210
E-mail: ic@ic.mchamber.org.mk

Publishers' Association of Macedonia

FRYOM
Address: Bulevar Sr Kliment, Ohridaki 68A, Skopje
Telephone: +389 91 111 332
Fax: +389 91 228 608
Chief officers: Mr D Basevski (General Secretary), Ms Z Sazdova (Director)

MALAWI

Hotels and Catering Trades' Association

Address: PO Box 284, Blantyre
Telephone: +265 6 205 88

MALAYSIA

Agriculture Institute of Malaysia

Address: 367-1 A Jln. Ampang, 50450 Kuala Lumpur
Telephone: +60 3 456 6590/451 1480
Fax: +60 3 451 1480

Association of Accredited Advertising Agencies

Address: AMC-Melewat Zecha Communications 1 Jln, Sri Semantan Satu, Damansara Heights, 50490 Kuala Lumpur
Telephone: +60 3 282 5477/254 5000
Chief officers: George Chen (President)

Association of Banks in Malaysia

Address: 17th Floor, UBN Tower, 10 Jalan P. Ramlee, 50250 Kuala Lumpur
Telephone: +60 3 238 8041
Fax: +60 3 238 8004

Association of Finance Companies of Malaysia

Address: 18 Lorong Medam Tuanku 1, 50300 Kuala Lumpur
Telephone: +60 3 298 7888
Fax: +60 3 298 2761
Activities: regulation; representation; liaison with government; information services; help and advice to finance companies
Chief officers: Y M Tunk Dato' Abdul Malek Tunka Kassim Kewagan Usaha Bersatu Berhad (Chairman); Elizabeth Yeap (Director)

Association of Malaysian Medical Industries

Address: c/o Burson-Marsteller (M) Sdn. Bhd, 11th. Floor, Bangunan Getah Asli (Menara), 148, Jalan Ampang, 50450, Kuala Lumpur
Telephone: +60 3 261 7900
Fax: +60 3 261 3828
Chief officers: Ms. Violet Hoe (Secretary)

Association of Merchant Banks in Malaysia

Persatuan Bank-Bank Saudagar Di Malaysia
Address: Suite 1501-1502, 15th Floor, Wisma Hangsam, Jalan Hang Lekir, 50000 Kuala Lumpur
Telephone: +60 3 238 3991/2, 3 230 1380
Fax: +60 3 230 1316
E-mail: zeti@ambm.po.my
Activities: political lobbying, promotes sound codes of practice and conducting training programmes; liaises with government institutions
Chief officers: Y B Tan Sri Dato' Azman Hashim (Chairman), Mr Cheah Tek Kuang (Alternate Chairman), Mr Mohad Azman Yahya (Treasurer), Zeti Marziana Muhamed (Executive Secretary)
Structure: chairman, alternate chairman, tresurer, executive secretary, sub-committees
Membership: 12 merchant banks in Malaysia
Notes: the Association does not publish any material

Association of Rubber Gloves Manufacturers of Malaysia

Address: 16-D, Lorong Medan Tuanku 1, 50300 Kuala Lumpur
Telephone: +60 3 774 8522
Chief officers: YB. Dato' S.S.Subramaniam

Association of the Malaysian Computer Industry

Address: 25/F, Menara Tun Razak, Jalan Raja Laut, 50350 Kuala Lumpur
Telephone: +60 3 292 0297

Fax: +60 3 291 1504/292 5136
E-mail: pikom@po.jaring.my

Automobile Association of Malaysia
Address: 25 Jln Yap Kwan Seng, 50450 Kuala Lumpur
Telephone: +60 3 242 5777
Fax: +60 3 248 5358

Automotive Federation of Malaysia
Address: c/o AMIN Holding Sdn. Bhd, Jalan Sesiku, 40000 Shah Alam, Selangor
Telephone: +60 3 550 7139
Fax: +60 3 559 4863

Chemical Industries' Council of Malaysia
Address: PO Box 12194, 17th Floor, Wisma Sime Darby, Jalan Raja Laut, 50770 Kuala Lumpur
Telephone: +60 3 293 1244
Fax: +60 3 293 5105
Chief officers: Encik Mohd Kassim Salleh (Chairman); Wong Chew Yin (honorary Treasurer)
Membership: 38

Cocoa Manufacturers' Group
Address: PO Box 12194, 17th Floor, Wisma Sime Darby, Jalan Raja Laut, 50350 Kuala Lumpur
Telephone: +60 3 293 1244
Fax: +60 3 293 2661
Year established: 1985
Activities: promotes co-operation among cocoa manufacturers in Malaysia; government liaison; compiles and disseminates information
Chief officers: D Selvaraj (Chairman), William Ng (Vice Chairman)
Membership: 7 cocoa bean grinders and chocolate product manufacturers

Electrical and Electronics' Association of Malaysia (TEEAM)
Persatuan Elektrik Dan Elektronik Malaysia
Address: 5-B Jalan Gelugor, Off Jalan Kenanga, Kuala Lumpur 55200
Telephone: +60 3 221 4417/221 2091
Fax: +60 3 221 8212
Year established: 1952
Activities: education and training, advising members on legislation, government liaison, organising meetings with local and overseas organisations and trade missions
Chief officers: IR Donald Lim (President), Khong Choy Tai (Executive Secretary)
Structure: council, various committees
Membership: 1,100 members in both manufacturing and trading
Publications:
• Suara TEEAM Newsletter
• TEEAM Directory: *listing of member companies - annual*

Federation of Malaysian Manufacturers (FMM)
Address: POB 12194, 17th Floor, Wisma Sime Darby, Jalan Raja Laut, Kuala Lumpur 50330
Telephone: +60 3 293 1244
Fax: +60 3 293 5105/2681
Year established: 1968
Activities: trade fairs; training programmes covering all aspects of management training; monthly government reports; manufacturing surveys; ad hoc survey (strictly for internal circulation)
Chief officers: Dato Mohamed Bin Sheikh Ibrahim

(President); Lee Cheng Suan (General Manager); Tank Keok Yin (Chief Executive)
Structure: working committees reporting to an executive committee
Membership: 1,470
Publications:
• FMM Food and Beverage Directory: *primarily a company directory listing Malaysian food and drinks companies, with contact details, products manufactured and brand names. However does contain an intoductory section which gives an overview of food markets in Malaysia including: breakdown of food and drinks manufacturers by size, growth rates of selected food manufacturing sub-sectors as well as three years export data for food and drinks - annual*
• FMM Forum: *annual*
• Malaysian Exporter: *annual*
• Malaysian Manufacturers' Directory: *annual*
• SMI Handbook: *annual*
• Trend, Direction and Outlook: *annual*

FMM Furniture Industry of Malaysia
Address: d/a Persekutuan Pekilang, 2 Malaysia, Tingkat 17, Wisma Sime Darby, Peti Surat 12194, Jln. Raja Laut, Kuala Lumpur 50350
Telephone: +60 3 293 1244
Fax: +60 3 293 5105
Chief officers: Mr. Michael Ng

General Insurance Association of Malaysia
Address: 3/F, Wisma Plam, Lot 150, Jin. Tun Sambanthan, 50470 Kuala Lumpur
Telephone: +60 3 274 7399
Fax: +60 3 274 5910

Institute of Marketing Malaysia
Address: 8086, Kelana Jaya, 46781 Petaling Jaya, Selangor Darul Ehsan
Telephone: +60 3 735 9677
Fax: +60 3 735 9284
Year established: 1979
Activities: training courses
Publications:
• Marketeer: *current marketing issues and blends both academic and practical approaches to Malaysia marketing. - quarterly*

Malayan Commercial Banks' Association
Address: 2/F, Bangunan Dato'Zainal, 23 Jalan Melaka, 50100 Kuala Lumpur
Telephone: +60 3 298 3736/298 3991

Malaysia Association of Hotels
Address: Malaysia Tourist Information Complex, 109 Jalan Ampang
Telephone: +60 3 238 1693/4
Fax: +60 3 248 8059

Malaysia Automotive Tyre Manufacturers' Industry Group
Address: 17/F, Wisma Sime Darby, Jalan Raja Laut, Kuala Lumpur 50350
Telephone: +60 3 293 1244
Fax: +60 3 293 5105

Malaysia Book Publishers' Association
Address: 10 Jalan 217, 46050 Petaling Jaya, Selangor Darul Ehsan

Telephone: +60 3 791 4108/825 3485
Fax: +60 3 791 0416/825 4575
Chief officers: Mr H Hasrom (Director)

Malaysia Cosmetics and Toiletries Industry Group
Address: 17/F, Wisma Sime Darby, Jalan Raja Laut, 50350 Kuala Lumpur
Telephone: +60 3 293 1244
Fax: +60 3 293 5105

Malaysia Fruit Exporters' Association (FEAM)
Address: Lot 19, Block B, 1st & 2nd Floors, Cycle & Carriage, Jalan 51A/219, 46100 Petaling Jaya
Telephone: +60 3 775 7488
Fax: +60 3 775 8084

Malaysia Garment Manufacturers' Association
Address: 9A & B, Jalan Lingkungan Brunei, Pudu, 55100 Kuala Lumpur
Telephone: +60 3 242 2491/242 2471
Fax: +60 3 242 2491

Malaysia Knitting Manufacturers' Association
Address: 205N, 16/F, Bangunan Choo Cheng Khay, Jalan Choo Cheng Khay
Telephone: +60 3 242 7108

Malaysia Paper Merchants' Association
Address: 134A, Jalan SS 24/2, Taman Megah, 47301 Petailing Jaya, Selangor Darul Ehsan
Telephone: +60 3 774 9842
Fax: +60 3 775 2463/775 2400

Malaysia Pulp and Paper Manufacturers' Association
Address: Bangunan MUDA, Lot 7, Jalan 51A/241, 46100 Petaling Jaya, Selangor Darul Ehsan
Telephone: +60 3 775 9549
Fax: +60 3 775 1519
Chief officers: Y. Bhg. Datuk Yahaya Bin Yeop Ishak (President), Mr Kevin Lai Tak Kuan (Vice President), Masu't A.Samah (Honorary Secretary General)
Structure: President, Vice President, Secretariat, Committee
Membership: 15 member companies
Publications:
• Malaysia Pulp and Paper Manufacturers Association Annual Report: *short summary of prevailing market conditions, members' contact details, products, annual production, no. of employees etc. Also includes a detailed statistical breakdown of imports and exports by sector over a seven year review period, and a comprehensive glossary of pulp and paper related terms - annual*

Malaysia Retailers' Association
Address: 102 Jalan Bangsar, 59200 Kuala Lumpur
Telephone: +60 3 282 7277
Fax: +60 3 282 6729

Malaysian Advertising Association
Persatuan Para Pengiklan Malaysia
Address: Secretariat, No 18 (1st Floor) Lorong Travers, 50480 Kuala Lumpur
Telephone: +60 3 282 5477/282 5492/282 5493
Activities: advises on legislative or regulative measures relating to advertising; has established the Audit Bureau of Circulations which provides advertisers with up-to-date and properly audited circulation figures; operates an Education Committee which runs Certificate and Diploma Courses in advertising
Chief officers: Dato Jaffar Bin Mohd Ali (President)

Malaysian Agricultural Chemicals' Association (MACA)
Address: 1 (2nd. Floor), 76c Jalan SS22/21 Taman Mayang Jaya, 47301 Petaling Jaya
Telephone: +60 3 704 8968/718 3295
Fax: +60 3 704 8964/718 6331
Chief officers: Mr. Bachu Ratilal

Malaysian Article Numbering Council (MANC)
Address: 17th Floor, Wisma Sime Darby, Jalan Raja Laut, 50350 Kuala Lumpur
Telephone: +60 3 293 1244
Fax: +60 3 293 2681

Malaysian Association of Tour and Travel Agents (MATTA)
Address: 109 Jalan Ampang, 50450 Kuala Lumpur
Telephone: +60 3 241 3768/3771
Fax: +60 3 243 1163/242 0613
Year established: 1975
Activities: travel trade fair; fosters ethical business practices and discourages unfair competition; education and research; conventions and seminars
Chief officers: Shireen Hingun (Executive Director)
Membership: 534

Malaysian Automotive Components and Parts Manufacturers' Association
Address: c/o Malaysian Sheet Glass Bhd, 21 KM 47000 Sungei Buloh
Telephone: +60 3 293 1244
Fax: +60 3 294 7290
Chief officers: Paul Low Seng Kuan

Malaysian Booksellers' Association (MBA)
Address: 45 Jalan Tun Mohd Fuad Tiga, Taman Tun Dr Ismail, 60000 Kuala Lumpur
Telephone: +60 3 719 3485
Fax: +60 3 718 1664
Year established: 1969
Chief officers: K Arul (Honorary Secretary)
Membership: 121
Publications:
• Malaysian Booksellers Directory: *annual*

Malaysian Ceramics Industry Group
Address: POB 12194, 17th floor, Wisma Sime Darby, Jalan Raja Laut, 50770 Kuala Lumpur
Telephone: +60 3 293 1244
Fax: +60 3 293 5105
Chief officers: Encik Mustafa Mansur (Chairman); Long Heng Kow (Deputy Chairman); Joseph Chua (Honorary Secretary); Tony Goh (Honorary Treasurer)
Membership: 15 ordinary, 9 associate

Malaysian Edible Oil Manufacturers' Association (MEOMA)
Address: 134-1 Jalan Tun Sambanthan, 50470 Kuala Lumpur
Telephone: +60 3 274 7420
Year established: 1961
Activities: laboratory and consultancy services; warehousing and bulkship
Chief officers: S H Lim (Executive Secretary)
Structure: general working committee; subcommittees
Membership: 75 members comprising palm kernel crushers,

palm oil refiners, oleochemical manufacturers, brokers, dealers/traders, surveyors, cooking oil packers, manufacturers of activated clay and sulphuric acid
Publications:
• MEOMA Bulletin: *monthly*
• MEOMA Handbook: *biennial*

Malaysian Electrical Appliances Industry Group (MEIG)
Address: c/o Federation of Malaysian Manufacturer 17th Floor, Wisma Sime Darby Jalan Raja Laut,, Kuala Lumpur 50350
Telephone: +60 3 293 2244
Fax: +60 3 293 5105
Chief officers: Seck Hong Chee

Malaysian Employers' Federation
Address: 11th Floor, Exchange Square, off Jalan Semantan, Kuala Lumpur
Telephone: +60 3 254 9422
Fax: +60 3 255 0830
Year established: 1959
Chief officers: Datuk Dr Mokhzani Bin Abdul Rahim (President)
Membership: private-sector organisation incorporating 11 member associations and 1,051 ordinary members

Malaysian Exporters' Association (MAME)
Address: P.O. Box 10285, 163A, Tingkat Satu, Jalan Ipoh, 51200 Kuala Lumpur
Telephone: +60 3 442 6788
Fax: +60 3 791 3727
Chief officers: Tuan HJ. Mohd. Ayub Hassan

Malaysian Food Canners' Association
Address: P.O. Box 51, 46700 Petaling Jaya
Telephone: +60 3 791 8737/550 1311
Fax: +60 3 791 7023/559 2692

Malaysian Food Manufacturing Group (MAFMAG)
Address: PO Box 385, Jalan Sultan, Selangor Darul Ehsan
Telephone: +60 3 755 4466
Fax: +60 3 755 0992
Chief officers: Tuan Haji Idid Wan Chik

Malaysian Footwear Manufacturers' Association
Address: P.O. Box 160 42008, c/o Marco Shoe Sdn. Bhd. Pandamaran Industrial Site, Port Klang
Telephone: +60 3 985 5382
Fax: +60 3 984 5664

Malaysian Frozen Seafood Processing Association
Address: c/o Butterworth Iceworks Sdn. Bhd, 85, Leboh pantai, 10300 Pulau Pinang
Telephone: +60 4 261 1516/261 1517
Fax: +60 4 331 9804
Chief officers: Tajuddin Kassim

Malaysian Furniture Industry Council (MFIC)
Address: 75-1, Jalan Mega Mendung, Kompleks Bandar, Batu 5, Jalan Klang Lama, 58200 Kuala Lumpar
Telephone: +60 3 780 8275/780 8277
Fax: +60 3 781 0355
Web site: www.mtc.com.my/mfic/mfic.htm
Web site notes: site includes an overview of the Malaysian furniture industry with statistics on imports and exports of furniture
Year established: 1978

Activities: government liaison; education and training; trade promotion
Chief officers: Oh Han Cheng (President)
Membership: 300 furniture manufacturers and exporters
Notes: Formally known as the Furniture Manufacturers and Traders Federation of Malaysia (FMTFM).

Malaysian Motor Traders' and Importers' Association
Address: 7th Floor, Block A, Wisma Yakin, Jalan Masjid India, 50100 Kuala Lumpur
Telephone: +60 3 755 0454
Fax: +60 3 755 0954

Malaysian Motor Vehicle Assemblers' Association
Address: d/a AMIN Holdings Sdn. Bhd., Jalan Sesiku, 40000 Shah Alam, Selangor.
Telephone: +60 3 550 7139/559 1601
Fax: +60 3 559 4863/559 6962
Chief officers: Tuan Haji Mohamad Khalid

Malaysian Newspaper Publishers' Association
Persatuan Penerbit-Penerbit Akhbar Malaysia
Address: c/o Corporate Secretarius, 5c Jalan Semarak, 54100 Kuala Lumpur
Telephone: +60 3 292 5492
Fax: +60 3 292 8804

Malaysian Organisation of Pharmaceutical Industries (MOPI)
Address: 5B Lorong Rahim Kajai 13, Taman Tun Dr Ismail, 60000 Kuala Lumpur
Telephone: +60 3 717 3486
Fax: +60 3 717 3487
Telex: MA 36313
Chief officers: Tong Yew Sum (President); Chin Sek Min, Tay Hong Teong (Vice Presidents); Alex Tan (Executive Secretary)
Membership: 28

Malaysian Pharmaceutical Trade and Manufacturers' Association (MPTMA)
Address: 75-3, Medan Setia 1 Bukit Damansara, 50490 Kuala Lumpur
Telephone: +60 3 256 2493/3 256 2494
Fax: +60 3 255 2143

Malaysian Printers' Association
Address: 14A Jalan Murai Satu, Batu Kompleks Off Jalan Ipoh, 51200 Kuala Lumpur
Telephone: +60 3 621 2187/621 2189
Fax: +60 3 621 8702

Malaysian Rubber Products Manufacturers' Association
Address: 52 B Jalan SS 21/58, Damansara Utama, 47400 Petaling Jaya, Selangor
Telephone: +60 3 718 8582
Fax: +60 3 718 8832
E-mail: mrpma@po.jaring.my
Year established: 1977
Activities: disseminates local and overseas trade information through circulars; statistical data and market reports; assists members to gain places on trade missions; advises on government incentives; gives information on legislation; consults and liaises with government agencies; liaises with similar associations in other countries; participates in international forums
Chief officers: Tan Sri Datuk Arshat Ayub (President)
Membership: 120

Publications:
• Annual Directory: *annual*

Malaysian Textile Manufacturers' Association (MTMA)

Address: POBox #42, 9th Floor West Block, Wisma Selangor Dredging, 142C Jalan Ampang, 50450 Kuala Lumpur
Telephone: +60 3 262 1454/1587/1879
Fax: +60 3 262 3953/5148
E-mail: textile@po.jaring.my
Year established: 1973
Activities: organising trade fairs, conferences and seminars; information dissemination; training and government liaison
Chief officers: Tan Sri Dato' Azman Hashim (President), Ms Lom Mei Liang (Executive Secretary), Choy Ming Bil (Executive Director)
Membership: 295 companies in the fibre, spinning, weaving, knitting, garment-making, industrial textile/accessories sector
Publications:
• MTMA Newsletter: *domestic and international trade related matters, exhibitions, trade fairs, news and views on the textile and apparel industry - bi-monthly*
• MTMA Textile Directory: *comprehensive profiles of member companies - biennial*

Malaysian Tourism Promotion Board

Address: POB 10328, Menara Dato'Onn, 24-27th Floor, Putra World Trade Centre, 45 Jalan Tun Ismail, 50480 Kuala Lumpur
Telephone: +60 3 293 5188
Fax: +60 3 293 5884
Activities: organises conventions and exhibitions on tourism; compiles statistics on tourism
Chief officers: En Zainuddin Mohd Zain (Acting Director General)
Structure: managed by a board
Publications:
• Annual Report of the Malaysian Tourism Promotion Board: *annual*

Motorcycle and Scooter Assemblers' Association of Malaysia

Address: d/a Suzuki Assembler (M) Sdn. Bhd, 1412, Plot No.281, Kompleks Perindusrian Prai, 13600 Prai, Pulau Pinang.
Telephone: +60 3 511 8818
Fax: +60 3 511 8641

National Tobacco Board

Address: PO Box 198, 15720 Kota Bahru, Kelantan
Telephone: +60 9 765 1182
Fax: +60 9 765 5640
Year established: 1973
Activities: tobacco statistics (Malaysia); research carried out by separate agency (Malaysian Agricultural Research and Development Institute)
Chief officers: Mohamed Bin Ismail (Director General); Teo Hui Bek (Deputy Director General - enforcement); Haji Abdullah bin Awang (Deputy Director General - development)
Structure: board members (officials from growers, curers etc); working committee
Membership: growers, curers and cigarette manufacturers, suppliers of inputs for tobacco production
Publications:
• Annual Report of the National Tobacco Board: *annual*

National Tourism Council of Malaysia

Address: Lot 109, Dewan Tuanku Abdul Rahman, Jalan Ampang, 50450 Kuala Lumpur
Telephone: +60 3 242 7877
Fax: +60 3 244 4966

Packaging Council of Malaysia

Address: 17/F, Wisma Sime Darby, Jalan Raja Laut, 50350 Kuala Lumpur
Telephone: +60 3 293 1244
Fax: +60 3 293 5105

Palm Oil Refiners' Association Malaysia

Address: 15th Floor, West Block, Wisma Selangor Dredging,142c Jalan Ampang, 50450 Kuala Lumpur
Telephone: +60 3 261 7791/7788
Fax: +60 3 261 8063
Year established: 1975
Chief officers: Datuk Robert W K Chan
Membership: 27

Toys and Giftware Malaysia (TAG)

Address: 17/F, Wisma Sime Darby, Jalan Raja Laut, 50350 Kuala Lumpur
Telephone: +60 3 293 1244
Fax: +60 3 293 5105

MALTA

Association of General Retailers and Traders

Address: Exchange Buildings, Republic Street, Valleta VLT 05
Telephone: +356 230 459/234 170
Fax: +356 246 925
Chief officers: Mr C. Cini (President), Mr V. Farrugia (General Director)

Association of Insurance Companies

Address: St. Paul's Buildings, 43A/2 West Street, Valleta VLT 12
Telephone: +356 232 640/240 609
Fax: +356 248 388
Chief officers: Mr W.G. Camilleri (President), Mr J.E. Grech (Vice President)

Association of Retail Travel Agents

Address: Exchange Buildings, Republic Street, Valleta VLT 05
Telephone: +356 233 873/247 233
Fax: +356 245 223
Chief officers: Mr A. Bonello (Chairman), Mr W. Chircop (Honorary Secretary)

Federation of Associations of Travel and Tourism Agents

Address: Exchange Buildings, Republic Street, Valleta VLT 05
Telephone: +356 237 622/233 873/247 233
Fax: +356 230 541
Chief officers: Mr J. Borg Olivier (President), Dr P.J. Galea (Secretary General)

Federation of Hotels, Pensions and Catering Establishments

Address: 293/13 Republic Street, Valleta VLT 04
Telephone: +356 246 195
Fax: +356 807 706
Chief officers: Mr L.D. Abela (President), Mr V. Camilleri (Vice President)

Malta Article Numbering Council (MANA)

Address: c/o Malta Confederation of Industry, Development House, St Anne's Street, Floriana VLT 01
Telephone: +356 234 428

Fax: +356 240 702
E-mail: foi@maltanet.net

Malta Hotels and Restaurants Association
Address: 66/1 Tower Road, Sliema
Telephone: +356 318 133
Fax: +356 336 477
Chief officers: Mr W. Zahra (President), Dr S.Tortell
(Secretary General)

Rent-A-Car Association
Address: 1st Floor, Msida Court, 61 Msida Sea Front, Msida
MSD 08
Telephone: +356 222 912/221 001/234 322
Fax: +356 230 414
Chief officers: Mr A. Meli (President), Dr E. Mallia (Secretary
General)

Tobacco Industry Advisory Council
Address: 2nd Floor, Regency House, Republic Street, Valleta
VLT 04
Telephone: +356 240 432
Fax: +356 236 959
Chief officers: Mr V. Scicluna (Chairman), Dr A. Borg
Cardona (Chief Executive)

Yacht Traders' Association
Address: 5 Cresta Flats, Imradd Street, Ta'Xbiex MSD 12
Telephone: +356 320 577/314 222
Fax: +356 332 259
Chief officers: Mr R. Darmanin (President), Mr E. Warrington
(Secretary)

MARTINIQUE

Tourism Board of Martinique
Address: BP 520, Fort de France Cédex
Telephone: +596 6 379 60
Fax: +596 7 366 93

MAURITIUS

Article Numbering Association (EAN Mauritius)
Address: c/o Mauritius Chamber of Commerce and Industry,
3 Royla Street, Port-Louis
Telephone: +230 208 3301
Fax: +230 208 0076

Association of Hotels and Restaurants of Mauritius (AHRIM)
Association des Hôtelieres et Restauranteurs de L'Ile Maurice
Address: Royal Road, Grand Bay
Telephone: +230 2 635 099/8971
Fax: +230 2 637 907
Chief officers: Mr E Goldsmith, Mr K Braunecker

Association of Mauritian Manufacturers
Address: C/o The Mauritius Chamber of Commerce &
Industry, 3, royal Street, Port-Louis
Telephone: +230 2 083 301
Fax: +230 2 080 076
E-mail: mccipl@bow.intnet.mu
Chief officers: Mr Bashir Currimjee

Mauritius Chamber of Merchants
Address: P.O. Box 300 , C/o Abdullasonco Ltd, 23, Louis
Pasteur Street, Port-Louis
Telephone: +230 2 401 477/241 0197
Fax: +230 2 407 088/242 1646
E-mail: abson@bow.intnet.mu
Chief officers: A. A. Ahmed (Director)

Mauritius Export Processing Zone Association (MEPZA)
Address: 42, Sir William Newton Street, Port Louis
Telephone: +230 2 085 212/212 1853
Fax: +230 212 1853

Small and Medium Size Industries Development Organisation (SMIDO)
Address: Royal Road, Coromandel
Telephone: +230 2 335 712/3/4/233 4877
Fax: +230 2 335 545

MEXICO

Association of the Mexican Toy Industry
Asociación Mexicana de la Industria del Juguete, AC
Address: Av San Antonio Nº 256 -8º piso, 03849 México DF
Telephone: +52 5 563 3400 Ext 376
Fax: +52 5 611 3899
Year established: 1990
Activities: information, trade fairs, international contacts
Membership: 195 toy manufacturers, distributors and
importers
Publications:
● Membership List

Automotive Parts' Manufacturers of Mexico (INA)
Industria Nacional de Autopartes, AC
Address: Amatlán Nº 19, Condesa, Delegación Cuauhtémoc,
06140 México DF
Telephone: +52 3 247 553 1936/553 2124
Fax: +52 3 286 4101
E-mail: autopartes@attmail.com
Web site: www.ina.com.mx
Web site notes: site includes statistics on the Mexican
automotive industry
Chief officers: Antonio Zarate Negrón (Presidente), Lic.
Oscar Vejar de la Barrera (General Director)
Notes: Amatlán No. 19, Col. Condesa, 06140, México, D.F.
Tel: 553-19-36/553-15-52/553-02-47/553-09-21 Fax: 286-41-01
No. de afiliación:

Brewers' Association (ANFACER)
Asociación de Fabricantes de Cerveza y de la Malta, AC
Address: Av Horacio Nº 1556, Colonia Chapultepec Morales,
11570 México DF
Telephone: +52 5 520 6283/5/280 9850/9911/9124
Fax: +52 5 202 1124/280 0201
Chief officers: Lic. Juan Sanchez Navarro Redo (President),
Lic.Andres Escobar y Cordova (General Director)
Membership: brewers

Business Co-ordinating Council (CCE)
Consejo Coordinador Empresarial
Address: Homero Nº 527, 6º piso, Chapultepec Morales,
11570 México DF
Telephone: +52 5 250 6977/7755/7304
Fax: +52 5 250 6995/4130
Telex: 1772948

Year established: 1974
Activities: represents and coordinates the activities of private enterprises
Notes: also houses the Consejo Mexicana de Hombres de Negocios (National Businessmen's Association)

Confederation of Mexican Industries (CONCAMIN)

Confederación de Cámaras Industriales de los Estados Unidos Mexicanos
Address: Manuel Maria Contreras N° 133, 8° piso, Cuauhtémoc, 06500 México DF
Telephone: +52 5 566 7822
Fax: +52 5 535 6871
E-mail: cetin@solar.sar.net
Web site: www.concamin.org.mx
Web site notes: site includes latest economic indicators
Year established: 1918
Chief officers: Alvaro Torre Prieto (Director General), Rene Espinosa y Torres Estrada (Foreign Trade), Amaya Lasa Arana (Communications)
Membership: 67 chambers of commerce and 28 industrial associations, which represent a total of some 380,000 concerns
Publications:
• Revista Industrial: *general information and confederation news - monthly*

Electrical Appliances Manufacturers' Association

Asociación Nacional de Fabricantes de Aparatos Domésticos, AC
Address: Homero N° 109, Desp. 1601, Colonia Polanco, 11560,México DF
Telephone: +52 5 545 0018/5450320
Fax: +52 5 545 8366
Chief officers: C.P. José Manuel Contreras Martínez (President), Lic. Guillermo Cochran Garza (General Manager)

Federation of Coffee Organisations (CNOC)

Coordinadora Nacional de Organizaciones Cafetaleras
Address: Tabasco 262-301, Colonia Roma, 06700 México DF
Telephone: +52 5 514 0205
Fax: +52 5 207 0508
E-mail: cnoc@laneta.apc.org
Web site: www.laneta.apc.org/cnoc/
Year established: 1988
Activities: promotes regional economic development with collective capital and strives to improve social welfare through the organisation of peasant families
Chief officers: Fidel Morales Meza (President), Abraham López Ramírez (Secretary), Felipe Francisco Reyes (Treasurer)
Membership: national network of 126 regional organisations representing 75,000 small coffee producers
Notes: CNOC exports its coffee via its sales office, Promotora Comercial de Cafés Suaves Mexicanos, S.A. de C.V. CNOC also has a marketing and sales office in San Francisco, California, which sells roasted and ground coffee throughout the United States using CNOC's own brand label: Aztec Harvests.

Mango Packaging Export Association (EMEX)

Asociación de Empacadoras de Mango de Exportación, AC
Address: Químicos 4897, Colonia Jardines de Guadalupe, 45030 Zapopan, Jalisco
Telephone: +52 3 620 4315/628 5778
Fax: +52 5 620 4187
E-mail: lacruz@infosel.net.mx
Web site: www.emex.org
Year established: 1991
Activities: carries out research; education and training and produces a variety of publications and market reports; advises member companies on export procedures and produces

statistics on imports, exports, prices, distribution and the US market for mangoes
Chief officers: Luis Villegas Murguia (President), Luis Alberto Cruz García (General Director), Reginaldo Baez Saudo (Executive Secretary of the Scientific-Technical Committee)
Membership: 66 mango producers and exporters
Publications:
• Boletín Informativo: *production statistics, commercial information and analysis, information on different sources related to the sector*
• Manejo Post-Cosecha de Mango: *annual*
• Manual para Cosechadores de Mango: *annual*
• Memorias del Segundo Seminario Nacional de Calidad en Mango: *annual*
• Norma de Calidad para el Mango Fresco: *information on quality rules for the production and packaging of goods - annual*
• Revista EMEX

Metal Packaging Producers' Association (AFEMAC)

Asociación de Fabricantes de Envases Metálicos, AC
Address: Bosques de Ciruelos N° 190 Nivel 3, Desp. B-301, Bosques de las Lomas, 11700 México DF
Telephone: +52 5 251 1998
Fax: +52 5 251 7668
Chief officers: Ing. Alberto Galvan Rodriguez (President), Ing. Alfonso de Leon Julian (General Director)
Membership: producers of metal containers

Mexican Advertising Agencies' Association (AMAP)

Asociación Mexicana de Agencias de Publicidad, AC
Address: 2ª Cerrada de Luz Saviñón N° 5, Colonia Del Valle, 03100 México DF
Telephone: +52 5 523 0980/682 6459
Fax: +52 5 543 6188
Activities: publishes information about the advertising sector in Mexico; annual statistical report; organises trade fairs
Chief officers: Lic. Eugenio Velazco William (President), Lic. Sergio López Zepeda (General Manager)
Membership: 47 advertising agencies nationwide
Publications:
• Boletín Informativo: *advertising industry report - monthly*
• Creativa: *magazine with information on advertising and the media - monthly*
• Media Data México: *statistical information - annual*
Notes: also at: Plaza Carlos J Finlay, #6, 4° piso, Col del Valle, México DF. Tel 5 535 0139, Fax 5 592 7139.

Mexican Association for Product Codification (AMECOP)

Asociación Mexicana del Código de Producto AC
Address: Horacio 1855, 6° piso, Colonia Chapultepec, 11570 Mexico D.F.
Telephone: +52 5 395 2044
Fax: +52 5 395 2038
E-mail: amecop@iserve.net.mx

Mexican Association of Car Dealers (AMDA)

Asociación Mexicana de Distribuidores de Automotores, AC
Address: Mercaderes N° 134, San José Insurgentes, 03900 México DF
Telephone: +52 5 593 2644/660 5870
Fax: +52 5 651 4599
Membership: new car distributors

Mexican Association of Gifts, Decorative Goods and Folk Art Producers (AMFAR)
Asociación Mexicana de Fabricantes de Artículos para Regalo, Decoración y Artesanías, AC
Address: Monterrey Nº 149, Colonia Roma, 06700 México DF
Telephone: +52 5 564 8961/564 4564/8938/8765
Fax: +52 5 574 9709
Activities: organises annual AMFAR EXPO REGALO trade fair
Chief officers: De la Paz Pani Carral (President), Angel Landeros Chávez (Vice President), Victoria de Murga Alvarez (Secretary)
Membership: manufacturers and wholesalers of gifts, decorations and handicrafts

Mexican Association of the Pharmaceutical Industry (AMIF)
Asociación Mexicana de Industriales Farmacéuticos, AC
Address: Brillante Nº 82, Col la Estrella-Delg, Gustavo A Madero, 07810 México DF
Telephone: +52 5 601 2739/688 9550
Fax: +52 5 601 1464

Mexican Automobile Association (AMA)
Asociación Mexicana Automovilistica, AC
Address: Orizaba Nº 7, Colonia Roma, 06700 México DF
Telephone: +52 5 208 8329/5116285
Fax: +52 5 207 4448/511 6285
Membership: companies in the automotive industry

Mexican Automotive Industry Association (AMIA)
Asociación Mexicana de la Industria Automotriz, AC
Address: Ensenada Nº 90, Colonia Condesa, 06140 México DF
Telephone: +52 5 272 1144/515 2542/516 0711
Fax: +52 5 515 2541/272 7139
Chief officers: César Flores (President), Sr Bernard Leissner (General Director), Lic. Fausto Cuevas Mesa (Administrative Director)
Membership: car manufacturers

Mexican Coffee Exporters' Association (AMEC)
Asociación Mexicana de Exportadores de Café, AC
Address: Av Insurgentes Sur Nº 682, 8º piso, Colonia Del Valle, 03100 México DF
Telephone: +52 5 536 7767/68/64
Fax: +52 5 523 8659
Chief officers: Lic Jorge Cisneros Salas (General Manager)
Membership: coffee exporters

Mexican Footwear Chamber (CICEG)
Cámara de la Industria del Calzado
Address: Blvd.Lopez Mateos 3401 OTE, Fracc. Julian de Obregon, 37290 León , Guanajato
Telephone: +52 4 711 5195
Fax: +52 4 711 4120
E-mail: ciceg@leon.intermex.com.mx
Web site: www.intermex.com.mx/ciceg/index.html
Year established: 1940
Activities: organises the SAPICA trade show on footwear products, leather goods, sporting goods and accessories
Chief officers: Lic. Luis Ernesto Ayala Torres (President), Lic. Francisco Ramirez Renteria (General Director)

Mexican Franchise Association
Associación Mexicana de Franchising
Address: Insurgentes Sur 1783, #303, Colonia Guadalupe Inn, CP 01020 Mexico City
Telephone: +52 5 255 248043
Fax: +52 5 255 248043

Chief officers: Adolfo Crespo (Director General)

Mexican Industrialists' Association (AIEM)
Asociación de Industriales del Estado de México, AC
Address: Av. Parque Chapultepec Nº 105, Naucalpan de Juárez, 53390 México
Telephone: +52 5 576 2111
Fax: +52 5 576 2080
E-mail: aiem@telesur.acnet.net
Web site: telesur.acnet.net/AIEM
Year established: 1945
Activities: government liaison in relation to industrial planning, education and training

Mexican National Hotel and Motel Association (AMHMRM)
Asociación Mexicana de Hoteles y Moteles de la República Mexicana, AC
Address: Balderas Nº 33, Desp 414- 4º piso, Colonia Central, Delegación Cuauhtémoc, 06040 México DF
Telephone: +52 5 510 8614/9062/8659
Fax: +52 5 510 8874
Year established: 1922
Activities: legal and tax advice, technical advice, training, educational and cultural programmes on subjects and areas of national importance; seminars etc.
Chief officers: Alfredo Tinajero Fontan (President), Manuel Lopez Palomino (Vice President), Javier Tapia Camou (2nd Vice President), Javier Pister Rueda (Secretary), Jorge Rosales Saade (Treasurer), Benjamín Aguilera Palancares (Executive Director)
Membership: 3,200 hotels and motels throughout Mexico, represented through 79 branches of the association
Publications:
● Análisis de la Reforma Fiscal
● Directorio Nacional de Hoteles: *information on members - annual*
● Hoteles Mexicanos: *hotel industry magazine - monthly*
● Marco Legal de la Hotelería
Notes: Member of the American Hotel and Motel Association, Washington DC, and the International Hotel Association, Paris.

Mexican Pharmaceutical Association (AFM)
Asociación Farmacéutica Mexicana, AC
Address: Adolfo Prieto Nº.1649 601, Colonia Del Valle, México D.F.03100
Telephone: +52 5 524 0993/5685/534 5397
Fax: +52 5 534 5098
Year established: 1966
Activities: analysis and discussion of different topics of interest to the association; such as Farmacopea de los Estados Unidos Mexicanos (FEUM) and Normas Oficiales; organises various events: Congreso Nacional de Ciencias Farmacéuticas (National Cogress of Pharmaceutical Sciences), Expofarma, Jornadas Nacionales de Ciencias Farmacéuticas, Encuentro Nacional de Calidad Farmacéutica
Chief officers: C Helgi Jung (President), José Manuel Cárdenas (General Director)
Membership: over 2,000 members: professionals, academics and students

Mexican Pulp and Paper Industries' Association (ATCP)
Asociación Mexicana de Técnicos de las Industrias de Celulosa y del Papel, AC
Address: Lafayette Nº 138, Colonia Azures, 01590 México DF
Telephone: +52 5 254 7990/7579/7700/7359
Fax: +52 5 203 8521
Year established: 1960
Activities: research, education and training
Chief officers: Raúl López Díaz (President), Raúl Cicero Fernandez (Vice President), Jose Antonio Peña (General

Manager)
Membership: 500 pulp and paper manufacturers, processors and recyclers' of secondary fibres
Publications:
• ATCP Magazine: *bi-monthly*

Mexican Travel Agencies' Association (AMAV)

Asociación Mexicana de Agencias de Viajes, AC
Address: Guanajuato N° 128, Colonia Roma, 06700 México DF
Telephone: +52 5 584 9300
Fax: +52 5 264 1486
Membership: travel agencies

National Association for Domestic Appliance Dealers (ANDAD)

Asociación Nacional de Distribuidores de Aparatos Domésticos, AC
Address: Zacatecas N° 155, Colonia Roma, 006700 México DF
Telephone: +52 5 584 8844
Fax: +52 5 584 8844/1360
Chief officers: C.P. José Manuel Contreras Martinez (President), Lic. Guillermo Cochran Garza (General Manager)
Membership: domestic appliance dealers

National Association for Importers and Exporters of the Republic of Mexico (ANIERM)

Asociación Nacional de Importadores y Exportadores de la República Mexicana, AC
Address: Monterrey N° 130, Colonia oma, 06700 México DF
Telephone: +52 5 564 9379/9218/8618/584 9522
Fax: +52 5 584 5317
Activities: database of company and market information, conferences, courses and seminars on international trade, research, trade documents
Chief officers: Carlos Viveros Figueroa (President), Martín Morell Miranda (services Manager), Reynaldo Díaz
Membership: ca. 1,000 importers and exporters nationwide
Publications:
• Carta Mensual con Demandas Concretas de Productos: *trade bulletin - monthly*
• Directory: *information on members - annual*

National Association of Agricultural Produce Trading Companies

Asociación Nacional de Empresas Comercializadoras de Productores del Campo, AC
Address: Miguel Angel de Quevedo No. 50-403, Colonia Agrícola Chimalistac, Delegación Alvaro Obregón, México DF
Telephone: +52 5 661 5914
Fax: +52 5 661 5909
E-mail: anec@laneta.apc.org
Web site: www.laneta.apc.org/anec

National Association of Bakery Products

Cámara Nacional de la Industria Panificadora y Similares
Address: Dr. Liceaga N° 96, 2° piso, Colonia Doctores, 06720 México DF
Telephone: +52 5 578 9277/578 9803
Fax: +52 5 761 8924
Chief officers: Lic. Carlos Sánchez Latiznere (President), Lic. José Luis Valenzuela Arce (General Director)
Membership: bread and related products manufacturers'

National Association of Bottled Water Producers (ANPAEAC)

Asociación Nacional de Productores de Aguas Envasadas, AC
Address: Paseo de la Reforma N° 195-1301, Cuauhtemoc, 06500 México DF
Telephone: +52 5 566 2244/566 2359/535 0374
Fax: +52 5 535 0374
Membership: bottled drinks producers'

National Association of Footwear Suppliers (ANPIC)

Asociación Nacional de Proveedores de la Industria del Calzado, AC
Address: Av Obreros N° 403, AP 1239, Fraccionamiento Industrial Julián de Obregón, 37290 León, Guanajuato
Telephone: +52 4 711 4042/113 567/112 012
Fax: +52 47 112 139
Telex: 120479 ANPIME
Chief officers: Lic. Ramón Flores Alcazar (President) , Patricia Pimentel García (General Manager)
Membership: suppliers to the shoe industry

National Association of Self-Service and Department Stores

Asociación Nacional de Tiendas de Autoservicio y Departamentales, AC
Address: Homero N° 109, piso 11, Colonia Polanco, 11560 Mexico DF
Telephone: +52 5 545 8803/203 4438/254 1714
Fax: +52 5 203 4495

National Association of Tanners (ANACU)

Asociación Nacional de Curtidores, AC
Address: Cuahutémoc N° 306- 107, 37320 Leon, Guanajuato
Telephone: +52 47 165 728/167077
Fax: +52 4 716 7077
Web site: www.intermex.com.mx/Anacu

National Association of the Edible Oils and Fats Industry (ANIAMC)

Asociación Nacional de Industrias de Aceites y Mantecas Comestibles, AC
Address: Praga N° 39, 3er piso, Juárez, Delegación Cuauhtémoc, 06600 México DF
Telephone: +52 5 207 0961/533 2846/7/8/9/59/525 7546
Fax: +52 5 525 5124
Year established: 1959
Activities: government liaison; 2 conferences each year; Mexican market statistics for oilseeds and edible oils and fats (monthly, available to members on request); analysis and strategy department; foreign trade assessment
Chief officers: Lic.Enrique Garcia Gómez (President), Lic. Amadeo Ibarra Hallal (Director)
Membership: 36 individuals; 6 crushing and refining companies
Publications:
• ANIAMC Magazine: *technical and economic analysis, cultural and other articles - quarterly*
• Noticias, el Mercado de la Soya y Canola: *opening and closing prices for soyabean and rapeseed on the Chicago market; Spanish graphics - daily*

National Association of the Mexican Publishing Industry (CANIEM)

Cámara Nacional de la Industria Editorial Mexicana
Address: Holanda N° 13, San Diego Chubrubusco, 04120 México DF 21
Telephone: +52 5 688 2011/2221/2434
Fax: +52 5 604 4347/3147

Chief officers: Lic. Jorge Velasco Felix (President), Lic. Rafael Servin Arroyo (Director General), JI Ortega,
Membership: publishing houses
Publications:
- Editores: *bulletin - monthly*
- Membership Directory: *annual*

National Association of the Tequila Industry

Cámara Nacional de la Industria Tequilera
Address: Calzada lázaro Cardenas Nº 3289, 5º piso, Colonia Chapalita, 45000 Guadalajara, Jalisco
Telephone: +52 9 131 215 021/215 113/215 060
Fax: +52 9 136 472031
Chief officers: Lic. Adolfo Reveron Cervantes (President), C.P. Sergio Laguna Legorreta (Director)
Membership: Tequila manufacturers and distributors

National Cable Television Association (CANITEC)

Cámara Nacional de la Industria de Televisión por Cable
Address: Monte Albán Nº 281, Colonia Navarte, 03020 México DF
Telephone: +52 5 682 0173/0298/669 3691
Fax: +52 2 682 0881
Chief officers: Mauricio Montaño (President), Enrique Castro y Amaya (Director General)
Membership: cable television companies
Publications:
- Cable Notas: *information bulletin - bi-monthly*
- Membership Directory: *information on members, with statistical section - annual*

National Carbonated Soft Drinks and Water Producers' Association (ANPRAC)

Asociación Nacional de Productores de Refrescos y Aguas Carbonatadoas, AC
Address: Moliere Nº 39 - 3º piso, Colonia Polanco, México DF
Telephone: +52 5 281 2496
Fax: +52 5 280 3353/ 2800652
Activities: participates in InterBev exhibition; annual general assembly
Chief officers: Jorge Zindel Mundet (President), Enrique C Molina, Miguel Barragón (Vice Presidents), Luis Regordosa (General Director), Luis Torija (Secretary)
Membership: producers of soft drinks and mineral water
Publications:
- Drinks (Bebidas - Publicación para México): *news and trends in the Mexican soft drinks industry - bi-monthly*

National Chamber for the Textile Industry

Cámara Nacional de la Industria Textil
Address: Plinio Nº 220, Chapultepec de los Morales, 11510 México DF
Telephone: +52 5 280 8637/6608/8262
Fax: +52 5 280 3973
Chief officers: César López (Director)
Membership: textile manufacturers

National Chamber of Air Transport

Cámara Nacional de Aerotransportes
Address: Paseo de la Reforma Nº 76, 17º, Colonia Juárez, Del Cuauhtémoc, 06600 México DF
Telephone: +52 5 535 1458/5924472
Fax: +52 5 535 1458
Chief officers: Lic. Alfonso Pasquel Barcenas (President), Lic. Gabriel Ortega Alcocer (General Director)
Membership: air transport companies

National Chamber of Consultancy Businesses (CNEC)

Cámara Nacional de Empresas de Consultoría
Address: Torre World Trade Center, Av de las Naciones Nº 1, piso 18-35, Colonia Nápoles, 03810 México DF
Telephone: +52 5 488 0522/3/4/5/6/7
Fax: +52 5 488 0522/3/4/5/6/7
E-mail: cnec95@mail.internet.com.mx
Web site: www.internet.com.mx/cnec/
Year established: 1985
Chief officers: José Antonio Cortina Suarez (President), Lic Alejandro Sánchez Quiroz (Manager)
Membership: publishers of market and private research
Publications:
- Boletín Informativo CNEC: *information report, details of the chamber's activities - monthly*
- Membership Directory: *annual*

National Chamber of Manufacturers (CANACINTRA)

Cámara Nacional de la Industria de la Transformación
Address: Av San Antonio Nº 256, piso 7, Ampliación Napoles, 03849 México DF
Telephone: +52 5 563 3400/563 3164
Fax: +52 5 611 0912/598 9467/598 6988
Web site: www.intermex.com.mx/canacintra
Year established: 1941
Activities: administrative assistance, technical support, education and training, government liaison
Chief officers: Ing.Carlos Gutierrez Ruiz (President)
Structure: public autonomous institution
Membership: 76,000 manufacturers in all sectors (mainly small and medium-sized companies)
Publications:
- Directorio de Exportadores CANACINTRA: *directory of members involved in exports - annual*
Notes: 71 delegations nation-wide

National Chamber of the Beer and Malt Industry

Cámara Nacional de la Industria de la Cerveza y la Malta
Address: Av Horacio Nº 1556, Chapultepec Morales, 11570 México DF
Telephone: +52 5 280 9850/9911/9124
Fax: +52 5 280 0201
Membership: beer and malt producers

National Chamber of the Cellulose and Paper Industry (CNICP)

Cámara Nacional de las Industrias de la Celulosa y del Papel
Address: Privada de San Isidro Nº 30, Reforma Social, Delegación Miguel Hidalgo, 11650 México DF
Telephone: +52 5 202 8603/540 4296
Fax: +52 5 202 1349
Year established: 1942
Activities: economic studies; information on quality; demand and prices of products on national and international markets; research; statistics on production; consumption; capacity; supply and demand; international trade and investment; conferences; seminars, courses, etc.
Chief officers: Guillermo Fernandez García (President), Jose Manuel Cuevas Valdés (Vice President), Martín Rincón Arredondo (Vice President), Ernesto Lippert Watty (Secretary), José I Garduño Malo (Treasurer)
Membership: 52 active members, 3 affiliated, 3 cooperating
Publications:
- Memoria Estadística: *detailed statistical overview of the Mexican pulp and paper industry; contains detailed production statistics by volume over a six year review period; imports-exports and international comparisons with major countries in both North and Latin America are also included - annual*

National Chamber of the Cinematographic Industry (CANACINE)
Cámara Nacional de la Industria Cinematográfica
Address: General Anaya Nº 198, San Diego Churubusco, 04210 México DF
Telephone: +52 5 688 0442/688 3258/8301
Fax: +52 5 688 8810
Activities: information service
Chief officers: C.P. Alfredo Nava Garduño (President). Sra Ofelia Dominguez Sosa (Subdirector), Hugo Chararría Ramírez (Dept. of Information and Statistics)
Membership: companies in the film and cinema industry
Publications:
• Membership Directory: *annual*

National Chamber of the Clothing Industry
Cámara Nacional de la Industria del Vestido
Address: Manuel Tolsa Nº 54, Colonia Centro, 06040 México DF
Telephone: +52 5 588 7822/3934/0698
Fax: +52 5 578 6210
E-mail: rtn0506@rtn.net.mx
Web site: www.cniv.org.mx
Web site notes: site includes statistics on the industry including production and retail sales
Year established: 1944
Activities: government liaison, information services on taxes, working conditions, foreign trade, etc
Chief officers: David Maauad Abud (President), Miguel Lozada (General Manager), Jorge Levy Bloch (Treasurer)
Membership: all manufacturers, garment assemblers and their accessories

National Chamber of the Construction Industry (CMIC)
Cámara Mexicana de la Industria de la Construcción
Address: Periférico Sur Nº 4839, Parques del Pederegal, 14010 México DF
Telephone: +52 5 665 0424/6440/652 3040
Fax: +52 5 606 8329/652 4372
Web site: www.cnic.org.mx
Activities: consultancy; technical and legal support; government liaison; statistical and cost engineering information related to the construction sector
Chief officers: Ing Fernando Acosta Martinez (President), Ing Mario Padilla Orozco (General Director)
Membership: building and building materials' companies
Publications:
• Construction Industry Report (Informe Trimestral del Sector Formal de la Industria de la Construcción (ITSFIC)): *report with statistical information covering production cost (classified by type of construction, company's size, institutional sector), purchase value and building material consumption, activities index, personnel (wages, payroll) - quarterly*
• Encuesta Nacional del Sector Formal de la Industria de la Construcción CMIC-INEGI (ENSFIC)
• Situación de la Industria de la Construcción: *annual (February)*

National Chamber of the Electrical and Electronic Communications Industries
Cámara Nacional de la Industria Eléctronica y de Comunicaciones Eléctricas
Address: Culiacán Nº 71, Hipódromo Condesa, 06100 México DF
Telephone: +52 5 574 7485/264 0808
Fax: +52 5 264 0808/0466
Chief officers: Eduardo Reyes Phillips (Director General)
Membership: electronics and electrical communications companies

National Chamber of the Fish Industry
Cámara Nacional de la Industria Pesquera
Address: Vito Alessio Robles Nº 240, Colonia Cuauhtémoc, Delegación Alvaro Obregón, 01030 México DF
Telephone: +52 5 661 9160/661 8495
Fax: +52 5 661 3398/8495/8509
Chief officers: Ing. José Antonio Ramirez Thomas (President), Lic. Alejandro Borja Marquez (General Director)

National Chamber of the Food Preservatives Industry
Cámara Nacional de la Industria de Conservas Alimenticias
Address: Calderón de la Barca Nº359-200, Colonia Polanco, 11560 México DF
Telephone: +52 5 250 9679/203 9587/531 5939/250 8929
Fax: +52 5 203 6798
Chief officers: Lic. Armando Cobos Pérez (General Director)
Membership: food processors

National Chamber of the Milk Industry
Cámara Nacional de la Industria de la Leche
Address: Benjamín Franklin Nº 134, Escandón, 11800 Mexico DF
Telephone: +52 5 271 3848/2884/2791/5166040/5514
Fax: +52 5 271 3798
Chief officers: Lic.Luis Miguel Hernandez Zamorano (President), Lic. Jose Garcia Gonzalez (General Director)

National Chamber of the Oils, Fats and Soaps Industry
Cámara Nacional de la Industria de Aceites, Grasas y Jabones
Address: Melchor Ocampo Nº 193-801, Torre A, 8º piso, Verónica Anzures, 11300 México DF
Telephone: +52 5 260 6589/203 1780/1713
Fax: +52 5 260 6925
Chief officers: Sr Lucio Argüello Burunat (President), Ing. Ramón Abad Ayala (Operations Manager)
Membership: manufacturers of oils, fats and soaps

National Chamber of the Perfume and Cosmetics Industries
Cámara Nacional de la Industria de Perfumería y Cosmética
Address: Gabreil Mancera Nº 1134, Colonia Del Valle, 03100 México DF
Telephone: +52 5 575 3108/1883/2111
Fax: +52 5 559 9018
Chief officers: Roberto Cadena (President), Federico Velez (Vice President)
Membership: cosmetics and perfume manufacturers

National Chamber of the Pharmaceutical Industry
Cámara Nacional de la Industria Farmacéutica
Address: Av Cuauhtemoc Nº 1481, Santa Cruz Atoyac, 03310 México DF
Telephone: +52 5 688 9477/9817/9616
Fax: +52 5 604 9808/688 9704
Chief officers: Ing. Eric Hagaster Gartenberg (President), Lic. Jorge Lanzagorta Darder (General Director)
Membership: pharmaceutical manufacturers

National Chamber of the Radio and Television Industry (CIRT)
Cámara Nacional de la Industria de Radio y Televisión
Address: Horacio Nº 1013, Colonia Polanco Reforma, 11550 México DF
Telephone: +52 5 250 2577/2221/726 9909
Fax: +52 5 545 6767/4165
Year established: 1941
Activities: information on advertising tariffs, regulations for television and radio, library (1,600 volumes, 35 periodicals) and photocopying service

Chief officers: Casio Carlos Narváez (President), César Hernández Espejo (Manager)
Membership: radio and television companies
Publications:
• Revista Antena: *bi-monthly*

National Chamber of the Restaurant and Food Seasoning Industries (CANIRAC)
Cámara Nacional de la Industria de Restaurantes y Alimentos Condimentos
Address: Aniceto Ortega N° 1009, Colonia Del Valle, 03100 México DF
Telephone: +52 5 604 0418/0238
Fax: +52 5 604 4086
Chief officers: C.P Jose Manuel Delgado Tellez (President), Lic. Pedor Villaseñor Baez (General Director)
Membership: restaurants all over Mexico - from small restaurants to chains

National Chamber of the Sugar and Alcohol Industries
Cámara Nacional de las Industrias Azucarera y Alcoholera
Address: Rio Niagara N° 11, Cuauhtemoc, 06500 México DF
Telephone: +52 5 533 3040/3004/3042
Fax: +52 5 511 7803/207 6592
Chief officers: C Artolozaga Noriega (President), A Lara Valerio (Director General)
Membership: sugar and alcohol producers

National Chemical Industry Association (ANIQ)
Asociación Nacional de la Industria Química, AC
Address: Av Providencia N° 1118, Colonia Del Valle, Del Benito Juárez, 03100 México DF
Telephone: +52 5 559 7833/7022/3001
Fax: +52 5 559 5589
Telex: 1764109
Web site: www.aiq.org.mx
Chief officers: Ing. Raul Millares Neyra (President), Ing. Jose Montemayor Dragone (General Director)
Membership: chemicals companies

National Chocolate and Confectionery Producers' Association (ANFCDSAC)
Asociación Nacional de Fabricantes de Chocolate, Dulces y Similares, AC
Address: Manuel Maria Contreras N° 133-310, Cuauhtémoc, 06500 México DF
Telephone: +52 5 546 1259/546 0974
Fax: +52 5 592 2497
Membership: sweet and chocolate manufacturers

National Coffee Association
Asociación Nacional del Café, AC
Address: Sierra de Picacho N°14, PB, Lomas de Chapultepec, 11000 México DF
Telephone: +52 5 259 1403/1528/5207994
Fax: +52 5 540 0429
Chief officers: Lic. Juan Martínez del Campo Herrero (Executive President), Lic. Jorge Cisneros Salas (General Gerente)
Membership: coffee processors and roasters

National Council of Packers of Prepared Meat Products
Consejo Nacional de Empacadores de Carnes Frías y Embutidos
Address: Miguel Angel de Quevedo N° 350, Coyoacán, 04310 México DF
Telephone: +52 5 658 1120/658 8347
Fax: +52 5 658 3688

Chief officers: Arq. Ricardo Antonio Metz Andrade (President),
Lic. Héctor Rodríguez Licea (General Director)

National Medicine Producers' Associations
Asociación Nacional de Fabricantes de Medicamentos, AC
Address: Eugenia N° 13-601, Colonia Nápoles, 03810 México DF
Telephone: +52 5 536 1405/6
Fax: +52 5 536 1405/669 3608
Chief officers: Lic. Guillermo Schiefefer (President), Ing. Rafael Gual Cosio (Executive President)
Membership: medicine manufacturers

National Paint and Ink Manufacturers' Association
Asociación Nacional de Fabricantes de Pinturas y Tintas, AC
Address: Gabriel Mancera N° 309, Colonia Del Valle, 03100 México DF
Telephone: +52 5 543 6488/682 7794
Fax: +52 5 682 7975/543 6488
Chief officers: Carlos Benitez de la Garza (President)
Membership: paint and dye manufacturers

National Plastics Industry Association (ANIPAC)
Asociación Nacional de Industrias del Plástico, AC
Address: Av Parque Chapultepec N° 66, Desp. 301, Colonia El Parque, 53390 Ciudad de México
Telephone: +52 5 576 5548/576 5547
Fax: +52 5 576 5548
Chief officers: Lic. Francesco Secchetti Peregrini (President), María del Socorro Sedano (General Director)
Membership: companies from the plastics industry

National Vintners' Association (ANVAC)
Asociación Nacional de Vitivinicultores, AC
Address: Calzada de Tlalpan N° 3515, Santa Ursula Coapa, 04650 México DF
Telephone: +52 5 666 1331/2298/606 9724
Fax: +52 5 606 5153
Chief officers: Ing. Jesús Bueno Pontigo (President), Rafael Almada Navarro (Director General)
Membership: wine producers

Pasta and Biscuit Manufacturers' Association
Asociación Nacional de Fabricantes de Galletas y Pastas Alimenticias, A.C
Address: Mariano Escobedo N° 53-B 8° Piso, Desp. 8-B, Chapultepec Morales, 11570 México DF
Telephone: +52 5 250 5478
Fax: +52 5 250 5478
Chief officers: C.P. Carlos Alavarez Morodo (President), Lic. Xochitl Medina Benavides (Administrative Coordinator)

Tequila Producers' Union
Unión Agrícola Regional de Pruductores de Mezcal Tequilero
Address: López Cotilla N° 2189, 44130 S.J., Guadalajara, Jalisco
Telephone: +52 3 825 7556/616 4451/853 1740/5907/2051
Fax: +52 3 853 1740/6154323
Chief officers: Lic. Justino Delgado Caloca, Lic. Joaquín Romero Soria
Membership: 1,425 producers of Agave, Amatitan, Tequila, Arandas, Tepatitlan, Jesús Mª Atotonilco and Ayotlan

MOLDOVA

Article Numbering Association (EAN Moldova)
Address: 63 Kogalnicheanu Street, 277014 Kishinev
Telephone: +373 2 443 253
Fax: +373 2 440 119
E-mail: mdean@cni.md

MOROCCO

Article Numbering Association (EAN Maroc)
Address: 11 Boleveard Emile Zola, Appt 17, Casablanca
Telephone: +212 2 447 350
Fax: +212 2 447 331

Moroccan Association of the Pharmaceutical Industry (AMIP)
Association Marocaine de l'Industrie Pharmaceutique
Address: Residence Amir, Place Division Leclerc, Boulevard Gerrada, Oasis, Casablanca
Telephone: +212 2 233 686/234 445
Fax: +212 2 234 090

Moroccan Clothing and Textiles Association (AMITH)
Association Marocaine des Industries Textiles et de l'Habillement
Address: 92, Angle Rue Ibn Attir et Moulav Rachid, Casablanca
Telephone: +212 2 942 084/86
Fax: +212 2 940 587
Telex: 45502
Year established: 1958
Chief officers: Lahlou Muhammad (President), Abdelali Berrada (Director General)
Membership: 700 members of the textile sector

National Federation of Travel Agencies of Morocco
Federation Nationale des Agences des Voyages du Maroc
Address: 10, rue de Foucauld, Casablanca
Telephone: +212 2 260 300
Fax: +212 2 277 963
Chief officers: Mr Fouad Lahbabi (President), Mr Idrissi Othman (Director General)

NAMIBIA

Association of Namibian Publishers (ANP)
Address: PO Box 21601, Windhoek
Telephone: +264 61 357 96/293 4388
Fax: +264 61 352 79/239 042
Chief officers: Mr P Reiner (Chairman)

Association of Namibian Travel Agents (ANTA)
Address: PO Box 100 or PO Box 20808, Windhoek
Telephone: +264 61 236 880/237 946
Fax: +264 61 225 430/225 932
Chief officers: Ms F Kreitz (Chairman)

Association of the Meat Trade and Industry of Namibia
Address: PO Box 428, Windhoek
Telephone: +264 61 261 211
Fax: +264 61 216 561
Chief officers: Mr U Eins (Chairman)

Bankers' Association of Namibia
Address: PO Box 31067, Windhoek
Telephone: +264 61291 223
Fax: +264 61 223 188
Activities: training courses, seminars, conferences, information service, advisory service
Chief officers: MR D.P. de Lange (President)
Membership: banks and bankers of Namibia

Book Trade Association of Namibia
Address: PO Box 1327, Windhoek
Telephone: +264 61 225 216
Fax: +264 61 225 011
Chief officers: Mr U Moegenburg (Chairman)

Car Rental Association of Namibia (CARAN)
Address: PO Box 2057, Windhoek
Telephone: +264 61 233 166
Fax: +264 61 223 072
Chief officers: MR u Kessler (Chairman)

Coastal Tourism Association
Address: PO Box 949, Swakopmund
Telephone: +264 6 414 994
Fax: +264 6 414 993

Federation of Namibian Tourism Associations (FENATA)
Address: PO Box 3900, Windhoek
Telephone: +264 61 240 240/3700
Fax: +264 61 249 391
Year established: 1991
Activities: serves as a communication vehicle between the government and members and actively participates in the drafting of the Tourism Plan for Namibia and various White Papers on Tourism; information service; training, seminars, conferences; marketing campaigns abroad
Chief officers: Mr Udo Weck (President)
Membership: umbrella organisation

Hotel Association of Namibia (HAN)
Address: PO Box 2862, Windhoek
Telephone: +264 61 233 145
Fax: +264 61 234 512
Activities: information service for members, training courses, promotes tourism in the region
Chief officers: Mr Tom Mutavdzic (Chairman)

Institute of Marketing Management of Namibia
Address: PO Box 23153, Windhoek
Telephone: +264 61 222 262
Fax: +264 61 222 262
Chief officers: Ms L Schwerdtfeger (Director)

Jewellers' Association of Namibia
Address: PO Box 946, Windhoek
Telephone: +264 61 236 100
Fax: +264 61 235 955
Chief officers: Mr P Adrian (Chairperson)

Journalists' Association of Namibia
Address: PO Bpox 21109, Windhoek
Telephone: +264 61 221 711
Fax: +264 61 230 578
Chief officers: Mr P Ndauendapo (Chairperson)

Karakul Producers' Association
Address: PO Box 13255, Windhoek
Telephone: +264 61 237 838
Fax: +264 61 220 193
Chief officers: MR JN Junius (Chairperson)

Meat Board of Namibia
Address: PO Box 38, Windhoek
Telephone: +264 61 233 280
Fax: +264 61 228 310
Year established: 1935
Activities: advises the authorities in all matters concerning the meat trade and the export of livestock; compiles statistics on meat imports and exports; develops marketing channels and offers price and statistical services to members
Chief officers: Mr H.L. Immelman (General Manager)
Membership: livestock marketing agents, livestock producers, meat manufacturers and traders

Motor Industries' Federation of Namibia
Address: PO Box 1503, Windhoek
Telephone: +264 61 237 970
Fax: +264 61 233 690
Chief officers: MR R Moens (President)

Namibia Federation of Business and Professional Women
Address: PO Box 2103, Windhoek
Telephone: +264 61 222 262
Fax: +264 61 222 262
Chief officers: Ms L Schwerdtfeger (President)

Namibia Insurance Association
Address: PO Box 2199, Windhoek
Telephone: +264 61 237 730
Fax: +264 61 235 716
Chief officers: Mr J Steele (Chairman)

Namibia Insurance Brokers' Association
Address: PO Box 20002, Windhoek
Telephone: +264 61 235 010
Fax: +264 61 225 971
Chief officers: Mr A Schiebler (President)

Namibia Taverns' Association
Address: PO Box 10917, Windhoek
Telephone: +264 61 211 747
Fax: +264 61 211 781

Namibian Chamber of Printing
Address: PO Box 363, Windhoek
Telephone: +264 61 237 905
Fax: +264 61 222 927
Chief officers: Mr S Timm (Chairperson)

Namibian Food and Catering Association
Address: PO Box 87, Swakopmund
Telephone: +264 6 412 864
Fax: +264 6 414 442
Chief officers: Mr S Klein (Chairperson)

National Book Development Council (NBDC)
Address: PO Box 21601, c/o Association of Namibian Publishers, Windhoek
Telephone: +264 61 235 796/221 134
Fax: +264 61 235 279
E-mail: nnb@granny.mac.com.na

Pharmaceutical Society of Namibia
Address: PO Box 1147, Windhoek
Telephone: +264 61 220 509
Fax: +264 61 231 701
Chief officers: Ms M Fourie (Chairperson)

Tour and Safari Association (TASA)
Address: PO Box 6850 or PO Box 11534, Windhoek
Telephone: +264 61 225 178/238 423/238 423
Fax: +264 61 233 332
Chief officers: Mr D Glaue (Chairperson)

Tourist Related Namibian Businesses Association (TRENABA)
Address: PO Box 24204 or PO Box 3837, Windhoek
Telephone: +264 61 235 053/224 578
Fax: +264 61 225 276/220 341
Chief officers: Ms B Herma-Herrle (Chairperson)

NETHERLANDS

Alliance of Potato, Vegetable and Fruit Retailers
Bond van Detailhandelaren in Aardappelen, Groenten en Fruit
Address: Prins Mauritsplein 1A, NL-2582 NA The Hague
Telephone: +31 70 351 2106
Fax: +31 70 351 2199
Year established: 1989
Chief officers: Ms K Weisfelt (Chairman), Mr M Korevaar (General Secretary)
Membership: 1,450 fruit and vegetable retailers
Notes: The Association does not produce any statistics or publications.

Alliance of Retailers in the Perfume Industry (BODEPA)
Bond van Detaillisten in Parfumeriehandel
Address: Postbus 765, Fontijenenburglaan 8, NL- 2270 AT Voorburg
Telephone: +31 70 398 9833
Fax: +31 70 390 8194
Year established: 1977
Activities: publication, collecting data about the perfume sector and market
Chief officers: C W Bosman, P F T Harmes
Membership: 150 retailers of perfumery goods
Publications:
● Handbook Voor Parfumerie en Schoonheidssalon: *annual*
● Kosmetiek: *monthly*

NETHERLANDS ANTILLES

Association of Importers of Pharmaceutical Products (VIPP)
Address: c/o Zuid West N.V./Hubert Salas, Kaya Buena Vista, Curaçao
Telephone: +599 9 696 533
Fax: +599 9 696 188
Chief officers: Mr. G.A. van Loon (Deputy President)
Membership: pharmaceutical manufacturers and importers

Association of Representatives of Importers and Exporters of Foods and Allied Products (VIGLEG)

Address: c/o Hector Henriquez B. In, Caracasbaaiweg 38, Curaçao
Telephone: +599 9 613 266
Fax: +599 9 616 972
Chief officers: Mr. G. Brandao (Treasurer)
Membership: food and drinks importers and exporters

Association of Small Entrepreneurs Curaçao

Address: c/o General Catering Services, Fransche Bloemweg/Hoek Sta. Rosaweg, Curaçao
Telephone: +599 9 369 365
Fax: +599 9 377 618
Chief officers: Mr G. Magdalena (President)

Curaçao Bankers' Association (CBA)

Address: P.O. Box 3785, c/o Banco di Caribe N.V., Schottegatweg Oost 20, Curaçao
Telephone: +599 9 617 000/616 499
Fax: +599 9 615 220
Membership: banks and bankers

Curaçao Exporters' Association

Address: ITC-Building, Lobby Unit 2, Curaçao
Telephone: +599 9 636 151
Fax: +599 9 636 451
Chief officers: Mr. O. Ergun (Chairman)
Membership: exporters

Curaçao Hotel and Tourism Association (CHATA)

Address: P.O. Box 6115, I.T.C. Building, Curaçao
Telephone: +599 9 636 260
Fax: +599 9 636 445
Chief officers: Mr F.N. Roelofsen (President)
Membership: hotel, catering, travel and tourism enterprises

Curaçao Trade and Industry Association (VBC)

Address: P.O. Box 49, Kaya Junior Salas 1, Curaçao
Telephone: +599 9 611 210/611 366
Fax: +599 9 615 652
Chief officers: Mr R.P.J. Lieuw (Executive Director)

Free-Zone Merchants' Association (FREZACUR)

Address: P.O. Box 618, c/o Palais Hindu, Curaçao
Telephone: +599 9 612 213
Fax: +599 9 616 315
Chief officers: Mr R. Daryanani (President)

Netherlands Antilles Automobile Dealers' Association (NAADA)

Address: c/o Saliña Trading Corporation, Grebbelinieweg z/n, Curaçao
Telephone: +599 9 614 122
Fax: +599 9 613 787
Chief officers: Mr. A. Moron (President)

St Marteen Hotel Association

Address: PO Box 486, Philipsburg, St Marteen
Telephone: +599 5 231 33
Fax: +599 5 254 03

St Marteen Tourist Board

Address: WJA Nisbeth Road, Philipsburg, St Marteen
Telephone: +599 5 227 34

NETHERLANDS

Association of Agents, Brokers and Valuers of Wine and Foreign Spirits

Vereniging van Agenten Commissionairs, Makelaars en Taxateurs in Wijn en Buitenlands Gedistilleerd
Address: Van Eeghenlaan 27, NL-1071 EN Amsterdam
Telephone: +31 20 673 0331
Fax: +31 20 664 5466
Activities: provides information on legal questions and keeps track of the number of businesses involved in the sector
Chief officers: F W Hanega
Membership: 23 agents and importers of foreign alcoholic drinks
Notes: The Association is an independent non-profit organisation associated with the Federation of Wine and Spirits Importers and Wholesalers, it does not produce any statistics or publications.

Association of Alcoholic and Non-Alcoholic Drinks Superstores

Vereniging van Grootwinkelbedrijven in Alcoholhoudende en Alcoholvrije Dranken
Address: POB 715, Engelandlaan 374, NL 2700 AS Zoetemeer
Telephone: +31 79 342 1501
Fax: +31 79 342 4648
Chief officers: M F A Zwartepoorte (Chairman), C A C M Emmen (Secretary)
Membership: retailers and wholesalers of alcoholic and non-alcoholic drinks

Association of Bread and Pastry Products Retailers

Brood en Banketbakkerij Ondernemers Vereniging
Address: Laan van Nieuw Oost-Indië 277, NL-2593 BS The Hague
Telephone: +31 70 347 7441
Fax: +31 70 383 8741
Chief officers: J van de Vall (President); L Volkeri (Secretary)
Membership: 1,700 retail bakers

Association of Butter and Butter-oil Wholesalers

Vereniging van Groothandelaren in Boter (VGB)
Address: Patrijsweg 58, 2289 EX Rijswijk
Telephone: +31 70 336 9450
Fax: +31 70 336 9454
Year established: 1951
Activities: provides information service
Membership: 20 butter wholesalers
Notes: No publications produced.

Association of Dutch Drinks Manufacturers' and Wholesalers (BBM)

Algemene Nederlandse Bond van Frisdrankenfabrikanten en Groothandelaren in Dranken
Address: Heemraadssingel 167, NL-3022 Rotterdam
Telephone: +31 10 477 4033
Fax: +31 10 425 9025
Publications:
• BBM Jaarverslag: *a review of the drinks sector covering mainly soft drinks and beer. A statistical section covers production, imports, exports, consumption of specific drinks for a series of years with comparative data for other EU areas - annual*

Association of Food Wholesalers (VGL)

Vereniging van Grootwinkelbedrijven in Levensmiddelen
Address: Postbus 715, Engelandlaan 374, NL-2700 AS Zoetemeer

Telephone: +31 79 342 1501
Fax: +31 79 342 4648
Activities: conferences and information service
Chief officers: J W Adrian (Director), K Dorsman (Chairman)
Membership: 15 food wholesalers

Association of Frozen Meat Importers

Vereniging van Importeurs van Bevroren Vlees
Address: Postbus 18506, 1e Sweelinckstraat 72, NL-2502 EM
The Hague
Telephone: +31 70 346 9667
Fax: +31 70 364 5107
Chief officers: J Hulsker, J A J M Heyning
Membership: 36 frozen meat importers

Association of Suppliers of Household Appliances in the Netherlands (VLEHAN)

Vereniging van Leveranciers van Huishoudelijke Apparaten in
Nederland
Address: P.O. Box 190, 2700 AD Zoetermeer
Telephone: +31 79 353 1371
Fax: +31 79 353 1365

Association of Textile and Clothing Retailers and Wholesalers (FENECON)

Vereniging van Grootwinkelbedrijven in Textiel
Address: Postbus 69265, Kon. Wilhelminaplein 13, NL-1060
CH Asterdam
Telephone: +31 20 512 1416
Fax: +31 20 617 0634
E-mail: fenecon@fenecon.nl
Activities: provides economic, legal and technical services
for the clothing and knitwear industry
Chief officers: JA Bekke Han (Secretary)
Membership: 320 manufacturers, wholesalers and large
retailers of textiles, knitwear and clothing
Publications:
● Annual Report: *annual*
● Members Directory: *biannual*

Association of Textile Retailers

Vereniging Mitex
Address: Vondelstraat 172, NL-1054 GV Amsterdam
Telephone: +31 20 683 2201
Fax: +31 20 616 2921
E-mail: meindert@mitex.nl
Activities: advice on economical and legal affairs;
negotiations with other organisations to achieve collective
contracts; information on legislation, wages and the clothing
market
Chief officers: Mrs A H van Arenthals-Kramer Freher
(President); Mr J J Meerman (Director)
Membership: approx. 3,400 members
Publications:
● Jaarboek: *information about members - annual*
● Schoenvisie: *monthly*
● Sportpartner: *monthly*
● Textielvisie: *monthly*

Association of the Dutch Chemical Industry (VNCI)

Vereniging van de Nederlandse Chemische Industrie
Address: Postbus 443, Vlietweg 16, NL-2260 AK
Leidschendam
Telephone: +31 70 337 8787
Fax: +31 70 320 3903
E-mail: roopramk@vnci.nl
Web site: www.vnci.nl
Activities: trade association for all chemicals manufacturers,
with sub-groups; organises conferences, provides information
and compiles statistics

Chief officers: P F Noordervliet (Director), W F Bohne
(Director of information and communication)
Membership: approx. 100 manufacturers, wholesalers and
importers in the chemical industry
Publications:
● Annual Report: *annual*
● Nederlandse Chemische Industrie: *fortnightly*

Association of the Dutch Pasta Industry

Vereniging Nederlandse Deegwarenindustrie
Address: Postbus 177, Schipholweg 7D, NL-2300 AD Leiden
Telephone: +31 71 522 4220
Fax: +31 71 522 5095
Chief officers: I Menkveld, K Herijgers
Membership: pasta manufacturers

Association of the Dutch Pharmaceutical Industry (NEFARMA)

Nederlandse Vereniging van de Innoverende Farmaceutische
Industrie
Address: P O Box 9193, Einsteindreef 123-125, 3506 GD
Utrecht
Telephone: +31 30 263 1800
Fax: +31 30 263 1830
E-mail: p.bossert@nefarma.nl
Web site: www.nefarma.nl
Activities: provides information on the pharmaceutical
industry in the Netherlands; collects statistics on annual
turnover, production and investments for annual report
Chief officers: Mr Ed Worm (Chairman)
Membership: 60 members
Publications:
● Annaul Report: *annual*
● We Invest in Tomorrow's Medicines: *information on the
pharmaceutical industry*

Association of the Publishers and Distributors of Audio, Video and Multimedia Software (NVPI)

Nederlandse Vereniging van Producenten en Importeurs van
Beeld - en Geluidsdragers
Address: Albertus Perkstraat 36, NL-1217 NT Hilversum
Telephone: +31 35 624 0951
Fax: +31 35 624 1954
E-mail: bas.de.wolf@nvpi.nl
Year established: 1972
Activities: collects statistics for the audio, video and
multimedia industry based on trade deliveries and market
research; represents the audio-visual sector
Chief officers: Paul Solleveld (Managing Director); Yvonne
Looye (Legal and General Affairs Director)
Membership: 76 members including 52 audio members, 10
video members and 14 multimedia members
Notes: NVPI is the co-founder of the Edison Foundation.
Produces several annual publications covering market, legal
and promotional affairs which are in Dutch and available free
of charge to non-members.

Association of Wholesalers in Milk Products (VGM)

Vereniging van Groothandelaren in Melkproducten
Address: Patrijsweg 58, 2289 EX Rijswijk
Telephone: +31 70 336 9450
Fax: +31 70 336 9454
Activities: provides information service
Membership: 29 wholesalers of milk powder and other milk
products
Notes: No publications produced.

Bakery and Confectionery Industries' Association

Vereniging vaoor de Bakkerij- en Zoetwarenindustrie
Address: Bankastraat 131-B, NL-2585 EL The Hague
Telephone: +31 70 355 4700
Fax: +31 70 358 4679
Chief officers: J W Hilbron (Chairman), Mrs JMC van der Bruggen (Secretary)
Membership: 90 manufacturers of cakes, rusks, biscuits, gingerbread and related products

Breweries Central Office (CBK)

Centraal Brouwerij Kantoor
Address: Postbus 3462, Herengracht 282, NL-1016BX Amsterdam
Telephone: +31 20 625 2251
Fax: +31 20 622 6074
Activities: statistics collected and produced in annual publication
Membership: 11 brewers
Publications:
• Facts and Figures: *statistical information covering the brewing industry - annual*

Central Alliance of Furniture Manufacturers (CBM)

Centrale Bond van Meubelfabrikanten
Address: Westerhoutpark 10, NL-2012 Haarlem
Telephone: +31 23 515 8800
Fax: +31 23 531 5538
Year established: 1912
Chief officers: J A A M Nuyens (Chairman); G N Nieuwenhuizen (Director)
Membership: 485 furniture manufacturers

Central Association of Dutch Wine Traders (CVNW)

Centrale Vereniging van Nederlandse Wijnhandelaren
Address: van Eeghenlaan 27, NL-1071 EN Amsterdam
Telephone: +31 20 673 0331
Fax: +31 20 664 5466
Year established: 1899
Activities: provides information to exporters of wine producing countries, and assistance for promotional activities of wine producers; statistical service available to members only
Chief officers: R J B Wallast Groenewoud (General Secretary)
Membership: 107 importers, wholesalers and retailers of wine
Publications:
• Bulletin: *monthly*

Central Office for Business and Trade in Food (CBL)

Centraal Bureau Levensmiddelenhandel
Address: Postbus 262, Overgoo 2, NL-2266 AG Leidschendam
Telephone: +31 70 337 6200
Fax: +31 70 317 6887
E-mail: cbl@worldonline.nl
Year established: 1960
Activities: umbrella organisation for the general grocery trade, retail and wholesale; consults with government, parliament, business associations, public corporations, consumer organisations, the press, etc.
Chief officers: J van den Broek (Chairman), M J Roos (Director)
Membership: 36 members including Co-op Marketing, Federatie van de Groothandel in Levensmiddelen (Food Wholesalers Federation) etc; see notes below
Notes: combines Het Vakcentrum (Professional Organisation of Grocery Retailers) and Vereniging van Grootbedrijven in Levensmiddelen (General Food Wholesalers Association)

Central Organisation of Meat Wholesalers (COV)

Centrale Organisatie voor de Vleesgroothandel
Address: Postbus 18506, Sweelinckstraat 72, NL-2517 GG's-Gravenhage
Telephone: +31 70 346 9667/363 2445
Fax: +31 70 364 5107
Chief officers: J J Ramekers and J A J M van de Heijning
Membership: meat wholesalers

Dairy Secretariat (GemZu)

Stichting Gemeenschappelijk Zuivelsekretariaat
Address: Patrijsweg 58, 2289 EX Rijswijk
Telephone: +31 70 336 9450
Fax: +31 70 336 9454
Activities: compilation of production data by product and prices (published regularly in the association's journal)
Membership: 8 dairy associations of wholesalers of butter, milk powder and cheese, cheese exporters, and manufacturers and wholesalers of butteroil and ghee
Publications:
• Zuivelnieuws (Dairy News): *800 examples per week - weekly*

Dutch Alliance of Tropical Fruits and other Imported Fruits Wholesalers and Dealers (FRUBO)

Nederlandse Bond van Grossiers in Zuidvruchten en ander Geïmporteerd Fruit
Address: Postbus 90410, 2509 LK Den Haag, Bezuidenhoutseweg 82, NL-2594 AX The Hague
Telephone: +31 70 385 0100
Fax: +31 70 347 5253
Year established: 1955
Chief officers: R Oringa (Chairman), I Wellsche (Secretary)
Membership: 1,500 wholesalers of exotic and other imported fruit

Dutch Article Numbering Association

Address: Postbox 90445, Tourniairestraat 3, NL-1065KK Amsterdam
Telephone: +31 20 511 3820
Fax: +31 20 511 3830
E-mail: info@eannl.com

Dutch Association of Bakeries (NVB)

Nederlandse Vereniging voor de Bakkerij
Address: Bankastraat 131-B, NL-2585 EL The Hague
Telephone: +31 70 354 9847
Fax: +31 70 354 8311
Chief officers: A Schipper, A Mandemaker
Membership: ca. 80 industrial bakeries

Dutch Association of Banks (NVB)

Nederlandse Vereniging van Banken
Address: Postbus 19870, Keizersgracht 706, NL-1000 GW Amsterdam
Telephone: +31 20 550 2888
Fax: +31 20 623 9748
Chief officers: P J Kalff (Chairman), L M Overmars (Director)
Membership: banks, insurance companies and credit companies.

Dutch Association of Cheese Exporters (VKE)

Nederlandse Vereniging van Kaasexporteurs
Address: Patrijsweg 58, 2289 EX Rijswijk
Telephone: +31 70 336 9450
Fax: +31 70 336 9454
Activities: provides information
Membership: 45 cheese exporters
Notes: No publications produced.

Dutch Association of Soap Manufacturers (NVZ)

Nederlandse Vereniging van Zeepfabrikanten
Address: PO Box 914, Waterigeweg 31, NL-3700 AX Zeist
Telephone: +31 30 692 1880
Fax: +31 30 691 9394
Activities: organises conferences, research and an information service; compiles industry statistics
Chief officers: Mr J H Burema (Director)
Membership: 30 manufacturing companies

Dutch Association of the Cosmetics Industry

Nederlandse Cosmetica Vereniging
Address: Brinkwal 15-A, NL-3432 GA Nieuwegein
Telephone: +31 30 604 9480
Fax: +31 30 604 9999
E-mail: nlcosver@pi.net
Year established: 1950
Activities: collects statistics on turnover at ex-factory prices
Chief officers: F de Koeijer (Secretary General); W A Pfeifer (Managing Director)
Structure: non-profit branch organisation
Membership: 75 members representing 90% of the industry's output in the Netherlands
Publications:
• Annual Report: *annual*

Dutch Association of Wholesalers in Cheese

Landelijke Vereniging van Kaashandelaren
Address: Patrijsweg 58, 2289 EX Rijswijk
Telephone: +31 70 336 9450
Fax: +31 70 336 9454
Activities: provides information
Membership: 138 cheese wholesalers

Dutch Association of Wholesalers of Beverages, Food and Non-Food (GDH)

Address: PO Box 26155, NL-3022 ED Rotterdam
Telephone: +31 10 477 4033
Fax: +31 10 425 9025
E-mail: bbmbbmnl@worldaccess.nl
Year established: 1950
Membership: 190 members
Publications:
• Yearbook of the Dutch Association of Wholesalers of Beverages, Food and Non-Food: *annual*
Notes: The Association does not produce statistics.

Dutch Bacon Producers Association

Vereniging van Nederlandse Bacon Fabrikanten
Address: Postbus 87936, Wagenaarweg 14, NL-2508 DH The Hague
Telephone: +31 70 352 4441
Fax: +31 70 350 3723
Activities: compiles sector statistics but not for publication; provides information service
Chief officers: H J Heier (Director)
Membership: 12 bacon manufacturing companies (making up 90% of the total bacon production in the Netherlands)
Notes: No publications produced.

Dutch Bakery Foundation (NBC)

Nederlandse Bakkerij Centrum
Address: PO Box 360, Agro Business Park 75-83, 6700 AJ Wageningen
Telephone: +31 317 424 344
Fax: +31 317 423 206
E-mail: nbc@globalxs.nl
Year established: 1881
Activities: education; promotion; economic and corporate consultancy
Chief officers: J H Diekema (Managing Director)
Structure: foundation
Membership: 1,000 small and medium-sized bakeries, both employers and employees
Notes: Collects statistics and produces publications but for members only.

Dutch Bakery Products' Association

Nederlandse Vereniging voor de Bakkers
Address: Bankastraal 131 B, NL-2585 EL Den Haal
Telephone: +31 70 354 9847
Fax: +31 70 358 4679
Year established: 1969
Membership: 66 member companies
Notes: The Association does not produce any publications or statistics.

Dutch Frozen Foods Association

Federatie Van de Nederlandse Diepvriesindustrie
Address: PO Box 177, NL-2300 Ad Leiden
Telephone: +31 71 522 4220
Fax: +31 71 522 5095
Chief officers: Mr Fred H.J. Van de Wetering
Notes: member of the Federation of the Associations of EU Frozen Food Producers (FAFPAS) based in Brussels (Belgium)

Dutch Fruit Growers' Organisation (NFO)

Nederlandse Fruittelers Organisatie
Address: POB 90607, Schiefbaanstraat 29, 2596 RC Den Haag, NL-2509 LP Den Haag
Telephone: +31 70 345 0600
Fax: +31 70 345 3902
Publications:
• Fruitteelt: *the Dutch fruit and vegetable growing industry - weekly*

Dutch General Alliance of Beauty Parlours (ANBOS)

Algemene Nederlandse Bond van Schoonheidsinstituten
Address: Postbus 1274, Bisonspoor 342-A, NL-3600 BG Maarssen
Telephone: +31 3465 68137
Fax: +31 3465 63184
Year established: 1983
Activities: collects information for its members
Chief officers: UAF Koch (Director)
Membership: over 200 beauty parlours
Publications:
• De Schoonheidsspecialist

Dutch Jewellery, Watch and Clock Makers Branch

Nederlandse Juweliers- en Uurwerkenbranche
Address: Postbus 904, Koningin Julianalaan 345, NL-2270 AX Voorburg
Telephone: +31 70 386 7777
Fax: +31 70 387 1047
Year established: 1989
Activities: helps jewellers with legal problems
Chief officers: Mr Rvuyk (Secretary)
Membership: 1,000 jewellery retailers

Dutch National Committee of the International Dairy Federation

Nederlands Nationaal Comité van de Internationale Zuivelbond
Address: Bleiswijkseweg, 35, 2712 PB Zoetermeer
Telephone: +31 79 343 03 21
Fax: +31 79 342 61 85
Chief officers: Mrs M.L. Bögemann (Secretary)

Dutch Newspapers' Association

Vereniging van Nederlandse Dagbladers
Address: Postbus 12040, Atlas Gebow Azië, Hoogoorddreef
5, 1100 AA Amsterdam-Zuidoost
Telephone: +31 20 430 9171
Fax: +31 20 430 9199
Chief officers: Mr Jan Willem Gast (General Secretary)

Dutch Pharmaceutical Wholesalers' Association (BG Pharma)

Bond van Groothandelaren in Het Pharmaceutische Bedriff
Address: Kuiperbergweg 50, 1101 AG Amsterdam Z-O
Telephone: +31 20 696 0876
Fax: +31 20 696 0986
Activities: public relations, project management, consultancy;
collects statistics on wholesale sales
Chief officers: Mr K M Hof (President and General Secretary);
Mrs M S Fluit (Executive Secretary)
Membership: 4 companies
Publications:
• Annual Report: *annual*
• Bulletin: *quarterly*

Dutch Publishers' Association

Address: Atlas Kantorenpark, Gebow Azië, Hoogoorddreef 5,
1100 AA Amsterdam-Zuidoost
Telephone: +31 20 430 91 50
Fax: +31 20 430 91 79
Chief officers: Mr H Spruijt (President), Mr RM Vrij (Director)

Dutch Retail Association (HBD)

Hoofdbedrijfschap Detail-Handel
Address: PO Box 90703, Nieuwe Parklaan 72-74, NL-2509 LS
The Hague
Telephone: +31 70 352 9800
Fax: +31 70 354 5435
E-mail: hbd@hbd.nl
Web site: www.hbd.nl
Activities: conducts research on the environment; labour
market; shop criminality; collective campaign for retail
business; collect statistcs including number of shops and
retailers, figures on the labour market and index numbers
Chief officers: E E van de Lustrgraaf (Director)
Membership: no actual members but all retailers (approx.
150,000) are obliged to pay a fee to HBD
Publications:
• Detailhandel Magazine

Dutch Soft Drinks' Association (NFI)

Address: PO Box 26155, NL-3002 ED Rotterdam
Telephone: +31 10 477 4033
Fax: +31 10 425 9025
E-mail: bbmbbmnl@worldaccess.nl
Year established: 1993
Activities: services in the following areas: packaging and the
environment; nutrition and commodities; legislation; statistics
covering production, consumption, imports and exports;
logistics; information on soft drinks and mineral waters;
distributing newsletters to members; conducting various
studies and investigations
Chief officers: H.G.L Comhhoff (Chairman)
Membership: 24 members
Publications:
• Statistical Leaflet of the Dutch Soft Drinks Industry: *annual*
• Yearbook of the Dutch Soft Drinks Industry: *annual*

Federation of Dutch Butchers' Alliances

Federatie van Nederlandse Slagersbonden
Address: Diepenhorstlaan 3, NL-2288 EW Rijswijk
Telephone: +31 70 390 6365
Fax: +31 70 390 4459
Year established: 1951
Activities: coordination of association's activities, meetings,
internal news-letter and a library
Chief officers: J Van Dalen (President)
Membership: 5 retail and wholesale butchers' associations
Publications:
• De Slager: *developments in the meat market and trade;
includes technical aspects and list of meat sales prices -
weekly*
Notes: Affiliated to the international butchers' association
COBCEE.

Federation of Organisations in the Wholesale Trade in Fish and Fish Processing

Federatie van Organisaties op het gebied van de Groothandel in
en Be- en Verwerking van Vis
Address: Postbus 72, Treubstraat 17, NL-2280 AB Rijswijk
Telephone: +31 70 336 9600
Fax: +31 70 399 9426
E-mail: p-vis@pvis.nl
Chief officers: L Zijp (Secretary General)
Membership: 7 organisations with 156 members
Notes: The Association does not produce any statistics or
publications.

Federation of Tourism-Related Firms in the Netherlands (TOERNED)

Federatie van Toeristische Bedrijven in Nederland
Address: Maaspromenade 27, NL-6211 HS Maastricht
Telephone: +31 43 325 4151
Fax: +31 43 321 7958
Chief officers: C van Stiphout (Chairman), A Diepenhorst
(Secretary)

Federation of Wine and Spirits Importers

Federatie Wijn/Importgedistilleerd
Address: Van Eeghenlaan 27, NL-1071 EN Amsterdam
Telephone: +31 20 673 0331
Fax: +31 20 664 5466
Year established: 1950
Chief officers: R J B Wallast Groenewoud
Membership: 113 wine and spirits importers
Publications:
• Bulletin: *monthly*

General Alliance of Dutch Fruit and Vegetable Exporters

Algemene Nederlandse Bond van Groenten en Fruit Exporteurs
Address: Postbus 90410, Bezuidenhoutseweg 82, NL-2509
LK The Hague
Telephone: +31 70 385 0100
Fax: +31 70 347 5253
Year established: 1968
Activities: compiles detailed statistics on the fruit and
vegetable market which are published annually; publishes a
trade magazine.
Chief officers: J van Es (Director)
Membership: ca. 470 fruit and vegetable wholesalers

General Association of Dutch Egg Traders (ANEVEI)

Algemene Nederlandse Vereniging van Eierhandelaren
Address: Postbus 503, 3700 AM Zeist, Zeisteroever 17,
NL-3704 GB Zeist
Telephone: +31 30 696 7205
Fax: +31 30 696 7250

Year established: 1951
Activities: library services and monthly publication
Chief officers: Mr J Van Noord (Chairman); Mr I A Mijs (Secretary General)
Structure: employers' organisation
Membership: 60 egg wholesalers and manufacturers
Publications:
• Anevei-News: *monthly*
Notes: The Association does not produce statistics.

International Association of Scientific, Technical and Medical Publishers

Address: Muurhuizen 165, 3811 EG Amersfoort
Telephone: +31 33 465 6060
Fax: +31 33 465 6538
Web site: www.stm.springer.de/
Chief officers: Mr D Goetze, Mr L Lefebvre (Director)

Netherlands Association of the Ice Cream Industry (NVC)

Nederlandse Vereniging van Consumptie-Ijsfabrikanten
Address: Postbus 165, Bleiswijkseweg 35, NL-2700 AD Zoetemeer
Telephone: +31 79 343 0321
Fax: +31 79 342 6185
Activities: provides information service; collects statistics but not for publication
Chief officers: M L J Bogemann (Secretary)
Membership: 9 ice cream manufacturing companies
Notes: No publications produced.

Netherlands Cocoa Association

Nederlandse Cacao en Cacaoproducten Vereniging
Address: Havengebouw, De Ruyterkade 7, 1013 AA Amsterdam
Telephone: +31 20 422 2727
Fax: +31 20 422 2726
Year established: 1935
Activities: compilation of sector statistics; library and information services
Chief officers: Dr T L Van der Waerden
Membership: 40 companies (industry, trade, warehouses)
Publications:
• Annual Report: *market surveys, international issues, prices, export information and members list - annual*

Netherlands Franchise Association

Address: Boomberglaan 12, NL-1217RR Hilversum
Telephone: +31 35 624 3444
Fax: +31 35 624 9194
Chief officers: Mr AWM Brouwer (Director)

Netherlands Oils Fats and Oilseeds Trade Association (NOFOTA)

Address: Postbus 190, Weena 666, 3012 CN (3000 AD) Rotterdam
Telephone: +31 10 404 2111
Fax: +31 10 404 2333
Chief officers: P W van Baal (Secretary/Treasurer)
Membership: 149 wholesalers of edible oils and fats and related products
Publications:
• Annual Report: *annual*
Notes: The Association does not produce statistics.

Netherlands Wholesale and International Trade Federation

Address: Postbus 29822, Adriaan Goekooplaan 5, NL-2502 LV The Hague
Telephone: +31 70 354 6811
Fax: +31 70 351 2777
Year established: 1911
Membership: 80 members (branch associations)
Notes: The Association does not produce any statistics or publications.

Textile Federation KRL

Textielvereniging KRL
Address: Postbus 518, De Schutterij 16, NL-3900 AM Veenendaal
Telephone: +31 318 564 488
Fax: +31 318 564 487
E-mail: krl@pi.net
Year established: 1906
Activities: organises study days and meetings about new developments and problems in the textile industry; brings together people involved in the textile industry: consumers, suppliers and manufacturers; collects statistics on turnover, employment, exports and investment
Chief officers: Mr Cees Lodiers (Secretary General); Mr Jef Wintermans (Secretary)
Structure: independent non-profit organisation affiliated to the international IFATCC
Membership: 70 textile manufacturers
Publications:
• Annual Report: *public annual report with economic data - annual*
• Infodex: *actual policy developments and activities - fortnightly*

NEW ZEALAND

Apparel and Textile Federation of New Zealand Inc.

Address: PO Box 11 543, Enterprise House, 3-9 Church Street, Wellington
Telephone: +64 4 473 3004
Fax: +64 4 473 3000
Activities: compiles statistics on clothing production by volume and value (broken down by clothing type)
Chief officers: Marcia Dunnett (Chief Executive)

Aviation Industry Association of New Zealand Inc.

Address: PO Box 2096, 2nd Floor Agriculture House, 12 Johnston Street, Wellington
Telephone: +64 4 472 2707
Fax: +64 4 471 1314
E-mail: aviation.industy@clear.net.nz
Activities: annual conference, government liaison
Chief officers: Capt J Jones (President), T A Riddell (Executive Director), V A Sleath (Secretary)
Membership: 300 commercial airlines
Publications:
• AIA Arrow: *monthly*

Book Publishers' Association of New Zealand

Address: PO Box 36-477, Northcote, Auckland 1039
Telephone: +64 9 480 2711
Fax: +64 9 480 1130
E-mail: cllbpanz@ns.planet.gen.nz
Activities: professional training; produces a statistical survey on school book spendings
Chief officers: Ms Wendy Harrex (Secretary), Ms K Sheat

(Executive Director)
Membership: 90 publishers
Publications:
• Publisher: *printing and publishing matters and issues of interest for members - 11 p.a.*

Electronic Appliance Guild Incorporated
Address: PO Box 3481, Unit 2, 59 Carbine Road, Mt Wellington, Auckland 1
Telephone: +64 9 573 1332
Fax: +64 9 573 1336
Chief officers: Dennis A. Amiss (Executive Director)

Federated Farmers of New Zealand Inc.
Address: PO Box 715, 6th Floor, Agriculture House, 12 Johnston Street, Wellington 1
Telephone: +64 4 473 7269
Fax: +64 4 473 1081
Telex: 312525
E-mail: nationaloffice@no.fedfarm.org.nz
Year established: 1945
Chief officers: Malcom Bailes (President), Alistair Polsen (Vice President), Tom Lambie (Vice President), Tony St.Clair (Chief Executive), Jeremy Harding (Policy Executive, International)
Structure: federation of 24 provincial organisations representing meat,wool,dairy,arable
Membership: 18,000 farming families
Publications:
• Annual Report: *annual*
• Report to Members: *federations activities - four p.a.*
• Straight Furrow: *bi-weekly*
Notes: The Association does not produce statistics.

Hospitality Association of New Zealand
Address: 8th Floor, West Block, Education House, !78-182 Willis Street, Wellington 6015
Telephone: +64 4 385 1369
Fax: +64 4 384 8044
Chief officers: Bruce H Robertson (Chief Executive)
Notes: The Association does not produce any statistics.

Information Technology Association of New Zealand
Address: PO Box 1710, Wellington
Telephone: +64 4 472 2731
Fax: +64 4 499 3318
E-mail: ttait@nzonline.ac.nz

Insurance Institute of New Zealand Inc.
Address: PO Box 1368, GRE House, 111-115 Customhouse Quay, Wellington 6001
Telephone: +64 4 499 4630
Fax: +64 4 499 4536
E-mail: ceo@iinz.org.nz
Web site: www.iinz.org.nz
Year established: 1937
Activities: tertiary education for general insurance subjects and continuing education; collects statistics on examination
Chief officers: Robyn Nation (President), Pam Taylor (Membership and Administration Manager)
Membership: 3,800 insurance industry staff, including general, life, savings, brokers, loss adjusters
Publications:
• Bulletin: *quarterly*

Jewellers and Watchmakers of New Zealand Inc.
Address: PO Box 386, Level 8, Norwich Building, CNR Queen and Durham Streets, Auckland 1000

Telephone: +64 9 309 2561
Fax: +64 9 309 7798

Magazine Publishers' Association of New Zealand
Address: PO Box 68213, Newton Auckland
Telephone: +64 9 358 3906
Fax: +64 9 308 9523
Chief officers: Janice Boswell (Executive Manager)
Publications:
• Magazines: *issues affecting New Zealand magazine publishers and advertising agencies - bi-monthly*
• New Zealand Magazine Market: Present Trends and Future Outlook: *household expenditure, advertising revenue, overall revenue, circulation trends and a brief market summary. Compiled from various sources - annual*

Motor Industry Association (MIA)
Address: PO Box 308, 2nd Floor, Timber Industry House, 219 Thorndon Quay, Wellington
Telephone: +64 4 473 6700
Fax: +64 4 473 1913
Year established: 1931
Activities: compiles statistics on production and monthly registrations by make and model for both passenger cars and commercial vehicles
Chief officers: Perry Kerr (Chief Executive Officer), Helen Wickens (Statistics, Information)
Membership: 32 corporate members including manufacturers, importers and assemblers
Notes: The Association does not produce any publications.

New Zealand Apple and Pear Marketing Board
Address: PO Box 3328, 11/17 Boltonst, Wellington
Telephone: +64 4 473 1420
Fax: +64 4 472 2980
Activities: producer board representing export marketers of NZ pipfruit; collects statistics on fresh fruit exports, financial performance, cash flows
Chief officers: Gary Smith (CEO), Heather Hayden (Communications Manager), Alasdair Robertson (General Manager Marketing), Bob Hudson (General Manager Global Logistics)
Publications:
• Annual Report: *analysis of the performance of the marketing of the board, with a mention to the activities of the Association, etc.. As well as statistical data on exports, statements of financial performance, financial position, statement of cash flows, statement of accounting policies - annual*
• Pipmark Grower News

New Zealand Berryfruit Growers Federation Inc.
Address: PO Box 10050, 2nd Floor, Agriculture House, 12 Johnston Street, Wellington 6036 N2
Telephone: +64 4 473 5387
Fax: +64 4 473 6999
E-mail: berry@xtra.com.nz
Year established: 1967
Activities: annual conference; provides information on the industry and updates; lobbying; servicing and administering
Chief officers: Bob Ferguson (Executive Officer), Antonia Crawford (Accounts Executive), Sharyn Hetaraka (Executive Assistant)
Membership: 490 commercial berryfruit growers and horticulture industry
Publications:
• Commercial Grower: *monthly*
Notes: The Association does not produce statistics.

New Zealand Employers' Federation (Inc.)

Address: PO Box 1786, 10th Floor, Clear Centre, 15-17 Murphy Street, Wellington 6015
Telephone: +64 4 499 4111
Fax: +64 4 499 4112
E-mail: nzef@nzef.org.nz
Year established: 1902
Activities: national representative of business interests, particularly in labour market issues. Offers an information service, publishes guides on legislation, carries out research, produces ad hoc publications on major issues. Also compiles statistics on labour market behaviour, training and investment in training, skill shortages, effects of legislation, resource management and environmental regulation, regulatory compliance costs etc.
Chief officers: Steve Marshall (Chief Executive Officer), Anne Knowles, (Dep Chief Executive), John McCaskey (Secretary)
Membership: 4 regional employers' associations representing 12,000 employers, 46 national industry organisations representing a further 81,000 employers
Publications:
• Employer (The): *innovations in business processes, international opportunities for business, education and training, political opinion etc. - 11 p.a.*

New Zealand Fruitgrowers' Federation

Address: PO Box 2175, 2nd Floor, Huddart Parker Building, Post Office Square, Wellington 6015
Telephone: +64 4 472 6559
Fax: +64 4 472 6409
Year established: 1985
Activities: Annual conference (November); promotes fruit industry development
Chief officers: Peter Silcock (Acting Chief Executive), Sue Pickering (Business Manager)
Membership: 4,500 fruit growers
Publications:
• Orchardist of NZ: *monthly*

New Zealand Honey Producers' Association

Address: PO Box 664, 57A Theodosia Street, Timaru
Telephone: +64 3 684 8882
Fax: +64 3 688 4859

New Zealand Library and Information Association

Te Rau Herenga o Aotearo
Address: PO Box 12 212, Level 6, Old Wool House, 135-141 Featherston St, Wellington
Telephone: +64 4 473 5834
Fax: +64 4 499 1480
E-mail: office@nzlia.org.nz
Web site: www.netlink.co.nz/~nzlia/
Activities: promotes the use and development of libraries and information service through publications, meetings, continuing education programmes and conferences; produces statistics on libraries including output, financial summaries, staff and loans
Chief officers: Sue Cooper (President), Steve Williams (Office Manager)
Membership: 1,000 individual members and 500 institutional members
Publications:
• Library Life: *monthly*
• New Zealand Libraries: *quarterly*

New Zealand Meat Board

Address: Box 121, Wellington
Telephone: +64 4 473 9150
Fax: +64 4 472 3172
E-mail: mpb@zephr.grace.cri.nz

Year established: 1922
Activities: service organisation to the New Zealand meat industry involved in access and trade policy, market development, research, technology transfer and dissemination of information. The Board produces statistics on production, exports, local consumption and livestock numbers etc.
Chief officers: John D Ackland (Chairman),
Membership: meat producers and processors
Publications:
• Annual Report: *annual*
• Meat News: *bi-weekly*
• Meat Producer: *6 times p.a.*

New Zealand Meat Industry Association

Address: PO Box 345 Wellington, Level 4, Wool House, 10 Brandon Street, Wellington 6015
Telephone: +64 4 473 6465
Fax: +64 4 473 1731
Year established: 1985
Activities: compile statistics on the New Zealand meat industry
Chief officers: Chris Jackson Jones (Economist)

New Zealand Meat Producers' Board

Address: POBox 121, 6th Floor, Seabridge House, 110 Featherston Street, Wellington
Telephone: +64 4 473 9150
Fax: +64 4 472 3172
E-mail: mpb@zephyr.grace.cri.nz
Activities: market access monitoring and negotiation, management of tariff rate quota, collection of statistical and industry information, market intelligence, market development and promotion
Chief officers: Neil Taylor (Chief Executive), Robyn Dalton (Statistics)
Publications:
• Annual Report: *analysis of trends and statistics on the New Zealand meat industry for the past year - annual*
• Meat Board News: *news and trends in the New Zealand meat industry. Includes statistics on per capita consumption and export production as well as a section on meat prices - bi-monthly*
• New Zealand Meat Producer: *company profiles, statistics and commentary on the New Zealand meat industry - quarterly*

New Zealand National Committee of International Dairy Federation

Address: P.O.Box 2526, c/o Ministry of Agriculture & Fisheries, MAF Regulatory Authority, Wellington
Telephone: +64 4 498 9874
Fax: +64 4 474 4240
E-mail: fawcetp@ra.maf.govt.nz
Chief officers: Mr P.R. Fawcet (Secretary)

New Zealand Pork Industry Board

Address: PO Box 4048, Level 4, Walsh Wrightson Tower, 94 Dixon St, Wellington
Telephone: +64 4 385 4229
Fax: +64 4 385 8522
E-mail: industryinfo@nzpib.co.nz
Year established: 1937
Activities: generic promotion of pork in New Zealand; conducts research; industry liaison; collects statistics on pig slaughtered, production , exports/imports, etc.
Chief officers: R E Jeffrey (Chairman), Brian Mulne (Chief Executive Officer), DJ Dobson (General Manager)
Membership: 600 registered pork producers
Publications:
• Annual Report: *annual*
• Pork at Look: *production oriented magazine - monthly*

• Pork Environment: *productionoriented, environmental issues - every six months*
• Pork Report: *bimonthly*
• Quarterly Report: *industry report with up-to-date statistical information - quarterly*
• World Pork News: *world-wide pork industry news - quarterly*

New Zealand Press Association

Address: PO Box 1599, 93 Boulcott Street, Wellington
Telephone: +64 4 472 7910
Fax: +64 4 473 7480/478 1625

New Zealand Retail Meat and Allied Trades Federation Inc.

Address: PO Box 12 126, Molesworth House, 101-103 Molsworth Street, Wellington
Telephone: +64 4 472 0807
Fax: +64 4 472 0804
Activities: education and training
Chief officers: David Lonsdale (Executive Director)

New Zealand Soft Drinks Manufacturers' Association Inc.

Address: PO Box 6549, 3rd Floor, CMC Building, 89 Courtenay Place, Wellington 6035
Telephone: +64 4 384 5939
Fax: +64 4 385 9237
Year established: 1920

New Zealand Tourism Board

Address: PO Box 95, 89 The Terrace, Wellington
Telephone: +64 4 472 8860
Fax: +64 4 478 1736
Web site: www.nztb.govt.nz
Year established: 1991
Activities: development, implementation and promotion of strategies for tourism; advises government and New Zealand tourism industry on related matters; consumer and trade promotions; information distribution; public relations; carries out research; receives monthly and annual statistics which summarise intentional visitor characteristics data from the New Zealand arrival card
Chief officers: Bryan Mogridge (Director's Chair), Paul Winter (Chief Executive), Chris Ryan (Deputy Chief Executive)
Publications:
• Annual Report of the New Zealand Tourism Board: *annual*
• Inbound Market Guide: *annual update on conditions in New Zealand's main tourism markets - annual*
• New Zealand Holiday Planner: *the Board's main consumer brochure*
• New Zealand International Visitors Survey: *examines the travel behaviour of visitors to New Zealand*
• New Zealand Tourism News: *news publication for the wider tourism industry that focuses on NZTB initiatives - bi-monthly*

New Zealand Vegetable and Potato Growers' Federation (VEGFED)

Address: PO Box 10232, 2nd Floor, Agriculture House, Johnston Street, Wellington 6036
Telephone: +64 4 472 3795
Fax: +64 4 471 2861
E-mail: Peter@vegfed.co.nz
Year established: 1958
Activities: annual conference; monitors government legislation and government liaison; funds the activities of 38 local associations; funds activities to promote vegetables; carries out vegetable research and research projects; monitors and informs on technical and marketing issues; assists local grower associations with submissions and

comments on local and regional government proposals; export development and market access; collects statistics
Chief officers: Max Lilley (President), Brian D Gargiulo (Vice President), Peter Silcock (Chief Executive Officer), Ken Robertson (Executive Officer), Ron Gall (Executive Officer)
Structure: the federation has seven product sectors: fresh vegetables, processed vegetables, potatoes, fresh tomatoes, asparagus, export squash and process tomatoes. Each sector is run by an autonomous committee. Sector representatives along with the President make up the Council, which deals with issues of common concern
Membership: 4,500 vegetable growers
Publications:
• New Zealand Commercial Grower Magazine: *short articles and issues relating to the vegetable industry, some statistical product information - 10 p.a.*

Pharmacy Guild of New Zealand Inc.

Address: Upper Willis Street PB 27139, 3rd Floor, Pharmacy House, 124-126 Dixon Street, Wellington 6037
Telephone: +64 4 385 9708
Fax: +64 4 384 8085
Year established: 1931
Chief officers: Neville Dickson (Manger, Contracts and Commercial Services)

Poultry Industry Association of New Zealand

Address: 1st Floor, Carlton Gore Road, Newmarket Auckland
Telephone: +64 9 309 2417
Fax: +64 9 307 3831
E-mail: ed@pianz.org.nz or bobd@pianz.org.nz
Web site: www.pianz.org.nz
Activities: collects statistics on the volume of egg and poultry meat production in New Zealand and Australia
Chief officers: Ed Catherwood (Executive Officer)

Recording Industry Association of New Zealand Inc. (RIANZ)

Address: PO Box 9241 (Te Aro), 6th Floor, Oticon House, 15 Courtenay Place, Wellington 6035
Telephone: +64 4 384 3523
Fax: +64 4 384 5060
Year established: 1982
Publications:
• RIANZ Yearbook: *in-depth profile of the New Zealand recording industry. Includes statistics on the retail and wholesale markets for the latest year. Also includes information on the world market - annual*

Researched Medicines Industry Association of New Zealand Inc. (RMI)

Address: PO Box 10447 (The Terrace), 1st Floor, Agriculture House, 12 Johnstone Street, Wellington 6036
Telephone: +64 4 499 4277
Fax: +64 4 499 4276
Chief officers: Mr K.B. Miles (Chief Executive)
Structure: 8 person board of directors; secretariat of 35 staff
Membership: 37 pharmaceuticals (research-based) companies
Publications:
• Investing in Future Health: *annual*

Retail and Wholesale Merchants' Association of New Zealand Inc.

Address: PO Box 12-086, 7th Floor, Molesworth House, 101-103 Molesworth Street, Thorndon, Wellington 6038
Telephone: +64 4 472 3733
Fax: +64 4 472 1071

Web site: www.mmlink.org.nz/rwma
Chief officers: Chris James (President); Doug McLaren (Chief Executive); David Lonsdale (Executive Director-administration and training); Anna Bruce (Executive Director- marketing and business development)
Structure: 3 sectors: administration and training; member servicing marketing; business development
Membership: 1,750 stores; 1,500 affiliated members
Publications:
● Merchant: *all aspects of retailing and wholesaling - monthly except January*
● Notes: *monthly*

Tobacco Institute of New Zealand Ltd
Address: PO Box 1582, Floor 15, West Plaza Building, 3 Albert Street, Auckland 1015
Telephone: +64 9 379 7393
Fax: +64 9 308 9053
Year established: 1980
Activities: collects statistics on taxation, population data, market data
Chief officers: Michael J Thompson (Executive Director)
Structure: limited liability company
Membership: 2 full, 1 associate; all tobacco manufacturers
Notes: no publication

Wine Institute of New Zealand Inc.
Address: Private Bag 90-276, Level 6, 47 Wakefield Street, Auckland 1030
Telephone: +64 9 303 3527
Fax: +64 9 302 2969
E-mail: winz@nzwine.com or feedback@nzwine.com
Web site: www.nzwine.com
Web site notes: site includes various statistics on the New Zealand wine industry. Also includes information on New Zealand producers as well as overseas wholesalers and retailers that import New Zealand wines
Year established: 1976
Publications:
● Annual Report: *provides a summary of the New Zealand wine industry. Provides information on domestic consumption as well as imports, exports, total area under cultivation and number of producers - annual*

NICARAGUA

Association of Consumer Products Distributors
Asociación de Distribuidores de Productos de Consumo de Nicaragua
Address: Carretera Norte Km 4-1/2, Módulo 12, Oficentro Norte, Antiguo local SOVIPE, Managua
Telephone: +505 2 490 045
Fax: +505 2 490 094
Chief officers: Lic. América de Urtecho (General Manager)

Association of Industries of Nicaragua (CADIN)
Cámara de Industrias de Nicaragua
Address: Aptdo. 1436, Semáforos de Plaza España 300 mts al sur, Donde fue TURNICA, Managua
Telephone: +505 2 668 847/51
Fax: +505 266 1891
E-mail: cadin@sgc.com.ni
Web site: www.sgc.com.ni/cadin.html
Activities: promotes relations with the government and its institutions, as well as with regional, pan-regional and international institutions and organisations
Chief officers: Alberto Chamorro Chamorro (President), Dr. Gilberto Solís Espinosa (Executive Secretary)
Membership: private industry

Association of Nicaraguan Travel and Tourism Agencies (ANAVYT)
Asociación Nicaragüense de Agencias de Viajes y Turismo
Address: Ciudad Jardín de la Inmobiliaria, 50 Varas al Este, Managua
Telephone: +505 5056 416 26/445 85

Association of Private Enterprises (COSEP)
Consejo Superior de la Empresa Privada
Address: Apdo 5430, TELCOR Zacarías Guerra 175 mts abajo, Managua
Telephone: +505 2 271 30/228 030/42
Fax: +505 2 282 041
Chief officers: Ing. Gerardo Salinas (President)
Membership: umbrella organisation encompassing the main private trade and industry business associations

Association of Small and Medium-Sized Businesses (UNIPYME)
Unión Nicaraguense de Pequeña y Mediana Empresas
Address: Ciudad Jardín L-16, Managua
Telephone: +505 2 497 695
Fax: +505 2 490 662
Chief officers: Lic. William Tefel (President)

Chamber of Small and Medium-Sized Industries (CONAPI)
Cámara Nacional de la Mediana y Pequeña Industria
Address: Centro de Exposiciones la Piñata, Managua
Telephone: +505 2 784 892/277 5910
Chief officers: Antonio Chavez (President)

Federation of Cattle Breeders' Associations (FAGANIC)
Federación de Asociaciones de Ganaderos de Nicaragua
Address: Entrada Principal, Centro Comercial Managua, Managua
Telephone: +505 2 772 976/277 2947
Fax: +505 2 670 084
Chief officers: Ing. José Ramón Kontorovsky (President)

Fishing Association of Nicaragua (CAPENIC)
Cámara de la Pesca de Nicaragua
Address: Camino de Oriente, Edificio B 2-6, Managua
Telephone: +505 2 787 091
Fax: +505 2 787 054
Chief officers: Lic. Miguel Marenco (General Manager)

Hotel Association of Nicaragua
Asociación Hotelera de Nicaragua
Address: Hotel Camino Real - Managua, Carretera Norte Km. 9 1/2, Managua
Telephone: +505 2 631 381/5
E-mail: ahn@sgc.com.ni
Web site: 207.158.206.20/ahn/
Year established: 1966
Chief officers: Lic. Miguel Romero P. (President), Lic. William Rodriguez (Secretary)

National Sugar Producers Committee (CNPA)
Comité Nacional de Productores de Azúcar
Address: Apdo. Postal No. 223, Sandy's Carretera a Masaya 1 c. arriba 1 c. al sur, Casa No. 51, Colonial Las Robles, Managua
Telephone: +505 2 678 202/277 5447
Fax: +505 2 670 197
Chief officers: Lic. Noel Chamorro (General Manager)

National Union of Agricultural Producers (UPANIC)

Unión de Productores Agropecuarios de Nicaragua
Address: Reparto San Juan No. 300, Detrás del Ginmasio
Hércules, Managua
Telephone: +505 2 783 382/84
Fax: +505 2 782 587/278 3291
Chief officers: Ing. Alejandro Raskowsky (Executive
Secretary)

Nicaraguan Association of Producers and Exporters of Non-Traditional Products (APENN)

Asociación Nicaragüense de Productores y Exportadores de
Productos No Tradicionales
Address: Hotel Intercontinental 2 c. al sur 2 c. al oeste,
Managua
Telephone: +505 2 665 038/266 9850/1
Fax: +505 2 665 039
Chief officers: Patrick Bolaños D. (General Manager)

Nicaraguan Private Banking Association (ASOBANP)

Asociación de Bancos Privados de Nicaragua
Address: Distribuidora Vicky 1 c. al sur 1 c. arriba, No. 235,
Managua
Telephone: +505 2 783 821
Fax: +505 2 783 820
Chief officers: Dr. Francisco Ortega (Executive Secretary)

NIGERIA

Cocoa Producers' Council (CPA)

Address: PO Box 1718, Western House, 11th Floor, 8-10
Broad Street, Lagos
Telephone: +234 1 263 5506/ 5574

Manufacturers' Association of Nigeria (MAN)

Address: PO Box 3835, MAN House, 77 Obafemi, Awolowo
Way, Ikeja, Lagos
Telephone: +234 1 967 482/932 343/900 600/900 609
Year established: 1971
Activities: advises, consults and takes up issues with
governmental and other bodies on matters affecting its
members; promotes export; public relations, press releases;
seminars, workshops and conferences
Chief officers: Dr Hassan Adamu (President)
Membership: 2000 manufacturing companies in the private
and public sector
Publications:
• Articles of Association: *explains the constitution of the
Association - annual*
• Half-Yearly Economic Review: *review of the national
economy based on field surveys of industrial enterprises
nationwide - every six months*
• MAN Information Booklet: *information about MAN's activities,
policies, objectives and news on the industry, membership
information*
• National Council Reports: *publication that highlights the
activities of MAN througout the year - annual*
• Nigeria Industrial Directory: *guide to manufacturing
companies their location, contact addresses, product lines
and annual turnover in Nigeria, also information on the age,
status and authorised share capitals of these companies as
well as their principal raw materials: includes useful
information on procedures for establishing an industry in
Nigeria - annual*

Nigerian Book Development Council (NBDC)

Address: 3 Jibowu Street, Yaba, Lagos
Telephone: +234 1 862 269

Nigerian Book Foundation (NBF)

Address: PO Box 1132, 4 Ezi-Ajana Lane, Umukwa Village,
Awka
Telephone: +234 46 551 403
Fax: +234 46 552 615
Chief officers: Professor Chukwuemeka Ike (President)

Nigerian Booksellers' and Stationers' Association (NBSA)

Address: PO Box 3168, Ibadan
Chief officers: Sam A. Olaniyan (Secretary)

Nigerian Enterprises Promotion Board

Address: 72 Campbell Street or 15-19 Keffi Street, SW Ikoyi,
Lagos
Telephone: +234 1 689 29

Nigerian Publishers' Association

Address: PO Box 2541, 14 Awosika Avenue, off Oshuntokun
Avenue, Old Bodija G.P.O., Ibadan
Telephone: +234 1 496 3007/22 810 2684
Fax: +234 1 496 4370/497 2217
Chief officers: Mr AO Echebiri (President), Mrs FO Onikan
(Director)

NORWAY

Article Numbering Association (EAN Norge)

Address: Spireaveien 6, 0580 Oslo 5
Telephone: +47 2 265 1000
Fax: +47 2 265 5621
E-mail: firmapost@ean-norge.telemax.no

Association of Consumer Goods' Retailers

Dagligvare Leverandoerenes Forening
Address: Postbox 6851, St. Olavs Plass, N-0130 Oslo 1
Telephone: +47 221 10343
Fax: +47 222 06044
Year established: 1972
Membership: general food retailers

Association of Norwegian Breweries and Soft Drinks Producers (NBMF)

Norsk Bryggeri-og Mineralvannindustris Forening
Address: PO Box 7087 Majorstua, Essendropsgate 6, N-0306
Oslo
Telephone: +47 22 961 210
Fax: +47 22 603 004
Activities: taxation; legislation; packaging; statistics;
international co-operation
Chief officers: Per Undrum
Membership: 21 members
Publications:
• Facts and Figures for Beverages in Norway: *a pocketbook
with basic data on the beverage industry in Norway over the
last few years - annual*

Association of Norwegian Clothing, Shoe, Textile, Leather and Sporting Goods Industries

Teko Landsforening
Address: PO Box 7086 Majorstua, N-0303 Oslo
Telephone: +47 22 596 680
Fax: +47 22 596 694
Activities: employers' federation; provides information on
trade policy; legislation; affairs concerning the industry

Chief officers: Oyvind Haugerud (Managing Director)
Membership: 130 members
Publications:
• Teko Tidende: *monthly*
Notes: The Association does not produce statistics.

Association of Norwegian Finance Houses
Finansieringsselskapenes Forening
Address: PO Box 1310 Vika, Fred Olsengate 1, N-0112 Oslo
Telephone: +47 22 014 180/429 830
Fax: +47 22 014 184
Year established: 1984
Activities: involved in lobbying activities; provides information on the legal framework and economic conditions; public relations; carries out professional work on technical issues concerning member financial products, etc.; training courses and seminars; collects statistics on member companies activities
Chief officers: Frank Myhre (Managing Director), Jan Fr. Harladsen (Deputy Director), Inger Linell (Consultant)
Membership: 29 financial companies active in leasing, factoring, credit cards, car loans, etc.
Notes: No official publications produced.

Co-operative Union and Wholesale Society
Address: POB 1173 Sentrum, N-0107 Oslo
Telephone: +47 22 8995 00
Fax: +47 22 41 14 42
Year established: 1906
Chief officers: Jarle Benum (Chairman), Rolf Ronning (Director)
Membership: 390 societies

Federation of Norwegian Commercial and Service Enterprises (Incorporating the Association of Commercial Agents in Groceries, Foodstuffs and Margarine)
Handels og Servicenæringens Hovedorganisasjon/Landsbransjeforeningen For Kolonial, Næringsmidler og Margarin
Address: PO Box 2483, Drammensveien 30, N-0202 Oslo
Telephone: +47 22 558 220
Fax: +47 22 558 225
Chief officers: Mr. Ulf Andersen (Chairman of the Board): Mr. Herman Thrap-Meyer (Secretary)
Structure: the Federation of Norwegian Commercial and Service Enterprises (HSH) (Handels og Servicenæringens Hovedorganisasjon) incorporates the Federation of Norwegian Commercial Agents (Norske Agenters Landsforbund) and the Association of Commercial Agents in Goceries, Foodstuff and Margarine (Landsbransjeforeningen For Kolonial, Næringsmidler og Margarin)
Membership: commercial agents or sole distributors of groceries and foodstuffs, represents foreign companies and Norwegian manufacturers

Federation of Norwegian Processing and Manufacturing Industries
Address: Stensberggt 27, N-0170 Oslo
Telephone: +47 22 96 10 00
Fax: +47 22 96 10 99

National Association of the Fishing Industry
Fiskeindustriens Landsforening
Address: N-9005 Tromso
Telephone: +47 77 658 033
Fax: +47 77 655 497
Year established: 1982
Activities: collects data concerning the fish processing

industry (generally only available to members)
Chief officers: T. Matnussen (Managing Director)
Membership: 250 fish processing and fish export companies
Publications:
• Fish Industry (Fiskeindustrien): *10 p.a.*

Norwegian Association of Advertising Agencies
Relilame-byraforeningen
Address: Box 2373 Solli, Wergelandsveien 23, N-0201 Oslo
Telephone: +47 22 601 404
Fax: +47 22 601 444
E-mail: sissel@rff.no
Web site: www.rff.no/
Activities: collect statistics about income based on commission and fees
Chief officers: Hilde Britt Melbye (Director); Sissel Sem Stoltenberg
Membership: 59 members including 44 agencies
Publications:
• Byranytt: *6 p.a.*

Norwegian Association of Car Dealers
Norges Bilbransjeforbund
Address: POB 7628 Skillebekk, Drammensveien 97, N-0205 Oslo
Telephone: +47 22 601 290
Fax: +47 22 561 050
Activities: information service, training
Chief officers: Eirik Hoien (Administrative Director); Thrane Steen (Chairman); Thor Ottersen (Editor)
Structure: council, chairman, various ad hoc subcommittees
Publications:
• Bilbjrbransjen: *11 p.a.*

Norwegian Association of Chocolate Manufacturers
Address: Postboks 5472, Majorstua, N-0305 Oslo
Telephone: +47 22 965 009
Fax: +47 22 965 099

Norwegian Association of Domestic Electrical Appliance Manufacturers
Norske Elektroleverandorers Landsforening
Address: Postboks 236, Skoyen, N-0212 Oslo
Telephone: +47 22 732 706
Fax: +47 22 732 704
Chief officers: Willy Saebo (Manager)
Membership: 20 members
Notes: The Association does not produce statistics or publications.

Norwegian Association of Electrical Manufacturers, Agents and Wholesalers
Elektroforeningen/Norske Elektrogrossister, -Agenter og -Produsenter
Address: Postbox 2864 Solli, Drammensveien 30, N-0230 Oslo
Telephone: +47 2 255 8140
Fax: +47 2 255 8433
Activities: administers a product database for the eletro-technical trade; collects key annual statistical figures; maintains link with official bodies
Membership: 161 members representing electrical/electronics manufacturers, importers and wholesalers
Publications:
• Newsletter: *12-15 p.a.*

Norwegian Association of Fruit and Vegetable Wholesalers

Norges Frukt-og Gronnsaksgrossisters Forbund
Address: PO Box 157 Okern, N-0509 Oslo
Telephone: +47 22 650 375
Fax: +47 22 631 924
Activities: information and statistics covering production, sales and imports
Chief officers: Oddmund Ostebo (General Secretary)
Membership: 52 fruit and vegetable wholesalers
Publications:
• Bulletin

Norwegian Association of Pharmaceutical Manufacturers (LMI)

Legemiddelindustrien
Address: Po Box 734 Sentrum, Grev Wedels Plass 9, N-0105 Oslo
Telephone: +47 22 417 676
Fax: +47 22 417 675
E-mail: lmi@lmi.no
Year established: 1966
Activities: provides general information and service activities; maintains close contacts with governmental bodies, health related institutions and media; collects retail sales statistics
Chief officers: Liv Slettvold (Vice President), Thor Krev-Jakobsen (General Director), Bodil Brodin (Secretary), Geir Bredesen (Chief of Economy), Tone Veiteberg (Advisor)
Membership: 40 member companies: 4 manufacturers and 36 retailers
Publications:
• Drugs and Health Facts and Figures: *general data on the pharmaceutical market and public expenditure trends on health. Based on a mixture of official data and figures supplied by the drugs companies - every two years*
• Drugs and Society (Legemidler & Samfunn): *industry related issues - 10 p.a.*
• LMI Newsletter: *6 p.a.*

Norwegian Association of the Brewing and Mineral Water Industries

Norsk Bryggeri-og Mineralvannindustris Forening
Address: PO Box 7087, Homansbyen, N-0306 Oslo
Telephone: +47 224 65620/229 61210
Fax: +47 226 03004
Year established: 1901
Activities: statistics covering alcohol consumption, production, outlets, home production etc. (free), information on Norwegian breweries and soft drinks manufacturers (free)
Chief officers: Odd Einar Foss-Skiftevik (Managing Director)
Structure: board, standing committees and ad hoc working groups
Membership: 27 breweries, mineral water and soft drinks producers
Publications:
• Membership List
• Norwegian Beer: *facts and figures - annual*
• Norwegian Carbonated Soft Drinks: *facts and figures - annual*

Norwegian Association of Tobacco Manufacturers

Address: AV 1901 Fr Nansens Plass 9, N-0160 Oslo
Telephone: +47 22 414 621
Fax: +47 22 334 010
Chief officers: Asbjoern Fr. Asbjoernsen (President), Oddbjorn Oddaker (Vice President)

Norwegian Bankers' Association

Bankforeningen
Address: PO Box 1489, N-0116 Oslo
Telephone: +47 22 833 160
Fax: +47 22 830 751
Year established: 1915
Activities: to observe economic and social developments and look after the interests of member institutions when dealing with government authorities, other organisation and the media; Service Bureau conducts studies and advisory and informational activities
Chief officers: Trond R Reinertsen (Managing Director); Anne Kari Edgren (Executive Secretary)
Membership: 23 member institutions and 4 subsidiary members
Publications:
• Annual Report: *annual*
• Okonomisk Revy: *a review of economic trends in Norway with commentary and statistics and some forecasts in selected issues - bi-monthly*

Norwegian Egg Producers' Association

Address: Postboks 4377, Torshov 04012 Oslo
Telephone: +47 2 222 23050
Fax: +47 2 222 22887
Chief officers: Ivar Meltvedt

Norwegian Electrotechnical Committee (NEK)

Norsk Elektroteknisk Komite
Address: PO Box 280 Skoeyen, Harbitzalleen 2A, N-0212 Oslo
Telephone: +47 22 526 950
Fax: +47 22 526 961
E-mail: firmapost@nek.telemax.no
Year established: 1912
Activities: information concerning implementation of Norwegian electrotechnical standards and ongoing standards work, generally available
Chief officers: B I Odegard (Manager)
Structure: council of representatives, board of directors, secretariat, approximately 130 standards committees
Membership: 15 corporate members; 450 expert members
Publications:
• NEK Catalogue of Norwegian Electrotechnical Standards: *annual*
• NEK Communications: *available standards and new projects - quarterly*
• Norwegian Electro Technical Committee Annual Report: *annual*
Notes: The Association does not produce statistics.

Norwegian Frozen Foods Institute

Dypfrysingskontoret
Address: PO Box 1494 Vika, Avokatfirma Lyng and Co, Fridtjof Nansens plass 7, N-0116 Oslo
Telephone: +47 22 008 010
Fax: +47 22 008 020
Membership: 9 member companies
Notes: Member of the Federation of the Associations of EU Frozen Food Producers (FAFPAS) based in Brussels (Belgium).

Norwegian Hospitality Association

Reiselivsbedriftenes Landsforening
Address: Postboks 5465, Majorstua, N-0305 Oslo
Telephone: +47 22 965 080
Fax: +47 22 569 620
Year established: 1894
Activities: general information for members, i.e. on new laws and regulations; occupancy statistics for Norway (monthly); economic results for the hospitality industry (annual)

Chief officers: Knut Almquist (Managing Director), Björn Ketilsson (Information Manager)
Structure: 9 local associations
Membership: approximately 2,250 members: hotels, restaurants, cafes, bars, camping sites, catering companies
Publications:
• Travel News Bulletin (Reiseliv): *covers the entire hospitality and travel industry - monthly*

Norwegian National Committee of International Dairy Federation
Nasjonalkomitéen for Norge av det internasjonale Meieriforbund
Address: P.O.B. 9051 Grønland, Breigt, 10, 0133 Oslo
Telephone: +47 2293 8800
Fax: +47 2217 8822
E-mail: rigmor.blix@tine.no
Chief officers: Ms Rigor Blix (Secretary)

Norwegian Newspapers' Association (NAL)
Norske Avisers Landsforening
Address: Stortovet 2, 0155 Oslo
Telephone: +47 22 861 200
Fax: +47 22 861 201
E-mail: nal@nal.no
Web site: www.nal.no
Web site notes: site includes circulation and readership data for Norwegian newspapers as well as international comparisons and a list of members
Chief officers: Kurt Borgen (Managing Director)
Membership: 168 members, of which 154 are newspapers. Member newspapers account for 98 per cent of total circulation in Norway

Norwegian Publishers' Association
Den Norske Forleggerforning
Address: Ovre Vollgate 15, 0158 Oslo 1
Telephone: +47 22 42 13 55
Fax: +47 22 33 38 30
Chief officers: Mr T Ramberg, Mr NK Jacobsen, Mr PM Rothe (Director)

Norwegian Pulp and Paper Institute
Papirindustriens Forskningsinstitutt
Address: POB 24, Blindern, N-0313 Oslo
Telephone: +47 22 140 090
Fax: +47 22 468 014
Activities: 6 meetings p.a.; technical lectures; congress in November, research
Chief officers: Jan H Oreli (President); Sissel Raunsborg (Research Director)
Membership: 25 members
Publications:
• Papirforskning: *information on the pulp and paper industry - 4 p.a.*

Norwegian Pulp, Paper and Board Industry Association
Treforedlingsindustriens Bransjeforening
Address: Stensberggaten 27, N-0170 Oslo
Telephone: +47 2296 1000
Fax: +47 2296 1089
Publications:
• Key Figures (Treforedlingsindustriens Bransjeforening): *tables and graphs presenting a range of figures on the Norwegian pulp, paper, and board sectors. Data includes production, sales, foreign trade, raw materials used, energy, industry structure, and employment. Many tables and graphs cover the latest five years - annual*

Soap and Detergent Industry Association
Felleskontoret for Vaskemiddelfabrikanter
Address: PO Box 6780, St Olavs Pl. Rozenkrantz Gate, 11, N-0130 Oslo
Telephone: +47 22 337 765
Fax: +47 22 331 350
Activities: maintains a library; produces statistics covering retail sales
Chief officers: Ms Ingrid Standal (President)
Membership: 6 members representing manufacturers, wholesalers and retailers

PAKISTAN

All Pakistan Cloth Exporters' Association
Address: Ground Floor, 30 Regency Arcade, The Mall, Faisalabad
Telephone: +92 41 615 563/615 564
Fax: +92 41 617 985
Telex: 43382
Year established: 1986
Activities: recording textile quota exports from Pakistan
Chief officers: Mohammad Siddique (Chairman), Mian Naeem Omer, (Senior Vice Chairman), Rana Khalid Javed (Vice Chairman), Mr Ehsan Elahi Sheikh (Vice Chairman), Mr Aftab Ahmad (Secretary)
Structure: chairman, vice chairmen, executive committee (24 members)
Membership: 350 member companies
Publications:
• Annual Report of the All Pakistan Cloth Exporters' Asociation: *available to members free of charge - annual*

All Pakistan Gem Merchants' and Jewellers' Association
Address: Gem & Jewellery Trade Centre, Blanken Street, off Zaibunnissa Street Saddar, Karachi
Telephone: +92 21 519 121/526 063/522 968
Fax: +92 21 568 2970

All Pakistan Textile Processing Mills' Association
Address: PO Box 5446, Principal Office, APTMA House, 44A, Lalazar, Moulvi Tamizuddin Khan Road, Karachi 74000
Telephone: +92 21 561 0191/92/95
Fax: +92 21 561 1301
Chief officers: Iftkhar Afzal (Secretary General)

Pakistan Banks Association
Address: NBP Building, II Chundrigar Road, Karachi
Telephone: +92 212 416 686
Fax: +92 212 415 221
Year established: 1963
Membership: 4 foreign banks; 9 Pakistani banks

Pakistan Beverage Manufacturers' Association (PBMA)
Address: SF-25, 26, Centre Point, Main Boulevard, Gulberg III, Lahore
Telephone: +92 42 575 7281
Fax: +92 42 575 9356
Chief officers: Shaukat Janjua (Secretary General)

Pakistan Footwear Manufacturers' Association
Address: 1345 1st Floor, Raja Centre Extension, Main Market, Gullberg 11, 53000 Lahore
Telephone: +92 42 575 0051
Fax: +92 42 575 0052

Pakistan Tea Association
Address: Muhammad Baksh Building, 1st Floor, 23 West Wharaf Road, Karachi
Telephone: +92 212 01415
Fax: +92 212 415209

Travel Agents Association of Pakistan (TAAP)
Address: 115 Central Hotel Building, Mereweather Road, Karachi 75530
Telephone: +92 2 156 827 48/568 4469
Fax: +92 2 156 827 48
Year established: 1974
Activities: tourism policy, legislation and other matters affecting the travel and tourism industry
Chief officers: Mr M Riaz Chugati (Chairman), Mr M.A.K. Nasiri (Secretary General)
Membership: travel agents and tour operators: 173 full members and 64 associate members

PANAMA

Association of Enterprises Executives of Panama (ADEPE)
Asociación Panameña de Ejecutivos de Empresa
Address: Edificio ADEPE, Calle 42 y Avenida Balboa, Bella Vista, Panamá
Telephone: +507 2 273 511
Fax: +507 2 271 872

National Private Enterprises' Council
Consejo Nacional de la Empresa Privada
Address: Calle 41, Bella Vista, Panamá
Telephone: +507 2 270 791
Fax: +507 2 252 663

Non-Traditional Exporters' Group of Panama (GANTRAP)
Grupo de Agroexportadores No Tradicionales de Panamá
Address: Chitré, Herrera, Panamá
Telephone: +507 9 960 561
Fax: +507 9 967 659

Panama Banking Association
Address: PO Box 4554, Banco Union Building, Samuel Lewis Avenue, Zona 5, 15/F, Panama
Telephone: +507 263 7044
Fax: +507 263 7783

Panama Foreign Trade Institute
Address: Apdo 55 2359 Paitilla 4/F, Banco Extrerior Building, Balboa Avenue, Panama
Telephone: +507 225 7244
Fax: +507 225 2193
Chief officers: Kenia Jaén Rivera (Executive Director)

Panamanian Exporters' Association (APEX)
Asociación Panameña de Exportadores
Address: Apdo 6 - 6527 El Dorado, Edificio Ricardo Galindo, Vía Ricardo J Alfaro, Quelquejeu, Panamá
Telephone: +507 2 300 169/341/260/482
Fax: +507 2 300 805
E-mail: sip@sinfo.net
Year established: 1972
Activities: gives legal advice; organises and participates in training, fairs, exhibitions, courses, seminars, conferences, etc; promotes Panama's foreign trade

Chief officers: Lic. Dario Pascal (President)
Membership: manufacturers, banks, couriers, database services, insurance companies, agricultural cooperatives, shippers, packers, etc
Publications:
• Balance Report (Informe Balance): *existence in the international market, updated and documented news about projects and actions - periodically*
• Exporters' Directory (Directorio de Exportadores): *information about Panama, the past year in business, directory of members, some statistics - annual*

Seafood Producers', Processors' and Exporters' Association
Asociación de Productores, Procesadores y Exportadores de Productos del Mar
Address: Vía Porras y Calle 52, Panamá
Telephone: +507 2 700 892
Fax: +507 2 700 892

Travel and Tourism Agencies' Association of Panama (APAVIT)
Asociación Panameña de Agencias de Viajes y Turismo
Address: Apartado Postal 55-1000, Paitilla
Telephone: +507 694 044
Fax: +507 614 592

PARAGUAY

Centre of Importers of Paraguay
Centro de Importadores
Address: Montevideo 671 c/E.V., Haedo, Asunción
Telephone: +595 21 490 291/411 295
Fax: +595 21 441 295
E-mail: centroimportador@quanta.com.py
Chief officers: Lic. Miguel Carrizosa Galiano (President)

Cotton Association of Paraguay
Cámara Algodonera del Paraguay
Address: Boggiani 4753, Asunción
Telephone: +595 21 600 739/605 445/609 272
Fax: +595 21 600 739/663 017
Chief officers: Roberto Lesli Antebi (President)
Membership: cotton growers and processors

Federation of Agroindustrial Exporters (FEDEXA)
Federación de Exportadores Agroindustriales
Address: Doggiani 4744, Asunción
Telephone: +595 21 609 272
Fax: +595 21 663 017
Activities: information service, legal advice, training and seminars, promotes exports from Paraguay
Chief officers: Lic. Juan Carlos Altieri (President)
Membership: export companies from agricultural sector

Federation of Production, Industry and Commerce (FEPRINCO)
Federación de la Producción, Industria y Comercio
Address: Edificio Unión Club, piso 3, Palma 751 y 15 de Agosto, Asunción
Telephone: +595 21 444 963/446 638
Fax: +595 21 446 638
Chief officers: Eduardo Talavera Goibru (President)
Membership: encompasses private manufacturing and trade enterprises

Paraguayan Association of Brewers (CAPAFACE)
Cámara Paraguaya de Fabricantes de Cerveza
Address: Av Juan Domingo Perón, K 10, Itá Enradmada, Lambaré, Asunción
Telephone: +595 21 212 836
Fax: +595 21 362 65
Chief officers: Blas N Riquelme (President)
Membership: brewers

Paraguayan Association of Cereals and Oils Producers (CAPECO)
Cámara Paraguaya de Exportadores de Cereales y Oleaginosas
Address: Avda Brasilia 840, Asunción
Telephone: +595 21 208 855/205 749/211 094
Fax: +595 21 213 971
Year established: 1980
Chief officers: José Luis Manzoni (President), José Omella (Vice President), Ignacio Santiviago (Manager)
Membership: 42 members, both producers and exporters

Paraguayan Association of Meat and Meat Derivatives Exporters
Cámara Paraguaya de Industriales Exportadores de Carne y Derivados
Address: Capitán Lombardo c/ Bañado, Asunción
Telephone: +595 21 293 735/201 534
Fax: +595 21 292 193/201 534
Chief officers: Ing Fernando Pfannl (President)
Membership: meat and meat products processors and exporters

Paraguayan Association of Travel and Tourism Agencies
Asociación Paraguaya de Agencias de Viajes y Turismo
Address: Edificio Helipuerto, 1er piso, oficina 106, Juan E O'Leary 650, Asunción
Telephone: +595 21 494 728/491 755
Fax: +595 21 491 755
Chief officers: César Adorno Casco (President)
Membership: travel agencies

Paraguayan Banks' Association
Asociación de Bancos del Paraguay
Address: Edificio Parapitil, Oficina 323, O'Leary 405, Asunción
Telephone: +595 21 490 485
Fax: +595 21 491 450

Paraguayan Codification Association
Asociación de Codificación de Paraguay (Asociación de Empresarios Cristianos)
Address: Antequera 611, esquina Azara, 1° piso, oficina 4, Asunción
Telephone: +595 21 442 108
Fax: +595 21 445 490
E-mail: eanpy@attmail.com

PERU

Association of Air-conditioning and Refrigeration (ATRAE)
Asociación de Refrigeración y Aire Acondicionado
Address: Av. La Marina 430, Pueblo Libre, Lima
Telephone: +51 1 462 2699
Fax: +51 1 461 9809
Chief officers: Ing. Luis Yamada

Association of Peruvian Exporters (ADEX)
Asociación de Exportadores del Perú
Address: Apdo 1806, Los Sauces 320, San Isidro, Lima 100
Telephone: +51 1 470 4485/471 8364/346 2530
Fax: +51 1 471 8364/712 478/346 1879
E-mail: postmast@adex.org.pe
Year established: 1973
Activities: technical advice, technical database, library, legal advice, training, courses, seminars, forums
Chief officers: Juan E Pendaris Perales (President), Carlos Bruce Montes de Oca (1st Vice President), Luis López Guerra (2nd Vice President), Julio Alvarado Mendoza (General Manager)
Structure: divisions for different industry sectors: agriculture, fishing, mining, textile, wood, paper, chemical, metals, manufacturing, commerce, handicrafts, cereals, coffee, fruit, horticulture, leather, jewellery, packaging, clothing, imports, etc.
Membership: exporters and importers from all sectors
Publications:
• Bulletin of the Andes Binational Chambers (Boletín Informativo de las Cámaras Binacionales Andinas): *bi-monthly*
• Bulletin of the Peruvian-Argentinean Chamber of Commerce (Boletín Informativo de las Cámaras de Comercio Peruano-Argentina): *quarterly*
• Expoagriculture Magazine (Revista Expoagro): *agricultural review of Peru - quarterly*
• Fishing Exports Magazine (Revista Expopesca): *a review of the fishing export industry of Peru - quarterly*
• International Law Magazine (Revista DFI, Distribución Física Internacional): *quarterly*
• Magazine and Bulletin of Academic Centres (CEADEX) (Revista y Boletín de los Centros Académicos): *quarterly*
• Peruvian Exporters' and Importers' Directory (Directorio de Exportadores e Importadores del Perú): *up-to-date information on Peruvian export products, manufacturers and import/export companies, overview of Peru's situation - annual*
• Peruvian Exporters' Bulletin (Boletín El Exportador Peruano): *weekly*
• Peruvian Wood Industries: *magazine - quarterly*

Association of Peruvian Market Research Companies
Asociación Peruana de Empresas de Investigación de Mercado
Address: República de Panamá 6380, Miraflores, Lima 18
Telephone: +51 14 452 846/982
Fax: +51 14 479 556
Chief officers: Alfredo Torres (President), Bernardo Verjovski (Vice President), Giovanna Peñaflor (Treasurer), Saúl Mankevich (Secretary)
Membership: 12 corporate members

Automobile Association of Peru
Asociación Automotriz del Perú
Address: PO Box 1248, Av. Dos de Mayo 299, San Isidro, Lima 27
Telephone: +51 1 440 4119/442 5673/440 0495
Fax: +51 1 442 8865
Telex: 25257
Chief officers: Antonio Meier Cresci (President), César Barreda Chávez (General Director)
Membership: 360 importers of cars and accessories

Clothing Manufacturers Committee
Comité de Prendas de Vestir
Address: Los Laureles 365, San Isidro, Lima
Telephone: +51 1 441 4759
Fax: +51 1 441 0984
Membership: clothing manufacturers
Notes: member of the International Apparel Federation

Foreign Press Association (APEP)

Asociación de Prensa Extranjera en el Perú
Address: Hotel Las Américas - Sala de Prensa Internacional
Lobby, Av. Benavides 415, Miraflores
Telephone: +51 1 446 5950
Fax: +51 1 446 5950
E-mail: apepsec@amauta.rcp.net.pe
Year established: 1964
Chief officers: Sally Bowen (Presidenta), María Luisa
Martínez (Secretaria)
Membership: 104 members

National Association of Bread and Bakery Manufacturers (ANIIP)

Asociación Nacional de la Industria del Pan y de la Pastelería
Address: Jr Emancipación 178 - 1A, La Florida, Cajamarca
Telephone: +51 4 442 4066 ext 134
Fax: +51 4 442 4071
Chief officers: Elvis Bustamante (Coordinator)
Membership: small, medium and large-scale bread and
pastry industries
Notes: affiliated to the Sociedad Nacional de Industrias

National Confederation of Private Business Institutions of Peru (CONFIEP)

Confederación Nacional de Instituciones Empresariales Privadas
del Perú
Address: Calle Vanderghan, 595, San Isidro, Lima
Telephone: +51 14 422 2675/442 9122/472 3195
Fax: +51 14 440 7702/441 5072
Web site: www.unired.net.pe/~confiep/
Year established: 1984
Chief officers: Arturo Woodman Pollit (President), Arturo Tello
Díaz (General Manager)
Membership: umbrella organisation: 21 professional
associations, 93 regional Chambers of Commerce, over
16,000 privately owned companies

National Fisheries Society (SNP)

Sociedad Nacional de Pesquería
Address: Calle Los Laureles No 381, San Isidro, Lima
Telephone: +51 1 442 3640/422 0724/44 7180/4418345
Fax: +51 1 442 7190
Chief officers: Javier Reátegui Roselló (President), Richard
Díaz González (General Manager)
Membership: central organisation of the the Peruvian fishing
industry

National Pharmaceutical Laboratories' Association (ALAFARPE)

Asociación Nacional de Laboratorios Farmacéuticos del Perú
Address: Calle 27, No 224, Urbanización Córpac, Lima 27
Telephone: +51 1 224 1486/2432/2433/2434
Fax: +51 1 224 1400
E-mail: alafarpe@rcp.net.pe
Chief officers: Manuel Podestá Ventura (President), Rafael
Fernández Stoll (Executive Director)
Membership: pharmaceutical laboratories

National Society of Exporters (SNE)

Sociedad Nacional de Exportadores
Address: Calle Bartolomé Herrera No 254, Miraflores, Lima
Telephone: +51 1 428 7840/446 4394/446 4355/446 3905
Fax: +51 1 446 7973
Web site: ekeko.rcp.net.pe/SNE/
Chief officers: Carlos Gilksman Latowicka (President), Luis
Chang Changfun (General Manager)
Membership: exporters

National Society of Industries (SNI)

Sociedad Nacional de Industrias
Address: Apdo 632, Los Laureles 365, San Isidro, Lima 27
Telephone: +51 1 440 8700/441 6560
Fax: +51 1 442 2573/403 395
Year established: 1896
Activities: international business missions; economic
research studies and surveys; training, seminars, courses,
conferences; legal advice on the following aspects: industrial
laws, labour laws, foreign trade laws, municipal laws, tax laws;
defence of trade associations; foreign trade; financing for
production, marketing and export credit insurance;
participation in non-commercial operations; publications;
Chief officers: Eduardo Farah Hayn (President), Guillermo
Iturriaga (General Manager), Emilio Navarro Castañeda
(Secretary)
Structure: organised into 80 autonomous Sectorial
Committees grouped in accordance with the International
Standard Industrial Classification. Each committee is
represented on the SNI Board of Directors by its
Chairman/President; SNI is structured by one general
assembly, a board of directors and an executive committee (1
Chairman, 1 Vice Chairman, 1 Secretary, 1 Deputy Secretary,
1 Treasurer, 1 Deputy Treasurer, 2 Members, 1 Past Chairman)
Membership: 2,500 industrial companies
Publications:
• Fortnightly Bulletin (Boletín Quincenal): *news bulletin
containing the latest events affecting the industry; in addition,
there are international and other comments related to the
industrial scene, such as the publication of laws and other
matters of general interest - fortnightly*
• Industrial Directory of Peru (Directorio Industrial del Perú):
*compact summary of domestic industrial products and
services - semi-annual*
• Peruvian Industry Review (Revista Industria Peruana):
*magazine containing topics the latest events affecting the
industry and the economy in general, as well as those related
to institutional policies and activities - monthly*

National Tourism Association (CANATUR)

Cámara Nacional de Turismo
Address: Santander 170 - Miraflores, Lima
Telephone: +51 1 422 7124/422 4954/446 2775
Fax: +51 1 446 2775/422 1278
E-mail: postmaster@canatur.org.pe
Web site: www.canatur.com
Activities: organises events, seminars and training courses;
promotes the tourism sector; represents the sector
nation-wide; provides administrative, economic and legal
information in relation to the tourist sector in Peru; maintains a
database of companies and individuals related to the industry;
liaises with the government
Chief officers: José Koechlin von Stein (President)
Membership: travel agencies, airlines, restaurants, hotels,
transport companies and other businesses as well as
individuals

Peruvian Banks' Association (ASBANC)

Asociación de Bancos del Perú
Address: Urbanización Córpac, Calle 41, Nº 975, San Isidro,
Lima
Telephone: +51 1 224 1715/1716/1718
Fax: +51 1 224 1707/224 1400
E-mail: postmaster@asbanc.org.pe
Activities: publishes and takes part in a variety of economic
and law studies in relation to banking, financial services and
taxation
Chief officers: Jorge Picasso Salinas (President), Lucrecia
Vivanco de French (General Manager)
Membership: banks

Peruvian Books Association
Cámara Peruana del Libro
Address: Av Cuba 247, Jeus Maria, Lima 11
Telephone: +51 14 472 9516
Fax: +51 14 265 0735
Chief officers: Mr JC Flores (General Secretary), Mr R Guerra (Director)

Peruvian Codes' Association (APC)
Asociación Peruana de Códigos
Address: Av Javier Prado Oeste 2150, San Isidro, Lima
Telephone: +51 1 221 1000
Fax: +51 1 440 0270
E-mail: apc@amauta.rcp.net.pe

Peruvian Construction Industry Association (CAPECO)
Cámara Peruana de la Construcción
Address: Av Paseo de la República n° 571, 12° piso, Lima
Telephone: +51 14 329 217
Fax: +51 14 330 188
E-mail: coll@capeco.org.pe
Web site: ekeko.rcp.net.pe/capeco/
Year established: 1958
Activities: organises congresses, conventions, forums and seminars; carries out research on the industry; maintains a database of economic statistics, pricing of materials, wages and prices readjustment, building prices, bidding advertisements, legal reports etc.
Chief officers: Ing. José Ortíz Rivera (President), Ing.Pablo Coll Calderón (General Manager)
Structure: Asamblea General de Asociados Junta General de Delegados, Directorio (in charge of management and administration of the Chamber)
Membership: construction companies, construction material producers' and traders', promotion and credit entities, and all institutions related to the sector
Publications:
• Anuarium de la Construcción: *major report on the activities of the construction sector - annual*
• Informativo Quincenal
• Revista "Construcción e Industria": *two attached publications "Indicadores Económicos" (Economics Indicators) and "Cuaderno Técnico" (Technical Notebook) - monthly*

Peruvian Newspapers' Association (ADIPE)
Asociación de Diarios del Perú
Address: Casilla Postal 270163, Lima 27
Telephone: +51 14 475 6420
Fax: +51 14 44 4901
Chief officers: J Pablo Caero-Egusquizas (General Director)

Peruvian Radio and Television Association (ARTV)
Asociación de Radio y Televisión del Perú
Address: Roma 140, San Isidro, Lima
Telephone: +51 1 470 3434
Fax: +51 1 472 5058
Chief officers: Humberto Maldonado Balbín (President), Daniel Linares Bazán (Executive Director)

Travel Agencies' Association of Peru
Asociación Peruana de Agencias de Viajes
Address: Antonio Roca 121, Santa Beatriz, Lima
Telephone: +51 4 331 111
Fax: +51 4 337 610

PHILIPPINES

Advertising Boards of the Philippines (Adboard)
Address: 2nd Floor, L & F Building, 107 Aguirre Street, Legaspi Village, Makati, Metro Manila
Telephone: +63 2 818 6158/817 7724
Fax: +63 2 818 7109
Chief officers: Winston A Marbella (Chairman), Andre S Kahn (Vice Chairman), Francisco S Zaldarriaga (Treasurer), Josie Tan-Magtoto (Secretary)
Publications:
• AdSpend: *breakdown of adspend by medium and by product category*

Association of Accessories' Manufacturers and Exporters of the Philippines
Address: c/o UDD Exports, #20 Alta Vista Drive, Loyola Heights, QC
Telephone: +63 2 921 1634
Fax: +63 2 921 1626
Chief officers: Mr Uldarico Deloso Jr. (President)

Association of Accredited Advertising Agencies - Philippines (4As)
Address: c/o Adboard Office, 2nd Floor, L & F B, 107 Aguirre Street, Legaspi Village, Makati, Metro Manila
Telephone: +63 2 818 6157/813 4397
Fax: +63 2 818 6157
Chief officers: Emily A Abrera (President), Francisco Roman (Chairman)

Association of Broadcasters in the Philippines (KBP)
Address: 6th Floor, LTA Building, 118 Perea Street, Legaspi Village, Makati, Metro Manila
Telephone: +63 2 815 1990-93/812 5913
Fax: +63 2 815 1989
Chief officers: Jose Escarer Jnr (President), Butch Canoy (Vice President), Eduardo Montilla (Chairman), Rino Basilio (Vice President of Television), Adrian Sisor (Secretary)

Association of Consolidated Automotive Parts Producers Inc. (ACAPP)
Address: 2nd Floor, Guieb Building, 961 President Quirino Avenue, Malate, Manila 1004
Telephone: +63 2 522 0533
Fax: +63 2 525 6664
Chief officers: George C Lim (President), Harald H. Hoffmann (Vice President), Fernando A. Romillano (Corporate Secretary)
Structure: President, Vice President, Corporate Secretary, Tresurer, Board of Directors, Technical Committee, Membership Committee
Notes: member of the Philppine Chamber of Commerce and Industry, Federation of Philippine Industry, Philippine Automotive Federation

Association of Philippine Leather Goods Exporters and Manufacturers (APLEM)
Address: 6157 Einthoven St. Palanan, Makati, Metro Manila 1235
Telephone: +63 2 831 8771-73
Fax: +63 2 833 3022
Chief officers: Vivian T. Uy (President)

Association of the Footwear Industries of the Philippines
Address: c/o Paramount Vinyl Products, 56 G de Jesus Street, Caloocan, Metro Manila

Telephone: +63 2 361 2760/8874
Fax: +63 2 361 7361
Chief officers: George T Barcelon (President); Cecille S Dino (Secretary)

Bankers' Association of the Philippines
Address: 11th Floor, Sagittarius Building, Salcedo Village, Makati, Metro Manila
Telephone: +63 2 832 0596/810 3859
Fax: +63 2 810 3860/812 2870
Chief officers: Rafael Buenaventura (President)

Book Development Association of the Philippines
Address: c/o Reyes Publishing, Mariwasa Building, 717 Aurora Blvd., Quezon, Metro Manila 1100
Telephone: +63 2 721 7492, 721 2041
Fax: +63 2 721 8782
Chief officers: Louie O. Reyes (President)

Ceramic Exporters' and Manufacturers' Association
Address: Suite 201 Fedman Suit, Salcedo Street, Legaspi Vill., Makati, M. M. 1229
Telephone: +63 2 813 5303-04
Fax: +63 2 813 5303
Chief officers: Renato M Pleno (President)

Ceramics Association of the Philippines
Address: c/o Saniwares 2/F Feliza Building, 108 Herrera Street, Legaspi, Makati, Metro Manila 1229
Telephone: +63 2 892 9801
Fax: +63 2 818 4884
Chief officers: Benito Chua (President)

Chamber of Furniture Industries of the Philippines (CFIP)
Address: Unit H, 9th Floor, Strata 100 Building, Emerald Avenue, Pasig, Metro Manila
Telephone: +63 2 631 2834/632 9007
Fax: +63 2 631 2977
Activities: the Association compiles some basic statistics on the Philippine furniture industry
Chief officers: Myma Natividad (President), Ms Malu Balano (Executive Director)

Chamber of Philippine Drug Manufacturers and Distributors Inc.
Address: C/O Asia Health Systems Inc., 377 Florida Street, East Greenhills, Mandaluyong City
Telephone: +63 2 700 031
Chief officers: Mr Benny P. De Guzman (President)

Chamber of the Cosmetics Industry of the Philippines
Address: Ste. 281, G/F Cosmopolitan Tower Cond., 134 Valero Street, Salcedo Vill., Makati City, M. M. 1227
Telephone: +63 2 741 4511/16
Fax: +63 2 732 0568
Chief officers: Ms. Melinda Pellicer (President)

Chemical Industries' Association of the Philippines
Address: c/o Mabuhay Vynil Corporation, 4th Floor, Gammon Centre, 126 Alfaro Street, Salcedo Village, Makati, Metro Manila
Telephone: +63 2 815 2088
Fax: +63 2 816 4785
Chief officers: Oscar A Barrera (President)

Coffee Exporters' Association of the Philippines
Address: Room 708, National Life Insurance Building, Ayala Avenue, Makati, Metro Manila
Telephone: +63 2 816 2942
Fax: +63 2 810 0543
Chief officers: Jose H Mercado (President)

Computer Distributors' and Dealers' Association (COMDDAP)
Address: 7/F SEDCCO 1 Building, Legaspi Cor. Rada Sts, Legaspi Village, Makati City
Telephone: +63 2 810 3814/815 6531/892 7947
Fax: +63 2 815 6531
Chief officers: Mr Wilton C. Ngo (President)

Confederation of Garments Exporters of the Philippines, Inc. (CONGEP)
Address: Suite 103, Mareic Building, 121 Tordesillas Street, Salcedo Village, Makati, Metro Manila
Telephone: +63 2 631 5213/817 6377/819 0373
Fax: +63 2 818 0224
Year established: 1985
Chief officers: Donald G Dee (President)
Membership: 56 regular members

Confederation of Small and Medium Enterprises
Address: Ground Floor, ABC Building, 2251 Pasong Tamo Street, Makati, Metro Manilla
Telephone: +63 2 811 2234 to 45

Consumer Electronics Products Manufacturers' Association
Address: c/o Solid Corporation, Solid House, 2285 Pasong Tamo Ext, Makati, Metro Manila
Fax: +63 2 816 0130
Chief officers: Peter Sen (President)

Electronic Industries' Association of the Philippines Inc.
Address: 12A, Project Cond. Building, J.P. Rizal Srreet, Project 4, Quenzon City
Telephone: +63 2 921 7563/922 2250/9226487
Fax: +63 2 922 8709
Chief officers: Mr Mario M. Rivero J.R. (President)

Employers' Confederation of the Philippines
Address: ECCH Building, 4th Floor, 355 Sen Gil J Puyat Ave, Makati, Manila
Telephone: +63 2 816 3813
Year established: 1975
Publications:
• Philippine Employer: *monthly*

Fashion Accessories Association of the Philippines (FAMA)
Address: Pelbel Building, Suite 303, 2019 Shaw Boulevard, Pasig, Metro Manila
Telephone: +63 2 673 7884
Fax: +63 2 631 4581
Membership: 27

Federation of Electrical and Electronics Suppliers and Manufacturers of the Philippines Inc.
Address: Room 213, Eva Building, 239 J. Luna Street, Binondo, Manila 1006

Telephone: +63 2 241 9501-4
Fax: +63 2 241 6949
Chief officers: George Go (President)

Federation of Fishing Associations
Address: 4/F Champ Building, Bonifacio Drive, Port Area, Manila 1018
Telephone: +63 2 481 929/ 477 888
Chief officers: Francisco Laurel (President)

Filipino-Chinese Bakery Association
Address: 1967 Rizal Avenue, Corner Camarines Street, Santa Cruz, Manila 1003
Telephone: +63 2 263 374/79/215 380
Fax: +63 2 215 380
Chief officers: Narciso Tan (President)

Financial Executives Institute of the Philippines Inc.
Address: c/o Secretariat, Room 310, 3rd Floor, Atrium Building, Makati Avenue, Makati, Metro Manila
Telephone: +63 2 817 5694/7464
Fax: +63 2 817 1338
Chief officers: Dennis Desena (President)

Footwear and Cooperation Development Office
Address: Marikina Municipal Building, Marikina, Metro Manilla
Telephone: +63 2 984 0027
Fax: +63 2 947 5228
Chief officers: Mr Delfin Estanislao

Foreign Buyers' Association of the Philippines (FOBAP)
Address: Room 514, 5th Floor, Cityland III, Corner Herrera/Ornaza/Esteban Streets, Legaspi Village, Makati, Metro Manila 1229
Telephone: +63 2 893 5126/1670
Fax: +63 2 817 4384
Activities: provides both pre and post order services to foreign buyers, and provides assistance to local manufacturers in meeting orders
Chief officers: Rodolfo C Mallari (President)
Membership: 72 regular, 14 associate members

Garment Business Association of the Philippines (GBAP)
Address: Room 2203, Cityland 10, Tower 1, H.V. Dela Costa Street Cor., Ayala Avenue, Makati City
Telephone: +63 2 819 1088 to 89
Fax: +63 2 819 1088
Chief officers: Dayana H.Santos (President)

Glass Manufacturers' Association of the Philippines
Address: C/O Union Glass and Container Corp., E. Rodriguez Junior Avenue, Bo. Ugong, Pasig City, M. M. 1604
Telephone: +63 2 673 1170-72
Fax: +63 2 673 6852
Chief officers: Peter M. Javier (President)

Guild of Philippine Jewellers Inc.
Address: C/O Union Glass and Container Corporation, E.Rodriguez Jr Avenue, Bo. Ugong, Pasig City
Telephone: +63 2 673 7440
Fax: +63 2 682 3083/673 1173
Year established: 1986
Chief officers: Mr Peter M. Javier (President)

Home Textiles Association of the Philippines
Address: c/o Q.C. Embroidery House Inc, Cecileville Building, 1205 Quezon Avenue, Quezon City
Telephone: +63 2 971 257/976 735/982 290
Fax: +63 2 982 290
Chief officers: Amparo O Medina (President)

Hotel and Restaurant Association of the Philippines (HRAP)
Address: Room 205, Regina Building, Trassiera corner Aguirre Streets, Legaspi Village, Makati, Metro Manila
Telephone: +63 2 815 4659/4661
Fax: +63 2 810 3821/815 4663
Telex: 66146 INFORM PU
Chief officers: Mr Leopoldo H. Prieto. Jr (President)

Information Technology Association of the Philippines
Address: Unit T-14, 3/F Milelong Building, Amorsolo Street, Legaspi Village, Makati, M. M. 1229
Telephone: +63 2 892 8895
Fax: +63 2 810 7391
Chief officers: German T. Gamboa (President)

Institute of Management Consultants of the Philippines (IMPHIL)
Address: C/O Valdez Consultant, 10/F Manila Bank Building, Ayala Avenue, Makati City
Telephone: +63 2 810 1078/818 1987/892 1993
Fax: +63 2 810 1024
Chief officers: MS Connie L. Manuel (President)

Lamps and Allied Electrical Products Manufacturers of the Philippines
Address: 3/F Ajinomoto Building, 331 Sen. G. Puyal Avenue, Makati, M. M. 1200
Telephone: +63 2 895 6081
Fax: +63 2 890 6663
Chief officers: Cayetano Ferreria (President)

Management Association of the Philippines
Address: 4th Floor, Ayala Life Building, Ayala Avenue, Makati, Metro Manila 1226
Telephone: +63 2 810 0721/0717
Fax: +63 2 817 7794
Chief officers: Edward S. Go (President)

Packaging Institute of the Philippines
Address: Room 216, 2nd Floor, Comfoods Building, Sen Gil Puyat Avenue, Makati, Metro Manila
Telephone: +63 2 817 2936/844 5661-69
Fax: +63 2 817 2936
Chief officers: Gonzalo U Marte (Chairman); Bemardino Paco (President)

Petroleum Association of the Philippines
Address: C/O 7/F Basic Petroleum Building, C. Palanca Jr St, Legaspi Village, Makati City
Telephone: +63 2 817 3329/631 8151/631 1801
Fax: +63 2 817 0191

Pharmaceutical and Healthcare Association of the Philippines (PHAP)
Address: PO Box 2248 MCPO, Unit 502, 1 Corporate Plaza, 845 Pasay Road, Makati, Metro Manila
Telephone: +63 2 815 0325/816 7334/ 816 7373/816 0618
Fax: +63 2 819 2702

Year established: 1946
Activities: intermediary and information services
Chief officers: Leo P Wassmer Jr (Executive Vice President and Chief Executive Officer); Jaime V. Castro (President)
Membership: 85 members, multinationals and local companies
Publications:
• Healthcare: *quarterly*
• Philippine Pharmaceutical Industry Fact Book: *comprehensive statistics and in-depth commentary on the Philippine Pharmaceutical Industry. Includes market size by volume and value, imports and exports, distribution, regional breakdowns, R&D, advertising expenditure, brand information etc. - triennial*

Pharmaceutical Association

Address: 10/F Stanisco Towers, 999 Pedro Gil cor. Agoncillo Sts., Ermita, Manila 1000
Telephone: +63 2 586 977/509 006
Fax: +63 2 526 4739
Chief officers: Lourdes T. Eschauz (President)

Philippine Article Numbering Council (PANC)

Address: #20 San Raffle Street, Bo. Kapitolyo, Passig City
Telephone: +63 2 893 2830
Fax: +63 2 892 4612
E-mail: panc@ibm.net

Philippine Association of Embroidery and Apparel Exporters (PAEAE)

Address: 30 San Pedro Street, Barrio Capitolyo, Pasig, Metro Manila
Telephone: +63 2 631 4667
Fax: +63 2 635 4446
Chief officers: Jose Montano Jr (President)

Philippine Association of Finance Companies Inc.

Address: G/F PCI Bank Building, Corinthian Gardens, Ortigas Avenue, Quenon City
Telephone: +63 2 772 654
Fax: +63 2 772 654
Chief officers: Mr Ricardo M. Della Tore (President)

Philippine Association of Meat Processors Inc.

Address: Suite 204 Sunrise Cond., Ortigas Avenue, Greenhills, San Juan, Metro Manila 1500
Telephone: +63 2 721 1813/721 2674
Fax: +63 2 721 2365
Chief officers: Nilo Penaflor (President)

Philippine Association of Service Exporters (PASEi)

Address: Ground Floor, RBAP Building, Andres Soriano Jr, Cor Arzobispo Sts, Intramuros, Manilla 1002
Telephone: +63 2 528 0315/19, 528 0324
Fax: +63 2 528 0315/19
Chief officers: Mr Loreto B.Soriano (President)

Philippine Automotive Association (PAA)

Address: Mantrade Building, EDSA Cor., Pasong Tamo, Makati City, M. M. 1231
Telephone: +63 2 843 7689
Fax: +63 2 816 0115
Activities: compiles statistics on new car sales in the Philippines
Chief officers: Francisco Aguilar (President)

Philippine Cable TV Association (PCTA)

Address: Room 203 - Centrum II Condo, 150 Valero St, Salcedo, Makati, Metro Manila
Telephone: +63 2 815 4406/815 0861-63
Fax: +63 2 817 5462
Telex: 63436
Year established: 1964
Chief officers: Reuel Dominguez (Chairman), Edmund Lopez (Secretary)

Philippine Chamber of Food Manufacturers

Address: Room 1216, 12/F Cityland X Tower II, Ayala Avenue cor. H. V. Dela Costa Street, Makati City, Metro Manila 1226
Telephone: +63 2 893 3893, 892 4163
Fax: +63 2 893 3893
Chief officers: Vicente Lim Jr. (President)

Philippine Chamber of the Handicraft Industry

Address: 544 3rd Street, Bacood, Sta. Mesa, Manila 1016
Telephone: +63 2 714 6647
Fax: +63 2 714 6651
Chief officers: Benjamin F.Kalalo Jr (President)

Philippine Coconut Oil Producers' Association

Address: 7th Floor, Citibank Centre, Paseo de Roxas, Makati, Metro Manila
Telephone: +63 2 892 4904
Fax: +63 2 819 1868
Telex: 22 630 AVA
Chief officers: Jeremias B Benico (Chairman); Jose Luis V Agcaoili (Secretary)

Philippine Electrical, Electronics and Allied Industries Federation

Address: 3rd Floor, Union Ajinomoto Building, 331 Sen. Gil Puyat Avenue, Makati City
Telephone: +63 2 876 081/89
Fax: +63 2 816 0402
Chief officers: MR Peter R. Sen (Chairman)

Philippine Electronics' and Telecommunications' Federation Inc.

Address: 3/F Electra House Building, Esteban Cor, Herera Sts, Legaspi Village, Makati City
Telephone: +63 2 816 0001/813 6398/815 8921/816 3101
Fax: +63 2 813 6397
Chief officers: Fortunato Pertas (President)

Philippine Exporters' Confederation Inc. (PHILEXPORT)

Address: Ground Floor, South Side, Philippine International Convention Centre,, CCP Complex, Roxas Boulevard, Pasay City, Manila
Telephone: +63 2 833 2531 to 34
Fax: +63 2 831 3707/831 0231
Year established: 1984
Activities: offers a range of services including: advisory and facilitation services; a trade reference library; Tradelink (computerised trade information system); training and technical advice; buyer-seller matching; basic promotion services; policy research and warehouse facilities
Chief officers: Mr Sergio Luis Ortiz Jr (President)
Membership: 2,000 members accounting for over 75% of the the total export earnings of the Philippines
Notes: private non-profit organisation and the largest exporters' organisation in the Philippines

Philippine Food Exporters' and Processors' Organisation (PHILFOODEX)
Address: Ground Floor, PICC Complex, Roxas Boulevard, Manila 1000
Telephone: +63 2 832 0309/480/7532/7512
Fax: +63 2 831 3707/0231
Chief officers: Edward David (President)

Philippine Industrial Estates Association
Address: c/o Carmelray Development Corporation, 7th Floor, Rufino Plaza, 6784 Ayala Avenue, Makati, Metro Manila
Telephone: +63 2 818 1831
Fax: +63 2 817 5051
Chief officers: Roberto Jose L Castillo (President)

Philippine Marketing Association, Inc.
Address: Cityland 10 Tower I, Unit 2414, Salcedo St. Cor., Ayala Avenue, Makati City, Manila
Telephone: +63 2 893 7127/982 3144/982 3291
Fax: +63 2 892 3261
Year established: 1954
Activities: government liaison; education and training
Membership: 324 members

Philippine Publishers' Association
Address: 84 P Florentino Street, Quenzon City
Telephone: +63 2 711 5702
Fax: +63 2 711 5412
Chief officers: Mr DD Buhain (Secretary), Mr JE Sibal (Executive Director)

Philippine Retailers' Association
Address: 2/F Collins Bldg, 167 EDSA, Mandaluyong City
Telephone: +63 2 532 5644/532 5677
Fax: +63 2 531 3894/1005
Chief officers: Evelyn Balmeo Salire (Secretary General)
Publications:
• Overview of the Phillipine Retail Industry: *detailed statistics and commentary on retailing in the Philippines including: number and type of retail establishment; gross value added to the retail trade; retail output vs GDP; personal consumer expenditure; retail sales; number of establishments broken down by sector of activity. Compiled from various sources - every 2 years*

Philippine Rubber Industries Association Inc.
Address: 78 Sgt. Rivera Street, Quezon City, M. M. 1400
Telephone: +63 2 641 5658 to 59
Fax: +63 2 641 4159
Chief officers: Ms Basiliza Ho (President)

Philippine Sugar Association
Address: 14th Floor, Pacific Bank Building, Ayala Avenue, Makati, Metro Manila
Telephone: +63 2 815 1279/810 1291
Fax: +63 2 810 1291
Chief officers: Jose Ma T Zabaleta (President)

Philippine Toy and Novelty Manufacturers' Association Inc.
Address: 1116 Kalayaan Ave., Guadalupe, Makati City
Telephone: +63 2 843 1884
Fax: +63 2 812 2757
Chief officers: Anicetas de Jesus (President)

Philippine Travel Agencies' Association (PTTA)
Address: Ste. 316 Secretariat Building PICC, CCP Cplx, Roxas Blvd., Metro Manila 1000
Telephone: +63 2 832 0309
Fax: +63 2 833 1462
Chief officers: Raquel Calma-Nakayama (President)

Philippine Wood Products Association (PWPA)
Address: 3rd Floor, LTA Condominium Building, 118 Perea Street, Legaspi Village, Makati, Metro Manila 1229
Telephone: +63 2 817 6751/6884-85
Fax: +63 2 817 6884
Chief officers: Ernesto Sanvictores (Chairman)

Philippines Association of Batteries Manufacturing, INC
Address: Yuasa Building, Ramcar Cmpd., Sct, Santiago cor. Marathon Street, Quezon, M. M. 1100
Telephone: +63 2 924 2928
Fax: +63 2 921 7238
Chief officers: Lourdes T. Eschauz (President)

Philippines Association of Electrical Industries, INC
Address: Ste. 712 Bank of PI Building, Plaza Cervantes, Binondo, Manila 1006
Telephone: +63 2 242 1144
Chief officers: Jimmy Ty (President)

Philippines Association of Multinational Companies, INC
Address: Room 1015 Cityland Cond. X Tower I, Dela Costa Street, Makati, M. M. 1200
Telephone: +63 2 810 8307/816 1549
Fax: +63 2 810 8307
Chief officers: Shameen Qurachi (President)

Philippines Association of Security Brokers and Dealers, INC.
Address: Unit 980 9/F SEC Building, EDSA, Greenhills, Mandaluyong, M. M. 1556
Telephone: +63 2 700 384
Fax: +63 2 700 384
Chief officers: Atty. Edgardo V. Guevara (President)

Philippines Association of Supermarkets Inc.
Address: Room 311, Mariwasa Building, Aurora Boulevard, Cubao, Quezon City
Telephone: +63 2 815 4107
Chief officers: Mr Jose A. Albert

Philippines Association the Record Industry
Address: Suite 1020 V. V. Soliven Building, EDSA, San Juan, M. M. 1554
Telephone: +63 2 722 8014/725 0770
Fax: +63 2 725 0786
Chief officers: Danilo Olivarez (President)

Philippines Plastics Industries Association, Inc.
Address: Rear Block, Solid Bank Building, 317 Rizal Avenue Ext. Grace Park, Kalookan, M. M. 1400
Telephone: +63 2 361 1160
Fax: +63 2 361 1168
Chief officers: Benjamin Co (President)

Printing Industries Association of the Philippines Inc.

Address: 1945 M Adriatico St, Malate, Manila 1004
Telephone: +63 2 521 4049
Fax: +63 2 521 4049
Chief officers: Jose Sandejas Sr (President)

Pulp and Paper Manufacturers' Association Inc.

Address: 12/F Room 1202, 1010 Building, A. Mabini Street, Ermita 1000, Manila
Telephone: +63 2 522 4266
Fax: +63 2 522 4266
Telex: 23313 NPC PH
Activities: promotes and protects the pulp and paper industry
Chief officers: Pedrito M Gragon (Chairman); Francisco P Monge (President); Cesar R Paglinawan (1st Vice-President)

Resort Association of the Philippines (RAPI)

Address: c/o LPL Towers, Suite 800, 112 Legaspi Street, Legaspi Village, Makati, Metro Manila
Telephone: +63 2 818 1083/817 6723
Fax: +63 2 810 3060

Soap and Detergents Association of the Philippines

Address: 7/F SGV II Building, 6758 Ayala Avenue, Makati, Metro Manila 1226
Telephone: +63 2 819 3011
Fax: +63 2 817 4193
Chief officers: Graeme Lane (President)

Textile Mills Association of the Philippines Inc. (TMAP)

Address: Ground Floor, Alexander House, 132 Amorsolo Street, Legaspi Village, Makati City 1229
Telephone: +63 2 818 6605/6601
Fax: +63 2 818 3107
Year established: 1956
Activities: promotes the modernisation and expansion of the Philippine textile industry; keeps track of developments which affect the industry; liaises with foreign groups involved in textiles and represents the local textile industry in such organisations as the Asian Federation of Textile Industries and Cotton Council International; organises seminars covering the latest developments in textile technology, as well as colour and fashion forecasts for textiles and garments; TMAP also maintains a library of the textile industry and houses the US Cotton Information Centre for the reference of its members and the general public
Chief officers: Hermenegildo C Zayco (President)
Membership: 23 textile manufacturer companies

Textile Producers Association of the Philippines, Inc.

Address: Room 513 Downtown Centre, 516 Q. Paredes street, Binondo, manila 1006
Telephone: +63 2 241 1162/241 1144
Chief officers: lorenzo Ku (President)

Tin Can Manufacturers Association of the Philippines, INC

Address: 1 Kalantiao cor. 20th Avenue, Cubao, Quezon, M. M. 1109
Telephone: +63 2 911 6504
Fax: +63 2 911 7036-39
Chief officers: Conrado S. Tiongson (President)

Tuna Canners' Association of the Philippines

Address: 106 Cabrera Building, 1130 Timog Avenue, Quezon City
Telephone: +63 2 921 2401

Tyre Manufacturers Association of the Philippines

Address: C/O Sime Darby Philippines, Ayala Ave Cor., Malugay Street, Makati City
Telephone: +63 2 844 9431
Fax: +63 2 817 9868

Wine and Spirits Importers' Association of the Philippines

Address: 7/F Builders Centre Building, 170 Salcedo St, Legaspi Village, Makati City
Telephone: +63 2 812 5233/818 5034
Chief officers: Joaquin F. Porta (President)

Wine Merchants' Association

Address: Tamaraw Studio Building, 2253 Aurora Boulevard, Pasay, M. M. 1300
Telephone: +63 2 832 2624
Fax: +63 2 832 3436
Chief officers: Ralph L. Joseph (President)

Wooden Gifts and Accessories Manufacturers' Association Inc. (WOODTAG)

Address: 6 South Bayview Drive, Sunset Village, Parañaque, Metro Manilla 1700
Telephone: +63 2 831 1316, 832 1633, 831 5355
Fax: +63 2 831 4806
Chief officers: Edgardo P. Oilvares (President)

POLAND

Article Numbering Association (EAN Poland)

Address: c/o Institute of Warehouse Management, Ul. Estkowskiego 6, 61-755 Poznan
Telephone: +48 61 527 681
Fax: +48 61 526 376
E-mail: ckk@ilim.poznan.pl

Chamber for Packaging

Address: ul. Konstancinska 11, PL-02-942 Warsaw
Telephone: +48 22 422 011
Fax: +48 22 422 303
Activities: liaison with the administration at all levels, collaborates with Polish, foreign and international professional organisations, associations and institutions, provides contact with both Polish and foreign partners
Chief officers: Jan Lekszycki (President)
Membership: over 130 companies, institutions and organisations dealing with packaging
Publications:
• Packaging Bulletin: *bimonthly*

Chamber of the Chemical Industry

Address: ul.Zurawia 6/12, PL-00-926 Warsaw
Telephone: +48 22 625 3178/629 8651
Fax: +48 22 625 3178
Chief officers: K. Chmielewski

Chamber of the Polish Book Industry

Address: ul Miodowa 10, PL-00-251 Warsaw
Telephone: +48 22 31 05 16
Fax: +48 22 26 71 63
Chief officers: Grzegorz Boguta (President), Ms RM Greda (Director)

Chamber of Tourism
Address: ul. Wierzbowa 9/11, PL-00-094 Warsaw
Telephone: +48 22 827 0166/622 8325
Fax: +48 22 621 7025
Chief officers: Wlodzimierz W Sukiennik (President)

Pharmaceutical Industry Association
Address: ul. Czarnieckego 48, PL-01-548 Warsaw
Telephone: +48 22 392 080
Fax: +48 22 392 080
Chief officers: Irena Rej (President)

Polish Association of Newspaper Publishers
Address: ul. Foksal 3/5, 00-366 Warsaw
Telephone: +48 22 27 87 18/277221
Fax: +48 11 27 87 18
Chief officers: Ms Anna Smolka (Managing Director)

Polish Franchise Association
Address: ul. Szpitalna 1 lok/ 5, 00-020 Warsaw
Telephone: +48 22 680 3039 ext 120/123
Fax: +48 22 625 6956
Chief officers: Jolanta Kramarz (Chairman)

Polish National Committee of International Dairy Federation
Address: c/o Olsztyn University of Agriculture and Technology, ul. Oczapowskiego 2, 10-957 Olsztyn
Telephone: +48 89 523 3650
Fax: +48 89 527 3908/523 3650/523 3402
E-mail: babuch@moskit.art.olsztyn.pl
Chief officers: Dr Andrzej Babuchowski (Secretary)

Polish Soap and Detergents Industry Association
Address: Ul. Marzalkowska 84/92, Pl-00 514 Warsaw
Telephone: +48 22 629 5976
Fax: +48 22 621 8466
Chief officers: Mr Andrzej Malina

Wool Federation
Address: ul.Klielecka 7, 81-303 Gdynia
Telephone: +48 58 209 501
Fax: +48 58 216 923
Telex: 054328

PORTUGAL

Adhesives Manufacturers' and Retailers' Association
Associação da Indústria e Comércio de Colas e Similares
Address: Avenida Guerra Junqueiro, 8,2°-E, P - 1000 Lisboa
Telephone: +351 1 849 4502
Fax: +351 1 849 4502

Association of Confectioners and Dairies of Northern Portugal
Associação das Confeitarias Pastelarias e Leitarias do Norte
Address: Rua de Fernandes Tomas 235, P-4000 Oporto
Telephone: +351 2 578 055
Fax: +351 2 510 3588
Membership: retail confectioners

Association of Cosmetics, Toiletries and Essential Oils Manufacturers
Associação dos Industriais de Cosmética, Perfumaria e Higiene Corporal e Oleos Essenciais
Address: Av António José d'Almeida, 7 - 2°, P-1000 Lisbon
Telephone: +351 1 799 1550
Fax: +351 1 799 1551
Year established: 1975
Activities: statistics, seminars and conferences
Chief officers: Engª Ana Maria Couras (Director General)
Membership: ca. 120 cosmetics manufacturers and importers
Publications:
● Bulletin (Boletim): *statistical information on the sector*

Association of Gold and Silversmiths and Jewellery Manufacturers of Northern Portugal (AIORN)
Associação dos Industriais de Ourivesaria e Relojoaria do Norte
Address: Avenida Rodrigues de Freitas 204, P-4000 Oporto
Telephone: +351 2 579 161/162/163
Fax: +351 2 573 292
Year established: 1943
Activities: compiles industry statistics; legal and economic advice; information centre; participation in national and international fairs; technical courses
Chief officers: Dr António Carlos Dias (Secretary General), David Garrido (Assistant Secretary General)
Membership: 636 (companies and individuals); these include gold and silversmiths and jewellery manufacturers
Publications:
● Directory of Members: *contact details and product information - annual*
● Newsletter (Boletim): *business opportunities, information about jewellery fairs, legislation applicable to the sector, etc. - regularly*

Association of Importers and Stockists of Chemical and Pharmaceutical Products
Associação dos Importadores Armazenistas de Produtos Químicos e Farmacéuticos
Address: Rua Faria Gimarães 679, P-4200 Oporto
Telephone: +351 2 551 0148

Association of Margarine and Vegetable Oils' Manufacturers (AMIGA)
Associação dos Industriais de Margarinas e Gorduras Alimentares
Address: Av António José d'Almeida 7, 2, P-1000 Lisbon
Telephone: +351 1 799 1550
Fax: +351 1 3799 1551
Year established: 1975
Activities: gives legal and technical advice and support; promotes studies and disseminates sector information and statistica data
Chief officers: Dr Luís Mesquita Dias (President), Dr Carlos M. Soares Marques (Vice President), Engª Ana Maria Couras (Director General)
Membership: 5 margarine and vegetable oils manufacturers and importers
Publications:
● Boletim Estatístico: *statistics*
Notes: no publications produced

Association of Soap, Detergents and Cleaning Products Manufacturers (AISDPCL)
Associação dos Industriais de Sabões, Detergentes e Produtos de Conservação e Limpeza
Address: Av António José d'Almeida 7, 2, P-1000 Lisbon
Telephone: +351 1 799 1550
Fax: +351 1 799 1551
Year established: 1975
Activities: gives legal advice and support; promotes studies

and disseminates sector information and statistical data
Chief officers: Dr Alberto da Ponte (President), Dr A. Escaja
Gonçalves, Engª Ana Maria Couras (Director General)
Membership: 47 soap, detergent and cleaning product
manufacturers and importers
Notes: no publications produced

Association of the Cereal and Oil Seed Stockists, Traders and Importers (ACICO)
Associação de Armazenistas, Comerciantes e Importadores de
Cereais e Oleaginosos
Address: Rua Braancamp 14 - 1º esq, P-1250 Lisbon
Telephone: +351 1 386 2896/2209
Fax: +351 1 386 4268
Year established: 1985
Activities: statistics, contacts
Membership: 16 warehouses, traders and importers of
cereals and oilseeds
Publications:
• Membership List

Association of the Glass Packaging Manufacturers (AIVE)
Associação dos Industriais de Vidrio de Embalagem
Address: Largo de Andaluz 16 - 1º dto, P-1050 Lisbon
Telephone: +351 1 354 9810
Fax: +351 1 354 9581
Chief officers: H Salles da Fonseca (Secretary General),
Manuel Faiao (Labour Matters), D Arlete (Sales)

Association of the Traders and Bottlers of Wines and Spirits from Northern Portugal (ANCEVE)
Associação do Norte de Comerciantes e Engarrafadores de
Vinhos e Bebidas Espirituosas
Address: Urbaniz Raione, Rua do Salgueiral 86, 2º pt 8,
P-4200 Oporto
Telephone: +351 2 597 055
Fax: +351 2 594 760
Activities: compiles sector statistics; market research studies
and provides an information service
Membership: producers, bottlers, merchants and exporters of
wines and spirits from the north of Portugal
Publications:
• Estatistica (ANCEVE): *detailed statistics on the production
and export of wines and spirits from suppliers in Northern
Portugal - annual*

Association of Tobacco Wholesalers, Importers and Exporters of Southern Portugal
Associação do Sul dos Depositários Importadores e Exportadores
de Tabacos
Address: Rua das Janelas Verdes, 13 - 2º esq, P-1200 Lisbon
Telephone: +351 1 396 4522
Fax: +351 1 396 4522
Year established: 1975
Chief officers: Francisco Carpinteiro
Membership: 116 wholesalers, importers and exporters of
tobacco

Association of Vehicle Assembly Industries (AIMA)
Associação das Industrias de Montagem de Automoveis
Address: Rua Palmeira 6, P-1200 Lisbon
Telephone: +351 1 347 0086
Fax: +351 1 342 0064
Year established: 1975
Activities: sponsorship and participation in the annual
International Motor Shows held in Oporto; information for
members on the national car assembly industry; monthly
statistics, annual report
Chief officers: João Anastácio (General Secretary), António

Cavaco (Statistical Department), J Costa Neves (Technical
Department)
Membership: 14 vehicle assembly companies
Publications:
• Magazine: *news of events in the automotive world - monthly*
• Portugese Automobile Statistics Digest: *annual statistics on
motor vehicle production, assembly, trade in Portugal based
on official statistics and some trade association data - annual*
• Revistacap : *monthly*

Association of Wholesalers of Chemical and Pharmaceutical Goods (GROQUIFAR)
Associação de Grossistas de Produtos Químicos e Farmacêuticos
Address: Av. António Augusto Aguiar, 118 - 1º, P-1050 Lisbon
Telephone: +351 1 317 2676/2672
Fax: +351 1 354 4510
Activities: professional training; information service; liaises
with national and international organisations
Chief officers: Eng. Luis Almeida Barros (President), Dr
Fernando Aires Miranda (Vice President), Dr Martins de
Castro (Secretary General)
Membership: 344 wholesalers of pharmaceutical and
chemical goods

Automotive Manufacturers' Association (AFIA)
Associação de Fabricantes para Indústria Automóvel
Address: Rua do Crasto 190, P-4150 Porto
Telephone: +351 2 617 2668
Fax: +351 2 610 1877
Activities: organises meetings; seminars and other events;
collects statistics covering turnover (total and by activity),
exports, national market, number of enterprises and
employees in the sector
Chief officers: Teresa Dieguez (General Manager)
Membership: 50 members
Publications:
• VDA Quality Manuals

Automotive Repair Enterprises' and Car Retailers' Association (ANECRA)
Associação Nacional das Empresas do Comercio e da
Reparação Automovel
Address: Calçada da Estrela nº 77
R.ALMEIDA BRANDÃO, Nº 2 - 1296 LISBOA, P-1296 Lisbon
códex
Telephone: +351 1 397 90 14
Fax: +351 1 397 85 14
E-mail: anecra@mail.telepac.pt
Web site: www.anecra.pt
Activities: regional meetings, professional training
Membership: 3303 members

Bakery and Confectionery Products' Association
Associação dos Industriais de Panificação e Pastelaria
Address: Apdo 1050, Rua de Tomar,11, P-3000 Coimbra
Telephone: +351 3 933 099
Fax: +351 3 933 099

Biscuit and Pasta Manufacturers' Association (AIBA)
Associação das Industrias de Bolachas e Afins
Address: Av. de República 62-F-6º, P-1000 Lisbon
Telephone: +351 1 796 6731
Fax: +351 1 793 8576
Year established: 1988
Activities: provides statistical and information service (for
members only); represents members in dealings with trade
unions and public authorities
Chief officers: David Vieira de Castro (President), Dr Barata
Simoes (General Secretary)
Membership: 9 biscuit and pasta manufacturing companies

Business Association of Oporto
Associação dos Comerciantes do Porto
Address: Av Rodrigues de Freitas, 200, P-4000 Oporto
Telephone: +351 2 574 148
Fax: +351 2 580 423
Activities: professional training, law and economical investment advice, seminars, conferences and other events, promotes commercial campaigns throughout the year (Christmas, Mother's Day, Father's Day, St Valentines' Day, etc.), statistics and studies of the trade industry
Chief officers: Dra Isabel Moreira (Secretary General)
Membership: ca. 5,000 members of different sectors of the trade industry in Portugal: clothing, footwear, cosmetics and toiletries, consumer electronics, personal goods, office stationary and equipment, food, optical goods
Publications:
• ACP Informs (ACP Informa): *monthly*
• Annual Report ACP (Anuário ACP): *annual*
• Oporto Commerce (Comercio Portuense): *bimonthly*

Central Association for Portuguese Agriculture (ACAP)
Associação Central da Agricultura Portuguesa
Address: Rua D Dinis, 2°, P-1250 Lisbon
Telephone: +351 1 388 2462
Fax: +351 1 388 0525
Year established: 1860
Activities: research and information
Chief officers: Eng José Nunes Mira Mexia
Membership: 400 individuals and cooperatives (agriculture, forestry, fishing)

Chemical Companies' Association (APEQ)
Associação Portuguesa das Empresas Químicas
Address: Av. D. Carlos I, 45 - 3°, P-1200 Lisbon
Telephone: +351 1 390 6796
Fax: +351 1 396 3052
Year established: 1963
Chief officers: Eduardo Mendes Leal (Secretary General), João Manuel Dotti (President), José Manuel Faria e Santos (Vice President)
Membership: industrial chemical companies

Chocolate and Confectionery Manufacturers' Association (ACHOC)
Associação dos Industriais de Chocolate e Confeitaira
Address: Av. de República 62 F - 6°, P-1050 Lisbon
Telephone: +351 1 796 9692/6731
Fax: +351 1 793 8576
E-mail: achoc@apan.pt
Year established: 1988
Activities: provides statistical and information service (members only), legislative advice, liaises CAOBISCO
Chief officers: Vasco Oliveira (President), Dr Barata Simões (Secretary General)
Membership: 9 chocolate and confectionery manufacturing companies
Publications:
• Annual Volume (Volume Anual): *turnover of the member companies and chocolate market figures for the past year - annual*

Coffee Roasting Companies' Association (ANT)
Associação Nacional dos Torrefactores
Address: Rua Padre Francisco Alvares, 1-1°Dto A, P-1500 Lisbon
Telephone: +351 1 774 1674/778 6321
Fax: +351 1 778 5344
Year established: 1975
Activities: compiles monthly export statistics and conducts market studies; organises annual conference

Chief officers: José Manuel Albuquerque (President), Luis Carvalho Neves (Secretary General)
Membership: 40 coffee processors
Publications:
• Informative Bulletin (Boletim Informativo): *legislative and economical information related to the coffee industry, coffee market analysis - quarterly*
• Trade Directory

Confederation of Portuguese Farmers (CAP)
Confederação dos Agricultores de Portugal
Address: Avenida do Colégio Militar - Lote 1786, P-1500 Lisbon
Telephone: +351 1 710 0000
Fax: +351 1 716 6122
Year established: 1975
Activities: regional and national meetings, professional training, seminars and Agricultural Information Centres Network
Chief officers: Eng. José Joaquim Lima Monteiro Andrade (President), Eng. José Manuel Rodrigues Casqueiro (Secretary General)
Structure: General Assembly is the main decision body which elects the Executive Committee of 7 members (the President, 5 Vice Presidents and the Secretary General), and the Plenary Committee with 10 full-time members
Membership: umbrella association which regroups over 300 federations and regional associations
Publications:
• Farmer's Journal (Revista do Agricultor): *articles on agricultural and economic policy and technical news - monthly*

Daily Newspapers' Association
Associação da Impresa Diaria
Address: Rua de Artilharia Um 69 - 2°, P-1297 Lisboa Codex
Telephone: +351 1 657 584
Chief officers: Carlos Eurico da Costa (General Secretary)

Dairy Industries' Association
Associação dos Industriais de Lacticínios
Address: Rua de Santa Teresa 2C, 2°, P-4050 Oporto
Telephone: +351 2 200 1229
Fax: +351 2 316 450
Activities: liaises with national and international entities (EDA, CIAA, FIL/IDF); acts as an employer association; training, seminars and courses; legal advice; collects statistics
Chief officers: José Castro (President), Dr Pedro Pimentel (Secretary General), Clara Moura Guedes (Secretary)
Membership: approx. 60 dairy products' manufacturers
Publications:
• Bulletin (Boletim): *statistical data, information of activities and events - monthly*

Direct Marketing Association (AMD)
Associação Portuguesa de Marketing Directo
Address: Estr. Nac. 91, Valejas, P-2795 Linda A Velha
Telephone: +351 1 436 6727
Fax: +351 1 436 7845
Activities: maintains contact with legislative organisations
Chief officers: Jorge D'Orey Pinheiro (President), João Novais de Paula (Secretary General)
Membership: 27 members

Fish Retailers' Association
Associação dos Comerciantes de Pescado
Address: Av Visconde Valmor 36-1°Esq, P-1050 Lisbon
Telephone: +351 1 797 4096
Fax: +351 1 795 1695
Year established: 1976
Activities: research; professional training and employment;

promotion and organisation of seminars, conferences and other information services; publishes material related to the industry
Chief officers: João Soeiro (Secretary General)
Membership: 220 companies and 38 individuals in the fish wholesale and retail sector

Food Distributors' Association (ADIPA)
Associação dos Distribuidores de Produtos Alimentares
Address: Rua Rodrigues Sampaio 31, 1°-D, P-1150 Lisbon
Telephone: +351 1 357 5296/7575
Fax: +351 1 352 4139
Activities: information service; education and training
Chief officers: Eduardo Vilarinho (President), Eng. Sinde Monteiro (Vice President), Camilo Pereira (Treasurer), José Luis Inverno (Director), António Carlos Costa (Director))
Membership: 443 wholesalers of food and beverages, toiletries, and household cleaning products

Food Retailers' Association (ARPA)
Associação Retalhistas de Produtos Alimentares
Address: Av Elias Garcia, 59 4°, P-1000 Lisbon
Telephone: +351 1 797 3283
Fax: +351 1 796 2470

Graphics and Paper Processing Association (APIGTP)
Associação Portuguesa das Indústrias Gráficas e Transformadoras do Papel
Address: Largo do Casal Vistoso, 2-D, Escritório B, P-1900 Lisbon
Telephone: +351 1 849 1020/9/4445
Fax: +351 1 847 0778
Year established: 1974
Activities: statistics, information service (for members); promotion and support of conferences and exhibitions
Chief officers: Durvalino Ribeiro Neto (President), Dr Jose Eduardo Carragosela (Secretary General)
Membership: over 1,000 companies
Publications:
• T & G Magazine: *quarterly*
• Yearbook: *details of members and their products*

Industrial Association of Oporto (AIP)
Associação Industrial Portuense
Address: Av da Boavista, 2671, P-4100 Oporto
P-4100 Oporto
Telephone: +351 2 617 2257
Fax: +351 2 617 6840
Web site: www.aiportuense/aip/
Year established: 1849
Activities: organises trade fairs, exhibitions and congresses; information services and technical support; consultancy, professional training; promotion of business and investment; Euro Info Centre
Chief officers: Eng. Ludgero Marques (President)
Publications:
• AIP Environment (AIP Ambiente): *articles and news on the environment and industry - monthly*
• Economics Newsletter (Relatório Mensal de Economia): *national and international information on economics, finance and politics - monthly*
• North Industry (A Indústria do Norte): *economic, political and social articles; information on trade fairs and articles on industrial projects - monthly*
• Projects' Supplement (Suplemento Missões): *information on different projects worldwide - monthly*

Knitwear Manufacturers' Association (APIM)
Associação Portuguesa das Industrias de Malha e Confecçâo
Address: Rua Guilhermina Suggia, 224 - 1° s.8, P-4200 Oporto
Telephone: +351 2 529 081/84
Fax: +351 2 529 210
Year established: 1965
Activities: gives legal and fiscal support; co-founded the following institutions: Centro de Formação Profissional da Indústria Téxtil (CITEX); Centro Tecnológico das Indústrias Têxtil e do Vestuário de Portugal (CITEVE); Centro de Estudos Técnicos Aplicados (CENESTAP); Centro de Design Têxtil e Moda (CDTM); provides information on the industry; maintains databases on the industry and compiles statistics
Chief officers: Joaquim de Sousa Coutinho (President), António Antunes dos Santos (General Director), Alvaro Manuel Vaz (Secretary General)
Membership: 500 knitwear manufacturers, most of which are small firms (70% of the total market)
Publications:
• Bulletin APIM (Boletim APIM): *mainly news items and features on technical and legal issues but some market statistics based on a combination of official and non-official sources - bimonthly*
• Directory APIM (Directório): *information on the previous and present year - annual*
• Employment Contract (Contrato Colectivo de Trabalho): *biannual*
• Knitwear Quality Brochure (Brochura sobre Qualidade nas Malhas): *regularly*

Leather Goods Manufacturers' Association
Associação Portuguesa dos Industriais de Curtumes
Address: Av.Femäo de Magalhães, 460 - 5° e, P-4300 Oporto
Telephone: +351 2 574 115
Fax: +351 2 572 065
Chief officers: Eng Jorge Melo da Costa (Chairman), Dr Eduardo da Sousa Campos (Secretary)
Membership: leather goods manufacturers

Leisure and Entertainment Companies' Association (APED)
Associação Portuguesa de Empresas de Diversoes
Address: Av Duque de Loulé 86 - 2° dto, P-1000 Lisbon
Telephone: +351 1 474 6405
Fax: +351 1 475 0713
Chief officers: José Marques (President), Dr Lima de Carlvalho (General Secretary)
Membership: leisure and entertainment companies

Metal Packaging Association (ANIEM)
Associação das Indústrias de Embalagens Metálicas
Address: Av. Defensores Chaves 35 - 6°, P-1000 Lisbon
Telephone: +351 1 315 9134
Fax: +351 1 315 9134
Chief officers: Arménio Cardo
Membership: metal packaging companies

National Association of Electrical and Electronics Companies (ANIMEE)
Associação Nacional dos Industriais de Material Eléctrico e Electrónico
Address: Av. Guerra Junqueiro, 11 - 2° esq, P-1000 Lisbon
Telephone: +351 1 849 4521
Fax: +351 1 840 5725
E-mail: animee@mail.telepac.pt
Web site: www.animee.pt
Year established: 1970
Activities: organises an exhibition every two years - The National Exhibition for the Development of Electrical and Electronic Industries

Chief officers: Eng Pedro Sena da Silva (President), Filipe dos Santos (Secretary General)
Structure: general assembly, board of directors, supervisiory board
Membership: 125 electrical and electronics companies in the private sector
Publications:
• ANIMEE Magazine (Revista ANIMEE): *bimonthly*
• Annual Directory (Anuário): *information on members - biennial*
• Report on the Industry (Monografia): *economic analysis of the industry - annual*

National Association of Food Products' Retailers and Manufacturers (ANCIPA)

Associação Nacional de Comerciantes e Industriais de Produtos Alimentares
Address: Largo Sao Sebastião da Pedreira 31, 1, P-1000 Lisbon
Telephone: +351 1 352 8803/25/27
Fax: +351 1 315 4665
Activities: information service, training courses, research and studies on the food industry
Chief officers: Dra Domitília Lopes de Almeida (Secretary General)
Membership: 600 food manufacturers, traders and distributors
Notes: Office in Oporto: Rua António Granjo, 157, 4300 Porto Tel 2 577779, Fax 2 560460

National Association of Fruit and Groceries Importers, Exporters and Warehouses (ANAIEF)

Associação Nacional dos Armazenistas, Importadores e Exportadores de Frutas e Produtos Hortícolas
Address: Rua Diogo Couto nº27 , 1º, P-1000 Lisbon
Telephone: +351 1 814 0521/357 4778
Fax: +351 1 352 0907
Membership: producers and exporters of fruit and fresh produce

National Association of Grain Millers

Associação Nacional dos Industriais de Moagem de Trigo, Milho e Centeio
Address: Av Elias Garcia 76, 1º-B, P-1050 Lisbon
Telephone: +351 1 796 1143
Fax: +351 1 793 1158
Membership: grain millers

National Association of Meat Processors' (ANICAR)

Associação Nacional dos Industriais de Carnes
Address: Ave Guerra Junqueiro 11, 1º-D, P-1000 Lisbon
Telephone: +351 1 840 0298
Fax: +351 1 840 0240
Chief officers: Luis Catarino Barbeiro (President)
Membership: meat processors

National Association of Paper Retailers

Associação Nacional dos Armazenistas de Papel
Address: Rua dos Industriais 29, 1ºE, P-1200 Lisbon
Telephone: +351 1 396 8456
Fax: +351 1 396 8456
Membership: stationery retailers

National Association of Poultry Processors (ANCAVE)

Associação Nacional dos Centros de Abate
Address: Av. Miguel Bombarda 120-3º, P-1050 Lisbon
Telephone: +351 1 796 6439
Fax: +351 1 796 6439
Year established: 1976
Activities: publishes monthly reports on prices, production

and consumption in association with FEPASA/Federaçâo Portuguesa das Associaçoes Avicolas (qv); operates information service for members and carries out promotional activities
Chief officers: José Antonio dos Santos (President), Albertino de Freitas Castro (Secretary)
Membership: 29 corporate poultry processors
Publications:
• Poultry and Eggs (Aves e Ovos): *future propects for the industry - monthly*

National Association of Supermarkets (ANS)

Associação Nacional Supermercados
Address: Campo Grande 286, 5º, P-1700 Lisbon
Telephone: +351 1 751 0920
Fax: +351 1 757 1952
Membership: supermarket operators

National Association of Young Businessmen (ANJE)

Associação Nacional de Jovens Empresários
Address: Casa do Farol, Rua Paulo da Gama, P-4150 Oporto
Telephone: +351 2 610 5210/7
Fax: +351 2 610 5218/9
E-mail: anje@mail.telepac.pt

National Canned Foods' Association

Associação Nacional dos Industriais de Conservas
Address: Rua Conde S. Salvador 352, 6º Salas 26/9, P-4450 Matosinhos
Telephone: +351 2 937 5213
Fax: +351 2 937 5805

National Food Traders' Association (ANACPA)

Associação Nacional de Comerciantes de Produtos Alimentares
Address: Av. Elias Garcia, 59 - 4, P-1000 Lisbon
Telephone: +351 1 797 3283/796 4166
Fax: +351 1 796 2470
Activities: information service; legal and fiscal advice; professional training, seminars; market reports and statistics
Chief officers: Manuel Lima Amorim (President), António Virgilio Mendes (Vice President, Marina Guedes (Secretary General)
Membership: 35,000 food retailers and wholesalers
Publications:
• ANACPA Journal (ANACPA Jornal): *quarterly*

National Motor Vehicle Association (ARAN)

Associação Nacional do Ramo Automóvel
Address: Rua Faria Guimarães, 631, P-4200 Oporto
Telephone: +351 2 592 761/591 053
Fax: +351 2 550 0174
E-mail: aran@mail.telepac.pt
Year established: 1940
Activities: provides an information service; statistics covering new registrations, imports, market size etc.; technical, legislative support; education and training
Chief officers: Dr Joaquim Daniel Costa Nerves (Secretary General), Eng. Paulo Jorge Pereira Lamelas (Statistical Department), Dr José Manuel Queiroz de Miranda e Barbosa (Public Relations Department)
Membership: 1,300 members: 1,200 motor traders and service companies, 40 manufacturers of spare parts and accessories, 60 vehicle manufacturers
Publications:
• ARAN Magazine (Revista ARAN): *statistical data, news on the automotive industry at national and international level - bimonthly*
• Bulletin (Boletim): *economic and financial information relating to the car repair industry, trade data*

• Technical Bulletins (Boletins Técnicos): *technical information on cars and automotives parts - regularly*

National Pharmacies' Association

Associação Nacional das Farmácias
Address: Praça do Principe Real 18, P-1200 Lisbon
Telephone: +351 1 340 0600/0630/347 2046
Fax: +351 1 347 2994
Web site: www.anf.pt
Activities: regional meetings (monthly); national meetings for community pharmacists (annual); post-graduate courses for both community and hospital pharmacists; Drug Information Centre
Chief officers: João Cordeiro (President of Board)
Membership: most pharmacies in Portugal
Publications:
• Farmácia Portuguesa: *information on future prospects - bi-monthly*
• Leaflet Series and Files of Drugs

National Rice Producers' Association (ANIA)

Associação Nacional dos Industriais de Arroz
Address: Ave da República 60, 5°-E, P-1050 Lisbon
Telephone: +351 1 796 8606
Fax: +351 1 793 5558
Telex: 62512 ANIA P
Membership: rice producers

National Wholesalers' Association (ANCG)

Associação Nacional dos Comerciantes Grossistas
Address: Edif. MAPFRE, Rua Gonçalo Cristóvão 347, 2ª sala, P-4000 Oporto
Telephone: +351 2 208 8085
Fax: +351 2 321 331

Non-Daily Press Association

Associação da Imprensa Não-Diária
Address: Rua Gomes Freire 183 - 4°E, P-1150 Lisbon
Telephone: +351 1 355 5092/6116
Fax: +351 1 314 2191

Paper Industry Association (CELPA)

Associação Portuguesa da Indústria Papeleira
Address: Rua Marquês Sá da Bandeira, 74 - 1°Esq, P-1050 Lisbon
Telephone: +351 1 796 0054
Fax: +351 1 795 9456/793 9054
Year established: 1993
Chief officers: Luis Bernardo Rolo (General Director), Armando Fialho, João Lança Rodrigues (Deputy General Managers)
Membership: 13 pulp and paper manufacturers
Publications:
• Bulletin of Statistics on the Portuguese Pulp and Paper Industry (Boletim Estatístico da Indústria Portuguesa de Celulose e Papel): *annual*
• Membership List

Photography Industry Association (ANIF)

Associação Nacional das Industriais de Fotografía
Address: Rodrigo Fonse 58, P-1250 Lisbon
Telephone: +351 1 386 0679
Fax: +351 1 387 7989
Chief officers: António Felix Marcs (President)

Port Wine Institute (IVP)

Instituto do Vinho do Porto
Address: Rua Ferreira Borges, P-4000 Oporto
Telephone: +351 2 207 1600
Fax: +351 2 208 0465
Chief officers: Fernando Bianchi de Aguiar (President), Louisa Fry (Public Relations)
Membership: port wine producers

Port Wine Shippers' Association (AEVP)

Associação das Empresas do Vinho de Porto
Address: Rua Barrao de Forrester, 412, P-4400 Vila Nova de Gaia
Telephone: +351 2 370 5395
Fax: +351 2 370 5400
E-mail: aevp@mail.telepac.pt
Web site: www.aevp.pt
Year established: 1975
Activities: consultancy; information and support services
Chief officers: António Jorge Ferreira Filipe (President), Maria Isabel MSC Fernandes Marrana (Executive Director)
Membership: 37 port wine producers and exporters

Portuguese Association of Animal Feed Manufacturers (IACA)

Associação Portuguesa dos Industriais de Alimentos Compostos para Animais
Address: Av 5 de Outubro 21 - 2° esq, P-1050 Lisbon
Telephone: +351 1 352 5091
Fax: +351 1 353 0387
E-mail: iaica@mail.telepac.pt
Year established: 1975
Activities: produces statistics covering production of animal feed and consumption of raw materials
Chief officers: Dr Jaime Lança de Morais (President), Sr Luis Elso Marques (General Secretary)
Membership: 70 certified feed manufacturers: individuals and companies
Publications:
• Animal Feed Magazine (Revista Alimentaçao Animal): *quarterly*
• IACA Annual Report (Anuário IACA): *yearbook and directory - annual*
• Weekly Information (Informaçao Semanal): *weekly*

Portuguese Association of Booksellers and Publishers

Associação Portuguesa dos Editores e Livreiros
Address: Av Estadoa Unidos da América, 97 - 6°E, P-1700 Lisbon
Telephone: +351 1 848 9136
Fax: +351 1 848 9377
E-mail: info@apel.pt
Web site: www.apel.pt
Year established: 1927
Activities: organises the trade fair Feiras do Livro de Lisboa e Porto; represents the Portuguese publishing industry at international events such as the book fairs of Frankfurt, Bologna, Sao Paulo and Rio de Janeiro; collects statistics covering production, imports/exports, etc; promotes training courses for librarians and book retailers
Chief officers: Mr JM Lello (President), Mr J Sá Borges (Director), Mr JM Guedes (Secretary)
Membership: booksellers and publishers
Publications:
• Books of Portugal (Livros de Portugal): *covers the Portuguese book market - monthly*
• Estudo sobre os Hábitos de Leitura em Portugal: *annual*
Notes: Office in Oporto: Livraria Lello e Irmao, Rua da Fábrica 38 - 4°, 4000 Porto Tel 2 200 2037

Portuguese Association of Clothing Manufacturers (APIV)

Associação Portuguesa dos Industriais de Vestuário
Address: Rua Castilho, 75 - 4º dto, P-1200 Lisbon
Telephone: +351 1 386 1259/1459/1059
Fax: +351 1 386 3672
Year established: 1975
Activities: participates in trade fairs and other national and international events; organises seminars, conferences; provides an information service; offers advice on legislation affecting the industry; provides training courses through the Gabinete Portugués de Moda and the Centro de Formação Profissional (CIVEC); produces statistics covering imports, exports, production, etc.
Chief officers: Teófilo Santos Pinto (President), Rui Teixeira Motta (Director), Maria de Fátima Tavares (Secretary)
Membership: 535 clothing manufacturers
Publications:
• To Dress (Vestir): *articles and news on the industry, information on training courses; statistics on the industry - quarterly*

Portuguese Association of Engineering Consultants' (APPC)

Associação Portuguesa de Projectistas e Consultores
Address: Av António Augusto de Aguiar 126-7, P-1000 Lisbon
Telephone: +351 1 352 0476
Fax: +351 1 356 3159
Chief officers: Raul Branco (General Secretary), J Caldeira Rodrigues (President)
Membership: consulting engineering companies

Portuguese Association of Footwear and Leather Goods Manufacturers (APICCAPS)

Associação Portuguesa dos Industriais de Calçado, Componentes e Artigos de Pele e seus Sucedâneos
Address: Rua Alves Redol, 372, P-4050 Oporto
Telephone: +351 2 550 6776
Fax: +351 2 524 997
E-mail: apiccaps@mail.telepac.pt
Web site: www.apiccaps.pt/apiccaps
Chief officers: Basilio Dias de Oliveira (President), Domingos Ferreira Neto (Secretary General)
Membership: 110 footwear and leather goods manufacturers

Portuguese Association of Identification and Codification of Products (CODIPOR)

Associação Portuguesa de Identificação e Codificação de Produtos
Address: Rua Prof. Fernando Fonseca 16, Lote B - 1ª F/G/H, P-1700 Lisbon
Telephone: +351 1 757 6254/757 2158
Fax: +351 1 759 9508
E-mail: codipor@codipor.mailpac.pt

Portuguese Association of International Trade (APCI)

Associação Portuguesa de Comércio Internacional
Address: Rua Saraiva de Carvalho, 1 - 5ºB, P-1200 Lisbon
Telephone: +351 1 397 3969
Fax: +351 1 395 3124
Membership: exporters and importers

Portuguese Association of Restaurants and Bars

Associação das Casas de Pasto e Vinho do Portugal
Address: Av Duque de Avila 75, P-1000 Lisbon
Telephone: +351 1 352 7060
Fax: +351 1 549 428
Membership: retail food and wine distributors

Portuguese Association of the Pharmaceutical Industry (APIFARMA)

Associação Portuguesa da Indústria Farmacêutica
Address: Rua Pero da Covilhã 22, P-1400 Lisbon
Telephone: +351 1 301 8264/8283
Fax: +351 1 301 8785
Membership: pharmaceutical companies

Portuguese Association of the Vehicle Trade (ACAP)

Associação do Comércio Automóvel de Portugal
Address: Rua Palmeira 6, P-1294 Lisbon
Telephone: +351 1 321 6400/347 0048
Fax: +351 1 342 0064
E-mail: acap@mail.telepac.pt
Web site: www.consiste.pt/acap
Year established: 1910
Activities: information service providing details of new legislation in the fields of law, technology and credit; conducts market surveys and publishes statistics; library (Monday - Friday, 09.30 - 18.00)
Chief officers: Anibal Bessa (President), Dr Helder Pedro (General Secretary)
Membership: 1700 companies
Publications:
• Auto-Catalógo: *members' directory, available to non-members*
• Guía do Comprador de Máquinas Industriais
• Membership List
• Portuguese Automotive Industry Statistics (O Comércio e a Industria Automóvel em Portugal): *statistics covering motor vehicles in Portugal with data on production, assembly, registration, and the motor vehicle parc broken down by types of vehicles. Some data for earlier years and a contents page in English - annual*
• Revistacap : *monthly*

Portuguese Association of Wholesalers and Importers of Watches, Clocks, Electric, Electronic and Photographic Material (AGEFE)

Associação Portuguesa dos Grossistas Importadores de Material Elétrico, Eletrónico, Eletrodoméstico, Fotográfico e de Relojaria
Address: Avenue João Crisóstomo 79 - 3º, P-1000 Lisbon
Telephone: +351 1 315 6608
Fax: +351 1 314 6367
Membership: wholesalers of electric, electronic and photograpic material, household appliances and watches

Portuguese Banks' Association

Associação Portuguesa de Bancos
Address: Avda de la República 35 - 5º, P-1050 Lisbon
Telephone: +351 1 357 9804
Fax: +351 1 357 9533
Membership: banks

Portuguese Brewing Industry Association (ACIP)

Associação da Industria Cervejeira Portuguesa
Address: Largo de Santos, 9 - 3º e, P-1200 Lisbon
Telephone: +351 1 397 8467/8468/8469
Fax: +351 1 602 996
Chief officers: Dr Cipriano Henao (President), Eng Soares da Fonseca (Vice President), Dr Emanuel Jardim Fernandes (Treasurer), Eng Américo Martins (Secretary General)
Membership: 4 brewing companies

Portuguese Broadcasting Association (APR)

Associação Portuguesa de Radiodifusão
Address: Av Descobertas 4, P-1400 Lisbon
Telephone: +351 1 301 6999/5453
Fax: +351 1 301 6536
Chief officers: José M Ignacio

Portuguese Confederation of Business and Services (CCP)

Confederação do Comércio e Serviços de Portugal
Address: Rua dos Correeiros, 79 - 1º/2º, P-1100 Lisbon
Telephone: +351 1 342 2160/3422047
Fax: +351 1 347 8638
E-mail: ccp.socinfo@mail.telepac.pt
Web site: www.ccp.pt/
Year established: 1976
Activities: to promote and coordinate professional training, seminars, market reports, statistics
Structure: General Assembly, Board of Directors, Fiscal Board, Presidents Board
Membership: over 100 regional and sectorial associatios, representing wholesalers, retailers and services activities and over 200,000 companies
Publications:
• Annual Questionaire to Business (Inquérito Anual às Empresas Comerciais): *annual survey of business with analysis of current trends in the industry - annual*
• Annual Trade Industry Enquiry (Inquérito Anual ao Comercio): *statistical data on retail and wholesale - annual*
• Commerce Issues (Os Números do Comércio): *compilation of statistical data related to the Business sector: general trade indicators, regional analysis, retail and wholesale trade figures and rankings - annual*
• Economics Bulletin (Boletim Económico): *articles on economic topics related to the industry - quarterly*
• Food Industry Bulletin (Brochura do Comércio Alimentar): *statistical information on the food industry*

Portuguese Dietetic Foods Association (APARD)

Associação Portuguesa de Alimentação Racional e Dietética
Address: Rua Padre Francisco 9, Salas 57/59, P-1350 Lisbon
Telephone: +351 1 414 4819
Fax: +351 1 396 1188

Portuguese Distributors' Association (APED)

Associação Portuguesa de Empresas de Distribução
Address: Campo Grande 286, 5, P-1700 Lisbon
Telephone: +351 1 751 0920/0929
Fax: +351 1 757 1952
Activities: promotes and organises seminars and conferences; provides training on marketing, the environment, human resources and other topics related to the sector; compiles statistics on food markets
Chief officers: José António Rousseau (General Director)
Membership: 30 members
Publications:
• Newsletter: *bimonthly*

Portuguese Edible Oils Association

Casa do Azeite- Associação do Azeite de Portugal
Address: Rua Castillo 69 - r/c esq, P-1250 Lisbon
Telephone: +351 1 386 3363/3054
Fax: +351 1 386 1970
Activities: compiles sector statistics on national market and exports; information service for members; participates in trade fairs and other events to promote the oil industry at a national and international level; market reports
Chief officers: Carlos Oilveira (President), Dra Maria Oliveira Fernandes (Secretary General)
Membership: 60 producers and distributors of edible oils

Portuguese Flour Millers' Association

Associação Porutguesa da Indústria de Moagem
Address: Rua Tomás Fonseca 1, 5C, P-1600 Lisbon
Telephone: +351 1 727 1610
Fax: +351 1 727 1609
Telex: 62707 AIM LISBOA

Chief officers: Dr Gomes Pereira (Director)
Membership: flour millers

Portuguese Franchising Association (APF)

Associação Portuguesa de Franchise
Address: Rua Castilho, nº 14 - 2º, Sala 4, P-1250 Lisbon
Telephone: +351 1 315 1845
Fax: +351 1 315 1845
Year established: 1988
Activities: promotes contact at national and international level between franchisers and franchisees; professional training and seminars; research studies; information service for members and non-members; collects sector statistics
Chief officers: Marcelino Pena Costa (President), Dra Margarida Telo Machado (General Director)
Membership: 30 members from different sectors such as food, clothing and textiles, insurance, banking, hotels and catering, travel and tourism etc.; national and international companies which have a franchise in Portugal and companies which want to expand through franchising
Publications:
• Franchise Annual Report (Anuário Franchise): *statistical information on the Portuguese franchising sector - annual*
• Franchising Newsletter (Franchising): *news on the sector with information on activities organised by APF: seminars, training and conferences - quarterly*

Portuguese Hotel Association

Associação dos Hotéis de Portugal
Address: Rua Ramalho Ortigão 3, 3, P-1070 Lisbon
Telephone: +351 1 385 5492
Fax: +351 1 385 5497
Year established: 1981
Activities: annual congress; legal, economic and fiscal services for members
Chief officers: Manuel Telles (President)
Membership: 181 hotels and travel agencies
Publications:
• Hotéis de Portugal: *hotel industry magazine; includes some statistics - every 2 months*

Portuguese Leasing Association (APELEASE)

Associação Portuguesa de Empresas de Leasing
Address: Edificio Aviz, Av. Fontes Pereira de Melo, 35 - 6ºB, P-1050 Lisbon
Telephone: +351 1 352 8509
Fax: +351 1 353 5373
Activities: provides assistance to memebers on fiscal, legal and accounting matters; media and public relations; provides statistics on the sector; maintains a client database
Chief officers: Dr António Mota (President), Dr António Beja Amaro (Vice President), Dr Carvalho e Silva (Vice President), Dra Margarida Ferreira (Secretary General)
Membership: 26 equipment/real estate leasing companies
Publications:
• Statistics (Estatísticas): *statistics on the Portuguese leasing sector which forms part of the annual study LEASEUROPE which covers the European equipment leasing market (machinery, computers, automotives, aviation) - annual*

Portuguese Meat Wholesalers' Association (AGROCAR)

Associação Portuguesa de Grossistas de Carnes
Address: Rua Cidade da Beira 22/B - r/c, P-1800 Lisbon
Telephone: +351 1 851 3700
Fax: +351 1 851 3700
Chief officers: Mario Raposo Almeida (President)
Membership: meat wholesalers

Portuguese Mineral Water Producers' Association (APIAM)
Associação Portuguesa dos Industriais de Aguas Mineriais e de Nascente
Address: Av Miguel Bombarda 110, 2º dto, P-1050 Lisbon
Telephone: +351 1 794 0575/0602/0574
Fax: +351 1 793 8233
Activities: statistics, seminars and conferences
Chief officers: Eng. Luis Leyva (President), Dr Furtado Mendoça (Secretary General)
Membership: 27 mineral water producers
Publications:
• Statistics (Estatísticas): *monthly*
• Water, Soft Drinks and Juices - Bulletin (Boletim - Aguas, Refrigerantes e Sumos): *quarterly*

Portuguese Petroleum Enterprises' Association (APETRO)
Associação Portuguesa de Empresas Petrolíferas
Address: R.A. Particular, Qtº do Figo Maduro, P-2685 Sacavém
Telephone: +351 9 417 428/75/1954
Fax: +351 9 418 671

Portuguese Phonographic Association
Associação Fonográfica Portuguesa
Address: Rua Augusto dos Santos 2, 4º e, P-1050 Lisbon
Telephone: +351 1 352 9189/9199
Fax: +351 1 314 7325
Activities: compiles rankings and statistics on the Portuguese phonographic market (quarterly, annual)
Chief officers: Carlos Pinto (President), Eduardo Simões (Director General)
Membership: 19 members

Portuguese Restaurants' Association
Associação dos Restaurantes e Similares de Portugal
Address: Av Duque de Avila, 75, P-1000 Lisbon
Telephone: +351 1 352 7060
Fax: +351 1 354 9428
Chief officers: Dra C Costa

Portuguese Textile Wholesalers' Association
Associação Portuguesa de Grossistas Texteis
Address: Rua da Picaria nº 36, 1º Salas 2 a 7, P- 4000 Oporto
Telephone: +351 2 316 317
Fax: +351 2 311 699
Membership: textile wholesalers: wool, cotton, silk and fibres

Portuguese Textiles and Clothing Association
Associação Portuguesa de Têxteis e Vestuario
Address: Rua Gonçalo Cristovao 96, 1-2, P-4000 Oporto
Telephone: +351 2 317 961/64
Fax: +351 2 310 343
Chief officers: Gradim Santos (Executive Director)

Private Label Association
Associação Centro Marca
Address: P-Lisbon
Telephone: +351 1 796 9692
Fax: +351 1 793 8576
Chief officers: Eng. João Pinto Ferreira

Shopping Centres' Association (APCC)
Associação Portuguesa de Centros Comerciais
Address: Rua Fialho de Almeida 1, 1ºDtº, P-1070 Lisbon
Telephone: +351 1 387 9757/8008
Fax: +351 1 385 3233
E-mail: apcc@mail.telepac.pt
Web site: www.apcc.pt:/apcc/
Year established: 1984
Activities: carries out studies and provides information on the industry; provides legislative and technical advice ; training, conferences and seminars; cooperation with the government in the preparation of specific legislation; maintains a database with information on Shopping Centres; provides the press and governmental institutions with up-to-date information on shopping centres; compiles statistics
Chief officers: Dr João Dias Coelho (President), Dr Fernando Figueiredo dos Santos (Vice-President), Dra Elsa Monteiro (Tresuarer), Dália Coutinho (Secretary)
Membership: 36 members which represent a total of 53 shopping complexes
Publications:
• APCC Newsletter (APCC Boletim): *information on the activiteis of the APCC and national and international news relevant to the sector - monthly*
• Directory (Directório): *directory of the sector with information on all shopping centres registered with the APCC - annual*
• Shopping and Departmental Stores (Shopping - Centros Comerciais em Revista): *articles, news and analysis of Portuguese retailing in general and shopping centre in particular - bimonthly*
Notes: Member of International Council of Shopping Centres.

Soft Drink and Fruit Juice Producers' Association
Associação Nacional dos Industriais de Refrigerantes e Sumos de Frutos
Address: Av Miguel Bombarda 110, 2º Dtº, P-1050 Lisbon
Telephone: +351 1 794 0574/0602
Fax: +351 1 793 8233
Membership: soft drinks and fruit juice producers

Tomato Canners and Purée Producers' Association
Associação Nacional dos Industriais de Tomate
Address: Avenue Casal Ribeiro 44, 4º, P-1000 Lisbon
Telephone: +351 1 356 1814/15
Fax: +351 1 356 1814
Year established: 1975
Chief officers: Dr Miguel Quemberses
Membership: tomato canners and purée producers

Travel and Tourism Agencies' Association (APAVT)
Associação Portuguesa das Agências de Viagens e Turismo
Address: Rua Duque de Palmela 2 - 1º dto, P-1250 Lisbon
Telephone: +351 1 352 9463
Fax: +351 1 352 5700
Telex: 14339 APAVT
Year established: 1950
Activities: quarterly general assemblies, circular letters with information for members
Chief officers: Dr Atílio Forte (President), José da Silva (Secretary General)
Membership: 441 travel agencies (plus 276 branches), 475 allied members (325 hotels, 28 air companies, 72 car-rental companies, etc.)
Publications:
• Membership List
Notes: Office in Oporto: Rua Stª Catarina, 1381 - 2º, 4000 Porto. Tel 2 495582/499738. Also has regional committees in Algarve, Madeira and Azores.

PUERTO RICO

Puerto Rico Manufacturers' Association
Asociación de Fabricantes de Puerto Rico
Address: Aptdo. 19577, Ave. Ponce de León 420, Halto Rey, P.R. 00918, San Juan
Telephone: +1 809 759 9445
Fax: +1 809 756 7670
Year established: 1928
Activities: promotes the investment of resources and the transformation of the manufacturing sector; Agency Service

ROMANIA

Article Numbering Association (EAN Romania)
Address: 10 Mexic Street, 1st Ward, 71206 Bucharest
Telephone: +40 1 212 1302
Fax: +40 1 121 1872
E-mail: ean@ean.ro

Romanian Franchise Association
Address: 86, Bd. Aviatorilor, Bucharest 1
Telephone: +40 1 210 4884
Fax: +40 1 210 4832
E-mail: mbas@bah.logicnet.ro
Chief officers: Mr Florin Dolea (President)

Romanian Press Editors' Association
Address: Centre International de Presa, Str. Batistei 14, Bucharest
Telephone: +40 1 210 0820/3120819
Fax: +40 1 211 9543
Chief officers: Mr Ion Raus (Executive Secretary)

RUSSIA

Agro-Industrial Union of Russia
Address: Orlikov per. 1/11, 107 139 Moscow
Telephone: +7 095 208 7224/208 5820
Fax: +7 095 208 5820
Year established: 1990
Activities: protection of its members, legal, social and economic support, internal communication
Chief officers: Starodubcev V. A. (Chairman)
Membership: companies engaged in agriculture and the processing of agricultural products
Publications:
• Information Bulletin: *2-3 times a year*

Association of International Pharmaceutical Manufacturers (AIPM)
Address: Slavjanskaya/Radisson Hotel, 2 Berezhovskaya nab., 121059 Moscow
Telephone: +7 095 941 8300
Fax: +7 905 941 8301/9418256
E-mail: aipm@online.ru

Association of Russian Automobile Dealers (ROAD)
Address: 64 Ysacheva St., 119048 Moscow
Telephone: +7 095 246 7561
Fax: +7 095 246 6709
Activities: liaison with governmental institutions; provides contacts with foreign companies; promotes investment in the Russian automotive industry and the creation of joint ventures; promotes the industry through fairs and exhibitions; collects statistics on the Russian automobile market
Chief officers: N.N. Soloshyn (President), V.A. Smirnov (Vice-President), S.E. Taraverdyev (Executive Vice-President)
Structure: association is a voluntary non-commercial unit of automobile dealers
Membership: 20 actual members, 10 associated members, among them Avto VAZ, newspaper Avto Review

Association of Russian Banks
Address: Skatertny per. 20, 121 069 Moscow
Telephone: +7 095 290 1000
Fax: +7 095 291 6666
Year established: 1991
Activities: liaison with governmental institutions, banking legislation and regulation
Chief officers: Egorov S. E.
Membership: 1,000 banks all over Russia
Publications:
• Information Bulletin: *3 times month*

Automatic Identification Association (UNISCAN)
Address: PO Box 10 UNISCAN, 117415 Moscow
Telephone: +7 095 432 4926
Fax: +7 095 431 0854
E-mail: info@ean.ru

Book Publishers' Association
Address: Bolshaya Nikitskaya 44b, (formerly Hersten str.), 202 1174 Moscow
Telephone: +7 095 202 1174
Fax: +7 095 202 3989
Year established: 1990
Chief officers: Mr M Shishigin (President)
Membership: 170 publishers

International Bureau for Information and Telecommunications
Address: POB 44, Leningradskiy Ave 80/2, Moscow 125190
Telephone: +7 095 158 8080/158 5665
Fax: +7 095 158 9680/158 5732
Publications:
• Goods and Services
• Russian Encyclopedia of Information and Telecommunications (INFOPARTNER)
• Russian Exporters and Importers

National Advertising Association
Address: 8, Neglinnaya Str., 103031 Moscow
Telephone: +7 095 921 3529
Fax: +7 095 923 7057
Year established: 1989
Activities: legal consulting and information services; research and educational programs; organises exhibitions and fairs in the advertising sector; government liaison
Chief officers: B.A. Shkolnikov (President), S. Igolkin (Executive Director)
Structure: the association includes the Russian Association for Public Relations (29 collective members) and the Association for Out-Door Advertising (15 collective members)
Membership: 36 member companies, including the largest advertising agencies (Premier SV, Intourreklama, Sasha, etc.) broadcasters such as Russkaya Troika, Airplane Centre Avgur and publishing companies
Notes: NAA is the member of the Chamber of Commerce of the Russian Federation and the co-founder of Reklama (Advertising) magazine.

Russian Association of Tourism

Address: Pl. Polsedi d. 2, Kor 2, Kw 34, 121293 Moscow
Telephone: +7 095 930 1580/4637/6805
Fax: +7 095 229 2637
Telex: 112916 URUS SE
Activities: liaises with international tourism organisations; organises the reception of foreign tourists and businessmen; conducts research on the industry; provides education and training
Chief officers: I.I.Laptev (President)
Membership: 298 enterprises (restaurants, cafes, bars, tourist complexes, hotels, etc.) and 72 regional Tourist-Excursion Executional Unions, firms, associations and joint-stock companies
Notes: The Association is a member of WTO..

Russian Editors' and Publishers' Association

Address: c/o Journalists Union of Russia, Subowsky boul. 4, 119021 Moscow
Telephone: +7 095 201 50 38
Fax: +7 095 201 35 47
Chief officers: Vladimir Kapelkin (Director)

Russian Federation National Committee of the International Dairy Federation

Address: c/o Ministry of Agriculture and Food, 3, Orlikov per., Moscow 107802
Telephone: +7 095 207 6391
Fax: +7 095 288 9580
Chief officers: Dr E.G. Konoplev (Secretary)

Society of Merchants and Industrialists of Russia

Address: Tokmakov per. 21/2, 107 066 Moscow
Telephone: +7 095 261 4106
Fax: +7 095 261 4106
Year established: 1992
Activities: collects statistical data (usually only available to members); publishes information bulletins
Chief officers: Garcev O. I.
Membership: 20,000 individuals, companies and organisations
Publications:
• Our Business: *monthly*

Union of Producers and Users of Pallets and Packaging Products (SOYUZUPACK)

Address: Sadovaya-Spaskaya 18, 107 807 Moscow
Telephone: +7 095 203 0547/975 3731
Fax: +7 095 203 0547
Year established: 1994
Activities: carries out scientific and industrial research; internal communications between producers and users of packaging products; information service; advice on marketing and advertising; professional training; publishes and distributes specialised literature, catalogues, directories and periodical publications; organises seminars and exhibitions
Chief officers: Smirenny Y. N. (President)
Membership: 218 companies and organisations in Russia, Kasakhstan, Uzbekistan, Belarus, Moldova, Ukraine and Latvia
Publications:
• Pallets and Packaging: *6 times a year*
Notes: Member of World Packaging Organisation.

Rwanda Coffee Board (OCIR)

Address: PO Box 104, Kigali
Telephone: +250 750 04/756 00/769 30
Fax: +250 739 92

Sierra Leone Produce Marketing Board

Address: PO Box 508, 508 Clinetown, Freetown
Telephone: +232 22 250 435/453/500 44/504 13
Telex: 3211 SILPROBOD

Advertising Media Owners' Association, Singapore

Address: c/o Lee Fook Hong and Company, #09-03/04 Asia Insurance Building, 2 Finlason Green, 049247
Telephone: +65 224 4521
Fax: +65 222 3041
Chief officers: Mr Tham Khai Wor (President), Mr Jack Wong (Hon Treasurer), Ms Loh Lai Ping (Hon Secretary)
Structure: president, treasurer, secretary, committee members
Membership: 37 full members and 5 associate members
Publications:
• Advoice: *covers advertising and the media*

Air Conditioning and Refrigeration Association

Address: 58 Kensington Park Road, Singapore 1955
Telephone: +65 288 5491
Chief officers: Joseph Kandathil (President); Fumiaka Okano (Vice President); Chan Kwang Meng (Honorary Secretary); T K Goh (honorary Treasurer)
Membership: 26 companies

Association of Banks in Singapore

Address: Floors 12-8, Mas Building, 10 Shenton Way, Singapore 0207
Telephone: +65 224 4300
Fax: +65 224 1785
Year established: 1973
Activities: education and training; represents Singapore banks on ASEAN Banking Council
Chief officers: Patrick Yeoh (Chairman); Ong-Ang Ai Boon (Director)
Membership: 156

Association Of Small and Medium Enterprises

Address: 8 Queen Street, #02-06, Singapore 188535
Telephone: +65 338 5868
Fax: +65 338 6859

Association of Telecommunications Equipment Suppliers (ATES)

Address: #08-12 Orchard Plaza, 150 Orchard Road, Singapore 238841
Telephone: +65 737 8526
Fax: +65 353 5559/737 8559
Chief officers: Ronnie Sim (President)

Association of the Electronics Industries of Singapore (AEIS)

Address: Blk 1003, Bukit Merah Central, Singapore 159836
Telephone: +65 278 1932
Fax: +65 278 7945

Direct Marketing Association of Singapore

Address: 100 Beach Road #27-05, Shaw Towers, Singapore 0718
Telephone: +65 297 0438
Fax: +65 299 8306
Year established: 1983
Activities: organises conferences and provides education and training
Chief officers: Andrew Chua Kim Poh (Chairman); Alex Har Yun Ling (Vice Chairman); Lee Lup Poon (Honorary Secretary)
Publications:
• Direct Marketer: *quarterly*

General Insurance Association of Singapore

Address: 13-07/08 Robina House, 1 Shenton Way, Singapore 0106
Telephone: +65 221 8788
Fax: +65 227 2051
Telex: RS 20814 TBA
Chief officers: Jennet Huang (Manager)

Institute of Management Consultants (Singapore)

Address: 9 Penang Road, #13-20, Park Mall, Singapore 238459
Telephone: +65 330 1213
Fax: +65 334 3668

Leasing Association of Singapore

Address: 15-04 Asia Insurance Building, 2 Finlayson Green, Singapore 0104
Telephone: +65 221 7379/221 7509
Fax: +65 221 9674
Telex: RS 26739 ALA
Chief officers: Steven Goh (Chairman); Lim Tiong Wee (Vice Chairman); R S Mohan (Honorary Secretary); Gregory Yeo (Honorary Treasurer)

Marketing Institute of Singapore

Address: 51 Anson Road, #03-53 Anson Centre, Singapore 079904
Telephone: +65 221 7788
Fax: +65 223 8785
Web site: sunsite.nus.sg/apmf/apmfhome.html
Year established: 1973
Activities: maintains international links to other national marketing bodies, including those in the UK, US, Japan, Hong Kong, Australia, New Zealand, Malaysia, Turkey and Greece
Structure: the institute is run by a full-time secretariat with an elected council as its policy-making body
Membership: 4000 members
Publications:
• Asian Journal of Marketing
• Marketing News: *Responding on MIS' activities and includes interesting marketing related information - bi-monthly*
• Singapore Market: *provides practical information on marketing - annual*

Master Printers' Association

Address: 68 Lorong, 16 Geylang, #04-02 Association Building, 398889
Telephone: +65 745 6913
Fax: +65 745 6916

Microcomputer Trade Association (Singapore)

Address: Institute of Micro-Electronics, 11 Science Park Road, Singapore Science Park 2, Singapore 117685
Telephone: +65 779 7522
Fax: +65 778 0136

Motor Traders' Association of Singapore

Address: 24 Leng Kee Road, 159096
Telephone: +65 474 2308
Fax: +65 475 9554
Publications:
• Monthly Vehicle Sales Statistics: *monthly motor vehicle sales data broken down by make and model. Based on data collected by the association. Includes a cumulative annual total - monthly*

National Association of Travel Agents in Singapore

Address: Hotel Miramar, Levels 4-6, 401 Havelok Road, Singapore
Telephone: +65 542 9976
Fax: +65 737 4834

National Book Development Council of Singapore

Address: c/o Bukit Merah Branch Library, Bukit Merah Central, Singapore 0315
Telephone: +65 273 2730
Fax: +65 270 6139
Year established: 1969
Chief officers: Vasantha Kumaree Siva (Executive Secretary)
Structure: executive committee elected from members of board
Membership: 43
Publications:
• Annual Report of the National Book Development Council of Singapore: *annual*

Radio and Electrical Traders' Association of Singapore

Address: Association Bldg, 68, Lor 16 Geylang, #04-01, Singapore 398889
Telephone: +65 747 0971
Fax: +65 744 7100
Chief officers: Toh Hock Chwee

Real Estate Developers' Association of Singapore (REDAS)

Address: 07-01 Singapore Shopping Centre, 190 Clemenceau Avenue, 0923
Telephone: +65 336 6655/223 1511
Fax: +65 337 2217
Year established: 1959
Chief officers: Amy Hsu (Project Executive)
Structure: management committee and subcommittees; research and development publications
Membership: 320 member companies
Publications:
• Property News: *bi-monthly*
• Property Review: *bi-monthly*

Seafood Industries' Association Singapore

Address: Blk 1003 #02-19/11, Bukit Merah Central, Singapore 159836
Telephone: +65 278 2538
Fax: +65 278 7518

Singapore Advertisers' Association

Address: Ngee Ann City, Tower A, #08-01, 391B Orchard Road, 238874

Telephone: +65 735 7792
Fax: +65 735 9692
Year established: 1974
Publications:
• Advoice: *monthly*

Singapore Association of Pharmaceutical Industries (SAPI)

Address: 02-13A/14 Manhattan House, 151 Chin Swee Road, #02-13A/14, Singapore 169876
Telephone: +65 738 0966
Fax: +65 738 0977
E-mail: sapi@cyberway.com.sg
Year established: 1966
Publications:
• SAPI News: *news and views on developments in the pharmaceutical industries of Singapore - quarterly*

Singapore Book Publishers' Association

Address: Blk 86 #03-213, Marine Parade Central, 440086
Telephone: +65 344 7801
Fax: +65 447 0897
E-mail: sbpa@sbpa.org.sg.
Web site: www.sbpa.org.sg
Activities: trade fairs and festivals; publishing and distribution of educational, consumer and trade magazines; import and distribution of books; sale and purchase of rights; arrangement of printing
Chief officers: K P Sivam (President); B C Poh (Treasurer); Tan Wu Cheng (Honorary Secretary)

Singapore Booksellers' and Stationers' Association

Address: #03-01 Midland House, 112 Middle Road, 188970 Singapore 188970
Telephone: +65 337 2768
Fax: +65 338 6826

Singapore Chinaware Merchants' Association

Address: 33, Lor 16 Geylang, Singapore 398873
Telephone: +65 747 2169
Fax: +65 747 2169
Chief officers: Peter Lek Ting Ngweng

Singapore Chinese Merchandise Importers' and Exporters' Association

Address: Golden Mile Tower, 6001, Beach Rd, #11-01, Singapore 199589
Telephone: +65 298 3622
Fax: +65 296 9492
Chief officers: Chen Mong Tse

Singapore Clock and Watch Trade Association

Address: Association Bldg, 68, Lor 16 Geylang, #05-05, Singapore 398889
Telephone: +65 746 5748
Fax: +65 743 3535
Chief officers: Tan Kien Lip

Singapore Coffee Association

Address: c/o Coopers & Lybrand, 9 Penang Road, #13-20 Park Mall, Singapore 238459
Telephone: +65 336 2344
Fax: +65 336 2539

Singapore Commodity Exchange

Address: 23-04/05 Peninsula Plaza, 111 North Bridge Road, Singapore 0617

Telephone: +65 338 5600
Fax: +65 338 9116/9640/9676
Year established: 1992
Activities: quarterly seminars; brochures on products traded and historical price data; price statistics for nominal fee; internal research on new contracts
Chief officers: Patrick Hays (Chairman); David Chin (Vice Chairman)
Structure: board of directors; committees
Membership: 112
Publications:
• Exchange Brochures

Singapore Confederation of Industries

Address: SMA House, 20 Orchard Road, 0923
Telephone: +65 338 8787
Fax: +65 336 5385
E-mail: scihq@sci.org.sg
Activities: plays intermediary role between government, semi-government organisations and members; provides information services relating to domestic and international government policies
Chief officers: Robert Chua (President), Tan Wah Thong (Honorary President), Bob Tan (Deputy President)
Structure: executive committee, functional committees, product group committees, secretariat, management committee, membership committee, local industries committee, production committee, trade development committee
Membership: 1,400 members
Publications:
• Annual Report of the Singapore Manufacturers' Association: *annual*
• Mailing List
• Manufacturers Link- SMA Mini Directory
• Singapore Manufacturer: *bi-annual*
• SMA News
• Tradelink: *annual*
Notes: formerly Singapore Manufacturers' Association

Singapore Cycle and Motor Traders' Association

Address: Blk 261 Waterloo Street, #03-09 Waterloo Centre, Singapore 180261
Telephone: +65 339 7648
Fax: +65 336 6181

Singapore Federation Of The Computer Industry

Address: 71 Science Park Drive, 118253
Telephone: +65 775 1927
Fax: +65 778 4968
E-mail: sfcii@singnet.com.sg
Web site: www.asianconnect.com/sfci
Year established: 1982
Activities: main activities include the following: liaison with the Asian Oceanian Computing Industry Organization (ASOCIO) and the government; Organisation of Singapore Informatics (trade fair); business surveys and an information technology salary survey
Chief officers: William Liu (Chairman), Mr Michael Fleming (Secretary), Mr. Chung Seng Hong (Executive Director)
Membership: members comprise IT vendor companies which have significant local value-added component in their product and services
Publications:
• A Guide to IT Agreements: *It covers key issues concerning the acquisition, maintenance and support of computer systems*
• SFCI Link: *newsletter of the SFCI. Its features include activities of the SFCI, trade missions, corporate news of members - bi-monthly*

Singapore Fish Merchant General Association

Address: 413 Fish Merchant Office Building, 35 Fishery Port
Road, Singapore 619742
Telephone: +65 265 0051
Fax: +65 266 2585

Singapore Food Manufacturers' Association

Address: 7 Teo Hong Road, Singapore 088324
Telephone: +65 221 2438
Fax: +65 223 7235

Singapore Footwear Merchants' Association

Address: 68 Lorong 16, Geylang, Association Building No.
05-01/02, Singapore 1439
Telephone: +65 747 3022

Singapore Fruit and Vegetables Importers' and Exporters' Association

Address: Blk 1 #02-07, Wholesale Centre, Singapore 100001
Telephone: +65 775 3676
Fax: +65 773 1336

Singapore Furniture Industries' Council (SFIC)

Address: #02-110/111, IMM Bldg, 2, Jurong East St 21,
Singapore 609601
Telephone: +65 568 2626
Fax: +65 568 2922
E-mail: sfic@pacific.net.sg
Web site: www.sfic.org.sg
Year established: 1981
Activities: organises trade fairs, furniture design
competitions, design seminars; consultancy service;
industry-wide computerisation programme; Good Furniture
Retailers' Scheme
Chief officers: Choo Yong Fee (President)
Membership: 280 manufacturers, exporters and suppliers
Publications:
• Singapore Furniture: *contact details and product information
on Singapore furniture manufacturers - annual*
• Singapore Furniture Industries Council Newsletter: *news and
industry trends in the Singapore furniture industry - quarterly*

Singapore Furniture Manufacturers' and Traders' Association

Address: 7500D, Beach Rd, #03-03, The Plaza,, 199594
Telephone: +65 295 2300
Fax: +65 296 2355
Activities: organises trade missions; market development
Chief officers: Paul Keng (President); Yew Tian Sam
(Honorary Secretary)
Structure: executive committee, working committees
Membership: 303 member companies
Publications:
• Singapore Furniture Directory

Singapore Glass Merchants' and Glaziers' Association

Address: 33 Geylang Lorong 4, Singapore 399824
Telephone: +65 747 1132
Fax: +65 747 1178

Singapore Hotel Association

Address: 37 Duxton Hill, Singapore 0208
Telephone: +65 227 7577
Fax: +65 227 9085
Telex: RS 35 235 SHA
Chief officers: Pakir Singh (Chief Executive officer)

Singapore International Franchise Association (SIFA)

Address: 71 Sophia Road, Singapore 228154
Telephone: +65 334 8200
Fax: +65 334 8211
E-mail: frantech@pacific.net.sg
Chief officers: Tan Thuan Seng (Chairman)

Singapore Merchant Bankers' Association

Address: 16-02 Clifford Centre, 24 Raffles Place, Singapore
0104
Telephone: +65 532 7565
Fax: +65 532 3390
Year established: 1975
Chief officers: Vicky Loke (Executive Secretary)
Membership: 68 member companies

Singapore Motor Cycle Trade Association

Address: 40 Sam Leong Road, Singapore 207930
Telephone: +65 297 1991
Fax: +65 297 1313

Singapore Packaging Council

Address: SMA House, 20 Orchard Road, 0923
Telephone: +65 338 8787
Fax: +65 338 3358
Year established: 1975
Activities: organises conferences and exhibitions; keeps
members informed of the latest trends and technologies
available; promotes the benefits of packaging to government
bodies and the public
Membership: 60 member companies
Publications:
• Singapore Packaging Industries' Directory: *contact details;
product and service information for member companies;
articles of interest to the packaging industry - annual*

Singapore Paint Manufacturers' Association

Address: 22 Song Lee Road, Singapore 608082
Telephone: +65 265 0677
Fax: +65 265 4775

Singapore Paper Merchants' Association

Address: c/o Permana Enterprise Pte Ltd, Blk 34 #06-14,
Commonwealth Lane, Singapore 149553
Telephone: +65 777 0677
Fax: +65 779 0704

Singapore Plastic Industry Association

Address: 15B, Lorong 4, Geylang, Singapore 399272
Telephone: +65 743 5571
Fax: +65 743 3309

Singapore Pulp and Paper Manufacturers' Association

Address: c/o Sanyen Paper Pte Ltd, 76 Kian Teck Road,
Singapore 2262
Telephone: +65 268 6188
Fax: +65 265 3338
Chief officers: T. S. Ong (President)

Singapore Retailers' Association

Address: #15-03, 2 Bukit Merah Central, Singapore 159835
Telephone: +65 272 3160
Fax: +65 271 3091
Chief officers: Penelope Phoon (Executive Director)

Singapore Textile and General Merchants' Association
Address: 148 Neil Road, Singapore 088877
Telephone: +65 223 8061
Fax: +65 222 3501

Singapore Textile Centre Merchants' Association
Address: 200 Jalan Sultan, #12-06 Textile Centre, Singapore 199018
Telephone: +65 295 4108
Fax: +65 299 1928

Singapore Tourist Promotion Board
Address: 250 North Bridge Road, 36-04 Raffles City Tower, 0617
Telephone: +65 339 6622
Fax: +65 334 6254
Publications:
• Annual Report on Tourism Statistics: *commentary and statistics on tourism trends including data on visitor arrivals, reasons for visit, type of transport, length of stay, accommodation, hotels, hotel building etc. - annual*
• Singapore Monthly Report on Tourism Statistics: *monthly summary statistics on tourism trends with data on visitor arrivals, country of origin, purpose of visit etc. - monthly*

Textile and Garment Manufacturers' Association of Singapore
Address: 60 Martin Road, Trade Mart Singapore Levels 07-61/17, 0923
Telephone: +65 735 8390
Fax: +65 735 8409
Activities: Liaison with government bodies; training.
Chief officers: Chris Koh (President); Wong Soi Yong (Secretary General)
Structure: management committee, 6 sub-committees
Publications:
• Members Directory: *annual*

SLOVAKIA

Article Numbering Association (EAN Slovakia)
Address: Predmestska ul.1, 010 01 Zilina
Telephone: +42 89 641 896
Fax: +42 89 641 897
E-mail: inform@ean.sk

Association of Textile, Clothing & Leather Industries (Slovakia)
Asociacia Textilneho a Odevenho Priemyslu
Address: Stefanikova 19, 91140 Trencin
Telephone: +42 1 831 437 811
Fax: +42 1 831 431 440
Chief officers: Rokasi Anton (President), Jan Hajmach (General Secretary)

Slovak Union of Newspaper Publishers (ANPS)
Address: Odboráske námestie 3, 812 71 Bratislava
Telephone: +42 7 689 157
Fax: +42 7 212 985
Chief officers: Dr Milos Nemecek (President)

SLOVENIA

Association for Engineering and Consulting
Address: Slovenska cesta 58, 61000 Ljubljana
Telephone: +386 61 317 287/131 3190
Fax: +386 61 312 569
Chief officers: Franc Zle (Secretary)

Association for the Construction Materials Industry
Address: Slovenska cesta 58, 61000 Ljubljana
Telephone: +386 61 133 6233/133 6259
Fax: +386 61 312 569
Chief officers: Joze Vucajink (Secretary)

Association for the Electrical and Electronics Industry
Address: Dimiceva 9, 61000 Ljubljana
Telephone: +386 61 301 133/132 7214
Fax: +386 61 218 380
Chief officers: Franc Gerbec (Secretary)

Association of Banks and Insurance Companies
Address: Subiceva 2, 61000 Ljubljana
Telephone: +386 61 215 076
Fax: +386 61 212 180
Chief officers: Srecko Korber (General Secretary)

Association of Entrepreneurs of Slovenia
Address: Slovenska cesta 71, 61000 Ljubljana
Telephone: +386 61 159 3241/159 3187
Fax: +386 61 559 270
Chief officers: Stefan Stepko Mioc (Secretary)

Association of Hotels and Restaurants and Tourism
Address: Chamber of Commerce and Industry of Slovenia, Slovenska 54, SI-1000 Ljubljana
Telephone: +386 61 132 8218/132 7283
Fax: +386 61 302 983
E-mail: pretnar@hq.gzs.si
Web site: www.gzs.si
Chief officers: Miro Pretnar (General Secretary)
Membership: 3,000 members
Notes: Association is he branch association of the Chamber of Commerce and Industry of Slovenia.

Association of the Chemical and Rubber Industry
Address: Dimiceva 9, 61000 Ljubljana
Telephone: +386 61 301 133/320 596
Fax: +386 61 218 380
Chief officers: Stefan Trajbaric (Secretary)

Banks Association of Slovenia
Address: Subiceva 2, 61000 Ljublijana
Telephone: +386 61 215 076
Fax: +386 61 125 2106
E-mail: info@zbs-giz.si
Activities: banking, publishing financial statements of Slovenian banks
Chief officers: Srecko Korber (General Manager), Miro Kos (Deputy General Manager
Membership: 31 banks

Food and Agriculture Association
Address: Chamber of Commerce and Industry of Slovenia, Dimiceva 9, 1504 Ljubljana
Telephone: +386 61 219 464

Fax: +386 61 218 380
E-mail: kavcic.@hq.gzs.si
Web site: www.gzs.si
Activities: information service to members; education and training; government liaison
Chief officers: Joze Kavcic (Secretary)
Membership: 516 large and medium-sized companies, 172 small companies
Notes: Association is the branch association of the Chamber of Commerce and Industry of Slovenia.

Importers and Exporters Association

Address: Chamber of Commerce and Industry of Slovenia, Slovenska cesta 54, SI-1504 Ljubljana
Telephone: +386 61 316 048/313 906
Fax: +386 61 317 443
Activities: trade promotion; liaison with state authorities; research; education and training
Chief officers: Metka Potocnik (Secretary)
Membership: 14,000 members, membership is obligatory for all enterprises engaged in the sector
Publications:
• Information: *taxation, customs, salaries, modification of legislation focus on direct and indirect influence on trade, sales methods - weekly*
Notes: Association is the branch association of the Chamber of Commerce and Industry of Slovenia.

Pulp, Paper and Paper Converting Industry Association

Address: Chamber of Commerce and Industry of Slovenia, Dimiceva 9, 61000 Ljubljana
Telephone: +386 61 329 198
Fax: +386 61 218 380
E-mail: hocevar.@hq.gzs.si
Activities: liaison with governmental institutions and trade unions; collects statistical data on production, exports, imports, employment, raw materials, etc.
Chief officers: Janez Hocevar (Secretary of the Board)
Membership: 20 big and medium and 60 small companies

Slovenian Article Numbering Association (SANA)

Address: WTC Ljubljana, Dunajska 156, 61000 Ljubljana
Telephone: +386 61 188 1350
Fax: +386 61 168 8312
E-mail: eanslov@perftech.si

Slovenian Publishers' Association

Slovenska Knjiga d.o.o.
Address: Litijska 38, 61000 Ljubljana
Telephone: +386 61 140 2008
Fax: +386 61 447 305
Web site: www.slo-knjiga.si/
Chief officers: Mr MJ Korinsek (Secretary), Dr M Znidersic (Director)

Textile, Clothing and Leather Processing Industries' Association

Address: Chamber of Commerce and Industry of Slovenia, Dimiceva 9, 1504 Ljubljana
Telephone: +386 61 301 133
Fax: +386 61 218 380
E-mail: grasic.@hq.gzs.si
Web site: www.gzs.si
Activities: provides all kinds of business information; education and training; business contacts, trade promotion
Chief officers: Franc Grasic (Secretary)
Membership: 106 large and medium-sized companies, 533 small companies

Publications:
• Barometer Tekstilcev in Usnjarjev: *statistics and analysis of the textiles, clothing and leather processing industries in Slovenia; information on the industry in other countries; information about the activities of the association and the Chamber of Commerce and Industry of Slovenia - monthly*
Notes: The Association is the affiliated to the Chamber of Commerce and Industry of Slovenia.

Transport and Communications Association

Address: Dimiceva 9, 61000 Ljubljana
Telephone: +386 61 301 133/342 795
Fax: +386 61 218 380
Chief officers: Viktor Trstenjak (Secretary)

SOUTH AFRICA

Aerosol Manufacturers' Association (AMA)

Address: PO Box 483, 180 Lever Road, Olifantsfontein 1665
Telephone: +27 11 315 2716
Fax: +27 11 318 1698
Year established: 1963
Activities: activities related to self-regulation of aerosol industry; promotion of the aerosol package; interaction with regulators; collects annual production statistics
Chief officers: Pierce Clarke (Chariman), Mike Naude (Executive Director), Marion Plint (Administrative Assistant)
Membership: 46 companies involved in the aerosol industry: suppliers, contract fillers, manufacturers
Publications:
• Bulletin: *regularly*
• Newsletter of the Aerosol Manufacturers Association (AMA): *news on events and developments in the aerosol industry - quarterly*

Animal Feed Manufacturers' Association (AMFA)

Address: PO Box 4473, Hingyip Building, c/o 9th Avenue & Wessel Road, Rivonia 2128
Telephone: +27 11 803 3128
Fax: +27 11 803 8148
E-mail: afma@icon.co.za
Year established: 1945
Activities: organises triennial congresses for the feed and related industries as well as regular symposia on topical issues for the industry; collects statistics on feed production and raw material utilisation
Chief officers: M Griessel (Chairman), Hansie Bekker (General Manager)
Structure: secretariat
Membership: 40 feed manufacturers and 4 premix manufacturers
Publications:
• AFMA MATRIX: *information for the feed and related industries - quarterly*
• Simposia and Congress Reports

Association of Plastics Processors of South Africa (APPSA)

Address: Private Bag X68, c/o Plastics Federation of South Africa, Halfway House 1685
Telephone: +27 11 314 4021
Fax: +27 11 314 3764
E-mail: enquiries@plasfed.co.za
Chief officers: Mrs L. Taylor (Secretary)
Membership: 165 manuafcturers of plastics user products

Association of South African Travel Agents (ASATA)

Address: PO Box 31742 Johannesburg 2000, 6th Floor, Field North, Jorissen Street, Braamfontein 2017
Telephone: +27 11 403 2923/403 2933
Fax: +27 11 403 3997
Activities: liaise with government on behalf of members
Chief officers: Mr Chris du Toit (Executive Director), Miss Jacqui McKinght (Administrative Manager)
Membership: 645 travel agents and tourism-related enterprises
Publications:
• ASATA News: *industry matters and issues of interest - monthly*

Audit Bureau of Circulation of South Africa (ABC)

Address: POBox 47189, 8th Floor, North Wing, Nedbank Gardens, 33 Bath Avenue, Parklands 2121
Telephone: +27 11 447 1264
Fax: +27 11 447 1269/11 447 1289
E-mail: pma.sa@johan.sprintlink.co.za
Web site: johan.sprintlink.co.za
Activities: produces detailed circulation data for South African and magazines and newspapers as well as cinema attendance figures
Chief officers: D.A Dickens (Chairman), MDW Short (Vice-Chairman), Mr PSC Pote (General Manager), Mrs S.Grundy (Secretary)
Membership: 545 newspapers, magazines advertising agencies, advertisers, cinema proprietors and distributors
Notes: The association does not produce any publications but does produce a report on circulation figures distributed to members.

Book Trade Association of South Africa (BTA)

Address: PO Box 109, Pietermaritzburg 3200
Telephone: +27 33 194 6830
Fax: +27 33 194 3096/ 33 427 419
Activities: statistical data
Chief officers: Jess Fourie
Membership: booksellers and publishers

Cape Wools SA

Address: PO Box 2191, North End, Port Elizabeth 6056
Telephone: +27 41 544 301
Fax: +27 41 546 760
Year established: 1946
Activities: wool promotion, produces market information and statistics
Chief officers: J.W. Gieselbach (Manager), A. Strydom (Information), P. Buys (Secretary), Mrs O. Viljoen (Public Relations)
Membership: non-profitmaking company serving the wool industry from producer level through to primary processing
Publications:
• Annual Report: *annual*
• Annual Statistics: *production, export, international wool prices and market movements - annual*
• Market Report: *weekly*

Chemical and Allied Industries' Association (CAIA)

Address: P O Box 91415, 2006 Auckland Park
Telephone: +27 11 482 1671
Fax: +27 11 726 8310
Activities: promotes efficiency, productivity and competitiveness of the chemical and allied industries in South Africa
Chief officers: Dr L Lotter (Executive Director)
Structure: board of directors, each of whom is a chief executive of a member company. The board is structured so as to represent small, medium and large companies

Clothing Federation of South Africa (CLOFED)

Address: PO Box 75755, Gardenview, 2047 Johannesburg
Telephone: +27 11 622 8125
Fax: +27 11 622 8316
Year established: 1945
Activities: dissemination of information on the South African clothing industry , training, arbitration
Chief officers: Hennie Van Zyl (Executive Director), P.L. Theron (Economist), Mrs ME Scott (Administration Manager)
Membership: 349 clothing manufacturers representing 57,610 employees
Publications:
• Newsletter: *issues affecting the South African clothing industry - quarterly*
• Product Directory: *clothing available from member companies - annual*

Commercial Employers' Association

Address: Private Bag 34, JCC House, Auckland Park 2006
Telephone: +27 11 726 5300
Fax: +27 11 726 8421/482 2000
Telex: 425594
Chief officers: Jean McKenzie (Chief Executive)
Membership: commercial employers

Consumer Electronics' Association

Address: PO Box 1084, Pinegowrie 2123
Telephone: +27 11 789 6770
Fax: +27 11 789 6645
Chief officers: RJ Van de Berg

Council of South African Banks (COSAB)

Address: 10th Floor, 17 Harrison Street, Johannesburg 2001
Telephone: +27 11 838 4978
Fax: +27 11 836 5509
Chief officers: B.J Swart (Chairman)
Membership: banks

Direct Selling Association

Address: Private Bag 34, JCC House, Auckland Park 2006
Telephone: +27 11 726 5300
Fax: +27 11 726 8421/482 2000
Telex: 4 25594
Year established: 1972
Chief officers: Avroy Shlain (Chairman), J Solomon (Secretary)
Structure: part of an international organisation with branches in 27 countries
Membership: retailers and wholesalers

Electronic Industries' Association (EIF)

Address: PO Box 1980, 338 16th Road, Randjespark, Halfway House 1685
Telephone: +27 11 315 1002
Fax: +27 11 315 1645
Chief officers: DH Botha (President), K Prins (Executive Director)

Federated Hospitality Association of South Africa (FEDHASA)

Address: PO Box 718, Randburg 2125
Telephone: +27 11 886 2394
Fax: +27 11 789 4811
E-mail: fedhasa@fedhasa.co.za
Year established: 1949
Activities: represents its members interests, disseminates information
Chief officers: Ken Forrester (President), Deon Vilioen

(Executive Director),Chris de Jager (Finance Chairman)
Membership: 2000 member companies
Publications:
• Cater Talk: *four p.a.*
• FEDHASA News: *four p.a.*
• FEDSAS Feedback (Self-catering Accommodation): *four p.a.*
• NHASA Newsline (Hotels): *four p.a.*
• SA Restaurant Guild Gazette: *four p.a.*
Notes: Represents the National Hotel Association of South
Africa (NHASA), the South African Restaurant Guild (Sarg), the
Caterers Guild of South Africa (CGSA), the Federation of the
South African Self-Catering Accomodation Industry (FEDSAS)
and the Associatied Clubs of South Africa (ACSA).

Furniture Traders' Association of South Africa (FTA)
Address: PO Box 1084, Pinegowrie 2123
Telephone: +27 11 789 6770
Fax: +27 11 789 6645
Year established: 1932
Activities: negotiates with government; liaises with consumer
bodies; monitors the association's code of conduct;
disseminates information to members
Chief officers: Frans Jordaan (Executive Director), Melanie
Crossley (Secretary)
Membership: 296 furniture, appliance, audio and television
retailers
Publications:
• FAS Retailer
Notes: The Association does not produce any statistics or
publications.

Grocery Manufacturers' Association of South Africa
Address: PO Box 34, Randburg 2125
Telephone: +27 11 886 3008
Fax: +27 11 886 5375
Activities: contact with consumer organisations and the media
Chief officers: Neville Isemonger (Chairman), Jeremy Hele
(Executive Director)
Membership: 10 producers, manufacturers and distributors of
grocery products
Notes: standing member of Food Legislation Advisory Group
(FLAG), and Cosmetics Legislation Advisory Group (COSLAG)

Hand Tool Manufacturers' Association
Address: PO Box 1338, Johannesburg 2000
Telephone: +27 11 883 6033
Fax: +27 11 838 1522
Chief officers: V A Mattysen (Secretary)
Membership: hand tool manufacturers

Health Products' Association of Southern Africa (HPA)
Address: P O Box 953, Northlands 2116, Gauteng
Telephone: +27 11 789 4464
Fax: +27 11 886 3047
E-mail: hpaofsa@iafrica.com
Web site: www.ehpm.org/members/south_af.htm
Year established: 1978
Activities: government liaison, organises annual trade
exhibitions
Chief officers: B.W. Dennison (President), Miss D. K. Allen

Independent Car Rental Association of South Africa
Address: P O Box 1195, Sea Point, 8001
Telephone: +27 21 448 0016
Fax: +27 21 448 2759
E-mail: comet@iafrica.com.za
Web site: africa.cis.co.za/cape/travel/rentcar/icrasoc.html
Web site notes: site includes a list of members
Membership: 20 independent car rental companies

Institute of Marketing Management
Address: PO Box 91820, Auckland Park 2006
Telephone: +27 11 482 1419
Fax: +27 11 726 3639

Institute of Packaging SA (IPSA)
Address: PO Box 56145, Pinegowrie 2123
Telephone: +27 11 782 1233
Fax: +27 11 782 4926
Activities: publishes educational and training information on
matters relating to packaging, conferences, seminars,
educational courses and bursaries, participates in and
supports the triennial Pakprocess packaging exhibition,
packaging design award scheme
Chief officers: Pierre Pienaar (Chairman), Henry Willis
(Secretary)
Membership: over 1,000 packaging companies
Publications:
• Packaging Review: *official journal - covers news and events
concerning the institute*

Malt Manufacturers' Association of South Africa
Address: PO Box 91267, Auckland Park 2006, JCC House,
Empire Road, Milpark 2092
Telephone: +27 11 482 2524
Fax: +27 11 726 1344/ 11 482 1281
Membership: Malt manufacturers

Master Butchers' Association
Address: Private Bag X3060, 147 Hendrick Verwoerd Drive,
Randburg 2125
Telephone: +27 11 886 7940
Fax: +27 11 886 7109
E-mail: davidson@icon.co.za
Year established: 1940
Chief officers: Lesley Dennison (Secretary)
Structure: executive committee appointed by general
membership
Membership: 1,500 retail meat traders
Publications:
• Meat (Vleis): *useful information on people and events in the
meat industry - bimonthly*
Notes: affiliated to the South African Federation of Meat
Traders

Meat Board
Address: PO Box 40051, Publishers of South African Meat
Trade, 556 Verr, Arcadia 0007, Pretoria
Telephone: +27 12 323 1515
Fax: +27 12 325 5753/323 3300
Activities: collects statistical information
Chief officers: Dr Kempen (General Manager)

Milk Board
Address: PO Box 1284, Pretoria 0001
Telephone: +27 12 804 4800
Fax: +27 12 804 4811
Year established: 1994
Chief officers: J. Haneicam (Deputy General Manager)
Structure: statutory marketing board
Membership: 8,500 producers and processors of milk
Publications:
• Dairy Mail

Motor Industries' Federation (MIF)
Address: PO Box 2940, Randburg 2125, 303 Surrey Avenue,
Randburg 2194

Telephone: +27 11 789 2542
Fax: +27 11 789 4525
Year established: 1910
Chief officers: Wietsche Fourie (Executive Director), Willem Schröeder (Deputy Executive Director)
Membership: 11 constituent associations representing 9000 industries
Publications:
• Newsletter
Notes: The Federation does not produce any statistics. The MIF is the hostbody for the following 11 constituent associations linked to the motor and related industries: NADA (representing vehicle car dealers), MTA (representing garages, service stations and some independent fleet owners), MDA (Motorcycle Dealers Association), TDA (representing retreaders and tyre dealers), ERA (Engineers and Engine Rebuilders Association), NMPEA (representing parts dealers of all kinds), ACRA (representing parts remanufacturers), SAVABA (Vehicle Body Builders Association), NAMTA (representing farm equipment dealers), SAMBRA (Panelbeaters and automotive refinishers), SADFIA (diesel pump room operators)

Motor Traders' Association (MTA)
Address: PO Box 2940, Randburg 2125, 303 Surrey Avenue, Randburg 2194
Telephone: +27 11 789 2542/3
Fax: +27 11 789 4525
Membership: The Association represents the service station and non-franchise workshop industry and specialist workshop establishments
Notes: The Association is attached to the Motor Industries' Federation

Motorcycle Dealers' Association (MDA)
Address: PO Box 2940, Randburg 2125, 303 Surrey Avenue, Randburg 2194
Telephone: +27 11 789 2542/3
Fax: +27 11 789 4525
Membership: The association represents the motorcycle industry
Notes: The Association is attached to the Motor Industries' Federation

National Association of Automobile Manufacturers of South Africa (NAAMSA)
Address: PO Box 40611, Arcadia 0007, 1st Floor, Nedbank Plaza, Cnr Church and Beatrix Streets, Pretoria 0002
Telephone: +27 12 323 2980/1/323 2003
Fax: +27 12 326 3232
Year established: 1935
Activities: monthly detailed sales statistics for cars and commercial vehicles sold in the Republic and exported to neighbouring countries; research by NAAMSA may be commissioned
Chief officers: N M W Vermeulen (Director), C A Z Pierides (Assistant Director), A J J Wessels (President)
Structure: executive committee, car/light commercial vehicle and heavy commercial vehicle divisions, and various specialist committees
Membership: 14 full members, 3 associate members, all manufacturers of cars, light, medium and/or heavy commercial vehicles
Publications:
• Annual Report of the National Association of Automobile Manufacturers of South Africa: *annual*
• Car and Commercial Vehicle Statistics: *monthly sales figures, by make and model, for cars and commercial vehicles in South Africa. Based on data collected by the Association - monthly*

• Quarterly Review (NAAMSA): *commentary and statistics covering trends in the South African automobile sector with regular statistics on production, registrations, sales, foreign trade, prices - quarterly*
• Review: *business conditions in the South African vehicle manufacturing industry - quarterly*

National Association of Automotive Component and Allied Manufacturers (NAACAM)
Address: PO Box 1398, 2nd Floor North, Dorbyl Park, 4 Skeen Boulevard, Bedfordview 2008, Johannesburg
Telephone: +27 11 455 3431/2
Fax: +27 11 455 1014/455 6045
E-mail: cbw@global.co.za
Web site: www.tradepage.co.za/naacam/
Year established: 1979
Activities: participation in international fairs, up-to-date information and advice
Chief officers: John Brandtner (President), Steve Wynne, Johan Meyer (Vice Presidents)
Membership: ca. 160 automotive companies
Publications:
• Newsletter of the National Association of Automotive Component and Allied Manufacturers: *up-to-date details on the South African automotive industry - monthly*

National Association of Pharmaceutical Wholesalers
Address: P.O. Box 30857, Braamfontein 2017
Telephone: +27 11 339 3576
Fax: +27 11 339 7307

National Automobile Dealers' Association (NADA)
Address: PO Box 2940, Randburg 2125, 303 Surrey Avenue, Randburg 2194
Telephone: +27 11 789 2542/3
Fax: +27 11 789 4525
Activities: training programme for sales and marketing personnel employed in member establishments
Membership: The association represents franchise holders for new vehicles and second hand motor vehicle dealerships
Notes: The Association is attached to the Motor Industries' Federation

National Federation of Meat Traders
Nasionale Federasie Van Vleishandelaars
Address: Private Bag X3060, 147 Hendrick Verwoerd Drive, Randburg 2125
Telephone: +27 11 886 7940
Fax: +27 11 886 7109
E-mail: davidson@icon.co.za
Year established: 1990
Chief officers: T G Davidson, R W Ward, Kim Manzocco
Structure: the Federation comprises: the South Africa Urban Retail Meat Traders, the South Africa Rural Retail Meat Traders and Corporate Members (wholesale meat traders and abattoirs); management committee consisting of five representatives appointed annually
Membership: c.a. 5,000 wholesale and retail meat traders
Publications:
• Meat (Vleis): *news and trends in the South African meat industry - bi-monthly*
Notes: Recognised by the authorities in the meat industry as the representative body in the retail trade; the Association does not produce statistics (collected by the Meat Board).

Packaging Council of South Africa
Address: PO Box 782205, Sandton 2146
Telephone: +27 11 783 4782

Fax: +27 11 883 7170
E-mail: packagec@cis.co.za
Year established: 1984
Activities: collects statistics on recycling of materials used in the packaging industry
Chief officers: Derrick Minnie (President), Owen C. Bryuns (Executive Director)
Membership: 40 raw materials' suppliers, packaging manufacturers, packaging users, retailers, packaging designers and consultants

Pharmaceutical Manufacturers' Association of South Africa (PMA)

Address: P. O. Box 12123, Building No 5, Momentum Business Park, Old Pretoria Road, Midrand, Vorna Valley 1686
Telephone: +27 11 805 5100
Fax: +27 11 805 5105/5109
E-mail: pma@iafrica.com
Year established: 1967
Activities: government liaison, informs members of legal, trade, labour and economic issues affecting the industry, negotiates with international pharmaceutical bodies in order to improve the South African industry
Chief officers: Mrs Ericka Pinto (Public Affairs Manager), Mrs Mirryéna Deeb (Chief Executive Officer)
Structure: the association is divided into 5 divisions: pharmaceutical, non-prescription medicines and cosmetics, medical devices, diagnostic, and veterinary
Membership: manufacturers and distributors of pharmaceuticals representing approximately 80% of the research based pharmaceutical manufacturers in South Africa

Plastics Federation of South Africa (PFSA)

Address: Private Bag X68, Halfway House, 1685 South Africa
Telephone: +27 11 314 4021
Fax: +27 11 314 3764
E-mail: enquiries@plasfed.co.za
Web site: www.plasfed.co.za
Year established: 1979
Activities: government liaison, training and education, dissemination of the latest technological information. Maintains a data base and provides information on the plastics industry
Chief officers: Mr R Crewe-Brown (President), Bill Naude (Executive Director)
Notes: PFSA is an umbrella organisation representing plastics material suppliers, plastics converters, associations and allied interest groups in the South African plastics industry. These include the following: Association of Plastics Processors of South Africa (APPSA), Composite Material Suppliers Group (CMSG), Plastics Institute of Southern Africa (PISA), representing individuals in the South African plastics industry, Plastics Manufacturers' Association of South Africa (PMA), Polifin, Sentrachem (including Safripol & Plastomark), South African Machinery Suppliers' Association for the Plastics, Printing, Packaging and Allied Industries (SAMPLAS), South African Polymer Importers' Association (SAPIA)

Plumbing and Sanitaryware Manufacturers' Association of South Africa

Address: Private Bag 34, JCC House, Auckland Park 2006
Telephone: +27 11 726 5300
Fax: +27 11 726 8421/482 2000
Chief officers: R A Russouw (Manager)
Membership: 15 manufacturers

Pottery Manufacturers' Association

Address: Private Bag 34, Auckland Park 2006
Telephone: +27 11 726 5300

Fax: +27 11 482 2000
E-mail: jcci@cis.co.za
Web site: www.jcci.co.za
Chief officers: Jean McKenzie (President)

Printing Industries Federation of South Africa

Address: PO Box 46125, 1084 Honeydew 2040, Orange Grove, Johannesburg 2119
Telephone: +27 11 794 3810/483 1275
Fax: +27 11 794 3964/483 1540
Year established: 1916
Activities: interest groups in the following areas: security printing, folding cartons, business forms, corrugated containers, graphic reproduction, flexible packaging, book printing
Chief officers: C W J Sykes (Executive Director), E Kühl (Director, commercial and technical services), W F Uys (Director)
Membership: all printing sectors, packaging
Notes: Southern African Printing College is a subsidiary of PIFSA. Nationally organised into chambers in the following regions: Johannesburg, Pretoria, Cape Town, Durban, Port Elizabeth, East London, and Bloemfontein.

Proprietary Dairy Industry Association

Address: PO Box 933, Showgrounds, Soutter Street, Pretoria
Telephone: +27 12 327 1487
Fax: +27 12 327 1501
Membership: dairies

Radio, Appliance and Television Association of South Africa (RATA)

Address: PO Box 1338, Metal Industries House, 42 Anderson Street, Johannesburg 2001
Telephone: +27 11 833 6033
Fax: +27 11 838 1522
Year established: 1942
Activities: an employer organisation dealing mainly with servicing in the industry
Chief officers: G Whiffler (Secretary)
Membership: 256 member companies

Road Freight Association (RFA)

Address: PO Box 7, Randburg 2125
Telephone: +27 11 789 1357
Fax: +27 11 789 1367
Activities: information service
Chief officers: Neil Wright (Chairman), Kerry Curtis (Vice Chairman), Herman Lemmer (Chief Executive)
Membership: small companies and large carriers
Publications:
• Focus on the Freight Industry: *monthly*
• Vehicle Cost Schedule: *biennial*

South African Advertising Research Foundation

Address: 98874, Sloan Park 2152
Telephone: +27 11 463 5340
Fax: +27 11 463 5010

South African Article Numbering Association (SAANA)

Address: PO Box 41417, Craighall 2024
Telephone: +27 11 447 6110
Fax: +27 11 447 4159
E-mail: saana@cis.co.za
Year established: 1982
Chief officers: Mr Pearcey (Executive Director)
Membership: 6000 companies from a wide range of market and industry sectors in South Africa

Publications:
• Newsletter: *four p.a.*
Notes: member of EAN International

South African Battery Manufacturers
Address: Private Bag 34, JCC House, Auckland Park 2006
Telephone: +27 11 726 5300
Fax: +27 11 726 8421/482 2000
Activities: information service, use of JHB Chamber of Commerce and Industry library, battery surcharge statistics published monthly by members
Membership: 4 battery manufacturers

South African Breweries' Association
Address: Private Bag 34, Auckland Park 2006
Telephone: +27 11 881 8111
Fax: +27 11 881 8030/31
Year established: 1927
Chief officers: L I Goldstone
Membership: brewing companies

South African Chamber of Baking
Address: PO Box 7408, 7 and 8 Centuria Park, 265 von Wielligh Str, Lyttelton, Centurion
Telephone: +27 12 663 1600/1/2/3
Fax: +27 12 663 1604
Activities: government liaison
Chief officers: P.J Cownie (Executive Director)
Membership: manufacturers, wholesalers and retailers of bread and confectionery

South African Chocolate and Sweet Manufacturers' Association
Address: PO Box 933, Showgrounds, Soutter Street, Pretoria
Telephone: +27 12 327 1487
Fax: +27 12 327 1501
Membership: confectionery manufacturers

South African Dairy Foundation
Address: PO Box 72300, Lynwood Ridge 0040
Telephone: +27 12 348 5345
Fax: +27 12 348 6284
Year established: 1945
Activities: financial, statistical, secretarial, administrative, public relations, economic, research and legal services available to members; collects statistics on milk production, consumption (sales), import, export
Chief officers: P.J. Theron (General Manager), S.W. van Coller (Secretary), D.J. Boghoff (Manager Business Economics)
Membership: 30 members form within dairy processing sector
Publications:
• Dairy Digits: *monthly*
• Dairy Review: *annual*
Notes: South African National Committee of IDF.

South African Direct Marketing Association
Address: PO Box 997, Auckland Park, Johannesburg 2000
Telephone: +27 11 482 6440
Fax: +27 11 482 1200
E-mail: dma@iafrica.com
Activities: promotes integrated marketing technologies
Chief officers: Mr Davy Ivins (Executive Director), Mrs Michelle Hardy (Communications Manager), Ms Gal Anderson (Councils), Mrs Lorna Mann (Administrative)
Membership: ca. 1,000 members from retail, banking, insurance, advertising agencies, etc.

Publications:
• Direct Marketing Journal
Notes: The Association does not produce statistics.

South African Federation of Soft Drinks Manufacturers
Address: Private Bag 34, JCC House, Auckland Park 2006
Telephone: +27 11 726 5300
Fax: +27 11 482 2000
Activities: a watchdog body for the soft drinks industry
Chief officers: Hennie Viljoen (President), J Potgieter (Secretary)
Membership: soft drinks manufacturers

South African Foreign Trade Organisation (SAFTO)
Address: PO Box 782706, Johannesburg Head Office, Export House, Cnr Maude and West Streets, Sandton 2146
Telephone: +27 11 883 3737
Fax: +27 11 883 6569/883 8273
E-mail: jscheepf@idc.co.za
Web site: www.safto.co.za
Year established: 1963
Activities: regularly organises conferences, exhibitions abroad (non-members may participate), library and international database information services, information on international trade, foreign markets, South African economy and trade, technical aspects of international trade; compiles statistics on South African trade; undertakes individual and group special research in South Africa and abroad
Chief officers: R A Norton (Chairman), Johan Scheepers (Chief Executive), Ann Moore (General Manager, Corporate Marketing), Liz Whitehouse (General Manager, Research and Information)
Membership: 800 member companies, mostly companies involved in export trade
Publications:
• Exporters Diary
• Foreign Trade Enquiry
• SAFTO Exporter
• SAFTO World Trader: *South African imports and exports, changes in legislation, analysis of SA trade statistics, exporters confidence surveys, foreign trade enquiries, analysis of foreign markets - monthly*

South African Fruit and Vegetable Canners' Association (Pty) Ltd
Address: PO Box 6175, Paarl 7620, 258 Main Street, Paarl 7646
Telephone: +27 22 116 11308/9
Fax: +27 21 125 930
Year established: 1954
Activities: collects statistics on production of canned deciduous fruit, government liaison
Chief officers: T R M Malone (Secretary)
Membership: 27 fruit and vegetable processors

South African Ice Cream Association
Address: PO Box 933, Showgrounds, Soutter Street, Pretoria
Telephone: +27 12 327 1487
Fax: +27 12 327 1501
Membership: ice cream producers

South African Margarine Manufacturers' Association
Address: PO Box 9126, Auckland Park 2006
Telephone: +27 11 482 2524
Fax: +27 11 726 1344
Membership: margarine manufacturers

South African Marketing Research Association

Address: PO Box 91879, Auckland Park, Johannesburg 2006
Telephone: +27 11 482 1419
Fax: +27 11 726 3639
Activities: annual convention, monthly functions, training courses, seminars
Chief officers: Shirley Harding (Chairwoman), Elaine Alder (Vice Chairwoman), Margarita Megson (Treasurer), Monica Waisman (Secretary)
Membership: 720 members (320 full, 330 associate, 20 student)
Publications:
• South African Marketing Research Association Newsletter: *quarterly*

South African Non-woven Manufacturers' Association

Address: PO Box 1506, 39 Field Street, Durban
Telephone: +27 31 3013692
Fax: +27 31 304 5255
Membership: manufacturers of non-woven materials

South African Petroleum Industry Association (SAPIA)

Address: P O Box 7082, Roggebaai 8012
Telephone: +27 21 419 8054
Fax: +27 21 419 8058
Web site: mbendi.co.za/sapia/index.htm
Year established: 1994
Activities: acts as a source of information on the industry as a whole
Chief officers: Mr S.D. Poole (Chairman), Colin McClelland (Director)
Structure: SAPIA operates under a Board of Governors drawn from the member companies
Membership: BP Southern Africa (Pty) Ltd, Caltex Oil (SA) (Pty) Ltd, Engen Petroleum Ltd, Shell South Africa (Pty) Ltd, Total South Africa (Pty) Ltd, Zenex Oil (Pty) Ltd
Publications:
• Press Release: *includes a summary of trends in the industry as well as sales figures for various petroleum products by volume - monthly*
• SAPIA Annual Report: *statistics and commentary on the petroleum industry in South Africa. Includes aggregate financial results of SAPIA members, sources of crude oil for SAPIA members for the latest year, inland consumption of major petroleum products, retail prices - annual*

South African Publishers' Association

Address: PO Box 116, St. James, 7946 Cape Town
Telephone: +27 21 788 6470
Fax: +27 21 788 6469
Web site: www.jutastat.com/pasa/index.1htm
Year established: 1945
Chief officers: Mr B van Rooyen, Ms E van Greunen (Admin)
Membership: book publishers

South African Sugar Association (SASA)

Address: Private Bag 507, Durban 4000
Telephone: +27 31 305 6161
Fax: +27 31 304 4939
Year established: 1936
Activities: actively promotes environmental awareness and conservation measures, conducts agricultural research and is involved in a wide range of educational and training programmes. The association compiles statistics on sugar production in South Africa
Chief officers: Michael J A Mathews (Executive Director), D W Hardy (Marketing Director)
Structure: non-profit governing body of the sugar industry
Membership: 2 member associations: the South African Cane

Growers' Association (SACGA) and the South African Sugar Millers' Association Limited (SASMAL)
Publications:
• SASA Annual Report: *annual*
• SASA Industry Directory: *general information and history of the South African sugar industry; information on the association and its members, statistics, addresses - annual*

South African Synthetic Resin Manufacturers' Association

Address: PO Box 1506, 39 Field Street, Durban
Telephone: +27 31 3013692
Fax: +27 31 304 5255
Membership: synthetic resin manufacturers

South African Wine and Spirit Exporters' Association

Address: PO Box 236, 154 Dorp Street, Stellenbosch 7599
Telephone: +27 21 887 0199
Fax: +27 21 883 8545
E-mail: sawsea@iafrica.com
Activities: publish statistics on exports of South African wines and spirits; promotes South Africa wines and spirits; publishes promotional material (brochures, leaflets, etc.) on wines and spirits of South Africa
Chief officers: Dr J le Retief (Chairman), AM Kruger (Director), Andries van Tonder (Administrative Manager)
Membership: 106 wine and spirit producers and exporters of South Africa

South African Wool and Mohair Buyers' Association

Address: PO Box 2201, North End, Port Elizabeth 6056
Telephone: +27 41 545 252
Fax: +27 41 545 629
Year established: 1953
Chief officers: Ms C Thomas (Chairman)
Membership: wool and mohair buyers

Textile Federation of South Africa

Address: PO Box 16278, Construction House, 121 Van Beek Street, Ellis Park, Doornfontein 2028
Telephone: +27 11 404 2423/4/5
Fax: +27 11 404 2101
E-mail: texfed@global.co.za
Activities: collects statistics on production, sales, import, export
Chief officers: Brian Brink (Executive Director), Helena Claassens (Marketing/Statistics), Cecile Auld (Communications/PR)
Membership: 80 companies representing 92% of all textile manufacturing in South Africa
Publications:
• Economic Review and Forecast: *annual*
• Newsletter: *textile topics - quarterly*
• Trade Directory: *names and details of companies*

Tobacco Board

Address: PO Box 26100, Tobacco Exchange Building, 529 Edmund Street, Arcadia, Pretoria 0001
Telephone: +27 12 323 4152
Fax: +27 12 323 7966
Chief officers: P F D Le Roux (Chairman), J S M L Venter (General Manager)

Tyre Dealers' Association (TDA)

Address: PO Box 2940, Randburg 2125, 303 Surrey Avenue, Randburg 2194
Telephone: +27 11 789 2542/3
Fax: +27 11 789 4525

Membership: importers of new tyres, the tyres retreating industry and tyre retailers
Notes: The Association is attached to the Motor Industries' Federation

Wheat Board
Koringraad
Address: PO Box 908, Pretoria 0001
Telephone: +27 12 325 1970
Fax: +27 12 216 448
Activities: compiles statistics on wheat and wheat products
Chief officers: Mrs A. Enslin (General Manager)

Yeast and Allied Products Manufacturers' Association of South Africa
Address: Private Bag 34, JCC House, Auckland Park 2006
Telephone: +27 11 726 5300
Fax: +27 11 726 8421/482 2000
Chief officers: Ms R. Aviges
Membership: yeast manufacturers

SPAIN

Air Conditioning Equipment Manufacturers' Association
Asociación de Fabricantes de Equipos de Climatización
Address: Francisco Silvela, 69 - 3°B, E-28028 Madrid
Telephone: +34 1 402 7383
Fax: +34 1 401 7927
Year established: 1977
Activities: research, export promotion
Chief officers: Rafael Budí (General Secretary)
Membership: 44 manufacturers of air conditioners, cooling plants, air treatment plants, terminal units, fans, air distribution equipment, cooling towers, energy recovery units, metering, regulation and control, thermal insulation and accessories

Association of Alcohol, Wine and Spirits Distillers
Asociación de Destiladores y Rectificadores de Alcohol y Aguardientes Vínicos
Address: Príncipe de Vergara 57-59 1°D, E - 28006 Madrid
Telephone: +34 1 561 7499
Fax: +34 1 562 6755
Chief officers: Juan Antonio López (President), Nestor Calvo (Secretary)
Membership: drinks distillers
Notes: Member of the Spanish Food and Drinks Industries' Federation (FIAB).

Association of Branded Drinks Distributors (ADIGRAM)
Asociación de Distribuidores de Grandes Marcas de Bebidas
Address: Juan Bravo, 10, 2°, 28006 Madrid
Telephone: +34 91 578 0164/56 341 046
Fax: +34 91 578 0164/56 346 081
E-mail: rgr@sister.es
Web site: www.sister.es/adigram.htm
Year established: 1992
Chief officers: Vicente Dalda
Membership: drinks distributors
Notes: Member of the Spanish Food and Drinks Industries' Federation (FIAB).

Association of Detergents and Related Products' Manufacturers (ADTA)
Asociación de Fabricantes de Detergentes, Tensioactivos y Productos Afines
Address: Profesor Waksmann, E-28036 Madrid
Telephone: +34 1 457 0044
Fax: +34 1 344 1584

Activities: provides production data for soaps and detergents (available to non-members, free of charge)
Chief officers: Luis Erice (General Manager), J M Mustieles (Technical Adviser)
Membership: 50 soap and detergent manufacturers

Association of Fish Retailers
Asociación de Empresarios Detallistas de Pescados
Address: Fernández de la Hoz, 32, E-28010 Madrid
Telephone: +34 1 319 7047
Fax: +34 1 319 3199
Year established: 1902
Activities: information and education (circulars, bulletins, telephone service), labour, legal, fiscal and trade advice
Chief officers: Domingo de Antonio Castillo (President), Fernando Martínez Gómez (Director General)
Membership: 1,500 members, who represent 2,000 establishments (95% of fish and seafood retailers)
Notes: Member of Federación Nacional de Asociaciones Provinciales de Empresarios Detallistas de Pescados, Confederación de Empresarios de Comercio al por Menor de la Comunidad de Madrid (CECOMA) and Confederación Empresarial de Madrid (CEOE).

Association of Hotel Owners of the Costa del Sol (AEHCOS)
Asociación Española de Empresarios Hoteleros de la Costa del Sol
Address: Apdo 396, Río Salazar 9, Torre 3, 3° planta (por Avda de los Manantiales), E-29620 Torremolinos
Telephone: +34 5 238 1700/30/46/47
Fax: +34 5 237 4026/2186
E-mail: aehcos@spa.es
Web site: www.costadelsol.spa.es/aehcos/
Activities: professional training for personnel of affiliated companies; promotion of the Costa del Sol region; implementation of a central reservation system; sector statistics
Chief officers: Migule Sánchez Hernández (President), Francisco Mena Navas (Secretary General)
Structure: Board of Management; Secretariat; advisory department; employment, legislative and industrial-technical matters; training department
Membership: 224 members: paradores (luxury hotels), hotels, apartments and villas complex, residential complex, bed and breakfast hotels, camping, nautical and sport clubs
Publications:
● Activities Report AEHCOS (Memoria de Atividades de AEHCOS): *the Associations activities, list of members, statistical data on occupations, categories of hotels - annual*
● Annual Report (Memoria): *summary of conferences and seminars - annual*
● Hotels, Apartments and Camping Guide - Costa del Sol (Guía de Hoteles, Apartamentos y Campings - Costa del Sol): *directory of members of AEHCOS, giving detail information of the location, capacity, amenities and contact details etc. - annual*

Association of Independent Hotels (HAI)
Hoteles Asociados Independientes
Address: Avda Alfonso XIII, 141, E-28016 Madrid
Telephone: +34 1 350 1708
Fax: +34 1 350 1692
Chief officers: José María Carbó Antón (President), Agustín Martínez Bueno, Luis Tusqyets Berronto, Philippe Mocquard (Vice Presidents), Ramón Buendía Perona (Manager)
Membership: 31 hotels

Association of Leather Exporters (ACEXPIEL)

Asociación de la Industria de la Piel para el Comercio Exterior
Address: Valencia 359, 3ª, E- 08009 Barcelona
Telephone: +34 3 459 3396
Fax: +34 3 458 5061
Year established: 1989
Chief officers: Alexandre Genis i Canal (President), Agustin Giralt Yglesias (Secretary)
Membership: 144 tanning companies (exporters and manufacturers of leather and leather goods)
Publications:
• Directory: *detailed information on member companies, including product information by type and final destination*

Association of Manufacturers (AFAMSA)

Asociación de Fabricantes de Artículos Manufacturados SA
Address: Av Francesc Cambo 14 - 5°, E-08003 Barcelona
Telephone: +34 3 310 3500
Fax: +34 3 310 4939
Year established: 1977
Activities: wholesale distribution, export and import of all kinds of goods.
Chief officers: Vicente Urrutia Nadal (President)
Membership: manufacturers

Association of Spanish Costume Jewellery Manauafcturers and Exporters (SEBIME)

Asociación Española de Fabricantes Exportadores de Bisutería
Address: Alquería Cremada s/n, Polígono Ind., E-07714 Mahon (Menorca)
Telephone: +34 71 360 313/365 0856
Fax: +34 71 360 566
Membership: manufacturers and exporters of costume jewellery

Association of Spanish Tobacconists

Unión de Asociaciones de Estanqueros de España
Address: Argensola, 2, E- 28004 Madrid
Telephone: +34 1 308 3666
Fax: +34 1 308 3713
Year established: 1992
Membership: retail tobacconists
Notes: Federación Nacional de Expendedores de Tabacos (National Federation of Tobacconists) y Timbres and Coordinadora de Expendedores de Tabacos y Timbres (Tobacconists Co-ordinating Committee) became Unión de Asociaciones de Estanqueros de España in 1992.

Clothing Industries Association

Industrias y Confecciones SA
Address: Tomás Bretón 60 - 62, E-28045 Madrid
Telephone: +34 1 528 4303
Fax: +34 1 467 8723
Chief officers: Isodoro Alvarez Alvarez (President), Luis Aveces Rodríguez (Vice President), Armando Pérez (Commercial Director)
Membership: 6 clothing manufacturers

Federation of Jerez Wine Producers (FEDEJEREZ)

Federación de Bodegas del Marco de Jerez
Address: Eguiluz, 2-1°, 11402 Jerez de la Frontera (Cadiz)
Telephone: +34 56 341 046
Fax: +34 56 346 081
Chief officers: Juan Luis Bretón (Secretary)
Notes: Member of the Spanish Food and Drinks Industries' Federation (FIAB).

Federation of Spanish Confectionery Associations (FEAD)

Federación Española de Asociaciones del Dulce
Address: Mallorca 286 Entio, 2ª, E-08037 Barcelona
Telephone: +34 3 207 2516
Fax: +34 3 207 1611
Activities: compiles statistics on the industry including data on production, imports and exports and consumption by type
Chief officers: Antonio García de Blas (President), Juan Manuel González-Serna (Vice President), Alfonso Bonmatí (Director)
Membership: members account for 70% of the total market for sugar confectionery and 96% of total chocolate sales. The Chocolate branch has 65 corporate members
Notes: Umbrella organisation of the Spanish confectionery industry incorporating the: Asociación Española de Fabricantes de Caramelos Y Chicles (Spanish Association of Sugar Confectionery and Chewing Gum Manufacturers); Asociación Española de Fabricantes de Chocolates Y Derivados del Cacao (Spanish Association of Chocolate and Cocoa Extracts' Manufacturers); and the Asociación Española de Fabricantes de Turrones Y Mazapanes (Spanish Association of Nougat and Marzipan Manufacturers), Asociación Profesional de Fabricantes de Galletas de España (Spanish Association of Biscuits Manufacturers), Asociación Española de Panificación y Pastelería de Marca (Spanish Association of Branded Pastry and Fine Bakery Products), Asociación Nacional de Prensadores de Cacao (National Association of Cocoa Processors)

Federation of Spanish Leather Products Associations (FECUR)

Federación de Asociaciones de Empresas Curtidoras de España
Address: Universidad, 4, E- 46003 Valencia
Telephone: +34 6 352 3878
Fax: +34 6 352 3413

Food Additives Manufacturers' and Traders' Association (AFCA)

Asociación de Fabricantes y Comercializadores de Aditivos y Complementos Alimentarios
Address: Bruc, 72-74, 6, E- 08009 Barcelona
Telephone: +34 3 487 55 74
Fax: +34 3 487 6520

General Association of Spanish Sugar Manufacturers (AGFAE)

Asociación General de Fabricantes de Azúcar de España
Address: Calle Montalbán, 11- 4, E- 28014 Madrid
Telephone: +34 1 522 8432/522 8624/522 8731/521 3814
Fax: +34 1 531 0608
Activities: compiles sector statistics covering production, import, export
Chief officers: Rafael Pastor (General Director)
Membership: 5 sugar refining companies:
EBRO-AGRICOLAS, Compañía de Alimentación, SA; Sociedad General Azucarera de España, SA; Azucareras Reunidas de Jaén, SA; Azucarera del Guadalfeo.
Notes: Member of the Spanish Food and Drinks Industries' Federation (FIAB).

Gift Manufacturers' and Wholesale Traders' Association

Asociación Empresarial de Fabricantes y Comerciantes Mayoristas de Artículos de Regalos
Address: Nuñez de Balboa 49 - 2° Izda 22, E-28001 Madrid
Telephone: +34 1 435 6096
Fax: +34 1 575 1785
Chief officers: Fernando Hueso Montón (President), Bernardo Corrochano Godoy (Vice President), José Cabanas Jorqueda

(Vice President)
Membership: manufacturers and wholesalers of gift items

Institute for Small and Medium Sized Companies (IMPI)
Instituto de la Pequeña y Mediana Empresa Industrial
Address: Paseo de la Castellana 141 - 2°, E-28046 Madrid
Telephone: +34 1 582 9300
Fax: +34 1 582 9375
Chief officers: Eugenio Triana (President), Jorge Orozco (Secretary)
Membership: small and medium-sized companies

Magazines' Association (ARI)
Asociación de Revistas de Información
Address: Claudio Coello 98, E-28006 Madrid
Telephone: +34 1 585 0038
Fax: +34 1 585 0039

Meat Processing Industries' Association of Spain (AICE)
Asociación de Industrias de la Carne de España
Address: General Rodrigo, 6 - Planta 12, E-28003 Madrid
Telephone: +34 1 554 7045/7848/7046
Fax: +34 1 554 7849
E-mail: aice@cestel.es
Web site: sun20.cestel.es/aice/aiceing.html
Web site notes: includes detailed statistics on the market for meat in Spain and other European countries. Some sections can only be accessed with a password
Chief officers: Antonio Roncal (Secretary)
Membership: 800 manufacturers of meat products representing 60% of total national production
Notes: Member of the Spanish Food and Drinks Industries' Federation (FIAB); member of CLITRAVI (Liaison Centre of the Meat Processing Industry in the EU).

Multisectoral Business Association (AMEC)
Asociación Multisectoral de Empresas
Address: Riera Sant Miquel, 3, E-08006 Barcelona
Telephone: +34 3 415 0422
Fax: +34 3 416 0980
E-mail: asoc@amec.es
Web site: www.amec.es
Year established: 1969
Chief officers: Miquel Lloveras Marti (President), Eduardo Gisbert Amat (Director General)
Structure: non-profit-making business organisation
Membership: 400 manufacturers and exporters in the Catalan area
Publications:
• Revista AMEC Export: *statistics, export-import information, reports by sector - quarterly*

National Association of Automatic Distributors' (ANEDA)
Asociación Nacional Española de Distribuidores Automáticos
Address: Puerto Rico 5 (bajo C), E-28016 Madrid
Telephone: +34 1 381 5386
Fax: +34 1 431 0655/457 3329
Membership: vending machine operators

National Association of Automobile Equipment and Component Manufacturers (SERNAUTO)
Asociación Nacional de Fabricantes de Equipo y Componentes para Automoción
Address: Castelló 120, 1°, E-28006 Madrid
Telephone: +34 1 562 1041/1595
Fax: +34 1 561 8437

Year established: 1967
Activities: information service and statistics
Chief officers: Miguel Angel Obregón Crespo (Director)
Membership: 197 manufacturers of car parts and equipment
Publications:
• Automotive Industry International: *international statistics on production, exports, registration and vehicles in use worldwide - annual*
• Automotive Industry: Its Figures: *domestic statistics on passenger cars, industrial vehicles, buses and coaches including exports by country of destination and the national vehicle parc - annual*
• Directory of Spanish Manufacturers of Automotive Equipment and Parts for the Automotive Industry: *full contact details of Spanish automotive equipment and parts manufacturers - annual*
• Equipment and Parts for the Automobile Industry: *vehicles market in Spain: Spanish parts industry, spare parts industry - annual*
• Handbook: *annual*
• Membership List
• MERCA-DATA: *bulletin of vehicle registration by make, model and type,, vehicle production and export by make and model - monthly*
• Newsletter of the National Association of Automobile Equipment and Component Manufacturers: *bi-monthly*
• Noticias Estadísticas: *a press release with production, import, and export figures for the vehicle equipment and component sector. Figures for the latest year with the percentage change over the previous year, based on the association's own survey. A brief commentary is included - annual*
• Quality Manuals

National Association of Automotive Dealers, Repair Outlets and Component Retailers (GANVAM)
Asociación Nacional de Vehículos a Motor, Reparación y Recambios
Address: Príncipe de Vergara 74 - 6°, E-28006 Madrid
Telephone: +34 1 411 3745/411 3663
Fax: +34 1 563 9081
Year established: 1963
Activities: International Automobile Show, legal consultancy (for members), vehicle registration statistics (monthly, for members only)
Chief officers: José Ruiz (Chairman), Tomás Herrera Ricoy (General Secretary)
Membership: 8,0000 motor vehicle dealers (new and used), garages, and retailers of spare parts and accessories
Publications:
• Boletín de Precios de Vehículos Nuevos y Usados: *price survey of new and used vehicles - quarterly*
• Brochure: *statistical survey on car sales - monthly*
• Bulletin: *vehicle ownership exchange rate - annual*
• Información GANVAM: *current information on the motor industry in Spain and the EU*

National Association of Baby Food Manufacturers (ANDI)
Asociación Nacional de Fabricantes de Productos de Dietética Infantil
Address: ABBOTT Laboratories SA, Josefa Valcárcel, 48, E-28027 Madrid
Telephone: +34 1 337 5200
Fax: +34 1 337 5306
Chief officers: Estrella Bengio Bengio (Secretary)
Notes: Member of the Spanish Food and Drinks Industries' Federation (FIAB).

National Association of Canned Seafood Manufacturers (ANFACO)

Federación Nacional de Asociaciones de Fabricantes de Conservas, Semiconservas y Salazones de Pescados y Mariscos
Address: Apdo. 258, E- 36200 Vigo
Telephone: +34 86 469 330
Fax: +34 86 469 269
Chief officers: Juan Vieites (Secretary)
Notes: Member of the Spanish Food and Drinks Industries' Federation (FIAB).

National Association of Chicken Producers (ANPP)

Asociación Nacional de Productores de Pollos
Address: Diego de León, 33, E- 28006 Madrid
Telephone: +34 1 562 42 93
Fax: +34 1 561 4471
Chief officers: Angel Martín (Secretary)
Notes: Member of the Spanish Food and Drinks Industries' Federation (FIAB).

National Association of Chilled Meat Warehouses and Abattoirs (ANAFRIC - GREMSA)

Asociación Nacional de Almacenes Frigoríficos de Carnes y Salas de Despiece
Address: Gran Vía de les Corts Catalanes 631, 6º, E- 08010 Barcelona
Telephone: +34 3 301 3374
Fax: +34 3 317 1644/412 26 68
Telex: 59100
Chief officers: Enric Capafrons Salas (President), José Millás (General Secretary)
Membership: cold storage warehouses

National Association of Cocoa Pressers

Asociación Nacional de Prensadores de Cacao
Address: Natra SA, Ctra. Nacional 111, Camino del Hornillo s/n, E- Quart de Poblet, Valencia
Telephone: +34 6 154 4761
Fax: +34 6 154 4453
Chief officers: Germán Sanjuán (President), Antonio Escuder (Secretary)
Notes: Member of the Federation of Spanish Confectionery Associations (FEAD).

National Association of Domestic Electrical Appliance Manufacturers (ANFEL)

Asociación Nacional de Fabricantes de Electrodomésticos
Address: Príncipe de Vergara 74, E-28006 Madrid
Telephone: +34 1 411 2705
Fax: +34 1 411 2964/411 2705
Membership: manufacturers of household electrical appliances

National Association of Electronics Industries (ANIEL)

Asociación Nacional de Industrias Electrónicas SA
Address: Príncipe de Vergara, 74- 4, E- 28006 Madrid
Telephone: +34 1 411 1661/562 0553
Fax: +34 1 411 4000
Chief officers: Jesús Banegas Nuñez (President), Gonzalo Caro Santa Cruz (General Director)
Publications:
• Spanish Electronics Directory: *member companies' contact details and product information - annual*

National Association of Finance Institutions (ASNEF)

Asociación Nacional de Entidades de Financiación
Address: Paseo de la Castellana 128, E-28046 Madrid
Telephone: +34 1 411 5465/564 0384

Fax: +34 1 562 1230/562 1230
Telex: 4678
Chief officers: Salvador Casanovas Martí (President), José María del Rey Villaverde (Secretary General)
Membership: finance houses and other financial institutions

National Association of Fish Processing Industries

Asociación Nacional de Industrias de Elaboración de Productos del Mar
Address: Alcalá, 115, E- 28009 Madrid
Telephone: +34 1 435 2081
Fax: +34 1 578 1260
Chief officers: José M Alló (Secretary)
Notes: Member of the Spanish Food and Drinks Industries' Federation (FIAB).

National Association of Manufacturers of Ingredients for Bakery, Pastry and Ice Cream Products (ASPRIME)

Asociación Nacional de Fabricantes de Materias Primas y Mejorantes para Panadería, Pastelería y Heladería
Address: Bonmacor- Mallorca, 286, E- 08037 Barcelona
Telephone: +34 3 207 2516
Fax: +34 3 207 1611
Chief officers: Agustín Roqué (Secretary), Luis Castell (President)
Membership: Bakery, pastry and ice cream manufacturers
Notes: Member of the Spanish Food and Drinks Industries' Federation (FIAB).

National Association of Medium-Sized and Large Retailers (ANGED)

Asociación Nacional de Grandes y Medianas Empresas de Distribución
Address: Alfonso XI, 3-1º, E-28014 Madrid
Telephone: +34 1 522 3004/532 8643/522 4523
Fax: +34 1 522 6125
Chief officers: José Serrano Carvajal (President), José Antonio García de Castro (General Secretary)
Membership: large and medium-sized retail companies and department stores

National Association of Nougat and Marzipan Manufacturers

Asociación Nacional de Fabricantes de Turrones y Mazapanes
Address: Bonmacor- Mallorca, 286, E- 08037 Barcelona
Telephone: +34 3 207 2516
Fax: +34 3 207 1611
Chief officers: Alfredo López (President), Alfonso Bonmatí (Secretary)
Notes: Member of the Spanish Food and Drinks Industries' Federation (FIAB).

National Association of OTC Pharmaceutical Products (ANEFP)

Asociación Nacional de Especialidades Farmacéuticas Publicitarias
Address: Juan Alvarez de Mendizábal 47, bajo A, E-28008 Madrid
Telephone: +34 1 559 7494/542 9471
Fax: +34 1 541 1443
Year established: 1978
Activities: provides information about non-prescription medicines; compiles market data, advertising data and self-medication studies (all for members only); also library service for members, which covers internal bulletin, articles on the health field in Spain, all regulations and health legislation etc.
Chief officers: Rafael García Gutierrez (Director General), Fernando Morán, Andrés Santos (Vice Presidents), Carmen Isbert (Technical Secretary)

Membership: 50 pharmaceutical companies, (manufacturers and distributors of non-prescription medicines)
Publications:
• ANEFP Bulletin: *members only*
• EFP/OTC: *professional magazine - in-house publication covering details of current and future developments in the industry - monthly*
• Membership List

National Association of Perfume and Related Products' Manufacturers (STANPA)
Asociación Nacional de Fabricantes de Perfumería y Afines
Address: Calle San Bernardo 23 - 3º, E-28015 Madrid
Telephone: +34 1 542 1616/523 2377/242 1616
Fax: +34 1 559 0137/542 2673
Chief officers: Ramón Merce Juste (President), Fernando González Hervada (Director)
Membership: 338 manufacturers of cosmetic and perfume products representing 95% of the industry
Publications:
• Perfume Manufacturers' Survey (Censo General de Fabricantes de Perfumería): *a survey of manufacturers of perfumes, scents and beauty products with data on production, sales, imports and exports by type - quarterly*
Notes: Address in Barcelona: Valencia 292, Barcelona Tel. 3 2153877, Fax. 3 4871813

National Association of Smoked Fish Products' Manufacturers
Asociación Nacional de Fabricantes de Productos de la Pesca Ahumados
Address: VENSY ESPAÑA SA - Pol. Ind. Guadalhorce, Hernest Hemingway, Parcela 20, E- 29004 Málaga
Telephone: +34 52 238 040
Fax: +34 52 170 583
Chief officers: María José Ramos (Secretary)
Notes: Member of the Spanish Food and Drinks Industries' Federation (FIAB).

National Association of Suppliers to the Shoe Industry (AEAC)
Asociación Nacional de Empresas Auxiliares del Calzado
Address: Capitán Antonio Mena, 25 Entlo. izda, 03201 Elche, Alicante
Telephone: +34 6 546 0158
Fax: +34 6 546 6033
E-mail: aeac@clavei.es
Web site: www.sho.es/aeac/

National Association of the Pharmaceutical Industry (FARMAINDUSTRIA)
Asociación Nacional Empresarial de la Industria Farmacéutica
Address: Fray Juan Gil, 5, E-28002 Madrid
Telephone: +34 1 563 1324
Fax: +34 1 563 7380
Membership: pharmaceutical companies

National Automobile Equipment, Aftermarket and Accessories Traders' Association (ANCERA)
Federación Nacional de Asociaciones de Comerciantes de Equipos, Recambios y Accessorios para la Automoción
Address: Príncipe de Vergara, 74, E-28006 Madrid
Telephone: +34 1 564 2386/564 2387
Fax: +34 1 561 8422
Year established: 1983
Activities: a list of companies in Madrid region; national listing available October 1995, a national listing available from October 1995
Chief officers: Jorge Belloo (President), Valentín Alonso (Director General)

Membership: motor vehicle component and accessory distributors and retailers: 17 provincial associations, 7 buying groups, 3 independent companies

National Business Association of the Spanish Beer Industry (Cerveceros de España)
Asociación Nacional Empresarial de la Industria Cervecera en España- Cerveceros de España
Address: Almagro, 24- 2 izda, E-28010 Madrid
Telephone: +34 1 308 6770
Fax: +34 1 308 6661
E-mail: info@cerveceros-es.com
Web site: www.cerveceros-es.com/
Web site notes: statistical data on national and European consumption, taxation, bier tax evolution, packaging
Activities: provides production data for beer and related products
Chief officers: Antonio Trujillo (President), Jacobo Olalla Marañón (Director)
Membership: 13 business groups which represent almost the 100% of the beer production in Spain
Publications:
• Produccion de Cerveza: *production statistics for beer and related products based on returns from member companies - annual*
Notes: Associations member of Cerveceros de España: Asociación de Investigación de Cerveza y Malta (IN.VES.CE.MA.) and Escuela Superior de Cerveza y Malta.

National Cheese Manufacturers' Association
Asociación Nacional de Fabricantes de Quesos
Address: Queserías Ibérica, Ctra. Toledo km 17,200, E-28940 Fuenlabrada - Madrid
Telephone: +34 1 690 7014
Fax: +34 1 697 2706
Chief officers: Antonio Ribera (Secretario)
Notes: Member of the Spanish Food and Drinks Industries' Federation (FIAB).

National Dairy Board (CNL)
Comité Nacional Lechero- Comité National Español de la FIL
Address: C/Ayala, 10 - 1º - izq., 28001 Madrid
Telephone: +34 1 576 2100
Fax: +34 1 576 2117
E-mail: cnl@tekres.com
Chief officers: Mr P. Valentín-Gamazo (Secretary)
Notes: National Committee of the International Dairy Federation.

National Federation of Bleach and Related Products Manufacturers' Associations (FENAYLD)
Federación Nacional de Asociacones de Fabricantes de Lejia y Derivados
Address: Gran Via 63, 3 izq, E-28013 Madrid
Telephone: +34 1 548 2345
Fax: +34 1 542 9952
Chief officers: Salvador Coromina Torras (Secretary General)

National Federation of Cosmetics and Perfume Retailers
Federación Nacional de Perfumistas y Drogueros de España
Address: Paz 13 - 3º, E-28012 Madrid
Telephone: +34 1 521 6086
Fax: +34 1 532 7089
Chief officers: Javier Arango Menéndez (President), Juan Tavora (General Secretary)
Membership: perfume retailers and druggists

National Federation of Importers and Exporters (FIE)

Federación Nacional de Importadores y Exportadores
Address: Trafalgar 4 - 4°, E-08010 Barcelona
Telephone: +34 3 317 9590/268 3069
Fax: +34 3 268 1489
Chief officers: Nuria Bigorra
Membership: importers and exporters

National Federation of Preserved Vegetables Industry Associations

Federación Nacional de Asociaciones de la Industria de Conservas Vegetales
Address: Princesa, 24, E- 28008 Madrid
Telephone: +34 1 547 5714
Fax: +34 1 559 1512
Chief officers: Arturo Díez Marijuan (Secretary)
Notes: Member of the Spanish Food and Drinks Industries' Federation (FIAB).

National Paper and Board Association (ASPAPEL)

Asociacion Nacional de Fabricantes de Papel y Cartón
Address: Alcalá 85, 4, E-28009 Madrid
Telephone: +34 1 576 3003/5763004
Fax: +34 1 577 4710
Year established: 1977
Activities: statistics covering production, consumption and trade in paper products in Spain
Chief officers: José Luis Asenjo (President), Jesús Garrido Arilla (Director), Armando García Mendoza Raso (Secretary General)
Publications:
• Annual Report of the National Paper and Board Association: *annual*
• Statistics: *monthly/quarterly*

National Soft Drink Manufacturers' Association (ANFABRA)

Asociación Nacional de Fabricantes de Bebidas Refrescantes Analcohólicas
Address: Avda Menéndez Pelayo 81, E-28007 Madrid
Telephone: +34 1 552 6275/552 6422
Fax: +34 1 551 9791
Chief officers: Julián Martínez Otamondi (President), Luis Fernando Escudero (Secretary)
Membership: producers of non-alcoholic drinks
Notes: Member of the Spanish Food and Drinks Industries' Federation (FIAB).

Olive Exporters' Association (ASEMESA)

Asociación de Exportadores de Aceitunas de Mesa
Address: Mesón del Moro, 1, E- 41001 Sevilla
Telephone: +34 5 422 9483
Fax: +34 5 422 3261
Chief officers: Antonio de Mora (Secretary)
Notes: Member of the Spanish Food and Drinks Industries' Federation (FIAB).

Sherry Producers' and Exporters' Association

Asociación de Criadores Exportadores de Sherry
Address: Eguiluz, 2- 1, E- 11402 Jerez de la Frontera
Telephone: +34 56 341 046
Fax: +34 56 346 081
Chief officers: José Luis García Ruiz (President), Juan Luis Bretón Abrisqueta (Director)

Small Domestic Electrical Appliance Manufacturers' Association (FAPE)

Asociación de Fabricantes de Pequeños Electrodomésticos
Address: Rocafort, 241- 4-3, E-08029 Barcelona
Telephone: +34 3 430 9903
Fax: +34 3 410 9105
Year established: 1980
Chief officers: José M Goiricelaya Echevaria (President)
Membership: manufacturers of household electrical appliances
Publications:
• Directory: *profiles of manufacturers and a brief overview of the small appliances sector in Spain*

Spanish Aerosols Association (AEDA)

Asociación Española de Aerosoles
Address: Balmes 189, 5 Dcha - 2A, E-08006 Barcelona
Telephone: +34 3 218 6920
Fax: +34 3 415 3012
Activities: conferences, information and research service, statistics
Membership: 92 aerosol manufacturers
Publications:
• News Bulletin

Spanish Alcoholic Drinks Manufacturers' Federation

Federación Española de Fabricantes de Bebidas Alcohólicas
Address: Villanueva 16-4°, Esquina Serrano, E-28001-Madrid
Telephone: +34 1 575 7002/0203
Fax: +34 1 576 0067
Year established: 1977
Chief officers: Javier Angúlo (Director General)
Membership: manufacturers of alcoholic beverages

Spanish Article Numbering Association (AECOC)

Asociación Española de Codificación Comercial
Address: Calle Mallorca 288, Entlo, 08037 Barcelona
Telephone: +34 3 207 53 62
Fax: +34 3 459 2152
E-mail: info@sede.aecoc.es

Spanish Association of Beer and Malt Technicians

Asociación Española de Técnicos de Cerveza y Malta
Address: Ramírez Prado, 8 - 1°F 2° esc, E-28045 Madrid
Telephone: +34 1 527 7255
Fax: +34 1 528 5507
Year established: 1964
Activities: annual assembly, scientific conferences and social events, education and training
Chief officers: Salvador Martín Aparicio (Director)
Membership: 800 beer manufacturers and technicians, 120 suppliers
Publications:
• Annual Report of the Spanish Association of Beer and Malt Technicians (Anuario): *annual*
• Beer News (Noticias Cerveceras): *news and industry trends in the Spanish beer market - monthly*
• Brewing Magazine (Cerveza y Malta): *articles and technical, scientific and professional information on the beer and malting industry - quarterly*

Spanish Association of Breakfast Cereal Manufacturers

Asociación Española de Fabricantes de Cereales en Copos o Expandidos
Address: Kellogg SA- Pol. Industrial s/n, E- 43800 Valls, Tarragona
Telephone: +34 77 603 114
Fax: +34 77 605 431
Chief officers: Mireia Bernat (Secretary)

Notes: Member of the Spanish Food and Drinks Industries' Federation (FIAB).

Spanish Association of Cider Manufacturers (AESI)
Asociación Española de Fabricantes Elaboradores de Sidras
Address: Consultores Asociados- Avilés, 4 - 5, E- 33207 Gijón
Telephone: +34 8 534 7742
Fax: +34 8 534 7742
Chief officers: Miguel González (Secretary)
Notes: Association member of the Spanish Food and Drinks Industries' Federation (FIAB).

Spanish Association of Egg Producers (ASEPRHU)
Asociación Española de Productores de Huevos
Address: Agustín de Bethencourt, 17-2°, E- 28003 Madrid
Telephone: +34 1 553 1969
Fax: +34 1 533 1969
E-mail: aseprhu@readysoft.es
Chief officers: Mª Mar Fernández (Secretary)
Notes: Member of the Spanish Food and Drinks Industries' Federation (FIAB).

Spanish Association of Flour and Semolina Manufacturers
Asociación de Fabricantes de Harinas y Sémolas de España
Address: Ayala, 13- 1 izda, E- 28001 Madrid
Telephone: +34 1 575 4004
Fax: +34 1 576 2944
Chief officers: Enrique Martín (Secretary)
Notes: Member of the Spanish Food and Drinks Industries' Federation (FIAB).

Spanish Association of Frozen Vegetable Manufacturers (ASEVEC)
Asociación Española de Fabricantes de Vegetales Congelados
Address: Moratín, 28, E-28014 Madrid
Telephone: +34 1 420 1821
Fax: +34 1 420 0881
Chief officers: Mr J.M. Aguilar (President)
Notes: member of the Federation of the Associations of EU Frozen Food Producers (FAFPAS) based in Brussels (Belgium)

Spanish Association of Fruit Juice, Citrus Fruit Concentrates and Related Products Manufacturers (AIZCE)
Asociación Española de la Industria de Zumos y Concentrados de Frutos Cítricos y sus Productos Derivados
Address: Hernán Cortés, 4, E- 46004 Valencia
Telephone: +34 6 352 5215
Fax: +34 6 394 4199
Chief officers: Víctor Pérez (Secretary)
Notes: Member of the Spanish Food and Drinks Industry Federation (FIAB).

Spanish Association of Health Products' Manufacturers and Distributors
Asociación Española de Fabricantes y Distribuidores de Productos de Nutrición Enteral
Address: Abbot Laboratorios, Josefa Valcárcel, 48, E- 28027 Madrid
Telephone: +34 1 337 5200
Fax: +34 1 337 0137
Chief officers: Isabel Pérez Magariños
Membership: manufacturers an distributors of health products
Notes: Member of the Spanish Food and Drinks Industries' Federation (FIAB).

Spanish Association of Ice Cream Manufacturers
Asociación Española de Fabricantes de Helados
Address: BONMACOR - Mallorca, 286, E-08037 Barcelona
Chief officers: Alfonso Bonmatí (Secretary)
Membership: ice cream and frozen confectionery industry
Notes: Member of the Spanish Food and Drinks Industries' Federation (FIAB).

Spanish Association of Jewellery, Silverware and Watch Exporters (JOYEX)
Asociación Española de Exportadores de Joyería, Platería, y Relojería
Address: Riera Sant Miquel, 3, E-08006 Barcelona
Telephone: +34 3 415 0422
Fax: +34 3 416 0980
E-mail: asoc@amec.es
Web site: www.amec.es
Year established: 1981
Chief officers: Octavio Sarda (President), Javier Tort (Director)
Membership: 44 manufacturers and exporters of jewellery, silverware, watches and clocks
Publications:
● Revista AMEC Exporta: *statistics, export-import information, reports by sector - quarterly*
Notes: member of Grupo AMEC

Spanish Association of Leather Manufacturers and Exporters (FECUREX)
Asociación Española de Comercio Exterior de Empresarios Fabricantes de Curtidos
Address: Hernán Cortés, 4 - 3e, E- 46004 Valencia
Telephone: +34 6 351 0153
Fax: +34 6 351 0081
Web site: www.sho.es/asociaciones/asocurtidores

Spanish Association of Manufacturers and Exporters of Cables and Electrical Materials (AMELEC)
Asociación Española de Fabricantes y Exportadores de Aparamenta, Cables y Material Eléctrico
Address: Santa Teresa 7, E-08009 Barcelona
Telephone: +34 3 415 0422
Fax: +34 3 416 0980
E-mail: asoc@amec.es
Web site: www.amec.es
Year established: 1980
Chief officers: Jaime Baldé (President), Javier Tort (Director)
Structure: non-profit-making business association
Membership: 58 industrial companies (manufacturers and exporters of electrical material)
Publications:
● AMEC EXPORT: *magazine - statistics, exports, imports - quarterly*
● Exports and Imports of Electrical Equipment: *imports and exports by product sector of electrical equipment. Based on central government data - quarterly*
Notes: Member of Grupo AMEC.

Spanish Association of Manufacturers of Branded Pastry and Fine Bakery Products
Asociación Española de Fabricantes de Pastelería de Marca y Panificación Especial Fina
Address: Bonmacor- Mallorca, 286, E- 08037 Barcelona
Telephone: +34 3 207 2516
Fax: +34 3 207 1611
Chief officers: Javier Argenté (President), Alfonso Bonmatí (Secretary)
Notes: Member of the Spanish Food and Drinks Industries' Federation (FIAB).

Spanish Association of Manufacturers of Chocolate and Cacao Products Manufacturers

Asociación Española de Fabricantes de Chocolates y Derivados del Cacao
Address: Bonmacor- Mallorca, 286, E- 08037 Barcelona
Telephone: +34 3 207 2516
Fax: +34 3 207 1611
Activities: statistical
Chief officers: Francesc Casals (President), Alfonso Bonmatí (Secretary)
Membership: manufacturers of chocolate and cocoa derivatives
Notes: Member of the Spanish Food and Drinks Industries' Federation (FIAB) and the Federation of Spanish Confectionery Associations (FEAD).

Spanish Association of Manufacturers of Packaging and Bottling Equipment (ENVASGRAF)

Asociación Española de Fabricantes de Maquinaria para Envase, Embalaje, Embotellado y su Grafismo
Address: Riera Sant Miquel, 3, E-08006 Barcelona
Telephone: +34 3 415 0422
Fax: +34 3 416 0980
E-mail: asoc@amec.es
Web site: www.amec.es
Year established: 1982
Activities: import/export statistics
Chief officers: Aleix Mas (President), Victor Pascual (Director)
Structure: non-profit-making business association
Membership: 55 industrial companies (manufacturers of packaging machinery)
Publications:
• Informe Coyuntura: *quarterly*
• Revista AMEC Exporta
Notes: member of Grupo AMEC

Spanish Association of Olive Oil Exporters (ASOLIVA)

Asociación Española de la Industria y Comercio Exportador de Aceite de Oliva
Address: José Abascal, 40, E-28003 Madrid
Telephone: +34 1 446 8812/16/50
Fax: +34 1 593 1918
E-mail: g5spons@dial.eunet.es
Web site: www.eunet.es/InterStand/cyberagentes/cyber_p0/news8_en/aso li_en.htm
Year established: 1928
Chief officers: Juan V Gómez
Membership: 84 companies dedicated to the export of olive oil, representing 95% of total national bottled oil and between 50% and 75% of bulk export
Notes: Member of the Spanish Food and Drinks Industries' Federation (FIAB).

Spanish Association of Orujo Oil Manufacturers

Asociación Española de Fabricantes de Aceite de Orujo de Aceituna
Address: El Portazgo, Ctra. Gijón-Sevilla km 676,200, E- Los Santos de Maimona, Badajoz
Telephone: +34 24 544 000
Fax: +34 24 544 195
Chief officers: Francisco Carrasco (Secretary)
Notes: Member of the Spanish Food and Drinks Industries' Federation (FIAB).

Spanish Association of Ready Meals Manufacturers

Asociación Española de Fabricantes de Platos Preparados
Address: Sociedad Nestlé, AEPA, Gran Vía, 16, E- 28013 Madrid
Telephone: +34 1 522 2915
Fax: +34 1 521 7750

Chief officers: Juan Camín (Secretary)
Notes: Mmember of the Spanish Food and Drinks Industries' Federation (FIAB).

Spanish Association of Sauces and Seasoning Manufacturers

Asociación Española de Fabricantes de Salsas, Condimentos Preparados y Similares
Address: Bonmacor- Mallorca, 286, E- 08037 Barcelona
Telephone: +34 3 207 2516
Fax: +34 3 207 1611
Chief officers: Agustín Roqué (Secretary)
Notes: Member of the Spanish Food and Drinks Industries' Federation (FIAB).

Spanish Association of Snack and Crisp Products Manufacturers

Asociación Nacional de Fabricantes de Patatas Fritas y Productos de Aperitivo
Address: Bonmacor- Mallorca, 286, E- 08037 Barcelona
Telephone: +34 3 207 2516
Fax: +34 3 207 1611
Chief officers: Agustín Roqué (Secretary)
Notes: Member of the Spanish Food and Drinks Industries' Federation (FIAB).

Spanish Association of Soluble Coffee Manufacturers

Asociación Española de Fabricantes de Café Soluble
Address: SEDA- Paseo de la Habana, 170, E- 28036 Madrid
Telephone: +34 1 359 2740
Fax: +34 1 350 9480
Chief officers: Juan de Dios Cruz (Secretary)
Notes: Member of the Spanish Food and Drinks Industries' Federation (FIAB).

Spanish Association of Stock and Soup Products Manufacturers

Asociación Española de Fabricantes de Caldos y Sopas
Address: Bonmacor- Mallorca, 286, E- 08037 Barcelona
Telephone: +34 3 207 2516
Fax: +34 3 207 1611
Chief officers: Agustín Roqué (Secretary)
Notes: Member of the Spanish Food and Drinks Industries' Federation (FIAB).

Spanish Association of Sugar Confectionery and Chewing Gum Manufacturers

Asociación Española de Fabricantes de Caramelos y Chicles
Address: Bonmacor- Mallorca, 286, E- 08037 Barcelona
Telephone: +34 3 207 2516
Fax: +34 3 207 1611
Chief officers: Celestino Alcaraz (President), Alfonso Bonmatí (Secretary)
Notes: Member of the Spanish Food and Drinks Industries' Federation (FIAB) and the Federation of Spanish Confectionery Associations (FEAD).

Spanish Association of Tea, Infusions and Herbal Products Manufacturers

Asociación Española de Envasadores de Infusiones de Té y Herboristeria
Address: Bonmacor- Mallorca, 286, E- 08037 Barcelona
Telephone: +34 3 207 2516
Fax: +34 3 207 1611
Chief officers: Agustín Roqué (Secretary)
Notes: Member of the Spanish Food and Drinks Industries' Federation (FIAB).

Spanish Association of the Meat Industry (ASOCARNE)

Asociación Española de Empresas de la Carne
Address: Calle Infanta Mercedes, 13 - 4°, E-28020 Madrid
Telephone: +34 1 571 6855/6/3
Fax: +34 1 571 6854
Year established: 1977
Activities: provides information service and collects sector statistics, gives information about legislation, markets, etc
Chief officers: Fernando Pascual (General Secretary)
Membership: 63 companies in the meat trade and industry (some of these are regional associations representing various meat companies)
Notes: Spanish representative on the EU pork industry's committee

Spanish Association of Vermouth, Bitter Soda and Fortified Wine

Asociación Española de Elaboradores y Distribuidores de Vermouths, Bitter Soda y Aperitivos Vínicos
Address: Apdo.14, Bacardi-Martini España SA, E- 08100 Mollet del Valles, Barcelona
Telephone: +34 3 570 6556
Fax: +34 3 593 9855
Chief officers: Enrique Fabregat Mayol (President)
Notes: Member of the Spanish Food and Drinks Industries' Federation (FIAB).

Spanish Association of Yoghurt and Dairy Products Manufacturers

Asociación Española de Fabricantes de Yogur y Postres Lácteos Frescos
Address: Sociedad Nestlé- AEPA- Gran Vía, 16, E- 28013 Madrid
Telephone: +34 1 522 2915
Fax: +34 1 521 7750
Chief officers: Juan Camín (Secretary)
Notes: Member of the Spanish Food and Drinks Industries' Federation (FIAB).

Spanish Biscuit Manufacturers' Association

Asociación Profesional de Fabricantes de Galletas de España
Address: Bonmacor- Mallorca, 286, E- 08037 Barcelona
Telephone: +34 3 207 2516
Fax: +34 3 207 1611
Chief officers: Antonio García de Blas (Presidente), Alfonso Bonmatí (Secretary)
Notes: Member of the Spanish Food and Drinks Industries' Federation (FIAB).

Spanish Bottled Water Association (ANEABE)

Asociación Nacional de Embotelladores de Aguas de Bebida Envasadas
Address: Serrano, 76 - 5ª dcha, E-28001 Madrid
Telephone: +34 1 575 9339/8226
Fax: +34 1 578 1816
Chief officers: Irene Zafra (Secretary), M Jesús Pérez Díaz
Membership: producers of bottled water and soft drinks
Notes: Member of the Spanish Food and Drinks Industries' Federation (FIAB).

Spanish Ceramic Tile and Paving Stone Manufacturers' Association (ASCER)

Asociación Española de Fabricantes de Azulejos, Pavimentos y Baldosas Cerámicas
Address: Guitarrista Fortea, 25 - 4E, E-12205 Castellón
Telephone: +34 64 223 012
Fax: +34 64 222 783
Activities: statistical service, monthly import and export data (free of charge)
Chief officers: Juan Pitarch Villareal (President), Manuel

González (Director)
Membership: manufacturers of ceramic tiles and paving stones

Spanish Chemical Cosmetics Society (SEQC)

Sociedad Española de Químicos Cosméticos
Address: Pau Claris 107 Pral, E-08009 Barcelona
Telephone: +34 3 488 1808
Fax: +34 3 488 3210
Activities: sponsors technical courses; lectures; maintains a database; conducts seminars
Chief officers: J Sisto Rovira (President), Jordi Quintas (General Secretary)
Membership: 610 members

Spanish Chemical Industry Federation (FEIQUE)

Federación Empresarial de la Industria Química Española
Address: Hermosilla 31- 1° dcha, E-28001 Madrid
Telephone: +34 1 431 7964/5758553
Fax: +34 1 576 3381
Telex: 45960 FEIQ E
Activities: statistical compilation and publication of data on production, imports, exports, consumption, etc.
Chief officers: Juan José Nava Cano (President), José Capmany Ferrer (Director General), Enrique Alas-Pumarino (Director of Technical and International Departments)
Membership: manufacturers of chemical products of all types
Publications:
● La Industria Química en Cifras: *quarterly statistics on the chemicals sector in Spain with data on production, imports, exports, consumption etc. - quarterly*
● Membership List

Spanish Coffee Group (ANCAFE)

Agrupación Española del Café
Address: Paseo de la Castellana, 140, E-28046 Madrid
Telephone: +34 1 457 6045
Fax: +34 1 457 9925
Telex: 41974
Chief officers: J M de Miguel (President), A H de la Quintana (Vice President)

Spanish Coffee Importers' Association (INCAFE)

Asociación Española de Importadores de Café
Address: Gran Vía, 31, E-28013 Madrid
Telephone: +34 1 522 7329
Membership: coffee importers and wholesalers

Spanish Coffee Roasters' Association (AETC)

Asociación Española de Torrefactores del Café
Address: General Alvarez Castro 20, E-28010 Madrid
Telephone: +34 1 448 8212
Fax: +34 1 448 8501
Chief officers: Luis Felipe Albert (Secretary)
Membership: coffee roasters
Notes: Member of the Spanish Food and Drinks Industries' Federation (FIAB).

Spanish Confederation of Animal Feed Manufacturers (CESFAC)

Confederación Española de Fabricantes de Alimentos Compuestos para Animales
Address: Diego de León, 54, 28006 Madrid
Telephone: +34 1 563 3413
Fax: +34 1 561 5992
E-mail: cesfac@bitmailer.net
Chief officers: Jacobo Olalla (Secretary)
Notes: Member of theSpanish Food and Drinks Industries' Federation (FIAB).

Spanish Confederation of Bakery Organisations (CEOPAN)

Confederación Española de Organizaciones de Panadería
Address: Palma 10-1, E-28004 Madrid
Telephone: +34 1 447 4887
Fax: +34 1 447 4363
Activities: research and compilation of statistics; information service and library
Chief officers: Emilio Madrid (President), José María Fernández de Vallado (Secretary)
Membership: bakeries
Publications:
• Agenda de Pan: *contains general and dietetic information; annual statistics - annual*

Spanish Confederation of Breweries

Confederación Empresarial de Cerveceros de España
Address: Almagro, 24 - 2 izda, E- 28010 Madrid
Telephone: +34 1 308 6770
Fax: +34 1 308 6661
Notes: Member of the Spanish Food and Drinks Industries' Federation (FIAB).

Spanish Confederation of Business Organisations (CEOE)

Confederación Española de Organizaciones Empresariales
Address: Diego de León 50 - 6°, E-28006 Madrid
Telephone: +34 1 563 9641
Fax: +34 1 562 8023/562 4035/564 0135
Chief officers: José María Cuevas (President), Arturo Gil (Vice President)
Membership: business associations

Spanish Confederation of Plastic Business (ANAIP)

Confederación Española de Empresarios de Plásticos
Address: Avenue Brasil 17, 13-A, 28020 Madrid
Telephone: +34 1 556 7575
Fax: +34 1 556 4992
Web site: www.edigital.es/anaip/anaip.htm
Chief officers: Fernando Galbis (President), José María Cavanillas (General Director)
Publications:
• Los Plásticos en España - Plastics in Spain: *an economic commentary section is followed by a section on trends over the last five years in the plastics sector and sections on specific plastics - commodity plastics, thermosetting plastics, engineering plastics, other plastics. Further sections cover plastic processing, processing and machinery, and plastics and the EC - annual*

Spanish Confederation of Small and Medium Sized Companies (COPYME)

Confederación Española de la Pequeña y Mediana Empresa
Address: Plaza Independencia, 5 - 2° Izq., E-28009 Madrid
Telephone: +34 1 411 6161/561 6757
Fax: +34 1 564 5269
Chief officers: José Agenjo Bielsa (President)
Membership: small and medium-sized businesses, and provincial business associations

Spanish Corn Processors' Association (HUMAIZ)

Asociación de Transformadores de Maiz por Via Húmeda
Address: Hermenegildo, 28 -2ªB, 28015 Madrid
Telephone: +34 1 542 0715
Fax: +34 1 541 6333
Chief officers: Luis Felipe Albert (Secretary)
Notes: Member of the Spanish Food and Drinks Industries' Federation (FIAB).

Spanish Edible Oils Industry Federation

Federación de Industrias Oleícolas de España
Address: Paseo Reina Cristina, 6, E- 28014 Madrid
Telephone: +34 1 501 8969
Fax: +34 1 551 5013
Chief officers: Primitivo Fernández (Director))
Membership: Asociación Española de Refinadores de Aceites (Spanish Association of Oil Refineries), Asociación Española de Extractores Independientes de Semillas Oleaginosas (Spanish Association of Independent Extractors of Oil Seeds) and Asociación Española de Extractores de Aceite de Orujo (Spanish Association of Orujo Oil Extractors).
Notes: Member of the Spanish Food and Drinks Industries' Federation (FIAB).

Spanish Federation of Clothing Companies

Federación Española de Empresas de la Confección
Address: Virgen de los Peligros 2, Planta 10, Madrid
Telephone: +34 1 522 0421/521 9535
Fax: +34 1 521 9525
Membership: 16 clothing manufacturers and retailers

Spanish Federation of Domestic Electrical Appliances Traders (FESCE)

Federación Española de Comerciantes de Electrodomésticos
Address: Abtao, 11- 1c, E- 28007 Madrid
Telephone: +34 1 551 3206
Fax: +34 1 501 2240
Chief officers: Juan Zurita (President)
Membership: household appliances and consumer electronics retailers
Publications:
• Informaciones Acerna: *includes sector statistics - every 2 months*

Spanish Federation of Olive Oil Producers (INFAOLIVA)

Federación Española de Industrias Fabricantes de Aceite de Oliva
Address: Madre Soledad Torres Acosta, 3A, 5°, E-23001 Jaen
Telephone: +34 53 262 003/24
Fax: +34 53 258 429
Year established: 1986
Activities: government lobbying
Chief officers: Luis Moncayo Liébana (President), Manuel Villén Jimenez (Secretary)
Membership: 650 olive oil producers

Spanish Federation of Producers and Exporters of Wines, Aromatic Wines, Sparkling Wines and Wine Vinegar

Federación Española de la Industria y el Comercio Exportador de Vinos, Vinos Aromatizados, Vinos Expumosos, Vinos de Licor Mostos, Mistelas y Vinagres
Address: Mártires Concepcionistas, 18 - 1, Esquina Serrano, E-28006 Madrid
Telephone: +34 1 576 2726
Fax: +34 1 575 1114
Chief officers: Pablo Roca (Secretary)
Membership: producers and exporters of all types of wine

Spanish Federation of the Footwear Industry (FICE)

Federación de Industrias del Calzado Español
Address: Edificio Eurocis, Oficinas 5-6, Núñez de Balboa 116 - 3°, E-28006 Madrid
Telephone: +34 1 562 7001/562 7002/5627003
Fax: +34 1 562 0094
Activities: provides statistical data
Chief officers: Rafael Calvo Rodriguez (President)
Membership: footwear manufacturers
Publications:
• Anuario del Calzado de España: *commentary and statistics*

on the Spanish footwear market and industry with data on industry structure, production, domestic consumption, foreign trade - annual
• FICE Press: *monthly*

Spanish Federation of the Wool Industry (FITEXLAN)
Federación de la Industria Lanera Española
Address: San Quirce 30, E-08201 Sabadell (Barcelona)
Telephone: +34 3 725 9311
Fax: +34 3 726 1526
Year established: 1977
Activities: annual statistical services
Chief officers: Francisco Llonch (President), Benito Armurgol Obrador (Secretary General)
Membership: 400 companies from the wool industry

Spanish Food and Drinks Industries' Federation (FIAB)
Federación Española de Industrias Alimentación y Bebidas
Address: C/ Diego de León, 44 - 1º, E-28006 Madrid
Telephone: +34 1 411 7211/411 7499/411 7111
Fax: +34 1 411 7344
E-mail: fiab@sister.es
Web site: www.sister.es/fiab.htm
Activities: information service and research
Chief officers: Arturo Gil Pérez-Andújar (President), Jorge Jordana Butticaz (General Secretary)
Membership: 62 sectoral associations comprising 30,000 companies

Spanish Food Industry Machinery Manufacturers' Association (ALIMENTEC)
Asociación Española de Fabricantes de Maquinaria para la Industria de la Alimentación
Address: Riera Sant Miquel, 3, E-08006 Barcelona
Telephone: +34 3 415 0422
Fax: +34 3 416 0980
E-mail: asoc@amec.es
Web site: www.amec.es
Year established: 1982
Chief officers: Marti Lloveras (President), Victor Pascual (Director)
Membership: 35 manufacturing companies (equipment for the food industry)
Publications:
• Revista AMEC Exporta: *statistics, export-import information, reports by sector - quarterly*
Notes: Member of Grupo AMEC.

Spanish Fruit Juice Association (ASOZUMOS)
Asociación Nacional de Fabricantes de Zumos
Address: Princesa, 24, E- 28008 Madrid
Telephone: +34 1 559 2452
Fax: +34 1 559 6649
Chief officers: Alfonso Mena (Secretary)
Notes: Member of the Spanish Food and Drinks Industries' Federation (FIAB).

Spanish Health and Herbal Products Manufacturers' Association (AFEPADI)
Asociación Española Fabricantes de Preparados Alimenticios Especiales, Dietéticos y Plantas Medicinales
Address: Calle Aragón 208-210/4A, 08011 Barcelona
Telephone: +34 3 454 8725
Fax: +34 3 451 3155
Activities: provides information about legislation, exhibitions, business prospects in Spain and overseas, annual statistics
Chief officers: Javier Santiveri (President), Teresa del Hoyo (General Secretary)
Membership: 32 manufacturers of health and dietary foods, and medicinal plant products

Notes: Member of the Spanish Food and Drinks Industries' Federation (FIAB).

Spanish Hotels Federation (FEH)
Federación Española de Hoteles
Address: Orense 32, E-28020 Madrid
Telephone: +34 1 556 7112/5567202
Fax: +34 1 556 7361
Chief officers: José María Carbo (President), Carlos Díaz (Secretary General), Dolores Mata (overseas area)
Membership: hotels

Spanish Jewellery, Silverware and Watches Association
Asociación Española de Joyeros, Plateros, y Relojeros
Address: Príncipe de Vergara, 74, E- 28006 Madrid
Telephone: +34 1 561 1450
Fax: +34 1 561 1456
Membership: manufacturers of jewellery, silverware, watches and clocks

Spanish Knitting Industries' Association
Agrupación Española de Fabricantes de Género de Punto
Address: Avda Diagonal 474 1esc B Desp 8-9, E-08006 Barcelona
Telephone: +34 3 415 1228
Fax: +34 3 416 0442
Year established: 1927
Chief officers: José M. Cañellas Fargas (President), Juan Canals (1st Vice President), Ramón Azpiroz (2nd Vice President), José Sánchez (3rd Vice President), Manuel Benach Olivella (General Secretary)
Membership: 948 members (284 companies, 664 individuals), manufacturers of all types of knitwear and knitted fabrics
Publications:
• Directory of Spanish Knitwear Manufacturers
• Statistics (Spanish Knitting Industries' Association) (Estadisticas): *key figures on the Spanish knitting industry based on a survey carried out by the association. Data on production, sales, trade, industry structure - annual*

Spanish Manufacturers' and Exporters' Association
Asociación Española de Fabricantes y Exportadores
Address: Riera Sant Miquel, 3, E- 08006 Barcelona
Telephone: +34 3 415 0422
Fax: +34 3 416 0980
E-mail: asoc@amec.es
Web site: www.amec.es
Year established: 1983
Activities: organises trade fairs world-wide including: Industry Hannover; Elec Paris; Electrotech Birmingham; Matelec Madrid; Elenex Thailand
Chief officers: Jaime Baldé Muxá (President), Alejandro Serrano (Vice President), Eduardo Gisbert (Director General), Jesús García Anadón (Secretary General), Javier Tort (Director)
Membership: 75 exporters and manufacturers of electrical equipment, lighting and cables
Publications:
• Catalogue: *every 3 months*

Spanish Margarine Manufacturers' Association (AEFMA)
Asociación Española de Fabricantes de Margarina
Address: Castelló, 115 - oficina 820, E-28006 Madrid
Telephone: +34 1 561 6171
Fax: +34 1 561 5901
Year established: 1978
Chief officers: Alfonso Martín (Secretary General)

Membership: 365 margarine manufacturers (350 individuals, 15 firms)
Notes: Member of the Spanish Food and Drinks Industries' Federation (FIAB).

Spanish Market Research and Opinion Association (AEDEMO)
Asociación Española de Estudios de Mercado y Opinión
Address: Conde de Urgell 152 - ático 2, E-08036 Barcelona
Telephone: +34 3 453 9810
Fax: +34 3 451 0015
Chief officers: Carlos Clavero (President), Juan Alos (Secretary)
Membership: 670 marketing and market research companies
Publications:
• Investigación y Márketing

Spanish Meat Confederation (CECARNE)
Confederación Española de la Carne
Address: Infanta Mercedes, 13, E- 28020 Madrid
Telephone: +34 1 571 6853
Fax: +34 1 571 6854
Chief officers: Fernando Pascual (Secretary)
Notes: Member of the Spanish Food and Drinks Industries' Federation (FIAB).

Spanish Motor Vehicle Manufacturers' Association (ANFAC)
Asociación Española de Fabricantes de Automóviles y Camiones
Address: Fray Bernardino Sahagún, 24, E-28036 Madrid
Telephone: +34 1 345 1054/359 7165
Fax: +34 1 345 0377/359 4488
E-mail: luis.valero@mx2.redestb.es
Year established: 1966
Activities: compiles statistical information covering production, exports and registrations
Chief officers: Juan José Sanz (President), Luis Valero (General Director), Carlos Mataix (Technical Director), Miguel Aguilar (Director of Economic Department)
Membership: 11 manufacturers of cars and trucks (Citroen Hispania, Fasa-Renault, Ford España, Iveco-Pegaso, Mercedes Benz España, Nissan Motor Iberica, Opel España, Peugot España, Renault V I España, Santana-Motor, Seat)
Publications:
• Annual Report: *statistics on exports, imports, production and new registrations by make - annual*
• New Registrations' Statistical Bulletin: *statistical data on new registrations - monthly*
• Statistical Bulletin: *contains detailed production and export statistics - quarterly*

Spanish Newspaper Editors' Association (AEDE)
Asociación de Editores de Diarios Españoles
Address: Espronceda 32, E-28003 Madrid
Telephone: +34 1 442 1992/442 8621
Fax: +34 1 442 8621
Chief officers: Pedro Crespo de Lara (Director), Vicente Montiel y Rodriguez de la Encina (President)
Membership: daily newspapers

Spanish Paint and Printing Inks Manufacturers' Association (ASEFAPI)
Asociación Española de Fabricantes de Pinturas y Tintas de Impresión
Address: Plaza de Castilla 3, planta 15, E-28046 Madrid
Telephone: +34 1 773 9012/7339146
Fax: +34 1 733 9304
Activities: statistics
Chief officers: Francisco Javier Sandeszate (President), José

Luis Mata (Secretary General)
Membership: manufacturers of paint and dyes
Publications:
• Bulletin: *bi-monthly*
• Statistical Review of Imports and Exports (Cuadro Estadístico Importación Exportación): *annual statistics on imports and exports of paints and printing inks with data for the latest six years. Based on official statistics - annual*

Spanish Pasta Manufacturers' Association (AEFPA)
Asociación Española de Fabricantes de Pastas Alimenticias
Address: Vía Layetana, 32 - 4 Dpto. 94, E- 08003 Barcelona
Telephone: +34 3 310 5597
Fax: +34 3 310 5597
Chief officers: Pedro Antonio Espona (Secretary)
Notes: Member of the Spanish Food and Drinks Industries' Federation (FIAB).

Spanish Pharmaceutical Centres' Association (ACFESA)
Asociación de Centros Farmacéuticos de España SA
Address: General Oraa, 70 - 4°, E-28006 Madrid
Telephone: +34 1 562 4025/5643464
Fax: +34 1 563 5976
Year established: 1930
Activities: distribution of pharmaceutical products
Chief officers: Antonio Peleteiro (General Secretary)
Membership: pharmacists

Spanish Phonographic and Videographic Association (AFYVE)
Asociación Fonográfica y Videográfica Española
Address: Pedro Muguruza,8, entreplanta izda, E-28036 Madrid
Telephone: +34 1 345 4150
Fax: +34 1 345 6674
Year established: 1978
Chief officers: Carlos Grude (President), Carmen Millán (Legal Adviser)
Membership: 51 recorded music and video producers

Spanish Restaurant, Café and Bar Federation (FER)
Federación Española de Restaurantes Cafes y Bares
Address: Camino de Las Huertas N°18, Pozuelo de Alarcon, E-28223 Madrid
Telephone: +34 1 352 9042
Fax: +34 1 352 8882
Activities: information service, compilation of statistics, research
Chief officers: Ines Galindo Mattas (head of international relations)
Structure: president, vice-presidents, board of directors, assembly, provincial association's presidents
Membership: national associations
Publications:
• IH Hostelería y Turismo: *weekly*

Spanish Spirits Manufacturers' Federation (FEFBE)
Federación Española de Fabricantes de Bebidas Espirituosas
Address: Villanueva 16-4°, Esquina Serrano, E-28001 Madrid
Telephone: +34 1 575 7002/03
Fax: +34 1 576 0067/57
Year established: 1977
Activities: information service for members only; statistics on export and national markets
Chief officers: Manuel Piñera Gil-Delgado (President), Felipe Sánchez Nogues, Javier Oniera Aguirre Gomez (Vice Presidents), Javier Angulo Gómez de Cadiñanos (General Director)
Membership: 187 manufacturers of alcoholic drinks

Publications:
• Annual Statistics (Estadísticas): *regular statistics on alcoholic drinks with data on the home market and export sales. Based on various sources - annual*
• News Circulars: *members only - weekly & fortnightly*

Spanish Textile Machinery Manufacturers' Association (AMTEX)
Asociación Española de Constructores de Maquinaria Téxtil
Address: Riera Sant Miquel, 3, E-08006 Barcelona
Telephone: +34 3 415 0422
Fax: +34 3 416 0980
E-mail: asoc@amec.es
Web site: www.amec.es
Year established: 1980
Chief officers: José Mª Dalmau (President), Javier Tort (Director)
Structure: non-profit-making business association
Membership: 53 manufacturers of textile machinery and equipment
Publications:
• Revista AMEC Exporta: *statistical information, exports/imports, reports by sector - quarterly*
Notes: member of Grupo AMEC

Spanish Toy Manufacturers' Association (AEFJ)
Asociacion Española de Fabricantes de Juguetes
Address: Torre de Valencia, O'Donnell 4 - 1°, E-28009 Madrid
Telephone: +34 1 575 4975
Fax: +34 1 435 6750
Activities: provides data on sales, exports, etc (published in the association's journal)
Chief officers: Salvador Miró Sanjuan (President), Salvador Miró (General Director), Luis Moreno (Secretary General)
Membership: 120 manufacturers of toys and games
Publications:
• Spanish Toys and Games (Juguetes y Juegos de España): *a quarterly review of the market for toys and games with some data on sales, foreign trade etc. - quarterly*

Spanish Travel Agencies' Association (AEDAVE)
Asociación Empresarial de Agencias de Viajes Españolas
Address: Plaza de Castilla 3, planta 18 E -2, E-28046 Madrid
Telephone: +34 1 314 1830
Fax: +34 1 314 1877
Year established: 1979
Chief officers: Félix Arévalo Sancho (Director General)
Membership: 265 travel agencies (with a total of 900 subsidiaries)
Publications:
• Boletín Informativo AEDAVE: *future developments of the travel industry - bi-monthly*

Spanish Vegetable Conserves Manufacturers' Group (AGRUCON)
Agrupación Española de Fabricantes de Conservas Vegetales
Address: Castelló 115, E-28006 Madrid
Telephone: +34 1 561 5994
Fax: +34 1 561 5901
Telex: 42461 - AGFMA
Chief officers: A Riano Lopez, F Bruckner, Alfonso Martín (Secretary)
Membership: fruit and vegetable processors
Notes: Member of the Spanish Food and Drinks Industries' Federation (FIAB).

Spanish Wine Federation (FEV)
Federación Española del Vino
Address: Castelló 95, 6B, E-28006 Madrid
Telephone: +34 1 576 2726/576 2728

Fax: +34 1 575 1114
E-mail: fevino@bitmailer.es
Web site:
www.eunet.es/InterStand/cyberagentes/cyber_15/asoliva.htm
Chief officers: Pablo Roca (Secretary)
Membership: member companies account for approximately 70% of domestic sales and more than 80% of Spanish wine exports by value
Notes: Member of the Spanish Food and Drinks Industries' Federation (FIAB).

Trade Press Association (APP)
Asociación de Prensa Profesional
Address: Rambal Cataluña, 10 - 4° 4a CIPB, E-08007 Barcelona
Telephone: +34 3 412 1388
Fax: +34 3 412 7749
E-mail: app@datalab.es
Web site: www.app.es
Web site notes: site includes a database of Spanish trade journals

Union of Domestic Electrical Appliance Manufacturers (UFESA)
Unión de Fabricantes de Electrodomésticos SA
Address: Larrañeta s/n, E-31820 Echarri-Arantaz (Navarra)
Telephone: +34 48 460 000
Fax: +34 48 460 533
Chief officers: Manuel Crespo de Vega (Export Manager)
Membership: manufacturers of household electrical goods

Union of Sparkling Wine Manufacturers (UCEVE)
Unión de Criadores Elaboradores de Vinos Espumosos
Address: Sant Antoni, 21, E-08770 San Sadurni de Noya, Barcelona
Telephone: +34 3 891 0236
Fax: +34 3 818 3392
Chief officers: José Luis Boner (President), Francisco Herrera (Director)

Vinegar Manufacturers' and Packers' Association
Asociación de Elaboradores y Envasadores de Vinagre
Address: Bonmacor- Mallorca, 286, E- 08037 Barcelona
Telephone: +34 3 207 2516
Fax: +34 3 207 1611
Chief officers: Agustín Roqué (Secretary)
Notes: Member of the Spanish Food and Drinks Industries' Federation (FIAB).

SRI LANKA

Coconut Producers' Association
Address: c/o The Ceylon Chamber of Commerce, 50 Navam Mawatha, Colombo 2
Telephone: +94 421 745/7
Fax: +94 449 352/437 477

National Chamber of Exporters of Sri Lanka
Address: Export Trade Centre, Lower Chatham Street, Colombo 1
Telephone: +94 445 040/445110
Fax: +94 445 040

Prawn Farmers Association of Sri Lanka
Address: c/o Aquatic Enterprises, 98 Kollupitiya Mawatha, Colombo 3

Telephone: +94 573 312/573 378
Fax: +94 576 241

Publishers' Association of Sri Lanka
Address: 112 S Mahinda Mawatha, Colombo 10
Telephone: +94 1 69 57 73
Fax: +94 1 69 66 53
Chief officers: Mr C Wijesuriya (President), Mr D Jayakody (Director)

Seafood Exporters' Association
Address: 96 Nawala Road, Narahenpita
Telephone: +94 436 562/585 488
Fax: +94 585 488

Spices and Allied Products Association
Address: c/o the Ceylon Chamber of Commerce, 50 Navam Mawatha Road, Colombo 2
Telephone: +94 421 745-7
Fax: +94 449 352

Sri Lanka Pharmaceutical Manufacturers' Association
Address: PO Box 274, 50 Navam Mawatha, Colombo 2
Telephone: +94 1 421 745/47
Fax: +94 1 449 352

ST KITTS AND NEVIS

Hotel and Tourism Association of St Kitts and Nevis
Address: PO Box 438, Liverpool Row, Bassetterre
Telephone: +1 809 465 5304
Fax: +1 809 465 7746

Nevis Board of Tourism
Address: Main Street, Charlestown, Nevis
Telephone: +1 809 469 1042/5521
Fax: +1 809 469 1066

St Kitts and Nevis Small Business Association
Address: PO Box 286, Bassterre
Telephone: +1 809 465 8630
Fax: +1 809 465 6661

ST LUCIA

St Lucia Tourist Board
Address: PO Box 221, Pointe Seraphine, Castries
Telephone: +1 809 452 4094/5968
Fax: +1 809 453 1121

SUDAN

Sudanese Publishers' Association
Address: PO Box 2771, HQ AL Ikhwa Building, Flat 7 - floor 7, Khartoum
Telephone: +249 11 750 51/791 80
Chief officers: Mr AA Khatir (Director)

SURINAME

Suriname Association of Trade and Industry
Address: Pprins Hendrikstraat 18, Paramaribo
Telephone: +597 475 286/287
Fax: +597 472 207

SWAZILAND

Hotel and Tourism Association
Address: PO Box 462, Mbabane
Telephone: +268 4 221 8

Insurance Brokers' Association of Swaziland
Address: PO Box A32, 4th floor Dhlan'Ubeke House, Walker Street, Mbabane
Telephone: +268 4 803 1/429 29
Fax: +268 4 525 4
Year established: 1983

Swaziland Citrus Board
Address: PO Box 343, Mbabane
Telephone: +268 4 426 6/442 67/63
Fax: +268 4 354 8
Year established: 1969

Swaziland Dairy Board
Address: PO Box 1789, Manzini
Telephone: +268 8 441 1/869 01/ 865 21
Fax: +268 8 531 3
Year established: 1990
Activities: provides a guaranteed market for milk producers; monitors the import and distribution of other dairy products (butter, cheese)
Membership: milk producers and dairy products manufacturers and traders

Swaziland Sugar Association
Address: PO Box 445, Mbabane
Telephone: +268 4 264 6/7
Fax: +268 4 500 5
Activities: provides administrative and financial support to members; provides information service; marketing orientated organisation which undertakes sugar storage, transportation and sales; professional training and education
Membership: sugar producers and manufacturers

SWEDEN

Association of Forestry Industries
Skogsindustrierna
Address: Box 5518, Storgt 19, S-11485 Stockholm
Telephone: +46 8 783 8400
Fax: +46 8 661 7306
Chief officers: Dr J. Remrod (Managing Director)
Structure: board of directors, secretariat, committees: forest policy, transport policy, environment and energy, products, sawmills
Membership: 16 companies
Publications:
• Forest Cycle Piece by Piece
• Skogens Kretsloppbitforbit: *annual*

Association of Pharmaceutical Manufacturers (LIF)
Läkemedelsindustriföreningen
Address: PO Box 17608, Medborgarplatsen 25, S-118 92
Stockholm
Telephone: +46 8 462 3700
Fax: +46 8 462 0292
E-mail: lif@ls.se
Year established: 1951

Association of Suppliers of Professional Audio, Video and Lightning Equipment in Sweden (LLB)
Leverantörsföreningen Ljud, Ljus och Bild för professionellt bruk
Address: Box 1416, S-111 84 Stockholm
Telephone: +46 8 240 700
Fax: +46 8 218 496
E-mail: llb@branschkansliet.se
Web site: www.llb.se
Web site notes: site includes a database of member
companies with information on the products/brands they
supply
Year established: 1990
Activities: advises members on new legislation, organises a
trade show, produces statistics on the industry
Membership: manufacturers and distributors of musical
instruments, professional audio, lightning, video, and
multimedia equipment representing 80% of the trade in
Sweden

Association of Swedish Brewers
Svenska Bryggareföreningen
Address: Box 26063, Baldersgatan 4, S-100 41 Stockholm
Telephone: +46 8 723 0180/660 1860
Fax: +46 8 791 8775/666 9965
E-mail: reception@swedbrewers.se
Web site: www.swedbrewers.se
Web site notes: site includes various statistics on the
Swedish beer, soft drinks and bottled water industries. It also
includes data on the following: consumption, imports and
exports, distribution, packaging, excise duties, etc.
Membership: 26 breweries, maltsters, soft drinks and bottled
water producers
Publications:
• Annual Report (Bryggaråret): *includes activities of the
Association over the past year, a list of members as well as
various statistics on the industry - annual*
• Bryggeri-Bulletin: *articles, graphs, news and comment on
the Brewing Industry - 3-6 times p.a.*

Association of Swedish Chemical Industries
Den Svenska Kemiindustrins Branschorganisation
Address: Box 5501, S-11485 Stockholm
Telephone: +46 8 783 8000
Fax: +46 8 663 6323
Web site: www.chemind.se:8000/Kemikontoret/
Chief officers: Owe Fredholm, Ulla Filliez

Association of Swedish Fruit and Vegetable Distributors
Sveriges Frukt- och Grönsaksdistributöreres Förening
Address: Box 5512, Grevgatan 34, S-11485 Stockholm
Telephone: +46 8 666 1100
Fax: +46 8 662 5518
E-mail: ake.nattochdag@stockholm.mail.telia.com
Activities: government relations, collection and dissemination
of information; collects statistics on imports of fruit and
vegetables by value, by type and by country of origin
Chief officers: Ake Natt Och Dag (Managing Director)
Membership: 20 fruit and vegetable distributors
Notes: No publications available to non-members.

Association of Swedish Shoe Retailers
Sveriges Skohandlarförbund
Address: Kungsgatan 19, S-10561 Stockholm
Telephone: +46 8 791 5453
Fax: +46 8 213 690
Year established: 1941
Chief officers: Åke Weyler
Membership: ca. 600 footwear retailers
Publications:
• Shoe Retailing (Skohandlaren): *monthly*

Association of Swedish Shoe, Textile and Clothing Retailers (STIL)
Sko & Textilhandlarna
Address: Kungsgatan 19, S-10561 Stockholm
Telephone: +46 8 791 5300
Fax: +46 8 213 690
Activities: sponsors the Stockholm Fashion Fair, which takes
place twice a year in February and late August, organised by
Stockholmsmassan (Tel: +46 8 749 4100); compiles data on
textiles; provides education and information for its members
Chief officers: Mr Åke Weyler (Managing Director)
Membership: approx. 900 corporate members, textile and
clothing retailing companies
Publications:
• Importnytt
• Membership List: *information on members - annual*
• Newsletters (Association of the Swedish Textile and Clothing
Retailers): *10 p.a.*

Association of Swedish Suppliers of Toy and Hobby Articles
Address: Box 5512, S-11485 Stockholm
Telephone: +46 8 667 4912
Fax: +46 8 665 4996
Activities: toy safety and environmental issues
Chief officers: Mr Johan Leffler (Managing Director)
Notes: No publications or statistics.

Association of Swedish Wholesalers of Automotive Parts and Accessories
Address: Box 5512, S-11485 Stockholm
Telephone: +46 8 666 1100
Fax: +46 8 667 8051
Chief officers: Goran Nilsson (Ombudsman), Lillemor
Vigstrom (Secretary)
Membership: 11

Federation of Swedish Fish Industries and Wholesalers
Address: Fiskhallsvagen 16-18, S-12044 Årsta 12044
Telephone: +46 8 811 400
Fax: +46 8 812 515
Year established: 1988
Membership: 70 companies (manufacturers and wholesalers)

Federation of Swedish Industries
Address: Box 5501, Storgatan 19, S-11485 Stockholm
Telephone: +46 8 783 8000
Fax: +46 8 662 3595
Activities: liaison with other Nordic industrial federations
Chief officers: Bo Rydim (Chairman); Bert-Olof Svanholm,
Harald Jahn (Deputy Chairman); Magnus Lemmel (Director
General)
Structure: board of directors, executive committee,
departments: administrative, information, economic policy,
trade policy, market and transport, environment and energy,
legal, fiscal policy
Membership: 6,000 companies, 17 trade associations

Publications:
• Conjectures (Konjunkturen): *forecasts, usually up to 18 months ahead, of economic and business trends in Sweden. Also includes some forecasts for other countries - quarterly*

Federation of Swedish Suppliers of Electrical Household Appliances

Elektriska Hushållsapparat Leverantörer
Address: PO Box 1416, S-11184 Stockholm
Telephone: +46 8 240 700
Fax: +46 8 218 496
E-mail: pwa@branschkansliet.se
Web site: www.branschkansliet.se/associations.htm
Year established: 1966
Activities: collects statistics for members only
Chief officers: Per Wallin (Managing Director); Christina Wirbing (Assistant Director)
Membership: 25 companies

National Association of Bicycle and Sports Equipment Retailers

Cykel-och Spothandlarnas Riksforbund
Address: Kungsgatan 19, S-10561 Stockholm
Telephone: +46 8 791 5440
Fax: +46 8 249 616
Year established: 1925
Membership: bicycles and sports goods retailers
Publications:
• Ftitidhandlaren Cykel och Sport: *monthly*

National Association of Confectionery Importers

Konfektyrimportorernas Riksforbund
Address: PO Box 5512, Grevgatan 34, S-11485 Stockholm
Telephone: +46 8 666 1100
Fax: +46 8 662 6548
Year established: 1969
Activities: government liaison, compilation of import statistics (monthly); compilation of press cuttings
Chief officers: Roland Nordlund (Director)
Membership: 12 companies
Publications:
• Monthly Import Statistics (National Association of Confectionery Importers): *detailed monthly import statistics for confectionery broken down by general product area - monthly*
Notes: No publications produced.

National Association of Tobacco Retailers

Tobaks and Servicehandelns Riksforbund
Address: Box 9025, S-126 09 Hagersten
Telephone: +46 8 681 0320
Fax: +46 8 199 526
Year established: 1910
Activities: information on relevant legislation
Chief officers: Susan Fritz (Managing Director)
Structure: executive board with managing director, editor and an economist
Membership: 900 retailers
Publications:
• Tobacconist (Tobakshandlaren): *information on legislation affecting tobacco retailing, reports from members of the Association and articles on the tobacco industry in general - 8 p.a.*

Shoe Suppliers' Association

Address: Box 5512, S-11485 Stockholm
Telephone: +46 8 666 1100
Fax: +46 8 662 7457
Chief officers: Lillemor Vigstrom (Secretary)

Swedish Advertisers' Association

Annonsörföreningen
Address: Box 1327, Drottninggatan 71 C, S-111 83 Stockholm
Telephone: +46 8 235 100
Fax: +46 8 235 510
E-mail: info@annons.se
Web site: www.annons.se

Swedish Advertising Association

Sveriges Reklamforbund
Address: PO Box 1420, Norrlandsgatan 24, S-111 84 Stockholm
Telephone: +46 8 679 0800
Fax: +46 8 679 0801
Activities: legal counselling; seminars; collects salary statistics (distributed to participants only)
Chief officers: Stefan Skogh; Henri Pagot
Membership: 320 member companies
Publications:
• Advertising Agencies in Sweden: *annual*

Swedish Aerosol Association

Svenska Aerosol Föreningen
Address: Box 61, S-18621 Vallentuna
Telephone: +46 8 511 72100
Fax: +46 8 511 73941
Activities: trade and branch organisation for aerosols in Sweden; collects statistics on production of filled aerosols
Chief officers: Par Lindell; Sune Haglund
Membership: 19 member companies

Swedish Article Numbering Association (EAN Sweden)

Address: Klarabergsviadukten 96, S-106 13 Stockholm
Telephone: +46 8 698 3040
Fax: +46 8 698 3049
E-mail: info@ean.se

Swedish Association of Bakers

Sveriges Bageriförbund
Address: Box 16141, S-10323 Stockholm
Telephone: +46 8 762 6000
Fax: +46 8 678 6664
E-mail: kansli@bageri.se
Web site: www.bageri.se
Year established: 1990
Activities: negotiates with unions and advises member companies; collects statistics on salaries for workers
Chief officers: Per Helgesson (Managing Director)
Membership: 700 member companies

Swedish Association of Cheese and Egg Wholesalers

Sveriges Ost- och Aggrossisters Forening
Address: Box 5512, Grevgatan 34, S-11485 Stockholm
Telephone: +46 8 666 1100
Fax: +46 8 662 6548
Year established: 1941
Activities: collects monthly import statistics
Chief officers: Roland Nordlund (Director), Eva Brunberg (Secretary)
Membership: 9 companies
Notes: No publications produced.

Swedish Association of Management Consultants (SAMC)

Address: Box 7470, S-103 92 Stockholm
Telephone: +46 8 661 5790
Fax: +46 8 661 5792
E-mail: Info@samc.se
Web site: www.samc.se

Swedish Bankers' Association
Address: Box 7603, Regeringsgatan 42, S-10394 Stockholm
Telephone: +46 8 453 4400
Fax: +46 8 676 0387

Swedish Book Publishers' Association
Svenska Bokförläggareföreningen
Address: Drottninggatan 97, S-113 60 Stockholm
Telephone: +46 8 736 1940
Fax: +46 8 736 1944
Web site: www.ihb.se:8001/
Chief officers: Mr L Bergstrom (President), Mr L Grahn (Secretary), Ms K Ahlinder (Director)

Swedish Chocolate and Confectionery Manufacturers' Association
Svenska Choklad-, Konfektyr-och Kexfabrikantföreningen
Address: PO Box 5501, Storgatan 19, S-11485 Stockholm
Telephone: +46 8 783 8000
Fax: +46 8 783 8273
Chief officers: G Holmqvist (Director)

Swedish Consumer Electronics Retailers' Association
Elektronikforbundet
Address: PO Box 6821, S-11386 Stockholm
Telephone: +46 8 441 5180
Fax: +46 8 441 5191
E-mail: fan@elektronikforbundet.se
Web site: www.elektronikforbundet.se
Year established: 1936
Activities: provides information, international contacts and cooperation; deals with environmental questions, consumer laws and education; collects sales statistics on brown goods
Chief officers: Sture Lundin (Managing Director); Jonte Johannisson (Development Manager)
Membership: approximately 1500 companies
Publications:
• El & Vitt: *4 p.a.*
• Rateko & Foto: *10 p.a.*

Swedish Cosmetic, Toiletry and Household Products Suppliers' Association (KTF)
Kemisk-Tekniska Leverantörförbundet
Address: Klarabergsviadukten 90, S-106 13 Stockholm
Telephone: +46 8 698 8120
Fax: +46 8 698 8129
E-mail: info@ktf.se
Web site: www.ktf.se
Activities: assists members in complying with legislation; establishes contact with authorities, retailers, consumers, media; initiates trade cooperation on joint issues; provides information service on safety of chemical products and legislation; research and statistical service including collecting annual official statistics on cosmetics; training courses and seminars; consulting
Chief officers: Dr Christina Mattsson (Secretary General); Camilla Fagerberg (Dept. of Cosmetics and Toiletries); Olof Holmer (Dept. of Household Products)
Membership: approx. 80 importers, manufacturers and dealers in toiletries, cosmetics and household products
Publications:
• KFT Newsletter
• KTF Regulatory News: *covering regulatory affairs for cosmetics*

Swedish Dairies' Association - Swedish National Committee of IDF
Address: c/o Swedish Dairies' Association, S-105 46 Stockholm

Telephone: +46 8 788 0300
Fax: +46 8 218 363
Chief officers: Ms M. Andersson (Secretary)

Swedish Food Retailers' Association
Sveriges Livsmedelshandlareförbund
Address: PO Box 1311, S-11183 Stockholm
Telephone: +46 8 141 870
Fax: +46 8 243 506
Membership: general food and beverage retailers
Publications:
• Livs: *the Swedish food retailing industry - 8 per year*

Swedish Franchise Association
Address: PO Box 5512, Stig Sohlberg, CEO/Legal Counsel, S-114 85 Stockholm
Telephone: +46 8 660 8610
Fax: +46 8 662 7457

Swedish Frozen Food Association
Djupfrysningsbyran
Address: Kavalleristen, Berga Allée, 1, S-254 52 Helsinborg
Telephone: +46 421 630 25
Fax: +46 421 525 80
Chief officers: Mr Kjell Olsson
Notes: Member of the Federation of the Associations of EU Frozen Food Producers (FAFPAS) based in Brussels (Belgium).

Swedish Furniture Industries' Association
Sveriges Möbelindustriförbund
Address: Box 14012, Grevgatan 5, S-10440 Stockholm
Telephone: +46 8 230 780
Fax: +46 8 783 0596
Membership: 200 companies
Publications:
• Good News from Sweden

Swedish Furniture Retailers' Association
Address: Kungsgatan 19, S-10561 Stockholm
Telephone: +46 8 791 5410
Fax: +46 8 791 5418
E-mail: furniture-a.stroemberg@swipnet.se
Year established: 1918
Activities: legal support; training and education; marketing services; market surveys and development projects; internal retail sales statistics
Chief officers: Anders Stromberg (Managing Director)
Membership: 300 companies including the four biggest furniture retailers' chains
Publications:
• Mobler och Miljo (Furniture and Milieu): *10 p.a.*

Swedish Hardware Dealers' Association
Sveriges Jarnhandlareforbund
Address: PO Box 24146, Torstenssonsgatan 12, S-104 51 Stockholm
Telephone: +46 8 663 5140
Fax: +46 8 667 7148
Activities: training; insurance; printing and selling company-profiled forms; trade information; contacts with politicians, authorities and suppliers; seminar arrangements; legal assistance; collects statistics covering turnover and profitability of member companies
Chief officers: Mr Roland Billme (Managing Director)
Membership: 400 members
Publications:
• Bygg & Jarnhandeln: *trade information - monthly*
• Jarninfo: *monthly*

Swedish Meat Trade Association

Köttbranschens Riksförbund
Address: Box 5093, S-121 16 Johanneshov
Telephone: +46 8 659 0005
Fax: +46 8 659 2182
E-mail: info@meattrade.se
Year established: 1916
Activities: collects statistics covering production, prices, sales
Chief officers: Mr Ake Rutegard (Managing Director)
Membership: 180 member companies involved in slaughtering, cutting and meat processing
Publications:
• Köttbranschen: *only publication concerning the Swedish meat industry, including regular trade statistics for meat - monthly*

Swedish Meat Wholesalers' Association

Sveriges Köttgrossister
Address: Box 5512, Grevgatan 34, S-11485 Stockholm
Telephone: +46 8 666 1100
Fax: +46 8 662 6548
Activities: collects import statistics
Chief officers: Roland Nordlund (Director)
Membership: 14 wholesale meat merchants
Notes: No publications produced.

Swedish National Organisation for Motor Retail Trade and Repairs (MRF)

Motorbranschens Riksforbund
Address: Box 5611, Karlavägen 14A, S-11486 Stockholm
Telephone: +46 8 701 6300
Fax: +46 8 244 401
E-mail: mrf@mrf.se
Web site: www.mrf.se
Year established: 1960
Activities: education and training, information service to members, government lobbying and arbitration
Membership: 2,000 car dealers, repair shops and car painters
Publications:
• Motor Trade (Motorbrauschen): *reports on new trends within different segments of the automotive industry. Also includes information on current trade issues and European legislation - 9 times p.a.*

Swedish Newspaper Association

Svenska Tidningsutgibareforeningen
Address: PO Box 22500, S-104 22 Stockholm
Telephone: +46 8 692 4600
Fax: +46 8 692 4638
E-mail: eric.castegren@tu.se or annemarie.gottfarb@tu.se
Web site: www.tu.se
Chief officers: Ms Barbro Fischerström (Managing Director)

Swedish Packaging Research Institute

Packforsk
Address: PO Box 9, Torshamnsgatan 24, S-164 93 Kista
Telephone: +46 8 752 5700
Fax: +46 8 751 3889
E-mail: packforsk@packforsk.se
Web site: www.packforsk.se
Activities: produces statistics on packaging consumption
Chief officers: Anders Soras (Managing Director); Carl Olsmats (Deputy Managing Director)
Membership: 250 member companies

Swedish Paint Trade Association

Sveriges Färghandlares Riksförbund
Address: Kungsgatan 19, S-10561 Stockholm
Telephone: +46 8 791 5390
Fax: +46 8 103 126

Activities: lobbying; study tours
Chief officers: Mrs Birgitta Nygren (Managing Director); Mrs Inga-Lill Fossum (Assistant)
Membership: 290 paint retailers
Publications:
• Svensk Färghandel: *news and analysis concerning people, products and events in the paint and wall paper trade - 7 p.a.*
Notes: The Association does not collect statistics.

Swedish Periodical Publishers' Association

Sveriges Tidskrifter
Address: Vasagatan 50, S-111 20 Stockholm
Telephone: +46 821 5302
Fax: +46 814 9865
E-mail: info@sverigestidskrifter.se
Web site: www.torget.se/svetid

Swedish Plastics and Chemicals Federation

Plast- och Kemibranscherma
Address: PO Box 101, Drottninggatan 68, S-101 22 Stockholm
Telephone: +46 8 402 1360
Fax: +46 8 411 4526
E-mail: por.pastkretsen@plast-kemi.se
Web site: www.plast-kemise.se
Activities: information service; trade policies; international cooperation; education of management and workers in the industry; carries out research activities; coordinates standardisation and common norms in the industry; advice and expert assistance to member companies; member list available on request
Chief officers: Mr Stieg Edlund (Managing Director), Ms Lena Johansson (Secretary)
Membership: 270 members importers, agents, manufacturers and trading companies within the plastic and chemical industry
Publications:
• Buyer's Guides
• Members List: *address, telephone and fax details of association members*
Notes: The Association does not produce statistics.

Wine Agents (UVOS)

UVOS - Vinagenterna
Address: PO Box 5512, Grevgatan 34, S-11485 Stockholm
Telephone: +46 8 666 1100
Fax: +46 8 662 7457
Activities: collects import statistics
Chief officers: Roland Nordlund (Director)
Membership: 22 representatives of foreign wine and spirits producers
Notes: No publications produced.

SWITZERLAND

Association of Cosmetics and Perfume Manufacturers, Importers and Distributors (ASCOPA)

Association des Fabricants, Importateurs, Fournisseurs de Produits de Cosmétique et Parfumerie
Address: CP 5278, Rue de St Jean 98, CH-1211 Geneva 11
Telephone: +41 22 715 3204
Fax: +41 22 715 3213
Web site: www.ascopa.ch
Activities: compilation of statistics (available to members only)
Chief officers: F Brühlmann (President), Nina Ricci (Secretary)
Structure: represents 130 brands of cosmetics and toiletries
Membership: ca.40 perfumery goods wholesalers and retailers

Association of Foreign Banks in Switzerland
Address: Stockerstrasse 38, CH- 8039 Zürich
Telephone: +41 1 283 80 50
Fax: +41 1 201 87 00
Year established: 1972
Chief officers: Max C. Schäfer (General Secretary)
Membership: 129 foreign-controlled banks organised under Swiss law, 11 foreign banks with Swiss branches, 17 foreign-controlled finance companies, 13 representative offices of foreign banks

Association of Roofing and Plumbing Contractors (SSIV)
Schweizerischer Spenglermeister- und Installateur-Verband
Address: Postfach 8023, Auf der Mauer 11, CH-8001 Zürich
Telephone: +41 1 251 7400
Fax: +41 1 251 3228
Chief officers: Max Meyer (Managing Director)

Association of Swiss Commercial and Asset Management Banks
Address: Selnaustrasse 30, CH-8021 Zürich
Telephone: +41 1 229 28 01
Fax: +41 1 229 28 33
Year established: 1981
Chief officers: Dr. Dieter Sigrist (Secretary)
Membership: 27 members, including 10 commercial banks and 17 Asset Management Banks, which together run approximately 15% of the funds managed by banks in Switzerland

Association of Swiss Specialist Wholesalers (VSSG)
Verband Schweizerischer Spezialitäten-Grossisten
Address: Postfach 401, Grand-Places 14, CH-1701 Freiburg
Telephone: +41 26 322 2228
Fax: +41 26 322 8087
E-mail: VSSG <Etude@cottier-associes.ch>
Activities: statistics
Membership: 8 wholesalers

Association of the Swiss Pulp, Paper and Cardboard Industry (ZPK)
Verband der Schweizerischen Zellstoff, Papier und Kartonindustrie
Address: Postfach 134, Bergstrasse 110, CH-8032 Zürich
Telephone: +41 1 261 9747
Fax: +41 1 252 3882
Activities: Technical Committee and Working Groups: eco-balance, waste paper, pulp, on waste disposal, energy, ad-hoc working groups; collects sector statistics: quarterly delivery statistics, annual statistics on imports, exports, consumption, annual waste paper statistics, annual energy statistics
Chief officers: Urs Widmer (President), Ansgar Gmür (Director)
Membership: 17 members of the paper industry
Publications:
• Brochures: *brochures about paper, recycling and other topics in relation to the paper industry - periodically*
• Common Annual Report (Jahresbericht): *annual statistics on production, demand, imports, exports on the paper and board industry in Switzerland (based on various sources) - annual*

Book Retailers' and Publishers' Association
Schweizerischer Buchhändler- und Verleger-Verband
Address: Postfach 9045, CH-8050 Zürich
Telephone: +41 1 318 6450
Fax: +41 1 318 64 62
E-mail: SBVV@dm.krinfo.ch
Membership: book retailers and publishers

Federation of Swiss Food Wholesalers (COLGRO)
Schweizerischer Verband des Lebensmittel-Grosshandels
Address: Guterstrasse 78, CH-4053 Basel
Telephone: +41 61 271 3385
Fax: +41 61 272 3039
Activities: collects sector statistics and operates information service
Chief officers: Herr Dieter Furstenberger (Senior Director)
Membership: ca. 25 food wholesalers

Federation of Swiss Importers and Wholesalers
Vereinigung des Schweizerischen Import- und Grosshandels
Address: Postfach 656, Centralbahnstrasse 9, CH-4010 Basel
Telephone: +41 61 271 3385
Fax: +41 61 272 3039
Membership: approx. 5,000 general importers and wholesalers
Publications:
• VSIG Pressedienst: *press releases on association activities; information brochures also available - irregular*

Food Manufacturers' Swiss Association (FIAL)
Branchengruppierung Schweizerischer Lebensmittelfabrikanten/ Fédération des Industries Alimentaires Suisses
Address: Elfenstrasse 19, CH-3000 Berne 16
Telephone: +41 31 352 1188
Fax: +41 31 352 1185
Year established: 1946
Activities: umbrella organisation for the Swiss food industry comprising 6 specialist groups each dealing with a specific sub-sector of the food industry; each group collects statistical data on their sector
Chief officers: Bernhard Hodler (Senior Director)
Membership: 54 food manufacturers
Publications:
• Annual Report of the Swiss Association of Food Manufacturers: *annual*
• Die Schweizerische Nahrungsmittel Zeitung: *issues affecting food production; new business development and product development etc. - weekly*

Ice Cream Manufacturers' Association
Verband Schweizerischer Glace und Eiscreme-Fabrikanten (Glace Verband)/Fédération Suisse des Glaces Alimentaires
Address: Postfach 246, Elfenstrasse 19, CH-3000 Berne 16
Telephone: +41 31 352 1188
Fax: +41 31 352 1185
Membership: 8 ice cream manufacturing companies

Pharmaceutical and Cosmetics Manufacturers' Association
Interessengemeinschaft für Pharmazeutische und Kosmetische Produkte
Address: Postfach 396, CH-8034 Zürich
Telephone: +41 1 383 1349
Fax: +41 1 383 1020
Activities: statistical service to members; conferences and exhibitions held; Rundschreiben (circulars) distributed to members every 2 months
Chief officers: Dr W Spillmann-Thulin (President)
Membership: 43 manufacturers and dealers in cosmetics and pharmaceuticals
Publications:
• Jahresbericht (Association of Pharmaceutical and Cosmetics Manufacturers): *in-house publication providing details of association activities and market information/product development*
Notes: represents medium- and small-sized firms

Soap and Detergent Manufacturers' Association (SWI)
Verband der Seifen- und Waschmittelfabrikanten
Address: Postfach 8027, Breitingerstrasse 35, CH-8002 Zürich
Telephone: +41 1 202 3386
Fax: +41 1 201 0985
Year established: 1899
Activities: organises conferences
Chief officers: Dr Kurt Gehri (Director)
Membership: 19 soap and detergent manufacturers
Publications:
• Annual Report of the Union of Soap and Detergent Manufacturers: *annual*

Swiss Article Numbering Association
Address: Dornacherstrasse 230, CH-4053 Basel
Telephone: +41 61 338 7000
Fax: +41 61 338 7099
E-mail: mail@ean.ch

Swiss Association of the Cigarette Industry
Communauté de l'Industrie Suisse de la Cigarette
Address: Case Postale 212, Pétrolles 5, CH-1701 Fribourg
Telephone: +41 2 632 141 21
Fax: +41 2 632 262 18
E-mail: Office@cisc.ch
Year established: 1933
Activities: collects statistics on the tobacco industry; various publications about tobacco and society
Chief officers: Hans-Ulrich Hunziker (Managing Director), Hans-Ruedi Huber (Head of Communications)
Membership: 4 companies of tobacco wholesalers
Publications:
• Annual Sales Volumes: *statistical data on the sales volume in Switzerland - annual*
• Annual Tax Volumes: *statistical data on tax volumes in relation with the tobacco industry in Switzerland over the past year - annual*
• Development of Market Shares: *statistical information on the development of market shares of tobacco companies and brands and their turnover, profits, assets over the past year - annual*
• Public Tobacco (Tabac Public): *news and opinion articles on the tobacco industry in Switzerland - regularly*
• Tobacco in Switzerland (Tabac en Suisse): *portrait of the Swiss industry*
• Tobacco in Switzerland (Tabac en Suisse): *factsheet of the tobacco industry in Switzerland*

Swiss Association of Asset Managers (SAAM)
Address: Südstrasse 11, CH-8034 Zürich
Telephone: +41 1 383 91 59
Fax: +41 1 383 91 74
Year established: 1986
Chief officers: Herr Viktor Sauter

Swiss Association of Bakers and Pastry Masters (SBKV)
Schweizerischer Bäcker- Konditorenmeister- Verband
Address: Seilerstrasse 9, CH-3001 Berne
Telephone: +41 31 381 7877
Fax: +41 31 382 1506
Activities: dissemination of information and statistics for members; provides services in entrepreneurial, political and economic areas for members
Chief officers: Rudi Steiner (President), Renaldo Ninzer (Director)
Membership: 4,390 master bakers and confectioners
Publications:
• Panissimo: *market news, trade fair information and employment vacancies - weekly*

• Swiss Baking Statistics: *statistics on consumption, production, etc*

Swiss Association of Distributors of Products for Hairdresser (LICOPHA)
Verband der Schweizerischen Lieferanten Kosmetischer und verwandter Produkte für das Coiffeurgewerbe
Address: Breitingerstrasse 35, CH-8002 Zürich
Telephone: +41 1 202 5107
Fax: +41 1 201 0985
Activities: information service for members
Chief officers: Dr Kurt Gehri (President), Marina Mannes (Secretary)
Structure: allied to the Association de l'Industrie Suisse de Cosmétiques (qv)
Membership: 14 distributors, wholesalers and importers of beauty products
Publications:
• Annual Report (Jahresbericht): *annual*

Swiss Association of French Language Books' Distributors (ASRDL)
Association Suisse Romande des Diffuseurs et Distributeurs de Livres
Address: 2 Avenue Agassiz, CH-1001 Lausanne
Telephone: +41 21 319 7111
Fax: +41 21 319 7910
Year established: 1975
Chief officers: Philippe Schibli (Secretary General)
Structure: part of an umbrella organisation which includes Association Suisse des Libraires de Langue Française and Association Suisse des Éditors de Langue Française
Membership: 18 booksellers in French-speaking Switzerland

Swiss Association of French-Language Libraries (ASLLF)
Association Suisse des Librairies de Langue Française
Address: 2 Avenue Agassiz, CH-1001 Lausanne
Telephone: +41 21 319 7111
Fax: +41 21 319 7910
Year established: 1866
Chief officers: Philippe Schibli (Secretary General)
Structure: part of an umbrella organisation which includes Association Suisse des Éditeurs de Langue Française and Association Suisse Romande des Diffuseurs et Distributeurs de Livres
Membership: 132 French-language bookshops

Swiss Association of German-Language Books Publishers (VVDS)
Buchverleger-verband der deutschsprachigen Schweiz
Address: Baumackerstasse 42, CH-8050 Zürich
Telephone: +41 1 318 6430
Fax: +41 1 318 64 62
Web site: www.swissbooks.ch/
Chief officers: Mr W Stocker (President), Mr E Raez (Director)

Swiss Association of Health and Dietary Foods Manufacturers
Vereinigung Schweizerischer Hersteller von Diät und Kraftnahrungen
Address: Elfenstrasse 19, CH-3006 Berne 16
Telephone: +41 31 352 1188
Fax: +41 31 352 1185
Chief officers: Herr Bert Hodler (Senior Director)
Membership: 11 manufacturers of health and dietary foods

Swiss Association of Patents and Trade Marks (PROMARCA)

Schweizerischer Markenartikelverband/Union Suisse de l'Article de Marque
Address: Münzgraben 6, CH-3000 Bern 7
Telephone: +41 31 312 5565
Fax: +41 31 312 3444
E-mail: promarca@bluewin.ch
Activities: collects statistics on private and public organisations; supports the favourable conditions for the production, marketing and sale of trade marks
Chief officers: Dr Jean-Bernard Bosset (Director), Valentin K Wepter (Communications Department)
Membership: 57 members
Publications:
● Annual Report (Jahresbericht): *anual*
● Membership Information (Mitgliederinfo): *10-12 p.a.*

Swiss Brewers' Association

Schweizerischer Bierbrauerverein/Société Suisse de Brasseurs/Societa Svizzera Dei Birrai
Address: Po Box 6325, Bahnhofplatz 9, CH-8023 Zürich
Telephone: +41 1 221 2628
Fax: +41 1 211 6206
E-mail: bierbrauerverein@spectraweb.ch or bier@bier.ch
Web site: www.bier.ch
Year established: 1877
Activities: compilation of industrial data, general information on brewing and the brewing industry for members and public, training services
Chief officers: Alexander Füglisaller (President), Konrad Studerus (Director)
Membership: 30 breweries
Publications:
● Brauerei- und Getränke-Rundschau: *actual, economic and technical information about Swiss bier industry, as well as information about the international bier and beverage industry - monthly*
● Brochures on Beer (Broschüren zum Thema Bier): *different brochures on beer topics: data of the association, Swiss bier, history of the bier, etc. (information about title, price and coverage available in the web page)*

Swiss Butter Union

Schweizerische Butter-Union
Address: Hotelgasse 1, CH-3011 Berne
Telephone: +41 31 311 1906
Fax: +41 31 311 1916
Activities: information and statistical service to members only
Chief officers: Frau Ruth Wenge (President and Senior Director)
Membership: 12 wholesalers
Publications:
● Annual Report of the Swiss Butter Union: *annual*

Swiss Cheese Exporters' Association (VSKE)

Verband Schweizerischer Käseexporteure/Syndicat des Exportateurs Suisses de Fromage
Address: Postfach 246, Elfenstrasse 19, CH-3000 Berne 16
Telephone: +41 31 352 2611/1188
Fax: +41 31 352 0065/1185
Year established: 1896
Activities: collects statistics published in association with the Swiss Cheese Union (Schweizerischen Käseunion AG); information service, collection of company reports (available on request)
Chief officers: Dr Guy Emmenegger (President), Pierre Gehring (Executive Director)
Membership: 20 cheese wholesalers and exporters
Publications:
● Annual Report of the Association of Swiss Cheese Exporters

(Jahresbericht): *annual (published in May)*
● Geschaftsbericht (VSKE): *data on the production, sales, imports, and exports of Swiss cheese with some data for earlier years. Also contains a review of the cheese sector - annual*

Swiss Cheese Union

Schweizerische Käseunion AG
Address: Postfach 8225, Montbijoustrasse 45, CH-3001 Berne
Telephone: +41 31 378 1111
Fax: +41 31 378 1116
Activities: collects production, sales, consumption, import and export data; operates information department
Chief officers: M Pierre Goetschi (Senior Director)
Membership: 30 members involved in cheese distribution
Publications:
● Annual Report (Jahresbericht): *annual*
● Market Report (Geschäftsbericht): *review and statistics on the cheese sector - annual*
Notes: Central joint organisation for the wholesale and export of Swiss cheese under the branded product names: Emmental Switzerland, Gruyere Switzerland, Sbrinz Switzerland.

Swiss Chocolate Manufacturers' Association (CHOCOSUISSE)

Verband Schweizerischer Schokoladefabrikanten/Union des Fabricants Suisses de Chocolat
Address: Postfach 84, Münzgraben 6, CH-3000 Berne 7
Telephone: +41 31 311 6494
Fax: +41 31 312 2655
Activities: collects annual general data on the production of and markets for chocolate confectionery in Switzerland (see below)
Chief officers: Dario Kuster (Director), Kurt Hunziger (Secretary)
Membership: 14 chocolate confectionery manufacturers
Publications:
● Annual Report (Jaresbericht): *includes some basic statistics - annual*
● Swiss Chocolate Industry Statistics/Chocosuisse Bulletin (Statistique de l'Industrie Chocolatière Suisse/Bulletin Chocosuisse): *general statistics on the production and markets for chocolate confectionery in Switzerland. Figures for the latest year and comparative figures for earlier years - annual*

Swiss Confectionery and Pastry Bakers' Association

Schweizerischer Konditor- Confiseurmeister-Verband/Union Suisse des Patrons Confiseurs-Pâtissiers-Glaciers
Address: PO Box 8494, Tramstrasse 10, CH-8050 Zürich
Telephone: +41 1 311 4166
Fax: +41 1 311 3982
Year established: 1898
Activities: advertising, marketing working contracts, insurance, PR work (all for members only)
Chief officers: Judith Irniger (General Manager), Benno Keller (General Secretary)
Membership: 1,000 (all small-medium sized independent producers of confectionery and chocolate products; retail trade)
Publications:
● Baker, The (Der Confiseur/Le Confiseur): *weekly*
● Panissimo

Swiss Cosmetics Industry Association (VSKI)

Verband der Schweizerischen Kosmetikindustrie/Association de l'Industrie Suisse de Cosmétiques
Address: Breitingerstrasse 35, CH-8027 Zürich
Telephone: +41 1 202 3386
Fax: +41 1 201 0985

Chief officers: Dr Kurt Gehri (President), Marina Mannes (Secretary)
Membership: 41 cosmetics producers and suppliers
Publications:
• Annual Report (Jahresbericht): *annual*

Swiss Dairy Products Industry Association (SMV)
Schweizerischer Milchwirtschaftlicher Verein
Address: Postfach 2687, Gurtenstrasse 6, CH-3001 Berne
Telephone: +41 31 311 6948
Fax: +41 31 312 5660
Activities: collects data on the milk industry and trade covering production, imports, exports, consumption, prices, etc. (published in the annual report)
Chief officers: Herr Viktor Schenker (Senior Director)
Membership: over 2,000 dairy farmers and dairy enterprises
Publications:
• Annual Report (Jahresbericht): *mainly text on trends in the milk indusry but some statistics in the text and a statistical section at the end covering production, foreign trade, consumption, prices etc. Most tables have data for earlier years - annual*

Swiss Department Stores' Association (VSWK)
Verband der Schweizerischen Waren- und Kaufhäuser
Address: Holbeinstrasse 22, CH-8032 Zürich
Telephone: +41 1 252 4040
Fax: +41 1 252 4097
Year established: 1939
Chief officers: Dr Klaus Hug (President and Director), Barbara Regli (Secretary General)
Membership: department stores and large retailers
Publications:
• Annual Report of the Association of Swiss Department Stores: *annual*

Swiss Food Importers' and Distributors' Association
Schweizerischer Verband von Comestibles-Importeuren und Händlern
Address: Postfach 113, Appenzellerstraße 4, CH-9424 Thal SG
Telephone: +41 33 654 1935
Fax: +41 33 654 1935
Activities: publishes information on new businesses, market data and statistics
Chief officers: Xaver Martin (Secretary)
Membership: ca. 70 importers and distributors of foodstuffs
Publications:
• Bericht von neuen Geschäften: *report on new businesses; covers sectors on fish, fowl and poultry - annual*
• Comestible: *in-house publication covering activities of association and some market data - 3 p.a.*

Swiss Food Retailers' Association
Schweizerischer Verband der Lebensmittel-Detaillisten/ Association Suisse des Détaillants en Alimentation
Address: Postfach 2740, Falkenplatz 1, CH-3012 Berne
Telephone: +41 31 311 6153
Fax: +41 31 312 5087
Year established: 1900
Chief officers: Gottfreid Sulser (Chairman), Peter Schütz, Pierre Hiltpold
Membership: 3,500 independent food retailers

Swiss Food Wholesalers' Association
Verband Schweizerische Agenten der Lebensmittel-Branche
Address: PO Box 219, Gustav Gerig AG, CH-8037 Zürich
Telephone: +41 1 271 3436
Fax: +41 1 271 3014

Year established: 1896
Chief officers: Wener Fehr (Secretary)
Membership: 14 food wholesalers, agents and exporters of food products

Swiss Franchise Association
Schwezerischer Franchise Verband
Address: Lowenstrasse 11, Ch-8039 Zürich
Telephone: +41 1 225 4757
Fax: +41 1 225 4777
Chief officers: Werner Kieser (President), Dr Christoph Wildhaber (Secretary)

Swiss Glass and China Trade Association (GPV)
Schweizerischer Glas- und Porzellanhandels- Verband
Address: Postfach 337, Seftgenstasse 301, CH-3084 Wabern
Telephone: +41 31 961 3894
Fax: +41 31 961 0187
Activities: publishes a consultative document; exchanges information; negotiates the delivery conditions, etc.
Chief officers: Fred Nufer (President), Georg Marugg (Vice President), Walter Wildeisen (Secretary)
Membership: 50 member firms
Publications:
• TAVOLA-Customers' Journal (TAVOLA-Kundenzeitschrift): *annual*

Swiss Hairdressing Association
Schweizerischer Coiffeurmeister-Verband
Address: Postfach 641, Moserstrasse 52, CH-3000 Berne 22
Telephone: +41 31 332 7942
Fax: +41 31 331 4500
Year established: 1888
Activities: organises conferences and exhibitions; professional education; political representation
Chief officers: Kuno Giger (President), Rolf Fauser (Chief Editor)
Membership: 4,000 hairdressers
Publications:
• Swiss Hair Professional: *information about fashion, hairstyles, new techniques in haircare, marketing - monthly*
• Swiss Hair Shop: *short articles about events, information about activities of the association, classified adverstisements - monthly*

Swiss Health Food and Dietetic Food Association (VSRD)
Verband Schweizer Reform- und Diätfachgeschäfte
Address: Ekkehardstrasse 9, CH-8008 Zürich
Telephone: +41 1 363 6040
Fax: +41 1 363 0193
Activities: organises conferences and operates information service; training courses for members
Chief officers: E Räz (Secretary)
Membership: ca. 450 health foods retailers
Publications:
• Healthy Life (Health Fürs Lieben): *Swiss dietetic - bi-monthly*

Swiss Livestock Importers' Association
Verband Schweizerischer Viehimporteure
Address: Postfach 309, c/o GVFI, Schutzengraben 35, CH-4003 Basel
Telephone: +41 61 264 5050
Fax: +41 61 261 5259
Membership: 190 livestock importers and meat wholesalers

Swiss Mineral Water and Soft Drink Producers' Association (SMS)
Verband Schweizerischer Mineralquellen und Soft Drink-Produzenten
Address: General Wille Strasse 21, CH-8027 Zürich
Telephone: +41 1 202 7078
Fax: +41 1 201 7542
Activities: produces internal annual report for members only
Chief officers: Dr Alex Kuhn (Secretary General)
Membership: 10 soft drinks producers
Publications:
• Annual Report (Jahresbericht): *annual*

Swiss National Committee of the International Dairy Federation
Comité National Suisse de la FIL- Commission Suisse du Lait
Address: Schwarzenburgstrasse 161, 3003 Liebefeld-Berne
Telephone: +41 31 323 8221
Fax: +41 31 323 8227
E-mail: melchior.schaellibaum@fam.admin.ch
Chief officers: Prof. Melchior Schällibaum (Secretary)

Swiss Paper Manufacturers' Association (ASPI)
Arbeitgeberverband Schweizerischer Papier-Industrieller
Address: Postfach 134, Bergstrasse 110, CH-8030 Zürich
Telephone: +41 1 261 9747
Fax: +41 1 252 3882
Activities: conferences; education; training; information; Personnel managers' Committee; Working Group for working security; Education Committee; Committee for paper technologists; Committee for commercial trainees; Commission for the General Agreement on Employment Contract; Conference on the General Agreement on Employment Contract
Chief officers: Herr Ansgar Gmür (Senior Director)
Membership: 11 members
Publications:
• Common Annual Report (Jahresbericht): *annual statistics on production, demand, imports, exports on the paper and board industry in Switzerland (based on various sources) - annual*

Swiss Perfume Association
Schweizerischer Parfümerie-Verband
Address: Merkurstrasse 34, CH-8032 Zürich
Telephone: +41 1 252 4522
Fax: +41 1 261 1986
Activities: the publication of the magazine "Pour Vous Madame"; special offers for members
Chief officers: Waltes Furres (President), Anschka Mares (Redaction), Ursula Maria Cormark (Advertising Department)
Membership: 115 perfumery retailers, druggists
Publications:
• For you Madam (Für Sie Madame/Pour vous Madame): *10 p.a.*

Swiss Photographic Trade Association
Schweizerischer Verband für Photo- Handel und Gewerbe
Address: Postfach 3348, Limmattalstrasse 164, CH-8049 Zürich
Telephone: +41 1 241 0757
Fax: +41 1 241 1409
Activities: information service and statistics
Chief officers: Peter Zomstein (Director)
Structure: part of the Landesverband freier Schweizer Arbeitnehmer
Membership: photographic equipment retailers
Publications:
• Die Schweizerische Arbeitzeitung: *general information on self-employed business trends*
• Schweizerische Photorundschau: *fortnightly*

Swiss Poultry Producers' Association (VSGH)
Verband Schweizerischer Geflügelhalter
Address: Burgerweg 24, CH-3052 Zollikofen
Telephone: +41 31 911 1945
Fax: +41 31 911 6460
Year established: 1932
Activities: collects statistics on production, consumption and trade and provides information service
Chief officers: Mettler Alois (General Manager), Herr A Rettler (General Secretary)
Membership: 300 poultry producers
Publications:
• Swiss Poultry Journal (Schweizerische Geflügelzeitung): *32 pages about poultry production and marketing - monthly*

Swiss Press Association
Schweizer Presse/Presse Suisse/Stampa Svizzera
Address: Baumackerstrasse 42, CH-8050 Zürich
Telephone: +41 1 318 6464
Fax: +41 1 318 6462
Activities: organises events, conferences, seminars
Chief officers: Peter Hartmeier (Director), Ch Brunnschweiler
Membership: 250 members
Publications:
• Flash (Flash): *fortnightly*

Swiss Radio and Television Retailers' Association (VSRT)
Verband Schweizerischer Radio-Televisions-Fachgeschäfte/Union Suisse des Installateurs Concessionnaires en Radio et Télévision (USRT)
Address: Postfach 729, Breitenrainplatz 38, CH-3000 Berne 22
Telephone: +41 31 331 1919
Fax: +41 31 331 6558
Activities: information, conferences and trade fairs; statistical service for members only
Chief officers: Herr Robert-Stephan Portmann (Director)
Membership: 407 domestic retailers and 111 foreign retailers
Publications:
• Video Audio Revue: *trade journal dealing with issues in the retailing of consumer electronic goods; some market data (national and international) - monthly*
Notes: represents domestic and international retail outlets

Swiss Retail Association (SDV)
Schweizerischer Detaillistenverband
Address: Postfach 8166, Schwartztorstrasse 26, CH-3001 Berne
Telephone: +41 31 381 7791
Fax: +41 31 382 2366
Activities: conferences and fairs designed to unite regional associations
Chief officers: Peter Kaufmann (Director)
Structure: umbrella organisation with sub-associations representing regions of Switzerland
Membership: 8 regional associations
Publications:
• Die Schweizerische Detaillistenzeitung: *up-to-date information regarding retail trade; new business developments etc. - 10 p.a.*

Swiss Retail Chemists' Association
Schweizerischer Drogisten-Verband/Association Suisse des Droguistes
Address: Postfach 924, Längfeldweg 119, CH-2501 Biel
Telephone: +41 32 342 5051
Fax: +41 32 342 5058
Chief officers: Daniel Fontolliat (President), Ernst Hutter (Director)
Membership: 960 retail chemists and druggists

Publications:
• Die Schweizerische Drogisten Zeitung: *association events and details of new members; new product and market developments; annual report - 10 p.a.*
• Drogisten-Zeitung: *fortnightly*
• Naturstern: *quarterly*

Swiss Shoe Industry Association
Verband Schweizerischer Schuhindustrieller
Address: Postfach 87, Parkstrasse, 36, CH-5012 Schönenwerd
Telephone: +41 62 849 2043
Fax: +41 62 849 3889

Swiss Shoe Traders' Association
Schweizerischer Schuhhändlerverband
Address: Resslegrasse 15, CH-4460 Jelterkindern
Telephone: +41 61 985 9600
Fax: +41 61 985 9603
Activities: organises trade fairs, provides training and educational service
Membership: 450 footwear manufacturers; 1,200 sales outlets
Publications:
• Der Schuhhandel: *issues affecting shoe retail trade - monthly*
• List of members

Swiss Society of Chemical Industries (SGCI/SSIC)
Schweizerische Gesellschaft für Chemische Industrie/Société Suisse des Industries Chimiques
Address: Postfach 328, Nordstrasse 15, CH-8035 Zürich
Telephone: +41 1 368 1711
Fax: +41 1 368 1770
E-mail: mailbox@sgci.ch
Year established: 1882
Activities: includes industry groups covering various branches within the Swiss chemical industry; conferences; information service; statistics
Chief officers: Mrs L Ritter
Membership: 263 member companies
Publications:
• Annual Report of the Swiss Society for the Chemical Industry: *in-house publication detailing association activities - annual*
• Infochemie: *periodical*
• List of members
• SGCI Facts and Figures: *an annual compilation of chemical statistics including data on turnover, production, employment, plant locations, prices, research, energy, foreign trade, environmental protection and some comparative international data. A number of tables give figures for the last five years. The statistics are preceded by a short commentary on the industry. Based on various sources - annual*
• Swiss Chemical Industry in Figures

Swiss Technical Distributors' Association (VSTH)
Verband Schweizerischer Technischer Händler
Address: Zelgstrasse 13, CH-8003 Zürich
Telephone: +41 1 461 5060
Fax: +41 1 462 9294
Activities: education and training services and information for members; list of members available; statistics (only available to members)
Chief officers: Dr Guido Imholz (President and Secretary)
Membership: 40 wholesalers and distributors
Publications:
• Annual Report (Jahresbericht): *annual*

Swiss Textile Association
Textilverband Schweiz
Address: Postfach 4838, Beethovenstrasse 20, CH-8022 Zürich
Telephone: +41 1 201 5755
Fax: +41 1 201 0128
Activities: statistics covering production, stocks, incoming orders for the spinning, weaving, etc.
Chief officers: Alexander Hafner (Director)
Membership: 400 members from the textile and clothing industry
Publications:
• Annual Report (Jahresbericht): *annual*
• Swiss Textile Country: *publicity brochure about the Swiss textile industry*
• Swiss Textiles Directory: *provides useful information about the member companies, product range, etc. - annual*

Swiss Videogram Association
Address: Badenerstrasse 555, 8048 Zürich
Telephone: +41 1 491 9756
Fax: +41 1 401 4420
Publications:
• Swiss Market for Video (Le Marché Suisse de la Vidéo): *video retailing information including statistical data on sales by type of video as well as information on Swiss retailers*

Swiss Wine Association
Schweizerischer Weinhändlerverband/Fédération Suisse des Négociants en Vins
Address: Box 207, Amthausgasse 1, CH-3000 Berne 7
Telephone: +41 31 311 4508
Fax: +41 31 312 1072
Year established: 1893
Activities: trade statistics
Chief officers: Ernest Dällenbach (Secretary)
Membership: retail wine and spirits stores
Publications:
• Schweizerische Weinzeitung/Journal Vinicole Suisse/Giomale Vinicole Svizzero: *includes market surveys and trade data and the association's annual report - fortnightly*

Swiss Wine Exporters' Association (SWEA)
Société des Exportateurs de Vins Suisses/Verband Schweizer Weinexporteure
Address: Case Postale 1346, Avenue Avant-Poste 4, CH-1001 Lausanne
Telephone: +41 21 320 5083
Fax: +41 21 312 7483
E-mail: info@swisswine.ch
Web site: www.swisswine.ch
Activities: organises conferences, exhibitions and gives out information to members, trade fairs, other promotion events, publishes information material, produces statistical data covering export, retail and production figures
Chief officers: Daniel Lehmann (Director)
Membership: 54 wine exporters
Publications:
• Annual Report of the Association for the Export of Swiss Wine: *annual*
Notes: German branch: Verband Schweizer Weinexporteure (SWEA), Büro Deutschland, Haus der Schweiz, Unter den Linden 24, D-10117 Berlin
Tel. (+ 49) 30 201 20 18, Fax (+ 49) 30 201 20 28.

Swiss Wine Wholesalers' Association
Société des Encaveurs de Vins Suisses
Address: Case Postale 3453, CH-1002 Lausanne
Telephone: +41 21 341 8111
Fax: +41 21 311 1351

Activities: organises conferences and exhibitions
Chief officers: François-Daniel Golay (Director)
Membership: 65 wine wholesalers

Swissfashion (Clothing and Textile Association)
Address: Postfach 265, Gotthardstrasse 61, CH-8027 Zürich
Telephone: +41 1 202 7161
Fax: +41 1 202 0651
Chief officers: Rolf Langenegger (Director)

Umbrella Manufacturers' Association
Verband Schweizerischer Schirmfabrikanten
Address: Steppackerstrasse 86, CH-8194 Hüntwangen, Zürich
Telephone: +41 1 229 2888
Fax: +41 1 229 2833
E-mail: dieter.siegrist@swx.ch
Year established: 1914
Chief officers: Edgar Strotz (Chairman), Dieter Sigrist (Secretary)
Membership: 6 companies

Union of Swiss Biscuit and Confectionery Manufacturers
Union Suisse des Fabricants de Biscuits et de Confiserie
Address: Münzgraben 6, CH-3000 Berne 7
Telephone: +41 31 311 6494
Fax: +41 31 312 2655
Publications:
• Bulletin: *members list and market data covering the confectionery and biscuit markets*

TAIWAN

Association of Accredited Advertising Agents Taiwan
Address: 18/F Union Century Building, 163 Keelung Road, Section 1, Taipei
Telephone: +886 2 746 9028
Fax: +886 2 766 4166

Bankers' Association of the ROC
Address: 8th Floor, 46 Kuan-chien Road, Taipei
Telephone: +886 2 361 6489
Fax: +886 2 383 1783
Chief officers: Lo Chi-tang (Chairman)

Chinese Federation of Industries (Taiwan)
Address: 12th Floor, 390 Fu-Hsing South Road, Section 1, Taipei
Telephone: +886 2 703 3500
Fax: +886 2 703 3982
Year established: 1942
Chief officers: C. Y. Kao (Chairman)
Structure: board of 45 directors and 15 alternate directors; 15 supervisors and 19 committees
Membership: 134 member companies

Chinese National Export Enterprises' Association (CNEEA)
Address: 6th Floor, 285 Nanking East Road, Section 3, Taipei
Telephone: +886 2 713 8153/6920
Fax: +886 2 713 0115
Chief officers: Hsiung Chi-fan (Chairman)

Edible Oil Traders' Association of ROC
Address: 7th Floor, 221 Chunghsiao East Road, Section 4, Taipei
Telephone: +886 2 778 0785
Fax: +886 2 741 9666
Chief officers: Chao Chung-San (Chairman)

Garment Industry Association of Taiwan
Address: 8th Floor, 22 Ai Kuo East Road, Taipei
Telephone: +886 2 391 9113
Fax: +886 2 391 9055
Chief officers: HT Lin (Chairman)

Manufacturers' Association of Daily Hygienic Chemical Products of Taiwan
Address: 5F, 136 Po-ai Rd, Taipei
Telephone: +886 2 381 9700
Fax: +886 2 361 1584

National Fabrics Traders' Association of ROC
Address: Suit 5, 32, Lane 190, Chungshan N. Road, Taipei
Telephone: +886 2 871 9185

Petrochemical Industry Association of Taiwan
Address: 9th Floor-2, 390 Fuhsing South Road, Section 1, Taipei 106
Telephone: +886 2 707 3175/3018
Fax: +886 2 755 5154
Chief officers: K A Hsu (Chairman); C P Yao (Executive Manager)
Membership: 42 companies
Publications:
• Petrochemical Industry in Taiwan: *annual*
• Petrochemical Industry Journal: *monthly*

Taiwan Association of Educational Material Industries
Address: 6F, 305 Nanking E. Road, Section 3, Taipei
Telephone: +886 2 514 7273
Fax: +886 2 712 9692

Taiwan Association of Frozen Food Industries
Address: Rm. 2, 11F, 103 Chungcheng 4th Rd, Kaohsiung
Telephone: +886 7 241 2053
Fax: +886 7 241 2055

Taiwan Association of Frozen Vegetable and Fruit Manufacturers
Address: Room 6, 11th Floor, 103 Chungcheng IV Road, Kaohsiung, Taipei
Telephone: +886 7 201 5694/251 7317
Fax: +886 7 221 0471

Taiwan Association of Leather Goods Manufacturers
Address: 6th Floor, 5-1 Nanking West Road, Taipei
Telephone: +886 2 521 0090
Fax: +886 2 567 7403

Taiwan Association of Machinery Industries
Address: 2nd Floor, 110 Hwai Ning Street, Taipei
Telephone: +886 2 381 3722/ 4
Fax: +886 2 381 3711
Year established: 1946
Activities: investigation, research and compilation of information on domestic and foreign machinery industries
Chief officers: K Chuang (Chairman), K L Chiou (General Secretary); C C Wang (Deputy General Secretary)

Structure: executive board; 20 special committees
Membership: 1,930
Publications:
• Directory of Textile Dyeing and Garment Machinery in Taiwan: *machinery manufacture - annual*
• Metal Working Machinery: *machinery manufacture - annual*
• Taiwan Food Processing, Packaging & Printing Machinery: *machinery manufacture - annual*
• Taiwan Plastic and Rubber Machinery: *machinery manufacture - annual*
• Who Makes Machinery?: *machinery manufacturing - annual*

Taiwan Automobile Repair Industry Association
Address: 6th Floor, Cheng-te Road, Section 3, Taipei
Telephone: +886 2 596 6965/596 4217
Fax: +886 2 595 3813

Taiwan Bicycle Exporters' Association
Address: Rm. 2C-11, 5 Hsinyi Rd, Section 5, Taipei
Telephone: +886 2 722 1551
Fax: +886 2 723 8019
Chief officers: King Liu (Chairman), Francis Liaw (President)

Taiwan Canners' Association
Address: 7th Floor, 170 Min-Sheng East Road, Section 2, Taipei
Telephone: +886 2 502 2666/502 2660/2669
Fax: +886 2 502 2667
Year established: 1954
Activities: conferences (4 per annum); provision of information on canning machines, packaging food hygiene, labour, transportation, trade, government regulation, etc.
Chief officers: K C Hsieh (Chairman); T K Chen (Secretary General); Jesse Wu (Business Director)
Structure: board of directors; standing committee; 4 sales committees
Membership: 130

Taiwan Chinese Motion Picture Studios Association
Address: 4F, 45 Chilin Rd, Taipei
Telephone: +886 2 523 7831
Fax: +886 2 563 7094

Taiwan Clothing Manufacturers' Association
Address: 8th Floor-3, 202 Nanking East Road, Section 5, Taipei
Telephone: +886 2 766 6661-2
Fax: +886 2 762 5722
Chief officers: T Y Lu (Chairman)

Taiwan Computer United Association
Address: 9F, 95-98 Changping Road, Section 1, Taichung
Telephone: +886 4 242 1717
Fax: +886 4 241 1030
Chief officers: Chen Chia-yi (Chairman)

Taiwan Confectionery, Biscuit and Flour-based Food Industry Association
Address: 9th Floor, 390 Fu Shing South Road, Section 1, Taipei
Telephone: +886 2 704 1662
Fax: +886 2 708 4429
Year established: 1969
Chief officers: Ho Chong-Sen (Chairman)
Structure: board of directors consisting of 27 directors and 9 supervisors

Membership: 110 manufacturers of confectionery, chewing gum, instant noodles, rice cookies, jam, etc.
Publications:
• Directory of Member Companies: *lists all major members of the association and includes contact details, factory address and main product categories offered - annual*

Taiwan Electric Appliance Manufacturers' Association
Address: 10th Floor, 10 Lane 609 Chung Hsin Road, Section 5, Sanchung City
Telephone: +886 2 999 2828
Fax: +886 2 999 2626

Taiwan Eyeglass Industry Association
Address: 2F, 206 Minchuan E. Rd., Section 2, Taipei
Telephone: +886 2 505 7583
Fax: +886 2 507 0260

Taiwan Food Industry Association
Address: 6th Floor, 10 Chungking South Road, Section 3, Taipei
Telephone: +886 2 371 9848
Fax: +886 2 381 7084
Chief officers: F S Chen (Chairman); S L Chi (Executive)

Taiwan Footwear Manufacturers' Association
Address: 13th Floor, 131 Sung Kiang Road, Taipei
Telephone: +886 2 506 6191/8
Fax: +886 2 508 1489
Chief officers: Frank Z Kung (General Secretary)

Taiwan Frozen Meat Industry Association
Address: 4th Floor, 19 Lane 118 Anchu Street, Taipei
Telephone: +886 2 733 9112
Fax: +886 2 735 4155
Chief officers: T T Kuo (Chairman); S Y Chung (Executive)

Taiwan Frozen Meat Packers' Association
Address: 12F, 18 Chinshan S. Rd., Section 2, Taipei
Telephone: +886 2 393 2306/393 2321
Fax: +886 2 393 2604

Taiwan Frozen Seafood Exporters' Association
Address: 3rd Floor, 29 Lane 30 Yung Chi Road, Taipei
Telephone: +886 2 765 7152/ 765 7082
Fax: +886 2 763 4259
Chief officers: Ming Chu (Chairman)

Taiwan Fruit and Vegetable Export Association
Address: 12F-3, 31-1 Hsinsheng N. Rd., Section 2, Taipei
Telephone: +886 2 571 5191
Fax: +886 2 562 8411

Taiwan Fruit and Vegetable Juice Manufacturers' Association
Address: 3rd Floor, 6 Lane 59 Yi Tung Street, Taipei
Telephone: +886 2 507 0830
Fax: +886 2 508 0516
Chief officers: C Lin (Chairman)

Taiwan Furniture Manufacturers' Association
Address: 9th Floor, Room 905, 100 Chung Hsiao East Road, Section 2, Taipei
Telephone: +886 2 321 5811
Fax: +886 2 395 1754

Chief officers: Hsiao Shu-shan (Chairman)

Taiwan Garment Industry Association

Address: 8th Floor, 22 Ai Kuo East Road, Taipei
Telephone: +886 2 391 9113
Fax: +886 2 391 9055
E-mail: tgia@ms5.hinet.net
Chief officers: Hse-Tseh Lin (Chairman), Young-Jieh Hong
(Secretary General)
Membership: 345 manufacturers of men's and boys' wear,
ladies' and girls' wear, infants' wear, sports' and casual wear

Taiwan Gas Appliance Manufacturers' Association

Address: 658 Chung Hsiao Road, Linkou, Taipei Hsien
Telephone: +886 2 609 1185
Fax: +886 2 600 2925

Taiwan Gift and Housewares Exporters' Association

Address: 6th Floor, 28 Alley 2, Lane 250, Nanking East Road,
Section 5, Taipei
Telephone: +886 2 769 7303
Fax: +886 2 761 5942

Taiwan Glass Industry Association

Address: 12th Floor-3, 22 Chungking North Road, Section 1,
Taipei
Telephone: +886 2 556 6018
Fax: +886 2 558 6765

Taiwan Glove Manufacturers' Association

Address: 4th Floor, 33-3 Lane 37, Yung kang St., Taipei
Telephone: +886 2 391 8396
Fax: +886 2 395 1532
Chief officers: Alex M. S. Lee (Chairman), Chia Mei Teng
(Secretary General)

Taiwan Hand Tools' Association

Address: 3rd Floor, 687-1 Mintsu East Road, Taipei
Telephone: +886 2 715 2250/713 0667
Fax: +886 2 715 2617

Taiwan Handbags Export Trade Association

Address: 12th Floor, 22 Ai Kuo East Road, Taipei
Telephone: +886 2 392 5305
Fax: +886 2 394 9253
Year established: 1978
Chief officers: Y Y Dei (Chairman), C C Lo (Executive
Officer), Wan Hsien-Chang (General Secretary)
Membership: 170

Taiwan Hat Exporters' Association

Address: 6th Floor, 22 Aikuo E. Rd, Taipei
Telephone: +886 2 393 7892
Fax: +886 2 396 3842
Chief officers: T. C. Yue (Chairman), Frank Kao (Secretary
General)

Taiwan Hosiery Manufacturers' Association

Address: 6th Floor, 22 Ai Kuo East Road, Taipei
Telephone: +886 2 391 3709/392 1483
Fax: +886 2 322 1744
Chief officers: Mei En Chung (Chairman), Pao Chu Chen
(Secretary General)

Taiwan Hotel Businesses Association

Address: 4th Floor, Chung Hwa Road, Section 1, Taichung
Telephone: +886 4 224 4868
Chief officers: C S Chen (Chairman); H C Chang (Executive)

Taiwan Importers' and Exporters' Association

Address: 14th Floor, 2 Fuhsing North Road, Taipei
Telephone: +886 2 773 1155
Fax: +886 2 773 1159
Chief officers: H P Yang (Chairman)

Taiwan Jewellery Industry Association

Address: Room B, 4F, 67 Changchun Road, Taipei
Telephone: +886 2 571 2639
Fax: +886 2 562 5639
Chief officers: Chen Jui-lin (Chairman)

Taiwan Knitwear Industry Association

Address: 7th Floor, 22 Ai Kuo East Road, Taipei
Telephone: +886 2 394 5121
Fax: +886 2 394 1356/1355
Chief officers: Thomas Hwang (Chairman), Po-Chiwn Chien
(Secretary General)

Taiwan Manufacturers' Association

Address: Room 905, 100 Chung Hsiao E Rd, Section 2, Taipei
Telephone: +886 2 321 5791
Fax: +886 2 395 1754
Chief officers: C T Alseih (Chairman)

Taiwan Margarine Industry Association

Address: 9F, 390 Fuhsing S. Rd., Section 1, Taipei
Telephone: +886 2 706 0839
Fax: +886 2 702 4302

Taiwan Musical Instruments Industrial Association

Address: 3rd Floor, 416-2 Ting Chou Road, Kuting District,
Taipei
Telephone: +886 2 392 6772
Fax: +886 2 393 2361
Chief officers: K H Huang (Chairman)

Taiwan Optical and Photographic Goods Industry Association

Address: 10 Alley 18, Lane 325, Chien Kang Road, Sungshan
District, Tapei
Telephone: +886 2 765 3196/746 0657/746 0419
Fax: +886 2 761 7873
Year established: 1978
Activities: quarterly conferences for directors/supervisors;
development of more advanced camera modules and
programming for cameras such as Date Imprinting Systems,
camera controllers, LCD Modules & Auto Focus Modules
Chief officers: Davis T W Hsia (Secretary General); Bill C P
Liu (Secretary); Jerry C L Huang (Section Chief)
Structure: Optometry Technology Development committee, 4
working groups
Membership: 81 members
Publications:
● Taiwan Optics Buyers Guide: *annual*

Taiwan Paint Industry Association

Address: 7th Floor, 8 Alley 1, Lane 75, Chung Hua Road,
Section 2, Taipei
Telephone: +886 2 331 1827/381 4249
Fax: +886 2 375 4258

Chief officers: C F Cheng (Secretary General)
Membership: 100 approx

Taiwan Paper Containers' Association
Address: 2nd Floor, 4-1 Lane 6, Ching Tien Street, Taipei
Telephone: +886 2 351 7469
Fax: +886 2 351 7292
Chief officers: Lim Wan-sheng (Executive Chairman); Julie Chu (Secretary General)

Taiwan Paper Industry Association
Address: 5th Floor, Taize Building, 20 Pa Teh Road, Section 3, Taipei
Telephone: +886 2 577 6352/577 8137
Fax: +886 2 578 8139
Activities: statistics on production, sales, exports/imports; technical seminar; international paper industry meeting and exhibition; group tours to visit foreign paper industries
Chief officers: Han Fen Chen (Secretary General); Yue- Yao Lin
Membership: 166

Taiwan Pharmaceutical Industry Association
Address: 3rd Floor, 267 Tunhwa South Road, Section 2, Taipei
Telephone: +886 2 738 7688/736 5838/5839
Fax: +886 2 738 7689
Chief officers: Tsai She-shong (Chairman)

Taiwan Plastic Industry Association
Address: 8th Floor, 162 Chang-an East Road, Section 2, Taipei
Telephone: +886 2 771 9111
Fax: +886 2 731 5021/5020
Chief officers: J T Hsieh (Chairman)

Taiwan Regional Association of Adhesive Tape Manufacturers
Address: 4B-14, 4F, 5 Hsinyi Rd., Section 5, Taipei
Telephone: +886 2 725 2217
Fax: +886 2 722 9244

Taiwan Regional Association of Ceramic Industries
Address: 12th Floor, 30 Peiping East Road, Section 2, Taipei
Telephone: +886 2 395 9858
Fax: +886 2 395 9608

Taiwan Regional Association of Cotton Fabrics Printing, Dyeing and Finishing Industries
Address: 12th Floor, 22 Ai Kuo East Road, Taipei
Telephone: +886 2 321 1095
Fax: +886 2 322 3522
Chief officers: James Cheng (Chairman), P. Y. Chiang (Secretary General)

Taiwan Regional Association of Dairy Processors
Address: 4th Floor, 27 Chang An East Road, Section 1, Taipei
Telephone: +886 2 531 1906
Fax: +886 2 531 1906

Taiwan Regional Association of Educational Materials' Industries
Address: 6th Floor, Ever Glory Building, No 305, Nanking East Road,, Section 3, Taipei
Telephone: +886 2 574 7273
Fax: +886 2 712 9692

Activities: stationery supplies for education purposes
Membership: 63

Taiwan Regional Association of Frozen Seafood Product Manufacturers
Address: Rm. 6, 8F, 103 Chungcheng 4th Rd, Kaohsiung
Telephone: +886 7 241 1894/2 251 8523
Fax: +886 7 251 9603

Taiwan Regional Association of Leather Goods Manufacturers
Address: Room B, 6th Floor, No 5-1 Nanking West Road, Taipei
Telephone: +886 2 521 0090/541 3472
Fax: +886 2 567 7403
Year established: 1957
Chief officers: Victor Lin (Executive), Hsueh Tsung Ho (General Secretary)
Membership: 62 factories
Publications:
• Members Directory
Notes: Close links with Taiwan Regional Tanneries Association.

Taiwan Regional Association of Preserved Fruits
Address: 6F-4, 36 Sanmin St, Yuanlin Chen, Changhua Hsieni
Telephone: +886 48 321 006
Fax: +886 48 321 280

Taiwan Regional Association of Rug Manufacturers
Address: RM. 207, 25 Po Ai Road, Taipei
Telephone: +886 2 381 0660
Fax: +886 2 383 1802
Chief officers: James W. P. Lin (Chairman), Chien-Chiou Kao (Secretary General)

Taiwan Regional Association of Synthetic Leather Industries
Address: 5th Floor, 30 Nanking West Road, Taipei
Telephone: +886 2 559 0204
Fax: +886 2 559 8823

Taiwan Rice Industry Association
Address: 4F-9, 18 Chungcheng N. Rd, Sanchung City, Taipei Hsieni
Telephone: +886 2 718 7484/987 4772/986 7375
Fax: +886 2 986 7375/987 4772

Taiwan Soap and Detergent Manufacturers' Association
Address: 9th Floor, 390 Fuhsing South Road, Section 1, Taipei
Telephone: +886 2 706 0839/702 4441
Fax: +886 2 702 4302

Taiwan Soy Sauce Manufacturers' Association
Address: 4th Floor-3, 24 Peiping East Road, Taipei
Telephone: +886 2 351 7726
Fax: +886 2 351 8475

Taiwan Sporting Goods Manufacturers' Association
Address: 8th Floor, 22 Tehnwei Street, Taipei
Telephone: +886 2 594 1864
Fax: +886 2 591 9396

Taiwan Surgical Dressings and Medical Instruments Industrial Association
Address: 8th Floor, 201-18 Tunhua North Road, Taipei
Telephone: +886 2 712 3070
Fax: +886 2 735 0286

Taiwan Sweater Industry Association
Address: 9th Fl, 22 Ai Kuo East Road, Taipei
Telephone: +886 2 394 5216
Fax: +886 2 397 5270
Chief officers: Thomas Huang (Chairman)

Taiwan Tape and Record Industry
Address: 2F, 115 Minchuan E. Road, Section 2, Taipei
Telephone: +886 2 504 5763
Fax: +886 2 504 5752

Taiwan Tea Export Trade Association
Address: 6th Floor, 24 Kanku Street, Taipei
Telephone: +886 2 555 2962
Fax: +886 2 555 0753

Taiwan Tea Manufacturers' Association
Address: Room 9, 10th Floor, 165 Nanking West Road, Taipei
Telephone: +886 2 558 6251
Fax: +886 2 559 6601
Chief officers: A Lee (Chairman)

Taiwan Textile Federation (TTF)
Address: TTF Building, 22 Ai Kuo East Road, Taipei 10726
Telephone: +886 2 341 7251
Fax: +886 2 392 3855
E-mail: service@www.textiles.org.tw
Web site: www.textiles.org.tw
Web site notes: site includes import and export statistics on the Taiwan apparel market as well as commentary on the industry
Year established: 1975
Activities: vocational training; fashion consulting service; information on quota management; trade negotiation; export promotion/ information network (TTFNET) has been established
Chief officers: C Y Liu (Secretary General)
Membership: 22
Publications:
• Textile Weekly

Taiwan Towel Industry Association
Address: 12th Floor, 22 Ai Kuo East Road, Taipei
Telephone: +886 2 321 0866
Fax: +886 2 341 0434
Chief officers: S. N. Chang (Chairman), Steve Tsai (Secretary General)

Taiwan Toy Manufacturers' Association
Address: 6th Floor, 42 Minsheng East Road, Section 1, Taipei
Telephone: +886 2 571 1264/6
Fax: +886 2 541 1061

Taiwan Vegetable Oil Manufacturers' Association
Address: 6th Floor, 27 Chang-an East Road, Section 1, Taipei
Telephone: +886 2 561 6351
Fax: +886 2 562 1745

Taiwan Vegetable Processing Association
Address: 3rd Floor, 6 Lane 59, Yitung Street, Taipei
Telephone: +886 2 507 0830
Fax: +886 2 508 0516

Taiwan Watch and Clock Industrial Association
Address: Room 1, 11th Floor, 40 Chang Chun Road, Taipei
Telephone: +886 2 565 2966/567 9494
Fax: +886 2 523 9529
Year established: 1972
Activities: attends main international fairs for watches and clocks; assists foreign buyers; handles Intellectual Property Rights; regulates the statistics for import and export of watches and clocks
Chief officers: K H Hong (President); Jason Han (Secretary General)
Structure: board of directors; board of supervisors; 7 committees
Membership: 253
Publications:
• Taiwan Watch & Clock: *annual*
• Taiwan Watch and Clock Industrial Association Newsletter: *monthly*
• Time Study: *quarterly*

Taiwan Wooden Furniture Industrial Association
Address: Room 905, 100 Chung Hsiao East Road, Section 2, Taipei
Telephone: +886 2 321 5791/5811
Fax: +886 2 395 1754

TANZANIA

Publishers' Association of Tanzania
Address: PO Box 1408, Dar Es Salaam
Telephone: +255 51 276 08/348 78
Fax: +255 51 462 22
Chief officers: Mr AE Musiba, Mr W Bgoya (Director), Mr Abdullah Saiwaad (Executive Officer)

Tanzania Coffee Marketing Board
Address: PO Box 732, Moshi
Telephone: +255 55 4011/3033
Telex: 43000 COBOT

THAILAND

Advertising Association of Thailand
Address: 12-14 Prachaniwesna 1 Road, Laryao, Chatuchak, Bangkok 10900
Telephone: +66 2 591 6461/65
Fax: +66 2 589 9470

Animal Health Products' Association
Address: 69/26 Soi Athens Theatre, Phayathai Road, Bangkok 10400
Telephone: +66 2 252 8773
Fax: +66 2 252 8793

Association of Domestic Tour Operators
Address: 133/20 Rajprarob Road, Makkasan, Bangkok 10400
Telephone: +66 2 245 2616/245 2687/245 5658
Telex: 82071 MAT TH

Association of Finance Companies
Address: 3rd Floor Sinthorn Building, Wireless Road, Bangkok 10500
Telephone: +66 2 255 9100

Association of International Trading Companies
Address: 394/14 Samsen Rd, Bangkok 10300
Telephone: +66 2 280 0951

Association of Members of the Securities Exchange
Address: 11th Floor, Unico House, 29/1 Soi Langsuan, Ploenchit Road, Bangkok 10330
Telephone: +66 2 251 0063/4

Association of Ready Meals Producers
Address: 578-80 Ploenchit Road, Bangkok 10330
Telephone: +66 2 255 3978/253 6791/4
Fax: +66 2 255 1479

Association of Thai Computer Industry
Address: 28/18-21 Sukhumvit 19, Phakhanong, Bangkok 10110
Telephone: +66 2 251 8245/ 255 2329
Fax: +66 2 251 8245

Association of Thai Travel Agents
Address: GPO Box 942, 94 Soi Langsuan, Ploenchit Road, Bangkok 10330
Telephone: +66 2 252 0069
Fax: +66 2 254 4809

Automotive Industries' Association
Address: 394/14 Samsen Road, Bangkok 10330
Telephone: +66 2 229 4255

Coffee Exporters' Association
Address: 61/1 Khasemraj Road, Prakhanong, Bangkok 10120
Telephone: +66 2 222 2501

Computer Association of Thailand
Address: 2nd Floor, Chulalongkron University, Alumni Building, Phayathai Road, Bangkok 10330
Telephone: +66 2 215 3546/215 3962

Cosmetic Manufacturers' Association
Address: 1091/22-23 Soi Charurat, Makkasan, Phetchaburi Road, Bangkok 10400
Telephone: +66 2 530 856/253 334/251 2404
Fax: +66 2 390 1823

Cosmetics Association
Address: 1765 Ramkhamhaeng Road, Huamark, Bangkok 10240
Telephone: +66 2 314 1415
Fax: +66 2 319 2053

Department Stores' Association
Address: 4th Floor, Imperial Department Store, 166/11-19 Sukhapibal 2, Bangkapi, Bangkok 10240
Telephone: +66 2 377 1141/377 0918

Druggists Association
Address: 1759/30 Soi Udomsap, Nakornchaisri Road, Bangkok Noi, Bangkok 10700
Telephone: +66 2 434 4261/433 6547
Fax: +66 2 433 6547

Federation of Thai Industries
Address: 394/14 Samsen Road, Wachira Dusit, Bangkok 10300
Telephone: +66 2 280 0951
Fax: +66 2 280 0959
Activities: represents members through separate 'industry clubs'; has branches throughout the country; holds annual industrial fair and participates in ASEAN trade fairs; promotes trade missions; broadcasts a regular TV programme "Pride in Thai Products"; Thailand's representative on the ASEAN Chamber of Commerce and Industry body; newsletters on specific industries
Chief officers: Sirayapa Buranapichet (Chief of Secretariat Office); Yupa Asavapol (Chief of Public Relations)
Membership: approximately 3,000 in 25 different industries
Publications:
• Annual Directory: *general coverage of the economy and industrial sector, plus details on member firms - annual*
• Trade and Investment Opportunities Journal

Fishery Association of Thailand
Address: 1575 Chareon Nakorn Road, Bangkok 10600
Telephone: +66 2 437 0158/62
Telex: 82812 THAISERI TH

General Insurance Association
Address: 223 Soi Ruamrudee, Wireless Road, Bangkok 10500
Telephone: +66 2 254 5326/254 5326
Fax: +66 2 254 5327

Glassware Products' Association
Address: 107 Asoke-Dindaeng Road, Samsen Nai, Bangkok 10400
Telephone: +66 2 246 3957
Chief officers: Charoon Techarungroj (President)
Membership: manufacturers, exporters, importers and wholesalers of glass products

Home Textile Association
Address: 11/16 Soi Somsoonsuk, Prachachuen Road, Dusit, Bangkok 10800
Telephone: +66 2 589 2967/589 5972
Fax: +66 2 580 1853/580 8412

Insurance Brokers' Association
Address: 4th Floor, 99 Rajdarmnoen Road, Pranakorn, Bangkok
Telephone: +66 2 281 0494
Activities: information service
Chief officers: Boonluen Tongsamuth (President)

Jewellers' Association
Address: 42/1 Soi Panumas, Banmoh Road, Bangkok 10100
Telephone: +66 2 221 4465/ 223 6951
Fax: +66 2 222 2727
Chief officers: Sunthorn Phornprakit (President)

Leather Association
Address: 2-4 Soi Phaisingto, Rama IV Road, Phrakanong, Bangkok 10100
Telephone: +66 2 250 1658/9

Marketing Association of Thailand
Address: 14th Floor, Lumpinee Tower, 1168 Sathorn Road, Yannawa, Bangkok 10120
Telephone: +66 2 285 5987/9
Fax: +66 2 285 5989
Activities: promotes knowledge and management skills in the field of marketing; conducts various types of seminars, intensive courses and talks each year

National Federation of Thai Textile Industries
Address: c/o The Thai Silk Co Ltd, 9 Surawong Road, Bangkok 10500
Telephone: +66 2 234 4900

Pharmaceutical Producers' Association (PPA)
Address: 8th floor, Land and Tower Building, 230 Ratchadapisek Road, Huay Kwang District, Bangkok 10310
Telephone: +66 2 274 0683/274 0685
Fax: +66 2 274 0686
E-mail: ppathai@ksc.th.com
Chief officers: Prof. Vanida Chitman (Executive Director)

Photographic Dealers' Association
Address: 96-98 Chula Soi 6, Rama IV Road, Bangkok 10500
Telephone: +66 2 215 4271

Poultry Promotion Association of Thailand
Address: Department of Livestock Development, Phayathai Road, Bangkok 10400
Telephone: +66 2 251 8205

Publishers' and Booksellers' Association of Thailand, The
Address: 320 Lat Phrao 94, Bankapi Bangkok 10310
Telephone: +66 2 559 3348
Fax: +66 2 538 1499
Chief officers: H. Nidda (General Manager)

Radio, Television and Sound System Traders' Association
Address: 119 Charasmuang Road, Bangkok 10500
Telephone: +66 2 251 4894
Fax: +66 2 251 8250

Rice Exporters' Association
Address: 37 Soi Ngamduplee, Rama IV Road, Yannawa, Bangkok 10120
Telephone: +66 2 287 2674/2677/286 6630/286 6633
Fax: +66 2 287 2678
Telex: 20565 RICEEXA TH
Chief officers: Smarn Ophaswongse (President)
Membership: exporters of rice and rice products

Small Industries Association
Address: 174/1 Soi Wat Mai-Amatoros, Visuthikasat, Bangkok
Telephone: +66 2 280 1235

Sports Goods Trade Association
Address: 80/2-4 Rama 1 Road, Patumwan, Bangkok 10330
Telephone: +66 2 214 1796/214 1546/214 1942

Sugar Dealers' Association
Address: 298/134 Lukluang Road, Bangkok 10100
Telephone: +66 2 223 6923

Sugar Industry Association
Address: 98/125 Soi Ongkarn Utsahakam Pamai, Ngamvongvan Road, Ladyao, Chatujack, Bangkok 10900
Telephone: +66 2 579 0630/0873/2870
Fax: +66 2 579 6840

Tea Traders' Association
Address: 7th Floor, Suankwantung Flat, 70 Rama IV Road, Bangkok 10100
Telephone: +66 2 221 4511/221 6416/222 0748

Telecommunications Association of Thailand
Address: 2nd Floor, 37/1 Lim Chareon Building 2, Viphavadee-Rangsit Road, Bangkok 10400
Telephone: +66 2 279 7311/3/279 9285 ext 121
Fax: +66 2 278 3373
Activities: education, training and research; monitoring of progress of telecommunications technology; information services; educational publications

Thai Bankers' Association
Address: 4th Floor, Lake Rajada Office complex, CDF house, 195-7 Rajadapisek Road, Klongtoey, Bangkok
Telephone: +66 2 264 0883/7
Fax: +66 2 264 0888
Chief officers: Pakorn Thauisin (Chairman)

Thai Battery Trade Association
Address: 3669/3-4 Rama IV Road, Phrakanong, Bangkok 10110
Telephone: +66 2 391 8991/392 4985

Thai Coffee Exporters' Association
Address: 1298 Songwad Road, Bangkok 10110
Telephone: +66 2 221 1264
Fax: +66 2 225 1962
Telex: 81111 SUSIN T
Chief officers: Susin Surattanakawikul (President)

Thai Electrical and Mechanical Contractors' Association
Address: 7th Floor, FILPN Tower, 216/6 Nanglinjee Road, Chongnonsri, Yannawa, Bangkok 10120
Telephone: +66 2 285 4287/4846-7
Fax: +66 2 285 4288
Year established: 1983
Activities: observes market movements domestically and abroad; serves as centre for the exchange of technical information among members; studies and research projects
Chief officers: Swake Srisuchart (President), Komol Wongpornpenpap, Charn Lerdsuwannakij, Poonphiphat Tantanasin, Apimook Nuntavitayaporn, Pongpol Tachavichitra (Vice Presidents), Phoemsin Sirirat-Usdorn (Secretary General), Raksa Phakdeesupharithi (Treasurer)
Structure: TEMCA committee board, executive board, honorary advisers
Membership: 268 ordinary members, 35 extraordinary members
Publications:
● Directory: *annual*

Thai Fertiliser and Agricultural Marketing Association

Address: 88/13-14 Pinklao Nakhon Chaisri Road, Bangkok 10700
Telephone: +66 2 434 2403
Fax: +66 2 434 2403

Thai Fishery and Frozen Products Association

Address: ITF Building, 12th Floor, 160/194-7 Silom Road, Bangkok 10500
Telephone: +66 2 235 5622/4
Fax: +66 2 235 5625
Telex: 21952 IT SILOM TH
Year established: 1968
Membership: 100 member companies

Thai Fishmeal Producers' Association

Address: 189 Soi Intamara 33, Suttisarn Road, Bangkok 10400
Telephone: +66 2 277 3330/4240
Fax: +66 2 277 4240

Thai Food Processors' Association

Address: 11th Floor, Mahuthun Plaza, 888/95 Ploenchit Road, Bangkok 10330
Telephone: +66 2 253 6791/4
Fax: +66 2 255 1479

Thai Footwear Industries' Trade Association

Address: 876-882 Pra-Cha-Uthit Road, Huaykwang, Bangkok 10320
Telephone: +66 2 274 4067
Fax: +66 2 274 4068
Chief officers: Chatree Cittkomut (President)
Membership: manufacturers, importers, exporters and wholesalers of footwear

Thai Furniture Industries' Association

Address: 1267/3 Soi Lardprao 35, Lardprao Road, Lardyao, Bangkok 10900
Telephone: +66 2 513 6262/1082
Fax: +66 2 513 1082
Chief officers: Somporn Sahawattana (President)

Thai Garment Manufacturers' Association

Address: 92/48 17th Floor, Sathorn Thani, Building 2, North Sathorn Road, Bangruk, Bangkok 10500
Telephone: +66 2 681 2222
Fax: +66 2 681 2223/681 0231
Telex: 21010 TGMA TH
Year established: 1973
Activities: information on the manufacture and marketing of garments; government liaison; support and assistance to members; to find new export markets
Chief officers: Viroj Amatakulchai (President); Seri Uahwatanasakul (Honorary President); Anan Vongsuraphicet, Eam Uahwatanasakul (Honorary Directors)
Structure: board of directors; subcommittees: general affairs, public relations, finance, foreign affairs
Membership: 29 members

Thai Gem and Jewellery Traders' Association (TGJTA)

Address: 15th Floor, Charn Issara Tower, 942/152 Rama IV Road, Bangrak, Bangkok 10500
Telephone: +66 2 235 3039
Fax: +66 2 235 3040
Year established: 1974
Activities: compilation of information and statistics, arbitration, government liaison

Chief officers: Anan Salwala (Senior President), Boonyong Assarasakorn (President), Mr. Parinya Tumwattana (Public Relations Chairman)
Membership: 1,104

Thai Glass Traders' Association

Address: 110-112 Chaokhumrop Road, Pomprab, Bangkok 10600
Telephone: +66 2 224 8167/221 5255

Thai Hotels' Association

Address: 203-209/2 Rajdamnoen Klang Avenue, Bangkok 10200
Telephone: +66 2 281 9496/9579
Fax: +66 2 281 4188
Telex: 21422 THAOFF TH
Year established: 1963
Activities: acts as a forum for exchange of business information among members; advises government authorities; gives information on policies affecting the industry; organises programmes and seminars; establishes standards; settles disputes
Chief officers: M L Somsak Kambhu (Manager)
Membership: 250
Publications:
• Hotel Directory: *annual*

Thai Life Assurance Association

Address: 36/1 Soi Sapanku, Rama 4 Road, Bangkok 10120
Telephone: +66 2 287 4596/8/679 7099/679 7825/6
Fax: +66 2 679 7100/679 7823
Chief officers: Sukhathep Chansrichawala (President), Poomchai Lamsam (Vice President), Kitti Pasukdee (Secretary General)

Thai Merchant Association

Address: 150 Rajbopit Road, Bangkok 10200
Telephone: +66 2 221 3300/222 2228/2229/6092

Thai Packaging Association

Address: 16th Floor, BB Building, 54 Asoke Road, Klongtoey, Bangkok 10110
Telephone: +66 2 260 7103/08
Fax: +66 2 260 7109
Telex: 22 030 xtradex th
Activities: organises Printing and Packaging Trade Exhibition
Chief officers: Manita Kamolsuan (President), Pun Kongcharoenkiaet, Withien Nildum (Vice Presidents), Kasem Yaemvathithong (Secretary), Puchapong Worapirangkul (Assistant Secretary)

Thai Pharmaceutical Manufacturers' Association

Address: 1759/30 Soi Udomsub, Pinklao-Nakornchaisri Road, Bangkok Noi, Bangkok 10700
Telephone: +66 2 424 8588
Fax: +66 2 433 6547
Year established: 1969
Chief officers: Preeya Sibunruang (President)

Thai Pharmacies Association

Address: 116 Prachatipok Road, Bangkok 10600
Telephone: +66 2 465 1876/8716/8707
Fax: +66 2 465 8707
Chief officers: Pichet Vetjathpron (President)

Thai Plastic Industries' Association

Address: 127/2 Phaya Mai Road, Somdej Chaophaya, Klongsarn, Bangkok 10600
Telephone: +66 2 223 6183/6
Fax: +66 2 437 2850
Activities: Joint organisers of THAIPLAS, exhibition of plasics and rubber technology
Chief officers: Pradit Hiranpradit (President)
Publications:
• THAIPLAS Programme: *annual*

Thai Printing Industry Association

Address: 4/1 Soi Jindatavin, Sipraya Road, Bangrak, Bangkok 10500
Telephone: +66 2 214 3982
Fax: +66 2 472 1552

Thai Pulp and Paper Industries' Association

Address: 394/14 Samsen Road, Dusit, Bangkok 10300
Telephone: +66 2 280 0951
Fax: +66 2 587 0738/2213
Telex: 72250 SKIC TH
Activities: statistics and market information on pulp and paper industries; research and development; participation in conferences; organises TPPIA conference; information service
Chief officers: Abdul Udol (President); Phairuch Mekapron (Secretary General)
Membership: 8 member organisations
Publications:
• Directory: *annual*

Thai Real Estate Association

Address: 2447 New Phetchaburi Road, Huaykwang, Bangkok 10310
Telephone: +66 2 318 2053/2054/0083

Thai Rice Association

Address: 89 Soi Yotha, New Road, Bangkok 10130
Telephone: +66 2 234 9187/237 3184

Thai Silk Association

Address: Industrial Service Division, Soi Kluaynamthai, Rama IV Road, Bangkok 10110
Telephone: +66 2 391 2896

Thai Soap and Detergents Manufacturers' Association

Address: 10th Floor, Kasemkij Building, 120 Silom Road, Bangkok 10500
Telephone: +66 2 233 9693

Thai Steel Furniture Association

Address: 357-363 Mahachai Road, Bangkok 10200
Telephone: +66 2 221 0362/221 6998
Fax: +66 2 384 0480
Chief officers: Uthai Tansiriwiwat (President)

Thai Sugar Manufacturing Association

Address: 4th Floor, Kiatnakin Building, 78 Captain Bush Lane, New Road, Bangkok 10500
Telephone: +66 2 233 4156/5858
Fax: +66 2 236 8438

Thai Sugar Producers' Association

Address: 8th Floor, Thai Ruam Toon Building, 794 Krung Kasem Road, Bangkok 10100
Telephone: +66 2 282 2022/0990

Thai Tapioca Trade Association

Address: 20th Floor, Sathorn Thani 2 Building, 92/58 Sathorn Nua Road, Bangkok 10500
Telephone: +66 2 234 4724/0620
Fax: +66 2 236 6084
Telex: 20522 TAPIOCA TH
Activities: special lectures; seminars on related subjects, tax, etc.; Market Review reports domestic and foreign prices
Chief officers: Santiparp Rakbamrung (General Manger)
Structure: tapioca starch sub-committees
Membership: 116 ordinary, 50 associate members
Publications:
• Market Review: *bi-monthly*
• Monthly Bulletin: *monthly*
• Yearbook

Thai Textile Manufacturing Association

Address: 454-460 Sukhumvit Road, Phrakanong, Bangkok 10110
Telephone: +66 2 258 2044, 258 2023
Fax: +66 2 260 1525

Thai Timber Exporters' Association

Address: 4th Floor, Ratchada Trade Centre, 10/73-6 Ratchadapisek Road, Bangkok 10310
Telephone: +66 2 277 1459/279 8149 Ext 14
Fax: +66 2 259 2920/0486

Thai Tourism Industry Association

Address: Naria Hotel, 222 Silom Road, Bangkok 10500
Telephone: +66 2 233 3350/233 6503 Ext 203

Thai Vegetable and Fruit Exporters' Association

Address: 3 Soi Achara, Sutthisarn Road, Huaykwang, Bangkok 10310
Telephone: +66 2 277 3062
Fax: +66 2 274 7291

Thailand Incentive and Convention Association

Address: 15th Floor, Room 1509/2, Bangkok Bank Building, 333 Silom Road, Bangkok 10500
Telephone: +66 2 235 0731/2
Fax: +66 2 235 0730

Thailand Leasing Association

Address: 19th Floor, Sathorn City Tower, 175 South Sathorn Road, Tung Mahamek, Sathorn, Bangkok 10120
Telephone: +66 2 679 6161
Fax: +66 2 679 6160
Year established: 1990
Chief officers: Pusadee Fuangfu
Membership: 20 (14 ordinary, 6 associate)

Thailand Management Association

Address: 276 Ramkhamhaeng 39 (Theplecla), Huamark, Bangkapi, Bangkok 10240
Telephone: +66 2 319 5675/8/319 7675/8
Fax: +66 2 319 5666

Tobacco Wholesalers' Association

Address: 185 Soi 4, Sukhumvit Road, Klongtoey, Bangkok 10110
Telephone: +66 2 251 2966

Toys Industries' Association
Address: 64 Soi Suksawittaya, North Sathorn Road, Bangkok 10500
Telephone: +66 2 237 0080
Fax: +66 2 236 9410

Trade Association for Electronic Industries
Address: 660 Rama IV Road, Bangkok 10500
Telephone: +66 2 233 1790/235 8033/235 9350

Union Textile Merchants' Association
Address: 3rd Floor, Sethi Building, 160 Sermsinka Road, Jakrawad, Bangkok 10100
Telephone: +66 2 223 3559/233 8843
Fax: +66 2 223 8843

Wheat Consumers and Traders Association
Address: T F Building, 2154/1 New Phetchaburi Road, Bangkok 10310
Telephone: +66 2 314 6021/9

TOGO

Association of Manufacturers of Togo
Groupement Interprofessionnel des Entreprises du Togo
Address: PO Box 346, Agetrac
Telephone: +228 213 513

Togo Coffee Marketing Board (OPAT)
Address: BP 1334, Lomé
Telephone: +228 214 471/77
Fax: +228 210 665

TRINIDAD & TOBAGO

Association of Trinidad and Tobago Insurance Companies (ATTIC)
Address: Maritime Building, 1 Ajax Street, Port of Spain
Telephone: +1 868 9 627 7979/80

Trinidad and Tobago Hotel and Tourism Association
Address: c/o The Travel Centre, Uptown Mall, Level 244-58, Edward Street, Port of Spain
Telephone: +1 868 6 243 928

Trinidad and Tobago Manufacturers' Association
Address: P.O. Box 971, 8a Stanmore Avenue, Port of Spain
Telephone: +1 868 6 231 029
Fax: +1 868 6 231 031
E-mail: lonsdale@trinidad.net
Web site: www.trinidad.net.londsdale/ttmahist.htm
Year established: 1956
Activities: encourages achievement of full potential in the areas of exports, investment, job and wealth creation; influences legislation and policy affecting its membership; education and training; provides timely information to the country's manufacturers; generates market expansion both regionally and internationally through the mounting of local, regional and international trade fairs and trade missions
Membership: 260 members from all sectors: food and beverages, clothing and textile, banking and finance, publishing, cosmetics and toiletries, pharmaceuticals and chemicals, building and construction

Publications:
- Manufacturer: *quarterly*
- TTMA Business Column: *an index of the articles of the TTMA which are published in the Trinidad Express Business Section*

TUNISIA

Association of Canned Fruit and Pulses
Chambre Syndicale de Conserves de Fruits et Legumes
Address: 38 rue d'Espagne, 1000 Tunis
Telephone: +216 1 241 394
Fax: +216 1 346 522

Association of Coffee Roasters
Chambre Syndicale de Torrefaction de Café
Address: 7 rue Dag Hammarskjoeld, 1000 Tunis
Telephone: +216 1 242 439
Fax: +216 1 342 872

Chemical Products Traders' Association
Chambre Syndicale Commercants des Produits Chimiques
Address: 28 rue 8601 Z.I. Charguia, 2035 Tunis-Carthage
Telephone: +216 1 788 100
Fax: +216 1 786 303

Confectionery Manufacturers' Association
Chambre Syndicale de Confectionneurs
Address: 41 rue 8601 la Charguia, 2035 Tunis-Carthage
Telephone: +216 1 789 928
Fax: +216 1 781 129

Couscous and Pasta Association
Chambre Syndicale de Pates Alimentaires et Couscous
Address: Rte de Sousse Km 4, 2014 Mégrine
Telephone: +216 1 493 609/493 963
Fax: +216 1 39 037

Dairy Products and Yoghurt Association
Chambre Syndicale de Yaourts et Similaires
Address: Rte de Mateur Km 8, 2010 la Manouba
Telephone: +216 1 521 000
Fax: +216 1 520 777

Detergents and Household Cleaning Products Manufacturers' Association (UTICA)
Chambre Syndicale des Fabricants de Produits d'Entretien et Détergents
Address: Av Liberté 103, 1002 Tunis-Belvédère
Telephone: +216 1 791 882
Fax: +216 1 791 882

Electronic Wholesalers' Association
Chambre Syndicale des Grossistes Electromenagers
Address: Cité Chaabane et Fils, 6000 Gabès
Telephone: +216 5 270 144
Fax: +216 5 272 387

Exporters' and Importers' Association
Chambre Syndicale des Exportateurs et Importateurs
Address: 50 Av Habib Bouguiba, 1000 Tunis
Telephone: +216 1 341 267
Fax: +216 1 350 438

Federation of Exporters (FEDEX)
Fédération des Exportateurs
Address: 103 Av de la Liberté, 1002 Tunis
Telephone: +216 1 780 366/725
Fax: +216 1 782 143

Fish Retailers' Association
Chambre Syndicale de Revendeurs de Poissons
Address: 3 rue Martin Luther King, 1000 Tunis
Telephone: +216 1 244 031
Fax: +216 1 343 782

Food Industry Association
Chambre Syndicale d'Industries de Produits Alimentaires
Address: 15 rue Ali Ben Khélifa, 6000 Gabès
Telephone: +216 5 271 163/275 511
Fax: +216 5 275 499

Food Wholesalers' Association
Chambre Syndicale Commercants Grossistes en Alimentation
Address: 3 rue Martin Luther King, 1000 Tunis
Telephone: +216 1 244 031
Fax: +216 1 343 782

Fruit and Pulses Retailers' Association
Chambre Syndicale Revendeurs de Fruits et Legumes
Address: 3 Martin Luther King, 1000 Tunis
Telephone: +216 1 244 031
Fax: +216 1 343 782

Fruit, Pulses and Dates Importers' and Exporters' Association
Chambre Syndicale de Fruits, Legumes, Dattes Import-Export
Address: 9 rue de Jérusalem, 2036 la Soukra
Telephone: +216 1 286 423/782 402
Fax: +216 1 788 860

General Food Retailers' Association
Chambre Syndicale de Detaillants en Alimentation Generale
Address: 103 Av de la Liberté, 1002 Tunis
Telephone: +216 1 780 366
Fax: +216 1 782 143

Hotel Federation
Fédération de Hotellerie
Address: 62 rue d'Iran, 1002 Tunis
Telephone: +216 1 287 200
Fax: +216 1 791 281

National Federation of Leather and Footwear
Address: 17, Rue Abderrahman Jaziri, 1002 Tunis
Telephone: +216 1 786 418
Fax: +216 1 787 740

National Textile Federation (FENATEX)
Fédération Nationale du Textile
Address: 116, Av. de la Liberté, 1002 Tunis Belvedere
Telephone: +216 1 780 358/781 514
Fax: +216 1 782 143/782 154
Chief officers: Sassi Bahri (Secretary General)

Pharmaceutical Industry Association
Chamber Syndicale d'Industries Pharmaceutiques
Address: Fondouk Choucha, 2040 Radès
Telephone: +216 1 381 222
Fax: +216 1 382 768

Seafood Products Association
Chambre Syndicale des Produits de la Mer
Address: 85 Av de Londres, 1000 Tunis
Telephone: +216 1 346 424
Fax: +216 1 350 116

Spirits Wholesalers' Association
Chambere Syndicale de Grossistes de Boissons Alcoolisees
Address: 8 Av Habib Bougatfa, 1005 Tunis
Telephone: +216 1 564 044
Fax: +216 1 564 044

Textile Industry Association
Chambre Syndicale d'Industrie Textile
Address: Cité PV. 1 App. no.11, 5000 Monastir
Telephone: +216 3 461 681
Fax: +216 3 460 682

Textile Retailers' Association
Chambre Syndicale de Detaillants en Textiles
Address: 6 rue d'Allemagne, 1000 Tunis
Telephone: +216 1 241 341

Tunisian Cheese Association
Chambre Syndicale de Fromage
Address: Av de la Mosqueé Erraoudha, 2036 la Soukra
Telephone: +216 1 765 146
Fax: +216 1 765 632

Tunisian Exporters' Club
Club des Exportateurs Tunisiens
Address: CTKD Building, 1st Floor, Complèxe El Mechtel, rue Ouled Haffouz, 1002 Tunis-Belvedere
Telephone: +216 1 788 347/789 234
Fax: +216 1 782 516

Tunisian Ice Cream Association
Chambre Syndicale des Glaces
Address: BP 53, Rte de Monastir Km 8, 4000 Sousse
Telephone: +216 3 266 066/266 140
Fax: +216 3 266 070

Tunisian Milk Association
Chambre Syndicale du Lait
Address: Rte de Mateur Km 8, 2010 la Manouba
Telephone: +216 1 521 000
Fax: +216 1 520 777

Tunisian Soft Drinks' Association
Chambre Syndicale des Boissons Gazeuses
Address: Z.I., 8030 Grombalia
Telephone: +216 2 255 807
Fax: +216 2 256 205

Tunisian Spirits Association
Chambre Syndicale des Boissons Alcoolisees
Address: 47 bis, rue d'Iran, 1002 Tunis
Telephone: +216 1 285 701/789 618
Fax: +216 1 786 406

Tunisian Union of Industry, Commerce and Handicrafts
Union Tunisienne pour l'Industrie, le Commerce et l'Artisanat
Address: 103 Av de la Liberté, 1002 Tunis
Telephone: +216 1 780 366
Fax: +216 1 782 143

TURKEY

Advertisers' Association
Reklamcilar Dernegi
Address: Yildiz Cicegi sok. No 19, 80630 Etiler-Istanbul
Telephone: +90 212 257 88 73
Fax: +90 212 257 88 70

Air Conditioners Manufacturers' Association(ISKID)
Isitma Sogutma Klima Imalatcilari Dernegi
Address: E-5 Cad. Yeniyol Sok. Etab Is Merkezi No. 18, 81020 Kadikoy-Istanbul
Telephone: +90 216 327 4110
Fax: +90 216 327 41 34
Year established: 1993
Activities: protects consumer rights, provides technical information to the manufacturers and importers, professional training, improves market conditions

Animal Feed Manufacturers' Association (YSB)
Yem Sanayicileri Birligi
Address: Halk Sok. No 20/7 Tuna Cad., Yenisehir-Ankara
Telephone: +90 312 431 1685
Fax: +90 312 431 2704
Year established: 1974

Association of Travel Agencies of Turkey (TURSAB)
Turkiye Seyahat Acentalri Birligi
Address: Gazeteciler Sitesi, Haberler Sokak, No 15, Esentepe-Istanbul
Telephone: +90 212 275 1397/212 275 1361
Fax: +90 212 275 0066
Year established: 1972
Activities: conducts marketing research; organises training courses and seminars; advises the Ministry; promotes tourism in the country
Chief officers: Mr Talha Camas (President), Mr M Cemil Baykal (Secretary General)

Association of Turkish Industrialists and Businessmen (TUSIAD)
Turk Sanayicileri ve Is Adamlari Dernegi
Address: Mesrutiyet Caddesi 74, Tepebasi, Istanbul
Telephone: +90 212 249 1929/212 249 5448/251 5313
Fax: +90 212 249 1350/0913
Year established: 1992
Membership: 350 members
Publications:
• An Econometric Model 1965-84
• Banking in the EC and Turkey: *Dec 1988*
• Görüs: *review of current economic developments*
• Inflation in Turkey and Conditions: *June 1986*
• Privatisation in Turkey: *Jan 1992*
• Privatisation, April 1987
• Problems Related to Population and Food: *July 1980*
• Report of State Economic Enterprises: *May 1982*
• Report on Education: *Sept 1990*
• Report on Financial Intermediaries: *Dec 1982*
• Short-term Econometric Model: *April 1987*
• Socioeconomic Situation and Outlook of the Turkish Household: *Dec 1987*
• Turkey Towards the 21st Century: *Nov 1992*
• Turkish Agriculture and Its Problems: *April 1981*
• Turkish Economy: *the social and economic aspects of the development of Turkey - annual*
• Tusiad Notlari: *brochure on current economic topics*
• TUSIAD's Leading Indicators for Turkish Economy
• TUSIAD, Members' Company Profiles: *March 1991*

Automotive Manufacturers' Association (OSD)
Otomotiv Sanayi Dernegi
Address: Altunizade Atilla Sok No. 8, Uskudar-Istanbul 81190
Telephone: +90 216 318 2994
Fax: +90 216 321 9497
Year established: 1974
Activities: seminars, information services (for members only); establishment of connections within the industry; conducts research studies on environment, quality management, relationship with EU, etc.; training and public relations
Publications:
• News from the Turkish Automotive Industry

Automotives Components' Association (TAYSAD)
Tasit Araclari Yan Sanayi Dernegi
Address: Hilmi Pasa Cad. No 32 D: 9-10, 81090 Kozyatagi-Istanbul
Telephone: +90 216 373 2275
Fax: +90 216 361 6284
Year established: 1978

Booksellers' Association
Kitapcilar Dernegi
Address: Cagaloglu Yokusu Evren Han, Kat 3 , No 56, Cagaloglu-Istanbul
Telephone: +90 212 511 3027
Fax: +90 212 511 3465
Year established: 1991
Activities: operates modern bookstores, protects members rights, promotes book retail trade, external communication with schools, academic institutes and government

Cosmetics Manufacturers' Association (KTMD)
Kozmetik ve Tuvalet Mustahzarlari Ureticileri Dernegi
Address: Degirmen Sok. Sasmaz Sitesi Duran Bey Sok No 19, Kat 3 D 9, 81090 Kozyatagi-Istanbul
Telephone: +90 216 416 7644/416 9439
Fax: +90 216 416 9218
Year established: 1993

Food Importers' Associations (TUGiDER)
Tum Gida Ithalatcilari Dernegi
Address: Buyukdere Cad. Nazmi Akbaci Is Merkezi No 235, Maslak-Istanbul
Telephone: +90 212 276 9348
Fax: +90 212 276 9133
Year established: 1992

Home Furnishing Association
Ev Tekstilcileri Dernegi
Address: Asirefendi Cad. Besler Han Kat 4, Sultanhamam-Istanbul
Telephone: +90 212 527 1567
Fax: +90 212 511 9255
Year established: 1991

Istanbul Stationery Manufacturers', Importers' and Wholesalers' Association (IKIT)
Istanbul Kirtasiye Imalatcilari, Ithalatcilari, Toptanticilari dayanisma Merkezi
Address: Tahtakale Cad. Menekse Is hani. D 67, 34460 Tahtakale-Istanbul
Telephone: +90 212 511 7657
Year established: 1986
Activities: dissseminates information among members, keeps records of customers' debt

Knitwear Manufacturers' Association (TRISAD)
Triko Sanayicileri Dernegi
Address: Abdi Ipekci Cad. Oluyol Osman Nuri Is Merkezi, No 29, Bayrampasa-Istanbul
Telephone: +90 212 612 8509
Fax: +90 212 612 7433
Year established: 1994

Leather Textile Manufacturers' Association
Deri Konfeksiyonculari Dernegi veya Dericiler Dernegi
Address: 58 Bulvar Cad. 48/1 Sok. Emek Ishani No 15, Kat 3, Zeytinburnu-Istanbul
Telephone: +90 212 665 2747
Fax: +90 212 546 7753
Year established: 1995

National Franchise Association of Turkey (UFRAD)
Ulusal Franchising Dernegi
Address: Selime Hatun Cami Sk 13/4, 80040 Findikli, Istanbul
Telephone: +90 212 252 55 61
Fax: +90 212 252 5561
Year established: 1991
Chief officers: Osman F Bilge (Vice President)

Plastic Manufacturers' Association
Plastik Sanayicileri Dernegi
Address: Kiztasi Caddesi. Gursoy Ishani No 7 Kat 4, Istanbul
Telephone: +90 212 635 4116
Fax: +90 212 635 4116
Year established: 1969

Shoe Manufacturers' Association
Ayakkabi Sanayicileri Dernegi
Address: M. Akif Cad. 1.Sk., Haydar Akin Is Merkezi No 25/10, Sirinevler-Istanbul
Telephone: +90 212 551 0950
Fax: +90 212 652 8972
Year established: 1985
Activities: collecting information; dealing with members problems and rights

Soaps and Detergents Manufacturers' Association (SDA)
Sabun ve Deterjan sanayicileri Dernegi
Address: Degirmen Sok. Sasmaz Sitesi Duran Bey Apt. No 19, Kat 3 Daire 9, 81090 Kozyatagi-Istanbul
Telephone: +90 216 416 7644
Fax: +90 216 416 9218
Year established: 1988
Chief officers: Mr Mustafa Bagan

Touring and Automobile Association of Turkey (TTOK)
Turkiye Turing ve Otomobil Kurumu Dernegi
Address: I. Oto Sanayi Sitesi Yani, No 2 Seyrantepe, Istanbul
Telephone: +90 212 282 8140
Fax: +90 212 282 8042
Year established: 1923

Turkish Association of Marketing and Public Opinion Research
Pazarlamaci ve Kamuoyu Arastirmacilari Dernegi
Address: Istiklal Cad. Imam Adnan Sok. no 1/2 Peva Han, Beyoglu 80060, Istanbul
Telephone: +90 212 251 0053
Fax: +90 212 251 3929
Year established: 1988

Turkish Banking Association (TBB)
Turkiye Bankalar Birligi
Address: Nispetiye Cad. Akmerkez B-3 Blok k 13-14, Etiler-Istanbul
Telephone: +90 212 282 0973
Fax: +90 212 282 0946
Year established: 1958

Turkish Ceramic Association (TSD)
Turk Seramik Dernegi
Address: Buyukdere Cad. No 193, Levent-Istanbul
Telephone: +90 212 248 2501
Fax: +90 212 279 8291
Year established: 1990

Turkish Chemical Manufacturers' Association (TKSD)
Turkiye Kimya Sanayicileri Dernegi
Address: Degirmen Sok. Sasmaz Sitesi Duran Bey Apt. No 19, K 3 Daire 9, 81090 Kozyatagi-Istanbul
Telephone: +90 216 416 7644
Fax: +90 216 416 9218
Year established: 1986

Turkish Clothing Manufacturers' Association (TGS)
Address: Yildiz Posta Caddesi No 48/18, Dedeman Is Ham, 80700 Gayrettepe, Istanbul
Telephone: +90 212 274 2525/5555
Fax: +90 212 274 4060
Year established: 1976
Chief officers: Erdemli Sabahnur (Secretary General)

Turkish Electronic Manufacturers' Association (TESID)
Turk Elektronik Saanayicileri Dernegi
Address: Bagdat Cad. No 477/4, 81070 Suadiye-Istanbul
Telephone: +90 216 386 0909/302 4594
Fax: +90 216386 0910
Year established: 1989

Turkish Film Industry Association (SESAM)
Turkiye Sinema Eseri Sahipleri Meslek Birligi
Address: Istiklal Cad. No.122, Beyoglu-Istanbul
Telephone: +90 212 245 4645
Fax: +90 212 247 4740
Year established: 1987

Turkish Food Service Association
Turkiye Lokantacilar, Kebapcilar, Pastacilar ve Tatlicilar Federasyonu
Address: Sanayi Cad. Sanayi Han No 23 d 46, Ulus 06550 Altindag-Ankara
Telephone: +90 312 312 4059/310 4172
Fax: +90 312 312 4059

Turkish Franchising Association
Address: Selilme Hatun Camii Sok, Ozlen Apt. No. 13/4, Gumussuyu, Istanbul
Telephone: +90 291 55 61
Fax: +90 291 55 61
Chief officers: Ms Pures Yoil (Secretary General)

Turkish Journalist Association (TGC)
Turkiye Gazeteciler Cemiyeti
Address: Basin Sarayi, Cagaloglu, Istanbul
Telephone: +90 212 513 8300
Fax: +90 212 526 8046
Year established: 1946

Turkish Libraries' Association (TKD)

Turk Kutuphaneciler Dernegi
Address: Necatibey Cad. Elgin Sok. 8/8, 06440 Ankara
Telephone: +90 312 230 1325
Fax: +90 312 230 1325
Year established: 1949

Turkish Milk, Meat and Food Manufacturers' Association (SET-BIR)

Turkiye sut, Et, Gida Sanayicileri ve Ureticileri
Address: Yildiz Posta Cad. Esengul Apt. No: 23 Kat 3 d: 22, 80280 Esentepe-Istanbul
Telephone: +90 212 272 0681
Fax: +90 212 275 5777
Year established: 1976

Turkish Newspaper Publishers' Association

Turkiye Gazette Sahipleri Sendikasi
Address: Cagaloglu Türkocagi Cad. Basin Sarayi 3, Kat 1, Istanbul
Telephone: +90 212 514 0692/93
Fax: +90 212 522 9834
Chief officers: Mr Barlas Küntay (General Secretary)

Turkish Pharmaceutical Manufacturers' Association (IEIS)

Address: Talatpasa Cad Ortabayir Mevkii 98/B, Gültepe, Istanbul
Telephone: +90 212 278 8540/278 8644
Fax: +90 212 278 7007/270 6998
Web site: pharmacy.ege.edu.tr/tiea/sanayi/ieis/english.html
Web site notes: site includes a list of members
Year established: 1964
Notes: The Association is a member of the following organisations: International Federation of Pharmaceutical Manufacturers' Associations (IFPMA), The European Proprietary Medicines Manufacturers' Association (AESGP) and an associate member of The European Federation of Pharmaceutical Industries' Associations (EFPIA).

Turkish Publishers' Association (YAY-BIR)

Turkiye Yayincilar Birligi Dernegi
Address: Kazim Ismail Gurkan Cad. Ortaklar Han 12/1, Cagaloglu-Istanbul
Telephone: +90 212 512 5602
Fax: +90 212 511 7794
Year established: 1985

Turkish Road Haulage's Association

Turkiye Nakliyeciler Dernegi
Address: Nakliyeciler Sitesi B Blok 328, 34780 Zeytinburnu-Istanbul
Telephone: +90 212 582 6033 or 212 664 1538
Fax: +90 212 510 50 04
Year established: 1947

Turkish Tourism Investors' Association (TYD)

Turkiye Turizm Yatirimcilari Dernegi
Address: Cumhuriyet Cad. Çelik Apt.nº 253 K.3, Elmadag Istanbul
Telephone: +90 212 234 52 45/241 7252
Fax: +90 212 231 1933/1845
Year established: 1988
Activities: project contracting, hotel management, marketing, production and representation, investment and finance
Chief officers: Mr Barlas Küntay (Chairman), Mr Sunuk Pasiner (Secretary General)
Membership: over 145,000 members in a range of sectors: accommodation sector, marinas, tourism oriented land, air transport, shopping centres, entertainment facilities and golf courses

Turkish Trade and Industries Association (TOBB)

Türkiye Ticaret ve, Sanayi Odalari ve Ticaret Borsalari Birligi
Address: 149 Atatürk Bulvari, Bakanliklar, Ankara
Telephone: +90 312 417 77 00 (9 lines)
Fax: +90 312 418 3268 /417 8235
Activities: central federation of commerce, industry and commodity exchanges

Union of Turkish Pharmacies (TEB)

Turk Eczacilar Birligi
Address: Farabi Sok. No 35, 06690 Cankaya-Ankara
Telephone: +90 312 467 2512 (4 lines)
Fax: +90 312 467 7585
Year established: 1956

Vegetables Oil Manufacturers' Association

Bitkisel Yag Sanayicileri Dernegi
Address: Yildiz Posta Cad. Yener Sok. No 3 D: 1, Esentepe-Besiktas-Istanbul
Telephone: +90 212 274 7557
Fax: +90 212 274 1257
Year established: 1975

White Goods Components Manufacturers' Association (BEYSAD)

Beyaz Esya Yan Sanayicileri Dernegi
Address: Inonu Caddesi, Turapoglu Sokak., Sumko Sitesi A4 Blok. Daire 14, Kozyatagi-Istanbul
Telephone: +90 216 445 0568
Fax: +90 216 445 0343
Year established: 1993
Activities: protects members rights

UGANDA

Uganda Manufacturers' Association (UMA)

Address: PO Box 6966, Lugogo Show Grounds, Kampala
Telephone: +256 41 220 285/221 034
Year established: 1960
Activities: information services and exchange, trade development activities (trade fairs, trade and investment conferences, etc), training courses
Chief officers: James Mulwana (Chairman)
Membership: over 450 members state- and privately-owned companies from the industrial and commercial sector
Publications:
• Manufacturer: *manufacturing and related matters, news and opinion articles, information about the acitivies of UMA - monthly*
• Manufacturers' Directory: *directory of the manufacturing companies of Uganda, with contact details, product lines, etc - annual*

Uganda Newspaper Editors' and Proprietors' Association (UNEPA)

Address: PO Box 4860, Kampala
Telephone: +256 41 242 764
Fax: +256 41 230 675
Chief officers: Mr Amos Kajoba (President)

Uganda Publishers' and Booksellers' Association

Address: PO Box 9536 or PO Box 7732, Globe Chambers, Plot 2C, Kampala Road, Kampala

Telephone: +256 41 235 922/259 163/251 112
Fax: +256 41 245 597/251 160
Chief officers: Mr James Tumisiine (President), Mr TWK Nakaana (Director)

UNITED KINGDOM

Advertising Association (AA)
Address: Abford House, 15 Wilton Road, London SW1V 1NJ
Telephone: +44 171 828 2771
Fax: +44 171 931 0376
E-mail: comments@adassoc.org.uk
Web site: www.adassoc.org.uk
Year established: 1926
Activities: the production and publication of statistics derived using surveys from the media, advertising agencies and advertisers; information centre open to members and non-members (by appointment only) containing reference books, statistics, periodicals, press cuttings; organises conferences and exhibitions
Chief officers: Andrew Brown (Director General), Debbie Harper (Secretary)
Structure: council; committees: executive, finance, information services, promotion of advertising, special issues, statistics working party, data protection and financial services advertising
Membership: 31 organisations
Publications:
• Advertising Association Newsletter: *quarterly*
• Advertising Forecast: *quarterly*
• Advertising Statistics Yearbook: *in-depth statistical profile of the UK advertising industry - annual*
• Annual Review of the Advertising Association: *annual*
• European Advertising and Media Forecast
• Marketing Product Book: *economic and demographic data; advertising expenditure; distribution; consumer expenditure - annual*
• Quarterly Survey and Expenditure Analysis: *quarterly*

Airport Operators' Association
Address: 3 Birdcage Walk, London SW1H 9JJ
Telephone: +44 171 222 2249
Fax: +44 171 976 7405
Activities: represents all UK airports
Chief officers: John Douthwaite (Chief Executive)
Membership: UK airports

Alliance of Independent Retailers (AIR)
Address: 5-9 St Nicholas St, Worcester WR1 IUW
Telephone: +44 1905 612733
Fax: +44 1905 21501
E-mail: kbi27dial.pipex.com
Year established: 1983
Activities: training, seminars, exhibitions, 24-hour legal helpline; professional consultants; discount facilities; marketing and promotion; political representation at government and EU levels. The Association does not produce any statistics.
Chief officers: Beryl Davis (Chief Executive), Gillian Davidson (Managing Director), Len Griffin (General Manager)
Structure: AIRB consists of three organisations: AIRB, National Retail Trade Centre, Independent Retailer Magazine
Membership: 10,000 member companies (retailers, businesspeople, manufacturers, distributors, suppliers and professional consultants)
Publications:
• Independent Retailer: *news and trends in the retailing sector with particular emphasis on issues affecting independents - monthly*

Notes: The National Retail Trade Centre, which is part of the Tri-Partite Independent Retailer organisation, provides a marketing and promotional arm for manufacturers and suppliers who wish to make direct contact with AIR members and readers of Independent Retailer magazine. The Alliance was formed by amalgamation and affiliation with a number of smaller organisations including the Association of Independent Retailers, the Amalgamated Restaurateurs, Caterers, Hoteliers and Innkeepers (ARCHI), the Decorative Lighting and Electrical Retailers' Associations, the Alliance of Video Retailers and the Asian Traders' Association.

Allied Brewery Traders' Association (ABTA)
Address: 85 Tettenhall Road, Wolverhampton WV3 9NE
Telephone: +44 1902 422 303
Fax: +44 1902 712 066
E-mail: intray@breworld.com
Web site: www.breworld.com:80/abta/index.html
Year established: 1907
Activities: organisation of conferences, seminars and trade fairs
Chief officers: Mr M J Rayner (Chief Executive)
Membership: companies trading with the brewing industry in the supply of raw materials and plant
Publications:
• ABTA - Annual Directory: *annual*

Aluminium Can Recycling Association Ltd (ACRA)
Address: 5 Gatsby Court, 176 Holiday Street, Birmingham B1 1TJ
Telephone: +44 121 633 4656
Fax: +44 121 633 4698
E-mail: alex.griffin@dial.pipex.com
Activities: collects sector statistics
Chief officers: Alex Griffin (National Manager)

Apparel Knitting and Textiles Alliance
Address: 5 Portland Place, London W1N 3AA
Telephone: +44 171 636 7788
Fax: +44 171 636 7515
Publications:
• Trends in Textile and Clothing Trade: *product import and export statistics for various types of clothing and textiles. Based on data from HM Customs and Excise - quarterly*

Article Numbering Association (ANA)
Address: 11 Kingsway, London WC2B 6AR
Telephone: +44 171 240 2912
Fax: +44 171 240 8149
E-mail: info@ana.org.uk
Web site: www.ana.org.uk
Year established: 1976
Activities: operating manuals for article numbering, barcoding and electronic data interchange standards; organises meetings; education and training; information and advice
Membership: 12,000 member companies in most trade and industry sectors

Association for Information Management (ASLIB)
Address: 20-24 Old Street, London EC1V 9AP
Telephone: +44 171 253 4488
Fax: +44 171 430 0514
E-mail: aslib@aslib.co.uk
Web site: www.aslib.co.uk
Year established: 1924
Activities: lobbying on all aspects of legislation concerning information, provides consultancy and information services, education and training, publishes journals, directories and

conference proceedings
Chief officers: Roger Bowes (Chief Executive)
Membership: 2,000 members in 70 countries
Publications:
• Aslib Directory of Information Sources in the United
Kingdom: *lists 9,400 information sources in the UK. Details
include type of organisation, its connections and affiliations,
special collections, subject coverage, information services
offered, trade and statistical information, printed publications,
electronic and video products - irregular*
• Aslib Membership Directory: *full contact listings for
corporate and affiliate members. Includes email and WWW
addresses, an industry index, and a products and services
directory - annual*
• Managing Information: *covers online, CD-ROM, Internet,
electronic publishing, copyright, library management systems,
document delivery and business information - monthly*

Association for Payment Clearing Services (APACS)

Address: Mercury House, 14 Finsbury Square, London EC2A
1BR
Telephone: +44 171 711 6200
Fax: +44 171 256 5527
Publications:
• Yearbook of Payment Statistics: *detailed statistics on UK
inter-bank clearings, automated clearings and clearings
between branches. Based on figures obtained from member
banks - annual*

Association of British Insurers (ABI)

Address: 51 Gresham Street, London EC2V 7HQ
Telephone: +44 171 600 3333
Fax: +44 171 696 8999
Web site: www.abi.org.uk
Web site notes: site includes comprehensive statistics on the
insurance market in the UK as well as business written by UK
insurers abroad
Year established: 1985
Activities: services include technical guidance, statistical
information, investment information and standards
Chief officers: A Bridgewater (Chairman), M Boleat (Director
General)
Structure: board and committees
Membership: 440 insurance companies in membership who,
between them, transact over 95% of the business of UK
insurance companies
Publications:
• AGM Statistics: *a press release giving key industry statistics
and the first provisional figures on the industry's performance
in the previous year - annual*
• Annual Report of the Association of British Insurers: *annual*
• General Insurance Statistics: Sources of Premium Income:
*an annual report on general business premiums and the
distribution channels used for sales - annual*
• Insurance Review: *presents key industry statistics for the
latest five years with commentary on key trends - annual*
• Insurance Statistics Yearbook: *annual statistics on general
and life insurance. Based largely on the Association's own
survey with a commentary accompanying the data - annual*
• Insurance Trends: *current issues plus various statistical
tables based on the Association's own surveys - quarterly*
• Long Term Insurance : New Business Results: *figures on
new life and pensions business written during the quarter -
quarterly*
• Sources of New Premium Income: *a report showing new
premium income sales and the distribution channels for sales -
quarterly*

Association of Contact Lens Manufacturers

Address: Meadowbank, 8 Twinoaks, Cobham Surrey KT11
2QP

Telephone: +44 1372 844 126
Fax: +44 1372 844 126
E-mail: psmeeth@compuserve.com
Web site: www.aclm.co.uk
Activities: liaises with government and European institutions
Chief officers: Peter Smeeth (Secretary General)
Membership: 35 member companies
Publications:
• Annual Statistics (Association of Contact Lens
Manufacturers): *contact lens sales and contact lens solution
sales based on a survey of members' sales - annual*
• Contact Lens Care and Information Brochure

Association of Household Distributors

Address: 36 Frogmore St, Tring, Herts, HP23 5AU
Telephone: +44 1442 890 991
Fax: +44 1442 890 992
Activities: collects statistics on revenue and volume of
door-to-door distribution annually; marketing members'
services
Chief officers: Ms Shelley Radice (Director)
Membership: 61 members
Publications:
• Door-To-Door Marketing Handbook: *introduction to using the
door-to-door medium; details of members' services and areas
to which they deliver - annual*

Association of Independent Businesses (AIB)

Address: 31 Bow Lane, London EC4M 9AY
Telephone: +44 171 329 0219
Fax: +44 171 329 3620
Year established: 1967
Activities: representation; lobbying; 24-hour legal banking;
taxation and accountancy; general/medical/property
insurance; management information; library facilities
Publications:
• AIB Annual Report: *annual*
• Independent Business

Association of Manufacturers of Domestic Electrical Appliances (AMDEA)

Address: Rapier House, 40-46 Lambs Conduit Street, London
WC1N 3NW
Telephone: +44 171 405 0666
Fax: +44 171 405 6609
Activities: the association produces statistics on the market
for domestic appliances in the United Kingdom
Chief officers: Peter Carver (Director General), John
Humphries (Technical Manager)
Membership: 90 manufacturers of domestic electrical
appliances
Publications:
• AMDEA Quarterly Statistics: *quarterly updates to the
Statistical Yearbook with statistics on deliveries and imports of
various domestic electrical appliances. Based largely on data
supplied by AMDEA members supplemented by some official
statistical data - quarterly*
• AMDEA Statistical Yearbook: *UK deliveries, and imports, of
domestic electrical appliances including white goods broken
down by product, and some electrical appliances. Also data
on prices and employment. Based primarily on data collected
by AMDEA from members with trade data supplemented by
official statistics - annual*
• Annual Report: *industry statistics, year review, technical
report - annual*

Association of Market Survey Organisations (AMSO)

Address: 16 Creighton Street, London N10 1NU
Telephone: +44 181 444 3692
Fax: +44 181 883 9953

Web site: www.amso.co.uk
Chief officers: Bill Blyth (Chairman), John Kelly (Honorary Secretary and Treasurer)
Structure: membership, council, sub-commitees
Publications:
● Research Industry Annual Turnover: *total annual turnover of member companies, including virtually all of the largest market research companies in the UK. Details of earnings in the UK and overseas. Based on a survey of members - annual*

Association of Master Upholsterers and Soft Furnishers (AMU)

Address: 102 Commercial Street, Newport Gwent, NP9 1LU
Telephone: +44 01633 215454
Fax: +44 01633 244488
E-mail: amu@easynet.co.uk
Web site: www.upholsterers.co.uk
Year established: 1947
Chief officers: Michael Spencer (Chief Executive Officer)
Membership: upholstery and soft furnishing manufacturers
Publications:
● AMU Journal (The): *news, technical articles and new product information for the soft furnisher and upholsterer - monthly*

Association of Publishing Agencies (APA)

Address: Queens House, 55/56 Lincoln's Inn Fields, London, WC2A 3LJ
Telephone: +44 171 404 4166
Fax: +44 171 404 4167
E-mail: Sarah@APA.co.uk
Web site: www.apa.co.uk
Web site notes: site includes a listing of APA member publications
Year established: 1993
Activities: the APA acts as a central source of information and industry advice for members and potential clients
Chief officers: Kim Conchie (Chairman), Sarah Farmer (Director)
Membership: 16 publishing agencies, who publish customer magazines for over 170 leading UK companies
Notes: Under the umbrella of the Periodical Publishers Association.

Association of the British Pharmaceutical Industry (ABPI)

Address: 12 Whitehall, London SW1A 2DY
Telephone: +44 171 930 3477
Fax: +44 171 747 1411
E-mail: IA@ABPI.demon.co.uk
Web site: www.abpi.org.uk
Year established: 1930
Activities: organises conferences and meetings; training and education; offers help and advice on commercial and legal affairs; library facilities; statistics
Structure: board of management; committees and working parties representing interests in medical specialities, biotechnology, general medicines and exports; four registers maintained by the associations; numerous committees, working parties, sub-committees, etc.
Publications:
● Annual Report of the Association of the British Pharmaceutical Industry: *medical, scientific, economic and commercial affairs; industry statistics - annual*

Association of Unit Trusts and Investment Funds (AUTIF)

Address: 65 Kingsway, London WC2B 6TD
Telephone: +44 171 831 0898
Fax: +44 171 831 9975

Activities: government lobbying, information service for members
Membership: 115 unit trust and investment fund managers which together have around £100 billion funds under management
Publications:
● Unit Trust and Pep Sales: *trends in sales of unit trusts and peps with data for the latest month and some previous months. Based on data collected by the Association - monthly*

Association of Wholesale Electrical Bulk Buyers Ltd (AWEBB)

Address: Rutland Court, Manners Industrial Estate, Ilkeston, Derby DE7 8EF
Telephone: +44 115 944 1088
Fax: +44 115 944 0837
Year established: 1972
Activities: information services
Chief officers: David Dunning (Chief Executive)
Structure: board 5 members
Membership: 36

Automatic Vending Association of Britain

Address: Bassett House, High Street, Banstead, Surrey SM7 2LZ
Telephone: +44 1737 357211
Fax: +44 1737 370501
Year established: 1929
Activities: provides statistical service for members but some general information available to non-members (no charge), enquiry service for vending products and services
Chief officers: Janette Gledhill (Director and Chief Executive)
Membership: 250 corporate members (manufacturers, distributors, dealers and contract operators of vending services)
Publications:
● Codes of Practice
● Directory
● Vendinform Census: *a census of the beverage and snack foods vending industry and market with data on number and types of machines, consumer spending, and products. Based on research commissioned by the Association - every few years*

Baby Products' Association (BPA)

Address: Erlegh Manor, Vicarage Rd, Pitstone, Leighton Buzzard, Beds, LU7 9EY
Telephone: +44 1296 662 789
Fax: +44 1296 662 789
Year established: 1960
Activities: promotion of the annual Baby and Child International Fair
Chief officers: Mr R Chantry-Price (Secretary)
Membership: 75 members
Publications:
● BPA Yearbook: *lists all major suppliers in the trade, and relevant British and European standards - annual*
● Catalogue for the Baby and Child International Fair: *annual*
Notes: The Association does not produce statistics.

Bakery Allied Traders' Association (BATA)

Address: 6 Catherine Street, London WC2B 5JJ
Telephone: +44 171 836 2460
Fax: +44 171 836 0580
Chief officers: Ms F A McLean, (Executive Secretary), Ms Anna Lancaster (Secretary)
Membership: 21 bakery and confectionery ingredients suppliers
Notes: The Association does not produce statistics or publications.

Biscuit, Cake, Chocolate and Confectionery Alliance

Address: 37-41 Bedford Row, London WC1R 4JH
Telephone: +44 171 404 9111
Fax: +44 171 404 9110
Year established: 1987
Activities: operates enquiry service; compiles 4-weekly statistical summaries covering manufacturers' dispatches of Alliance products (available for sale to non-members; details on application), technology conference
Chief officers: JE Newman (Director)
Membership: 150 UK based manufacturing companies and 20 overseas companies; only manufacturers of Alliance products are eligible for membership
Publications:
• Annual Review of the Biscuit, Cake, Chocolate and Confectionery Alliance: *annual*
• Four-Weekly Summaries (Biscuit, Cake, Chocolate and Confectionery Alliance): *a series of individual reports on specific sectors of the confectionery market, biscuits, chocolate confectionery, sugar confectionery. Detailed breakdowns by type of product in each report. Based on returns from member companies - monthly*
• Newsletter of the Biscuit, Cake, Chocolate and Confectionery Alliance: *quarterly*
• Statistical Yearbook (Biscuit, Cake, Chocolate and Confectionery Alliance): *annual data on deliveries to the home and export market of biscuits, chocolate confectionery and sugar confectionery. Statistics on specific products and historical data over a 20-30 year period. Based on returns from members - annual*

Booksellers' Association of Great Britain and Ireland

Address: Minster House, 272 Vauxhall Bridge Road, London SW1V 1BA
Telephone: +44 171 834 5477
Fax: +44 171 834 8812
E-mail: 100437.2261@ compuserve.com
Web site: www.bic.org.uk/~bic/batrain.html
Year established: 1895
Activities: The Changing Face of Retail Bookselling conference (annual); information on trade practice; technological developments
Chief officers: Tim Godfray (Chief Executive)
Structure: council, finance and general purposes committee
Membership: represents 96% of all bookshops throughout Great Britain and Ireland
Publications:
• Bookselling - Journal of Booksellers Association: *quarterly*
• Charter Group Economic Survey : *regularly updated*
• Directory of Book Publishers, Wholesalers and Distributors: *annual*
• Directory of Book Trade Sidelines and Services: *annual*
• Directory of Booksellers Association Members: *annual*

Brewers and Licensed Retailers' Association (BLRA)

Address: 42 Portman Square, London W1H 0BB
Telephone: +44 171 486 4831
Fax: +44 171 935 4358
E-mail: prmail@blra.co.uk
Web site: www.blra.co.uk
Year established: 1904
Publications:
• Beerfacts: *free leaflet containing selected information from the Statistical Handbook*
• Cross-Channel Trade in Beer: *the market and impact of cross channel trade*
• UK Statistical Handbook (Brewer's and Licensed Retailers Association): *contains production, consumption, industry structure, and price statistics plus data on brewing materials, duties, licensing data, drunkenness and some international comparisons. Based largely on central government data - annual*

Brewers Guild

Address: 8, Ely Place, Holborn, London, EC1N 6SD
Telephone: +44 171 405 4565
Fax: +44 171 831 4995
E-mail: 106026.1571@compuserve.com
Membership: 1,800 members made up of technical brewers, brewery production directors, plant managers, bottling and packaging managers, maltsters, chemists, engineers and beer service managers
Publications:
• Brewer: *review of the international brewing industry with emphasis on beer production - monthly*

British Aerosol Manufacturers' Association (BAMA)

Address: Kings Building, Smith Square, London SW1P 3JJ
Telephone: +44 171 828 5111
Fax: +44 171 834 8436
E-mail: Bama@compuserve.com
Web site: tecweb.com/bama/bama.htm
Activities: technical legislative, promotional activities on behalf of the industry; compiles UK production statistics by sector
Chief officers: Mrs Sue Rodgers (Director), Miss Sarah Ross (PR Manager)
Membership: 75 member companies
Publications:
• BAMA Annual Report: *mainly commentary on the industry but some statistics on the number of aerosols filled by product category. Based on information supplied by member companies - annual*

British Agrochemical Association (BAA)

Address: 4 Lincoln Court, Lincoln Road, Peterborough PE1 2RP
Telephone: +44 1733 349 225
Fax: +44 1733 625 23
E-mail: kreke@baa.prestel.co.uk
Web site: www.baa.org.uk
Activities: produces statistics covering UK and export sales
Chief officers: Dr Anne Buckenham (Director General)
Membership: 40 members
Publications:
• BAA Annual Review Handbook: *mainly commentary on the Association's activities but it also includes a statistical section with aggregate data on agrochemical sales and pesticide usage by type of pesticide, in the UK. Summary data on the international agrochemicals market. Based on a survey of members - annual*

British Apparel and Textile Federation

Address: 5 Portland Place, London W1N 3AA
Telephone: +44 171 636 7788
Fax: +44 171 636 7515
E-mail: batc@dial.pipex.com
Activities: represents the industry, provides information about UK clothing
Chief officers: John Wilson (Director General)
Membership: 80% of the UK clothing and textile industry
Publications:
• Industry Statistical Overview (British Apparel and Textile Federation): *a general review of the industry with statistics on sales, employment, production, investment and trade - annual*
• Quarterly Bulletin of Statistics, Woollen and Worsted (British Apparel and Textile Federation): *contains a range of statistics on textiles and clothing including production, sales, imports, exports, balance of trade and employment data. Based on various sources - quarterly*

• Quarterly Export Data, all textiles and made up items: *quarterly*
• Quarterly Import Data, all textiles and made up items: *quarterly*
• Quarterly Production Data, Cotton and Allied Textiles: *quarterly*
• Quarterly Review of Trade Statistics, Woollen and Worsted: *quarterly*
• Quarterly Statistical Review, Cotton and Allied Textiles (British Apparel and Textile Federation): *contains a range of statistics on textiles and clothing including production, sales, imports, exports, balance of trade and employment data. Based on various sources - quarterly*
• TRENDATA: *statistical overview for both apparel and textiles. Contains key figures on imports and exports, production, consumer expenditure and employment, as well as more detailed analysis of each sector within the industry - quarterly*

British Association for Chemical Specialities (BACS)
Address: The Gatehouse, White Cross, Lancaster LA1 4XQ
Telephone: +44 1524 849 606
Fax: +44 1524 849 194
Year established: 1977
Chief officers: Dr Karen E Duff (Chairman), Richard J Farn (Director)
Membership: 160 companies operating in the field of speciality and performance chemicals, particularly maintenance products for institutional, industrial and consumer use, biocides (including water treatment chemicals), disinfectants and speciality surfactants. Represents manufacturers and marketers as well as supermarket chains marketing their own branded products

British Association of Beauty Therapy and Cosmetology Ltd (BABTAC)
Address: Parabola House, Parabola Road, Cheltenham, Glos GL50 3AH
Telephone: +44 1242 570 284
Fax: +44 1242 222 177
Year established: 1976
Activities: organises 2 large congresses/exhibitions each year
Chief officers: Mrs Dawn Mernagh-Ward (Chairperson), Mrs Jane Crebbin-Bailey (Vice Chairperson), Miss Deborah Williams (Executive Manager)
Membership: ca. 3,000 UK and overseas highly-qualified beauty therapists
Publications:
• In Touch: *news on the beauty industry - quarterly*

British Association of Canned and Preserved Food Importers and Distributors (BACFID)
Address: London
Telephone: +44 171 253 9421
Fax: +44 171 250 0965
Year established: 1974
Activities: collects import statistics (also available to non-members - price on application); information service on trade matters
Chief officers: Walter J Anzer (Secretary General)
Membership: 65 corporate members (importers and distributors)
Notes: Member of the Fédération Européenne du Commerce en Fruits Secs, Conserves, Epices et Miel.

British Association of Convenience Stores (ACS)
Address: Federation House, 17 Farnborough Street, Farnborough, Hants GU14 8AG
Telephone: +44 1252 515 001
Fax: +44 1252 515 002
E-mail: ACS@acs.org.uk

Web site: www.acs.org.uk
Activities: lobbying at a national and European level, retail services and communication; undertakes surveys and other research on an ad-hoc basis but results are only available to members
Chief officers: Trevor Dixon (Chief Executive), James Lowman (Public Affairs Manager)
Membership: independent retailers, convenience store multiples and wholesale groups representing 1,000 stores
Publications:
• ACS News: *the Association's activities and developments in the industry - bi-monthly*

British Association of Leisure Parks, Piers and Attractions (BALPPA)
Address: 25 Kings Terrace, London NW1 0JP
Telephone: +44 171 383 7942
Fax: +44 171 383 7925
Year established: 1936
Activities: government lobbying
Chief officers: John Wilkes (General Secretary)
Membership: 210 member companies
Notes: The Association does not produce any publications or statistics on the industry.

British Association of Pharmaceutical Wholesalers
Address: 19A South Street, Farnham, Surrey GU9 7QU
Telephone: +44 1252 711 412
Fax: +44 1252 726 561
Chief officers: Mr J M Watts (Executive Director); Mr K I Mentzel (Secretary)
Membership: 18 members (full line wholesalers in UK)
Publications:
• Membership Directory: *listings of members - annual*

British Association of Toy Retailers (BATR)
Address: 24 Baldwyn Gardens, London W3 6HL
Telephone: +44 181 993 2894
Fax: +44 181 248 2701
Web site: www.shopcity.co.uk/batr.html
Web site notes: site includes basic statistics on retail sales of toys in the UK, as well as some information on distribution and trends in the industry
Year established: 1950
Activities: liaison with DTI and EU agencies; information services; lobbying; insurance and legal services; liaison with British Toy and Hobby Association
Chief officers: Gerald Masters (Secretary/Press Officer)
Structure: council, sub-committees
Membership: 430 members representing around 1,500 outlets
Publications:
• BTHA Handbook
• Toy Trader: *monthly*

British Audio Dealers' Association (BADA)
Address: P O Box 229, London N1 7UU
Telephone: +44 171 226 4044
Fax: +44 171 359 6720
E-mail: 100761.1550@compuserve.com
Web site: www.bada.co.uk
Year established: 1982
Membership: 100 specialist hi-fi separates retailers

British Bankers' Association (BBA)
Address: 10 Lombard Street, London EC3V 9AP
Telephone: +44 171 623 4001
Fax: +44 171 283 7037
Web site: www.bba.org.uk
Web site notes: site includes a list of members

Year established: 1919
Activities: produces specialist publications e.g. market standards, circulars and reports on topical issues and regulatory matters; conducts various surveys on the banking sector and compiles statistics
Structure: Director General, Council, Working Parties
Membership: 300 banks including all major UK high street banks
Publications:
• Abstract of Banking Statistics: *annual statistics on the UK banking sector with sections on clearing statistics, credit cards, branches and banking groups. Historical data in many tables - annual*
• Annual Report of the British Bankers' Association: *annual*
• Monthly Statement (British Bankers Association): *regular statistics on the UK banking sector based largely on data supplied by member banks - monthly*
• Sterling Lending: *trends in sterling lending with data for the latest month and some cumulative data. Based on data supplied by members - monthly*

British Bathroom Council

Address: Federation House, Stoke-on-Trent, Staffs ST4 2RT
Telephone: +44 1782 747074
Fax: +44 1782 747161
Year established: 1988
Activities: information service; dealing with consumer enquiries
Membership: 20 full members, 1 associate member
Publications:
• Factfile

British Battery Manufacturers' Association

Address: Cowley House, 9 Little College St, London SW1P 3XS
Telephone: +44 171 222 0666
Fax: +44 171 233 0335
Year established: 1986
Activities: publishes information concerning battery issues (free); collects statistics: quarterly unit shipment data and sales; safety and environmental campaigns
Chief officers: Mr Paul Duke (Secretary General)
Membership: 7 members: Duracell Batteries, Ever Ready Ltd, Panasonic Industrial Europe, Philips Electronics Ltd, Rayovac Eurpe Ltd, Saft Nife UK Ltd, Varta Ltd

British Box and Packaging Association

Address: 5 Dublin Street, Edinburgh EH1 3PG
Telephone: +44 131 558 9986
Fax: +44 131 554 6416
Activities: annual conference; newsletters; annual design competition; lobbying; liaison; information on legislation
Chief officers: Tom Bullimore (Secretary)
Structure: executive council, area sections, regional committees
Membership: 100
Publications:
• Newsletter of the British Box and Packaging Association: *bi-monthly*
Notes: The Association does produce statistics on the industry but these are normally only available to members.

British Branded Hosiery Group

Address: c/o Charnos plc, Corporation Road, Ilkeston, Derbyshire, DE7 4BP
Telephone: +44 115 932 2191
Fax: +44 115 932 0722
Chief officers: Mr D Hutchinson (Director)

British Brush Manufacturers' Association

Address: Brooke House, 4 The Lakes, Bedford Rd, Northampton, NN4 7YD
Telephone: +44 1604 22023
Fax: +44 1604 31252

British Carpet Manufacturers' Association

Address: 5 Portland Place, London W1N 3AA
Telephone: +44 171 580 7155
Fax: +44 171 580 4854
Activities: education and training, produces statistics on the industry, provides an information service to members, liaises with government, international and other official bodies
Chief officers: Hugh G.W. Wilson (Executive Director)
Membership: 28 British carpet manufacturers
Publications:
• Annual Report (British Carpet Manufacturers Association): *includes a statistical section with data on carpet sales by type of carpet plus import and export statistics. Also some information on the fibres used in carpet surface yarns. Based mainly on official statistics - annual*
• Newsletter: *activities of the association, news and trends in the United Kingdom carpet industry - monthly*

British Ceramic Confederation

Address: Federation House, Station Road, Stoke on Trent, Staffs ST4 2SA
Telephone: +44 1782 744 631
Fax: +44 1782 744 102
E-mail: bcc@ceramfed.co.uk
Activities: produces statistics on the industry including: production; sales; overseas trade; energy consumption; costs; employment; health and safety
Chief officers: Mr Christopher Hall (Commercial and Public Affairs Director), Kevin Farrell (Chief Executive)
Membership: 250 ceramics manufacturers
Publications:
• Annual Report: *annual*
• Quarterly Report: *Quarterly*

British Chemical Distributors' and Traders' Association (BCDTA)

Address: Suffolk House, George Street, Croydon CR0 0YN
Telephone: +44 181 686 4545
Fax: +44 181 688 7768
Year established: 1923
Chief officers: Leslie Napier (President), Colin J D Wainwright (Director and Secretary)
Membership: chemical and dyestuff traders

British Chicken Association

Address: Imperial House, 15-19 Kingsway, London WC2B 6UA
Telephone: +44 171 240 9889
Fax: +44 171 240 7757
E-mail: bpmf@bpmf.co.uk
Activities: political lobbying, public relations, research and development
Chief officers: Miss Yvonne Sired (Secretary)
Membership: growers and packers of chicken

British Clothing Industry Association (BCIA)

Address: 5 Portland Place, London W1N 3AA
Telephone: +44 171 636 7788
Fax: +44 171 636 7515
Year established: 1982
Activities: sponsors exhibitions to promote British made clothing; statistics on trade, UK clothing industry including employment; research into manufacturing networks and

production
Chief officers: James McAdam (Chairman), John Wilson
(Chief Executive)
Structure: executive council and committees: industrial
relations, international development, finance, premier
menswear
Membership: clothing manufacturers
Publications:
• Annual Report of the British Clothing Industry Association:
annual
• BCIA Newsheet: *monthly*

British Contract Furnishing Association (BCFA)
Address: The Business Design Centre, 52 Upper Street,
Islington Green, London N1 0QH
Telephone: +44 171 226 6641
Fax: +44 171 288 6190
E-mail: enquiries@bcfa.org.uk
Web site: www.tradeworld.co.uk/bcfa/
Year established: 1975
Activities: offers a UK and export sales lead service,
sponsors trade fairs, advises on exporting, arbitration and
networking, maintains a library
Publications:
• Contract Furnishing Directory: *comprehensive directory of
2,000 providers of products and services across the
furnishings market - annual*
• Contract Furnishing Magazine: *the activities of the
Association as well as news and trends in the British
furnishings market - quarterly*

British Council of Shopping Centres
Address: 1 Queen Anne's Gate, Westminster, London, SW1H
9BT
Telephone: +44 171 222 1122
Fax: +44 171 222 4440
Activities: conferences, seminars, research, awards, lobbying
Chief officers: Mr P Lewis (Senior Vice-President), Keith
Redshaw (President), Michael D. Taplin (Head of Secreteriat)
Membership: 870 member companies
Publications:
• Checkout: *ownership and management, design and
construction, property, legislation and finance - quarterly*
• Research Papers: *a series of reports on issues affecting
shopping centres and retailing in the United Kingdom -
periodically*
Notes: The Association does not produce statistics.

British Dental Association (BDA)
Address: 64 Wimpole Street, London W1M 8AL
Telephone: +44 171 935 0875
Fax: +44 171 487 5232
E-mail: Enquiries@bda-dentistry.org.uk
Web site: www.bda-dentistry.org.uk

British Disposable Products' Association
Address: Rivenhall Rd, Westlea, Swindon, SN5 7BD
Telephone: +44 131 556 9986
Fax: +44 131 557 6716
Chief officers: Mr T Bullimore (Chairman)

British Egg Information Service
Address: Bury House, 126-128 Cromwell Road, Kensington,
London SW7 4ET
Telephone: +44 171 580 7425
Fax: +44 171 580 7430
Publications:
• Eggs Facts and Figures: *retail egg sales by region, value of

the egg market, consumption, breakdown of the egg
production system and number of flocks - annual*

British Egg Products Association
Address: Suite 101, Albany House, 324-326 Regent Street,
London W1R 5AA
Telephone: +44 171 580 7172
Fax: +44 171 580 7082
Chief officers: Mike Ring
Publications:
• Breaking and Production (British Egg Products Association):
*production and breaking statistics for the latest months
available with some figures for earlier months - ten issues per
year*
• Import and Export Statistics: *UK imports and exports of eggs
and egg products with data for the latest months and
comparative data for earlier months. Based on official
statistics - ten issues a year*

British Energy Association
Address: 34 St James's Street, London SW1A 1HD
Telephone: +44 171 930 1211
Fax: +44 171 925 0452
Publications:
• British Annual Energy Review: *commentary and statistics on
UK energy trends with data on specific energy sectors. Based
on various sources - annual*

British Essence Manufacturers' Association
Address: 6 Catherine Street, London WC2B 5JJ
Telephone: +44 171 836 2460
Fax: +44 171 836 0580
Year established: 1942
Activities: government lobbying
Chief officers: Mrs J.Clarke (Executive Secretary), Mr G.
White (Chairman)
Structure: executive committee, technical committee,
environmental health and safety
Membership: 40 manufacturers of flavourings for food and
non-food applications
Publications:
• Reports: *annual and half-yearly*
Notes: The association does not produce publications or
statistics.

British Exporters' Association
Address: 16 Dartmouth Street, London SW1H 9BL
Telephone: +44 171 222 5419
Fax: +44 171 799 2468
Year established: 1940
Activities: conferences, meetings, information services,
lobbying, establishing contacts between manufacturers and
export houses
Chief officers: H W Bailey (Director)
Structure: council, membership
Membership: 100 companies
Publications:
• Directory of Export Houses
• Export Enquiry Circular

British Federation of Audio (BFA)
Address: Landseer House, 9 Charing Cross Road, London
WC2H 0ES
Telephone: +44 171 930 3206
Fax: +44 171 839 4613
E-mail: info@british-audio.org.uk
Web site: www.british-audio.org.uk/
Activities: compiles statistics on the industry, available free of
charge to members who submit figures

Membership: members represent 75% of UK hi-fi loudspeaker production and a large proportion of UK electronics manufacture

British Food Export Council

Address: 301-344 Market Towers, 1 Nine Elms Lane, London SW8 5NQ
Telephone: +44 171 233 5111
Fax: +44 171 233 9515
Activities: organises trade exhibitions, promotional visits, etc.; compiles export statistics and provides information service
Chief officers: Charlotte Lawson
Membership: about 300 companies
Publications:
• Annual Report of the British Food Export Council: *annual*
• Bulletin: *monthly*

British Footwear Association (BFA)

Address: 5 Portland Place, London W1N 3AA
Telephone: +44 171 580 8687
Fax: +44 171 580 8696
E-mail: bfa@easynet.co.uk
Web site: www.shoeworld.co.uk/bfa
Web site notes: site includes statistics and analysis of the UK footwear industry, as well as a list of members with product descriptions
Activities: advises on legislation, marketing and exporting, government lobbying, joint ventures to overseas fairs, disseminating information
Chief officers: Niall Campbell (Chief Executive), Denis Bowen (Statistics)
Membership: 70 footwear manufacturers
Publications:
• Footwear for Special Needs: *consumer publication listing retailers*
• Footwear Industry Statistical Review: *annual statistics on the structure of the footwear industry, plus data on production, consumption, sales, foreign trade. Based on various sources - annual*
• Monthly Statistics (British Footwear Manufacturers Federation): *general economic indicators for the footwear industry covering deliveries, retail sales, foreign trade, employment, prices - monthly*
• Quarterly Statistics (British Footwear Manufacturers Federation): *detailed production, consumption and foreign trade data for specific sectors of the footwear industry. Based mainly on official statistics - quarterly*

British Forging Industry Association

Address: 245 Grove Lane, Handsworth, Birmingham B20 2HB
Telephone: +44 121 554 3311
Fax: +44 121 523 3696
E-mail: ukforgers@aol.com
Web site: www.birmingham.co.uk/britishforgers
Activities: development of industry business potential; technology transfer; self-improvement programmes; statistics on market data
Chief officers: Neil Marshall (Director General); Mike Baker (Secretary)
Membership: 250 members
Publications:
• Annual Report of the British Forging Industry Association: *a section contains summary statistics covering trends in the forging industry. Based primarily on extracts from surveys undertaken by the Association - annual*
• Statistical Bulletin (British Forging Industry Association): *current statistical information on the forging industry including market trends, deliveries, prices. Some European data also included. Based primarily on the Association's own survey - annual*

British Fragrance Association (BFA)

Address: 6 Catherine Street, London, WC2B 5JJ
Telephone: +44 171 836 2460
Fax: +44 171 836 0580
Year established: 1942
Chief officers: Knut Rossbach (Chairman), Karin Goodburn (Secretary)
Membership: companies involved in marketing fragrance compounds and aroma chemicals to manufacturers of perfumed consumer or industrial products

British Franchise Association (BFA)

Address: Thames View, Newtown Road, Henley on Thames RG9 1HG
Telephone: +44 1491 578 050
Fax: +44 1491 573 517
Web site: www.lds.co.uk/franchise/BFA/
Year established: 1977
Publications:
• BFA/Nat West Survey: *a review of trends in the UK franchise sector with data on the number and type of franchises broken down by sector. Also includes details of numbers employed in franchising. Comparative figures for the previous year are also included in a survey based on research by the Association - annual*

British Frozen Food Federation

Address: 3rd Floor, Springfield House, Springfield Road, Grantham, Lincs NG31 7BG
Telephone: +44 1476 515 300
Fax: +44 1476 515 309
Activities: compiles and publishes statistics on the frozen food market with over 50% of the data collected from the Federation's surveys supported by data from other non-official sources and government statistics
Membership: over 300 companies
Publications:
• British Frozen Food Yearbook: *review of the frozen food market with a statistical section including general data on consumption, expenditure and freezer ownership, and specific data on the markets for ice cream, vegetables, fish, meat and gateaux. Other figures cover retail and catering trends and some international statistics are included - annual*

British Furniture Manufacturers (BFM Ltd)

Address: 30 Harcourt Street, London, England, W1H 2AA
Telephone: +44 724 0851
Fax: +44 706 1924
E-mail: enquires@bfm.org.uk
Web site: www.bfm.org.uk
Activities: sourcing furniture, sponsoring shows, market research, organising shows, industry training, personnel and business matters, industry promotion, and government links. The Association produces statistics on production and trade
Chief officers: Roger Mason (Managing Director), Laraine Janes (Exhibitions)
Membership: 220 furniture manufacturers
Publications:
• Furniture Focus: *industry issues, product updates and training - monthly*

British Glass Manufacturers' Confederation

Address: Northumberland Road, Sheffield S10 2UA
Telephone: +44 114 268 6201
Fax: +44 114 268 1073
Web site: www.britglass.co.uk
Year established: 1988
Activities: information service open to members and non-members; produces accident, commercial and glass recycling statistics

Chief officers: Alistair Mair (President)
Structure: council, committees: finance and general purposes, research, container group, marketing, environment, market research, domestic glass group, pollution, health and safety
Membership: approximately 40 full members, 71 associate members
Publications:
• British Glass Annual Review: *overall review of both the trade association activities and technical services - annual*

British Goose Producers' Association

Address: Imperial House, 15-19 Kingsway, London WC2B 6UA
Telephone: +44 171 240 9889
Fax: +44 171 240 7757
E-mail: bpmf@bpmf.co.uk
Activities: political lobbying, public relations
Chief officers: Mr JM Walker (Secretary)

British Hardware and Housewares Manufacturers' Association (BHHMA)

Address: 35 Billing Road, Northampton NN1 5DD
Telephone: +44 1604 22023
Fax: +44 1604 31252
Web site: www.zipmail.co.uk/bhhma
Web site notes: site includes a product guide with contact details of member companies and a short summary of the products they produce
Activities: sponsor of the International Hardware Fair and Housewares International, compiles market information
Chief officers: Sydney Levy (President)
Membership: 700 UK manufacturers and suppliers of housewares, hardware, DIY and gardening products
Publications:
• Business Trends Survey (British Hardware and Housewares Manufacturers Association): *a quarterly opinion survey of Association members providing information on sales, orders, stocks, margins, investment. Trends over the last three months and expectations for the next three months - quarterly*

British Hardware Federation (BHF)

Address: 225 Bristol Road, Edgbaston, Birmingham B5 YUB
Telephone: +44 121 446 6688
Fax: +44 121 446 5215
Year established: 1899
Activities: provides advice on financial issues, statistics, merchandising, legislation, technical aspects, shop design services, etc; National Conference and AGM (May); 5 annual regional conferences; fact sheets on a variety of topics; interim comparison scheme (members only)
Chief officers: Jonathan Swift (Managing Director), Alan Hawkins (Deputy Managing Director), David Brawn (Sales and Marketing Director), Maisie Slater (Information Officer)
Structure: board of management, committees: finance and general purposes, building supplies division executive, marketing, legal and parliamentary, development, enterprise team
Membership: 4,500 companies
Publications:
• Architectural & Building Ironmongery Catalogue: *annual*
• Hardware Today: *news and features - monthly*
• Members Handbook and Directory: *annual*
• New Grey List: *monthly*

British Hospitality Association

Address: Queen's House, 55-56 Lincoln's Inn Fields, London WC2A 3BH
Telephone: +44 171 404 7744

Fax: +44 171 404 7799
E-mail: bha@bha.org.uk
Web site: www.bha-online.org.uk
Activities: lobbying, education and training
Chief officers: Jeremy Logie (Chief Executive), Robert Hunter (Chairman)
Membership: hotels, restaurateurs, contract caterers, clubs, transport caterers, theatres, attraction, outside caterers, universities, suppliers to the industry representing 25,000 establishments
Publications:
• Hospitality Matters: *the activities of the Association - monthly*
• UK Contract Catering Industry: *annual statistics and analysis of the UK contract catering sector with data on outlets by sector, businesses, turnover, catering costs, meals served. Catering turnover is broken down into UK and overseas turnover. Based on a survey by the Association - annual*

British Importers' Association

Address: Suite 8, Castle House, Castlereagh Street, London W1H 5YR
Telephone: +44 171 258 3999
Fax: +44 171 724 5055
Year established: 1972
Activities: government lobbying, provision of an information and advice service to UK importers
Membership: 100 member companies
Publications:
• Directory of British Importers (The): *information about British importing companies - annual*
• Importing Today: *customs procedures; import opportunities; freight logistics; import related sourcing; insurance - bi-monthly*
• Worldtrade: A Practical Guide to Doing Business in Overseas Markets: *sourcing overseas; customs matters; transportation; trade finance; information systems; legal issues - annual*
Notes: The Association does not compile statistics.

British Insurance and Investment Brokers' Association (BIIBA)

Address: 14 Bevis Marks, London EC3A 7NT
Telephone: +44 171 623 9043
Fax: +44 171 626 9676
E-mail: enquiries@biiba.org.uk
Web site: www.biiba.org.uk
Year established: 1977
Activities: offers an advice service to members
Membership: insurance brokers and financial advisors

British Interactive Multimedia Association (BIMA)

Address: 61 Ravenscourt Road, London W6 OUJ
Telephone: +44 181 741 5522
Fax: +44 181 563 9443
E-mail: enquiries@bima.co.uk
Web site: www.bima.co.uk
Year established: 1985
Activities: government liaison, education and training, maintains a database of multi-media products and companies, organises an awards event
Chief officers: Norma Hughes (Secretary)
Membership: users, application developers, hardware manufacturers, distributors, lawyers, publishers, consultants and disc pressers
Publications:
• BIMA Newsletter: *quarterly*
• Directory of Members: *contact details of member companies - annual*

British Interior Textile Association

Address: Reedham House, 31 King St West, Manchester, M3 2PN
Telephone: +44 0161 832 8684
Fax: +44 0161 833 1740
Chief officers: Mr C Smith (Director and Secretary)

British International Freight Association (BIFA)

Address: Redfern House, Browells Lane, Feltham, Middlesex, TW13 7EP
Telephone: +44 181 844 2266
Fax: +44 181 890 5546
E-mail: Bifasec@msn.com
Web site: www.bifa.org
Activities: international relations, training and education, public relations and publicity, political matters
Chief officers: Ted Sangster (Director General)
Membership: BIFA is the trade association for companies engaged in the international movement of freight to and from the UK by all modes of transport, road, rail, sea and air. It incorporates the Institute of Freight Forwarders (IFF), the professional organisation for individuals engaged in the international trade and transport sector of industry.

British Jewellers' Association

Address: Export Services Department, Federation House, Birmingham, BIS 6LT
Telephone: +44 121 237 1115
Fax: +44 121 237 1118
Activities: advice and information on the jewellery, giftware and affiliated industries in the UK and assistance in sourcing suppliers of British goods
Chief officers: Mrs Ruth E Budd

British Jewellery and Giftware Federation (BJGF)

Address: 10 Vyse Street, Birmingham B18 6LT
Telephone: +44 121 236 2657
Fax: +44 121 236 3921
Chief officers: Julian Henwood (Chief Executive)
Publications:
• British Jeweller: *includes a monthly Market Report section with news and statistics on precious metal and gold prices - monthly*
• British Jewellery Yearbook: *a directory of the jewellery industry with a statistical section giving fine gold prices for the last 15 years - annual*
Notes: The BJGF is the umbrella organisation of the British Jewellers' Association and the Giftware Association.

British Knitting and Clothing Export Council (BKCEC)

Address: 5 Portland Place, London W1N 3AA
Telephone: +44 171 636 5577
Fax: +44 171 636 7515
Web site: www2.fashionweb.co.uk/fashionweb/bkcec.html
Membership: clothing and knitwear manufacturers and exporters
Publications:
• Exporter: *export opportunities, overseas promotions and BKCEC activities - monthly*

British Marine Industries' Federation

Address: Meadlake Place, Thorpe Lea Road, Egham TW20 8HE
Telephone: +44 1784 473377
Fax: +44 1784 439678
E-mail: bmif@aboard.co.uk
Web site: www.aboard.co.uk:80/bmif
Chief officers: Tony Beechey (Executive Chairman)

Publications:
• National Survey of Boating and Watersports Participation: *statistics on the number participating in boating and watersports and analysis by type of activity. Other data on expenditure on relevant activities, equipment ownership, services used, visitors to water, etc. A consumer profile of boating and watersports enthusiasts is also included - annual*

British Office Systems and Stationery Federation (BOSS)

Address: 6 Wimpole Street, London W1M 8AS
Telephone: +44 171 637 7692
Fax: +44 171 436 3137
Chief officers: Mr L Demetriou, (Deputy Director)
Publications:
• BOSS Survey of Manufacturers' Turnover: *turnover details for three sectors of the market: office furniture, office machines, office products. The survey is based on returns from member companies and data is given for the latest quarter and some previous quarters - quarterly*

British Paper and Board Industry Federation (BPBIF)

Address: Papermakers House, Rivenhall Road, Westlea, Swindon, Wilts SN5 7BD
Telephone: +44 1793 886 086
Fax: +44 1793 886 182
Year established: 1990
Activities: houses the Pulp and Paper Information Centre, a central source of information relating to the industry; monthly, annual and ad hoc statistics available for purchase
Publications:
• BPBIF Grey Book : *monthly*
• British Paper and Board Industry Facts : *annual*

British Phonographic Industry Ltd (BPI)

Address: 25 Saville Row, London W1X 1AA
Telephone: +44 171 287 4422
Fax: +44 171 287 2252
E-mail: general@bpi.co.uk
Web site: www.bpi.co.uk
Web site notes: site includes statistics on UK music sales including volume and value data on LP's, CD's and cassettes over a three-year review period. The site also includes data on the top ten selling singles and albums over the past year, as well as a breakdown of classical music sales
Membership: 200 member companies which together account for over 90% of UK record sales
Publications:
• BPI Survey: *statistics on the UK recorded music market. Data is compiled by tracking shipments from distributors to retailers, clubs, mail order companies and wholesalers. Also included are direct sales to consumers which do not go through conventional distributors - quarterly*
• BPI Yearbook: *an annual review of the audio equipment and software market with data on production, imports, exports, deliveries, sales, prices, advertising expenditure, ownership relating to CDs, tapes, and records plus hardware. Also general statistics on leisure market trends - annual*
• Market Information Sheets (British Phonographic Industry Ltd): *brief commentary and statistics on trends in the audio industry and market with data on hardware and software - quarterly*

British Plastics Federation (BPF)

Address: 6 Bath Place, Rivington Street, London EC2A 3JE
Telephone: +44 171 457 5000
Fax: +44 171 235 8045
E-mail: bpf@dial.pipex.com
Web site: www.bpf.co.uk
Membership: 400 manufacturers of polymers, additives and

machinery as well as all types of plastics processors and fabricators

Publications:
● BPF Statistics Handbook: *annual statistics on production, consumption, imports, and exports of plastics and plastic materials. Also data on end-user sectors. Primarily based on data collected by the Federation - annual*
● Business Trends Survey (British Plastics Federation): *a survey of member companies providing data on sales, orders, stocks, exports, prices, profits, investment, and capacity utilisation. Includes information for the previous quarter and expectations for the next quarter - biannual*
● International Status Report: *trade statistics covering twenty countries, compiled with information from the world's Plastics Associations. Includes statistics on production, consumption, imports, and exports of plastics materials. In addition, it details sales of plastics products, the size and distribution of the processing industry and trade in plastics processing machinery - annual*

British Poultry Breeders' and Hatcheries' Association

Address: Imperial House, 15-19 Kingsway, London WC2B 6UA
Telephone: +44 171 240 9889
Fax: +44 171 240 7757
E-mail: bpmf@bpmf.co.uk
Activities: political lobbying
Chief officers: Mr JM Walker (Secretary)
Membership: broiler chicken hatcheries and producers

British Poultry Meat Federation

Address: Imperial House, 15-19 Kingsway, London WC2B 6UA
Telephone: +44 171 240 9889
Fax: +44 171 240 7757
E-mail: bpmf@bpmf.co.uk
Activities: political lobbying
Chief officers: Miss Yvonne Sired (Secretary)
Membership: producers, breeders, growers, slaughterers, processors

British Printing Industries' Federation (BPIF)

Address: 11 Bedford Row, London WC1R 4DX
Telephone: +44 171 242 6904
Fax: +44 171 405 7784
Year established: 1903
Activities: employment affairs (members only); information, law, technical matters, economics and statistics, health and safety, available to non-members at a premium on a consultancy basis; large selection of technical information
Chief officers: Colin Stanley (Director General)
Structure: national board of management; standing committees: industrial relations, education and training, development and technology, government and industry; 6 regional offices; 9 specialist trade sections (including British Carton Association)
Membership: 2,500 companies
Publications:
● British Printing Industries Federation Annual Review
● Economic Trends Survey: *quarterly*
● Printing Industries: *10 p.a.*
Notes: New services available to members only; free industrial tribunals insurance: free negotiating seminars; free quick response on site employment affairs consultancy.

British Radio and Electronics Equipment Manufacturers' Association (BREEMA)

Address: Landseer House, 19 Charing Cross Road, London WC2H 0ES
Telephone: +44 171 930 3206
Fax: +44 171 839 4613
Publications:
● Annual Report of the British Radio and Electronics Equipment Manufacturers Association: *a supplement to the report has basic data on the consumer electronics industry - annual*
● Deliveries of Selected Consumer Electronics Products: *deliveries to the trade of televisions, videos, teletext and music centres. Based on data supplied by members - quarterly*
● Market for Consumer Audio Equipment: *detailed analysis and statistics on the UK market for audio equipment with data on sales, production, foreign trade, deliveries, consumer offtake, stocks - annual*
● Market for Domestic Television Receivers: *detailed analysis and statistics on the UK market for television sets with data on production, foreign trade, deliveries, consumer offtake, stocks - annual*
● Market for Videography: *detailed analysis and statistics on the UK market for video equipment with data on production, foreign trade, deliveries, consumer offtake, stocks - annual*

British Retail and Professional Florists' Association Ltd

Address: 3 Alexandra Rd, Gorseinon, Swansea, SA4 4NW
Telephone: +44 1792 892 629
Fax: +44 1792 894 457
Chief officers: Major D Morgan (President)

British Retail Consortium

Address: Bedford House, 69-79 Fulham High Street, London SW6 3JW
Telephone: +44 171 647 1500
Fax: +44 171 647 1599
Membership: multiple retailers and department stores
Publications:
● Retail Crime Costs Survey: *an analysis of retail crime with figures on costs, crime by retailer type, and types of crime. Based on a survey of over 53,000 retail outlets - annual*
● Retail Sales: *monthly figures on the volume and value of retail sales based primarily on an analysis of government statistics. Some data from non-official sources - monthly*
● Retail World: *commentary and statistics covering all aspects of retailing including crime, product development, retail outlets, etc. - quarterly*

British Road Federation

Address: Pillar House, 194-202 Old Kent Road, London SE1 5TY
Telephone: +44 171 703 9769
Fax: +44 171 701 0029
Chief officers: Richard Diment (Director and Chief Executive)
Membership: 85 members
Publications:
● Basic Road Statistics: *statistics on roads and transport covering traffic, expenditure, energy, taxation, accidents. Some international comparative statistics are also included - annual*
● Briefing: *summary of road development issues - monthly*

British Robot Association (BRA)

Address: Aston Science Park, Love Lane, Birmingham B7 4BJ
Telephone: +44 121 628 1745
Fax: +44 121 628 1746
E-mail: bra@globalnet.co.uk
Web site: www.bra-automation.co.uk
Activities: statistics on robot installations within the UK
Chief officers: Mr M Wilson (President); Mr J D'Angelillo (Chairman)
Membership: over 100 members

Publications:
• BRA Datafile: *details of robot specifications from most of the major suppliers - regular*
• Robot Facts: *UK investment in robot automation in manufacturing industry - annual*

British Sandwich Association (BSA)
Address: 29 Market Place, Wantage, Oxfordshire OX12 8BG
Telephone: +44 1235 772207
Fax: +44 1235 769044
E-mail: tesa@martex.co.uk
Web site: www.martex.co.uk/bsa
Web site notes: site includes a directory of sandwich manufacturers and retailers

British Security Industry Association
Address: Security House, Barbourne Road, Worcester WR1 1RS
Telephone: +44 1905 214 64
Fax: +44 1905 613 625
E-mail: info@bsia.co.uk
Activities: security incorporating alarms, CCTV, physical and manned; statistics regarding industry turnover and wage surveys
Chief officers: David Fletcher (Chief Executive); Catherine Park (Policy/PR Manager)
Membership: 300 company members
Publications:
• CCTV Market Survey: *an annual review of the closed-circuit television security market based on a combination of turnover figures from member companies operating in this sector and some commissioned research - annual*
• Wage Survey (British Security Industry Association): *a salary survey relating to various security occupations including security guards, alarm installation staff, and central station staff. Based on a survey of member companies - biannual*

British Shops' and Stores' Association (BSSA)
Address: Middleton House, 2 Main Rd, Middleton Cheney, Banbury, Oxon, OX17 2TN
Telephone: +44 1295 712 277
Fax: +44 1295 711 665
Activities: organises meetings, conferences and exhibitions, training courses, etc.; provides information, research and statistics on retail wages
Chief officers: Mr A A Sayers (Chief Executive), John Astill (Commercial Director)
Membership: 2,500 retailers representing 10,000 non-food outlets
Publications:
• Retail Wages Survey: *an annual survey of retail wages in the non-food sector - annual*

British Soft Drinks Association Ltd (BSDA)
Address: 20-22 Stukeley St, London WC2B 5LR
Telephone: +44 171 430 0356
Fax: +44 171 831 6014
Activities: information service; technical assistance; assistance with legislation; meetings; conferences; exhibitions; training; regional groups
Membership: manufacturers, factors and franchisors of soft drinks (both still and carbonated) concentrates, freeze drinks, fruit juices and packaged waters
Publications:
• Newssheet
• Soft Drinks: *soft drinks market information in the UK, some European and international coverage, soft drinks marketing, company and individual profiles - monthly*
• Soft Drinks Industry Legal Handbook: *codes of practice, videos and other specialist booklets and leaflets are published*

by and obtainable from the Association
• Soft Drinks Today Factsheets: *brief commentaries and statistics on the soft drinks market covering soft drinks flavours, soft drinks sales, fruit juices, bottled waters, low calorie soft drinks, packaging of sparkling soft drinks, employment and the European consumption of carbonates - annual*

British Toy and Hobby Association (BTHA)
Address: 80 Camberwell Road, London SE5 0EG
Telephone: +44 171 701 7271
Fax: +44 171 708 2437
E-mail: admin@btha.co.uk
Web site: www.btha.co.uk
Year established: 1944
Activities: lobbying, statistics on domestic and international markets
Chief officers: David Hawtin (Director General), Wendy Pluckrose (Toy Fair Organiser)
Membership: 219 companies and individuals
Publications:
• British Toy and Hobby Briefing: *news and trends in the United Kingdom toys and games market - monthly*
• BTHA Handbook: *a small section of the handbook contains statistics on the sales of toys and games plus import and export data. Some figures for earlier years. Based on a combination of official and non-official statistics - annual*
• Toy and Hobby Statistics: *retail sales data for the total toys and games market in the United Kingdom as well as a breakdown by type and by outlet - annual*
• Toy Industry in the United Kingdom

British Turkey Federation
Address: Imperial House, 15-19 Kingsway, London WC2B 6UA
Telephone: +44 171 240 9889
Fax: +44 171 240 7757
E-mail: bpmf@bpmf.co.uk
Activities: political lobbying, public relations, research and development
Chief officers: Mr JM Walder (Secretary)
Membership: turkey breeders and processors

British Vehicle Rental and Leasing Association (BVRLA)
Address: River Lodge, Badminton Court, Amersham, Bucks HP7 0DD
Telephone: +44 1494 434 747
Fax: +44 1494 434 499
Web site: www.bbi.co.uk/bvrla
Web site notes: site includes statistics on the BVRLA member fleets and estimates of the total UK rental fleet, as well as a membership directory
Activities: government lobbying, education and training, providing members with information on the market
Chief officers: Norman Donkin (Secretary General), Robin MacKonochie (External Affairs Manager)
Membership: car and commercial vehicle rental, leasing, contract hire and fleet management companies. Its members operate in excess of 1.2m vehicles
Publications:
• BVRLA Annual Statistical Survey: *detailed annual statistics on the size of the rental and leasing vehicle sectors. Based on data collected from members operating fleets. A detailed analysis of the figures supports the text - annual*
• Residual Value Survey: *details of the residual value of fleets operated by members of the Association - quarterly*
• Vehicle Rental and Leasing: *news and trends in the UK vehicle rental, leasing, contract hire and fleet management industry - monthly*

British Venture Capital Association (BVCA)

Address: Essex House, 12-13 Essex Street, London, WC2R 3AA
Telephone: +44 171 240 3846
Fax: +44 171 240 3849
E-mail: bvca@bvca.co.uk
Web site: www.brainstorm.co.uk/bvca/welcome.html
Web site notes: site includes key facts and statistics on the venture capital market in the UK.
Year established: 1983
Activities: lobbying, education and training, provision of information on venture capital and its sources
Membership: BVCA represents every major UK source of venture capital which invests principally in the UK, accounting for over 95% of the industry
Publications:
● Directory of Members: *lists venture capital firms' contact details and their investment preferences, including the minimum and maximum amounts of venture capital they invest, and financing stage, industry sector and location of companies they may consider for investment. Also lists experienced venture capital advisers' contact and other details - annual*
● Performance Measurement Survey: *analyses the aggregate net returns to investors from independent venture capital funds raised from 1980, by year and type of fund - annual*
● Report on Investment Activity: *investment trends and activities of member companies over the previous year. Contains commentary and statistics with data collected from members - annual*

British Video Association (BVA)

Address: 167 Great Portland Street, London W1N 5FD
Telephone: +44 171 436 0041
Fax: +44 171 436 0043
E-mail: bva@itl.net
Web site: www.bva.org.uk
Web site notes: site includes a full list of members with links to their home pages
Year established: 1980
Activities: lobbying, public relations, market research
Chief officers: Lavinia Carey (Director General)
Membership: 36 manufacturers and distributors of pre-recorded video cassettes for sale or rental (chiefly the video divisions of the major US and British film companies)
Publications:
● British Video Association Yearbook: *analysis and statistics covering the video sales and rental markets with detailed statistics on sales, prices, distribution channels, best sellers, regional trends and a demographic breakdown. The rental section also includes data on the source of rentals, frequency of rentals and viewing trends. Additional data available on video equipment, cinema admissions and employment in the industry - annual*

British Waste Paper Association

Address: Alexander House, Station Road, Aldershot, Hants GU11 1BQ
Telephone: +44 1252 344454
Fax: +44 1252 23417
Year established: 1921
Activities: information on the collection of waste paper; produces statistics (simple year on year)
Chief officers: G L Jones (national Secretary)
Structure: president and council, working groups as required
Membership: 69 members, 12 associate member companies
Publications:
● Waste Paper Paste

British Woodpulp Association

Address: 9 Glenair Avenue, Lower Parkstone, Poole BH14 5AD
Telephone: +44 1202 738732
Fax: +44 1202 738747
Publications:
● Annual Report of the British Woodpulp Association: *mainly commentary on the activities of the Association, but a statistical section has data on production, consumption, imports of pulp, paper and board - annual*
● Digest of Woodpulp Import Statistics: *volume import data for wood pulp for paper making coming into the UK. Based on official statistics - monthly*

British Wool Marketing Board

Address: Oak Mills, Station Road, Bradford BD14 6JD
Telephone: +44 1274 882 091
Fax: +44 1274 818 277
Web site: www.britwool.co.uk
Activities: collects, grades and auctions all UK fleece wool; promotes the wool industry; produces statistics on production, prices and marketing costs
Chief officers: Ian M. Hartley (Managing Director), David Nunn (Financial Director)
Membership: 82,000 registered wool producers in the UK
Publications:
● Annual Statistics (British Wool Marketing Board): *annual statistics covering wool production, weight of wool taken up, and the number of registered producers in the UK. Based on a regular survey by the Board - annual*
● Basic Data (British Wool Marketing Board): *brief details of key trends in the wool industry with data on sheep population, registered producers, and production. Based on key results of board surveys - annual*

Building Societies' Association (BSA)

Address: 3 Saville Row, London W1X 1AF
Telephone: +44 171 437 0655
Fax: +44 171 734 6416
Activities: provision of information on mortgages and savings markets
Chief officers: Adrian Coles (Director General)
Membership: 70 member societies
Publications:
● Building Societies Yearbook: *a statistical section includes statistics on housing finance trends with data on mortgages, loans, assets, commitments, repossessions, etc. Based mainly on data collected by the association - annual*
● Building Society Annual Accounts Data: *members' accounts for the current year - annual*
● Directory of Members: *contact details of member societies - annual*

Cable Telecommunications Association (CATA)

Address: POBox 1005, 3950 Chain Bridge Road, Fairfax VA 22030-1005
Telephone: +44 703 691 8875
Fax: +44 703 691 8911
Web site: www.catanet.org
Web site notes: site includes general statistics on the industry
Chief officers: Stephen R. Effros (President), Anne Cowan (Vice President of Communications)

Cable Television Association (CTA)

Address: 5th Floor, Artillery House, Artillery Row, London SW1P 1RT
Telephone: +44 171 222 2900
Fax: +44 171 799 1471
Year established: 1934
Activities: Annual Cable Convention; Convention and

Exhibition (open to anyone, members receive a reduced rate); organises various workshops and seminars; PR information department for industry related queries; freephone telephone line to inform potential customers of cable availability in their area; compilation of cable development statistics from cable operators in UK; totals published in booklet of current cable statistics, updated monthly, available free on request
Chief officers: Richard Woolam (Director General)
Structure: various committees covering programming, telecommunications, engineering, marketing and administration
Membership: 24 full members (major system operators, companies); 46 affiliate members
Publications:
• Cable Companion: *book/database in form of regularly updated ring binder; includes information on cable history and developments, how cable works, legislation and regulation, finance, location, statistics and contracts*
• Cable Statistics: *statistics cover cable household penetration, TV sets and ownership and details of the cable companies - regular*
Notes: Originally established as British Relay Association.

Camping and Outdoor Leisure Association (COLA)
Address: Morrit House, 58 Station Approach, South Ruislip, Ruislip, Middx, HA4 6SA
Telephone: +44 181 842 1111
Fax: +44 181 842 0090
Year established: 1961
Activities: organises the national outdoor leisure trade shows
Chief officers: Mr C R J Southcott (Director), Pat Edwards
Membership: 360 members
Publications:
• COLA Bulletin
• COLA News
Notes: The Association does not produce statistics.

Can Makers
Address: 1 Chelsea Manor Gardens, London SW3 5PN
Telephone: +44 171 349 5024
Fax: +44 171 352 6244
Year established: 1981
Activities: information service; commissions research and publishes the results; occasional papers; produces statistics on can production
Chief officers: Patricia Braun (Head of Information)
Membership: 15 manufacturers of drinks cans and their raw material suppliers
Publications:
• Can Makers Report: *a review of the market for beer and soft drinks cans with a general commentary on trends in the sector. Based on original data collected by the service - biannual*
• Can Makers Update: *can recycling trends and policies*
• Newsletter of the Can Makers' Information Service: *2 p.a.*

Catering Equipment Distributors' Association of Great Britain (CEDA)
Address: 7 Stafford Place, Weston-super-Mare, BS23 2QZ
Telephone: +44 0956 701 248
Fax: +44 0934 641 175
Web site: www.ceda.co.uk
Web site notes: site includes a list of members
Year established: 1972
Activities: annual AGM and conference; information service from secretary (business hours)
Chief officers: Peter W.W. Nisbet (Secretary), J.D. Carter (Chairman), N.J. Howe (Vice Chairman)
Structure: chairman (elected bi-annually), council of 6

members
Membership: 65 member companies
Publications:
• CEDA Handbook: *annual*
• CEDANews: *activities of the Association and news on the industry - quarterly*

Catering Equipment Suppliers' Associations
Address: Carlyle House, 235/237 Vauxhall Bridge Road, London SW1V 1EJ
Telephone: +44 171 233 7724
Fax: +44 171 828 0667
Year established: 1994
Activities: cooperation with similar associations at home and abroad; government lobbying; technical committee plays a leading role in liaising with organisations such as BSI and British Gas, in maintaining standards for commercial catering equipment; carries out detailed studies of EU legislation
Chief officers: Walter G Hill (Chairman), Bryan Whittaker (Director)
Structure: elected council which meets 6 times per year, and 4 standing committees covering technical, exports, statistics and promotions
Membership: 100 members, covering the full range of manufactured and imported food service equipment
Publications:
• Newsletter of the Catering Equipment Suppliers Associations
Notes: Formerly Catering Equipment Importers Association (CEIA). Present association created in October 1994 out of a merger of CEIA and CEMA (Catering Equipment Manufacturers Association).

Chamber of Shipping
Address: Carthusian Court, 12 Carthusian Street, London EC1M 6EB
Telephone: +44 171 417 8400
Fax: +44 171 626 8135
E-mail: postmaster@british-shipping.org
Web site: www.british-shipping.org/
Activities: represents British shipping to the government and internationally; monitors and liaises with other maritime services; acts for industry on policy issues including shipbuilding, safety and environment; collects all shipping statistics, especially figures for industry earnings in the context of the balance of payments
Chief officers: Anthony Cooke (President); Raul Skinner (Vice President); Admiral Sir Nicholas Hunt (Director General)
Membership: 137 members
Publications:
• Annual Review: *annual*
• Making Waves: *quarterly*

Chartered Institute of Marketing (CIM)
Address: Moor Hall, Cookham, Maidenhead, Berks SL6 9QH
Telephone: +44 1628 427 500
Fax: +44 1628 427 499
E-mail: marketing@cim.co.uk
Web site: www.cim.co.uk
Activities: training; professional qualifications; Infomark library and information service; membership services; conferences; accommodation facilities
Publications:
• Connections (Chartered Institute of Marketing): *members newsletter - quarterly*
• Journal of Marketing Management: *academic marketing journal - 8 times p.a.*
• Marketing Business: *covers the activities of the association and marketing trends - 10 times p.a.*
• Marketing Success: *CIM student newsletter and study factsheets - quarterly*
• Marketing Trends Survey: *marketing and sales report*

forecasts (national and regional trends report)
● State of the Market: *CIM's economic report - quarterly*

Chemical Industries' Association

Address: Kings Building, Smith Square, London SW1P 3JJ
Telephone: +44 171 834 3399
Fax: +44 171 834 4469
Publications:
● Activities Report: *annual*
● Basic International Chemical Industry Statistics: *a selection of tables and graphs on the chemical industry in EU and EFTA countries plus USA and Japan. Historical data covers a 30-year period - regular*
● Chemicals: *directory and buyers' guide of chemicals on the UK market*
● Economics Bulletin (Chemical Industries Association): *a regular monitor of the UK chemical industry based on a compilation of data from various sources - 3 p.a.*
● Investment Intentions Survey: *a survey of CIA member company investment intentions covering capital expenditure in the last 12 months and a review of investment intentions for the next year - annual*
● UK Chemical Industry Facts: *a leaflet with basic statistics on the UK chemical industry, including historical data for a ten-year period - annual*

Chilled Food Association (CFA)

Address: 11 Yewfield Road, London NW10 9TD
Telephone: +44 181 451 0503
Fax: +44 181 459 8061
Chief officers: Kaarin Goodburn

Cleaning and Hygiene Suppliers' Association

Address: P O Box 770, Marlow, Bucks, SL7 2SH
Telephone: +44 1628 478 273
Fax: +44 1628 478 286
Activities: education and training
Chief officers: Mr K Baker (Chairman), Mr G Fletcher (General Secretary)
Membership: 200 member companies
Notes: The Association does not produce any statistics or publications.

Computing Services and Software Association (CSSA)

Address: Hanover House, 73-74 High Holborn, London WC1V 6LE
Telephone: +44 171 405 2171
Fax: +44 171 404 4119
E-mail: cssa@cssa.co.uk
Web site: www.cssa.co.uk/cssa
Web site notes: site includes a list of member companies
Membership: 520 companies in the UK based software, IT services and information industries
Publications:
● Annual Report of the Computing Services and Software Association: *includes a survey of business conditions and trends in the computing services sector based on a survey of member companies. Data on their business activities in the previous 12 months, revenues by business sector, profits and outlook - annual*

Confederation of British Industry (CBI)

Address: Centre Point, 103 New Oxford Street, London WC1A 1DU
Telephone: +44 171 379 7400
Fax: +44 171 836 5856
Web site:
www.brainstorm.co.uk/CBI/public/cbinewshomepage.html
Year established: 1965

Activities: statistical publications; conferences; information service; library; representation; export promotion; negotiation services covering pay and conditions of employment
Chief officers: Sir Colin Marshall (President), Adair Turner (Director General)
Membership: 250,000 companies from every sector of UK business, and more than 200 trade associations, employer organisations and commercial associations
Publications:
● CBI Distributive Trades Survey: *a survey of distributive outlets in 22 distribution sectors with data on sales volume, orders, stocks, employment, investment, prices and business expenditure. Based on a CBI survey - monthly*
● CBI News: *a wide range of business topics, including commercial and industrial property, conferences and exhibitions, vehicle leasing, etc. - monthly*
● CBI/Cooper and Lybrand Financial Services Survey: *a survey of the various sectors of the financial services industry. Based on a CBI survey - quarterly*
● Industrial Trends Survey: *trends in orders, output, stocks, expenditure, exports, costs and labour in 44 industry groups covering 1,700 companies - monthly*

Confederation of British Wool Textiles

Address: Merrydale House, Roydsdale Way, Bradford BD4 6SB
Telephone: +44 127 465 2207
Fax: +44 127 468 2293
Chief officers: Mr J. Lambert (Secretary General)

Consumer Credit Trade Association

Address: 1st Floor, Tennyson House, 159-163 Great Portland Street, London W1N 5FD
Telephone: +44 171 636 7564
Fax: +44 171 323 0096
Activities: education and training, advising members on the law, standard contract documemts
Chief officers: John Patrick (Director), Anthony Sharp (Deputy Director)
Membership: 615 member companies
Publications:
● Consumer Credit: *commentary and statistics on consumer credit trends with comparative data for earlier years - six issues per year*

Cosmetic, Toiletry and Perfumery Association Ltd (CTPA)

Address: Josaron House, 5/7 John Princes Street, London W1M 9HD
Telephone: +44 171 491 8891
Fax: +44 171 493 8061
Year established: 1945
Activities: information service for members only; annual conference in the autumn (members only); DTI Joint Venture Cosmoprof Exhibition (open to non-members); ad hoc workshops and seminars; technical and legislative information service (members only)
Chief officers: Marion Kelly (Director General)
Structure: council, commercial committees including packaging, legal environment, perfumery; scientific committees including cosmetic colourants, cosmetic ingredients, hair preparations, health and safety, toxicology, sun products, talc
Membership: 150 companies including manufacturers, raw material suppliers and contract laboratories
Publications:
● Cosmetic, Toiletry & Perfumery Association Annual Report: *personnel; environmental issues; export reviews; report and accounts - annual*

• Cosmetic, Toiletry & Perfumery Association Ltd Newsletter: *monthly*

Council for Travel and Tourism

Address: Vigilant House, 120 Wilton Road, London SW1N IJZ
Telephone: +44 171 630 6686
Fax: +44 171 630 6656
Year established: 1977
Activities: networking and political lobbying
Chief officers: Barry F I Goddard (Executive Director)
Membership: 19 member companies
Notes: The Association does not produce any statistics or publications.

Council of British Cotton Textiles

Address: Reedham House, 31 King Street West, Manchester M3 2PF
Telephone: +44 161 834 7871
Fax: +44 161 833 1740
Year established: 1989
Chief officers: Colin Shone (Secretary)
Membership: companies and industrial groups
Notes: members represent UK interests in EU sectoral bodies in Brussels - Eurocoton and AIUFFASS - and ITMF in Zurich

Council of Mortgage Lenders

Address: 3 Saville Row, London W1X 1AF
Telephone: +44 171 437 0655
Fax: +44 171 734 6416
Publications:
• Compendium of Housing Finance Statistics: *a compilation of historical statistics relating to the UK housing market. Based on various sources - regular*
• Housing Finance: *articles on the UK housing market. A statistical section contains data on house building, mortgages, lending, prices, transactions, etc. - quarterly*

Dairy Industry Federation

Address: 19 Cornwall Terrace, London NW1 4QP
Telephone: +44 171 486 7244
Fax: +44 171 487 4734
Year established: 1933
Activities: information, advice, lobbying, training, national pay and employment negotiations
Chief officers: Mr R.E.K. McKeith (Company Secretary)
Structure: council, committees: strategy, accounts, industrial relations, transport, marketing, scientific advisory, technical policy, environmental
Membership: all major UK dairy companies
Publications:
• Annual Report of the Dairy Trade Federation: *annual*
• Dairy Review: *bi-monthly*
• Training News: *quarterly*

Direct Marketing Association (DMA) (UK) Ltd

Address: Haymarket House, 1 Oxendon Street, London SW1Y 4EE
Telephone: +44 171 321 2525
Fax: +44 171 321 0191
E-mail: dma@dma.org.uk
Web site: www.dma.org.uk
Year established: 1992
Activities: agencies seminar (4 p.a.); legal and commercial advice (members only); information on industry and member companies; industry research (on-site library); leaflets (free)
Chief officers: Colin Lloyd (Chief Executive), Martin Bartle (Communications Manager)
Structure: board, committees: government and legislative affairs, postal affairs, self-regulation, telecommunications, public relations, membership, events
Membership: 670 member companies
Publications:
• Census of the UK Direct Marketing Association: *a census of the direct marketing sector with data on number and size of companies, sales, postings. Based on original research by the Association - annual*
• Direct Marketing Statistics: *a compilation of statistics, from various sources, on direct marketing trends in the UK - annual*
• Who's Who in Direct Marketing: *contact details of DMA members - annual*

Direct Selling Association (DSA)

Address: 29 Floral Street, London WC2E 9DP
Telephone: +44 171 497 1234
Fax: +44 171 497 3144
Web site: www.dsa.org.uk
Year established: 1965
Activities: publishes a full statistical survey annually on direct sales of consumer goods in the UK; produces an annual Code Administrators report; offers legal advice relating to direct sales; organises seminars and conferences
Structure: council, membership services sub-committee, MLM sub-committee, public relations sub-committee, standard of code committee
Membership: 20 associate members; 45 companies
Publications:
• Advice Sheet: *legal and financial advice*
• Code of Business Conduct: *code of conduct between members and their salespeople*
• Consumers Guide to Shopping at Home: *consumer advice on home shopping. Members' responsibilities to consumers*
• Direct Selling in the UK: *an annual report on the direct selling sector with statistics on total value of the sector and a product breakdown. Based on a survey of members - annual*
• Direct Selling in the United Kingdom: *statistics on the value and range of products sold, sales personnel, selling methods, volume of retail sales - annual*

Duck Producers' Association

Address: Imperial House, 15-19 Kingsway, London WC2B 6UA
Telephone: +44 171 240 9889
Fax: +44 171 240 7757
E-mail: bpmf@bpmf.co.uk
Activities: political lobbying
Chief officers: Miss Yvonne Sired (Secretary)
Membership: processors of duck

Electrical Wholesalers' Federation (EWF)

Address: Greener House, 66-68 Haymarket, London SW1Y 4RF
Telephone: +44 171 930 2002
Fax: +44 171 930 4102
Year established: 1914
Chief officers: Nigel Ellis (Director of Administration)
Structure: council, executive, sections
Membership: 48

Electronic Commerce Association (ECA)

Address: Ramillies House, 1-9 Hills Place, London W1R 1AG, UK
Telephone: +44 171 432 2500
Fax: +44 171 432 2501
E-mail: ops@eca.org.uk
Web site: www.eca.org.uk
Web site notes: site includes a list of members
Activities: provides information on electronic commerce, maintains a library
Chief officers: Dr. Roger Till (Chief Executive), Jeremy Arnold

(Manager Electronic Commerce Projects)
Membership: membership covers a wide range of industries and all sizes of company. Members are existing practitioners of Electronic Commerce, companies intending to implement EC systems, and suppliers of products and services
Publications:
• ECA Digest: *summary of the latest industry and Association news - monthly*
• Electronic Commerce and Communications Magazine: *latest news and trends in electronic commerce - 10 times p.a.*

Envelope Makers' and Manufacturing Stationers' Association (EMMSA)
Address: Rushley Walls, Sugar Lane, Whiteley Green, Macclesfield, Cheshire, SK10 5SL
Telephone: +44 1625 572 282
Fax: +44 1625 574 478
Chief officers: Peter J. Middleton (Secretary)
Membership: 30 full members and 18 associated companies
Publications:
• Annual Report: *activities of the Association - annual*
Notes: The Association does produce statistics on the market, but these are normally only available to contributing companies.

Federation of Bakers
Address: 20 Bedford Square, London WC1B 3HF
Telephone: +44 171 580 4252
Fax: +44 171 255 1389
Web site: www.bakersfederation.org.uk
Year established: 1942
Activities: government lobbying, research, public relations, education and training; compiles production statistics on the industry
Chief officers: Mr. A. Casdagli (Director), Mrs. A Lineham (Assistant Director)
Membership: 70 bread manufacturers, wholesalers and retailers; members account for 80% of bread production the UK
Publications:
• Annual Report: *mainly a summary of the activities of the Association and a directory of members but includes some statistics on bread production and consumption by type - annual*
• British Bread Market: *a fact sheet with a short summary of current trends in consumption. Includes statistics on the value and volume of the UK bread market as well as distribution and percentage sales by type etc. - annual*

Federation of Fresh Meat Wholesalers
Address: 227 Central Markets, London EC1A 9LH
Telephone: +44 171 329 0776
Fax: +44 171 329 0653
E-mail: scott@ffmw.demon.co.uk
Year established: 1934
Activities: political pressure group; membership advice and representation; secretariat
Chief officers: Mr P G Scott
Membership: 100 members representing slaughterhouses, meat wholesalers, cutting and processing plants (red meat only)
Notes: The Association does not produce any statistics or publications.

Federation of Ophthalmic and Dispensing Opticians (FODO)
Address: 113 Eastbourne Mews, London W2 6LQ
Telephone: +44 171 258 0240
Fax: +44 171 724 1175

Year established: 1985
Activities: general meetings (2 p.a. June and November); information service
Chief officers: Robert Hughes (General Secretary)
Structure: FODO council, committees: negotiation and Europe, way ahead, education and professional standards, house and finance
Membership: 129 members (dispensing and opthalmic practices)
Publications:
• FODO News: *quarterly*
• FODO Update: *latest developments and decisions in the optical world and in FODO - 5 p.a.*
• Optics at a Glance: *basic data on the opthalmic market including the number of opticians, and spectacle prices. Based on various sources including some survey results from the Federation - annual*

Federation of the Electronics Industry (FEI)
Address: Russell Square House, 10-12 Russell Square, London WC1B 5EE
Telephone: +44 171 331 2000
Fax: +44 171 331 2040
E-mail: feedback@fei.org.uk
Web site: www.fei.org.uk
Year established: 1993
Activities: education and training, sponsorship of international trade shows, lobbying,
Chief officers: Anthony Parish (Director General), John Park (Director Office Products and Furniture)
Structure: Divisions include the Mailing Equipment Manufacturers Organisation (MEMO), the Office Furniture and Filing Manufacturers Association (OFFMA) and the Office Products and Reprographics Association (OPERA)
Membership: over 200 companies in the UK IT, electronics, communications, business equipment and office furniture sectors
Publications:
• CMAIL Newsletter: *digest of current affairs, events and activities in the field of electronic components and manufacturing - bi-monthly*
• EECA Annual Report: *overview of the European electronics industry and statistics, together with information on the work of the European Electronic Component Manufacturers' Association (EECA) - annual*
• Electronic Component Manufacturing in the UK: *lists UK electronic component manufacturers by category - annual*
• European Information Technology Observatory (E.I.T.O): *market analysis and statistical data on the information and communications technology industry in Europe. Includes special studies on technological trends, standardisation, the information society, new networks and applications, and distribution channels - annual*
• FEI Annual Review: *focuses on the developments and achievements of FEI, its members and UK industry, with an in-depth statistical analysis of the UK market - annual*
• FEI EUROBYTES: *FEI news forum covering new developments, current affairs, legislative and regulatory proposals in the areas of standards, environment and trading - monthly*
• Interface: *dedicated platform for communication between FEI industries, government and world commerce; Interface carries news of FEI initiatives and members' activities, along with informative articles, guidelines to legislation and industry innovations - quarterly*
• Mailing Room Equipment: *produced for the Mailing Equipment Manufacturers Organisation (MEMO), a division of FEI, the report analyses the UK market by product - quarterly*
• MEMO FLASH: *regular news update on the UK mailing equipment market from the industry's official representative, MEMO, a division of FEI - monthly*
• OFFCUTS: *focuses on the UK furniture sector with regular*

news updates and market analysis from the Office Furniture and Filing Manufacturers Association (OFFMA), a division of FEI - monthly
- Office Furniture: *produced for the Office Furniture and Filing Manufacturers Association (OFFMA), a division of FEI, the report analyses the UK market by product - quarterly*
- OPERA NOTES: *industry news, views and market analysis from the Office Products and Reprographics Association (OPERA), a division of FEI*
- Overview Report on Semiconductor Annual Statistics: *a summary of the UK and Eire semiconductor market, based on the detailed market statistics and future projections published in the Semiconductor Annual Memorandum - annual*

Federation of the Retail Licensed Trade
Address: 91 University St, Belfast, BT7 1HP, N Ireland
Telephone: +44 1232 327578
Fax: +44 1232 327578
Chief officers: Mr B Gray (General Secretary)

Federation of Wholesale Distributors (FWD)
Address: 1st Floor, Berkeley House, 26 Gildredge Road, Eastbourne, East Sussex BN21 4SA
Telephone: +44 1323 724 952
Fax: +44 1323 732 820
Year established: 1918
Activities: annual conference; annual events Drinksummit (May) and Catersummit (October)
Chief officers: Alan Toft (Director General)
Membership: approx. 450 wholesale companies in the food and drinks sector
Publications:
- Pro Wholesaler: *coverage of the cash and carry and delivered grocery and drinks sector - monthly*

Fertiliser Manufacturers' Federation
Address: Greenhill House, Thorpe Road, Peterborough PE3 6GT
Telephone: +44 1733 332 904
Fax: +44 1733 332 909
E-mail: fma@farmline.com
Activities: provides educational material; collects statistics on overall fertiliser use; produces leaflets offering guidance for farmers
Chief officers: Mrs Jane Salter
Membership: 38 members
Publications:
- Fertiliser Review: *mainly text on the trends in the fertiliser industry but also includes statistics on crop area, consumption of fertilisers, and the use and application rates of fertilisers. Based largely on statistics collected by the association - annual*

Finance and Leasing Association (FLA)
Address: 18 Upper Grosvenor Street, London W1X 9PB
Telephone: +44 171 491 2783
Fax: +44 171 629 0396
Activities: produces monthly, quarterly, and annual consumer and business statistics; also undertakes government lobbying and networking
Chief officers: Martin Hall (Director General), David Lewis (Director of Corporate Affairs)
Membership: 105 full members and 54 associate members in the finance and leasing sector
Publications:
- Annual Report of the Finance and Leasing Association: *mainly commentary on the leasing industry but also includes statistics on consumer credit, motor leasing, etc. Based on returns from member companies - annual*
- Annual Survey of Business Finance: *annual*

Flexible Packaging Association
Address: 4 The Street, Shipton Moyne, Tetbury, Glos GL8 8PN
Telephone: +44 1666 880 406
Fax: +44 1666 880 495
Chief officers: Mr M I H Unwin (Secretary)

Flour Advisory Bureau
Address: 21 Arlington Street, London SW1A 1RN
Telephone: +44 171 493 2521
Fax: +44 171 493 6785
Publications:
- Bread at Work - Market Report: *commentary and statistics on the UK bread market including figures on consumption, speciality breads and traditional bread, catering sales, dietary issues, and consumer preferences and attitudes - annual*

Flowers and Plants Association
Address: Covent House, New Covent Garden Market, London, SW8 5NX
Telephone: +44 171 738 8044
Fax: +44 171 622 5307
E-mail: press-office@flowers.org.uk
Web site: www.flowers.org.uk
Web site notes: site includes a list of the top ten flowers and houseplants by sales value
Activities: promotes sales of cut flowers and indoor plants on behalf of its members; PR, editorial, media liaison, information phone-lines and exhibitions; collates and distributes statistics on all areas of the cut flower and indoor plant markets
Chief officers: Ms Veronica Richardson (Secretary)
Membership: 160 companies and 3 organisations (representing a further 6,000 companies) drawn from across the horticultural industry
Publications:
- Consumer Survey: *a consumer survey on the UK market for cut flowers and house plants. Covers buying behaviour of consumers and market trends in the industry - annual*

Food and Drink Federation
Address: Federation House, 6 Catherine Street, London WC2B 5JJ
Telephone: +44 171 836 2460
Fax: +44 171 836 0580
Year established: 1986
Activities: publishes annual production and sales statistics for specific foods and drinks; also import and export data and employment trends (see under publications); information service for members only
Chief officers: Michael Mackenzie (Director General)
Membership: 35 serviced members and 12 independent associations
Publications:
- Annual Report of the Food and Drink Federation: *annual*
- FDF Annual Statistics
- Feedback

Food from Britain
Address: 123 Buckingham Palace Road, London SW1W 9SA
Telephone: +44 171 233 5111
Fax: +44 171 233 9515
Chief officers: Charlotte Lawson
Publications:
- Annual Report of Food from Britain: *a review of trends in the food industry plus specific data on UK export trends for food. Based on official statistics - annual*

Footwear Distributors Federation

Address: 5 Grafton St, London, W1X 3LB
Telephone: +44 171 647 1500
Fax: +44 171 647 1599
Chief officers: Mr J May (Secretary), A Robinson (Director General)

Furniture Industry Research Association (FIRA International Ltd)

Address: Maxwell Road, Stevenage SG1 2EW
Telephone: +44 1438 313433
Fax: +44 1438 727607
E-mail: fira@ttlchiltern.co.uk
Activities: research, testing, information services, consultancy in relation to design, marketing, manufacturing, quality and the environment; produces statistics on various aspects of the industry via government sources as well as ad-hoc market research, which is sometimes client-based
Chief officers: Mr Hayden Davies (Managing Director), Libby Tooley (Information Services Manager)
Membership: 700 member companies
Publications:
● FIRA Bulletin: *a quarterly update of the annual statistical digest with some statistics on sales, foreign trade, deliveries, and prices. Based largely on official sources - quarterly*
● Furniture Industry in the United Kingdom - A Statistical Digest: *statistics on the UK furniture industry and market covering turnover, sales, deliveries, consumption, foreign trade, prices, and advertising expenditure. Based on official statistics - annual*

Futures and Options Association (FOA)

Address: Aldgate House, 33 Aldgate High Street, London EC3N 1EA
Telephone: +44 171 426 7250
Fax: +44 171 426 7251
Activities: member services including seminars and training, regulatory advice, information and surveys
Chief officers: Sir Michael N H Jenkins (Chairman); Anthony M Belchambers (Chief Executive Officer); Lucinda Campbell-Gray (Director of Operations)
Membership: 200 members representing international banks and financial institutions, commodity trade houses, brokerage houses, fund managers and exchanges
Publications:
● An Option on Your Future: *introduction to futures and options, overview of markets, information on careers available in the industry and list of useful contacts*
● Compliance Officers Manual: *comprehensive and practical overview of the role of a compliance officer working in a derivatives environment*
● FOA Master Netting Agreement for Exchange-Traded (and Related) Transactions: *provides greater legal certainty to firms' netting arrangements*
● Futures and Options: a Forward Look: *summarises views of 107 market participants on likely changes to the industry over the next 5-10 years*
● Guidance on Performance Reporting by Derivative Fund Managers: *guidelines setting out a method for calculating and reporting performance of derivative funds*
● Impact of Technology on the Future and Options Industry: *study of the range of technology issues facing the futures and options industry*
● Managing Derivatives Risk: Guidelines for End-Users: *comprehensive and practical guide to procedures, controls and documentation required for a company using derivative products*
● Series 32 Workbook: *workbook to assist individuals to pass the series 32 examination as required by the US National Futures Association; provides an overview of US futures and options regulation*

● Uniform Give-Up Agreement: *standard agreement accepted for use on all UK and US markets*
● Update: *overview of association's work and current issues - quarterly*

Garden Industry Manufacturers' Association (GIMA)

Address: 225 Bristol Road, Edgbaston, Birmingham B5 7UB
Telephone: +44 121 446 6688
Fax: +44 121 446 5215
Activities: education and training, awards, technical committees; collects statistics on the retail value of garden products in the UK
Chief officers: Adrian Dick (President), Peter Marsh (Director), Maisie Slater (Secretary)
Membership: 60 member companies
Publications:
● Garden Industry Compilation Study
Notes: The Association sponsors the Garden Industry Statistics Compilation Study.

General Products Association

Address: 6 Catherine Street, London, WC2B 5JJ
Telephone: +44 171 836 2460
Fax: +44 171 836 0580
Chief officers: Ms G O'Shea (Secretary)

Gin and Vodka Association of Great Britain (GVA)

Address: Strangford, Amport, Andover, Hampshire SP11 8AX
Telephone: +44 1264 773 089
Fax: +44 1264 773 085
E-mail: 106530.3221@compuserve.com
Year established: 1944
Activities: secretariat deals with queries on the industry; statistics on the industry are produced each year covering production, UK sales and exports
Chief officers: Clive Wilkinson (Director)
Structure: council with approximately 10 members; committees: vodka, trade and public relations
Publications:
● Annual Report of the Gin and Vodka Association of Great Britain: *annual*
● Newsletter of the Gin and Vodka Association of Great Britain: *monthly*
● Returns for the Four Half Years Ended 31st December: *gin and vodka production in the UK plus sales within the UK and exports by country. Based on returns from member producers - annual*

Greeting Card Association

Address: 41 Links Drive, Elstree, Herts, WD6 3PP
Telephone: +44 181 236 0024
Fax: +44 181 236 0024
Year established: 1929
Chief officers: Mr R Cousins (Chief Executive)

Guild of Fine Food Retailers

Address: P O Box 1525, Gillingham, Dorset, SP8 5TA
Telephone: +44 1963 371 271
Fax: +44 1963 371 270
Chief officers: Mr R J Farrand (National Director), Mr John Shepard (Chairman)
Membership: independent fine food retailers
Publications:
● Fine Food Directory: *contact details of fine food retailers - annual*
● Good Food Retailing: *bi-monthly*
Notes: The Association does not produce statistics.

Home Decoration Retailers' Association

Address: P O Box 44, Walsall, W Midlands, WS3 1TD
Telephone: +44 1922 31134
Fax: +44 1922 723 703
Chief officers: Ms Diana Truman, (Company Secretary)
Membership: 766 independent home decoration retailers
Publications:
• Home Decor: *news and trends in home decoration retailing -
7 issues p.a.*
Notes: The Association does not produce statistics.

Horticultural Trades' Association (HTA)

Address: 19 High Street, Theale, Reading, RG7 5AH
Telephone: +44 118 930 3132
Fax: +44 118 932 3453
E-mail: hta@martex.co.uk
Web site: www.martex.co.uk/hta.htm
Year established: 1898
Activities: education, training and research, lobbying;
maintains a database of statistics on retail sales together with
consumer purchase and attitude information
Chief officers: Mr D Gwyther (Director General)
Membership: 1,600 nurserymen, retailers, suppliers and
manufacturers within the ornamental plants industry,
representing over 2,200 outlets
Publications:
• HTA News: *the activities of the Association as well as
up-to-date news, views, events and promotions in the industry
- monthly*
• Membership Directory: *contact details of member
companies - annual*

Hotel and Catering International Management Association (HCIMA)

Address: 191 Trinity Road, London SW17 7HN
Telephone: +44 181 672 4251
Fax: +44 181 682 1707
E-mail: sabine@hcima.org.uk
Web site: hcima.org.uk
Activities: collects statistics on hospitality education
worldwide; CD Rom concerning worldwide hospitality and
tourism trends (WHATT) for hospitality researchers, planners
and students
Chief officers: David Wood (Chief Executive); Tony
Lainchbury (Business Manager)
Membership: 23,000 members in 100 countries worldwide
Publications:
• European Business Link Newsletter: *European legislation,
education and training initiatives with particular reference to
the hospitality industry - monthly*
• Hospitality: *international hospitality management and
educational issues - 10 p.a.*
• Hospitality Yearbook: *a directory of the hotel and catering
industry which includes an Annual Review feature providing
commentary and statistics on market and industry trends over
the previous 12 months - annual*
• Market Forecasts (HCIMA): *brief trends and forecasts for
150 consumer markets covered in more detail in various
market reports throughout the year. Included for each market
sector is a five-year forecast - annual*

Incorporated National Association of British and Irish Millers Ltd

Address: 21 Arlington Street, London SW1A 1RN
Telephone: +44 171 493 2521
Fax: +44 171 493 6785
Year established: 1878
Activities: compiles statistics relating to the UK flour milling
industry, including wheat usage and source, flour production
by type, number of mills, comparison with other EU industries
and limited nutritional information; Flour Help Line (171
4936786); educational material
Chief officers: Mr John Murray (Director General); Mr Philip
Neill (Secretary)
Structure: executive committee, functional committee
covering wheat, industrial relations committee, scientific
committee, food legislation committee
Membership: 32 members (flour millers)

Incorporated Society of British Advertisers (ISBA)

Address: 44 Hertford Street, London W1Y 8AE
Telephone: +44 171 499 7502
Fax: +44 171 629 5355
E-mail: ISBA@dial.pipex.com
Web site: www.isba.org.uk
Activities: represents the interests of British advertisers on
anything connected with marketing and communications;
information service for members
Chief officers: Jackie Marlow (Marketing Services Manager)
Membership: 290 member companies who invest money in
marketing communications, advertising, direct marketing,
sponsorship, sales promotion and exhibitions
Publications:
• Direct Marketing Survey: *ISBA members' direct marketing
activities, organisation of agency relationships and
expenditure - annual*
• Exhibition Expenditure Review: *based on a survey of 2,000
exhibitors in the UK, this report provides details of their
expenditure by venue and by media. Includes an analysis of
both consumer and trade events - annual*

Independent Footwear Retailers' Association (IFRA)

Address: 24 Fairlawn Grove, Chiswick, London, W4 5EH
Telephone: +44 181 994 6259
Fax: +44 181 742 2396
Chief officers: Mr A F Spencer Bolland (Secretary)
Membership: 260 independent footwear retailers
Publications:
• Footprint: *activities of the Association as well as footwear
retailing issues in general - monthly*
Notes: The Association does not produce any statistics.

Independent Healthcare Association (IHA)

Address: 22 Little Russell Street, London WC1A 2HT
Telephone: +44 171 430 0537
Fax: +44 171 242 2681
Activities: political lobbying, representation of sector,
information provision, advisory service to members; compiles
various statistics on healthcare in the independent sector
Chief officers: Barry Hassell (Chief Executive)
Membership: 1,100 member companies
Publications:
• Survey of Acute Hospitals in the Independent Sector: *an
annual review of the private healthcare sector in the UK with
data on turnover, hospital numbers, patients, Figures for the
UK market as a whole and some regional data - annual*

Institute of Brewing

Address: 33 Clarges Street, London W1Y 8EE
Telephone: +44 171 499 8144
Fax: +44 171 499 1156
Web site: www.breworld.com:80/iob/index.html
Year established: 1886
Activities: research, education and training
Membership: 3700 members worldwide, covering the whole
spectrum of disciplines concerned with brewing, distilling,
wine, cider and vinegar making and a wide selection of allied
activities

Publications:
• Ferment: *scientific and technological articles as well as news about both the Industry and the Institute - bi-monthly*

Institute of Grocery Distribution (IGD)
Address: Grange Lane, Letchmore Heath, Watford WD2 8DQ
Telephone: +44 1923 857 141
Fax: +44 1923 852 531
Activities: research, education and training, conferences; compiles statistics on the food industry in the UK and Europe and maintains the IGD Stores Database of over 7,000 grocery stores in the UK
Chief officers: J.A. Beaumont (Chief Executive), Ms J. Denney (Business Director)
Membership: 360 corporate members drawn from every stage of the supply chain
Publications:
• Account Management Series: *detailed analysis of leading gorcery retailers. Includes information on market share, corporate strategy, customer profiles, store portfolio, buying, marketing etc - annual*
• Convenience Tracking Programme: *detailed study of the UK convenience market - annual*
• Distribution Services: *detailed analysis of the UK contract distribution marke - annual*
• European Fact File: *analysis and statistics on the European grocery sector with data on specific countries. Based on various sources - annual*
• Food Industry Statistics Digest: *data on the national economy plus food and retailing consumption and expenditure trends. Trends by market sector, company, region, and retailing and wholesaling. Some historical data and based on various sources - monthly*
• Forecourt Retailing: *detailed analysis and statistics of forecourt retailing in the UK - annual*
• Grocery Market Bulletin: *news items, features, and statistics on the UK grocery trade. Based on various sources - monthly*
• Grocery Retailing: *a report on UK food retailing with data on turnover, retail outlets, consumer trends, and new developments. Based on various sources - annual*
• Grocery Wholesaling: *analysis and statistics on UK grocery wholesaling with data on turnover, outlet numbers, employment, etc - annual*
• IGD Stores Directories: *series of four directories with information on all multiple, co-operative and independent chain stores with sales araes over 3,000 sq ft - annual*
• Retail Distribution: *detailed analysis and statistics of the distribution activities of major retailers in the UK - annual*
• Supplier Opportunities in the Food Service Sector: *detailed analysis of the food service sector in the UK with emphasis on opportunities for suppliers. The three main sub-sectors covered are Hotels, Public Houses and Fast Food - annual*

Institute of Packaging
Address: Sysonby Lodge, Nottingham Rd, Melton Mowbray, Leics, LE13 ONU
Telephone: +44 1664 500 055
Fax: +44 1664 641 64
E-mail: info@iop.co.uk
Year established: 1947
Activities: education; training
Chief officers: Mr Gerry Berragan (Chief Executive), Mrs Moira Hart (Marketing Manager)
Membership: 3600 members
Publications:
• Panorama: *6 p.a.*
Notes: The Association does not produce statistics.

Institute of Petroleum (IP)
Address: 61 New Cavendish St, London W1M 8AR
Telephone: +44 171 467 7100

Fax: +44 171 255 1472
E-mail: ip@petroleum.co.uk
Web site: www.cityscape.co.uk/users/eq61
Web site notes: site includes a brief summary of the Retail Marketing Survey in the form of a press release
Year established: 1913
Activities: a wide variety of meetings held at branch level; technical conferences; full library information services (available also to non-members at increased charge); desk research; on-line searches
Chief officers: Ian Ward (Director General), John Hayes (Technical Director)
Structure: council, committees: oil industry liaison, technical, non-technical; discussion groups
Membership: 8,000 individual members and 400 corporate members
Publications:
• IP Information Folder: *information on what the IP does and information on membership*
• IP Statistics Folder: *a folder with data sheets containing summary information on the key indicators relating to the UK petroleum sector. Based mainly on the Institute's own data - regular*
• Petroleum Review: *advances, trends, changes and events throughout the international oil industry. In addition to the magazine, regular surveys look at sectors such as retail marketing and independent bulk storage - monthly*
• Ten-Year Cumulation Booklet: *historical statistics covering the main indicators in the UK petroleum sector - regular*
• UK Petroleum Industry Statistics: Consumption and Refinery Production: *statistics on petroleum deliveries, production and end-uses with most tables covering the latest two years. A brief commentary supports the data collected by the Institute - annual*
• UK Retail Marketing Survey: *commentary and statistics on the UK retail market for petrol with data on sales, sites, company performance, new outlets - regular*
• World Oil Statistics: *various fact sheets on world petroleum trends including data on reserves, production, consumption, trade - regular*
• World Statistics: *international statistics covering reserves, production, refinery capacity, consumption, tanker tonnage and the oil trade. Based on various sources - annual*

Jewellery Distributors' Association of the United Kingdom (JDA)
Address: Federation House, 10 Vyse Street, Birmingham B18 4BR
Telephone: +44 121 236 2657
Fax: +44 121 236 3921
E-mail: jda.secretariat@teg.co.uk
Web site: www.teg.co.uk/teg/jda/index.html
Chief officers: Lynn Snead (Secreatry)
Membership: wholesalers, distributors, importers and exporters of precious and fashion jewellery, watches, clocks and other items to the Jewellery and Allied Trades
Notes: Affiliated to the British Jewellery and Giftware Federation.

Library Association (LA)
Address: 7 Ridgmount Street, London WC1E 7AE
Telephone: +44 171 636 7543
Fax: +44 171 436 7218
E-mail: info@la-hq.org.uk
Web site: www.la-hq.org.uk
Activities: information on employment related issues, education and training
Structure: Council, Standing Committees and Sub-Committess
Publications:
• Library Association Record: *news sections and features in all*

sectors, including public, health, academic, industry, business and the media - monthly

Mail Order Traders' Association (The)

Address: 100 Old Hall Street, Liverpool L3 9TD
Telephone: +44 151 227 4181
Fax: +44 151 227 2584
Year established: 1941
Activities: finance; personnel and training; consumer protection; appropriate information provided on request
Chief officers: K M Tamlin (Director General)
Membership: 74 members
Publications:
• Code of Practice: *code of practice and list of members*

Malt Distillers Association of Scotland

Address: 1 North Street, Elgin, Moray IV30 1UA
Telephone: +44 1343 544 077
Fax: +44 1343 548 523
Year established: 1874
Activities: minimum wage negotiator; information services for members; liaison with UK government departments on matters concerning production, including environmental legislation, C&E, distillery animal feeds
Chief officers: W.P. Mennie
Membership: 23 member companies covering 94 Pot Still Malt distilleries in Scotland
Publications:
• Bulletin: *2 p.a.*

Maltsters Association of Great Britain

Address: 31b Castlegate, Newark-on-Trent, NG24 1AZ
Telephone: +44 1636 700781
Fax: +44 1636 701836
Year established: 1827
Structure: executive committee, five standing committees
Membership: 23 member companies: Sales maltsters, selling malt on the open market, and Brewer and Distiller malters, who make malt for brewing and distilling in house

Management Consultancies Association (MCA)

Address: 11 West Halkin Street, London SW1X 8JL
Telephone: +44 171 235 3897
Fax: +44 171 235 0825
E-mail: mca@mca.org.uk
Web site: www.mca.org.uk
Web site notes: site includes a directory of members with links to members' home pages
Activities: government liaison, media promotion; publishes reports, pamphlets, directories and other literature
Publications:
• Annual Report (Management Consultancies Association): *a statistical section gives details of the turnover of the management consultancy sector plus data on the number of clients for UK consultants, consultants employed and a turnover breakdown by service area. Based on a survey of the Association's members - annual*

Market Research Society (MRS)

Address: 15 Northburgh Street, London EC1V 0AH
Telephone: +44 171 490 4911
Fax: +44 171 490 0608
Year established: 1946
Activities: annual conference (usually in March); education and training leading to diploma of the Market Research Society; education courses; information services; statistics; publications
Structure: council, committees: professional standards, publications, training and education, conferences, field and

international; regional and interest groups
Membership: 7,500 individual members
Publications:
• Journal of the Market Research Society: *quarterly*
• Market Research Abstracts: *marketing and advertising research; statistics; psychology; economics; sociology; other fields relevant to market research - bi-annual*
• Market Research Abstracts: *abstracts from about 40 English language journals, covering all fields of marketing and advertising research. The emphasis is on the theory and techniques of marketing and advertising, with sections on topics such as survey techniques, advertising and media research, new product development, etc. - semi-annual*
• Market Research Abstracts: *bi-annual*
• Market Research Society Yearbook 19..: *details about the society; useful addresses; code of conduct; list of members; organisations providing market research services in the UK - annual*
• Orgs Book 19..: *information on organisations and individuals providing market research services. Includes information on turnover, services, personnel, etc - annual*
• Research: *appointments, companies, issues, news, letters - monthly*
• Research Magazine: *10 p.a.*

Metal Packaging Manufacturers' Association (MPMA)

Address: 19 Elmshott Lane, Slough SL1 5QS
Telephone: +44 1628 605 203
Fax: +44 1628 665 597
Activities: government lobbying, industry standards; compiles and analyses statistics on total industry sales
Chief officers: Mr R.S. Davis (Director)
Membership: 27 manufacturers of light metal containers, closures and components
Publications:
• Annual Review of the Metal Packaging Manufacturers' Association: *an annual report with a review of sales of packaging materials over the year. Includes a breakdown of end-user sectors and sales by type of packaging. Based primarily on returns from members - annual*

Motor Cycle Industry Association (MCI)

Address: Starley House, Eaton Road, Coventry CV1 2FH
Telephone: +44 1203 227 427
Fax: +44 1203 229 175
Year established: 1910
Activities: organises International Motorcycle Show (NEC, annual); collects statistics on new motorcycle registrations by capacity, style and country, and publishes general trade information (free to members)
Chief officers: Mr T. Waterer (Executive Director), Mr F. Finch (Marketing Services Manager)
Structure: board of directors elected annually with an honorary post of president
Membership: approx. 135 companies comprising motorcycle manufacturers and importers, factors, motorcycle marketing services, off road retailers and associated companies in the motorcycle industry
Publications:
• Annual Report of the Motor Cycle Industry Association (MCI): *annual*
• MCI Statistics: *covers the United Kingdom motor cycle industry. Includes data on production, number of vehicles in use, registrations by capacity, registrations by type and imports-exports - monthly*
• Monthly Statistics Booklet: *covers new motorcycle registrations by capacity, style and country and general trade information - monthly*

Motor Cycle Retailers' Association

Address: 201 Great Portland Street, London W16AB
Telephone: +44 171 580 9122
Chief officers: Kevin Kelly (Director), Sue Robinson (Public Relations Manager)
Membership: 700 retail motorcycle dealers representing 75% of all new motorcycle sales
Notes: The Motor Cycle Retailers Association is a division of the Retail Motor Industry Federation.

Music Industries' Association

Address: PO Box 249, London W4 5EX
Telephone: +44 1753 511 550
Fax: +44 1753 539 200
Web site: www.mia.org.uk
Year established: 1893
Activities: organises trade fairs and public shows, compiles statistics on retail sales of musical instruments and associated products
Chief officers: Bob Kelley (Secretary General), Linda Mitchell (Membership Secretary)
Membership: 250 musical instruments manufacturers and retailers
Publications:
• Music World: *monthly*

Music Publishers' Association Ltd

Address: 18-21 York Buildings, London WC2N 6JU
Telephone: +44 171 839 7779
Fax: +44 171 839 7776
Publications:
• Summary of Printed Music Sales: *results from a survey by the Association of printed music sales in the UK and abroad. Figures for the latest year and comparative data from the previous year - annual*

National Association of Catering Butchers

Address: 217 Central Markets, London EC1A 9LH
Telephone: +44 171 489 0005
Fax: +44 171 248 4733
Chief officers: A G Gordon (Executive Director); C J Gadsden (Secretary General)
Membership: 79 members
Publications:
• Guidelines for Inspections of Catering Butchery Plants
Notes: The Association does not produce statistics.

National Association of Cider Makers

Address: 6 Catherine Street, London WC2B 5JJ
Telephone: +44 171 836 2460
Fax: +44 171 836 0580

National Association of Estate Agents

Address: Arbon House, 21 Jury Street, Warwick CV34 4EH
Telephone: +44 1926 496 800
Fax: +44 1926 403 958
E-mail: naea@pipex.com
Chief officers: Hugh Dunsmore-Hardy (Chief Executive)
Membership: 9,500 member companies
Publications:
• Estate Agent: *industry news and trends - every six weeks*
• Market Trends (National Association of Estate Agents): *a monthly analysis of housing market trends with data on sales, prices, mortgages, etc. Based largely on members' returns, but also includes data from other sources - monthly*

National Association of Health Stores

Nr Devizes
Address: Wayside Cottage, Urchfont, Cuckoo Corner, Wiltshire, SN10 4RA
Telephone: +44 1380 840 736
Fax: +44 1380 840 133
E-mail: nahs1@aol.com
Chief officers: Mr Richard Mistlin (Secretary), Sue Maconie (Secretariat)
Membership: 400 member companies
Publications:
• Health Store News: *developments in health store retailing*
Notes: The Association does not produce statistics.

National Association of Master Bakers

Address: 21 Baldock Street, Ware, Herts SG12 9DH
Telephone: +44 1920 468 061
Fax: +44 1920 461 632
E-mail: dsmith@dial.pipex.com
Year established: 1887
Activities: annual conference; information service for members, covering legal and business matters
Chief officers: David Smith Chief (Executive)
Structure: 60 local associations each elect representatives to serve on one of 9 regional councils, the regional councils elect members to serve on one of 3 main national committees (financial, parliamentary, training and education), the president is elected for one year at the AGM (held in May)
Membership: 2,000 bakery businesses as full members, 430 associate members (companies and individuals)
Publications:
• Bakers Review: *monthly*
• Handbook & Buyers' Guide: *annual*

National Association of Shopkeepers (NAS)

Address: Lynch House, 91 Mansfield Road, Nottingham NG1 3FN
Telephone: +44 115 947 5046
Fax: +44 115 950 9139
Year established: 1942
Activities: provides advice and/or information on any issue relevant to the retail distributive trade to association members and to persons who want to purchase or operate a business; legal advice; insurance; representation in Wages Councils
Chief officers: T D Hiley (National President) ; A Widdowson-Toone (General Secretary); W O Booth (National Treasurer)
Membership: ca. 3,000 retail and service businesses
Publications:
• Newsletter of the National Association of Shopkeepers (NAS)

National Dried Fruit Trade Association (NDFTA)

Address: Kemp House, 152-160 City Road, London EC1V 2NP
Telephone: +44 171 253 9421
Fax: +44 171 250 0965

National Federation of Fishmongers

Address: Pisces, London Road, Feering, Colchester, Essex CO5 9ED
Telephone: +44 1376 571391
Fax: +44 1222 383303
Chief officers: John Adams (General Secretary)
Membership: 600 fishmongers
Publications:
• Fish Trader: *quarterly*
Notes: The Association does not produce statistics.

National Federation of Meat and Food Traders

Address: 1 Belgrove, Tunbridge Wells, Kent TN1 1YW
Telephone: +44 1892 541 412
Fax: +44 1892 535 462
Publications:
• Meat Trader: *market news, legislation information and trade fair news covering the meat and poultry sector - monthly*

National Market Traders' Federation

Address: Hampton House, Hawshaw Lane, Hoyland, Barnsley, South Yorks S74 0HA
Telephone: +44 1226 749 021
Fax: +44 1226 740 329
Year established: 1899
Activities: information, representation, legal advice, insurance
Chief officers: D E Feeny (General Secretary); J Burton (Marketing Director)
Membership: 26,000 retailers
Publications:
• Federation News: *6 p.a.*
• Federation World: *annual*
Notes: The Association does not produce statistics.

National Pharmaceutical Association (NPA)

Address: Mallinson House, 40-42 St Peter's Street, St Albans, Herts AL1 3NP
Telephone: +44 1727 832161
Fax: +44 1727 840858
E-mail: npa@cix.co.uk
Web site: www.npa.co.uk
Year established: 1921
Activities: business services, insurance, training, public relations, advisory service on legal, pharmaceutical, business and financial topics; library for members, conference on Drugs in Society and a telephone information service
Structure: board of directors elected by members
Membership: 7,500 members
Publications:
• Supplement: *monthly*

National Retail Trade Centre

Address: 5-9 St Nicholas St, Worcester, WR1 2RU
Telephone: +44 1905 61310
Fax: +44 1905 21501
Year established: 1974
Chief officers: Mrs B L Davis (Chief Executive), Mrs G I Davison (Operations Director)

National Tyre Distributors' Association (NTDA)

Address: Elsinore House, Buckingham Street, Aylesbury, Bucks HP20 2NQ
Telephone: +44 1296 395933
Fax: +44 1296 88675
E-mail: ntda@ndirect.co.uk
Web site: www.ntda.co.uk
Web site notes: site includes a directory of members
Year established: 1930
Activities: bi-annual conference held abroad and in the UK; general telephone enquiry service; tyre wholesalers group supply line; monthly market monitor for members only
Chief officers: Richard Edy (Director)
Structure: national association led by executive council and president; 8 working committees; association divided into 9 regions throughout the UK
Membership: 400 individual companies representing some 2,800 tyre retail outlets and fast fit centres
Publications:
• Directory of Members and Yearbook: *information on the Association and contact details of member companies - annual*
• Market Monitor: *statistics of sales of new car tyres, retreads,*

exhausts and batteries - monthly
• NTDA News: *news and trends in the UK tyre market - monthly*

Newspaper Publishers' Association

Address: 34 Southwark Bridge Road, London SE1 9EC
Telephone: +44 171 928 6928
Fax: +44 171 928 2067
Year established: 1906
Activities: organises meetings; training; examinations; research and study groups; services include statistical collection, information, library and negotiation of pay and conditions of employment
Chief officers: David Pollock (Director)
Membership: 12 corporate members, representing national morning, evening and Sunday newspapers (including their Manchester editions)

Newspaper Society (NS)

Address: Bloomsbury House, 74-77 Great Russell Street, London WC1B 3DA
Telephone: +44 171 636 7014
Fax: +44 171 631 5119
E-mail: lynne@newspapersoc.org.uk
Web site: www.newspapersoc.org.uk
Web site notes: site includes detailed data on the UK regional newspaper publishing industry, including information on the following: top 20 regional press publishers; all regional press publishers ranked by weekly circulation; major regional press acquisitions; regional press births and deaths; advertising expenditure by medium; readership profiles, etc.
Year established: 1836
Activities: the Association maintains an industry database of regional media and marketing information in the UK (the database can be accessed without charge from the Internet)
Chief officers: Chris Stanley (Marketing Director)
Membership: regional and local newspaper publishers representing 1,400 regional, daily and weekly titles
Publications:
• Reaching the Regions: *structure of the regional press, readership, advertising statistics, training matters, employment trends, newsprint consumption, production and printing technology, multimedia, press freedom and regulatory issues - annual*

Paper Federation of Great Britain

Address: Papermakers House, Rivenhall Road, Swindon, Wiltshire SN5 7BD
Telephone: +44 1793 886 086
Fax: +44 1793 886 182
E-mail: info@paper.org.uk
Web site: www.paper.org.uk
Web site notes: site includes statistics on the UK paper and board industry including consumption, production, imports and exports, number of companies, etc.
Activities: lobbying and representation, education and training, trade and environment, communications and statistics, employee relations, international links with EU and CEPI
Structure: Headquarters in Swindon, with offices in London and Bury
Membership: represents large and small companies, covering over 90% of paper manufacturing in the UK
Publications:
• Annual Survey of Capacity: *capacity trends in the industry over the last three years and forecasts for the next three years - annual*
• Annual Survey of Energy Use and Costs: *a detailed annual review of energy trends in the paper industry and cost trends over a number of years - annual*
• Fact Card: *brief data on the paper industry based on various*

sources - annual
● Industry Key Figures: *basic monthly figures on production, consumption, and a brief analysis - monthly*
● Market Statistics (Paper Federation of Great Britain): *detailed monthly statistics on the paper industry based on various sources. Includes statistics on production, consumption, sales, foreign trade - monthly*
● Paper Federation of GB Annual Review: *review of the year plus list of members - annual*
● Paper, Naturally: *review of the papermaking process and the industry's use of raw materials and resources*
● Pulp, Paper and Board Mills: *map showing location of all pulp, paper and board mills (federated and non-federated) within the UK*
● Reference Statistics: *detailed statistics on the paper industry and market with figures over the last ten years. Based on various sources - annual*
● Who Makes What ?: *a directory of the UK paper mills and their products.*
Notes: Runs The Pulp and Paper Information Centre, which provides Government departments, media, schools and the public with authoritative facts and information about pulp and paper.

Periodical Publishers' Association (PPA)

Address: Queens House, 28 Kingsway, London WC2B 6JR
Telephone: +44 171 404 4166
Fax: +44 171 404 4167
E-mail: info1@ppa.co.uk
Web site: www.ppa.co.uk
Web site notes: site includes comprehensive statistics on magazines in the UK, including the top 100 magazines by circulation, total sales over a six year review period and distribution by type of outlet, profitability, etc.
Chief officers: Phil Cutts (Statistics)
Membership: 200 members representing over 80% of magazines published in the UK
Publications:
● Handbook of Statistics on the Magazine Industry: *various statistics on the magazine and journals markets in the UK collected from various sources - annual*

Pet Care Trust (PTIA)

Address: Bedford Business Centre, 170 Mile Road, Bedford MK42 9TW
Telephone: +44 1234 273 933
Fax: +44 1234 273 550
Year established: 1985
Activities: media information service; members' information service; staff training programmes; legal helpline (members only); conferences; trade fairs; seminars
Chief officers: Barry Huckle (Secretary)
Structure: board of directors, livestock advisory panel, working groups: dog grooming, kennels, medicines, cat litter, pesticides, education
Membership: 1,400 members
Publications:
● Pet Care magazine: *consumer magazine - bi-monthly*
● UK Pet Care Industry Year Book and Buyers Guide: *association information and membership lists; listings of manufacturers, wholesalers, importers, exporters, livestock suppliers, dog groomers, boarding kennels, catteries, brand names and product categories - annual*

Pet Food Manufacturers' Association (PFMA)

Address: Suite 1/2, 12-13 Henrietta Street, London WC2E 8LH
Telephone: +44 171 379 9009
Fax: +44 171 379 8008/3898
E-mail: pfma-uk@dial.pipex.com
Year established: 1970
Activities: represents the prepared pet food industry;

compiles statistics on pet population, sales of pet food in the UK and other pet food market data by food type
Chief officers: Ms Lyn Francis Roberts, Ms Barbara Shaw, Ms Nyree Connell, Ms Margaret Gordon
Membership: 69 member companies
Publications:
● PFMA Profile: *statistics covering the UK pet food market including market size for prepared pet foods and some data on pet ownership. Some commentary accompanies the data which is based on the Association's own survey - every few years*

Pizza, Pasta and Italian Food Association

Address: 29 Market Place, Wantage, Oxon OX12 8BG
Telephone: +44 1235 772 207
Fax: +44 1235 769 044
Activities: annual awards and exhibition; information service to members; undertakes research on an occasional basis for specific statistical projects
Chief officers: Jim Winthip (Director)
Structure: retail and supplier committees
Membership: 1,250 manufacturers, retailers, suppliers and foodservice outlets
Publications:
● Pizza, Pasta and Italian Food Magazine: *news and market information, special features and reports, profiles, new products, suppliers' guide - bi-monthly*
Notes: The Association does not produce regular industry statistics.

Private Label Manufacturers' Association

Address: Lindum Lodge, Dean Lane, Cookham Dean, Berks, SL6 9AH
Telephone: +44 1628 471 535
Fax: +44 1628 890 779
Chief officers: Mr H Burnham (Chairman)

Proprietary Articles Trade Association (PATA)

Address: 5 Caxton Way, Watford Business Park, Watford, Herts WD1 8UA
Telephone: +44 1923 211 647
Fax: +44 1923 211 648
Year established: 1896
Activities: monitors resale price maintenance for OTC products on behalf of individual manufacturers
Chief officers: G Harraway (Director)
Membership: 9,500 members
Publications:
● Newsletter: *the activities of the Association - annual*

Proprietary Association of Great Britain (PAGB)

Address: Vernon House, Sicilian Ave, London WC1A 2QH
Telephone: +44 171 242 8331
Fax: +44 171 405 7719
E-mail: pagb@pagb.org.uk
Year established: 1919
Activities: provides commercial, legal and regulatory guidance to industry; administers PAGB Code of Standards of Advertising Practice; promotes cooperation between manufacturers; liaises with government on industry regulation; regulates advertising on OTC; provides information service; also produces statistics on the OTC medicine market size and conducts research on consumer attitudes and behaviour towards self-medication
Chief officers: Sheila Kelly (Executive Director), Michael Baker (Head of Commercial Affairs)
Structure: executive committee is main policy board, commercial affairs committee (reports to executive), other committees: GP project team, pharmacy plan group and consumer working party

Membership: 70 full company members, 60 associate company members
Publications:
• Annual Report: *deals with major issues rather than financial statements - annual*
• Bulletin: *the activities of the Association and trends in the OTC market - monthly*
• Everyday Healthcare: *consumer study of self-medication in Britain - annual*
• Information or Communication: *consumer study of television advertising - annual*
• Monitor: *news on legislation affecting the OTC market - quarterly*
• OTC Directory: *reference guide to products available without prescription - annual*
• OTC Update: *trends in the the UK OTC market - monthly*

Publishers' Association (PA)
Address: 19 Bedford Square, London WC1B 3HJ
E-mail: mail@publshers.org.uk
Web site: www.publishers.org.uk
Year established: 1896
Activities: AGM (members), annual conference (members and non-members), trade fairs (members and non-members), education exhibitions (members and non-members); a wide selection of publications on copyright, network agreement, production and distribution, UK market, electronic publishing, export market
Chief officers: Sir Roger Elliott (President), Clive Bradley (Chief Executive and Secretary)
Structure: PA council, international division, educational publishers council, council of academic and professional publishers, many committees, groups and working parties
Membership: 180 companies
Publications:
• Annual Report of the Publishers Association, The: *annual*
• Book Industry Performance Summary
• Book Trade Yearbook: *comprehensive collection of statistics and commentary on the market for books - annual*
• Book Trade Yearbook: *a commentary plus detailed statistics on the industry structure, markets, output, turnover, imports, exports, distribution, prices, consumer and institutional expenditure. Statistics cover a number of years and are based on various sources - annual*
• CAPP Brief: *newsletter for academic, business and professional publishers*
• Directory of Publishing
• EPC Brief: *newsletter for educational publishers*
• Publishers Association Brief: *newsletter for members*

Radio, Electrical and Television Retailers' Association (RETRA)
Address: RETRA House, St John's Terrace, 1 Ampthill Street, Bedford MK42 9EY
Telephone: +44 1234 269 110
Fax: +44 1234 269 609
Year established: 1942
Activities: annual conference (April); regional and local meetings (quarterly); legal and business advice
Chief officers: F. Round (Chief Executive), S. Kurpita (Information Executive)
Structure: council (directors), management committee, action teams
Membership: 1,300 member businesses
Publications:
• Alert: *monthly*
• Annual Report of the Radio, Electrical and Television Retailers Association (RETRA): *annual*
• Code of Practice
• Members List

• Safety in Electrical Testing
• Yearbook: *annual*

Retail Motor Industry Federation (RMI)
Address: 201 Great Portland Street, London W1N 6AB
Telephone: +44 171 580 9122
Fax: +44 171 580 6376
E-mail: press@rmif.co.uk
Web site: www.rmif.co.uk
Membership: represents thousands of businesses which distribute, service and repair new and used cars, commercial vehicles and motorcycles, petrol retailers, vehicle recovery operators and those who provide specialist engineering services
Publications:
• Engine and Repair: *technical magazine providing information and practical advice on everything from diagnostics to MOT testing equipment. - bi-monthly*
• Forecourt: *news on the retail petrol trade - monthly*
• Monthly Statistics (RMI): *monthly statistics on new car sales, in volume terms, with a breakdown into general sales and sales to companies - monthly*
• Motor Retailer: *in-depth coverage of the latest trends in motor retailing. It includes the RMI's own news, views, profiles and features on all areas of the trade from the largest franchised dealers and motorcycle retailers to independent garages and cherished numbers specialists - monthly*
• New Car Sales: *details of annual car sales, in volume terms, with data for specific regions and counties of the UK. Sales split between total sales and sales to companies with comparisons with sales in the previous year - annual*
• Recovery Operator: *news, views, profiles and special reports looking at the key issues facing the recovery industry - quarterly*

SATRA Technology Centre
Address: SATRA House, Rockingham Road, Kettering, Northants NN16 9JH
Telephone: +44 1536 410 000
Fax: +44 1536 410 626
E-mail: admin@satra.co.uk
Year established: 1919
Activities: research and information services (including statistical) for footwear, furniture and clothing; compiles statistics on production, number of employees and wage rates in world footwear markets
Chief officers: R.H. Turner (Deputy Chief Executive), Dr Ron E. Whittaker (Chief Executive)
Structure: governed by board of directors
Membership: 1,200 member companies in 65 countries
Publications:
• Footwear Business International: *trends and statistics on international footwear markets - monthly*
• Footwear Digest International: *not really an abstracting journal, but includes digests from other publications; includes sections on world industry, market information and company news - 6 times a year*
• How Shoes are Made
• How to Fit Footwear
• SATRA Bulletin: *monthly*
• Settling Footwear Complaints

Scotch Whisky Association
Address: 17 Half Moon Street, London W1Y 7RB
Telephone: +44 171 629 4384
Fax: +44 171 493 1398
E-mail: enquiries@swa.org.uk
Web site: www.scotch-whisky.org.uk
Web site notes: site includes a directory of members with full contact details, including e-mail addresses and hyperlinks to their sites. It also gives comprehensive information on all the

members' brands and statistics on sales volume and value for selected world markets
Membership: 69 distillers, blenders, brand owners, brokers and those engaged in the wholesale and export trade in Scotch Whisky. Members represent over 95% of the Scotch Whisky market
Publications:
• Questions and Answers; Spirit of Scotland
• Statistical Report: *data on whisky production and exports, whisky stocks, duties paid, worldwide sales - annual*
• Statistical Report (Scotch Whisky Association): *statistics on the whisky industry including production, exports, stocks, and duty paid. Figures for latest year and earlier years based almost entirely on Central Government data - annual*

Scottish Dairy Association
Address: Phoenix House, South Avenue, Clydebank G81 2LG
Telephone: +44 141 951 1170
Fax: +44 141 951 1129
Web site: www.efr.hw.ac.uk/SDA
Year established: 1988
Chief officers: Jim Murphy (President)
Membership: representative body for the milk processing industry in Scotland

Scottish Grocers' Federation
Address: 222-224 Queensferry Rd, Edinburgh, EH4 2BN
Telephone: +44 131 343 3300
Fax: +44 131 343 6147
Year established: 1918
Activities: produces statistical reports; collates data on the Scottish and UK grocery trade; information service; VAT, payroll and accountancy services; shop-related services (site assessment, site analysis, shopfitting, layout)
Chief officers: Lawrie Dewar (Chief Executive)
Membership: 600 individual members; 2,800 corporate members
Publications:
• Retail News: *newsletter - monthly*
• Retail Outlook: *members yearbook - annual*
Notes: The Federation is the Scottish branch of the Institute of Grocery Distribution (IGD) and is affiliated to the International Federation of Grocers' Associations (IFGA).

Scottish Licensed Trade Association
Address: 10 Walker Street, Edinburgh EH3 7LA
Telephone: +44 131 225 5169
Fax: +44 131 220 4057
Year established: 1880
Chief officers: EW Ridehalgh (Secretary)

Silk Association of Great Britain Ltd
Address: 5 Portland Place, London W1W 3AA
Telephone: +44 171 636 7788
Fax: +44 171 636 7515
E-mail: sagb@pipex.dial.com
Year established: 1970
Activities: compiles statistics on imports and exports of silk raw materials, yarns, fabrics and garments
Chief officers: A Gaddum (Chairman)
Membership: 35 member companies
Publications:
• Serica: *newsletter - monthly*
• Silk Education Services

Snack, Nut and Crisp Manufacturers' Association
Address: Swiss Centre, 10 Wardour Street, London W1U 3HG
Telephone: +44 171 439 2567
Fax: +44 171 439 2673

Publications:
• Sales Data (Snack, Nut and Crisp Manufacturers Association): *sales data on various snack products, including crisps, savoury snacks and nuts, based on returns from member companies - monthly*

Soap and Detergent Industry Association (SDIA)
Address: PO Box 9, Hayes Gate House, 3-5 Clair Road, Hayes, Middlesex UB4 0JD
Telephone: +44 1444 450 884
Fax: +44 1444 450 951
Year established: 1939
Chief officers: Mrs Jan Lewis
Membership: 70 manufacturers and marketers of consumer, institutional or industrial soap or detergent products
Publications:
• Fact Sheet on the Market (Soap and Detergent Industry Association): *basic statistics on market trends with data on production, consumption, foreign trade. Based on a summary of Association surveys and official statistics - regular*
• SDIA News

Society of Film Distributors Ltd (SFD)
Address: 22 Golden Square, London W1R 3PA
Telephone: +44 171 437 4383
Fax: +44 171 734 0912
Year established: 1915
Activities: cooperates with all other film organisations and government agencies where distribution interests are involved
Chief officers: J R C Higgins MBE (President), D C Hunt (General Secretary)
Membership: 12 distribution companies including all major distribution companies and several independant companies in the UK
Notes: The Association does not produce any statistics or publications on the industry.

Society of Motor Manufacturers and Traders Limited (SMMT)
Address: Forbes House, Halkin Street, London SW1X 7DS
Telephone: +44 171 235 7000
Fax: +44 171 235 7112
Telex: 21628
E-mail: smmt@dial.pipex.com
Web site: www.autoline.org:80/smmt.org.html
Year established: 1902
Activities: statistical analyses
Chief officers: Ernie Thompson (Chief Executive), Ted Patterson (ADS department)
Publications:
• Monthly Statistical Review (SMMT): *latest figures on production, new registrations (by make and country of origin), imports, exports etc - monthly*
• World Automotive Statistics: *covers the world automotive industry, including production, registration, exports of motor vehicles, etc - annual*

Solvents Industry Association
Address: 57 Mymms Drive, Brookmans Park, Hatfield, Herts AL9 7AE
Telephone: +44 1707 655 461
Fax: +44 1707 655 461
Year established: 1973
Activities: government lobbying, information, advice and services within the industry on technical, environmental and legal matters; collects and circulates statistics relating to the industry
Chief officers: Dr T H Farmer (General Secretary)

Tableware Distributors' Association

Address: c/o HG Stephenson Ltd, Kennerley Works, 161 Buxton Rd, Stockport, Cheshire, SK2 6EQ
Telephone: +44 161 483 6256
Fax: +44 161 483 2385

Telecommunications Industry Association (TIA)

Address: 20 Drakes Mews, Crown Hill, Milton Keynes MK8 0ER
Telephone: +44 1908 645 000
Fax: +44 1908 632 263
Year established: 1984
Activities: organises conferences and meetings; training and exams; information service
Chief officers: Alan P Cobb (Director General), Mrs Diane Read (Office Manager)
Membership: 300 network service providers, customer equipment manufacturers and installation, maintenance and consultancy service companies
Publications:
• TIA Digest: *6 p.a.*
• TIA Userlink: *3 p.a.*
• TIA Yearbook: *annual*
Notes: The Association does not produce statistics.

Timber Trade Federation

Address: 26-27 Oxendon Street, London SW1Y 4EL
Telephone: +44 171 839 1891
Fax: +44 171 930 0094
Publications:
• Yearbook of Timber Statistics: *detailed statistics on production, consumption, foreign trade, stocks, of various types of timber and wood products. Most tables give figures for the latest two years available. Based primarily on official statistics - biennial*

Tobacco Manufacturers' Association (TMA)

Address: 55 Tufton Street, London SW1P 3QF
Telephone: +44 171 544 0108
Fax: +44 171 544 0117
Web site: www.thetma.org.uk
Web site notes: site includes some basic statistics on the UK market for tobacco and the importance of the industry to the British economy
Activities: produces statistics on employment, tax, price, sales distribution, market share, prevalence, clearances, production, sales, consumption, revenue, expenditure (all based on government or industry sources)
Chief officers: David Swan (Chief Executive), John Carlisle (Executive Director/Industry Affairs)
Publications:
• Tobacco Facts: *published every few years, the report presents commentary and statistics on the tobacco market with tables on market trends, employment, sponsorship, advertising, prices, and taxes. Compiled from various sources - regular*
Notes: The Association also publishes a series of briefing papers on issues affecting the industry, i.e. advertising, sponsorship, taxation, etc.

United Kingdom Association of Frozen Food Producers

Address: 1 Green Street, Grosvenor Square, London W1Y 3RG
Telephone: +44 171 629 0655
Fax: +44 171 499 9095
Chief officers: Ms K.L. Cheesman, Mrs K. Cooke
Notes: Member of the Federation of Associations of EU Frozen Food Producers (FAFPAS), based in Brussels.

United Kingdom Dairy Association

Address: c/o National Dairy Council, 5-7 John Princes Street, London, WIM 0AP
Telephone: +44 171 499 7822
Fax: +44 171 491 0529
Activities: serves as the United Kingdom National Committee of the International Dairy Federation (IDF) and represents U.K. dairying interests at other international bodies
Chief officers: I. Wakeling (Secretary), Dr D. Stewart (Chairman)
Membership: dairy trade and producers as well as academic and research establishments

Wholesale Confectionery and Tobacco Trade Alliance Ltd

Address: 17 Stoneyfield, Farnham, Surrey GU9 8DU
Telephone: +44 1252 727 769
Fax: +44 1252 727 779
Year established: 1892
Activities: compilation of industry data; information service; exhibitions, conferences and trade education
Membership: 160 full members; 120 associate members (manufacturers, wholesalers and agents)
Publications:
• Wholesale Confectionery and Tobacco Alliance Yearbook: *contains a brief overview of the UK markets for confectionery, soft drinks, salty snacks, batteries and cigarettes. Includes data on market size, market shares, manufacturers, distribution, etc. Also includes a directory of members - annual*

Wine and Spirit Association of Great Britain and Northern Ireland

Address: Five Kings House, 1 Queen Street Place, London EC4R 1XX
Telephone: +44 171 248 5377
Fax: +44 171 489 0322
Year established: 1830
Activities: general circulars and enquiry service; specialist reports covering waste management, trade marks, product recall, EU legislation
Chief officers: Peter Lewis (Director)
Structure: executive committee, council
Membership: 300 companies: importers of wine and spirits, manufacturers of wines (including 20+ companies and national associations outside the UK)
Publications:
• Annual Review: *role of the association, market report and analysis and review of the association's activities - annual*
• Checklists (Covering Labelling, Importing, Bottling, and Packaging): *guide to EU legislation on wine and spirits*
Notes: The Association does not produce statistics.

URUGUAY

Article Numbering Association of Uruguay (CUNA)

Centro Uruguayo de Numeración de Artículos
Address: Agr. German Barbato 1363/903, 11200 Montevideo
Telephone: +598 2 983 534
Fax: +598 2 931 382
E-mail: cuna@adinet.com.uy

Association of Importers and Warehouse Wholesalers

Asociación de Importadores y Mayoristas de Almacén
Address: Rincón 454, Montevideo
Telephone: +598 2 956 103
Fax: +598 2 960 796/921 739
Membership: importers and warehousers

Association of Manufacturers and Importers of Tobacco and Cigarettes
Asociación de Fabricantes Importadores de Tabacos y Cigarrillos
Address: Asunción 1159, Montevideo
Telephone: +598 2 940 710/05/18
Fax: +598 2 943 991
Chief officers: Luis Gianlopi (President)
Membership: cigarette and tobacco producers and exporters

Chamber of Agroindustries and Exports
Cámara Mercantil de Productos del País
Address: Av. Gral. Rondeau 1908 piso 1, Montevideo
Telephone: +598 2 940 644
Fax: +598 2 940 673
E-mail: cmpp@davanet.com.uy
Year established: 1891
Chief officers: Simón Pierre Berkowitz (President), Christian Bolz (Vice President), Heinz Rippe (Secretary), Gonzalo González Piedras (General Director)
Structure: Directive Committee with President, Vice President, Secretary and Treasurer
Membership: The following trade associations conform the Chamber: Uruguayan Association of Cereal Producers, Wool and Skin Consignees and Sellers Association, Millers Union Committee, Uruguayan Association of Wool Exporters, Noodle Producers Union Committee, Cereals and Oilseeds Exporters Centre, Balanced Feed Producers Union, Hide Exporters and Traders Union, Wool Exporting Industrialists Association, Wool Consignees and Auctioneers of Uruguay, Association of Grain Traders, Livestock Consignees Association, Uruguayan Chamber of Seeds, Exporters of Agricultural Products of Uruguay
Notes: The member associations can be contacted through the Chamber.

Knitwear Clothing Manufacturers' Association of Uruguay (PIU)
Asociación de Fabricantes de Prendas de Tejidos de Punto del Uruguay
Address: Cámara de Industrias del Uruguay, Av Gral Rondeau 1655, 11000 Montevideo
Telephone: +598 2 923 402
Fax: +598 2 922 567
Year established: 1974
Activities: promotes relations with Argentina, Brazil, Paraguay and other countries to study business opportunities for its members; close contact with pan-regional and international clothing and trade bodies; information service; market reports; collects on a regular basis statistical data on national retail sales, imports, exports, etc.; promotional and advertising campaigns; organises and participates in trade fairs at a national and international level
Structure: Directive Committee elected by members
Membership: 50 member companies from the clothing sector: hand-knitted, industrial knitwear, wool, cotton, synthetic fibre, fine hairs
Publications:
● PIU Bulletin (Boletín PIU): *information and documentation in relation to trade matters and sector related news - regularly*

Newspapers' Association of Uruguay
Asociación de Diarios del Uruguay
Address: Río Negro 1308 - piso 6, Montevideo
Telephone: +598 2 907 651
Fax: +598 2 905 852
Chief officers: Dr Daniel Scheck (President), Enrique Arzúa (Director)

Pharmaceutical Products Association (CEFA)
Cámara de Especialidades Farmacéuticas y Afines
Address: Plaza de la Cagancha 1342, 2° piso, esc 9, Montevideo
Telephone: +598 2 913 395/985 156
Fax: +598 2 916 816
Membership: pharmaceutical companies

Union of Exporters of Uruguay
Unión de Exportadores del Uruguay
Address: Rinón 454, piso 2, oficina 222, Montevideo
Telephone: +598 2 970 105/06
Fax: +598 2 961 117
E-mail: ueu@mti6000.zfm.com
Web site: www.zfm.com/ueu
Year established: 1967
Activities: analyses economic, financial, administrative and legal matters related to exports; information service; promotes the foreign investment; import-export information databases with economic and financial profiles of foreign importing firms; Market Surveys on products in different countries; courses and seminars; close contacts with other chambers, specially on foreign trade matters; collects statistics on foreign trade
Chief officers: Daniel Soloducho (President)
Structure: Board of Directors from a range of associations
Membership: exporters

Uruguay Book Association
Cámara Uruguaya del Libro
Address: Juan D Jackson 1118, 11200 Montevideo
Telephone: +598 2 415 732
Fax: +598 2 411 860
Chief officers: Mr H Raviolo, MS AC Rodriguez (Director)

Uruguay Industrial Association (CIU)
Cámara de Industrias del Uruguay
Address: Av. Libertador Lavalleja1672, 11100 Montevideo
Telephone: +598 2 923 402/915 000
Fax: +598 2 922 567
E-mail: sipe@ciu.com.uy
Web site: www.ciu.com.uy

Uruguayan Association of Travel Agencies (AUDAVI)
Asociación Uruguaya de Agencias de Viajes
Address: San José 942, piso 2, oficina 201, Montevideo
Telephone: +598 2 912 325/326
Fax: +598 2 921 972
Chief officers: José Rodrigo Marimón (President), Mónica W de Raij (Manager)
Membership: 100 travel agencies, 20 adherent members (hotels, car rental companies, etc)

USA

Adhesive and Sealant Council, Inc. (ASC)
Address: 1627 K Street, NW, Suite 1000, Washington, DC 20006
Telephone: +1 202 452 1500
Fax: +1 202 452 1501
Web site: www.ascouncil.org

Advertising Council
Address: 11th Floor, 261 Madison Avenue, New York- NY 10016
Telephone: +1 212 922 1500
Fax: +1 212 922 1676
E-mail: adcouncil@prodigy.com

Web site: www.adcouncil.org
Membership: advertising agencies, media, corporations and foundations
Notes: The Advertising Council is a private, non-profit organisation of volunteers who conduct advertising campaigns for the public good. The Council is the largest source of public service advertising

Advertising Research Foundation (ARF)
Address: 641 Lexington Avenue, New York, NY 10022
E-mail: email@arfsite.org
Web site: www.amic.com/arf
Year established: 1936
Activities: research
Chief officers: James Spaeth (President)
Membership: represents more than 350 advertisers, advertising agencies, research firms, media companies, educational institutions and international organisations

Agricultural Retailers' Association (ARA)
Address: Suite 110, 11701 Borman Drive, St Louis, MO 63146
Telephone: +1 314 567 6655
Fax: +1 314 567 6808
E-mail: amills@agretailerassn.org
Web site: www.agretailerassn.org
Year established: 1954
Chief officers: Paul E Kindinger (President and CEO)
Structure: permanent staff, board
Membership: 1,000 dealers, manufacturers and suppliers of fertilisers
Publications:
• Connections (Agricultural Retailers' Association): *bi-monthly*
• Membership Directory and Buyer's Guide: *annual*

Air and Waste Management Association
Address: Box 2861, 3rd Floor, 1 Gateway Center, Pittsburgh, PA 15222
Telephone: +1 412 232 3444
Fax: +1 412 232 3450
E-mail: tpedder@awma.org
Web site: www.awma.org
Year established: 1907
Activities: provides a neutral forum for discussion of environmental management issues; compiles statistics; sponsors educational programs
Chief officers: Martin Rivers (Executive Vice President)
Structure: permanent staff; chapters; board; committees
Membership: 17,000 environmental and technical professionals
Publications:
• Journal of the Air and Waste Management Association: *technical journal covering air pollution control and waste management issues - monthly*

Air Conditioning and Refrigeration Institute
Address: Suite 425, 4301 N Fairfax Drive, Alington VA 22203
Telephone: +1 703 524 8800
Fax: +1 703 528 3816
E-mail: ari@dgsys.com
Web site: www.ari.org
Web site notes: site includes statistics on factory shipments of air conditioning equipment
Chief officers: Clifford H. "Ted" Rees, Jr. (President), Dave Martz (Vice President of Administration and Statistics)
Membership: manufacturers and of air conditioning and refrigeration products
Publications:
• ARI Statistical Profile: *annual*
• International Statistical Profile: *annual*
• News Release of the Air Conditioning and Refrigeration Institute: *commentary and statistics on US shipments of air conditioners and heat pumps. Based on the Institute's own survey - monthly*

Air Transport Association
Address: 1301 Pennsylvania Avenue, NW, Suite 1100, Washington, DC 20004-1707
Telephone: +1 202 626 4257
Fax: +1 202 626 4081
E-mail: rfcrum@air-transport.org
Web site: www.air-transport.org
Web site notes: site includes financial highlights of member companies as well as various statistics on air transport in the US, including passenger transport, cargo traffic, fuel costs and consumption, etc.
Year established: 1936
Activities: coordinates industry and government safety programs, and serves as a focal point for industry efforts to standardise practices and enhance the efficiency of the air transport system
Structure: councils, committees, subcommittees and task forces, composed of experts from member airlines, which are formed to address industry issues
Membership: 21 U.S. airline members and 3 foreign flag carrier associate members
Publications:
• Air Transport: *significant facts and figures drawn from all areas of the industry including financial data, domestic and international traffic statistics for both cargo and passenger operations, safety data, individual airline and aircraft operating statistics etc. - annual, June*
• Air Travel Survey: *current trends in air travel demographics, including a breakdown by purpose of trip, the number of trips taken annually and destination data - annual*
• Origin and Destination Survey Report (Air Transport Association): *statistics for airline scheduled service that show passenger trip origin and destination and volume of traffic by routing in terms of carriers and transfer points*
• Preliminary Scheduled Cargo Traffic Statistics: *preliminary monthly statistics on cargo, freight, express and mail trends transported by US airlines - monthly*
• Preliminary Scheduled Passenger Transport Statistics: *preliminary statistics on passenger travel trends on internal US routes and international routes - monthly*
• State of the US Airline Industry: *recent trends for US air carriers in the areas of aircraft orders/deliveries, air fares, capacity, costs, employment, load factors, net income, regulations, taxes and traffic*

Aircraft Electronics' Association (AEA)
Address: PO Box 1963, Independence, MO 64055
Telephone: +1 816 373 6565
Fax: +1 816 478 3100
E-mail: aea@microlink.net
Web site: www.aeaavnews.org/
Year established: 1957
Activities: promotes uniform regulations; collects technical data; professional certification; compiles statistics
Chief officers: Monte Mitchell (President)
Structure: permanent staff
Membership: 1,000 electronic aviation equipment and systems companies
Publications:
• Avionics News: *monthly*

American Accounting Association (AAA)
Address: 5717 Bessie Drive, Sarasota, Florida 34233-2399
Telephone: +1 941 921 7747
Fax: +1 941 923 4093
E-mail: AAAhq@aol.com

Web site: www.rutgers.edu/Accounting/raw/aaa
Year established: 1916

American Advertising Federation (AAF)

Address: 1101 Vermont Avenue. NW, Washington - DC 2005
Telephone: +1 800 999 2231
E-mail: aaf@aaf.org
Web site: www.aaf.org
Membership: 50,000 members including corporate advertisers, agencies, media companies, suppliers and academia

American Apparel Contractors' Association (AACA)

Address: PO Box 720693, Atlanta, GA 30358
Telephone: +1 404 843 3171
Fax: +1 404 256 5380
E-mail: sourcing@aaca.com
Web site: www.apparelsource.org

American Apparel Manufacturers' Association

Address: Suite 301, 2500 Wilson Boulevard, Arlington, VA 22201
Telephone: +1 703 524 1864
Fax: +1 703 522 6741
Year established: 1962
Activities: operates the Apparel Foundation; compiles statistics
Chief officers: Larry Martin (President)
Structure: permanent staff; board of directors; committees
Membership: 434 manufacturers of men's, women's and children's clothing; 381 suppliers of fabric, equipment, services
Publications:
• American Apparel Manufacturers' Association Newsletter: *monthly*
• Apparel Industry Economic Profile: *biennial*
• Apparel Plant Wages Survey: *annual*
• Apparel Sales/Marketing Compensation Survey: *annual*
• College Directory: *biennial*
• Committee Manual: *biennial*
• Directory of Members and Associate Members: *annual*
• Focus: An Economic Profile of the Apparel Industry: *an overview of the industry is followed by detailed statistics on production, retail sales, deliveries, employment, financial trends, etc, Relatively long runs of historical data. Based on various sources - annual*
• Import Digest: *annual*
• Personnel Policy Survey: *biennial*
• Research Notes: *periodical*
• Technical Advisory Committee Bulletin: *periodical*
• Washington Letter: *every 3 weeks*

American Association of Advertising Agencies (AAAA)

Address: 405 Lexington Avenue, New York, NY 10174-1801
Telephone: +1 212 682 2500
Fax: +1 212 682 8391
E-mail: aaaa@commercepark.com
Web site: www.commercepark.com/AAAA
Activities: provides an information service for members on the agency business, products and services, markets and industries and current advertising procedures and regulations; also provides information on foreign media and agencies as well as international statistical data
Chief officers: O. Burtch Drake (President and CEO), Kathy Galvin (Board Secretary)
Membership: 575 agencies representing 75 percent of all agency-produced national US advertising

American Association of Exporters and Importers (AAEI)

Address: 11 West 42nd Street, New York NY 10036
Telephone: +1 212 944 2230
Fax: +1 212 382 2206
E-mail: membership@aaei.org
Web site: www.aaei.org
Year established: 1921
Membership: 1,000 exporters, importers, distributors and manufacturers of a broad spectrum of products, including chemicals, electronics, machinery, footwear, autos/parts, food, household consumer goods, toys, speciality items, textiles and apparel. In addition, membership includes many organisations serving the international trade community including customs brokers, freight forwarders, banks, attorneys, insurance firms and carriers
Publications:
• International Trade Alert: *recent developments affecting international business as well as the latest news in the international trade sphere - weekly*
• Weekly Textile and Apparel Quota Report: *status of all textile quotas, embargoes, visas and bilateral agreements - weekly*

American Association of Meat Processors (AAMP)

Address: Box 269, One Meating Place, Elizabethtown, PA 17022
Telephone: +1 717 367 1168
Fax: +1 717 367 9096
E-mail: aamp@aamp.com
Web site: www.aamp.com
Year established: 1939
Activities: government lobbying, education and training, publishes a range of bulletins on the industry
Chief officers: Stephen F Krut (Executive Director)
Structure: permanent staff; state groups; board; committees
Membership: 1,800 medium-sized and smaller meat, poultry and food business: slaughterers, packers, processors, wholesalers, in-home food service business, retailers, deli and catering operators, and industry suppliers
Publications:
• AAmplifier (American Association of Meat Processors): *newsletter - bi-weekly*
• American Association of Meat Processors Membership Directory: *semi-annual*

American Automobile Manufacturers' Association (AAMA)

Address: Suite 900, 1401 H Street NW, Washington DC 20005
Telephone: +1 202 326 5500
Fax: +1 202 326 5567
Web site: www.aama.com
Web site notes: site includes comprehensive statistics on the automotive market in the USA
Year established: 1903
Activities: compiles statistics; conducts research programs; monitors regulations
Chief officers: Andrew H. Card, Jr., (President and CEO)
Structure: comprises three operating units: Government Affairs, Engineering Affairs and Law Divisions
Membership: Chrysler Corporation, Ford Motor Company, General Motors Corporation
Publications:
• Directory of Motor Vehicle Related Organisations: *a guide to transportation related associations containing addresses, telephone numbers and descriptive information - annual*
• Economic Indicators (AAMA): *quarterly data on motor vehicle production, sales and registrations - quarterly*
• Motor Vehicle Facts and Figures: *comprehensive statistical publication of the U.S. motor vehicle industry which covers production, sales, registrations, ownership, usage and various other industry and economic data - annual*

• Motor Vehicle Identification Manual: *photographs of Chrysler, Ford and GM passenger cars, multipurpose vehicles and light trucks designed primarily for law enforcement and accident investigation agencies - annual*
• World Motor Vehicle Databook: *statistics covering the production, assembly, registrations, imports, exports of vehicles by make, model, engine capacity in various countries. Data available can vary from country to country. Summary world information is also included and some tables give historical data - annual*

American Bakers' Association (ABA)

Address: 1350 I Street, NW , Suite 1290, Washington, DC 20005-3305
Telephone: +1 202 789 0300
Fax: +1 202 898 1164
E-mail: 102135.1520@compuserve.com
Web site: www.sosland.com/aba/
Chief officers: Paul C. Abenante (President and CEO), Nancy Render (Communications Manager)
Membership: wholesale baking industry

American Bankers' Association (ABA)

Address: 1120 Connecticut Avenue NW, Washington, DC 20036
Telephone: +1 202 663 5000
Fax: +1 202 296 9258
E-mail: custserv@aba.com
Web site: www.aba.com
Year established: 1875
Activities: conducts educational programs and serves as a clearing house for information; carries out research; legal action, legislative liaison; lobbying
Chief officers: Don Ogilvie (Executive Vice President)
Structure: permanent staff; board; committees
Membership: 11,000 commercial banks and trust companies
Publications:
• Bank Card Industry Survey Report: *in-depth statistical profile of bank cards in the U.S. Includes data on combined VISA and MasterCard statistics by type on 5 years of credit and debit card business - annual*
• Statistical Information on the Financial Services Industry (Factbook): *includes statistics on the following: trends in payment systems and retail delivery channels; capital markets; financial sector capital, earnings, and structure; economic trends and demographics; government credit operations; international banking; sources and uses of funds; trends in assets, liabilities, financial flows of non-financial sectors and consumer attitudes - annual*

American Booksellers' Association

Address: 828 S Broadway, Tarrytown, NY 10591-5112.
Telephone: +1 800 637 0037/914 591 2665
Fax: +1 914 631 8391
E-mail: aba-info@bookweb.org
Web site: www.ambook.org:80/aba/
Year established: 1900
Activities: works for improvement and maintenance of favourable trade conditions and sound bookseller/publisher relations; conduces seminars; sponsors promotional campaigns
Chief officers: Bernard E. Rath
Membership: independents, speciality, franchise, college and university stores, chains and others with a special interest in bookselling
Publications:
• ABA Book Buyers' Handbook: *trade, discount and return prices of publishers - annual*
• ABA Newswire: *weekly*
• American Bookseller: *monthly*
• Basic Book List: *biennial*

• Book Buyers Handbook: *annual*
• Newswire: *weekly*
• Sidelines Directory: *biennial*

American Brush Manufacturers' Association (ABMA)

Address: 1900 Arch Street, Philadelphia, PA 19103-1498
Telephone: +1 215 564 3484
Fax: +1 215 564 2175
E-mail: assnhqt@netaxs.com
Web site: www.abma.org
Activities: publishes a newsletter as well as statistics on the industry

American Chemical Society

Address: 1155 16th Street NW, Washington DC 20036
Telephone: +1 202 872 4600
Fax: +1 202 872 4615
E-mail: webmaster@acs.org
Web site: www.acs.org
Year established: 1876
Activities: scientific and educational society; conducts research; monitors legislation; continuing education programs
Structure: permanent staff; board; committees; local groups
Membership: 144,500 chemists and chemical engineers
Publications:
• Chemical and Engineering News: *scientific, technical, educational, business, and governmental aspects of chemistry - weekly*

American Council of Life Insurance (ACLI)

Address: 1001 Pennsylvania Avenue NW, Washington DC 20004 - 2599
Telephone: +1 202 624 2000
Fax: +1 202 624 2319
Web site: www.acli.com
Membership: 557 legal reserve life insurance companies
Publications:
• Life Insurance Fact Book: *statistics on life insurance purchases, ownership of schemes and benefit payments, insurance company reserves, income, assets, obligations, number of establishments, etc. Historical data and mainly based on surveys by the Council - biennial*

American Crop Protection Association

Address: Suite 400, 1156 15th Street NW, Washington DC 20005
Telephone: +1 202 296 1585
Fax: +1 202 463 0474
E-mail: webmaster@acpa.org
Web site: www.acpa.org/
Web site notes: site includes various statistics on pesticide sales, exports etc.
Year established: 1933
Activities: government relations; regulatory oversight
Chief officers: Jay J Vroom (President)
Structure: permanent staff; board; committees; councils
Membership: 75 agricultural chemical manufacturers, formulators and distributors of agricultural crop protection and pest control products
Publications:
• Bulletin: *irregular*
• Growing Possibilities: *quarterly*

American Dietetic Association

Address: 216 W. Jackson Boulevard, Chicago, Illinois 60606
Telephone: +1 312 899 0040
Fax: +1 312 899 1979
E-mail: webmaster@eatright.org.

Web site: www.eatright.org
Year established: 1917
Membership: 70,000 members (75 percent registered dietitians (RDs) 4% dietetic technicians)

American Egg Board (AEB)

Address: 1460 Renaissance Drive, Park Ridge, Illinois 60068
Telephone: +1 847 296 7043
Fax: +1 847 296 7007
E-mail: aeb@aeb.org
Web site: www.aeb.org
Web site notes: site includes statistics and commentary on the market for eggs in the US
Chief officers: Lou Raffel (President), Joanne Ivy (Senior Vice President Industry and Market Development)
Publications:
• American Egg Board Annual Report: *activities of the Association over the past year as well as accounts - annual*

American Electronics' Association

Address: 1225 I Street, NW Suite 950, Washington, DC 20005
Telephone: +1 202 682 9110
Fax: +1 202 682 9111
E-mail: CSC@aeanet.org
Web site: www.aeanet.org
Year established: 1943
Chief officers: William Archey (President)
Membership: 3,000 electronics and information companies, from semiconductors and software to mainframe computers and telecommunication systems
Publications:
• AEA Directory: *annual*
• American Electronics Association Update: *newsletter - bi-monthly*

American Farm Bureau Federation

Address: 225 Touhy Avenue, Park Ridge, IL 60068
Telephone: +1 312 399 5700
Fax: +1 312 399 5896
E-mail: davel@fb.com (Media Relations)
Web site: www.fb.com
Year established: 1919
Chief officers: Dean R Kleckner (President), C. David Mayfield (Secretary)
Structure: permanent staff, board
Membership: 4 million family farms and state farm bureaus
Publications:
• Farm Bureau News: *weekly*

American Feed Industry Association (AFIA)

Address: Suite 1100, 1501 Wilson Boulevard, Arlington, VA 22209
Telephone: +1 703 524 0810
Fax: +1 703 524 1921
E-mail: mailafia@tomco.net
Web site: www.afia.org
Year established: 1909
Activities: compiles statistics
Chief officers: David A Bossman (President), Barbara Estridge (Vice President/Secretary)
Structure: permanent staff; state groups; board; committees
Membership: 740 manufacturers of formula feed and suppliers
Publications:
• Membership Directory and Buyer's Guide: *detailed information on over 700 member companies - annual*

American Fibre Manufacturers' Association (AFMA)

Address: 150 Seventeenth Street, NW, Suite 310, Washington, DC 22036

Telephone: +1 202 296 6508
Fax: +1 202 296 3052
E-mail: Afma@aol.com
Web site: www.apparelnet.com:80/afma/index.html
Year established: 1933
Membership: U.S. producers of more than 90 percent of domestic production of manufactured fibers, filaments and yarns

American Forest and Paper Association (AF&PA)

Address: 2nd floor, 1250 Connecticut Avenue, Washington, DC 20036
Telephone: +1 202 463 2700
Fax: +1 202 463 2785
E-mail: Info@afandpa.ccmail.compuserve.com
Web site: www.afandpa.org
Year established: 1932
Activities: collects statistics; monitors government regulation and legislation; acts as government liaison
Chief officers: Henson Moore (President and CEO)
Structure: permanent staff; regional groups
Membership: represents member companies engaged in growing, harvesting, and processing wood and wood fibre, manufacturing pulp, paper, and paperboard products from both virgin and recycled fibre, and producing engineered and traditional wood products
Publications:
• Newsprint Division Annual Statistical Summary: *detailed statistics on newsprint supply and demand. A compilation from various sources with historical runs of data in many tables - annual*
• Paper, Paperboard, Pulp Capacity: *industry capacity by product grade with additional data on the geographical distribution of capacity and world capacity. Historical data in many tables - annual*
• Statistical Roundup (American Forest and Paper Association (AFC): *summary statistics on timber production, shipments, consumption, foreign trade, and employment. Mainly based on data compiled by the Association - monthly*
• Statistics of Paper, Paperboard and Wood Pulp: *detailed statistics on the paper and pulp sectors including production, consumption, trade, and employment. Many tables have long runs of historical data - annual*

American Frozen Food Institute (AFFI)

Address: 2000 Corporate Ridge, Suite 1000, MacLean VA 22102
Telephone: +1 703 821 0770
Fax: +1 703 821 1350
E-mail: affi@pop.dn.net
Web site: www.affi.com
Web site notes: site includes various statistics on the U.S. frozen food market including retail sales by type, food service value sales and distribution by channel, etc.
Membership: members account for approximately 90 percent of the total production of frozen food in the U.S.
Publications:
• AFFI Letter: *covers legislative and regulatory issues affecting the frozen food industry. AFFI Letter also reports on AFFI activities in distribution, international trade, research and technical services, conventions and industry trends - biweekly*
• Cold Storage Report: *information on frozen products from the U.S. Department of Agriculture's (USDA) monthly report on stocks in cold storage - monthly*
• Frozen Food Pack Statistics: *production statistics for various frozen foods with data over a five-year period - annual*
• Frozen Food Report: *government relations, research and technology, distribution and logistics and international trade - annual*
• Year 2000 Forecast: Impact Assessment of New Processing

Technologies Upon the Frozen Food Industry: *future trends in packaging and processing techniques - irregular*

American Furniture Manufacturers' Association (AFMA)

Address: PO Box HP-7, High Point, NC 27261
Telephone: +1 910 884 5000
Fax: +1 910 884 5303
Year established: 1984
Activities: compiles statistics; conducts market research; conducts employee development programs
Chief officers: Douglas L Brackett (Executive Vice President)
Structure: permanent staff; board
Membership: 350 furniture manufacturers
Publications:
• Membership Directory: *annual*

American Gas Association (AGA)

Address: 1515 Wilson Boulevard, Arlington VA 22209
Telephone: +1 703 841 8400
Fax: +1 703 841 8406
E-mail: webmaster@aga.com
Web site: www.aga.com/
Publications:
• Gas Facts: *statistics on gas reserves, supply, storage, distribution, transmission, consumption, customers, sales, revenues, appliances, prices, finance and employment. Detailed statistics for the latest year and summary statistics for 20-25 years - annual*
• Gas Statistics: *summary statistics on gas supply and demand with figures for the latest period and earlier periods - quarterly/monthly*
• Residential Natural Gas Market Surveys: *an annual survey of consumption trends, costs, prices, bills in the household gas market - annual*

American Hardware Manufacturers' Association (AHMA)

Address: 801 North Plaza Drive, Schaumburg, IL 60173-4977
Telephone: +1 847 605 1025
Fax: +1 847 605 1093
E-mail: ahma@ahma.org
Web site: www.ahma.org
Chief officers: William P. Farrell (President and CEO), Ruth E. Arredia (Executive Assistant), Jack Kelleher (Communications)

American Health and Beauty Aids Institute (AHBAI)

Address: 24th Floor, 401 North Michigan Avenue, Chicago, IL60611
Telephone: +1 312 644 6610
Fax: +1 312 527 6658
E-mail: ahbi@sba.com
Web site: www.ahbai.org
Web site notes: site includes a directory of members
Year established: 1981
Activities: monitors for legislation and regulation and acts as lobbying group; provides information and education for business development
Chief officers: Geri Duncan Jones (Executive Director)
Structure: board; committees; permanent staff
Membership: 18 companies that manufacture ethnic hair care and beauty related products
Publications:
• Membership Directory: *annual*

American Hotel and Motel Association (AHMA)

Address: Suite 600, 1201 New York Avenue NW, Washington, DC 20005
Telephone: +1 202 289 3100
Fax: +1 202 289 3199
E-mail: comments@ahma.com
Web site: www.ahma.com/
Web site notes: site lists the world's 50 largest hotel franchisors, owners/operators and associations (also lists the number of properties operated)
Year established: 1910
Activities: conducts training courses and promotional programs; compiles statistics
Chief officers: William P.Fisher (President and CEO)
Structure: permanent staff; committees; board
Membership: over 10,000 hotel and motel operators/owners
Publications:
• Directory of Hotel and Motel Systems: *annual*

American Institute of Food Distribution

Address: 28-12 Broadway, Fair Lawn, NJ 07410
Telephone: +1 201 791 5570
Fax: +1 201 791 5222/201 794 7648
E-mail: btodd@foodinstitute.com
Web site: www.foodinstitute.com and www.register.com/food
Web site notes: includes the on-line version of the Food Institute Report
Year established: 1928
Activities: collects statistics; acts as information service for industry
Chief officers: Rick Pfaff (President), Mary Ann Rizzitello (Information and Research)
Structure: permanent staff; board
Membership: 2,500 companies in all sectors of the food distribution system
Publications:
• Food Business Mergers and Acquisitions: *annual*
• Food Institute Report: *news on the U.S. food industry including market reports, mergers and acquisitions, industry statistics and the latest company results - weekly*
• Food Retailing Review: *an annual review of food retailing trends with commentary and statistics, by type of food, on sales, consumption, etc - annual*

American International Automobile Dealers' Association (AIADA)

Address: 99 Canal Center Plaza, Suite 500, Alexandria, VA 22314
Telephone: +1 703 519 7800
Fax: +1 703 519 7810
E-mail: goaiada@aiada.org
Web site: www.aiada.org
Year established: 1970
Chief officers: Wayne Williams (Chairman)
Membership: franchised new car and truck dealers selling international models
Publications:
• International Automobile Dealer (IAD): *information on industry trends, the dealership business and association news - bi-monthly*

American Library Association (ALA)

Address: 50 East Huron Street, Chicago, Illinois 60611
Telephone: +1 312 944 6780
Fax: +1 312 944 3897
E-mail: ala@ala.org
Web site: www.ala.org
Publications:
• Statistical Report: Public Library Data Service: *an annual report on library operations and financial trends in the USA and Canada. Based on a survey of almost 700 libraries - annual*

American Management Association (AMA)

Address: 1601 Broadway, New York NY 10019
Telephone: +1 212 586 8100
Fax: +1 212 903 8168
E-mail: amapubs@aol.com
Web site: www.amanet.org
Activities: management training and development; human resources planning; international links
Publications:
● Management Review: *management information, professional management issues - monthly*
Notes: AMA has established international management centres in Canada, Latin America, Japan and the Middle East.

American Marketing Association (AMA)

Address: 250 S. Wacker Dr. Suite 200, Chicago - IL 60606
Telephone: +1 312 648 0536
Fax: +1 312 993 7542
E-mail: info@ama.org
Web site: www.ama.org
Year established: 1937
Activities: education and training, maintains a reference centre
Chief officers: Michael J. Etzel (Chairman)
Membership: 45,000 worldwide members in 92 countries and 500 chapters throughout North America
Publications:
● AMA International Member and Marketing Services Guide: *comprehensive guide of marketing services and AMA members - annual*
● AMA Marketing Journals: *marketing theory and research - quarterly*
● Marketing Management: *marketing strategy - quarterly*
● Marketing News: *marketing, marketing research, advertising, sales and sales management, promotion, etc. - bi-weekly*
● Marketing Research: *in-depth articles on research methods and new technologies for the research professional - quarterly*

American Meat Institute (AMI)

Address: PO Box 3556, Washington, DC 20007
Telephone: +1 703 841 2400
Fax: +1 703 527 0938
Web site: www.meatami.org
Year established: 1906
Activities: education of members in industrial processes; research into marketing methods
Chief officers: J Patrick Boyle (President)
Structure: permanent staff, baord, committees
Membership: 1,300 meat packers, processors, suppliers, canners etc representing 70% of the American meat market
Publications:
● American Meat Institute Newsletter: *weekly*
● Meat and Poultry Facts: *statistics on livestock and poultry production, slaughterings and the production, consumption and trade in various types of meat and poultry. Also data on household expenditure and nutrition. Long runs of historical data going back to the 1920s. Based mainly on official statistics - annual*

American Pet Products Manufacturers' Association (APPMA)

Address: 511 Harwood Building, Scarsdale, NY 10583
Telephone: +1 203 532 0000
Fax: +1 203 532 0551
E-mail: fundaappma@aol.com
Web site: www.appma.org
Web site notes: site includes a summary of the APPMA annual Pet Owners Survey
Year established: 1959
Activities: organises the APPMA Annual National Trade Show, undertakes education and training, government lobbying, public relations and produces market research reports, periodicals and industry alerts
Chief officers: William D. Schoolman (Executive Vice President), Funda Alp (Director of Public Relations)
Structure: permanent staff; board; committees
Membership: 350 manufacturers and importers of pet products
Publications:
● APPMA's Legislative Affairs Alert: *pending legislation affecting the pet industry - monthly*
● National Pet Owners Survey: *extensive pet product research report summarising the buying habits of U.S. pet owners - annual*
● Newbriefs (American Pet Products Manufacturers Association): *industry specific information on market trends, point-of-purchase issues and news regarding pet product consumers - quarterly*

American Petroleum Institute (API)

Address: 1220 L Street NW, Washington, DC 20005
Telephone: +1 202 682 8000
Fax: +1 202 682 8232
E-mail: pr@api.org
Web site: www.api.org
Year established: 1919
Activities: government liaison; promotes international trade in petroleum products and the interests of the petroleum industry; provides information services; conducts research
Chief officers: Charles J DiBona (President)
Structure: permanent staff; board; committees
Membership: 300 producers, refiners, marketers and transporters of crude oil and petroleum products
Publications:
● Basic Petroleum Data: *a compendium of statistics on US and world petroleum trends with data in most tables going back to 1947. Chapters cover energy, reserves, exploration, drilling, production, prices, demand, finance, refining, imports, exports, offshore, transportation. Based on various sources - 3 p.a.*
● Guide to Petroleum Statistical Sources: *the petroleum, petrochemical, natural gas and energy industries. It contains almost 900 statistical features that appear in more than 100 energy and chemical industry publications from 61 worldwide sources - annual*
● Imports and Exports of Crude Oil and Petroleum Products: *detailed data on the imports and exports of crude oil and petroleum products. Details include importer of record, port of entry, country of origin, recipient, destination, quantity and API gravity (except residual fuel oil) and sulfur content (for crude oil and residual fuel oil) - monthly*
● Joint Association Survey on Drilling Costs: *a survey of wells, footage and related expenditure for each active drilling area. Data is given by state and area and for offshore and onshore areas - annual*
● Monthly Completion Report/Quarterly Completion Report (American Petroleum Institute): *number of drilling completions and related footage by month and year for the current year and the previous two years. The quarterly report has more detailed information on drilling plus estimates of the total number of wells drilled - monthly/quarterly*
● Monthly Statistical Report (American Petroleum Institute): *analyses and comments on recent trends relating to major products, production, imports, refinery operations and inventories. Monthly statistics on all these areas, based on API estimates, are also included - monthly*
● Sales of Natural Gas Liquids and Liquefied Refinery Gases: *annual sales to consumers, and internal company use, of ethane, propane, butane and pentanes plus. Data are categorized by state and by type of use, i.e., residential and commercial, industrial, chemical, etc - annual*
● Sales of Natural Gas Liquids and Liquefied Refinery Gases:

annual sales to consumers, and internal company use, of ethane, propane, butane and pentanes plus. Data are categorised by state and by type of use, i.e., residential and commercial, industrial, chemical, etc. - annual
• Weekly Statistical Bulletin (American Petroleum Institute): reports total US and regional data relating to refinery operations and the production of the major petroleum products: leaded and unleaded motor gasoline, naphtha and kerosene jet fuel, distillate and residual fuel oil. Based on data collected by the Institute - weekly
Notes: To order publications e-mail publications@api.org, telephone 202 682 8375 or fax 202 962 4776.

American Pharmaceutical Association (APhA)

Address: 2215 Constitution Ave., N.W., Washington, DC 20037-2985
Telephone: +1 202 628 4410
Fax: +1 202 783 2351
E-mail: webmaster@mail.aphanet.org
Web site: www.aphanet.org
Activities: government lobbying
Membership: retail pharmacists
Publications:
• Handbook of Non-prescription Drugs: guide to non-prescription medicines - annual
• Journal of the American Pharmaceutical Association: monthly

American Rental Association (ARA)

Address: 1900 19th Street, Moline IL 61265
Telephone: +1 800 334 2177/309 764 2475
Fax: +1 309 764 1533
E-mail: ara@ararental.org
Web site: www.ararental.org
Web site notes: site includes a list of retail outlets
Chief officers: James R. Irish (Executive Vice President), Diane Hamann (Information Center Coordinator)
Publications:
• Cost of Doing Business Survey: a report reviewing the financial performance of equipment rental companies and outlets. Data usually for the last five years. Results based on a survey of over 380 companies - annual

American Risk and Insurance Association (ARIA)

Address: PO Box 9001, Mount Vernon, NY 10552
Telephone: +1 914 699 2020
Fax: +1 914 699 2025
E-mail: webmaster@aria.org
Web site: www.aria.org
Year established: 1932
Membership: membership is comprised of academics, individual insurance industry representatives and institutional sponsors

American Soybean Association

Address: Box 419200, 540 Maryville Center Drive, St Louis, MO 63141
Telephone: +1 314 576 1770
Fax: +1 314 576 2786
E-mail: bcallanan@soy.org
Web site: www.oilseeds.org/asa
Web site notes: site includes Soystats, a comprehensive statistical publication on the US soy bean industry
Year established: 1920
Chief officers: Dennis Sharpe (CEO)
Structure: permanent staff, board
Membership: 30,000 soybean producers
Publications:
• Leader Letter: contains news about ASA member recruitment, ASA leader activities on issues of trade policy and legislation, updates on ASA staff activities in the US and abroad, and program updates on contract work in International Marketing of soybeans - weekly
• Soya Bluebook: the Bluebook gives data on soya production, processing, prices, utilisation, imports, exports. It includes some historical data back to the 1920s and some international data. Most of the data is reproduced from the US Department of Agriculture (USDA) - annual
• SoyStats: in-depth statistical profile of the U.S. soy bean industry. Includes data on production and consumption - annual

American Speciality Toy Retailing Association (ASTRA)

Address: 206 6th Avenue - Suite 900, Des Moines, Iowa 50309-4018
Telephone: +1 515 282 8192
Fax: +1 515 282 9117
E-mail: astra@assoc-mgmt.com
Web site: www.assoc-mgmt.com/users/astra/astra.html
Membership: retailers, manufacturers of speciality toys

American Sugarbeet Growers' Association (Sugar Association)

Address: Suite 600, 1101 15th Street, NW, Washington, DC 20005
Telephone: +1 202 785 1122
Fax: +1 202 785 5019
E-mail: ASGA@aol.com
Web site: member.aol.com/asga/sugar.htm
Year established: 1949
Activities: promotes research; conducts educational seminars
Structure: permanent staff; board
Membership: 25 processors and refiners of beet sugar and cane sugar
Publications:
• On Your Mark: newsletter on nutrition and fitness - quarterly
• Sugar Note and News: general interest newsletter - quarterly

American Textile Manufacturers' Institute (ATMI)

Address: 1130 Connecticutt Avenue NW, Suite 1200, Washington, DC 20036-3954
Telephone: +1 202 862 0500
Fax: +1 202 862 0570
Web site: www.apparelex.com/atmi/
Publications:
• Textile Fact File: summary data on the US textile industry including production, consumption and trade figures - annual
• Textile Hi-Lights: a short commentary on the industry is followed by statistics on fibre consumption, unfilled orders, investment, retail sales, production of special textiles, prices, imports, exports, employment. Mainly based on official statistics - quarterly
• Textile Trends: weekly news items and statistics on the US textile industry and market - weekly

American Wholesale Marketers' Association (AWMA)

Address: 1128 16th Street, NW, Washington, DC 20036
Telephone: +1 202 463 2124
Fax: +1 202 467 0559
E-mail: davids@awmanet.org (President)
Web site: www.webplus.net/awma/
Activities: conducts research and educational programs
Chief officers: David E Strachan (President)
Structure: permanent staff; board
Membership: 3,000 companies involved in the distribution, manufacture and retail sale of convenience products. Members consist of wholesalers, manufacturers, retailers, brokers and others involved in the convenience products industry
Publications:
• Distribution Channels: issues affecting convenience product

distribution, warehousing, marketing, ECR, product merchandising, new products, news. Also special retailer section - 10 p.a.
• Distribution Channels Buying Guide and Membership Directory: AWMA's members, including ordering and shipping information for manufacturers and regional/state breakdowns of wholesalers and brokers - annual
• Peer Resource Networking Directory: listings of experts in the convenience store industry ranging from technology to sales, warehousing to merchandising - annual
• Quick Topics Newsletter: convenience store wholesaling. Topics covered range from the latest industry ideas and tips to position listings - monthly
Notes: Formerly the National Candy Wholesalers' Association and the National Association of Tobacco Distributors. AWMA members represent the full convenience product line, including candy, tobacco, grocery, HBC, general merchandise and deli/foods.

American Wine Society
Address: 3006 Latta Road, Rochester, NY 14612
Telephone: +1 716 225 7613
Fax: +1 716 225 7613
Web site: www.ricon.net/aws
Year established: 1967
Activities: liaises with government on labelling issues; sponsors educational programs including testings and field trips
Chief officers: Angel Nardone (Executive Director)
Structure: permanent staff; committees; board
Membership: 5,000 winegrowers, winemakers, merchants
Publications:
• American Wine Society: quarterly
• AWS News: Association news - quarterly

Amusement and Music Operators' Association (AMOA)
Address: 401 N Michigan Avenue, Chicago, IL 60611-4267
Telephone: +1 312 245 1021
Fax: +1 312 245 1085
E-mail: amuseus@aol.com
Web site: www.amoa.com
Year established: 1948
Activities: marketing and promotion programs as well as government lobbying
Membership: companies from the amusement, music, entertainment and vending industries
Publications:
• AMOA Location: association activities and industry news - bimonthly
• Annual Report: association's activities during the previous year as well as financial information - annual
• Membership Directory: names, addresses and phone numbers of all AMOA members. It also includes detailed listings on AMOA committees, officers, directors, state association contacts and staff - annual

Association of American Publishers (AAP)
Address: 71 Fifth Avenue, New York, NY 10003-3004
Telephone: +1 212 255 0200
Fax: +1 212 255 7007
E-mail: mckee@aap.publishers.org
Web site: www.publishers.org
Web site notes: site includes commentary and statistics on retail book sales by sector over a five year review period. The site also includes a list of members
Year established: 1970
Activities: conducts seminars and workshops on copyright, sales and educational publishing; compiles statistics
Chief officers: Nicholas A Veliotes (President), Thomas D. McKee (Executive Vice President)

Structure: permanent staff; board; committees
Membership: 220 member companies
Publications:
• Association of American Publishers' Monthly Report: newsletter - monthly
• Industry Statistics (Association of American Publishers): annual statistics on trends in the US publishing sector with data on sales of books by type, subject, and customer category. Data on volume and value sales with historical runs in many tables - annual

Association of American Railroads (AAR)
Address: 50F Street NW, Washington, DC 20001-1564
Telephone: +1 202 639 2100
Fax: +1 202 639 2986
Web site: www.aar.org
Year established: 1934
Activities: coordinating and research agency of the American railway industry; compiles statistics
Chief officers: Joyce Koeneman (President)
Structure: permanent staff; board
Membership: 71 railroads
Publications:
• Rail News Update: newsletter - bi-weekly
• Railroad Facts: a pocket-sized statistical guide to US railroad operations with data on traffic, revenues, expenses, equipment, employment and fuel consumption - annual

Association of Brewers
Address: PO Box 1679, Boulder, CO 80306-1679
Telephone: +1 303 447 0816
Fax: +1 303 447 2825
E-mail: info@aob.org
Web site: www.aob.org
Year established: 1977
Activities: collection and dissemination of beer and brewing information
Publications:
• North American Brewers Resource Directory: names, contact people, phone numbers and addresses of North American breweries. It also has listings for consultants, publications, associations, suppliers, manufacturers and distributors in the craft-brewing industry - annual
Notes: The association has four seperate divisions: American Homebrewers Association, Institute for Brewing Studies, Brewers Publications, Great American Beer Festival.

Association of Food Industries
Address: PO Box 776, 5 Ravine Drive, Matawan, NJ 07747
Telephone: +1 908 583 8188
Fax: +1 908 583 0798
Year established: 1906
Activities: liaises with government; acts as arbitrator in industry conflicts; provides information services
Chief officers: Richard J Sullivan (Executive Vice President)
Structure: permanent staff; board; divisions by products
Membership: 370 food processors, importers, brokers, exporters
Publications:
• Association of Food Industries Newsletter: bi-monthly

Association of Home Appliance Manufacturers (AHAM)
Address: 20 North Wacker Drive, Chicago, IL 60606
Telephone: +1 312 984 5800
Fax: +1 312 984 5823
E-mail: @aham.org
Web site: www.aham.org
Web site notes: site includes various statistics on the US appliance industry including annual sales volume and value by type over a three year review period

Year established: 1966
Activities: government relations, certification programs, appliance performance standards, compiles statistics (unit shipments), undertakes consumer and market research; provides a fax-back information service
Chief officers: Robert Holding (President)
Structure: permanent staff; board
Membership: 173 major appliance manufacturers
Publications:
• AHAM Major Appliance Factory Shipment Report: *provides monthly, year-to-date, and quarterly shipment data in "units" for current periods and percentage increase from previous year. Covers 12 product categories - monthly*
• AHAM Major Appliance Industry Factbook: *comprehensive reference book on the US major home appliance industry. Includes tables providing key industry data - annual*
• AHAM Membership Directory: *listing of member companies within the three divisions of AHAM - annual*
• Global Appliance Report: *digest of international news affecting the home appliance industry - monthly*
• Major Appliance Factory Shipment Historical Data: *listing of industry shipments by product (including exports) - monthly*

Association of International Automobile Manufacturers Inc. (AIAM)

Address: 1001 19th Street North, Suite 1200, Arlington Virginia 22209
Telephone: +1 703 525 7788
Fax: +1 703 525 8817
Web site: www.aiam.org
Web site notes: site includes detailed statistics on automotives in the US
Activities: government liaison, acts as a clearing house of industry-related information
Membership: U.S. subsidiaries of international automobile companies

Association of Managing Consulting Firms (ACME)

Address: 521 5th Avenue, New York, NY 10169
Telephone: +1 212 697 9693
Fax: +1 212 949 6571
E-mail: info@acmeworld.org
Web site: www.acmeworld.org/
Year established: 1929
Publications:
• Directory of Members: *full page description of the firm, practice areas, office and branch locations. Firms are cross-indexed according to specialty and industry - annual*
• Multi-Client Research Study on The Management Consulting Profession: *a world-wide research study of the management consulting profession - annual*
• Surveys of United States and European Key Management Information: *track vital management issues such as fee arrangements, financial operations, recruiting and staffing practices, compensation and business development costs. The US edition evaluates all data according to specialty, annual billing revenues, size of professional staff, typical project size, number of domestic offices and for all responding firms. The European edition analyses the data by country, size of professional consulting staff and for all responding firms - annual*

Association of Manufacturing Technology

Address: 7901 Westpark Drive, McLean VA 22102
Telephone: +1 703 893 2900
Fax: +1 703 893 1151
Publications:
• Economic Handbook of the Machine Tool Industry: *detailed production, trade, and consumption statistics covering the machine tool sectors in the USA and the rest of the world - annual*

Association of the Nonwoven Fabrics Industry (INDA)

Address: 1001 Winstead Drive, ste. 460, Cary, NC 27513
Telephone: +1 919 677 0060
Fax: +1 919 677 0211
Web site: www.inda.org
Activities: organises an annual trade fair, undertakes marketing, shared technology, interpretation of governmental and international trade regulations
Membership: 200 non-woven fabric manufacturers
Publications:
• International Nonwovens Directory: *contact details and details of products offered by the membership of non-woven associations world-wide - annual*

Audit Bureau of Circulation (ABC)

Address: 900 Meacham Road, Schaumburg, IL 60173
Telephone: +1 847 605 0909
Fax: +1 847 605 0483
E-mail: service@accessabc.com
Web site: www.accessabc.com
Activities: maintains the ABC Circulation Data Bank which provides electronic access to circulation data on nearly 1,500 daily and weekly newspapers and more than 1,000 periodicals in North America
Membership: 5,000 advertisers, advertising agencies, business and farm publications, consumer magazines, and daily and weekly newspapers
Publications:
• Audit Reports: *provide audited verification of circulation data as well as circulation increase or decrease - annual*
• Canadian Newspaper Circulation Factbook: *circulation figures for all Canadian Daily and Weekly Newspaper members by market, county and province. The report includes a ranking by circulation size of all Daily Newspaper members and five-year circulation trends data for all dailies in census metropolitan areas. The report also includes a county analysis showing the combined coverage of dailies and weeklies - annual*
• Magazine Market Coverage Reports: *offer county-based circulation information from ABC's Circulation Data Bank on more than 200 Consumer Magazines, Farm Publications and Business Publications - annual*
• Magazine Trend Reports: *provides five years of circulation data needed to determine magazine sales trends and magazine subscriber interest for over 700 Consumer Magazines - annual*
• Supplemental Data Reports: *demographic data for publication readership based on ABC-monitored research studies - annual*

Automotive Industry Action Group (AIAG)

Address: Suite 200, 26200 Lahser Road, Southfield, M1 48034
Telephone: +1 810 358 3570
Fax: +1 810 358 3253
Web site: www.aiag.org
Year established: 1981
Activities: government liaison, tackles industry issues in supply, manufacturing, engineering, quality and finance
Structure: permanent staff; board; committees
Membership: 800 North American vehicle manufacturers and suppliers
Publications:
• Actionline (Automotive Industry Action Group): *newsletter - monthly*

Automotive Parts and Accessories Association (APAA)

Address: 4600 East-West Hwy.,Suite 300, Bethesda, MD 20814
Telephone: +1 301 654 6664
Fax: +1 301 654 3299
E-mail: apaa@apaa-po.apaa.sprint.com
Web site: www.apaa.org
Web site notes: site includes a statistical overview of car aftermarket in the US
Activities: providing information on federal/state legislation and regulations affecting the independent aftermarket; by monitoring international trade policy for automotive products; by conducting market research on aftermarket sales, trends, and export trade; and by compiling statistics
Chief officers: Al Gaspar (President), Yvonne Dock (Senior Director, Marketing and Membership)
Membership: 1,700 members made up of automotive parts and accessories retailers, distributors, manufacturers, and manufacturers' representatives including 300 international members in 50 countries
Publications:
• APAA Aftermarket Factbook: *data on size of the retail aftermarket by segment, distribution channels, merger activity, consumer do-it-yourself activity and aftermarket purchases, service repair, employment, imports and exports plus state-by-state vehicle registrations. Includes data on the Canadian and Mexican aftermarkets - annual*
• APAA Mini-Monitor: *latest data on the size of the retail aftermarket, including sales of replacement parts, chemicals, accessories and service repair. Also includes updates on the motor vehicle market, vehicle operating trends, automotive retail and service outlets, consumer purchases, employment, manufacturing and trade - annual*
• Brazilian Market for Automotive Parts and Accessories: *data on size of the automotive parts and accessories market, motor vehicle sales and registrations and lists of key contacts in Brazil such as manufacturers, distributors and retailers. Also includes details on Mercosul and other trade agreements, economic trends, tariffs and taxes, distribution channels, pricing, customs regulations, banks etc. - annual*
• Latin American Buyers Directory: *directory of over 625 Mexican and other Latin American retailers, distributors, wholesalers, importers and manufacturers. Listings include: contact name, title, company name and address, type of business, phone and fax (if available), products sold, territory covered and U.S. suppliers represented. Most also provide the number of years in business, sales volume and number of employees - annual*
• Light Truck/Sport Utility Market: *national surveys of recent purchasers of new and used light trucks and for the aftermarket with information on dealer vs. aftermarket purchases of light truck accessories, demographics of pickup truck, van and sport utility vehicle owners, purchase decision factors, accessories and parts purchasing patterns and future plans for repair and maintenance — DIY vs. professional. Also includes light truck sales and market shares, registrations, and forecasts for the future of the light truck market - annual*
• Mexican Market for Automotive Parts and Accessories: *comprehensive study of the Mexican automotive marketplace covering demographics, vehicle fleet, import statistics, distribution channels, the retail aftermarket, legal environment, top buyers, tariff schedules, plus supplementary information on NAFTA, banks, visa requirements, etc. - annual*
• Retail Market Trends - What's Hot, What's Not in Aftermarket Distribution: *detailed research project on aftermarket sales and distribution, combines a distribution channel analysis with three separate reports detailing the results of a study of 25 individual aftermarket product lines - irregular*
• Venezuelan Market for Automotive Parts and Accessories: *information on the size of the automotive market by segment; vehicle production, sales and exports; vehicle registrations by make and model; lists of auto parts manufacturers, automotive assembly plants and parts distributors. Plus a detailed section on establishing an office in Venezuela that covers pricing, distribution channels, selling techniques, franchising, joint ventures and licensing, customs regulations, tariffs and taxes, economic trends, banks, etc. - annual*

Automotive Parts Rebuilders' Association (APRA)

Address: 330 Lexington Drive, Buffalo Grove, IL 60089-6933
Telephone: +1 847 541 7025
Fax: +1 847 541 5808
E-mail: apramail@aol.com
Web site: www.apra.org
Membership: 2,000 member companies that rebuild automotive related "hard" parts, such as starters, alternators, clutches, transmissions, brakes, drive shafts, and numerous other parts for passenger cars, trucks, off-road, equipment and industrial uses
Notes: Included in the association: (AERA) Engine Rebuilders Association, (PERA) Production Engine Remanufacturers Association.

Automotive Service Association (ASA)

Address: PO Box 929, Bedford, Texas, 76095-0929
Telephone: +1 817 283 6205
Fax: +1 817 685 0225
E-mail: asainfo@asashop.org
Web site: www.asashop.org
Chief officers: Donald C. Seyfer (Chairman), Michael Lund (General Director)
Membership: 12,000 mechanical, collision and transmission service companies

Automotive Service Industry Association (ASIA)

Address: 25 Northwest Point #425, Elk Grove Village, IL 60007-1035
Telephone: +1 708 228 1310
Fax: +1 708 228 1510
E-mail: research@aftmktusa.org
Web site: www.aftmkt.com:80/MISG/associations/ASIA/
Year established: 1959
Activities: compiles statistics; holds educational and research programs
Chief officers: Gene A Gardner (President), Gary D. McCoy (Director of Communications)
Structure: board; committees
Membership: 2,000 executives from auto industry
Publications:
• Aftermarket Today: *latest developments and trends the U.S. car aftermarket - quarterly*

Automotive Warehouse Distributors' Association (AWDA)

Address: 9140 Ward Parkway, Kansas City, Mo 64114
Telephone: +1 816 444 3500
Fax: +1 816 444 0330
E-mail: jennie@awda.org
Web site: www.awda.org
Chief officers: Raymond T. Walker (Chairman), Art Fisher (Secretary), John F. Creamer (President)

Bank Marketing Association (BMA)

Address: Suite 300, 1120 Connecticut Avenue NW, Washington, DC 20036
Telephone: +1 202 663 5268/800 433 9013
Fax: +1 202 828 4540
Web site: www.bmanet.org
Web site notes: site includes a facts and figures section with information on the number of retail banking branches in operation, bank marketing expenditure, customer service survey results, services provided by bank call centres, retail

bank fees and services trends as well as a summary of a consumer survey on the image of banks
Year established: 1915
Activities: compiles statistics; provides marketing information to banking industry; conducts research; offers education courses
Structure: permanent staff; board
Membership: 3,000 marketing executives for banking industry
Publications:
• Analysis of Bank Marketing Expenditures: *a report of bank marketing expenditure with data by function, i.e. advertising, sales promotion, training, public relations etc. Also data by type of service advertised - annual*
• Bank Marketing Magazine: *financial marketing sector - monthly*
• Marketing Update (Bank Marketing Association): *newsletter - monthly*
• Membership Directory: *annual*

Barbecue Industry Association

Address: Suite 113, 710 E. Ogden, Naperville, IL 60563
Telephone: +1 708 369 2404
Fax: +1 708 369 2488

Battery Council International (BCI)

Address: 401 North Michigan Avenue, Chicago, IL 60611
Telephone: +1 312 644 6610
Fax: +1 312 321 6869
E-mail: ann_noll@sba.com
Year established: 1924
Activities: compiles statistics; recommends industry standards
Chief officers: Edward M Craft (Executive Secretary)
Structure: permanent staff; board; committees
Membership: 215 battery manufacturers and recyclers, marketers and retailers, suppliers of raw materials and equipment, plus industry consultants
Publications:
• Battery Council International - News: *newsletter, industry and association news - irregular*
• Battery Replacement Data Book: *statistics - annual*

Biscuit and Cracker Manufacturers' Association (B&CMA)

Address: Suite 400, 1400 L Street NW, Washington, DC 20005
Telephone: +1 202 898 1636
Fax: +1 202 898 1668
E-mail: bcmabake@aol.com
Web site: www.net-link.net/bcma/
Year established: 1901
Activities: sponsors education programs; monitors government legislation and regulation
Chief officers: Francis P Rooney (President)
Structure: permanent staff; board
Membership: 220 biscuit and cracker bakers and suppliers
Publications:
• B&CMA Bulletin: *information on legislation and regulatory issues affecting the industry - monthly*
• Directory of Members: *names and addresses of all the Regular, International and Allied Members of the Association and the products or services offered - annual*

Business and Institutional Furniture Manufacturers' Association (BIFMA)

Address: 2680 Horizon SE, Ste. A-1, Grand Rapids, MI 49546-7500
Telephone: +1 616 285 3963
Fax: +1 616 285 3765
E-mail: email@bifma.com
Web site: www.bifma.com
Web site notes: site includes comprehensive statistics on the US market for office furniture including: market value over a 15-year review period; annual shipments by product category; imports and exports; industry trends; distribution and forecasts. Also includes links to member organisations' home pages
Membership: BIFMA International is an association of office furniture manufacturers and their associates

Business Products Industry Association (BPIA)

Address: 301 North Fairfax Street, Alexandria, 22314-2696
Telephone: +1 703 549 9040
Fax: +1 703 683 7552/800 542 6672
E-mail: beboken@aol.com
Web site: www.bpia.org
Activities: offers a comprehensive research service to members, education and training
Chief officers: Mr. Robert Kennedy (Chairman), Mr. Bill Crawford (Secretary/Treasurer)
Publications:
• BPIA Office Products Industry Sourcebook: *information about office products shipments, white collar employment, producer price indexes, the cost of living and the performance of public office products firms - annual*
• Industry Report: *latest news, events and trends affecting the office products industry. Includes financial news, a Wall Street stock report, featured columnists and in-depth reports on topics of interest to the industry in general - bi-weekly*
• Introduction to the Office Products Industry: *detailed introduction to the office supplies and related industries, as well as an overview of the industry. It describes the various trade channels, gives profiles of the major players and details the revenue and cost structure of different types of manufacturers, wholesalers and resellers - annual*
• Office Supplies Distribution Trends Report: *tracks shipments of office supplies to different types of reseller categories for a panel of U.S. manufacturers. Also includes buying group information, and data on exports and shipments for four size groupings of manufacturers - annual*
• Source Guide: *comprehensive directory of dealers, wholesalers, manufacturers, rep firms and sales and marketing reps in North America. Also includes cross-references to more than 550 manufacturers' product categories - annual*
• Stockwell Report: *comprehensive quarterly research report focusing on office products marketing and distribution trends and developments - quarterly*
• Wholesalers In Transition: *profiles over 35 leading international, national and regional wholesalers. Includes both traditional office products and microcomputer and related products distributors in the U.S. and Europe. Discusses recent past, achievements and growth, current marketing strategies and the future of office products wholesaling - irregular*
Notes: Formerly the National Office Products Association the BPIA is the umbrella organisation of a number of organisations including: Business Products Wholesalers Alliance; Furniture Manufacturers Alliance; Office Furniture Dealers Alliance; Office Products Dealers Alliance; Office Products Manufacturers Alliance; Office Products Representatives Alliance.

Business Products Wholesalers' Alliance (BPWA)

Address: 301 North Fairfax Street, Alexandria, VA22314-2696 Alexandria, VA 22314-2696
Telephone: +1 703 549 904/800 542 6672
Fax: +1 703 683 7552
E-mail: sdegroot@bpia.org
Web site: www.bpia.org/alliances/bpwa.htm
Chief officers: Simon DeGroot (Director)

Notes: The Association is part of the Business Products Industry Association.

Cellular Telecommunications Industry Association (CTIA)

Address: Suite 200, 1250 Connecticut Avenue NW, Washington, DC 20036
Telephone: +1 202 785 0081
Fax: +1 202 785 0721
E-mail: wowcom@ctia.org
Web site: www.wow-com.com/consumer/
Year established: 1984
Activities: offers educational courses; conducts seminars; monitors government regulation and legislation; compiles statistics
Structure: permanent staff; board; committees
Membership: 450 individuals and companies involved in cellular communications
Publications:
• Cellular Industry Report: *monthly*
• Industry Data Survey: *semi-annual*
• Roamer Review: *newsletter - quarterly*

Chemical Manufacturers' Association (CMA)

Address: 2501 M Street NW, Washington, DC 20037
Telephone: +1 202 887 1100
Fax: +1 202 887 1237
Web site: www.cmahq.com
Year established: 1872
Activities: conducts advocacy and research in areas important to members, especially environmental issues
Structure: permanent staff; board, committees
Membership: 185 chemical manufacturers
Publications:
• Chemical Manufacturers' Association News: *newsletter - 10 p.a.*
• CMA Directory: *annual*

Chemical Specialities Manufacturers' Association (CSMA)

Address: 1913 Eye Street NW, Washington, DC 20006
Telephone: +1 202 872 8110
Fax: +1 202 872 8114
E-mail: CSMA@Juno.com
Web site: www.csma.org
Year established: 1914
Activities: liaises with government agencies; conducts surveys; provides information
Chief officers: Ralph Engel (President), Connie Neuman (Communications Director)
Structure: permanent staff; committees; council; board
Membership: 425 companies engaged in the manufacture, formulation, distribution and sale of consumer products for household, institutional and industrial use
Publications:
• Aerosol Pressurized Products Survey: *provides comprehensive statistics and insights into the state of the American aerosol industry over the past 10 years, gives aerosol production in areas including animal products; food products; insect sprays; paints and finishes; automotive and industrial products; household products; and personal products - annual*
• Chemical Times and Trends: *corporate management, research and development, sales and marketing, purchasing, production, legal and public affairs, and safety testing in the industry - quarterly*
• Consumer Products Handbook - A Comprehensive Guide to Today's Household Chemical Products: *profile of the chemical specialties industry and its products, including an informative historical overview of consumer household products - irregular*

• Ethylene Glycol Base Antifreeze Survey: *sales of various anti-freeze products - annual*
• Polishes and Floor Maintenance Products Bi- Annual Survey: *survey covering production of: floor polish, polymer and wax-based; products designed for concrete, terrazzo or other mineral surfaces; polish and wax stripper products - bi-annual*
• Propylene Glycol Base Antifreeze Survey: *survey data in a number of end-use categories, including statistics and sales volume - annual*
• Vendors to the Trade: *classified listings of all vendors to the chemical specialties industry - by products and services - as well as a membership directory of the Association with addresses, phone and fax numbers and names of the CSMA representatives - annual*

Chilled Foods Association

Address: Suite 500G, 5775 Peachtree Dunwoody Road, Atlanta, GA 30342
Telephone: +1 404 252 3663
Fax: +1 404 252 0774
Year established: 1988
Activities: promotes chilled foods industry; acts as lobbying group; monitors government regulation and legislation; supports research
Chief officers: Richard Cristol (Executive Director)
Structure: board; permanent staff
Membership: 22 manufacturers, retailers, distributors, suppliers
Publications:
• Technical Handbook for the Chilled Foods Industry: *irregular*

Chocolate Manufacturers' Association of the USA (CMA)

Address: 7900 Westpark Drive, McLean VA 22102
Telephone: +1 703 790 5750
Fax: +1 703 790 5752
E-mail: info@candyusa.org
Web site: www.candyusa.org/who_cma.html
Web site notes: site includes statistics on the US chocolate market with some international per capita consumption data
Year established: 1923

Clothing Manufacturers' Association of the USA

Address: Suite 1061, 1290 Avenue of the Americas, New York, NY 10104
Telephone: +1 212 529 0823
Fax: +1 212 541 4012
Year established: 1933
Activities: assists members with labour, government and supplier relations; sponsors seminars; compiles statistics
Chief officers: Robert A Kaplan (Executive Director)
Structure: permanent staff; board
Membership: 200 manufacturers of menswear
Publications:
• Members News Bulletin: *weekly*
• Statistical Report on Production, Sales, and Profit Trends: *annual statistics, with historical data, on production, sales and profit trends in the mens' and boys' tailored clothing sector - annual*

Commercial Finance Association (CFA)

Address: Suite 1815, 225 West 34th Street, New York, NY 10122
Telephone: +1 212 594 3490
Fax: +1 212 564 6053
Web site: www.cfa.com
Year established: 1943
Activities: compiles statistics; offers seminars; conducts surveys; monitors government legislation and regulation
Chief officers: Bruce H. Jones (Deputy Executive Director)

Structure: permanent staff; regional groups; board; committees

Membership: commercial finance companies factors banks and other financing agencies engaged in the asset-based financial services industry

Publications:
• Secured Lender: *lender liability, sales and marketing, financial controls and budgeting, legal and legislative developments, industry software and management functions - bi-monthly*

Commercial Refrigerator Manufacturers' Association

Address: 1200 19th Street, N.W., Suite 300, Washington, DC 20036
Telephone: +1 202 857 1145
Fax: +1 202 857 1186

Composite Can and Tube Institute (CCTI)

Address: 1630 Duke Street, Alexandria, VA 22314
Telephone: +1 703 549 2233
Fax: +1 703 549 4912
E-mail: cctiwdc@cctiwdc.org
Web site: www.cctiwdc.org
Year established: 1933
Activities: compiles statistics; monitors government regulation and legislation, education and training
Chief officers: Kristine Garland (Executive Vice President)
Structure: permanent staff; board; committees
Membership: manufacturers of composite paperboard cans, tubes, cores, fibre drums, cones, spools, ribbon blocks, bobbins and related products for commercial sale, as well as suppliers of paperboard products, machinery and other materials and services

Publications:
• Cantube Bulletin: *information about issues affecting the industry globally as well as updates on CCTI activities. includes information on the following; environmental issues, legislative updates, member company news, and safety and human resources information - bimonthly*
• Industry Directory: *list of all known manufacturers in this industry worldwide. It includes product descriptions, contact names, plant addresses, phone and fax numbers - annual*
• Tube and Core Statistical Report: *sales data of composite cans, tubes and cores as well as paperboard tonnage - monthly*

Consumer Electronics Manufacturers' Association (CEMA)

Address: 2500 Wilson Boulevard, Arlington Virginia 22201-3834
Telephone: +1 703 907 7674
Fax: +1 703 907 7601
E-mail: cessales@eia.org
Web site: www.cemacity.org
Web site notes: site includes statistics on the US market for consumer electronics
Activities: sponsor and producer of The Consumer Electronics Shows
Publications:
• US Consumer Electronics Industry Today: *an annual report aimed at the general public covering the consumer electronics sector. It includes a detailed history of the sector, and key statistics for various sectors including video, audio, communication and information products, multimedia and CD-ROM, personal electronics, accessories, mobile electronics. Statistics are primarily from the association - annual*

Contact Lens Manufacturers' Association (CLMA)

Address: 4400 East-West Hwy, Suite 33, Bethesda, MD 20814
E-mail: clma@mindspring.com
Web site: www.contact.inter.net/
Web site notes: site includes some general statistics on contact lenses in the US
Year established: 1961
Membership: represents contact lens laboratories as well as material, solution and equipment manufacturers in the U.S. and abroad

Cosmetic, Toiletry and Fragrance Association (CTFA)

Address: 1101 17th Street, NW, Suite 300, Washington, DC 20036
Telephone: +1 202 331 1770
Fax: +1 202 331 1969
Web site: www.ctfa.org
Year established: 1894
Activities: public service and educational activities
Chief officers: Robert Phillips (Chairman), Charles G Cooper (Vice Chairman and Treasurer), John Saxton (Secretary)
Structure: CTFA is governed by a Board of Directors, and the Chairman of the Board is the chief elected officer of the Association
Membership: 500 members worldwide (although the majority are in the US) - active members are manufacturers and distributors of finished personal care products and associate members include suppliers of ingredients, raw materials, packaging materials and services used in the production and marketing of finished products, as well as consumer and trade publications
Publications:
• CFTA Compendium of Cosmetic Ingredient Composition: *cosmetic raw material specifications, four volumes - 1990*
• Cosmetic, Toiletry and Fragrance Association News: *newsletter - bi-weekly*
• CTFA International Buyers' Guide: *worldwide listing of cosmetic raw materials and their suppliers, identifying more than 1000 suppliers in 23 countries - annual*
• CTFA International Resource Manual: *laws and regulations in 70 countries, including new countries in South America, Eastern Europe and the Middle-East, with detailed analyses on registration requirements, labeling rules, ingredient restrictions, packaging issues, testing requirements, and more - 4th edition, 1995*
• CTFA Labeling Manual: *U.S. regulations governing the labeling of cosmetics, professional products and over-the-counter drugs - 1990*
• CTFA List of Japanese Cosmetic Ingredients: *listing of ingredients approved for cosmetic use in Japan - 2nd edition, 1992*
• International Cosmetic Ingredient Dictionary: *contains 7,500 ingredients cross-referenced to more than 31,000 trade names and other technical names, and identifies the names and addresses of 630 cosmetic raw material suppliers from 28 countries. Provides the accepted nomenclature required for labeling in the U.S., the EU and many other countries - 6th edition, 1995*
• International Cosmetic Ingredient Handbook: *information to assist users in understanding the purpose of an ingredient in a formulation, with details on the chemical class, functions, and reported product categories of use for the 7,500 ingredients - 3rd edition, 1995*
• Occupational and Environmental Safety and Health Guidelines: *Material Safety Data Sheets, General Safety Training, and Laboratory Safety, addressing issues such as Hazardous Waste Management, Occupational Health Surveillance, Hearing Conservation, Respiratory Protection, Powered Equipment, Lockout/Tagout, Dust, Fume and Vapour Control, Personal protective Equipment, and more - 1995*
• Who's Who - CTFA: *complete listings of all CTFA member companies. Listings include company contact information,*

names and titles of key executives, complete address, phone and fax numbers and a description of products and services - annual

Direct Marketing Association

Address: 14th Floor, 1120 Avenue of the Americas, New York, NY 10036-6700
Telephone: +1 212 768 7277
Fax: +1 212 302 6714
E-mail: lrc@the-dma.org
Web site: www.the-dma.org
Chief officers: H. Robert Wientzen (President and CEO)
Publications:
● DMA Surveys: a series of regular surveys on specific aspects of the direct marketing sector in the USA. Based on surveys carried out by the Association - regular
● Statistical Fact Book (Direct Marketing Association): detailed statistics and market data on the direct mail industry including demographic characteristics, buying behaviour, comparisons with other advertising methods, number of mailings, etc. Also includes a list of companies and various features - annual

Direct Selling Association (DSA)

Address: Suite 1010, 1666 K Street NW, Washington, DC 20006-2808
Telephone: +1 202 293 5760
Fax: +1 202 463 4569
E-mail: info@dsa.org
Web site: www.dsa.or
Web site notes: site includes statistics on the US direct sales market taken from the Direct Selling Industry Wide Growth and Outlook Survey. Included is data on retail sales, number of salespeople, sales by method, location of sales and percentage sales by product group. Also includes a list of members with links to home pages
Year established: 1910
Activities: compiles statistics; conducts research; offers educational programs
Structure: permanent staff; board; committees
Membership: 140 companies that manufacture and distribute goods and services sold directly to consumers
Publications:
● Data Tracker: statistics - quarterly
● Direct Selling Industry Wide Growth and Outlook Survey: in-depth statistical profile of the U.S. direct sales market. Includes data on retail sales, number of sales people, sales by method, location of sales and percentage sales by product group. Based on a survey by the Association - annual
● International Directory: annual
● Membership List: quarterly
● Newsletter of the Direct Selling Association: monthly
● Status Report: statistics - weekly

Distilled Spirits Council of the United States (DISCUS)

Address: Suite 900, 1250 I Street, NW, Washington, DC 20005
Telephone: +1 202 628 3544
Fax: +1 202 682 8888
E-mail: webmaster@discus.org.
Web site: www.discus.health.org
Activities: compiles statistics; conducts educational programs; monitors government regulation and legislation
Chief officers: F A Meister (President)
Structure: permanent staff; board; committees
Membership: 24 producers and marketers of distilled spirits
Publications:
● Annual Statistical Review (Distilled Spirits Council of the United States): current and historical data on the distilled spirits industry covering production, shipments, distribution, stocks, withdrawals, sales, consumption, trade, bottles, etc. - annual

● Summary of State Laws and Regulations Relating to Distilled Spirits: biennial

Door and Hardware Institute (DHI)

Address: 14170 Newbrook Drive, VA 20151-2232
Telephone: +1 703 222 2010
Fax: +1 703 222 2410
E-mail: publications@dhi.org or membership@dhi.org
Web site: www.dhi.org
Year established: 1975
Activities: sponsors research; conducts management and employee training
Chief officers: Richard M Hornaday (Executive Vice President)
Structure: permanent staff; board; committees
Membership: 5,000 distributors and manufacturers of doors and builders' hardware
Publications:
● Blueprint: newsletter - monthly
● DHI Buyer's Guide: 600 manufacturers of products in the architectural openings area - annual
● Doors and Hardware: builders hardware, doors, electronic security devices, technology, fire and life safety equipment, codes and ADA issues, washroom accessories and many specialty products. The magazine covers the operation and technical aspects of the architectural openings industry, construction-related subjects, changes and growth within the industry, as well as non-technical concerns such as management, financial matters and sales techniques - monthly

Electronic Industries' Association (EIA)

Address: 2500 Wilson Blvd, Arlington VA 22201-3834
Telephone: +1 703 907 7500
Fax: +1 703 907 7501
E-mail: PublicAffairs@eia.org
Web site: www.eia.org
Year established: 1924
Activities: conducts regular surveys, publishes a broad range of statistical and analytical publications and special reports, including an annual statistical yearbook on the industry. In addition, the Department also analyses industry trends, works with outside firms on market research studies, and operates an in-house information centre/specialised library. This centre offers access to hundreds of on-line databases and provides the ability to conduct customised information searches
Chief officers: Peter F McCloskey (President)
Structure: board; permanent staff; committees; councils
Membership: EIA represents 1,200 manufacturers involved in the design and manufacture of electronic components, parts, systems and equipment for communications, industrial, government and consumer uses
Publications:
● Annual Report: reports on the activities of the association as well as providing commentary and statistics on the various sectors of the U.S. electronics industry - annual
● Electronic Market Trends: short articles and statistics on various electronics markets. Each issue has figures for electronic factory sales, imports, exports and employment. Based mainly on official sources - monthly
● Electronics Market Data Book: sales, production, trade, employment and R&D statistics for the electronic industry and for specific products in the following areas: consumer electronics, components, government electronics, industrial electronics and telecommunications - annual
● US Consumer Electronics Industry in Review: annual report covering general trends in the electronics sector plus a production breakdown. Based on various sources - annual

Envelope Manufacturers' Association

Address: 300 N. Washington St, Ste. 500, Alexandria, VA 22314-2530

Telephone: +1 202 347 0055
Fax: +1 202 347 0789
E-mail: donnah@amma.org
Web site: www.americapost.com/ema/
Web site notes: site includes statistics on retail sales of envelopes in the US as well as other industry statistics
Chief officers: Maynard Benjamin, (President)
Publications:
• Outlook for Envelopes: *six-month market forecast and analysis of current trends in the envelope manufacturing industry - semi-annual*

Flavour and Extracts Manufacturers' Association

Address: Suite 925, 1620 Eye Street, NW, Washington, DC 20006
Telephone: +1 202 293 5800
Fax: +1 202 463 8998
Year established: 1909
Activities: monitors government regulation and legislation; helps set safety standards for products
Chief officers: Daniel R Thompson (Executive Secretary)
Structure: permanent staff; board; committees
Membership: 130 manufacturers, wholesalers and suppliers

Food Marketing Institute (FMI)

Address: Suite 500, 800 Connecticut Avenue NW, Washington DC 20006
Telephone: +1 202 452 8444
Fax: +1 202 429 4519
E-mail: fmi@fmi.org
Web site: www.fmi.org
Year established: 1977
Activities: liaises with government and consumers; conducts research programs; continuing education
Chief officers: Timothy M Hammonds (President)
Structure: permanent staff; board
Membership: 1,500 grocery retailers and wholesalers
Publications:
• Annual Financial Review (Food Marketing Institute): *a review of the financial performance of the supermarkets sector in the USA with financial data over a five-year period. Based on a survey of members - annual*
• Consumer Attitudes and the Supermarket: *a survey of approximately 1,000 households obtaining consumer views on general economic issues, supermarkets, industry performance, shopping patterns. Seperate issues covering the following: U.S; Canada; Puerto Rico; Mexico; Australia and Europe - annual*
• Cumulative Index: *annual*
• Facts about Store Development: *examines areas such as new store size, costs of building and opening new stores, store remodelling and rental and leasing data for both new and existing stores. Based on data collected by the Institute - annual*
• Food Marketing Industry Speaks: *two volumes covering the food wholesaling and retailing trade with data on sales and production in the USA and Canada. Volume 1 has a commentary on the sector with summary data and Volume 2 contains the detailed statistics. Based on a combination of sources - annual*
• Food Retailing and Distribution: Issues And Opportunities Around the World: *detailed information on key industry issues identified by supermarket CEOs around the world. Issues highlighted include competition, consumer lifestyles, the economy, environmental issues, financial trends, government, labour, nutrition/food safety, operations and technology. Results are examined globally and for the following regions: Australia, New Zealand, Japan, other Pacific Rim countries, North America, Latin America, Continental Europe, the United Kingdom and Africa, Middle East - annual*
• Issues Bulletin: *monthly*

• Operating Results of Independent Superstores: *an annual review of the financial performance of independent superstores based on a survey by the Institute - annual*
• Supermarket Facts: *information package presents the industry's view of major food issues. Separate sections discuss such issues as food prices, food and nutrition, food safety, competition and profits, marketing costs, productivity and consumers' views - annual*
• Supermarket Industry Financial Review: *annual*
• Supermarket Operations In Latin America: *study of retail food operations in Latin America examines many areas of supermarket retailing, including productivity and operations results, product mix and human resource concerns - irregular*
• Washington Report: *weekly*

Foodservice and Packaging Institute (FPI)

Address: 1901 North Moore Street, Suite 918, Arlington, Virginia 22209
Telephone: +1 703 527 7505
Fax: +1 703 527 7512
E-mail: foodserv@crosslink.net
Web site: www.fpi.org
Web site notes: site includes statistics on disposable food-service products, including retail sales volume and value
Year established: 1933
Activities: government lobbying, compiles statistics on the industry
Chief officers: Celia T. Besore (Manager, Communication Technologies), Ann Mattheis (Director and Public Affairs)
Membership: manufacturers, raw-material suppliers, machinery suppliers, and distributors of food service disposable products. These products consist of single-use cups, plates, bowls, bags, wraps, cutlery, trays, egg cartons, nested dairy and salad containers and other disposable items
Publications:
• Foodservice Disposables and Packaging Product Directory: *foodservice products manufactured by FPI member companies as well as raw materials and a list of machinery suppliers and foodservice product distributors - annual*
• Indispensable Info: *trends in the foodservice industry - quarterly*
• Product Directory: *lists all FPI members' products - annual*

Footwear Distributors and Retailers of America (FDRA)

Address: 1319 F Street NW, Suite 700, Washington, DC 20004-1153
Telephone: +1 202 737 5660
Fax: +1 202 638 2615
E-mail: fdra@fdra.org
Web site: www.fdra.org
Chief officers: Peter Mangione (President), Faith Lewis (Statistical Services)

Footwear Industries of America (FIA)

Address: 1420 K Street, NW Suite 600, Washington DC 20005
Telephone: +1 202 789 1420
Fax: +1 202 789 4058
E-mail: mbrshp@fia.org
Web site: www.fia.org
Web site notes: site includes detailed statistics on the US footwear market
Year established: 1982
Activities: compiles statistics, organises the annual trade show Global Leather
Structure: permanent staff; board, committees
Membership: US manufacturers, suppliers, retailers, importers and distributors of footwear
Publications:
• Shoestats: *detailed commentary and statistics on the U.S. footwear market. Includes statistics on production, retail sales, distribution, brand availability, imports, exports, etc. - annual*

Fragrance Foundation
Address: 14th Floor, 145 East 32nd Street, New York, NY 10016
Telephone: +1 212 725 2758
Fax: +1 212 779 9058
E-mail: info@fragrance.org.
Web site: www.fragrance.org
Year established: 1949
Activities: public relations to promote use and care of perfume and like products
Chief officers: Annette Green (Director)
Structure: permanent staff; board
Membership: 170 perfume manufacturers, suppliers
Publications:
• Fragrance Forum: *newsletter - quarterly*
• Fragrance, Fashion and Lifestyle Trends Forecast: *overview of lifestyle and fashion trends for both men and women, and an in-depth report on fragrance trends - bi-annual*

Furniture Manufacturers' Alliance (FMA)
Address: 301 North Fairfax Street, Alexandria, VA 22314
Telephone: +1 703 549 904/800 542 6672
Fax: +1 703 683 7552
E-mail: dsolomon@bpia.org
Web site: www.bpia.org/alliances/fma.htm
Chief officers: David Solomon (Associate Executive Director)
Notes: The Association is part of the Business Products Industry Association.

General Merchandise Distributors' Council (GMDC)
Address: 1275 Lake Plaza Drive, Colorado Springs, CO 80906
Telephone: +1 303 576 4260
Fax: +1 303 375 1859
Web site: www.gmdc.com
Year established: 1970
Activities: research, compilation of statistics and conferences
Membership: 650 wholesalers of non-food items
Publications:
• Newsletter of the General Merchandise Distributors Council: *monthly*
• Occasional legal briefings

Glass Packaging Institute (GPI)
Address: Suite 800, 1627 K Street NW, Washington, DC 20006
Telephone: +1 202 887 4850
Fax: +1 202 785 5377
E-mail: gpiwest@aol.com
Web site: www.gpi.org
Year established: 1945
Activities: conducts promotional activities; liaison with government; monitors government regulation and legislation; conducts research
Chief officers: Mr. Joseph J. Cattaneo (Executive Vice President)
Structure: permanent staff; board; committees
Membership: member companies produce glass containers for food, beer, soft drinks, wine, spirits, cosmetics, toiletries, medicine, etc. In addition to serving domestic companies that manufacture glass containers, GPI also represents Canadian and Mexican glass container companies, numerous suppliers and closure manufacturers

Grocery Manufacturers of America (GMA)
Address: Suite 900, 1010 Wisconsin Avenue, NW, Washington, DC 20007
Telephone: +1 202 337 9400
Fax: +1 202 337 4508
E-mail: webmaster@gmabrands.com
Web site: www.gmabrands.com
Year established: 1908
Activities: monitors government legislation and regulation; lobbies; provides advice on distribution practices
Chief officers: C Manly Molpus (President and CEO)
Structure: permanent staff; board; committees
Membership: represents companies accounting for 90% of all food and consumer packaged goods sold in the U.S
Publications:
• GMA Directory: *annual*
• Grocery Manufacturers of America Executive Letter: *newsletter - monthly*
• Washington Report: *summary of important legislative and regulatory developments, issue briefs and other relevant information concerning federal governmental actions affecting grocery manufacturers - monthly*

Health Insurance Association of America (HIAA)
Address: 555 13th Street NW, Washington, D.C. 20004
Telephone: +1 202 824 1600
E-mail: drandolph@hiaa.org
Web site: www.hiaa.org
Year established: 1956
Activities: government lobbying, research and education programs on health care and health insurance
Chief officers: Christos Orestis III (Director of External Affairs), Richard Coorsh (Manager of Media Relations)
Membership: 250 members include commercial insurers and businesses that provide products and services to the health insurance industry
Publications:
• Source Book of Health Insurance Data: *an annual review of health insurance coverage, benefits, premium income, health care programmes, costs, etc. Historical data in many tables - annual*

Hobby Industry Association (HIA)
Address: P.O. Box 348, 319 East 54th Street, Elmwood Park, N.J. 07407
Telephone: +1 201 794 1133
Fax: +1 201 797 0657
E-mail: hia@ix.netcom.com
Web site: www.hobby.org/hia/
Year established: 1940
Activities: organises the world's largest craft and hobby trade show each January in the U.S. and the largest European trade market dedicated exclusively to crafts and hobbies in the Netherlands in March. The Association also sponsors the Craft and Hobby Information Bureau (which provides the consumer press with industry information) and conducts market research
Membership: 4,100 member companies

Hospitality Sales and Marketing Association International (HSMAI)
Address: Suite 800, 1300 L Street NW, Washington, DC 20005
Telephone: +1 202 789 0089
Fax: +1 202 789 1725
E-mail: rsmythe@hsmai.org
Web site: www.hsmai.org
Chief officers: Robert A. Gilbert (Executive Vice President), Kenneth Esthus (Marketing Director)
Structure: permanent staff; board; committees
Membership: 4,000 multinational hospitality professionals
Publications:
• HSMAI - Update: *membership newsletter with coverage of the Associations activities - bi-monthly*
• HSMAI Marketing Review: *latest trends in the in U.S. hospitality sales and marketing - quarterly*

Independent Bankers' Association of America (IBAA)
Address: Suite 950, One Thomas Circle, NW, Washington, DC 20005

Telephone: +1 800 422 8439
Fax: +1 202 659 9216
E-mail: info@ibaa.org
Web site: www.ibaa.org
Year established: 1930
Activities: acts as government liaison and monitors legislation and regulation; sponsors educational seminars; provides group purchasing programs
Chief officers: Robert Forbus (Director of Communications), Kenneth A. Guenther (Executive Vice President)
Structure: permanent staff; board; committees
Membership: IBAA represents 5,500 independent community banks
Publications:
• Community Bank Director Quarterly: *newsletter - quarterly*
• Independent Banker: *journal - monthly*
• Washington Weekly Report: *newsletter - weekly*

Independent Cosmetic Manufacturers and Distributors (ICMAD)

Address: 1220 W Northwest Highway, Palatine, IL 60067
Telephone: +1 847 991 4499
Fax: +1 847 991 8161
E-mail: picmad@aol.com
Web site: www.trainingforum.com/ASN/ICMAD
Year established: 1974
Activities: monitors government regulations and legislation in relation with product testing and product liability; provides group product liability insurance
Chief officers: Penni Jones (Executive Director)
Structure: permanent staff; board
Membership: ICMAD membership is composed of over 600 small to medium size cosmetic companies from 37 states and 12 foreign companies. They represent all segments of the cosmetic and beauty industry including manufacturers, distributors, marketers, retailers, consultants, educators, R&D labs, chemists and suppliers
Publications:
• ICMAD Digest: *a synopsis of matters current and important to the cosmetic industry - 10 p.a.*

Independent Grocers' Alliance (IGA)

Address: 8725 W. Higgins Road, Chicago, Illinois 60631-2773
Telephone: +1 773 693 4520
Fax: +1 773 693 1271
E-mail: talm@igainc.com
Web site: www.igainc.com/homepage.stm
Year established: 1926
Chief officers: Paulo G. Goelzer (President)
Membership: 3,600 supermarkets

Independent Petroleum Association of America (IPAA)

Address: 1101 16th Street NW, Washington, DC 20036
Telephone: +1 202 857 4722
Fax: +1 202 857 4799
E-mail: lmeyer@ipaa.org
Web site: www.ipaa.org
Web site notes: site includes comprehensive statistics on the US petroleum industry
Year established: 1929
Activities: compiles statistics; acts as lobbying group; monitors government regulation and legislation
Chief officers: Kate Hutcheons (Communications)
Structure: permanent staff; board; committees
Membership: 8,000 independent crude oil and natural gas explorers/producers in the United States
Publications:
• Domestic Oil and Gas Trends: *includes statistics for supply and demand trends, oil and natural gas data with prices, employment, etc. Also includes quarterly well completion data*

and footage drilled, wholesale prices for gasoline, kerosene, distillate and residual fuel oil - monthly
• IPAA Supply and Demand Committee Report (Short and Long-Run Forecasts): *forecasts U.S. supply and demand for petroleum products and natural gas on a quarterly basis. It also includes projections for other energy sources and general macroeconomic conditions - monthly*
• Petroleum Independent - The Oil and Gas Producing Industry in Your State: *the Association's journal, published regularly throughout the year. One issue per year has an annual review of the US petroleum sector with statistics for the USA in total and by individual state. Statistics cover production, reserves, drilling, prices, employment, costs, supply of petroleum products. Summary data is given for a number of years - annual*
• Profile of Independent Producers: *statistical portrait of independent oil and natural gas producers. It includes demographic, financial and operating information as well as accompanying tables and graphs. The data is broken down by size of company to show the variations from small to large firms - annual*
• State of the Industry: *one page overview of industry positions and trends. Includes latest statistics on employment, imports, production, drilling, and reserves - annual*
• United States Petroleum Statistics: *up-to-date annual data for the U.S. oil and natural gas business. Covers exploration, drilling, reserves, supply, demand, prices, costs, industry employment, financial indicators etc. - annual*

Information Technology Association of America (ITAA)

Address: Suite 1300, 1616 North Ft Myer Drive, Arlington, VA 22209
Telephone: +1 703 522 5055
Fax: +1 703 525 2279
E-mail: bcohen@itaa.org
Web site: www.itaa.org
Year established: 1960
Activities: compiles statistics; conducts research; monitors government regulation and legislation; offers educational seminars
Chief officers: Bob Cohen (VP, Communications), Mr Harris Miller (President)
Structure: permanent staff; board; committees
Membership: 700 information technology companies
Publications:
• DATA Newsletter: *bi-monthly*
• ITAA Membership Directory: *annual*

Information Technology Industry Council (ITIC)

Address: Suite 200, 1250 I Street NW, Washington, DC 20005
Telephone: +1 202 737 8888
Fax: +1 202 638 4922
E-mail: hsayadian@itic.nw.dc.us
Web site: www.itic.org
Web site notes: site includes some statistics on US PC shipments
Year established: 1916
Activities: compiles industry statistics; liaises with government; monitors government regulation and legislation
Chief officers: Helga Sayadian (Director, Industry Statistics Programs)
Structure: permanent staff; board; committees
Membership: 25 manufacturers of information processing and business equipment
Publications:
• Information Technology Industry Databook: *in-depth statistics on the following: U.S. information technology industry performance and the national economy; U.S. employment and earnings, education and establishment distribution; U.S. market analysis (product shipments); tariff, trade and customs information; international statistics on information technology*

industry markets, major economic indicators, employment, R&D, and trade. Also includes an index of information sources as well as historical and forecast data - annual

Institute for Brewing Studies
Address: PO Box 1679, Boulder, CO 80306-1679
Telephone: +1 303 4470816
Fax: +1 303 4472825
E-mail: service@aob.org
Activities: publishes a bi-monthly magazine, The New Brewer; presents the annual National Craft-brewers Conference and Trade Show
Membership: 1500 members
Publications:
• New Brewer: *brewing industry statistics, home-brewing news and suggestions, all matters relating to home-brewing - bi-monthly*

Institute of Management Accountants (IMA)
Address: 10 Paragon Drive, Montvale- NJ 07645 - 1760
Telephone: +1 800 638 4427
Fax: +1 800 638 4427
E-mail: lestelle@imanet.org
Web site: www.rutgers.edu/Accounting/raw/ima/ima.htm
Membership: 80,000 members
Publications:
• IMA Focus: *IMA activities and issues affecting the accounting profession - bi-monthly*
• Management Accounting: *articles on the latest finance and accounting techniques - monthly*

International Association of Business Communicators
Address: 1 Hallidie Plaza Suite 600, San Francisco - CA 94102
Telephone: +1 415 433 3400
Fax: +1 415 362 8762
E-mail: service_centre@iabc.com
Web site: www.iabc.com
Year established: 1970
Activities: provides products, services, activities and networking opportunities to help people and organisations achieve excellence in public relations, employee communication, marketing communication, public affairs and other forms of communication; offers the Communication Bank, a comprehensive information service to members
Chief officers: Don Brunn (Chairman), Elizabeth Allan (President CEO)
Membership: 12,500 worldwide
Publications:
• Communication World: *marketing communication, media relations, employee communication, career advice, work in the corporate, agency and freelance spheres, how to harness technology, how to communicate globally, strategic planning - monthly*

International Dairy-Deli-Bakery Association (IDDA)
Address: PO Box 5528, Madison, WI 53705-0528
Telephone: +1 608 238 7908
Fax: +1 608 238 6330
E-mail: IDDA@iddanet.org
Web site: www.iddanet.org
Year established: 1964
Activities: professional dialogue, education, exchange of industry data and selling opportunities, organises the annual trade fair Dairy-Deli-Bake
Membership: manufacturers, retailers, distributors, brokers
Publications:
• Consumers In The Bakery: Who, What, When, Why, and Where They Buy and How to Get Them to Buy More: *in-depth statistical report covering consumption trends of breads, sweet goods, desserts and bakery products. Also covers*

consumer dietary habits, purchasing patterns, etc. - annual
• Consumers In The Deli: Who, What, When, Why and Where They Buy and How to Get Them to Buy More: *covers: prevalence of deli users; delis in supermarkets; where deli shoppers make most of their deli purchases; frequency of deli shopping; why people shop at delis; household consumption of various deli items; shopping and consumption behavior of deli users; importance of dietary and other factors with respect to purchase behaviors; opinions about foods from delis and satisfaction with variety, quality, and price; deli services and characteristics - annual*
• Dairy-Deli-Bake Digest: *new management trends, new products, reports, reviews, association news, features, and consumer attitudes and trends - monthly*
• Dairy-Deli-Bake Wrap-Up: *covers IDDA's seminars, expositions, member news, awards, programs and services - quarterly*
• IDDA Legis-Letter: *highlights recent legislative bills and reports, FDA activities, and topical issues - monthly*
• IDDA's What's In Store: *in-depth statistical profile of bakery and dairy consumption. Includes trends in the industry and consumer lifestyle trends*

International Food Information Council (IFIC)
Address: 1100 Connecticut Avenue N.W., Suite 430, Washington D.C. 20036
E-mail: foodinfo@ific.health.org
Year established: 1985
Activities: promotes the exchange and dissemination of scientifically-based information on food safety and nutrition
Membership: leading food and beverage companies

International Music Products' Association (NAMM)
Address: 5790 Armada Dr, Carlsbad, CA 92008
Telephone: +1 760 438 8001
Fax: +1 760 438 7327
E-mail: namm@namm.com
Web site: www.namm.com
Year established: 1901
Activities: collects statistics
Chief officers: Larry Herrmann (Information Services Manager), John Maher (Communications Director)
Structure: permanent staff; board
Membership: 6,000 music products retailers, manufacturers, distributors, wholesalers and publishers located in the United States and in more than 100 other countries
Publications:
• Music USA - A Statistical Review of the US Music Products Industry: *an annual review of the music industry including product sales, retail trends, prices, etc. Based on the Association's own surveys, including an opinion survey of consumers and a survey of music dealers - annual*
• National Association of Music Merchants News: *monthly*

International Swimwear and Activewear Market (ISAM)
Address: 110 E. 9th Street A-727, Los Angeles, CA 90079
Telephone: +1 213 630 3610
Fax: +1 213 624 9368
Web site: www.apparelnet.com/isam
Year established: 1978
Chief officers: Barbara Brady (ISAM Coordinator)

Intimate Apparel Council (IAC)
Address: c/o The Bromley Group, 150 Fifth Avenue, Suite 510, New York, NY 10011
Telephone: +1 212 807 0978
Web site: www.apparelnet.com/iac
Activities: conducts consumer and retail research to explore industry trends and opportunities
Membership: lingerie manufacturers, distributors and retailers

Notes: A division of the American Apparel Manufacturers Association.

Investment Counsel Association of America (ICAA)

Address: Suite 725, 1050 17th Street, NW, Washington, DC 20036-5503
Telephone: +1 202 293 4222
Fax: +1 202 293 4223
E-mail: ICAA@icaa.org
Web site: www.icaa.org
Year established: 1937
Membership: 215 investment adviser firms

Jewellers of America, Inc. (JA)

Address: 30th Floor, 1185 Avenue of the Americas, New York, NY 10036
Telephone: +1 212 768 8777
Fax: +1 212 768 8087
E-mail: jewelersam@aol.com
Web site: www.jewelers.org
Activities: conducts surveys and compiles statistics, offers scholarships
Chief officers: Matthew Runci (Executive Director), Eileen Farrell (Director of Marketing and Communications)
Structure: permanent staff; board
Membership: 15,000 retailers

Juvenile Products Manufacturers' Association (JPMA)

Address: 236 Route 38 West, Suite 100 Moorestown, NJ 08057
Telephone: +1 609 231 8500
Fax: +1 609 231 4664
E-mail: jpma@ahint.com
Web site: www.jpma.org
Year established: 1962
Activities: organises a trade show; conducts research and surveys; provides information on international trade, produces statistics
Structure: permanent staff; board
Membership: 250 manufacturers of infant products such as cribs, car seats, strollers, bedding, and a wide range of accessories and decorative items

Leather Industries of America

Address: Suite 515, 1000 Thomas Jefferson Street, Washington, DC 20007-3805
Telephone: +1 202 342 8086
Fax: +1 202 342 9063
Chief officers: Charles S Myers (President)
Publications:
• US Leather Industry Statistics: *statistics on leather production and foreign trade, livestock slaughterings, footwear, non-rubber shoe market, tanning, hide prices. Historical data is given in most tables - annual*

Luggage and Leather Goods Manufacturers of America Inc. (LLGMA)

Address: Suite 2624, 350 Fifth Avenue, New York, NY 10118
Telephone: +1 212 695 2340
Fax: +1 212 643 8021
E-mail: llgma@llgma.org
Web site: www.llgma.com
Year established: 1938
Activities: organises the annual International Travelgoods, Leather and Accessories Show, maintains a file of all trade names registered in the luggage and leather goods industry
Chief officers: Robert K Ermatinger (Executive Vice President)
Structure: permanent staff; board

Membership: 240 manufacturers and wholesalers of luggage, handbags, novelties and other leather goods
Publications:
• Customs and Trade Newsletter: *trade and customs matters,including trade with China, changes to textile quotas (including a quota bulletin report), labeling issues, classification issues, and customs compliance measures. Also provides information for exporters including: relevant trade show listings; opportunities for travelgoods products in other markets, information on trading over the Internet and relevant Internet addresses - monthly*
• FTC Industry Guides: *latest information on FTC rules covering "Made in USA" labeling and advertising, leather and imitation leather labeling, and advertising allowances and other merchandising payments and services - annual*
• LLGMA Exporting Guide: *information necessary to export, find profession assistance, and provide basic export information on luggage, flat goods, handbags, belts and luggage carts - annual*
• NAFTA Export Guide: *provides an overview of the treatment of luggage and personal leather goods in NAFTA - annual*
• Showcase: *covers new products and trends in the U.S. luggage and leather goods markets - bi-monthly*
• Statistical Reports: *detailed information on imports and exports of luggage and leather goods - quarterly*

Marketing Research Association

Address: 2189 Silas Deane Hwy. Suite 5, Rocky Hill, CT 06067-0230
Telephone: +1 203 257 4008
Fax: +1 203 257 3990
E-mail: email@mra-net.org
Web site: www.mra-net.org
Publications:
• Alert: *industry events, legislative and management issues, and Association news - monthly*
• MRA Blue Book: *detailed information on market research companies and their services - annual*

Milk Industry Foundation (MIF)

Address: Suite 900, 1250 High Street NW, Washington DC 20005
Telephone: +1 202 737 4332
Fax: +1 202 331 7820
E-mail: jrice@idfa.org
Web site: www.foodexpo.com/orgs/mif/
Publications:
• Milk Facts (Milk Industry Foundation): *annual statistics on the milk industry covering production, sales, consumption, trade, industry structure, employment. Historical statistics are included along with some international statistics - annual*

Mohair Council of America

Address: P.O. Box 5337, 516 Norwest Bank Building, San Angelo, Texas 76902
Telephone: +1 915 655 3161
Fax: +1 800 583 3161
E-mail: mohair@airmail.net
Web site: www.mohairusa.com
Chief officers: Duery Menzies (Executive Director)

Mortgage Bankers' Association of America (MBA)

Address: 1125 15th Street NW, Washington, DC 20005
Telephone: +1 202 861 6500
Fax: +1 202 429 1672
Web site: www.mbaa.org
Year established: 1914
Activities: collects statistics; conducts research; offers continuing education programs; acts as government liaison
Chief officers: Warren Lasko (Executive Vice President)

Structure: permanent staff; board; committees
Membership: 2,700 corporations involved in mortgage finance
Publications:
• MBA Directory of Members: *information on key personnel, branch office locations, ownership, and activity volume - annual*
• Mortgage Banking: *monthly trends in the mortgage market with data on housing construction, sales, lending, etc. "Vital Statistics" section in each issue - monthly*
• Mortgage Banking Performance Report: *contains a balance sheet, income statement, and key performance ratios for mortgage banking companies - annual*
• Mortgage Banking Sourcebook: *reference guide to regulatory, legislative, tax and accounting, and educational information on the mortgage lending industry. It serves as a comprehensive directory to federal and state government agencies, as well as private sources of information on mortgage lending - weekly*
• Mortgage Finance Review: *industry trends, including housing starts and sales, origination volume and market share, trends in delinquencies, movements of refinancing activity etc. - quarterly*
• Mortgage Market Scan: *lists the top 30 lenders ranked by dollar volume of origination's and provides each lender's share of the overall purchase, refi, jumbo, government, and conventional markets; evaluates MSA approval and denial rates for applicants by race and controlling for income; provides a demographic report, housing report, and population overview. - annual*
• National HMDA Databook: *provides number and dollar volume of loan applications and originations for the nation categorized by loan purpose and loan type - annual*
• Real Estate Finance Today: *news reports on events and trends affecting the residential and commercial mortgage markets - monthly*
• Weekly Survey of Mortgage Applications: *average loan sizes, contract interest rates, and corresponding points for six popular mortgage products and their share of market volume - weekly*

Motor and Equipment Manufacturers' Association (MEMA)

Address: PO Box 13966, 10 Laboratory Drive, Research Triangle Park, NC 27709
Telephone: +1 919 549 4800
Fax: +1 919 549 4824
E-mail: info@mema.com
Web site: www.aftmkt.com/MISG/associations/MEMA
Year established: 1904
Activities: conducts market research, monitoring of legislation and regulations, representation on major legislative and regulatory issues, periodic informational bulletins on the industry and in-depth information on foreign markets and market opportunities
Chief officers: Robert R Miller (President)
Structure: permanent staff; board, committees
Membership: 700 manufacturers

National Agri-Marketing Association (NAMA)

Address: Suite 205, 11020 King Street, Overland Park, KS 66210
Telephone: +1 913 491 6500
Fax: +1 913 491 6502
E-mail: agrimktg@nama.org
Web site: www.nama.org
Year established: 1957
Activities: organises the annual Agri-Marketing Conference, education and training
Chief officers: Eldon J White (Executive Director), Jenny Conrad (Communications Director)
Structure: permanent staff, local groups

Membership: 2,500 individuals involved in agricultural marketing
Publications:
• NAMA Directory of Members: *includes full contact details of member companies - annual*
• National Agri-marketing Association News: *newsletter - bi-weekly*

National Association of Beverage Importers

Address: 1025 Vermont Avenue North West, Washington DC 20005
Telephone: +1 202 638 1617
Fax: +1 202 638 3122
Publications:
• NABI Annual Statistical Report: *annual statistics on the imports of wine, spirits and beer with data on specific types of drink. Most tables have historical data back to the 1950s and, in some cases, the 1930s. Based largely on official statistics - annual*

National Association of Beverage Retailers

Address: 5101 River Rd., #108, Bethesda, MD 20816
Telephone: +1 301 656 1494
Fax: +1 301 656 7539

National Association of Broadcasters

Address: 1771 North Street NW, Washington DC 20036
Telephone: +1 202 429 5300
Fax: +1 202 429 5343
E-mail: kcrum@nab.org
Web site: www.cmmnet.com
Year established: 1922
Activities: legislative lobbying; employment clearinghouse; provides grants for broadcasting related research
Chief officers: Edward O Fritts (CEO and President)
Structure: permanent staff; board, committees
Membership: 7,500 representatives of radio and TV stations, networks and suppliers
Publications:
• America's Watching: Public Attitudes Towards Television: *based on interviews with 2,000 adults aged over 18, a survey of attitudes with comparative data from earlier years - biennial*
• Conference Proceedings: *annual*
• Member Services Catalogue: *annual*
• RadioWeek: *weekly*
• Television Financial Report: *financial and employment data for commercial TV broadcasting stations, by station category, market size, revenue size - annual*
• TV Today: *weekly*

National Association of Chain Drug Stores (NACDS)

Address: PO Box 1417-D49, 413 N. Lee Street, Alexandria, Virginia 22313-1480
Telephone: +1 703 549 3001
Fax: +1 703 836 4869
E-mail: info@nacds.org
Web site: www.nacds.org
Web site notes: site includes an industry facts section
Year established: 1933
Activities: maintains a library, tracks and interprets government action in the drug field; sponsors meetings and seminars on marketing, administrative operations, etc.
Chief officers: Thomas M. Ryan (Chairman)
Structure: permanent staff; board; committees
Membership: 30,000 community retail pharmacies, and chain-operated community retail pharmacies representing 60% of prescriptions dispensed in the United States
Publications:
• Executive Newsletter (National Association of Chain Drug Stores): *news about the chain drug store industry, coverage of*

NACDS meetings, and information on NACDS members, programs, and resources - bi-monthly
• NACDS Membership Directory: *lists the chain and associate members with key personnel; product categories of manufacturers, distributors and service providers; retail buyers by product category and warehousing information - annual*
• NACDS Source Book: *lists industry organisations and publications, state pharmacy associations, state boards of pharmacy, schools of pharmacy, state retail/chain drug store associations, key U.S. Government offices and U.S. House and Senate committees - annual*

National Association of Chemical Distributors (NACD)
Address: Suite 750, 1525 Wilson Boulevard, Arlington, VA, 22209
Telephone: +1 703 527 6223
Fax: +1 703 527 7747
E-mail: mail@nacd.com
Web site: www.nacd.com

National Association of Convenience Stores (NACS)
Address: 1605 King Street, Alexandria, VA 22314
Telephone: +1 703 684 3600
Fax: +1 703 836 4564
E-mail: nacs@cstorecentral.com
Web site: www.cstorecentral.com/public/nacs/05.htm
Year established: 1961
Activities: government liaison; compiles statistics; conducts education programs; conducts seminars
Chief officers: Kerley Le Boeuf (President), Teri Richman (Research and Information)
Structure: permanent staff; board; committees
Membership: 2,000 retail companies operating over 68,000 convenience stores in the United States and all over the world
Publications:
• Convenience Store Fact Book: *survey of the convenience store sector, giving a 10 year back file of data on industry trends*
• Convenience Store Industry Fact Book: *a report with ten years' worth of data on convenience store industry trends. Includes data on store sales, profits, merchandising categories, labour costs, gasoline operations, etc - annual*
• National Association of Convenience Stores SCAN: *newsletter - monthly*
• National Association of Convenience Stores: Membership and Services Directory: *annual*
• State of the Convenience Store Industry Report: *an annual compilation of convenience store data including statistics on gas and non-gas sales, operating costs, expenses, initial outlay for land, building, equipment and inventory. The report also contains product category breakdowns illustrating dollars/sales percentages and gross margins for each category. Based on a survey of approximately 67,000 stores - annual*
• Washington Report: *bi-weekly*

National Association of Electrical Distributors Inc. (NAED)
Address: 45 Danbury Road, Wilton, CT 06897
Telephone: +1 203 761 4900
Fax: +1 203 762 0324
E-mail: lhealy@naed.org (Information or Publications)
Web site: www.naed.org
Year established: 1908
Activities: government liaison; collects statistics; offer educational programs and seminars; improves member networking
Chief officers: R. Lee Hite (Chairman)
Structure: permanent staff; regional groups; board;

committees
Membership: 4,000 manufacturers, wholesale distributors of electrical supplies and equipment
Publications:
• Membership Directory: *annual*
• TED (The Electrical Distributor Magazine): *news, opinions, commentary and market trends on the U.S. electrical distribution industry - monthly*

National Association of Export Companies (NEXCO)
Address: P.O. Box 1330, New York, NY 10156
Telephone: +1 212 725 3311
Fax: +1 212 725 3312
E-mail: info@nexco.org
Web site: www.imex.com/nexco
Year established: 1965
Activities: maintains the NEX-Connection database of 4,500 export trade intermediaries (management and trading companies, agents, distributors, wholesalers and representatives) in the U.S. providing a wide range of products and services to U.S. manufacturers and overseas importers and buyers
Chief officers: Land Grant (President), Peter Robinson (Executive Director)
Membership: export management and export trading companies, manufacturing exporters, export service providers and individual entrepreneurs with an interest in exporting

National Association of Home Builders of the United States (NAHB)
Address: 1201 15th Street NW, Washington, DC 20005
Telephone: +1 202 822 0200
Fax: +1 202 822 0559
E-mail: info@nahb.com
Web site: www.nahb.com
Web site notes: site includes Housing Facts and Figures with detailed statistics on US housing
Year established: 1942
Activities: lobbies on behalf of housing industry and conducts public affairs activities relating to housing and its relationship to the economy; collects statistical information, sponsors seminars and workshops on building practices and technology
Chief officers: Kent W Colton (Executive Vice President)
Structure: permanent staff; local groups; board; committees
Membership: 164,000 builders/contractors and others
Publications:
• Home Builders Forecast: *short-term forecasts of trends in the US housing market - monthly*
• Housing Economics: *a monthly analysis of various subjects related to housing. Regular features include the Housing Outlook, a review of the latest data on housing starts and other measures of housing activity. Every issue has a special feature - monthly*
• Housing Market Statistics: *detailed monthly statistics on housing starts, completions and other measures of housing activity - monthly*

National Association of Hosiery Manufacturers
Address: 447 S. Sharon Amity Road, Charlotte NC 28211
Telephone: +1 703 365 0913
Fax: +1 703 362 2056
E-mail: nahminc@aol.com
Web site: www.nahm.com
Web site notes: site includes detailed statistics and analysis on the US hosiery market including production and retail sales
Chief officers: Chuck Brooks (Executive Vice President), Sally F. Kay (Vice President and Secretary)
Publications:
• Annual Statistics: *figures on US hosiery production and other statistics on shipments, inventories, per capita consumption,*

imports, exports, number of companies, plants, and
employment. Production and shipment figures cover a
ten-year period with data for specific product categories.
Based on various sources - annual
• Directory of NAHM Member Hosiery Mill Suppliers: *company
name, address and phone number of the suppliers are listed.
Products, services and companies are cross-referenced -
annual*
• Hosiery News: *contains articles and information regarding,
industry announcements, personnel changes, foreign trade,
financial data and retail sales trends - monthly*
• NAHM's Directory of Hosiery Manufacturers and Distributors:
*detailed directory on U.S. hosiery. Includes addresses,
telephone numbers and key personnel as well as product
information - annual*
• Quarterly Statistics: *comprehensive report that details
production/shipments, sales, international trade and NAFTA
data for the entire hosiery industry - quarterly*

National Association of Independent Insurers (NAII)
Address: 2600 Driver Road, Des Plaines, IL 60018
Telephone: +1 847 297 7800
Fax: +1 847 297 5064
E-mail: badaire@naii.org
Web site: www.naii.org
Membership: 560 independent insurance companies

National Association of Manufacturers (NAM)
Address: Suite 600, 1331 Pennsylvania Avenue NW,
Washington DC 20004
Telephone: +1 202 637 3000
Fax: +1 202 637 3182
E-mail: manufacturing@nam.org
Web site: www.nam.org
Year established: 1895
Chief officers: Jerry J Jasinowski (President)
Structure: permanent staff; board, committees
Membership: 14,000 member companies and subsidiaries
representing 85 percent of U.S. output of manufactured goods
Publications:
• Briefing: *developments in legislation affecting manufacturing
industry - irregular*
• Exporter: *details on implementation of GATT rules, European
Union developments, general legal and regulatory issues
affecting trade, etc. - irregular*
• Harris Manufacturers Directory, Volumes I & II: *company
profiles; key contacts with titles, addresses, telephone and fax
numbers; employment figures; import/export information;
product descriptions; computer make; annual sales; facility
size, etc. - annual*
• World Trade: *covers a broad array of trade topics, including
export licensing, barter and trends in trade practices - 8 p.a.*
• World Trade and Customs Directory: *directory of trade and
customs officials around the globe - annual*

National Association of Margarine Manufacturers (NAMM)
Address: Suite 202, 1101 15th Street NW, Washington, DC
20005
Telephone: +1 202 785 3232
Fax: +1 202 223 9741
E-mail: namm@assnhq.com
Web site: www.margarine.org/namm.htm
Year established: 1936
Activities: acts as government liaison; monitors government
regulation and legislation; promotes margarine products
Chief officers: Belva Jones (Director)
Structure: permanent staff; board
Membership: 30 margarine manufacturers, distributors and
suppliers

Publications:
• Advocate: *newsletter - quarterly*

National Association of Recording Merchandisers (NARM)
Address: Suite 140, 11 Eves Drive, Morlton, NJ 08053
Telephone: +1 609 596 2221
Fax: +1 609 596 3268
E-mail: web_mstr@narm.com
Web site: www.narm.com
Web site notes: site includes the Association's annual survey
with detailed statistics and analysis of the US music and
pre-recorded entertainment software market
Year established: 1958
Activities: networking, annual convention, government
relations and public affairs, education and training, compiles
statistics on the industry
Chief officers: Pamela Horowitz (President), Jim Donio (Vice
President of Communications and Events)
Structure: permanent staff; board; committees
Membership: 1,200 retailers and wholesalers of music and
other pre-recorded entertainment software
Publications:
• Annual Survey of the National Association of Recording
Merchandisers: *detailed statistics and analysis of the U.S.
market for music and entertainment software. Includes
statistics on the following: album and single sales by type;
video sales by type; retail sales transactions; distribution
breakdown by type of outlet; sales by genre; sales by age and
by gender, etc. Also includes information detailed information
on retailers - annual*

National Association of Sporting Goods Wholesalers (NASGW)
Address: PO Box 11344, Chicago, IL 60611
Telephone: +1 312 565 0233
Fax: +1 312 565 0233
Web site: www.nasgw.org
Year established: 1954
Activities: compiles statistics
Chief officers: Rebecca A Maddy (Executive Director)
Structure: small permanent staff
Membership: 450 wholesalers and manufacturers of sporting
goods
Publications:
• Membership Directory: *annual*
• Sporting Goods Wholesaler: *bi-monthly*

National Association of Wholesale Distributors (NAW)
Address: 3rd Floor, 1725 K Street NW, Washington, DC 20006
Telephone: +1 202 872 0885
Fax: +1 202 785 0586
Year established: 1946
Activities: acts as liaison with federal government; monitors
government legislation and regulation; conducts public
relations; offers courses
Chief officers: Dirk Van Dongen (President)
Structure: permanent staff; board; committees
Membership: 45,000 national, state and regional associations
and wholesaler-distributor firms
Publications:
• NAW Report: *general interest - bi-monthly*

National Automatic Merchandising Association (NAMA)
Address: Suite 3500, 20 North Wacker Drive, Chicago IL
60606
Telephone: +1 312 346 0370
Fax: +1 312 704 4140
Web site: www.vending.org
Year established: 1936

Activities: compiles statistics; conducts research
Chief officers: Anna Cummings (President)
Structure: permanent staff; state groups; board
Membership: 2,400 membership is comprised of service companies, equipment manufacturers, suppliers of products and services, also includes distributors, brokers and other industry-related companies
Publications:
• Current Industrial Report: Vending Machines: *lists quantity and value of vending machines manufactured - annual*
• Directory of Members: *listing of over 2,200 vending and foodservice management firms that are NAMA members. Including independent firms and branches of national operating companies. Listed by state and city, identifies products vended by each firm and other services provided - annual*
• National Automatic Merchandising Association Newsletter: *bi-monthly*
• National Automatic Merchandising Association State Legislative Review: *newsletter - irregular*
• Vending Machine Shipments: *tabulation of vending machine shipments by type of machine, number and dollar value - annual*

National Automobile Dealers' Association (NADA)

Address: 8400 Westpark Drive, Mclean VA 22102
Telephone: +1 703 821 7000
Fax: +1 703 821 7075
E-mail: nada@nadanet.com
Web site: www.nadanet.com
Year established: 1917
Membership: represents 19,000 automotive retailers
Publications:
• American Truck Dealer Division Newsletter: *monthly*
• Automotive Executive Magazine: *monthly*
• NADA Data: *commentary and statistics on franchised new car and truck dealer operations and finances. Historical figures in many tables - annual*

National Beer Wholesalers' Association (NBWA)

Address: 1100 South Washington, Alexandria, VA 22314
Telephone: +1 703 683 4300
Fax: +1 703 683 8965
Web site: www.nbwa.org
Year established: 1938
Activities: conducts specialised education
Chief officers: Ronald R Sarasin (President)
Structure: permanent staff; board; committees
Membership: 800 independent wholesalers of beers and affiliates in malt beverage industry
Publications:
• Beer Perspectives: *weekly*
• Distributor Productivity Report: *triennial*
• NBWA Handbook: *annual*

National Bicycle Dealers' Association (NBDA)

Address: 2240 University Drive, #130, Newport Beach, CA 92660
Telephone: +1 714 722 6909
Fax: +1 714 722 1747
E-mail: bikeshops@aol.com
Web site: cyclery.com:80/NBDA/index.html

National Cable Television Association (NCTA)

Address: 1724 Massachussetts Avenue NW, Washington DC 20036
Telephone: +1 202 775 3669
Fax: +1 202 775 3696
Web site: www.ncta.com
Web site notes: site includes comprehensive statistics on the

US cable industry, including number of subscribers by region
Year established: 1952
Activities: serves as information and research clearing house; organises an annual trade show; lobbies on behalf of the industry; conducts research on cable television, technical and other issues; compiles statistics
Chief officers: S Decker Anstrom (President)
Structure: permanent staff, board, committees
Membership: 3,100 franchised cable operators, programmers, networks and suppliers
Publications:
• Linking Up: *quarterly*
• Newsletter of the National Cable Television Association: *irregular*
• Producer's Sourcebook: A Guide to Cable TV Program Buyers: *annual*
• Report: *irregular*
• Techline: *10 p.a.*

National Candle Association

Address: 1200 G. Street, Ste 760, Washington, DC 20005
Telephone: +1 202 393 1780
Web site: www.candles.org
Web site notes: site includes general statistics on the US candle market, including retail sales, distribution etc.
Membership: candle manufacturers and suppliers of wax, wicks, fragrance, machinery, moulds, dyes, packaging and container materials and other industry related products and services

National Candy Brokers' Association (NCBA)

Address: 710 East Ogden Avenue, Suite 600, Naperville,IL60563-8603
Naperville, IL 60563-8603
Telephone: +1 630 369 2406
Fax: +1 630 369 2488
E-mail: ncba@b-online.com
Web site: www.candynet.com
Web site notes: site includes online directory of US confectionery manufacturers
Membership: brokers who represent manufacturers and importers of confectionery and other related products either as individual brokers or salespeople who are employed by brokers
Publications:
• Candy Dish: *activities of the NCBA and member companies as well as news on the confectionery industry in general - quarterly*
• NCBA Membership Roster: *comprehensive directory includes all brokers, manufacturers and distributor members. In addition to the alphabetical listing, brokers members are also indexed by their territories - annual*

National Cheese Institute (NCI)

Address: 1250 H Street, NW, Washington DC 20005
Telephone: +1 202 737 4332
Fax: +1 202 331 7820
E-mail: jrice@idfa.org
Web site: www.foodexpo.com/orgs/nci/
Notes: Constituent organization of the International Dairy Foods Association (IDFA).

National Coffee Association of USA

Address: 13th Floor, 110 Wall Street, New York, NY 10005
Telephone: +1 212 344 5596
Fax: +1 212 425 7059
Year established: 1911
Activities: promotes increased coffee consumption; collects statistics; monitors government regulation and legislation
Chief officers: Robert N DeChillo (Secretary)

Structure: permanent staff; board; committees
Membership: 220 coffee importers, brokers, processors
Publications:
• Membership Directory: *annual*
• Newsletter of the National Coffee Association of USA: *weekly*

National Community Pharmacists' Association

Address: 205 Daingerfield Road, Alexandria, VA 22314
Telephone: +1 703 683 8200/800 544 7447
Fax: +1 703 683 3619
E-mail: info@ncpanet.org
Web site: www.vais.net/~ncpa/
Year established: 1898
Activities: offers comprehensive service covering advice on legal and insurance matters and product information; provides student assistance and professional qualification guidelines
Chief officers: Charles M West
Membership: 30,000 independent pharmacies
Publications:
• Almanac: *annual*
• Calendar: *annual*
• Journal: *monthly*
• Newsletter of the National Association of Retail Druggists: *fortnightly*
Notes: Formerly the National Association of Retail Druggists (NARD).

National Confectioners' Association of the United States (NCA)

Address: Suite A320, 7900 Westpark Drive, McLean VA 22102
Telephone: +1 703 790 5750
Fax: +1 703 790 5752
E-mail: info@candyusa.org
Web site: www.candyusa.org
Web site notes: site includes statistics on the US confectionery market and per capita trends worldwide
Year established: 1884
Activities: offers education and leadership in manufacturing, technical research, public relations, retailing practices, government relations, and statistical analyses
Chief officers: Lawrence T Graham (President)
Structure: permanent staff; board; committees
Membership: 69 confectionery manufacturing firms
Publications:
• Confectionery News Bulletin: *newsletter - irregular*

National Corn Growers' Association

Address: Suite 105, 1000 Executive Parkway, St Louis, MO 63141-6397
Telephone: +1 314 275 9915
Fax: +1 314 275 7061
E-mail: corninfo@ncga.com
Web site: www.ncga.com
Web site notes: site includes various statistics on US corn as well as world corn production
Year established: 1957
Activities: conducts research and educational programs, compiles statistics
Chief officers: Jeffrey W Gain (CEO)
Structure: permanent staff; state and local groups, board, committees
Membership: 26,000 corn growers
Publications:
• National Corn Grower: *newsletter - monthly*
• NCGA Membership Directory: *annual*

National Cotton Council of America

Address: PO Box 12285, 1918 North Parkway, Memphis TN 38182
Telephone: +1 901 274 9030

Fax: +1 901 725 0510
E-mail: info@cotton
Web site: cotton.rd.net/ncc/index.htm
Web site notes: site includes retail sales value of US Agricultural Commodities and information on the economic outlook for cotton
Year established: 1938
Activities: conducts public relations, economic, technical and government relations activities
Chief officers: Tom W. Smith (Chairman), Phillip C Burnett (Executive Vice President)
Structure: board, committee, permanent staff
Membership: 300 delegates from other cotton organisations
Publications:
• Cotton Counts it's Customers: *an annual review of the end user markets for cotton with a commentary and statistics on overall trends and the situation in specific end user sectors - annual*
• Cotton Economic Review: *newsletter, economic developments in industry - monthly*
• Cotton's Week: *newsletter, council activity - weekly*

National Customs Brokers' and Forwarders' Association of America, Inc.

Address: 1200 18th Street, N.W, #901 - Washington, DC 20036
Telephone: +1 202 466 0222
Fax: +1 202 466 0226
E-mail: staff@ncbfaa.org
Web site: www.tradecompass.com/fabnet

National Electrical Manufacturers' Association (NEMA)

Address: Suite 1847, 1300 North 17th Street, Rosslyn, Virginia 22209
Telephone: +1 703 841 3200
Fax: +1 703 841 3300
E-mail: rae_hamilton@nema.org (Communicationss Director)
Web site: www.nema.org
Activities: activities include the development of technical standards, the establishment and advocacy of industry policies on legislative and regulatory matters and the collection, analysis and dissemination of industry data
Chief officers: R. Hamilton (Director, Communications), Linden J. (Statistical Manager)
Membership: 600 member companies
Publications:
• Facts and Figures: *statistics on domestic shipments electrical equipment, imports, exports, etc. - annual*
• Survey of Business Trends: *statistics on orders, shipments, and unfilled orders for six electrical equipment sectors - power, industry, lighting, building, insulated wire and cable, electrical insulating material - quarterly*

National Farmers' Organisation (NFO)

Address: 2505 Elwood Drive, Ames, Iowa 50010-2000
Telephone: +1 515 292 2000
Fax: +1 515 292 7106
E-mail: NFO@netins.net
Web site: nfo.org
Web site notes: site includes information on sales of livestock (cattle and pigs)

National Fashion Accessories Association, Inc. (NFAA)/Fashion Accessories Shippers' Association, Inc. (FASA)

Address: 330 Fifth Avenue, Suite 205, New York, NY 10001 USA
Telephone: +1 212 947 3424
Fax: +1 212 629 0361
E-mail: info@nfaa-fasa.org

Web site: www.nfaa-fasa.org
Membership: 100 handbags, belts, small leather goods, gloves and luggage firms
Notes: Incorporates the Fashion Accessories Shippers Association, Inc.

National Field Selling Association (NFSA)
Address: 1900 Arch Street, Philadelphia, PA 19103-1498
Telephone: +1 215 564 3484
Fax: +1 215 564 2175
E-mail: assnhqt@netaxs.com
Web site: www.nfsa.com/
Year established: 1987
Chief officers: Andrew S. Hortatsos (President), Robert W.Lake, Jr. (Secretary)

National Fisheries Institute (NFI)
Address: Suite 700, 1901 North Fort, Myer Drive, Arlington, VA 22209
Telephone: +1 703 524 8880
Fax: +1 703 524 4619
E-mail: office@nfi.org
Web site: www.nfi.org
Web site notes: web site includes statistics on per capita consumption of the top ten types of fish over a six-year review period
Year established: 1945
Activities: monitors for regulations and legislation, compiles statistics
Chief officers: Lee J Weddig (Executive Vice President)
Structure: board; committees
Membership: 1,000 producers, distributors, processors, canners, wholesalers, importers and exporters
Publications:
• Blue Book: *membership directory - annual*
• Flashes: *newsletter - monthly*

National Food Brokers' Association (NFBA)
Address: Suite 400, 2100 Reston Parkway, Reston, VA 22091
Telephone: +1 703 758 7790
Fax: +1 703 758 7787
Year established: 1904
Chief officers: Robert C Schwarzo (President and CEO)
Structure: permanent staff; board
Membership: 1,500 food brokers
Publications:
• Directory of Members: *annual*
• Food Broker Quarterly: *monthly*
• Newsline (National Food Brokers Association): *newsletter - monthly*

National Food Processors' Association (NFPA)
Address: Suite 400, 1401 New York Avenue NE, Washington, DC 20005
Telephone: +1 202 639 5900
Fax: +1 202 639 5932
E-mail: nfpa@nfpa-food.org
Web site: www.nfpa-food.org
Year established: 1909
Activities: operates research laboratories, conducts research programs on new food technologies and labelling issues
Chief officers: John R Cady (President)
Structure: permanent staff
Membership: NFPA's members process and package fruits, vegetables, meat, fish, and speciality food and beverage products using a variety of technologies including canning, freezing, refrigeration, dehydration and aseptic manufacturing
Publications:
• Annual Report of the National Food Processors' Association: *contains some statistics on canned foods by type of food -*

annual
• Information Letter: *update on current issues affecting the U.S. food industry, including new legislation and regulations, consumer issues etc. Includes Washington Report, a monthly update on federal legislation - bi-weekly*
• State Legislative Report: *bi-weekly*
• Washington Report: *monthly*

National Frozen Food Association Inc. (NFFA)
Address: Suite 300, 4755 Linglestown Road, Harrisburg, PA 17112
Telephone: +1 717 657 8601
Fax: +1 717 657 9862
E-mail: lori@nffa.org (Publications)
Web site: www.nffa.org
Year established: 1945
Activities: education and training, research, government relations, compiles statistics on the industry
Chief officers: Nevin B Montgomery (President), Lori B. Pohlman (Vice President Publications and New Media)
Structure: permanent staff; board; committees
Membership: 700 member companies including: manufacturers, distributors, brokers, warehousers, suppliers, retailers and foodservice operators
Publications:
• Annual Membership Directory: *information about NFFA member companies and the frozen food industry - annual*
• Frozen Food Executive: *Association information, government legislation affecting the industy, market and industry trends, market statistics and research and regional news and views - monthly*

National Grocers Association (NGA)
Address: 1825 Samuel Morse Drive, Reston, VA 22090
Telephone: +1 703 437 5300
Fax: +1 703 437 7768
E-mail: dawnb@eidolongroup.com
Web site: www.onetoone.com/nga/
Year established: 1982
Activities: acts as government liaison; helps develop programs to improve productivity and operating efficiency; sponsors seminars and training programs
Structure: permanent staff; state and local groups
Membership: independent food retailers and wholesale food distributors
Publications:
• National Grocer: *in-depth articles on issues affecting retailers, wholesalers, manufacturers and suppliers in the grocery industry - quarterly*

National Home Furnishings Association (NHFA)
Address: PO Box 2396, High Point, NC 27261
Telephone: +1 800 888 9590
Fax: +1 910 883 1195
E-mail: nhfaa@homefurnish.com
Web site: www.homefurnish.com:80/NHFA/home.htm
Year established: 1920
Activities: maintains research and development fund; conducts seminars and warehouse workshops
Chief officers: Don Earles (Executive Vice President)
Structure: permanent staff; board; committees
Membership: 13,500 retailers of furniture, carpeting and related products
Publications:
• Home Furnishings Executive: *in-depth features, market trends and retailer profiles - monthly*

National Housewares Manufacturers' Association (NHMA)

Address: Suite 650, 6400 Shafer Court, Rosemont, IL 60018
Telephone: +1 847 292 4200
Fax: +1 847 292 4211
E-mail: dteschke@nhma.com or hchantos@nhma.com
Web site: www.housewares.org
Web site notes: site includes a directory of members
Year established: 1938
Activities: compiles statistics; conducts market research
Chief officers: Deborah Teschke (Manager and Media Relations and Communications), Helen Chantos (Director and International Services)
Structure: permanent staff; board
Membership: 1,900 manufacturers and distributors of housewares and small appliances
Publications:
• Housewares Indexes: *tracks product purchase data and consumer trends in the U.S., U.K. and Asia - quarterly*
• Internal Intelligence Survey: *detailed information concerning common challenges and financial benchmarks by product category - annual*
• Membership Directory: *lists all NHMA members with complete company and product information. Companies are also cross-referenced by product categories, as well as by brand names and licensed products - annual*
• NHMA Reports: *Association news, education, informative articles and "Link-Up", a classified ad service for members - bi-monthly*
• NHMA State of the Industry Report: *broad overview of the housewares industry. Includes trends by product category and by retail distribution channel - annual*

National Ice Cream and Yoghurt Retailers' Association (NCYRA)

Address: Suite 210, 1429 King Avenue, Columbus, OH 43212
Telephone: +1 614 486 1444
Fax: +1 614 486 4711
E-mail: NICYRA@aol.com
Web site: www.nicyra.org
Web site notes: site includes a supplier membership directory
Year established: 1933
Chief officers: Frank E.P. Conyngham
Structure: permanent staff; board
Membership: retailers, manufacturers and suppliers of ice cream, frozen yoghurt, speciality products, cones, nuts, toppings, serving and food preparation equipment. Members represent over 2,500 outlets
Publications:
• Bulletin: *monthly*
• Yearbook: *annual*

National Independent Automobile Dealers' Association (NIADA)

Address: 2521 Brown Boulevard, Arlington, TX 76006
Telephone: +1 817 640 3838
Fax: +1 817 649 5866
E-mail: maryann@niada.com.
Web site: www.niada-online.com
Year established: 1946
Activities: collects and disseminates information; represents members before regulatory and legislative agencies; conducts seminars, meetings and training programs
Chief officers: Don A Harris (Executive Vice President)
Structure: permanent staff; board, committees
Membership: 12,500 companies and individuals lisensed to buy, sell or auction motor vehicles
Publications:
• Used Car Dealer: *covers management, marketing and legislative issues - monthly*

National Juice Products' Association

Address: PO Box 1531, Suite 2300, 111 East Madison Street, Tampa, FL 33602
Telephone: +1 813 273 6572
Fax: +1 813 273 4397/6
E-mail: tga@macfar.com / dck@macfar.com
Year established: 1957
Activities: promotion and research; technology; trade matters; uniform standards of quality, advertising and labelling practices; communication within the industry; organises annual meetings; disseminates to its members current information affecting the food industry, including regulatory actions, pending legislation, marketing data, commodity information, anti-trust development, etc.
Chief officers: David C.G. Kerr (Executive Director), Tammy G. Andis (Executive Secretary)
Structure: permanent staff; board; committees
Membership: 93 regular members (processors, packers of juice, drinks and bases), 63 associate members (suppliers, container, closures and ingredients)
Publications:
• Membership Roster: *annual*
Notes: The Association does not produce statistics.

National Kitchen and Bath Association (NKBA)

Address: 687 Willow Grove Street, Hackettstown, NJ 07840
Telephone: +1 908 852 0033
Fax: +1 908 852 1695
Web site: www.nkba.org
Year established: 1963
Activities: operates seminars and runs design contests
Chief officers: Paul A Kohmescher (Executive Director)
Structure: permanent staff; councils
Membership: 5,200 manufacturers and suppliers to retail of kitchen equipment and other designers and manufacturers of allied products
Publications:
• Directory of Accredited Members: *annual*
• Directory of Certified Kitchen and Bathroom Designers: *annual*
• Perspective (National Kitchen and Bath Association): *newsletter - monthly*

National Knitwear and Sportswear Association

Address: 386 Park Avenue South, New York, NY 10016
Telephone: +1 212 683 7520
Fax: +1 212 532 0766
E-mail: ktwrseth@aol.com
Web site: www.apparelsource.org

National Licensed Beverage Association (NLBA)

Address: 4214 King Street, West, Alexandria, VA 22302
Telephone: +1 703 671 7575
Fax: +1 703 845 0310
Year established: 1950
Activities: monitors government regulations and legislation; conducts education programs
Chief officers: Debra A Leach (Executive Director)
Structure: permanent staff; board
Membership: 20,000 bars, restaurants, liquor stores and other locations selling alcoholic beverages
Publications:
• Membership Directory: *annual*
• NLBA News: *bi-monthly*

National Meat Association (NMA)

Address: 1970 Broadway, Suite 825, Oakland, CA 94612
Telephone: +1 510 763 1533
Fax: +1 510 763 6186
E-mail: nma@hooked.net

Web site: www.hooked.net/users/nma/
Membership: 600 meat packers and processors, as well as equipment manufacturers and suppliers who provide services to the meat industry
Publications:
• Herd on the Hill: *latest developments on legislationof the meat and poultry industry - weekly*
• Lean Trimmings: *industry regulations, technology, exporting, international news, labor issues, and business news - monthly*

National Milk Producers' Federation (NMPF)
Address: 1840 Wilson Boulevard, Arlington, Virginia 22201
Telephone: +1 703 243 6111
Fax: +1 703 841 9328
E-mail: nmpf@aol.com
Web site: www.nmpf.org
Year established: 1916
Activities: NMPF deals with milk quality and standards, animal health and food safety issues, dairy product labelling and standards, and legislation affecting the dairy industry
Chief officers: James P. (Tom) Camerlo, Jr. (President), Edward T. Coughlin (Acting Chief Executive Officer), Clyde E. Rutherford (Secretary), Sandra L. Grimes (Director of Administration)

National Music Publishers' Association (NMPA)
Address: 711 Third Avenue, New York, NY 10017
Telephone: +1 212 370 5330
Fax: +1 212 953 2384
E-mail: mdrum@nmpa.org
Web site: www.nmpa.org
Year established: 1917
Chief officers: Margaret Drum, (Vice President)
Membership: 600 music publishers
Publications:
• International Survey of Music Publishing Revenues: *a survey of the world music publishing market compiled from sources in over a hundred countries. Includes an international review of the previous year as well as revenue by type of royalty income. Based on a survey conducted by the Association - annual*

National Newspaper Association (NNA)
Address: 1525 Wilson Boulevard, Suite 550, Arlington VA 22209
Telephone: +1 703 907 7900
Fax: +1 703 907 7901
E-mail: TheNNA@aol.com
Web site: www.oweb.com/nna
Year established: 1885
Activities: compiles statistics, sponsors competitions
Chief officers: Tonda F Rush (CEO)
Structure: permanent staff, board, committees
Membership: 4,200 editors and publishers of weekly and regional newspapers
Publications:
• National Newspaper Exchange (NNX): *fax information to the approximately 8,000 community newspapers - annual*

National Paint and Coatings Association (NPCA)
Address: 1500 Rhode Island Ave NW, Washington, DC 20005
Telephone: +1 202 462 6272
Fax: +1 202 462 8549
E-mail: npca@paint.org
Web site: www.paint.org
Web site notes: site includes statistics on the US paint market including a detailed breakdown of value sales by product type, per capita sales by volume, employment in the industry, wages and company size

Membership: 400 paint and coatings manufacturers, raw materials suppliers and distributors

National Paper Trade Association (NPTA)
Address: 111 Great Neck Road, Great Neck NY 11021
Telephone: +1 516 829 3070
Fax: +1 516 829 3074
Web site: www.papertrade.com
Year established: 1903
Membership: distributors and suppliers of paper, plastics, packaging, chemicals and allied products
Publications:
• Annual Business Forecast: *detailed survey of members to determine prospects for the industry in the coming year - annual*
• Distribution Sales and Management Magazine: *monthly*
• Performance Analysis Report: *analysis and statistics for the latest survey year and earlier years covering sales, profitability, personnel productivity, costs, and assets. A general overview is followed by sections on specific sectors of the industry. Based on a survey by the Association - annual*

National Paperbox Association (NPA)
Address: 801 N. Fairfax Street, #211, Alexandria, VA 22314
Telephone: +1 703 684 2212
Fax: +1 703 683 6920
E-mail: boxmaker@erols.com
Web site: www.paperbox.org
Year established: 1918
Activities: represents industry before government regulation and legislative bodies; compiles statistics; conducts workshops and seminars
Chief officers: R Mickey Gorman (President)
Structure: permanent staff; board; committees
Membership: 300 independent manufacturers of paper boxes and suppliers
Publications:
• Key Ratios: *two reports covering the folding carton industry and the rigid paper box industry. Both reports give financial and operating statistics with figures for the latest year and some earlier years. Based on a survey by the Association - annual*
• Membership Directory: *key business leaders in the Paperbox Industry - annual*
• Monthly Reports: *sales statistics which include regional breakouts, year-to-year comparisons, Regional and National rankings - monthly*
• Packet: *trends in the box-making industry worldwide - bi-monthly*

National Pasta Association
Address: Suite 920, 2101 Wilson Boulevard, Arlington, VA 22201
Telephone: +1 703 841 0818
Fax: +1 703 528 6507
E-mail: npa-admin@ari.net.
Web site: www.ilovepasta.org
Year established: 1904
Activities: conducts research; promotes manufacturer and supplier efficiency
Chief officers: Jula J Kinnaird (President)
Structure: permanent staff, board, committees
Membership: 75 pasta manufacturers and suppliers to the industry
Publications:
• Pasta Industry Directory: *annual*
• Pasta Journal: *bi-monthly*

National Petroleum Council (NPC)

Address: 1625 K Street N.W., Washington D.C.
Telephone: +1 202 393 6100
Fax: +1 202 331 8539
E-mail: info@npc.org
Web site: www.npc.org
Publications:
• Marginal Wells: *domestic oil and gas marginal well production and the access to potential reserves that those wells provide. Evaluations of marginal well contributions to the national, state, and local economies as well as to the oil and gas industries are provided. Detailed economic analyses on an after tax basis are presented as well as federal regulatory issues - irregular*
• Oil Pollution Act-Issues and Solutions: *examines the legal background, the potencial impact on U.S oil and gas production and the impact on the insurance and financial communities and other parties - irregular*

National Pork Producers' Council

Address: PO Box 10383, Des Moines, IA 50306
Telephone: +1 515 223 2600
Fax: +1 515 223 2646
E-mail: pork@nppo.org
Web site: www.nppc.org
Year established: 1954
Activities: research programs, consumer education, advocacy; compiles statistics
Chief officers: Russ Sanders (Executive Vice President)
Structure: board, committees
Membership: 85,000 pork producers in 43 affiliated state associations
Publications:
• Annual Research Review: *annual*
• Newsletter of the National Pork Producers Council: *monthly*
• Pork Report: *bi-monthly*

National Restaurant Association

Address: 1200 17th Street NW, Washington, DC 20036-3097
Telephone: +1 202 331 5900/800 424 5156
Fax: +1 202 331 5946
E-mail: isal@restaurant.org
Web site: www.restaurant.org
Year established: 1919
Activities: supports research and education; offers training programs; produces training films and other advice and information; maintains large library
Chief officers: William P Fisher (Executive Vice President)
Structure: permanent staff; board; committees
Membership: represents 175,000 food service outlets
Publications:
• Foodservice Numbers: *sales, purchases and number of units for more than 50 separate sectors of foodservice. Also highlights statistics on industry figures, operating ratios and costs, industry trends, consumer behaviour and attitudes*
• Menu Analysis: *an annual review of menu developments and patterns based on a survey of restaurants - annual*
• National Restaurant Association Foodservice Industry Forecast: *overview of consumer and industry trends, includes an economic outlook and projections for sales and purchases by industry sectors. Tables provide state-by-state sales forecasts - annual*
• Restaurant Industry Operations Report: *overview of consumer and industry trends, includes an economic outlook and projections for sales and purchases by industry sectors. Tables provide state-by-state sales forecasts - annual*
• Restaurants USA Magazine: *legislative and regulatory fronts in Washington, industry trends and statistics, features - monthly*
• Table Service Restaurant Trends: *compiled from several surveys, explores restaurant computer use, reservation policies, remodelling and a host of employee issues-ranging from training trends to turnover. Also popular menu items and customer expectations regarding service, atmosphere and food quality - annual*
• Washington Weekly: *political and legislative developments relating to the restaurant industry - weekly*

National Retail Federation (NRF)

Address: Suite 1000, 325 7th Street NW, Washington, DC 20004
Telephone: +1 202 783 7971
Fax: +1 202 737 2849
E-mail: webmaster@nrf.com
Web site: www.nrf.com
Year established: 1990
Activities: conducts conferences; monitors government regulation and legislation
Chief officers: Allen Questrom (Chairman and CEO), Karen Shunk (International Member Relations)
Structure: permanent staff; board; committees
Membership: department, specialty, discount, mass merchandise and independent stores, as well as 32 national and 50 state associations
Publications:
• Dictionary of Retailing and Merchandising: *vocabulary of buying, merchandising and visual display, catalogue marketing, retail advertising and more - irregular*
• Electronic Retailing Market: *detailed exposition of demographic, socio-economic, and other trends in the retail market, and their significance to electronic shopping - irregular*
• Financial and Operating Results of Retail Stores: *statistical data of retail store performance based on a survey of retail stores. Provides expense trends for various categories of department and speciality stores and offers industry averages of retail sales growth, mark-downs, operating performance, expenses and inventory productivity and profitability - annual*
• Management of Retail Buying: *guide on how to choose merchandise and how to negotiate the best deal. Covers every aspect of the retail buyer's job, including: planning and managing the merchandise assortment and flow; the buyer's role in marketing, selling, sales promotion, and inventory management - irregular*
• Merchandising and Operating Results of Retail Stores: *statistical data of operating results of retail stores. Represents the results of a survey of retail companies and offers overall trends in sales, merchandising and inventory, inventory productivity and space productivity in department and speciality stores. The MOR also provides specific data on these trends by merchandise category - annual*
• Software Directory for Retailers: *complete source of retail software package alternatives available, containing over 300 vendors and 750 packages - irregular*
• Specialty Store Human Resource Directors' Wage and Benefit Survey: *covers incentive plans, compensation by position, compensation by metropolitan area, turnover/recruiting statistics, benefits checklist, health plan design, disability income plan, estate plans - annual*
• Stores: *latest news on: technology, information systems, operations, credit, loss prevention, marketing, shopping centre development, logistics, store design, merchandising and physical supports - monthly*
Notes: The largest retail trade association in the world.

National Retail Hardware Association

Address: 5822 W 74th Street, Indianapolis IN 46278
Telephone: +1 317 290 0338
Fax: +1 317 328 4354
E-mail: nrha@iquest.net.
Web site: www.nrha.org
Web site notes: site includes a report on the US retail hardware market
Year established: 1900

Activities: government lobbying, education and training, retail market research, dissemination of industry information
Membership: 46,000 hardware stores, home centres and lumber/building material retailers in more than 10,000 cities and towns in the United States and Canada
Publications:
• Benchmarks for Success: *study of merchandising trends offers a sales profile and performance benchmarks for core hardware/home improvement departments and products - annual*
• Cost of Doing Business Survey: *detailed operating information including income statements, balance sheets and performance ratios for hardware stores, home centers and consumer-oriented lumber outlets - annual*
• DIY Retailing: *marketing, management and merchandising information and interpretation of distribution trends - monthly*
• Market Measure Annual Report: *in-depth statistical overview of the American hardware/home improvement industry - annual*
• Merchandising Report: *profiles 23 major product categories in hardware stores, home centers, lumber outlets. Provides average performance ratios including sales, inventory and gross margin per square foot, sales to inventory ratio, gross margin percentage, and GMROI for each department by type of store - annual*
Notes: Affiliated with the Canadian Retail Hardware Association and the International Federation of Ironmongers' and Iron Merchants' Associations.

National Shoe Retailers' Association (NSRA)

Address: 9861 Broken Land Parkway, Columbia, MD 21046
Telephone: +1 800 673 8446
Fax: +1 410 381 1167
E-mail: info@nsra.org
Web site: www.apparelnet.com/nsra
Year established: 1912
Activities: offers training programs; compiles statistics; co-sponsors National Shoe Fair
Chief officers: William Boettge (President), Phyllis Endrich (Vice President)
Structure: permanent staff; board; committees
Membership: 1,800 specialty stores and independent retailers
Publications:
• Shoe Retailing Today: *newsletter - bi-monthly*

National Soft Drink Association (NSDA)

Address: 1101 16th Street NW, Washington DC 20036
Telephone: +1 202 463 6732
Fax: +1 202 463 8178
E-mail: mariec@nsda.com
Web site: www.nsda.org
Year established: 1919
Activities: maintains the NSDA Information Center which contains books, magazines, studies, reports, statistics, consumer information and the latest on-line data
Chief officers: Robert W. Anania
Structure: permanent staff; board; committees; state groups
Membership: represents hundreds of soft drink bottling firms, franchise companies and support industries
Publications:
• Membership Directory and Buyer's Guide: *annual*
• NSDA News: *legislative, association news - monthly*

National Sporting Goods' Association (NSGA)

Address: 1699 Wall Street, Mount Prospect IL 600056
Telephone: +1 847 439 4000
Fax: +1 847 439 0111
Web site: www.nsga.org
Web site notes: site incudes a database of members with company, product and brand information
Publications:
• Cost of Doing Business for Retail Sports Goods Stores:

financial performance indicators for sports goods retailers, with data by type of store and other variables - annual
• Lifestyle Characteristics of Sporting Goods Consumers: *statistics on the lifestyle characteristics of consumers in 12 broad social groups. Based on a sample of 80,000 consumers. A detailed analysis accompanies the data - annual*
• NSGA Sports Retail: *retail and industry news for corporate executive members of the association - monthly*
• Sporting Goods Market: *statistics on consumer purchases and value retail sales for the last 12 years plus volume data for the latest year. A range of sporting equipment, clothing and footwear with data by store type, demographic groups, local data, etc. - annual*
• Sports Participation: *data on sports participation, frequency, expenditure on clothing and other goods. Includes analysis by geographical area and demographic groups. Based on a sample of 20,000 households - annual*

National Wholesale Druggists' Association (NWDA)

Address: PO Box 2219, Suite 400, 1821 Michael Faraday Drive, Reston, VA 20190-5348
Telephone: +1 703 787 0000
Fax: +1 703 767 6930
E-mail: industry@nwda.org
Web site: www.nwda.org
Year established: 1876
Activities: compiles statistics; sponsors research; offers educational seminars; monitors government regulation and legislation
Chief officers: Ronald J Streck (President and CEO)
Structure: permanent staff; board; committees
Membership: 450 wholesalers and manufacturers of drug and toiletry products
Publications:
• Fact Book of the National Wholesale Druggists Association (NWDA): *statistics and trends within NWDA member companies and the health care industry - annual*
• Institutional Marketing, Distribution, and Procurement of Pharmaceuticals Through Drug Wholesalers: *covers the entire process, including bid solicitation, bid award, bid award notification, purchasing, chargebacks, return of goods, contract termination and hospital group administration fees - annual*
• Membership Directory: *listing of active, associate and international members; NWDA officers, directors, staff and committees; drug trade press; drug industry associations; and colleges of pharmacy - annual*
• National Wholesale Druggists Association Executive Newsletter: *news on association programs and services, the membership and the industry - monthly*
• Operating Survey: *comprehensive report of financial and operating ratios for the wholesale drug industry, as aggregated from confidential data submitted by participating wholesalers - annual*
Notes: To order publications e-mail pubs@nwda.org.

National Yoghurt Association (NYA)

Address: Suite 1000, 2000 Corporate Ridge, McLean, VA 22102
Telephone: +1 703 821 0770
Fax: +1 703 821 1350
Activities: NYA sponsors scientific research regarding the health attributes of live and active culture yoghurt consumption
Chief officers: Leslie G. Sarasin (President)
Membership: manufacturers of refrigerated and frozen yoghurt products containing live and active cultures, as well as the suppliers to the industry

Neckwear Association of America, Inc. (NAA)

Address: 51 Lexington Avenue, New York, NY 10016
Telephone: +1 212 683 8454
Fax: +1 212 686 7382
Web site: www.apparel.net/naa
Year established: 1947
Activities: promotes tie wearing with consumers through an active public relations program
Membership: member firms in the United States, Canada and Europe

Newspaper Association of America (NAA)

Address: Suite 600, 1921 Gallows Road, Vienna, VA, 22182
Telephone: +1 703 902 1600
Fax: +1 703 917 0636
E-mail: naainfo@naa.org
Web site: www.naa.org
Web site notes: includes comprehensive statistics on all aspects of newspapers in the USA
Chief officers: John J. Curley (Chairman)
Membership: 1,500 member newspapers (approximately 87 percent of US daily circulation)
Publications:
• Facts about Newspapers: *a brief commentary is followed by statistics on the number of daily and weekly newspapers, circulation, sales prices, advertising volume, newsprint consumption and prices, employment, US newspaper companies. Also data on the Canadian newspaper market. Based largely on non-official sources - annual*
• Presstime: *journal - monthly*
• Update (Newspaper Association of America): *newsletter - quarterly*

Non-prescription Drug Manufacturers' Association (NDMA)

Address: Suite 1200, 1150 Connecticut Avenue NW, Washington, DC 20036
Telephone: +1 202 429 9260
Fax: +1 202 223 6835
Year established: 1881
Activities: monitors government regulation and legislation; promotes information on scientific discoveries; conducts labelling review service
Chief officers: James D Cope (President)
Structure: permanent staff; board; committees
Membership: 225 marketers of non-prescription drugs and suppliers
Publications:
• Compilation of Laws Affecting Proprietary Drug and Allied Industries: *annual*
• Directory: *annual*
• Executive Newsletter (Non-prescription Drug Manufacturers' Association): *weekly*
• Scientific News Bulletin: *irregular*

North American Association of Food Equipment Manufacturers (NAFEM)

Address: 401 N. Michigan Ave, Chicago, IL 60611
Telephone: +1 312 644 6610
Fax: +1 312 527 6658
E-mail: nafem_hq@sba.com
Web site: www.nafem.org
Membership: 700 companies throughout the United States, Canada and Mexico that manufacture commercial foodservice equipment and supplies. NAFEM members account for 85 per cent of all foodservice equipment and supplies sold in the United States
Publications:
• Available Foodservice Market Research Sources: *provides a description of various sources for foodservice industry*

research and lists contact information for obtaining the materials - annual
• Foodservice Industry Yellow Pages: *directory of foodservice companies in North America - annual*
• Trends and Forecasting Seminar Proceedings: *300 pages of slides and summary data from the day-long seminar. Headings include macro economic overview, foodservice market segment outlook, current menu/food trends, the world of foodservice, doing business in Latin America and international trends in foodservice equipment and supplies manufacturing - annual*

North American Meat Processors' Association (NAMP)

Address: 1920 Association Drive, Suite 400, Reston, VA 22091-1547
Telephone: +1 703 758 1900
Fax: +1 703 758 8001
E-mail: nami@foodexpo.com
Web site: www.foodexpo.com/orgs/namp/
Chief officers: Mr. Deven Scott (Executive Vice President)
Notes: Formerly the National Association of Meat Purveyors.

North American Telecommunications' Association (NATD)

Address: 1045 East Atlantic Avenue, Delray Beach, Florida 33483
Telephone: +1 561 266 9440
Fax: +1 561 266 9017
E-mail: jmarion@ix.netcom.com
Web site: www.natd.com
Chief officers: Ann Marie Murphy (Secretary)
Membership: NATD members specialise in telecommunications equipment in the secondary market

Office Furniture Dealers' Alliance (OFDA)

Address: 301 North Fairfax Street, Alexandria, VA 22314
Telephone: +1 703 549 904/800 542 6672
Fax: +1 703 683 7552
E-mail: dsolomon@bpia.org
Web site: www.bpia.org/alliances/ofda.htm
Chief officers: David Solomon (Associate Executive Director)
Notes: The Association is part of the Business Products Industry Association.

Office Products Dealers' Alliance (OPDA)

Address: 301 North Fairfax Street, Alexandria, VA 22314-2696
Telephone: +1 703 549 904/800 542 6672
Fax: +1 202 637 3182
E-mail: swilliams@bpia.org
Web site: www.bpia.org/alliances/opda.htm
Chief officers: Sandra Williams (Director)
Notes: The Association is part of the Business Products Industry Association.

Office Products Manufacturers' Alliance (OPMA)

Address: 301 North Fairfax Street, Alexandria, VA 22314-2696
Telephone: +1 703 549 9040/800 542 6672
Fax: +1 703 683 7552
E-mail: rhorshok@bpia.org or tmccafferty@bpia.org
Web site: www.bpia.org/alliances/opma.htm
Chief officers: Randy Horshok (Interim Executive Vice President
Notes: The Association is part of the Business Products Industry Association.

Office Products Wholesalers' Association

Address: 5024-R Campbell Blvd., Baltimore, MD 21236
Telephone: +1 410 931 8100

Fax: +1 410 931 8111
E-mail: OPWA@aol.com
Web site: www.podi.com/opwa/
Membership: trade association for organizations or individuals who are engaged in the manufacture, production, and wholesale distribution of office and related products

Personal Communications Industry Association (PCIA)

Address: Suite 700, 500 Montgomery Street, Alexandria, VA 22314-1561
Telephone: +1 703 739 0300
Fax: +1 703 836 1608
E-mail: FerraraV@PCIA.COM
Web site: www.pcia.com
Web site notes: site includes statistics on the wireless communications industry in the US as well as international summaries. Includes current data and forecasts to 2001
Year established: 1949
Activities: acts as liaison with government; monitors government regulation and legislation; compiles statistics and disseminates information; offers educational programs; sponsors and produces of the annual Personal Communications Showcase
Chief officers: Jay Kitchen (President)
Structure: board of directors and an elected membership council
Membership: 2,000 companies in the personal communications industry: PCS, paging, cellular, ESMR, SMR, mobile data, cable, computer, manufacturing, local and interexchange sectors of the industry, as well as technicians, wireless systems integrators, communications site owners and manufacturers, distributors and service professionals and private corporate system users
Publications:
• An Overview of the Personal Communications Services Industry: *general background of regulatory and legislative activities related to PCS as well as an overview of technical and marketing issues related to the development and licensing for new personal communications services - annual*
• PCIA Bulletin: *provides in-depth coverage of legislation that affects the industry - bi-weekly*

Pet Foods Institute

Address: Suite 700, 1101 Connecticut Avenue NW, Washington, DC 20036
Telephone: +1 202 857 1120
Fax: +1 202 857 1186
Year established: 1958
Chief officers: Duane H E Kedhal (Executive Director)
Structure: board, committees; permanent staff
Membership: 130 manufacturers of commercially prepared pet foods
Publications:
• Directory: *annual*
• Monitor: *monthly*

Pet Industry Joint Advisory Council (PIJAC)

Address: 1220 19th Street, NW, Washington, DC 20036
Telephone: +1 202 452 1525
Fax: +1 202 293 4377
E-mail: PIJAC@CIS.CompuServe.Com
Web site: www.pijac.org
Activities: represents members on international, national, state and local policy issues affecting the industry; acts as a national advocate for the industry on matters of public policy; develops minimum standards for the housing, maintenance and care of companion pets; sponsors educational programs; provides media relations and maintains an information centre (Pet Information Bureau) that collects and distributes statistical and general pet industry data
Chief officers: Howard Deardorff (Director Education and

Research), Geri Mitchell (Director of Communication)
Membership: retailers, wholesalers, companion animal suppliers, manufacturers, manufacturers representatives, hobbyist groups and other trade associations
Publications:
• PetAlerts: *legislation and regulations affecting the pet industry including summaries of proposals and recommended action*
• PetLetter: *news and trends in the U.S. pet market as well as key PIJAC activities and calendar of events - monthly*
• PIJAC Updates: *information on trends, detailed current status of pending legislation and regulations - monthly*

Petroleum Marketers' Association of America (PMAA)

Address: Suite 1200, 1901 North Ft Myer Drive, Arlington, VA 22209
Telephone: +1 703 351 8000
Fax: +1 703 351 9160
E-mail: info@pmaa.org
Web site: www.pmaa.org
Year established: 1941
Structure: permanent staff; board; committees
Membership: PMAA is a federation of 41 state and regional trade associations representing 10,000 independent petroleum marketers in the United States. Members account for around 50% of petrol, 60% diesel fuel and 80% of the home heating oil consumed in the U.S. annually
Publications:
• Journal of Petroleum Marketing: *monthly*
• Petroleum Marketing Databook: *statistics - bi-annual*
• PMAA Directory: *annual*

Pharmaceutical Manufacturers' Association

Address: Suite 900, 1100 15th Street, NW, Washington, DC 20005
Telephone: +1 202 835 3400
Fax: +1 202 785 4834
Year established: 1958
Activities: lobbying group; monitors government regulation and legislation; encourages research
Chief officers: Gerald J Mossinghoff (President)
Structure: permanent staff; board
Membership: 87 manufacturers of pharmaceutical and biological products
Publications:
• Annual Report of the Pharmaceutical Manufacturers' Association: *annual*
• Fact Book: *statistics - annual*
• Newsletter of the Pharmaceutical Manufacturers' Association: *weekly*
• PMA Annual Survey Report: *a financial report on US and foreign operations of US-based pharmaceutical companies. Based on an annual survey of member firms with estimates for non-members - annual*
• PMA Statistical Fact Book: *every few years*

Pharmaceutical Research and Manufacturers of America (PHRMA)

Address: 1100 Fifteenth Street, NW, Washington, DC 20005
Telephone: +1 202 835 3400
Fax: +1 202 835 3413
E-mail: hbale%phrma@mcimail.com
Web site: www.phrma.org
Web site notes: site includes an in-depth statistical profile of the US pharmaceutical industry
Chief officers: Alan F. Holmer (President), Charles A. Heimbold, Jr. (Chairman)
Membership: 100 U.S. companies engaged in pharmaceutical reseach

Plastic Bag Association
Address: 1817 E. Carson St, Pittsbugrh, PA 15203
Telephone: +1 800 438 5856
Fax: +1 412 381 8890
E-mail: pbainfo@aol.com
Web site: www.plasticbag.com
Membership: 60 manufacturers and suppliers of plastic bags

Polystyrene Packaging Council
Address: Suite 600K, 1801 K Street, Washington D.C. 20006-1301
Telephone: +1 202 974 5321
Fax: +1 202 296 7354
E-mail: ikusek@socplas.org
Web site: www.polystyrene.org
Chief officers: Mike Levy (Executive Director), Laurie Kusek (Director of Communications)

Private Label Manufacturers' Association (PLMA)
Address: 3rd Floor, 369 Lexington Avenue, New York, NY 10017
Telephone: +1 212 972 3131
Fax: +1 212 983 1382
Web site: www.plma.com
Year established: 1979
Activities: promotes private label industry through consumer education; compiles statistics; conducts research, organises trade shows
Chief officers: Brian Sharoff (President)
Structure: permanent staff; board
Membership: 1,400 manufacturers, brokers and suppliers
Publications:
• Scanner: *newsletter - bi-monthly*

Produce Marketing Association (PMA)
Address: PO Box 6036, 1500 Casho Mill Road, Newark DE 19714-6036
Telephone: +1 302 738 7100
Fax: +1 302 731 2409
E-mail: pma@mail.pma.com
Web site: www.fruitnet.com/FruitnetDirectoryFR.html
Year established: 1949
Chief officers: Bryan Silbermann (President), Grant M. Hunt (Secretary/Treasurer)
Membership: 2,500 members who market fresh fruits, vegetables and floral products worldwide. Its members are involved in the production, distribution, retail and foodservice sectors of the industry

Public Relations Society of America (PRSA)
Address: 3rd Floor, 33 Irving Place, New York, NY 10003
Telephone: +1 212 995 2230
Fax: +1 212 995 0757
E-mail: hdq@prsa.org
Web site: www.prsa.org
Year established: 1947
Activities: conducts professional development programs
Structure: permanent staff; local groups; board; committees
Membership: 17,000 members represent business and industry, counselling firms, government, associations, hospitals, schools, professional services firms and non-profit organisations
Publications:
• PR Tactic: *news and trends in public relations - monthly*
• Public Relations Strategist: *issues and trends in public relations - quarterly*

Retail Confectioners' International (RCI)
Address: Suite 204, 1807 Glenview Road, Glenview, IL 40025
Telephone: +1 800 545 5381
Fax: +1 847 724 2719
E-mail: rciinfo@retconint.org
Web site: www.retconint.org
Year established: 1917
Activities: monitors government legislation and regulations; offers training, organises an annual trade fair
Chief officers: Evan N Billington (Executive Director)
Structure: permanent staff, board
Membership: 600 confectionery manufactacturing retailers
Publications:
• Kettle Talk: *newsletter - monthly*
• Membership Directory: *annual*
• RCI Directory: *directory of members of the Retail Confectioners International trade association - annual*
• RCI Magazine: *quarterly*
• RCI Magazine: *quarterly*
• Retail Confectioners International - Membership Directory and Buyers' Guide: *lists over 550 manufacturing retail confectioners and their outlets (around 15,000). Arranged alphabetically - annual*

Rubber Manufacturers' Association (RMA)
Address: 1400 K Street NW, Washington, DC 20005
Telephone: +1 202 682 4800
Fax: +1 202 682 4854
E-mail: kristen@tmn.com
Web site: www.rma.org
Chief officers: Donald B. Shea (President)
Membership: manufactures of tyres, tubes, roofing, sporting goods, mechanical and industrial products
Publications:
• Monthly Rubber Report: *detailed rubber statistics broken down by type. Covers total industry and producer stocks, production, imports, exports and apparent US consumption - monthly*
• Monthly Tire Report: *presents total industry data for passenger, light truck, medium and wide base truck and heavy truck tyres. Includes data on: manufacturer shipments to original equipment vehicle manufacturers; replacement shipments to all segments of the tyre aftermarket; tyre trade data; import and export shipments; total tyre shipments and US tyre production. Additionally, the report presents shipments and production of inner tubes, broken down by type - monthly*
• Monthly Trade Reports: *import and export activity for various rubber products. In most cases the reports reflect both units and value of shipments by country by month. The report presents imports by the country of origin and exports by the country of destination for each item included - monthly*
• Tire Industry Fact Book: *extensive information on the US tyre industry compiled from data supplied by companies which constitute over 90% of the market. The Fact Book features shipment and production data for various tyre categories, natural and synthetic rubber usage, tyre plant locations, tyre size popularity, time line chart on major events in the tyre industry and information regarding North American (Canada and Mexico) tyre activity - annual*

Satellite Broadcasting and Communications Association (SBCA)
Address: Suite 600, 225 Reinekers Lane, Alexandria, VA 22314
Telephone: +1 703 549 6990
Fax: +1 703 549 7640
E-mail: ccole@sbca.org
Web site: www.sbca.com
Year established: 1986
Activities: compiles statistics; conducts research; offers

educational programs; liaises with to government and rest of communications industry; monitors government regulations and legislation
Chief officers: Charles C Hewitt (President), Margaret J. Parone (Vice President of Communications)
Structure: permanent staff; board; committees
Membership: 2,500 satellite manufacturers, system operators, equipment manufacturers, distributors, retailers, DBS companies, encryption vendors and programmers
Publications:
• Satellite Retail Report: *news, product information and trends in the satellite retailing industry - monthly*
• SkyREPORT: *statistical newsletter on the satellite industry - monthly*

Securities Industry Association (SIA)
Address: 120 Broadway, New York, NY 10271-0080
Telephone: +1 212 608 1500
Fax: +1 212 608 1604
E-mail: info@sia.com
Web site: www.sia.com
Web site notes: site includes a directory of members and a summary of the Association's Investor Survey
Year established: 1972
Chief officers: Margaret G. Draper Manager (Corporate Communications), Stephen L. Carlson (Assistant Vice President and Director/Surveys)
Membership: 750 member securities firms throughout North America
Publications:
• Investment Today: *varied aspects of investing, includes a long-term perspective on securities ownership - monthly*
• Investor Survey: *provides comprehensive opinion research of investor's attitudes toward the securities industry, brokerage services and investing in general - annual*
• Securities Industry Trends: *an analysis of trends in the securities industry with data on fund sales, stock market performance, etc. - two-monthly*

Ski Industries America (SIA)
Address: 8377-B Greensboro Drive, Mclean, VA 22102-3587
Telephone: +1 703 556 9020
Fax: +1 703 821 8276
Web site: www.snowlink.com/sia/sia/index.html
Web site notes: site includes statistics on the US ski apparel and equipment industries
Membership: snow product suppliers, sales reps, retailers, and ski area operators
Publications:
• SIA Ski, Snowboard, and Outdoors Sports Show Directory: *850 SIA members with their addresses, telephone numbers, and key staff. The SIA Directory covers over 3,000 brands of on-snow, in-line skate and other outdoor products and has a complete product index listed by category and brand name - annual*

Snack Food Association (SFA)
Address: Suite 1, 1711 King Street, Alexandria, VA 22314
Telephone: +1 703 836 4500
Fax: +1 703 836 8262
E-mail: sfa@sfa.org
Web site: www.usii.net/sfa/
Year established: 1937
Activities: educational programs, seminars and trade show; governmental relations; industry information, public relations, communications
Chief officers: James W Shofelt
Structure: permanent staff, board, committees
Membership: 900 manufacturers and suppliers of potato chips, pretzels, processed nuts, etc.

Publications:
• Consumer Snacking Behavior Report: *annual*
• SFA State of the Industry Report: *annual commentary and statistics on snack food sales, consumption, prices and distribution. Tables on specific snack foods. Based on an SFA annual survey and Nielsen data - annual*
• Snack World: *the snacks market in the USA - monthly*

Soap and Detergent Association (SDA)
Address: 475 Park Avenue South, New York, NY 10016
Telephone: +1 212 725 1262
Fax: +1 212 213 0685
Web site: www.sdahq.org
Web site notes: site includes a list of members with links to members' home pages
Year established: 1926
Activities: conducts environmental research; liaises with government agencies, provides consumer information
Structure: permanent staff; board, committees
Membership: 135 manufacturers of household, industrial and institutional cleaning products, the ingredients used in cleaning products, and finished packaging. Members account for 90% of the cleaning products marketed in the U.S.
Publications:
• Cleanliness Facts: *bi-monthly*
• Detergents-in-Depth Symposium Proceedings: *periodic*
• Newsletter of the Soap and Detergent Association: *monthly*

Society of the Plastics Industry (SPI)
Address: Suite 400, 1275 K Street NW, Washington, DC 20006-1301
Telephone: +1 202 371 5200
Fax: +1 202 296 7005
E-mail: feedback@socplas.org
Web site: www.socplas.org
Web site notes: site includes statistics on production and sales by type for the US plastics industry
Year established: 1937
Activities: government liaison, sponsors major trade shows, proposes industry standards; compiles statistics; supports research
Structure: permanent staff; regional groups; board
Membership: 2,000 manufacturers and suppliers
Publications:
• Facts and Figures of the U.S. Plastics Industry: *production, sales, markets, end uses and growth rates for major resins and includes statistical information on plastics machinery, reinforced plastics shipments, vinyl siding and soffit shipments and other financial data - annual*
• Financial and Operating Ratios Survey for Plastic Processing Companies: *survey of SPI member processing companies. Measures F&O ratios such as assets and liabilities, net sales, pre-tax and after-tax income, cost of sales, overhead, depreciation, inventory and administrative expenses - annual*
• SPI Membership Directory and Buyer's Guide: *directory with contact details of 2,000 SPI members. Also includes a detailed listing of products and services - annual*

Software Publishers' Association
Address: Suite 700, 1730 M Street, NW, Washington, DC 20036
Telephone: +1 202 452 1600
Fax: +1 202 223 8756
E-mail: krakestraw@spa.org/ jsanders@spa.org
Web site: www.spa.org
Year established: 1984
Activities: acts as liaison with government; monitors government regulation and legislation; compiles statistics; conducts research; offers educational programs; operates campaign to protect intellectual property rights
Chief officers: Ken Wasch (President), Kathleen Rakestraw

(Director of Communications), James Sanders (Director of Research)
Structure: permanent staff; board; committees
Membership: 1,000 software manufacturers and associates
Publications:
● Consumer Survey: *annual end user study quantifies the penetration of U.S. households using personal computers and/or video game players. Profiles the hardware installed, types of software used and household demographics. Based on telephone interviews and compares results with earlier surveys - annual*
● SPA Membership Directory: *detailed information on the 1,200 SPA member firms: software publishers/developers, hardware companies, online services, distributors, resellers, consultants and vendors. Detailed listings include company descriptions and key contact names - annual*
● Upgrade: *news and trends in the industry. Also includes a software top-seller list, industry events calendar and information on SPA activities, programs and services - monthly*

Special Libraries' Association
Address: 1700 Eighteenth Street, NW Washington DC, 20009
Telephone: +1 202 234 4700
Fax: +1 202 265 9317
E-mail: john@sla.org or david-b@sla.org
Web site: www.sla.org
Activities: government liaison, public relations, research, maintains an information resource centre
Chief officers: David Bender (Executive Director)
Membership: 15,000 information resource experts employed by corporations, private companies, government agencies, technical and academic institutions, museums, medical facilities and information management consulting firms
Publications:
● Information Outlook: *international trends in information management - monthly*
● Who's Who in Special Libraries: *lists members alphabetically by last name and indexes unit affiliations - annual*

Speciality Coffee Association of America (SCAA)
Address: One World Trade Center, Suite 1200, Long Beach, California 90831-0800
Telephone: +1 1 310 624 4100
Fax: +1 1 310 624 4101
E-mail: coffee@scaa.org
Web site: www.scaa.org
Activities: organises an annual exhibition and conference
Membership: 2,400 companies comprised of retailers, roasters, roaster/retailers, producers, exporters, importers, green coffee brokers, manufacturers of coffee processing-roasting-brewing equipment and other allied products
Publications:
● SCAA Membership Directory: *member's addresses, company information, a list of the significant products and the services that they offer - annual*

Specialty Equipment Market Association (SEMA)
Address: PO Box 4910, 1575 South Valley Vista Drive, Diamond Bar, CA 91765
Telephone: +1 909 396 0289
Fax: +1 909 860 0184
E-mail: membership@sema.org
Web site: www.sema.org
Web site notes: site includes an online directory of aftermarket company products and services. It also includes commentary and statistics on the US aftermarket
Year established: 1963
Activities: lobbying group; coordinates and conducts research; compiles statistics; assists in developing industry standards

Chief officers: Charles R Blum (President)
Structure: permanent staff; board; committees
Membership: 2,500 firms in specialty vehicle industry
Publications:
● Membership Directory: *annual*
● SEMA News: *prevailing market conditions and trends in the U.S. aftermarket sector - monthly*

Sporting Goods Manufacturers' Association (SGMA)
Address: 200 Castlewood Drive, North Palm Beach, FL 33408
Telephone: +1 407 842 4100
Fax: +1 407 863 8984
Web site: www.sportlink.com
Chief officers: John Riddle (President and Executive Officer), Maria Stefan (Executive Director)
Publications:
● American Sports Analysis Participation Summary Report: *tracking study on Americans' participation in sports and recreation activities. The study identifies and analyses general patterns, trends and relationships among 58 sports/activities - annual*
● Health Club Trend Report: *based on national consumer surveys, covers health club membership including frequency of participation by sex, age, income, region, and types of equipment used by facility. Health club membership fee data also included - annual*
● Market for Physical Fitness and Exercise Equipment: *retail market, institutional market forecasts, profiles of marketers and trends - annual*
● National Soccer Participation Survey: *comprehensive overview of soccer participation in the continental U.S. designed to identify and analyse general patterns, trends and relationships within a full range of demographic variables - annual*
● Retail Soccer USA: *directory of soccer specialty retailers, team dealers and general sporting goods stores with strong soccer sales. About 1000 listings - annual*
● SGMA Athletic Footwear Market Index by FMI: *total market trends among women, men and children. Includes shoe sales trends by shoe type, price point, retail outlet, sale versus regular prices, branded and primary usage is detailed. An annual report on the demographics of purchasers is also included in the annual subscription - tri-annual*
● SGMA Licensed Sports Products Market Report: *brief four page review of market size with breakouts by major sports leagues and discussion of market trends - annual*
● SGMA Membership Directory: *information for the approximately 2,000 member companies of the SGMA - annual*
● SGMA Recreation Market Report: *brief report on the overall size of the sports/recreation industries and its product components. Contains a statistical summary in wholesale dollars for the industry and its products in the U.S. for the past two years - annual*
● SGMA Sports Apparel Market Index and Active Sports Reports by NPD: *data from their ongoing consumer purchase diary panel on sports apparel sales trends. Based on a survey 16,000 households every month it covers consumer preferences for key sports apparel/active wear items. Includes information on sweatpants, sweatshirts, jogging/sweatsuits, shorts, thermals, athletic socks, jackets, swimwear, sport shirts and T-shirts - annual*
● SGMA State of the Industry Report: *an eight page report highlighting the key trends in the industry with statistical information on industry sales and outlooks for major product segments - annual*
● Sports Brand Intelligence Report: *based on a study of 5,000 US households by American Sports Data, this study measures consumer awareness and ownership of 186 sports brands. Volume 1 provides demographic analysis of brand recognition and ownership and volume II cross-analyses brand awareness by sports participation, product ownership, magazine readership, TV viewership and sports spectatorship*

• Sports Media Index: *national consumer mail panel survey of 5,000 people over the age of 13 monitoring magazine readership of 45 consumer publications by American Sports Data. TV viewership of 15 sports; in-person spectatorship of 13 sports; consumer recognition and ratings of 50 celebrity athletes. All media cross-analysed by other media, demographics (including black and Hispanic markets), sports participation, and sports product ownership - annual*
• State of the Industry Report Human Powered Outdoor Recreation: *overview of participant trends, demographics and attitudes; economic value of outdoor recreation; trends - annual*
• TIA Tennis Market Study: *information on racquets, tennis balls, strings, shoes, and clothing. Includes information on opinions and attitudes of tennis players and factors influencing their purchase decisions - annual*
• US Athletic Footwear Market Today: *report highlighting athletic footwear history and growth, market data, consumer attitudes and buying habits and marketing facts and trends - annual*

Synthetic Organic Chemical Manufacturers' Association (SOCMA)

Address: Suite 1090, 1100 New York Avenue NW, Washington, DC 20005
Telephone: +1 202 414 4100
Fax: +1 202 289 8584
E-mail: earmstrong@socma.com
Web site: www.socma.com
Year established: 1921
Activities: continuing education program; monitors government relations and legislation
Chief officers: Ed Armstrong (Communications)
Structure: permanent staff; board; committees
Membership: 280 manufacturers of synthetic organic chemicals
Publications:
• SOCMA Membership Directory: *annual*
• Synthetic Organic Chemical Manufacturers' Association Newsletter: *issue oriented - bi-monthly*

Telecommunications Industry Association (TIA)

Address: 2500 Wilson Boulevard, Arlington, VA 22201
Telephone: +1 703 907 7700
Fax: +1 703 907 7727
E-mail: tia@tia.eia.org
Web site: www.industry.net/tia
Year established: 1988
Activities: government relations, market support activities such as trade shows and trade missions, standards setting activities and educational programs. TIA also maintains a database of member companies' products and services (this information is available to members and non-members for direct mail programs)
Chief officers: Matthew J. Flanigan (President), Sharon Grace (Communications Manager)
Structure: permanent staff; board
Membership: 600 member companies in the communications and information technology industry
Publications:
• Annual Report: *includes a report on the telecommunications industry with statistics on sales of communications equipment, exports, etc. - annual*
• Industry Beat: *news bulletin sent via fax covers TIA action, upcoming meetings and notices of importance to all those with an interest in the telecommunications industry - weekly*
• Industry Pulse: *association activities and industry trends. Also covers business opportunities, seminars, conferences and outside publications available to members; new TIA member listings; an industry calendar and a variety of other features - monthly*

• TIA Telecom Trade Statistics: *includes a broad sector breakdown on sales of telecommunications equipment by type over a two year period as well as the top ten import sources/export markets for U.S. equipment - annual/monthly*
Notes: TIA represents the communications and information technology industry in association with the Electronic Industries Association.

Tobacco Manufacturers' Association of the United States (TMA)

Address: PO Box 8019, Princeton N.J. 08543-8019
Telephone: +1 609 275 4900
Fax: +1 609 275 8379
Web site: www.tma.org
Year established: 1915
Activities: maintains trademark records; compiles statistics
Chief officers: Farrell Delman (President)
Structure: permanent staff, board
Membership: 14 manufacturers of tobacco products and suppliers
Publications:
• Executive Summary (Tobacco Merchants' Association of the United States): *newsletter - weekly*
• Issues Monitor: *newsletter - quarterly*

Tortilla Industry Association (TIA)

Address: 16000 Ventura Blvd. - Suite 500, Encino, CA 91436
Telephone: +1 818 981 2547
Fax: +1 818 907 0327
Web site: www.tortilla-info.com/
Web site notes: site includes statistics on the US market for tortillas
Year established: 1990
Membership: 130 tortilla manufacturers, industry suppliers and distributors

Toy Manufacturers of America (TMA)

Address: 200 Fifth Ave., Suite 740, New York, NY 10010
Telephone: +1 212 675 1141
Fax: +1 212 633 1429
E-mail: info@toy-tma.com
Web site: www.toy-tma.com:80/
Web site notes: comprehensive statistics on the market for toys in the US
Year established: 1916
Activities: compiles statistics; monitors government regulation and legislation on safety and trade issues; conducts educational programs; organises the annual American International Toy Fair
Chief officers: Charles Riotto (Executive Director)
Structure: permanent staff; board
Membership: 240 American toy manufacturers
Publications:
• American International Toy Fair Official Directory: *lists more than 1,600 domestic and foreign manufacturers who participated in American International Toy Fair. Includes names of toy companies, reps, addresses, telephone and fax numbers and a brief description of each companies products - annual*
• Monthly Market Trend Reports (Toy Manufacturers of America, TMA): *a survey of approximately 40 toy manufacturers provides summary data on toy shipments - monthly*
• National Statistics Program: Shipments: *volume and value shipments of toys by product type for the latest two years. Based on a survey of toy manufacturers - annual*
• Toy Industry Factbook: *in-depth statistical profile of the U.S. toy market. Includes 10 years of data on manufacturers shipments and retail sales by product type - annual*

Travel and Tourism Research Association (TTRA)
Address: Suite 304, 10200 West 44th Avenue, Wheat Ridge, CO 80033
Telephone: +1 303 940 6557
Fax: +1 303 422 8894
E-mail: careyl@mgtserv.com
Web site: www.ttra.com
Year established: 1970
Activities: annual conference and trade show, quarterly newsletter, quarterly journal of travel research, awards program for excellence in travel and tourism research and marketing, proceedings of the annual conference
Chief officers: Lisa Carey (Executive Director)
Structure: permanent staff; board; committees; chapters
Membership: 900 members (made up of providers and consumers of travel and tourism research)
Publications:
• Journal of Travel Research: *articles on travel research and marketing - quarterly*
• Research Handbook
• Travel, Tourism and Hospitality Research: *comprehensive collection of the many methodologies used in travel, tourism and hospitality research - irregular*
• TTRA Membership Directory: *lists over 900 travel and tourism research and marketing professionals. The directory includes the name, company name, address, phone/fax number and email address of the TTRA membership - annual*

Travel Industry Association of America (TIA)
Address: Suite 450, 1100 New York Avenue NW, Washington, DC 20005-3934
Telephone: +1 202 408 8422
Fax: +1 202 408 1255
E-mail: feedback@tia.org
Web site: www.tia.org
Web site notes: site includes a brief statistical profile of the US travel industry
Year established: 1969
Activities: conducts domestic and international promotions; compiles statistics
Chief officers: William S. Norman (TIA President and Chief Executive Officer), Dr. Suzanne Cook (Senior Vice President Research)
Structure: permanent staff; board; committees; councils
Membership: 1,900 travel industry executives; government officials
Publications:
• "Selling Too" Report Series: *a series of manuals containing information for marketing travel products in specific markets worldwide. Includes a general overview of each market; a statistical profile of outbound travellers from that markets including information on number of trips taken, trip characteristics and demographics; detailed descriptions of the structure of the travel industry in each country, including a list of the names and addresses of in-country tour operators - annual*
• National Travel Survey: *estimates of U.S. resident travel volume and characteristics based on telephone interviews from a national probability sample of adults - monthly*
• Newsletter of the Travel Industry Association of America: *monthly*
• Outlook for Travel and Tourism: *forecast trends for industry sectors and popular market segments such as domestic and international visitors, business and leisure travel, air and auto travel and accommodations - annual*
• TIA's International Pow Wow Market Update: *current market trends and statistics for 54 different countries. Complete with economic and political forecasts - annual*
• TIA's Market Share Indicators (MSI): *top 14 countries of origin for travel to the United States. Examines prevailing market conditions within each country to determine its impact on U.S. arrivals and overall market share. These indicators are*

Gross Domestic Product, unemployment, consumer prices, real private consumption and exchange rate - annual
• Travel FORECAST: *forecasts of both domestic and international visitation and expenditures, as well as travel price inflation for the next four years - annual*
• Travel Industry Association of America Directory of Membership and Services: *contact details of member companies and services offered - annual*
• Travel Market Report: *overall trends and events affecting the domestic travel industry along with details for the complete calendar year. Includes analysis of tourism conditions by region, transportation mode, trip distance and duration, purpose of trip, types of lodging used, income, age and other demographics, use of rental car, package tour and travel agent. Based on a survey conducted by the Association - annual*
• Travelometer: *seasonal forecast about what Americans think about the U.S. economy and their own financial situation and how it will relate to their travel plans. Other information includes seasonal traveller spending, length of trip and travelling companions, top 10 pleasure destinations, and intended activities - quarterly*
• Weekend Travel Report: *comprehensive data and analysis on the weekend traveller. Includes information on travel regions, purpose of trip, distance travelled, mode of transportation, travel party size, trip duration, lodging types, travel agent use, package tour use and demographics are included for weekend travellers - annual*

United Dairy Industry Association
Address: O'Hare International Center, Suite 900, 10255 W Higgins Road, Rosemont, IL 60018
Telephone: +1 708 803 2000
Fax: +1 708 803 2077
Year established: 1970
Activities: sponsors activities of the American Dairy Association, Dairy Research Inc. and the National Dairy Council
Chief officers: Thomas Gallagher (CEO)
Structure: permanent staff; board
Membership: 60 members

United Egg
Address: Suite 200, 1303 Hightower Trail, Atlanta, Georgia
Telephone: +1 770 587 5871
Fax: +1 770 587 0041
E-mail: info@unitedegg.org
Web site: www.unitedegg.org
Web site notes: site includes a profile of the US egg industry as well as up-to-date statistics on production, consumption and distribution over a three year period
Year established: 1982
Activities: government relations; EGGPAC funding; market information; egg trading; exporting; statistics; product and service programs; communications; quality assurance programs for food safety, environment and animal well-being
Chief officers: Albert E Pope (President), Dr. Donald McNamara (Executive Director of Egg Nutrition Center)
Structure: board; committees
Membership: egg producers, packers and processors
Publications:
• New Yolk Times: *newsletter - quarterly*
Notes: United egg is an alliance of four separate organisations providing services to the egg industry. The four organisations are: United Egg Producers (UEP); UEA Further Processor Division; UEA Allied Industry Division; UEA Producer/Packer Division.

United Fresh Fruit and Vegetable Association
Address: 727 North Washington Street, Alexandria, VA 22314
Telephone: +1 703 836 3410
Fax: +1 703 836 7745
Year established: 1904
Activities: liaises with government; monitors government legislation and regulation; conducts marketing programs and education
Chief officers: Thomas E Stenzel (President)
Structure: permanent staff; board; committees
Membership: 2,100 growers, shippers, brokers, wholesalers, distributors and retailers
Publications:
• United Newswire: *newsletter, general information - bi-weekly*

US Hide, Skin and Leather Association
Address: 1700 N Moore, Suite 1600, Arlington, VA 22209-1989
Telephone: +1 703 841 5485
Fax: +1 703 841 9656

Wheat Foods Council
Address: 5500 South Quebec, Ste #111, Englewood, Co 80111 USA
Telephone: +1 303 694 5828
Fax: +1 303 694 5807
E-mail: wfc@wheatfoods.org
Web site: www.wheatfoods.org

Wine and Spirits Shippers' Association (WSSA)
Address: Suite 332, 11800 Sunrise Valley Drive, Reston, VA 22091
Telephone: +1 703 860 2300
Fax: +1 703 860 2422
Year established: 1976
Activities: offers members reduced ocean freight
Chief officers: Howard Rappin (President)
Structure: permanent staff; board
Membership: 385 importers and distillers of alcoholic beverages
Publications:
• WSSA Grapevine: *bi-monthly*

Wine and Spirits Wholesalers of America (WSWA)
Address: 4th Floor, 1023 15th Street NW, Washington, DC 20005
Telephone: +1 202 371 9792
Fax: +1 202 789 2405
Web site: www.wswa.org
Year established: 1943
Activities: promotes interests of members; monitors regulation
Chief officers: Douglas W Metz (Managing Director), David W. Dickerson (Vice President and Public Affairs and Communications)
Structure: permanent staff; councils
Membership: 250 wine and spirits wholesaler companies accounting for 90% of all wine and spirit's sold at wholesale in the United States
Publications:
• Upfront (Wine and Spirits Wholesalers of America): *newsletter - bi-monthly*
• WSWA Member Roster and Industry Directory: *annual*

VENEZUELA

Association of Chemical Product Manufacturers
Asociación de Fabricantes de Productos Químicos
Address: PO Box 6632, Caracas 1010 A, Edificio Centro Solano, piso 1 - oficina 1 A, Av Francisco Solano López, Chacaito, Caracas 1050
Telephone: +58 2 762 5485/5104/4911/721 911/5101/0597
Fax: +58 2 762 0597
Telex: 28574
Chief officers: Pedro Carmona Uzcanga (President)
Membership: chemicals companies
Notes: Also located at: Edificio Fedecamaras, piso 4, oficina A1, Avenida El Empalme, Urbanizació El Bosque, Caracas.

Association of Edible Oils and Fats Manufacturers (ASOGRASAS)
Asociación de Industriales de Aceites y Grasas Vegetales Comestibles
Address: PO Box 50342, Caracas 1050 A, Centro Comercial La Florida, Oficinas 2 y 3, Av Avila c Calle Coello, Ur La Florida, 1050 Caracas
Telephone: +58 2 742 626/662
Fax: +58 2 744 916
Telex: 28354 GRASAS
Chief officers: Jesús Manuel Rojas Salazar (President)
Membership: manufacturers and refiners of vegetable oils and edible vegetable fats

Association of Exporters (PROMEXPORT)
Asociación de Exportadores
Address: Edf Fedecámaras, 4° piso, ofcina F 4, Av El Empalme, Urb El Bosque, 1050 Caracas
Telephone: +58 2 731 1089/774 2853/5687/6903
Fax: +58 2 747 158
Activities: database to identify markets and points of sale, strategy planning, information on regulations and laws in Venezuela and abroad, financial advice, puts members in contact with potential overseas companies
Structure: civil association
Membership: exporters

Association of the Graphic Arts Industry (AIAG)
Asociación de Industriales de Artes Gráficas
Address: Apdo 14405, Caracas 1011 A, Centro Empresarial Senderos, piso 1, of 107 B, Av Principal c/ 2ª Transversal, Urb Los Cortijos de Lourdes, Caracas 1071
Telephone: +58 2 239 3322/3543/3132/3710
Fax: +58 2 239 3322/3921
Telex: 24453 CAINC VC
Chief officers: Jorge Furtado (President)
Membership: graphics companies

Automotive Components Manufacturers' Association
Cámara de Fabricantes Venezolanos de Productos Automotores
Address: Edificio Cámara de Industriales, piso 7, oficina A, Esquina Puente Anáuco, La Calendaria, Caracas, DF
Telephone: +58 2 571 5091/3698

Automotive Industry Association
Cámara de la Industria Automotriz
Address: Cámara de Industriales del Estado Miranda, piso 1, ofic.12, Av Ppal de Chuao, Caracas, Miranda
Telephone: +58 2 921 128/923 886
Fax: +58 2 923 886

Book Association of Venezuela
Cámara Venezolana del Libro
Address: Apdo 51858, Torre Oeste, Piso 11- oficina 112-0,
Avda Andrés Bello, 1050 A Caracas
Telephone: +58 2 793 1347
Fax: +58 2 793 1368
Chief officers: Mr W Rodriguez, Ms MP Vargas (Director)

Canned Fish Manufacturers' Association
Cámara Venezolana de Enlatadores de Pesca
Address: Torre Beta, piso 1- oficina 110, Calle Los
Laboratorios, Los Ruices, Miranda, Caracas
Telephone: +58 2 238 1711
Fax: +58 2 239 0464
Telex: 21513 PISCE VC

Cheese Industry Association (ANIQUESOS)
Asociación de Industriales del Queso
Address: Edificio Fedecámaras, piso 4- oficina D, Calle El
Empalme, El Bosque, Caracas, DF
Telephone: +58 2 721 838
Telex: 29890 FEDECAM

Cocoa Processors' Association (APROCAO)
Asociación de Industriales de Procesadores de Cacao
Address: Apdo 112 Caracas 1010-A, Calles 5 y 7, P. B3-01,
Urb La Urbina, Frente a Ipostela - Quintas Prefabricadas,
Caracas 1071
Telephone: +58 2 241 5856/5173
Fax: +58 2 242 1826
Telex: 25369 CRESTA
Chief officers: Sigfredo Mathison (President)
Membership: cocoa processors

Coffee Industries' Association (ANICAF)
Asociación Nacional de Industriales del Café
Address: Edificio Cámara de Industriales, Esq. Puente
Anáuco, Caracas
Telephone: +58 2 571 5010/5920

Flour Industry Association
Cámara de la Industria de la Harina
Address: Edif. Casa de Italia, Piso 4, Ofc. 3, Av. Las
Industrias, San Bernardino, Caracas
Telephone: +58 2 571 4509

Food Industry Association (CAVIDEA)
Cámara de la Industria de Alimentos
Address: Edificio Ctro. Empresarial Los Ruices, piso 5- oficina
510, Av Ppal Los Ruices, 5109 Carmelitas, Caracas
Telephone: +58 2 239 0918/9818/5294/234 2226
Fax: +58 2 234 2226/238 3268
Telex: 21488 CAVID VC

Furniture and Related Industries' Association (ANIMA)
Asociación de Industriales del Mueble y Afines
Address: Edificio Ciemi, Av El Cafetal, Chuao, Miranda,
Caracas
Telephone: +58 2 571 4210/4368

National Advertisers' Association (ANDA)
Asociación Nacional de Anunciantes-Venezuela
Address: Resd. Primavera, piso B, oficina B, 1 Av de Santa
Eduvigis, Urb. Santa Eduvigis, Caracas
Telephone: +58 2 284 1163/286 1732/283 6553
Fax: +58 2 283 6553
E-mail: anda@telcel.net.ve

Web site: www.andaven.org/
Year established: 1957
Activities: legal advice, ethical committee, professional
training, collects statistics and research studies, link to
government and international bodies
Chief officers: José Nuñez (President), Fini de Otero (Vice
President), Thais Hernández (Executive Director)
Membership: 87 advertisers from different industry sectors:
food and drinks, automotive, departmental stores,
communication, cosmetics and toiletries, construction,
domestic electrical appliances, office equipment,
pharmaceutical, banking and finance, miscellaneous,
tobacco, travel and tourism
Publications:
• ANDA Newsletter (Anda Al Día): *bulletin distributed to
members with issues related to the advertising industry,
information about the events and activities of the Association -
regularly*

National Association of Importers and Distributors of Automotive Components
Cámara Nacional de Importación y Distribución de Repuestos
Automotrices
Address: Edif. Cámara de Comercio de Caracas, piso 5, Av.
Este 2. No. 215, Los Caobos, Caracas, D.F.
Telephone: +58 2 571 0122/2824/0265
Telex: 28386

National Fish Retailers' Association
Cámara Nacional de Detallistas y Expendedores de Pescado
Address: Ctro. Profesional Urdaneta, Ofc. 4-D, Av. Urdaneta,
Esq. La Pelota, Caracas
Telephone: +58 2 562 2070/6124/8728
Telex: 21859

National Rugs and Carpets Manufacturers' Association
Cámara Nacional de Fabricantes de Alfombras y Afines
Address: Edificio Pascal, Torre B, piso 13-oficina 133, Av
Romulo Gallegos, Sta. Eduvigis, 3706 Caracas 1010-A,
Miranda
Telephone: +58 2 284 8388/8577
Telex: 25361 PAGUA

Packaging Association
Cámara Venezolana del Envase
Address: Edificio Torre Beta, piso 3-oficina 301, Calle Los
Laboratorios, Los Ruices, Caracas
Telephone: +58 2 238 3061/345 125
Fax: +58 2 345 125

Small and Medium-Size Traders' Association
Cámara de Pequeños y Medianos Comerciantes
Address: Edf. Karam, Piso 6, Ofc. 607, Av. Urdaneta, Esq.
Ibarras a Pelota, Caracas
Telephone: +58 2 561 5455/564 1619

Spirits Manufacturers' Association
Cámara Venezolana de Licoristas
Address: Edif. Bomplant, Piso 1, oficina 103, Gradillas a
Sociedad, No. 15, Caracas
Telephone: +58 2 545 7813

Sugar Producers' Association (UPAVE)
Unión de Productores de Azúcar
Address: Edificio Ctro. Empresarial Los Ruices, piso 5-ofic.
510, Av Ppal de Los Ruices, Caracas
Telephone: +58 2 239 9518/7882
Fax: +58 2 354 456

Membership: sugar producers and manufacturers

Toys Manufacturers' Association
Cámara Venezolana de Fabircantes de Juguetes
Address: Edif.Ctro.Solano, P.5,Ofc.5-A, Av.Fco.Solano, Cruce con 3a. calle, Las Delicias, Caracas
Telephone: +58 2 721 202/1456

Traders' and Retailers' Association
Cámara de Comerciantes-Detallistas
Address: Edificio Central, Esquina Las Ibarras, Caracas
Telephone: +58 2 563 1505/564 1619

Venezuelan Pharmacist Association
Cámara Venezolana de Farmacia
Address: Urb Valle Abajo, Av Atabapo c/c Calle Orinoco, Caracas 1040
Telephone: +58 2 626 122
Fax: +58 2 617 186
Chief officers: Dr Darío Rigaud Smith (President)
Membership: pharmacies and chemists shops

Venezuelan Alcoholic Industry Association
Cámara de la Industria Venezolana de Especies Alcohólicas
Address: Centro Plaza, Torre C- oficina 11-F, Av Francisco Miranda, Los Palos Grandes, Caracas, Miranda
Telephone: +58 2 284 8289/285 1919/2687
Fax: +58 2 262 1931

Venezuelan Association for the Import and Distribution of Motorcycles Components and Related Products
Cámara Venezolana de Importación y Distribución de Repuestos para Motocicletas y Afines
Address: Edif. Oriol, Piso 2, Ofc. 18, Calle El Progreso, Las Acacias, Caracas
Telephone: +58 2 641 367/628 049

Venezuelan Association of Brewers (CAVEFACE)
Cámara Venezolana de Fabricantes de Cerveza
Address: PO Box 66654, Caracas 1061 A, Edif. Distribuidora Polar, Mezzanina, Urb Los Cortijos de Lourdes, 2ª Transversal c/c Calle La Gruta, Caracas 1071
Telephone: +58 2 239 9298/9507/203 3535
Fax: +58 2 239 9507
Chief officers: Antonio Aldazoro B (President)
Membership: brewers

Venezuelan Association of Manufacturers of Electrical and Electronic Household Goods
Cámara Venezolana de Fabricantes de Artefactos Domésticos y de la Industria Eléctrica y Electrónica
Address: Centro Parque Carabobo, Torre A- piso 3, of 309-310, Pte Victoria a Ño Pastor-La Candelaria, Caracas 1011
Telephone: +58 2 575 2619/4878/2616/6519
Fax: +58 2 576 2617/2645
Chief officers: Ing Hernán Suarez Flamerich (President)
Membership: manufacturers of household appliances, electric and electronic goods

Venezuelan Association of Medicines (CAVEME)
Cámara Venezolana del Medicamento
Address: Calle Villaflor, Centro Profesional del Este, Piso 12 - oficina 124, Av Casanova, Sector Sabana Grande, Caracas 1050
Telephone: +58 2 762 6421/761 7183/761 5173/763 4789
Fax: +58 2 762 5376
Activities: permanent relation with public and private institutions; political lobbying; prepares position papers on

critical issues; regular information to associates
Chief officers: Raúl Mejuto (Chairman), Piero Bertolucci (Vice Chairman), Ulrich Steuer (Treasurer)
Membership: 32 members
Publications:
• Annual Report (Anuario): *annual*
• Monthly Report (Informe Mensual): *news and short articles on medical and pharmaceutical issues - monthly*

Venezuelan Association of Metallurgical and Mining Industrialists (AIMM)
Asociación de Industriales Metalúrgicos y de Minería de Venezuela
Address: Apdo 14504 Caracas 1011 A, Edficio Cámaras de Industriales, piso 9, Esq Puente Anáuco, La Candelaria, Caracas 1011
Telephone: +58 2 571 5009/5310/5808/4210/4368
Fax: +58 2 571 3120/5750186
Telex: 27396 AIMM
Chief officers: Lic Tomás Avellin (President), Dra Michelle Rodriguez (Executive President)
Membership: metal and metallurgy companies
Notes: also at:C C C Tamanaco, 1ª etapa, piso 3, of 325, Urb Chauo, Caracas 1060, Tel 2 9799511, Fax 2 978093

Venezuelan Association of Packaging
Cámara Venezolana del Envase
Address: Torre Beta, piso 3, of 301, Calle Los Laboratorios, Urb los Ruices, 1071 Caracas
Telephone: +58 2 238 3061/239 4626/23 45125
Fax: +58 2 234 5125
Telex: 21339
Chief officers: Ing Manuel Antonio Sosa (President)
Membership: packaging companies

Venezuelan Association of the Clothing Industry
Cámara Venezolana de la Industria del Vestido
Address: 1054, Ed Gral Urdaneta, piso 2º, oficina 23, Marron a Pelota, 1054 Caracas
Telephone: +58 2 561 4763/6390/4743
Fax: +58 2 561 4321
Chief officers: Luis Vicente León Vivas (President)
Membership: clothing manufacturers

Venezuelan Association of the Hygiene, Personal Care, Perfume, and Cosmetics Products Industries (CAVEINCA)
Cámara Venezolana de la Industria de Productos de Higiene, Cuidado Personal, Perfumería, Cosméticos y Afines
Address: Apdo 3004/3577, Edificio IASA, piso 1, oficina 106-108, Plaza de la Castellana, Final Av Rómulo Gallegos, 3757 Caracas 1010-A
Telephone: +58 2 333 004/331 293/917 444/266 3004
Fax: +58 2 331 293/239 9533
Chief officers: Mariano Bernal (President), Dr Fedor Sladivia (Executive President)
Membership: cosmetics companies

Venezuelan Association of the Paper, Pulp and Cardboard Industries (APROPACA)
Asociación Venezolana de Productores de Pulpa, Papel y Cartón
Address: Edif Johnson & Johnson, 2º piso, of 2B, An Rómulo Gallegos, Los Dos Caminos, Caracas DF
Telephone: +58 2 234 3130/1/2/3/4
Fax: +58 2 234 6541
Telex: 24453 CAINC VC
Activities: CICELPA Assembly of the Latin American Pulp and Paper Industry Confederation
Chief officers: Donald Nelson (President)
Membership: 13 paper and pulp manufacturers

Notes: another office: Edificio Cámara de Industriales, piso 6, Puente Anáuco, Caracas DF, Venezuela/ Tel:(2) 572 5398/5402

Venezuelan Association of the Plastics Industries (AVIPLA)
Asociación Venezolana de Industrias Plásticas
Address: Edificio Multicentro de Macaracuay, 7° piso, ofic. 7-9, Avenida Principal de Macaracuay, 1070 Caracas
Telephone: +58 2 256 3345/4192/1632/3680
Fax: +58 2 256 2867/0418
Telex: 21509 AVIPL
Year established: 1965
Activities: information service, studies and research, technical events and courses
Chief officers: Roberto Roca (President), Francisco Massott (Vice President), Ivano Romano (Treasurer), Carlos Eduardo Villegas (Executive Director)
Structure: board of directors, 3 regional committees, 9 working committees
Membership: full (manufacturers of plastic products and prime materials; associate (people or companies allied to the plastics industry; honorary (people who through their work in research, teaching and technology are chosen by the association)
Publications:
● Internal Informative Bulletin (Boletín Informativo Interno): *periodically*
● Venezuela in Plastic (Venezuela en Plástico): *industry news, association news, international news, information on prices and legislation, recycling, services, international offer and demand section, fairs and conference news and information - bi-monthly*

Venezuelan Bakery Industrials' Association
Cámara Venezolana de Industriales de la Panificación
Address: Urb. Los Chorros, Av. El Rosario, No. 4-15-2-25, Caracas
Telephone: +58 2 239 6439/6653
Telex: 25569 CADA

Venezuelan Chamber of Air-conditioning, Refrigeration and Related Industries (VENACOR)
Cámara Venezolana de las Industrias de la Ventilación, Aire Acondicionado, Refrigeración Afines y Conexas
Address: Central Parque Carabobo,Torre B, Piso 22, Oficina 2, Avenida Este 6, Equina nõ Pastor a Puenta Victoria, Caracas
Telephone: +58 2 577 3874
Fax: +58 2 577 1627
Chief officers: Eloy Sardiñas (President)

Venezuelan Decorators and Furniture Manufacturers' Association
Cámara Venezolana de Fabricantes del Mueble, Decoradores y Afines
Address: Edif. Freites, P.1, Av Libertados con Av Santiago de Chile, Urb. Los Caobos, Caracas
Telephone: +58 2 781 8846

Venezuelan Department Stores' Association
Asociación Venezolana Tiendas Departamentos
Address: Torre Olímpica, Av Principal de la Urbina, Caracas
Telephone: +58 2 241 0176
Fax: +58 2 241 8240/762 9185
Chief officers: Cándido Rodríguez (President), William Cohen (Vice President), Dr Osvaldo Carrasquero (Executive Director)
Membership: department stores

Venezuelan Editors' Association (CAVE)
Cámara Venezolana de Editores
Address: Edif. Belvel, Piso 4, Ofc. 4-3, Pte. Yanez a Tracabordo No.80-82, 14234 Caracas
Telephone: +58 2 572 5453

Venezuelan Federation of Advertising Agencies (FEVAP)
Federación Venezolana de Agencias Publicitarias
Address: Apdo 14283, Edf Roraima, Penthouse A, Av Francisco de Mirando, Urb Campo Alegre, Caracas1060
Telephone: +58 2 263 7158/261 3986/8936
Fax: +58 2 261 8936/2637158
E-mail: webmaster@cyberven.com
Web site: www.cyberven.com/fevap/
Activities: legal advice, information service, training courses and seminars
Chief officers: Jose Antonio Vazquez-Figueroa (President), Franklin Whaite (Vice President), Ana Paula de Souza (Executive Director)
Membership: 49 advertising agencies
Publications:
● Newsletter (Informe Mensual): *news related to the advertising industry and information about conferences and activities of the Federation - monthly*

Venezuelan Insurance Companies' Association
Cámara de Aseguradores de Venezuela
Address: Edificio Fedecámaras, psio 2- oficina A y B, Urb El Bosque, Caracas
Telephone: +58 2 732 851/3852/3853
Telex: 23593 CAVEN VC

Venezuelan Knitwear Association
Cámara Venezolana de Tejidos de Punto
Address: Edificio Tip-Top, Urb Industrial San Martín, 2a Calle, Caracas
Telephone: +58 2 421 831/411 832

Venezuelan Radio Broadcasting Association
Cámara Venezolana de la Radiodifusión
Address: Calle Josá A Istúriz, 3a, Entre AV Mohedano y Contry Club, La Castellana, 3955 Caracas
Telephone: +58 2 320 930/312 653/265 0930/2672653

Venezuelan Spirits Association
Cámara Venezolana de Licoristas
Address: Edificio Bomplant, piso 1- oficina 103, Gradillas a Sociedad n° 15, Caracas
Telephone: +58 2 545 7813

Venezuelan Television Broadcasting Association
Cámara Venezolana de la Televisión
Address: Torre La Previsora, 7° piso, Av Abraham Lincoln, Sabana Grande, Caracas
Telephone: +58 2 781 4608/781 4886
Fax: +58 2 793 7528
Chief officers: Hector Ponsdomenach (President), Ibsen Garcia (Vice President)
Membership: television stations

Venezuelan Textile Association (ATV)
Asociación Textil Venezolana
Address: Edificio Karam, piso 5 - oficina 503, Ibarras a Maturín, Caracas
Telephone: +58 2 561 6851/6922

Venezuelan Toys Distributors' Association
Cámara Venezolana de Distribuidores de Juguetes
Address: Edif. Pas de Calais, Piso 5. Ofc B, Veroes a Jesuita, Caracas
Telephone: +58 2 562 4726

Venezuelan Travel and Tourism Agencies' Association (AVAVIT)
Asociación Venezolana de Agencias de Viajes y Turismo
Address: Apdo 51247 Caracas 1050 A, 6ª Avenida #17, entre Calles 6ª y 7ª, Transversal Quinta, Altamira, 1050-A Caracas
Telephone: +58 2 261 1845/37/7861
Fax: +58 2 261 0821
Telex: 24791 AVAVT VC
Chief officers: Arturo Tenorio Ciffoni (President)
Membership: travel agencies

VIETNAM

Central Council of Cooperative Union and SMEs of Vietnam
Address: 77 Nguyen Thai Hoc Street, Hanoi
Telephone: +84 4 843 1768/823 4488
Fax: +84 4 823 4488/843 1883
Chief officers: Hoang Minh Thang (Chairman)

Cooperatives Association Vietnam
Address: 213 Le Thanh Ton Street, Ho Chi minh City
Telephone: +84 8 822 3664
Chief officers: Tran Thanh Lam (Chairman)

Cooperatives Union Council of Hanoi
Address: 15 Quan Thanh Street, Hanoi
Telephone: +84 4 843 4411/843 4334
Fax: +84 4 843 4411
Chief officers: Pham Van Khue (Chairman)

Hanoi Investment Development Group
Address: 90 To Hien Thanh Street, Hanoi
Telephone: +84 4 821 6812
Fax: +84 4 826 1702

Hanoi Union of Association of Industry and Commerce
Address: 95 Ly Nam De Street, Hanoi
Telephone: +84 4 843 4794
Fax: +84 4 843 4794
Chief officers: Dang Duuy Phuc (Chairman)

Non-State Economic Development Centre
Address: 62 Giang Vo Street, Hanoi
Telephone: +84 4 823 4456
Fax: +84 4 823 6382
Chief officers: Nguyen Tuan Quan (Director)

Non-State Transportation Association
Address: 10 Bat Co Street, Hanoi
Telephone: +84 4 825 2677
Chief officers: Bui Quang Tan (Chairman)

SMEs Promotion Centre of VCCI
Address: 33 Ba Trieu Street, Hanoi
Telephone: +84 4 825 0883
Fax: +84 4 825 6446
Chief officers: Phan Tat Dinh (Chairman)

SMEs Scientific and Technological Promotion Centre
Address: 62 Giang Vo Street, Hanoi
Telephone: +84 4 823 6368
Fax: +84 4 823 6382
Chief officers: Nguyen Van Thanh (Director)

Vietnam Banks' Association
Address: 193 Ba Trieu Street, Hanoi
Telephone: +84 4 821 8673
Fax: +84 4 821 8732
Chief officers: Le Dac Cu (Chairman)

Vietnam Young Entrepreneur Association
Address: 64 Ba Tricu Street, Hanoi
Telephone: +84 4 822 8227
Fax: +84 4 825 0796
Chief officers: Nong Quoc Tuan (Secretary General)

VIRGIN ISLANDS

Hotel Association of St Croix
Address: PO Box 3869, Christiansted, St Croix
Telephone: +1 809 773 1435
Fax: +1 809 773 8172

Hotel Association St Thomas-St John
Address: PO Box 2300, 00803 St Thomas
Telephone: +1 809 774 6835

Tourist Board of Virgin Islands
Address: PO Box 136, Road Town, Tortola
Telephone: +1 809 494 3134
Fax: +1 809 494 3866

YUGOSLAVIA

Independent Media Association of the Federal Republic of Yugoslavia
Address: 7 trg Nikole Pasica, 11000 Belgrade
Telephone: +38 11 324 8871/338 226/340 221
Fax: +38 11 324 8871/338 226/340 221
Chief officers: Mr Branislav Milosevic (Chairman of the Coordination Board)

Mineral Water Association
Udruzenje Mineralnih Voda Doo
Address: Lomina 8-10, 11000 Belgrade
Telephone: +38 11 662 966
Fax: +38 11 668 362

Yugoslavian Article Numbering Association (YANA)
Address: Terazije 23/V, soba 531, 11000 Belgrade
Telephone: +38 11 324 8392
Fax: +38 11 324 8754

Yugoslavian Editors' Association
Association des Éditeurs Yougoslaves
Address: Kneza Milosa 25/1, 11000 Belgrade
Telephone: +38 11 64 22 48
Fax: +38 11 64 63 39
Chief officers: Ms M Popovic (Director)

ZAIRE

Bankers' Association of Zambia
Address: PO Box 33611, c/o Zambia National Commercial Bank, Lusaka
Telephone: +243 221 418/221 174
Chief officers: JY Ngoma

Coffee Board of Zaire (OZACAF)
Office Zairois du Café
Address: BP 8931, ave Général Bobozo, Kinshasa I
Telephone: +243 12 77144/222 736
Fax: +243 7 814 4
Telex: 20062
Year established: 1979
Activities: state agency for coffee and also cocoa, tea, quinquina and pyrethrum
Chief officers: Feruzi Wa Ngenda (Commercial Director), Noel Munga, Juma Badjoko (Executives), Munga Wa Mbasa (Chief Executive)

ZAMBIA

Clothing and Allied Industries' Association of Zambia
Address: PO Box 71464, c/o FN Kayula, Ndola
Fax: +260 650 172
Chief officers: RC Mistry

Export Board of Zambia
Address: PO Box 3064, Lusaka
Telephone: +260 228 106/7
Fax: +260 222 509

Gemstones Corporation of Zambia
Address: PO Box 30815, Ndeke Hotel, Lusaka
Telephone: +260 252 779
Chief officers: Theo Bull

Hotel and Catering Association of Zambia
Address: PO Box 30815, Ndeke Hotel, Lusaka
Telephone: +260 229 074/5
Chief officers: G Rossi

Leather Industry Association of Zambia (LIAZ)
Address: PO Box 33922, Keembe States, Lusaka
Telephone: +260 222 210/225 797
Chief officers: C.A. Sypon

Master Printers and Newspapers Proprietors' Association of Zambia
Address: PO Box 36655, Zambia Printing Company, Lusaka
Telephone: +260 224 261
Fax: +260 611 171
Chief officers: B Lubumbashi

Motor Traders' Association
Address: PO Box 70646, c/o A.D. Pulford, Ndola
Telephone: +260 614 017
Chief officers: George S. Donkin

Textile Producers' Association of Zambia
Address: PO Box 71846, Swarp Spinning Mills Ltd, Ndola
Telephone: +260 650 821
Fax: +260 650 111

Chief officers: R.J. Patel

Travel Agents' Association of Zambia
Address: Lubi Travel and Tours Ltd, Lusaka
Telephone: +260 225 650/223 964
Fax: +260 223 216
Chief officers: S. Konie

Young Entrepreneurs' Association of Zambia
Address: PO Box 735171, Lusaka
Chief officers: Paul Lupunga

Zambia Association of Manufacturers (ZAM)
Address: PO Box 71564, Crown Cork Ltd, Lusaka
Telephone: +260 252 369/650 261
Telex: 40124 ZA
Chief officers: Tommy Simmonds

Zambia Coffee Growers' Association
Address: PO Box 35388, TAZ House, Ground Floor, Chachacha, Ciparamba Roads, Lusaka 10101
Telephone: +260 1 223 120
Fax: +260 1 222 736/223 249
Telex: 40693 ZCGA

Zambia Export Growers' Association
Address: PO Bpox 31705, Lusaka
Telephone: +260 262 806/822

ZIMBABWE

Agricultural Marketing Authority
Address: PO Box 8094, Royal Mutual House, 45 Baker Avenue, Causeway, Harare
Telephone: +263 4 700 221
Fax: +263 4 730 948
Membership: farmers, marketing executives in agriculture, government

Booksellers' and Publishers' Association of Zimbabwe (BAZ)
Address: PO Box 31762, Room 6, Lotti House, Cairo Road, Lusaka
Telephone: +263 1 222 647
Fax: +263 1 225 282
Chief officers: Christine Kasonde (Executive Secretary)

Booksellers' Association of Zimbabwe
Address: PO Box 3916, Harare
Telephone: +263 4 750 282
Fax: +263 4 751 202
Chief officers: Maxwell Nyamangara (Secretary)

Coffee Growers' Association
Address: PO Box 4382, 113 Leopold Takawira Street, Harare
Telephone: +263 4 750 238
Fax: +263 4 750 754
Telex: 22084 CFU 2W
Chief officers: R J Fennell, G J Shaw (Executives)

Commercial Farmers' Union
Address: PO Box 1241, Agriculture House, Leopold Takawira Street, Harare

Telephone: +263 4 723 945/8
Fax: +263 4 750 754
Membership: farmers, agriculturists

Confederation of Zimbabwe Industries (CZI)

Address: PO Box 3794, 4th Floor, Fidelity Life Tower, Cnr Raleigh, Luck Streets, Harare
Telephone: +263 4 739 833
Fax: +263 4 702 873
Membership: umbrella organisation for private and public manufacturing companies and trade associations
Notes: Various trade associations affiliated to the Confederation of Zimbabwe Industries (CZI) can be contacted directly through the CZI: Agricultural Chemical Industry Association, Battery Manufacturers' Association, Federation of Master Printers, Food Manufacturers' Association, Footwear and Tanners' Association, Furniture Manufacturers' Association, Master Bakers' Association, Metal Merchants' Association, Plastics Manufacturers' Association, Steel Importers' Association, Vehicle Industry Association, Zimbabwe Association of Packaging and Zimbabwe Chemical Manufacturers' Association.

Grain Marketing Board

Address: CY 77 Causeway, Kurima House, 89 Baker Avenue, Harare
Telephone: +263 4 732 011/20
Fax: +263 4 732 038
Telex: 22217/22336 GMB2W
Chief officers: R M Gasela, P M Jongwe

Horticulture Promotion Council

Address: PO Box 1241, Agriculture House, Leopold Takawira Street, Harare
Telephone: +263 4 750 754
Fax: +263 4 750 547

Hotel and Restaurant Association of Zimbabwe

Address: HG 306, 9th Floor, Travel Centre, Jason Moyo Avenue, Highlands, Harare
Telephone: +263 4 733 211
Fax: +263 4 794 015/6

Ostrich Producers' Association of Zimbabwe

Address: Private Bag 7220, 1 Mallis Court, Glenroy Shopping Centre off Glenara Avenue, Harare
Telephone: +263 4 495 062/498 456
Fax: +263 4 498 456

Timber Council of Zimbabwe

Address: PO Box 3645, Riembarta House, 256 Samora Machel Avenue, Harare
Telephone: +263 4 746 645
Fax: +263 4 746 013

Transport Operators' Association

Address: PO Box 2002, Harare
Telephone: +263 4 722 356/725 310/724 116
Fax: +263 4 722 356

Zimbabwe Association of Tour and Safari Operators

Address: PO Box 7240, 9th Floor Travel Centre, Harare
Telephone: +263 4 733 211
Fax: +263 4 794 015

Zimbabwe Book Development Council (ZBDC)

Address: PO Box CY 1179, 78 Kaguvi Street, Causeway, Harare
Telephone: +263 4 750 282
Fax: +263 4 751 202
Chief officers: Miriam Bamhare (Executive Director)

Zimbabwe Book Publishers' Association

Address: PO Box CY 1179 Causeway, 78 Kaguvi Street, Harare
Telephone: +263 4 750 282/739 681
Fax: +263 4 751 202
Chief officers: Mr EL Luphahla, Mrs Tainie Mundondo (Executive Director)

Zimbabwe Cereals Producers' Association

Address: PO Box 592, Agriculture House, Leopold Takawira Street, Harare
Telephone: +263 4 791 881
Fax: +263 4 750 754/753 578/9

Zimbabwe Clothing Council

Address: PO Box 4557, c/o Wisdom Services (Pvt) Ltd, 107 Leopold Takawira Street, Harare
Telephone: +263 4 752 120

Zimbabwe Farmers' Union

Address: PO Box 3755, Reliance House, Leopold Takawira Street/Speke Avenue, Harare
Telephone: +263 4 737 733/4
Fax: +263 4 750 456

Zimbabwe International Dairy Federation Committee

Address: P.O. Box CY 2026, c/o ZDHIA, Causeway
Telephone: +263 4 791 881
Fax: +263 4 728 317
Chief officers: Ms P.A. Borland (Secretary)

Zimbabwe Wholesalers' Association

Address: PO Box 323, Harare
Telephone: +263 4 752 018/9
Telex: 22082 HAROB ZW
Activities: monitors trade practices
Chief officers: G Tselentis, Y Hussein, C H Arnott
Membership: 36 members, representative body for Zimbabwe wholesalers

General Index

Index of Trade Associations by Sector

AEROSPACE

AGRICULTURE

ANIMAL FEEDS

AUTOMOTIVES

AUTOMOTIVE COMPONENTS

BATTERIES

BRANDED GOODS

BROADCASTING

BUILDING AND CONSTRUCTION

BUSINESS SERVICES

CHEMICALS

CHILDREN AND YOUTH

CLOTHING AND TEXTILES

CONSUMER ELECTRONICS

AUDIO

RADIO

CONSUMER SERVICES

COOPERATIVES

COSMETICS AND TOILETRIES

DISPOSABLE PAPER PRODUCTS

DIY AND HARDWARE

DOMESTIC ELECTRICAL APPLIANCES

SMALL ELECTRICAL APPLIANCES

DRINKS

WINE

ECONOMICS

ELECTRICAL ENGINEERING

ELECTRONIC ENGINEERING

ENERGY AND WATER

GAS

OIL

ENGINEERING

ENVIRONMENT

FILM INDUSTRY

FISHING

FLAVOURS AND FRAGRANCES

FOOD

DELICATESSEN FOODS

DRIED FOODS

EDIBLE OILS AND FATS

FISH

FROZEN FOODS

HEALTH FOODS

HONEY

HOT BEVERAGES

JAMS AND PRESERVES

MEAT (FRESH)

SUGAR

FOOTWEAR

FOREIGN TRADE

FORESTRY

FRANCHISING

GENERAL BUSINESS

GENERAL LIBRARY

GLASS

HOTELS AND CATERING

FAST FOOD

HOUSEHOLD CHEMICALS

INFORMATION TECHNOLOGY

INSURANCE

LABOUR AND EMPLOYMENT

LAW

LEASING

PHOTOGRAPHIC GOODS

RECORDS AND TAPES

LIVESTOCK

MANAGEMENT SCIENCES

MARINE CONSTRUCTION

MARKET RESEARCH

MECHANICAL ENGINEERING

MEDIA

MEDICAL SUPPLIES AND EQUIPMENT

MEDICINE

METALS

MINING AND QUARRYING

OFFICE EQUIPMENT AND SUPPLIES

OPTICAL GOODS

PACKAGING

PATENTS AND TRADE MARKS

PERSONAL GOODS

GIFTWARE

JEWELLERY

MUSICAL INSTRUMENTS

PERSONAL STATIONERY

PETS

TRAVEL GOODS

WATCHES AND CLOCKS

WRITING INSTRUMENTS

PETROLEUM

PHARMACEUTICALS/OTC

VETERINARY PRODUCTS

PHOTOGRAPHIC SERVICES

PLASTICS

PRINTING AND PUBLISHING

PRIVATE LABEL

PUBLIC RELATIONS

PULP, PAPER AND BOARD

TOBACCO

CIGARETTES

CIGARS AND CIGARILLOS

TRADE DEVELOPMENT BODY

TRADE FAIRS

TRANSPORT AND COMMUNICATION

TRAVEL AND TOURISM

VENDING

VINICULTURE

WHOLESALE AND RETAIL TRADE

RETAILING

WHOLESALING